T0189198

Lecture Notes of the Institute for Computer Sciences, Social-Informatics and Telecommunications Engineering 10

Elisa Bertino   James B.D. Joshi (Eds.)

Collaborative Computing: Networking, Applications and Worksharing

4th International Conference, CollaborateCom 2008
Orlando, FL, USA, November 13-16, 2008
Revised Selected Papers

 Springer

Volume Editors

Elisa Bertino
Purdue University, Department of Computer Science
LWSN 2142G, 656 Oval Drive, West Lafayette IN 47907, USA
E-mail: bertino@cs.purdue.edu

James B.D. Joshi
University of Pittsburgh, School of Information Sciences
Department of Information Sciences and Telecommunications
135 North Bellefield Avenue, Pittsburgh, PA 15260, USA
E-mail: jjoshi@mail.sis.pitt.edu

Library of Congress Control Number: Applied for

CR Subject Classification (1998): I.2.6, K.3.2, K.3.1, H.5.3, K.4.3, C.2.4

ISSN   1867-8211
ISBN-10   3-642-03353-9 Springer Berlin Heidelberg New York
ISBN-13   978-3-642-03353-7 Springer Berlin Heidelberg New York

springer.com

© ICST Institute for Computer Science, Social-Informatics and Telecommunications Engineering 2009
Printed in Germany

Typesetting: Camera-ready by author, data conversion by Scientific Publishing Services, Chennai, India
Printed on acid-free paper   SPIN: 12712380   06/3180   5 4 3 2 1 0

Preface

CollaborateCom is an annual international forum for dissemination of original ideas and research results in collaborative computing networks, systems, and applications. A major goal and feature of CollaborateCom is to bring researchers from networking, systems, CSCW, collaborative learning, and collaborative education areas together. CollaborateCom 2008 held in Orlando, Florida, was the fourth conference of the series and it reflects the accelerated growth of collaborative computing, both as research and application areas.

Concretely, recent advances in many computing fields have contributed to the growing interconnection of our world, including multi-core architectures, 3G/4G wireless networks, Web 2.0 technologies, computing clouds, and software as a service, just to mention a few. The potential for collaboration among various components has exceeded the current capabilities of traditional approaches to system integration and interoperability. As the world heads towards unlimited connectivity and global computing, collaboration becomes one of the fundamental challenges for areas as diverse as eCommerce, eGovernment, eScience, and the storage, management, and access of information through all the space and time dimensions. We view collaborative computing as the glue that brings the components together and also the lubricant that makes them work together. The conference and its community of researchers demonstrate the concrete progress we are making towards this vision.

The conference would not have been successful without help from so many people. We would like to thank the Organizing Committee for their hard work in putting together the conference. First, we would like to express our deep gratitude to our Program Chairs: James Joshi from the University of Pittsburgh, USA and Elisa Bertino, from Purdue University, USA. Together with their Program Committee, they assembled a strong program from submissions and invited papers. The other committee members made similarly important contributions, including the Panel Chairs: Dimitrios Georgakopoulos of CSIRO, Australia, and Ling Liu, Georgia Institute of Technology, USA; Workshop Program Chairs: Gail-Joon Ahn of Arizona State University, USA, and Lakshmish Ramaswamy of University of Georgia, USA; Industry Program Chairs: Claudio Bartonlini of HP and Yuecel Karabulut of SAP; Tutorial Chairs: Barbara Carminati of University of Insubria, Italy, and Bugra Gedik of IBM; Publication Chair Anna Squicciarini of Penn State University, USA; and Publicity Chair Youna Jung of University of Pittsburgh, USA.

Finally, we would like to express our special thanks to our Local Organization Chair, Lotzi Boloni of University of Central Florida, USA, and conference coordinator and Finance Chair, Karen Decker of ICST, who did all the hard work. We also thank the Steering Committee of CollaborateCom, particularly Imrich Chlamtac of University of Trento, Italy (Chair), and Ling Liu of Georgia Institute of

Technology, USA. Without the support and dedication from these volunteers, we would not be able to assemble such an interesting and attractive conference program

Calton Pu
Heri Ramampiaro

Message from the Program Chairs

On behalf of the Program Committee of the 4th International Conference on Collaborative Computing: Networking, Applications and Worksharing (CollaborateCom-2008), we welcome you to the proceedings CollaborateCom-2008 which was held in Orlando, Florida. It was a great pleasure as Program Committee Co-chairs to help organize this year's impressive scientific and technical program and technical proceedings. The proceedings contain papers selected as well as invited for presentation at the conference and two workshops. We hope these proceedings will serve as a valuable reference for the research community.

This year's conference was jointly sponsored by Create-Net, ACM SIGCHI and the International Communication Sciences and Technology Association (ICST). *CollaborateCom* serves as the principal international forum for bringing together academic and industrial researchers, practitioners, and students interested in systems, networks, and applications that support collaboration. This year, *CollaborateCom* received 70 submissions. The Technical Program Committee selected 26 papers (acceptance rate of 37.14%) after a rigorous review and a brief follow-up discussion. Most of the papers were reviewed by three or four referees. The authors were asked to address each and every comment made by the referees to improve the quality of their papers. Our program this year included two keynote speeches, one panel, one industrial session, three tutorials and 12 technical sessions.

We would like to thank many dedicated people who contributed to the success of this event. In particular, we want to express our gratitude to the Program Committee members and the external referees. Their diligent work in reviewing the papers and participating in a follow-up discussion was instrumental in raising the quality of the accepted papers. We extend our sincere and deepest gratitude to the Panel Chairs: Dimitrios Georgakopoulos of CSIRO, Australia, and Ling Liu, Georgia Institute of Technology, USA; Workshop Chairs: Gail-Joon Ahn of Arizona State University, USA and Lakshmish Ramaswamy of University of Georgia, USA; Industry Program Chairs: Claudio Bartonlini of HP and Yuecel Karabulut of SAP; Tutorial Chairs: Barbara Carminati of University of Insubria, Italy, and Bugra Gedik of IBM; Publication Chair Anna Squicciarini of the Pennsylvania State University, USA; and Publicity Chair Youna Jung of University of Pittsburgh, USA. Most importantly, we want to thank the authors for submitting excellent papers; it is because of their work that we had an outstanding program covering a variety of important topics in the area of collaborative systems and technologies.

Our deepest appreciation also goes to the Keynote Speakers Ravi Sandhu of the University of Texas, San Antonio and Taieb Znati of the University of Pittsburgh who is currently the Division Director of NSF CNS program for sharing their insights and experiences with the conference attendees, and to the workshop organizers for their effort in organizing the event. We also extend special thanks to the organizers of the

TrustCol-2008 and CoNGN-2008 workshops, and the organizers of the three tutorial sessions.

We would like to express our deepest thanks to the General Chairs, Calton Pu of Georgia Institute of Technology, USA and Heri Ramampiaro of NTNU, Norway, as well as the Steering Committee of *CollaborateCom*, in particular Imrich Chlamatac of Unviersity of Trento, Italy (Chair) and Ling Liu of Georgia Institute of Technology, Tech, USA for their continuous help/feedback and unequivocal support throughout the year without which this conference could not have been brought to fruition. Finally, our sincere appreciation and gratitude to our Local Organization Chair, Lotzi Boloni of University of Central Florida, USA, conference coordinator and Finance Chair, Karen Decker of ICST, and other members of the ICST technical and publication team, who did all the hard work.

November 2008   Elisa Bertino
                                                                James Joshi

Table of Contents

Full Papers

A Distributed Collaborative Filtering Recommendation Model for P2P Networks

Jun Wang[1], Jian Peng[1,2], and Xiaoyang Cao[3]

[1] School of Computer Science, Sichuan University, Chengdu 610065, China
[2] Department of Computer Science, University of Maryland, MD 20742, USA
[3] Chengdu University of Information Technology, 610225, China

Abstract. Conventional collaborative filtering(CF) recommendation applies the user-based centralized architecture. This architecture has some problems of sparsity and scalability, in addition to not fit the current popular P2P architecture. Therefore, this paper proposes a distributed model to implement the CF algorithm by maintaining the user's record information distributedly in each nodes throughout the network, constructing a DHT, applying the Chord algorithm to realize locating of the record and designing the corresponding communication policy to obtain data needed.

Keywords: collaborative filtering, probabilistic relevance model, distributed, Chord.

1 Introduction

With the rapid development of network technology and the continuous increase of resources, users need a more personalized service to help users to find the information they need from enormous resources. The so-called personalized service considers the need and choice of individual users, applies different strategies for different users and meets the users' personalized needs by providing pertinent content. The most prevailing and effective way is to use collaborative filtering(CF). CF is based on the fact that, if different users' rating of the information which has already been judged is similar, then their rating of other information which has not been judged should be similar. Thus, basing on other users' evaluation and combining target user's personal history record, the collaborative filtering recommendation system provides the user with the information he may interest most.

In the past, most of the collaborative filtering systems search and maintain relevant information in a central server. This centralized architecture has two major problems. One is data sparsity. In e-commerce or other applications, the number of items and users is enormous, therefore, even the active users only rate a very small part of the items and even the hot items are only rated by a very small part of the total users. In such a sparse circumstance with large amount of data, it's difficult to judge the similarity of different users. Another problem is the system's scalability. The time complexity of user-based Collaborative filtering algorithm, in the worst-case scenario, is the O(MN),where M denotes the

E. Bertino and J.B.D. Joshi (Eds.): CollaborateCom 2008, LNICST 10, pp. 1–10, 2009.

number of users and N denotes the number of items. Thus, with the increase of users and items, the amount of computation will dramatically increase. Besides that, P2P networks have become a popular way of sharing resources and, taking into account of system robustness and issue about intellectual property rights, pure P2P architect does not include a central server or central router to control the entire network, Such as Gnutella, Freenet file system. Therefore, this paper proposes a distributed collaborative filtering recommendation model applicable to the P2P architecture.

2   A Distributed Collaborative Filtering Recommendation Architecture

Conventional collaborative filtering recommendation system is as shown in Figure 1. The central server runs an application to response the request from the clients. When receiving a client's request, the server searches the data needed from the user data set and the item data set, sends the data to CF module, gets the recommendation set through the recommendation algorithm set by the system and finally sends the result back to the client. This centralized approach makes the process simple and has a high efficiency when the number of users and items is not very great. However, such a centralized structure is not applicable to P2P network, besides the problems of the data sparsity and poor scalability. Some studies propose the cluster model. By measuring the similarity of users, the cluster model divides the user base into different clusters and each cluster is a collection of the most similar users. Its purpose is to assign the user to the cluster containing users most similar to itself. By calculating the similarity only with the users in the same cluster, thus it greatly reduces the dimensions of the user-item matrix and greatly improves the scalability and the performance of collaborative filtering algorithm.[7] However, the grouping for the user base is not very precise, largely affecting the recommendation's accuracy. If applying more precise cluster in order to improve the accuracy, expenses produced will largely offset the improvement brought by the decrease in dimensions of user-based matrix[4]. Therefore, by storing the data

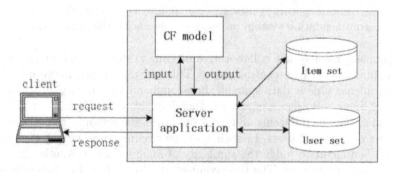

Fig. 1. A centralized CF architecture

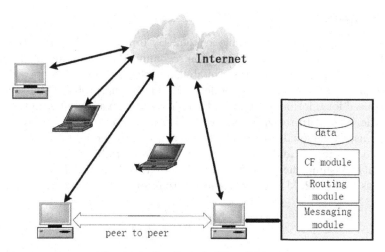

Fig. 2. A distributed CF architecture

and performing computing in each node, this paper proposes a distributed CF recommendation system architecture.

Unlike the centralized architecture, in the distributed architecture as shown in Figure 2, data is scattered throughout the network and the corresponding computing is also performed in each node. All the nodes in the system are linked together orderly in accordance with a certain rule, and each node shares records it maintains. The target node in the system needs to collect the necessary data to calculate the corresponding recommendation set, so every node needs to achieve the following four modules.

User data module: user data module keeps user's own downloading record, which is a collection of movie names the user has downloaded. This record not only reflects the tendency of the user's preference, but is also part of data source which other users use to calculate its own user-item relevance.

CF module: When the target collects all the necessary data, as the input source, the probabilistic relevance model is used to calculate the relevance between the user and the item. And according to the relevance, return 15 items with the highest relevance as the recommendation set for the target user.

Routing module: Compared to a centralized server, which all the data is stored in a central database server, in the distributed architecture, user's data is maintained by each node alone. Since it needs to search and locate other users' record when calculating the recommendation set for target user, routing module uses the chord algorithm to build a distributed hash table(DHT) in the whole system with each node responsible for maintaining one small part, and to provides a highly effective way to achieve the locating for the necessary records.

Message processing module: message processing module is mainly to handle the inter-node message, responsible for the registration and deregistration of nodes' records, the corresponding work for requesting data from other nodes or sending data to other nodes, thus achieve the objective that the data can be shared in all nodes.

2.1   CF Module

CF module is the core of the whole system. By inputting relevant data to calculate the user-item relevance, obtain the recommendation aiming at the user's preference. In this paper, we use probabilistic relevance model proposed in [9] to build the user-item relevance model . Originally, the probabilistic relevance model is used for information retrieval, judging the relevance between the query and the document. In recommendation system, the user's history record represents the user's personal preference, so we can regard the user's history record as the model's input, and introduce two random variables r (relevant) and $\bar{r}$ (irrelevant). Assume there are N items, denoted as $I_a(a=1,2,,N)$,and M users, denoted as $U_b(b=1,2,,M)$. the relevance of item for user is denoted as follow

$$R_{I_a,U_b} = log\frac{P(r|I_a,U_b)}{P(\bar{r}|I_a,U_b)} \tag{1}$$

$P(r|I_a,U_b)$ denotes the relevance probability between I_a and U_b, $P(\bar{r}|I_a,U_b)$ denotes irrelevance probability between I_a and U_b. Factorize $P(r|I_a,U_b)$ with $P(U_b|I_a,r)P(r|I_a)/P(U_b|I_a)$

$$R_{I_a,U_b} = log\frac{P(r|I_a,U_b)}{P(\bar{r}|I_a,U_b)} = log\frac{P(U_b|I_a,r)}{P(U_b|I_a,\bar{r})} + log\frac{P(r|I_a)}{P(\bar{r}|I_a)} \tag{2}$$

To simplify the model without affecting its generality, we only care about the positive relevance and remove the irrelevance terms. Then the equation will become as follow:

$$R_{I_a,U_b} \propto logP(U_b|I_a,r) + logP(r|I_a) \tag{3}$$

The items that the user have interacted with(downloading, watching or browsing) before reflect the positive interest of user for those items. Let L_b denote the downloading list of U_b. If I_a is a member of the downloading list of U_b, then $L_b(I_a)=1$, otherwise $L_b(I_a)=0$. Therefore, the item set the downloading list keeps can represent the user's preference and can be used to calculate the relevance as the input source. Assuming each item in downloading list is irrelevant, the equation(3) becomes:

$$R_{I_a,U_b} \propto \sum_{\forall I_i:I_i \in L_b} logP(I_i|I_a,r) + logP(r|I_a) \tag{4}$$

Apply the Bayers in equation(4):

$$R_{I_a,U_b} \propto \sum_{\forall I_i:I_i \in L_b} log\frac{P(r|I_a,I_i)}{P(r|I_a)} + logP(r|I_a) \tag{5}$$

As the equation(5) shows, calculation of the item-user relevance is converted into calculation of the probability of an item and the relevance probability between items. If a user likes item A and item B at the same time, a certain correlation is established between them. Therefore we can calculate the probability of the relevance between two items, namely $P(r|I_a, I_i)$, through the frequency of those two items appearing in the same downloading list and calculate the probability of an item, namely $P(r|I_a)$, through the frequency of this item in the downloading list as follow.

$$P(r|I_a, I_i) = (\sum_{n=i}^{M} L_n(I_a) \wedge L_n(I_i))/M \tag{6}$$

$$P(r|I_a) = (\sum_{n=i}^{M} L_n(I_a))/M \tag{7}$$

Different from user-based collaborative filtering algorithm, this is a item-based collaborative filtering algorithm. The item-based recommendation model uses users' downloading records to reflect relationship between the items, reducing the impact caused by data sparsity by avoiding calculating the adjacent user set.

2.2   Routing Module

In the distributed environment, user data is all scattered throughout the network. So, before providing users recommendation values, the system must obtain other users' downloading lists from other nodes. Therefore we use the Chord algorithm as system's routing and search algorithm, building a DHT to quickly search and locate nodes. The first P2P routing algorithm, which each node maintains a routing table, randomly stores some other nodes as the neighbor nodes. When needing to search resources in the network, the node sends the query message to every neighbor node stored in the routing table, and then according to the routing information of the neighbor nodes, forward the query message to other nodes in the network alike, which is a broadcasting method to search the nodes needed. This manner is suitable for small and medium-sized networks, but, as the network expands, the searching time will increase dramatically. In addition, the broadcasting message will put burden on the network and, due to TTL, message's searching will be limited to a certain extent, which can not guarantee that the records needed will be found. Therefore, the system uses DHT to locate the nodes the system needs. DHT provides a distributed search service. All the index entries constitute a big hash table, in which every index entry is denoted as a key-value pair, namely, pair(K, V). K denotes keywords, which is the hash of file name or other descriptive information of the file, and V denotes the node's IP address or other descriptive information of the node which actually stores the file. Following certain rules, each participating node maintains part of the whole hash table. Through the query message, Nodes can route to the corresponding node according to the keyword, obtaining all the addresses of the nodes which stores this file. In this way, the changes of the nodes only have a small impact on the network, and the system has good scalability.

In this collaborative filtering model, through building a distributed hash table, we link the item name with the address which have downloaded that item already and achieve the fast locating. In the system, each keyword and node has a m-bit

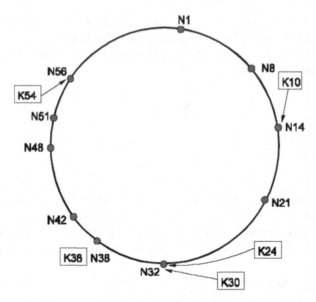

Fig. 3. Chord ring

identifier respectively. Using a hash function SHA-1, hash the keyword (Here is the file name) as the keyword identifiers, and hash node's IP address as the node identifier. All the nodes are arranged along a logical ring clockwise in ascending order according to its node identifier. The item whose keyword identifier is equal to K, is indexed in the node whose identifier is equal to K or this node's successor. The successor node in the Chord ring is the node nearest to and bigger than node K clockwise, denoted as successor (K)[3]. As shown in Figure 3, the item with identifier 10 stores at the node with identifier 14, the items with identifier 24 and 30 stores at the node with identifier 32. Each node contains a reference to its successor node, when search the file name, the query message is transferred through the successor node along the ring until arriving at the corresponding nodes indexing the record.

In order to speed up searching speed, routing algorithm uses the extended algorithm to achieve O(logN) search performance. Each node needs to be responsible for the maintenance of a routing table known as the finger table. For The node n, the ith reference in its finger table points to the node m which is at lest 2^{i-1} greater than node n in the Chord ring, m = successor $(n + 2^{i-1})$. The fist entry in the finger table points to the direct successor of node n in the ring, that is, successor $(n +1)$. If node n's finger table does not contain successor(k), node n finds the node f which is closest to successor(k)in the finger table and sends a query request to node f. Node f proceeds the search in the same way and this process will continue, recursively, until arriving the node in accordance with keyword k.

Since node joining/exiting have an impact on the system, routing algorithm also establishes a policy to overcome the impact of system changes. When a new node joins the network, firstly the new node n calculates the node identifier according to IP, through the node identifier finds its successor node and inserts it between its successor nodes and successor's previous precursor nodes. At the same time, due to system change, part of the index entries originally maintained by its successor will be transferred to the hash table that the new node maintains, and then will be removed in the successor. Similarly, when node leaves, in addition to need to inform the successor node and precursor node re-points its precursor and successor respectively, it needs to transfer the index entries it maintains to its successor.

2.3 Messaging Module

The routing algorithm just achieves distributed data search, in order to achieve distributed collaborative filtering algorithm, and ensure the node can access the data needed from other nodes, every node also needs to achieve the corresponding inter-node message processing function for different events.

Event I. registration of downloading records: For collaborative filtering recommendation system, each item in downloading list can be regarded as a shared resource, namely, K in (K, V) pair. Each node maintains a hash table as part of the whole DHT. When new node joins, in addition to transfer corresponding (K,V) entries of the successor node to the new node, the new node needs to share its own downloading records. For each download record, namely file name, it gets the keyword identifier K after being hashed, and locates the corresponding node according to K. The new node traverse each item in the downloading list, sends the request to the corresponding node according to K and creates corresponding index entries in the harsh table on the corresponding node. In this way, the downloading records of the new nodes become a part of DHT, exposed to the entire network. Other nodes can find and access to the downloading records of the new node.

Event II. request for records: In order to calculate preference value between the target user and item, need to obtain item data associated with items in the target user's downloading list, that is, by analyzing other users' downloading lists which also include the item that the target node has downloaded before, calculate the user-item relevance according to the probabilistic relevant model mentioned above. In the entire network, we build a DHT. Due to the property of DHT, the same items in various downloading list are registered and indexed in the same node which is decided by identifier K(the hash of the file name). Therefore, through the node (like node B in Figure 4) in accordance with identifier K, the system can obtain all addresses of nodes (like nodes C, D, E in Figure 4)which have downloaded this item, and through these nodes which have downloaded this item, the system can obtain these nodes' downloading records, which are the basis for calculating the relevance between target item and other items. As shown in Figure 4, a node needs to complete corresponding work in the process of requesting records. Assuming the number of the nodes is n, since Node A can only send message to most n nodes and receive message from most n nodes, the message complexity is $O(n)$

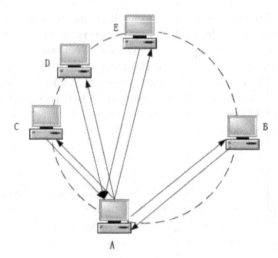

Fig. 4. The process of request record

Algorithm of the protocol is represented as followed:

For each item I_a in node A of user U_1
  For each Node N_1 which has downloaded I_a
        send the data of its downloading list to Node A
  For each item I_b which is in the downloading list of
  nodes which has downloaded I_a
        compute the relevance between I_a and I_b

For each item I_c which is collected from other nodes
 mentioned above
      compute the relevance between I_c and U_1
Get the top n relevant items of user U_1

Event III. deregister the downloading records: When the node withdraws, the downloading records maintained by this node in its hash table will not be available. Therefore, when node exits the network, the target node should send deregistration message to all the nodes which index the target node's downloading record. The corresponding nodes will delete the corresponding entry in the hash table it maintains when receiving the message. The algorithm is as follows: when the target node leaves the network, for every entry of the downloading list, hash the item name to obtain the identifier K, send deregistration request to the corresponding node according to K.

3   Experiment

In order to verify the performance of distributed collaborative filtering model, we built a system with 30 nodes, each node maintaining 20 to 30 downloading

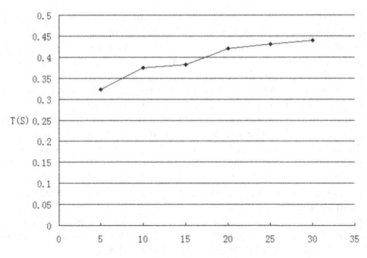

Fig. 5. The experimental result

records. Experiments are divided into six groups. At first, only five nodes participate, and each time increase 5 more nodes to participate in the system. In each experiment, a fixed node is chose to record required time to get the recommendation set. Each group of experiments was conducted five times, calculating the average as experimental result.

As show in figure 5, that node can get the recommendation set in a short period. And with the increase of the number of participating nodes, the time of obtaining recommendation set grows in a low rate, which proves that system has a very good scalability and is applicable to P2P network.

4   Conclusion

Collaborative filtering systems in e-commerce and other applications are more and more widely used. Addressing the sparsity and scalability of the centralized collaborative filtering algorithm, this paper proposes a distributed architecture. By maintaining the user downloading records in various nodes, using Chord as the routing algorithm for data search, designing corresponding inter-node message processing policy to enable the node to access the data needed by searching the DHT, and calculating the user-item relevance according to the equation derived from the probabilistic relevance model, the user can obtains the personalized recommendation set from other users without a central server.

References

1. Karypis, G.: Evaluation of item-based top-n recommendation algorithms. In: Proc. of the tenth international conference on Information and knowledge management, pp. 247–254 (2001)

2. Tveit, A.: Peer-to-peer based recommendation for mobile commerce. In: Proc. of the First International Mobile Commerce Workshop, pp. 26–29 (2001)
3. Stoica, I., Morris, R., Karger, D., Kaashoek, F., Balakrishnan, H.: Chord: A Scalable Peer-to-Peer Lookup Service for Internet Applications. In: Proc. ACM SIGCOMM Conf., pp. 149–160 (September 2001)
4. Linden, G., Smith, B., York, J.: Amazon com recommendations: Item-to-item collaborative filtering. IEEE Internet Computing, 76–80 (2003)
5. Balakrishnan, H., FransKaashoek, M., Karger, D., Morris, R., Stoica, I.: Looking up data in P2P systems. Communications of ACM 46(2), 43–48 (2003)
6. Peng, H., Bo, X., Fan, Y., Ruimin, S.: A scalable p2p recommender system based on distributed collaborative filtering. Expert systems with applications, 203–210 (2004)
7. Xue, G., Lin, C., Yang, Q., Xi, W., Zeng, H., Yu, Y., Chen, Z.: Scalable collaborative filtering using cluster-based smoothing. In: Proc. of the 28th Annual Int'l ACM SIGIR Conf., pp. 114–121 (2005)
8. Shakery, A., Zhai, C.: A probabilistic relevance propagation model for hypertext retrieval. In: Proc. of the 15th ACM International Conference on Information and Knowledge Management (CIKM 2006), pp. 550–558 (2006)
9. Wang, J., Pouwelse, J., Lagendijk, R., Reinders, M.R.J.: Distributed Collaborative Filtering for Peer-to-Peer File Sharing Systems. In: Proc. of the 21st Annual ACM Symposium on Applied Computing (2006)

Access Control for Cooperation Systems Based on Group Situation

Minsoo Kim[1], James B.D. Joshi[2], and Minkoo Kim[1]

[1] Graduate School of Information and Communication, Ajou University
Suwon, Korea (South)
{visual,minkoo}@ajou.ac.kr
[2] School of Information Science, University of Pittsburgh, PA, USA
jjoshi@mail.sis.pitt.edu

Abstract. Cooperation systems characterize many emerging environments such as ubiquitous and pervasive systems. Agent based cooperation systems have been proposed in the literature to address challenges of such emerging application environments. A key aspect of such agent based cooperation system is the group situation that changes dynamically and governs the requirements of the cooperation. While individual agent context is important, the overall cooperation behavior is more driven by the group context because of relationships and interactions between agents. Dynamic access control based on group situation is a crucial challenge in such cooperation systems. In this paper we propose a dynamic role based access control model for cooperation systems based on group situation. The model emphasizes capability based agent to role mapping and group situation based permission assignment to allow capturing dynamic access policies that evolve continuously.

Keywords: Group Situation, Access Control, Cooperation System.

1 Introduction

A cooperation system involves a group of diverse entities interacting with each other for achieving common goals. Cooperation based approaches have been recently being pursued as a promising way to build large and complex ubiquitous or pervasive application environments. Several cooperation based approaches such as Gaia [1] and community computing [2] have been proposed in the literature. These approaches focus on the design and implementation of cooperation systems in highly dynamic environments. In these approaches, the concept of role is used to define interactions among agents. This idea gives well-recognized advantages to system developers with regards to separation of concerns between algorithmic issues and the interaction issues, reuse of solution and experience, and dynamic system management of operation [3, 4].

Group situation based cooperation model was proposed as a model for designing cooperation using roles similar to approaches mentioned above by Kim et al. [5]. The main contribution of this model is to design interactions among roles by defining group situations. All agents perform their own action(s) and interaction(s) with others

E. Bertino and J.B.D. Joshi (Eds.): CollaborateCom 2008, LNICST 10, pp. 11–23, 2009.

based on the current group situation and, eventually, the goal of the group is achieved by such a situation flow [5]. The group situation is expressed by aggregation of context of agents within the group.

Situation-awareness in systems is an emerging technology that goes beyond context-awareness that makes pervasive systems more dynamic [5, 19]. Context, which refers to any useful information for the operation of an application, has become one of the key requirements of current and emerging systems, such as web services, ubiquitous systems, and business enterprises [9]. Context-awareness in such application provides capability for fulfilling user and environmental requirements. Moreover, in systems composed of multiple entities, for example multi-agent systems, awareness of group situation as well as individual situation is very crucial. For instance, one agent can decide to perform a certain authorized action based on its context, but the overall group context may require the interruption of that action. In summary, the group situation based cooperation model emphasizes appropriate cooperation among agents to ensure that the cooperation goal is achieved.

Existing models do not address security issues and in particular access control requirements within such cooperation systems. Access control refers to the process of limiting access to the resources of a system only to authorized programs, processes, or other systems so as to ensure that confidentiality, integrity and availability requirements are met [10]. Within a cooperation system there can be two types of access control requirements for cooperation systems. One is an access control to ensure authorized access to resources and information shared by agents, the other is access control related to the authorized interactions among agents.

Role-Based Access Control (RBAC) [10] and its variations have been found to be the most promising approaches for addressing access control issues related to complex and emerging systems. RBAC approach is very desirable in terms of powerful functions and flexibility for addressing the security needs of systems and applications. Moreover, it provides a mechanism for reducing the complexity, time, and potential security faults within the organization. To avail of these advantages of RBAC, various systems such as large enterprises and web services are adopting RBAC. Recently, Attribute-Based Access Control (ABAC) [11][12], Rule-Based RBAC (RB-RBAC) [13] and Context-RBAC [14][15] models that support dynamic user-role and role-permission assignments using knowledge about users and systems have been proposed.

Access control in cooperation system should consider the group situation in addition to individual context. For example, one agent has permission to an object, but sometimes the group might limit the permission depending on group situation. The main contribution of this paper is towards addressing this idea; i.e. *establishing access control mechanism based on group situation in cooperation system*. In this paper, we propose a group situation driven RBAC (GS-RBAC) model, which has the following key distinguishing characteristics.

- *Automatic user-role mapping.* In the cooperation systems, roles are subjects that perform their actions and interact with others, so user-role mapping is a process which finds the best user who can play the role. Therefore, capability of user is an important property in the mapping process, and capability matching methods such as agent matchmaking can be used for mapping users to roles dynamically and automatically.

- *Dynamic role-permission assignment based on group situation.* On a given group situation, each agent that is mapped to role performs its own actions and/or and engages in cooperative interactions for achieving common goals. To ensure success of these actions and interactions, proper permissions are given to proper roles depending on group situation.
- *Constraints for user-role mapping are different from those for role-permission assignment.* The former is context-based constraints to find a best user who can play a role, while the latter is group situation based constraints to assign permissions to the role. While the mapped roles to users do not change during cooperation, permissions are dynamically changed depending on changes of group situation.

The remainders of the paper are structured as follows. In section 2 we describe motivating example, and in section 3 we introduce situation-related researches and the group situation based cooperation model. In section 4, we present our proposed GS-RBAC model. Illustrative examples are described in section 5, and finally the conclusions and future work are discussed in section 6.

2 A Motivating Example – *Preparing Presentation*

Scene 1. John, head of personnel section, receives directions from his boss. He has to prepare a presentation within next 8 hours about a performance rating of all the employees in the company. This will involve the following tasks - analyzing employee data, researching sections, creating statistics, and preparing a presentation document.

Scene 2. John selects members to form a cooperation group to prepare the presentation - two for analyzing employee data, one for researching sections, one for statistics for the ranking, and one member for preparing a presentation document. They cooperate with each others, works individually. John has to make a schedule - when members need to cooperate and when they work alone. Each member has daily regular work that he/she has to do.

Scene 3. Member m_1 is analyzing employee data by using an employee database. He interacts with member m_2 who is researching sections. Member m_3 needs to work on the statistics and to interact with m_1 and m_2, and can access the employee database after m_1 finishes using.

Cooperation is frequently required for solving complex problem in computer systems as well as in human society. As shown in above examples, there are several issues in cooperation. First, which tasks are needed for cooperation should be analyzed - *cooperation process* (scene 1) should be identified. This process indicates which agents can engage in what type of interaction with which other agents and when. Second, it needs to find agents that are engaged in the defined cooperation - which can be referred to as the *organizing process* (scene 2). Note that cooperation dynamically assigned tasks of agents. Therefore, it is important to find agents that can perform cooperative takes defined in a cooperation process. Finally, access control needs to be defined to ensure that agents engage in authorized interactions and make only authorized access to resources shared among agents - which is basically the *access control process* (scene 3). Even though all the members in a group have permissions to access a resource, sometimes it needs to limit use of those permissions in order to ensure the success of cooperation.

3 Context, Situation, and Group Situation

3.1 Context and Situation

Attribute, context and situation are concepts representing knowledge about objects or systems and hence, at times it is difficult to clearly distinguish among them. Generally, an attribute is a specification that defines a property of an object, computing elements or system - e.g. size of file and age of human. Context is referred to as 'any information that can be used to characterize the situation of an entity (i.e. whether a person, place or object) that are considered relevant to the interaction between a user and an application, including the user and applications themselves'. [9]. Therefore, any attribute of a system can be a context and can be used for *manipulating* context. In other words, context is more conceptualized as a set of attributes. For example, aggregation of attributes *temperature* and *humidity* can manipulate context *weather*. We can say 'it is so hot' when temperature is 95F and humidity is 80%. Using context, the status of system can be represented in a more comprehensive form and made more human understandable.

The situation research has long history and now it has been re-focused to represent systems more comprehensively. Situation has several different definitions. First, McCarthy, the originator of the situation calculus, defines situation *'is the complete state of the universe at an instant of time'* [6]. Reiter formalized the situation calculus and argues situation *'is a finite sequence of actions. It's not a state, it's not a snapshot, it's a history'* [7]. In researches and systems which adopted McCarthy' definition, a situation is described by using properties of systems such as variables, attributes and context. In contrary, if a situation is a history, for example in GOLOG which is a programming language for describing situation calculus, the state of the world is described by functions and relations (fluent) relativized to a situation.

Recently, Stephan Yau et al. defines situation in the context of pervasive environment as follows [8]:

The situation of an application software system is an expression on previous device-action record over a period of time and/or the variation of a set of contexts relevant to the application software on the device over a period of time. Situation is used to trigger further device actions.

This definition seems to combine McCarthy and Reiter' definitions and provide a more comprehensive understanding. First, the concept of context which is one of major requirements of pervasive computing is inserted into situation. Second, they refer the purpose of situation which means to trigger the further actions of systems. Of course this is not a new, but it provides comprehensive way to researches for developing systems having ability of situation-awareness. However, this definition does not show what differences between context and situation are and what meaning (semantic) of situation is (situation is not just expression).

We define situation as follows:

Situation is a problematic state of a computational element. The problem is recognized by being aware context information, and it needs to plan (a sequence of actions) for solving the problem on the situation. Context information includes changes of context, relations between context as well as individual context.

Situation is a concept which includes planning as well as context awareness. Context information characterizes problem which has to be solved on a given situation, and a sequence of further actions are specified to solve the problem on the situation. Situation does not use to trigger actions, but the actions are triggered by recognizing a set of context information (context-awareness) and history of actions (planning). Therefore, situation-awareness means to recognize problem by context-awareness and to discover (plan) a sequence of actions for solving problem. One important difference between context and situation is that the former is domain dependent and the latter is system-dependent. In other words, situation is specified by each system while context may be shared by applications on same domain (sometimes on most systems). For example, 'hot' or 'temperature is 95F' may be understood as same meaning on most systems, but situation may be specified as different ways (different problems, different plans).

3.2 Group Situation Based Cooperation

To explain a group situation, we first define a cooperative group [5]. A group situation includes aggregation of individual context, relationship among those context, and relationship among individuals (agents). A group is a metaphor of cooperation system which is composed of multiple entities (agents), common goals, and a cooperation process. Moreover, when considering the dynamic environment such as a ubiquitous environment, dynamic group organization is required. Therefore we define the cooperative group including organization process in [5].

Definition of *group situation* is composed of two parts; context information and a sequence of cooperative actions. Context information means a status of agents, relation between agents, and changes of context within a group. Moreover it works as pre-conditions for cooperative actions with history of cooperation.

On a given situation s_i, each agent within a group performs actions listed in f_i. The result of agents' actions makes changes of group situation to s_j, and then agents perform actions in f_j. After all, a goal can be achieved by following group situations from s_0 to s_g (s_0 is a start situation when group organizes and s_g is a goal situation when cooperation ends). More detail description about group situation based cooperation model is described in [5]. Applications and examples using group situation based cooperation is shown in [2] with community computing paradigm which was proposed for building dynamic cooperation systems in ubiquitous environment.

4   Group Situation Based Access Control

The key idea behind group situation based cooperation model is that a group situation can be defined by aggregating agents' context and a cooperation process can be defined for each group situation. However, this model does not consider the access control issues for ensuring security for shared resources among agents. We propose an access control method that controls accesses to resources and agents based on group situation so that the agents and resources involved in the cooperation are protected while the cooperation goals are achieved. Existing RBAC variations do not support group context and fine-grained situation awareness, especially for agent-based cooperation environments. In the proposed secure cooperation model, actions of agent required for cooperation is driven by group situation. That is, the permissions required for performing agents' actions and interactions (i.e. cooperation) are driven by group situation.

For the proposed GS-RBAC model, we define following sets by extending the standard RBAC model [10].

- USERS: a set of users or autonomous software/hardware agents.
- ROLES: a set of roles defined within a cooperative group.
- OBJS: a set of objects within a cooperative group
- OPS: a set of applicable operations on OBJS
- PERS: a set of permissions, PERS $\subseteq$ OBJS × OPS
- UM: a many-to-many user-to-role mapping, UM $\subseteq$ USERS × ROLES
- PA: a many-to-many permission-to-role assignment, PA $\subseteq$ PERS × OLES

Additionally, for user-role mapping there are three constraint sets.

- CAPS: a set of capability of roles and users
- CONTEXTS: a set of context of role and users
- QOSS: a Set of QoS parameters of capabilities

4.1   User-Role Mapping

In the group situation based cooperation model [5], the group organizing process can be considered as user-role assignment process in traditional RBAC. When organizing a group, however, all agents are not assigned to roles, but only best agents are mapped to roles. In other words, the agent-role mapping process is to find the best agents that can play a given role. This is similar to the agent match-making and service discovery processes. Three constraints are used for user-role mapping in our model.

Capability Matching. To map a user to a role, a user should have capabilities that are depicted in the role descriptions. Role description includes role's capabilities for cooperating with others, and the cooperation process. Therefore, an agent should be able to act or interact with others according to the cooperation process which is required by the cooperative group.

Context-based constraints. Only users that satisfy context-based constraints can be candidates for final mapping to a role. These constraints come into effect only when a group is organized. Note that role-mapping in the cooperation model is a group organizing process. Therefore, if a user is mapped to a role, then this relation is not changed until the cooperative group is dissolved.

QoS filtering. There may be many users having same capability in large scale environments, so several users can be candidates for assuming a role. Therefore, we need to select proper agents among them. QoS (Quality of Service) is a popular way to filter or prune bad ones during agent matchmaking and web service discovery. Hence, for role-mapping we adopt this method and use the following QoS parameters introduced in [17]: *agent trustworthiness, reliability, availability, robustness* of capabilities, and *response time*.

4.2   Role-Permission Assignment

Standard RBAC supports only static role-permission assignment, and hence is not adequate for the dynamic computing environment where permissions need to be assigned dynamically. More recent extended RBAC models have focused on capturing context information and hence support dynamic assignments.

A key aspect of the proposed model is that the permission assignment is dynamically driven by changes of group situations. Since objects within a group are shared among agents, conflicts and security problems can result during cooperation, if only static permission assignment is considered and proposed situation information is not incorporated in the access control policy. Even though several RBAC variations support dynamic role-permission assignment, they are not applicable for cooperation systems because only context of individual agent is considered for the assignment. Each agent works for cooperation by grasping status of others and group. Therefore role-permission assignment should support cooperation among agents. In order to do this, we propose role-permission assignment based on group situation. This means that the role-permission assignment should support all agents' actions on a given situation, because each agent takes actions as cooperation in group situation based cooperation model. All permissions that are required for performing cooperation are given to agents within the group in a given situation. Given the start situation s_0 and the goal situation s_g, while user-role mapping is done once in s_0, role-permission assignment is done in every intermediate group situation.

Table 1 lists status predicates of the group situation based access control model. First column describes predicates, second column specifies evaluation domain for predicates, and third column describes semantics of the predicates.

Predicate *u_mapped (u, r, c, s)* refers to user-role mapping in situation *s*, and *u_mapped (u,r,c,s)*, *u_mapped (u, r, c, x, s)*, and *u_mapped (u, r, c, x, q, s)* refer to user-role mapping with matching capability *c*, satisfying context-based constraints *x*, and filtering QoS parameter *q*. Each constraint can be a set, for example *u_mapped (u_1, r_1, {c_1, c_2,}, {x_1, x_2, x_3}, q_1)* indicates "user u_1 is mapped to r_1 with capabilities {c_1, c_2 | move(), compute()}, context-based constraints {x_1, x_2, x_3 | time=3p.m., age>30, location=inBuilding}, and QoS parameter {q_1, reliability>80}".

Now we introduce the following axioms, based on those earlier proposed by Joshi et al. in GTRBAC [20], to capture the key relationships among status predicates in Table 1. In our cooperation model, especially, user-role mapping is only accomplished in the starting situation s_0, and de-mapped in the goal situation s_g. This means that users mapped to roles can activate the roles in all situations (from s_0 to s_g).

Table 1. Status predicates of group situation based RBAC

Events	Predicates	Evaluation Domains	Semantics
P: set of permissions, R: set of role, U: set of users, C: set of capabilities, Q: set of QoS parameters, X: set of user context, S: set of group situation, $r \in R$, $p \in P$, $u \in U$, $c \subset C$, $q \subset Q$, $x \subset X$, $s \in S$			
Role Enabling	enabled (r, s)	R×S	r is enabled in s
User-Role Mapping	u_mapped (u, r, s)	U×R×S	u is mapped to r in s
	u_mapped (u, r, c, s)	U×R×C×S	u is mapped to r with c in s (c is a sub-set of C)
	u_ mapped (u,r,c,x,s)	U×R×C×X×S	u is mapped to r with c and x in s (x is a sub-set of X)
	u_ mapped (u,r,c,x,q,s)	U×R×C×X×Q×S	u is mapped to r with c, x, and q in s (q is a sub-set of Q)
Role-Permission Assignment	p_assigned (p, r, s)	P×R×S	p is assigned to r in s
Run-Time Events	can_activate (u,r,s)	U×R×S	u can activate r in s
	can_acquire (u, p, s)	U×P×S	u can acquire p in s
	r_can_acquire (u,p,r,s)	U×P×R×S	u can acquire p through r in s
	can_be_acquired (p,r,s)	P×R×S	p can be acquired through r in s
	acquires (u,p,t)	U×P×T	u acquires p in s
	r_acquires (u,p,r,s)	U×P×R×S	u acquires p through r in s

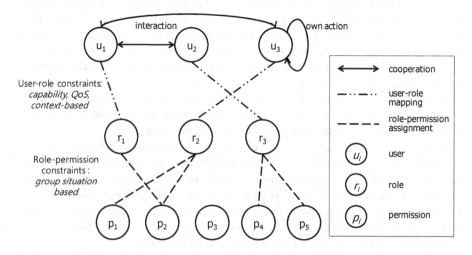

Fig. 1. Group situation based access control in cooperation system. In run time, users mapped to roles cooperate with each other according to the cooperation process described for roles. Capability matching, context-based constraints, QoS parameters are used for user-role mapping, and role-permission assignment is accomplished depending on changes of group situation.

Next axioms show semantic relations between status predicates.

Axioms. For all $r \in$ ROLES, $p \in$ PERS, $u \in$ USERS, $s \in$ SITUATIONS, the following implications hold:

1. u_mapped $(u,r,s) \rightarrow$ can_activate(u,r,s)
2. u_mapped $(u,r,s_0) \rightarrow$ can_activate (u,r,s_i), $i \in \{0, \ldots, g\}$, $s_0 =$ starting situation, s_g=goal situation
3. p_assigned $(p,r,s) \rightarrow$ can_be_acqured(p,r,s)
4. can_activate$(u,r,s) \wedge$ can_be_acquired$(p,r,s) \rightarrow$ can_acquire(u,p,s)

Fig.1 illustrates the basic operations of group situation based cooperation model. Users are mapped to roles based on capability matching and QoS parameters filtering as well as context-based constraints. Users mapped roles are assigned proper permissions to cooperate with each other depending on changes of group situations.

5   Illustrative Examples

In this Section, we revisit the scenarios depicted in Section 2 to illustrate the proposed model. Fig. 2 shows role description for the example.

```
Role presenter
    capability: present();
    context-constraints : age>30, position= departmentManager;
    QoS: trustiness>90, reliability>90; availability=100;
Role dataAnalyzer
    capability: useDatabase();
    context-constraints: part = data-analysis part, availableTime > 5;
    QoS: trustiness>80, availability=70;
Role statistician
    capability: takeStatistics(), useStatisticsProgram(), useDatabase();
    context-constraints : part=statistics, availableTime>7, position > sectionChief;
    QoS: trustiness>90, reliability>80; availability=80;
Role sectionResearcher
    capability: none;
    context-constraints : availableTime>5;
    QoS: trustiness>60, availability=80;
Role documentWriter
    capability: useDatabase(), makePresentationFile(), useDrawingProgram()
    context- constraints: position > sectionChief, availableTime>7
    QoS: trustiness>90, reliability>90; availability=90;
```

Fig. 2. Role Description of '*preparing presentation*' example

Five roles are designed for achieving the common goal, and four group situations are defined to cooperation among roles. In the starting situation s_0, all roles are mapped to roles, and permissions are assigned to roles based on group situation. As we can see in cooperation description, a group situation is expressed by user context.

Table 2. Elements in *'preparing presentation'* example

USERS	$\{u_1,...,u_6$ I John, Daniel, James, David, Jack, Joe$\}$
ROLES	$\{r_1,...,r_5$ I Presenter, Data analyzer, statistician, section researcher, document writer $\}$
OBJS	$\{o_1,...,o_6$ I employ-database, presentation-file, statistic-file, data-analyzing-file, research-section-file, presentation-room$\}$
OPS	$\{op_1, ...,op_5$Iread, write, modify, delete, enter$\}$
PERS	$\{p_1,...,p_{13}$I(op$_1$,o$_1$), (op$_2$,o$_4$), (op$_2$, o$_5$), (op$_1$,o$_4$), (op$_3$,o$_4$), (op$_1$,o$_5$), (op$_2$,o$_3$), (op$_3$,o$_5$), (op$_2$, o$_2$), (op$_1$, o$_2$), (op$_3$, o$_2$), (op$_5$, o$_6$),(op$_3$,o$_4$) $\}$
SITUATIONS	$\{s_0,s_1,s_2,s_g$IStarting, TakingStatistics, MakingPresentationFile, Presentation$\}$
CAPS	$\{c_1,...,c_6$Ipresent(), useDatabase(), takeStatistics(), useStatisticsProgram(), makePresentationFile(), useDrawingProgram()$\}$
CONTETS	$\{x_1,...,x_4$Iage,position,part,time$\}$
QOSS	$\{q_1,...,q_3$Itrustworthyness, reliability, availability$\}$

Users mapped to roles share objects within the group, and permissions for those objects may change with time. For example, presentation file is authorized to Joe (r_4) for writing operation in s_2, and to John and Joe for reading operation in s_g. This dynamic permission assignment supports the success of cooperation - each user can act or interact without any limitation for accessing the objects or without conflicts with other's accesses. Table 2 lists elements shown in the example.

Predicate-expressions are listed by separated situation in Table. 3. Second column shows run-time events indicated by axioms described in chapter 4.

Table 3. Predicate expression of example 'preparing presentation'

Situation	Assignment(mapping)	Run-time Event
s_0	u_mapped $(u_1, r_1, c_1, (x_1,x_2), (q_1,q_2,q_3), s_0)$	can_activate(u_1,r_1,s_0)
	u_mapped $(u_2, r_2, c_2, (x_3,x_4), (q_1, q_3), s_0)$	can_activate(u_2,r_2,s_0)
	u_mapped $(u_3, r_2, c_2, (x_3,x_4), (q_1, q_3), s_0)$	can_activate(u_3,r_2,s_0)
	u_mapped $(u_4, r_3, (c_2,c_3,c_4), (x_2,x_3,x_4), (q_1,q_2,q_3), s_0)$	can_activate(u_4,r_3,s_0)
	u_mapped $(u_5, r_4, \emptyset,x_4, (q_1, q_3), s_0)$	can_activate(u_5,r_4,s_0)
	u_mapped $(u_6, r_5, (c_2,c_5,c_6), (x_2,x_4), (q_1,q_2,q_3), s_0)$	can_activate(u_6,r_5,s_0)
		can_acquire(u_2,p_1,s_0)
		can_acquire(u_3,p_1,s_0)
	p_assigned(p_1,r_2,s_0)	can_acquire(u_3,p_2,s_0)
	p_assigned(p_2,r_2,s_0)	can_acquire(u_3,p_2,s_0)
	p_assigned(p_3,r_4,s_0)	can_acquire(u_5,p_3,s_0)

Table 3. (*continued*)

Situation	Assignment(mapping)	Run-time Event
s_1	p_assigned(p_4,r_2,s_1) p_assigned(p_5,r_2,s_1) p_assigned(p_1,r_3,s_1) p_assigned(p_4,r_3,s_1) p_assigned(p_6,r_3,s_1) p_assigned(p_7,r_3,s_1) p_assigned(p_6,r_4,s_1) p_assigned(p_8,r_4,s_1) p_assigned(p_9,r_5,s_1)	can_acquire(u_2,p_4,s_1) can_acquire(u_3,p_4,s_1) can_acquire(u_2,p_5,s_1) can_acquire(u_3,p_4,s_1) can_acquire(u_4,p_1,s_1) can_acquire(u_4,p_6,s_1) can_acquire(u_4,p_7,s_1) can_acquire(u_3,p_6,s_1) can_acquire(u_5,p_8,s_1) can_acquire(u_6,p_9,s_1)
s_2	p_assigned(p_{10},r_1,s_2) p_assigned(p_{11},r_1,s_2) p_assigned(p_{12},r_2,s_2) p_assigned(p_{13},r_3,s_2) p_assigned(p_{12},r_4,s_2) p_assigned(p_{11},r_5,s_2)	can_acquire(u_1,p_{10},s_2) can_acquire(u_1,p_{11},s_2) can_acquire(u_2,p_{12},s_2) can_acquire(u_3,p_{12},s_2) can_acquire(u_4,p_{13},s_2) can_acquire(u_5,p_{12},s_2) can_acquire(u_6,p_{11},s_2)
s_g	p_assigned(p_{10},r_1,s_g) p_assigned(p_{10},r_5,s_g)	can_acquire(u_1,p_{10},s_g) can_acquire(u_6,p_{10},s_g)

6 Conclusions and Future Works

In this paper, we have addressed the issues of access control in cooperation systems. We focused mainly on group situation beyond individual context as a key aspect of cooperation systems. Being aware of the group situation is an emerging requirement for cooperative systems such as MAS. Since objects are shared within the group, there might be conflicts or limitation of accesses to resources during cooperation. For achieving the goal of a cooperative group successfully, permissions which are required during cooperation should be given to users within the group. In the proposed model users cooperate with others based on group situation, moreover permission assignment is also based on group situation. Each user in the group acts or interacts with others on a given situation (cooperation), and permissions are given to users on same situation for supporting users' actions (permission assignment). We showed a feasible example based on proposed model with status predicates.

We plan to extend the proposed model in several directions. First, role-hierarchy introduced some RBAC models can be considered for efficient role and permission management. Moreover, for cooperation among users hierarchical relationship can be helpful. Second, we plan to extend the policy specification - language to conform with web-standard.

Acknowledgments. This research is supported by Foundation of ubiquitous computing and networking project (UCN) Project, the Ministry of Knowledge Economy (MKE) 21st Century Frontier R&D Program in Korea and a result of subproject UCN 08B3-S2-10M and this research also supported by the US National Science Foundation award IIS-0545912.

References

1. Wooldridge, M., Jennings, N.R.: The Gaia Methodology for Agent-oriented Analysis and Design. Autonomous Agents and Multi-Agent Systems 3, 285–312 (2000)
2. Jung, Y., Lee, J., Kim, M.: Community Computing Model supporting Community Situation based Cooperation and Conflict Resolution. In: Obermaisser, R., Nah, Y., Puschner, P., Rammig, F.J. (eds.) SEUS 2007. LNCS, vol. 4761, pp. 47–56. Springer, Heidelberg (2007)
3. Cabri, G., Leonardi, L., Zambonelli, F.: BRAIN: A Framework for Flexible Role-based Interactions in Multi-agent Systems. In: Meersman, R., Tari, Z., Schmidt, D.C. (eds.) CoopIS 2003, DOA 2003, and ODBASE 2003. LNCS, vol. 2888, pp. 145–161. Springer, Heidelberg (2003)
4. Kim, M., Jung, Y., Lee, J., Kim, M.: Context-based Cooperation Architecture for Ubiquitous Environment. In: Youn, H.Y., Kim, M., Morikawa, H. (eds.) UCS 2006. LNCS, vol. 4239, pp. 171–182. Springer, Heidelberg (2006)
5. Kim, M., Lee, J., Kim, M.: Group Situation based Cooperation Model. In: 2nd International Conference on Convergence Information Technology, pp. 1372–1377. IEEE Computer Society Press, Los Alamitos (2007)
6. McCarthy, J., Hayes, P.J.: Some Philosophical Problems from the Standpoint of Artificial Intelligence. Machine Intelligence 4, 463–502 (1969)
7. Reiter, R.: The situation Calculus Ontology. Electronic News Journal on Reasoning about Actions and Changes (1997),
   http://www.ida.liu.se/ext/etai/rac/notes/1997/09/note.html
8. Yau, S.S., Wang, Y., Karim, F.: Development of Situation-Aware Application Software for Ubiquitous Computing Environments. In: 26th Annual International Computer Software and Applications Conference, pp. 233–238. IEEE Computer Society Press, Los Alamitos (2002)
9. Dey, A.K.: Understanding and Using Context. Personal and Ubiquitous Computing, Special Issue on Situated Interaction and Ubiquitous Computing 5(1), 4–7 (2001)
10. Sandhu, R.S., Coyne, E.J., Feinsteing, H.L., Younman, C.E.: Role-Based Access Control Models. IEEE computer 29(2), 38–47 (1996)
11. Yuan, E., Tong, J.: Attributed based Access Control (ABAC) for web services. In: IEEE International Conference on Web Services, pp. 561–569. IEEE Computer Society Press, Los Alamitos (2005)
12. Priebe, T., Dobmeier, W., Kamprath, N.: Supporting Attribute-based Access Control with Ontologies. In: 1st International Conference on Availability, Reliability and Security, pp. 465–472. IEEE Computer Society Press, Los Alamitos (2006)
13. Kern, A., Walhorn, C.: Rule Support for Role-Based Access Control. In: 10th ACM Symposium on Access control models and Technologies, pp. 130–138. ACM, New York (2005)
14. Kulkarni, D., Tripathi, A.: Context-Aware Role-based Access Control in Pervasive Computing Systems. In: 13th ACM Symposium on Access control models and Technologies, pp. 113–122. ACM, New York (2008)
15. Kuamr, A., Karnik, N., Chafle, G.: Context Sensitivity in Role-Based Access Controls. ACM SIGOPS Operating Systems Review 36(3), 53–66 (2002)
16. Yau, S.S., Yao, Y., Banga, V.: Situation-Aware Access Control for Service-Oriented Autonomous Decentralized Systems. In: International Symposium on Autonomous Decentralized Systems, pp. 17–24. IEEE Computer Society Press, Los Alamitos (2005)

17. Maximilien, E.M., Singh, M.P.: A Framework and Ontology for Dynamic Web Services Selection. IEEE Internet Computing 8(5), 84–93 (2004)
18. Barwise, J., John, P.: Situations and Attitudes. Journal of Philosophy 77, 668–691 (1981)
19. You, S.S., Huang, D., Gong, H., Seth, S.: Development and runtime support for situation-aware application software in ubiquitous computing environment. In: 28th International Conference on Computer Software and Applications, pp. 452–472. IEEE Computer Society Press, Los Alamitos (2004)
20. Joshi, B.D.J., Bertino, E., Ghafoor, A.: Temporal Hierarchies and Inheritance Semantics for GTRBAC. In: 7th ACM Symposium on Access control models and Technologies, pp. 74–83. ACM, New York (2002)

Web Canary: A Virtualized Web Browser to Support Large-Scale Silent Collaboration in Detecting Malicious Web Sites*

Jiang Wang, Anup Ghosh, and Yih Huang

Center for Secure Information Systems,
George Mason University,
Fairfax VA 22030, USA
{jwanga,aghosh1}@gmu.edu, huangyih@cs.gmu.edu

Abstract. Malicious Web content poses a serious threat to the Internet, organizations and users. Current approaches to detecting malicious Web content employ high-powered honey clients to scan the Web for potentially malicious pages. These approaches, while effective at detecting malicious content, have the drawbacks of being few and far between, presenting a single snapshot in time of very dynamic phenomena, and having artificial test data. To address these problems, we developed a virtualized Web browser that uses large-scale collaboration to identify URLs that host malicious content on a continuing basis by building in an elective reporting system. The system, which we call a Web canary, runs a standard Web browser in a known, pristine OS every time the browser starts. Users not only report malicious URLs but also benefit from protection against malicious content. Experimental results show that it can detect the malicious Web pages effectively with acceptable overhead.

Keywords: Web browser security, honey client, malicious code, spyware, botnets, virtualization.

1 Introduction

Malicious Web content is a common vector for stealthy malicious software to infect and compromise a user's computer without his or her knowledge. In an organization, if one user's computer is compromised, the attacker can use that machine as a stepping stone to attack other computers within the organization. Some websites will deliberately host malicious content to attack users' machines in order to hijack their machines to serve as bots in a botnet, spam relays, or for fraud and other computer crime purposes. On the other hand, a website may unintentionally host malicious content, via third-party arrangements, such as Google AdSense software, user-contributed content, such as blog sites, and

---

* This work was supported in part by DARPA under contract W31P4Q-07-C-0244 and the National Science Foundation under grant CNS-0716323.

E. Bertino and J.B.D. Joshi (Eds.): CollaborateCom 2008, LNICST 10, pp. 24–33, 2009.

third-party software, such as visitor counters [10]. In addition, a compromised website may also host malicious code. Hosting third party content, especially advertising, is very common on the Web today, and makes finding, tracking, and black-listing websites challenging.

To actively detect these malicious websites, researchers have devised honey clients [1]. Unlike a honeypot that sits passively waiting for attacks, a honey client is usually a well-provisioned computer (or computers) driven by a program to crawl the Internet and detect malicious Web servers. It has high accuracy and can detect zero-day attacks. On the other hand, current honey clients also suffer from: 1) inadequate data about which URLs to visit; 2) temporal dynamics – they capture a snapshot in time only for the sites they visit; 3) sites that use CAPTCHAs or passwords to foil automated Web crawling; 4) following links embedded in multi-media content (such as Adobe flash or Microsoft Silverlight); 5) scalability – it is hard to crawl the entire Internet within a short time interval.

One drawback of the current honey clients is that they are driven programmatically, and cannot mimic some human behavior. In addition, honey clients tend to be few and far between because most of them are only deployed in some research laboratories. To address these issues, we employ the power of silent collaboration through Web browsing: we give the end user a honey client disguised as a Web browser. The user uses it as his or her normal browser, while our software determines if the Web browser downloaded any malicious content to the virtual machine (VM) it transparently runs in. If malicious content is detected, we notify the user, report the website to a server on the Internet, then revert the VM to its pristine state.

We take advantage of virtualization to run a snapshot of the pristine operating system (OS) every time the browser is launched. The VM has only one active application – the Web browser. So it is easy to apply anomaly detection. Perhaps more significantly, by distributing it as a Web browser, we have the ability to form a very large distributed honey client network with millions of users. While the user participates in this community of distributed honey clients, the user is also protected from the malicious content infecting his or her own OS.

We call this kind of personal honey client a 'Web canary' after the birds used in coal mines to detect poisonous gases. In our case, when the Web canary dies, or more appropriately notifies the user that an unauthorized change has been made to the VM, we capture and report the offending URL and revert the VM back to its pristine state with user approval. The Web canary browser behaves identically to a normal Web browser, except that it runs in its own VM transparently to the user.

Since the VM is restored from a snapshot when the browser is launched, it is feasible to detect malicious changes to the OS. We pre-define the normal system interaction activities of the Web browser, such as caching and cookies. The Web canary browser signals when anything else on the system changes after the browser visited a URL. Sometimes, a user may open multiple browser windows at once. In order to determine which Web page is malicious among those, we perform time correlation heuristics to correlate the unauthorized changes to the most closely time-correlated URL. In addition, we collect these malicious URLs and send them, with user permission, to a server to record all the malicious URLs visited by Web canaries. This information, in turn, can be used by organizations, such as the Anti-Phishing Working Group, or OpenDNS to label URLs as malicious.

To demonstrate the feasibility of the Web canary idea, we built a prototype Web canary using Microsoft®Internet Explorer (IE) running on Windows XP, and VMware®Workstation. In Section 2, we describe related work and how our approach leverages prior work as well as the contribution of our work. Section 3 describes the design of Web canaries, and Section 4 describes its implementation. We evaluate the performance of Web canaries in Section 5. Section 6 concludes the paper with discussion of results.

2   Related Work

A honeypot is a trap set to attract, detect, deflect, capture, or in some manner counteract attempts at unauthorized use of information systems. Most early honeypots are server honeypots that run vulnerable software to lure attackers into attacking those servers. Recently, honey clients were developed by researchers to check Web servers for client-side exploits, such as HoneyMonkey [1], MITRE's HoneyClient [2],Capture – HPC [3] and [10].

All of above honey clients suffer from the problem that it is difficult to mimic human behavior to get past CAPTCHAs and authentication mechanisms. In addition, honey clients tend to be few and far between and only capture a snapshot of the Web in time. Given the fast-changing, dynamic nature of not only the Web, but also threats, a solution is needed that can be widely distributed while continuously capturing malicious activity from websites people are actually visiting. Web canaries enable this solution by letting the end user actually be the driver.

Since the Web canary is implemented as a Web browser, it has the potential to be widely distributed on an Internet scale. Also, Web canaries get around CAPTCHAs and authentication issues that honey clients normally suffer. Finally, the URLs visited by Web canaries represent ground truth on meaningful URLs since they represent the actual websites users visit.

Related work on sandboxing browsers can be divided into two classes: weak isolation, such as IE 7 protected mode [14], ZoneAlarm®Force Field [13], Google Chrome[20], and strong isolation, such as browser virtual appliance [17] and browser operating system [11]. Web canary provides strong isolation because of the whole system virtualization approach and also provides a detection mechanism to detect and report malicious URLs.

In addition, some researchers work in programming language analysis and browser-level add-ons to enhance the browser security, such as [6] [7] [8] [15] [18] [16]. They are complementary to the Web canary since we mainly focus on the OS level. Also, King et.al [21] are attempting to build a secure browser from scratch and SpyProxy [12] uses execution-based analysis to protect users.

Another related class of work focuses on how to use the log files from firewall collaboratively to generate black lists of potentially malicious sites based on their firewall intrusion attempts [19]. We think collaboration on intrusion records enables greater understanding of adversarial methods. However, the work in [19] focuses on firewall records, which will record blind attempts to access open ports behind firewalls, while our approach will share records about actual intrusions against a VM on end hosts.

3   Design

The goal of the Web canary is to detect and collect the malicious URLs without any specific knowledge of attacks themselves. To this end, we leverage virtualization technologies to run the common and vulnerable Web browser in a VM. Although a VM is equipped with a complete (guest) OS, its use is restricted to the browser application. Any other applications launched in the VM will be flagged as potentially malicious activity. The VM starts from a suspended state in pristine condition when the user launches the browser. This method provides fast start-up time as well as ensures the VM starts from a known good state. As the browser runs, we monitor system events in the VM. We also set up a specific folder for files downloaded by the user. Any other changes to the guest OS are treated as intrusion and we need to record the offending URL and report it to a central server.

3.1   System Monitoring and Filtering Module

Similar to other honey client solutions, a key requirement for the Web canary is a reliable and comprehensive monitor for file system and process creation events to detect potentially malicious behavior. We prefer a kernel-level monitor, because sufficient context is available in the kernel for detecting malicious websites and it is more difficult to subvert. Also, the monitor module should be able to filter out the normal behaviors of the Web browser.

3.2   URL Collecting Module

Once an unauthorized event is detected, we attempt to associate it with a particular website or URL. For this purpose, we create a browser add-on to capture the URLs requests made by the browser. Upon receiving system change events and visited URLs, we correlate them together. Correlating URLs to system changes is straightforward when Web pages are loaded one after another singly. In the presence of concurrent sessions, however, we cannot absolutely determine which one(s) of them cause malicious events. Instead, we list all the concurrently opening URLs as potentially malicious. A user can subsequently visit the listed URLs one by one in the Web canary (or use a pure honey client) and check the results. Note that there is a subtle difference between the state of multiple Web pages opened and the action of opening multiple pages at the same time. The former happens more frequently while the latter happens less frequently. Only the latter will incur some difficulties for correlating URLs to the events.

3.3 Auto-Reversion

When a malicious website is detected, the Web canary notifies the user, reports the offending website to our server on the Internet, and asks permission to revert the VM to its pristine state. We also provide an option to schedule an auto-reversion of the VM to its pristine state upon the detection of unauthorized events.

3.4 Persistent Storage

When reverting the VM after malware is detected, no information can be kept for that VM. This may cause problems if the user wants to save certain data. To address this problem, we introduce persistent storage (PS), a shared directory accessible by the VM that resides on the host file system or a networked file system. We restrict the portion of the host system visible to the guest OS only to the shared directory. This limits the access of a malicious or compromised guest OS to only the shared directory.

This approach ensures users can save documents from the temporary guest OS on to the host OS while not exposing the rest of the host system to the untrusted guest. Likewise, we use this shared directory to store our log files of monitoring module and URL collecting module running in the guest OS. In addition, we save personal browser data such as bookmarks, history, cookies by copying it to the PS before reversion and restore it after reversion.

3.5 Attacks That Web Canaries Cannot Detect

Since the web canary detects the malicious websites by detecting the abnormal changes in the guest OS, it cannot detect malicious activities that do not change system state, e.g. phishing attacks. One limitation of the current implementation is that we do not report in-memory changes to the browser process itself that stay resident (*i.e.*,changes that do not crash the browser or spawn new processes). We note that these exploits are removed after the browser is terminated or its VM reverted. In addition, our current approach may mistakenly attribute a URL as malicious when there is a time bomb and the user opened multiple Web pages.

4 Implementation

In this section, we describe how the system is implemented for Microsoft Windows XP host and Windows XP guest, using IE 6.x as the browser. Fig. 1 is the architecture for the Web canary. We use VMware Workstation^{TM} as the virtualization layer, because it is easy to install, support Windows and have live snapshot function. We also developed different versions using the free VMware server and VMware player to reduce the cost of deployment. The browser and monitor module ("Capture Client" in the Fig. 1) are running inside a VM. This implementation has two advantages: 1) the virtual machine monitor provides

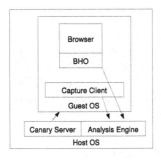

Fig. 1. Architecture of Web canary   **Fig. 2.** User Interface of Canary Server

strong isolation between the host OS and the guest OS. Even if the guest OS is compromised by malware, it is difficult for malware to penetrate the virtual machine monitor and infect the host OS; 2) after the Web canary detects the malware inside the guest OS, it can easily remove the malware by reverting the VM to a pristine state (snapshot). The main components for the Web canary browser shown in Fig. 1 are as follows:

1. A Brower Helper Object (BHO) which can capture all the URLs visited by IE. It then writes the URLs to a log file in PS.
2. Capture Client [3] which is able to monitor files, processes and registry changes in the Windows OS at kernel level. It also supports exclusion lists to filter out the normal changes.
3. Analysis Engine which reads the log files of the BHO and Capture Client and correlates system changes to the URL according the rule described in §3.2.
4. Canary Server which shows the health state of the guest OS (whether malware is detected or not) and can start, stop or revert the VM automatically. Fig. 2 is the GUI of the Canary Server. Canary Server can also send the detected malicious URLs to a remote central server with user's permission. The central server then saves it into a database. Currently, the central server does not authenticate the client (Canary Server) for ease of use. The central server could enforce a maximum traffic from a given user to mitigate the effect of malicious users who try to launch a DoS attack.
5. Persistent Storage (PS) which is a shared folder between the guest OS and the host OS. In the guest OS, only the BHO and Capture Client can write to this folder.

5   Evaluation

In this section, we present experimental evaluation results of the Web canary to measure its ability to detect malicious content as well as its performance overhead on a physical machine. The Web canary has not yet been released for download, so we are not able to measure its large-scale detection performance.

5.1   Testbed

Our test-bed is a Dell Precision 690 workstation with Dual-core 3.0 GHz CPU and 8GB memory. The host OS is Window XP Professional x64 edition with SP2, and the guest OS is Windows XP Professional with SP2. We use VMware Workstation 6.03. For the VM, we allocate 256 MB memory and 8 GB disk space, and installed VMware tools to support shared folder and improve user experience. The browser application is IE 6 with SP2.

5.2   Effectiveness to Detect Malicious Web Pages

To test the effectiveness of Web canaries in detecting malicious Web pages, we visited some known malicious Web pages with both the Web canary browser and the Capture Honey Client, which serves as a baseline for detection of malicious URLs. Then we compare the results.

First, we used the Capture Honey Client to find active malicious Web pages, from the potential list of malicious URLs obtained from [9] (which was scanned by Capture Honey Client one year ago). Interestingly, among all the 1937 Web pages that were previously classified as malicious by the Capture Honey Client (CHC), only 66 of them are still malicious now. This verifies our assertion that malicious websites change frequently, and using the powerful, but single honey client only provides a snapshot in time. Among the 1937 Web pages, we select all the malicious Web pages detected by CHC as well as others randomly chosen for a total of 302 Web pages. Then we use the Web canary browser and CHC to visit them one by one. The results are shown in Table 5.2.

Table 5.2 shows the number of Web pages in each class. "Malicious" is the Web pages classified as malicious by either Web canary or CHC. "Benign" means no malicious behavior detected. "Removed" means the Web page has been taken down. From Table 5.2, we can see that the Web canary browser detected all the malicious Web pages that are also detected by CHC. The numbers for benign and removed Web pages for web canary and CHC are different because CHC uses network response to attribute a Web page as "Removed" when it gets error codes 404 or 403. It cannot detect that a Web page is replaced by a removal notice page or redirect to the parent domain. However, the web canary is used by a human, so we report websites as removed when we observe this.

This experiment shows that all the malicious Web pages detected by the CHC are also detected by the Web canary. However the processes are quite different. For CHC, it first knows the URL and then visits that URL to see if anything malicious happens. For the Web canary, one of the authors inputs the URLs

Table 1. Web pages visited by the Web canary browser and Capture Honey Client

	Malicious	Benign	Removed	Total
Web canary	66	110	126	302
Capture Honey Client	66	203	33	302

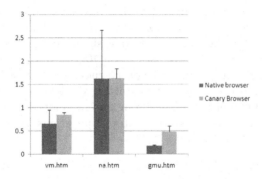

Fig. 3. Delays when loading a Web page

to visit the Web pages (one by one), then Canary Server reports detection of malicious Web pages. However, this is not the normal envisioned use of the Web canary, but rather a crafted experiment to allow us to compare detection capabilities. Normally, a user will use the Web canary as his or her regular browser. As a result, the Web canary will detect Web pages that are visited by users including those that require authentication or CAPTCHA challenges.

5.3 Performance Evaluation

Our solution is designed for personal everyday use by any user. As a result, our solution should not introduce significant delays in using a Web browser or the user will not use it. There are two types of execution performance overhead we consider: (1) the start-up time to load the VM and the browser and (2) page load time. The start-up penalty is taken every time the user starts the browser, but not for every website the user visits.

We first test page load time. The result is shown in Fig. 3. To minimize the effect of variability in network traffic between tests, we downloaded three Web pages from vmware.com, nationalgeographic.com and gmu.edu; saved it to a local Web server, and then visited each of them six times. The Fig. 3 shows the average time and the standard deviation. The black bar shows the delay for loading the Web page from a native IE 6 browser running on the host. The gray bar shows the delay for loading a Web page from the Web canary browser. The unit is sec. The Web canary browser introduces a small delay when loading vm.htm and ng.htm. The delay for loading gmu.htm from Web canary browser is bigger than that of native browser but still within 0.5 sec.

Table 2. Delays when reverting a virtual machine

	Delay for cold start (s)	Delay for warm start (s)
Web canary browser	12	7
Native browser	3.0	0.7

Table 2 shows performance results in starting the Web canary from a cold start and a warm start and similar performance measures for starting the browser natively on the host OS. The Web canary has significantly longer start-up time than the native browser (4x for cold start and 10x for warm start) because the VM software and a 256 MB memory file of the guest OS loads before the browser starts. This penalty is taken only when starting the browser for the first time, not during normal browser operation. From a user standpoint, the starting time is still on par with the times to start desktop applications, however.

6   Conclusion

In this paper, we present a system that can leverage a large, distributed network of users, who simply by using a standard Web browser, silently collaborate to detect and report malicious Web pages. In contrast to traditional honey clients, the user drives the browser as normal, but in the process, the Web canary will actively detect malicious Web content, while reporting the Web pages to a server on the Internet. The advantages of this method are that it can get meaningful URLs from users and easily visit Web pages that require CAPTCHAs or passwords. Another significant advantage is the user's machine is protected from malicious Web content that he or she may have loaded. To determine the viability of the approach, we built a prototype of Web canary. This prototype runs IE in a VMware VM, uses the client part of Capture to monitor the OS states, and a Browser Helper Object to capture URLs. We also developed an Analysis Engine to correlate the unauthorized changes to the URLs. Once a malicious Web page is detected, we provide an auto-revert feature to revert the VM to its pristine state. We also provide a persistent storage via a shared directory on the host for users to save data.

The experimental results presented here show that the Web canary can detect all the malicious Web pages detected by Capture Honey Client. It can be also used to detect the websites requiring password authentication or CAPTCHAs. In the future, we will try to correlate the unauthorized changes with particular URLs accurately even if users open multiple Web pages concurrently. We are also building a Web canary browser for Linux and other browsers such as Firefox so that it can be released and re-distributed for widespread adoption.

References

1. Wang, Y.-M., Beck, D., Jiang, X., Roussev, R., Verbowski, C., Chen, S., King, S.: Automated Web Patrol with Strider HoneyMonkeys: Finding Web Sites That Exploit Browser Vulnerabilities. In: 13th Annual Network and Distributed System Security Symposium, Internet Society, San Diego (2006)
2. MITRE HoneyClient, http://www.honeyclient.org/trac
3. Capture HPC client honeypot, https://projects.honeynet.org/capture-hpc
4. VMware, http://www.VMware.com
5. Sapuntzakis, C., Lam, M.: Virtual appliances in the collective: A road to hassle-free computing. In: Workshop on Hot Topics in Operating Systems, pp. 55–60 (2003)

6. Jackson, C., Bortz, A., Boneh, D., Mitchell, J.: Protecting Browser State from Web Privacy Attacks. In: Proc. WWW (2006)
7. Ross, B., Jackson, C., Miyake, N., Boneh, D., Mitchell, J.: Stronger Password Authentication Using Browser Extensions. In: Proc. USENIX Security (2005)
8. Zhang, Y., Egelman, S., Cranor, L.F., Hong, J.: Phinding Phish: Evaluating Anti-Phishing Tools. In: Proceedings of the 14th Annual Network & Distributed System Security Symposium (NDSS 2007), San Diego, CA (2007)
9. Know Your Enemy: Malicious Web Servers,
   http://www.honeynet.org/papers/mws/
10. Provos, N., McNamee, D., Mavrommatis, P., Wang, K., Modadugu, N.: The Ghost In The Browser -Analysis of Web-based Malware. In: Proceedings of the 2007 HotBots, Usenix, Cambridge (2007)
11. Cox, R., Gribble, S., Levy, H., Hansen, J.: A safety-oriented platform for Web applications. In: Proceedings of the 2006 IEEE Symposium on Security and Privacy, Washington, DC (May 2006)
12. Moshchuk, et al.: SpyProxy: Execution-based Detection of Malicious Web Content - Usenix 2007 (2007)
13. ForceField (August 2008),
    http://download.zonealarm.com/bin/forcefield_x/index.html
14. IE7 Protected Mode (August 2008),
    http://www.microsoft.com/windows/windows-vista/features/
    IE7-protected-mode.aspx
15. Chong, S., Liu, J., Myers, A.C., Qi, X., Vikram, K., Zheng, L., Zheng, X.: Secure web applications via automatic partitioning. In: Proceedings of the 21st ACM Symposium on Operating Systems Principles (SOSP 2007) (October 2007)
16. Howell, J., Jackson, C., Wang, H.J., Fan, X.: MashupOS: Operating system abstractions for client mashups. In: Proceedings of the Workshop on Hot Topics in Operating Systems (May 2007)
17. Browser Appliance (August 2008),
    http://www.vmware.com/appliances/directory/815
18. Reis, C., Dunagan, J., Wang, H.J., Dubrovsky, O., Esmeir, S.: BrowserShield: vulnerability-driven filtering of dynamic HTML. In: Proceedings of the 7th conference on USENIX Symposium on OSDI, Seattle, WA, November 6-8 (2006)
19. Zhang, J., Porras, P.: Highly Predictive Blacklisting. In: Proceedings of 17th USENIX Security Symposium (July 2008)
20. Barth, A., Jackson, C., Reis, C.: The Security Architecture of the Chromium Browser, Technical report (2008)
21. Grier, C., Tang, S., King, S.T.: Secure Web Browsing with the OP Web Browser. In: Proceedings of the 2008 IEEE Symposium on Security and Privacy, Oakland (May 2008)

CalSWIM: A Wiki–Based Data Sharing Platform

Yasser Ganjisaffar, Sara Javanmardi, Stanley Grant,
and Cristina Videira Lopes

University Of California, Irvine, USA
{yganjisa,sjavanma,sbgrant,lopes}@uci.edu

Abstract. Organizations increasingly create massive internal digital data repositories and are looking for technical advances in managing, exchanging and integrating explicit knowledge. While most of the enabling technologies for knowledge management have been used around for several years, the ability to cost effective data sharing, integration and analysis into a cohesive infrastructure evaded organizations until the advent of Web 2.0 applications. In this paper, we discuss our investigations into using a Wiki as a web–based interactive knowledge management system, which is integrated with some features for easy data access, data integration and analysis. Using the enhanced wiki, it possible to make organizational knowledge sustainable, expandable, outreaching and continually up–to–date. The wiki is currently under use as California Sustainable Watershed Information Manager. We evaluate our work according to the requirements of knowledge management systems. The result shows that our solution satisfies more requirements compared to other tools.

Keywords: Knowledge Management, Wikis, Data–Sharing.

1 Introduction

In today's increasingly unstable and competitive environment, knowledge is widely considered the main source of competitive advantage for organizations. As a consequence, organizations have become progressively more concerned with the concept of knowledge management, since nurturing organizational assets potentially could enable long-term competitive advantage [1,2].

Traditionally, knowledge management systems (KMSs) are controlled by a small number of individuals and any non-trivial changes to the system require intervention of software experts. Only users who feel more comfortable with web technologies are more likely to engage in electronic knowledge exchanges [3]. The problem gets worse when organizations have some publicly available data, but there is no simple interface for data sharing or any tool for data aggregation and analysis. To access the data, researchers or professionals usually need to download the data, which is not always the most updated data, and use their own analytical tools for data aggregation and analysis. In this way, it is not easy to share and discuss the results with others.

E. Bertino and J.B.D. Joshi (Eds.): CollaborateCom 2008, LNICST 10, pp. 34–43, 2009.

With the emergence of web 2.0 tools, such as wikis, mashups, blogs and RSS feeds, theorists have explored these social and collaborative web tools as knowledge management enablers. They believe that web 2.0 tools specifically wikis are undemanding and affordable tools for communication and knowledge management, and they have the potential to offer the features of complex and expensive IT-solutions [4]. One of the key characteristics of the wiki software is that it allows very low cost collective content creation through a regular web browser and a simple markup language. This feature makes wiki software a popular choice for content creation projects where minimizing overhead in creating new or editing and accessing already existing content is of high priority. Although Openness, participation and decentralization in wikis have made wikis suitable targets for effective knowledge management [5], not all of the requirements of KMSs can be satisfied through the current wiki engines – specifically when user needs to access organizational data for data integration and analysis purposes.

In this work, we show how a wiki can be used in organizations as a web-based interactive KMS in order to make their knowledge *sustainable, expandable, outreaching*, and *continually up-to-date*. We describe our investigations into enhancing an open source wiki called XWiki [1] with advanced knowledge management features, including databases, GIS layers, and other forms of digital data. In this way it is possible to (a) fetch and process historical and real-time data from different sources such as local or remote databases; (b) provide data analysis tools integrated with the wiki, which permit the seamless merging, analysis and presentation of the data; (c) share and discuss the reports and the results of analysis. The enhanced wiki is currently used as California Sustainable Watershed Information Manager (CalSWIM) [2]. We evaluated our solution with other solutions to knowledge management in organizations according to the KMS requirements [6]. The results show that our solution satisfies more requirements compared to other knowledge management tools.

The remainder of this paper is as follows: Section 2 summarizes some of the relevant related work. Section 3 illustrates CALSWIM wiki and the extended features. In section 4, we describe the evaluation of the work according to the knowledge management requirements. Finally, section 5 draws some conclusions and future research work.

2 Background and Related Work

With the emergence of the Internet and increase in the availability of information, web–based KMSs enabled organizations to take advantage of heterogeneous data: structured (e.g. relational), semi–structured (e.g. HTML, XML) and unstructured (e.g. plain text, audio/video) data [7]. In the web 1.0 era, using web mark–up languages such as XML reduced the obstacles to data sharing among diverse applications and databases [8]. Ashly *et al.* [6] explains some of the significant information challenges facing organizations and discuss how web–based

---

[1] http://www.xwiki.org/xwiki/bin/view/Main/WebHome
[2] http://calswim.org

technologies such as content management servers, portals, or document management systems lower information barriers. Alavi *et al.* [9] have addressed the requirements of KMSs; their survey shows that KMSs in general require a variety of technological tools in three areas: database and database management, communication and messaging, browsing and retrieval. They also highlight the need for seamless integration of the various tools in these three areas.

With the advent of web 2.0, collaborative and social technologies have made a significant impact on knowledge sharing. In contrast to the previous web 1.0 tools that passed on information to an inactive and receptive users, collaborative applications enable users to create and publish their own content [10]. Collaborative technologies can enhance collaboration between employees as well as sharing the organizational information and knowledge [2]. According to Sauer *et al.* [4], blogs and wikis are undemanding and affordable tools for communication and knowledge management. It is suggested that their rather unsophisticated structure can facilitate integration into already existing intranet and internet solutions. They go further by stating that web 2.0 tools such as blogs and wikis have the potential to offer all the features of complex and expensive IT-solutions.

Some research have studied the use of wikis as KMSs (so called corporate wikis), in corporations [11,12]. Wei *et al* [13] define corporate Wiki as an open community process that encourages multiple iterations in the creation of a knowledge repository. Pfaff *et al.* [12] explain participatory organizational processes of creation, accumulation and maintenance of knowledge, and analyze Wiki as a mediating employee-based knowledge management tool for democratizing organizational knowledge. They also have addressed quality issues in corporate wikis. They also believe that unlike radically open wikis (e.g. Wikipedia), which raises questions whether the information is authoritative and credible, corporate wikis contains more reliable information; employees who make contributions to the corporate Wiki are employed by the organization as specialists whose opinions will be highly regarded by their organizations as trusted and authoritative. Some work like [14] also shows that how in open wikis trustworthiness of users can be estimated by tracking users' actions over time.

The idea of using web 2.0 applications such as wikis, blogs and RSS feeds has been implemented in a commercial Mindroute Software [3], where organizational users use blogs for writing their comments, and wikis for sharing their knowledge (e.g. derived from meetings) in the organizations.

In this work, we discuss our investigations on enriching an open source wiki, XWiki, for knowledge management purposes. The wiki is designed for both organizational and volunteer users (e.g. researcher and professionals) in public. The new features integrated into the wiki enable users to retrieve data from local/remote relational databases or data spreadsheets. In addition, users can do data integration and analysis in a seamless way. The wiki (CalSWIM), which is currently used as California Sustainable Watershed/Wetland information Manager satisfies the requirements of an effective KMS.

---

[3] http://www.corporatewiki.us/?id=689

3   CalSWIM Wiki

CalSWIM is an ongoing project with the goal of facilitating open, coordinated, integrated, and informed decisions for those interested in water resources. With initial focus on California, CalSWIM provides a framework for engaging water management professionals, scientists, and the general public in the process of sharing information about water resources; therefore benefiting from critical open supervision of the content, and from valuable volunteer contributions that cannot occur in a closed infrastructure. The current work aims at creating a public and easily update–able information infrastructure of "all things watershed" that includes all watersheds in California.

CalSWIM is designed both as a public forum for exploring local watersheds and as a web location to help coastal managers make cost-effective and scientifically justifiable decisions regarding the monitoring, management, and alteration of coastal urban wetlands and their associated watersheds. To enable CalSWIM to scale up to its visionary goal, the first design goal has been being easily editable by environmental experts who are not software experts.

CalSWIM has three types of stakeholders:

1. *Organizations*, who have databases of historical and real–time data from their monitoring sites. CalSWIM enables organizations to link their databases to the wiki system in order to make the data accessible by public. Data is hosted on the organizational servers and only meta–data including read–only access credentials is registered in CalSWIM (Fig. 1). CalSWIM connects to these databases on demand to fetch the requested data.
2. *Environmental Experts*, who use the wiki system for retrieving data from the linked databases and processing it. They can share the results by creating new wiki pages, which can be accessible by other users.
3. *General Public*, who may use the CalSWIM wiki as a source of information or voluntarily contribute to it (for example by sampling environmental data and reporting the results in the wiki pages).

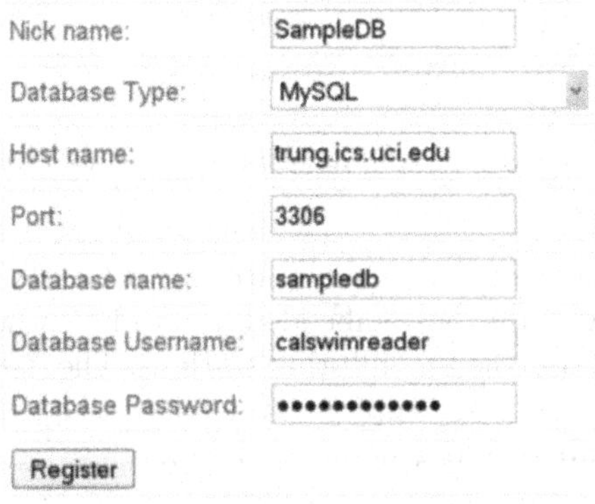

Nick name:	SampleDB
Database Type:	MySQL
Host name:	trung.ics.uci.edu
Port:	3306
Database name:	sampledb
Database Username:	calswimreader
Database Password:	••••••••••••

Register

Fig. 1. Database Registration in CalSWIM

CalSWIM wiki aims at providing an infrastructure integrated with useful features in order to facilitate interactions among these parties. Currently, most of the organizations collecting environmental data either do not publish the data on the Web or have their own customized websites. Typically, users who are interested in accessing the data, need to go through several online forms in order to get the data.

The problem with this type of data sharing is that users need to download data and convert it to an understandable data model for their analytical tools. Then, they can share the result on the web. The goal of CalSWIM project is to streamline this Download–Analyze–Publish process. It enables users to insert standard queries into the wiki pages to retrieve the data from the linked databases. Users can then use the visualization and analysis tools integrated with the wiki in order to process the data and make the result accessible to the wiki users. The main advantage of this approach is that results are always up–to–date. As soon as data in linked databases is updated, content of CalSWIM pages is also updated. Fig. 2 shows the knowledge management stream in CalSWIM wiki.

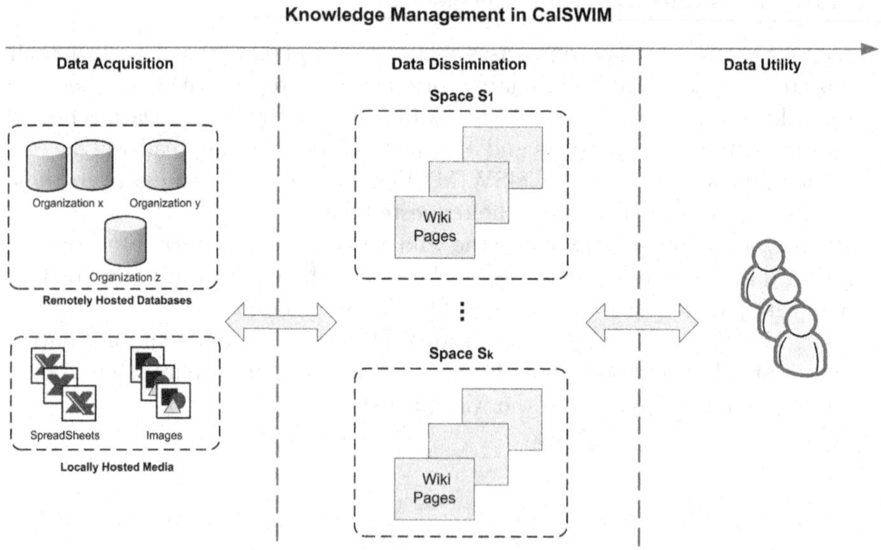

Fig. 2. Knowledge Management in CalSWIM

An example of visualization tools integrated with CalSWIM wiki is the map tool. Fig. 3 shows how a user has embedded a map into a wiki page. The map shows the location of watershed monitoring stations. The data is extracted from a linked database. The following snippet is used in a wiki page for for extracting the data from the database and generating the map:

```
#mapFromDB("StateWaterDB", "Select Name,
           Latitude, Longitude FROM Station")
```

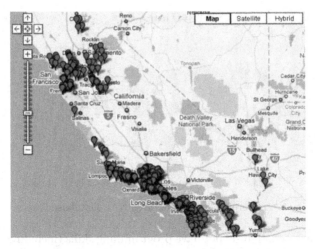

Fig. 3. A Map Generated by a Database Query

The first parameter is the database nick name linked to the wiki and the second parameter is a standard SQL query which retrieves data from the database.

In addition to database retrieval tools, users can also extract data from attached spreadsheets and display them on wiki pages. For example, the same map as Fig. 3 can be generated if the data is in an attached Excel file using the following line of code:

```
#mapFromExcel("locations.xls", "Sheet1", "A1-C16")
```

The first parameter is the name of the attached Excel spreadsheet, the second parameter is the name of the sheet, and the third parameter is the range which contains data.

Charting tool is another visualization tool integrated with CalSWIM. Charts enable users to display real–time data extracted from online databases in the wiki pages. Inserting the following code snippet generates a chart as shown in Fig. 4.

```
{chart:
 source=type:query;
 dbnickname:StateWaterDB;
 command:SELECT Date, Result FROM sample
          Where StationCode = 'D7'|
 type=time|
 title=Sample Time Chart|
}
```

The following of this section, describes some of the other features of CalSWIM.

3.1   Content Creation

Content creation in CalSWIM is very easy. Users can use both WYSIWYG editor and wiki editor. The WYSIWYG editor is similar to popular word processors in which users see how what they type is rendered. In the wiki editor, users should use a simple wiki syntax for formatting their content. Our experiments showed

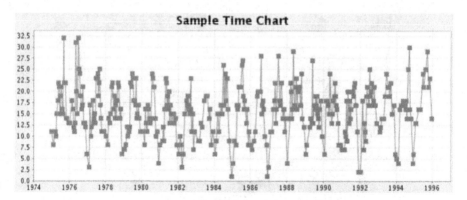

Fig. 4. A Sample Chart Generated by a Database Query

that most of the users that do not have programming skills (including most of the researchers) prefer WYSIWYG editor. These types of users are very reluctant to using codes. Even they hesitate in using very simple markups. Therefore we made the WYSIWYG editor the default editor of our wiki platform and extended it to provide simple forms for embedding maps, charts and other objects that are specific to CalSWIM.

3.2 Version Control

In CalSWIM, any change made to a document is automatically saved by Version Control component. It enables users to see how information has changed over time and gives them the ability to rollback documents to previous versions if needed.

3.3 Content Structure

CalSWIM allows users to organize pages into a set of *Spaces*. Wiki spaces are collections of related pages. Contributors can create new spaces, and add pages in them, at any time.

3.4 Access Control

CalSWIM has a three–level hierarchical access control mechanism. Access rights can be page–level right, space–level rights or global rights. Page–level rights override space–level rights and space–level rights override global rights. Rights can be assigned or denied from individuals or groups of users. Our experiments in CalSWIM showed that most of the experts only contribute in restricted spaces and pages that can only be edited by them. But are open for comments and discussion by others. Their argue is that if pages are going to be publicize their research and results of their work (with their name somewhere on them), they cannot accept them to be editable by others. In fact, while we want high school students looking at pages created by scientists and domain experts and detecting eventual mistakes, we do not want those students to change the content. Therefore CalSWIM is a mixture of Open and Closed content. But comments are always open for allowing general public to share the opinions.

4   Evaluation

To evaluate the effectiveness of our solution, in this section we compare our solution with other tools currently used in KMSs. Major requirements of KMSs have been discussed in [9,6]. Fig. 5 compares CalSWIM with other current solutions according to the requirements. The following is the summary of each requirement:

	File Server	Web Server	CMS	DMS	Wikis	Portals	Databases	CalSWIM
Easy Info. Creation	YES	NO	YES	YES	YES	PART	NO	YES
Easy Info. Access	PART	YES	YES	YES	YES	YES	NO	YES
Find-Grained Access Control	NO	NO	YES	NO	NO	PART	PART	PART
Automatic Integrated Version Control	NO	NO	YES	YES	YES	YES	NO	YES
Easy Collaboration	NO	NO	NO	NO	PART	PART	NO	PART
Fine-grained reuse	NO	NO	NO	NO	NO	NO	PART	PART
Integrated Productivity tool functionality	PART	NO	NO	NO	NO	PART	NO	PART
Full Content Search	PART	YES	YES	YES	YES	PART	PART	YES

Fig. 5. Comparison of CalSWIM with other knowledge management systems

Easy Information Creation and Access:
   Like other wikis, Calswim provides a user friendly platform to create and access information. Users can contribute with the system via almost every web browser.

Automatic Version Control:
   Like other Wikis, CalSWIM has a built–in version control component. This component enable users to view the previous versions of a document as well as the name of their editors and the timestamps. Users can rollback the current revision of a document to an older version if needed. In addition, they can use the diff functionality to view the difference between two versions of a document.

Easy Collaboration:
   CalSWIM Wiki provides some tools for data aggregation and analysis, and let users attach different types of files to a Wiki page. It make the collaboration easier compared to traditional wiki softwares; but wikis are not still perfect tools for user collaboration [6].

Full Content Search:
   CalSWIM supports two types of content (a) the content in the Wiki Pages (b) the content accessible from the linked databases. For the content in the Wiki pages, users can use full content search feature. However, the search is limited to the pages and the spaces they have access to. They can also narrow down their search to some special spaces. To search in the content available through the linked databases, users can use SQL queries, which enable them to formulate complex data retrieval queries.

Fine–grained access control:
Unlike traditional wiki software, CalSWIM provides page and space level access control. The most granular access rights can be defined on a Wiki page. Access control can be enhanced if we apply access rights on different sections of a wiki page as well as on inset and delete actions.

Integrated Productivity Tool Functionality:
CalSWIM allows users to attach any kind of files to pages and either reference to the attached file or use its content in creating part of the page content. For example, users can attach an Excel spreadsheet and use a simple interface to instruct the wiki to retrive data from this attachment and display it as a table in the page.

5   Conclusions and Future Work

In this paper we presented CalSWIM as a tool, which uses Wiki technology in knowledge acquisition, dissemination and utilization. It enables organizations to link their databases to the wiki engine, and make them accessible to public by defining suitable access rights. Using the integrated tools, users can (a) Fetch data from these databases; (b) Perform processing on the data; (c) Display or visualize the results and share them with others.

Currently, users need to use SQL queries to retrieve data from databases and represent it in the wiki pages, or to feed it to the analytical tools. According to the initial feedback of users, writing SQL queries is not easy for most of them. To overcome this problem, we are developing an easy to use query builder tool. In addition, some researchers want to import their documents in different formats such PDF, TeX and MS–Word in order to receive some comments from other users. A challenge in publicizing this type of content in CalSWIM wiki is to convert these documents to the wiki format. In addition, we aim at extending the CalSWIM to understand TeX markup, and use it as an alternative to its wiki markup.

Acknowledgement

This work has been partially supported by NSF grant OCI-074806 and by the Orange County Stormwater Program.

References

1. Bolloju, N., Khalifa, M., Turban, E.: Integrating knowledge management into enterprise environments for the next generation decision support. Decis. Support Syst. 33(2), 163–176 (2002)
2. Fried, C., Edlund, A.: Web 2.0: It and knowledge management in the 21st century: A case study of mindroute software ab. Uppsala University, Tech. Rep. (2007)

3. Staples, D.S., Jarvenpaa, S.L.: Using electronic media for information sharing activities: a replication and extension. In: ICIS 2000: Proceedings of the twenty first international conference on Information systems, pp. 117–133. Association for Information Systems, Atlanta (2000)
4. Sauer, M., Bialek, D., Efimova, E., Schwartlander, R., Pless, G., Neuhaus, P.: "blogs" and "wikis" are valuable software tools for communication within research groups. Artificial Organs 29(1), 82–83 (2005)
5. Wan, L., Zhao, C.: Construction of a knowledge management framework based on web 2.0. In: WiCom 2007: International Conference on Wireless Communications, Networking and Mobile Computing, pp. 5341–5344. IEEE, Los Alamitos (2007)
6. Aitken, A.: Managing unstructured and semi-structured information in organizations. In: ICIS 2007: 6th IEEE/ACIS International Conference on Computer and Information Science, pp. 712–717. IEEE, Los Alamitos (2007)
7. Abiteboul, S., Buneman, P., Suciu, D.: Data on the web: From reltions to semistructured data and xml. Science Press (1999)
8. Seligman, L., Rosenthal, A.: Xml's impact on databases and data sharing. Computer 34(6), 59–67 (2001)
9. Alavi, M., Leidner, D.E.: Knowledge management systems: issues, challenges, and benefits. Commun. AIS, 1 (1999)
10. Abiteboul, S., Buneman, P., Suciu, D.: Coming to terms with web 2.0. Reference Reviews 21, 5–6 (2007)
11. Hasan, H., Meloche, J.A., Pfaff, C.C., Willis, D.: Beyond ubiquity: Co-creating corporate knowledge with a wiki. In: Ubicomm, pp. 35–40 (2007)
12. Pfaff, C., Hasan, H.: Can knowledge management be open source? In: OSS, pp. 59–70 (2007)
13. Wei, C., Maust, B., Barrick, J., Cuddihy, E., Spyridakis, J.H.: Wikis for supporting distributed collaborative writing. In: Proceedings at the Society for Technical Communication, pp. 204–209 (2005)
14. Javanmardi, S., Lopes, C.: Modeling trust in collaborative information systems. In: Proceedings of the 3rd International Conference on Collaborative Computing: Networking, Applications and Worksharing (November 2007)

Examining a Bayesian Approach to Personalizing Context Awareness in Ubiquitous Computing Environments

Yaser Mowafi, Dongsong Zhang, and Guisseppi Fogionne

Department of Information Systems
University of Maryland, Baltimore County, Baltimore, MD 21250, USA
{ymowafi,zhangd,forgionn}@umbc.edu

Abstract. There is a growing interest in the use of context-aware systems, which can recognize user's situational context and accordingly provide a desirable interaction with the user. However, the design, development, evaluation and deployment of context-aware systems are still at its infancy. In this paper, we propose an operational mechanism approach to context acquisition driven by the relevant dependency between users' ongoing activities and context in ubiquitous computing environments. We present a Bayesian model to classify and predict users' activities and associated context that offers more interactive and construed context awareness to users. The model performance is examined in terms of its classification accuracy in predicting users' activities and the associated context trends. The results demonstrate that such probabilistic models can provide an effective and feasible approach to learning and predicting users' context that can yield further the development of deployable context-aware systems.

Keywords: Context-aware computing, mobile and ubiquitous computing, context modeling, context inference, context history, machine learning, Bayesian networks.

1 Introduction

Proliferation of ubiquitous computing in humans' everyday life combined with the significant advancement of mobile technologies and wireless networks have taken Human Computer Interaction (HCI) beyond desktop computers level. Amid this evolving trend, context-aware computing that aims at sensing clues about user's context to enable desired interaction with the users has gained increasing recognition as one of the emerging technologies for the next generation of personal computing. However, the design, development, evaluation and deployment of context-aware systems are still facing many challenges.

While much of the literature on the context and context awareness has broadly focused on the context extraction from users' surrounding environment and interpretation, the discrepancy between real world context perceived by humans and context aware systems poses a big challenge. For example, attuning a system to a

E. Bertino and J.B.D. Joshi (Eds.): CollaborateCom 2008, LNICST 10, pp. 44–55, 2009.
© ICST Institute for Computer Sciences, Social-Informatics and Telecommunications Engineering 2009

limited set of real contextual circumstances might contain irrelevant inputs that are unintentionally included in the context-aware service trained context, leading to a mismatch between user anticipation and the context-aware system actions. Such unresolved mismatch, or so called "ambiguity" in both sensed and interpreted context, has received some attention. For example, Bellotti et al. [1] argued that traditional HCI fundamentals and Human-Human-Interface (HHI) "do not fare well", and urged for the need of real collaboration between social science and HCI researchers to provide a systematic framework for the design of sensing-based systems. Some researchers [2-4] also questioned the viability of the conventional notion of context awareness as a representational problem that is mainly focused on encoding and presenting the environmental surroundings in a software system. They suggested to rethink context awareness as an interactional problem, rather than a representational problem, of users' ongoing activities to directly build their relevant information.

In this article, we discuss some of the unresolved issues in this field and propose some solutions. We first introduce fundamental concepts of context and context awareness. Then, we present a user-centered context awareness approach, in which we propose an operational mechanism of context acquisition based on the relevant dependency between users' activities and ongoing tasks with their context. Finally, we examine the performance of our proposed model and conclude the paper with future work.

2 Related Work

The dynamic nature of context has granted the definition of context a "slippery" characteristic that keeps the context schema subject to researchers' context of interest and their intention of context utilization [3]. Among many context definitions [5-8], we adopt the one proposed by Dey and Abowd [5]: *"Any information that can characterize the situation to an entity that is considered relevant to the interaction between the user and the application. An entity is a person, place, or object that is considered relevant to the interaction between user and the application, including the user and applications themselves (p.3)."* The unconstrained boundaries of context have led to a taxonomy approach to context categorization in the literature, context is broadly classified into user context (e.g., activity, identity, etc.), and physical context (e.g., location, lighting, noise level, etc.) [9-11]. Much of the context awareness research has broadly separated the synthesis of the physical context (also called sensor-based context) from the user context [12, 13]. While most of the context-aware applications considered a few types of sensed context by and large location and time; interestingly, few have captured the user activity as part of their addressed context of interest domain. Similar findings were compiled in earlier literature surveys of context-aware applications [5, 6, 14]. Remarkably, [6] voiced a motivating concern about whether other contexts are difficult to be sensed or are viewed to be not useful.

Of the many schemes that have been proposed to categorize context-aware systems, context-aware systems can be broadly classified into explicit and implicit systems. Explicit systems normally behave based on users' direct input and setting commands, while implicit systems proactively provide users with certain awareness behaviors over time and place [5, 15, 16]. While the former approach leaves the definition of the context scope exclusively to the user interface (UI) that is usually predefined by users, this approach ignores the intelligent adaptive characteristics that are mainly sought for by context-aware systems. Alternatively, the latter approach ignores the natural dialogue between users and context-aware systems to uphold users' aspect in the context-awareness process. In this work, we attempt to take a different stance in addressing these limitations from the following aspects:

- The need for integration of implicit and explicit means of context-awareness. Such integration will bring users and context-aware systems closer and define a common awareness background based on the users' needs and tasks. This idea has been proposed in personalized information systems and goal-driven theories for information-related-activity in context user-modeling [9, 17].
- Context-awareness needs to be interpreted or abstracted from a user's perspective to extend context-aware systems' ability of parsing user context. This will enable a context-aware system to incorporate some of the contextual information already abstracted by users, rather than solely relying on the system's inference of user's actual context. We draw such an analogy from "embodied action" view of context in interaction [3].

A number of research efforts have been made to resolve the discrepancy between context-aware systems' synthesis and users' understanding of their surrounding context, mainly by integrating the users' cognizance into context-aware systems' intention of conduct [13, 18, 19]. Some researchers proposed a user-mediation approach to resolving the ambiguity of the sensor-based physical context [14, 20, 21]. Although those approaches aimed at bridging the gap between the physical context and user context, their scope was broadly limited to the user's input as a filtering criterion mainly to reduce the ambiguity of the sensor-based context acquisition. Of significant importance to our work is the Artificial Intelligence (AI) research on collaboration of users' interaction information with decision support systems to enable such systems to draw better conclusions and recommend appropriate courses of actions. Of these efforts are the initiatives that aimed at extending the functionality of interpersonal communication tools, such as Instant Messaging (IM) and Groupware Calendar Systems (GCS's) with users' presence and availability [22-25]. Other initiatives proposed probabilistic models to predict users' decisions based on historical information about their interaction with their daily calendaring events [26, 27]. For example, Horvitz et al. [28, 29] examined the potential cost of users' interruption of incoming messages based on users' availability and business status. While the aforementioned initiatives have broadly attempted to address the collaboration between users and their computing systems to infer some form of user context in very specific computer tasks, many questions related to the inference of the users' social situations beyond the computer activity domain remain not answered.

This work also touches on some of the key challenges for achieving the utility purpose of context awareness, highlighted by Abowd and Mynatt [30] who identified the following challenges of providing an augmented context information to couple users' natural interactions with their surrounding context in all, the failure of context-aware systems to 1) incorporate users' interpretation or input of their activities for the "what" part of context information; 2) incorporate user identity information in dealing with the "who" part of user context; 3) associate the "who" and "what" with the other

"W's" of context information, such as "when" and "where"; 4) go beyond using time as an index of records' capturing rather than an indicator of a general task or user interest for the "when" part of context information; and finally, 5) explore "why" users are interested in the context beyond the "what" part of context information. These and other issues presented earlier led us to propose a user-centered context awareness approach, in which we view user's daily activities and tasks as natural sensors of user context. The approach aims at enriching the context acquisition with user's ongoing social situations. The theoretical basis of our work comes from the theory of informal communication between users and personal computing artifacts [31], which aims to capture some of the abstracted information defined by users themselves rather than solely relying on the computing systems' deduction of users' actual intentions.

3   User-Centered Context Awareness

We propose a user context awareness model that inherits the uncertainty of users' context in their daily recurring activities. We apply Bayesian networks for learning and predicting user context based on users' daily interactions with system applications running on their ubiquitous computing devices, like calendaring and tasks management tools currently available on most mobile and handheld devices. This approach complies with Dey and Abowd [5]'s definition of context, in which they characterized context information according to its relevance with the interaction between the user and an application.

3.1   A Bayesian User Context Model

Bayesian networks are directed graphs of joint probability distributions over certain problem domain variables with some conditional independence relationships among those variables. One of the primary advantages of Bayesian networks, among many probabilistic models and inference techniques, is their ability of modeling causal relationships under uncertainty [32, 33]. Given the continuous updates to the joint probability distributions within their structure, Bayesian networks have been successfully deployed for inferring users' activity patterns [26, 27, 34]. Simply put, a Bayesian network $N = (X, G, P)$ consists of an acyclic, directed graph $G(V, E)$ with nodes V and a set of directed links E, over a set of mutually exclusive and exhaustive variables $X \in V$, with a set of conditional probability distributions P [35]. For each variable X, there is a conditional probability distribution $P(X_{child} \mid P(X_{parent}))$, which satisfies the Markov Model condition that the likelihood of a certain variable occurrence depends on previously occurred ones. Applying the chain rule of probability to repetitively decompose the conditional distribution over the network N, with a set of variables X_i for $i = 1,...,n$ and Pa_i to present the parents of X_i yields the generalized probability distribution function for X, given all possible observations:

$$P(X) = \prod_{i=1}^{n} P(X_i \mid Pa_i). \tag{1}$$

Learning Bayesian networks becomes a task of identifying the problem domain within an acyclic, directed graph G, with nodes $V = (V_1,...V_n)$, that captures the skeleton of directed links E, between the network nodes for each variable $X \in V$. Applying the chain rule of probability rule to all the conditional probability distributions over V when $G(V, E)$ yields:

$$P(V) = \prod_{X \in V} P(X \mid Pa(X)). \tag{2}$$

Once the network structure is built with the complete joint probability distributions (JPD) between its node variables, one can perform probabilistic reasoning analyses for all possible inference queries of interest.

3.2 Building and Training the Model

To construct the network structure of our model, we conducted a series of informal interviews with a group of five graduate students within an academic department at an east-coast university of the United States. The goal of the interviews was to solicit and collect the factors considered by the interviewees in defining the naming convention of the context of their ongoing daily activities. With this in mind, the interviewees were asked to objectively define their activities' context domain, such as locations or places, activity types and attendees, as well as to define the relationship among the defined activities' context domain. In particular, the interviewees were asked to define the relationship between place and activity, activity and attending personnel or accompany, accompany and place, etc. The next step was to define a context profile that characterized the users' defined activities. To reflect the relevance of the context to the users' activities, as well as to provide context presentation decisions that better match the user's activity needs, we classified the context profiles according to the cognitive states, the interviewees thought to be normally associated with their defined activities. More specifically, we distinguished between the following context profiles, high-attention activity, medium-attention activity, and low-attention activity.

Fig. 1 illustrates the network nodes that represent the identified variables in the model, namely user activity, time of the day, place, weekday, accompany, activity recurring frequency, duration, and user context. The directed links between the nodes represent the causal relationships between the nodes. The model nodes consist of mutually exclusive and exhaustive variables that inherent the likelihood of the user context of a certain activity based on the influencing variables influencing the user activity. More specifically, time of the day (e.g., 8am-10am, 10am-12pm etc.); place (e.g., home, work, outdoor, etc.); accompany (e.g., individual, coworkers, family, friends, etc.); day of the week (e.g., weekday, weekend); duration of the user activity (e.g., 1 hour, 2 hours, 4 hours, etc.); and recurring types of the activity (e.g., daily, weekly, biweekly, monthly, etc.). The user activity is defined as busy, free, tentative,

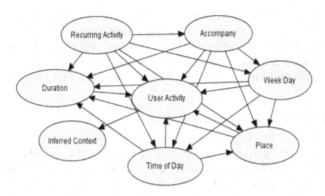

Fig. 1. A Bayesian network for user context inference

office, meetings, etc. As stated earlier, the users' context profiles associated with their activities are defined as high-attention activity, medium-attention activity, and low-attention activity. The model was constructed using Hugin Developer decision support systems software package [36].

We trained the model on three months worth of daily activities of a single user, with approximately 400 individual and group activities (382 observations). Previous research found that applying personalized Bayesian models derived from one or more user to another would yield poor performance [34]. To enable a realistic set-up, we chose Google calendar for mobile devices to observe and log the user daily activities and the causal influential variables defined in the model network structure, as shown in Fig. 2. In addition to its free shared calendaring web-based anytime anywhere service, Google calendar events format (i.e. events creation properties mainly centered around: what, who, where, and when type of questions), complied with our model structure data compilation requirements. Like any learning system, given the

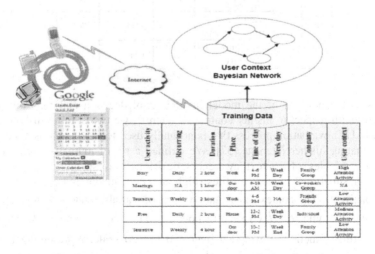

Fig. 2. A user context awareness data compilation diagram

user context association sensitiveness to the user activity influencing variables, the user context likelihood is propagated to provide a context profile that best matches the user activity influencing variables. As new findings are obtained, the probability distribution of each relevant node in the network will be updated, and thus the network beliefs about the user context likelihood will be adjusted accordingly.

4 Evaluation of Model Performance

To examine the model performance, we used the general cross-validation evaluation technique to test the model power of accuracy of the user activity and associated context. The collected data were divided into 90% of training data, and the remaining 10% for testing. Table 1 presents the confusion matrix of user context inference accuracy, in pursuit of the model influential variables. The rows present the generated case values and the columns present the predicted values. The un-shaded diagonal cells present the correctly predicted cases, and the sum of these correctly predicted percentages present the overall classification accuracy of the model. The model showed a classification accuracy of 92% of user context inference with an average Euclidian distance of 0.007. Euclidian distance ranges from 0 for the perfect classifier and sqrt(2) for incorrect classification.

Table 1. Confusion matrix for user context inference

		Predicted User Context		
		High-attention Activity	Medium-attention Activity	Low-attention Activity
Actual User Context	High-attention Activity	30%	1%	1%
	Medium-attention Activity	1%	31%	1%
	Low-attention Activity	1%	1 %	33%

To assess the benefits of the model in support of decision making from a user satisfaction with respect to his/her context of interest; we used Multi-attribute utility theory (MAUT) evaluation process that is normally used to evaluate a user's consent when estimating his/her interests [37]. We defined a set of mutually exclusive and exhaustive variables of context awareness decisions corresponding to the earlier defined user situational context profiles (high-attention, medium-attention, and low-attention activity). The context presentation decision variable state, Di, is associated with a utility outcome, $u(Di, Cj)$, corresponding to the model context inference state Cj. The utility function is weighed over a 0 to 100 scale, representing the user satisfaction with the context awareness decisions. That being said, the expected utility

(EU) of the inferred context presentation decision obtained from the cumulative contribution to the total utility function outcomes is,

$$EU(Di) = \sum_j u(Di, Cj) P(Cj|\varepsilon). \tag{3}$$

Where $P(Cj \mid \varepsilon)$ is the probability of each context inference state Cj conditioned on the given observations at hand ε. To enable a context presentation decision that couples the user situational context at hand with his/her tolerance of interruption of the earlier defined context profiles, we defined two context presentation states associated with the user's context profiles namely, interruptible or not interruptible context preference. The network belief about the user context likelihood was then evaluated based on the interrupting presentation decision that is weighed by the utility function outcome. The results showed that the model decision classifier performed fairly well in predicting the user cognitive situational context related to a given activity. For example, for the "meeting" activity of high-attention context profile, the model provided a utility value of 20% for an interrupting presentation decision, and 80% for a non-interrupting presentation decision. In contrast, for the "free" activity case of low-attention context profile, the model showed an equal utility weight of 20% for providing an interrupting or a non- interrupting presentation decision. The equal-weight decision indicated that neither decision has effect on the user satisfaction with respect to his/her current situational context.

In addition to studying the model classification accuracy, we are also interested in investigating the model sensitivity to the competing combinations of the network structure influencing variables (e.g. place, accompany, time, and duration). Examining the variables with higher contribution value to the overall context awareness value can lead to defining a base model with sets of variables in order to enhance the model accuracy and shorten the model learning time. A key feature of Bayesian models is their capability of computing the power degree of each variable over the remaining set of variables in the network using entropy reduction metrics [36], by calculating the posterior probability, in a form of a likelihood distribution over the remaining set of variables in the network, also known as the evidence function. Interested readers are encouraged to refer to any machine learning text, such as [38]. Using Hugin software, we reproduced multiple trials of the model learning association features from the earlier collected training data. For most theoretical probability distributions, simulation can be used to generate many observations, thereby reproducing population-like distributions [39]. Moreover, according to the central limit theorem, empirical measurements will tend to move toward a normal distribution asymptotically as the sample size increases [40]. That being said, we examined the model's classification accuracy given a distinct evidence function for each of the model influential variables at a time. We used the computed classification accuracy values to address the following question and hypothesis:

Question: Which competing approach (place, accompany, time, duration, etc.) provides the best context awareness value?

Hypothesis: There is a difference in the context awareness value provided by the competing influencing variables.

To examine the significance of each influential variable on the overall context awareness value, we used Analysis of Variance (ANOVA) parametric test. The results partially confirmed our hypothesis. The results showed that both place (P=0.0018) and accompany (P=0.0013) evidence variables performed significantly better (P<0.01) in determining the overall context awareness value. While weekday showed to be significant (P=0.0461<0.05), the activity duration showed insignificant (P=0.0756, P>0.05), and the recurring activity was noticeably not significant (P=0.4992) to the overall context awareness value. The significance of both place and accompany in determining the user context value also indicated their importance in enhancing the model classification accuracy at early stages of the model training.

5   Conclusion and Future Work

Looking back to Weiser's [41] view where people daily lives will become augmented with invisible computational resources to provide information and services when and where desired, in a way that such computational systems are interwoven into people life. In this article, we have presented a user-centered approach to context awareness, in which we perceive users' daily activities and tasks as natural sensors of their situational context. Our goal is to facilitate a simple yet practical approach to context awareness directly based on users' crafting of their personal activities and ongoing tasks. We have created a Bayesian model that inherits the uncertainty of users' context of their daily recurring activities, and provides context awareness inference driven by users' context of interest. We have demonstrated the model through developing an informed personal user context profile drawn from user's daily informal communication with the built-in calendar on his/her mobile handheld device. We have also assessed the potential value of our model in providing a context presentation decisions that better match user's situational context or context of interest for a given activity, such as users' defined tolerance of interruption of their situational context.

We found our preliminary evaluation results promising as a step forward towards building context inference and making context presentation decisions that are more relevant to users' context. Although we believe that the demonstrated model network variables and scenarios do not cover all users' social and mental states that might occur in reality, we think that the model will help in developing more deployable context awareness features relevant to the users' needs in reality. In contrast to the earlier work of Horvitz et al. [28, 29] and Mynatt et al. [26, 27] who examined models of users' availability and attendance mainly to facilitate and support users' scheduling activities and potential interruptibility, our proposed model intended to provide to mobile users a mechanism for developing an informed context-aware service beyond those normally dealt with in desktop applications.

Given the results presented in this paper, we have identified some potential future research to further validate and extend our proposed user context model. One issue of particular interest is to assess the overall context awareness value of incorporating both the sensor-based and user-centered context inputs. From a decision making perspective, we believe that the sensor-based approach and the user-centered contribute different measures to the overall context awareness value. In particular, we are interested in comparing our model context awareness prediction with the context detection of a sensor-based context determined value. A popular methodology that facilitates such analysis falls within the framework of Multiple criteria decision making (MCDM) [42], we are currently exploring to determine the context awareness value of incorporating the competing approaches of context acquisition, as well as to explore the measures that most contribute to context awareness from each competing approach.

Acknowledgements

The authors thank all the people who have participated in this study.

References

1. Bellotti, V., et al.: Making sense of sensing systems: five questions for designers and researchers. In: Proceedings of the SIGCHI conference on Human factors in computing systems: Changing our world, changing ourselves, Minneapolis, Minnesota, USA. ACM Press, New York (2002)
2. Barkhuus, L.: The context gap: An essential challenge to context-aware computing. In: Computer Science. The IT University of Copenhagen, Copenhagen (2005)
3. Dourish, P.: What we talk about when we talk about context. Personal Ubiquitous Comput. 8(1), 19–30 (2004)
4. Jones, G.J.F.: Challenges and Opportunities of Context-Aware Information Access. In: Proceedings of the International Workshop on Ubiquitous Data Management. IEEE Computer Society, Los Alamitos (2005)
5. Dey, A.K., Abowd, G.D.: Towards a Better Understanding of Context and Context-Awareness. In: The Workshop on The What, Who, Where, When, and How of Context-Awareness, as part of the 2000 Conference on Human Factors in Computing Systems (CHI 2000), The Hague, The Netherlands (2000)
6. Chen, G., Kotz, D.: A Survey of Context-Aware Mobile Computing Research. TR2000-381, Dept. of Computer Science, Dartmouth College (2000)
7. Schilit, B., Theimer, M.: Disseminating Active Map Information to Mobile Hosts. IEEE Network 8(5), 22–32 (1994)
8. Schmidt, A., et al.: Advanced Interaction in Context. In: Proceedings of the 1st international symposium on Handheld and Ubiquitous Computing, Karlsruhe, Germany. Springer, Heidelberg (1999)
9. Ranganathan, A., Campbell, R.H.: An infrastructure for context-awareness based on first order logic. Personal Ubiquitous Comput. 7(6), 353–364 (2003)
10. Razzaque, M.A., Dobson, S., Nixon, P.: Categorisation and modelling of quality in context information. In: Proceedings of the IJCAI 2005 Workshop on AI and Autonomic Communications (2005)
11. Jones, G.J.F., Brown, P.J.: Context-Aware Retrieval for Ubiquitous Computing Environments. In: Mobile and Ubiquitous Information Access, pp. 227–243. Springer, Heidelberg (2004)

12. Dey, A.K.: Understanding and Using Context. Personal Ubiquitous Comput. 5(1), 4–7 (2001)
13. Chen, G., Kotz, D.: Context Aggregation and Dissemination in Ubiquitous Computing Systems. In: Proceedings of the Fourth IEEE Workshop on Mobile Computing Systems and Applications. IEEE Computer Society, Los Alamitos (2002)
14. Dey, A.K., Mankoff, J.: Designing mediation for context-aware applications. ACM Trans. Comput.-Hum. Interact. 12(1), 53–80 (2005)
15. Schilit, B., Adams, N., Want, R.: Context-Aware Computing Applications. In: IEEE Workshop on Mobile Computing Systems and Applications, Santa Cruz, CA. IEEE Computer Society, Los Alamitos (1994)
16. Pascoe, J.: Adding Generic Contextual Capabilities to Wearable Computers. In: ISWC 1998: Proceedings of the 2nd IEEE International Symposium on Wearable Computers. IEEE, Los Alamitos (1998)
17. Perugini, S., Ramakrishnan, N.: Personalizing Interactions with Information Systems. In: Advances in Computers. Information Repositories, vol. 57, pp. 323–382 (2003)
18. Pärkkä, J., et al.: Activity classification using realistic data from wearable sensors. IEEE Information Technology in Biomedicine 10(1), 119–128 (2006)
19. Wu, H., Siegel, M., Ablay, S.: Sensor Fusion for Context Understanding. In: IEEE International Measurement Technology Conference (IMTC 2002), Anchorage, USA (2002)
20. Gellersen, H.W., Schmidt, A., Beigl, M.: Multi-sensor context-awareness in mobile devices and smart artifacts. Mob. Netw. Appl. 7(5), 341–351 (2002)
21. Cheverst, K., et al.: Exploiting context to support social awareness and social navigation. SIGGROUP Bull. 21(3), 43–48 (2000)
22. Perttunen, M., Riekki, J.: Inferring Presence in a Context-Aware Instant Messaging System. In: 2004 IFIP Int. Conference on Intelligence in Communication Systems (INTELLICOM 2004), Bangkok, Thailand (2004)
23. Perttunen, M., Riekki, J.: Introducing Context-Aware Features into Everyday Mobile Applications. In: Strang, T., Linnhoff-Popien, C. (eds.) LoCA 2005. LNCS, vol. 3479, pp. 316–327. Springer, Heidelberg (2005)
24. Fogarty, J., Lai, J., Christensen, J.: Presence versus availability: the design and evaluation of a context-aware communication client. International Journal of Human-Computer Studies 61(3), 299–317 (2004)
25. Sen, S., et al.: FeedMe: a collaborative alert filtering system. In: 2006 20th anniversary conference on Computer supported cooperative work, Banff, Alberta. ACM Press, New York (2006)
26. Mynatt, E., Tullio, J.: Inferring calendar event attendance. In: 6th international conference on Intelligent user interfaces, Santa Fe, New Mexico, United States. ACM Press, New York (2001)
27. Tullio, J., et al.: Augmenting shared personal calendars. In: ACM Symposium on User Interface Software and Technology (UIST 2002), Paris, France (2002)
28. Horvitz, E., Koch, P., Apacible, J.: BusyBody: creating and fielding personalized models of the cost of interruption. In: 2004 ACM conference on Computer supported cooperative work, Chicago, Illinois, USA. ACM Press, New York (2004)
29. Horvitz, E., et al.: Bayesphone: Precomputation of Context-Sensitive Policies for Inquiry and Action in Mobile Devices. In: User Modeling 2005, Edinburgh, Scotland (2005)
30. Abowd, G.D., Mynatt, E.D.: Charting past, present, and future research in ubiquitous computing. ACM Trans. Comput.-Hum. Interact. 7(1), 29–58 (2000)

31. Kraut, R.E., et al.: Informal Communication in Organizations: Form, Function, and Technology. In: Oskamp, S., Spacapan, S. (eds.) Claremont symposium on applied social psychology, pp. 145–199 (1990)
32. Heckerman, D.: A Tutorial on Learning with Bayesian Networks. In: Jordan, M. (ed.) Learning in Graphical Models. MIT Press, Cambridge (1999)
33. Horvitz, E.J., Breese, J.S., Henrion, M.: Decision Theory in Expert Systems and Artificial Intelligence. International Journal of Approximate Reasoning 2, 247–302 (1998)
34. Horvitz, E., Apacible, J.: Learning and reasoning about interruption. In: 5th international conference on Multimodal interfaces, Vancouver, British Columbia, Canada. ACM Press, New York (2003)
35. Jensen, F.V.: An Introduction to Bayesian Networks. Springer, New York (1996)
36. Lite, H.: Hugin Expert Probabilistic Graphical Models Software. In: Expert, H. (ed.) Hugin Expert A/S, Aalborg, Denmark,, http://www.hugin.com/
37. Dyer, J.S., Fishburn, P.C., Steuer, R.E., Wallenius, J., Zionts, S.: Multiple Criteria Decision Making, Multiattribute Utility Theory: The Next Ten Years. Management Science 38(5), 645–654 (1992)
38. Mitchell, T.M.: Machine Learning. McGraw-Hill, New York (1997)
39. Zeigler, B.P., Praehofer, H., Kim, T.G.: Theory of Modeling and Simulation. Academic Press, London (2000)
40. Tijms, H.: Understanding Probability: Chance Rules in Everyday Life. Cambridge University Press, Cambridge (2004)
41. Weiser, M.: The Computer for the 21st Century. Scientific American 165(3), 94–104 (1991)
42. Saaty, T.L.: Decision Making for Leaders: The Analytic Hierarchy Process for Decisions in a Complex World, Pittsburgh, Pennsylvania. RWS Publications (1999)

Smart Homes for All: Collaborating Services in a for-All Architecture for Domotics

Tiziana Catarci[1], Febo Cincotti[2], Massimiliano de Leoni[1],
Massimo Mecella[1], and Giuseppe Santucci[1]

[1] Dipartimento di Informatica e Sistemistica
SAPIENZA - Universita di Roma, Italy
{catarci,deleoni,mecella,santucci}@dis.uniroma1.it
[2] Fondazione Santa Lucia, Rome, Italy
f.cincotti@hsantalucia.it

Abstract. Nowadays, control equipments such as automobiles, home appliances, communication, control and office machines, offer their functionalities in the form of services. Such service pervasivity is particularly evident in immersive realities, i.e., scenarios in which invisible embedded systems need to continuously interact with human users, in order to provide continuous sensed information and to react to service requests from the users themselves. The SM4ALL project, which will be presented in this paper, is investigating an innovative middleware platform for collaborating smart embedded services in immersive and person-centric environments, through the use of composability and semantic techniques.

1 Introduction

Embedded systems are specialized computers used in larger systems or machines to control equipments such as automobiles, home appliances, communication, control and office machines. Such pervasiveness is particularly evident in immersive realities, i.e., scenarios in which invisible embedded systems need to continuously collaborate with human users, in order to provide continuous sensed information and to react to service requests from the users themselves. Examples of such scenarios are digital libraries and eTourism, automotive, next generation buildings and infrastructures, eHealth, domotics.

This human-service collaboration poses many new challenges to current technologies, in terms of *(i)* dynamism, *(ii)* scalability and dependability, and *(iii)* security and privacy. Indeed sensors/devices/appliances/actuators offering services are no more static, as in classical networks, (e.g., for environmental monitoring and management or surveillance), but the overall distributed system needs to continuously adapt on the basis of the user context, habits, etc. That is done by adding, removing and composing on-the-fly basic elements, that are the offered services. Moreover, in order to really immerse the users in the system, the number of sensors/devices/appliances/actuators should be huge, at least an order of magnitude more than the current situations. As an example, the current best-in-class smart houses count for tenths of sensors/devices/appliances/actuators, the

E. Bertino and J.B.D. Joshi (Eds.): CollaborateCom 2008, LNICST 10, pp. 56–69, 2009.

next generation smart houses for all will count hundreds of devices. Finally, when users make public their sensible data, the security of the overall invisible environment is crucial. Indeed if the system were hacked, it could potentially provide any sensible information of users. And that is especially critical when users have some diseases, disabilities, etc.). In the light of that, the design of the collaborating system should take into consideration privacy preservation. It should be built-in in the system, and not added-on later, as in current design practices.

The paper intends to describe the European-funded project SM4ALL (Smart hoMes for All - http://www.sm4all-project.eu), started on September 1st, 2008 and finishing on August 31st, 2011. SM4ALL aims at studying and developing an innovative platform for the collaboration of human-based and software smart embedded services in immersive and person-centric environments through the use of composition and semantic techniques. This is applied to the challenging scenario of private home and building in presence of users with different abilities and needs (e.g., young, elderly or disabled people).

In order to introduce the novel idea of collaborating services underlying SM4ALL, the reader should consider the following scenario: a person is at home and decides to take a bath. He/she would like to simply express this goal to the house (e.g., through a touch screen, but we will see later on other possible interfaces are being considered in the project) and have the services of the house collaborate in order to move the house itself to a new state which is the desired one. The temperature in the bathroom is raised through the heating service, the guardrobe in the sleeping room is opened in order to offer the bathrobe, the bath is filled in with 37 °C water, etc. If we suppose the person is a disabled one, some services cannot be directly automated, e.g., the one of helping the person to move into the bath. In this case, a service still exists, but it is offered by a human, e.g., the nursery, which is doing her job in another room, and that at the right moment is notified – through her PDA or any other device – to go into the bath and help the patient. Maybe this service is offered also by the son of the patient (or any other person), living in a nearby house, which is notified at the right moment, and if the nursery is not present at home, to help the patient. The scenario shows the idea of a society of services, some offered in a completely automated way through sensors/appliances/actuators, other realized through the collaboration of other persons, which moves continuously from a desired state to a new one, in order to satisfy user goals. Clearly, as in all societies, there are trade-offs to be considered (the goal of the person willing a relaxing bath is in contrast with the availability of the nursery/son offering the "help" service), which in our case are handled by suitably composing the most appropriate services, and possibly adapting their involvement during the runtime.

In this paper, after giving an overall insight of the SM4ALL architecture, we will outline a couple of techniques adopted in SM4ALL: Brain-Computer Interaction and Service Composition.

Brain-Computer Interaction (BCI) is a specific set of techniques, based on the interplay of hardware and software, that allows people to interact with a screen "through their mind". The project envisions the possibility of selecting a desired goal, which a user in the house would like to reach, among possible ones in the given state of the house. Such goals are proactively offered by the SM4ALL system on the basis of the available services and the current user context, which are perceived through the sensors and a profiling of previous actions and goals. Therefore, BCI interfaces are considered in the project as a suitable solution for disabled persons in order to drive the house.

Service Composition plays also an important role. We aims at proposing techniques to define the most suitable way of coordinating the available collaborating services, and will deploy such an orchestration specification on top of the infrastructure, through which the services interact each other in order to deliver some final composite service to the user. Such a composite service can effectively satisfy the user's goal, or can take the infrastructure "closer" to it.

Section 2 describes research works related to the intends of SM4ALL. Section 3 describes, firstly, the overall architecture and, then, details the initial techniques for BCI and Services' Composition. Finally, Section 4 concludes the paper, delineating the future work direction for the project.

2   Related Work

Presently, we are assisting at a blooming of research projects on domotics for assisting people with physical or mental disabilities.

For instance, at Georgia Tech a domotic home has been built for the elder adult with the goals of compensating physical decline, memory loss and supporting communication with relatives [1]. This study also considers issues of acceptability of domotics identifying key issues for the adoption of the technology by the end user. Acceptability, dangers and opportunities are also surveyed in [2]. At Carnegie Mellon people's behavior is studied by automatic analysis of video images [3]. This is fundamental in detecting anomalies and pathologies in a nursing home where many patients live. Pervading the environment with active landmarks, called Cyber Crumbs, aims at guiding the blind by equipping him/her with a smart badge [4]. A number of projects to give virtual companion's to people, to monitor people's health and behavioral patterns, to help Alzheimer patients are presented in [5]. The social dimension is considered in [6], where social networks are used to model the social relationships of the user. This network is used for providing information or issuing alarms related to the home. The Gator Tech Smart House [7] is a programmable approach to smart homes targeting the elder citizen. The idea is to have a service layer based on OGSi [8] in order to enable service discovery and composition. This work is close to what we propose as for the SOA spirit, though it does not commit to any open standard or XML based technology hindering openness and dynamic scalability of the approach. No reference is made to the communication model adopted in the home and, most notably, there is no attention toward brain interfaces.

As far as service composition, there are been in the last years several works addressing it from different point of views. So far, the work on services has largely resolved the basic interoperability problems for service composition (e.g., standards such as WS-BPEL and WS-CDL exist and are widely supported in order to compose services, even if their applicability in embedded systems is still to be demonstrated), and designing programs, called orchestrators, that execute compositions by coordinating available services according to their exported description is the bread and butter of the service programmer [9].

The availability of abstract descriptions of services has been instrumental to devising automatic techniques for synthesizing service compositions and orchestrators. Some works have concentrated on data-oriented services, by binding service composition to the work on data integration [10]. Other works have looked at process-oriented services, in which operations executed by the service have explicit effects on the system. Among these approaches, several consider *stateless* (a.k.a., atomic) services, in which the operations that can be invoked by the client do not depend on the history of interactions, as services do not retain any information about the state of such interactions. Much of this work relies on the literature on Planning in AI [11,12,13]. Others consider *stateful* services which impose some constraints on the possible sequences of operations (a.k.a., conversations) that a client can engage with the service. Composing stateful services poses additional challenges, as the composite service should be correct w.r.t. the possible conversations allowed by the component ones. Moreover, when dealing with composition, data usually play an important role: typically they are sent back, forwarded during operation invocations and manipulated by the service. This work relies on research carried out in different areas, including research on Reasoning about Actions and Planning in AI, and research about Verification and Synthesis in Computer Science [14,15,16,17].

In SM4ALL, we focus on composition of process-oriented stateful services, in particular we aim at considering and extending the framework for service composition adopted in [18,19,20,21,22,23], sometimes referred to as the "Roman Model" [24]. In the Roman Model, services are represented as transition systems (i.e., focusing on their dynamic behavior) and the composition aims at obtaining an actual composite service that preserves such an interaction. The composite service is expressed as a (virtual) target service specifying a desired interaction with the client.

Finally, we would like to point out that some projects (e.g., EU-PUBLI.com [25] in an e-Government context and WORKPAD [26] in emergency management) have considered the issue of collaborating services, in which some services actually are not classical software applications, but human operators which executing actions are abstracted by the system as services and therefore seamlessly integrated into a general architecture.

3   Architecture

The vision of collaborating services pursued by SM4ALL requires that the following features are enforced:

Person-centric awareness. Humans are at the heart of new immersive environments and all efforts to develop such environments should be initiated and motivated by needs to provide interesting and/or novel experiences to users. This requires novel technologies for *(i)* data dissemination, *(ii)* their integration, *(iii)* user profiling, *(iv)* context computation.

Globally distributed, service-centric functionalities. The middleware and provided infrastructure services (e.g., storage and retrieval of service descriptions, communication, etc.) should be managed in a widely distributed manner to guarantee dynamism, scalability and dependability.

Openness and maximum-reuse. For economy of scale, reusability and extensibility, generic embedded middleware should be developed that capture all common aspects of the immersive scenarios. Openness is also worthy as it allows to consider any service for integration.

Figure 1 shows the SM4ALL architecture, consisting of different components:

Sensors and devices. Sensors are devices for the measurement of physical quantities. There is an ever increasing variety of sensor types, ranging from simple thermometers to self-calibrating satellite-carried radiometers. They are in charge of measuring properties of the area surrounding the sensor or at a certain distance. SM4ALL points to a vast plethora of sensors without

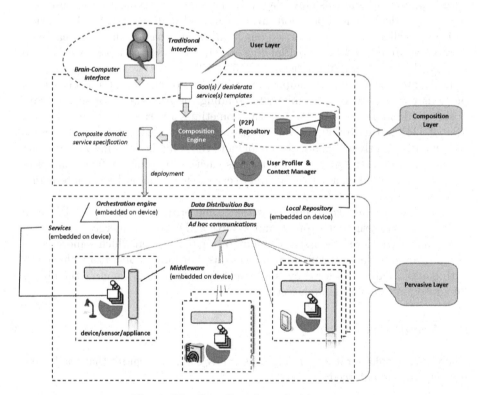

Fig. 1. The Overall SM4ALL Architecture

putting any limit. There exists, then, other devices (e.g., typical home appliances) that act on the environment for changin its properties (e.g., an appliance for opening the window can change the luminosity value sensed by a sensor).

Services. Both sensors and devices make their functionalities available according to the service oriented paradigm. Such embedded services can be either synchronous (e.g., when requesting an operation to a domestic appliance) or asynchronous (e.g., the service offered by a sensor sending the fridge temperature at regular interval). Moreover, asynchronous services can be arranged according to a publish & subscribe paradigm, in a direct-querying one, etc. Therefore, in SM4ALL, the full-fledged merge of SOAs (Service Oriented Architectures) and EDA (Event Driven Architectures) will be realized, on the basis of the standard Web service stack [27]. In order to be dynamically configured and composed, embedded services need to expose semantically rich service descriptions, comprising *(i)* interface specifications, *(ii)* specifications of the externally visible behaviors, *(iii)* offered QoS and *(iv)* security requirements.

Moreover, human actors acting in the environment can be abstracted as services, and actually "wrapped" in order to include them in the general architecture and make them collaborate with the software ones for pursuing a certain goal. Also these human-based services should be semantically described in order to include them in the more appropriate way. Their metrics can be derived through a continuous monitoring of their "performances" and user-profiling techniques); for instance, if the nursery is quite far away from a disabled person, the service "help" may present low response time and therefore, during a particular composition, may not be the best solution for reaching a given goal).

Embedded middleware. Devices, appliances and sensors are inter-connected in a wireless ad-hoc fashion, and a specific middleware needs to be available for allowing the effective interoperability among the offered services.

Embedded distributed orchestration engine. Collaboration of services needs to be carried out by a specific orchestration component. As the middleware, also this component is not centralized (as it currently happen with WS-BPEL engines in eBusiness and eGovernment scenarios), but need to be embedded in a P2P fashion in all devices/appliances/sensors of the house.

Composition engine. When the user selects a desired goal (e.g., expressed as a state of the house she would like to have realized), some automatic techniques need to synthesize the right orchestration of services able to satisfy such a goal. These techniques are realized by a composition engine, which is deployed on a special node of the infrastructure, and which is able, after the synthesis, to automatically deploy the orchestration specification on the orchestration engine for execution. Section 3.1 is devoted to give more details on this concern.

Repository of service description. Service descriptions, in order to be available during the synthesis process, need to be stored on some repository in a decentralized fashion.

Context-aware user profiler. The SM4ALL system aims at continuously profiling users and houses in order to anticipate their wishes and wills before
users explicitly express them. That is supported by the composition engine
as well as by BCI techniques. Morevoer, user profiling is crucial for deriving
QoS metrics describing human-based services.

User interface. The user is able to interact with her own house through many
interfaces, either centralized (e.g., in a home control station) or distributed
and embedded in specific interface devices. User Interfaces exploits Brain-
Computer-Interaction techniques in order to allow specific user categories
(e.g., disable or elderly people) to access and interact with the domotic in-
frastucture.

Figure 1 depicts also the deployment of the components described above in order
to highlight the pervasive and embedded nature of most of them. In order to
provide a better integrated vision of the overall SM4ALL system, we grouped
components in three layers: Pervasive, Composition and User layer.

3.1   Service Composition

Sensors and devices provide information about the environment that is remarkable to offer the best service to the user. Context-aware computing allows the
dynamic adaptation of applications and services to guarantee an optimum usage
of device and network resources, and to properly handle runtime requirements
of applications in order to provide added-value services or to carry out complex
activities. A context model should provide an unambiguous definition of the
context's semantics and usage. The context-awareness needs this model to cope
with context information belonging to heterogeneous context sources.

The user selects a desired goal expressed as a state of the environment (e.g.,
the house he/she would like to have realized). Later, some automatic techniques
are needed to synthesize the right orchestration of services able to satisfy such a
goal. These techniques are realized by a composition engine, which is deployed
on a special node of the infrastructure, and which is able, after the synthesis, to automatically deploy the orchestration specification on distributed (i.e.,
embedded into the sensors/devices/appliances/actuators) orchestration engines
for execution. The composition engine will discover available services from the
repository and compose new services as desired by the customers.

More in details, Figure 2 shows the adopted framework. The synthesis, given
the requirements of the target goal and the service descriptions of the available
services, produces a skeleton of the process of the composed service realizing
the target. Service descriptions comprise both functional features (including the
specification of the behaviour, e.g., expressed as a transition system over the
operations offered by the service) and non-functional ones, such as QoS, cost,
performance, etc. The skeleton of the composite service, together with the non
functional requirements of the target service and of the orchestration, is used
at execution-time by the orchestration and the monitoring for dynamically coordinating the available services. Specifically, the orchestration is in charge of

interacting with the client and scheduling service invocations, whereas the monitoring is in charge of monitoring the matches of the available services with respect to the specification, possibly substituting them with more suitable ones or performing remedial actions.

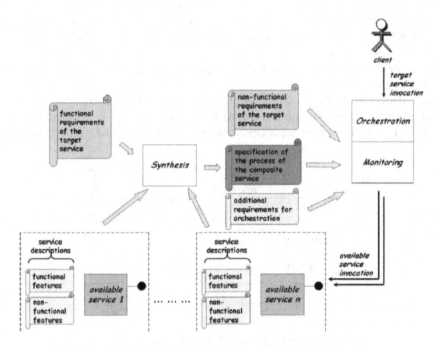

Fig. 2. The Service Composition Subsystem

3.2 Brain-Computer Interaction

Brain-Computer Interfaces (BCIs) allow individual people to communicate by detecting the user's neural activity, thus with no involvement of his/her muscles [28]. In fact, such systems are considered the only possible aid for persons with severe motor disabilities. Compared to other user interfaces, a BCI allow a reduced communication speed (up to some tens of bits per minute).

A BCI relies on the automatic detection of the user's intent, based on the classification of patterns of her brain waves. In SM4ALL, we are considering 4 steps to achieve such a detection:

Collection. Bioelectrical signals are collected from the surface of the scalp using electrodes, whose number ranges from 2 (simple applications) to 128 (brain mapping studies). These signals, whose amplitude is just a few microvolts, are amplified, digitized and sent to a processor.

Processing. Relevant features are extracted from bio-signals. Processing may consist in averaging over a few repetitions of the same response of the brain to an external stimulus (as in the case of BCIs based on P300), or in the analysis of spectral properties of the electroencephalographic signal (as in the case of BCIs based on sensorimotor rhythms).

Translation. This is a two-step process. First, features of the biological signal are combined (linearly or nonlinearly) into a logical signal, which may either be an analogical signal (e.g., a degree of displacement from baseline values), or a discrete output (e.g., an actual classification). Second, the logical signal is further transformed into a semantic signal, which is meaningful for the application control interface (e.g., in the case of a computer application, how many pixels a cursor should be displaced, which command was selected in a menu, etc.).

Application Control. Semantic symbols are finally translated into physical controls for the actual application, which may consist of, for instance, a computer program, an assisting device, a robot, or a whole a domotic enviromnemt.

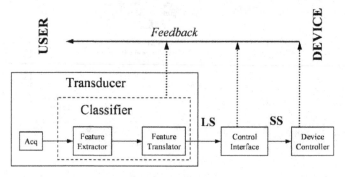

Fig. 3. Functional model of a BCI system [29]

The above steps are supported by a typical BCI architecture (see Figure 3, [30,31]) consisting of a commercial electroencephalographic (EEG) system connected to a personal computer running software that implements, processes, interfaces and communicates with the applications. An EEG can record a positive deflection in voltage at a latency of roughly 300 ms. This event related potential (ERP) is named *P300 (P3) potential* wave and is typically measured most strongly by the electrodes covering the parietal lobe. The presence, magnitude, topography and time of this signal are often used as metrics of cognitive function in decision making processes. While the neural substrates of this ERP still remain hazy, the reproducibility of this signal makes it a common choice for psychological tests in both the clinic and laboratory.

Figure 4 shows the current prototypal version developed in Fondazione Santa Lucia. The figure depicts a user who controls home appliances using a Brain Computer Interface. Electrodes fixed on the user's head measure brain potentials, which are processed by a PC (not shown). The visual interface shows an icon based cascading menu. When a certain icon is flashing and a P300 potential is recognized, that means the user is concentrating on it.

Fig. 4. A prototype developed in Fondazione Santa Lucia

After the command is recognized by the BCI, a command is sent to the target switch to enable/disable specific domotics features (light, fan, motorized armchair, etc).

In particular, the BCI system currently utilized in the SM4ALL project is composed by the following parts:

Acquisition hardware. A portable 8-channel EEG amplifier (g.Mobilab, gTec GmbH, Austria) collects brain potentials from an array of electrodes mounted on the user's head by means of an elastic cap. The signal is amplified, digitized and preprocessed (e.g., bandpassed) and transmitted wireless over a Bluetooth connection.

Processing hardware/software. Feature extraction and translation is performed by means of the BCI2000 software [32] running on a portable PC. Feature extraction consists in the analysis of short (500 ms) segments of EEG following each cue on the Control Interface screen (see below), in order to detect whether a P300 potential is present. P300 reveals that the user was in fact concentrating on that specific cue, thus detecting his intention.

Control interface. The control interface (CI) prompt the user with a set of possible choices, and delivers the stimulation (cue) which may trigger a P300 wave. The CI builds the current set of choices based on: (i) previous selections, thus acting as a multi-layer menu, and (ii) information from the SM4ALL architecture (through the Application Interface), which holds the user profile and the current state of the environment.

In SM4ALL, a bi-directional interface provides connection between the BCI and the rest of the system. From the BCI point of view, it provides information about the state of the environment; this information is used by the Control Interface to build up the set of possible selections, which is thus dynamically linked to the most probable choices (i.e., the possible target that the user would like to reach and the system realized by composing and orchestrating the services).

As for the user interaction, in general she will be able to interact with the house through many interfaces, either centralized (e.g., in a home control station) or distributed and embedded in specific interface devices. Specifically, the BCI system will provide interfaces particularly suited to some specific categories of users (disabled, etc.), allowing them to exploit almost all services offered by the platform.

Concerning the users, we have to characterize their roles (end users, doctors, relatives, etc.), their needs and capabilities, and their usual behaviour, in order to activate the right UI functionalities and to suitably adapt the interface. As for the system, a formal description of available devices, in terms of I/O operations and bandwidth is needed, together with a characterization of the environment hosting the user, in terms of topology, installed sensors, people and object locations, equipment (TV, radio, phone, etc.). In this way, the system is aware of the actual user role, needs, and capabilities, and knowing the environment and the installed sensors and devices, it is able to compute the actual state (e.g., temperature value, end user watching the tv, phone ringing, etc.), selecting the applicable commands and controls and presenting them to the user according to her role and capabilities and the installed UI I/O channels. As an example, when the phone rings, the system activates an icon on the PC screen interface and two flashing lights, one in the kitchen and another one near the phone.

Adaptivity is the key feature to allow an effective interaction between user and system through a low-speed communication channel like BCI. The adaptation involves both the way in which the interface commands are presented to the user (e.g., large icons, pop up menus, physical buttons or switches, etc.) and their order (as an example, the command *open the door* is presented as a first choice when the door is ringing). This implies to build and instantiate a user profile able to capture user preferences and capabilities and an environment profile, corresponding to the house status (temperature, light, phone/door ringing, and so on). Moreover, a set of parameters/constraints will model some relationships among users, interface, and environment. As an example, it could be possible to pose some temporal constraints on the maximum time of action completion (e.g., the answering time for an incoming phone call must not exceed 10 seconds) or to model the fact that the average selecting time of an icon using a low-speed communication channel, for a given user, is 4.5 seconds (and variance is 1.4 seconds). Such figures allow to define some quality metrics and give precise indications and constraints on how to arrange the interface command order (e.g., putting the *answer the phone* command on the third menu level may result in an answering time exceeding the 10 second constraint). On the other end, the adaptation mechanism should not be invasive, allowing the user to quickly switch the interaction to a prefixed, static, behavior. This is quite useful when contrasting happened situations unforeseen and the user wants to override the automatic system choices. Roughly speaking, the system should allows to associate each user to a static and optimized interface and to a set of rules/metrics allowing to adapt the static structure to the context and, at same time, leaving the user free to switch between the two modalities at any time.

4   Conclusions

In this paper we have outlined the SM4ALL project, which aims at studying and developing a pervasive service oriented architecture, in which the collaboration of services (either software-based or human-based) seamlessly allow users (including those ones with disabilities) to continuously interact with the environment.

The project, recently started, is expected to follow a User-Centered Design approach, in which continuous interactions with concrete users is pursued through the development of mock-ups, prototypes, etc. till the final system. Concurrently, a deep analysis over available sensors/actuators/devices/appliances and their capabilities to host services is undertaken, in order to better characterize the possible performance level that may be obtained.

Acknowledgements. The work is partly supported through the FP7-224332 SM4ALL project. The authors would like to thank the other project partners for useful discussions, and BTicino for providing the hardware equipments currently used in some experimentations.

References

1. Mynatt, E., Melenhorst, A., Fisk, A., Rogers, W.: Understanding user needs and attitudes. IEEE Pervasive Computing 3, 36–41 (2004)
2. Roberts, J.: Pervasive health management and health management utilizing pervasive technologies: Synergy and issues. The Journal of Universal Computer Science 12, 6–14 (2006)
3. Hauptmann, A., Gao, J., Yan, R., Qi, Y., Yang, J., Wactlar, H.: Automatic analysis of nursing home observations. IEEE Pervasive Computing 3, 15–21 (2004)
4. Ross, D.: Cyber crumbs for successful aging with vision loss. IEEE Pervasive Computing 3, 30–35 (2004)
5. Joseph, A.: Successful aging. IEEE Pervasive Computing 3, 36–41 (2004)
6. Consolvo, S., Roessler, P., Shelton, B., LaMarca, A., Schilit, B., Bly, S.: Technology for care networks of elders. IEEE Pervasive Computing 3, 22–29 (2004)
7. Helal, S., Mann, W.C., El-Zabadani, H., King, J., Kaddoura, Y., Jansen, E.: The gator tech smart house: A programmable pervasive space. IEEE Computer 38, 50–60 (2005)
8. Tuecke, S., Foster, I., Frey, J., Graham, S., Kesselman, C., Maquire, T., Sandholm, T., Snelling, D., Vanderbilt, P.: Open service grid infrastructure (2003)
9. Alonso, G., Casati, F., Kuno, H., Machiraju, V.: Web Services. Concepts, Architectures and Applications. Springer, Heidelberg (2004)
10. Michalowski, M., Ambite, J.L., Knoblock, C.A., Minton, S., Thakkar, S., Tuchinda, R.: Retrieving and semantically integrating heterogeneous data from the web. IEEE Intelligent Systems 19, 72–79 (2004)

11. Wu, D., Parsia, B., Sirin, E., Hendler, J.A., Nau, D.S.: Automating DAML-S Web Services Composition Using SHOP2. In: Fensel, D., Sycara, K.P., Mylopoulos, J. (eds.) ISWC 2003. LNCS, vol. 2870, pp. 195–210. Springer, Heidelberg (2003)
12. Blythe, J., Ambite, J.L. (eds.): Proceedings of ICAPS 2004 Workshop on Planning and Scheduling for Web and Grid Services. ICAPS (2004)
13. Cardoso, J., Sheth, A.: Introduction to semantic web services and web process composition. In: Cardoso, J., Sheth, A.P. (eds.) SWSWPC 2004. LNCS, vol. 3387, pp. 1–13. Springer, Heidelberg (2005)
14. Bultan, T., Fu, X., Hull, R., Su, J.: Conversation specification: a new approach to design and analysis of e-service composition. In: Proceedings of the Twelfth International World Wide Web Conference, WWW, pp. 403–410 (2003)
15. Pistore, M., Traverso, P., Bertoli, P.: Automated composition of web services by planning in asynchronous domains. In: Proceedings of the Fifteenth International Conference on Automated Planning and Scheduling (ICAPS 2005), pp. 2–11 (2005)
16. Gerede, C.E., Hull, R., Ibarra, O.H., Su, J.: Automated composition of e-services: lookaheads. In: Service-Oriented Computing - ICSOC 2004, Second International Conference, Proceedings, pp. 252–262 (2004)
17. McIlraith, S.A., Son, T.C.: Adapting golog for composition of semantic web services. In: Proceedings of the Eights International Conference on Principles and Knowledge Representation and Reasoning (KR 2002), Toulouse, France, April 22-25, pp. 482–496 (2002)
18. Berardi, D., Calvanese, D., Giacomo, G.D., Lenzerini, M., Mecella, M.: Automatic composition of e-services that export their behavior. In: Orlowska, M.E., Weerawarana, S., Papazoglou, M.P., Yang, J. (eds.) ICSOC 2003. LNCS, vol. 2910, pp. 43–58. Springer, Heidelberg (2003)
19. Berardi, D., Calvanese, D., De Giacomo, G., Lenzerini, M., Mecella, M.: Automatic service composition based on behavioral descriptions. International Journal of Cooperative Information Systems (IJCIS) 14, 333–376 (2005)
20. Berardi, D., Calvanese, D., De Giacomo, G., Mecella, M.: Composition of services with nondeterministic observable behavior. In: Benatallah, B., Casati, F., Traverso, P. (eds.) ICSOC 2005. LNCS, vol. 3826, pp. 520–526. Springer, Heidelberg (2005)
21. Muscholl, A., Walukiewicz, I.: A lower bound on web services composition. In: Seidl, H. (ed.) FOSSACS 2007. LNCS, vol. 4423, pp. 274–286. Springer, Heidelberg (2007)
22. Giacomo, G.D., Sardiña, S.: Automatic synthesis of new behaviors from a library of available behaviors. In: Proceedings of the 20th International Joint Conference on Artificial Intelligence (IJCAI 2007), pp. 1866–1871 (2007)
23. Sardina, S., Patrizi, F., De Giacomo, G.: Behavior composition in the presence of failure. In: Proceedings, Tenth International Conference on Principles of Knowledge Representation and Reasoning (KR 2008) (2008)
24. Hull, R.: Web services composition: A story of models, automata, and logics. In: Proceedings of the IEEE International Conference on Web Services (ICWS 2005), Orlando, FL, USA, July 11-15 (2005)
25. Contenti, M., Mecella, M., Termini, A., Baldoni, R.: A Distributed Architecture for Supporting e-Government Cooperative Processes. In: Böhlen, M.H., Gamper, J., Polasek, W., Wimmer, M.A. (eds.) TCGOV 2005. LNCS, vol. 3416, pp. 181–192. Springer, Heidelberg (2005)
26. Catarci, T., de Leoni, M., Marrella, A., Mecella, M., Salvatore, B., Vetere, G., Dustdar, S., Juszczyk, L., Manzoor, A., Truong, H.: Pervasive Software Environments for Supporting Disaster Responses. IEEE Internet Computing 12, 26–37 (2008)

27. Aiello, M., Dustdar, S.: Are our homes ready for services? a domotic infrastructure based on the web service stack. Pervasive and Mobile Computing 4, 506–525 (2008)
28. Wolpaw, J.R., Birbaumer, N., McFarland, D.J., Pfurtscheller, G., Vaughan, T.M.: Brain-computer interfaces for communication and control. Clinical neurophysiology 113, 767–791 (2002)
29. Bianchi, L., Quitadamo, L.R., Garreffa, G., Cardarilli, G.C., Marciani, M.G.: Performances evaluation and optimization of brain computer interface systems in a copy spelling task. IEEE Transaction on Neural Systems and Rehabilitation Engineering 15, 207–216 (2007)
30. Mason, S.G., Birch, G.E.: A general framework for brain-computer interface design. IEEE Transaction on Neural Systems and Rehabilitation Engineering 11, 70–85 (2003)
31. Mason, S.G., Bashashati, A., Fatourechi, M., Navarro, K.F., Birch, G.E.: A comprehensive survey of brain interface technology designs. Annals of Biomedical Engineering 35, 137–169 (2007)
32. Schalk, G., McFarland, D.J., Hinterberger, T., Birbaumer, N., Wolpaw, J.R.: BCI2000: a general-purpose brain-computer interface (BCI) system. IEEE Transaction on Neural Systems and Rehabilitation Engineering 51, 1034–1043 (2004)

Archer: A Community Distributed Computing Infrastructure for Computer Architecture Research and Education

Renato J. Figueiredo[1], P. Oscar Boykin[1], José A.B. Fortes[1], Tao Li[1],
Jie-Kwon Peir[1], David Wolinsky[1], Lizy K. John[2], David R. Kaeli[3],
David J. Lilja[4], Sally A. McKee[5], Gokhan Memik[6], Alain Roy[7],
and Gary S. Tyson[8]

[1] University of Florida, Gainesville, FL, USA
[2] University of Texas, Austin, TX, USA
[3] Northeastern University, Boston, MA, USA
[4] University of Minnesota, Twin Cities, MN, USA
[5] Cornell University, Ithaca, NY, USA
[6] Northwestern University, Evanston, IL, USA
[7] University of Wisconsin, Madison, WI, USA
[8] Florida State University, Tallahassee, FL, USA
http://archer-project.org

Abstract. This paper introduces Archer, a community-based computing infrastructure supporting computer architecture research and education. The Archer system builds on virtualization techniques to provide a collaborative environment that facilitates sharing of computational resources and data among users. It integrates batch scheduling middleware to deliver high-throughput computing services aggregated from resources distributed across wide-area networks and owned by different participating entities in a seamless manner. The paper discusses the motivations that have led to the design of Archer, describes its core middleware components, and presents an analysis of the functionality and performance of the first wide-area deployment of Archer running a representative computer architecture simulation workload.

Keywords: virtualization, computer architecture, simulation, collaborative environments, Grid computing.

1   Introduction

Modern computer architecture research is driven by quantitative analysis. Leading-edge research requires detailed, cycle-accurate evaluation of many benchmark applications with several simulated configurations and is thus tightly dependent on the availability of high-throughput computing (HTC) systems. Many research groups are hindered in their ability to perform research because of lack of access to such resources. This is because, in addition to hardware costs, the investment of time and funds to train and educate students and staff to deploy,

E. Bertino and J.B.D. Joshi (Eds.): CollaborateCom 2008, LNICST 10, pp. 70–84, 2009.

maintain and effectively use such systems presents a significant barrier of entry, especially for small- to medium-sized research groups. This paper describes Archer, a community-based computing resource for computer architecture research and education. Archer integrates technologies for resource virtualization, batch job schedulers, and multi-institution collaboration, in order to create:

- *A computing infrastructure which scales in capacity with community buy-in*: Archer starts from a seed set of cluster resources deployed at the Florida State University, Northeastern University, University of Texas at Austin, Northwestern University, University of Minnesota, Cornell University, and University of Florida. In addition to this seed set, each new user joining Archer with one or more desktops or servers seamlessly contribute to its aggregate capacity.
- *A system that is easy for non-experts to join and use*: Archer relies on packaging and distribution of high-throughput computing software environments as self-configuring virtual networks of virtual machine (VM) "appliances". System virtual machines [19] (such as VMware, VirtualBox) are easily installed by individual users in their own resources and can coexist with existing software in a non-intrusive manner. VM appliances allow packaging of complex system software in images that are easy to deploy [18,21]. Surveys shows that users with no prior experience with VMs can typically install and use the appliances upon which Archer is built within 30 minutes.
- *A community-based repository of simulation environments*: Archer allows sharing not only of hardware resources, but also of full-fledged software simulation modules consisting of application executables, support scripts, input and output data sets, and usage documents. In doing so, Archer facilitates the dissemination of useful tools and data sets, and foster creation of reproducible simulation experiments.

The system architecture and design choices made in Archer significantly differentiate it from related infrastructures such as the Open Science Grid (OSG) and TeraGrid, in three important ways. First, Archer enables seamless addition of resources by the community, at a fine grain (at a minimum a single desktop computer by an individual user), within minutes. This is in contrast to OSG and TeraGrid, where individual resources cannot be easily incorporated. Second, Archer deployments are virtualized and can be easily replicated, both at a smaller scale within an institution, and at a multi-institution scale by research communities. Such replicability enables research groups to easily bring up (using Archer software) local resource pools and be assured of preemptive access to their resources when needed, while providing opportunistic cycles to the community. This is in contrast to OSG and TeraGrid, which are large-scale shared physical resources not easily replicable at a small scale on local resources. Third, Archer empowers entry-level users to quickly learn HTC skills, from basic to advanced, with an interactive graphical interface hosted on their own workstations. This is in contrast to OSG and TeraGrid, where entry-level users need to learn how to operate resources that are hosted remotely, using non-interactive sessions and unfamiliar interfaces for data transfer, login, and job scheduling.

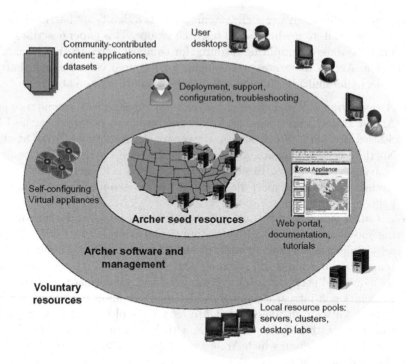

Fig. 1. Overview of Archer. The seed resources consist of seven clusters at Cornell, Florida State, Northeastern, Northwestern, U. Minnesota, U. Texas at Austin, and U. Florida. In addition to the hardware infrastructure, Archer provides virtual appliance (U. Florida) and job scheduling (U. Wisconsin) software and ready access to user-contributed data and applications. Users from non-seed sites build upon these elements to increase available resources when they join the system.

The technology in Archer provides a way to swiftly create grids of medium size, which is complementary to these projects. Figure 1 presents an overview of the Archer infrastructure.

2   Background and Motivations

In modern computer architectures, processor performance, power consumption and cost are significantly affected by design parameters and target workloads. Thus, researchers rely on simulation environments to evaluate the merit of a new idea before it is implemented in hardware. In addition, computer architects depend on high-fidelity, cycle-accurate simulation environments (including the simulators themselves and associated tools such as compilers and datasets). Because these are complex and time-consuming to develop, researchers have relied on extensible simulation environments, benchmarks and datasets developed by others in the community — such as SimpleScalar [6], SESC [17], Simics [2], among others — as well as on modules that plug in to commercial systems, such as GEMS for Simics. The broad needs of computer architecture researchers to access high-performance resources and share simulation environments are addressed in an integrated manner by Archer. We believe that the availability of Archer encourages collaboration among groups by greatly simplifying the dissemination of applications, and increases the competitiveness of smaller research groups by providing seamless access to hardware resources and software environments. To illustrate use cases and the unique capabilities enabled by Archer, consider the scenarios described in Table 1 and illustrated by the following three fictional examples:

- *Scenario 1: High-throughput cycles for research*: Graduate student Maria at Florida State U. is preparing a paper on a novel cache design for submission to a conference. She has developed a simulator which models her design. Each simulation takes on average 12 hours to complete on her desktop, and she wishes to analyze 10 configurations on 16 SPEC CPU benchmarks. The time to run this experiment on her desktop is prohibitively large (80 days). She downloads, instantiates an Archer appliance, copies her Linux simulator binary to the VM, prepares a Condor job file (building on a tutorial), and queues 160 jobs. Archer resources are utilized at 75% capacity by other jobs; still, her simulations are expected to finish within a day.

- *Scenario 2: Local resource pooling and community sharing*: A group at Northeastern University has a local set of resources, time-shared and scheduled by students via scripts. Because the scripts do not provide load balancing, often resources become contended. They try out the Archer VM appliance and decide to join. Interacting with Archer management, they set up a local Condor pool. Their resources are load-balanced, and when not in use, they become available to other Archer users through Condor flocking.

- *Scenario 3: Collaborative development and dissemination of tools and experiments*: A joint project between Cornell and Northwestern entails the development of an environment with extensions to the SESC simulator. Graduate students Carol at Cornell and John at NWU begin development by downloading code from the SESC software repository onto Archer appliances. Carol implements and tests new features in the simulator within her VM, creates Condor scripts that vary a parameter of interest, and places her code and scripts in a shared repository. John uses Carol's code to perform experiments of his own. After several iterations, they gather data for their experiments and publish a paper highlighting their findings. They make the source code snapshot, benchmarks, and Condor scripts available on the Archer Wiki as well as on an Archer NFS (Network File System) repository which is accessible to the entire virtual network, enabling others to repeat and build upon their experiment.

Table 1. Scenarios in which users with different levels of expertise can use Archer

User	Scenario	Resources/interfaces used
Novice	Casual/trial usage of the system e.g. homework assignments in undergraduate classes	Access pre-built tools, tutorials, educational modules through interactive Web portal. No local software required but Web browser
Entry level	Small-scale experiments on Archer resources; graduate class projects	Baseline Archer appliance installed on personal workstation. Reuse tools, datasets and scripts, and pre-packaged tutorials.
Advanced	Graduate research; run medium to large-scale experiments on Archer Develop/modify simulation tools	User builds simulation tools and scripts of their own. Software installation time: 15-30 minutes
Research group	Use Archer software to manage local resources (e.g. desktop grids); deploy local/multi-site Archer pools with high priority for users belonging to research group.	Customized Archer appliance installed on PCs of researchers, lab PCs, servers and clusters. Customization and installation times: hours to days.

3   Archer Infrastructure

3.1   Overall Design Approach

The key motivations for the Archer infrastructure to be a distributed system are scalability, sustainability and dependability: new resources that join increase system capacity, the infrastructure is sustained by the community and does not overburden a single site with hosting, and the system can withstand hardware/software failures in individual sites. A distributed system, however, poses challenges in management which need to be addressed. Our system design builds on virtualization and autonomic computing techniques that specifically target ease of management. They make it possible to have effective centralized management of decentralized resources, similarly to successful infrastructures such as PlanetLab [15]. The Archer middleware integrates easy-to-install, self-configuring virtual machine appliances with virtual networks to create scalable community pools of virtual resources. Each Archer resource is a virtual appliance that is preconfigured with an installation of a Linux O/S and distributed computing middleware (Condor [16]). Archer virtual appliances are interconnected by the IPOP [9] self-configuring virtual network overlay. The choice of virtual appliances, virtual networks and Condor is motivated by the following reasons:

1. *Ease of deployment*: Virtual appliances can be easily deployed on typical x86-based machines regardless of their existing hardware/software configuration. Today's VM technologies are mature and several free virtualization options exist for Windows, Linux and MacOS systems (including VMware Player/Server, KVM, VirtualBox and Xen). Experiments with our prototype environment show that Archer virtual appliances can be deployed typically within 30 minutes by entry-level users.

2. *Software compatibility*: Virtual appliances can run unmodified, binary software, including a wealth of existing computer architecture simulators and support tools. Representative examples include SESC, SimpleScalar, PTLsim and Simics.

3. *Seamless connectivity*: The IPOP virtual network overlay which runs on Archer appliances provides bidirectional IP connectivity across all appliances. The virtual network supports nodes behind firewalls and network address translators (NATs) typically found in educational institutions and Internet service providers. The virtual network is self-organizing and packaged with the virtual appliance in a way that does not require any configuration from end users.

4. *Scalable and robust job scheduling*: Condor is a robust job scheduler used in thousands of resources across the world. It supports both unmodified binaries and Condor-linked applications, facilitates the queuing and management of large numbers of jobs, and has been successfully demonstrated to be effective in supporting a variety of computer architecture simulation workloads.

5. *Isolation*: Virtual appliances are isolated from their hosts. Undesirable behavior is confined to a VM, which can be easily shut down and restarted from scratch by its user.

3.2   Archer Core Middleware

Virtual Machines

Archer builds on the Grid appliance system [21], which is a self-configuring virtual machine appliance that packages, in an easy-to-deploy image: a Linux distribution trimmed for size, the Condor high-throughput computing scheduler [16], the IPOP [9] virtual network, and system management scripts that automate the process of joining the Archer virtual network. Figures 2 and 3 show screenshots of the Grid appliance.

Classic system VMs were originally developed to enable efficient time-sharing of mainframe computers by multiple independent applications and O/Ss [12,19]. They are implemented by means of VM monitors (also known as hypervisors), which are responsible for intercepting and emulating the execution of privileged instructions that deal with shared resources: CPU, memory and I/O. VM technologies have evolved quite rapidly in recent years [8]. VMs now can achieve performance on par with non-virtualized systems [5], and are increasingly pervasive in commodity systems; virtualization extensions are shipped with all Intel and AMD x86 processors, virtualization software is available from a variety of vendors (VMware, Microsoft, Parallels) and in the open source realm (Xen, KVM, which has already been integrated with the Linux kernel, and VirtualBox). The isolation and decoupling properties of VMs are particularly attractive in distributed systems [7]. Virtual machines assist in the deployment of compute nodes because of their decoupling from the operating system running on the physical machine. VMs offer unique opportunities for load balancing and fault tolerance that build upon growing support for checkpointing and live migration of running VMs. Furthermore, the ability to package VM software in easy-to-deploy virtual appliances [18] is attractive as a means to disseminate (and maintain) complex, preconfigured software and middleware stacks.

Virtual Networks

Archer VMs are decoupled not only from the physical hosts by means of the VM monitor, but also from the physical network by means of tunneling. Once instantiated, an Archer VM appliance is able to self-configure and maintain connections to other appliances via IPOP tunnels. The resulting system is akin in functionality to a Network of Workstations (NOW [4]); we term it a Wide-area Overlay of virtual Workstations (WOW [10]) because both compute nodes and network links are virtualized, and resources are distributed across wide-area domains.

Complementary to VMs, virtual networking enables isolated multiplexing of private networks providing the TCP/IP environment for communication among participating nodes. Network virtualization techniques for distributed grid computing [20,9,10,13] have been shown to provide applications their native network environments, despite the idiosyncrasies of the real physical network — in particular, the increasing use of Network Address Translation (NAT) and IP firewalls, recognized as a hindrance to programming and deploying distributed computing applications, does not impede the use of virtual network-based systems. Central to the scalability of Archer are peer-to-peer techniques for resource discovery, virtual network routing, and NAT traversal, which are described in detail in [10].

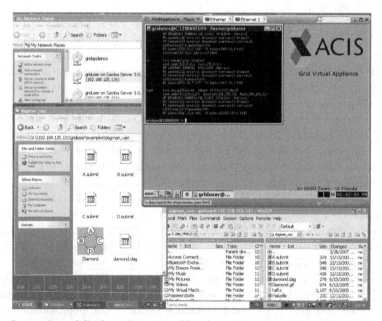

Fig. 2. Screenshot of Grid appliance in a Windows host. Top right: Grid appliance X11 user interface; top and bottom left: loop-back Samba file share allows simple browsing and drag-and-drop movement of files from host to appliance; bottom right: loop-back SSH server allows login and file transfers to the appliance.

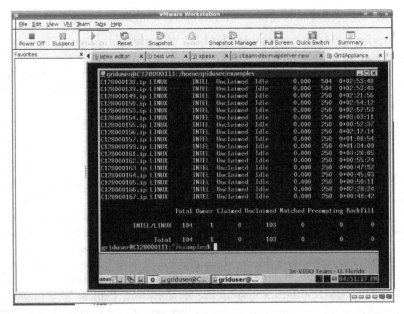

Fig. 3. The screenshot shows the Grid appliance graphical user interface and the output of the condor_status command

Condor

Condor provides easy access to large amounts of dependable and reliable computational power over prolonged periods of time by effectively harnessing all available resources, including both dedicated compute clusters and non-dedicated machines under the control of interactive users or autonomous batch systems.

Condor is an established distributed computing environment appropriate for building an ad-hoc high-throughput computing grid like Archer. Throughout this time, Condor has evolved from a local batch management system into a full-fledged distributed computing environment capable of supporting wide-area grids, complex workflows, compute-intensive applications, and data placement reliably, scalably, and with fault tolerance. It has facilities for resource monitoring, job scheduling, and workflow supervision. Current statistics show that Condor has been deployed on well more than 100,000 computers in well more than 1400 Condor pools. An important feature of the Archer system is that it creates an incentive for sites to join the infrastructure with several nodes. The pre-packaged Archer VMs provide an easy way to set up local Condor pools to manage jobs submitted by local users of a site, which are guaranteed to gain high-priority access to their resources and access to external Archer resources through flocking, while making their resources available to remote Archer users when they are idle. This kind of deployment with multiple shared pools where local control and priority is retained by individual groups has been an important feature of the GLOW infrastructure at Wisconsin, and we expect it to create further incentives for the growth of Archer.

3.3 Collaboration and Sharing

Collaboration in Archer is enabled by both the distributed virtualized infrastructure and a centralized Web-based server. The Archer Web presence includes a content management system and Web portal, with a user registration system, a Wiki (where Archer users can share documentation on how to use simulation tools in the system), and user discussion groups.

In addition to the Web-based framework for collaboration, the wide-area network of Archer virtual machines provides a basis for the deployment of file-system based data sharing frameworks that are widely used in systems, such as the Network File System (NFS). In the computer architecture field, it is desirable to use experimental data sets that include checkpointed disk and memory images containing representative benchmark workloads to drive execution-driven simulators. These disk/memory images can be large (of the order of GBytes each), as they encapsulate entire operating systems and application benchmarks. Nonetheless, in many instances these images are sparse and only a fraction of the data (few MBytes) is referenced during a simulation. Archer provides a framework for on-demand, block-level data transfer that builds on the Network File System (NFS) de-facto distributed file system implementation. Typical NFS implementations target local-area environments; Archer provides a tunneling framework that allows the deployment of wide-area NFS file systems over the encrypted tunnels enabled by IPOP. The current NFS-based deployment provides users with an automatically configured "export" folder in their appliance, where they can copy datasets that are then available via on-demand, auto-mounted read only NFS mounts.

3.4 Deployment Modes

Recognizing that the the infrastructure is used in different ways by different kinds of users, Archer supports three main deployment modes: Express, Global and Local.

Archer Express: The main purpose of Archer Express is to make it as simple as possible for a user with little background on VMs, Linux, or Condor to get started with a hands-on experiment with Archer in less than 30 minutes. Archer Express includes a small-scale public resource test pool, and a self-configuring VM appliance that does not require registration and authentication with the database of registered users.

Archer Global: The main purpose of Archer Global is to serve as the production, large-scale resource pool for the computer architecture community at large. Unlike Archer Express, where the key goals are quick deployment and ease of use, Archer Global strives to achieve scalability with strong security guarantees, by creating a private pool connecting resources of registered Archer users.

Archer Local: The main purpose of Archer Local is to allow users who wish to deploy a private Archer pool — i.e. one that runs on their own resources and is fully decoupled from Archer Global and Archer Express. With Archer Local, users are in control of the entire configuration and management of their local cluster, independently from other Archer resources.

3.5   Security Considerations

By utilizing VMs, virtual networks and Condor, Archer provides several levels of isolation among users and with respect to the physical infrastructure. The only access that external users have to any Archer VM is through Condor, as an unprivileged user "nobody" — no direct logins are allowed. The VM runs only essential middleware services to minimize the possibility of privilege escalation within the VM. Even if privilege escalation does happen, users are confined to a virtual machine sandbox and do not have direct access to the underlying physical resources. The TCP/IP traffic that is generated by a VM is completely confined to the virtual network, as described in [21]. Archer hosts are authenticated and traffic is encrypted end-to-end by deploying a security stack in each VM based on public key cryptography (PKI). In other words, Archer VMs are only able to communicate with other Archer VMs, preventing the use of Archer resources to initiate denial of service or other kinds of attacks to physical resources. There are a couple of exceptions to this rule, which are necessary for Archer VMs to be accessible from physical resources so users can interact with them. We establish communication channels between Archer VMs and physical hosts using host-only virtual networks (software-emulated networks confined to a single host) that are carefully controlled to provide only two types of services: secure shell logins, and access to user data within the VM through Samba and NFS file systems. In a typical usage case of a Windows-based desktop, a user deploys an Archer VM on their desktop, interacts with the X11-based graphical user interface in the VM through its console, logs into the VM from the physical host using SSH, and browses a Samba network share exported by the appliance (accessible only within the host) to copy data to and from the VM. Security patches are regularly applied to the baseline Archer VMs and made available for upgrades; the process of upgrading VM appliances is facilitated by the use of UnionFS stacked file systems, whereby it is possible for users to upgrade the base system configuration of the appliance by simply replacing a virtual disk file and rebooting the system. User data and local configurations remain unmodified in the VM after the upgrade as they are stored in different stacks of the file system.

3.6   Performance Considerations

The advantages in isolation, security and management provided by VMs connected over virtual networks have associated performance overheads due to the VM and virtual network tunneling. However, these overheads are often small for CPU-intensive applications which are typical in computer architecture simulation. Studies have quantified this overhead under different scenarios, showing that the overhead CPU-intensive applications such as SPEC benchmarks is a few percent points [5], and in [21] it has been shown that the virtual/physical overhead for a Xen VM connected to a virtual network approximately 1% for a 37-minute Condor-scheduled SimpleScalar run (sim-cache, "go" benchmark). The following experiment illustrates the capabilities and performance of the middleware and software of Archer in the context of computer architecture research and education. We have run a simulation experiment in our prototype Archer deployment, in which 200 jobs were submitted from a virtual appliance. Each job consisted of a cache simulation running 1 billion instructions of the SPEC benchmark "go" for different cache configurations arising from varying level-1 and level-2 cache sizes and associativities. The jobs were submitted from a laptop running the Archer virtual appliance behind a broadband (1MB/s) network provider. The virtual appliances in which the jobs executed were distributed across five universities (including U. Florida, U. Minnesota, Northwestern University), making up a pool of 56 VMs.

The total execution time to finish all 200 jobs was approximately 7.5 hours. If these jobs were to be executed on a single node, the execution time would have been 9.5 days assuming the median single job times measured across the 56 heterogeneous resources. Figure 4 shows a plot of the cumulative distribution of number of jobs completed as a function of time. The virtualization overhead for this application using VMware-based VMs was measured to be 11 percent, which is acceptable given the goal of achieving high throughput. Reducing the overhead introduced by

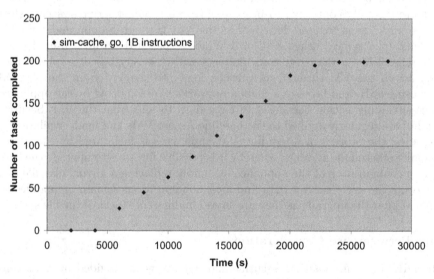

Fig. 4. Distribution of simulation completion times for an experiment with 200 SimpleScalar sim-cache jobs executed on a 56-node prototype Archer system. The median and average single job execution times are 4080 and 4320 seconds, respectively. In steady state the system was completing jobs at an approximate rate of one job every 90 seconds, compared to the throughput of one job per 42 minutes of a single job running on a single resource.

virtual machines is an active area of research and development in academia and industry, and the expected trend is for these overheads to be reduced.

4   Related Work

Inspired by projects which have been extremely successful at bringing large number of voluntary resources, such as SETIhome [3] and other BOINC-based (Berkeley Open Infrastructure for Network Computing) projects, Archer also allows nodes to join the infrastructure seamlessly. The key difference in Archer is that, in BOINC-based systems, applications need to be modified to use their application programming interfaces, and users are constrained to donating resources only. In contrast, in the Archer infrastructure, the computing node sandboxes are system VMs capable of running existing, unmodified binary applications, which is critical for adoption by the computer architecture community. Furthermore, users are able to both donate and make use of Archer resources through their virtual appliances.

Archer is closely related to PlanetLab [15] with respect to how resources are distributed and managed. PlanetLab is also a distributed system where individual researchers across many sites contribute to the overall aggregate capacity of the system by providing locally managed physical hardware (805 nodes at 402 sites worldwide, as of July 2007, while the middleware and software is managed in a centralized manner (by PlanetLab Central). However, Archer differs fundamentally from PlanetLab in purpose. PlanetLab is a generic testbed for experimental networking research and does not support load balancing of jobs, while Archer targets compute-intensive applications. Archer is also different in that it does not require dedicated non-firewalled physical machines.

RAMP (Research Accelerator for Multiple Processors [1]) is a related resource for the computer architecture community. The focus of RAMP is on the use of programmable logic to speed up the simulation of large-scale multiprocessors. While RAMP provides the potential for large speedups over software simulation, it requires users to develop their simulation infrastructure to match the specific RAMP software and hardware stack. Archer, in contrast, is general-purpose and supports a wealth of unmodified single- and multi-processor simulation tools that computer architecture researchers already use in their own local environments (e.g. SimpleScalar, SESC, Simics), offering a lower barrier of entry to its use. Nonetheless, Archer and RAMP are complementary resources in that they focus on different aspects of quantitative computer architecture research: general-purpose simulation in Archer, high-performance multi-processor simulation in RAMP.

Archer is related to Open Science Grid, where resources are pooled across institutions using a consistent software base packaged for ease of configuration, deployment and maintenance of middleware (Virtual Data Toolkit, VDT), and TeraGrid, a high-performance infrastructure well-suited to run large parallel jobs. Aside from the fundamental differences in goals, Archer differentiates from these systems with respect to its technology: the use of VM-based appliances for software distribution and self-configuring virtual networking to facilitate the addition of resources to the infrastructure. Also, Archer is targeted at serving a single rather than multiple communities, which enables its content to be tailored to the interest of computer architects by the architecture community.

Archer is similar to the Intel NetBatch infrastructure in its support for high-throughput simulation workloads. NetBatch is also a distributed system consisting of CPUs distributed across multiple sites, managed by an in-house batch scheduler. It has been highly successful in providing batch computing cycles for a variety of applications at Intel: it started with hundreds of computers in 1990, and over the course of ten years grew to 10,000 nodes across 25 sites, logging 2.7 million jobs per month in their queues [11]. Archer is different from NetBatch in that it is not internal to a private corporate network, allowing individuals to easily join and contribute resources to the system.

5 Conclusions and Future Work

This paper describes a novel infrastructure that integrates virtual machine appliances interconnected by virtual networks with Grid high-throughput scheduling to create wide-area collaborative environments for sharing of CPU cycles, data sets and documentation. An initial deployment of Archer with 56 CPUs began in the Summer of 2008 and has been successfully exercised with representative open-source and commercial computer architecture simulators (SESC, SimpleScalar, and Simics). The infrastructure is being extended with three distributed clusters (112 cores and 4TB of storage each) in the Fall of 2008.

The work described in this paper focuses on the infrastructure as tailored to the needs and tools of the computer architecture community. Nonetheless, the approach taken in Archer can be applied to other areas of engineering and science. As an example, related work also uses the core virtualization in Archer (the Grid appliance) in support of simulation tools for a community of coastal and estuarine scientists (SCOOP).

Directions for future work in Archer include the ability to incorporate performance and availability enhancements on top of the baseline NFS data sharing infrastructure through user-level caching proxies, request redirection to replica servers, and resource discovery using IPOP's distributed hash table. In addition, a complementary approach for cooperative whole-file transfers using a FUSE virtual file system with BitTorrent transport is being developed.

Another area of future work involves the integration of social networking frameworks with Grid appliances, which will enable the creation of a fourth deployment mode for the infrastructure — Archer Social — where ad-hoc groups of users will be able to easily bring up resource pools by leveraging Web-based online social networking infrastructures to enable simple creation of social virtual private networks and clusters [14]. We have a prototype of the Grid appliance integrated with Facebook APIs aimed at facilitating the creation and management of local and cross-domain private pools dedicated to groups of collaborators.

Acknowledgments

This work is sponsored by the National Science Foundation under CRI collaborative awards 0751112, 0750847, 0750851, 0750852, 0750860, 0750868, 0750884, and 0751091. Any opinions, findings and conclusions or recommendations expressed in this material are those of the authors and do not necessarily reflect the views of the NSF.

References

1. Ramp web site, http://ramp.eecs.berkeley.edu (accessed, October 2008)
2. Virtutech simics web site, http://www.virtutech.com (accessed, October 2008)
3. Anderson, D., Cobb, J., Korpella, E., Lebofsky, M., Werthimer, D.: Seti@home: An experiment in public-resource computing. Communications of the ACM 11(45), 56–61 (2002)
4. Anderson, T., Culler, D., Patterson, D.: A case for network of workstations: Now. IEEE Micro (February 1995)
5. Barham, P., Dragovic, B., Fraser, K., Hand, S., Harris, T., Ho, A., Neugebauer, R., Pratt, I., Warfield, A.: Xen and the art of virtualization. In: Proceedings of the nineteenth ACM symposium on Operating systems principles, Bolton Landing, NY, pp. 164–177 (2003)
6. Burger, D., Austin, T., Bennett, S.: Evaluating future microprocessors - the simplescalar toolset. Technical Report 1308, Computer Science Dept. University of Wisconsin (July 1996)
7. Figueiredo, R., Dinda, P., Fortes, J.: A case for grid computing on virtual machines. In: Proceedings of the 23rd IEEE International Conference on Distributed Computing Systems (ICDCS), Providence, Rhode Island (May 2003)
8. Figueiredo, R., Dinda, P., Fortes, J.: Resource virtualization renaissance. Guest Editor's Introductionm, in special issue on Virtualization 38(5), 28–31 (2005)
9. Ganguly, A., Agrawal, A., Boykin, P.O., Figueiredo, R.: IP over P2P: Enabling self-configuring virtual IP networks for grid computing. In: Proceedings of the IEEE International Parallel and Distributed Processing Symposium (IPDPS), Rhodes, Greece (June 2006)
10. Ganguly, A., Agrawal, A., Boykin, P.O., Figueiredo, R.: WOW: Self-organizing wide-area overlay networks of virtual workstations. In: Proceedings of the IEEE International Symposium on High Performance Distributed Computing (HPDC), Paris, France (July 2006)
11. Gelsinger, P.: Keynote speech, intel developers forum, Fall (August 2000), http://www.intel.com/pressroom/archive/speeches/pg082400.htm (accessed November 2008)
12. Goldberg, R.: Survey of virtual machine research. IEEE Computer Magazine 7(6), 34–45 (1974)
13. Jiang, X., Xu, D.: Violin: Virtual internetworking on overlay infrastructure. In: Cao, J., Yang, L.T., Guo, M., Lau, F. (eds.) ISPA 2004. LNCS, vol. 3358, pp. 937–946. Springer, Heidelberg (2004)
14. St Juste, P., Wolinsky, D., Xu, J., Covington, M., Figueiredo, R.: On the use of social networking groups for automatic configuration of virtual grid environments. In: Proceedings of Grid Computing Environments (GCE) Workshop, Austin, TX (November 2008)

15. Culler, D., Peterson, L., Anderson, T., Roscoe, T.: A blueprint for introducing disruptive technology into the internet. In: Proceedings of HotNets-I 2002 (October 2002)
16. Litzkow, M., Livny, M., Mutka, M.: Condor - a hunter of idle workstations. In: Proc. 8th IEEE International Conference on Distributed Computing Systems (ICDCS) (June 1988)
17. Renau, J., Fraguela, B., Tuck, J., Liu, W., Prvulovic, M., Ceze, L., Sarangi, S., Sack, P., Strauss, K., Montesinos, P.: Sesc simulator web site, http://sesc.sourceforge.net (accessed, October 2008)
18. Sapuntzakis, C., Lam, M.: Virtual appliances in the collective: A road to hassle-free computing. In: Proceedings of 9th Hot Topics in Operating Systems (HotOS) (May 2003)
19. Smith, J., Nair, R.: Virtual Machines: Versatile Platforms for Systems and Processes. Morgan Kaufmann, San Francisco (2005)
20. Tsugawa, M., Fortes, J.A.B.: A virtual network (vine) architecture for grid computing. In: Proceedings of the IEEE International Parallel and Distributed Processing Symposium (IPDPS), Rhodes, Greece (June 2006)
21. Wolinsky, D., Agrawal, A., Boykin, P.O., Davis, J., Ganguly, A., Paramygin, V., Sheng, P., Figueiredo, R.: On the design of virtual machine sandboxes for distributed computing in wide-area overlay of virtual workstations. In: First IEEE Workshop on Virtualization Technologies in Distributed Computing (VTDC) (2006)

Collaborative Search and User Privacy: How Can They Be Reconciled?

Thorben Burghardt[1], Erik Buchmann[1], Klemens Böhm[1], and Chris Clifton[2]

[1] Universität Karlsruhe (TH), IN-F, 76131 Karlsruhe, Germany
{burgthor,buchmann,boehm}@ipd.uka.de
[2] Dept. of Computer Science/CERIAS, Purdue University, West Lafayette,
IN 47907-2107, USA
clifton@cs.purdue.edu

Abstract. Collaborative search engines (CSE) let users pool their resources and share their experiences when seeking information on the web. However, when shared, search terms and links clicked reveal user interests, habits, social relations and intentions. In other words, CSE put privacy of users at risk. This seriously limits the proliferation and acceptance of CSE. To address the problem, we have carried out a qualitative study that identifies the privacy concerns of CSE users. In particular, our study reveals the range and type of concerns when sharing query terms and search results with different social groups, e.g., family members or colleagues. To control the information shared, the participants of our study have called for anonymity and reciprocity in combination with time- and/or context-dependent conditions. To facilitate the specification of privacy preferences, we define a general policy structure to express privacy needs in the context of CSE. We also give an approach to address the reciprocity condition identified in the study, and we discuss options to anonymize sharing of query terms.

Keywords: Collaborative Search, Privacy, Policy.

1 Introduction

Collaborative Search Engines (CSE) enhance web search by sharing query terms, search results and links clicked among users. Examples include I-SPY [1], MUSE and MUST [2], SearchTogether [3] and Fireball LiveSearch [4]. CSE let knowledge workers synchronize efforts, provide guidance for inexperienced searchers, and offer Web-2.0-style information on Internet activities of friends/colleagues. So far, collaborative search has been done by hand [5], e.g., by sending emails with search results. CSE are more efficient in this respect. However, as queries and the results clicked can reveal the habits, interests, social relationships and intentions of the searcher [6], CSE are problematic from a privacy perspective.

Current CSE either state that any search information will be visible to others, and/or leave it to the user to manually invite individuals to benefit from a particular piece of information [3]. CSE require that information is shared automatically, or that people can subscribe to information generated by others, in

E. Bertino and J.B.D. Joshi (Eds.): CollaborateCom 2008, LNICST 10, pp. 85–99, 2009.
© ICST Institute for Computer Sciences, Social-Informatics and Telecommunications Engineering 2009

the spirit of friendfeed.com. Acceptance of such an environment will depend on the appropriateness of privacy mechanisms. It is challenging to determine what constitutes a suitable privacy mechanism. CSE are about supporting other individuals; privacy laws that regulate how organizations can collect and use private information do not really fit. Web privacy mechanisms such as P3P [7] focus on the user-provider relationship, while CSE support sharing between individuals; the privacy needs are likely to be different. Also, privacy is a highly emotional issue; previous studies have shown that humans do not necessarily reveal their true privacy needs in laboratory experiments and/or questionnaires [8].

To tackle these challenges, we have conducted a user study with 27 computer science graduate students. Therefore, we constructed a CSE with mock-up privacy mechanisms to observe the true privacy needs of the users. Since CSE are a new technology, we familiarized the participants with CSE concepts and usage. The mock-up privacy mechanisms let the participants specify their privacy preferences for collaborative search in natural language. Asking for policies in natural language rules out any technical limitations, e.g., limited expressiveness of a specific formal language. Questions we wanted to answer include: (i) What are the **parameters** of polices, e.g., "at work", "not before 8 pm", used to control disclosure of search information? (ii) Which **groups**, e.g., friends, family or colleagues, do CSE users address in their policy definitions? (iii) Is there a common **structure** of the policies so that they can easily be transformed to a machine readable representation? (iv) Do the users express different privacy needs for the query terms and the links followed from the query result?

Our evaluation yields interesting insights (described briefly in [9]): Individuals are concerned most about what friends, colleagues and family might learn from their queries. This is particularly interesting given that SearchTogether [3] found that these are the people individuals want to collaboratively search with. We also found that participants express their privacy needs with policies of simple structure, but refer to different kinds of constraints. Our participants also defined reciprocal conditions, i.e., they take characteristics of other users into account, like having similar search interests, or distinguish between users registered for a long time and new ones. This is noteworthy, as we are not aware of privacy preference specification languages that incorporate this concept. Furthermore, most users do not distinguish between sharing query terms and sharing links.

Finally, we outline how a CSE supporting privacy could be constructed. Some of the expressed policies would be difficult to guarantee if the CSE manages privacy. This is because the authority that would control the CSE may be the very authority to whom some policies prevent disclosure. We describe techniques for decentralized search, collaboration, and policy management that could be used to overcome this limitation.

Paper structure: We review related work in Section 2, and we describe the methodology and key design decisions of this study in Section 3. Section 4 features the study results together with a policy specification language that can represent the user requirements. We present approaches to enforce these policies in Section 5; Section 6 concludes.

2   Related Work

While people are willing to share information [10], they distinguish between individuals, e.g., friends, relatives, or colleagues [3]. General studies have shown that approximately 90% of participants are concerned about privacy [11]. Privacy studies, e.g., [12], do not focus on the unique traits of CSE. Technology-independent studies [10,11] reveal the general willingness to share personal information if privacy mechanisms are available, but do not give us any hints on how to design such mechanisms for CSE.

User studies [13,5,14] have shown that individuals already collaborate for complex search tasks, e.g., holiday planning or homework; [5] shows that more than 85% of their "relatively sophisticated web searchers" share results of a web search, with over 25% cooperating on a weekly basis and over 75% monthly. They share using approaches such as email or instant messaging; the "push" nature of such sharing allows users to implicitly enforce their privacy policies; these studies provide little insight into user privacy requirements.

While some CSE exist, e.g., I-SPY [1], SearchTogether [3], MUSE [2], or Fireball LiveSearch, we are not aware of any research on the privacy issue. For instance, SearchTogether shares query histories, personal comments on pages and information on pages visited automatically, without any restriction regarding privacy. The design goals of SearchTogether are *Awareness, Division of Labor* and *Persistence*. Awareness of the search processes and search results of others means that people can learn from experienced searchers and work together on a search project without explicitly asking for information on pages visited or search terms tried; this prevents the automatic/implicit self-enforcement of privacy preference in push-based collaboration. SearchTogether makes search sessions persistent, including the query history, links clicked and comments provided. Evaluation shows SearchTogether to be more efficient than conventional methods. A study of MUSE, which has a similar structure, has focused on communication in the context of CSE [2] and has shown that users frequently wish to communicate. SearchTogether, MUSE and I-SPY let the user manually select which information should be shared with whom, based on search sessions or groups. While this allows users to enforce their privacy policies, it also requires them to manually ensure that they do so: within a session, any user (even one joining later) can see the whole search history.

People also share information with open communities. With the Fireball LiveSearch, the search engine displays all query terms it is currently processing. There are around 250,000 visits of Live Search per month. Fireball satisfies the curiosity of others, it allows users to learn, and it provides suggestions for future queries. The information displayed is not restricted to certain topics or users.

Few existing single-user search engines feature privacy mechanisms. The AskEraser of Ask.com deletes all information on past search activities and turns off all personalization features. This involves a tradeoff: Simply deactivating logging increases the privacy of the users, but can reduce effectiveness of the search [15,16,17,18].

3   Study Design and Environment

We now describe the key design decisions behind our study, and the environment
developed to support these decisions.

3.1   Study Design Decisions

Skilled Participants. Understanding the information flow and ways to build privacy profiles for queries and links shared requires a thorough knowledge of information systems. Our study participants are graduate students in computer
science with a focus on information systems, making them skilled Internet users
and knowledge workers, a target group of CSE [3].

Training on CSE. Currently, only research prototypes and early implementations of CSE exist; we did not expect participants to possess in-depth knowledge
of CSE. As competence is required to obtain meaningful study results [19], we
implemented a CSE prototype ourselves and ensured that participants have familiarity with its use and technical details. To avoid influencing the results of the
study, we did no training on privacy threats or privacy-enhancing technologies.

Observing the Behavior. Since users adapt their behavior to the technology
available [19], it is problematic to obtain real privacy needs by means of abstract questionnaires or synthetic experiments. We implemented mock-up privacy mechanisms that allow us to observe the privacy needs of participants
working with an operational CSE.

Plaintext Policies. A final design decision was to let the participants specify
policies in natural language instead of using a machine-readable policy language.
First, this does not restrict the expressiveness of policies. Second, it is intuitive;
if the participants had to learn and use a formal language unfamiliar to them,
the added effort could limit the number of policies obtained. Third, use of an
open-ended natural language interface ensures that the mechanism used does
not influence the policies specified, supporting our goal of learning all criteria
users find important to privacy in CSE.

3.2   Study Environment and Methodology

We now briefly outline the methodology used for our study, including the components of the CSE and the training approach used to satisfy the design decisions
of the previous section. Today's CSE consist of three main components [3,2]:
a search engine where users can enter their information needs, an integrated
mechanism that allows users to exchange query terms as well as links clicked
and to make them persistent for future search sessions and other users, and a
way to communicate between the collaborating parties. In the first three of five
three-week phases, participants implemented a portion of each component (as
projects in a database course) to ensure familiarity with the technology.

Introduction Phase (P1). To generate a basic understanding how CSE work, we prepared a presentation introducing the functionality and let the participants search for common topics individually. We built our CSE on top of Google, because our participants were familiar with the use, layout, and quality of the search result. Furthermore, [1] showed that the effectiveness of the collaboration strongly depends on the reference search engine; they achieved best results using Google. The queries and query metadata were stored in a relational database; during Phase 1 the participants wrote small programs to access the search data, such as SQL queries to find searches similar to their own.

Query Phase (P2). We then activated collaborative aspects of the CSE, specifically a window that displays similar query terms (calculated using an Unweighted Vector Space retrieval model [20]) and clicked links without the name of the issuer (as with I-SPY [1]). The participants used these to find information to solve the training tasks. We also enabled logging of clicks on similar queries and links. As working with the database was part of the training task, the participants knew in detail what information was stored and processed by our CSE.

User Awareness Phase (P3). This phase incorporated user identity into the interface (previously seen by participants through access to the database as part of their training tasks.) The participants developed a Skype plugin to subscribe to query terms of other participants, giving subscribers a notification containing the query term, links clicked, name of the issuer, and the time of the query. This interface enabled messenger-based collaboration when searching. The Skype feature "asynchronous communication" was leveraged to cache messages when others are offline; the history function gave persistence of the communication.

Policy Definition Phase (P4). We then asked participants to enter their policies using a plaintext (natural language) policy editor. When using the CSE, users selected a (self-defined) policy (e.g., "being at work") from a list; if a policy is selected, the current query term and links clicked are available only for users that match (as implemented by study administrators based on the natural language policy.) The policy stays active until the user switches to another one.

While we did suggest that policies should encompass in *which context* they would or would not share *which query terms and clicked links* with *whom*, the policies were specified in natural language to give users the freedom to realize their own notions and ideas when specifying their privacy needs. As policies can be sensitive [21,22], we kept all policy definitions private. To avoid overtaxing the participants and to allow for a structured evaluation, this phase had three steps: 1) policies to protect query terms, 2) policies to protect links clicked, and 3) three weeks of CSE use to give the opportunity to refine policies.

Survey Phase (P5). We closed with a survey 1) asking the participants control questions, to guarantee the representativeness of our CSE, and 2) to obtain information about their general privacy attitude. This information was used in interpretation of our results. To motivate participation in the final survey we drew two Amazon vouchers among the participants; participation in phases P1–P3 was ensured as the tasks were graded course requirements. We did not give grades or inducement on defining policies (P4) to avoid influencing the results. Supplementary information on the CSE and study methodology is available on an accompanying web page [23].

3.3 Study Representativeness

Before describing the outcome, we outline the background of participants and why we feel the results are representative of typical CSE users. The 27 graduate students in the study were enrolled in a practical course in database systems at the University of Karlsruhe. All participants had a fundamental understanding of information systems, complex search tasks, and are interested in data analysis and KDD; but as the goal of the course was knowledge of database systems, we did not expect them to be particularly biased toward or against CSE. The students represent a range of cultural backgrounds, covering seven nationalities (ten German, six Hungarian, four Bulgarian, three Chinese, two Ukrainian, and one each from Belorussia and Romania.) We had 7 female and 20 male participants, with age ranging from 20 to 34 years (avg 24).

To gauge the privacy attitude of our participants, we asked their usual practices regarding privacy policies, registering at search engines, and querying personal information on the Internet. 66% said they have read the privacy policy of at least one web site, 27% stated they read them frequently (but not always) when registering. We found it interesting that 81% said they had never read a search engine privacy policy while 78% have registered with a search engine for further services like email or a messenger account. 59% expected that their search engine can link their identity to each of their queries. The results indicate that participants had no extreme privacy attitudes, and while not naïve, are probably not fully aware of privacy threats in the context of search engines.

To evaluate if our prototypical CSE is representative and if the participants represent individuals likely to use CSE, in Phase 5 we asked the participants how they perceived its components. On a 5 point Likert scale over 70% found our CSE and the links proposed medium (10), useful (9) or very useful (1). Asked if they would use the CSE for a learning group, three stated no, four rather not, but 67% stated rather yes (15) or absolutely yes (3). We see this as a confirmation that the CSE is useful and that the study has not been biased by technical limitations. 59% (16) of the participants have investigated query terms of others by browsing the search history of specific users. Reasons for those who did not are "no interest in searches by others" (4), "finding Google recommendations sufficient" (3), "finding searches by others not good enough", or "no need for this functionality" (1). Four participants stated that the effort necessary to select a policy before a search was very easy (grade 1), 6 gave a 2, 9 chose the middle, and 4 each chose grade 4 and 5. This gives us confidence that participants felt the privacy mechanism realistic.

We conclude that participants deemed our CSE useful. Many would continue to use it, and are willing to share query information within the constraints of privacy preferences. Thus, we can expect realistic results from our study.

4   Study Evaluation

We now describe the results of our study, i.e., we analyze the policies provided by our participants. We obtained 247 policy definitions from the 27 users. 142 policies consider sharing of query terms, and 105 address the links clicked. We first analyze the policies assigned to the query terms. We investigate (1) how these policies are structured, (2) the contexts they refer to, (3) which social groups are mentioned, and (4) the form of the policy predicates. We then investigate how the policies for the links clicked differ.

4.1   Policy Structure

We found that the plaintext policies of the participants can all be expressed using the following general structure:

[ALWAYS | IF <conditions>] [DO NOT] DISCLOSE <objects> [TO <groups>]

Conditions, objects and groups were composed of one or more terms connected with AND or OR, e.g., "If I am at work OR time between 7 am and 6 pm DO NOT DISCLOSE query terms to my friends AND family". Some policies followed this structure literally; the rest could be transformed to fit the structure.

While some policies allow or prohibit information disclosure without conditions ("ALWAYS DO..."), most refer to one or more of the following:

1. *context* (e.g., "while I am at work")
2. *content* ("the query contains adult material")
3. *time* ("between 7 am and 6 pm")
4. *reciprocity* ("if the other user has similar query terms")
5. *query-result dependency* ("show the query term if the clicked link refers to a newspaper site")

The difference between context and content condition is that the former relates to the user, the latter to the wording of the query. In the policies formulated by the participants, the *object* can either be a query term, a clicked link, or both. The *group* specifies individuals that may/may not access a certain object.

The conditions, addressed groups, and objects are orthogonal to each other, i.e., we did not see one group mentioned only in combination with a specific context, etc. Therefore, we now evaluate these aspects separately.

4.2   General Policies

The simplest variant of policies allows or forbids the disclosure of the query term without specifying conditions or persons, similar to "ALWAYS DO NOT DISCLOSE anything TO anybody". 12 of our 27 participants created a policy that always prohibits the disclosure of the query term, 5 defined a policy that discloses the query term to everyone. This is similar to studies on other technology; 90% of the participants in [11] are moderately or very concerned about privacy.

4.3   Conditions

For policies with a condition, 39% (56) refer to a context, 11% (16) to the query term (content condition), 7 to characteristics of the person who wants access (reciprocal condition), and 3 are time-dependent (time condition). In general, policies were simple. The vast majority had only one condition. A few combined (at most two) different conditions, e.g., "If I am at work, and the time is between 7am and 6pm". Policies did not differentiate between sharing the query term and the metadata of the query such as query issuer or the time the query was issued, although one participant did express a desire for anonymous sharing.

Contexts. The context describes the current situation of the query issuer, e.g., at work, planning holidays, etc. 39% (56) of the 142 query term policies can be assigned to a concrete context (see Table 1; the accompanying web page [23] contains examples of each group.) The remaining 86 policies apply to all contexts.

Table 1. User Contexts

Context	Frequency
Being at work	21
Private surfing at work	10
Searching for adult material	5
Searching provider related content (e.g., "youtube videos")	5
Online shopping	4
Searching for disease	3
Searching for jobs	2
Planning holidays	2
Searching for dating sites	1
Searching for person names	1
Searching for sports issues	1
Money management	1

Participants defined policies for many contexts not explicitly addressed by law, e.g., by the EU directives [24]. Laws typically specify contexts relevant to information sharing between an individual and an organization, such as medical issues or employer-employee relationships. Our participants also specified more personal contexts such as holiday planning or searching for persons of interest.

Content Conditions. Content conditions refer to the query term. However, as the content of the query and the context that motivated the user to issue that query are closely related, some policy definitions overlap. 11% (16) of all policies defined at least one policy comparable to *"If I issue a query containing <some keywords>, (do not) show the query to <some persons>"*. 5 policies refer to a provider name, e.g., youtube or newspapers, 3 refer to person names, 3 to technical issues and 2 to sex and porn. See [23] for the full list.

    A rather surprising content condition relates to the structure of the query. Participants stated 5 policies where query terms are (not) published if they consist of less (more) than a certain number of words. We conclude that the participants intend to restrict the level of detail, i.e., they assume that longer search terms carry more or more sensitive information than shorter terms.

Time Conditions. Three policies from different users define conditions based on time and date. For example, one policy forbids disclosing search information during working hours (this was to prevent competitors benefiting from the person's work.) Another participant allowed sharing query terms with friends only between 6pm and 8pm. One policy used date; it forbid sharing search terms with friends before Christmas while shopping for presents.

We were surprised that no participant generated a policy that takes the sequential order of the queries into account or requires a certain delay between the time the query was issued and the time the query is shown to another person. Instead, the participants preferred to either share the query terms at once or prohibit access completely. As with ALWAYS (DO NOT)-Policies, this is another hint that users want to keep policies simple.

Reciprocal Conditions. Reciprocal conditions depend on characteristics of other persons when deciding if a certain piece of information should be disclosed. Three users defined a total of 7 reciprocal policies: (i) Five share query terms if other users have previously issued similar queries, e.g., by requiring a number of identical words in the query term, (ii) One allows sharing the query term with users who registered to the CSE before the issuer of the query, and (iii) One participant requires that a query can be shown to someone else as long as this other person does not learn the issuer's identity from the query term.

The results indicate that some users are willing to share information with like-minded people only, e.g., if they suffer from the same disease. Further, one participant explicitly called for anonymization, i.e., sharing query terms and links only if identity is not revealed. Reciprocity conditions indicate that other technologies cannot readily be transferred to CSE. For example, no formal privacy-preference language we are aware of considers reciprocity conditions.

4.4 Groups

A group defines which individuals are allowed (or prohibited) to see a query term. We were interested which social relationships and classes of social groups (like *friends* or *family*) participants address in their policies. One insight is that social groups can be divided into (i) groups containing only individuals which are personally known or (ii) groups with unspecified members. For example, *family members* are known personally, while *children* stands for an unspecified group. Our participants defined 106 policies referring to various social groups, cf. Table 2. 60% (82) relate to Class (i), 40% (42) to Class (ii). 83% (88) policies only address one group per policy, 17% (18) policies address multiple groups.

The most common group in Class (ii) was "colleagues". This was not surprising given policies that address topics like "job search" that one would expect need protection from colleagues that are not close friends. Regarding Class (i),

Table 2. Social Groups

Group	Class	Frq	Acc.	Prohib.
Friends	known	35	8	27
Family	known	19	8	11
Acquaintance	known	12	7	5
Boy/Girlfriend	known	4	1	3
Supervisors	known	4	3	1
Doctors	known	3	0	3
Teacher	known	3	3	0
Parents	known	1	0	1
Landlord	known	1	1	0
Colleagues	unspec	26	6	20
(Fellow) Students	unspec	6	2	4
Children	unspec	3	3	0
Male/Female	unspec	3	0	3
Official Persons	unspec	3	3	0
Fellow Citizen	unspec	1	1	0

participants addressed friends (33%) and family (18%) most often. 20 of 27 (74%) participants have specified a policy that allows sharing queries with friends.

Further, we explore if these groups are used to restrict or increase the set of individuals allowed to see a query. We differentiate between policies used to grant access to information, e.g., *"show my query to my colleagues and friends"*, and groups used for the reverse, e.g., *"do not let my boss see my query"*. In our study, participants used both variants frequently and even combined them, e.g., *"give access to my friends but not to my family"*. 64% (68) of our 106 group-based policies grant access, and 36% (38) use groups to prohibit access to query information (Table 2). Our study indicates that individuals are concerned about what friends, colleagues or family members might learn from their query terms. This is interesting: [3] shows that it is exactly these individuals people want most to search with collaboratively.

4.5 Link Policies

With our setup, the object specified in the policy can be a query term or the link clicked. The 142 policies analyzed so far address the query terms; we now investigate the 105 policies that refer to the links clicked. 81 policies on links are copies of policies referring to query terms. 7 new policies have been defined. 17 policies originate from policies on queries, but have been extended. Three participants have not specified any policy on links clicked.

Those 23% (24) that differ are either general *ALWAYS DO NOT*-policies, policies that have been further restricted, e.g., by specifying additional *groups* that may (not) see the links, or define *content conditions* on the URLs or descriptions of the websites displayed as part of the query result. Interesting are 6 policies with a *time condition*: 3 require that information on links clicked be disclosed to others for some days only. These policies allow participation in the CSE, but rule out the derivation of long term profiles. Three policies allow sharing the last n links clicked only. Four policies define so-called *query-result dependencies*. Such dependencies are a new class of conditions: They share query terms depending on the links clicked, e.g., "Do not share query terms except when a link clicked leads to a newspaper site".

4.6 Discussion

We found that policies fit a simple structure consisting of one or more conditions, objects and groups of persons. Policies do not contain conditions from more than two different classes. Participants have created very specific policies, e.g., in order to prevent family members from learning about presents before Christmas, as well as abstract policies like "prohibit any access". Since we did not discuss possible privacy threats or existing privacy-enhancing technologies, the set of policies is probably incomplete. However, the policies reveal the spectrum of requirements that users deem useful, i.e., a privacy mechanism should at least comprise. This includes lists of keywords, although providing and maintaining a comprehensive list of sensible words is a daunting task. WordNet [25] or other thesauri could help to address word concepts instead of individual words. Policies also refer to social groups that roughly correspond to the social relationships of the query issuer. One approach to simplify group definition could be extracting relationships from social network sites or messenger services [26]. Identifying unspecified members of groups, e.g., colleagues or children, without raising new privacy threats by additionally revealing data like age or employer, will be much more difficult, although issues of such group membership are a problem for identity management in general. Further, policies address time and content constraints, reciprocal constraints that take into account characteristics of other users, and distinguish between query terms and links clicked.

5   Enforcing CSE Policies

A CSE provider learns much about each user. This is particularly critical if the provider not only supports collaborative search, but also manages user privacy. Suppose a CSE in a corporate setting to support collaborative search among an engineering team. Asking the corporation CSE to enforce the policy "do not let my boss see my query" is problematic.

In this section, we assume a distributed, anonymized system architecture, and we propose mechanisms to manage policies at the client. Each of the CSE components identified in Section 3.2 can be realized by using existing tools and techniques, e.g., anonymous instant messaging such as TorChat, anonymous information sharing such as FreeNet, and anonymous web search tools such as PWS [27]. This allows separating collaboration from the search engine, thus allowing use of public search engines while supporting collaboration on a local server only when user policy allows, or even through a peer-to-peer network.

Most policies can be enforced locally at the user's machine: The policy context, content, time, and query-result dependency either allow the query to be shared or not. Two types of policies cannot: reciprocity and anonymity. We now describe how these policies could be enforced through collaboration between parties, enabling privacy preference handling without the help of third parties.

5.1 Reciprocity

Reciprocity means that a user wants to share only if the recipient has certain characteristics, e.g., a compatible policy or similar interests. Complicating this is the fact that the conditions themselves may be sensitive. For example, a law enforcement officer may only be willing to share searches about a suspect with other officers who already know of the suspect; revealing the suspect to determine if other officers are searching for that suspect is nearly as compromising as revealing the search. In the following, we focus on typical reciprocity policies that require both parties to be willing to share similar content, while revealing query terms to determine if other parties are willing to share inherently violates that policy. Extension of the approaches presented to conditions such as "share only with people who have issued similar queries in the past" is straightforward. We sketch how this could be accomplished for reciprocity conditions requiring equality tests on context, content, time, and query-result dependency; for conditions that are too complex to efficiently map into a set of equality tests, trust negotiation approaches can be used (e.g., [28]).

Using commutative encryption, reciprocity conditions involving exact match of conditions can be tested in a peer-to-peer fashion that ensures nothing is learned except the conditions that match. The basic idea behind commutative encryption is that $E_a(E_b(m)) = E_b(E_a(m))$. If m is a tuple consisting of context, content, time, and query-result dependency, each party encrypts the tuple m with its own key, then passes the encrypted tuple to the other party. Each party then encrypts the encrypted tuple with its own key; the parties can now share the (doubly) encrypted tuple. If the doubly-encrypted tuples are the same, then the conditions match (see [29] for more details and proof that nothing is revealed.)

In practice, the users have to compare sets of policies. For example, "share queries using these terms only if the recipient agrees to sharing similar queries." means that multiple combinations of the terms specified must be compared. Our approach can be used to find a set of matching policies, then both parties can decrypt the matching policies to expose them (note that both parties must agree to and participate in the decryption.) Alternatively, the test can be performed on a per-collaboration basis: One party encrypts all relevant policies and the query terms relevant to that policy, the other encrypts the particular policies and terms that apply to the particular collaboration. If there is a match, then the parties have reciprocity.

5.2 Anonymous Collaborative Search

One user explicitly called for anonymous sharing. This is challenging, as the query terms and links may inherently be identifying [30]. We propose a model based on k-anonymity [31,32]: users agree to share query terms if at least k users have issued a query with the same terms. This can be checked using the same commutative encryption ideas above, see [29] for a more secure approach.

Note that everyone needed to form such a group of k users must have a policy of only sharing those terms/links anonymously. Otherwise, a query could be used to form such an anonymous group, then the user could reveal they had issued it; then only $k - 1$ users would remain anonymous, violating their anonymity constraint. However, it is likely that the types of searches where some users desire anonymity will be ones where many will (e.g., non-work-related searches performed at work, politically or legally sensitive topics), so this is likely to be a reasonable constraint in practice.

If any term in a query is covered by an anonymous sharing policy, all terms that are shared must meet the k constraint, not just the content condition in the policy. This is because terms not covered by the policy may be the ones that are inherently identifying. For example, one could say that a query "computing jobs available" could be revealed only anonymously; then issue a query "computing jobs available near Fasanenplatz". Even if k users issued "computing jobs available" queries, it would not be safe to disclose the query including address unless at least k individuals had issued a query with the same address.

It would be possible to share only the subset of query terms / links clicked that meet the k constraint. As with reciprocity, techniques from distributed privacy-preserving data mining (in particular, [29]) can be used to anonymously determine when sharing is possible in a peer-to-peer fashion. This is similar to the commutative encryption approach above, except that a final cryptographic protocol is used to disclose only if the number of users issuing each term meets the k threshold. Further study is needed to determine:

- How large a community of collaborators is needed to generate a pool of identical query terms sufficient to meet the k constraint? This study had 23 participants who generated at least one query, with an average of 61 queries per user. The queries averaged just under three terms. We had five 3-term and 26 2-term subsets that were 3-anonymous, and 11 4-term, 49 3-term, and 138 2-term subsets that were 2-anonymous (for comparison, there were 277 distinct 3-term queries and 391 distinct 2-term queries.) The users did have common tasks, so overlap is to be expected; this would be likely in envisioned collaborative search environments such as within a company. While a larger user base is needed to obtain a reasonably high percentage of anonymous queries, we can see that k-anonymous collaborative search is plausible.
- Is sharing a subset of a query as effective in supporting user search as sharing an entire query? (Eleven of the 49 3-term 2-anonymous queries exactly matched real 3-term queries, the rest were subsets of larger queries.)
- Does anonymous sharing provide value, or is knowledge of who has performed a search necessary to give credibility to the process?

6 Conclusions

Collaborative search engines (CSE) are an important new trend in Internet search. Information shared by CSE can put privacy of users at risk. To gain insight into this important issue (the privacy needs of CSE users), we implemented a CSE and used it during a one-semester course to give 27 study participants a thorough understanding of CSE technology. This let us observe the real privacy needs of users with an operational system.

While a few individuals define "don't care" policies, most define policies for various contexts addressing different social groups. The groups friends, colleagues and family most frequently addressed in policies are the ones people want most to search with collaboratively. This underlines the importance of privacy mechanisms for CSE. Further, individuals make use of different conditions in their policies but tend to keep the policies simple. Some users call for reciprocal conditions that depend on characteristics of others. This is noteworthy, as we are aware of no privacy approaches that consider this issue. Fortunately, these needs can be addressed: we have outlined a policy structure and mechanisms for enforcement that support development of privacy mechanisms for future CSE.

Acknowledgments. This work was partly funded by DFG BO2129/8-1 and the Graduate School IME, Universität Karlsruhe (TH).

References

1. Smyth, B., Balfe, E., Boydell, O.: A Live-User Evaluation of Collaborative Web Search. In: IJCAI (2005)
2. Reddy, M.C., Jansen, B.J., Krishnappa, R.: The Role of Communication in Collaborative Information Searching. In: ASTIS (2008)
3. Morris, M.R., Horvitz, E.: SearchTogether: An Interface for Collaborative Web Search. In: UIST (2007)
4. Fireball (2008), http://www.fireball.de/
5. Morris, M.R.: Collaborating Alone and Together: Investigating Persistent and Multi-User Web Search Activities. Technical report, Microsoft Research (2007)
6. EU Data Protection Working Party. Opinion on Data Protection Issues Related to Search Engines (2008)
7. W3.org (2002), www.w3.org/TR/P3P-preferences/
8. Cvrcek, D., et al.: A study on the Value of Location Privacy. In: WPES (2006)
9. Burghardt, T., Buchmann, E., Böhm, K.: Discovering the Scope of Privacy Needs in Collaborative Search. In: Web Intelligence (2008)
10. Olson, J.S., Grudin, J., Horvitz, E.: A Study of Preferences for Sharing and Privacy. In: CHI (2005)
11. Acquisti, A., Grossklags, J.: Privacy and Rationality in Individual Decision Making. IEEE Security and Privacy (2005)
12. Consolvo, S., et al.: Location Disclosure to Social Relations: Why, When, & What PeopleWant to Share. In: SIGCHI (2005)
13. Large, A., Beheshti, J., Rahman, T.: Gender Differences in Collaborative Web Searching Behavior: An Elementary School Study. In: Information Processsessing and Management (2002)
14. Twidale, M.B., Nichols, D.M., Paice, C.D.: Browsing is a Collaborative Process. In: Information Processing and Management (1997)
15. Glance, N.S.: Community Search Assistant. In: Workshop on AI for Web Search AAAI (2001)

16. Kriewel, S., Fuhr, N.: Adaptive Search Suggestions for Digital Libraries. In: Goh, D.H.-L., Cao, T.H., Sølvberg, I.T., Rasmussen, E. (eds.) ICADL 2007. LNCS, vol. 4822, pp. 220–229. Springer, Heidelberg (2007)

17. Teevan, J., et al.: Information Re-Retrieval: Repeat Queries in Yahoo's Logs. In: SIGIR (2007)

18. White, R.W., Morris, D.: Investigating the Querying and Browsing Behavior of Advanced Search Engine Users. In: SIGIR (2007)

19. Babbie, E.R.: The Practice of Social Research, 10th edn. Academic Internet Publ., London (2007)

20. Salton, G., Wong, A., Yang, C.S.: A vector space model for automatic indexing. Commun. ACM (1975)

21. Yu, T., Winslett, M.: A Unified Scheme for Resource Protection in Automated Trust Negotiation. In: SP (2003)

22. Zou, D., Liao, Z.: A new Approach for Hiding Policy and Checking Policy Consistency. In: ISA (2008)

23. IPD Privacy Web Site (2008), http://privacy.ipd.uni-karlsruhe.de/

24. Directive 95/46/EC of the European Parliament and of the Council of 24 October 1995 on the protection of individuals with regard to the processing of personal data and on the free movement of such data (1995)

25. Fellbaum, C. (ed.): WordNet: An Electronic Lexical Database (Language, Speech, and Communication). The MIT Press, Cambridge (1998)

26. Leskovec, J., Horvitz, E.: Planetary-Scale Views on a Large Instant-Messaging network. In: WWW (2008)

27. Saint-Jean, F., et al.: Private Web Search. In: WPES, Alexandria, Virginia, October 29, pp. 84–90. ACM Press, New York (2007)

28. Bertino, E., Ferrari, E., Squicciarini, A.C.: Trust-x: A peer-to-peer framework for trust establishment. In: TKDE (2004)

29. Vaidya, J., Clifton, C.: Secure set intersection cardinality with application to association rule mining. Journal of Computer Security (2005)

30. Barbaro, M., Zeller Jr., T.: A Face Is Exposed for AOL Searcher No. 4417749 (2006)

31. Samarati, P.: Protecting respondent's privacy in microdata release. In: TKDE (2001)

32. Sweeney, L.: K-anonymity: a model for protecting privacy. International Journal on Uncertainty, Fuzziness and Knowledge-based Systems (2002)

Defending against Attribute-Correlation Attacks in Privacy-Aware Information Brokering

Fengjun Li[1], Bo Luo[2], Peng Liu[1], Anna C. Squicciarini[1], Dongwon Lee[1], and Chao-Hsien Chu[1]

[1] College of Information Science and Technology, The Pennsylvania State University
[2] Dept. of Electrical Engineering and Computer Science, The University of Kansas

Abstract. Nowadays, increasing needs for information sharing arise due to extensive collaborations among organizations. Organizations desire to provide data access to their collaborators while preserving full control over the data and comprehensive privacy of their users. A number of information systems have been developed to provide efficient and secure information sharing. However, most of the solutions proposed so far are built atop of conventional data warehousing or distributed database technologies.

Recently, information brokering systems have been proposed to provide privacy-preserving information sharing among loosely federated data sources. However, they are still vulnerable to attribute-correlation attacks during query routing, due to the lack of protection of the routed queries. In this paper, we investigate the problems caused by such an attack, and propose a countermeasure by limiting the view of query content at each intermediate broker. We show that the proposed content-based XPath query routing scheme with level-based encryption and commutative encryption can effectively prevent an attribute-correlation attack originated by compromised brokers, with reasonable overhead.

Keywords: information brokering, attribute correlation attack, privacy, XML.

1 Introduction

Today's organizations often operate across organizational boundaries. They raise strong needs for efficient and secure information sharing to facilitate extensive collaborations. However, early approaches on information sharing, which mainly focus on providing transparency and interoperability among heterogeneous system, fall short of satisfying new requirements of these inter-organizational collaborations.

To better understand such requirements, we overview the unique needs of such interorganization collaboration by considering an example in the healthcare domain. Large-scale health information infrastructures, such as Regional Health Information Organization (RHIO), are being developed to share medical information (e.g., patient records) collected by collaborative health providers (e.g., hospitals) via protected "channels". First, there is no centralized authority to

E. Bertino and J.B.D. Joshi (Eds.): CollaborateCom 2008, LNICST 10, pp. 100–112, 2009.

coordinate the data in different hospitals. Each health provider is authorized by its patients to collect medical information independency, and stores it across multiple local data servers. Since the data is private and sensitive, the health providers are responsible for not leaking patient records to irrelevant parties. The health providers desire to share their data to fulfill collaboration, however, they prefer to do it in a restricted and controlled fashion. Data requestors, such as doctors, need to be able to retrieve the medical records with precision and not be distracted by "noisy" data. Finally, the RHIO should be able to maintain a large number of data servers, considering the participant population. In general, such interorganization collaboration application requires an information sharing system that offers full autonomy to underlying databases, preserve data security and privacy comprehensively, and provides good scalability.

Recently, information brokering systems (IBS) [8,13] have been proposed to meet the above requirements. In an IBS, geographically distributed data sources within a consortium are linked through a set of brokers to provide unified data access to all the users in the consortium. No third party is required to keep a centralized copy of data from local databases. Each data source maintains full control over its data and has great flexibility to grant, restrict, and revoke access of a particular user to certain data. Moreover, in order to achieve the desired query expressiveness, XML data model is widely adopted. Brokers are linked in a peer-to-peer fashion that makes IBS a scalable system.

Although IBS systems meet most of the requirements in current interorganizaion information sharing, they suffer from many attacks to privacy. In [13], we gave an insightful analysis of types of privacy involved in on-demand distributed information access as well as the risks. We proposed an automaton based approach for comprehensive privacy protection, however, it still suffered from a major privacy threat. In databases, data is represented as a set of records and each record can be viewed as a set of *attributes* with distinct values. Thus, the content of a query may be simply viewed as a sequence of query conditions (or predicates): each condition/predicate involves a specific attribute. Although the queries are sent through secure tunnels, an intermediate broker can view every XML query routed through it. If no proper privacy control is enforced, an enroute broker, when compromised or turned into a malicious insider, could easily extract query conditions and *correlate* the attributes to infer sensitive information about the data owner. The attack is known as *attribute-correlation attack*. Moreover, the results from attribute-correlation attacks may facilitate further inferences such as the re-identification attack.

In this paper, we define the attribute-correlation attack in information brokering systems, and provide solutions. More specifically, we design a content-based query routing scheme which uses encryption scheme to protect query content from attribute-correlation attacks by limiting broker's view of query content. Through insightful analysis, we show that no private information leaks even if some brokers collude. To the best of our knowledge, this is the first solution that protects an IBS against attribute-correlation attacks launched by compromised brokers.

The rest of the paper is organized as follows. We first summarize the related work in Section 2. Then, in Section 3, we briefly introduce IBS and the attribute-correlation attack problem in IBS. We propose the details of our scheme in section 4, including broker tree construction, content-based routing, and level-based and commutative encryptions. Privacy and performance analysis is given in section 5. And we conclude in Sections 6.

2   Related Work

A number of information integration approaches had been developed to support business applications since 1980's. However, most of the early approaches focus on providing transparency and interoperability among heterogeneous system but neglect the needs for autonomy, scalability and privacy-preserving.

In early 90's, Wiederhold proposed the well-known mediator architecture [16,17], in which an additional layer of mediators was added between clients and back-end databases. The mediators, exploiting encoded knowledge about data, execute and enforce regulations over both query and data bidirectionally. However, the mediator approach was not designed for large scale federations, so it is only practical for systems with a small number of components.

The data warehousing and data store approaches [10,5] provide another way for information integration and sharing. However, they all request to pour the data into a centralized repository so as to provide a global view to the user. Therefore, these approaches fall short to meet the autonomy needs of individual organizations.

Federated database systems have the requested capabilities of autonomy and supporting large-scale data distribution. However, the current designs neglect comprehensive privacy considerations.

Other approaches, such as pub/sub approaches in [3,18], mesh-based overlay network proposed in [15], and peer-to-peer (P2P) systems that support content-based routing of XPath queries [6,11], all implement the *information push* model, thus they are not suitable for the applications focused in this paper, in which information access is typically in the *information pull* model.

3   Information Brokering Overview

An IBS system is a peer-to-peer overlay network consisting of data owners, brokers and end users (i.e. data requestors). This type of architecture is employed in an interorganization scenario, where multiple organizations have strong needs of cross-organizational information sharing.

More specifically, we define IBS as agent-based systems across loosely federated XML or XML-supported databases. XML data model and XML query languages are adopted to achieve the desired query expressiveness. Local databases are autonomous systems geographically distributed across multiple domains. Certain agents, namely brokers, are employed to link data sources (i.e. databases) and data requestors, where data sources and data requestors of each domain are connected to a local broker. Then, brokers are linked in a peer-to-peer fashion to provide transparent data access to data requestors. The flexible topology of broker overlay may ease the on-and-off maintenance as well as reduce the cost when the number of databases scales.

In this work, we focus on read-only querying access to various data sources, which enables a data requestor with no priori knowledge about the requested data distribution to send a query to a local broker and to receive answers from data sources sitting in different organization domains.

To guide a query to data sources with the requested data, a broker(s) needs certain knowledge about data distribution. Such knowledge is represented as *routing rules*, describing which data source (i.e. `location`) holds which data objects.

In a distributed setting, regardless of the network topology and routing protocol adopted by the IBS [12], one broker only holds a partial set of all routing rules. Thus, multiple brokers should collaborate in routing an XML query to its destined data source(s).

3.1   The Attribute-Correlation Attack

A major function of an IBS is to route XML queries from data requestors to relevant data sources by means of routing rules. Routing rules are metadata of the form R = {subject, location}, where `subject` is an XPath [4] expression denoting a set of data objects and `location` is a list of IP addresses[1]. Routing rules could be expressed at different level of specificity. Two example routing rules are shown as follows.

```
Rule1:{//recordTarget//patient//*, {206.132.1.18, 206.132.1.19}},
Rule2:{//ClinicalDocument//Date[@value='041207']//*, 206.132.1.110}.
```

To route a query, a broker extracts the XPath expression from the `subject` field and compares with its routing rules. If the XPath expression matches one of its routing rules, the broker will forward the query to the address(es) in the `location` field of the routing rule; otherwise, the broker will deny the routing request and drop the query. Obviously, in order to fulfill the routing task, the involved brokers should be allowed to view the query in clear-text.

The main body of a query is an XPath expression consisting of a sequence of steps. Each step is an axis specification followed by a node test and a predicate (optional). Two steps are separated by a "/". A query always contains one or several predicates in some of its steps, which act as query conditions. Each predicate involves a specific attribute that may represent sensitive and private data of its owner (e.g. name, SSN or credit card number, etc.). If there are more than one predicate in a query, one can associate the corresponding attributes to infer sensitive information about the data owner. This attack is known as *attribute correlation attack*.

---

[1] In this work, we adopt XPath as a format to express XML queries and routing rules. XPath is a restricted variation of regular path expressions, which can refer to all or part of the nodes in an XML document. However, our system is applicable to any regular path expression and any query language based on it.

Next, we elaborate on the vulnerability with an example. Assume a data requestor, doctor Bob, requests all medical records that are relevant to blood cancer of a patient named Alice. Bob creates an XML query:

```
q=/report[//patient/@name='Alice']//code[@displayname='BloodCancer']//*.
```

This query has two query conditions (i.e. `name = 'Alice'` and `displayname = 'BloodCancer'`) on attributes of XML nodes `patient` and `code`, respectively. Without further protection, one could easily extract the two query conditions and correlate the two attributes to infer "Alice has blood cancer", a highly sensitive information of Alice.

The problem of correlated attributes in XML query was not considered as severe in early information brokering systems, due to the fact that query content is only viewable to intermediate brokers that are typically assumed trusted. However, as large amount of local data sources join the system, this assumption becomes more and more weak. When joining the system, a member organization either contributes with its own servers to be used as local databases or local brokers, or it delegates it to a third party. It is unrealistic to assume full trust to the brokers, especially if the IBS is used for privacy-sensitive applications.

To defend against the problem caused by attribute correlation, our goal is to limit or at least minimize the capability of any intermediate broker's view of non-empty statement in the sub-queries.

4   New Privacy-Preserving IBS Design

The most intuitive approach to address the problem of attribute-correlation problem is to rely on trustworthiness of the brokers. It is believed that the chance of the attacker will be greatly reduced if we limit the interactions only among trusted brokers, which are less likely to be malicious or compromised. However, fully trusting a broker either exposes to unexpected risks in case it gets compromised or it introduces expensive costs on continuously monitoring its status. Moreover, the set of brokers trusted by any given organization needs to capture a complete copy of routing rules in order to fulfill the routing task. In the worst case, when every single organization only trusts its own broker, each broker needs to store all routing rules. As a conclusion, the trust-based solution is neither practical nor scalable.

A more effective solution is to let multiple entities share responsibility for query routing, so that the trust assumption on each entity could be lowered to a more reasonable level. We assume the brokers are semi-honest, i.e. brokers will faithfully obey the rule but curiously infer the private data as much as they can.

Our approach is to split the routing responsibility into multiple brokers so that they can fulfill the routing task by cooperating together, but a single broker is no longer capable of launching the attribute-correlation attack. More specifically, our approach is characterized by two main components: (1) constructing a broker-tree overlay atop of current topology by decomposing each routing rule into segments and assigning each routing segment to one broker; and (2) splitting each query into segments accordingly and wrapping each segment with a special key. We present the details in the following subsections.

4.1   Broker Tree Construction

Since our work is orthogonal to information integration, we simply assume a global integrated schema (e.g. HL7) is shared among all organizations in a consortium. The schema is a structural description of the syntax of XML documents. If we model the schema as a tree, every node denotes an element or attribute of the schema and the edge between two nodes represents the parent-child relationship. Taking XMark[2] as example, its schema graph is shown in Figure 1(a).

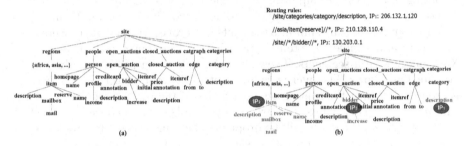

(a)   (b)

Fig. 1. (a) The schema graph of XMark DTD; (b) Filtering routing rules against the schema

Routing rules are collected from distributed data sources (by means of query searching) based on the global schema. Considering the XPath expression in the subject field of a routing rule, it denotes a set of nodes in XML documents. We can locate a subtree by filtering the subject field of a routing rule against the global schema. Then, we attach the address(es) in the location field to the root of the subtree. In this way, we create a centralized *routing schema* for query routing, similar as in [13]. An example in Figure 1(b) shows that the addresses (i.e. IP_1, IP_2 and IP_3) are attached to the roots of three subtrees (i.e. nodes description, item and bidder) when three routing rules are filtered against the XMark schema.

Next, we divide the routing schema into multiple sub-trees (namely *routing segments*) in a way that every leaf-node of a subtree points to the root of its child subtree. We allow flexible granularity in schema dividing : a more fine-grained schema dividing results in less nodes in a routing segment, which indicates well-protected privacy but increased maintenance cost. For each broker, we assign a unique routing segment to it, and attach its address to the leaf-nodes of the parent routing segments. In this way, the brokers are connected in a tree structure

---

[2] XMark is an XML benchmark modeling data from Internet auction applications with a single DTD. We use it as an example in the following discussions.

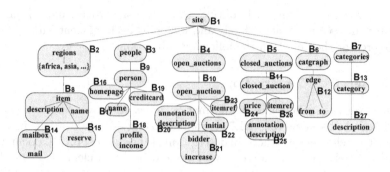

Fig. 2. A broker-tree is constructed with 27 subtrees

according to the relationship of their routing segments. Figure 2 shows a broker tree consists of 27 routing segments based on the routing schema in Figure 1(b).

Since routing rules are split into segments in a broker tree, several brokers need to cooperate to complete the routing task. Let us denote by $q=\{q_{seg_1}||...||q_{seg_n}\}$ an XML query with n segments. The content based routing process can be simply described as follows. The query q is first sent to the root broker B_1, where q_{seg_1} is processed against the routing segment at B_1. If the routing segment matches with q_{seg_1}, the query will be forwarded to the broker whose address is attached at B_1; otherwise, the query will be dropped. The same process follows until the query is dropped by some broker or reaches the final data source.

4.2   Query Segment Encryption

As introduced in the previous section, the first step of our solution consists of sharing the routing responsibility among multiple brokers by constructing a broker tree. Next, we design query segment encryption schemes to guarantee each broker can only decrypt one query segment of a encrypted query. More specifically, for any query segment q_{seg_i} of $q=\{q_{seg_1}||...||q_{seg_n}\}$, the responsible broker B_i is only allowed to view q_{seg_i} in clear-text, while both the processed segments $\{q_{seg_1}||...||q_{seg_{i-1}}\}$ and the unprocessed segments $\{q_{seg_{i+1}}||...||q_{seg_n}\}$ are still encrypted beyond the capability of B_i.

We propose a *level-based encryption* scheme for general cases. As we return later in the paper, this solution is not yet satisfactory, since the wildcard "//" introduces mismatch among the level keys. As such, a new *commutative encryption* scheme is proposed to solve this problem.

Level-based Encryption Scheme. A simple solution to meet the encryption requirement is to encrypt each query segment with the public key of the responsible broker. For example, assume an input query q=/site/regions/asia/item[@id= 10028]/name. If q is processed through the broker tree in Figure 2, the query segments /site, /regions/asia, and /item[@id='10028']/name will be processed by brokers B_1,B_2, and B_8, respectively. So, we can encrypt the three query segments, each with the related public key.

However, a fundamental problem in the proposed PKI-based solution occurs since we assume no centralized routing authority exists after offline broker tree construction process. For any query, the route through the broker tree is unpredictable since neither the brokers enroute nor their public keys to decrypt portions of the route are known.

Therefore, we propose a more effective solution, which encrypts query segments while mitigating the dependency of routing, namely *level-based encryption scheme*. Instead of assigning a pair of public and private keys to each broker, we assign them to all the brokers in the same $level^3$. The concept of level is defined as the distance from a node to the root of the tree. Taking the broker tree in Figure 2 as an example, brokers B_2, B_3, B_4, B_5, B_6, and B_7 are all belonging to level 1. Moreover, if a routing segment contains nodes belonging to more than one levels, all the relevant private level key will be assigned to that broker. Since an XPath expression in an XML query is a location path consisting of s sequence of steps, we will encrypt the XPath steps with corresponding public level keys, e.g. encrypting the ith step with the public key of level i.

Commutative Encryption Scheme. The level-based encryption scheme works well unless the input query contains the *descendant-or-self* axis in its XPath expression. According to the level-based encryption scheme, a broker of level i can view and only view the ith XPath step of any given query. However, if a *descendant-or-self* axis (denoted as "*//*") shows at the ith XPath step, the brokers behind level i may have chance to view some steps after the ones they are authorized to view. We refer to this issue as the *mismatching problem*.

We employ a simple example (as shown in Figure 3(a)) to further elaborate on the mismatching problem. We denote by E_i the encryption process with public level key Pu_i and D_i the decryption process with private level key Pr_i. The input query is Q_2 = /site//item/name. Three XPath steps of Q_2 are encrypted with the public keys of level 1, level 2, and level 3, respectively. If we send Q_2 into the global schema tree of Figure 1, the XPath step "/name" is an XPath node of level 5, which should be processed by broker B_8 along the path "/site/regions/{africa|asia|...}/item/name" in Figure 2. However, following the level-based encryption scheme, broker B_2, with the private level keys of level 2 and 3, will first decrypt the XPath step "//item" at the node "regions" and add a step "/regions" to the original query. Then, it will decrypt the XPath step "/name" at the node "/{Africa|Asia|...}" and add another step "Asia" to the query. As a result, B_2 will uncover the XPath step (i.e. /name) that it is not authorized to access.

To tackle this problem, we propose a new encryption scheme based on well-known *commutative encryption algorithms* [2,7,14]. Commutative encryption is a collection of algorithms that have the property of being *commutative*. In short, an encryption algorithm $E(.)$ is commutative if for any two keys e_1 and e_2, $E_{e_1}[E_{e_2}[m]] = E_{e_2}[E_{e_1}[m]]$, where m is the message to be encrypted. We adopt

---

[3] We adopt the broadcast encryption scheme [9,1] to create public and private level keys so that the public key of any given level is generated based on the private keys of all the brokers at this level.

Pohlig-Hellman exponentiation cipher with modulus p as our commutative encryption function.

We employ the commutative encryption algorithm in order to make flexible switching of decryption sequence possible. The commutative-based encryption scheme introduces a commutative symmetric key for each level, namely *commutative level key* C_i. Besides being issued to brokers of level i, C_i is also issued to all the brokers at level C_{i+2}. The public and private level keys Pr_i and Pu_i, as defined in level-based encryption scheme, are also defined and assumed to be commutative. Moreover, a pointer p is introduced to indicate the XPath step to be processed by the current broker. A broker will always decrypt the XPath step marked by the pointer with its private level key, and move the pointer to the next XPath step.

Commutative encryption scheme is an improver for the level-based encryption scheme. In general, the brokers process XPath steps of a query in the same way as they do following the level-based scheme. When encountering a step with wildcard "//", and the token in wildcard step does not match with the one in its routing segment, the broker will launch the special commutative encryption process, which is summarized as follows: first, the broker starts the set wildcard processing stage by setting a flag $f = 1$. Then, it encrypts all the following unprocessed XPath steps with its commutative level key. With respect to the example in Figure 3(a), the XPath step "/name" is encrypted with key C_2 at the node "regions" of B_2. The following brokers compare the wildcard token with the one in its routing segment. If they do not match, the broker, says B_j, will apply two symmetric commutative keys onto all the XPath steps in the query. This additional encryption guarantees every unprocessed XPath segments are protected by the commutative keys of the current level and its upper level. If they match with each other, B_j will set $f = 2$ to indicate post-wildcard processing. In this stage, a broker encrypts all the unprocessed steps with C_j and decrypts them with C_{j-2}. As shown in Figure 3(b), B_2 wraps unprocessed query step /name with the commutative level key C_2 and C_3. Then, when B_8 finds "//item"

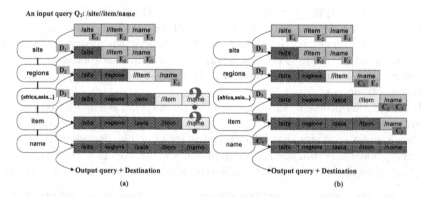

Fig. 3. Example of (a) the mismatching problem caused by the descendent-or-self axis in a query; (b)the solution based on commutative encryption scheme

matches with the token in its routing segment, it decrypts /name with C_2 and C_3, accordingly.

5   Analysis

The main purpose of this work is to protect the privacy of the data owners while authorized organizations collect the data from them and share with other collaborators. More specifically, we protect the content of the query from the malicious or compromised intermediate servers during information brokering process. Therefore, we evaluate our system with two metrics: the *privacy* preserved with the proposed schemes, and the overhead introduced in the querying access of distributed data.

5.1   Privacy Analysis

If the honest-but-curious assumption about the brokers holds, the proposed level-based and commutative encryption schemes can guarantee that no intermediate broker views the complete query content while the brokers fulfilling the query routing function. Risks exist only when one or multiple brokers are abused by the insiders or compromised by the outside adversaries.

The threats caused by malicious or compromised brokers depend on the number of hostile brokers as well as their relative positions in the schema tree. Here, we classify possible cases as the threat under *one hostile broker* and *collaborate brokers*, and briefly discuss as follows.

One hostile broker. In the proposed IBS, a broker is assigned with a routing schema, which is part of the global schema tree, and with level keys (i.e. one private level key and two commutative level keys). With the level keys, a hostile broker can always uncover the corresponding XPath step(s) of an input query. However, the XPath step may at most contain one attribute. Thus, a single hostile broker cannot conduct attribute correlation attack with the restricted view of the query content.

However, a hostile broker may locate the relative position of the routing schema it holds in the global schema tree by looking it up in the global schema tree. From the relative location, it can further guess the routing schemas of the brokers right before and next to it. This information itself is not sensitive, although it may help colluded brokers to determine the next-step target to be compromised.

Collusive brokers. Hostile collusive brokers at different level are capable to uncover different XPath steps of an input query. Whenever a hostile broker receives a query, it can intercept the query and forward it to colluded brokers for decryption. In this case, the compromised broker will view multiple segments of the query instead of one, so its chance to successfully launch the attribute correlation attack increases. In our approach, the risk is however still restricted due to two reasons: first, when a query is intercepted by a broker, only its unprocessed part is at risk since processed XPath steps of the query are encrypted using preassigned public keys of the data servers. So the attacker's chance to succeed depends on the position of the hostile broker that first intercepts the query. If the hostile brokers are near the leaf brokers, the unprocessed query segments are very limited. Therefore, possible countermeasure is to strategically assign the routing schemas of higher levels to more trusted brokers. Secondly, the risk is also related to the number of levels that collusive brokers can cover. Since an attacker may not compromise all the brokers in a limited time interval, his view of the query content is still incomplete.

5.2   Performance Analysis

The overhead introduced by our routing scheme mainly includes computational cost and communication overhead. The former denotes the cost introduced by cryptography operations and query segment matching, and the latter represents the overhead in the end-to-end query brokering time due to distributed routing.

Computational Cost. Assume the cost of asymmetric encryption and decryption as C_{ae} and C_{ad}, respectively, and the cost of commutative encryption and decryption as C_{ce} and C_{cd}, respectively. Since Pohlig-Hellman method requires almost the same number of exponentiation operations and modulus operations as RSA method, we adopt C_e and C_d to denote the cost of encryption and decryption in general, where C_e and C_d are at millisecond level.

For each XML query with m XPath steps, the computational costs of our scheme include asymmetric encryption cost $m \cdot C_e$ at the user-side, asymmetric decryption cost of C_d at each intermediate broker, and additional commutative encryption and decryption cost $C_e + C_d$ at each broker when encountering query segment with wildcard. At each broker, the query segment is matched against the routing schema carried by the broker. We adopt a similar approach as in [13], which implemented query segment matching and routing table look-up using hash table. It results in an average query segment matching time as 1ms[4].

Communication Cost. Since the computational cost at each intermediate broker is at millisecond level, the overhead in end-to-end query brokering is mainly caused by the direct IP latency in overlay routing. The latency is measured using round trip time (RTT), where data from Internet traffic report [5] shows average IP latency is about 200ms.

An important parameter that determines the RTT of a particular query is the *number of hops* experienced by the query. It is related to how we split the global schema tree. If the finest granularity splitting is taken, the number of hops is exactly the depth of the query, providing that the query has no wildcard. When there exists a wildcard, the number of hops cannot be measured accurately, but we know it should be smaller than the depth of the path, a branch of the global routing schema, along which it is routed. As a result, we can estimate the *average*

---

[4] The result is based on simulations with synthetical XML queries and XPath routing rules that are generated atop of the XML benchmark [4].

[5] http://www.internettrafficreport.com

number of hops with the average depth of the global routing schema. Considering the setting as in [13], this value is 5.7.

Therefore, the average overall overhead is around $5.7 \times 100ms$, which is reasonable considering the preserved privacy.

6 Conclusion

We have described an application of content-based information brokering to defend against attribute-correlation attacks. A commutative encryption based scheme is further designed to protect query content from irrelevant brokers. Performance overhead is evaluated and results show that the performance degradation is insignificant.

The privacy of query content is enhanced with the proposed scheme, however, it is not without limitation - the privacy of query content is at risk in some extreme cases when a specific set of brokers collude. We plan to further explore this vulnerability in the future work and to devise possible mitigation techniques.

References

1. Abdalla, M., Kiltz, E., Neven, G.: Generalized key delegation for hierarchical identity-based encryption. In: Biskup, J., López, J. (eds.) ESORICS 2007. LNCS, vol. 4734, pp. 139–154. Springer, Heidelberg (2007)
2. Agrawal, R., Evfimievski, A., Srikant, R.: Information sharing across private databases. In: SIGMOD 2003: Proceedings of the 2003 ACM SIGMOD international conference on Management of data, pp. 86–97. ACM, New York (2003)
3. Altinel, M., Franklin, M.J.: Efficient filtering of XML documents for selective dissemination of information. The VLDB Journal, 53–64 (2000)
4. Berglund, A., Boag, S., Chamberlin, D., Fernndez, M.F., Kay, M., Robie, J., Simon, J.: XML path language (XPath) version 2.0 (2003),
   http://www.w3.org/TR/xpath20/
5. Calvanese, D., Giacomo, G.D., Lenzerini, M., Nardi, D., Rosati, R.: Source integration in data warehousing. In: DEXA Workshop, pp. 192–197 (1998)
6. Chan, C.-Y., Felber, P., Garofalakis, M., Rastogi, R.: Efficient filtering of XML documents with XPath expressions. In: ICDE, San Jose, pp. 235–244 (2002)
7. Clifton, C., Kantarcioglu, M., Vaidya, J., Lin, X., Zhu, M.: Tools for privacy preserving distributed data mining. ACM SIGKDD Explorations 4(2) (2003)
8. De Capitani, S., Samarati, P.: Authorization specification and enforcement in federated database systems. Journal of Computer Security 5(2), 155–188 (1997)
9. Fiat, A., Naor, M.: Broadcast encryption. In: Stinson, D.R. (ed.) CRYPTO 1993. LNCS, vol. 773, pp. 480–491. Springer, Heidelberg (1994)
10. Hammer, J., Garcia-Molina, H., Widom, J., Labio, W., Zhuge, Y.: The stanford data warehousing project. IEEE Data Engineering Bulletin 18(2), 41–48 (1995)
11. Koloniari, G., Pitoura, E.: Content-based routing of path queries in peer-to-peer systems. In: Bertino, E., Christodoulakis, S., Plexousakis, D., Christophides, V., Koubarakis, M., Böhm, K., Ferrari, E. (eds.) EDBT 2004. LNCS, vol. 2992, pp. 29–47. Springer, Heidelberg (2004)

12. Koudas, N., Rabinovich, M., Srivastava, D., Yu, T.: Routing XML queries. In: Proceedings of 20th International Conference on Data Engineering, p. 844 (2004)
13. Li, F., Luo, B., Liu, P., Lee, D., Chu, C.-H.: Automaton segmentation: A new approach to preserve privacy in XML information brokering. In: ACM CCS 2007, pp. 508–518 (2007)
14. Lu, H.Y.S.: Commutative cipher based en-route filtering in wireless sensor networks. In: Vehicular Technology Conference, vol. 2, pp. 1223–1227 (September 2004)
15. Snoeren, A.C., Conley, K., Gifford, D.K.: Mesh-based content routing using XML. In: Symposium on Operating Systems Principles, pp. 160–173 (2001)
16. Wiederhold, G.: Mediators in the architecture of future information systems. Computer 25(3), 38–49 (1992)
17. Wiederhold, G.: Value-added mediation in large-scale information systems. In: DS-6: Proceedings of the Sixth IFIP TC-2 Working Conference on Data Semantics, London, UK, pp. 34–56 (1995)
18. Yan, T.W., Garcia-Molina, H.: The SIFT information dissemination system. ACM TODS 24(4), 529–565 (1999)

Incentive and Trust Issues in Assured Information Sharing

Ryan Layfield, Murat Kantarcioglu, and Bhavani Thuraisingham

Computer Science Department, University of Texas at Dallas
{layfield,muratk,bxt043000}@utdallas.edu

Abstract. Assured information sharing among different organizations in a coalitional environment is an important first step in accomplishing many critical tasks. For example, different security agencies may need to share intelligence information for detecting terrorist plots. At the same, each organization participating in the assured information sharing process may have different incentives. In this paper, we explore the effects of different incentives and potential trust issues among organizations on the assured information sharing process by developing an evolutionary game theoretic framework. In addition, we provide extensive simulation analysis that illustrates the impact of various different information sharing strategies.

1 Introduction

Many current challenges require different organizations to share critical information. Defending against the threats of international terrorism presents this scenario in an alarming manner. Countries that are concerned about an attack on native soil must frequently consider assailants that have collaborators which span the globe. A single country rarely has the necessary resources and jurisdiction to continuously investigate every possible suspect. Even if the resources are available, unless attacks are expected to have a considerable impact, it is not likely that the investment is cost-effective. Thus, a variety of agreements have been created in the course of history to attempt to unite multiple governing bodies under a common threat by exchanging information with their allies.

Unfortunately, in the scope of international politics, the only governing factor that ensures members of an alliance will always cooperate fully lies in their individual incentives. Unless information can be verified, there are no guarantees that the information supplied will be truthful. In addition, in some cases, there exists the potential for increasing gain from an information exchange by presenting false knowledge. In such cases, if the other party's knowledge is truthful, and the malicious party is not caught, a one-sided gain could occur. Thus, one of the biggest challenges in such endeavors is how to encourage honest assured information sharing.

The study of game theory deals directly with the motivations of participants, known as players, attempting to achieve some known goal and the choices they must make to do so. Out of all options available, game theory assumes that each participant wishes to maximize their own personal benefit in a rational manner. At any given

E. Bertino and J.B.D. Joshi (Eds.): CollaborateCom 2008, LNICST 10, pp. 113–125, 2009.
© ICST Institute for Computer Sciences, Social-Informatics and Telecommunications Engineering 2009

time in an information exchange, both participants have the option of telling the truth, providing false data or providing no data. While it may seem obvious that all parties would collectively benefit from the truth, each individual is often only concerned with their own gains [14]. If that gain comes at the expense of another participant with no threat of retribution, there is little encouragement to do otherwise.

However, when games are repeated, new constraints begin to emerge on a player's strategies. If a participant chooses to lie, they run the risk of being caught, leading to a potential net loss. When a central authority can observe actions and affect the payout a player receives, enforcement of the agreement often becomes a simple manner of finding an appropriate punishment. When considering agreements between multiple sovereign governing entities, there is not necessarily any central authority that can enforce such punishments. In such cases, the burden of ensuring an ideal situation is created is shifted to the collective actions of the group.

One option a player has within such a scenario is to simply refuse to participate. This can include all members, or just a selection of those that are not giving the desirable responses. If one player has information that is highly desirable to the rest, with little dependence on others, they can potentially influence the choices by the entire group. On a level playing field, where no player has information that is significantly more valuable, a single player which no longer communicates with the rest can be sacrificed with little trouble. Clearly, collective action must be taken by a significant number of participants to have any effect on group. Thus, several players must be willing to isolate the same player with undesirable behavior in the hopes that the malicious participant will change their ways.

Another more indirect method of enforcing behavior is to base punishment indirectly on the level of trust shared by the players. Normally, each player already has opinions of the rest, but they lack a broader view of the situation and must assume that how a player deals with them is how they deal with everyone else. Eigentrust [22] provides a means of collectively allowing each individual player to form accurate opinions of the group by providing ratings of their own experiences. Such opinions can be gathered in a distributed manner and provide the rough equivalent of an 'omniscient' view of the rest.

Several of these factors have already been explored in other works (e.g., [21]). However, a factor that has not always been considered is the cost of determining whether or not information is correct. While there is certainly data that can easily be verified, that nature of certain kinds of information requires a much more in-depth review. Thus, the cost of verification should always be considered in situations where the net gain of the interactions is paramount to the success or failure of an exchange.

The goal of our work is to explore the potential of punishment via isolation with regards to the introduction of trust computations. We wish to determine whether or not such methods are viable in large games with multiple players with different incentive structures, and consider various scenarios that such logic may face. Success of such a method would prove useful in a variety of decentralized assured information sharing platforms.

Our paper is organized as follows. Section 2 describes existing work on the subject, including our own. Section 3 describes our model. Section 4 discusses how we setup our experiments while section 5 details our results. Finally, we share our own conclusions on the subject in section 6 and consider future directions of the field.

2 Related Work

One closely related area to our current work is the research on incentive issues in peer-to-peer file sharing networks. Within these file sharing systems, independent players join and leave at their leisure, seeking to download a file or files with the help of other participants. Problems arise when a new participant joins the network and download a resource from other peers and never actually contribute to the group. This process, known as leeching, has been a large problem in piece-meal file sharing protocols such as the popular BitTorrent. The work of Gupta et al. [20] and Buragohain et al. [19] both deal with this behavior by creating a system of incentives for further contribution.

In our previous work [21], we provide a simpler model that excludes distributed trust from behavior influence and focuses on how individual agents indirectly can contribute towards achieving a common goal in a virtual game of assured information sharing. Agents were permitted to shift their behavioral choices to more effective means through analysis at a fixed interval. The LivingAgent (more on this later) was introduced as a competitive alternative to the Tit-for-Tat strategy, and the former worked well in the constraints provided. However, it still suffered from a need for 'critical mass' of the behavior's presence before it was effective.

A great deal of research has dealt with trust in the realm of distributed systems. Information exchange methods have been particularly useful in the formation of ad-hoc networks. Seredynski et al. [1] used the concept of an evolving genetic algorithm to enhance security and trust in a wireless network among multiple nodes relaying data packets. Other works have taken a purely game-theoretic approach to trust. The work of Cascella [2] performed analysis of an infinitely repeated form of the prisoner's dilemma with regard to persistent players randomly selected. They found the introduction of a reputation system allowed punishment systems based on discriminating between good and bad reputations succeeded as long as players were sufficiently patient to achieve the results. Other works have attempted to apply peer-to-peer trust in scenarios involving military joint cooperation in the field [3]. Given a military body as a dividable resource, they attempt to address the problem of resource allocation in situations where either a central authority is not robust enough or the resources span multiple international owners. The core issues they addressed were dealing with malicious reports attempting to sabotage trust ratings and attempting to give more control to an agent's own rating.

3 Our Model

Our previous work on the subject of behavior enforcement in distributed information sharing focused solely on the feasibility of the verification and punishment process. Several experiments proved conclusively that the LivingAgent behavior outlined in [21] both helped to eliminate malicious agents and eventually become the dominate strategy in an adaptive game. We plan to build upon the success of that agent by integrating distributed trust metrics into the decision making process.

The scenario for our information exchange strategies is based on a loose alliance with no central authority to enforce behavior. Consider multiple nations that have learned of an impending terrorist attack. They do not have conclusive data to suggest when or where the attack will occur, but each country has reason to believe it may occur on their own soil. Their objective is to attempt to thwart the current threat. However, given an indefinite time span in which the attack could occur and limited resources, they have each determined they must ask other countries for help. After discovering each of them had a common goal, they have formed an alliance in which they exchange information they have collected both at home and abroad. The nature of the game is one which occurs repeatedly for an indefinite amount of time.

Information is exchanged between members of the alliance individually at a regular interval. The transaction occurs between two countries in such a way that the data is swapped simultaneously; both countries must decide on their strategy before the transaction is complete. Each of these transactions occurs between all possible pairs of countries simultaneously, assuming each pair agrees to do business. The value of the information fluctuates within predictable boundaries, and no player has a considerable advantage over the rest.

Each player faces that challenge that they do not know of the kind of behavior the members will engage in. While all countries involved are assumed to have a common goal, they may also see an opportunity to advance other political statements. For example, one country may wish to keep what they know a secret from the rest, in the hopes of learning more at no real cost.

The strategies chosen by each country is determined by the overall behavior they have chosen. Each country wishes to find the optimal strategy to reduce the impact of defense on their national budget. We assume thus that countries are willing to adapt by altering the behavior to reflect the one they believe has performed the best. At the same time, as behaviors shift, the payouts of strategy choices may shift as well, leading to a dynamic balance of power. For example, a behavior to always lie may perform well when other countries are not verifying, but as others learn of the benefits of the behavior, others may follow suit. This would result in several liars always lying to each other and never gaining any information.

Determining whether or not the data is received is legitimate is the responsibility of the country itself. Since the data is primarily intelligence, verifying it has a substantial cost due to the resources, manpower, and time required. In our scenario, verification is always less than the value of the information itself, which means consistently doing so will still result in a net gain. However, it is not necessarily the most efficient.

The use of adaptation to improved behaviors within a game raises an interesting point about the duration of punishment. One option is to punish a deviating agent indefinitely. When this is done, any future benefit from that agent is simply not possible, potentially allowing more forgiving agents to flourish. Instead, punishment in our game is done in such a way that the other player simply loses a significant amount of their own potential earnings, reducing their net gain from the game. This indirectly makes the ideal behaviors much more likely to be chosen. Eventually, if this is practiced widely enough, overall behavioral choices yield an ideal environment where everyone can benefit. Likewise, when we have a fixed interval when agents may take the opportunity to change behaviors, we would potentially discourage what may otherwise be an excellent source of profit; thus, forgiveness must be performed by all agents during this round. An example of this would be when a government agency has a new leader or a business comes to the end of a fiscal quarter.

Determining reputations within a distributed network can be a difficult endeavor. Since it is possible for a malicious participant to deal honestly with some players and dishonestly with others, a trust value must extend beyond a local perspective. This necessitates querying others for their opinions on opponents within the game, which introduces the possibility of the same malicious agents simply telling others they have an outstanding rating while their peers have just the opposite. This introduces the additional possibility that different players will come to separate conclusions, based on the 'noise' introduced by the subversion. Sepandar [22] et al. devised the EigenTrust algorithm as an answer to these problems.

The algorithm itself is relatively straightforward. Each player queries every other player for their opinion on the rest. This forms a matrix of relative trust, based on a score built from history among individual agents. From here, a normalized matrix is constructed, then evaluated with the Eigenvalue Decomposition technique. When all players perform this properly, they will all come up with the same left-principle eigenvector. This vector represents the Eigentrust rating of each player. The algorithm has been well received as a foundation for more robust distributed systems, though trust itself needs further refinement to be properly defined [7]. In real distributed system deployments, Eigentrust would be done in a distributed fashion [22].

Table 1. Utilities for various actions

		Play (agent j)		Do Not Play
		Truth	Lie	
Play (Agent i)	Truth	$\left(\dfrac{\delta_{min}+\delta_{max}}{2}\right)-C_v(P_i+t_j)\sigma_i$ $\left(\dfrac{\delta_{min}+\delta_{max}}{2}\right)-C_v(P_j+t_i)\sigma_j$	$-C_v(P_i+t_j)\sigma_i$ $\left(\dfrac{\delta_{min}+\delta_{max}}{2}\right)-C_v(P_j+t_i)\sigma_j$	0 0
	Lie	$\left(\dfrac{\delta_{min}+\delta_{max}}{2}\right)-C_v(P_i+t_j)\sigma_i$ $-C_v(P_j+t_i)\sigma_j$	$-C_v(P_i+t_j)\sigma_i$ $-C_v(P_j+t_i)\sigma_j$	0 0
Do Not Play		0 0	0 0	0 0

Given these ingredients, the basics of each round of our game can be described with an immediate snapshot of the game matrix. There are essentially three choices every player can choose: lie, tell the truth, or stop playing with the other player. The potential benefit from the truth is an average of δ_{min} and δ_{max}, the upper and lower bounds of what the information is worth. A lie of course carries no value, but checking as to whether a piece is legitimate or not does carry a cost. The expected cost of verification is determined by the cost of verification C_V times the probability that verification will occur coupled. The probability of verification is determined by three factors: (i) the type of the agent i (σ_i) (ii) the minimal probability of verification for agent i (P_i) (iii) the Eigentrust value t_j assigned to the opponent j. However, certain behaviors never consider verification as a possibility, regardless of trust, and as such the verification has no effect on the result. For example, a player may want to accept the provided information without any verification. In that case, we can set the σ_i as 0. The table 1 summarizes the payoff matrix for each information exchange transaction.

3.1 Behaviors

In our analysis, we considered various different types of agent behaviors. The Honest behavior takes a naïve approach to other players. Truth is the only strategy ever chosen, and it never verifies the strategies of other players. It has the advantage of never incurring the cost of verification, and it always maximizes the potential gains with other players by never severing the links. An example may be a country that wishes to set an example, or perhaps is simply under significant amounts of scrutiny. While this may prevail against behaviors that perform even the slightest verification, they will always lose in a competition with the Dishonest behavior. Essentially serving as the opposite of the Honest behavior, this behavior simply chooses the Lie strategy regardless of the outcome.

Not every player may believe that a predictable behavior is optimal. The Random behavior picks either Truth or Lie with equal probability. No punishment or verification is ever performed. Countries that wish to avoid being anticipated may choose this strategy. It carries the same benefits as the Dishonest behavior, but potentially only gains at most half the benefit.

In our prior work [21], we encountered a unique yet simple approach to dealing with undesirable behavior known as the Tit-for-Tat behavior. Devised by Anatol Rapoport [13, 14], it follows a simple strategy selection process. Initially, it selects the desirable strategy (Truth). From that point on, it simply selects the same strategy as its' opponent within the game. This was proven quite effective against all but the most sophisticated collaborative opponents [23]. In our simulation, however, being able to mimic the opponent's actions requires constant verification.

Our devised behavior from our prior work is the LivingAgent. Initially, like Tit-for-Tat, the Truth strategy is chosen. During each transaction, there is a probability P_i that the player will verify whether or not the other player told the truth. If a lie was told, the other player is punished by severing the link for R_S rounds. This is a sacrifice in the sense that, if the other player is telling the truth for at least part of the time, further opportunity will be lost. The goal with this behavior is to place a high price on deviation. A country which behaves in this manner may be attempting to send a message to the rest of the participants, or may simply be unwilling to waste time with participants whom are equally unwilling to share valid information.

A variant on this behavior is the SubtleLiar, which obeys the same principle but has a threshold in which it will automatically choose the Lie strategy. The net effect is a behavior which can take advantage of a low P_i and net a slightly larger gain in information. An example of this behavior may be countries that believe their fellow members trust them enough to be taken advantage of.

Finally, we have the Liar. This behavior is almost identical to that of LivingAgent, with one notable exception. Is called Liar simply because it essentially tries to pass itself off as a honest participant while consistently trying to take advantage of the right situations. Assuming that the value of the information about to be received is known in advance by both, the Liar will always lie if the received value is within a certain threshold of maximum value. Thus, this agent appears to capitalize on advanced information by attempting to only take a risk when the gain appears to be sufficient. This threshold is determined by the constant $\delta_{valuable}$.

4. Experimental Setup

Our experimental setup involves creating an alliance of 100 virtual countries. They begin with equal levels of trust, and hold all of their peers in the same regard. Each experiment begins by distributing initial behaviors based on a configuration file. The behaviors are assigned to each player based on the distribution specified within the file. During each round of the simulation, a transaction is executed between all possible combinations of players through a virtual link. After this round, the trust metrics are updated, history files are recorded, and agents receive their payoff based on the results. This payoff is used to directly determine the performance of the agent itself. The value of the information varies between $\delta_{min} = 3$ and $\delta_{max} = 7$. If the information provided is false, it has no value. In the event verification is performed, it comes at a cost C_V, set to a value of 2. Thus, even if all information is verified, a net gain is still possible. When verification occurs, and no lie was told, it is noted as waste. The overall score a player receives is simply the total value of all information sans any cost incurred. The threshold for Liar to lie is at 6.9.

All players are assumed to be willing to change their behavior to a more effective one, based on the performance of their neighbors. To simulate this, every 5,000 rounds, each agent is assigned a new behavior based on a weighted probability assigned based on the total gain achieved. For example, if the Honest agent has an total net payoff of 10,000, while Dishonest has a total net payoff of 20,000, each agent has a 33% chance of choosing Honest and a 67% chance of choosing Dishonest. Thus, the new distribution reflects the relative performance of all agents. Note that while this method does not necessarily guarantee an ineffective behavior will be eliminated, it will ensure that any effective choice will be much more likely to emerge victorious. The simulation ends when either 100,000 rounds have passed or all players have chosen the same behavior, the latter considered a 'win' by the behavior adopted by the rest.

There are several verification rates possible for a LivingAgent-derived behavior. To ensure a larger search space is explored during the experiment, a small mutation rate is introduced on P_i for each player behavior that is copied. This allows players to adapt over time and consider reducing the potential waste as the system approaches an equilibrium in which all participants tell the truth.

5 Experimental Results

The LivingAgent performed admirably against Tit-for-Tat, even when the latter behavior began in the experiment with twice as many players adopting it. Out of all experiments, neither the Dishonest nor the Tit-for-Tat behavior ever successfully became the dominant behavior. However, the LivingAgent behavior only won the

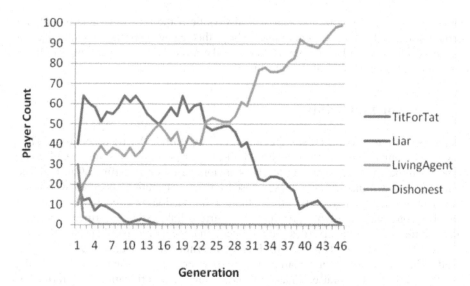

Fig. 1. Success of various strategies against LivingAgent

game 87% of the time, while Liar won the rest. The average verification rate was 14.8% in the final behavior tally, while the average standard deviation was only 2%, taking an average of 15 generations to declare a winner.

In figure 1, we see that LivingAgent successfully achieved the majority behavior despite beginning as a much smaller population. At first, Liar benefits from the fact that it and the rest of the behaviors engage in punishment. Those that leave the Dishonest behavior go towards both LivingAgent and Liar, with more towards Liar. However, Dishonest is no longer being used, Tit-for-Tat begins to help LivingAgent by working slightly against Liar. A trend in the results is that once LivingAgent achieves half of the population, the Liar behavior rapidly loses ground to the point of complete loss. This appears to be the critical mass for the behavior in such a situation.

When Tit-for-Tat was able to sustain itself for at least 10 generations, LivingAgent often benefited from this indirectly. The Liar players, even when they initially surged ahead, would usually observe that Tit-for-Tat was a better choice. As Tit-for-Tat increased, LivingAgent took some losses, but the efforts ended up working in concert to reduce the threat of a lying behavior. Ultimately, once Tit-for-Tat was no longer in play, LivingAgent needed only to compete with a smaller pool of malicious players.

Another trend that made itself apparent is that the verification rates of the LivingAgent did not correlate directly with the number of malicious agents present. In many instances, as the number of Liars increased, the average rate continued to drop. In these cases, it appears that players simply cannot afford to refuse doing business with other players that ran the risk of lying. Essentially, the punishment method ended up only punishing the enforcer.

In order to demonstrate the effectiveness of the LivingAgent approach, we ran experiments involving all behaviors not derived from it (Figures 2 and 3). The behaviors here were only Dishonest, Honest, Tit-for-Tat, and Random. The first thing we noticed is that there was automatically a large increase in the number of iterations

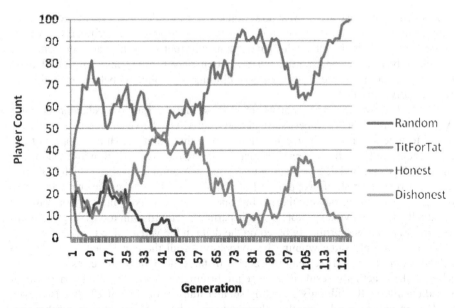

Fig. 2. Evolution of various strategies without LivingAgents: Honest behavior winning case

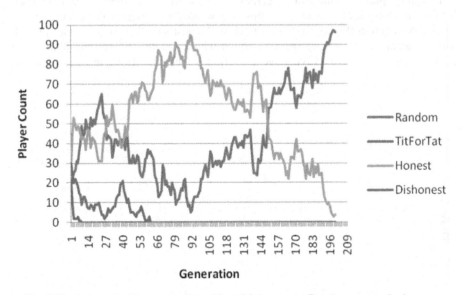

Fig. 3. Evolution of various strategies without Livingagents: Random agent winning case

necessary. The winner was not always clear, and it appeared that the fluctuation in the payoffs alone caused some agents to benefit more than others. The biggest competitor to Honest was strangely Dishonest, even though both used the polar extremes of selecting a strategy, and neither made any efforts to check information validity.

Another issue that arose was how quickly Tit-For-Tat was eliminated at times within the first generations. This, however, was no surprise; the verification costs no doubt came at a high toll to the payouts. It contributed to the game by removing malicious behaviors consistently, but this often only resulted in a surge of Honest behavior adoptions. Once Tit-for-Tat was eliminated, malicious behaviors again rose substantially in numbers.

Figure 3 shows an experiment where we find that the Random behavior has won. Again, Tit-for-Tat helps Honest surge ahead briefly, but the verification costs cause it to fail to function after only 7 generations. From that point on, Honest appears to be the certain victor, eliminating Dishonest. At generation 92, Random begins to succeed. Essentially, because Random does not discriminate against which players it lies to, it runs the risk of dropping off at just shy of 50% of the player market. This happens twice during the simulation, but due to fluctuations in information value, it eventually achieves victory. Note that this particular equilibrium took 197 generations to achieve, and it was primarily based on the delta in the value gained.

There were only three winning behaviors out of all the experiments. The Honest behavior only achieved the majority 26.1% of the time. Out of those instances, only 84% of them actually resulted in an equilibrium behavior. The Random behavior faired equally well, with only a slightly smaller number of wins at 23.3%. However, the Dishonest behavior beat both of them twice as often at 53.3% as either of them.

In reality, players within these games can vary widely in their ulterior motives, beliefs, and decisions. To observe this, we wanted to observe all of the devised behaviors in action (Figure 4). Unsurprisingly, Honest won 99% of all games played. The abundance of malicious agents, coupled with a roughly 3:1 starting ratio to the Honest behavior, allows LivingAgent to flourish briefly. However, as malicious

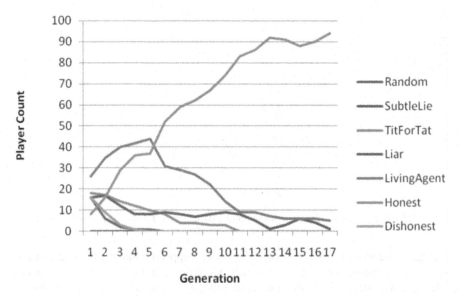

Fig. 4. Evolution of all possible strategies together

agents begin to disappear due to lack of relative performance, the appeal of the Honest approach eventually coerces a majority of agents away from it. The loss of Dishonest and Random predictably caused a 25% drop in.

On the surface, it may appear that our own LivingAgent is a failure under these circumstances. If our goal was simply to find the 'perfect' behavior, this would indeed be true. However, our constructed behavior helps to create an environment in which the Honest behavior can flourish. Thus, the end result is still the ideal, truth-telling environment. Since previous results demonstrated that Honest would normally fail against the malicious competitors, the introduction of our behavior has acted as an indirect policing force within the system. The Honest behavior achieved the majority roughly 97% of the time within our initial experiments, over three times what it achieved under similar conditions on its' own.

Additional experiments were performed to observe the minimum behavioral mix necessary to ensure Honest would succeed, performed in the form of ratios between LivingAgent and Honest. When equal parts of both behaviors were present, Honest won 86% of the time. Increasing the ratio of LivingAgent to Honest to 2:1, it increased to 92% of the time. At a ratio of 3:1, an effectiveness of nearly 100% was achieved. Thus, although LivingAgent benefited the rest of the group in achieving a truth-telling majority, significant numbers of LivingAgent were needed to guarantee it.

6. Conclusions

The overall experiment was a relative success. When enough players choose a behavior that reflects our approach to punishment, the malicious behaviors were successfully eliminated from consideration. The underlying nature of LivingAgent allowed it to defeat even variants of its' own behavior involving light amounts of deviation. However, the same nature of the persistent verification meant that the behavior did not succeed against the Honest behavior, which performed no verification whatsoever despite the circumstances. Even in these circumstances, the ideal situation still arose, allowing players to conclude that honesty is indeed the best choice.

We hope to increase the robustness of our punishment method in scenarios closer to reality. In real life, information cannot always be verified with 100% accuracy, nor do even the best intelligence agencies guarantee that information provided will be completely true. Such inadvertent mistakes would result in a system which potentially punish otherwise trustworthy players. This can be addressed with a mixture of a higher tolerance for lies and a slightly more relaxed punishment. Our future work will explore this problem in depth.

The growing size of networks such as the internet and the increasing use of distributed systems suggest that centralized authority approaches will be insufficient. Insuring behavioral choices by members of peer-to-peer networks requires an approach which can scale as much as the system itself. We believe our work offers a solution to the problem of encouraging behavior when players become responsible for their own outcome.

References

1. Seredynski, M. Bouvry, P. Klopotek, M.A.: Modelling the Evolution of Cooperative Behavior in Ad Hoc Networks using a Game Based Model. Computation Intelligence and Games, 96–103 (2007)
2. Cascella, R.G.: The "Value" of Reputation in Peer-to-Peer Networks. In: Consumer Communications and Networking Conference, 516–520. (2008)
3. Oh, J.C., Gemelli, N., Wright, R.: A Rationality-based Modeling for Coalition Support. Intelligent Systems, 172–177 (2004)
4. Li, X.: A Grassroots Approach in P2P Reputation Studies. In: Distributed Computing Systems Workshops, p. 234 (2008)
5. Yi, X., Han, J., Yu, P.: Truth Discover with Multiple Conflicting Information Providers on the Web. IEEE Transactions on Knowledge and Data Engineering, 796–808 (2007)
6. Eckel, C., Wilson, R.: The Human Face of Game Theory: Trust and Reciprocity in Sequential Games. In: Trust Working Group Meeting (1999)
7. Morselli, R., Katz, J., Bhattacharjee, B.: A Game-Theoretic Framework for Analyzing Trust Inference Protocols. In: Workshop on Economics of Peer-to-Peer Systems (2004)
8. Cascella, R., Battiti, R.: Social Networking and Game Theory to Foster Cooperation, http://www.enisa.europa.eu/doc/pdf/Workshop/June2007/Papers/reputation/REP_UniversityTrento.pdf
9. De Paola, A., Tamburo, A.: Reputation Management in Distributed Systems. In: 2008 IEEE Symposium on Game theory, evolutionary approach, distributed systems (March 2008)
10. Song, S., Hwang, K., Zhou, R., Kwok, Y.: Trusted P2P Transactions with Fuzzy Reputation Aggregation. IEEE Internet Computer, 24–34 (November 2005)
11. Agarwal, N.: Equilibrium Game Theory Under the Conditions of Repeatability. In: Proceedings of the 10th International Conference on Extending Database Technology, pp. 240–256 (2006)
12. Andrade, N., Mowbray, M., Lima, A., Wagne, G., Ripeanu, M.: Influences on cooperation in BitTorrent communities. In: Proceedings of the 2005 ACM SIGCOMM workshop on Economics of peer-to-peer systems, pp. 111–115 (2005)
13. Axelrod, R.: The Evolution of Cooperation. Basic Books, New York (1984)
14. Fudenberg, D., Tirole, J.: Game Theory. MIT Press, Cambridge (1991)
15. Mahajan, R., Rodrig, M., Wetherall, D., Zahorjan, J.: Experiences applying game theory to system design. In: Proceedings of the ACM SIGCOMM workshop on Practice and theory of incentives in networked systems, Portland, Oregon, pp. 183–190 (2004)
16. Monderer, D., Tennenholtz, M.: Distributed games: from mechanisms to protocols. In: Proceedings of the sixteenth national conference on Artificial intelligence and the eleventh Innovative applications of artificial intelligence conference innovative applications of artificial intelligence, Orlando, Florida, pp. 32–37 (1999)
17. Myerson, R.: Game Theory: Analysis of Conflict. Harvard University Press, Cambridge (1991)
18. Riolo, R., Worzel., B.: Genetic Programming Theory and Practice. Kluwer Academic, Boston (2003)
19. Buragohain, C., Agrawal, D., Suri, S.: A Game Theoretic Framework for Incentives in P2P Systems. Peer-to-Peer Computing, 48–56 (2003)
20. Gupta, M., Judge, P., Ammar, M.: A Reputation System for Peer-to-Peer Networks. In: Proceedings of the 13th international workshop on Network and operating systems support for digital audio and video, Monterey, CA, pp. 144–152 (2003)

21. Layfield, R., Kantarcioglu, M., Thuraisingham, B.: Enforcing Honesty in Assured Information Sharing Within a Distributed System. In: Barker, S., Ahn, G.-J. (eds.) Data and Applications Security 2007. LNCS, vol. 4602, pp. 113–128. Springer, Heidelberg (2007)
22. Kamvar, S., Schlosser, M., Garcia-Molina, H.: The Eigentrust algorithm for reputation management in P2P networks. In: Proceedings of the 12th international conference on World Wide Web, Budapest, Hungary, pp. 640–651 (2003)
23. Grossman, W.: New Tack Wins Prisoner's Dilemma. Wired Magazine, http://www.wired.com/culture/lifestyle/news/2004/10/65317

Combining Social Networks and Semantic Web Technologies for Personalizing Web Access[*]

Barbara Carminati, Elena Ferrari, and Andrea Perego

DICOM, Università degli Studi dell'Insubria, Varese, Italy
{barbara.carminati,elena.ferrari,andrea.perego}@uninsubria.it

Abstract. The original purpose of Web metadata was to protect end-users from possible harmful content and to simplify search and retrieval. However they can also be also exploited in more enhanced applications, such as Web access personalization on the basis of end-users' preferences. In order to achieve this, it is however necessary to address several issues. One of the most relevant is how to assess the trustworthiness of Web metadata. In this paper, we discuss how such issue can be addressed through the use of collaborative and Semantic Web technologies. The system we propose is based on a Web-based Social Network, where members are able not only to specify labels, but also to rate existing labels. Both labels and ratings are then used to assess the trustworthiness of resources' descriptions and to enforce Web access personalization.

1 Introduction

The availability of metadata describing Web resources' has been considered as a key issue as soon as the Web became a public information space. Originally, the idea was to use metadata to protect end users from inappropriate and/or harmful content. Released by the W3C in 1996, PICS [1] was the first attempt to define a standard format for such metadata, referred to as *content labels*. Despite PICS has been quickly implemented by MS Internet Explorer and the Netscape browser, resource labeling has not gained success, mainly due to the following reasons. First, resource labeling requires content providers to spend time to describe their resources, and such an effort can be justified only if labels bring real marketing benefits to a content provider. Second, since Web resources' content may frequently change, it is necessary to update content labels accordingly, to be sure that they actually describe the resources they refer to.

However, in recent years the situation has changed, and Web metadata are currently seen by content and service providers as a means to assure the quality of online information. One of the outcomes of such new attitude has been the establishment of the POWDER (Protocol for Web Description Resources) W3C Working Group,[1] aiming at the definition of a new generation of content

---

[*] The work reported in this paper is partially funded by the European Community under the QUATRO Plus project (SIP-2006-211001) and by the Italian Ministry of University, Education and Research under the ANONIMO project (PRIN-2007F9437X_004).

[1] Working Group page: http://www.w3.org/2007/powder

E. Bertino and J.B.D. Joshi (Eds.): CollaborateCom 2008, LNICST 10, pp. 126–144, 2009.

labels making use of Semantic Web technologies. Moreover, there currently exist several Web-based Social Networks (WBSNs) providing their members the ability of specifying and sharing metadata (referred to as *tags*), such as, for instance, del.icio.us (`http://del.icio.us`), RawSugar (`http://rawsugar.com`), Flickr (`http://flickr.com`), and Last.fm (`http://last.fm`). Such practice, also known as *social* or *collaborative tagging* [2,3], has the purpose of collecting and sharing opinions about Web resources, and simplifying resource retrieval by organizing resources according to a tag-based browsing criterion.

Although, currently, labels and tags (which we refer to as *Web metadata*) are used, respectively, for quality assurance and tag-based resource classification and browsing, we think that they can have more enhanced applications. In particular, they can be the basis for enhancing access personalization to Web resources. In such a scenario, end users can specify policies determining the actions to be performed by a user agent upon detection of resources associated with given Web metadata. However, in order to achieve this, it is necessary first of all to devise mechanisms able to assess the trustworthiness of Web metadata. We think that collaborative environments and Semantic Web technologies can provide a solution to such issue. In fact, the availability of WBSNs consisting of thousands of users would help not only in increasing the number of labeled/tagged resources, but also in assessing their trustworthiness, based, for instance, on the percentage of labels providing identical descriptions of a resource. Additionally, if WBSN members can express their agreement/disagreement with the descriptions provided by existing labels, this would further help in selecting the most appropriate descriptions for a given resource. By elaborating on these ideas, in this paper we propose a system for collaborative resource labeling and label rating, and we show how it can be exploited for Web access personalization. In our approach, we use the notion of *descriptor* instead of the one of tag, and we denote a *label* as a set of descriptors, modeled according to the POWDER definition. Besides labeling resources, WBSN members can express their dis/agreement about existing labels, by specifying ratings on the contained descriptors. Labels are then statistically analyzed in order to assess the trustworthiness of the contained descriptors. Additional key features of our system are the support for (a) trust policies, making each WBSN member able to denote who he/she considers trustworthy about given topics and/or resource properties, and (b) user preferences, which allow WBSN members to state which actions must be performed on the requested resource, on the basis of the associated descriptors and their trustworthiness. An implementation of our framework is currently carried on in the context of the QUATRO Plus EU project (`http://www.quatro-project.org/`), whose overall goal is to set up an integrated environment for the creation, distribution, and usage of Web metadata.

To the best of our knowledge, currently there does not exist any online service supporting all the features of our proposal. Indeed, most of the existing online communities can be basically considered as recommender systems [4], in that users share resources that they consider relevant, and express personal opinions on them with the purpose of making easier resource retrieval. Examples of these communities are MovieLens [5] and PHOAKS [6]. In order to simplify the search of shared resources, in the last years several online communities have also provided support for *collaborative tagging*. However, as far as we know, no online community gives its users the possibility of expressing their dis/agreement about existing ratings and tags, with the only exception of MovieLens, where a user can rate (positively or negatively) existing tags. Moreover, none of the above-mentioned communities support user preferences for access personalization.

Trust computation is a feature which is supported by some online communities, mainly in order to refine recommendations. Examples are LinkedIn, Orkut, and RepCheck, for personal/professional reputation, FilmTrust, for movie recommendation [7], Moleskiing, for safe skiing [8], and MyWOT (`http://mywot.com`), for Web resource reputation. FilmTrust and Moleskiing are particularly relevant for the scope of our paper. FilmTrust gives its members the possibility of specifying *trust relationships*, denoting how much they trust the opinions on movies of the people they know. Such trust relationships are then used to compute the transitive trust of existing members, in order to weight the relevance of their ratings. Moleskiing adopts a similar approach to personalize recommendations concerning safer skiing. Our trust policies extend the features provided by these online communities, by allowing a user to specify how much he/she trusts another user, in general or with respect to specific descriptors and/or topics. Moreover, trust policies are not only specified in terms of personal relationships existing among WBSN users, but also on user credentials and/or credential attributes.

Finally, user preferences are supported only by MyWOT, an online community for collecting and sharing ratings concerning Web site reputation. MyWOT provides a browser extension allowing subscribed users to associate Web sites with a score concerning the following Web site properties: *trustworthiness, vendor reliability, privacy*, and *child safety*. Such data are then elaborated by a Bayesan-based algorithm in order to compute an average reputation score. My-WOT allows its members to specify preferences concerning the actions to be performed by the browser, (i.e., *block* or *warning*) upon detection of a Web site with given characteristics. The approach adopted by MyWOT is similar to ours, but some relevant differences are present. First of all, it supports just four descriptors (i.e., trustworthiness, vendor reliability, privacy, and child safety), and it does not give users the possibility of expressing their dis/agreement with claims made by other users. Moreover, differently from our proposal, explicit trust policies or trust relationships are not supported, in that the trustworthiness of rating authors is computed by the system itself.

The remainder of this paper is organized as follows. Section 2 provides a general overview of our approach and describes its architecture. Section 3 introduces our social network model, users' credentials and relationships, and the notions of labels and ratings. Section 4 illustrates trust policies, whereas Section 5 introduces user preferences. Section 6 describes how user preferences are enforced. Finally, Section 7 concludes the paper and outlines future research directions.

2   Overview of the Proposed Approach

In this section, we first introduce the overall framework for a collaborative labelling and rating environment supporting Web access personalization. Then, we discuss the architecture of the proposed system.

2.1   Overall Framework

To support WBSN-based Web access personalization, we propose a framework consisting of five layers (see Figure 1). The Web metadata and ratings layers contain, respectively, resource descriptions and the ratings concerning such descriptions, whereas the users' credentials and relationships layer stores personal information concerning the authors of both Web metadata and ratings. These three layers, as a whole, provide the data used by the upper layers, namely, the trust policies and user preferences layers, which store the rules for determining, respectively, the trustworthiness of Web metadata and the action to be performed by the user agent upon detection of resources associated with Web metadata with given characteristics and trustworthiness.

Each layer in our framework can be seen as a black box, providing a given (set of) service(s) to the upper layers. As such, the only requirement is that layers adopt a standard format for exchanging data, so that they can be implemented by using different technologies. For instance, Web metadata can be encoded by using a variety of formats, but they must be provided to the upper layers by using a standard one. Similarly, as far as the ratings and trust policies layers are concerned, we do not pose any constraint about how reputation and trust are computed, which is totally transparent to the upper layers, which "see" just the results of such computation. The same applies to user preferences.

Such framework has two main advantages. First, our approach can be applied to existing content labeling and collaborative rating systems, by supplying the layers they do not support. For instance, a typical collaborative tagging service supports just the Web metadata layer and, possibly, the one concerning users' credentials and relationships. Ratings, trust policies, and user preferences layers can then be added to enhance its features by exploiting information already stored by the service. The second advantage is that our framework can be used

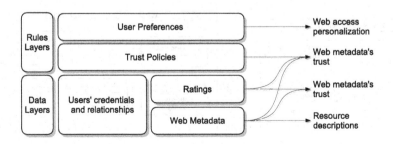

Fig. 1. Layers of the WBSN-based Web access personalization framework

to give end users integrated access to a variety of services. In fact, it may be often the case that an end user is member of several WBSNs and/or online communities, where data are represented by using specific formats, and accessed through specific interfaces. As a consequence, end users can access only separately the resources and services they provide. In contrast, our framework makes it possible to make such systems interoperable by supporting a standard interchange format and a standard set of interfaces, so that end users can transparently access them by using a single tool.

Although there currently exist several frameworks which can be used to enforce the trust policies and user preferences layers of our approach, such as Protune [9] and WIQA [10], in this paper we investigate Semantic Web technologies as the basis of the standard interchange format between our layers. More precisely, RDF/OWL will be used to encode users' credentials and relationships, labels and ratings, whereas trust policies and user preferences will be represented and enforced through N3Logic rules [11].

2.2   System Architecture

The overall architecture of the proposed system is depicted by Figure 2. For simplicity, in the figure, we have omitted the modules in charge of user registration and authentication and those concerning the specification of relationships, labels, ratings, trust policies, and user preferences.

The architecture consists of two main components: the WBSN Management System (WMS) and a WBSN User Agent (WUA). Besides carrying out user registration and authentication, the WMS provides WBSN members the possibility of creating/revoking relationships with other members, specifying *labels* describing the content/characteristics of Web resources, and expressing, by means of *label ratings*, their dis/agreement with existing labels. In contrast, the WUA is in charge of evaluating the trustworthiness of the descriptors contained into the existing labels and notifying such results to WBSN members. Moreover, it allows WBSN members to specify trust policies and user preferences, and it provides an interface to the WMS.

In order to become a WBSN member, a user must register through the registration service provided by the WMS. Then, he/she can provide personal

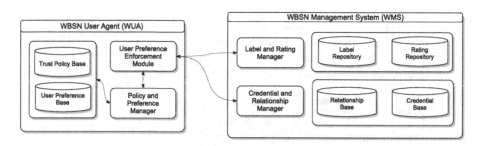

Fig. 2. System architecture

information by importing in the WMS only those of his/her credentials containing information he/she wishes to make publicly available to WBSN members. Users can then create relationships with other WBSN members, specify labels for Web resources, as well as rating existing labels. All this information is stored by the WMS in specific repositories, managed by the *Credential and Relationship Manager* and the *Label and Rating Manager* (see Figure 2).

Resource labels may be of two different types: *owner-defined labels*, that is, labels specified by the owner of the resource(s) they apply to, and *user-defined labels*, that is, labels specified by WBSN members not owning the corresponding resource(s) (see Section 3 for more details). Labels and ratings available in the WBSN are then used to select among those available the most accurate descriptions of the resource content. Such process can be customized by both resource owners and WBSN members through the specification of trust policies (see Section 4).

Finally, WBSN members can specify *user preferences* determining the action to be performed by the WUA when the user tries to access a resource associated with a given set of labels and ratings (e.g., block the access to such resource). User preferences are stored by the WUA in the local *User Preference Base*, which is managed, along with the *Trust Policy Base*, by the *Policy and Preference Manager* (cfr. Section 4). The WUA uses the trust policies in order to determine which descriptors/ratings should be considered when computing descriptors' trust values. In addition, when a WBSN member requests access to a resource, the WUA verifies whether it satisfies the existing user preferences, and performs the corresponding action. These tasks are carried out by the *User Preference Enforcement module* of the WUA (see Figure 2).

3   Users' Credentials and Relationships, Web Metadata and Ratings

In this section, we illustrate the first three layers of our framework (the *data layers*), namely, users' credentials and relationships, Web metadata, and ratings.

3.1   Users' Credentials and Relationships

Typically, in WBSNs a user is associated with two types of information, namely, personal data (such as, first and last name, email address, nationality) and the relationships he/she has with other WBSN members. Therefore, we assume that each WBSN member is denoted by a set of properties (attribute-value pairs), encoded by credentials. Each member of the WBSN may hold one or more credentials. Besides the certified properties, a credential contains the IDs of the Certification Authority (CA) and of the member whom the credential refers to. Finally, the credential is signed by the CA releasing it.

Users' credentials can be modeled by using the FOAF vocabulary [12]. FOAF (Friend of a Friend) is a widely used Semantic Web technology which allows the specification of personal information. In addition, FOAF profiles can be signed to grant their authenticity, and thus they can be effectively used as certified credentials.

As far as users' relationships are concerned, we model a WBSN $\mathcal{SN}$ as a labeled directed graph, whose nodes denote WBSN members, whereas the labeled edges denote the type of the relationships existing between them. We say that two WBSN members participate in a relationship of a given type rt, if there exists a path connecting them consisting only of edges labeled with relationship type rt. We refer to the length of such path as the *depth d* of the corresponding relationship. If $d = 1$, we say that the relationship is *direct*; if $d > 1$, we say that the relationship is *indirect*. In order to model such notion of relationship, it is possible to use the REL-X ontology[2], which defines an OWL class for the notion of relationship (relx:Relationship), and properties denoting the members (relx:hasMember), type (relx:type), and depth (relx:depth) of a relationship.

An example of WBSN is presented in Figure 3, where nodes correspond to four WBSN members (Alice, Bob, Carol, and David), whereas edges to the relationships existing between them. In the figure, the arrows at both ends of an edge are a shortcut to denote mutual relationships, i.e., the existence of two edges between the same pair of nodes, associated with the same label, and having opposite direction. E.g., the edge connecting A to B denotes the existence of two edges with the same label, one exiting from A and entering in B, and one exiting from B and entering in A.

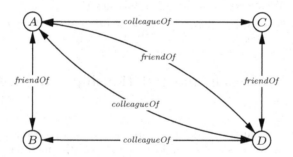

Fig. 3. A small portion of a WBSN

3.2   Web Metadata

As discussed in the previous sections, there exist a variety of Web metadata, adopting different formats and vocabularies. The Web metadata layer in our framework does not put any restriction about the type of supported Web metadata. However, in order to support different Web metadata sources, it is fundamental that they can be transformed into a standard representation. For this purpose, in our framework, we adopt POWDER as an interchange format for Web metadata [13]. POWDER can be used to associate any type of descriptor with a group of resources, and, additionally, to provide meta information about

---

[2] Namespace URI: http://www.dicom.uninsubria.it/dawsec/vocs/relx

such descriptors (such as, who have specified them, when they have been issued, which is their validity period), which can be used as a basis for assessing their trustworhiness. In what follows, we use the traditional term *label* to denote a set of descriptors encoded according to the POWDER format.

Labels describe the content and/or characteristics of a (set of) resources and can be specified by resource owners, or by users belonging to the WBSN. They are identified by a URI and contain a set of *resource descriptors* $rd_1, \ldots, rd_n$, which may be of two different types, namely, *resource property descriptors* and *resource content descriptors*. Resource property descriptors are used to model specific characteristics of the resource (such as the author's name, its title, the language used). They are modelled as pairs $pn = pv$, where pn denotes the name of a resource property and pv denotes the value of pn. In contrast, resource content descriptors are used to denote the relevance of a given topic for describing a resource, and they are expressed as pairs $t = \rho$, where $\rho \in [0, 1]$ denotes the relevance of topic t in describing the considered resource. The set of resources to which a label refers to is denoted by a *URI pattern*, by which it is possible to express statements like "all the resources hosted by `www.example.org`, where the URI path component starts with `foo`".[3] Besides resource descriptors, a label contains the ID of the WBSN member who created it, a timestamp, and, optionally, the validity period for the label.

Example 1. Table 1 presents examples of resource labels, where, for simplicity, the timestamp and validity period have been omitted. Moreover, we denote by LB_n the URI of label n. Labels LB_1 and LB_2 describe all the resources hosted by `www.example.org`. Label LB_1 has been specified by Alice, and it states that she is the author of such resources, that the used language is English, and that topic sport has a relevance equal to 80% in describing their content. Label LB_2 has been specified by Bob, and it states that topic medicine has a relevance equal to 40%. Labels LB_3 and LB_4 describe all the resources having a URI starting with `http://www.example.org/boxing`. Label LB_3, specified by Alice, states that such resources are authored by David, that their title is "Boxing", and that the topic fighting has a relevance equal to 100%, whereas topic violence has a relevance equal to 60%. Finally, label LB_4 is specified by Bob, and it states that such resources are authored by Alice, and topic movies has a relevance equal to 20%, whereas topic violence has a relevance equal to 40%.

Table 1. Examples of labels

URI	Author	URI Pattern	Property Descriptors	Content Descriptors
LB_1	Alice	`http://www.example.org*`	author = Alice, lang = en	sport = 0.8
LB_2	Bob	`http://www.example.org*`	∅	medicine = 0.4
LB_3	Alice	`http://www.example.org/boxing*`	author = David, title = Boxing	fighting = 1.0, violence = 0.6
LB_4	Bob	`http://www.example.org/boxing*`	author = Alice	movies = 0.2, violence = 0.4

---

[3] URI patterns are specified by using a simplified regular expression syntax, where the wildcard (∗) matches a string of $0, \ldots, n$ URI characters.

```
1   @prefix      rdfs:  <http://www.w3.org/2000/01/rdf-schema#> .
2   @prefix       owl:  <http://www.w3.org/2002/07/owl#> .
3   @prefix      wdrs:  <http://www.w3.org/2007/05/powder-s#> .
4   @prefix  property:  <http://www.example.com/property#> .
5   @prefix      base:  <http://mynet.net/labels/lb1#> .
6   @prefix         :   <http://mynet.net/members/> .

8   base: a owl:Ontology; wdrs:issuedby  :Alice; wdrs:issued "2008-02-12";
        wdrs:validFrom "2008-02-12"; wdrs:validUntil "2009-02-12"  .

10  _:lriset a owl:Class; rdfs:subClassOf [ a owl:Restriction; owl:onProperty
        wdrs:matchesregex; owl:hasValue "http:\/\/www\.example\.org.*" ]  .

12  _:D1 a owl:Class; rdfs:subClassOf [ a owl:Restriction; owl:onProperty
        property:author; owl:hasValue :Alice ]  .
13  _:D2 a owl:Class; rdfs:subClassOf [ a owl:Restriction; owl:onProperty
        property:lang; owl:hasValue "en" ]  .
14  _:D3 a owl:Class; rdfs:subClassOf [ a owl:Restriction; owl:onProperty
        property:sport; owl:hasValue "0.8" ]  .

16  _:lriset rdfs:subClassOf _:D1, _:D2, _:D3  .
```

Fig. 4. OWL-encoding of LB$_1$ in Table 1

Figure 4 shows the RDF/OWL encoding of LB$_1$ in Table 1, by using the N3 syntax and according to the POWDER specifications. The ontology header at line 8 encodes the information about who issued the label, when it has been issued, and its validity period. By contrast, the class description at line 10 denotes all the resources having a URI starting with http://www.example.org, whereas the class descriptions at line 12-14 denote the resources having Alice as author (line 12), those written in English (line 13), and those where the relevance of topic sport is equal to 80% (line 14). Finally, line 16 states that all the resources having a URI starting with http://www.example.org are a subset of those authored by Alice, written in English, and where the relevance of topic sport is equal to 80%. In the RDF/OWL encoding of POWDER, this is how the relationship between a set of resources, denoted by their URIs, and their description is modeled.

3.3 Ratings

According to the proposed interchange format, ratings applying to descriptors in the same label are grouped into a *label rating*. The structure of a label rating is very similar to the one of a label, with the difference that the URI pattern always corresponds to a single resource—i.e., the label being rated—, and no validity period is specified. A rating is considered valid if it has been created after the label it refers to, and such label is not yet expired.

Example 2. Table 2 reports examples of ratings for the labels in Table 1, where the timestamp component of each rating has been omitted for brevity. As in Example 1, we assume that LB$_1$, ..., LB$_4$ correspond to the URIs of the labels in Table 1. Rating RT$_1$ is specified by Bob on label LB$_1$, and it expresses Bob's agreement about the descriptors stating that Alice is the resource's author (i.e., (Author = Alice, 1)), and that the topic sport has a relevance equal to 80% (i.e., (sport = 0.8, 1)). Also

Table 2. Examples of label ratings

ID	Author	Label's URI	Ratings on Property Descriptors	Ratings on Content Descriptors
RT_1	Bob	LB_1	(author = Alice, 1)	(sport = 0.8, 1)
RT_2	David	LB_1	∅	(sport = 0.8, 1)
RT_3	Carol	LB_2	∅	(medicine = 0.4, 1)
RT_4	David	LB_3	(author = David, 0)	(fighting = 1.0, 1), (violence = 0.6, 0)
RT_5	David	LB_4	(author = Alice, 1)	(violence = 0.4, 1)
RT_6	Carol	LB_4	∅	(movies = 0.2, 0), (violence = 0.4, 1)

rating RT_2 applies to LB_1: it has been specified by David, who agrees that the topic sport has a relevance equal to 80%. Ratings RT_3 and RT_6 have been specified by Carol and they apply to labels LB_2 and LB_4, respectively. In RT_3, Carol agrees that the topic medicine has a relevance equal to 40%. Whereas in RT_6 she disagrees on the fact that the topic movies has a relevance equal to 20%, but she agrees that the topic violence has a relevance equal to 40%. Finally, David specifies also ratings RT_4 and RT_5 concerning labels LB_3 and LB_4, respectively. In RT_4, he disagrees on the fact that he has been claimed to be the author of the labeled resources, and that the relevance of topic violence is equal to 60%, but he agrees that topic fighting has a relevance equal to 100%. In contrast, in RT_5, David agrees that Alice is the author of the labeled resources, and on the fact that topic violence has a relevance equal to 40%.

Figure 5 shows the N3 encoding of RT_1 in Table 2. In order to associate a rating to the statements in label LB_1, they are enclosed into *quoted formulae,*[4] and then the rating (voc:rating)[5] is specified on them. Thus, lines 11-14 specify the rating about the statement according to which Alice is the author of the resource having a URI starting with http://www.example.org, whereas lines 15-18 specify the rating about the relevance of topic sport for the same set of resources. Quoted formulae are then used also to specify when the ratings have been issued (line 19), and who issued them (line 20).

As we have discussed in the previous sections, the main purpose of supporting collaborative labeling and rating of Web resources is to identify the most objective descriptions of a resource, to be then used for Web access personalization purposes. This is achieved by aggregating all labels associated with a resource *rsc*, and by computing a *trust value* for each descriptor *rd* contained in the selected labels. Several formulae may be used for trust computation, which might depend also on the possible values used for ratings (e.g., ratings can be binary or scalar, using either discrete or continuous values) and are outside the scope of this paper. Our framework is independent from the adopted one. For that reason, hereafter, we assume the existence of a generic function $T(rd, rsc)$, which

---

[4] In N3, quoted formulae are statements delimited by curly brackets, used to represent multiple, and possibly nested, RDF graphs into the same document. This allows one to specify "statements describing other statements", thus providing an alternative to RDF reification.

[5] Here and in the remainder of the paper we use the voc namespace prefix for properties and classes needed to model the notions of our approach.

```
1   @prefix      rdfs : <http :// www.w3.org /2000/01/ rdf—schema#> .
2   @prefix       owl : <http :// www.w3.org /2002/07/ owl#> .
3   @prefix      foaf : <http :// xmlns .com/ foaf /0.1/> .
4   @prefix   dcterms : <http :// purl .org/dc/ terms/> .
5   @prefix      wdrs : <http :// www.w3.org /2007/05/ powder—s#> .
6   @prefix  property : <http :// www.example .com/ property#> .
7   @prefix       voc : <http :// mynet .net/voc#> .
8   @prefix           : <http :// mynet .net/ members/> .

10  {
11    {
12      {[] a owl:Class ; rdfs:subClassOf
13        [ a owl:Restriction ; owl:onProperty wdrs:matchesregex ; owl:hasValue
             " http :\/\/www\.example \.org.*" ],
14        [ a owl:Restriction ; owl:onProperty property:author ; owl:hasValue
             : Alice ]
15      } voc:rating "1" .
16      {[] a owl:Class ; rdfs:subClassOf
17        [ a owl:Restriction ; owl:onProperty wdrs:matchesregex ; owl:hasValue
             " http :\/\/www\.example \.org.*" ],
18        [ a owl:Restriction ; owl:onProperty property:sport ; owl:hasValue " 0.8"
             ]
19      } voc:rating "1" .
20    } dcterms:issued "2008—07—11" .
21  } wdrs:issuedby :Bob .
```

Fig. 5. OWL-encoding of RT₁ in Table 2

takes as input a descriptor rd and the corresponding resource rsc, and returns it trust value.

4   Trust Policies

Similarly to other collaborative systems, where the collected data are statistically analyzed to assess their reliability, the proposed framework computes the trustworthiness of resources' descriptions based on the associated labels and corresponding ratings. However, in addition to this, our framework makes a user able to explicitly specify which labels/ratings have to be considered during trust computation. In particular, we have identified two different criteria for labels/ratings selection. The first raises by the consideration that a user might prefer to select, for a given resource, only labels/ratings specified by those WBSN members he/she considers trustworthy. For example, for a given Web site, a user might consider trustworthy only his/her direct friends, or only selected colleagues. Moreover, a user might further specify which are the resource topics or properties for which he/she considers trustworthy a given user. For instance, for a given Web site, a user might consider trustworthy with respect to 'sport' only a subset of his/her friends, and, for another topic, say 'music', a different selection of friends.

The second criteria for labels/ratings selection arises by the fact that a resources' owner might wish to suggest those members he/she considers trustworthy with respect to the description/rating of his/her resources. As an example, suppose that a WBSN member owns a Web site dealing with medicine. As resource owner, he/she may wish to allow only medical experts to specify labels for such Web site, and/or rate the associated labels. Providing the resources' owner with the capability of suggesting trustworthy members brings to the other criteria supported by our framework. Indeed, the second criteria supported by our system is to follow the resource owner suggestions, that is, to select only labels/ratings specified by those members considered trustworthy by the resource owner.

To implement both these criteria of labels/ratings selection, our framework exploits *trust policies*. In particular, it supports two different kinds of trust policies, namely, *user-defined trust policies* and *owner-defined trust policies*. User-defined trust policies implement the first criteria, making thus a user able to specify which are the members he/she judges enough trustworthy, with respect to given topics and/or resource properties, to consider their labels/ratings during the trust computation. In contrast, owner-defined trust policies implement the second criteria, that is, they make a resource owner able to specify which are the members he/she judges enough trustworthy to associate a label/rating with one of his/her resources. How and if these two criteria have to be combined, that is, how user and owner-defined trust policies have to be enforced, depends on the considered scenario. In our approach, to be as flexible as possible, we allow members to specify through their user preferences (cfr. Section 5) whether and how user- and owner-defined trust policies should be combined.

It is interesting to note that, even if user-defined and owner-defined trust policies have different semantics, i.e., the first specify user preferences, whereas the second owner suggestions, syntactically they are similar in that both of them identify a set of members whose labels/ratings have to be considered trustworthy wrt a particular topic/property on a given resource. As such, we make use of a unified syntax to represent both user-defined and owner-defined trust policies. According to this syntax, a user/owner-defined trust policy has to specify the following information: (1) a *URI pattern*, denoting the set of resources to which the policy applies to; (2) *trustworthy members*, that is, a set of WBSN members; (3) a set of *topics* for which the labels/ratings on resources denoted by *URI pattern* and specified by *trustworthy members* are considered trustworthy; (4) a set of *property names* for which the labels/ratings on resources denoted by *URI pattern* and specified by *trustworthy members* are considered trustworthy.

Moreover, the *trustworthy members* can be denoted in three different ways: the first is based on members' IDs, that is, by listing the IDs of those members that have to be considered trustworthy; alternatively, it is possible to exploit relationships existing in the WBSN, that is, to pose constraints on the relationships a user must have in order to be considered trustworthy; finally, another way is by specifying constraints on members credentials. For example, by these three different options, a user is able to (a) state that Ann and Bob are trusted (assuming that names are defined as IDs); (b) identify as trustworthy members those having a "friend of" relationship with Ann of maximum depth 2; or (c) specify as trustworthy members only those whose credentials contain the attribute 'organization' equal to 'University of Insubria'.

Example 3. Table 3 reports examples of trust policies, all applying to the resources hosted by www.example.org. TP$_1$ states that Alice considers trustworthy her direct friends for any topic and for resource property author. In contrast,

Table 3. Examples of trust policies concerning resources having a URI matching pattern `http://www.example.org*` (the URI pattern component has been omitted due to space constraints)

ID	Author	URI Pattern	Trustworthy Members	Topics	Properties
TP$_1$	Alice	http://www.example.org*	(Alice, $friendOf$, 1)	*	author
TP$_2$	Bob	http://www.example.org*	Alice	sport	author
TP$_3$	Carol	http://www.example.org*	expertise = parental_control	violence	*
TP$_4$	David	http://www.example.org*	(David, $friendOf$, 1), (David, $colleagueOf$, 2)	*	*

TP$_2$ states that Bob considers Alice trustworthy for topic sport and for resource property author, whereas TP$_3$ states that Carol considers trustworthy for topic violence and for any resource property only those WBSN members who are experts in parental control. Finally, TP$_4$ specifies that David considers trustworthy for any topic and resource property only the WBSN members who are, at the same time, David's direct friends, and David's colleagues with a maximum depth equal to 2 (i.e., Alice and Carol, according to Figure 3).

Figure 6 shows the encoding of TP$_1$ in Table 3 into an N3 rule. More precisely, lines 12-16 correspond to the antecedent of the rule, stating the constraints on the URI pattern (line 13), trustworthy members (line 14), and property/content descriptors (line 15). If such constraints are satisfied, then a label or rating is marked as trustworthy (line 16). Finally, line 17 states that the author of such trust policy is Alice.

Based on such policies, when their authors access a resource rsc having a URI matching `http://www.example.org*`, the WUA verifies which descriptors and ratings match the policies (see Table 4). Then, it computes the trust values of the descriptors concerning resource rsc by using function $T(rd, rsc)$ evaluated only on the matching descriptors and ratings.

```
1   @prefix        voc: <http://mynet.net/voc/#> .
2   @prefix        relx: <http://www.dicom.uninsubria.it/dawsec/vocs/relx#> .
3   @prefix        owl: <http://xmlns.com/foaf/0.1/> .
4   @prefix        foaf: <http://xmlns.com/foaf/0.1/> .
5   @prefix        log: <http://www.w3.org/2000/10/swap/log#> .
6   @prefix        string: <http://www.w3.org/2000/10/swap/string#> .
7   @prefix        math: <http://www.w3.org/2000/10/swap/math#> .
8   @prefix        wdrs: <http://www.w3.org/2007/05/powder-s#> .
9   @prefix property: <http://www.example.com/property#> .
10  @prefix        : <http://mynet.net/members/> .

12  {
13    {
14      ?Resource a foaf:Document; log:uri [ string:startsWith
              "http://www.example.org" ]  .
15      ?Relationship a relx:Relationship; relx:hasMember ?Author, :Alice;
              relx:type relx:FriendOf; relx:depth [ math:notGreaterThan "1"]  .
16      ?LabelOrRating a [ owl:unionOf ( voc:Label voc:Rating ) ]; wdrs:issuedby
              ?Author; log:includes {[] a owl:Restriction; owl:onProperty
              property:author}  .
17    } log:implies {?LabelOrRating voc:isTrustworthy "true"}
18  } wdrs:issuedby :Alice .
```

Fig. 6. N3-encoding of TP$_1$ in Table 3

Table 4. Labels and ratings in Tables 1 and 2 satisfying (Y) or not satisfying (N) the trust policies in Table 3

	LB$_1$	LB$_2$	LB$_3$	LB$_4$	RT$_1$	RT$_2$	RT$_3$	RT$_4$	RT$_5$	RT$_6$
Alice	Y	Y	Y	Y	Y	Y	N	Y	Y	N
Bob	Y	Y	Y	Y	Y	N	N	N	N	N
Carol	N	N	N	Y	Y	N	Y	N	N	Y
David	Y	N	Y	N	N	Y	Y	Y	Y	Y

5   User Preferences

Labels' descriptors make end users aware of the content/characteristics of re-sources. Moreover, the associated trust values, computed based on labels/rat-ings selected according to user trust policies, make user aware also of descriptor correctness. All these information can then be used by users to decide how a given resource has to be managed, that is, whether it has to be filtered or not. For instance, a user might prefer to block all resources whose labels state that their content is pornographic with trust value at least equal to 80%.

In the proposed framework, this is achieved by means of *user preferences*. These allow a user to specify one or more conditions on resources' descriptors and corresponding trust values, and to state which action has to be performed in case at least one of the specified condition is satisfied. In general, a user preference can be applied to all resources a user is going to access, as well as only to selected resources. Thus, a first component of a user preference is its *scope*, specified as a URI pattern, which forces the system to evaluate the preference whenever a resource denoted by the URI pattern is required. Moreover, user preferences support two types of actions: *block*, which denies the access to resources satisfying at least one of the conditions stated in the user preference; and *notify*, which allows the access, but it forces the system to notify the end user that the resource matches one or more of his/her user preferences.

Regarding the conditions a user can specify, user preferences support con-straints on both the property and content descriptors. The former, called *prop-erty constraints*, pose conditions on the resource properties and the correspond-ing trust values. Thus, for instance, it is possible to state that a given resource has to be blocked if the associated descriptors concerning property author, and having a trust value greater than 50%, have a value equal to `Alice`. By means of property constraints, a user is also able to specify conditions on the distri-bution of property descriptors. For instance, a user can enhance the previous preference by specifying that the resource has to be blocked if at least 50% of the author descriptor have a trust value greater than 50% and state that Alice is the authors.

Thus, *property constraints* are defined as triples (pc, tc, dc), where: pc is a property constraint of the form pn OP pv, where pn is a property name, pv is a property value, whereas OP is a comparison operator compatible with pn's domain; tc is a trust constraint of the form tv OP τ, where $\tau \in [-1, +1]$ denotes the trust value of the descriptors satisfying pc, and OP $\in \{=, <, >, \leq, \geq\}$; dc is a distribution constraint of the form dv OP δ, where $\delta \in [0,1]$ denotes the required percentage of descriptors satisfying pc, and OP $\in \{=, <, >, \leq, \geq\}$;

In contrast, *content constraints* make a user able to specify conditions on content descriptors and the corresponding trust values. As an example, these constraints allow users to specify that a given resource has to be blocked if the content descriptors with trust value greater than 70% state that topic violence has a relevance greater than 50% in describing the resource.

To support these conditions, *content constraints* consist of two components: a resource content constraint of the form t OP ρ, where t is a topic, $\rho \in [0,1]$ denotes the relevance of topic t, OP $\in \{=, <, >, \leq, \geq\}$, and a trust constraint of the form tv OP τ.

Besides specifying constraints on property and content descriptors, user preferences give WBSN members the capability to state how user- and/or owner-defined trust policies have to be taken into account when evaluating descriptors' trustworthiness. More precisely, a user can state whether only user-defined or owner-defined policies, or both/neither of them, must be considered to select the labels and ratings used to evaluate descriptors' trustworthiness. If both user- and owner-defined trust policies must be used, it is also possible to specify whether the descriptors and ratings denoted by user- and owner-defined trust policies must be combined by using union or intersection operator. In addition, we give the end user the possibility of deciding whether all or only some of the owner-defined policies must be taken into account. These preferences are specified by means of the *settings* component, whose syntax is omitted.

Example 4. Table 5 reports examples of user preferences. Preference UP_1, specified by David, requires to block the access to the resources hosted by www.example.org, if (a) at least 50% ($dv \geq 0.5$) of the associated descriptors concerning property author, and having a trust value greater than 50% ($tv > 0.5$), have a value equal to Alice (author = Alice); (b) the content descriptors having a trust value greater than 60% ($tv > 0.6$) state that topics sport and fighting have a relevance greater than 50% (sport > 0.5, fighting > 0.5). Preference UP_1 also states that the descriptors and ratings to be considered when computing descriptors trustworthiness are only those satisfying at least one policy among the owner- and user-defined trust policies (i.e., (all, all, $\cup$)). Differently from UP_1, preference UP_2, specified by Alice, does not include content constraints, and it states that, when evaluating descriptors' trustworthiness, the WUA must select only the descriptors and ratings satisfying at least one policy among (a) the user-defined trust policies or (b) those owner-defined policies selected at run-time by Alice (this is denoted by (all, some, $\cup$)). Preference UP_3, specified by Bob, includes both property and content constraints, and it states that, when evaluating descriptors trustworthiness, only the descriptors and ratings satisfying at least (a) one among the owner-defined trust policies and (b) one among the user-defined trust policies must be considered (i.e., (all, all, $\cap$)). Finally, preference UP_4, specified by Carol, includes just content constraints, and it asks the WUA to perform a 'block' action in case it is satisfied. For evaluating

Table 5. Examples of user preferences

ID	Author	Scope	Property Constraints	Content Constraints	Settings	Action
UP_1	David	`http://www.example.org*`	(author = Alice, $tv > 0.5$, $dv \geq 0.5$)	(sport > 0.5, $tv > 0.6$), (fighting > 0.5, $tv > 0.6$)	$(\texttt{all}, \texttt{all}, \cup)$	`block`
UP_2	Alice	`http://www.example.org*`	(author = Bob, $tv = 1.0$, $dv = 1.0$)	*	$(\texttt{all}, \texttt{some}, \cup)$	`notify`
UP_3	Bob	`http://www.example.org*`	(author $\neq$ Alice, $tv > 0.5$, $dv > 0.5$)	(sport > 0.4, $tv > 0.8$), (medicine > 0.8, $tv > 0.8$)	$(\texttt{all}, \texttt{all}, \cap)$	`notify`
UP_4	Carol	`http://www.example.org*`	*	(violence > 0.8, $tv > 0.2$)	$(\texttt{all}, \texttt{none}, \cup)$	`block`

descriptors' trustworthiness, UP_4 states that only user-defined trust policies must be considered (i.e., $(\texttt{all}, \texttt{none}, \cup)$).

Figure 6 shows the encoding of UP_1 in Table 5 into an N3 rule. More precisely, line 12 denotes the trust policies to be considered (in this case both owner- and user-defined, combined by using OR). If, after having evaluated the rules corresponding to the selected trust policies, their conclusions (i.e., the statements inferred from the rules) satisfy the constraints on property/content descriptors in the user preference (lines 13-18), then the WUA is asked to perform the "block" action (line 19). Finally, line 20 states that the author of such user preference is David.

6   User Preference Enforcement

In general, when a member requests access to a resource, the WUA verifies whether the requested resource satisfies one or more of his/her user preferences, if any. If this is the case, WUA performs the action(s) specified in the satisfied user preference(s). In particular, if the satisfied user preferences specify different actions, we assume that the 'block' action prevails over the 'notify' one. In case no user preferences are satisfied, the WUA performs the *default action*, which can be either `block` or `notify`, and it is set by the end user in the WUA's configuration parameters.

User preference enforcement starts by retrieving the set of user preferences specified by the member requesting the resource. Among these user preferences, the WUA considers only those that apply to the requested resource, that is, those whose scope includes the requested resource. In case there do not exist any user preferences applying to the requested resource, the WUA authorizes the access. Otherwise, user preferences are evaluated to determine the set of actions ACTs to be performed. In case ACTs is empty, then the default action is performed. In case it contains at least a block action, the resource is blocked; otherwise the WUA performs the notify action.

The main steps carried out to evaluate each user preference are depicted in Figure 8.

```
1    @prefix       voc: <http://mynet.net/voc/#> .
2    @prefix       owl: <http://xmlns.com/foaf/0.1/> .
3    @prefix      foaf: <http://xmlns.com/foaf/0.1/> .
4    @prefix       log: <http://www.w3.org/2000/10/swap/log#> .
5    @prefix    string: <http://www.w3.org/2000/10/swap/string#> .
6    @prefix      math: <http://www.w3.org/2000/10/swap/math#> .
7    @prefix      wdrs: <http://www.w3.org/2007/05/powder-s#> .
8    @prefix  property: <http://www.example.com/property#> .
9    @prefix         : <http://mynet.net/members/> .

11   {
12     { ?TrustPolicy a [ owl:unionOf (voc:UserDefinedTrustPolicy
                          voc:OwnerDefinedTrustPolicy) ];
13       log:supports {
14         ?Resource a foaf:Document; log:uri [ string:startsWith
                    "http://www.example.org"] .
15         { ?Resource a foaf:Document; property:author :Alice . } voc:trustLevel
                   [ math:greaterThan "0.5"]; voc:distribution [ math:notLessThan
                   "0.5"] .
16         { ?Resource a foaf:Document; property:sport [ math:greaterThan "0.5"]
                   . } voc:trustLevel [ math:greaterThan "0.6"] .
17         { ?Resource a foaf:Document; property:fighting [ math:greaterThan
                   "0.5"] } voc:trustLevel [ math:greaterThan "0.6"] .
18       } .
19     } log:implies { voc:Wua voc:action voc:Block } .
20   } wdrs:issuedby :David .
```

Fig. 7. N3-encoding of UP_1 in Table 5

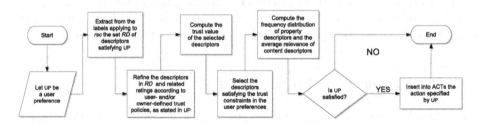

Fig. 8. Main steps of user preference enforcement

In particular, given a user preference UP, the first step retrieves those property and content descriptors, that are relevant for the property and content constraints specified in UP.

For instance, consider user preference UP_1 in Table 5, and suppose that David requests access to a resource *rsc* having URI http://www.example.org/boxing/, owned by Alice. In order to determine the action to be performed on *rsc*, the WUA first retrieves the associated labels, and then extracts from them the set of descriptors concerning property author or topics sport and fighting (i.e., some descriptors of labels LB_1, LB_3, and LB_4 in Table 1).

In the second step, the retrieved property and content descriptors are refined according to the owner and user-defined trust policies, combined together according the setting specified in UP. The enforcement also retrieve ratings of refined descriptors by enforcing again the owner and user-defined trust policies.

As example, according to the settings in UP_1, WUA selects only the descriptors and associated ratings satifying one among David's trust policies (i.e., TP_4) or the owner-defined trust policies (i.e., TP$_1$)—see Table 3. In this case, all the descriptors selected in the previous phase satisfy TP$_1$ or TP$_4$, whereas the selected ratings are RT$_1$, RT$_2$, RT$_4$, and RT$_5$ (see Table 2).

Once gathered all ratings satisfying the trust policies, the WUA computes the trust values of those descriptors resulting from second step (see third step in Figure 8). Then, it further refines the descriptors by removing those that do not satisfying the trust constrains specified in the UP. Note that both the property and content constraints pose conditions on trust value, thus this refinement is performed on both the property and content descriptors. To determine whether UP is satisfied or not, it is necessary to compute also the average relevance of the content descriptors as well as the frequency distribution of the property descriptors. These computations are performed in the fifth step in Figure 8.

Thus, referring to our example, the WUA computes (a) the trust value $tv_{rd,rsc}$ of each selected descriptor rd for resource rsc, (b) the average relevance $\overline{\rho}_{cc}$ of the topic in each selected content descriptor cc, and (c) the percentage $\delta_{\text{author=Alice}}$ of the set of property descriptors having a trust value greater than 50% and satisfying author = Alice. For the purposes of our example, we assume the following values: $tv_{rd,rsc} = +1$, if rd corresponds to sport = 0.8, fighting = 1.0, or author = Alice; $tv_{rd,rsc} = -1$, if rd corresponds to author = David; $\overline{\rho}_{cc} = 0.8$, if cc concerns topic sport; $\overline{\rho}_{cc} = 1.0$, if cc concerns topic fighting; $\delta_{\text{author=Alice}} = 1.0$.

Finally, the WUA verifies if all the property and content constraints are satisfied. If this is the case, the corresponding action is inserted into ACTs, and the process ends. Otherwise, the process ends without inserting a new action into ACTs.

In our example, UP$_1$ is satisfied, the WUA blocks the access to resource rsc.

7   Conclusions and Future Work

In this paper, we have presented a WBSN environment supporting collaborative labeling and rating, where the labels/ratings specified by its members are used to compute the trust value of resources' descriptors and to enforce Web access personalization. Key features of our system are the support for (a) trust policies, making each WBSN member able to denote who he/she considers trustworthy about given topics and resource properties, and (b) user preferences, which allow WBSN members to determine which action must be performed by the user agent on the requested resource, upon detection of descriptors with given characteristics and a given trust value.

An implementation of our framework is currently carried on in the context of the QUATRO Plus EU project (http://www.quatro-project.org/), whose overall goal is to set up an integrated environment for the creation, distribution, and usage of Web metadata.

In order to improve the accuracy of trust computation, an issue we plan to address concerns how the *specificity* of a label should affect the trustworthiness of the contained descriptors. For instance, labels LB$_1$,..., LB$_4$ in Table 1 all apply to the same resource rsc, having URI http://www.example.org/boxing/.

More precisely, such labels apply to two sets of resources, denoted, the former, by URI pattern http://www.example.org* (LB_1 and LB_2), and the latter by http://www.example.org/boxing* (LB_3 and LB_4). Since the latter is included in the former, we say that it is more *specific* with respect to *rsc*'s URI. In such a case, it should be reasonable that the descriptors in LB_3 and LB_4 are considered more trustworthy than those in LB_1 and LB_2. Note that such specificity principle may be also applied to user preferences, in order to determine which action should be performed by the user agent on the requested resource. A deep study of these issues will be part of our future work.

References

1. Resnick, P., Miller, J.: PICS: Internet access controls without censorship. Commun. ACM 39(10), 87–93 (1996)
2. Golder, S.A., Huberman, B.A.: The structure of collaborative tagging systems. The Computing Research Repository (CoRR) abs/cs/0508082 (2005)
3. Voß, J.: Tagging, folksonomy & Co – Renaissance of manual indexing? The Computing Research Repository (CoRR) abs/cs/0701072 (2007)
4. Adomavicius, G., Tuzhilin, A.: Toward the next generation of recommender systems: A survey of the state-of-the-art and possible extensions. IEEE Transactions on Knowledge & Data Engineering 17(6), 734–749 (2005)
5. Sen, S., Lam, S.K., Rashid, A.M., Cosley, D., Frankowski, D., Osterhouse, J., Harper, F.M., Riedl, J.: Tagging, communities, vocabulary, evolution. In: CSCW 2006, pp. 181–190 (2006)
6. Terveen, L., Hill, W., Amento, B., McDonald, D., Creter, J.: PHOAKS: A system for sharing recommendations. Commun. ACM 40(3), 59–62 (1997)
7. Golbeck, J.A.: Generating predictive movie recommendations from trust in social networks. In: iTrust 2006, pp. 93–104 (2006)
8. Avesani, P., Massa, P., Tiella, R.: A trust-enhanced recommender system application: Moleskiing. In: 2005 ACM Symposium on Applied Computing (SAC 2005), pp. 1589–1593 (2005)
9. Bonatti, P.A., Olmedilla, D.: Driving and monitoring provisional trust negotiation with metapolicies. In: POLICY 2005, pp. 14–23. IEEE CS, Los Alamitos (2005)
10. Bizer, C., Cyganiak, R., Maresch, O., Gauss, T.: The WIQA – Web Information Quality Assessment framework. Technical report, Freie Universität Berlin (2006), http://www4.wiwiss.fu-berlin.de/bizer/WIQA/
11. Berners-Lee, T., Connolly, D., Kagal, L., Scharf, Y., Hendler, J.: N3Logic: A logical framework for the World Wide Web. Theory and Practice of Logic Programming 8(3), 249–269 (2008)
12. Brickley, D., Miller, L.: FOAF vocabulary specification 0.91. RDF Vocabulary Specification (November 2007), http://xmlns.com/foaf/0.1
13. Archer, P., Smith, K., Perego, A.: Protocol for Web description resources (POWDER): Description resources. W3C Working Draft, World Wide Web Consortium (October 2008), http://www.w3.org/TR/powder-dr

Evaluating Security Policies in Pervasive Mobile Environments Using Context Information

Carlos Sánchez[1], Le Gruenwald[1], and Mauricio Sánchez[2]

[1] The University of Oklahoma, School of Computer Science, Norman OK USA
{maletas,ggruenwald}@ou.edu
[2] IMTEC Corporation a 3M Company, Ardmore OK USA
mauricio.sanchez @imtec.com

Abstract. Due to both the number of entities and the nature of the interactions and collaborations amongst them, conventional security models are inadequate for regulating access to data and services in a pervasive mobile computing environment. Since many of these interactions occur between entities that have not interacted with each other previously, new security paradigms rely on context information in order to arrive at a security and decision. However, these new systems fail to take into account the variability, correlation and uncertainty of the context variables composing a security policy when making a security decision. In this paper, we propose a Monte Carlo based framework to evaluate security policies that are based on the changes in multiple context variables. In this framework, context variables are modeled and risk in security decisions is measured.

Keywords: Security, integrity and protection, risk, context data, pervasive mobile environments.

1 Introduction

With ever increasing number of information sources, a modern collaboration system needs to not only rapidly assemble a set of disparate information systems into a coherently interoperating whole, but also make sure that the interactions amongst different entities participating in the system are secure. That is, strong security measures must be available to enforce data integrity and protect sensitive information. In addition, collaboration systems must take into account the environment in which not only no or few fixed infrastructure nodes exist, but also access to information depends on some context information (i.e. location) by the requesting entity. Because of the lack of fixed infrastructures and the variability of context data, it is unreasonable to expect that every entity in the collaboration system stores not only a reference (identity) to but also relevant context data relating to any other entity it may interact with as a way to enforce access control. It is for these reasons that traditional security implementations, such as access control lists (ACL) [28] and role base access controls (RBAC) [22], [23], are ill equipped to handle security operations since not only they expect the identity of the accessing entities to be known, but also they were not originally designed to support context based access. Moreover systems (i.e. [32], [36])

E. Bertino and J.B.D. Joshi (Eds.): CollaborateCom 2008, LNICST 10, pp. 145–161, 2009.

that have been expanded with context variable predicates (i.e. location, power resource, and connection type) to define security policies fail to take into account the fast changing nature of context information. This variability introduces uncertainty, which in turn introduces risk when a security decision is made. In addition, once the security decision is made, current security models do not revaluate the security decision after a specific time frame even though the context data is likely to change (i.e. the security decision would stand firm regardless of future changes in the context data) [26]. Therefore [secure] collaboration in dynamic communities that use context data to enforce access control should develop risk models to help an entity decide when access to sensitive data should be authorized.

To illustrate a secure collaboration, let us expand the scope of the interaction between a soldier and his commander in the example given in [26]. In this example, a soldier that moves about in the battlefield and dynamically retrieves enemy data from his nearby commander. In order to receive intelligence data, a soldier must first identify himself with his company commander and his platoon leader (data is restricted according to identity). The intelligence data is delivered provided that the soldier and his commanders (company and platoon leader) are within a 25-kilometer radius of a passing ScanEagle [2] UAV. Moreover, in order to avoid leaks, the platoon leader has to be within 150 meters of the company commander. To make sure that all the data is delivered, the soldier's mobile unit must have a minimum of 60% power availability. Finally, in order to receive any data, the connection rate amongst the soldiers needs to be above a specific threshold to guarantee that the communications are not being jammed (again data transfer is limited to a specific connection mode).

As the example points out, the security implementation that allows the soldier to receive the intelligence data must take into account the variability and correlation of the commanders and the UAV location information, the communication connection rate and power of his mobile unit. Thus, in order to make a reliable security decision, the security system should try to predict how much the different variables (i.e. commanders and UAV location, etc) would change by the time the enemy data is delivered to and used by the soldier, since by the time the data is delivered, any of the entities (solider, commanders or UAV) may have moved to a new place making the security decision invalid. Moreover, the security system should be able to detect, tolerate and ignore invalid context assertions made by compromised or hostile entities. Furthermore, the security implementation should be able to use a certain amount of data history for each of context variables in order to not only predict future values but also to measure the degree of change (volatility) of the context variables in order to arrive at a more accurate security decision [26]. In addition, the security system needs to determine the risk involved when making a security decision because of the changeability and correlations of the context variables. Finally, due to the dynamic nature of a context variable, each security decision should hold only for a certain degree of time.

In this paper, we extend our previous work ([26]) to model the behavior of context variables in a security policy using a random walk framework that takes into correlations amongst them. Finally, the model in [26] is further expanded to include a risk measure for the overall change in a policy according to the changes of its constituting context variables.

The remainder of this paper is organized as follows. Section 2 details a random walk framework to model context variables. Section 3 describes the Monte Carlo method used in our framework. Section 4 describes the measure of risk when evaluating a security policy. Section 5 describes a context security policy. Section 6 reviews related work in this area. Finally Section 7 concludes the paper and presents future research.

2 Modeling Context Variables

In a pervasive mobile environment, context variables of a user may change in a non-predetermined way. That is, context variables follow a stochastic process since their values may change over time in an uncertain way. Using a stochastic process model gives us a risk-measuring tool to characterize the future change in a process' value.

One stochastic process that can be employed as a risk-measuring tool is the random walk. In the random walk, forecasts for each of the context variables' future value changes - using only its past variations – can be constructed. However, before defining the random walk model we need to introduce the concepts of a context variable time series and variable return (In order to have an unified model, in this work we assume that all context variables can be modeled using a random walk even though, many context variables can display deterministic models).

Context Variable Time Series. A context variable time series is a collection of observations indexed by the time of each observation. An entity collects the context variable data beginning at a particular time (e.g. t=1) and ending at another (e.g. t=N). Formally, a time series for context variable a context variable V is represented in a vector form as follows [11], [13]:

$$\{V_t\}_{t=1}^{N} = (V_1, V_2, \ldots, V_i, \ldots V_N)$$

where Vi is the observation made at time I and VN is the observation made at time N.

One-Time (Single Period) Value Return Horizon. The change in the value of a variable can be expressed in a variety of forms, such as, absolute value change, relative value change, and log value change. When a value change is defined relative to some initial value, it is known as a return [13]. That is, the changes over time of a variable's value can be measured and modeled in terms of continuously compounded returns (log value changes). Table 1 shows the definition of Absolute, Relative and Log value change for a context variable V between time t and t-1 (denoted as V_t and V_{t-1}).

Table 1. Definitions of absolute, relative and log changes of a variable

Absolute value change	Relative value change	Log value change (return)
$D_t = V_t - V_{t-1}$	$R_t = \dfrac{V_t - V_{t-1}}{V_{t-1}}$	$r_t = \ln(1+R_t) = \ln\left(\dfrac{V_t}{V_{t-1}}\right) = (v_t - v_{t-1})$ where vt = ln(Vt)

Random Walk Model for One Context Variable. A random walk is a formalization of the idea of taking successive steps, each in a random direction. It may be thought of as a model for an individual walking on a straight line who, at each point of time, takes one step either to the right or to the left with different probabilities [34]. Random walk models have been applied in several fields. For instance, in economics, a random walk is used to model shares prices and other factors and in wireless networking, they are used to model node movement. Formally, a single value random walk model for a context variable can be stated as follows.

$$V_t = \mu + V_{t-1} + \sigma_t \varepsilon_t, \varepsilon_t \sim IIDN(0,1) \tag{2.1}$$

or

$$V_t - V_{t-1} = \mu + \sigma_t \varepsilon_t, \varepsilon_t \sim IIDN(0,1) \tag{2.2}$$

where IID stands for "identically and independently distributed", and N(0,1) stands for the normal distribution with mean 0 and variance 1. That is, at any point in time the current value Vt depends on one fixed parameter μ (mean), one time based parameter σt (standard deviation), the last period's value Vt-1, and a normally distributed random variable εt. The assumption that context values are normally distributed is helpful because 1) we only need the mean and variance to describe the distribution, 2) the sum of multiple normal context variables is also normally distributed, and 3) normality is the central assumption of the mathematical theory of errors [33].

Since returns not only have more attractive statistical properties than values, but also are often preferred to absolute value changes because the latter do not measure changes in terms of the given values [13], it is better to model the log value Vt (Table 1) as a random walk with normally distributed changes, that is:

$$v_t = v_{t-1} + \mu + \sigma_t \varepsilon_t, \varepsilon_t \sim IIDN(0,1) \tag{2.3}$$

Therefore, since we are modeling log changes, the expression for values is simply obtained by taking the inverse of the logarithm (ex), that is

$$V_t = V_{t-1} e^{\mu + \sigma_t \varepsilon_t}, \varepsilon_t \sim IIDN(0,1) \tag{2.4}$$

In [13] three core assumptions are made. First of all, returns in different periods are not auto correlated. Secondly, the variance of the returns (volatility) scales with time (it remains constant for different time horizons). Finally, the random walk model is relaxed by assuming that log values have a mean μ set to zero (in [15], it is shown that for short horizon periods, the volatility is much larger than the expected return; thus, the forecast of the future return distribution is dominated by the volatility estimate. In other words, when dealing with short horizons, using a zero expected return assumption is as good as any other mean estimate). Therefore, the model can be represented as:

$$v_t = v_{t-1} + \sigma_t \varepsilon_t, \varepsilon_t \sim IIDN(0,1) \tag{2.5}$$

in terms of returns

$$r_t = \sigma_t \varepsilon_t, \ \varepsilon_t \sim IIDN(0,1) \tag{2.6}$$

The standard deviation (volatility) at time t - σ_t - can be computed using an Exponential Moving Average (EMA) [6] of past observations, that is, for a given set of K (where K=t-1) returns, the variance can be defined as follows:

$$\sigma_t^2 = \frac{\sum_{i=1}^{K} \alpha^{i-1} (r_{t-i})^2}{\sum_{i=1}^{K} \alpha^{i-1}} \tag{2.7}$$

where the parameter α ($0 < \alpha <=1$) (*smoothing factor*) determines the relative weights applied to the observations (returns), thus, allowing the latest observations to carry the highest weight, while still not discarding older observations entirely in the standard deviation estimate. In addition, when K→∞, and using the convergence property of the geometrics series:

$$\sum_{i=1}^{T} \alpha^{i-1} \cong \frac{1}{1-\alpha} \quad 0 < \alpha < 1$$

equation (2.7) can be rewritten as follows

$$\sigma_t^2 = (1-\alpha) \sum_{i=1}^{\infty} \alpha^{i-1} r_{t-i}^2 \tag{2.8}$$

In a recursive manner, equation (2.8) can be rewritten as:

$$\sigma_t^2 = \alpha \sigma_{t-1}^2 + (1-\alpha) r_t^2 \tag{2.9}$$

Equation (2.9) represents one time-unit (e.g. 1 minute) calculation of the variance defined over the period t-1 through t, where each t represents one time-unit. Therefore, in order to make forecasts for horizons greater than one-time unit, and taking the assumption stated previously, the variance estimate of a context variable data return for H time units is stated as follows:

$$\sigma_H^2 = H\sigma_t^2 \tag{2.10}$$

The equation above gives a simple way to calculate the volatility of H time units (e.g. hour) from the 1 time unit (e.g. minute) volatility.

Random Walk Model for Multiple Context Variables. In a context-based security policy with M context variables, the behavior of the returns of each of the context variables can be described as:

$$r_{1,t} = \sigma_{1,t} \varepsilon_{1,t}, \ r_{2,t} = \sigma_{2,t} \varepsilon_{2,t} \ \dots. \ r_{M,t} = \sigma_{M,t} \varepsilon_{M,t}$$

Since the context variables may be related to one another, we have to account for their movements relative to one another (that is, the context variables may be statistically dependent). Thus, the linear association between each pair of returns must be quantified. These movements are captured by pair-wise correlations. Therefore, the ε_t's should come from a multivariate normal (MVN) distribution [27] then:

$$
\begin{bmatrix} \varepsilon_{1,t} \\ \varepsilon_{2,t} \\ \dots \\ \varepsilon_{N,t} \end{bmatrix} \sim MVN \left(\begin{bmatrix} \mu_1 \\ \mu_2 \\ \dots \\ \mu_M \end{bmatrix}, \begin{bmatrix} 1 \rho_{12,t} \cdots \rho_{1M,t} \\ \rho_{21,t} 1 \cdots \rho_{2M,t} \\ \dots \\ \rho_{M1,t} \rho_{M2,t} \cdots 1 \end{bmatrix} \right) \quad or \; \varepsilon \sim MVN(\mu_{G,t}, R_t) \tag{2.11}
$$

where R_t represents the correlation matrix of $(\varepsilon_1, \varepsilon_2, \dots \varepsilon_N)$ and the mean and variance are represented by [13]:

$$
\mu_{G,t} = \sum_{i=1}^{M} w_i \mu_i \; and \; \sigma_{G,t}^2 = \sum_{i=1}^{M} w_i^2 \sigma_i^2 + 2 \sum \sum_{i<j} w_i w_j \sigma_{ij,t}^2
$$

Moreover, the term σ_{ij}^2 represents the covariance between returns for the context variables i and j. We must remember that the covariance of two random variables X and Y is defined as:]

$$
\sigma_{XY}^2 = E[(X - \mu_X)(Y - \mu_Y)] = E(XY) - E(X)E(Y)
$$

Since E(X)=μx and E(Y)=μy (E is the mathematical expectation), both of which are equal to zero according to our model, then the covariance is simply defined as

$$
\sigma_{XY}^2 = E(XY)
$$

Finally, let's recall that the correlation coefficient of two random variables X and Y can be calculated as follows [19]:

$$
\rho_{XY} = \frac{\sigma_{XY}^2}{\sigma_X \sigma_Y} \backslash
$$

where σ_X and σ_Y are the standard deviations of X and Y, respectively.

Using the Exponential Moving Average (EMA) [6], an expression to estimate the covariance and correlation of context variable log changes (returns) can be constructed. As such the covariance formula is defined as [19]:

$$
\sigma_{XY|t}^2 = \frac{\sum_{i=1}^{T} \alpha^{i-1} \left(r_{X,t-i} - \bar{r}_1 \right) \left(r_{Y,t-i} - \bar{r}_2 \right)}{\sum_{i=1}^{T} \alpha^{i-1}} \tag{2.12}
$$

3   The Monte Carlo Method

Given a set of M context variables, we use the Monte Carlo method as a computational algorithm to repeatedly construct scenarios to produce future values (equations 2.4 and 2.11) for each of different context variables. We will first introduce the Monte Carlo algorithm when M=1 to later define the general case.

4   The Monte Carlo Method for One Context Variable

Given a time series $\{V_t\}_{t=1}^{N}$ of N observations for a context variable V, the procedure to produce scenarios is to generate standard normal variates and use equation 2.4 to produce future values. The algorithm to simulate future values for one context variable is described below [26].

One stochastic process that can be employed as a risk-measuring tool is the random walk. In the random walk, forecasts for each of the context variables' future value changes - using only its past variations – can be constructed. However, before defining the random walk model we need to introduce the concepts of a context variable time

Table 2. Scenario Generation Algorithm for One Context Variable

Input: $\{V_t\}_{t=1}^{N}$
1. Choose the number of scenario trials T and smoothing factor α
2. Compute the *N-1* log value changes (i.e. returns) from $\{V_t\}_{t=1}^{N}$. The result of this calculation is a time series of returns of the form $\{r_t\}_{t=2}^{N}$
3. Using $\{r_t\}_{t=2}^{N}$ compute the variance series $\{\sigma_t^2\}_{t=2}^{N}$ using equation (2.7). Compute the *volatility* (standard deviation) at time *t=N*, that is $\sigma_N = \sqrt{\sigma_N^2}$
4. In order to simulate values for the next H time units (evaluation horizon), use equation (2.10) to compute the horizon *volatility* $\sigma_H = \sigma_N \sqrt{H}$
5. Define a time series $\{S_t\}_{t=1}^{T}$ to store the context variable simulated values.
6. For each trial *k (1≤ k ≤ T)*
6.1. Compute the simulated log return *R* as follows:
$R = \sigma_N \cdot \sqrt{H} \cdot Z$, where $\sigma_N \sqrt{H}$ represents the horizon volatility (used to simulate values for the next H time units (evaluation horizon)), and Z is a generated IID normal value Z, that is, Z = ~N(0,1)
6.2. Compute the kth simulated value S_k as follows:
$S_k = V_N \exp(R)$ where *exp(x) = e^x* (equation 2.4) and V_N is the value of the context variable at time N
Output: $\{S_t\}_{t=1}^{T}$

series and variable return (In order to have an unified model, in this work we assume that all context variables can be modeled using a random walk even though, many context variables can display different deterministic models).

5 The Monte Carlo Method for Multiple Context Dependent Variables

In the previous section, an algorithm was derived to apply the Monte Carlo method to one context variable. For the case of multiple context variables, we need to take into account the correlation amongst the context variables when generating future values. The table below describes the modified algorithm [26].

Table 3. Scenario Generation Algorithm for Multiple Context Dependent Variables

Input: $\left(\{V_1\}_{t=1}^N, \{V_2\}_{t=1}^N \cdots \{V_M\}_{t=1}^N\right)$

1. Choose the number of scenario trials T and smoothing factor α

2. For each context variable time series i $(1 \le i \le M)$

   2.1 Compute the $N\text{-}1$ returns from $\{V_{i,t}\}_{t=1}^N$. The result of this calculation is a time series of returns of the form $\{r_{i,t}\}_{t=2}^N$

   2.2 Using $\{r_{i,t}\}_{t=2}^N$ compute the variance series $\{\sigma_{i,t}^2\}_{t=2}^N$ using equation 3.7 and then compute the *volatility* (standard deviation) at time $t=N$, that is $\sigma_{i,N} = \sqrt{\sigma_{i,N}^2}$

   2.3 Define a time series $\{S_{i,t}\}_{t=1}^T$ to store the context variable simulated values

      2.4 For each trial j $(1 \le j \le T)$

         2.4.1 Compute the simulated log return R^*

         2.4.2 Compute the jth simulated value S_j as follows:

         $$S_j = V_N^i \exp(R^*)$$ where $exp(x) = e^x$ and V_N^i is the value of context variable i at time N

Output: $S_G = \left(\{S_1\}_{t=1}^T, \{S_2\}_{t=1}^T \cdots \{S_M\}_{t=1}^T\right)$

The simulated log R* needs to be computed in such a way that the correlations amongst the context variables returns are maintained. For instance, by using the

Cholesky factorization [10], it can be shown that the formulae to generate the simulated returns for three context variables would be as follows:

$$R_1 = \sigma_1 Z_1, \, R_2 = \sigma_2 \left(\rho_{12} Z_1 + \sqrt{1 - \rho_{12}^2} \, Z_2 \right),$$

$$R_3 = \sigma_3 \left(\rho_{13} Z_1 + \frac{\rho_{23} - \rho_{12}\rho_{13}}{\sqrt{1 - \rho_{12}^2}} Z_2 + \sqrt{1 - \rho_{13}^2 - \frac{(\rho_{23} - \rho_{12}\rho_{13})^2}{1 - \rho_{12}^2}} Z_3 \right)$$

where σ_i is the volatility (standard deviation) for context variable i, ρ_{ij} is the correlation between context variables i and j and each Z is a generated IID normal value.

In general, generating correlated variates for M context variables can expressed as follows [25]:

$$R_1 = a_{1,1} Z_1 + a_{1,2} Z_2 + a_{1,3} Z_3 + ... + a_{1,n} Z_n$$
$$R_2 = a_{2,1} Z_1 + a_{2,2} Z_2 + a_{2,3} Z_3 + ... + a_{2,n} Z_n$$

$$...$$

$$R_M = a_{M,1} Z_1 + a_{M,2} Z_2 + a_{M,3} Z_3 + ... + a_{M,n} Z_n$$

or in matrix form

$$R = \begin{pmatrix} R_1 \\ R_2 \\ ... \\ R_M \end{pmatrix}, Z = \begin{pmatrix} Z_1 \\ Z_2 \\ ... \\ Z_M \end{pmatrix}, A = \begin{pmatrix} a_{1,1} \, a_{1,2} \, a_{1,3} \, ... \, a_{1,n} \\ a_{2,1} \, a_{2,2} \, a_{2,3} \, ... \, a_{2,n} \\ .... \\ a_{M,1} \, a_{M,2} \, a_{M,3} \, ... \, a_{M,n} \end{pmatrix} \equiv R = AZ$$

The matrix A must satisfy the covariance requirements. By eliminating the random vectors R and Z, we have the following:

$$R \qquad = AZ$$
$$RR^T \qquad = AZ(AZ)^T = AZZ^T A^T$$
$$E[RR^T] \, = E[AZZ^T A^T] = AE[ZZ^T]A^T$$
$$E[RR^T] \, = AIA^T$$
$$\Sigma \, = AA^T$$

Several methods can be used to solve the set of equations for AT and generate correlated variates, for instance, Cholesky Decomposition [10], Singular Value Decomposition [10] and Return Space Decomposition [1]. The authors in [25], [20, [1] showed that the matrix A can be expressed as follows: matrix A must satisfy the covariance requirements. By eliminating the random vectors R and Z, we have the following:

$$A = \frac{1}{\sqrt{\sum\limits_{i=1}^{n} \alpha^i}} \begin{pmatrix} \alpha^{\frac{1}{2}} r_{1,1} & \alpha^{\frac{2}{2}} r_{1,2} & \alpha^{\frac{3}{2}} r_{1,3} \dots \alpha^{\frac{n}{2}} r_{1,n} \\ \alpha^{\frac{1}{2}} r_{2,1} & \alpha^{\frac{2}{2}} r_{2,2} & \alpha^{\frac{3}{2}} r_{2,3} \dots \alpha^{\frac{n}{2}} r_{2,n} \\ \dots & \dots & \dots \quad \dots \\ \alpha^{\frac{1}{2}} r_{M,1} & \alpha^{\frac{2}{2}} r_{M,2} & \alpha^{\frac{3}{2}} r_{M,3} \dots \alpha^{\frac{n}{2}} r_{M,n} \end{pmatrix}$$

where n=N-1 is the number of log returns, α is the smoothing factor and $r_{i,j}$ is the return of context variable i at time j.

The advantages of using the Return Space Decomposition (RSD) over the Cholesky and SVD factorizations can be summarized as follows [25]:

- In both, Cholesky and SVD factorizations, the decomposed matrix does not easily provide an intuitive understanding of how the future values are generated and the change of a single value of a context risk factor requires a new decomposition. Finally, the Cholesky factorization requires that the correlation matrix be PD (positive definite), and SVD requires PSD (positive semi-definite).
- Volatilities and correlations do not have to be computed when using Return Space Decomposition.

Table 4 describes the modified algorithm for M context dependent variables using the Return Space Decomposition:

Table 4. Scenario generation algorithm for multiple dependent context dependent variables using Space Return Decomposition

Input: $\left(\{V_1\}_{t=1}^{N}, \{V_2\}_{t=1}^{N} \dots \{V_M\}_{t=1}^{N} \right)$
1. Choose the number of scenario trials T and smoothing factor α
2. Compute the α weights vector $lwv = \left(\alpha_1^{\frac{1}{2}}, \alpha_2^{\frac{2}{2}}, \alpha_3^{\frac{3}{2}}, \dots, \alpha_n^{\frac{n}{2}} \right)^T$ and the $ssq = \dfrac{1}{\sqrt{\sum\limits_{i=1}^{n} \alpha^i}}$

Table 4. (*continued*)

3. For each context risk factor time series i $(1 \le i \le M)$

3.1 Compute the A Matrix, where each
$$a_{ij}, (1 \le i \le M, 1 \le j \le N) = r_{ij} \cdot lmv \cdot ssq \text{ where } r_{ij} \text{ is the return of}$$
context variable i at time j.

3.2 Define a time series $\left\{ S_{i,t} \right\}_{t=1}^{T}$ to store the context variable simulated values

3.3 For each j trial $(1 \le j \le T)$

3.3.1 Compute an N size vector
$$Z = (z_1, z_2, z_3, \ldots, z_n)^T, z_i \sim IID\ N(0,1)$$

3.3.2 For each context variable k $(1 \le k \le M)$, compute
$$SLR = (A_k \circ Z) \cdot \sqrt{H} \text{ where } A_k \text{ is the row-vector corresponding}$$
to context variable k and the evaluation horizon H.

3.3.3 Compute the jth simulated value S_j as follows:
$$S_{i,j} = V_N^i \exp(SLR) \text{ where } exp(x) = e^x \text{ and } V_N^i \text{ is the value for}$$

the context variable i at time N 2.1 Compute the N-1 returns

from $\left\{ V_{i,t} \right\}_{t=1}^{N}$. The result of this calculation is a time series of returns

of the form $\left\{ r_{i,t} \right\}_{t=2}^{N}$

Output: $S_G = \left(\{S_1\}_{t=1}^{T}, \{S_2\}_{t=1}^{T} \ldots \{S_M\}_{t=1}^{T} \right)$

6 Risk

Due to the dynamic nature of context variables, we will measure the *risk* of each
context variable (and for a group of context variables) as the maximum *error* amount
that is incurred in the estimation of future values (for each context variable) during an
evaluation horizon for a given confidence level. In this framework, to measure the
risk of a context variable, the following is assumed:

1. Risk can be measured according to the changes of the context variables *(e.g.
   location, power resource, etc...)*.
2. Without loss of generality, the values of a context variable are always positive.
   Moreover, the [log] changes in the context variables can be modeled using as a
   random walk (following a normal distribution).

To calculate the maximum *error* amount for each context variable, we need to create a set of time series $E = \left(\{E_{1,t}\}_{t=1}^{T}, \{E_{2,t}\}_{t=1}^{T}, \ldots, \{E_{i,t}\}_{t=1}^{T}, \ldots \{E_{M,t}\}_{t=1}^{T} \right)$, where $\{E_{i,t}\}_{t=1}^{T}$ is the estimation error series for context variable i and defined as follows:

$$\{E_{i,t}\}_{t=1}^{T} = S_{i,j} - V_{N}^{i}$$

where V_{N}^{i} is the value for the context variable i at time N.

To measure the risk, we use the **percentile** function to determine the proportion of values in the time series $\{E_{i,t}\}_{t=1}^{T}$ that a specific magnitude will not be exceeded by a specific magnitude. This means that, for a context variable, this measure is the maximum error amount (*risk*) that would be incurred in the estimation during the evaluation horizon H for a given *confidence level (γ)*. Formally, the pth percentile of the $\{E_{i,t}\}_{t=1}^{T}$ values is defined as the magnitude that exceeds p percent of the values, that is:

$$risk_{i,P} = \left| percentile\left(\{E_{i,t}\}_{t=1}^{T}, (1-\gamma) \right) \right|$$

Because of the assumption that context values are *normally distributed*, mathematically, the pth percentile (denoted by α) of a continuous probability distribution is given by the following formula [13]:

$$p = \frac{1}{\sqrt{2\pi}} \int_{-\infty}^{\alpha} e^{-x^2/2} dx$$

Finally, assuming that the context variables can be linearly aggregated (Section 2.4) and given that the sum of normal random variables is itself normally distributed [19], then, the overall change time series of a group of M context variables is the weighted sum of M underlying returns and can be stated as follows:

$$\{E_G\}_{t=1}^{T} = \left(\sum_{i=1}^{M} \frac{E_{i,1}}{c_i}, \sum_{i=1}^{M} \frac{E_{i,2}}{c_i}, \ldots, \sum_{i=1}^{M} \frac{E_{i,T}}{c_i} \right)$$

where $E_{i,j}$ is the simulated error for context variable i at trial j, c_i is the scaling amount for context variable i. Then, the overall change (risk) of a group of context variables is

$$risk_{G,P} = \left| percentile\left(\{E_G\}_{t=1}^{T}, (1-\gamma) \right) \right|$$

7 Security Policies

In our army scenario, a simple security policy can be stated as follows: a Soldier can receive the location of his unit members, provided his *proximity* to the company commander (Captain) is no less than 70 meters. Moreover, the proximity between the Captain and the soldier's unit leader Sergeant) needs to be no less than 50 meters (The Sergeant and the Soldier are within line of sight of each other). The commanding officer requires that the location of the Soldier and the Sergeant be reported every minute and that the *volatility* (standard deviation) of the data not exceed 0.01. Every minute the policy is reevaluated ($H = 1$). The commanding officer (Captain) uses a smoothing factor of 0.95 ($\alpha = 0.95$) and generates 100 Monte Carlo scenarios ($T = 100$) before returning a decision. Table 5 shows the description of the example Context Based Security Policy described above.

Table 5. Example of the context based security policy

Name: Unit member location access policy.

Description: A soldier can access location of his unit members according to his current position and proximity of his commanding officer.
Entities:
    1) *so*: Soldier, 2) *co*: Commanding Officer, 4) se: Sergeant 3) *LD*: Location data
Context policy parameters:
    1) $H = 1$ minute, 2) $T = 200$, $y = \alpha = 0.95$, $N = 10$

Access to *LD* is granted to *so* iff
    1. *proximity(so, co)* < 70 meters & proximity(co, se) < 50 meters & proximity (so, se) < 5meters
    2. *volatility (proximity(so,co,N))* <= 0.01 & *volatility (proximity(co,se,N)) <=0.01*
    3. *error(proximity(so,co,N)) <=0.6*
***Functions*:**
    • *proximity(x,y): returns the proximity between entities x and y*
    • *proximity(x,y,n): returns a time series with the last n proximity values between x and y .*
    • *volatility(ts): returns the volatility of the time series ts*
    • *error(ts): returns the estimation error through a Monte Carlo simulation for time series ts.*

Security Policy Evaluation. Under the Random Walk - Monte Carlo method framework presented in Sections 3, 4 and 5, a context based security policy requires the following parameters to be defined and evaluated:

1. Smoothing factor (α)
2. The number of scenario trials (T)
3. Evaluation horizon (H)
4. Time series frequency (F)
5. Number of observations required in a context variable time series (N)
6. The confidence level (γ) to be used for risk evaluation
7. For each context variable in the policy, a risk (error) tolerance is defined.

The following steps are used to evaluate the policy:

1. A soldier so sends a request to his commanding officer co for the location of his unit members.

2. The co retrieves the locally stored security policy, reads it and determines which context variables (i.e. proximity) are necessary for the evaluation of the policy
3. The co sends a request asking both the so and the se for their proximity information. Such a request contains:
    a. The context variable to be gathered (e.g. proximity)
    b. The number of past observations (N) in the context variable time series.
4. Upon receiving the requests both the so and se return the required time series information to the co.
5. The co runs the modified Monte Carlo algorithm (Table 3) to calculate the 1-minute volatility. It then calculates the risk of the context variables (proximity) with the specified confidence level (y) using the percentile function.
6. Once the data is computed the co determines if access to the data LD can be granted for the next 1 minute (H = 1) before the policy needs to be revaluated.

8   Related Work

There are several research efforts in developing security systems that use context variables to either solely render a security decision or expand Role Based Access Control (RBAC) implementations and policies. For instance, [12] defines a security system that only uses context data to arrive at a security decision while keeping the anonymity of the accessing users. However the system does not use any context data history to render a more accurate security decision. In [21] a theoretical model to formalize and represent situation-based security policies using context graphs is proposed. However, no provision for the use of historical context data in the enforcement of security is given. The system in [17] defines a programming interface to handle inexact information from multiple sources while checking the honesty of the input context data; however it assumes that security of the data must be handled by the application using the interface.

The grammar explained in [32] allows the expansion of traditional RBAC policies with location-dependent data. However, the grammar does not include predicates to validate or use history of context data. The model in [36] expands the role based access control (RBAC) paradigm while a user agent adjusts role permissions based on context data. However, the system does not provide for a way to invalidate erroneous context claims, which may cause information leaks.

There are several systems that use the concept of trust and risk to deliver a security decision. For instance, the model in [7] characterizes an outcome-based approach to allow trust reasoning and calculate cost data per-outcome basis, instead of relying on a simple risk metrics value. Trust is then computed using current evidence along previous observations and recommendations. However, the system has not been fully validated for pervasive mobile environments. In [16] a model that takes into account the trust dynamics of past experiences, including intentions or beliefs is presented. The model requires each entity to count its own positive and negative evidences about others. However, the trust scheme does not use any context information to refine trust values.

The preliminary work done in [14] attempts to model the relationship between risk and trust in order to derive a computational model that integrates the two concepts. It uses the probability of success in a transaction between two entities. However, the system does not formally describe or model the risk in terms of context information. The research described in [3] uses Kalman-Filter equations to calculate trust between a client and a service provider based on the discrepancies found amid the service advertised quality values and the client's measurements. However, since the model is outcome based, it does not use context information to refine the trust measures. The research described in [29] illustrates a mechanism to compute trust between entities based on their own direct interaction experiences as well as recommendations. However, trust calculations do not take into account the entities' context information.

The work described in [37] extends the RBAC model with spatial and location-based information where spatial entities are used to model objects and user positions. In this system, security roles are activated based on the positional information from a user. Although very useful security system for geographical information systems (GIS), the system cannot be easily adapted to small mobile devices or implemented in a mobile ad-hoc network (MANET) environment.

The preliminary work in [26] introduces the random walk presented in Section 2.6 and the use of the percentile function to calculate the risk of a context variable in a security policy. However, this work does not take into account the correlations amongst different context variables in a policy.

9 Conclusions and Future Work

In this paper we presented a framework to model context variables that takes into account the relationships amongst them for secure collaborations. In this framework, security decisions are reached by measuring the risk of each context variable according to its value changes. To reach such a decision, we introduced a novel method called space return decomposition to evaluate a context-based security policy without calculating correlations and volatilities. In addition, we presented an example of a real world policy where our framework can be applied.

For future work, more investigation is necessary to include or derive a trust measure from the context data for the entity (user) requesting access permission. Finally, analysis is necessary to determine the appropriate amount of history to keep (or for bootstrapping) before a reliable computation can be made.

References

1. Benson, P., Zangari, P.: A General Approach to Calculating VaR without Volatilities and Correlations. JPMorgan/Reuters RiskMetrics Monitor (Second Quarter 1997)
2. Boeing. "ScanEagle." The Boeing Corporation, All rights reserved, http://www.boeing.com/defense-space/military/scaneagle/index.html (accessed, November 2007)
3. Capra, L., Musolesi, M.: Autonomic Trust Prediction for Pervasive Systems. In: International Conference on Advanced Information Networking and Applications, vol. 2, pp. 481–488 (2006)

4. Castelli, G., et al.: A Simple Model and Infrastructure for Context-Aware Browsing of the World. In: IEEE International Conference on Pervasive Computing and Communications, pp. 229–238 (March 2007)
5. Chong, C.-Y., Kumar, S.P.: Sensor Networks: Evolution, Opportunities and Challenges. Proceedings of the IEEE 91(8), 1247–1256 (2003)
6. Chou, Y.L.: Statistical Analysis. Copyright © 1975 Holt International (1975) ISBN 0030894220
7. Dimmock, N., Belokosztolszki, A., Eyers, D.: Using Trust and Risk in Role-Based Access Control Policies. In: ACM Symposium on Access Control Models and Technologies, pp. 156–162 (June 2004)
8. Dimmock, N., Bacon, J., Ingram, D., Moody, K.: Risk Models for Trust Based Access Controls (TBAC). In: Herrmann, P., Issarny, V., Shiu, S.C.K. (eds.) iTrust 2005. LNCS, vol. 3477, pp. 364–371. Springer, Heidelberg (2005)
9. FAS Military Network Analysis. "Land Warrior." Federation of American Scientists, http://www.fas.org/man/dod-101/sys/land/land-warrior.htm (accessed, January 2007)
10. Golub, G.H., Van Loan, C.F.: Matrix Computations, Section 4.2, 3rd edn., pp. 140–152. Johns Hopkins University Press (1996) ISBN 0-8018-5414-8
11. Hamilton, J.D.: Time Series Analysis. Copyright © 1994. Princeton University Press, Princeton (1994)
12. Hulsebosch, R., Salden, A., Bargh, M., Ebben, P., Reitsma, J.: Context Sensitive Access Control. In: ACM Symposium on Access control models and technologies, pp. 111–119 (June 2005)
13. JPMorgan/Reuters. RiskMetrics™ – Technical Document 4th Edition. RiskMetrics Group, New York (1996), http://www.riskmetrics.com
14. Jøsang, A., Presti, S.L.: Analyzing the Relationship between Risk and Trust. In: Jensen, C., Poslad, S., Dimitrakos, T. (eds.) iTrust 2004. LNCS, vol. 2995, pp. 135–145. Springer, Heidelberg (2004)
15. Kim, J., Malz, A.M., Mina, J.: LongRun. Technical Document, RiskMetrics Group (1999)
16. Korpipää, P., Mäntyjärvi, J., et al.: Managing Context Information in Mobile Devices. IEEE Pervasive Computing 2(3), 42–51 (2003)
17. Lin, C., Varadharajan, V., Wang, Y., Pruthi, V.: Trust Enhanced Security for Mobile Agents. In: IEEE International Conference on Ecommerce Technology, pp. 231–238 (July 2005)
18. Litterman, B.: Modern Investment Management: An Equilibrium Approach (Hardcover). In: Copyright © 2003, Goldman Sachs Inc., John Wiley & Sons Inc., Chichester (2003)
19. Mendenhall, W., Scheaffer, R.L., Wackerly, D.D.: Mathematical Statistics with Applications. Copyright © 1986, 3rd edn. PWS Publishers (1996) ISBN 0-87150-939-3
20. Mina, J., Xiao, J.Y.: Return to RiskMetrics: The Evolution of a Standard. RiskMetrics Group (April 2001)
21. Mostefaoui, G.K., Brezillon, P.: Modeling Context-Based Security Policies with Contextual Graphs. In: IEEE Annual Conference on Pervasive Computing and Communications Workshop, pp. 28–33 (March 2004)
22. Neumann, G., Strembeck, M.: Access Control: Design and Implementation of a Flexible RBAC-Service in an Object-Oriented Scripting Language. In: ACM Conference on Computer and Communications Security, pp. 58–67 (November 2001)
23. Park, J.S., Costello, K.P., Neven, T.M., Diosomito, J.A.: Access management for distributed systems: A composite RBAC approach for large, complex organizations. In: ACM Symposium on Access Control Models and Technologies, pp. 163–172 (June 2004)

24. riskglossary.com "Return." Copyright © Contingency Analysis, 1996 - current (1996), http://www.riskglossary.com/link/return.htm (accessed, December 2006)

25. RiskMetrics Group. "Risk University." RiskMetrics Group, http://riskuniversity.org/ (accessed, May 2006)

26. Sanchez, C., Gruenwald, L., Sanchez, M.: A Monte Carlos Framework to Validate Context-Based Security Policies in Pervasive and Mobile Environment. In: ACM SIGMOD International Conference on Data Engineering for Wireless and Mobile Access (MobiDE) (June 2007)

27. Rose, C., Smith, M.D.: The Multivariate Normal Distribution. In: Section 6.4 in Mathematical Statistics with Mathematica, pp. 216–235. Springer, New York (2002)

28. Swift, M., Hopkins, A., Brundrett, P., Dyke, C.V., Garg, P., Chan, S., Goertzel, M., Jensenworth, G.: Improving the granularity of access control for Windows 2000. ACM Transactions on Information and System Security 5(4), 398–437 (2002)

29. Teacy, W.T.L., Patel, J., Jennings, N.R., Luck, M.: TRAVOS: Trust and Reputation in the Context of Inaccurate Information Sources. Journal of Autonomous Agents and Multi-Agent Systems 12(2), 183–198 (2006)

30. Uryasev, S.: Introduction to the Theory of Probabilistic Functions and Percentiles (Value-at-Risk). In: Probabilistic Constrained Optimization: Methodology and Applications, pp. 1–25. Kluwer Academic Publishers, Dordrecht (2000)

31. Want, R.: Introduction to RFID Technology. IEEE Pervasive Computing 5(1), 25–33 (2006)

32. Wedde, H.F., Lishka, M.: Role-Based Access Control in Ambient and Remote Space. In: ACM Symposium on Access Control Models and Technologies, pp. 21–30 (June 2004)

33. Weisstein, E.W.: Normal Distribution. From MathWorld–A Wolfram Web Resource, http://mathworld.wolfram.com/NormalDistribution.html (accessed, August 2006)

34. Weisstein, E.W.: Random Walk–1-Dimensional. From MathWorld–A Wolfram Web Resource, http://mathworld.wolfram.com/RandomWalk1-Dimensional.html (accessed, August 2006)

35. Chou, Y.-L.: Moving Average. Statistical Analysis for Business and Economics. Holt Rinehart and Winston Publishers (January 1989) ISBN 978-0444013019

36. Zhang, G., Parashar, M.: Context-aware Dynamic Access Control for Pervasive Applications. In: Communication Networks and Distributed Systems Modeling and Simulation Conference, 2004 (January 2004)

37. Bertino, E., Damián, M., Catania, B., Perlasca, P.: GEO-RBAC: a spatially aware RBAC. ACM Transactions on Information Systems and Security 10(1) (February 2007)

Towards Continuous Workflow Enactment Systems

Panayiotis Neophytou, Panos K. Chrysanthis, and Alexandros Labrinidis

University of Pittsburgh, Pittsburgh, PA 15260, USA
{panickos,panos,labrinid}@cs.pitt.edu

Abstract. Traditional workflow enactment systems and workflow design processes view the workflow as a one-time interaction with the various data sources, executing a series of steps once, whenever the workflow results are requested. The fundamental underlying assumption has been that data sources are passive and all interactions are structured along the request/reply (query) model. Hence, traditional Workflow Management Systems cannot effectively support business or scientific monitoring applications that require the processing of data streams. In this paper, we propose a paradigm shift from the traditional step-wise workflow execution model to a continuous execution model, in order to handle data streams published and delivered asynchronously from multiple sources.

Keywords: workflow, continuous workflows, patterns, data streams.

1 Introduction

Many Enterprises use workflows to automate their operations and integrate their information systems and human resources. Workflows have also been used to facilitate outsourcing or collaboration beyond the boundaries of a single enterprise, for example, in establishing Virtual Enterprises [1]. Recently, workflows have been used in the context of scientific exploration and discovery to automate repetitive, complex and distributed scientific computations that often require the collaboration of multiple scientists [4,7,9].

A common class of applications in both business and scientific domains is monitoring applications that involve the processing of continuous streams of data (updates) [3]. Examples include financial analysis applications that monitor streams of stock data to support decision making in brokering firms and environmental analysis applications that collect and analyze sensor data to support discovery of air and water pollution.

Most recent workflow enactment/management systems orchestrate the interactions among activities within a workflow along the lines of web services [18]. Several business process modeling languages have been designed to capture the logic of a composite web service, including WSCI [19], BPML [2], BPEL4WS (with the latest update WS-BPEL 2.0 [8]), BPSS [15] and XPDL [20]. However, these interactions are usually one-shot interactions between the sender and the

E. Bertino and J.B.D. Joshi (Eds.): CollaborateCom 2008, LNICST 10, pp. 162–178, 2009.

receiver of the request and it is not clear whether or not these existing workflow management systems and languages are suited for monitoring applications.

Our goal in this paper is to examine the capability of current workflow models and workflow management systems to support business and scientific monitoring applications. We will base our examination on the Workflow Pattern framework which was developed in [17]. This framework proposed a set of 20 common workflow patterns and a set of 6 communication patterns in [13]. This framework was used to evaluate the capabilities of the languages mentioned above in [22] and [10], showing that these languages could not support nearly half of the 20 workflow patterns, and also 2 of the communication patterns. These 2 communication patterns are Publish/Subscribe and Broadcast which, interestingly, are essential for enabling monitoring applications. YAWL [16], which is a more recent workflow definition language, makes the effort to support all the workflow patterns, but there is no reference in its definition for the support of the two communication patterns which are prevailing in monitoring applications.

The two missing communication patterns from existing workflow models are a direct result of the fundamental assumption that data sources in workflows are passive (e.g., stored in databases or data files) whereas data consumers (users, tasks) are both active and passive. These two missing communication patterns assume that some data sources are active, supporting continuous data streams.

In order to address the lack of support for continuous data streams in existing workflow models, in this paper, we consider a paradigm shift towards the idea of "continuous" workflows (analogous to the recent data processing shift from Database Management Systems to Data Stream Management Systems). The main difference between traditional and continuous workflows is that the latter is continuously (i.e., always) active and continuously reacting on internal streams of events and external streams of updates from multiple sources at the same time at any part of the workflow network.

The key contributions of this paper are:

1. Identify the limitations of the current workflow model in terms of supporting streams of data events, internally and externally.
2. Propose a new Continuous Workflow model and introduce two key primitives to support it, namely, queues and window operators.
3. Illustrate how the 20 existing workflow patterns could be implemented in order to support data streams.
4. Identify 4 new Continuous Workflow patterns.
5. Illustrate the expressive power of our continuous workflow model, in terms of simplicity and flexibility, by comparing the implementation of a monitoring application in our model and using a Timed Petri net implementation [6].

The rest of the paper is organized as follows: Section 2 sets the stage by providing background to existing workflow systems. We also discuss the Workflow Pattern framework that was used to evaluate the abilities of these existing systems. In Section 3, we study the need for continuous workflow constructs and then propose the new workflow model for Continuous workflows in Section 4. We finally conclude and give our directions for future work in Section 5.

2   Existing Workflow Model

A *workflow* (also referred to as workflow process) is defined as the automation of a business process, in whole or part, during which documents, information or tasks are passed from one participant to another for action, according to a set of procedural rules. A *workflow management system* (WfMS) is one that defines, creates and manages the execution of workflows through the use of software, running on one or more workflow engines, which is able to interpret the process definition, interact with workflow participants (human or machine) and, where required, invoke the use of IT tools (databases, job schedulers etc.) and applications. A *workflow process* can be defined by set of sub-processes which form part of the overall process. Multiple levels of sub processes may be combined to form a workflow hierarchy.

A *workflow activity* is a description of a piece of work that forms one logical step within a process. An activity may be a manual activity, which does not support computer automation, or an automated activity. A workflow activity requires human and/or machine resources(s) to support process execution; where human resource is required an activity is allocated to a workflow participant. A workflow activity is specified in terms of name, preconditions, actions, rules of exception handling, completion and temporal constraints. Every workflow specification formalism is built around a set of control flow relationships and concepts, such as those defined in [21]. Examples include simple one-to-one precedence constraints to denote *sequential* execution, or *OR* and *AND* relationships to denote *parallel* execution. These are subdivided into *OR-split* and *AND-split* to specify branching and, *OR-join* and *AND-join* to specify convergence to initiate the next activity in the workflow.

A comprehensive study [17] enumerates the various control patterns required by workflow applications. A pattern "is the abstraction from a concrete form which keeps recurring in specific nonarbitrary contexts" [12]. The 20 patterns studied in [17] include more complex control structures, than the ones described by WfMC [21], such as XOR-split, Differed Choice, Multiple Instances etc. These help to define the workflow model in more detail and down to specific imperative workflow requirements. The study also elaborates on which of these patterns could be realized in workflow management systems and languages, available at the time of the study. Some of the patterns mentioned cannot be realized by these systems because their design did not take them into consideration. They then proposed a new workflow language [16] that is able to implement these patterns.

Workflow events are distinguished into internal and external events. External events, are relevant input workflow data, pushed into the workflow as a response to a request, from applications, users, databases and other entities external to the workflow. Internal events are workflow control data, as defined in [21], but limited to internally exchanged data between activities. This does not include the engine state data store in the WfMS database. Usually internal events mark the completion of an activity and signal the execution of the next one.

A *workflow request* is the initiating event of a workflow. Once it is received by the WfMS it creates a new instance of the workflow. The request includes

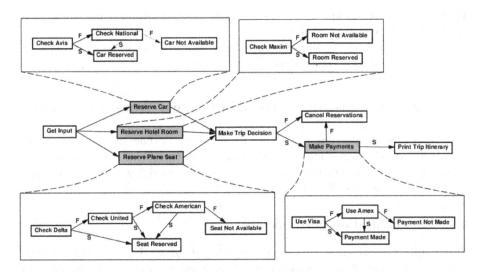

Fig. 1. Continuous Workflow enabling architecture

relevant data and constraints defined by the requester. This is the first piece of
information being fed to a workflow instance.

Most workflow languages model workflows either as State charts or Petri nets.
Figure 1 represents the state chart of a vacation trip booking workflow from [5],
where AND-splits (and AND-joins) are implicit when more than one arrow orig-
inates from (or is coincident to) a node. For example, *Get Input* represents an
AND-split and *Make Trip Decission* represents an AND-join. OR-splits and OR-
joins are depicted with arrows annotated with selection conditions. For example,
Make Payments represents an OR-split with condition **S** (Success) and **F** (Fail-
lure). There is also the case where conditions are not mutually exclusive and
more than one branches is activated. The workflow patterns observed in this
workflow, are defined as WP1-WP5 in [17]. One can also discern some activities
being defined as sub-processes.

Regarding the execution of activities, according to the transition definition in
[21], any two activities in the same sequence cannot run in parallel. The first one
will give the thread of execution to the next one. That means that if we have
two activities A and B where A comes before B in a sequence, then B cannot
start running (even on partial results from A) unless A is completely terminated
(Figure 2).

An attempt was made, by using Time Petri nets, to apply temporal constraints on events in [6]. The effort covers some cases of workflow patterns for
monitoring supply chains and reacting on events such as "Out of stock" and
"Order arrived". The Petri net approach is difficult to implement and although
is able to capture operations on multiple events, it cannot do it for an arbitrary
number of events, known only at runtime. Also events are consumed whenever an
activity is activated, and they have to be replaced if there is a need to reprocess
them. These are all considerations that the designer has to make before hand.

We will take their example and show an easier way to implement the supply line patterns described, in Section 4.

In the next section we will examine if the existing workflow model is suitable to support monitoring applications.

3 From the Existing to the Continuous Workflow Model

In this section we examine the ability of existing workflow models to support monitoring applications. This analysis is based on the communication patterns described in [22] and how those can be used inside a workflow using the internal workflow patterns described in [17].

3.1 Communication Patterns

Communication patterns are divided into two categories: Pull and Push. In the pull model the data consumer gets at most one reply per request. Three patterns from [17] follow this model. (1) Request/Reply, where a sender makes a request to the receiver and waits for a reply before continuing execution; (2) One-Way, where the sender makes a request to the receiver and waits for an acknowledgment reply before continuing execution; and (3) synchronous polling, where a sender makes a request to a receiver and continues processing. It then periodically checks to see if a reply was sent by the receiver. When it detects a reply it stops polling.

In the push model the data consumer receives multiple data items per request. Two patterns interest us which follow this model. Publish/Subscribe is a form of asynchronous communication where a request is sent by a process and the receivers are determined by a previous declaration of interest. The declaration of interest could also express constraints on the kind of replies each receiver is interested in. Lastly, Broadcast, is a form of asynchronous communication in which a request is sent to all participants, the receivers, of the network. Each participant determines whether the request is of interest by examining the content.

From the aforementioned patterns current workflow management systems and languages provide support for just the pull model communication patterns. In the best of our knowledge no system provides support for either of the two push model communication patterns.

3.2 Ability of Existing Workflows to Support Push Input

As we have mentioned in the introduction, monitoring applications monitor continuous streams of data. The only way to receive updates as soon as they happen is by using a Push mechanism such as Publish/Subscribe. In existing WfMSs the only point in a workflow that is able to handle push data is at the initial activity, where the request to instantiate a workflow comes in. This way, each event belonging to a stream will be individually handled by an instance of the workflow.

The workflow is able to notify humans or machine resources in the case that a specific event needs further handling.

An alternative processing model would be to use pipelined execution of the workflow. Since a high volume of events is expected from the data stream, a pipeline model could be used to save resources. In pipelined workflow enactment, activity instances are being shared by multiple workflow instances. Each activity is thought of as a pipeline stage. Buffering takes place between steps to independently handle individual events. The control flow is handled in the same way as in the case of multiple instances of the workflow.

There two problems with the pipeline approach. First, only one stream can be supported. Second, no multiple events can be handled together since each event runs on a separate instance or pipeline stage, thus the requirement that a monitoring application needs to run on a history of events in real time, is not met.

We will now examine how existing workflow models could support monitoring of multiple streams, and see where they fall back. Consider Figure 2. In this example, activity C is required to get continuous updates from a streaming data source. Since there are currently no constructs to allow for activity C to receive events directly from a data stream and act upon them immediately, let's assume that there is a buffer between activity C and the data stream. Now activity C is polling the buffer to get the new updates. In most systems, activity D cannot run on intermediate results of C since C has to terminate and then activate D. This is the case of synchronous polling, as described in Section 3.1. To alleviate this problem one can use loops (Figure 2.b.) We set activity C to query the buffer once and return the results to D. D then might split the results to G and back to C (for it to query the buffer once again). Now since G is an AND-join, and branch E-F was activated only once (not a loop), then G will only run once, consume the event that came from E-F, and then block. It will not be able to process all the results coming out of the loop. This problem could be solved by having G feed back the same event to its input, every time it executes, so that it will process it together with the results from the loop. This implementation, although it does not provide real-time monitoring of a data stream, it shows how a workflow system can monitor a buffer of a data stream, and internally produce a stream of events using a loop. There exist though workflow definition languages like BPEL, that do not allow loops that have an output on every iteration, like the one described above. The most common loops allowed have one input and one output.

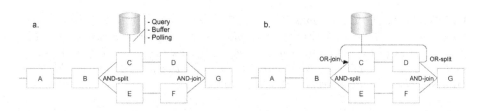

Fig. 2. Abstract Workflow example

If the designer adds another similar loop to the E-F branch then two internal asynchronous streams will be created, being joined at activity G. The results on random pairs of events would probably not make any sense. Also the two streams could have a big volume difference in number of events per unit of time, thus one of them would either drop events or should have means of buffering them. Introducing queues to the inputs of the joins should workout this problem. Moreover the results would probably make more sense if there was a way to synchronize the two streams in terms of temporal and value based functions on windows of these data, similar to the ones found in continuous queries [11].

We saw that polling is one way to monitor a stream, but this approach does not allow for real time reaction to the incoming stream, and in fact, even this is only allowed in systems where arbitrary loops are allowed. This makes us come to the conclusion that parallel execution of sequential activities is required to process streams of events, much like in the pipelined execution, because consecutive activities need to be continuously active processing the events. The difference here is that buffering of multiple events in the stream is required to be able to satisfy the requirement of monitoring applications to run on subsets of the history of the stream.

Another operation that monitoring applications need to be able to make on workflows processing data streams, is event invalidation. For example, if you have a stream from an airline which publishes fares, and a new fare update comes in that invalidates a previous fare, then the earlier update should be invalidated downstream, in order to avoid processing a fare that is invalid. Invalidation or otherwise known as cancelation is supported in YAWL [16] but it is not possible to selectivly invalidate events in the workflow, since they consider each workflow instance independent for each event and they do not support data streams.

4   Continuous Workflow Model

During our analysis in the previous section we made some observations on the functional and expressive ability of existing workflow languages and models. In light of those observations we now present our definition of "Continuous Workflows" and then elaborate on how this new workflow model can be applied to existing workflow patterns. We also identify 4 new patterns which we consider essential for new classes of applications, that require interaction with data streams either internally or externally.

Definition 1. *A "Continuous Workflow", is a workflow that supports enactment on multiple streams of data, by pipelining the flow and processing into various parts of the workflow. Continuous workflows can potentially run for an unlimited amount of time, constantly monitoring streams. To achieve that, the proposed Continuous Workflow Model introduces:*

1. *Concurrent execution of sequential activities, in a pipelined way.*
2. *Queues on the inputs of activities to buffer data in between activities.*

3. *Windows and window functions on the queues to allow the definition of synchronization semantics between multiple data streams. Windows are also used on multiple invocations of a single execution pipeline whose results are buffered in a queue. This means that an event can be considered as part of multiple pipeline invocations.*
4. *Interactions between pipeline steps. That is, the ability to notify a downstream or upstream activity of an update and cancel its execution.*

In order to introduce new synchronization semantics into Continuous Workflow we define the notion of event waves, as follows:

Definition 2. *A wave of internal events is created at a split node (or when initiating multiple instances) and it is synchronized at a join node (or when merging multiple instances). A split creates a wave of events that are disseminated in multiple branches that run in parallel. When these branches merge at a synchronizing join then all of the events in the wave must be joined and processed together. Even if an activity produces multiple events as a result of one invocation (or multiple invocations as part of a loop), then these are marked and considered part of the same wave. An event within a wave may create sub waves, creating a hierarchy of waves that need to be synchronized. These can be taken care by the system with appropriate instrumentation of the waves.*

4.1 Windows

A *window* is generally considered as a mechanism for adjusting flexible bounds on an unbounded stream in order to fetch a finite, yet ever-changing set of events, which may be regarded as a temporary bundle of events. We are introducing the notion of windows on the queues of events which are attached to the activity inputs. The windows are calculated by a window operator running on the queue. Windows are defined in terms of an upper bound, lower bound, extend and mode of adjustment as time advances. The upper and lower bounds are the timestamps of the events at the beginning and the end of the window. The extend is the size of the window. This can be defined in two measurement units: (a) Logical units, which are time based, and define the maximum time interval between the upper and lower bound timestamps. (b) Physical units, which are count based, and define the number of events between the upper and lower bounds. The mode of adjustment, also known as *window step*, defines the period for updating the window. If a step is not defined, then the window is evaluated every time a new event comes into the queue. This makes the window operator more accurate in terms of reacting to events on time, but in cases of high event rates this could seriously diminish the overall system performance. A flag called "delete_used_events" is also defined to denote if events that were used in the window that triggered the firing of an activity should be deleted from the queue. The signal to delete used events from queues comes as part of the post-conditions of an activity.

Another feature introduced for windows, is that every queue has two outputs: (1) the current window, as it is calculated according to the window constraints,

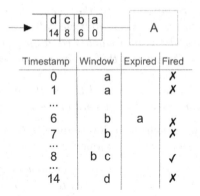

Timestamp	Window	Expired	Fired
0	a		✗
1	a		✗
...			
6	b	a	✗
7	b		✗
...			
8	b c		✓
...			
14	d		✗

Fig. 3. Window operator example

and (2) the events that are being expired with every recalculation of a window. For example, if an order is waiting in a queue and for some reason was delayed, the window might expire it and it will be transferred to a different queue to be handled as a delayed order.

To better understand the window operator we describe an example with the help of Figure 3. Letters represent events and numbers represent timestamps (in minutes). The window attributes are: Size=5 minutes, Step=1 minute, Delete used events=true. Firing of the activity depends on the contents of the window and the preconditions of the activity which could be dependent on the contents. Assume the preconditions include *if (window.length >= 2) then activate*. The window is calculated for every step (of 1 minute). If there is a change to the window operator's results then the preconditions of the activity are evaluated to determine whether the activity should be fired. If the activity is fired, then the events pushed are deleted from the queue. Notice in the example in Figure 3, that a was not used in firing activity A and that at timestamp 6, a does not fall inside the window, thus it was expired and returned to the expired output of the queue. However at timestamp 8, where the window pushed includes events b and c, the activity is fired and once it is completed these events are both deleted from the queue.

4.2   Workflow Patterns in Continuous Workflows

In this section, we consider the 20 workflow patterns presented in [17] whose implementation changes with the introduction of continuous workflow enactment, but their semantics remain the same. That means that continuous workflows are backward compatible with the existing workflows. The reader can easily verify that the examples in [17] are still valid for the patterns described here. All of the patterns except WP11 (Implicit termination) can be implemented using continuous workflows. We also introduce 4 new patterns that are unique to continuous workflows.

Basic Control Flow Patterns. These patterns capture the elementary aspects of process control. These patterns closely match the definitions of elementary control flow concepts covered in [21]. **WP 1,2** and **4** (Sequence, Parallel split and XOR-split) do not require any modifications to fit our continuous workflow model since they can be scheduled to execute without any synchronization dependencies on consecutive events.

In **WP3**, multiple parallel branches converge into a single thread of control (AND-join), thus synchronizing multiple threads. The join will be activated once all the branches have completed.

In continuous workflows, the assumption that a branch cannot be completed again before the execution of the join is relaxed, since the workflow reacts on streaming events. Events produced by multiple executions of a branch can be buffered in the join's queues. Figure 4.a shows that two data events were produced by activity A while activity B is still processing and may eventually drop the item. Given the AND-join semantics, activity C blocks until both queues have a result. Activities belonging to a branch that has already finished processing can be scheduled to execute on the next wave of events.

In **WP5**, two or more alternative branches come together without synchronization (XOR-join). The assumption in this pattern is that only one branch is activated. That means that each wave of events has only one event propagated through the only activated branch. The joining activity runs once on each wave coming into the queue.

Advanced Branching and Synchronization Patterns. This subsection includes more advanced patterns for branching and synchronization. Again the assumption for this set of patterns is that the activating stream is the same for each branch thus we use notion of waves. **WP6** (Multi-choice) and **WP8** (Multi-Merge) from this set are the same in the continuous setting, since no synchronization among events of the same wave is needed.

In **WP7**, multiple branches converge into a single thread (Synchronized Join). The join activity has to wait for all of the activated branches to finish and then execute. Some branches may not activate in which case a *null* event is propagated to the join. Figure 4.b shows a case where we have a branch (A) that has finished processing 2 events, branch (B) which is still processing the first event and branch (C)

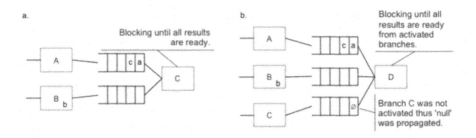

Fig. 4. (a) Pattern 3: AND-join and (b) Pattern 7: Synchronized-Merge

which was not activated and the *null* event was propagated. Activity D will only execute if all activated branches have finished.

In **WP9** (Discriminator) multiple branches merge and execution is initiated on the first result to arrive. Multiple branches are activated per wave. To avoid mixing of events from multiple waves, a cancellation signal is triggered for the specific wave after the join is finished executing. We present more details on cancellation in the WP19 pattern.

Structural Patterns. This set includes patterns for arbitrary cycles and work-flow termination. Cycles are categorized in structured cycles which in program-ming languages resemble WHILE loops, and interleaved cycles which resemble GOTO loops, where loops can be interleaved. Termination can be explicit (a set of conditions are met) or implicit (the workflow terminates when nothing is left to process).

WP10 (Arbitrary Cycles). In the continuous workflow model arbitrary cycles can be implemented, both structured (Figure 5.a) and interleaved cycles (Figure 5.b). Arbitrary cycles make the understanding of semantics difficult since more complicated situations can arise, thus the workflow designer must be able to understand the risks and possible confusion that may arise from such a design especially in the continuous workflow model.

WP11 (Implicit termination). This patterns captures the behavior of tradi-tional workflow systems when nodes can be terminated when activity ceases. This pattern is not directly supported by the continuous workflow model since streams of data are infinite and the only way to terminate the execution is only by defining a set of termination parameters. However, we could essentially im-plement similar functionality by relying on some sort of punctuations from the data sources [14].

Patterns Involving Multiple Instances. The patterns in this subsection involve cases where multiple threads of execution share the same definition. The number of instances could be known a priori or at runtime. We refer to a bundle as the set of instances required for a data event. If the results of the instances

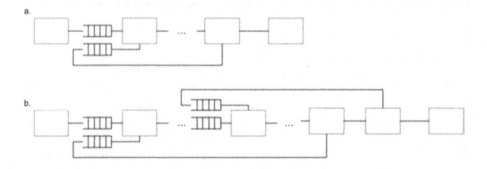

Fig. 5. Cycle patterns: (a) structured cycle and (b) interleaved cycle

of a bundle are needed for the execution of the rest of the workflow, then these results are gathered in a single queue at the activity joining the instances. The activity then runs on a window with the size of the number of instances. In the continuous model there are two cases to consider. The first one is running a number of bundles that were caused by the same number of events in parallel. The second case is running the bundles serially. When running serially, each event executes on the same bundle where the previous event was executed. The bundle will expand or shrink accordingly. Note the each bundle must finish execution before the next event can run on the same bundle.

WP12 (MI without Synchronization): This pattern refers to executing the instances in each bundle in parallel; their results are not required to be synchronized. Careful consideration must be taken if the results of an instance trigger the execution of the rest of the workflow. In the case of parallel bundles, results from multiple instances that correspond to one event can interleave with results that correspond to another event.

In **WP13-WP15** (MI with synchronization), instances within a bundle are synchronized once they end their execution. In WP13 the number of instances for each event/bundle is known at design time, in WP14 the number is known at runtime and in WP15 the number of instances is dynamic. In these cases the window size of the join node can be set to the number of instances, if the instances bundle is per-stream. If the instances bundle is per event then before moving on to the next step in the workflow each bundle has to synchronize internally and then forward the results. For WP15 to work, the process that creates the bundles has to also update the size of the windows at the corresponding queues inside the bundles.

State-Based Patterns. There are three state based patterns.

In **WP16** (Deferred choice), several branches have been activated (by AND-split or OR-split) but only one should execute. The decision is delayed until the occurrence of some event, where the one that finally executes sends cancel signals to the rest. In continuous workflows, since events are queued and the execution happens once some preconditions on the queues are met, the cancellation signal can be acted by removing the event from the activity's queue.

In **WP17** (Interleaved parallel routing), a set of activities is executed once, in an arbitrary order decided at runtime but no two activities can run at the same time for the same event. To achieve this, a list of mutual exclusion semaphores, (one for each wave of events) keeps the activities from running concurrently. The semaphore shows the wave id, a flag showing if some branch is acting on this event and a number for the active branches remaining to act on this wave. Once the number reaches 0 then the semaphore is removed from the list.

In **WP18** (Milestone), an activity can only run if a certain milestone is reached and has not expired. A milestone is a point in the process where a given activity A has finished processing an event, and a subsequent activity B has not yet started. It is important to keep track of which events have reached a certain milestone and if that milestone has expired. A similar approach to the one in WP17 is taken, where a list is used to keep track of the waves of events.

Cancellation Patterns. There are two cancellation patterns. **WP19** and **WP20** refer to the canceling of an activity and the withdrawal of the whole workflow respectively. Activity cancellation in Continuous workflows works much like in [16], but instead of flushing everything in the queues, events are canceled only if they belong to the same wave as the event that triggered the cancellation. To cancel an activity on a specific event, you have to either remove it from the queue of the activity, or if the activity is running on that event, notify the scheduler to terminate the execution of the activity. Withdrawal of a workflow instance can only happen once the termination conditions are met, or if the user has requested to terminate the execution of the continuous workflow.

Continuous Workflow Patterns. In addition to the somewhat radical changes to the previously mentioned patterns, we now describe 4 patterns that are required in the context of Continuous Workflows.

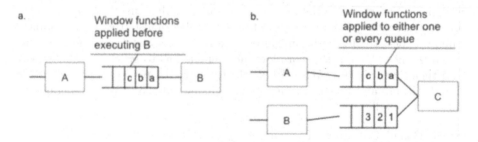

Fig. 6. (a) CWP1: Sequential aggreate and (b) CWP2: Stream-join

CWP1 Sequential Aggregate: A point in a workflow where two activities are to be run sequentially on a stream of events, one after the other. The later activity may need to run on the result of multiple invocations of the previous activity. The event results of the first activity are buffered in the second activity's queue. A function and/or window operations can be performed on a set of the resulting events as those are stored in the queue. The events in the queue can be involved in multiple invocations of the second activity until they are expired by the function. **Example:** Activity analyze_last_hour will analyze a one hour buffer of results produced by receive_temperature. The window function can also define the interval between invocation of the analysis part, like every 30 minutes.

CWP2 Stream-join: This pattern covers the case where each branch of the join activity is activated by a different stream of events. In this pattern the notion of event waves is not considered since the two streams are not synchronized. Again in this case the workflow can define functions on the individual queues. **Example:** In a travel agency application, activities receive_fares and receive_hotel_prices are joined into one stream by adding the prices.

CWP3 Stream-synch: A point in the workflow where two or more different event streams meet to get synchronized. The result is waves of events that are synchronized. This pattern is used to feed these waves to branches that require waves of events (see WP1-WP18). In CWP3, usually the slowest stream gives the pace and the other streams get sampled on some window of their events. **Example**: In a travel agency application, activities receive_fares and receive_hotel_prices are synchronized according to some window definitions, and split into pairs where the $hotel.price + fare.price < 300$. They are then handled individually but are considered part of the same wave.

CWP4 Workflow data view: This pattern refers to the ability to extract any kind of data being exchanged inside the continuous workflow and streamlining them into a separate event stream that can be used as an input to another workflow. An example usage of this pattern is to monitor the execution of the workflow and to debug it. Usually the views are not known at design time thus incorporating them into the workflow is not feasible. The view can be expressed as a set of predicates that can be evaluated on any arbitrary set of the data inside the workflow network. **Example**: Somewhere in the workflow an activity produces a result that is above expected values. The designer can add a view that will give her the message/event with the outlier value as soon as it is produced (i.e. $value > 100$). The message is annotated with meta-data regarding the activity it was last processed by.

4.3   Applicability of Continuous Workflow Patterns

We have evaluated the expressiveness of our continuous workflow model over a set of patterns which applies to the supply chain monitoring applications introduced in [6]. With the introduction of queues and window operators, designing those patterns is made much easier and it is more flexible.

In Figure 7, you can see two versions of the same pattern implemented using a Petri net approach and a Continuous Workflow approach. The pattern concerns the case where multiple occurrences of one event within a certain time period cause another event to occur. In the example shown if two out-of-stock events occur within a time period of T2 then a notification to the Supply Chain manager will be initiated. In Figure 7.a, transitions $t2$ and $t3$ wait for time interval $T2$ before consuming an event from either $e'1$ or $e''1$. This is used for expiring events that occurred time T2 ago. A notification by $t1$ is only fired if two events are allowed to coexist in $e'1$ and $e''1$.

In continuous workflows (Figure 7.b) this can be implemented by simple having a queue for Out-of-stock events and a window operator on that queue, which constructs windows of size $T2$. No step is defined thus the window is calculated for every new Out-of-stock event, and a notification is fired only if the window has two events in it (according to the precondition). Events are not deleted once used but they are eventually expired and handled by another activity, thus keeping the semantics of the two implementations the same. You can see that our implementation is much simpler. Moreover, if the designer wants to change the semantics and requires 3 out-of-stock events to happen before notifying the

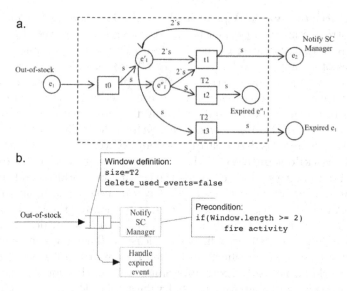

Fig. 7. (a) Petri net of "repeat cause-one effect" (b) Continuous workflow of "repeat cause-one effect"

supply chain manager, then, in the Petri net case she would have to add another transition like $t3$ and another like $t2$ and change the numbers on the arcs going to $t1$, from 2 to 3. In the continuous workflow case she would only have to change the precondition to $window.length >= 3$.

5   Conclusions and Future Work

In this paper we analyzed current workflow management systems' ability to enable the development of monitoring applications. A class of applications where it is possible for organizations to share resources and publish events, in order to enable real-time reaction management. We have shown where the existing WfMS's are lacking in functionality and proposed a new workflow enactment system which is capable of fulfilling the requirements of these applications. The new enactment model constitutes a paradigm shift from the traditional reactive model to one that is proactive towards multiple streams of events behaving in an almost random fashion.

Next on our agenda is to develop an architecture capable of enacting this new model, in an efficient and application centric way, and achieve the requested Quality of Results, in terms of response time, throughput and data quality. Three major challenges in this task: (1) Finding proper scheduling policies, that are able to handle different workflows and workloads, (2) Enable backwards compatibility with existing workflow definitions, in order to make the transition to the new model as smooth as possible, (3) Try to achieve maximum resource utilization in distributed environments, by integrating multiple workflow enactment systems and multiple resource providers (such as Grid computing platforms), thus enabling further inter-organizational collaborations, and (4) Provide a user interface to enable the participant of a collaboration, to collectively build and maintain collections of continuous workflows.

Acknowledgement

This research was supported in part by NIH-NIAID grant NO1-AI50018 and NSF grant IIS-0534531.

References

1. Berfield, A., Chrysanthis, P.K., Tsamardinos, I., Pollack, M.E., Banerjee, S.: A scheme for integrating e-services in establishing virtual enterprises. In: RIDE, pp. 134–142 (2002)
2. BPMI. Process modeling language (bpml) (2002), www.bpmi.org (accessed, november 2002)
3. Carney, D., Cetintemel, U., Cherniack, M., Convey, C., Lee, S., Seidman, G., Stonebraker, M., Tatbul, N., Zdonik, S.: Monitoring streams: A new class of data management applications. In: VLDB (2002)
4. Churches, D., Gombás, G., Harrison, A., Maassen, J., Robinson, C., Shields, M.S., Taylor, I.J., Wang, I.: Programming scientific and distributed workflow with triana services. Concurrency and Computation: Practice and Experience 18(10), 1021–1037 (2006)
5. Ramamritham, K., Chrysanthis, P.K.: Advances in concurrency control and transaction processing. IEEE Computer Society Press, Los Alamitos (1997)
6. Liu, R., Kumar, A., van der Aalst, W.M.P.: A formal modeling approach for supply chain event management. Decision Support Systems 43(3), 761–778 (2007)
7. Ludäscher, B., Altintas, I., Berkley, C., Higgins, D., Jaeger, E., Jones, M., Lee, E.A., Tao, J., Zhao, Y.: Scientific workflow management and the kepler system. Concurrency and Computation: Practice and Experience 18(10), 1039–1065 (2006)
8. OASIS. Web services businedd process execution language, http://docs.oasis-open.org/wsbpel/2.0/os/wsbpel-v2.0-os.html
9. Oinn, T.M., Addis, M., Ferris, J., Marvin, D., Senger, M., Greenwood, R.M., Carver, T., Glover, K., Pocock, M.R., Wipat, A., Li, P.: Taverna: a tool for the composition and enactment of bioinformatics workflows. Bioinformatics 20(17), 3045–3054 (2004)
10. Aalst Marlon Dumas, W.M.P., Arthur, H.M., Hofstede Petia, W.: Pattern based analysis of bpml (and wsci)
11. Patroumpas, K., Sellis, T.K.: Window specification over data streams. In: Grust, T., Höpfner, H., Illarramendi, A., Jablonski, S., Mesiti, M., Müller, S., Patranjan, P.-L., Sattler, K.-U., Spiliopoulou, M., Wijsen, J. (eds.) EDBT 2006. LNCS, vol. 4254, pp. 445–464. Springer, Heidelberg (2006)
12. Riehle, D., Züllighoven, H.: Understanding and using patterns in software development. TAPOS 2(1), 3–13 (1996)
13. Ruh, W.A., Maginnis, F.X., Brown, W.J.: Enterprise application integration: A wiley tech brief (2001)
14. Tucker, P.A., Maier, D., Sheard, T., Fegaras, L.: Exploiting punctuation semantics in continuous data streams. IEEE Trans. Knowl. Data Eng. 15(3), 555–568 (2003)

15. UN/CEFACT and OASIS. ebxml business process specification schema,
    www.ebxml.org/specs/ebbpss.pdf
16. van der Aalst, W.M.P., ter Hofstede, A.H.M.: Yawl: yet another workflow language.
    Inf. Syst. 30(4), 245–275 (2005)
17. van der Aalst, W.M.P., ter Hofstede, A.H.M., Kiepuszewski, B., Barros, A.P.:
    Workflow patterns. Distributed and Parallel Databases 14(1), 5–51 (2003)
18. W3C. Web services glossary, http://www.w3.org/tr/ws-gloss/
19. W3C. Service choreography interface (wsci) 1.0 (2002), www.w3.org/tr/wsci
20. WfMC. Workflow process definition interface - xml process definition language,
    http://www.wfmc.org/
21. WfMC. Workflow management coalition: Terminology & glossary (wfmc- tc-1011)
    (1999)
22. Wohed, P., van der Aalst, W.M.P., Dumas, M., ter Hofstede, A.H.M.: Analysis of
    web services composition languages: The case of bpel4ws. In: Song, I.-Y., Liddle,
    S.W., Ling, T.-W., Scheuermann, P. (eds.) ER 2003. LNCS, vol. 2813, pp. 200–215.
    Springer, Heidelberg (2003)

The RiverFish Approach to Business Process Modeling: Linking Business Steps to Control-Flow Patterns

Devanir Zuliane[1], Marcio K. Oikawa[1], Simon Malkowski[2], José Perez Alcazar[1], and João Eduardo Ferreira[1]

[1] Department of Computer Science, University of São Paulo,
Rua do Matão 1010, 05508-090 São Paulo, Brazil
{devanirz,koikawa,jperez,jef}@ime.usp.br
[2] Center of Experimental Research in Computer Systems,
Georgia Institute of Technology,
266 Ferst Drive, 30332-0765 Atlanta, USA
simon.malkowski@cc.gatech.edu

Abstract. Despite the recent advances in the area of Business Process Management (BPM), today's business processes have largely been implemented without clearly defined conceptual modeling. This results in growing difficulties for identification, maintenance, and reuse of rules, processes, and control-flow patterns. To mitigate these problems in future implementations, we propose a new approach to business process modeling using conceptual schemas, which represent hierarchies of concepts for rules and processes shared among collaborating information systems. This methodology bridges the gap between conceptual model description and identification of actual control-flow patterns for workflow implementation. We identify modeling guidelines that are characterized by clear phase separation, step-by-step execution, and process building through diagrams and tables. The separation of business process modeling in seven mutually exclusive phases clearly delimits information technology from business expertise. The sequential execution of these phases leads to the step-by-step creation of complex control-flow graphs. The process model is refined through intuitive table and diagram generation in each phase. Not only does the rigorous application of our modeling framework minimize the impact of rule and process changes, but it also facilitates the identification and maintenance of control-flow patterns in BPM-based information system architectures.

Keywords: business process management, conceptual schema, control-flow patterns, information systems, process modeling.

1 Introduction

With the advent of internet services a new way of making business has been introduced in many important markets. Today, numerous transactions that could

E. Bertino and J.B.D. Joshi (Eds.): CollaborateCom 2008, LNICST 10, pp. 179–193, 2009.
© ICST Institute for Computer Sciences, Social-Informatics and Telecommunications Engineering 2009

previously only be carried out in person (e.g., purchasing books, paying electricity bills, or participating in auctions) are readily available online. In order to remain competitive in the market, modern enterprises must adapt to this new way of making business in an effective way. However, the gathering of conceptual knowledge involved in the business processes of an enterprise is highly dependent on a clearly formulated acquisition framework and its rigorous enactment [7]. In other words, implementing business processes as workflows in information systems without thorough understanding of Business Process Management (BPM) methodology may result in severe problems.

This new business environment imposes particularly great challenges on large corporations with highly complex information system. Characteristically, these systems are composed of heterogeneous components that require collaboration to achieve high-level objectives. In this context, one of the major problems of classical business process languages is their implicit representation of hierarchical business step classification. Commonly, business steps are defined as atomic units of business processes, and they are inherently difficult to identify and classify correctly. We address this challenge through conceptual modeling, which is well established for mapping models and their relationships. Conceptual schema link the understanding of an organizational structure on various levels of abstraction and can incorporate different modeling concepts (e.g., the entity-relationship model or the UML class model [5]). Hence, they allow the specification of concept hierarchies and offer the necessary expressiveness for hierarchical business rule definition. Consequently, our approach introduces an explicit domain-layer that is well-structure, independent of framework, and independent of actual workflow implementation.

The main contribution of this paper is a new approach to business process modeling with direct integration of conceptual design. As an alternative to classical business process modeling, we base our work on a conceptual schema that enables the hierarchical classification of business process building blocks. This structured derivation of business steps is used for the identification of control-flow patterns in the underlying business processes. Concretely, we formulate the *RiverFish Conceptual Schema* based on our previous work on the RiverFish architecture [7,10]. We present a methodical step-by-step identification of underlying business steps, control-flow patterns, and business processes. The output of this approach constitutes the key input of successful business process implementation.

This five section paper is organized as follows. Section 2 discusses related works in the areas of business process and workflow management. In Section 3 we introduce our methodical foundation and describe the proposed conceptual schema along with the notion of control-flow patterns. Section 4 presents the guidelines that lead to the identification of control-flow patterns and business processes starting from the conceptual schema. We exemplify the application of this method in a simplified real collaborative information system case study. Finally, Section 5 concludes our findings and touches upon ongoing research.

2   Related Work

The representation and execution of business rules is a widely researched area. The predominant approaches are the design of specialized workflow languages [2, 3, 9] and large unifying methods of effective management of business processes [1, 13]. A workflow management system defines, creates, and manages the execution of workflows through the use of software running on one or more platforms [15]. Such systems are capable of interpreting the definition of processes, interacting with the participating users, and making (potentially necessary) external calls to tools and applications. Weske presents a comprehensive overview of the main concepts of BPM [13] . The emphasis lays on business process modeling, orchestration, and choreographies as well as business process properties, such as data dependencies and structural soundness. However, the derivation phase of business processes remains largely ambiguous in these references. They do not offer structured details about the identification of control-flow patterns or the composition of business steps into business processes. The methods used to quantify the actual business process flow in an enterprise are not explicitly discussed in any of these works. To this date, the identification of control-flow patterns has largely relied on the know-how of highly specialized and highly paid domain experts.

The necessity for rigorous methodologies in the BPM domain is well established and well understood. Hofstede et al. established three reasons for using the Petri net formalism in workflow specification [9]. Petri nets are formal; associate sophisticated analysis techniques with workflows; and are based on states rather than events. A detailed description of control-flow patterns based on Petri nets can be found in [3]. Nevertheless, the specification of all dependencies in control-flows remains a complex task and has led to the development of specifications such as Yet Another Workflow Language (YAWL) [4]. The latter addresses these challenges explicitly and emphasizes formal semantics in the transition systems.

Van der Aalst et al. have previously identified four different basic mechanisms in process management: sequence, selection, parallelism and iteration [3]. All of them are common in practice, and the authors infer that comprehensive real-world workflow functionality can be exhaustively modeled using these four mechanisms. The authors' main goal is to enable a comparative analysis between all major languages for business process specification and aid in business process modeling. Accordingly, they classify the control-flow patterns into six categories: basic control-flow; advanced branching and synchronization; structural; multiple instance; state-based; and cancellation. This work led to the foundation of the Workflow Patterns Initiative (www.workflowpatterns.com) at the 4th International Conference on Cooperative Information Systems (IFCIS 99). Today, many academic and technological results have contributed to the growth of the control-flow pattern repository, which spans over 100 patterns in control-flow, data and resource approaches. These patterns helped to define evaluations of UML 2.0 Activity Diagrams and Business Process Modeling Notation (BPMN) [14]. Although these efforts are closely related to the research presented in this paper, our work is orthogonal. While we focus on the methodological identification of control-flow in a real information system environment, the previously discussed approaches deal with the comparison and definition of workflow structures. Although control-flow patterns have had a significant impact on the field of workflow technology, their derivation and design remain a loosely structured process in the cited references. In general, there has been very little concern with the derivation and classification of business processes and rules. Even large initiatives such as BPMN [14] do not address this issue.

3   Foundation

3.1   Control-Flow Patterns

The notion of categorizing workflow management systems through patterns identified by four basic mechanisms in the process structure was introduced by van der Aalst et al. [3]. The authors argue that their systematic methodology enables reasoning about suitability and expressiveness of workflow frameworks. We utilize this method and adopt van der Aalst's approach in our work. Therefore, understanding the implications of control-flow patterns is an important prerequisite to understanding the RiverFish Conceptual Schema. Unfortunately, it is not an easy task to provide a thorough explanation using only few pages. Interested readers should refer to the original reference [3] for a comprehensive presentation and a detailed discussion. We confine ourselves to a sampled overview in Figure 1 and three brief examples in the following.

1. Patterns 4 and 16 in Figure 1 are called *Exclusive* and *Deferred Choice*, respectively. If the choice is exclusive, one of several activity branches is chosen based on decision or on workflow data. If the choice is deferred, it is not made explicitly. All alternatives are offered to the environment, which chooses only one of them for execution.
2. Pattern 8 in Figure 1 represents the *Multi-Merge*. This pattern constitutes "[...] a point in a workflow process where two or more branches re-converge without synchronization. If more than one branch gets activated, possibly concurrently, the activity following the merge is started for every activation of every incoming branch" [3].
3. Pattern 9 in Figure 1 is called the *Discriminator*. According to [3] it represents "[...] a point in a workflow process that waits for one of the incoming branches to complete before activating the subsequent activity. From that moment on it waits for all remaining branches to be completed and ignores them".

3.2   RiverFish Conceptual Schema

The RiverFish Conceptual Schema is founded on the concepts of the River-Fish architecture [7, 10] and on the classification of business rules proposed by von Halle [8]. A business rule is a declaration that restricts certain aspects of a business in order to define its structure or control its behavior [12]. Business rules are inherent to any type of business process and can be classified in the following four types [8].

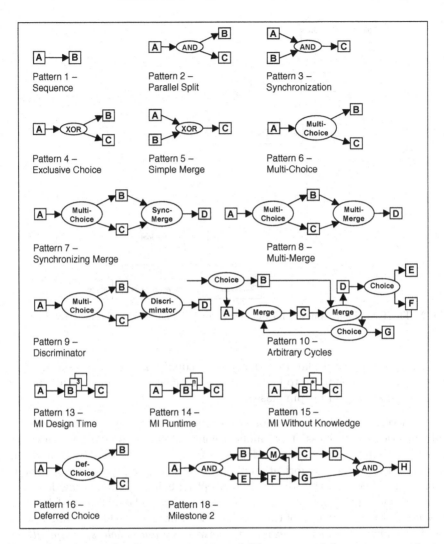

Fig. 1. Sample graphical representations of fifteen control-flow patterns adapted from [3]

1. A *constraint* is a declaration that expresses an unconditional circumstance, which must be either true or false (e.g., to be selected, a company must be authorized).
2. An *action enabler* is a declaration that verifies conditions, and some action is initiated in case the conditions are true (e.g., if the contributor's record is not on file, then execute the filling of the record).
3. A *computation* is a declaration that supplies an algorithm to calculate a term after verifying some conditions (e.g., if there is a record for the selected model, then consider the initial numbering to be the increment of the previous number).

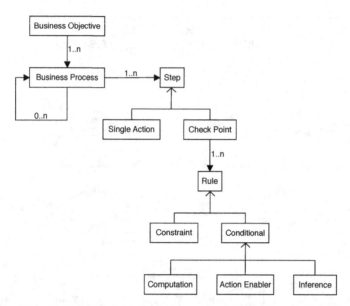

Fig. 2. The RiverFish Conceptual Schema, which extends the original RiverFish approach

4. An *inference* is a declaration that tests a condition and declares a new fact if it finds the condition to be true (e.g., if a client is a regular client, then he gets a discount on his purchases).

The RiverFish architecture represents request processing through modeling and execution of business steps under a common business goal [10]. However, RiverFish itself does not detail the differences between rules, validations and constraints. As such, the categorization of business rules in a given process remains ambiguous. Therefore, the RiverFish Conceptual Schema extends the definition of the business process *check point* using a common classification of business rules [8]. Careful evaluation of this classification approach yields the understanding of the inherent structural similarity between *action enablers, computations,* and *inferences*. Their characteristic similarity can be expressed in an intuitively clear format; i.e., If <condition>, Then <action>. Consequently, it is possible to group all types of business rules into solely two categories from the conceptual point of view; i.e., *constraints* and *conditionals*. Constraints can be modeled and defined by a single validation; i.e., "a certain condition must be true". Hence, this validation can easily be represented using first order logic or logic based on frames. On the other hand, the only difference between rules that are conditionals (i.e., action enabler, computation and inference) lays in the action to be executed in case the condition is true. The resulting schema is illustrated in Figure 2.

By comparing the conceptual schema approach to the initial RiverFish architecture, it becomes apparent that the adaptation occurred only at the rule level, preserving the entire previous structure. This is justified by the fact that the

Table 1. The characteristics and details of all business rule types

Rule Type	Conditional Type	Structure	Detail
Constraint	%	`<condition> =` `true or false`	`<condition>` is a logical expression
Conditional	Action Enabler	`If <condition>` `Then <action>`	`<action>` executes a procedure
	Computation	`If <condition>` `Then <action>`	`<action>` calls an algorithm for computation
	Inference	`If <condition>` `Then <action>`	`<action>` calls an execution to enable another rule

original architecture proposed a generic approach to controlling the processing of business rules. The details of all rule types of are given in Table 1.

4   From Business Steps to Control-Flow Patterns

To illustrate the proposed guidelines we present a simplified case study with an appropriate level of complexity to allow some scenario diversity. The electronic AIDF (a Portuguese acronym for Authorization to Print Fiscal Documents) is a large authorization system. Contributors make requests to the Finance Ministry of the state of São Paulo (SEFAZ) to print authorized fiscal documents. SEFAZ receives all requests from all contributors and chooses to approve or to decline them after a selective analysis. Because of space constraints, details about this process were omitted in this paper. Tables 2 to 5 present the main aspects of the AIDF case study.

Despite the RiverFish Conceptual Schema providing the hierarchy of business steps, checkpoints, and rules, this is not sufficient to identify the execution ordering for the entire business process. More concretely, there is a transition gap between conceptual schema and control-flow patterns. We provide this missing link through a phase model summarized in Figure 3. The main characteristics of the guidelines are listed in the following.

1. Separation of business process modeling in seven phases that characterize and delimit the business and information technology expertise;
2. Step-by-step application of these phases to generate the complex control-flow graphs;
3. Derivation of the process model through tables and diagrams generated in each phase.

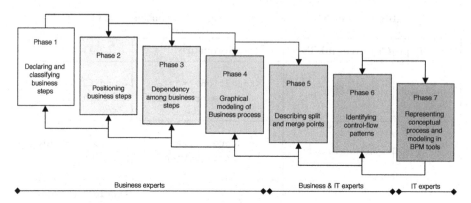

Fig. 3. Guidelines for business process conceptual modeling

In the rest of this section we give details for each of the seven phases and describe them in the context of the AIDF case study.

4.1 Declaring and Classifying Business Steps (Phase 1)

The first phase has the objective to declare and to classify the business steps of the RiverFish Conceptual Schema described in Section 3.2. The declaration of business steps seeks to turn all the steps that compose a business process explicit without worrying about the identification of control-flow structures (such as operators of sequences and alternative compositions). Table 2 presents an example of a purchasing business process with several steps composed in an arbitrary order.

After the declaration of business steps, they are classified into single actions and checkpoints. Checkpoints can be either constraints or conditional rules. In the business process example presented in Table 2, step D (i.e., "Validate driver ID") is a constraint rule because the validation is impossible without ID following

Table 2. Declaration of business steps

Step	Declaration
A	Generate data form
B	Fill out and send data form
C	Store data form
D	Validate driver ID
E	Update user data
F	Generate list of products for sale
G	Prohibit sale for younger than 18
H	Inform customer's fidelity
I	Calculate saving for customer
J	Calculate the purchase total
K	Finish the purchase

Table 3. Classification of business steps

Step	Declaration	Classification
A	Generate data form	Single action
B	Fill out and send data form	Single action
C	Store data form	Single action
D	Validate driver ID	*Constraint*
E	Update user data	Single action
F	Generate list of products for sale	Single action
G	Prohibit sale for younger than 18	*Constraint*
H	Inform customer's fidelity	Single action
I	Calculate saving for customer	Single action
J	Calculate the purchase total	Single action
K	Finish the purchase	Single action

Table 4. Step recomposition

Step	Declaration	Classification
A	Generate data form	Single action
B	Fill out and send data form	Single action
C	Store data form	Single action
D	Validate driver ID	*Constraint*
E	Prohibit sale for younger than 18	*Constraint*
F	Re-submission in case of invalid ID or younger than 18	Single action
G	Update user data	Single action
H	Generate list of products for sale	Single action
I	Inform customer's fidelity	Single action
J	Calculate saving for customer	Single action
K	Calculate the purchase total	Single action
L	Finish the purchase	Single action

a purchase. On the other hand, step H (i.e., "Inform customers fidelity") is a conditional rule. If step H is true then the computation step I (i.e., "Calculate saving for customer") is taken. Step G is another constraint-checkpoint because it prohibits the sale based on age limit. The classification of business steps directly aids in the business process control-flow ordering. Nevertheless, during the first phase only the constraint steps are clearly identified. In our example, all other steps are classified as single actions in order to facilitate the notation. Table 3 presents the resulting classification of business steps belonging to Table 2.

4.2 Positioning Business Steps (Phase 2)

A step classified as constraint check point can generate interrupts in the execution of business control-flows. This kind of check point only allows true responses to continue. The main goal in this phase is repositioning constraint-checkpoints whenever possible to the beginning of a control-flow. In our case study, the new step F is added for the handling of a false answers. Its sole purpose is to jump back to the start. This step repositioning reduces the effects caused by false answers at constraint check points. Table 4 shows the effect of step repositioning in the case study.

4.3   Dependency among the Business Steps (Phase 3)

This phase identifies the interdependencies among all steps. Table 5 presents the business step dependencies in our example. The notation X→Y defines Y as dependent on X. According to Table 5, steps C, D, E, and G have more than one dependency. Hence, they are called split points.

4.4   Graphical Modeling of Business Process (Phase 4)

In this phase, we use four basic connectors (illustrated in Figure 4) to generate the graphical modeling of business processes. With the help of these operators each business step has to be linked according to its dependency relationships. Figure 5 shows the results of this phase in the case study. This visual insight clearly reveals sequential and parallel business steps. However, it does not show the details for selection and synchronism mechanisms determining split and merge points. Capturing and declaring the behavior of split and merge points is fundamental to identifying and classifying underlying control-flow patterns. Nevertheless, in this phase we simply confine the labeling to integer numbers and leave the detailed identification for the next phase.

Table 5. Examples of business step dependencies

Step	Declaration	Classification	Dependency
Start			(Start)→A
A	Generate data form	Single action	A→B
B	Fill out and send data form	Single action	B→C
C	Store data form	Single action	C→D and C→E
D	Validate driver ID	*Constraint*	D→G or D→F
E	Prohibit sale for younger than 18	*Constraint*	E→G or E→F
F	Re-submission in case of invalid ID or younger than 18	Single action	F→(Start)
G	Update user data	Single action	G→H or G→J
H	Generate list of products for sale	Single action	H→I
I	Inform customer's fidelity	Single action	I→L
J	Calculate saving for customer	Single action	J→K
K	Calculate the purchase total	Single action	K→L
L	Finish the purchase	Single action	L→(End)
End			

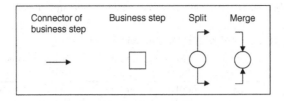

Fig. 4. Four basic connectors

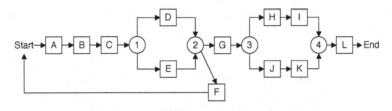

Fig. 5. Control-flow with dependencies

4.5   Describing the Split and Merge Points (Phase 5)

In general, split and merge points are classifieded by their selection mechanism. For instance, there are many possibilities for split execution of steps D and E.

1. D and E initialize in any order;
2. D and E initialize simultaneously;
3. E initializes after D;
4. D initializes after E.

The same applies to merge synchronization after the execution of D and E. There are the following four possibilities.

1. Waiting for the simultaneous execution of D and E to enable F or G;
2. Waiting for the execution of D or E enables F or G;
3. Waiting for the execution of D enables F or G without waiting for E;
4. Waiting for the execution of E enables F or G without waiting for D.

Table 6 describes the actual behavior for each point in our case study.

4.6   Identifying Control-Flow Patterns (Phase 6)

For Phase 6, it is important to understand the behavior of the control-flow patterns introduced in Section 3.1 and depicted in Figure 1. Using these patterns and the descriptions in Table 6, each split and merge point is matched to the best-fitting control-flow pattern. The resulting matching is shown in Table 7.

After identification, the corresponding control-flow pattern numbers are added to the dependency graph as shown in Figure 7. This graphical representation shows

Table 6. Behavior declaration for split and merge points

Label	Split	Merge	Behavior Declaration
1	√		Steps D and E can be executed simultaneously or in any order.
2		√	After executing D and E, it is possible to enable G. If either D or E are not true, F is enabled.
3	√		We can choose steps H after J, J after H, or the simultaneous execution of H and J and any possible combination of I and K afterwards.
4		√	If I, K, or I and K execution has completed, it is possible to enable L.

Table 7. Identification of control-flow patterns

Label	Control-flow Pattern	Number
1	Parallel split	Pattern 2
2	Synchronizing merge	Pattern 7
3	Multi choice	Pattern 6
4	Multi merge	Pattern 8

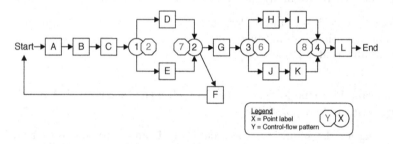

Fig. 6. The final result of the business processes modeling

the final output of the classification and identification process. These business processes can now be used as input of the implementation in information systems.

4.7 Representing Process Modeling in BPM Tools (Phase 7)

The implementation of the case study in phase 7 was carried out using BPM tools; however, it is out scope of this paper to show all details of this implementation. Instead, Table 8 lists all steps that were part of the actual implementation. All described steps are part of the authorization process for each AIDF request. The alias in the first column of Table 8 was established to facilitate the rule

Table 8. Steps of the AIDF business process

Alias	Description	Type
R1	The selected print shop must be **active** in SEFAZ;	Constraint
R2	The CNPJ of the print shop must be **valid**;	Constraint
R3	If the request is centralized, put the appropriate rules into action;	Action enabler
R4	The selected print shop must be **active** in SEFAZ;	Constraint
R5	The contributor must be **active** in SEFAZ;	Constraint
R6	If the contributor does not have a concluded record, verify that his record is on file;	Inference
R7	If the contributor has a record on file that is not concluded, execute the conclusion of the record;	Action enabler
R8	The selected print shop must be certified for the selected document;	Constraint
R9	If the models for the selected documents are allowed by the contributors National Classification of Economic Activities (CNAE), execute rule R10;	Inference
R10	If there is a record for the filtered models and the emission process is electronic, load the information on model, series, and subseries that are recorded in the Electronic System of Data Processing (SEPD);	Action enabler
R11	If there is a record for the filtered models, and the emission process is *not* electronic, load the information on the series and subseries;	Action enabler
R12	If there is a record for the selected model, series, and subseries, the initial Number equals the last printed number incremented by one;	Computation
R13	If the amount of copies informed is lower than the default amount recorded for the chosen model, execute rule R14;	Inference
R14	The contributor must have a justification to request unusual number of copies;	Constraint
R15	The operation field must be formatted with the default of the chosen model;	Constraint
R16	When emitted using the manual process, the fiscal documents in series B, C, D, and F must inform the destination of the subseries per operation as per the table;	Computation
R17	If the type of print-out is a PAD, the information Receipts per receipt pad should equal 20, 25, 30, 40, 50, or 100;	Computation
R18	The Amount of receipt pads should be equal to the amount of fiscal documents divided by the number of receipts per receipt pad;	Constraint
R19	If the counting process is **simple**, message one must be printed into the document;	Computation

Table 8. (*continued*)

Alias	Description	Type
R20	If the counting process is `electronic`, messages two and three must be printed onto the document;	Computation
R21	If the counting process is `electronic` and the request is `distributed`, message four must be printed onto the document;	Computation
R22	If the previous process executes `ok`, make the final number equal to the initial number plus the requested amount minus one.	Computation

manipulation. All rules were identified, grouped together, and classified according to von Halle [8]. The classification is listed in the third column of the table.

5 Conclusion

This paper has presented an alternative for classification of business processes and control-flow pattern identification, which constitutes the starting point for the implementation of business processes. We have adopted an approach based on conceptual modeling through conceptual schemas. This allows representing, analyzing, and documenting business processes in an application independent layer. Through the RiverFish Conceptual Schema, we avoid the coupling of rules and processes with code. This facilitates the adaptation and the handling of rules and processes in the actual application.

Another benefit of this approach is the formal representation of business rules that allows their systematic manipulation and automation. The methodology proposed in this work divides the complex task of business process modeling into seven phases and clearly delimits the actions taken by experts from different areas (i.e., business or IT). A step-by-step discovery of business dependencies allows identification of control-flow patterns, and resolves the complex identification of control-flows in business processes.

Our ongoing work includes the development of semi-automated algorithm planners and pattern recognition techniques for identifying control-flow patterns in business process modeling.

Acknowledgment

This work has been partially supported by FAPESP (São Paulo State Research Foundation) and CAPES (Brazilian Coordination for Improvement of Higher Level Personnel).

References

1. ABLE Project Team IBM T. J. Watson Research Center: ABLE Rule Language, User's Guide and Reference, Version 2.0.1 (October 2003)
2. van der Aalst, W.M.P., Berens, P.J.S.: Beyond workflow management: product-driven case handling. In: GROUP 2001: Proceedings of the 2001 International ACM SIGGROUP Conference on Supporting Group Work, pp. 42–51. ACM, New York (2001)
3. van der Aalst, W.M.P., ter Hofstede, A.H.M., Kiepuszewski, B., Barros, A.P.: Workflow patterns. Distributed and Parallel Databases 14(1), 5–51 (2003)
4. van der Aalst, W.M.P., ter Hofstede, A.H.M.: YAWL: Yet another workflow language. Inf. Syst. 30(4), 245–275 (2005)
5. Batini, C., Ceri, S., Navathe, S.B.: Conceptual database design: an Entity-relationship approach. Benjamin-Cummings Publishing Co., Inc., Redwood City (1992)
6. Braghetto, K.R., Ferreira, J.E., Pu, C.: Using control-flow patterns for specifying business processes in cooperative environments. In: Cho, Y., Wainwright, R.L., Haddad, H., Shin, S.Y., Koo, Y.W. (eds.) SAC, pp. 1234–1241. ACM, New York (2007)
7. Ferreira, J.E., Takai, O.K., Pu, C.: Integration of collaborative information system in internet applications using riverfish architecture. In: CollaborateCom. IEEE, Los Alamitos (2005)
8. Halle, B.V.: Business Rules Applied: Building Better Systems Using the Business Rules Approach. John Wiley & Sons, Inc, New York (2001); Foreword By-Ronald G. Ross.
9. Hofstede, A.H.M.T., Weske, M.: Business process management: A survey. In: van der Aalst, W.M.P., ter Hofstede, A.H.M., Weske, M. (eds.) BPM 2003. LNCS, vol. 2678, pp. 1–12. Springer, Heidelberg (2003)
10. Ferreira, J.E., Takai, O.K., Braghetto, K.R., Pu, C.: Large scale order processing through navigation plan concept. In: IEEE SCC, pp. 297–300. IEEE Computer Society Press, Los Alamitos (2006)
11. Motta, E.: Reusable Components for Knowledge Modelling: Case Studies in Parametric Design Problem Solving. IOS Press, Amsterdam (1999)
12. The Business Rules Group: Defining business rules - what are they really? (July 2000), http://www.businessrulesgroup.org
13. Weske, M.: Business Process Management: Concepts, Languages, Architectures. Springer, Heidelberg (2007)
14. White, S.: Business process modeling notation (BPMN). Business Process Management Initiative (BPMI)–Version 1.0–BPMI.org (2004)
15. Workflow Management Coalition (WfMC): resource page (September 2008), http://www.wfmc.org

A Federated Digital Identity Management Approach for Business Processes

Elisa Bertino, Rodolfo Ferrini, Andrea Musci, Federica Paci,
and Kevin J. Steuer

CS Department and CERIAS, Purdue University, West Lafayette IN 47907, USA
{bertino,rferrini,amusci,paci,ksteuer}@cs.purdue.edu

Abstract. Business processes have gained a lot of attention because of
the pressing need for integrating existing resources and services to better
fulfill customer needs. A key feature of business processes is that they
are built from composable services, referred to as *component services*,
that may belong to different domains. In such a context, flexible multi-
domain identity management solutions are crucial for increased security
and user-convenience. In particular, it is important that during the execution of a business process the component services be able to verify the
identity of the client to check that it has the required permissions for
accessing the services. To address the problem of multi-domain identity
management, we propose a multi-factor identity attribute verification
protocol for business processes that assures clients privacy and handles
naming heterogeneity.

Keywords: identity management, business process, naming heterogeneity, interoperability.

1 Introduction

Business processes have gained a lot of attention because of the pressing need
for integrating existing resources and services to better fulfill customer needs.
A key feature of business processes is that they are built from composable services, referred to as *component services*, that may belong to different domains. In
such a context, flexible multi-domain identity management solutions are crucial
for increased security and user-convenience. In particular, it is important that
during the execution of a business process the component services be able to
verify the identity of the client to check that it has the required permissions for
accessing the services. Clients identity consists of data, referred to as *identity
attributes*, that encode relevant-security properties of the clients. The management of identity attributes in business processes raises however a number of
challenges. On one hand, to enable authentication, the propagation of client's
identity attributes across the component services should be facilitated. On the
other hand, identity attributes need to be protected as they may convey sensitive information about a client and can be target of attacks. Moreover, because
business processes orchestrate the functions of services belonging to different domains, interoperability issues may arise in client authentication processes. Such

E. Bertino and J.B.D. Joshi (Eds.): CollaborateCom 2008, LNICST 10, pp. 194–206, 2009.

issues range from the use of different identity tokens and different identity negotiation protocols, such as the client-centric protocols and the identity-providers
centric protocols, to the use of different names for identity attributes. The use of
different names for identity attributes, that we refer to as *naming heterogeneity*,
typically occurs because clients and component services use a different vocabulary to denote identity attribute names. In this case, whenever a component
service requests from a client a set of identity attributes to verify its identity,
the client may not understand which identity attributes it has to provide.

To address the problem of multi-domain identity management, we propose a
multi-factor identity attribute verification protocol for business processes that
assures clients privacy and handles naming heterogeneity. The protocol uses an
identity attribute names matching technique based on look-up tables, dictionaries and ontology mapping, to match component services and clients vocabularies
and aggregate zero knowledge proofs of knowledge (AgZKPK) cryptographic
protocol to allow clients to prove with a single interactive proof the knowledge
of multiple identity attributes without the need to provide them in clear.

The rest of the paper is organized as follows. Section 2 introduces a running
example that is used throughout the paper to illustrate the discussion. Section
3 discusses the main issues related to digital identity management for business
processes. Section 4 introduces the notions on which our multi-factor identity
attribute verification protocol is based. Section 5 presents the multi-factor identity attribute verification protocol. Section 6 discusses the system architecture.
Section 7 reports experimental results. Finally, Section 8 concludes the paper
and outlines some future work.

2   Running Example

In this section we introduce an example of business process that implements a loan
approval process (see Figure 1). Customers of the service send loan requests. Once

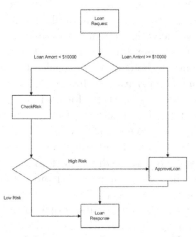

Fig. 1. A loan approval process specification

a request is received, the loan service executes a simple process resulting in either a "loan approved" message or a "loan rejected" message. The decision is based on the amount requested and the risk associated with the customer. For amounts lower than 10,000\$ a streamlined process is used. In the streamlined process low-risk customers are automatically approved. For higher amounts, or medium and high-risk customers, the credit request requires further processing. For each request, the loan service uses the functions provided by two other services. In the streamlined process, used for low amount loans, a *risk assessment* service is used to obtain a quick evaluation of the risk associated with the customer. A full *loan approval* service (possibly requiring direct involvement of a loan expert) is used to obtain an assessment about the customer when the streamlined approval process is not applicable. Four main activities are involved in the process:

- `Loan Request` allows a client to submit a loan request to the bank
- `Check Risk` (provided by *risk assessment* service) computes the risk associated with the loan request
- `Approve Loan` (provided by *loan approval* service) determines if the loan request can be approved or rejected
- `Loan Response` sends to the client the result of the loan request evaluation process

risk assessment and *loan approval* services require a set of identity attributes from the client who has submitted the loan request. The risk assessment service asks *DrivingLicense*, *CarRegistration* and *EmployeeID*, whereas the loan approval service requires *EmployeeID* and *CreditCard*.

3   Identity Management for Business Processes

Managing and verifying clients identity in a business processes raise a number of challenging issues. A first issue is related to how the client's identity attribute have to be managed within the business process. The client of a business process is not aware that the business process that implements the required service invokes some component services. The client thus trusts the composite service but not the component services. Therefore, every time the component services have to verify the client's identity, the composite service has to act as an intermediary between the component services and the client. Moreover, since the client's identity attributes may contain sensitive information and clients usually do not trust the component services, the client's identity attributes should be protected from potential misuse by component services.

Another issue is related to how the identity verification process is performed. Because component services belong to different domains, each with its own identity verification policies, the sets of identity attributes required to verify client's identity may partially or totally overlap. Therefore, the client has to prove several times the knowledge of the same subset of identity attributes. It is thus important to take advantage of previous client identity verification processes that other component services have performed.

Finally, another issue is the lack of interoperability because of naming heterogeneity. Naming heterogeneity occurs when component services define their identity verification policies according to a vocabulary different from the one adopted by clients. Therefore, component services and clients are not able to have "meaningful" interactions because they do not understand each other. Thus, it is also necessary that client identity verification process supports an approach to match identity attribute names of component services and clients vocabularies. In such respect, a first question to be addressed is which matching technique to use, which in turn depends from the types of variation in identity attribute names. A second question is related to the matching protocol to use, that is, by which party the matching has to be performed and whether the fact that a client has already performed a matching with a component service may help in a subsequent matching.

To address such issues we propose a multi-factor identity attribute verification protocol for business processes that supports a privacy usage of clients identity attributes and that guarantees interoperable interactions between clients and component services. In what follows, we provide more details about our approach.

4   Preliminary Concepts

To enable multi-factor identity attribute verification, clients have to register their identity attributes to a *registrar* [1]. The registrar is an additional component in digital identity management systems that stores and manage information related to identity attributes. For each client's identity attribute m, the registrar records an identity tuple $(\sigma_i, M_i, tag, validity - assurance, ownership - assurance, \{W_{ij}\})$. Each identity tuple consists of tag, an attribute descriptor, the Pedersen commitment [5] of m, denoted as M_i, the signature of the registrar on M, denoted as σ_i, two types of assurance, namely *validity assurance* and *ownership assurance* and a set of weak identifiers $\{W_{ij}\}$. M_i is computed as $g^m h^r$, where g and h are generators in a group G of prime order q. G and q are public parameters of the registrar and r is chosen randomly from $\mathbb{Z}_q$. Validity assurance corresponds to the confidence about the validity of the identity attribute based on the verification performed at the identity attribute's original issuer. Ownership assurance corresponds to the confidence about the claim that the principal presenting an identity attribute is its true owner.

Weak identifiers are used to denote identity attributes that can be aggregated together to perform multi-factor authentication. The identity tuples of each registered client can be retrieved from the registrar by the component services or the registrar can release to the client a certificate containing its identity record.

We assume that each of the component services define their identity verification policies by specifying a set of identity attribute names that have to be required from the client.

Because of naming heterogeneity, clients may not understand component services identity verification policies. The type of variations that can occur in clients and component services identity attribute names can be classified in: *syntactic*, *terminological* and *semantic* variations.

- *Syntactic variations* arise because of the use of different character combinations to denote the same term. An example is the use of "CreditCard" and "Credit_Card" to denote a client's credit card.
- *Terminological variations* refer to the use of different terms to denote the same concept. An example of terminological variation is the use of the synonyms "Credit Card" and "Charge Card" to refer a client's credit card.
- *Semantic variations* are related to the use of two different concepts in different knowledge domains to denote the same term.

Syntactic variations can be identified by using look up tables. A look up table enumerates the possible ways in which the same term can be written by using different character combinations. In detecting terminological variations, dictionaries or thesaurus such as WordNet[6] can be exploited. Finally, semantic variations can be determined by using ontology matching techniques. An ontology is a formal representation of a domain in terms of concepts and properties with which those concepts are related. Ontologies can be exploited to define a domain of interest and for reasoning about its features. Ontology mapping is the process whereby two ontologies are semantically related at conceptual level; source ontology concepts are mapped onto the target ontology concepts according to those semantic relations [4]. Typically an ontology matching algorithm takes in input two ontologies O_i and O_j, and returns a set of triples of the form $\langle c_i, c_j, s \rangle$, where c_i is a concept belonging to ontology O_i, c_j is a concept belonging to ontology O_j that matches concept c_i, and s is a *confidence score*, that is, a value between 0 and 1, indicating the similarity between the matched concepts.

To enable the matching of identity attributes by using the above techniques, we make the following assumptions. Component services' identity verification policies are defined according to their domain vocabulary ontology. Moreover, they track existing mappings with other component services' ontologies. Such mappings are formally represented by tuples of the following form:

$$\langle O_{CS}, CS', O_{CS'}, \{\langle c_1, c_2, s_{1,2} \rangle, \ \ldots, \langle c_l, c_m, s_{l,m} \rangle\} \rangle$$

where O_{CS} is the ontology of a component service CS, CS' is a component service whose ontology $O_{CS'}$ matches ontology O_{CS} and $\{\langle c_1, c_2, s_{1,2} \rangle, \ldots, \langle c_l, c_m, s_{l,m} \rangle\}$ is the set of concepts mappings $\langle c_i, c_j, s_{i,j} \rangle$ where $c_i \in O_{CS}$ and $c_j \in O_{CS'}$. Moreover, each component service keeps a look up table containing alternative character combinations and store a set of synonyms, denoted as *Synset*, for each of the identity attribute names used for expressing its identity verification policies. Finally, since we want to avoid that the client proves several times the possession of a same set of identity attributes, we assume that component services have a PKI infrastructure that allows them to issue certificates to clients. These certificates (see Definition 1 below) assert that an identity attribute by a client matches an identity attribute by a component service and that the component service has verified that the client owns the attribute. Clients can use these certificates to prove that they own a set of identity attributes without going through the authentication process during the execution of the same business process instance in which the certificates have been released. Instead, clients can use the certificates in business processes different from the one in which the certificate have been issued to prove there is a mapping between a set of client's attributes and a service's ontology. This distinction is motivated by the fact that there is a trust relationship between the component services in the same business process instance, that may not exist with services external to the process.

Definition 1 (Proof-of-Identity Certificate). *Let S be a component service participating to a business process BP and C be a client. Let O_S be the ontology describing the domain of S and $AttrSet$ be the set of C's identity attribute names. The proof of identity certificate released by S to C upon a successful verification is a tuple $\langle Issuer, Owner, OID, Mappings, IssuanceDate \rangle$ where: Issuer is the identifier of S, Owner is the identifier of C, OID is O_S ontology identifier, $Mappings$ is a set of tuples of the form $\langle Attr, Concept \rangle$ where $Attr \in AttrSet$ and $Concept \in O_S$, and IssuanceDate is the release date of the certificate.*

Besides being stored by the clients, proof-of-identity certificates released during the execution of a business process instance are stored in a local repository, denoted as $CertRep$, by the composite service for the whole process execution.

5   Interoperable Multi-factor Authentication

In this section, we present a multi-factor authentication protocol for business processes. The protocol takes place between a client, the composite service and a component service. Since the client is not aware of the component services, the composite service has to mediate the interactions between them. The protocol consists of two phases that make use of the notion of proof-of-identity certificate introduced in the previous section (see Figure 2). In the first phase, the component service matches the identity attributes of clients vocabulary with its own attributes to help the client understand its identity verification policy. In the second phase, the client carries out an aggregate ZKPK protocol to prove to the component service the knowledge of the matched identity attributes. Algorithm 1 summarizes the different phases of the protocol.

5.1   Identity Attribute Matching Protocol

The technique that we have developed for matching identity attribute names from different vocabularies is based on the combined use of look-up tables, dictionaries, and ontology mapping.

As we have already mentioned, an important issue is which party has to execute the matching. In our context, the matching can be executed by the client, the composite service or the component services. Performing the matching at the client has the obvious drawback that the client may lie and asserts that an identity attribute referred to in the component services policy matches one of its attribute, whereas this is not the case. The matching process cannot be performed by the composite service because it should have access to information which are local to the component services. Therefore, in our approach, the matching is performed by the component services. Notice that because of the privacy-preserving protocol that we use (see next section), the composite service and the component services will not learn the values of the identity attributes of the client and therefore do not have incentives to lie.

Algorithm 1: Multi-factor verification protocol

Input: $CertRep$: proof-of-identity certificates repository
$AttrProof$: set of identity attributes requested from the client
Output: c_i: proof-of-identity certificate

(1)   **foreach** $a_i \in AttrProof$
(2)   **if** $\exists c_j \in CertRep$ such that c_j prove the knowledge of a_i
(3) a_i is verified
(4)   **else**
(5)   Match a_i with client's proof-of-identity certificates
(6)   Verify AgZKPK
(7)   Release new proof-of-identity certificate c_i
(8)   Store c_i in $CertRep$

A second issue is how to take advantage of previous interactions that the client has performed with other component services. It is also important to exploit mappings that can exist between ontologies by different component services. To address such issue, the matching protocol relies on the use of the proof-of-identity certificates and matching techniques. We assume that $AttrProof$ is the set of identity attributes that a component service asks to a client to verify its identity. The identity attribute name matching process is carried out between the client, the component service and the composite service when some attributes in $AttrProof$ do not match any of the attributes in $AttrSet$, the set of clients' identity attributes. We refer to the set of component service's identity attributes that do not match a client attribute name to as $NoMatchingAttr$. The matching process consists of two main phases. The goal of the first phase is to match the identity attributes that have syntactical and terminological variations. During this phase, the component service sends to the composite service, for each identity attribute a_i in the $NoMatchingAttr$ set, the set $Synset_i$ that contains a set of alternative character combinations and a set of synonyms. Thus, the composite service sends the sets $Synset_i$ to the client. The client verifies that for each identity attribute a_i, there is an intersection between $Synset_i$ and $AttrSet$. If this is the case attribute a_i is removed from $NoMatchingAttr$. Otherwise, if $NoMatchingAttr$ is not empty, the second phase is performed. During the second phase the client sends $CertSet$, the set of its proof-of-identity certificates to the composite service that forwards them to the component service. Thus, in the second phase of the matching process the component service tries to match the concepts corresponding to the identity attributes the

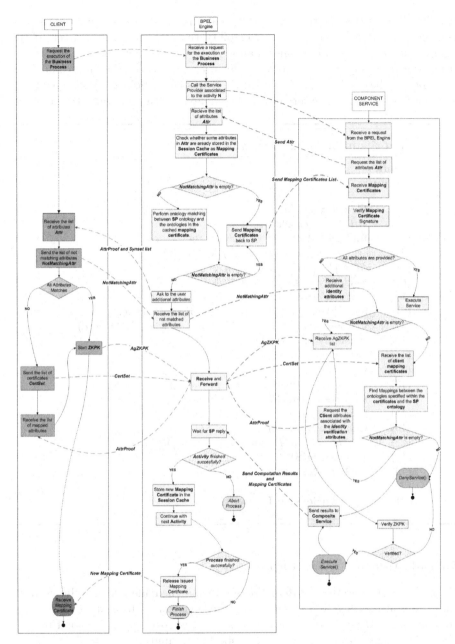

Fig. 2. Approach schema

client is not able to provide with concepts from the ontologies of the services which have issued the proof-of-identity certificates. Only matches that have a confidence score s greater than a predefined threshold are selected. The acceptance threshold is set up by the component service to assess the matches' validity. The greater the threshold, the greater is the similarity between the two concepts and thus higher is the probability that the match is correct. If the component service is able to find mappings for its concepts, it then verifies by using the information in the proof-of-identity certificates that each matching concept matches a client's attribute *Attr*. If this check fails, the component service notifies the composite service that terminates the interaction with the client.

Algorithm 2: Verification()

Input:
Output:

(1)   **C:** Receive($Match$)
(2) $AttrMathces$.**Add**($Match$)
(3)   **foreach** $\langle Attr, Id_i \rangle \in AttrMatches$
(4) $\{M_i, \sigma_i\} :=$ **Select**($RegCert, Attr$)
(5) $M = \prod_{i=1}^{n} M_i$
(6)   randomly picks $y, s \in [1..q]$
(7) $d = g^y h^s \pmod{p}$
(8)   **Send**($\{M_1, \ldots, M_n\}, \{\sigma_1, \ldots, \sigma_n\}, M, \sigma, d$);
(9)   **CS:** Receive($\{M_1, \ldots, M_n\}, \{\sigma_1, \ldots, \sigma_n\}, M, \sigma, d$)
(10)   randomly picks $e \in [1..q]$
(11)   **Send**(e)
(12)   **C:** Receive(e)
(13) $u := y + em \pmod{q}$ where $m = m_1 + m_2 + + m_n$
(14) $w := s + er \pmod{q}$ where $r = r_1 + r_2 + \ldots + r_n$
(15)   **Send**(u, w)
(16)   **CS:** Receive(u, w)
(17)   **if** $g^u h^w == dM^k \pmod{p} \wedge \sigma == \prod_{i=1}^{t} \sigma_i)$
(18)   Execute(**S**);
(19)   IssueCertificate();
(20)   **else**
(21)   **Send**(**Service Denied**)

5.2   Multi-factor Authentication

Once the client receives $Match$, the set of matched identity attributes from the composite service, it retrieves from the registrar or from its $RegCert$ the commitments M_i satisfying the matches and the corresponding signatures σ_i. The client aggregates the commitments by computing $M = \prod_{i=1}^{n} M_i = g^{m_1 + m_2 + \ldots + m_i} h^{r_1 + r_2 + \ldots + r_i}$ and the signatures into $\sigma = \prod_{i=1}^{n} \sigma_i$, where σ_i is the registrar's signature on the committed value $M_i = g^{m_i} h^{r_i}$. According to the ZPK protocol, the client randomly picks y, s in $[1, ..q]$, computes $d = g^y h^s \pmod{p}$, and sends $d, \sigma, M, M_i, 1 \leq i \leq t$, to the composite service that on in turn sends these values to the component service. The component service sends back a random challenge $e \in [1, .., q]$ to the client. Then the client computes $u = y + em$

(mod q) and $v = s + er$ (mod q) where $m = m_1 + \ldots m_t$ and $r = r_1 + \ldots r_t$ and sends u and v to the composite service. The composite service forwards u and v to the component service. The component service accepts the aggregated zero knowledge proof if $g^u h^v = dc^e$. If this is the case, the component service checks that $\sigma = \prod_{i=1}^{n} \sigma_i$. If also the aggregate signature verification succeeds, the component service releases a proof of identity certificate to the client. The certificate states that client's identity attributes in the $Match$ set are mapped onto concepts of the component service ontology and that the client has successfully proved the knowledge of those attributes. The composite service sends the proof-of-identity certificate to the client and stores a copy of the certificate in its local repository $CertRep$. The proof-of-identity certificate can be can be provided by the composite service to another component service to allow the client to prove the knowledge of an attribute without performing the aggregate ZKP protocol. The component service that receives the certificate has just to verify the validity of the certificate.

Example 1. Assume that a user Bob submits a loan request to the loan service introduced in Example 1. The risk assessment service wants to verify Bob identity and it asks him to provide *DrivingLicense*, *CarRegistration* and *EmployeeID* identity attributes. Bob provides to the loan service the aggregate proof of *DrivingLicense*, *CarRegistration* and *EmployeeID* to the loan service, that forwards them to the risk assessment service. The risk assessment service verifies by carrying out an aggregate ZPK protocol with Bob that he owns *DrivingLicense*, *CarRegistration* and *EmployeeID* and release to Bob a proof-of-identity certificate that asserts Bob has *DrivingLicense*, *CarRegistration* and *EmployeeID* identity attributes. Therefore, when the loan approval service requires Bob to prove the possession of *EmployeeID* and *CreditCard* identity attributes, the loan service requests to Bob only to provide *CreditCard* identity attribute and sends the proof-of-identity certificate released by the risk assessment service to the loan approval service.

6   System Architecture and Implementation

In this section we discuss the system architecture that supports our multi-factor identity attributes authentication for business processes. We assume that our processes are implemented as WS-BPEL business processes, that is, as business processes in which each component service is implemented by a Web service. The main components of the architecture are: the BPEL engine, the `Identity Attribute Requester` module, the `Client`, the `Registrar`, the `Identity Verification Handler` module, and the component Web services. The WS-BPEL engine is responsible for scheduling and synchronizing the various activities within the business process according to the specified activity dependencies, and for invoking Web services operations associated with activities. The `Identity Attribute Requester` module extends the WS-BPEL engine's functions by carrying on the communication with the client asking for new identity attributes whenever necessary. The `Identity Attribute Requester` keeps in a

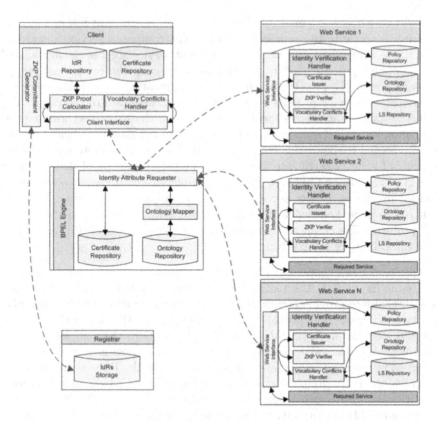

Fig. 3. System architecture

local repository the mapping certificate associated with previous clients identity verifications. The `Client` supports the functions to trigger the execution of the WS-BPEL business process, to select the identity attributes matching the ones requested by the component services, and to generate the aggregate ZKP of the matched attributes. The `Registrar` component provides functions for storing the clients' identity records and retrieving the public parameters required in the AgZKPK protocol. The `Identity Verification Handler` intercepts the components services invocation messages and provides functions for matching client identity attribute names and performing the aggregate ZKP verification. Finally, the component Web services support the operations that are orchestrated by the business process.

The `Identity Attribute Requester`, the `Identity Verification Handler` modules, and the component Web services have been implemented in JAVA. The `Identity Verification Handler` implements the identity attribute name matching protocol using the Falcon-AO v0.7 [2,3] ontology mapping API and WordNet 2.1 English Lexical database [6]. The `Client` application has been implemented in JSP while the `Registrar` has been implemented as a JAVA servlet. As BPEL engine we have chosen ODE. Finally, we have used Oracle 10g DBMS to store clients' identity records, ontology mappings, set of synonyms, session data and mapping certificates.

7   Experimental Evaluation

We have performed several experiments to evaluate the AgZKPK process that characterize the proposed approach to multi-factor identity verification and the identity attribute names matching process. To execute the tests we have developed a BPEL process composed by four component Web services and we have created a set of ontologies with an average cardinality of 60 concepts. We have carried out the following experimental evaluations:

- we have measured the time taken by a component Web service to perform the two different phases of the identity attribute names matching process by varying the number of identity attributes that have to be matched from 1 to 8. (Figure 4(a));
- we have measured the time taken by a component Web service to generate the aggregate ZKP by varying the number of identity attributes being aggregated from 1 to 50. (Figure 4(b));
- we have measured the time taken by a component Web service for aggregate ZKP verification execution time varying the number of identity attributes being aggregated from 1 to 50. (Figure 4(b));

The execution time has been measured in CPU time (milliseconds). Moreover, for each test case we have executed twenty trials, and the average over all the trial execution times has been computed.

Figure 4(a) shows the execution times of the two phases of the matching protocol for varying values in the number of identity attributes verified by a component service. The execution time of the first phase (green line) slightly increases and is around 60 ms. Instead, the time of the second phase is constant because even if the number of identity attributes to be match increases, this phase performs always the same operation, that is, matching two ontologies. Figure 4(b) reports the times to create an AgZKP and to verify it for varying values in the number of identity attributes being aggregated. The execution time to generate the AgZKP

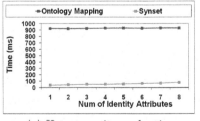
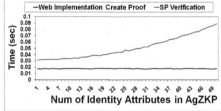

(a) Heterogeneity evaluation   (b) AgZKPK Verification versus Creation

Fig. 4. Experimental results

(represented by the blue line in the graph) is almost constant for increasing values in the number of identity attributes. The reason is that the creation of AgZKP only requires a constant number of exponentiations. By contrast, the time that the component Web service takes to perform identity attributes verification linearly increases with the number of identity attributes to be verified. The reason is that during the verification the component Web service is required to multiply all the commitments to verify the resulting aggregate signature.

8   Concluding Remarks

In this paper we have proposed a digital identity management approach for business processes. Our approach uses a combination of techniques from the area of semantic web and security protocols. We plan to extend this work in several directions. One direction is related to deal with heterogeneous identity negotiation protocols. The second direction is related to the definition of a language for identity verification policies that would allow service providers to specify conditions on identity attributes. We also plan to extend the AgZKPK protocol to verify that identity attribute's commitments satisfies such conditions.

References

1. Bhargav-Spantzel, A., Squicciarini, A.C., Bertino, E.: Establishing and Protecting Digital Identity in Federation Systems. Journal of Computer Security 14(3), 269–300 (2006)
2. Choi, N., Song, I.Y., Han, H.: A survey on ontology mapping. SIGMOD Record 35 (3), 34–41
3. Falcon, http://iws.seu.edu.cn/projects/matching/
4. Kalfoglou, Y., Schorlemmer, M.: Ontology mapping: the state of the art. The Knowledge Engineering Review 18(1), 1–31 (2003)
5. Pedersen, T.P.: Non-Interactive and Information-Theoretic Secure Verifiable Secret Sharing. In: Feigenbaum, J. (ed.) CRYPTO 1991. LNCS, vol. 576, pp. 129–140. Springer, Heidelberg (1992)
6. WordNet, http://wordnet.princeton.edu/

SelectAudit: A Secure and Efficient Audit Framework for Networked Virtual Environments

Tuan Phan and Danfeng (Daphne) Yao

Department of Computer Science
Rutgers University, Piscataway, NJ 08854
{tphan,danfeng}@cs.rutgers.edu

Abstract. Networked virtual environments (NVE) refer to the category of distributed applications that allow a large number of distributed users to interact with one or more central servers in a virtual environment setting. Recent studies identify that malicious users may compromise the semantic integrity of NVE applications and violate the semantic rules of the virtual environments without being detected. In this paper, we propose an efficient audit protocol to detect violations of semantic integrity through a probabilistic checking mechanism done by a third-party audit server.

Keywords: networked virtual environments, algorithm, audit, integrity.

1 Introduction

Networked virtual environments (NVE) [10,11] refer to the category of distributed applications that allow a large number of distributed users to interact with one or more central servers in a virtual environment setting. For example, Second Life is a social NVE application [17]. Second Life is also called as a massive multiplayer online role-playing game, so is World of Warcraft [18] where a player assumes the role of a fictitious character in the game. Multiplayer online games enjoy great popularity around the world with the revenue exceeding one billion dollars in western countries [8]. For a conventional single-player local game, the graphics are rendered and simulated on the player's local machine. For multiplayer online games with a client-server model, when the number of players are small, it is still possible for the game server to centrally compute the graphics simulations and send them back to the players. However, for massively multiplayer online games, the main graphics renderings need to be done on the client's machines in order to reduce the workload of the game servers. Therefore, the server no longer has the entire control over what gets to be computed and displayed on the client's machine. Vulnerabilities and flaws in game designs are exploited by cheating players to unfairly take advantages of other players. Cheating behaviors discourage honest players from participating in the games [16] that hinders the development of game industry [5].

Multiplayer games can have two types of architectures: client-server or peer-to-peer. In most client-server models, a client sends to the server updates that affected the client's local state. The server then coordinates the global state

E. Bertino and J.B.D. Joshi (Eds.): CollaborateCom 2008, LNICST 10, pp. 207–216, 2009.
© ICST Institute for Computer Sciences, Social-Informatics and Telecommunications Engineering 2009

and adjusts the interactions between players. In comparison, a peer-to-peer is serverless [12] and relies on game players to coordinate their interactions and states among themselves. In this paper, we focus on the security of the client-server architecture.

The architecture of multiplayer games needs to be scalable to accommodate the interactions among a large number of players. In particular, the workload on the central server or a cluster of central servers need to be kept efficient to ensure responsiveness to clients (players)'s updates and requests. Because graphics rendering is computationally intensive, it is infeasible to make the central servers to perform the rendering for each player. Therefore, typical multiplayer online game servers only maintain abstract states of each player and the concrete outcome of simulation is performed and kept on the player's computer. The concrete state information captures the settings, contexts, environments, visual effects of the player at a given point. The abstract state can be thought of as a digest of the concrete state.

Both client-server and peer-to-peer architectures have potential vulnerabilities for cheating. As defined by Baughman *et al.* [1,2], cheating occurs when a player causes updates to game state that defy the rules of the game or gain an unfair advantage. For example, the game player may attempt to intercept and access hidden information, collude with his friend to learn secret information of his opponent [1], or lookahead cheat where a player simply waits until all other players have sent their decisions. Several cheating behaviors have been studied and solutions have been proposed by the research community, including lockstep protocols [1,4] for lookahead cheats, a secure online Bridge game design by [19], fair message ordering protocol [3], and an audit framework to prevent cheating on semantic rules [9]. From the game industry, cheating in multiplayer online games have been intensively discussed and studied [5,16].

Unlike most of the existing anti-cheat work, we study the semantic integrity of multiplayer games in the client-server architecture. Our goal is to develop a general and efficient audit framework to detect and deter this type of cheating. *Semantic integrity* of multiplayer online games is defined as that all the game players must observe and follow the logical rules that govern the simulation and interactions specified by the server.

The attacks on semantic integrity in the client-server architecture are due to several reasons. First, the client software can be modified by participants, which is easy for open-source games. Even for proprietary games, client modification is sometimes possible through reserve engineering. Therefore, a security solution should not assume that all clients are trusted. Second, due to the large scale of the game, the central server typically only keeps an abstract state of each player. Third, there is a difference between the central server's abstract state and the player's concrete state. For example, the central server may only store the coordination of a few points on a client's moving path, instead of the entire

---

[1] Certain online Bridge game allows one to join as a bystander and thus can view the cards of all players [19]. Therefore, a cheater can make his friend a bystander who can pass other players' cards information onto the cheater.

trajectory. This distinction is called *semantic gap* first by [9], as the state of a game player contains the semantic meanings. Recently, researchers have identified that semantic gaps may be exploited by malicious players to violate semantic rules of the game without being detected.

The main challenge in designing an audit framework for massively multi-player online games is to prevent the audit server from becoming a performance bottleneck. Jha *et al.* proposed to use an audit server to catch cheating players by recomputing all of the audited players' previous game states. Their approach is simple and easy to implement. However, the heavy workload of the audit server is likely to create a bottleneck in the auditing process, as the recomputation of hundreds of thousands of game states is expensive. One easy mitigation is to deploy multiple audit servers to distribute the workload. Even with multiple audit servers, operations on each single auditor need to be optimized for efficiency as auditing needs to take place in real time to detect cheating players as quickly as possible.

In this paper, we develop a novel and efficient audit framework for multi-player online games through the use of Merkle hash tree and a random verification mechanism. Our solution is designed for the client-server architecture. We propose a scalable algorithm that allows an audit server to periodically examine clients' game states to detect cheating events. The main feature of our solution is that under reasonable assumptions, an audit server only needs to recompute a constant number of game states of a client in order to catch a potential cheating client with a high probability. Therefore, the auditing protocol is scalable to hundreds of thousands of clients as typically seen in popular multi-player online games. (E.g., World of Warcraft currently has 8 million registered players.) Because of the use of Merkle tree [13,14], once caught, a cheating client cannot refute the evidences produced by the audit server.

2   An Example

Here, we show a simple example of semantic integrity violation. Table 1 illustrates the distribution of game information between the players and the central game servers.

Table 1. A table shows the distribution of game information between the players and the central game server

Type of an entity	Stores/computes	Where
Player	Concrete game state of the player	Player's local machine
Central game server	Abstract states of all players' states	Central game server

Example 1. To reduce storage requirements, the central game server may only keep the coordinates of the two end points of a moving player as part of the abstract state of the player, for example, in the right figure, point a at (x_1, y_1) and point b at (x_2, y_2). As a result, a cheating player may violate the game rules by

walking through walls (the red path) without being detected by the state server! A correct path is to follow the green path. Without an secure audit mechanism, the central game server is unable to detect this type of cheating events.

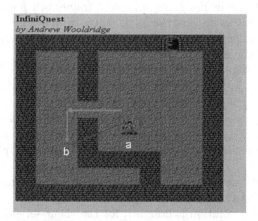

Fig. 1. Walking through walls: an example of semantic integrity violation. The central game server only keeps the coordinates of the two end points of a moving player as part of the abstract state, point a at (x_1, y_1) and point b at (x_2, y_2). A cheating player may violate the game rules by walking through walls (the red path) without being detected by the state server.

Other possible semantic integrity attacks include seeing hidden objects, shooting from the back, and reversing explosion damages, just to name a few. In some cases, semantic integrity violation is a result of other types of attacks such as reflex augmentation. For example, shooting from one's back (without seeing the target) is due to the use of aiming bot that is a program that automatically shoots once the target position is obtained (mostly by examining network packets). Therefore, catching semantic violations may also reduce other attacks in multi-player online games.

How to define semantic integrity rules that are to be enforced is specific to an application, which is out of the scope of this paper. However, open questions remain as to the complexity of such set of rules and how to easily generate these semantic rules by designing automatic tools. Our approach to detect semantic violations is to use an audit server to audit players by selectively recomputing and verifying players' concrete states, which is presented in the next Section. In what follows, we assume that the audit server has already obtained a set of semantic rules that it needs to enforce.

3   Preliminaries

In this section, we introduce the preliminary knowledge needed to understand our protocol. We briefly explains Merkle hash tree and the necessary cryptographic primitives that are used by us. We also briefly describe a simple audit approach that will be compared to our protocol.

We use Merkle hash trees for authentication of values $a_1, \ldots, a_n$. Merkle hash tree is for efficient authentication of a large number of items. This simple and elegant data structure has previously been used in various occasions [6,7]. A binary Merkle hash tree is a tree where an internal node h_0 is computed as the hash value $H(h_1, h_2)$ of two child nodes h_1 and h_2. In our construction, the order of inputs in the hash function matters and represents the node position in the tree, e.g., h_1 is the left node. The root hash y of the tree represents the digest of all the values at the leaf nodes, which are values $a_1, \ldots, a_n$. To authenticate that leaf a_i is in the hash tree, the proof is a sequence of hash values corresponding to the siblings of nodes that are on the path from a_i to the root. To verify the proof, anyone can recompute the root hash with a_i and the sequence of hash values in the proof. In our SelectAudit protocol, the Merkle tree can be thought of as the commitment on the game information by a player. Given a leaf node on a Merkle hash tree, the *proof nodes* refer to the minimum set of nodes that are required to construct the root hash. In other words, proof nodes consist of the sibling nodes of the leaf node on the path from the root to the leaf node.

The root hash of the Merkel tree needs to be authenticated with a digital signature using a public key signature scheme or a keyed-hash message authentication code (HMAC) with a shared secret key between the signer and the verifier. For online game settings, public key signature scheme is not suitable as a player may not possess a public and private key pair. Therefore, a shared secret session key is usually generated between the player and the central server, then the player uses the shared key to create HMAC on the root hash for authentication purpose. Our protocol assumes the existence of a collusion-resistance one-way hash function that (1) it is hard to compute the input of the hash function from the hash value and (2) it is hard to find two distinct messages that give the same hash values.

For the ease of discussion, we refer to the audit protocol presented in [9] as the SimpleAudit protocol. In SimpleAudit, each audited player has to compute HMAC on *all* of the update messages and send them to the auditor for verification. The auditor detects violation by performing the following three main operations.

1. To verify the MAC of each update message to ensure message authenticity.
2. To render *each* concrete game state corresponding to each update.
3. To verify the compliance of each concrete state according to the semantic rules of the game.

We describe our protocol SelectAudit in the next section.

4 Our Approach

In this section, we show how to apply cryptographic tools to prevent semantic integrity violation attacks in NVE. Our audit protocol reduces the computation costs at the audit server and the communication costs between the client and the audit server by using Merkle hash trees. Our aim is to improve the performance of the audit server so that it can efficiently audit a large number of players simultaneously.

Table 2. Notations in our SelectAudit protocol

k	Shared secret key between Client and AuditServer
$HMAC(k, M)$	HMAC of a message M by using a key k
S_0	Beginning concrete state of an audit cycle
Q_0	HMAC on S_0
S_c^t	Concrete state at the time t in the audit cycle c
Δ_i	Update on Client's concrete game state at epoch i
δ_i	Abstraction corresponding to Δ_i (i.e., update on abstract state)
Root hash	Root hash of Client's Merkle hash tree
Q_c	HMAC of root hash
$\hat{S}_i$	Concrete state of Client at epoch i recomputed by AuditServer

4.1 Overview

There are three types of entities in our protocol: Client, StateServer, and Audit-Server. StateServer is the central state server that coordinates the players and maintains the abstract states of all the players. AuditServer does auditing on all the players. Client refers to a player. AuditServer and StateServer are mutually trusted by each other. Client is not assumed to be trusted by the servers. To avoid requiring AuditServer to recompute *every* concrete state corresponding to an update of an audited client, we design a sampling technique. AuditServer only checks the semantic integrity associated with m updates out of n updates in an auditing cycle. By choosing a reasonably large m, a cheating player can be detected with high probability. We call our audit protocol *SelectAudit*.

An audit cycle refers to a time period specified by the game, during which a client's game records are examined by the audit server. The audit cycle is agreed upon by all the entities in the game system. An audit cycle consists of n number of epoches, each is associated with an update on the client's game state. During each cycle, each client constructs a Merkle hash tree on the update messages (no matter he is under audit or not). At the end of the cycle, the client computes the root hash of the tree and a message authentication code on the root hash. The client saves these values. If at a later point of time, the audit server decides to audit the client for a previous cycle, part of the stored Merkle tree corresponding to that cycle is sent to the auditor for verification. Without loss of generality, we choose n to be power of 2 for the ease of building the Merkle tree by the client.

For example, suppose the audit cycle consists of 8 epoches. A client joins the game at epoch 1. At each epoch from 1 to 8, he constructs the Merkle hash tree incrementally based on his game state information, and computes a MAC on the root hash at the end of epoch 8. At epoch 10, the audit server notifies the client that he is under audit. The client then engages in the audit protocol using the Merkle tree that he previous generated.

4.2   Our SelectAudit Protocol

Our SelectAudit protocol has three components: INITIALIZE, STATEUPDATE, and AUDIT, each of them is a protocol itself that is run. In what follows, we assume that the StateServer and AuditServer have a secure channel for communicating messages.

Initialize: This protocol is run among the StateServer, the AuditServer, and the Client when the Client first joins the online game. The StateServer sends the initial *concrete state* for the client based on the client's profile. As it is chosen by the StateServer, this initial concrete state of the client satisfies the semantic integrity of the game. The client also commits to AuditServer on the initial state by sending it a HMAC of the initial state. ASTATE is a shorthand for abstract state.

1. Client and AuditServer exchange a secret session key k, that is used to generate HMAC values in the updating phases and the auditing phases.
2. Client initializes $t = 0$ and sends an initialization request to StateServer.
3. StateServer chooses a concrete state S_0 for the client based on his profile. StateServer sends to the client the initial state S_0.
4. Client computes and stores $Q_0 = \text{HMAC}(k, S_0)$ along with the concrete state S_0 for audit purpose.

StateUpdate: This protocol is mainly run by the Client and StateServer to compute an updated game state for each epoch t of the game. The client also maintains the Merkle hash tree in case he gets audited later on. The Merkle hash tree is built on top of updates $\{\Delta_i\}$. The Merkle tree can be thought of as the commitment on the updates by the Client. For each epoch t in an audit cycle c,

1. Client computes a desired status update Δ_{t+1} and its corresponding abstraction δ_{t+1}.
2. Client sends δ_{t+1} to the StateServer.
3. Upon receiving δ_{t+1}, StateServer computes a new δ'_{t+1} and updates its abstract state accordingly.
4. StateServer sends the following to both Client and AuditServer: $(\delta'_{t+1} \parallel t + 1 \parallel Client_{id})$.
5. Client chooses and stores the concrete update $\Delta'_{t+1} \in \gamma(S_c^t, \delta'_{t+1})$ and computes the new concrete state $S_c^{t+1} = S_c^t + \Delta'_{t+1}$.
6. Client inserts Δ'_{t+1} into the Merkle tree corresponding to the current audit cycle.
7. Client increments t. At the end of cycle c, i.e., $t == n$ where n is the number of epoches in an audit cycle,
   (a) Client computes the corresponding new concrete state S^c.
   (b) Client computes $Q_c := \text{HMAC}(k, \text{root hash})$, then sends Q_c to Audit-Server. Note that this step is required for each Client for each cycle.
   (c) Client initializes for the next audit cycle by setting $t := 0$ and beginning concrete state $S_0 := S_c^n$. Client computes and stores $\text{HMAC}(k, S_0)$ along with the beginning concrete state S_0 for audit purpose.

Audit: To audit a previous cycle c on Client, AuditServer and Client engage in a protocol that allows the AuditServer to verify that (1) game renderings based on the beginning concrete state S_0 and updates at *selective* epochs satisfy semantic integrity, (2) the beginning concrete state and updates submitted by Client are authentic.

1. AuditServer informs Client that he is under audit for an earlier cycle c.
2. Client sends to AuditServer all the concrete updates $\{\Delta_i'\}$ in the audit cycle for all $i \in [1, n]$, and the beginning concrete state S_0 of cycle c, and its HMAC Q_0.
3. AuditServer checks whether VerifyHMAC(k, root hash, Q_c) = TRUE and VerifyHMAC(k, S_0, Q_0) = TRUE. These two steps are to verify the authenticity of the root hash of Merkle tree and the beginning concrete state S_0 that are received from Client. Recall that Q_c and root hash are sent by Client to AuditServer in Protocol STATEUPDATE.
4. AuditServer randomly picks m numbers from $[1, n]$ that represent the indices of epochs to be audited in audit cycle c. These numbers form the challenges for Client and are denoted by *challenge_set*. AuditServer sends the *challenge_set* to Client.
5. Client prepares a response message M that includes the proof nodes on Merkle tree corresponding to Δ_j' where $j \in$ *challenge_set*. Recall that proof nodes defined in Section 3 consist of the sibling nodes of the leaf node on the path from the root to the leaf node. Client sends to AuditServer: $M \parallel$ HMAC(k, M).
6. AuditServer verifies the HMAC on M. Then, for each challenge $i \in$ *challenge_set*:
   (a) Auditor verifies the authentication of Δ_i' by reconstructing the root hash of the Merkle Tree from Δ_i' and its proof nodes. If the reconstructed root hash should be the same is the one sent in STATEUPDATE.
   (b) Auditor re-computes the concrete state of Client associate with epoch i by $\hat{S}_i = S_0 + (\Delta_1' + \Delta_2' + ... + \Delta_i')$, i.e., to compute the concrete state by applying accumulated updates.
   (c) Auditor checks whether Δ_i' chosen from $\gamma(\hat{S}_i, \delta_i')$ is compliant with the rules of the game. How to define the rules of game depend on the specific NVE application and is out of the scope of this paper. Recall that δ_i' is obtained from StateServer in Step 4 in Protocol STATEUPDATE.
7. AuditServer accepts the computation of Client if and only all the above tests pass. Client may delete the stored audit records.

AuditServer needs to maintain the auditing schedule of each client, i.e., when to audit which subset of clients. The process of choosing which subset of clients to audit should be randomized as opposed to following a predictable pattern. Otherwise, a cheating client can predict the cycles that he will be audited and cheats for the rest of the time. Ideally, for each audit cycle, every client is audited, which gives the best guarantee on detecting semantic integrity violations. However, this type of scheduling gives the audit server a heavy workload. Thus, there is a tradeoff between efficiency and detectability.

Theorem 1. *Assuming the existence of collision-resistance one-way hash function, our SelectAudit protocol preserves the semantic integrity of NVE and is secure against probabilistic polynomial-time adversaries in NVEs in the following attacks: message tampering and forgery, audit replay attacks, refuting audit results attacks, collision attacks, reordering attacks, and tailored update attacks.*

Theorem 2. *Let n be the number of updates in an audit cycle, m be the number of updates the audit server challenges a player, and r be the honest ratio that is defined as the probability that a player does not cheat. Also let ϵ be the maximum allowed probability of cheating without being caught. Then in SelectAudit, the following formula captures the upper bound on m.*

$$m < \frac{\log \epsilon}{\log r}$$

Due to space limit, we omit the detailed security and performance analysis. We refer readers to the full version of our paper for more information [15].

Comparison with SimpleAudit. Jha *et al.* conducted the first study on the semantic integrity of multi-player online games [9]. The SimpleAudit protocol in Section 3 captures the essence of their protocol. Our SelectAudit improves SimpleAudit in terms of both audit server efficiency and communication overhead. In [9], when a player is audited for a previous time period t, he needs to send all of the game updates and their message authentication code (MAC) associated with t to the audit server. In our solution, the MAC is only computed *once* for time period t. This simplification not only saves the communication overhead between the players and the audit server, but also lowers the computation overhead for the players. In [9], the audit server needs to recompute all of the concrete game states of each player who is under audit. Because game rendering is expensive, this recomputation is a significant overhead, especially when the number of players to be audited is large. In comparison, our audit server only needs to recompute a selective number of concrete states for each player, in order to have a high detection probability.

5   Conclusions

We have described a general and scalable audit framework for massive multi-player online games and for networked virtual environments in general. We are able to develop a distributed and efficient audit protocol that is run by the audit server to periodically examine the semantic integrity of clients' game states. The audit server is able to quickly detect cheating players and provide irrefutable proofs on the cheating behavior. The main advantage of our random checking algorithm is that the audit server only needs to perform a small number of rendering operations in order to catch cheaters with a high probability. This randomization significantly saves the computation costs for the audit server.

References

1. Baughman, N.E., Levine, B.N.: Cheat-proof playout for centralized and distributed online games. In: IEEE INFOCOM, pp. 104–113 (2001)
2. Baughman, N.E., Liberatore, M., Levine, B.N.: Cheat-proof playout for centralized and peer-to-peer gaming. IEEE/ACM Trans. Netw. 15(1), 1–13 (2007)
3. Chen, B.D., Maheswaran, M.: A cheat controlled protocol for centralized online multiplayer games. In: Proceedings of the 3rd Workshop on Network and System Support for Games (NETGAMES), pp. 139–143. ACM Press, New York (2004)
4. Chen, B.D., Maheswaran, M.: A fair synchronization protocol with cheat proofing for decentralized online multiplayer games. In: 3rd IEEE International Symposium on Network Computing and Applications (NCA), pp. 372–375 (2004)
5. Davis, S.B.: Why cheating matters. In: Game Developer's Conference (2003), http://www.secureplay.com/papers/docs/WhyCheatingMatters.pdf
6. Du, W., Jia, J., Mangal, M., Murugesan, M.: Uncheatable grid computing. In: International Conference on Distributed Computing Systems (ICDCS), pp. 4–11
7. Haber, S., Hatano, Y., Honda, Y., Horne, W., Miyazaki, K., Sander, T., Tezoku, S., Yao, D.: Efficient signature schemes supporting redaction, pseudonymization, and data deidentification. In: Proceedings of the 2008 ACM Symposium on Information, Computer and Communications Security (ASIACCS), pp. 353–362 (2008)
8. Harding-Rolls, P.: Western world MMOG market: 2006 review and forecasts to 2011, Management Report. Screen Digest (March 2007)
9. Jha, S., Katzenbeisser, S., Schallhart, C., Veith, H., Chenney, S.: Enforcing semantic integrity on untrusted clients in networked virtual environments. In: IEEE Symposium on Security and Privacy, pp. 179–186 (2007)
10. Joslin, C., Giacomo, T.D., Magnenat-Thalmann, N.: Collaborative virtual environments: From birth to standardization. IEEE Communications Magzine, 28–33 (April 2004)
11. Joslin, C., Pandzic, I.S., Magnenat-Thalmann, N.: Trends in networked collaborative virtual environments. Computer Communications 26(5), 430–437 (2003)
12. Knutsson, B., Lu, H., Xu, W., Hopkins, B.: Peer-to-peer support for massively multiplayer games. In: IEEE INFOCOM (2004)
13. Merkle, R.: Protocols for public key cryptosystems. In: Proceedings of the 1980 Symposium on Security and Privacy, pp. 122–133. IEEE Computer Society Press, Los Alamitos (1980)
14. Merkle, R.C.: A certified digital signature. In: Brassard, G. (ed.) CRYPTO 1989. LNCS, vol. 435, pp. 218–238. Springer, Heidelberg (1990)
15. Phan, T., Yao, D.: Select audit: A secure and efficient audit framework for networked virtual environments. Technical Report DCS-TR-642, Rutgers University (2008)
16. Pritchard, M.: How to hurt the hackers: The scoop on internet cheating and how you can combat it, http://www.gamasutra.com/features/20000724/pritchard_pfv.htm
17. Second Life, http://secondlife.com/
18. World of Warcraft, http://www.worldofwarcraft.com/index.xml
19. Yan, J.: Security design in online games. In: ACSAC 2003, Washington, DC, USA, p. 286. IEEE Computer Society, Los Alamitos (2003)

Collaborative Attack vs. Collaborative Defense
(Extended Abstract)

Shouhuai Xu

Department of Computer Science, University of Texas at San Antonio
shxu@cs.utsa.edu

Abstract. We have witnessed many attacks in the cyberspace. However, most attacks are launched by individual attackers even though an attack may involve many compromised computers. In this paper, we envision what we believe to be the next generation cyber attacks — collaborative attacks. Collaborative attacks can be launched by multiple attackers (i.e., human attackers or criminal organizations), each of which may have some specialized expertise. This is possible because cyber attacks can become very sophisticated and specialization of attack expertise naturally becomes relevant. To counter collaborative attacks, we might need collaborative defense because each "chain" in a collaborative attack may be only adequately dealt with by a different defender. In order to understand collaborative attack and collaborative defense, we present a high-level abstracted framework for evaluating the effectiveness of collaborative defense against collaborative attacks. As a first step towards realizing and instantiating the framework, we explore a characterization of collaborative attacks and collaborative defense from the relevant perspectives.

Keywords: cyber security, cyber attack, collaborative attack, collaborative defense.

1 Introduction

Both academic cyber (or Internet) security research and commercial cyber security defense have mainly focused on understanding and combating *individual* cyber attacks. For example, we all should install, and frequently update, computer virus scanners or spyware detectors so as to protect our computers as well as important information stored on them (e.g., personal data files, private communications, credit card numbers, social security numbers, and bank account passwords). Individual attacks have caused severe damages and, for example, there have reportedly many stolen digital identities such as credit card numbers.

In this paper we envision a new class of cyber attacks, called *collaborative attacks*, which might represent the next generation cyber attacks. Collaborative attacks are characterized by the prevalence of coordination before and during attacks. Distributed Denial-of-Service (DDoS) attacks can be seen as a simple

E. Bertino and J.B.D. Joshi (Eds.): CollaborateCom 2008, LNICST 10, pp. 217–228, 2009.
© ICST Institute for Computer Sciences, Social-Informatics and Telecommunications Engineering 2009

example of collaborative attacks in that they involve a large number of compromised computers, which however are often controlled by a *single* attacker (e.g., a botnet master). Collaborative attacks in general would involve multiple human attackers or criminal organizations that have respective adversarial expertise but may not fully trust each other.[1] Intuitively, collaborative attacks are more powerful than the sum of the underlying individual attacks that can be launched by the individual attackers independently. As an analogy, we may think collaborative attacks as "chemical reactions" and individual cyber attacks as "chemical elements." Just like new (or fatal) materials can result from carefully designed chemical reactions, severe damage can be caused by well-coordinated less-powerful cyber attacks. In other words, collaborative attacks can exhibit the "1 + 1 > 2" phenomenon.

1.1 Our Contributions

In this paper, we make the following contributions:

– We envision the need to consider collaborative attacks. We also envision the need to defend collaborative attacks with collaborative defense because collaborative defense cal certainly exhibit the "1+1>2" phenomenon as well. This is not only because different defenders may have different expertise, but also because sharing information between the defenders would play a crucial role in successfully and effectively defending collaborative attacks.
– We present a conceptual framework for understanding, characterizing, and evaluating the effectiveness of collaborative defense against collaborative attacks. Within the framework we can ask interesting questions such as: How may we deincentivize the attackers from launching collaborative attacks, and how can we incentivize the defenders to collaborate on defense?
– Towards a full-fledged realization of the afore-mentioned framework, we explore the attributes of collaborative attacks and the attributes of collaborative defense. It is interesting to note that essentially the attributes of collaborative attacks mirror the attributes of collaborative defense.

The research problems introduced in the present paper may be more important than the content itself. Thus, we certainly hope that the paper will inspire more research activities towards solving them.

---

[1] In traditional cryptographic and security models, we often assume that all the compromised participants are controlled by a single attacker (for free). This assumption is legitimate when we talk about specific goals (e.g., when we discuss security of a digital signature scheme, we allow the attacker to compromise any private keys other than the one in question) within a relatively small-scale system (e.g., when we discuss security in a mobile ad hoc network). When we talk about attacks in the cyberspace in general, this assumption does not always hold. Indeed, there are likely many cyber criminal organizations that might have different expertise and might be (e.g., economically) motivated to launch collaborative attacks without having any centralized authority whatsoever. As such, collaborative attacks may be seen as a sort of *emergent property*.

1.2   Related Work

We are not aware of any prior work on dealing with collaborative attacks, except [5] in which we explore a modeling of coordinated internal and external attacks. Nevertheless, it is worthwhile to note that a somewhat related problem known as *alert correlation* has been extensively studied. However, alert correlation is different from collaborative attacks because it is motivated by the problem that IDSs often overload their human operators with a large number of simple alerts of low-level security-related events, while not being able to provide the often more important succinct and high-level view of multi-stage intrusion incidents [9,8,2]. Various approaches have been proposed for alert correlation, such as temporal correlation [7], spatial correlation for identifying attack sources [4,1], root cause detection [3], prerequisites-consequences correlation [6], and logical correlation [10]. As such, alert correlation mainly deals with attacks launched by a single attacker, rather than dealing with attacks launched by multiple attackers that may have different attack "fingerprints" that facilitate correlation. Nevertheless, alert correlation may be able to help deal with collaborative attacks to some extent as well.

Outline. The rest of the paper is organized as follows. In Section 2 we present a high-level framework for evaluating the effectiveness of collaborative defense against collaborative attack. In Section 3 we elaborate the characterization of collaborative attack, and in Section 4 we elaborate the characterization of collaborative defense. In Section 5 we conclude the paper with open problems for future research.

2   Collaborative Attack vs. Collaborative Defense: An High-Level Evaluation Framework

A networked system S_i may consist of a set of elementary components, which may be specific to the system properties we care. For example, when we only care about which private digital signing keys are compromised in a networked system, we may only take into consideration the software and hardware component instances that could directly or indirectly cause the compromise of the private keys. As a result, a set of individual systems $S_1, \ldots, S_n$ can compose a larger system $S = \cup_{1 \le i \le n} S_i$, where S_i is the set of component instances in the ith system. Note that the system space may impose a partial order over the power set of the set of the elementary component instances.

For system S, we have a set of assets or targets (e.g., private digital signing keys, passwords or digital identities) whose security is our concern. Let Ω be the power set of the set of the elementary assets. As a consequence of a successful cyber attack, some assets $\omega \in \Omega$ are compromised.

Let $\gamma_i \in \Gamma$ denote the defense resources (or mechanisms) in a networked system S_i, and $\mathcal{D}(\gamma_i)$ the actual defense strategy and tactics used by the defender with defense resources γ_i. Given individual defense γ_i in system S_i, where $i \in I$ for some index set I, the resources for collaborative defense $\cup_{i \in I} \gamma_i$ is well-defined with respect to the composed system $\cup_{i \in I} S_i$. It should be clear that the defense space, Γ, may impose a partial order over the power set of the set of the elementary defense resources. As such, $\mathcal{D}(\cup_{i \in I} \gamma_i)$ is the collaborative defense given resources $\cup_{i \in I} \gamma_i$. Note that $\mathcal{D}(\cdot)$ is indeed a class of algorithms for computing the defense, although $\mathcal{D}(\cdot)$ may not (always) produce the optimal defense.

Let $\theta_i \in \Theta$ denote the resources used by an individual attack against a networked system S_i with defense resources γ_i and defense algorithm $\mathcal{D}$, and $\mathcal{A}(\theta_i, \mathcal{D}(\gamma_i))$ the actual attack strategy and tactics used by the attacker with attack resources θ_i. To accommodate the worst-case scenario, we can assume that $\mathcal{A}(\theta_i, \mathcal{D}(\gamma_i))$ is the optimal attack against system S_i, where optimization intuitively means that it will cause the worst (from the defender's perspective) outcome, and will become fully specified later. Given that, $\mathcal{A}(\cdot, \cdot)$ is indeed a class of algorithms computing the optimal attacks based on given attack resources, defense resources and defense algorithm.

Given individual attack resources θ_i against system S_i with defense resources γ_i and defense algorithm $\mathcal{D}$, where $i \in I$ for some index set I, the resources for collaborative attack $\cup_{i \in I} \theta_i$ is well-defined against the composed system $\cup_{i \in I} S_i$. It should be clear that the attack resource space Θ may impose a partial order over the power set of the set of elementary attack resources. Similarly, based on the combined attack resources $\cup_{i \in I} \theta_i$, the optimal collaborative attack is given by $\mathcal{A}(\cup_{i \in I} \theta_i, \mathcal{D}(\cup_{i \in I} \gamma_i))$.

Ultimately, we want to fully specify the function $f_{\mathcal{D}, \mathcal{A}} : \Theta \times \Gamma \times \{S\} \to \Omega$ such that

$$f_{\mathcal{D}, \mathcal{A}}(\theta, \gamma, S) \mapsto \omega,$$

where $\mathcal{A}(\theta, \mathcal{D}(\gamma))$ is an attack against a system S with defense $\mathcal{D}(\gamma)$, and $\omega \in \Omega$ is the outcome of launching attack $\mathcal{A}(\theta, \mathcal{D}(\gamma))$ against system S. Note that $\mathcal{A}$ is optimal if for any $\mathcal{D}$ and $\mathcal{A}'$, and for all θ, γ and S, we have

$$f_{\mathcal{D}, \mathcal{A}'}(\theta, \gamma, S) \subseteq f_{\mathcal{D}, \mathcal{A}}(\theta, \gamma, S).$$

Since f may impose a partial order over Ω, the above definition of optimization may be adjusted as

$$\mathsf{payoff}(f_{\mathcal{D}, \mathcal{A}'}(\theta, \gamma, S)) \leq \mathsf{payoff}(f_{\mathcal{D}, \mathcal{A}}(\theta, \gamma, S))$$

where payoff is an appropriate payoff function.

Unfortunately, it may be very difficult to fully specify the function $f_{\mathcal{D}, \mathcal{A}}$, which means that we may have to approach it through various "approximations." Still, there is a plenty of interesting questions that can be asked.

– Fixing (collaborative or non-collaborative) defense algorithm $\mathcal{D}$, attack resources $\theta \in \Theta$ and a system S, is $f_{\mathcal{D}, \mathcal{A}}(\theta, \gamma, S)$ a decreasing function of (collaborative or non-collaborative) defense resources γ? Under what conditions the function $f_{\mathcal{D}, \mathcal{A}}(\theta, \gamma, S)$ is convex, concave, linear, or exhibits a phase transition with respect to γ? Note that in general $f_{\mathcal{D}, \mathcal{A}}(\theta, \gamma, S)$ may impose a partial order, meaning that we may need to resort to some payoff function as discussed above.

- Fixing (collaborative or non-collaborative) defense resources $\gamma \in \Gamma$, defense algorithm $\mathcal{D}$ and a system S, is $f_{\mathcal{D},\mathcal{A}}(\theta, \gamma, S)$ an increasing function of (collaborative or non-collaborative) attack resources θ? Under what conditions the function is convex, concave, linear, or exhibits a phase transition with respect to θ? Note that $f_{\mathcal{D},\mathcal{A}}(\theta, \gamma, S)$ may impose a partial order in general, meaning that we may resort to some payoff function as mentioned before.
- Fixing a system S, when both (collaborative or non-collaborative) attack and (collaborative or non-collaborative) defense resources are adaptively determined, meaning that both θ and γ are functions of time t and denoted by $\theta(t)$ and $\gamma(t)$, what are the dominating factors that determine the outcome $f_{\mathcal{D},\mathcal{A}}(\theta(t), \gamma(t), S)$? In particular, for a given $\theta(t)$, how can we optimally select adaption methods $\gamma(t)$, perhaps with minimal extra effort, so as to minimize $f_{\mathcal{D},\mathcal{A}}(\theta(t), \gamma(t), S)$? Note that $f_{\mathcal{D},\mathcal{A}}(\theta(t), \gamma(t), S)$ may impose a partial order in general, meaning that we may resort to some payoff function as mentioned before.
- For a given (collaborative or non-collaborative) defense resources $\gamma \in \Gamma$ in a system S, what is the minimal attack α in order for a (collaborative or non-collaborative) attacker to achieve an attack goal $\omega \in \Omega$? In other words, we need to identify the minimal attack effort corresponding to collaborative attack θ such that

$$\alpha = \min\{\theta : f_{\mathcal{D},\mathcal{A}}(\theta, \gamma, S) \mapsto \omega\}.$$

Note that since the collaborative attack space may impose a partial order, there may be multiple such α's. Nevertheless, if we are able to define a payoff function on the attack space Θ, it is possible to reduce the size of the set of collaborative attacks corresponding to the minimal attack efforts.

- Fixing (collaborative or non-collaborative) defense $\gamma \in \Gamma$ in a system S, it is important to characterize under what conditions we have

$$\cup_{i \in I} f_{\mathcal{D},\mathcal{A}}(\theta_i, \gamma, S) \subseteq f_{\mathcal{D},\mathcal{A}}(\cup_{i \in I} \theta_i, \gamma, S)$$

or

$$\mathsf{payoff}(\cup_{i \in I} f_{\mathcal{D},\mathcal{A}}(\theta_i, \gamma, S)) \leq \mathsf{payoff}(f_{\mathcal{D},\mathcal{A}}(\cup_{i \in I} \theta_i, \gamma, S))$$

based on an appropriate payoff function payoff. This allows us to disrupt the power of collaborative attacks so as to ensure an "$1 + 1 \leq 2$" effect and to deincentivize the attackers from launching collaborative attacks.

- For a given (collaborative or non-collaborative) attack $\theta \in \Gamma$ against a system S, what is the minimal attack β in order for a (collaborative or non-collaborative) defense to successfully protect asset $\omega \in \Omega$? In other words, we need to identify the minimal defense effort corresponding to collaborative attack θ such that

$$\beta = \min\{\gamma : f_{\mathcal{D},\mathcal{A}}(\theta, \gamma, S) \mapsto \omega\}.$$

Note that since the collaborative defense space may impose a partial order, there may be multiple such β's. Nevertheless, if we are able to define an investment function on the defense space Γ, it is possible to reduce the size of the set of collaborative defense corresponding to the minimal investment.

– Fixing (collaborative or non-collaborative) attack $\theta \in \Theta$ against a system S, it is important to characterize under what conditions we have

$$\cup_{i \in I} f_{\mathcal{D},\mathcal{A}}(\theta, \gamma_i, S) \subseteq f_{\mathcal{D},\mathcal{A}}(\theta, \cup_{i \in I} \gamma_i, S)$$

or

$$\mathsf{payoff}(\cup_{i \in I} f_{\mathcal{D},\mathcal{A}}(\theta, \gamma_i, S)) \leq \mathsf{payoff}(f_{\mathcal{D},\mathcal{A}}(\theta, \cup_{i \in I} \gamma_i, S))$$

based on an appropriate payoff function payoff. This gives the defenders incentives to collaborate in defending cyber attacks.

In order to answer the above questions, we need to fully specify the attack space and the defense space. As a first step towards this goal, in what follows we present a characterization of collaborative attack and collaborative defense.

3   A Characterization of Collaborative Attack

We believe that collaborative attack and collaborative defense have much in common, especially they need some kinds of Command & Control (C&C) for coordinating attack and defense, respectively. Given that, we characterize them from the same five perspectives. Specifically, for collaborative attacks we consider the time-aspect of collaborative attack C&C, the space-aspect of collaborative attack C&C, the effect of collaborative attack, the information exchange during collaborative attack, and the privacy aspect of collaborative attack. Figure 1 highlights the perspectives.

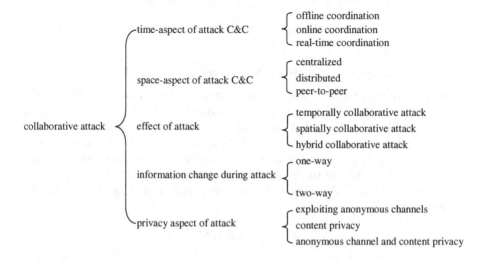

Fig. 1. A characterization of collaborative attack

Attribute 1: Time-aspect of collaborative attack C&C. C&C mechanisms are used for coordinating collaborative attacks. There is a spectrum of coordination methods from a time perspective, ranging from the least sophisticated off-line coordination to the most sophisticated real-time coordination. Various on-line coordination methods reside in between.

- Off-line coordination: The attackers command a set of adversarial computers (e.g., bots) to launch a future attack against some predetermined target. During the attack, there are no communications between the attackers and the adversarial computers, nor communications between the adversarial computers themselves. This means that the course of the attack process will not be adjusted according to the situation. Distributed Denial-of-Service (DDoS) attacks are often launched via an off-line coordination method.
- On-line coordination: In addition to off-line coordination, during an attack there may be communications between the attackers and the adversarial computers, or communications between the adversarial computer themselves. Moreover, newly compromised computers can become adversarial computers and launch attacks against other computers. On-line coordination gives the attackers extra power because the attackers can more effectively utilize their resources. For example, when the attackers realized that the same effect can be achieved with a subset of the adversarial computers, the attackers can withdraw some of them so as to reduce the chance they are caught (and punished).
- Real-time coordination: In this case, both the attackers and the adversarial computers, initially and later compromised alike, are always updated with the current global system state information (e.g., which computers have yet to be compromised). As such, the attackers can arbitrarily orchestrate an ongoing attack through a real-time C&C mechanism. Therefore, the attackers can command any adversarial computer to attack any target computer in a real-time fashion.

In general, off-line coordination is less powerful than on-line coordination, which in turn is less powerful than real-time coordination because off-line coordination does not accommodate any situational awareness in the cyberspace, whereas real-time coordination accommodates the most situational awareness in the cyberspace. In particular, attacks under on-line or real-time coordination can be made stealthy by avoiding any heavy or unnecessary use of resources of (compromised) computers and networks.

Attribute 2: Space-aspect of collaborative attack C&C. This captures the whereabouts of the C&C system. There are three kinds: centralized, distributed, and peer-to-peer.

- Centralized C&C: In this case, there is a single attacker that is coordinating the collaborative attacks, which may involve the adversarial computers controlled by multiple attackers (e.g., multiple attackers designate a single commander to exploit their botnets to launch attacks). Traditional IRC-based botnet C&C can be seen as a special example of centralized C&C.

- Distributed C&C: In this case, there are multiple attackers for commanding the adversarial computers to launch attacks. The commanding attackers may formulate some topology, which may reflect the relationship between them. For example, there may be a hierarchical structure (e.g., a tree) between the commanding attackers such that the "leaf" attackers actually deliver commands to the adversarial computers.
- Peer-to-peer C&C: In this case, there are multiple attackers that play equal roles. They can formulate a logical (i.e., a command is approved by multiple of them) and/or physical (i.e., the network connecting them formulates a graph) peer-to-peer network. Clearly, it is difficult to shut down such C&C networks, which have recently been exploited by some botnets.

In general, centralized C&C is less sophisticated than distributed C&C, which in turn is less sophisticated than peer-to-peer C&C. An important research problem is to identify and exploit the weaknesses of distributed and peer-to-peer C&Cs, if any, to better defend against them.

Attribute 3: Effect of collaborative attacks. The effect of collaborative attacks can be classified as spatially collaborative attacks, temporally collaborative attacks, and hybrid collaborative attacks.

- Spatially collaborative attacks: The set of adversarial computers, which are located in different geographic or network places, are coordinated to launch attacks against a target at (roughly) the same time. DDoS attacks often bear this characteristic.
- Temporally collaborative attacks: The attack may proceed in a well orchestrated fashion. For example, the first step is to shut down the IDS employed in the target system by one attacker, the second step is to disable the virus scanners installed at the target system by another attacker, and the final step is to launch the real attack against the target by yet another attacker (e.g., stealing confidential data from a data center without being noticed by the defender). Each step may be accomplished through a different set of adversarial computers, which may reside at different geographic or network places.
- Hybrid collaborative attacks: These attacks bear the characteristics of the spatially collaborative attacks and temporally collaborative attacks.

In general, spatially collaborative attacks are not compatible with temporally collaborative attacks. However, both of them are not as sophisticated as hybrid collaborative attacks.

Attribute 4: Information exchange during collaborative attacks. During an collaborative attack, information may be exchanged between the commanding attackers, between the commanding attackers and the adversarial computers, and between the adversarial computers. There are two kinds of information exchanges.

- One-way: In this case, information may only be sent from one participant to another (e.g., the adversarial computers always report to the respective commanding attackers about their progress), but not in the other direction (i.e., the commanding attackers may not send direct commands to the adversarial computers). This is possible because sending information to the adversarial computers, which is often a large number, may increase the chance that the commanding attackers or the adversarial computers are detected.

- Two-way: In this case, information may be sent from any computer to any other. This allows the sharing of situational awareness, which may be needed in order to launch sophisticated attacks.

In general, one-way information exchange is less powerful and less sophisticated than two-way information exchange.

Attribute 5: Privacy aspect of collaborative attacks. Attackers may abuse some advanced techniques to launch more sophisticated attacks. For example,

- Exploiting anonymous channels: In this case, the attackers exploit anonymous channels or their variants, which may or may not be deployed for legitimate uses, to conduct stealthy communications.
- Enforcing content privacy: In this case, the attackers exploit cryptographic techniques or their variants to protect the content of their communications (e.g., commands for attacks).
- Exploiting anonymous channels and enforcing content privacy: The attackers may exploit anonymous channels and enforce content privacy.

In general, attack exploiting such techniques are often difficult to deal with.

4   A Characterization of Collaborative Defense

In parallel to the characterization of collaborative attacks, we characterize collaborative defense from the same five perspectives, namely the time-aspect of collaborative defense C&C, the space-aspect of collaborative defense C&C, the effect of collaborative defense, the information exchange during collaborative defense, and the privacy aspect of collaborative defense. Figure 2 highlights the perspectives.

Attribute I: Time-aspect of collaborative defense C&C. C&C mechanisms are used for coordinating collaborative defense. There is also a spectrum of coordination methods.

- Off-line coordination: The defenders coordinate their defenses regardless of the specific attacks.
- On-line coordination: In addition to off-line coordination, there may be communications between the defenders during an attack so as to share information about situational awareness.
- Real-time coordination: In this case, the defenders are always updated with the current global system state information. As such, the defenders can orchestrate an ongoing defense through a real-time C&C mechanism.

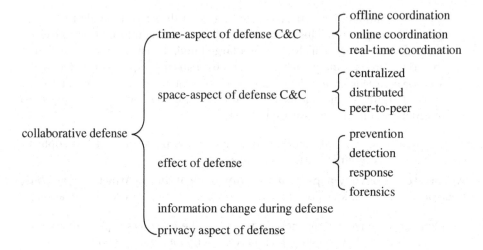

Fig. 2. A characterization of collaborative defense

In general, off-line coordination is less powerful than on-line coordination, which in turn is less powerful than real-time coordination because off-line coordination does not accommodate any situational awareness in the cyberspace, whereas real-time coordination accommodates the most situational awareness in the cyberspace. It is stressed, however, that the situational awareness may be misleading when sophisticated attackers can exploit deception to fool the detection sensors, and thus cause severe problems.

Attribute II: Space-aspect of collaborative defense C&C. This captures where the C&C system is located.

- Centralized C&C: In this case, there is a designated defender that is coordinating the collaborative defense, which may involve the resources of multiple defenders.
- Distributed C&C: In this case, there are multiple defenders that may formulate some topology, which may reflect the relationship between the defenders. For example, there may be a hierarchical structure (e.g., a tree) between the defenders.
- Peer-to-peer C&C: In this case, there are multiple defenders that play equal roles. They can formulate a logical (i.e., a command is approved by multiple of them) and/or physical (i.e., the network connecting them formulates a graph) peer-to-peer network.

In general, centralized C&C is less robust than distributed C&C, which in turn is less robust than peer-to-peer C&C.

Attribute III: Effect of collaborative defense. Collaborative defense should apply to the whole lifecycle of networked systems.

- Collaborative prevention: The defenders collaboratively prevent attackers from launching successful attacks.
- Collaborative detection: Defenders can share information about suspicious activities against their own networked systems so as to detect attacks that may be launched by multiple collaborative attackers.
- Collaborative response: During an attack, the defenders can collaboratively deal with attacks by allocating defense resources. For example, one defender's network may have been recruited as a botnet to launch attacks against another defender's network. Shutting done the botnet computers would help eliminate the attacks against the victim.
- Collaborative forensics: After the fact that multiple networks have been attacked, the defenders can share information so as to answer questions such as: When did an attack occur? How did it occur? How long did the attack last? What are the consequences (e.g., Which computers were broken? What information was stolen?) What are the possible attackers, supposing we know that different attackers have their fingerprints in, for example, their malware?

Attribute IV: Information exchange during defense. During defense, information may be exchanged between the defenders. In general, the information exchange should be two-way, meaning that any defender can send information to any other defender.

Attribute V: Privacy aspect of defense. There may be privacy issues when the defenders collaborate in defending attacks. In particular, one defender may not be willing to share some information about their assets (e.g., their internal network configurations).

5   Summary and Future Work

We envisioned what we believe to be the next generation cyber attacks, called collaborative attacks. To counter collaborative attacks, we might need collaborative defense. We presented a framework for understanding, characterizing and evaluating the effectiveness of collaborative defense against collaborative attacks. As a first step towards realizing and instantiating the framework, we explored a characterization of collaborative attacks and collaborative defense from the relevant perspectives.

As demonstrated in the paper, there are many challenging and important research problems. Thus, we hope that this paper will inspire active research toward understanding and adequately addressing collaborative attacks.

Acknowledgement. The chemical reaction analogy of collaborative attacks was inspired by a conversation with Bharat Bhargava.

The work was supported in part by AFOSR and NSF. The views and opinions contained in the paper are those of the author and should not be interpreted as, in any sense, the official policies or endorsements of the government or the agencies.

228   S. Xu

References

1. Allman, M., Blanton, E., Paxson, V., Shenker, S.: Fighting coordinated attackers with cross-organizational information sharing. In: HOTNETS 2006 (2006)
2. Green, J., Marchette, D., Northcutt, S., Ralph, B.: Analysis techniques for detecting coordinated attacks and probes. In: Proceedings of the Workshop on Intrusion Detection and Network Monitoring, pp. 1–9 (1999)
3. Julisch, K.: Clustering intrusion detection alarms to support root cause analysis. ACM Trans. Inf. Syst. Secur. 6(4), 443–471 (2003)
4. Katti, S., Krishnamurthy, B., Katabi, D.: Collaborating against common enemies. In: Proceedings of the 5th ACM SIGCOMM conference on Internet Measurement (IMC 2005), p. 34 (2005)
5. Li, X., Xu, S.: A stochastic modeling of coordinated internal and external attacks (manuscript in submission)
6. Ning, P., Cui, Y., Reeves, D.: Constructing attack scenarios through correlation of intrusion alerts. In: Proceedings of the 9th ACM conference on Computer and communications security (CCS 2002), pp. 245–254 (2002)
7. Ourston, D., Matzner, S., Stump, W., Hopkins, B.: Coordinated internet attacks: responding to attack complexity. Journal of Computer Security 12(2), 165–190 (2004)
8. Valdes, A., Skinner, K.: Probabilistic alert correlation. In: Proceedings of the 4th International Symposium on Recent Advances in Intrusion Detection (RAID 2000), pp. 54–68 (2001)
9. Valeur, F., Vigna, G., Kruegel, C., Kemmerer, R.: A comprehensive approach to intrusion detection alert correlation. IEEE Trans. Dependable Secur. Comput. 1(3), 146–169 (2004)
10. Zhou, J., Heckman, M., Reynolds, B., Carlson, A., Bishop, M.: Modeling network intrusion detection alerts for correlation. ACM Trans. Inf. Syst. Secur. 10(1), 4 (2007)

Learning Models of the Negotiation Partner in Spatio-temporal Collaboration

Yi Luo and Ladislau Bölöni

School of Electrical Engineering and Computer Science
University of Central Florida, Orlando, Florida, USA
yiluo@mail.ucf.edu, lboloni@eecs.ucf.edu

Abstract. We describe an approach for learning the model of the opponent in spatio-temporal negotiation. We use the Children in the Rectangular Forest canonical problem as an example. The opponent model is represented by the physical characteristics of the agents: the current location and the destination. We assume that the agents do not disclose any of their information voluntarily; the learning needs to rely on the study of the offers exchanged during normal negotiation. Our approach is Bayesian learning, with the main contribution being four techniques through which the posterior probabilities are determined. The calculations rely on (a) feasibility of offers, (b) rationality of offers, (c) the assumption of decreasing utility, and (d) the assumption of accepting offer which is better than the next counter-offer.

1 Introduction

Spatio-temporal negotiation is a specific case of multi-issue negotiation where the issues under negotiation can be spatial or temporal values. In previous work [7,8], we have shown that spatio-temporal negotiation has differentiating properties which require specific negotiation protocols and offer formation strategies.

In most practical negotiation problems, incomplete information is the default assumption. The self-interested negotiation partners disclose preferences only in the degree they believe that it allows them to reach a more favorable agreement. Naturally, a better knowledge of the opponent's preferences allows an agent to form better offers, and ultimately to reach a more favorable deal. Thus, in the recent years, a relatively lively research area deals with learning opponent preferences from the exchange of offers in the course of normal negotiation. In addition, argumentation techniques allow a more controlled way for agents to share a specific part of their preferences.

The preferences of the agent participating in spatio-temporal negotiation are defined in terms of physical properties such as current physical location, desired destination, current and maximum velocity, remaining fuel, desired trajectories and so on. This requires a different approach compared to worth oriented or task oriented domains.

In this paper, we outline a technique which allows an agent participating in a spatio-temporal negotiation to learn the preferences of the opponent agent. The

E. Bertino and J.B.D. Joshi (Eds.): CollaborateCom 2008, LNICST 10, pp. 229–243, 2009.
© ICST Institute for Computer Sciences, Social-Informatics and Telecommunications Engineering 2009

negotiation protocol we assume is a simple exchange of binding offers - that is, there are no arguments exchanged, the agent needs to infer the preferences of the opponent from its offers, or from the rejection of its own offers by the opponent. We are using the Children in the Rectangular Forest canonical problem as our working assumption, being a simplified environment, which however, represents all the properties of general spatio-temporal negotiations.

Our approach is based on Bayesian learning which was previously used for multi-agent negotiations by Zeng and Sycara [10], Li and Cao [6] and others. The agent updates its beliefs about the opponent's preferences after each negotiation round.

The main contributions of this paper are the specific techniques which need to be used to calculate the posterior probabilities considering the spatial and temporal nature of the preferences, and the specific dependencies between the preferences. In addition, in contrast with most previous work in preference learning, we do not assume that the opponent uses a specific negotiation strategy.

The only assumptions about the opponent are those dictated by common sense: (a) that it does not make binding offers which are not feasible for itself (b) that is does not make binding offers which are not rational for itself (they are worse than the conflict deal) (c) that from a pool of available offers it presents the ones with the higher utility for itself before the ones with the lower utility, and (d) that it doesn't reject the offer which is better than the counter offer it plans to propose next round. Note that the third requirement does not necessarily imply a uniform concession. There is a very large space of possible strategies which verify these requirements. These four assumptions translate into three algorithms for the computation of the posterior probabilities in the Bayesian learning.

The remainder of this paper is organized as follows. We succinctly describe the CRF problem in Section 2. Then we introduce the theory of Bayesian learning in Section 3. We design three ways to determine the posterior probabilities of preference in learning agent. In Section 4, we design two strategies with different parameters for the opponent agent, and show the experimental study about the performance of learning. We talk about the related work in Section 5 and conclude in Section 6.

2   Justifying the CRF Problem

Children in the Rectangular Forest (CRF) is a canonical problem designed to study spatio-temporal negotiations. It states that two children in the physical map go from their sources to destinations with their own speed. There is a rectangular forest in front of them. If the children join together, they can traverse the forest as a team with the speed of the slower child. Otherwise they have to go around the forest independently (see Figure 1). The key point for this problem is that the two children should negotiate and find a common path which potentially saves time compared to the case when they travel independently.

Many real life applications can be abstracted into the CRF problem, such as co-operative control of unmanned air vehicles (scouting and convoy) [9], multi-agent

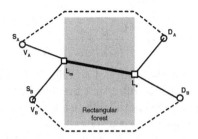

Fig. 1. The CRF problem: two children A and B try to move from sources S_A and S_B to destinations D_A and D_B with their own speed V_A and V_B. The dashed line indicates the trajectory of their conflict deals, and the solid line indicates the trajectory of an agreement.

routing [11], RoboCup soccer (when and where the robot receives the ball, and when and where it passes the ball to teammates), and so on.

In previous work [7,8], we found that the optimal trajectories of the conflict deal and the collaboration deal should be a sequence of straight lines, and the meeting and splitting locations should be at the edges of the forest. So the offer between two agents contains at least four issues: the meeting location L_m, the meeting time t_m, the splitting location L_s and the splitting time t_s.

When an agent receives an offer from its opponent, it should check if the offer is feasible and rational for itself. The offer is not feasible if the agent can not get to the designated locations on time. The offer is not rational if it is worse than the conflict deal. To evaluate the offer, the cost function is defined as the time to arrive destination. Mathematically, for an offer $\mathbf{O} = (L_m, t_m, L_s, t_s)$, agent A (going from S_A to D_A with speed of v_A) can arrive the destination at

$$C^{(A)}(O) = \begin{cases} +\infty, & if\ \frac{dist(S_A, L_m)}{v_A} \geq t_m \\ +\infty, & if\ \frac{dist(L_m, L_s)}{v_A} \geq t_s - t_m \\ t_s + \frac{dist(L_s, D_A)}{v_A}, & otherwise \end{cases} \tag{1}$$

where the $dist(S_A, L_m)$ means the spatial distance between source location S_A and meeting location L_m. The first two conditions in Equation 1 indicate the agent couldn't reach the meeting location and splitting location on time. So the cost of the offer will be infinity.

The cost of the conflict deal ($C^{(A)}_{conflict}$ for the agent A) is the time to arrive the destination if the agent doesn't negotiate. Obviously, such value is a criterion to decide whether the opponent's offer is rational or not. In addition, each agent has a best offer $O^{(A)}_{best}$ whose trajectory is a straight line between source and destination, and the corresponding cost $C^{(A)}_{best}$ is the ideal time it can arrive the destination. However, in most cases, the best offer for an agent may be neither feasible nor rational for the opponent. In this paper, the utility of an offer is defined by the time the agent can save, divided by the time saved by the best offer.

$$U^A(O) = \frac{C^A_{conflict} - C^A(O)}{C^A_{conflict} - C^A_{best}} \quad (2)$$

There are three states for the utility of an offer in Equation 2: (a) the utility is minus infinity, which means the offer isn't feasible for the agent; (b) the utility is a negative number, which means the offer isn't rational for the agent; and (c) the utility is a positive number between zero and one, which means that the offer is a potential deal for both negotiators. Thus, the objective of the negotiation is to find a deal between two agents, which is feasible and rational, and its utility is maximized in agent point of view.

For a negotiation with incomplete knowledge, it is hard for an agent to find an offer which is also feasible and rational for the opponent, unless it knows the opponent's preference. Such preference includes the opponent's source, destination and its speed. In the next section, we will start to discuss how the learning agent guesses these information from a sequence of offers proposed by the opponent.

3   Bayesian Learning of Preferences

The nature of the offer discloses some velocity information between agents. Specifically, for an offer by the opponent, the agent can easily calculate the common speed that the opponent wants to use to traverse the forest. This speed can not exceed the maximum speed of opponent, because it will not propose an offer which is not feasible for itself. In this way, to guess the speed of opponent, the learning agent just needs to calculate the maximum common speed from all the previous offers it received from the opponent. Moreover, it should add some time buffers in the splitting time field (if necessary) when proposing the next counter offer to the opponent.

To guess the source location and destination of the opponent, the map is divided into grid. The combination of a grid in the source area and another one in destination area is called a location model. The learning agent tries to guess the location model of the opponent, by updating the probabilities (belief) of all these combinations. Initially, each location model has equal probability, and the sum of these probabilities equals to one. From time to time, these probabilities are updated along the number of offers the learning agent receives from the opponent.

3.1   Bayesian Learning

Bayesian learning is the classical method to update the belief based on evidences [6,10]. Mathematically, the probability that the opponent is in the location model $\{sx, sy, dx, dy\}$ (the coordinates of the grid cells), when receiving a new evidence O_t (receiving an offer from opponent) can be calculated based on Bayes' theorem.

$$Pr(\{sx, sy, dx, dy\}|O_t) = \frac{Pr(O_t|\{sx, sy, dx, dy\})Pr(\{sx, sy, dx, dy\})}{\sum_{i,j,k,l=0}^{i,j,k,l=grid-1} Pr(O_t|\{i,j,k,l\})Pr(\{i,j,k,l\})} \quad (3)$$

where *grid* is the number of pieces the learning agent divides the map in each dimension, and t is the order of the offers it receives from the opponent. The formula shows that the posterior probability of a location model can be calculated by the prior probability times the probability to propose the offer given the opponent is indeed in the specific location model, and then normalized by all the updated probabilities. The learning algorithm is shown in algorithm 1.

Algorithm 1. Algorithm for the learning agent

1: initialize all location models and assign them equal probability;
2: **for** $t = 1$ to *theEndOfNegotiation* **do**
3:     get the opponent's offer O_t;
4:     **for all** location models $\{i, j, k, l\}$ **do**
5:         calculate $Pr(O_t|\{i, j, k, l\})$;
6:         updated posterior probability $Pr(\{i, j, k, l\}|O_t)$;
7:     **end for**
8:     normalize all the updated probabilities;
9:     propose next offer to opponent;
10: **end for**

3.2   Determining the Posterior Probabilities

In this subsection, we will discuss how the learning agent calculates $Pr(O_t|\{i, j, k, l\})$ - the probability to propose the offer O_t, given that the opponent is in location model $\{i, j, k, l\}$. First, we establish four basic rules according to the assumptions of opponent agent. We let the learning agent eliminate nonrational location models which break these rules. Next, the learning agent will calculate the expected utility of opponent at a specific negotiation round, and increase the probabilities of the location models whose actual utilities of the offer are close to the expected one. At last, we introduce a half Gaussian approach to overcome the case where the learning agent doesn't know the expected utility for the opponent.

The four basic rules

We are going to make four basic assumptions about the behavior of the opponent agent in the negotiation. First, the opponent will not propose an offer which is not feasible for itself. Second, the opponent will not propose an offer which is not rational for itself, (otherwise, it will arrive the destination later than its conflict deal). The third assumption is the opponent will propose a counter offer whose utility for itself is less or equal than the previous offers. This means that at each round of negotiation, the opponent should concede or at least insist on its last offer. The last assumption is that the opponent will accept the agent's offer if its utility is higher than the next counter offer. If the opponent in an assumed location model proposed an offer which breaks these rules, the learning agent will eliminate the possibility of that location model.

Practically, the value of $Pr(O_t|\{i, j, k, l\}) = 0$ if the opponent was assumed at location model $\{i, j, k, l\}$ but its last O_t breaks the four basic rules. All the other location models in the learning agent's belief share the same probability. Next, the learning agent will continue to discriminate these rational models and finds the one more likely.

Updating belief based on expected utility

A self-interested agent will not only act rational, but also propose the most profitable offers at first, and concede to less profitable ones later. Using this idea, the learning agent can calculate the expected utility at a specific negotiation round, and assign more probabilities to those location models for which the utility of the offer is close to the expected one. In practice, the learning agent assumes that the opponent proposes offers with utilities starting from 1.0 at the first call and linearly decreasing during the negotiation.

$$EU(t) = 1 - \alpha \times t \qquad (4)$$

where t is the order of the offers by the opponent and α is the conceding speed. At each negotiation round, the location model whose utility of the offer O_t is close to $EU(t)$, will have its probabilities increased based on the Gaussian p.d.f.

$$Pr(O_t|\{i,j,k,l\}) = \frac{1}{\sigma\sqrt{2\pi}}e^{-\frac{(U_t(O_t,\{i,j,k,l\})-EU(t))^2}{2\sigma^2}} \qquad (5)$$

where $U_t(O_t, \{i, j, k, l\}))$ is the utility of the opponent's offer O_t when it is assumed in location model $\{i, j, k, l\}$, and σ is the coefficient of confidence. There are several approximations for this approach. The first one is we transfer a four-dimensional vector (offer $\mathbf{O_t}$) into a value (utility U_t) and assume they have the same posterior probabilities.

$$
\begin{aligned}
&Pr(O_t|\{i,j,k,l\}) \\
&= \frac{Pr(U_t|\{i,j,k,l\}) \times Pr(O_t|U_t,\{i,j,k,l\})}{Pr(U_t|O_t,\{i,j,k,l\})} \quad (Bayes'theorem) \\
&= Pr(U_t|\{i,j,k,l\}) \times Pr(O_t|U_t,\{i,j,k,l\}) \ (definition\ of\ utility) \\
&= Pr(U_t|\{i,j,k,l\}) \quad\quad\quad\quad\quad\quad\quad\quad\quad (assumption)
\end{aligned}
$$

The equation assumes that $Pr(O_t|U_t, \{i, j, k, l\}) = 1$. In general, an agent may find many offers given a specific utility, and the assumption is not true for those strategies which want to try out every possible offer before conceding the utility. However, considering the negotiation time is crucial, we assume the opponent can only select one offer given a specific utility.

Another approximation for this approach comes from the four basic rules. The learning agent eliminates the probability of non-rational location models whose utilities are negative or greater than the utility of the opponent's last offer. Such elimination cuts off the Gaussian p.d.f (see Figure 2(a)), and the integral of the remaining part doesn't equal one. The assumption here is we ignore these parts because all the probabilities will be normalized later, and we just need a discriminant value to judge the distance between the actual utility and the expected one. In the mean time, we can also change the variance of Gaussian p.d.f to reduce the impact of this approximation.

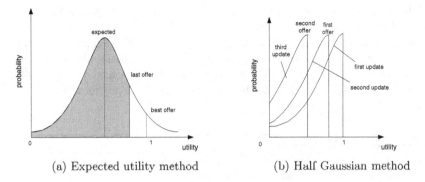

(a) Expected utility method   (b) Half Gaussian method

Fig. 2. Two methods to discriminate location models in the learning agent: 2(a): it updates belief based on Gaussian p.d.f which center at the expected utility and 2(b): it updates the probabilities based on half Gaussian p.d.f with the center at the utility of last offer.

The main deficiency of this approach is the difficulty to find a correct conceding speed to calculate the expected utility. If the opponent uses a different strategy which is not linear concession in utility, the learning agent may make a wrong guess. To overcome this problem, we need to model the opponent's strategy and calculate the expected utility based on the probabilities of strategy models [5] (we leave it in the future work), or we can apply it in a save way which we will discuss next.

Updating belief based on the half-Gaussian distribution
The idea of this approach is that an agent will concede step by step. At each step, it will give up a small amount of utility and see if the opponent accepts it. In this way, if the opponent which is assumed in a location model proposes two adjacent offers which have a big difference in utilities, the probability that the opponent is in that location model should be small.

Figure 2(b) depicts the way the learning agent calculates the conditional probability $Pr(O_t|\{i, j, k, l\})$. As we discussed above, the offer O_t is first transferred into utility U_t, given the assumption that the opponent is in location model $\{i, j, k, l\}$. Then, the learning agent calculates the probability of the offer based on utility and half Gaussian p.d.f, in which the mean of the Gaussian is at the utility of the last offer given the opponent is in the same location model.

4   Experimental Study

4.1   Strategies Used by the Opponent

Before we study the performance of the learning, we introduce several simple strategies which the opponent might use in the CRF game. The first strategy is called Monotonic Concession in Space (MCS), which is parameterized by the conceding pace at each side of the forest (C_{meet}, C_{split}). The MCS agent proposes its best offer at first, and then concedes in spatial fields to the opponent's last offer. The meeting time field is tightly calculated based on the agent's own speed, and the splitting time field is added some time buffer according to the maximum common speed in opponent's previous offers. When the MCS agent doesn't have space to concede its offer or the next concession breaks the rationality constraint, the agent quits the negotiation. On the other hand, if the next conceded offer is worse than the opponent's last offer in utility, the MCS agent will agree the opponent's offer (see Algorithm 2.)

Algorithm 2. The MCS agent

1: the agent receives an offer O_t from the opponent;
2: calculates conceded offer O_{next} according to (C_{meet}, C_{split});
3: **if** not exist O_{next} **then**
4:     **if** O_t is rational and feasible **then**
5:         agree the opponent's offer O_t;
6:     **else**
7:         quit the negotiation;
8:     **end if**
9: **else**
10:     **if** $U(O_t) \geq U(O_{next})$ **then**
11:         agree the opponent's offer O_t;
12:     **else**
13:         propose counter offer O_{next};
14:     **end if**
15: **end if**

The second strategy is called Uniform Concession (UC), which is parameterized by the conceding speed λ. The idea is the MCS strategy doesn't test all the combinations of meeting and splitting locations across the forest, nor add any time buffer in the meeting time field. In this way, it may omit some potential deals. The UC agent, however, searches the offers in the whole spatio-temporal domain, and uniformly concedes in utilities of those offers. Specifically, the agent proposes an offer based on a range of utility. The length of the range is the conceding speed λ. The higher boundary of the range is initialized as one (the utility of the best offer), and it decreases with the amount of λ at the next time. To calculate the next counter offer, the UC agent searches all possible combinations whose utilities are in the current utility range, and selects the one which is most similar to the opponent's last offer. The similarity between two offers is defined by the sum of squared difference for each issues $||\mathbf{O}_{next} - \mathbf{O}_{opponent}||^2$. When the lower boundary of the utility range is less than zero, the agent quits the negotiation without agreement. When the utility of the opponent's offer is greater than the lower boundary of the utility range, the UC agent agrees the opponent's offer (see Algorithm 3.)

4.2   Performance of Learning

In this subsection, we focus on the accuracy of learning by comparing the opponent's actual location model with the probabilities of location models in the

Algorithm 3. The UC agent

1: the agent receives an offer O_t from the opponent;
2: Create $Set\langle offer\rangle$ to hold all possible offers;
3: **while** $Set\langle offer\rangle$ is empty **do**
4:     $lower = lower - \lambda$;
5:     **if** $lower \leq 0$ **then**
6:         quit the negotiation;
7:     **end if**
8:     find all $Offer$ that $U(Offer) \in (lower, lower + \lambda)$;
9:     add all $Offer$ in $Set\langle offer\rangle$
10: **end while**
11: find $O_{next} \leftarrow \arg\min_{Set\langle offer\rangle} Similar(offer, O_t)$;
12: **if** $U(O_t) \geq lower$ **then**
13:     agree the opponent's offer O_t;
14: **else**
15:     propose O_{next}
16: **end if**

learning agent's belief. At first, we generate a typical scenario and see how the probabilities are updated during the negotiation. Then, we study the statistical performance in random generated scenarios.

A typical scenario
Figure 3 shows a typical scenario, where the opponent is located at the centers of grids in a specific location model and the learning agent is located at the lower corners of the forest. We let the learning agent use different methods to update the posterior probabilities. The opponent uses MCS strategy with parameter of

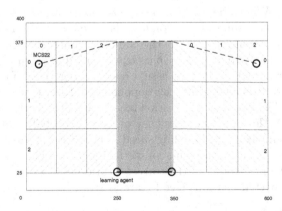

Fig. 3. A typical scenario: both the source and the destination area is divided into 3 × 3 girds, which corresponds to 81 location models. The opponent agent is located at the center of grid (0,0) and wants to move to the center of grid (0,2) with the speed of 1.0. The learning agent is located at the lower-left corner of the forest, insists its best offer until the end of negotiation.

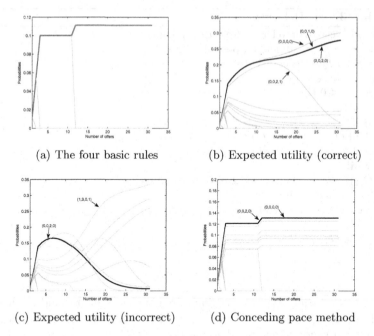

(a) The four basic rules   (b) Expected utility (correct)

(c) Expected utility (incorrect)   (d) Conceding pace method

Fig. 4. The probabilities are updated along the number of offers from the opponent, the bold line is the opponent's actual location model in the learning agent's belief. The learning agent use: 4(a): four basic rules, 4(b): expected utility with correct conceding speed, 4(c): expected utility with incorrect conceding speed, 4(d): half Gaussian method, to determine the posterior probabilities.

(2,2). Figure 4 shows the updating progress in the learning agent's belief. For all these three methods, 81 location models are initialized as equal probabilities at the beginning. When the learning agent uses four basic rules to update the posterior probabilities, some of location models are eliminated when the learning agent believes them non-rational. At the end of learning process, there are still 9 models it couldn't decide. So they share equal probabilities in learning agent's belief (see Figure 4(a)). Then, we assign a conceding speed for the learning agent to calculate expected utility by opponent, and let it negotiate with the same opponent. The 9 remaining location models are then further discriminated (see Figure 4(b)). However, the deficiency of using expected utility is disclosed when we assign an incorrect conceding speed in the learning agent's assumption (see Figure 4(c)). At last, half Gaussian method gives a relatively compromised outcome, with the probability of the correct location model between the correct and incorrect Expected methods (see Figure 4(d)).

A statistical study

We enumerate all the other combinations where the opponent's source and destination are initialized at the centers of grids. We let the opponent use simple strategies we discussed above and the learning agent use the four basic rules to update the belief. We calculate the averaged number of opponent models remained in the belief over all the combinations of grids and we increase the grid resolution in the map (see Table below):

	MCS $C_{meet}=2$, $C_{split}=2$	UC $\alpha=0.02$
grid=3, 81(models)	5.271	4.099
grid=4, 256(models)	9.731	7.016
grid=5, 625(models)	17.733	11.9936

The next question is how to decide whether the error tolerance due to the resolution of the grids is not high enough, and the opponent is not at the centers of the grids. Intuitively, the learning agent may eliminate the correct opponent model based on the four basic rules if the opponent is not at the center of the grids. This is a trade-off between the correctness and the accuracy of learning. The correctness of learning is defined by the number of experiments that the correct location model is still remained in the learning agent's belief, over the total number of experiments. The accuracy of learning is the averaged probabilities of the correct model in all the experiments. If the error tolerance is too small, the correct location model may be eliminated, so its probability will be zero. On the other hand, if it is too large, the number of location models remained in the belief is also large, so the probability of the correct location model will be very low too. In the experiment, we generate 1000 random scenarios, we let the learning agent use the four basic rules negotiating with a MCS agent. We calculate the correctness of these 1000 learning, and the accuracy of the learning. In addition, we change the value of error tolerance as well as the grid number to see the tendency of correctness and accuracy (see Figure 5). From the experiment, by increasing the error tolerance until the amount of time for the opponent travels a half length of grid diagonal, both correctness and accuracy are balancing. That's because if the opponent's source and destination are at the edge of grids, it is still believed as rational as it is located at the centers.

With a balanced error tolerance, we continue to study the performance of learning in 1000 random generated scenario when the learning agent use each of three methods to update the belief, and with opponent use simple strategies with different parameters (see Figure 6).

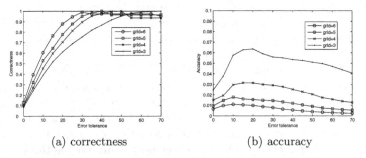

(a) correctness   (b) accuracy

Fig. 5. The values of correctness and accuracy in the function of error tolerance in 1000 random generated scenarios

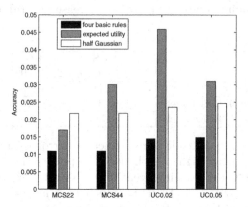

Fig. 6. The statistical study about the three learning approaches, when the opponent use the MCS22, MCS44, UC0.02, and UC0.05 strategies respectively. The results come from 1000 random generated scenario with learning agent's grid number of 6, error tolerance of 10. The learning agent which uses expected utility method assume the opponent's conceding speed is 0.03.

4.3   Performance of Negotiation with or without Learning

This subsection investigates how to apply the output of learning to accelerate the speed of negotiation. We design a strategy which is similar with the UC, but has full-knowledge about the opponent's preference (UCF). Contrasting to search offers within the small utility range, the UCF agent just has a conceding level. When proposing the next offer, it will choose the offer whose utility is higher than the current level and providing the opponent best utility. If there no such offer exists, the level is decreased. If the opponent doesn't accept the offer, it will also decrease the level in the next round. When the level is less than zero, the agent quits the negotiation.

In the experiment, we generate 1000 random scenarios, letting the learning agent select its next counter offer in the same way as the UCF agent. The difference is it guesses the opponent as in the most probable location model in its current belief. If it couldn't find any offer satisfy the requirements, it doesn't decrease the level but continue to search by changing the assumption that the opponent in the second most probable location model. After a certain round of search (a certain amount of probabilities in belief have been searched), it decreases the utility level until find the next offer. The story behind this approach is that the learning agent initially doubts the correctness of its own belief before it concedes the utility level, which in other words, it updates the subjective things it can control before concede the objective things it can not control (such as the opponent's strategy, and the nature of scenario).

We compare the averaged number of negotiation rounds, and the average utility of the testing agent as well as the opponent gains, among the UCF agent (an agent with full knowledge), the UC agent (an agent without knowledge and without learning), and the learning agent (an agent which uses half Gaussian

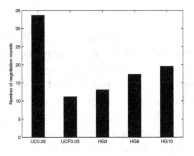 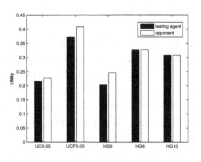

(a) Number of negotiation rounds   (b) Averaged utilities

Fig. 7. The benefit of learning: UC0.05, UCF0,05, HG3, HG6 and HG9 negotiate with another UC0.05 in 1000 random scenarios

method, without knowledge but with learning), when each of them negotiates with another UC agent as a fixed opponent (see Figure 7). From the experiment, we can see: (a) the number of negotiation rounds is dramatically decreased if the agent is learning; (b) the utility of the deal is also improved if the agent learns; and (c) the effect of the first two observations are more obvious when the learning agent increase the grid resolution of the map.

5 Related Work

Fatima et al. [4] used the shrinking pies model to investigate the multi-issue negotiation problem with deadlines. They assume a common preferences pool that both agents know in advance. During the negotiation, the agent assumes that the opponent uses the same strategy, and it guesses which type of preference in the common pool that the opponent is. In this paper, we also divide the preference into discrete representations of grids, and we remove the non-rational opponent model in the same way. However, we don't assume the learning agent knows the opponent's offering strategy, but we try to abstract the offer into the utility point of view to update the probabilities.

Hindriks et al. [2] used the Bayesian learning to study the opponent's type for each issue. They apply the probabilistic guess over a set of hypothesis and update the probabilities based on the distance between the opponent's expected bid and its actual bid. In this paper, we also try to guess the expected utility of opponent's offer, but we found that it is difficult to arbitrarily decide the conceding speed in the spatio-temporal negotiations. Moreover, issues of the offer in our problem are inter-dependent and the utility function is non-linear. Thus, we update the probability based on the expected utility and we design the half Gaussian method to compromise the risk of incorrect guess.

In addition, this paper also introduces some similar strategies which apply the learning result to improve the negotiation outcome, like the meta strategy introduced by Faratin et al. [3], the Bazaar model introduced by Zeng et al.[10], the learning strategy introduced by Bui et al. [1] and others.

6   Conclusion

In this paper, we applied the Bayesian learning in the spatio-temporal negoti-ation problem. The learning agent guesses the opponent's preference from the sequence of offers it received. We designed three approaches to update the prob-abilities of opponent's location models in learning agent's belief. First of all, for those non-rational models in which a rational opponent will not propose the of-fer, we eliminate their possibilities immediately. Then we continue to distinguish location models based on the expected utility for a specific negotiation time. At last, half Gaussian method is introduced to punish those models whose utilities of two adjacent offers have large difference. At the end of this paper, we evalu-ate these approaches and show the accuracy of learning by statistical analysis, then we show the benefit of learning when it negotiates with a fixed opponent in random scenarios.

Our future work is to continue the learning for the opponent's strategy mod-els, or the belief about belief if the opponent is also learning. Combining the preference model with the strategy model will lead the negotiation to a decision-making problem, which gives the learning agent much more advantageous than its opponent. We will also apply the output of strategy models to help the agent calculate the next expected offer (instead of calculating the expected utility in this paper). In this way, the preference models can be further updated.

Acknowledgments

This work was partially funded by NSF Information and Intelligent Systems division under award 0712869.

This research was sponsored in part by the Army Research Laboratory and was accomplished under Cooperative Agreement Number W911NF-06-2-0041. The views and conclusions contained in this document are those of the authors and should not be interpreted as representing the official policies, either ex-pressed or implied, of the Army Research Laboratory or the U.S. Government. The U.S. Government is authorized to reproduce and distribute reprints for Government purposes notwithstanding any copyright notation heron.

References

1. Bui, H.H., Kieronska, D., Venkatesh, S.: Learning other agents' preferences in mul-tiagent negotiation. In: Proceedings of the National Conference on Artificial Intel-ligence (AAAI 1996), pp. 114–119. AAAI Press, Menlo Park (1996)
2. Dmytro Tykhonov, K.H.: Opponent modelling in automated multi-issue negotia-tion using bayesian learning. In: Seventh International Conference on Autonomous Agents and Multiagent Systems (AAMAS 2008), pp. 331–338 (2008)
3. Faratin, P., Sierra, C., Jennings, N.R.: Using similarity criteria to make issue trade-offs in automated negotiations. Artificial Intelligence 142, 205–237 (2002)
4. Fatima, S.S., Wooldridge, M., Jennings, N.R.: Multi-issue negotiation with dead-lines. Journal of Artificial Intelligence Research 27, 381–417 (2006)

5. Ficici, S., Pfeffer, A.: Simultaneously modeling humans' preferences and their beliefs about others' preferences. In: Seventh International Conference on Autonomous Agents and Multiagent Systems (AAMAS 2008), pp. 323–330 (2008)
6. Li, J., Cao, Y.-D.: Bayesian learning in bilateral multi-issue negotiation and its application in mas-based electronic commerce. Iat, 437–440 (2004)
7. Luo, Y., Bölöni, L.: Children in the forest: towards a canonical problem of spatio-temporal collaboration. In: The Sixth Intl. Joint Conf. on Autonomous Agents and Multi-Agent Systems (AAMAS 2007), pp. 986–993 (2007)
8. Luo, Y., Bölöni, L.: Collaborative and competitive scenarios in spatio-temporal negotiation with agents of bounded rationality. In: Proceedings of the 1st International Workshop on Agent-based Complex Automated Negotiations, in conjunction with the The Seventh Intl. Joint Conf. on Autonomous Agents and Multi-Agent Systems (AAMAS 08), pp. 40–47 (2008)
9. Tim McLain, R.W.B.: Unmanned air vehicle testbed for cooperative control experiments. In: American Control Conference, Boston, MA, pp. 5327–5331 (2004)
10. Zeng, D., Sycara, K.: Bayesian learning in negotiation. Int. J. Hum.-Comput. Stud. 48(1), 125–141 (1998)
11. Zheng, X., Koenig, S.: Reaction functions for task allocation to cooperative agents. In: Seventh International Conference on Autonomous Agents and Multiagent Systems (AAMAS 2008), pp. 559–566 (2008)

Protecting Sensitive Information in Directory Services Using Virtual Directories

William Claycomb[1] and Dongwan Shin[2]

[1] Sandia National Laboratories, P.O. Box 5800, MS 0823, Albuquerque, NM,
87185-0823, USA
wrclayc@sandia.gov
[2] Computer Science Department, New Mexico Tech, Socorro, NM, 87801, USA
doshin@nmt.edu

Abstract. Directory services are commonly used to store information related to individuals, and often act as a source for security services, such as authentication and access control, in collaborative applications within/across organizations. Hence, there is an urgent need to protect the sensitive information they contain. Existing solutions offer minimal protection against insider attacks, a growing threat to both government and industry data services. In this paper we present a solution for data protection that leverages virtual directories and data encryption to provide a user-centric approach to data protection, delegation, and collaboration. A security architecture is presented, along with the discussion of the benefits and vulnerabilities of our approach. We also discuss a proof-of-concept implementation and performance testing results.

Keywords: Access controls, Cryptographic controls, Data encryption, Public key cryptosystems, Privacy, Information resource management, Data dictionary/directory.

1 Introduction

Directory services are used to store information about objects within an organization, such as users, computers, etc., and are organized in a hierarchical structure. Often, directory services (or simply, *directories*) are used as authoritative data sources for many collaborative applications that require user information, such as instant messaging, workflow systems, and social applications. In some cases, the information contained in a directory is considered confidential, such as employee ID number, clearance level, or other *personally identifiable information (PII)*. While techniques exist to protect this information, they do not adequately prevent a user with administrative privileges from unauthorized access. Moreover, many organizations have several directories, some containing duplicate information. This can arise from inadequate information planning, applications requiring proprietary data sources, or the need to protect specific information at different levels. Determining authoritative data sources and synchronizing data across directories is a challenging and ongoing task for many corporations.

E. Bertino and J.B.D. Joshi (Eds.): CollaborateCom 2008, LNICST 10, pp. 244–257, 2009.

Each object in a directory is described by a set of *attributes*. Examples include name, address, email, or manager name. Access control lists (ACLs) or marking attributes *confidential* [1] are two commonly practiced techniques to protect attribute data in a directory from ordinary users. In general, however, directories are used to share information, and rarely enforce access controls beyond simple user authentication (only users with accounts on the system may access the data). An insider threat, someone with authorized access, could potentially retrieve personal information about every object in the directory. The malicious activities possible with such information could include selling information to competing companies, foreign governments, or spammers, or even worse - the targeted attack of specific individuals within the company, such as domain-level administrators, known as *context aware attacks*, or *spear phishing* [2].

The threat of unauthorized access of sensitive data by employees or other authorized users, known as "dedicated insiders", is well documented [3,4,5]. In January 2008, the U.S. Secret Service and CERT issued a report titled "Insider Threat Study: Illicit Cyber Activity in the Government Sector" [3]. This study outlines a multi-year project, started in 2002, that explores the activity and threats posed by insiders. Among the key findings of this study are the following:

– Most of the insiders had authorized access at the time of their malicious activities
– Access control gaps facilitated most of the insider incidents, including:
  • The ability of an insider to use technical methods to override access controls without detection
  • System vulnerabilities that allowed technical insiders to use their specialized skills to override access controls without detection

In this paper we present a solution for data protection that leverages the concept of a virtual directory and data encryption to provide a user-centric approach to sensitive information protection, delegation, and collaboration. Specifically, we discuss an architecture for protecting individual attributes in directory services from unauthorized access. In standard configurations for directory data usage, clients communicate directly with directory services using the Lightweight Directory Access Protocol (LDAP). Clients connect to a specific port on a specific server, and may authenticate using various methods, including providing a username and password, if necessary. Our architecture is based on a middle layer placed in between the client and server, called a virtual directory, to handle LDAP transactions between them. A data protection component within the virtual directory is introduced and it relies on information provided by the client to encrypt sensitive information. While other solutions have proposed encrypting attribute information, our architecture provides this capability without requiring additional software or hardware on either the client or destination server.

The remainder of this paper is organized as follows. Section II presents an analysis of background material and related solutions. Section III describes our architecture in detail. In Section IV, we analyze the results of our implementation testing. Section V discusses the architecture, including various advantages, as well as attack models. Section VI concludes this paper with a glimpse of future work.

2   Background and Related Work

2.1   Directory Services

Directories are collections of information related to objects in an organization. These objects often include users, computers, or contacts. *Directory Services* are the services which make this data available for use by others. Frequently, the intention is to provide a single point of access for various applications and individuals to find information about users and other objects for different purposes including collaboration within/across organizations. The information contained within the directory may come from direct input, and can be manually maintained, but also may be referenced and managed indirectly from other corporate data repositories, such as databases and other information stores. Commonly used directory services are Microsoft Active Directory [6], IBM Tivoli [7], Apple Open Directory [8], Novell eDirectory (formerly called Novell Directory Services) [9], OpenLDAP [10], Fedora Directory Server [11], and Sun Java System Directory Server [12].

2.2   Protecting Information in Directory Services

A few techniques exist for protecting the information stored within a directory itself. In general, access control lists (ACLs) can be used to implement some form of protection in most directories. For instance, in OpenLDAP, ACL protection can be applied to individual objects, groups of objects, specific LDAP filters, or a list of attributes [13]. Other techniques are almost exclusively implementation-specific.

Microsoft Active Directory [6] provides additional access control features through the use of *confidential attributes* [1]. This is a setting applied to the *searchFlags* component of individual attributes, and is only supported on Microsoft Windows Server 2003 SP1 and later. When processing confidential attributes, the directory server checks for additional access control rights associated with the requesting user. This particular type of access, called "CONTROL_ACCESS," is granted to administrative accounts by default, but can be delegated to other accounts individually.

Another approach to protecting attributes is encrypting them. Fedora Directory Server [11] has the capability to encrypt all instances of specified attributes. This means that for every object containing such attributes, the data in that attribute is encrypted using a symmetric key known to the directory server. Various encryption methods can be configured, and different attributes can be encrypted using different ciphers. Encryption and decryption are handled by the directory server itself, so access to attributes is not controlled by this method. However, data would be protected from unauthorized access if the directory data was stolen or otherwise compromised.

A third approach to protecting directory attributes is described in [14]. This method is not dependent on a particular directory implementation. Rather, it uses public key infrastructure (PKI) to allow users to control the encryption of attributes related to their own directory information. This solution describes different methods for using PKI to ensure either data authenticity alone, or data authenticity combined with confidentiality. Specific solutions are proposed for scalability and usability purposes.

Additionally, [15] proposes encrypting directory information for users based on a *unique-id* chosen for each user. This method applies primarily to public directory servers, and does not address the issue of preventing unauthorized access so much as it addresses the issue of preventing access to the entire directory. For instance, a company could share contact information publicly, and provide selected clients with appropriate unique-ids, without worrying that the entire directory would be scanned for email addresses. One important aspect of the work is to choose a unique-id well, so that it cannot be easily guessed, but can still be easily shared with authorized users.

2.3   Metadirectories and Virtual Directories

One way to protect personal information is to reduce the number of different data stores containing personal information. This can be a complicated task, particularly for businesses with many disparate data sources. The International Data Corporation (IDC) and Gartner Groups have found that large corporations may have in excess of 100 data stores containing user information [16]. Additionally, proprietary systems often do not interact with other data sources. Consolidating data into a single data source is often not possible, due to constraints on who may have access to specific information. Technology has emerged to address these issues, specifically by referencing the underlying data sources and presenting end-users with customized views of the data they require, and by synchronizing data between different data sources. Two similar but distinct methods of handling these tasks are *virtual directories* and *metadirectories*.

Metadirectories. Analyzing the origin of the word "metadirectory," we see the Greek phrase "meta-" which means "after," or "beyond." In modern English, this term often describes abstraction. Thus, a metadirectory is an abstraction of an actual directory. In this sense, it acts as a directory in some instances, by providing user interaction via LDAP, but does not act as a directory in other instances, because it is not the actual authoritative source of directory information. A metadirectory is used to abstract data from other directories into a single source, which can be used for two purposes.

The first use is for end user reference. Users may access the data collected by a metadirectory via LDAP. In particular, this not only reduces the number of data sources an end user connects to, but enables customization of directory data for individual uses. Therefore, in one sense a metadirectory is a real directory - information is actually stored locally, and is queried directly by end users.

However, this repository is not the authoritative source of the data. Rather, data synchronization must occur between the metadirectory and source directories to ensure consistency and accuracy of the data. It is the synchronization of data which is its second purpose. When different data sources must store the same information, it is desirable to have a single source of authoritative data, which is synchronized with other data sources. For example, if the HR department is the authoritative source for a user's telephone number, but the company directory application, which uses its own data source, also requires a telephone number to be stored, a metadirectory could be used to automatically synchronize the data from the original source (HR). A more advanced use of metadirectories is for *user provisioning*, which is a modified version of synchronization, where new user accounts are created and prepared for use, based on data in an authoritative source, such as an account database. Examples of metadirectory implementations include Microsoft Identity Lifecycle Manager 2007 [17], Sun ONE Meta-Directory [18], and Critical Path Meta-Directory Server [19].

Virtual Directories. "A virtual directory functions as an abstraction layer between applications and data repositories." [20] In contrast to metadirectories, *virtual directories* do not maintain the data in a standalone data source (though some offer *data caching*, which does store data locally for improved performance). Rather, virtual directories reference various data sources and present a consolidated view to the end user. This has the advantage of not requiring data synchronization - the data presented is always real-time, directly from the source. Most virtual directory implementations have the additional capability of acquiring data from sources other than directories, such as databases, and presenting this information to end users via LDAP.

Virtual directory instances can be highly customized to modify, or *transform*, data prior to client use. Additionally, some products offer data synchronization as well, which when coupled with a virtual directory instance, could be used for user provisioning in much the same way as a metadirectory. Virtual directory products currently in use include Radiant Logic's RadiantOne [21], Symlabs Virtual Directory Server [22], and Oracle Virtual Directory [23].

3   Our Approach

Our approach to protecting sensitive information in directory services is to encrypt that information using user-controlled keys and to provide access to that data using user-controlled delegation. This user-centric approach follows current trends in computer security and privacy, but should not interfere with more traditional approaches to access control. Our approach also maintains usability with existing client applications and source directories. To better understand the overall picture of our solution, it is first important to understand various key components.

3.1   Data Encryption

Encrypting sensitive information to protect it from misuse is hardly a new concept. In the simplest application towards protecting information in directory services, an end user would simply encrypt sensitive information and then store the encrypted data in a directory.[1] To share information, the user would share the

---

[1] Note that encryption here is orthogonal to that of secure LDAP (or LDAPs). The former is for data protection in data stores while the latter is for network communication protection. It is assumed that LDAPs is supported for better security in our approach.

encryption/decryption key with another user, who would obtain the encrypted form from the directory and decrypt it locally.

However, this approach presents several usability and security problems. First of all, the confidentiality of the data relies entirely on the shared key. If a malicious user were to obtain this key, or if an authorized user were to share it with an unauthorized party, the information could be compromised. Data confidentiality could be provided by using an asymmetric encryption algorithm, such as RSA, but this still does not protect the data from unauthorized access.

Secondly, this approach requires the user to perform encryption and decryption before and after retrieving the information from the directory. At best, this could be accomplished by a custom application, which interfaced directly with the client LDAP application. At worst, existing client LDAP applications would need to be rewritten to incorporate encryption and decryption. This is an undesirable situation for which a simple solution exists: add a third party, between the client and server, to handle encrypting and decrypting the data.

The third party component could be a custom component written specifically for the purpose of handling encryption and decryption of information between the client and directory. However, we find it much more useful to leverage the existing technology of virtual directories to provide the third party component to the model. The benefits of doing so are numerous, and will be discussed in detail later.

3.2   System Architecture

If we consider a virtual directory as the container of the third party component - the one responsible for encrypting and decrypting data - we must consider several key aspects, namely: how does the virtual directory obtain key information from the client, how does the virtual directory perform pass-through authentication to destination directories, and how does the virtual directory manipulate the data in the destination directory? The system architecture, shown in Figure 1, is proposed to address those questions.

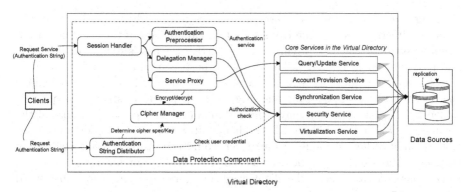

Fig. 1. System Architecture for Protecting Sensitive Information in Directory Service using Virtual Directory

Obtaining Client Key Information. When LDAP communications occur between a client and server, several standard pieces of information are transmitted. These components are generally configured by the client application, and can be changed by the end user. They are: username, password, and destination server name and port. We leverage these components to pass encryption information to the server as follows. The destination server and port are replaced with the destination server name and port of the virtual directory. This configures the client to communicate with the virtual directory, instead of the original destination directory. Note that the original destination directory is transparent to the client through virtualization, which is one of the core services in virtual directories, as shown in Figure 1. The password remains the same as the original password used to authenticate to the original destination directory.[2] We replace the username component with a string which is the concatenation of the following: the client username, ID_c, the hash of the original user password, $H(pwd_c)$, and a symmetric key between the client and virtual directory, K_{cv}. The last two components are encrypted using a secret key known only to the virtual directory server, K_v. The addition of these last components requires additional setup, performed by the Authentication String Distributor shown in Figure 1 with access to the virtual directory key, K_v, and is also discussed in detail later. The resulting string is called an *authentication string (AS)*:

$$ID_c|\{K_{cv}|H(pwd_c)\}_{K_v}$$

Performing Pass-Through Authentication. We do not ignore traditional authentication and access control methods with this solution. Unless configured for anonymous authentication (also called *anonymous bind*), the destination LDAP server will expect a client to authenticate prior to data retrieval. Some Virtual Directory implementations allow a static username and password to be used for every transaction, but this defeats the purpose of fine-grained access control. Rather, we will pass the original client username and password, obtained from the AS and password provided by the client, to perform an initial bind prior to data retrieval. If this bind is not successful, then no data transmission occurs between the virtual directory and the client.

Storing the Data. Once the user has successfully authenticated to the destination directory, we use the transformation capabilities of the Authentication Preprocessor module in our architecture to extract the user's symmetric key, K_{cv}, and password hash, $H(pwd_c)$. The password hash is used as an additional measure of security against an attack where a malicious administrator may change the user's password and, using the original authentication string, masquerade as the user. While this step may seem redundant, it is necessary because of the nature of LDAP clients. Many LDAP clients allow users to cache login information, including the username. An attacker would need to have no knowledge of the client secret key, K_{cv}, if he used a cached authentication string and a newly-reset password. However, if the client were configured to prompt for a password

---

[2] Pass-through authentication is more commonly practiced than single-sign-on, in virtual directories.

every time, while still retaining a cached authentication string, the user's password hash could be checked against the password hash encrypted by the virtual directory's secret key in the AS. In this instance, a changed user password would cause a failure, because its hash would not match the original hash in the AS.

Once verified, the user's secret key, K_{cv}, is used to perform encryption or decryption of data stored in the directory. The protocol for reading an encrypted attribute is shown in Figure 2, and the protocol for writing an encrypted attribute is shown in Figure 3.

3.3   Collaboration and Delegation

One of the key components to our approach, as shown in Figures 2 and 3, is the capability of the user to delegate access to attributes, enabling collaboration with other users. We modify a traditional Access Control List (ACL) model, by identifying the access control entry principal by password hash. If another user is delegated permission to access a particular attribute, the corresponding password hash, $H\{pwd_c\}$, must exist (read and/or write) in the ACL attached to the attribute when stored in the destination directory. Alternatively, if the attribute owner attempts to access the attribute, identified by $H\{pwd_o\}$, full access is granted. The ACL is managed by the virtual directory server, and again would require additional interaction by the attribute owner to manage. This is supported by the Delegation Manager in our system architecture.

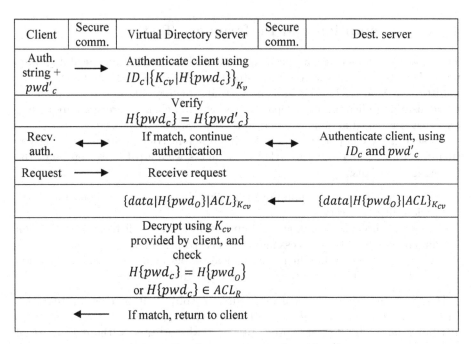

Fig. 2. Reading an encrypted attribute

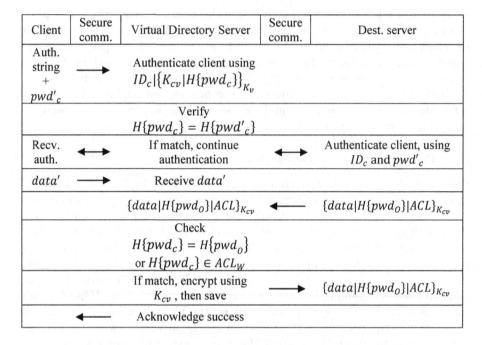

Client	Secure comm.	Virtual Directory Server	Secure comm.	Dest. server
Auth. string + pwd'_c	$\longrightarrow$	Authenticate client using $ID_c\lvert\{K_{cv}\lvert H\{pwd_c\}\}_{K_v}$		
		Verify $H\{pwd_c\} = H\{pwd'_c\}$		
Recv. auth.	$\longleftrightarrow$	If match, continue authentication	$\longleftrightarrow$	Authenticate client, using ID_c and pwd'_c
$data'$	$\longrightarrow$	Receive $data'$		
		$\{data\lvert H\{pwd_o\}\lvert ACL\}_{K_{cv}}$	$\longleftarrow$	$\{data\lvert H\{pwd_o\}\lvert ACL\}_{K_{cv}}$
		Check $H\{pwd_c\} = H\{pwd_o\}$ or $H\{pwd_c\} \in ACL_W$		
		If match, encrypt using K_{cv} , then save	$\longrightarrow$	$\{data\lvert H\{pwd_o\}\lvert ACL\}_{K_{cv}}$
	$\longleftarrow$	Acknowledge success		

Fig. 3. Writing an encrypted attribute

4   Implementation and Performance Testing

The system architecture has been implemented for testing and usability purposes. Directory servers were represented using Microsoft Active Directory Administration Mode (ADAM) [24]. The Virtual directory component was modeled via a custom application on a separate system, and clients were simulated using directory services functions in Microsoft Visual Studio .NET 2008.

To accurately compare results of testing different configurations of using virtual directories, three separate ADAM instances were created, to represent the following situations:

– No virtual directory - communication directly between the client and destination directory server
– A virtual directory handing communication between client and destination directory server, but processing no encrypted attributes
– A virtual directory handing communication between client and destination directory server, and processing some encrypted attributes

Data was simulated using real-world directory objects from a corporate Active Directory instance. For each test, 10,000 user objects were created, with 25 attributes populated for each user. Testing both with and without the virtual directory server, as well as with and without encrypted attributes was performed. When using encryption to protect attributes, three attributes per user were stored encrypted. The time to perform each operation was recorded, as well as the overall size on disk of each directory instance.

Creating New Objects. Creating new objects in a directory service, known as *account provisioning*, involves two distinct steps: creating the new object, and populating the attributes of that object. For testing purposes, this was measured as one atomic operation. Table 1 shows the average time necessary for each testing configuration to create new accounts.

Table 1. Average new account creation time (ms)

Configuration	Time (ms)
No virtual directory - no encryption	92
Virtual directory - not encrypting	99
Virtual directory - encrypting	205

Modifying an Non-Encrypted Attribute. When modifying an attribute, the virtual directory server is able to detect whether or not the attribute is encrypted. If the attribute is not encrypted, the virtual directory simply passes through the modification request from the client to the destination directory server. The time to modify an non-encrypted attribute is shown in Table 2.

Table 2. Average time to modify a non-encrypted attribute (ms)

Configuration	Time (ms)
No virtual directory - no encryption	6
Virtual directory - not encrypting	12
Virtual directory - encrypting	12

Modifying an Encrypted Attribute. To modify an encrypted attribute, the virtual directory is required to decrypt the authentication string, extract the shared secret key of the client, K_{cv}, and check to see if the requesting client is either the data owner, or listed as an authorized user of that particular object attribute. In some cases, the performance is dependent on whether or not the attribute is blank or has been previously populated. The time to complete these tasks is shown in Table 3.

Table 3. Average time to modify encrypted attributes (ms)

Configuration	Time (blank attribute (ms))	Time (populated attribute (ms))
No virtual directory - no encryption	5	6
Virtual directory - not encrypting	12	12
Virtual directory - encrypting	106	100

Table 4. Average time to retrieve an attribute (ms)

Configuration	Time (non-encrypted attribute (ms))	Time (encrypted attribute (ms))
No virtual directory - no encryption	3	3
Virtual directory - not encrypting	6	6
Virtual directory - encrypting	6	98

Table 5. Directory size on disk (MB)

Configuration	Beginning size (MB)	Final size (MB)
No virtual directory - no encryption	6.3	56.6
Virtual directory - not encrypting	6.3	56.6
Virtual directory - encrypting	6.3	77.6

Retrieving an Attribute Value. Retrieving an attribute also depends on the particular configuration and whether or not the attribute is encrypted. The time to retrieve an object attribute is Table 4.

Directory Size on Disk. The disk space necessary to store a directory services instance can be easily measured when using ADAM. Table 5 shows the beginning and ending size of the file used to store the directory for each test configuration. The final file size was recorded after all test accounts had been created and all test attributes modified.

5 Discussion

Analyzing our solution should be approached from several angles. First, what are the advantages to using a virtual directory as the encryption provider? Next, what are the benefits and limitations of using encryption to protect the data in directory services? No analysis of data protection would be complete without discussing vulnerabilities and attack models. Finally, how well does the solution perform, particularly in real-world situations?

5.1 Advantages of Using Virtual Directories

Virtual directories allow us to use existing technology to overcome barriers such as application reliability and security. Additionally, many virtual directory implementations compliment existing access control methods, by specifying yet another level at which users may be granted permission to access specific objects. Another distinct advantage is that virtual directories are client and destination independent. That is, any LDAP client can be configured to use a virtual directory, and virtual directories can be connected to almost any type of directory service, as well as other types of data sources, such as databases.

One additional advantage could be gained by incorporating a metadirectory service into the solution as well. By using the data synchronization component of metadirectories, we can ensure that all instances of a particular attribute related to a certain user are encrypted. This takes data protection one step further, by eliminating the need to individually protect data in each separate data source.

5.2   Advantages of Using Encryption

Allowing the user to maintain the encryption/decryption key used in this solution is a user-centric approach [25,26,27] to data protection and identity management. In general, user-centric identity management is a method of managing user identities where the users themselves control what information is stored, the actual content of that information, and who is allowed to view the information. One motivation for this concept is privacy, accomplished by giving users the choice about what is shared, and with whom it is shared. [14]. Allowing the users to control the key provides them with complete control over the content of the data, and by including a user-specified ACL in the model, we allow users to specify who is allowed to access that data.

This is a particular advantage when considering one possible threat to conventional ACL-based access control. Administrative users may have permissions to modify ACLs on directory objects, and could grant themselves permission to read attributes intended to be confidential. By encrypting this data, we mitigate this particular threat.

5.3   Vulnerabilities

Of course, it's still possible for a dedicated attacker to compromise this system by gaining administrative access to the virtual directory server. This type of attack is difficult to prevent in any architecture. However, the type of attack which would compromise the data stored using our solution would be a more sophisticated attack, require more technical knowledge, and be more risky in terms of detection. No longer is a simple ACL modification necessary, now an attacker must either compromise the virtual directory application and intercept unencrypted data in transit, or he must compromise the data during transit or storage, by attacking the SSL connection. This is a much harder attack to undertake, and the risk of detection by network monitoring tools is greater.

A much simpler attack on this solution would be to compromise the user's secret key. However, this would be useless without also compromising the user's original password. Tools such as keystroke logging and administrative access to the user's computer could be used to mount such an attack, but again, this requires more technical skill, and comes with a higher risk of detection.

5.4   Performance Analysis

Examining the performance tables shown in Section IV seems to reveal a large difference between the time it takes to manage encrypted attributes versus the time to manage unencrypted attributes. This is hard to avoid - encryption is not computationally easy - but we believe this large difference is not functionally detrimental to the overall performance of the directory. Often, attributes which need to be protected are rarely accessed. A difference of 100ms is hardly noticeable when the attribute is only accessed a few times per day.

More significant to the performance of the solution in the real world is the user interaction required. An initial interaction with the Authentication String Distributor is necessary to establish the authentication string. This could be done via secure web services, for example, but still requires user configuration of the local LDAP client. Additionally, any authorized password change would require a new authentication string to be issued.

Collaboration and delegation would also be an application management issue. To add a user to the object ACL, the owner would need to interact with the Delegation Manager, and would need to have access to the hash of the delegatee's password. Again, password changes would require a modification of the ACL stored on the directory object. For large-scale delegation, this could become unwieldy. However, for sharing information with a few select sources, the benefits of this solution appear to outweigh the administrative overhead.

6   Future Work and Conclusion

We have presented an architecture for protecting sensitive information in directory services, which often work as a data hub for collaborative applications. This architecture leverages the existing technology of virtual directories as a layer between client and directory service applications. This middle layer is responsible for handling communication between client and server, and manages encryption and decryption routines with information provided by the client. The client provides the information using standard LDAP client fields, requiring only a reconfiguration - not a recode - of client applications. By allowing users to control and protect encryption keys, we enable a user-centric model of data protection, and we reduce the threats posed by dedicated insider attacks.

Future work will include additional real-world implementation and testing. Integration with existing PKI infrastructure may also pose an interesting approach, and could help to eliminate some of the overhead associated with user key and password management. Finally, by examining existing data stores and the applications that utilize them, we may come to a better understanding of how sensitive information is distributed over an enterprise-level environment, and may discover new approaches to information protection based on such knowledge.

References

1. How to mark an attribute as confidential in windows server 2003 service pack 1, support.microsoft.com/kb/922836
2. Jakobsson, M.: Modeling and preventing phishing attacks. In: Phishing Panel at Financial Cryptography (February 2005)

3. Kowalski, E., Cappelli, D., Conway, T., Willke, B., Keverline, S., Moore, A., Williams, M.: Insider threat study: Illicit cyber activity in the government sector, U.S. Secret Service and CERT, Tech. Rep. (January 2008)
4. Keeney, M., Capelli, D., Kowalski, E., Moore, A., Shimeall, T., Rogers, S.: Insider threat study: Computer system sabotage in critical infrastructure sectors, U.S. Secret Service and CERT/SEI, Tech. Rep. (May 2005)
5. Shaw, E., Ruby, K., Post, J.: The insider threat to information systems. Security Awareness Bulletin 2-98 (September 1998)
6. Windows server 2003 active directory, www.microsoft.com/windowsserver2003/technologies/directory/activedirectory/default.mspx
7. Ibm tivoli directory server, www-306.ibm.com/software/tivoli/products/directory-server/
8. Mac os x server open directory, www.apple.com/server/macosx/opendirectory.html
9. Novell edirectory, www.novell.com/products/edirectory/
10. Open ldap, www.openldap.org/
11. Fedora directory server, directory.fedoraproject.org/
12. Sun java system directory server, www.sun.com/software/products/directory_srvr/home_directory.xml
13. Carter, G.: LDAP System Administration. O'Reilly, Sebastopol (2003)
14. Claycomb, W., Shin, D., Hareland, D.: Towards privacy in enterprise directory services: A user-centric approach to attribute management. In: Proceedings of the 41th IEEE International Carnahan Conference on Security Technology, Ottawa, Canada (2007)
15. Berger, A.: Privacy protection for public directory services. Computer Networks and ISDN Systems 30, 1521–1529 (1998)
16. Chacon, M.: Unifying diverse directories. Network Magazine 16, 70–75 (2001)
17. Microsoft identity lifecycle manager 2007 (2007), www.microsoft.com/windowsserver/ilm2007/default.mspx
18. Sun one meta-directory, www.sun.com/software/products/meta_directory/home_meta_dir.xml
19. Critical path meta-directory server, www.criticalpath.net/pdf/MetaDirectory.pdf
20. I. Radiant Logic, Using virtualization to leverage your investment in active directory, Radiant Logic, Inc., Tech. Rep.
21. Radiant logic, Inc., http://www.radiantlogic.com/main/
22. Symlabs virtual directory server, http://symlabs.com/products/virtual-directory-server
23. Oracle virtual directory, http://www.oracle.com/technology/products/id_mgmt/ovds/index.html
24. Windows server 2003 active directory application mode, www.microsoft.com/windowsserver2003/adam/default.mspx
25. Koch, M., Worndl, W.: Community support and identity management. In: Seventh European Conference on Computer-Supported Cooperative Work - ECSCW 2001, Bonn, Germany (September 2001)
26. Koch, M.: Global identity management to boost personalization. In: Ninth Research Symposium on Emerging Electronic Markets, Basel, Switzerland (September 2002)
27. Josang, A., Pope, S.: User centric identity management. In: Asia Pacific Information Technology Security Conference, AusCERT 2005, Austrailia (2005)

TeleEye: An Awareness Widget for Providing the Focus of Attention in Collaborative Editing Systems

Mauro C. Pichiliani, Celso M. Hirata, Fabricio S. Soares,
and Carlos H.Q. Forster

Instituto Tecnologico de Aeronautica, Praca Marechal Eduardo Gomes 50,
12228-900 Sao Paulo, Brazil
{pichilia,hirata,p2p,forster}@ita.br

Abstract. Awareness is the knowledge about present and past group's activities and it is a relevant issue for cooperative work. There are many devices that supply awareness information in synchronous collaborative editing systems. However, the current awareness devices have restrictions to both accomplish effective awareness and show the focus of attention identifying the exact place of the participants' attention. This paper presents an awareness widget for synchronous collaborative editing systems called TeleEye that provides information about the localization of the participants' attention during a collaborative session by means of eye tracking.

Keywords: awareness, attention, eye tracking.

1 Introduction

The CSCW (Computer Supported Cooperative Work) area has many goals including the exploration of the necessary means to accomplish effective awareness in group work. One of the means used in this exploration is the search for new awareness devices that provide information on the participants' actions and the sense of presence during group work.

The devices used to provide awareness information in Collaborative Editing Systems (CES) allow the participants to obtain knowledge of the group activities to know what happened, what is happening and what will happen, and also to provide details about the work and the group. However, the current awareness devices have restrictions to accomplish effective awareness and are not able to inform the exact place where the participants' focus of attention is during group work. The restrictions include the need of explicit actions to provide awareness, the effort required to obtain awareness and the need to occupy additional space of the shared workspace.

Being able to know the participants' focus of attention is important to preserve the smoothness of the group work and also contributes to communicate the participants' actions under current execution. Moreover, the awareness of the attention plays a key role in any form of cooperation, since the abilities to know, recognize and understand someone's attention are a major aspect of human interaction and communication.

E. Bertino and J.B.D. Joshi (Eds.): CollaborateCom 2008, LNICST 10, pp. 258–270, 2009.

According to Yarbus [19], a person's gaze direction is one of the factors that identify his focus of attention. Motivated by this assertion, we investigate how the gaze direction can be used to improve awareness in CES.

The goal of this paper is to present an awareness widget that provides information about the place of visual attention based on the detection of gaze direction. This paper also presents a comparison between the proposed widget and the current visual awareness widgets used in CES.

The rest of the paper is organized as follows. Section 2 describes the current awareness devices used in CES to provide information of the participants' actions and the sense of presence during group work. Section 3 presents four eye-tracking mechanisms used to detect the user's point of regard. Section 4 details the proposed awareness widget used to obtain information about the place of visual attention based on the use of an eye tracking mechanism. In the Section 5, we make a comparison of the proposed widget with some visual awareness devices discussed in Section 2. Finally, Section 6 presents the conclusions, comments and future work.

2 Awareness in CES

The support of group work in CES is a necessary factor to create a common context among the participants. This context prevents that a specific participant feels isolated of the group, thus blocking his contributions and distancing himself from the work being accomplished. Pinheiro et al. [13] define awareness as the supply of common context to the participants of a group. Awareness is also the understanding of past activities while knowing what happened, what is happening and what will happen as well as the knowledge of the group participants' and the work to be done [13].

In CES, awareness is responsible to provide the sense of presence and actions of the group to remote participants. This means that awareness allows each participant of the group to coordinate and organize his work, since he has information that allows the understanding of what the others are doing. The awareness also provides the opportunity to both enhance communication, either informal or not and support the social protocol used while the work is being produced.

When the group is working to complete a task, it is common to expect actions being made to objects placed in a workspace shared by the groups' participants. The objects and the shared workspace are important elements that affect the performance of the group as a whole because the cooperation and the interactions among the group occur through the manipulations of the objects. The awareness of what is happening in the shared workspace is called workspace awareness and it is similar to the perception that a participant has of each other and the work when they are sitting around a table during physical meetings. Workspace awareness is defined as the up-to-the-moment understanding of another person's interaction with a shared workspace and involves knowledge about where others are working, what they are doing, and what they are going to do next [9].

The sense of presence of the participants is the most traditional type of awareness information provided by the CES. This information leads to the current state of the participants and their activities, since the knowledge of who is active facilitates the identification of who is working, where the work is being made and if it is being made simultaneously or concurrently. Because of what can be inferred by the sense of presence it is closely related to the workspace awareness regarding the knowledge of who and where the participants are interacting with the group, and it is an essential type of information that can be used during group work.

The information about the sense of presence and workspace awareness is provided by awareness devices that show details about the individual actions of the participants. The devices offer the opportunity to understand the meaning of the actions and can be used to coordinate activities and enhance the communication. In CES, the visual awareness devices that provide information about the sense of presence and workspace awareness are called awareness widgets and are designed as elements of the user interface.

Fig. 1 shows six awareness widgets. They are: (i) Telecarets; (ii) Telepointers; (iii) Multi-user scrollbars; (iv) RadarView; (v) Read and Write Shadows and (vi) FishEyeView. Although the widgets presented in Fig. 1 does not form a complete list of awareness devices used in CES, they are traditionally mentioned in the literature of the CSCW area.

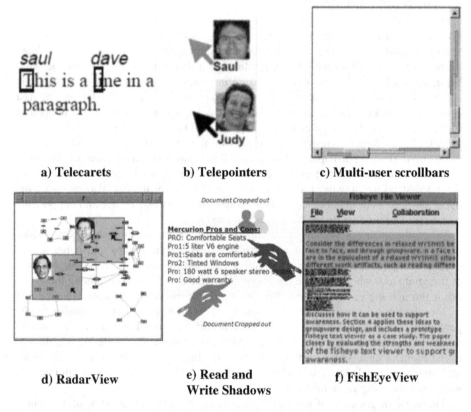

a) Telecarets   b) Telepointers   c) Multi-user scrollbars

d) RadarView   e) Read and   f) FishEyeView
                      Write Shadows

Fig. 1. Awareness widgets: a) Telecarets [6], b) Telepointers [5], c) Multi-user scrollbars [10], d) RadarView [7], e) Read and Write Shadows [15] and f) FishEyeView [4]

Telecaret [6] is an awareness widget that shows the area around the caret used in collaborative text editing. Every time a user edits the text, select a character or navigates among the words the caret's position is automatically replicated to the other participants of the collaborative session by means of a visual cue called Telecaret. With this widget the participants can see the exact position of the user's caret showing to them where in the text the user is working at the moment.

Using the same concept of Telecaret, Telepointer provides the remote position of the cursor used to represent the movements of the user's mouse pointer in the shared workspace. Telepointer can also show semantic information that identifies the current action being executed [5] by changing the form, the color or the image used in the cursor.

Multi-user scrollbars are awareness widgets created from the traditional horizontal and vertical scrollbars used in graphical user interfaces that are based on the windows metaphor. Those widgets show the visible part of the shared workspace that can be seen by each user through the visualization of individual view-ports in small colored rectangles added to the scrolling area of the widget. Multi-user scrollbars are included in the MAUI (Multi-User Awareness User Interface) [10] toolkit, which is a set of individual components designed to provide awareness information in CES. The toolkit has many components, however only the Multi-user scrollbars provide information about the sense of presence and workspace awareness at the same time.

RadarView [7] is a widget that displays a miniature view of the shared workspace. This widget presents the location of each user's view-port superimposed in the miniature allowing the group to see which part of the workspace is visible to each user. Every modification made to the objects contained in the shared workspace is immediately visible using RadarView, which also shows the position of the user's Telepointers. It is also possible to use RadarView to navigate through the shared workspace by changing the position of the user's view-port.

Read and Write Shadows [15] are widgets that provide read and write awareness during collaborative text editing, respectively. The write shadow widget indicates the exact place where the user is editing the text and is represented by the icon of a right hand placed near the last changed character. The right hand icon is filled with a color that identifies the user and is presented as a left hand icon in the shared workspace of the other users. The read shadow widget indicates the part of the text that the user is reading and is pictured by the icon of the user's silhouette filled with the user's color positioned in the part of the text that is visible to the user, i.e. the paragraph that is visible on the screen.

FishEyeView [4] is an awareness widget that changes the visualization of the shared workspace modifying the size of the objects contained in the document, such as words in a text or drawing elements in a diagram. When a user is located in a specific place of the document, named focal point, every object near this point has its sizes increased while other objects that are far from the focal point have their sizes reduced. With this visualization the users see the shared workspace distorted, since the objects near the focal point become bigger and the objects far from the focal point become smaller.

RadarView and FishEyeView are not the only widgets that provide the sense of presence and workspace awareness by a modified visualization of the shared workspace. Gutwin and Greenberg [8] present the dragmag view, a virtual magnifying glass that increases the size of all objects placed on a chosen point. The two-level view, also presented by Gutwin and Greenberg, superimposes RadarView allowing the user to see an overview of the workspace, with the details view of the magnifying class, allowing the user to see the details of objects. This visualization combines two layers of information in the same window.

The information about the sense of presence and workspace awareness is not provided only by visual awareness widgets. Gaver [3] proposed the use of different audio cues to represent the actions and types of activities done by the users in the objects of the shared workspace. Another example of audio used in CES to provide awareness is found on the project Kansas [16] in which activity sounds were used to indicate the distance and location of user's actions by changing volume and direction.

All the awareness devices discussed so far allow the users of a CES to obtain information about the sense of presence and workspace awareness aiming at reproducing the real world interaction found in physical meeting. Whereas they provide valuable awareness information, they are not able to inform the exact place where the participants' focus of attention is during group work. This focus of attention is part of the concept of gaze awareness [9], which is defined as the specific place of the shared workspace where the users are looking at.

The connection between the focus of attention and the place where a person is looking at is presented by Yarbus [19]. By conducting psychological experiments and studying its results, Yarbus provided evidence that the user's point of regard, which can be calculated by the projected trajectory of the gaze direction, is one indicator of his focus of attention. Based on this assumption, the gaze direction can be used to indicate the exact place containing the user's current focus of attention.

However, the CSCW literature contains few studies about the focus of attention based on the direction of gaze, probably because of the needed requirements to set up an eye tracking mechanism that detects the eye position. One of these studies is presented by Vertegaal and Ding [18], in which the authors discuss how to simulate the eye contact found in physical meetings. This study evaluates a system composed of an eye tracker and a video conference to support the collaboration during specific tasks. The authors concluded that the eye contact simulated by the system increased in 46% the performance of the tasks completed. Nevertheless, in that study the authors did not investigate the direct focus of attention of the users in order to provide awareness information.

3 Eye Tracking Mechanisms

The developments of mechanisms that track the eye position and detect the gaze direction have been evolving from many years. One of the main motivations to develop this technology is the possibility to improve the interaction capability of people with physical disabilities, allowing individuals that can only move the eye use the computer and have better communication with other people.

There are mechanisms that allow the human interaction with computers based on the detection of face and eye movements and using techniques provided by photo-and video-oculography, which allows the detection of the user's iris from images and real-time video. Fig. 2 presents four examples of eye trackers that represent the state of the art to detect gaze direction.

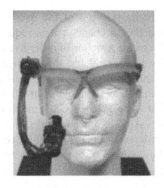

a) Portable eye tracker   **b) MCMO prototype**

c) REGT prototype   **d) Tobii eye tracker**

Fig. 2. Examples of eye tracking mechanisms: a) Portable eye tracker [11], b) MCMO prototype [2], c) REGT prototype [1] and d) Tobii Eye tracker [17]

The eye tracker proposed by Li et al. [11] is a portable mechanism based on open software and hardware that can be built from low cost components. It is composed of two cameras embedded in a pair of glasses and connected to a laptop inside a backpack. This mechanism has the estimation error for the point of regard of one degree of visual angle.

In order to facilitate the interface with the computer for people with motion disabilities that cannot speak and can only move the eyes, Foggiatto [2] proposes the MCMO (Mouse Controlled by Eye Movement) prototype, which is composed of an infrared camera inserted in the place of the left eye lens of a pair of glasses. The author did not provide data about the degree of visual angle error of this mechanism, however empirical experiments presented by the author suggest that the users adapted very fast to the mechanism and were able to properly communicate and to use a computer when using the mechanism.

Coutinho and Morimoto [1] propose a REGT (Remote Eye Gaze Tracking) prototype, which is an eye tracking mechanism that allows head movement without losing track of the eye's position. The mechanism uses a camera that is placed in front of the user with a set of infrared light in its optical axis. This mechanism has also motion engine that move the camera according to the position of the user's head, which is tracked by a classifier algorithm. To use the mechanism it is required to attach four infrared lights in the four frontal corners of the monitor in order to create a polygon that illuminates the user's iris. According to the authors, the average gaze estimation error of the mechanism is between 0.91 and 2.4 degrees of visual angle.

Tobii eye tracker [17] is a commercial product that detects the gaze direction as a complete solution. The mechanism has the format of a 17 inch CRT monitor and contains an infrared camera bellow the front screen. Among other features, Tobii eye tracker allows the user to wear glasses and contact lenses, supports head movements in a 30x15x20 cm space, transmits in real time the position of the eye's coordinates on screen via a TCP/IP connection and has the estimation error of less than one degree of visual angle.

The recent decrease of costs in devices that capture video, such as webcams, and the advances of the Computer Vision area motivated the development of unexpensives eye trackers. However, the current approaches based on webcams still lack precision and require many enhancements before they can be used in real eye tracking applications. We hope that in a near future the mechanisms reach a state where they are economically viable and technologically acceptable.

4 An Awareness Widget for Providing the Focus of Attention Using the User's Point of Regard

The eye trackers presented have the goal to find the user's point of regard or the estimation of his visual line of view using eye tracking techniques. With this information, the mechanisms map the approximate position of the eye to coordinates of the screen after a calibration phase. Most of the mechanisms require that the user keeps looking at fixed points in the screen for a short period of time. Once the calibration phase is completed, the mechanism is ready to provide the coordinates of the screen where the user is looking at in real time.

Having the coordinates of the point on the screen that the user is looing at, it is possible to display an icon to provide a visual feedback to the user in order to facilitate the navigation on the screen. However, for the proposed awareness widget the coordinates of the screen that show where the user is looking at must be presented only to the others participants of the collaborative session and not to the user that is generating the coordinates. This setting will provide the sense of presence and workspace awareness to the remote participants that are using the CES.

After the evaluation of the existing eye trackers we decide to develop an awareness widget that does not depend on any specific eye tracker. The proposed awareness widget is called TeleEye and is based on the existing Telepointer and Telecaret implementations that provide awareness information of the mouse pointer and the text caret positions, respectively.

A prototype of TeleEye was implemented in an existing CES in order to evaluate the feasibility of this awareness widget. The CES chosen was CoArgoUML [12], a CASE (Computer Aided Software Design) tool modified to support the synchronous collaborative modeling of UML (Unified Modeling Language) diagrams. Aiming to test TeleEye, a home made eye tracking mechanism was assembled using a video

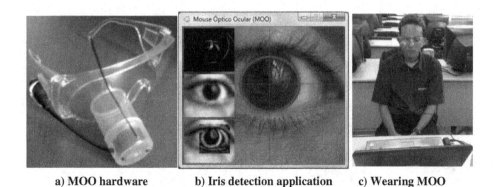

a) MOO hardware   **b) Iris detection application**   **c) Wearing MOO**

Fig. 3. Eye tracking mechanism used to test TeleEye: a) The MOO hardware, b) Screenshot of the iris detection application and c) An user testing the MOO

capture device that was mounted in front of the right eyeglass lens of a pair of plastic safety glasses. This prototype is called MOO (Ocular Optical Mouse) and uses an algorithm that detects circles based on the Hough Transformation. However, the MOO is not able to compensate user's head movements because it is fixed on the face and does not have the ability to detect background movements. The MOO hardware, the application that detects the user's iris and a user wearing MOO is shown in Fig. 3.

Although the eye tracking mechanism built does not provide precise estimation of the gaze direction, it was a suitable alternative to test TeleEye's prototype. Fig. 4 presents Telepointers and TeleEyes for two modelers, A and B, in their shared workspace during collaborative modeling of a Class diagram.

Fig. 4 shows an example in which TeleEye can be used with Telepointer. In the upper shared workspace of Fig. 4 the modeler A sees the Telepointer icon of the modeler B as a black cross placed on the left side, near the Binding class. The TeleEye icon of the modeler B, depicted as a circumference with the name of the modeler on the upper left side, is placed between the relationships connecting the abstract class *ModelElement* and the class Dependency.

Modeler B, whose shared workspace can be seen in the lower part of Fig. 4, sees a dark gray cross that represents the Telepointer icon of modeler A placed on the lower right side near the Abstraction class. Modeler B also sees the TeleEye icon of the modeler A depicted as a dark gray circumference placed on the center, near the Binding class.

In the scenario presented in Fig. 4 it is reasonable to assume that alhtough the mouse pointer of the modeler A is placed on the lower right side near the Abstraction class, the focus of his attention probably is in the Binding class, since he is looking at that class. The base for this assumption is the fact that TeleEye identifies the focus of attention of the modeler whereas Telepointer indicates the likely place of the next or previous mouse position. Likewise, the focus of attention of modeler B probably is in the relationships between the abstract class *ModelElement* and the class Dependency, because his TeleEye icon is near those relationships, and he is not focusing his attention in the empty space bellow the *ModelElement* class where his mouse pointer is placed.

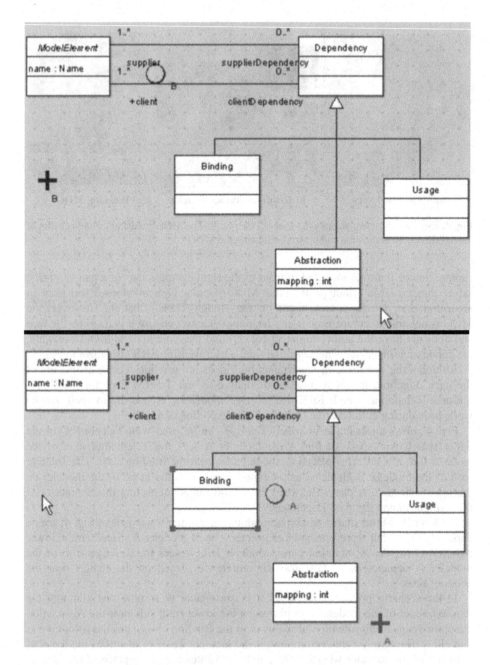

Fig. 4. Shared workspaces, Telepointers and TeleEyes of two modelers, A and B, on a collaborative modeling session of a Class diagram in CoArgoUML. The upper workspace is the user A screen and the lower workspace is the user B screen.

Another example in which TeleEye can be used is during the explanation of details in a collaborative session. While one participant explains the details of a specific part of a shared document he can be aware of where is the visual focus of the other participants through the TeleEye icons. He can check if they are paying attention in the visual details being explained or not. With this information the participant that is explaining the details can take an action to have the attention of the group. In this scenario TeleEye provide an important information for the group coordination.

TeleEye can also be combined with other awareness widgets to enhance the sense of presence and workspace awareness. For instance, TeleEye can replace Telepointer when a participant stops moving his mouse for a specific period of time. Another possible combination of awareness widget is to insert the TeleEye icon inside the miniaturized view of RadarView, providing information about the focus of attention in any place of the shared workspace.

5 Comparison of Awareness Widgets

This section presents a comparison of the awareness widgets discussed in Section 2 and TeleEye based on the affordance of the sense of presence and workspace awareness. We claim that a comparative analysis of the objective features can provide a base for the evaluation of TeleEye as a visual awareness widget.

The comparison between the visual awareness widgets and TeleEye is based on the three awareness principles proposed by Sasa et al. [15], which are: (i) The first principle, labeled *No Explicit Actions*, states that the awareness widget must automatically gather information about the user; in particular, the user must not be required to perform explicit actions to provide awareness to the observer; (ii) The second principle, labeled as *Least Effort*, states that the awareness widget must minimize interpretation difficulties compared to other competitive tools; in particular, the observer must be able to obtain awareness of the user with the least effort; (iii) The third principle, labeled as *No Additional Space*, states that the awareness widget should be in-place; that is, it should not occupy additional screen space. The adherence to these three principles is the first three criteria used in the comparison of the visual awareness widgets.

A fourth criterion, we call *Attention Focus*, is used in order to compare how the widgets provides the sense of presence and workspace awareness through the indication of the focus of attention. Only the widget that shows where the user's focus of attention inside the shared workspace is compliant with this criterion. Table 1 shows the comparison of the awareness widgets and TeleEye based on the four criteria. The comparative values for all the widget with the exception of TeleEye were obtained by Sasa et al. [15], which compares the existing widgets with the Read and Write Shadows according to the three awareness principles.

The comparison presented in Table 1 shows that TeleEye is the only widget that complies with the four criteria used in the comparison. However, it is important to stress that all the awareness widgets provide information about the current user action or the view-port in shared workspace that the participant is working on, but only TeleEye can identify the exact place of the participant's focus of attention.

Table 1. Comparison of the visual awareness widgets

Widget	No Explicit Actions	Least Effort	No Additional Space	Attention Focus
Telecarets		✓	✓	
Telepointers		✓	✓	
Multi-user Scrollbars		✓		
RadarView	✓	✓		
FishEyeView, Dragmag View and Two-level View	✓		✓	
Read and Write Shadows	✓	✓	✓	
TeleEye	✓	✓	✓	✓

The criterion *No Explicit Actions* indicates that Telecarets, Telepointers and Multi-user Scrollbars widgets requires explicit actions from the user to provide awareness. The actions are the pressing of the keyboard's keys that change the text caret's position, the mouse movements that change the mouse pointer and the scrolling actions that change the coordinates of the user's view-port, respectively. The eye movement is not classified as an explicit action since the user must naturally move his eyes while working with the computer.

The *Least Effort* criterion indicates that the widgets FishEyeView, Dragmag view and Two-level view require a considerable amount of effort to obtain awareness of the users. The reason for such effort is due to the fact that the understanding and comprehension of the information from a distorted shared workspace require more cognitive effort than the effort required in normal shared workspace, assuming that the users are not accustomed to work in a distorted workspace.

The criterion *No Additional Space* classified the widgets Multi-user Scrollbars and RadarView as widgets that occupy additional screen space. As presented in Section 2, RadarView requires a window to display the miniaturized view of the shared workspace. Multi-user scrollbars demands the space occupied by the scrolling area and elevator components of this widget.

6 Conclusions, Comments and Future Work

In this paper, we propose a visual awareness widget named TeleEye that provides information about the sense of presence and workspace awareness. The goal of TeleEye is to show the location of the participant's attention during a collaborative session by means of eye tracking. Using an eye tracker it is possible to find a reasonable accurate region on the screen that the user is looking at, which is calculated by the projected trajectory of the gaze direction.

The awareness devices used to obtain information about the sense of presence and workspace awareness in CES were presented, followed by a brief description of their use in order to contextualize TeleEye. In order to better understand how to capture the focus of attention, the paper discusses the technology and the characteristics of some eye-trackers available to detect the gaze direction.

We also compare TeleEye with other visual awareness widgets. The comparison indicates that TeleEye is the only awareness widget that does not require (i) explicit actions to provide awareness, (ii) extra effort to be used, and (iii) additional screen space. Besides it can also identify the location of the participant's focus of attention. However, one important limitation is that TeleEye can only be used with an eye tracking mechanism that detects the gaze direction.

Future work includes the evaluation of TeleEye with users in a collaborative application in order to assess the effectiveness of visual awareness widget. The study could also include comparison of usage of widgets discussed in this paper. The user study can also provide valuable information on how the participants communicate and coordinate their activities when they know where is the focus of attention of each participant of the group.

We believe that a significant contribution of TeleEye is its integration with the HCI (Human Computer Interface) area, which opens new opportunities to use non standard input devices to provide awareness information during collaborative work. More specifically, TeleEye provides a new environment to test and evaluate how eye tracking mechanisms can be used when more than one individual obtain information provided by the widget, i.e. see the patterns of the user's eyes movements, find the locations that capture the visual attention and even discover if the user is looking at the CES or not, which may indicate that the collaborative work might be doing concurrently with another task.

The awareness widget presented in this paper provides a novel approach to obtain additional awareness, the focus of attention, in collaborative sessions. With the new awareness information provided it is possible to enhance the coordination and communication of actions between the participants of collaborative sessions, giving them awareness information similar to the ones found in physical meetings.

References

1. Coutinho, F.L., Morimoto, C.H.: Free Head Motion Eye Gaze Tracking Using a Single Camera and Multiple Light Sources. In: Proceedings of the 19th Brazilian Symposium of Graphic Computing and Imaging Processing, Manaus, Brazil, pp. 1–10 (2006)
2. Foggiatto, M.N.S.: Mouse Controlado pelos Olhos. Master's Thesis, Universidade Tecnológica Federal do Paraná, Paraná, Brazil (2002)
3. Gaver, W.W.: Sound Support for Collaboration. In: Proceedings of the 2nd European Conference on Computer Supported Cooperative Work, Amsterdam, Netherlands, pp. 293–308 (1991)
4. Greenberg, S., Gutwin, C., Cockburn, A.: Awareness Through Fisheye Views in Relaxed-WYSIWIS Groupware. In: Proceedings of the 1996 Graphics Interface, Toronto, Canada, pp. 28–38 (1996)
5. Greenberg, S., Gutwin, C., Roseman, M.: Semantic Telepointers for Groupware. In: Proceedings of the 6th Australian Conference on Computer-Human Interaction, Hamilton, New Zealand, pp. 24–27 (1996)

6. Greenberg, S., Marwood, D.: Real Time Groupware as a Distributed System: Concurrency Control and its Effect on the Interface. In: Proceedings of the 5th ACM Conference on Computer Supported Cooperative Work, North Caroline, USA, pp. 207–217 (1994)
7. Greenberg, S., Roseman, M.: Groupware Toolkits for Synchronous Work. John Wiley & Sons, New York (1998)
8. Gutwin, C., Greenberg, S.: Focus and Awareness in Groupware. In: Video Proceedings of the 7th ACM Conference on Computer Supported Cooperative Work, Washington, USA (1998)
9. Gutwin, C., Greenberg, S.: A Descriptive Framework of Workspace Awareness for Real-time Groupware. Journal of Computer Supported Cooperative Work 11(3), 411–446 (2002)
10. Hill, J., Gutwin, C.: The MAUI Toolkit: Groupware Widgets for Group Awareness. Journal of Computer Supported Cooperative Work 13(5-6), 539–571 (2004)
11. Li, D., Babcock, J., Parkhurst, D.J.: OpenEyes: A Low-cost Head-mounted Eye-tracking Solution. In: Proceedings of the 4th ACM Symposium on Eye Tracking Research & Applications, California, USA, pp. 95–100 (2006)
12. Pichiliani, M.C., Hirata, C.M.: A Guide to Map Application Components to Support Multi-user Real-time Collaboration. In: Proceedings of the 2nd International Conference on Collaborative Computing: Networking, Applications and Worksharing, Georgia, USA, pp. 1–5 (2006)
13. Pinheiro, M.K., Lima, J.V., Borges, M.R.S.: Awareness em Sistemas de Groupware. In: Proceedings of the 4th Iberoamerican Workshop of Requirements Engineering and Software Environments, San Jose, Costa Rica, pp. 323–335 (2001)
14. Roseman, M., Greenberg, S.: Building Real Time Groupware with GroupKit, a Groupware Toolkit. ACM Transactions on Computer-Human Interaction 3(1), 66–106 (1996)
15. Sasa, J., Dewan, P., Rui, Y.: Read, Write, and Navigation Awareness in Realistic Multi-View Collaborations. In: Proceedings of the 3rd International Conference on Collaborative Computing: Networking, Applications and Worksharing, New York, USA, pp. 494–503 (2007)
16. The Kansas Project, http://research.sun.com/ics/kansas.html
17. Tobii Eye Tracker, http://www.tobii.com/corporate/start.aspx/
18. Vertegaal, R., Ding, Y.: Explaining Effects of Eye Gaze on Mediated Group Conversations: Amount or Synchronization? In: Proceedings of the 9th ACM Conference on Computer Supported Cooperative Work, Louisiana, USA, pp. 41–48 (2002)
19. Yarbus, A.L.: Eye Movements and Vision. Plenum Press, New York (1967)

Informa: An Extensible Framework for Group Response Systems

Matthias Hauswirth

University of Lugano, 6904 Lugano, Switzerland
Matthias.Hauswirth@unisi.ch
http://www.inf.unisi.ch/faculty/hauswirth

Abstract. Classroom clickers, also called group response systems, represent a form of technology-enhanced learning. An instructor can pose a question to the class during a lecture, and students can use their clicker devices to submit their answers. The system immediately aggregates the submissions and presents feedback to the instructor (and possibly the class).

This paper describes Informa, an extensible framework for building software-based group response systems. Informa is implemented as a distributed Java RMI application and distinguishes itself from traditional clickers in two key aspects: First, it allows for plug-ins to define the kinds of problems that can be posted (beyond the common multiple-choice). Second, it provides several levels of session anonymity, from completely anonymous sessions where the teacher does not know which student submitted which answer, all the way to authenticated sessions where students need to login when they join.

We have evaluated Informa in a pilot study during an undergraduate programming course, and we have found it to greatly enhance our insight into the students' understanding of the material.

Keywords: technology-enhanced learning, classroom response systems.

1 Introduction

Lecturing is probably the most often used teaching method in higher education. However, lecturing is not easy, and many lectures are evaluated as largely ineffective by students [1]. In his seminal book [2], Penner states that the problem is not the lecturing method, but its poor execution. In particular, he emphasizes the importance of continuous feedback from students to the lecturer. He goes as far as declaring invalid the methodology of a study, where (for the purpose of repeatability) taped lectures were played back to students, thereby completely inhibiting any feedback ("Blind flight" scenario in **Figure 1**).

The effectiveness of a lecture greatly depends on the education (in the subject matter as well as in pedagogy) and the personality of the teacher. Teachers often solicit feedback from students by asking questions ("Question" in Figure 1). However, even a well educated teacher with a well-suited personality is limited in

E. Bertino and J.B.D. Joshi (Eds.): CollaborateCom 2008, LNICST 10, pp. 271–286, 2009.
© ICST Institute for Computer Sciences, Social-Informatics and Telecommunications Engineering 2009

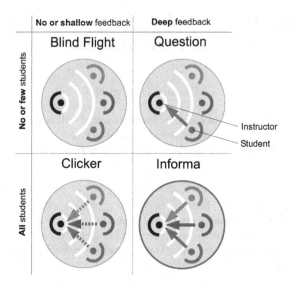

Fig. 1. Four Scenarios for Feedback in a Classroom

getting representative feedback. The problem in continuously evaluating how well the students understand the presented material is twofold. (1) With a large class size, there generally is not enough time to continuously assess every student's understanding, and (2) some students are reluctant to let the instructor or fellow students know that they have problems following the presentation.

Recent innovations in educational technology address these two issues. Group response systems [3,4], also called "classroom clickers", are a technological intervention for the continuous gathering and evaluation of feedback about student learning ("Clicker" in Figure 1). Clickers are little remote controls distributed to students before class. During the lecture, students are repeatedly asked multiple-choice questions which they answer using their clickers. The results are immediately tabulated and can be presented to the class, usually anonymized in the form of histograms.

The pedagogical motivations for using clickers are manifold: Clickers allow a more interactive teaching style even with very large class sizes; they allow for anonymous and immediate feedback from students; they increase class participation of shy students; they allow (or force) students to submit an answer even if they are not sure about a point; and they allow the instructor to regularly measure the standing of all students, not just the good ones.

Traditional clicker devices are special purpose remote controls with a limited user interface consisting of only a small number of buttons (corresponding to the maximum number of choices in a multiple-choice question). Some educators have used laptops instead of clicker devices [5], an approach that can easily be adopted at institutions where all students bring laptops to class. Other researchers have used programmable calculators [6], and one can envision other ubiquitous devices being used as clickers, such as mobile phones or PDAs. On devices that can execute arbitrary applications, a clicker can be implemented as a software application, and can thus provide capabilities that go far beyond the classical clicker device.

However, to our knowledge, the potential of such software-based clickers has not been fully exploited so far: While hardware clickers are limited to multiple-choice questions, software clickers allow students to submit much richer information ("Informa" in Figure 1). Moreover, software clickers enable several degrees of anonymity, from completely anonymous sessions where the teacher does not know which student submitted which answer, all the way to authenticated sessions where students need to login to join.

In this paper we introduce a system we call Informa (Integrated Formative Assessment). Informa enables the most desirable of the four scenarios shown in Figure 1: A classroom where the instructor gets *deep feedback* from *all students*. In Section 2 we outline our design goals. Section 3 describes Informa, and Section 4 presents a usage example. In Section 5 we define the different types of anonymity useful for a classroom response system, and in Section 6 we discuss Informa's extensibility through problem-type plug-ins. Section 7 presents the results of a pilot study using Informa, Section 8 discusses related work, and Section 9 concludes.

2   Goals

The primary goal of this work is the development of an effective pedagogical approach. The purpose of the infrastructure we present in this paper is to fulfill that goal. We thus do not strive to provide a framework that drives entire lectures, and we avoid the known problem of *over-scripting* [7], but we aim at a blended learning approach using technological support only where needed.

Given this premise, it is essential that our infrastructure has a low cost in terms of deployment and that it is easy to use. Students and teachers should not have to spend excessive amounts of time installing and maintaining the collaborative learning infrastructure. It should be possible for students to quickly install and run the student software during the first lecture of a course. Instructors should be able to install the software by simply downloading and running a program, without the need for any configuration or complicated server setup. The software, both the student and the instructor applications, should work on any platform commonly used by teachers or students.

Moreover, the software should gracefully handle latecomers, allowing students to connect or reconnect to a session at any time. This aspect is important in two ways: Besides addressing the issue of students who arrive late for classes, this also overcomes problems with students who terminate their application (e.g. because of a system crash, or because they accidentially close the application).

We strive for an infrastructure that is extensible along several axes: (1) teachers should be able to choose an anonymity level for a given session, (2) teachers should be able to compose problem sets for their lectures and create new problems, and (3) developers should be able to develop plug-ins to support new types of problems (e.g. beyond simple multiple-choice questions).

3   Informa

In this section we describe the Informa framework including its architecture, its communication protocol, and the pedagogical script behind its use.

3.1   Architecture

Figure 2 shows the system architecture of Informa. Informa consists of two applications. The *student* application, which students run on their laptops, represents the actual "clicker" and allows students to solve the posted problems and to submit their solutions. The *instructor* application runs on the instructor's computer and maintains the database of problems, manages sessions, and aggregates students' answers. Moreover, it provides a user interface for the instructor to manage and post problems, and to visualize the aggregated student solutions.

The student applications communicate with the instructor application over the (possibly wireless) network. We have implemented Informa as a distributed system using Java RMI. Using Java allows us to run on most operating systems installed on student laptops. Moreover, unlike a web-based application, a rich Java application enables the use of an extensive collection of open source libraries for implementing rich direct-manipluation GUIs for editing and solving problems.

3.2   Pedagogical Script

A teacher uses Informa in two contexts: (1) before class to prepare a session, and (2) in the classroom during a lecture to run a session. In both cases the teacher runs the Informa instructor application. The functionality available in both contexts is the same: a teacher can compose problem sets and create new problems during preparation as well as during class.

In the classroom, the teacher starts an Informa session at the beginning of class. An Informa session consists of one or more steps. Each step represents the execution of the following pedagogical script in which students are to solve a

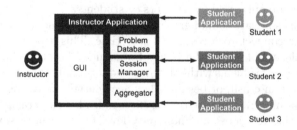

Fig. 2. System Architecture

solve   discuss   reveal

Fig. 3. One Step in an Informa Session

given problem. A step is partitioned into the three phases shown in **Figure 3**: First, in the "solve" phase, the teacher puts up a problem for the students to solve at their computers. Students work individually on their solutions and submit them when they are done. Second, after all submissions are in, or when the teacher decides the time is up, the teacher displays an aggregate visualization of all submitted solutions. In this "discuss" phase she moderates a discussion with the goal of identifying and explaining the good and bad solutions. Finally, in the "reveal" phase, the teacher reveals the correct solution and explains it to the class.

As Figure 3 shows, the students work independently during the "solve" phase. We intentionally designed our approach this way to encourage each student to think deeply about the given problem. The collaborative aspect of our approach manifests itself in the "discussion" phase. After each student has spent some time working on the problem, they now see how their individual solution relates to the overall view of the class. Note that at this point the correct solution is not revealed as yet, so the class is left on their own to collaboratively determine the correct solution. It is this phase that triggers the pedagogically most valuable discussions. After this discussion, the teacher may "reveal" the correct solution (or an example of one of many correct solutions), and explain any remaining issues.

Note that Informa does not require that a problem has correct solutions. Thus, a teacher may run a step to poll the students about their opinions on a given issue, or to gather their subjective judgements.

3.3   Protocol

In Informa, the instructor application is responsible for maintaining the session state. It is usually running during the entire duration of a lecture. Students are able to join or leave a session at any time, but they usually join at the beginning and leave in the end.

Figure 4 shows a high-level view of the RMI-based protocol between the instructor and student applications. It shows the following four scenarios:

Student joins session. Student applications join a session by contacting the instructor application. They find the instructor (an RMI remote object) by looking it up in an RMI registry at a well known port on the instructor's computer. The student application prompts the student for the IP address or hostname of the instructor's computer (the instructor application displays this address on the classroom beamer).

Once student applications have a reference to the instructor RMI object, they try to join the currently active session (see "Student joins session" in

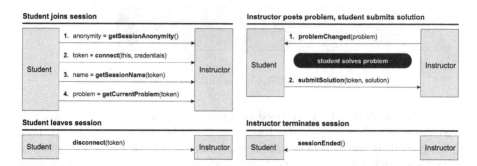

Fig. 4. RMI-based protocol between instructor and students

Figure 4). For this, they first enquire about the current session's anonymity approach (e.g. anonymous, or requiring login). Then they prompt the user for the necessary credentials depending on the given anonymity (e.g. user name and password for a session requiring a login) and connect to the session using these credentials. If the connection request is successful (e.g. user name and password are valid), the instructor returns a token that uniquely identifies the student and allows the student to participate in the session (all further methods of the instructor require a valid token). The student can then request the name of the current session (and other information), and retreive the currently active problem.

Using this approach, latecomers will retrieve the currently active problem, but will not have access to the previously posted problems. In general, the history of past problems is not retained in the student applications, since the intention of Informa is to drive a face-to-face classroom situation. However, the instructor application keeps a history of past problems and submitted solutions. In the future we might make this history available for students to review after class.

Instructor posts problem, student submits a solution. An instructor using Informa can decide to post a problem at any time. This leads to the instructor application notifying all students (`student.problemChanged()`) about the new problem. The student applications then present the new problem to the students, and the students spend some time solving the problem. Once a student is done, he can submit his solution, leading to a call of `instructor.submitSolution()`.

Student leaves session. A student may leave the session at any time. The instructor maintains a list of all students in the session in order to post new problems to all students. If a student explicitly disconnects (by calling `disconnect`), or if a student is unreachable when the instructor posts a problem, the instructor removes that student from the list.

Instructor terminates session. Finally, at the end of the lecture, the instructor terminates the session, notifying all the students with a call to `sessionEnded`.

Notice that both the student *and* the instructor application initiate remote method calls. This is necessary to allow the instructor to post new problems to the students without the students polling for updates. It also allows the instructor to notify students when it wants to terminate the session.

4 Example Usage Scenario

This section introduces the Informa system and the related teaching methodology with an example: the preparation and teaching of a lecture in a Java programming course.

4.1 Preparation

The instructor prepares for her lecture by building a set of problems she intends to post during class. She uses the instructor application to prepare her problem set. This tool allows her to manage existing problems in her database and to interactively create new problems of any supported type. She can also import problems from existing problem databases, for example from a similar course she taught before.

Figure 5 shows Informa with a list of problems related to Java programming. The selected problem, a multiple-choice question, is previewed below the list. The instructor decides to modify this problem and Informa invokes the problem editor specific to multiple-choice questions shown in **Figure 6**. In addition to changing this problem, the instructor creates a few additional problems of various types before finishing her preparation by saving her problem database.

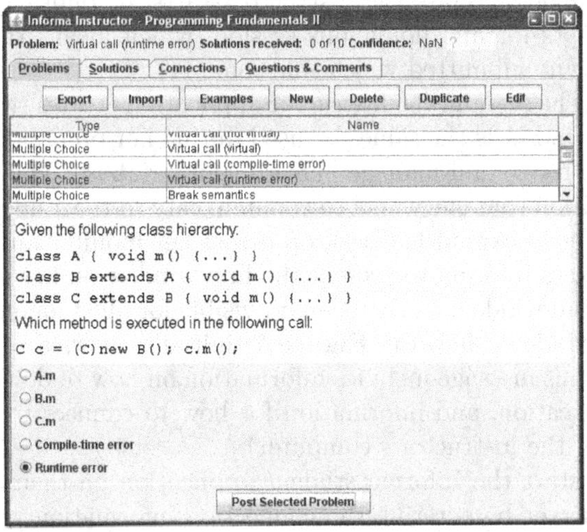

Fig. 5. Managing and Posting Problems

Fig. 6. Editing a Multiple Choice Problem

4.2   Classroom

At the beginning of the class the instructor starts an Informa session on her computer. She opts for an anonymous session, which means that she will not know which student submitted which solution.

After starting the session, the instructor application creates two different windows. The first window is the same she used during her preparations (Figure 5): it allows her to browse and manage her problem database. The second window presents information that she wants to communicate to the students. She configures her computer to extend her desktop across her monitor and the classroom beamer. This allows Informa to present the first window on her monitor while it projects the second window on the beamer, visible for all students.

The beamer window, shown in **Figure 7**, initially shows a welcome message for the session. This message includes information on how to download and start the student application, and information for how to connect to the server (i.e. the IP address of the instructor's computer).

The students start the Informa student application on their computers and connect to the server by entering the connection information presented on the beamer. Since the session is anonymous, they don't have to provide any additional login information.

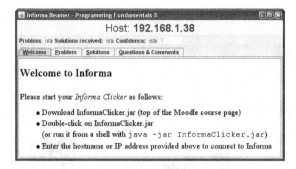

Fig. 7. Welcome Message on Beamer

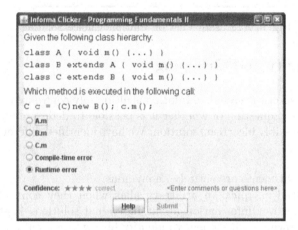

Fig. 8. Student Solving a Multiple-Choice Problem

Now the instructor picks and posts a problem to the class. All students will immediately see that problem on their screens, and they will be prompted to solve it (**Figure 8**). Since the instructor posted a multiple-choice question, the students just need to select the correct answer and submit.

The instructor can see the submitted solutions on her monitor, and she can see the number of outstanding solutions. She can close the problem before receiving all submissions, or she can wait until all students have submitted their solution.

We consider the next step the most valuable aspect of this teaching approach: The instructor application can project a visualization that summarizes all submitted solutions to the classroom beamer. **Figure 9** shows this visualization for the multiple-choice question she posted. It shows a histogram with the number of students who picked each of the choices. The instructor uses this histogram to prompt a discussion in class. Since the visualization does not reveal the correct answer, students can be asked to defend their choices or to explain whether and why an unpopular choice is correct. At the end of this discussion the instructor may reveal the correct answer(s) and provide clarifications and deeper explanations where necessary.

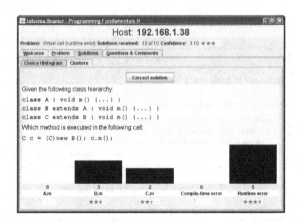

Fig. 9. Aggregate View of Multiple-Choice Solutions

5   Anonymity and Grouping

A classroom response system like Informa is ultimately confronted with the issue of anonymity: the question of whether it is possible to determine which student submitted a (possibly incorrect) solution. We have identified different approaches to anonymity:

Anonymous. Students are entirely anonymous.

User alias. Students pick an arbitrary alias when they connect. This alias is used whenever information about individual solutions is shown on the beamer, allowing each student to identify his own information.

User name. Students log in with a user name assigned to them by the instructor. This allows all students and the instructor to identify information about each individual student.

User name & password. Students connect with a user name and password. This type of session allows instructors to use Informa to keep class attendance information, or to conduct graded quizzes.

Group alias. Students enter a group alias of their choice. Unlike with a user alias, with a group alias multiple students are expected to enter the same alias (the alias of their group). While a user alias allows students to compete within a group of friends, a group alias allows students to compete between groups (e.g. the "skiers" vs. "snowboarders"). The specific group membership is irrelevant from the point of view of the instructor. The only purpose of forming groups is to increase motivation by fostering competition.

Group name. Students enter a group name assigned to them by the instructor.

Group pick. Students pick a group from a set of known groups.

The main goal of Informa is to enable *all* students to participate. Students are more inclined to answer a question if they feel comfortable making a mistake. Some students, even in the friendliest classroom, are reluctant to offer a solution in which they lack confidence. The anonymity provided by the anonymous, user alias, and group alias approaches eliminates this barrier. The group name and group pick approaches, with small group sizes, lead to a certain loss of anonymity, but have the benefit of providing more information (e.g. the "Pascal programmers" group understands information hiding better than the "C programmers" group). On the other end of the spectrum, the two user-name-based approaches, user name and user name & password, have the advantage of automatically tracking specific students' progress. This allows the early detection of challenged students, enabling instructors to help these students before it is too late.

The aspect of anonymity is related to the aspect of competition. If students are completely anonymous there is little means for competition. The more information about a student is known, the more competitive the session becomes. Except for anonymous, all of the above approaches foster competition. Moreover, in group-based appoaches (group alias, group name, and group pick), submissions are aggregated and visualized by group instead of over the entire class, exposing the specific performance of each group. This enables competition *between* groups, providing a motivating setting without exposing indiviual students directly.

With Informa, the instructor decides on an anonymity approach at the start of the session. Depending on the approach, students connecting to the session will then be prompted for the required information.

6   Problem Types

Traditional classroom clickers focus on multiple-choice questions: the instructor offers a set of predetermined answers, of which the student has to choose the correct subset. In Informa, multiple-choice questions represent just one supported problem type. Informa is an extensible framework, where problem types are defined in plug-ins. In this section we describe two problem types in more detail, the standard multiple-choice questions and our new text highlighting problems.

Each problem-type plug-in provides editors for creating new problems (for the instructor), GUIs for solving a problem (for the students), and visualizations that aggregate the submitted solutions (for showing on the beamer). Developers can easily develop new plug-ins for new types of questions.

6.1   Multiple-Choice Questions

Section 4 shows the support for multiple-choice questions available in Informa. Figures 8 and 9 show a student's view of the problem and the aggregate view of all submitted solutions in the form of a histogram. Informa allows questions with an arbitrary number of choices. A given question can be configured as either a single or a multiple answer question. When designing the question, the instructor also indicates which choices are correct. Informa uses this information to highlight the correct answers in the histogram aggregating the submitted solutions. Since giving away the correct solution may not be the pedagogically most effective approach, the highlighting of correct answers is initially disabled. The instructor can use the histogram to prompt a discussion with the students and highlight the correct answers only at the end of that discussion.

6.2   Text Highlighting Problems

This problem type consists of a text and a question that asks the student to highlight certain parts of that text. The example problem shown in **Figure 10** asks the students to highlight the name of each instance variable that has a reference type. The student has already highlighted `dateOfBirth`, is currently adding `mother`, and has not (yet) identified `name`.

While a multiple-choice problem has a fixed number of incorrect answers (distractors), text highlighting is a more open type of problem: a student is free to highlight any area(s) of the text he likes. Because it provides the student with less support (no choices to pick from), it may help uncover issues of understanding that would not have been detected with multiple-choice problems. Since the number of possible answers is large, the aggregation approach used for multiple-choice questions (i.e. histograms) becomes impractical.

For this reason we have developed the aggregation visualization shown in **Figure 11**. This visualization superimposes all solutions, leading to highlights with different intensity. The intensity of the highlights represents the number of solutions that highlighted the corresponding text. Intense highlights thus correspond to the majority solution, while divergences by small numbers of students (often corresponding to errors) show up either as faint highlights or as highlights of less-than-full intensity. The instructor can take action if the intensely highlighted text segments do not correspond to her expectations. In the case of minor issues like in Figure 11, the instructor may decide to explain that `String`

Fig. 10. Student Solving a Text Highlighting Problem

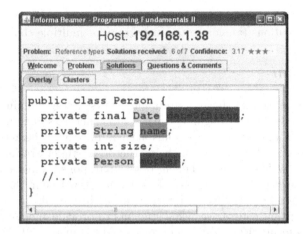

Fig. 11. Aggregate View of Text Highlighting Solutions

is a reference type, and she may comment that students were expected to select the name of the variable (not its type).

6.3 Writing New Problem Type Plug-Ins

To create a new problem type, a developer first has to decide how to store the information defining a problem and a solution by writing implementations of Informa's **Problem** and **Solution** interfaces. These classes are usually relatively lightweight. For example for the multiple choice problem type, the Problem class stores the question text and the list of possible choices. The Solution class stores the index (or indices) of the selected choices.

The Problem and the Solution class have to be serializable. This allows Informa to pass problems from the instructor to the student, and to return solutions from the student to the instructor. Moreover, it enables Informa to store problems in a file (the problem database is essentially a file containing serialized **Problem** objects).

```
public interface ProblemType {
    String getName ();
    ProblemEditor createProblemEditor ();
    SolutionEditor createSolutionEditor ();
    SolutionAnalysisView [] createSolutionAnalysisViews ();
}
```

Fig. 12. The ProblemType interface

Besides implementing these two model classes, supporting a new problem type also requires the developer to write an implementation of the **ProblemType** interface (see Figure 12), and to develop the necessary **ProblemEditor** and **SolutionEditor** GUI components. Moreover, the developer needs to develop one or more `SolutionAnalysisView` to visualize the aggregate information over all submitted solutions (analog to the histogram for multiple choice solutions).

7   Evaluation

We evaluated Informa in a Java programming course (Programming Fundamentals II) at the University of Lugano (USI). All informatics students at USI bring laptops to class, and all our classrooms are equipped with beamers and wireless networks. At USI we have a high instructor to student ratio, allowing for small class sizes. While the main benefit of group response systems is to improve teaching with larger classes, we have found that even in our class of thirteen undergraduate students the use of Informa can be beneficial.

At the end of that course, we asked students to provide anonymous feedback on the use of Informa. Eleven students responded to our request. Most students saw benefits in using Informa, providing comments like:

> My answers were almost all wrong. After that I've started to read and prepare myself more.

> After answering the questions we would get the right answer and that sticks better to your mind.

Students also provided significant feedback for improving Informa. They ranged from bug reports (e.g. student applications that dropped connections) over feature requests (e.g. way to review problems and solutions after class) to pedagogical issues (e.g. difficulty of the problems).

The most important limitation the students identified was an issue with our pedagogical script: at the end of the first phase ("solve") in each step, the faster students have to wait for the slower ones. This serialization issue also was of great concern to the instructor. We plan to address this issue by allowing the instructor to post a batch of related questions at once. Another approach would be to provide students who have submitted the answer to their problem with extra reading material or bonus problems.

A practical issue that surfaced early on in the semester was that each latecomer had to ask the instructor for connection information (the IP address of the instructor's computer). We solved this problem by always displaying connection information on the beamer. Another solution would involve the use of a service discovery protocol to allow student applications to automatically find instructor applications.

We found Informa's extensibility to be really useful. We developed several specific problem-types for our course (e.g. for matching regular expressions, or for identifying the type of a Java expression). However, writing a new problem-type plug-in requires some effort. Over time we thus identified more general problem-type plug-ins, such as the text highlighting plug-in described in Section 6.2. We believe that, as we continue to use and extend Informa, we will end up with a collection of problem types that are broadly applicaple across course topics.

8   Related Work

Trees and Jackson [8] conducted a study involving 1500 students showing how the use of clickers can improve the effectiveness of large lectures. Our pilot experiment provides a first indication that our approach, which involves problem types beyond traditional multiple-choice, can also be beneficial in a lecture with a small number of students.

Roschelle et al. [9] survey clicker-related research and connect it to the broader educational literature. They argue that next generation clickers should focus on formative assessment (Informa's focus) and on effective means to visually aggregate student answers (which they do using overlaid plots of submitted polynomial equations [6], and we do e.g. with our text highlighting problem).

A more recent survey by Fies and Marshall [10] confirms these issues. It also points out the logistical difficulties to instructors and the cost of purchasing clickers for students. Our free, lightweight software solution mitigates these problems in situations where networked computers that run Java (desktops, laptops, PDAs, cell phones) are available in classrooms.

The "Classroom Learning Partner" (CLP) project at MIT uses pen-based Tablet-PCs to allow students to submit answers to questions. CLP proposes to aggregate student answers, but the CLP publications [11,12] only report on a tool that does not support aggregation. Our work differs from CLP in several ways. CLP has to correctly interpret the electronic ink before being able to reason about and compare answers. Because Informa's solution editors constrain the space of possible answers, the semantics of a solution are always unambiguous, and "freak solutions" (solutions that do not fit the context in which the problem was posed) are avoided. Moreover, CLP requires (expensive) special hardware and is based on proprietary software (Microsoft PowerPoint).

9   Conclusions

Informa is an extensible framework for group response systems. Using Informa in a classroom allows the instructor to get *deep feedback* from *all students*. Informa enables getting deep feedback about the understanding of students because of its pluggable problem types. Developers can create new plug-ins that require students to solve problems that go far beyond the selection of a choice in a multiple-choice question. Informa enables getting feedback from all students, because of its different student anonymity approaches which allow the instructor to pick a tradeoff between anonymity and competitiveness. We have successfully used Informa in our own courses. We plan to further improve the system and to release it as an open source product.

Acknowledgments. We would like to thank the anonymous reviewers for their insightful comments and the students at the University of Lugano for their feedback on improving Informa.

References

1. Bligh, D.A.: What's The Use of Lectures. Jossey-Bass (2000)
2. Penner, J.G.: Why many college teachers cannot lecture: How to avoid communication breakdown in the classroom. C.C. Thomas (1984)
3. Abrahamson, A.L.: An overview of teaching and learning research with classroom communication systems (CCSs). In: Proceedings of the International Conference of the Teaching of Mathematics (June 1998)
4. Duncan, D.: Clickers in the Classroom. Pearson Education, London (2005)
5. Draper, S.W., Cargill, J., Cutts, Q.: Electronically enhanced classroom interaction. Australian Journal of Educational Technology 18(1), 13–23 (2002)
6. Roschelle, J., Vahey, P., Tatar, D., Kaput, J., Hegedus, S.: Five key considerations for networking in a handheld-based mathematics classroom. In: Proceedings of the 27th Conference of the International Group for the Psychology of Mathematics Education (July 2003)
7. Dillenbourg, P.: Over-scripting CSCL: The risks of blending collaborative learning with instructional design, pp. 61–91. Open Universiteit Nederland, Heerlen (2002)
8. Trees, A.R., Jackson, M.H.: The learning environment in clicker classrooms: Student processes of learning and involvement in large courses using student response systems. Learning, Media and Technology 32(1), 21–40 (2007)
9. Roschelle, J., Penuel, W.R., Abrahamson, L.: Classroom response and communication systems: Research review and theory. In: Annual Meeting of the American Educational Research Association (April 2004)
10. Fies, C., Marshall, J.: Classroom response systems: A review of the literature 15(1), 101–109 (2006)
11. Koile, K., Singer, D.: Development of a tablet-pc-based system to increase instructor-student classroom interactions and student learning. In: Workshop on the Impact of Pen-based Technology on Education (April 2006)
12. Koile, K., Singer, D.: Improving learning in cs1 with tablet-pc-based in-class assessment. In: Second International Computing Education Research Workshop (submitted)

Secure and Conditional Resource Coordination for Successful Collaborations

Dongxi Liu, Surya Nepal, David Moreland, Shiping Chen, Chen Wang, and John Zic

Networking Technologies Lab, CSIRO ICT Center, Marsfield, NSW 2122, Australia
firstname.lastname@csiro.au

Abstract. Successful completion of collaborations is necessary for collaborating participants to achieve their prescribed collaboration purposes. In this paper, we address the problem of successful completion of collaborations under a new model, called collaborative resource model. This model is graph-based, allowing participants to describe different ways to contribute and require resources for collaborations and the dependency relations among these resources. Resources in this model are protected by access control policies declared not only by resource providers but also by resource requestors. The requestors policies state how they will redistribute the acquired resources and thus increase the confidence of the providers to share resources. Except access control policies, resources are also constrained by usage conditions to reflect the fact, for instance, that a resource might be available only at some time. Based on this model, we present a coordination mechanism. Successful coordination means that all participants can get the necessary resources to complete their collaborations.

Keywords: Secure Resource Model, Robust Collaboration, Resource Coordination, Access Policies.

1 Introduction

Recently, a communication trend has clearly emerged for resources to be able to dynamically collaborate with each other within a distributed environment for various application scenarios, such as health, education and emergencies. This type of *collaborative environment* is rapidly becoming a commonplace means for enabling a collective of entities to deliver significantly bigger, better and more beneficial outcomes than they otherwise could by themselves. All collaborations are established for certain beneficial purposes. In order to achieve these purposes, it is necessary to guarantee the collaborations can be completed successfully by all participants. In particular for mission-critical collaborations, such as collaborative medical operations and collaborative military actions, the failure of such collaborations may cause great damages or losses.

The failures of collaboration can be caused by various reasons based on the fact that collaborations always involve resource sharing among participants with particular business protocols. For example, a failure can happen if one participant uses a protocol mismatched with the protocol used by other participants [1,2]. However, in this paper, we focus on the reason where some participants fail to get the necessary resources for continuing the current collaboration either because the resources are not available or

E. Bertino and J.B.D. Joshi (Eds.): CollaborateCom 2008, LNICST 10, pp. 287–303, 2009.

they do not have the privileges to access the resources. For example, suppose an operation is being collaborated by doctors from several hospitals. If during this operation one doctor from outside needs to access the medical records managed by the local hospital, but without enough rights, then the operation may have to get stopped. This will be a disaster for the patient.

In this paper, we first propose a collaborative resource model, and then based on this model we give a secure resource coordination mechanism. Before a collaboration begins, the involved resources are coordinated. A successful coordination guarantees that all participants can obtain the necessary resources to complete their collaboration.

1.1 Overview of the Collaborative Resource Model

In our collaborative resource model, participants not only contribute resources, but also require resources from other participants to complete collaborations. The resources contributed or required may be dependent on each other and the model allows participants to express such dependency relations among resources. For example, participants can express in this model what resources they will contribute according to what resources they can acquire from other participants. There are different reasons for this: the contributed resources cannot function correctly unless the dependent resources can be acquired, or participants do not feel fair if they think they contribute valuable resources, but others do not. For another example, when some resource is offered, a participant may want to offer another resource because these two resources must be used together and the second resource is dependent on the first one. This model is graph-based so that the dependency relations among resources can be captured naturally. Collaborations based on this model are said resource centric.

On the other hand, even though participants would like to contribute resources for collaborations, it does not mean that they would like every participant to access their resources freely since some participants may be competitors. Our model allows participants to protect their resources by specifying certificate-based policies and the authorization is based on the certificates the resource requestor can provide. This access control mechanism follows the widely accepted principle of trust management [3,4] for the distributed environment where participants belong to different administrative domains and maybe do not know each other in advance. It is worth mentioning that in our access control mechanism not only the resource providers but also the resource requestors can or need to define access control policies. For example, when a hospital requires the medical records from a patient, it needs to specify policies to show who in the hospital can access these data, and the patient releases the medical records only when the policies of the hospital are strong enough for the patient.

Another aspect about the collaborative resource model is that each resource has some conditions to restrict the usage of resources. For example, in a dynamic collaboration, a resource is available only from Monday to Tuesday, and the usage condition of this resource can help reflect this fact.

1.2 Overview of the Resource Coordination Mechanism

For a collaboration, we hope all participants can get their needed resource, so that the collaboration is robust and can complete successfully. A collaboration becomes

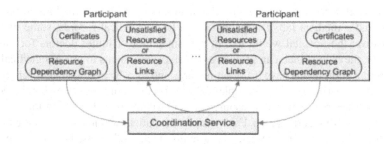

Fig. 1. The Framework of Resource Coordination

complex if it involves a lot of participants and the resources contributed and required by each participant have complex dependency relations and are protected and restricted by complex policies and usage conditions. For a complex collaboration, it is not straight-forward to check manually whether this collaboration can complete successfully or not. To address this problem, we give an automatic resource coordination mechanism based on the collaborative resource model, shown in Figure 1. The coordination service is used to check whether the resource requirements of all participants are satisfied before collaborations begin. The coordination service takes as input the certificates and resource descriptions of all participants. As introduced before, the resources of a participant is described in a graph. If the coordination succeeds, a set of resource links is returned to each participant. A resource link connects a resource requirement to a set of available resources, implying that the requestor has enough rights to access the resources and the usage conditions of these resources are satisfied by the requestor. For example, a resource link may state that a requirement for a special medical device can be satisfied by two such devices, each covering different time periods. Resource links can be incorporated into eContracts [5,6] to express resource agreements among participants. If the coordination fails, the coordination service specifies the unsatisfied resources to the participants requiring such resources. However, this paper focuses on the coordination mechanism and algorithm, and how to effectively use resource links as agreements and how to resolve the coordination failure are our future work.

The remainder of this paper is organized as follows. In Section 2, we introduce a scenario to motivate the resource centric collaborations. The collaborative resource model is introduced in Section 3 and a coordination mechanism based on state-space exploration is presented in Section 4. Section 5 gives an implementation algorithm for the coordination mechanism. Section 6 discusses the related work and finally Section 7 concludes the paper.

2   A Scenario for Resource Centric Collaboration

The collaborations we concern here are resource centric in the sense that all collaborating participants focus on what resources they will provide and what resources they can get from other participants to achieve their collaboration purposes. The following scenario illustrates this kind of collaborations.

Suppose in a collaborative medial diagnosis, the participants include a patient, a hospital and a medical lab. The patient has a lot of medical records, some of which are sensitive; the hospital would like to appoint senior or junior doctors for this collaboration; the medical lab can provide expensive equipments to process medical data, and different equipments have different features and may be available at different time. That is, every participant has multiple choices to contribute resources for the collaboration. For a participant, what resources to contribute may depend on the resources available from other participants. For example, the patient would like to release his sensitive medical records if he is treated by a senior doctor, otherwise he wants to provide only the insensitive medical records; the hospital would like to assign a senior doctor if the medical lab can offer an equipment with advanced features at the working time of the senior doctor, otherwise a junior doctor is assigned; the medical lab provides its equipments according to what data to be processed. The resources shared in collaboration are protected by security policies and restricted by usage constraints. For example, the patient wants to protect his sensitive medical records before and even after these data are released to the hospital. The usage constrains of resources impose conditions of using the resources. For example, the medical lab may ask an equipment must be run under certain temperature.

3   The Collaborative Resource Model

In this section, we present the collaborative resource model. A collaboration is always carried on by participants. In our model, these participants collaboratively contribute or require resources to achieve their collaboration purposes. The resources contributed or required by a participant may have dependency relations.

The model is compromised of a set of tuples, each of which describes a participant. Each tuple has the form of $(p, Cert, ResG)$, where p is a participant, $Cert$ a set of certificate instances describing the profile of p, and $ResG$ a graph describing the resources contributed or required by p and the dependency relations among these resources. Note that a participant p in our work can be an individual or an organization, and if p is an organization, it can redistribute the acquired resources to its members. In what follows, we will describe the certificates and the resource dependency graph in this model.

3.1   Certificates and Certificate Patterns

Collaborations may occur among participants belonging to different administrative domains. In order to regulate access to resources in collaborations, we should make authorization decisions according to requestors' attributes [3,4]. As usual, this model uses certificates to characterize the attributes of participants.

A certificate is defined with the form $cert^p(p')$, meaning that the principal p (may or may not be a participant in the current collaboration) issues the certificate $cert$ about the participant p'. For example, the certificate $doctor^H(Tom)$ means that Tom is a doctor certified by the hospital H; the certificate $nurse^{Tom}(Alice)$ means that Tom certifies Alice as his nurse. Certificates can be extended to include more information, such as Alice's address and telephone. For brevity, we ignore such extensions in this work.

Certificates represent certified attributes of principals, as shown by the above examples. They are however too rigid when used to express access policies (defined later). For example, if we want to formulate a policy to allow any doctor to access some confidential data, then we have to explicitly grant each doctor this privilege based on his or her doctor certificate. In this model, we use certificate patterns (like parameterized roles [4]) to make policy definition more convenient.

For a certificate $cert^p(p')$, if any of its parts $cert$, p or p' is replaced by a variable (represented by x, y or z), then it becomes a certificate pattern. A certificate pattern denotes a set of certificates which match this pattern. For example, the certificate $\texttt{doctor}^H(\texttt{Tom})$ matches the pattern $\texttt{doctor}^H(x)$, which means any doctor x certified by the hospital H, and also matches the pattern $\texttt{doctor}^y(x)$, which means any doctor x certified by any hospital y.

Certificate patterns can be ordered in terms of the number of certificates they can include. The order relation of certificate patterns will be used later to check whether the policies specified by the resource requestors are stronger than the policies given by the resource providers. The largest certificate pattern is $z^y(x)$, which can be matched by any certificate, and a certificate is also a pattern containing only itself. In the following definition, three placeholders $\square$, $\odot$ and $\boxdot$ are used to describe the shape of certificate patterns, where $\square$ is either a certificate or a variable, and $\odot$ and $\boxdot$ are either a participant or a variable. For simplicity, we assume $\square$, $\odot$ and $\boxdot$, if they are variables, are different variables in a certificate pattern.

Definition 1 (Order of Certificate Patterns). *Suppose CP_1 and CP_2 are two certificate patterns with the shapes $\square^\odot(\boxdot)$ and $\square'^{\odot'}(\boxdot')$, respectively. We say CP_2 is larger than CP_1, written as $CP_1 \sqsubseteq_\Theta CP_2$, if $\square \sqsubseteq_{\Theta_1} \square'$, $\odot \sqsubseteq_{\Theta_2} \odot'$ and $\boxdot \sqsubseteq_{\Theta_3} \boxdot'$, with $\Theta = \Theta_1 \cup \Theta_2 \cup \Theta_3$. The relation $\sqsubseteq_\Theta$ are determined by the following rules.*

- *$cert \sqsubseteq_\emptyset cert$, or $cert \sqsubseteq_{\{x/cert\}} x$;*
- *$p \sqsubseteq_\emptyset p$, or $p \sqsubseteq_{\{x/p\}} x$;*
- *$y \sqsubseteq_{\{x/y\}} x$.*

In the above definition, Θ is a set of substitutions generated when comparing two patterns. The substitution $x/cert$ means the variable x is to be replaced with $cert$, and similarly for the substitutions x/p and x/y. The substitutions will be used in Section 3.3 when comparing two policies. A policy is defined with a set of certificate patterns, and using substitutions can help check whether the link information captured by the same variables among patterns in the policy of resource providers is also kept by certificate patterns in the policy of resource requestors. For example, a policy consisting of patterns $\{\texttt{nurse}^x(y), \texttt{doctor}^H(x)\}$ means that y is the nurse of x who is a doctor of the hospital H. When it is compared with a policy containing patterns $\{\texttt{nurse}^{\texttt{Tom}}(y), \texttt{doctor}^H(\texttt{Tom})\}$, we obtain $\texttt{nurse}^{\texttt{Tom}}(y) \sqsubseteq_{\{x/\texttt{Tom},y/y\}} \texttt{nurse}^x(y)$ and $\texttt{doctor}^H(\texttt{Tom}) \sqsubseteq_{\{x/\texttt{Tom}\}} \texttt{dcotor}^H(x)$, which indicate that the link information captured by x is kept by the second policy since both x are replaced with the same value Tom in the second policy. In later sections, we will not distinguish between certificates and certificate patterns; when we want to mean certificates we say certificate instances.

3.2 Resource Dependency Graph

Participants always need to contribute resources and at the same time require resources from other participants to achieve their collaboration purposes. The resources a participant would like to contribute or require may depend on what resources he can contribute or acquire during collaborations. For example, in a collaboration between a patient and a hospital about medical consultation, the patient may contribute all his medical records if a medical expert is appointed for his consultation, or he may contribute only a part of his medical records if a doctor just graduated is appointed.

The usage of resources, whether they are being contributed or required, is controlled by access polices and conditions in our model. An interesting point is that when participants require resources they also need to specify policies for these resources. These policies tell the resource provider how these resources will be used by the requestor (and its members if the requestor is an organization). For example, a hospital may specify a policy that says only senior doctors are permitted to access the medical records acquired from a patient. In order to get a resource from a provider, the requestor's policies must be stronger than the the provider's policies. This increases the confidence of participants about how their resources are used by other participant during collaborations.

In our model, the resources contributed and required by a participant, their dependency relations, and their access policies and conditions are all captured by the resource dependency graph, which is a directed acyclic graph. Before defining resource dependency graphs, we first describe the resources in our model.

A resource is specified by a pair (r, Att), where r is the name of the resource and Att is a set of attributes characterizing the resource. An attribute has a name and a value. For example, a resource `doctor` could have a `position` attribute with the value `senior`. Attributes are needed when checking whether an offered resource matches the required resource. We use R to denote the pair (r, Att). The operator $\sqsubseteq$ is overloaded to reresent resource match (and other order relations later).

Definition 2 (Resource Match). *Let $R_1 = (r_1, Att_1)$ and $R_2 = (r_2, Att_2)$. If $r_2 = r_1$ and $Att_2 \subseteq Att_1$, then R_1 matches R_2, denoted as $R_2 \sqsubseteq R_1$.*

A resource dependency graph $ResG$ is described by a pair $(N, \rightarrow)$, where N is a set of nodes, and $\rightarrow$ is a set of directed edges. The details of nodes and edges are given below.

A node $n \in N$ has two forms $(-, R, Pol, con)$, or $(+, R, Pol, con)$. That is, n is either a negative node or a positive node. The negative node means that the resource R is being required, while the positive node means that R is being contributed. The policies Pol are used to protect the required or contributed resources, and the condition con specifies the condition of using the resource. The polices and conditions are introduced in the next two sections, respectively. For a node n, we write $\mathtt{sign}(n) = -$ or $\mathtt{sign}(n) = +$, depending on whether n is a negative node or a positive node. For each resource dependency graph, we specify a special node `sta` as the start node and a special node `end` as the end node. The unique start and end nodes make it convenient later to define the initial and the final states for the coordinating mechanism.

An edge $(n_1, n_2) \in \rightarrow$ means that only after the resource described in n_1 is contributed or acquired, the participant would like to contribute or needs to require the resource in n_2. We also write $n_1 \rightarrow n_2$ for $(n_1, n_2) \in \rightarrow$. For example, if $\mathtt{sign}(n_1) = -$

and $\mathtt{sign}(n_2) = +$, the edge $n_1 \rightarrow n_2$ means the participant first needs a resource in n_1, and then contributes the resource in n_2. Note that positive nodes and negative nodes in a resource dependency graph do not necessarily appear alternately. For example, if $\mathtt{sign}(n_1) = -$ and $\mathtt{sign}(n_2) = -$, the edge $n_1 \rightarrow n_2$ means the participant first wants a resource in n_1, and then another resource in n_2.

A node n may have more than one child nodes and parent nodes. We write $\mathtt{cnodes}(n)$ for the set of child nodes of n, and $\mathtt{pnodes}(n)$ for the set of its parent nodes. Suppose $\mathtt{cnodes}(n) = \{n_1, ..., n_m\}$. Then after the resource in n is contributed or required, any node n_i $(1 \leq i \leq m)$ can be chosen to let the collaboration proceed. That is, the edges $n \rightarrow n_i$ $(1 \leq i \leq m)$ are mutually exclusive for one collaboration; choosing different edges implies collaborations with different resources involved. Similarly, if $\mathtt{pnodes}(n) = \{n_1, ..., n_m\}$, then the resource in n is processed when any parent node $n_i (1 \leq i \leq m)$ is chosen to provide or require resources. Therefore, each path in a resource dependency graph represents a possible way of contributing and requiring resources for a participant in a collaboration.

3.3 Access Polices

In our model, resources, whether they are being contributed or being required, are all protected by a set of policies *Pol*, specified in each node of resource graphs. In the following, we assume the policies *Pol* is specified in a node n for the resource R.

A policy $pol \in Pol$ has the form $Cert \rightarrow (op, Cert')$, meaning that the participants with certificates $Cert$ have the right to access the resource R and after getting R they can delegate the operation op on R to users having certificates $Cert'$. If $Cert$ and $Cert'$ are the same certificates, then the participants getting and using the resources are the same. This special case corresponds to the traditional access policies, where the authorized users get and use resource by themselves. One operation op may be protected by more than one policies in *Pol* for different authorization cases. A resource user can execute op on R if there exists a policy $pol \in Pol$ that authorizes the user for this operation. For example, suppose a patient defines the following two policies in the policy set *Pol* to protect his medical records:

$$\{\mathtt{hospital}^{\mathtt{Gov}}(\mathtt{H})\} \rightarrow (\mathtt{read}, \{\mathtt{doctor}^{\mathtt{H}}(x)\})$$
$$\{\mathtt{hospital}^{\mathtt{Gov}}(\mathtt{H})\} \rightarrow (\mathtt{read}, \{\mathtt{nurse}^x(y), \mathtt{doctor}^{\mathtt{H}}(x), \mathtt{senior}^{\mathtt{H}}(x)\})$$

The first policy means the hospital H can access the medical records and let its doctors to read these data, and similarly for the second policy.

When a participant obtains resources during collaboration, this participant may redistribute this resource to other users. This case is common when the participant is an organization, such as a hospital, and it needs its affiliated members to use the resources to carry on the current collaboration, as shown in Figure 2. Hence, in order to let resource providers be willing to release their resources for successful collaborations, the resource requestors must have not only enough certificates to get themselves authorized, but also policies stronger than the polices desired by resource providers. Thus, if a user can provide certificates to access resources from the participant who is redistributing resources, then the certificates provided by this user are also enough to pass the policies of the resource provider. A stronger policy is defined with a set of stronger certificates, which is defined below.

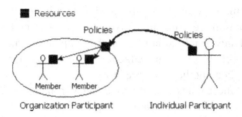

Fig. 2. Redistribution of Acquired Resources

Definition 3 (Order of Certificate Sets). *Suppose $Cert_1$ and $Cert_2$ are two sets of certificates. We say $Cert_1$ is stronger than $Cert_2$, written as $Cert_1 \sqsubseteq Cert_2$, if the following two conditions hold.*
- $Cert_2 = \emptyset$;
- *Let $Cert_2 = \{cert_2\} \cup Cert_2'$. Then, there exists $cert_1 \in Cert_1$, such that $cert_1 \sqsubseteq_\Theta cert_2$ and $Cert_1' \sqsubseteq \Theta(Cert_2')$, where $Cert_1' = Cert_1 \setminus \{cert_1\}$.*

In the above definition, the notation $\Theta(Cert_2')$ denotes a set of certificates obtained by applying all substitutions in Θ to all certificates in $Cert_2'$.

Definition 4 (Order of Policies). *Suppose pol_1 and pol_2 are two policies, and Cert is a set of certificate instances. Let $pol_1 = Cert_1 \rightarrow (op_1, Cert_1')$ and $pol_2 = Cert_2 \rightarrow (op_2, Cert_2')$. If $op_1 = op_2$, $Cert_1 \sqsubseteq Cert_2$, $Cert \sqsubseteq Cert_2$ and $Cert_1' \sqsubseteq Cert_2'$, then pol_1 is stronger than pol_2 when enhanced with Cert, written as $pol_1 \sqsubseteq_{Cert} pol_2$.*

In the relation $pol_1 \sqsubseteq_{Cert} pol_2$, pol_1 and pol_2 are policies specified by the resource requestor and providers, respectively, and $Cert$ is the profile certificates of the requestor. Two policies are comparable only when they both concern the same operation.

In order to get the needed resource, each policy specified by resource requestors must have a corresponding policy specified by resource providers, with the former stronger than the latter, so that resource providers have the confidence that their resource will be redistributed in ways not violating their polices. Two sets of policies are compared by the following definition.

Definition 5 (Order of Policy Sets). *Suppose Pol_1 and Pol_2 are two sets of policies, and Cert is a set of certificate instances. If for every $pol_1 \in Pol_1$ there exists $pol_2 \in Pol_2$, such that $pol_1 \sqsubseteq_{Cert} pol_2$, then Pol_1 is stronger than Pol_2 when enhanced with Cert, written as $Pol_1 \sqsubseteq_{Cert} Pol_2$.*

Continuing with the above example, we suppose the patient wants to collaborate with the hospital H. The hospital knows Tom is a doctor and owns the certificate $hospital^{Gov}(H)$, and defines the following policies to protect the medical records of the patient:

$$hospital^{Gov}(H) \rightarrow (read, \{doctor^H(Tom)\})$$
$$hospital^{Gov}(H) \rightarrow (read, \{nurse^{Tom}(y), doctor^H(Tom), senior^H(Tom)\})$$

According to the above definition, these policies are stronger than the policies specified by the patient since they only allow the doctor Tom and the nurse of Tom to access the patient's medical records. And when the hospital acquires the medical records, it does not release to other organizations as specified in these polcies.

3.4   Access Conditions

In our model, each resource is attached with a condition *con*, which imposes restrictions to resource accesses based on collaboration context parameters. For example, a condition may state that a resource is accessible between Monday and Tuesday or on Friday. A condition is a logical formula. True is a condition that is always satisfied, and False is a condition that cannot be satisfied. So if a resource is attached with True, then this resource can be used under any condition; if it is attached with False, then it actually cannot be used by anybody.

We use a differentiation operator diff to manipulate conditions. Given two conditions, con_1 and con_2, the operation $\mathtt{diff}(con_1, con_2)$ returns a new condition *con*, meaning that if the condition con_2 holds, then *con* implies con_1. The definition of diff depends on particular collaboration contexts. However, the following laws hold in all collaboration contexts:

$$
\begin{aligned}
\mathtt{diff}(con, con) &= \mathtt{True}, \text{if } con \neq \mathtt{False} \\
\mathtt{diff}(con \vee con', con'') &= \mathtt{diff}(con, con'') \vee \mathtt{diff}(con', con'') \\
\mathtt{diff}(con \wedge con', con'') &= \mathtt{diff}(con, con'') \wedge \mathtt{diff}(con', con'') \\
\mathtt{diff}(\mathtt{False}, con) &= \mathtt{False} \\
\mathtt{diff}(con, \mathtt{False}) &= con \\
\mathtt{diff}(con, \mathtt{True}) &= \mathtt{True}, \text{if } con \neq \mathtt{False}
\end{aligned}
$$

For example, in a collaboration, suppose a participant needs a device from 10am to 5pm (con_1). If such a device is offered with the condition True (i.e., it can be used anytime), then $\mathtt{diff}(con_1, \mathtt{True})$ returns True, meaning that the participant's requirement can be satisfied by this offer; if such a device can be used from 11am to 1pm (con_2), then $\mathtt{diff}(con_1, con_2)$ returns a conjunctive condition, specifying the time periods from 10am to 11am and from 1pm to 5pm. That is, if there are the same devices available during these two periods, the participant's requirement can be satisfied. Note that not all conditions can be divided. For example, if a condition specifies a temperature of 1000°C, we may not divide it into two 500°Cs. If a condition con_1 is indivisible, then $\mathtt{diff}(con_1, con_2)$ simply returns con_1 if con_2 cannot cover con_1. That is, the availability of resources with the condition con_2 has nothing to do with the requirement of the same resources with the condition con_1.

3.5   Resource Satisfaction

For a successful collaboration, all participants must be able to get their needed resources. In the following, we introduce step by step what resource satisfaction means for collaborations in our model.

A collaboration generally involves many resource requests from all participants. Here, we starts from the satisfaction problem of a single request. If a request of one participant is possible to be satisfied, then there must be other participants who contribute the requested resources. The predicate support defined below captures the necessary conditions on a set of positive nodes for satisfying a request in a negative node.

Definition 6 (Support Nodes). *Given a negative node n and a set of certificate instances Cert, a set of nodes $N = \{n_1, ..., n_k\}$ is a set of support nodes of n with respect to Cert, written as* support$(N, n, Cert)$, *if the following conditions hold:*

- $\texttt{sign}(n') = +$ for all $n' \in N$;
- $n.R \sqsubseteq n'.R$ for all $n' \in N$;
- $n.Pol \sqsubseteq_{Cert} n'.Pol$ for all $n' \in N$;
- $\texttt{diff}(n.con, n_1.con \vee ... \vee n_k.con) = \texttt{True}$.

Having support nodes does not mean a negative node can be satisfied definitely. This is because its support nodes may have negative parent or ancestor nodes that need to be satisfied first. Recall that a path in a resource graph represents a possible way to contribute and require resources for a participant in a collaboration. A well supported node n defined coinductively below asks every support node n' to be in a path from a resource graph with all negative parent and ancestor nodes also well supported. Thus, a well supported node can be satisfied definitely by its support nodes. In the definition below, $\texttt{pnodes}^+$ means the transitive closure of $\texttt{pnodes}$. Note that a node has only one parent node on a path.

Definition 7 (Well Supported Nodes). *Given a set of paths P from resource graphs and a set of certificate instances Cert, a negative node n is well supported in the set P with respect to Cert if there exists a set of nodes N from P such that* $\texttt{support}$ *$(N, n, Cert)$ and the following conditions hold for all $n' \in N$.*

- *for all $n'' \in \texttt{pnodes}^+(n')$, if $\texttt{sign}(n'') = -$, then n'' is well supported.*

Finally, based on the concept of well supported nodes, the resource satisfaction for collaborations in our model is defined below.

Definition 8 (Resource Satisfaction). *Suppose a collaboration consists of m participants $(p_i, Cert_i, ResG_i)$ $(1 \leq i \leq m)$. The resource requests in this collaboration are satisfiable if there exists a set of paths $\{path_i | 1 \leq i \leq m\}$, where $path_i$ comes from the graph $ResG_i$ with $\texttt{sta}$ and $\texttt{end}$ as its start and end nodes respectively, such that for all j $(1 \leq j \leq m)$ all negative nodes on $path_j$ are well supported in the set $\{path_i | 1 \leq i \leq m\}$ with respect to $Cert_j$.*

The following two sections will give the mechanism and algorithm to find the paths in a set of resource graphs that all have well supported negative nodes.

4   Coordination Based on State-Space Exploration

In this section, we present the coordinating mechanism to check whether collaborations in our model can be completed successfully or not. In our model, the reason for collaboration failures is that some participants fail to obtain the resources necessary for continuing the current collaboration. Since a resource in our model may be contributed depending on the availability of other resources and protected by access policies and conditions, we cannot simply say it is available to other participants because of its positive presence in some resource graphs. Our coordination mechanism is based on state-space exploration, which is widely used for computer-aided verification. A state represents a resource coordinating status, like what resources have been contributed and what resource requirements have been satisfied or are being proposed. A state transition indicates the coordination enters a new state because a resource is contributed or a resource requirement is satisfied.

4.1   States

A coordinating state has the form (RB, PS, RL), where RB is the resource base containing all resources currently offered by participants, PS describes the resource status of each participant and RL means resource links indicating how resource requirements are satisfied at this state. An element in RB has the form (p, n), where $\text{sign}(n) = +$, meaning that the participant p contributes the resource described by the node n in $p's$ resource dependency graph. The status of each participant in PS is also described by the pair (p, n), where $\text{sign}(n) = +$ or $\text{sign}(n) = -$, meaning that p is waiting to contribute or require the resource in n, a node in $p's$ resource dependency graph. Note that we can move to the children nodes of n by using the cnodes operator when changing $p's$ status. A resource link in RL has the form $((p, n), \{(p_1, n_1), ..., (p_m, n_m)\})$, where $\text{sign}(n) = -$ and $\text{sign}(n_i) = + \ (1 \leq i \leq m)$, meaning that the resource requirement n of p can be satisfied by combining the resources $n_1,..., n_m$ offered by participants $p_1,..., p_m$. For example, suppose p wants a device from 1pm to 5 pm. Then this requirement is satisfiable if p_1 and p_2 can collaboratively provide the device from 1pm to 2pm and from 2pm to 5pm, respectively.

The coordination procedure starts from an initial state. Suppose a model consists of $(p_i, Cert_i, ResG_i)$ $(1 \leq i \leq m)$ for m participants. Then the initial state for this model is $(\emptyset, \{(p_1, \text{sta}), ..., (p_m, \text{sta})\}, \emptyset)$. Recall that every resource graph $ResG_i$ starts with the special node sta. In the initial state, each participant has not begun to contribute and require resources, so there is no contributed resources, nor resource links.

For a collaboration, if the resources involved cannot be coordinated to a final state, then this collaboration will not be possible to complete. A final state has the form $(RB, \{(p_1, \text{end}), ..., (p_m, \text{end})\}, RL)$, where no participant has resources to contribute and require. The resource links RL contain the information of how to satisfy all resource requirements in collaborations. This information can be used at collaboration time to route resource requests. Hence, in a final state, if a resource appears in RB but not referred to in RL, then this resource is redundant for this collaboration and can be removed safely.

4.2   State Transitions

The state transitions of coordination are caused by the status change of participants. For example, a state changes when a participant contributes a resource or have a resource request satisfied. To help define how state transitions occur, the operator reduce (RB, p, n) in Figure 3 is used to check whether the resource request in the negative node n from the resource graph of p can be satisfied by the resource base RB. In this definition, $\text{certs}(p)$ means the certificate instances for the profile of p. This operator returns a pair with its first component being a node or a special value ϵ and its second component being a set of nodes. If the first component is ϵ, then it means that the requested resource of n can be satisfied and the second component contains the support nodes of n, otherwise the first component is a node whose satisfaction implies the satisfaction of n.

$$\text{reduce}(\emptyset, p, n) = (n, \emptyset)$$

$$\text{reduce}(\{(p', n')\} \cup \text{RB}, p, n) = \begin{cases} \text{reduce}(\text{RB}, p, n) & \text{if } n.R \not\sqsubseteq n'.R \text{ or } n.Pol \not\sqsubseteq_{\text{certs}(p)} n'.Pol \\ \text{reduce}(\text{RB}, p, n) & \text{if } n.R \sqsubseteq n'.R, \ n.Pol \sqsubseteq_{\text{certs}(p)} n'.Pol, \\ & \quad \text{diff}(n.con, n'.con) = n.con \\ (n'', \{(p', n')\} \cup S) & \text{if } n.R \sqsubseteq n'.R, \ n.Pol \sqsubseteq_{\text{certs}(p)} n'.Pol, \\ & \quad \text{diff}(n.con, n'.con) = con' \text{ and } con' \neq n.con \\ & \quad \text{with } (n'', S) = \text{reduce}(\text{RB}, p, (-, n.R, n.Pol, con')) \\ (\epsilon, \{(p', n')\}) & \text{if } n.R \sqsubseteq n'.R, \ n.Pol \sqsubseteq_{\text{certs}(p)} n'.Pol \\ & \quad \text{and } \text{diff}(n.con, n'.con) = \text{True} \end{cases}$$

Fig. 3. The reduce Operator

Proposition 1. *Given a resource base RB and a node n from the resource graph of participant p with* $\text{sign}(n) = -$, *if* $\text{reduce}(RB, p, n) = (\epsilon, S)$ *and let* $N = \{n' | (p', n') \in S\}$, *then N is a set of support nodes of n, that is,* $\text{support}(N, n, \text{certs}(p))$ *holds.*

In the following, we describe first from the perspective of a participant how state transitions occur, and then from the perspective of all participants.

Suppose the current state is $st = (RB, PS, RL)$ and $(p, n) \in PS$. The next states caused by the status change of p, denoted as $\text{next}^{(p,n)}(st)$, are generated according to the following rules.

- Rule 1: $n = \text{sta. next}^{(p,n)}(st) = \{(RB, PS' \cup \{(p, n')\}, RL) | n' \in \text{cnodes}(n)\}$, where $PS' = PS \setminus \{(p, n)\}$.
- Rule 2: $\text{sign}(n) = +. \text{next}^{(p,n)}(st) = \{(RB', PS' \cup \{(p, n')\}, RL) | n' \in \text{cnodes}(n)\}$, where $RB' = RB \cup \{(p, n)\}$ and $PS' = PS \setminus \{(p, n)\}$.
- Rule 3: $\text{sign}(n) = -, \text{reduce}(RB, p, n) = (n', S)$ and $n' \neq \epsilon. \text{next}^{(p,n)}(st) = \{st\}$.
- Rule 4: $\text{sign}(n) = -$ and $\text{reduce}(RB, p, n) = (\epsilon, S)$. $\text{next}^{(p,n)}(st) = \{(RB, PS' \cup \{(p, n')\}, RL') | n' \in \text{cnodes}(n)\}$, where $RL' = RL \cup \{((p, n), S)\}$ and $PS' = PS \setminus \{(p, n)\}$.
- Rule 5: $n = \text{end. next}^{(p,n)}(st) = \{st\}$.

For a state $st = (RB, PS, RL)$, its next states from the perspective of all participants, written as $\text{next}(st)$, are obtained by composing all next states from the perspective of each participant.

$$\text{next}(st) = \bigcup_{(p,n) \in PS} \text{next}^{(p,n)}(st)$$

4.3 Correctness

In this section, we show that the correctness of the above coordination mechanism for checking the resource satisfaction in collaborations. For this purpose, we need to extend the use of next operator in the following two aspects.

First, the next operator is extended to a set of states *ST*.

$$\text{next}(ST) = \bigcup_{st \in ST} \text{next}(st)$$

Second, the next operator can be applied iteratively many times, say m times, to a state st (or a set of states), written as $\text{next}^m(st)$.

$$\text{next}^1(st) = \text{next}(st)$$
$$\text{next}^{m+1}(st) = \text{next}(\text{next}^m(st))$$

Theorem 1 (Correctness of Coordination). *Given an initial state st for a collaboration, there exists some integer m such that $\text{next}^{m+1}(st) = \text{next}^m(st)$, that is, $\text{next}^m(st)$ is a fixed point of the operator* next. *If there is a final state in $\text{next}^m(st)$, then the resource requests in this collaboration are satisfiable.*

The next section will give an algorithm to compute the fixed point of the next operator, which is then used to check the resource consistency in collaborations.

5 A Coordination Algorithm

In this section, we present an algorithm that implements the previous coordination mechanism. The main code of the algorithm is SPExplore, shown in Figure 4, which computes the fixed point of the next operator by iteratively calling the subroutine ONext in the same figure. The code ONext implements the transition rules of next operator defined in the previous section but with some optimization. By this optimization, when a negative node is checked against a resource base *RB* to test its satisfaction with the reduce operator, the current check arguments and results are memoized if its request is not satisfied completely by the current resource base *RB*. And then, if *RB* is extended with new contributed resources in the later stage of coordination, it is not needed to check this negative node against the whole resource base, and instead the result of last check is reused and only the newly contributed resources are tested. Hence, this optimization can avoid repeating comparisons of resources, access policies and usage conditions during state transitions.

The optimization used in this implementation is based on the following proposition, which lays the foundation of using the resource base incrementally to test the satisfaction of resource requests.

Proposition 2. *Let $RB = RB_1 \cup RB_2$. For a node n from the resource graph of participant p with $\text{sign}(n) = -$, if $\text{reduce}(RB, p, n) = (n', S)$, $\text{reduce}(RB_1, p, n) = (n_1, S_1)$ and $\text{reduce}(RB_2, p, n_1) = (n_2, S_2)$, then $n' = n_2$ and $S = S_1 \cup S_2$.*

In the following, we will introduce how this optimization is implemented. The point of this optimization is to memoize the intermediate check results and reuse them for the further checks when the resource base is extended. The memoization is implemented by a mapping, called *RBMemo* or *RBMemo'* in the code, which maps p and n to $(RB, (n', S))$ if the mapping is defined on p and n. It means that the request in n has been tested against the existing resource *RB* but not satisfied completely, and if the request in n' can be satisfied by some newly contributed resources, then the request in n will be completely satisfied and S is a part of the final support nodes for n. An empty mapping is denoted by •, which is undefined for every p and n. The notation $RBMemo[(p, n) \mapsto (RB, (n', S))]$ means a new mapping obtained by updating the value

```
Function SPExplore( st)
Input:
  st=(∅,  PS,  ∅): an initial state
Output:
  WL: a set of states
  begin
    WL  =  {( st, •)}
    OldWL  =  WL
    NewWL  =  ∅
  while OldWL  ≠  NewWL do
    NewWL  =  ∅
    ST  =  ∅
    for each (st', RBMemo) ∈ WL do
      AST  =  ONext(st', RBMemo)
      NewWL  = NewWL ∪ AST
      ST  = ST ∪ { st'}
    endfor
    OldWL  =  WL
    WL  =  NewWL
  endwhile
  return  ST
end
Function ONext( st, RBMemo)
Input:
  st=(RB,  PS,  RL): a state
  RBMemo: a mapping from (p, n) to ( RB, (n, S))
Output:
  AST: a set of pairs of state and RB memo
  begin
  AST = ∅
  for each (p, n) ∈ PS do
    PS'  =  PS \ (p, n)
    if n =  sta then
      ST'  = {( RB, PS' ∪ {(p, n')}, RL)|n' ∈ child(n)}
      AST'  =  ST' × { RBMemo}
    else if sign(n) = + then
      RB'  =  RB ∪ {(p, n)}
      ST'  = {( RB', PS' ∪ {(p, n')}, RL)|n' ∈ child(n)}
      AST'  =  ST' × { RBMemo}
    else if sign(n) = − then
      if RBMemo(p, n)  =  ( RB', (n', S')) then
        (n'', S) = reduce(RB\RB', p, n')
        if n'' ≠ ϵ then
          RBMemo'= RBMemo[(p, n) ↦ ( RB, (n'',  S ∪ S'))]
          AST' = {( st, RBMemo')}
        else
          RBMemo'= RBMemo[(p, n) ↦ undefined]
          RL'  = RL ∪ {((p, n), S ∪ S')}
          ST'  = {( RB, PS' ∪ {(p, n')}, RL')|n' ∈ child(n)}
          AST'  =  ST' × { RBMemo}
      else if RBMemo(p, n)  = undefined then
        if reduce(RB, p, n) = (n', S)&&n' ≠ ϵ then
          RBMemo'= RBMemo[(p, n) ↦ ( RB, (n',  S))]
          AST' = {( st, RBMemo')}
        else if reduce(RB, p, n) = (ϵ, S) then
          RL'  = RL ∪ {((p, n), S)}
          ST'  = {( RB, PS' ∪ {(p, n')}, RL')|n' ∈ child(n)}
          AST'  =  ST' × { RBMemo}
    else if n =  end then
      AST' = {(st, RBMemo)}
    endif
    AST = AST ∪ AST'
  endfor
  return  AST
end
```

Fig. 4. The Coordination Algorithm

of (p, n) in *RBMemo* to $(RB, (n', S))$, that is, the new mapping returns $(RB, (n', S))$ for (p, n), and returns $RBMemo(p, n)$ otherwise.

The subroutine ONext implements all rules of state transitions for the next operator. Only in the rule concerning negative nodes, the mapping *RBMemo* is updated and referenced. For example, for a negative node n of participant p, if (p, n) is mapped to $(RB', (n', S'))$ in *RBMemo*, then the request test is done by the operation reduce $(RB \backslash RB', p, n')$, that is, only part of the whole resource base RB is checked and the check works on the node n' from last check. Based on this check, if the request of n is still not satisfied, that is reduce$(RB \backslash RB', p, n') = (n'', S)$ and $n'' \neq \epsilon$, then the mapping *RBMemo* on (p, n) is updated by $RBMemo[(p, n) \mapsto (RB, (n'', S \cup S'))]$ to incorporate the result of this check, otherwise the mapping of (p, n) is changed into undefined in *RBMemo*.

6 Related Work

The collaboration failures can also be caused by mismatched business protocols between participants. This problem can be addressed by adapting interactions among participants [1,2]. Our work is complementary to these work since we focus on resource satisfaction for collaborating participants, rather than on protocol consistency.

There are various access control mechanisms for collaborations among different organizations [7,8,9,10]. However, these mechanisms do not consider how they affect the successful completion of collaborations. For example, maybe a participant defines too strong security policies, and hence there are actually no possibility for other participants to access its resources intended for sharing. It is also similar for the work of enhancing business processes with authorization constraints [11]. Two process may collaborate well, but after enhanced with authorization constraints, they probably fail to work together.

The work [12,13] studies how to specify and solve authorization constraints on workflow systems, so as to make sure there are possible successful executions of workflow patterns. Their work focuses on tasks, concerning workflow tasks in the same organization, while our work focuses on resources, coordinating resources from different organizations.

The work [14] proposes an architecture to protect an object (or a resource) by enforcing the object owner's policy in the requestor's platform. This architecture is based on the special hardware for trusted computing. It is not clear whether this architecture can be scaled to the distributed collaboration environments where some participants may not have such special platforms. Access control in our resource has no special requirements on platforms by trusting the requestors faithfully enforce the policies they declare for requiring resources.

As surveyed in [15], graphs can be used to represent the allocation and request status of resources at a system state for checking deadlocks. For that purpose, those graphs have only one kind of nodes representing the resources being allocated and requested. The resources being offered for collaborations cannot be represented in those graphs.

For participants, offering resources can be regarded as their obligations for making collaborations successful. A centralized model has been proposed in [16] to analyze whether a system state can lead to another system state in which a subject cannot fulfill his obligation within the time window or at the deadline of the obligation. Our collaborative resource model is distributed in the sense that each participant has his own obligations to fulfill and his obligations may affect the ability of other participants to perform their obligations.

7 Conclusion

In this paper, we address the problem of whether collaborations can be completed successfully, so as to achieve the prescribed collaboration purposes. The collaborations we concern here is resource centric and we proposed a collaborative resource model for this kind of collaborations. This model can capture the dependency relations among resources offered or required by participants. This feature gives participants flexible strategies to choose resources for collaborations. Resources in this model are protected by security policies based on certificates and restricted by usage conditions. The certificates based access control mechanism is suitable for participants who do not know each other in advance in a distributed environment. Moreover, this model allows the resource requestors to declare policies, stating how the requestors will redistribute the acquired resources, and thus enables the resource owners to gain more confidence to contribute their resources. The usage condition can be used to model, for instance, dynamic collaborations, where participants may join and leave in the middle of collaborations. Based on the collaborative resource model, we proposed the coordination mechanism. Successful coordination means that there must be a possible way to satisfy the resource requirements of all participants during collaborations.

In the future, we will consider other principles of access control mechanisms, such as separation of duty and binding of duty, and other kind of resources, like consumable resources.

References

1. Nezhad, H.R.M., Benatallah, B., Martens, A., Curbera, F., Casati, F.: Semi-automated adaptation of service interactions. In: WWW 2007: Proceedings of the 16th International Conference on World Wide Web, pp. 993–1002 (2007)
2. Desai, N., Chopra, A.K., Singh, M.P.: Business process adaptations via protocols. In: SCC 2006: Proceedings of the IEEE International Conference on Services Computing, pp. 103–110. IEEE Computer Society, Los Alamitos (2006)
3. Blaze, M., Feigenbaum, J., Lacy, J.: Decentralized trust management. In: Proceedings of the 1996 IEEE Symposium on Security and Privacy, pp. 164–173 (1996)
4. Li, N., Mitchell, J.C., Winsborough, W.H.: Design of a role-based trust-management framework. In: SP 2002: Proceedings of the 2002 IEEE Symposium on Security and Privacy, pp. 114–130. IEEE Computer Society, Los Alamitos (2002)
5. Chan, J., Rogers, G., Agahari, D., Moreland, D., Zic, J.: Enterprise collaborative contexts and their provisioning for secure managed extranets. In: WETICE 2006: Proceedings of the 15th IEEE International Workshops on Enabling Technologies: Infrastructure for Collaborative Enterprises, pp. 313–318. IEEE Computer Society, Los Alamitos (2006)

6. Chan, J., Nepal, S., Moreland, D., Hwang, H., Chen, S., Zic, J.: User-controlled collaborations in the context of trust extended environments. In: WETICE 2007: Proceedings of the 16th IEEE International Workshops on Enabling Technologies: Infrastructure for Collaborative Enterprises, pp. 389–394. IEEE Computer Society, Los Alamitos (2007)

7. Gong, L., Qian, X.: The complexity and composability of secure interoperation. In: Proceedings of the 1994 IEEE Symposium on Security and Privacy, p. 190 (1994)

8. Shehab, M., Bertino, E., Ghafoor, A.: Secure collaboration in mediator-free environments. In: CCS 2005: Proceedings of the 12th ACM Conference on Computer and Communications Security, pp. 58–67 (2005)

9. Warner, J., Atluri, V., Mukkamala, R., Vaidya, J.: Using semantics for automatic enforcement of access control policies among dynamic coalitions. In: SACMAT 2007: Proceedings of the 12th ACM Symposium on Access Control Models and Technologies, pp. 235–244 (2007)

10. Zhang, X., Nakae, M., Covington, M.J., Sandhu, R.: A usage-based authorization framework for collaborative computing systems. In: Proceedings of the eleventh ACM symposium on Access Control Models and Technologies, pp. 180–189 (2006)

11. Bertino, E., Crampton, J., Paci, F.: Access control and authorization constraints for ws-bpel. In: ICWS 2006: Proceedings of the IEEE International Conference on Web Services, pp. 275–284 (2006)

12. Bertino, E., Ferrari, E., Atluri, V.: The specification and enforcement of authorization constraints in workflow management systems. ACM Trans. Inf. Syst. Secur. 2(1), 65–104 (1999)

13. Tan, K., Crampton, J., Gunter, C.A.: The consistency of task-based authorization constraints in workflow systems. In: CSFW 2004: Proceedings of the 17th IEEE workshop on Computer Security Foundations, p. 155. IEEE Computer Society, Los Alamitos (2004)

14. Sandhu, R., Zhang, X.: Peer-to-peer access control architecture using trusted computing technology. In: SACMAT 2005: Proceedings of the tenth ACM symposium on Access control models and technologies, pp. 147–158 (2005)

15. Coffman, E.G., Elphick, M., Shoshani, A.: System deadlocks. ACM Comput. Surv. 3(2), 67–78 (1971)

16. Irwin, K., Yu, T., Winsborough, W.H.: On the modeling and analysis of obligations. In: Proceedings of the 13th ACM Conference on Computer and Communications Security (2006)

RiBAC: Role Interaction Based Access Control Model for Community Computing

Youna Jung[1], Amirreza Masoumzadeh[1], James B.D Joshi[1], and Minkoo Kim[2]

[1] School of Information Sciences, University of Pittsburgh
{yjung,amirreza,jjoshi}@sis.pitt.edu
[2] College of Information Technology, Ajou University, Korea
minkoo@ajou.ac.kr

Abstract. Community computing is an agent-based development paradigm for ubiquitous computing systems. In a community computing system, ubiquitous services are provided by cooperation among agents. While agents cooperate, they interact with each other continuously to access data of other agents and/or to execute other agent's actions. However, in cases of security-critical ubiquitous services such as medical or military services, an access control mechanism is necessary to prevent unauthorized access to critical data or action. In this paper, we propose a family of *Role interaction Based Access Control* (RiBAC) models for Community Computing, by extending the existing RBAC model to consider role interactions. As a basic model, we propose the core RiBAC model. For the convenience of management and to provide more fine-grained access control, we propose Hierarchical RiBAC (H-RiBAC), Constrained RiBAC (C-RiBAC), and Constrained Hierarchical RiBAC (CH-RiBAC) models. Finally, we extend the existing community computing framework to accommodate the specification and enforcement of RiBAC policies.

Keywords: Cooperation, Community computing, Role interaction, Role-based Access Control, Multiagent system.

1 Introduction and Motivation

The capacity and intelligence of newly developed computing elements are growing day by day. For highly complex problems requiring diverse capabilities, an approach based on cooperation among elements can be an efficient solution [1]. Many researchers have tried to fulfill application requirements using cooperation among individual computing elements. For example, ubiquitous computing systems are often developed using cooperation among computing elements because such systems require, in general, many different capabilities of various computing elements. Because such a cooperation based approach involves continuous and rich interactions, multiagent technology is frequently used to design and develop cooperation based ubiquitous computing systems. In addition, agents' characteristics such as intelligence and autonomy are suitable for developing intelligent ubiquitous computing systems that can adapt to dynamically changing situations.

E. Bertino and J.B.D. Joshi (Eds.): CollaborateCom 2008, LNICST 10, pp. 304–321, 2009.

Jung *et al.* [2] propose Community Computing (CC) as an agent-based development paradigm for ubiquitous computing systems. The objective of CC framework is to provide ubiquitous services through dynamic cooperation among agents. The CC approach focuses more on cooperation compared to the other multiagent methodologies. As part of the CC approach, Jung *et al.* have proposed a cooperation model and two different CC models. However, security of such a CC based multiagent system has not been addressed in the literature.

Ubiquitous services are currently being expanded to various applications such as u-healthcare, u-government, u-city, etc. Security and performance issues are some key challenges to the deployment of such emerging ubiquitous systems, and hence a CC system for ubiquitous applications should incorporate efficient security mechanisms. In order to guarantee a secure CC system, first of all, the system should authenticate agents. During cooperation, agents interact with other agents to get information or request execution of other agents' actions, which may be critical. To ensure security of such critical actions or data, we need a proper access control mechanism to ensure that agents are engaged in only authorized activities.

In this paper, we propose a family of role interaction based access control (RiBAC) models that extend the standard RBAC models by incorporating authorized role-based interactions among agents. We define two types of interaction permissions to capture authorized interactions among agents. Moreover, we extend the CC specification framework to include the RiBAC policy specification and enforcement capabilities.

The remainder of this paper is organized as follows. In Section 2, we present the background on the CC model. In section 3, we propose the family of RiBAC models. In Section 4, we present the extended CC framework that includes the core RiBAC policy specification for communities. In Section 5, we discuss related work and in Section 6, we present our conclusions and discuss future work.

2 Community Computing

In this section, we briefly introduce the CC approach used for developing ubiquitous systems, where cooperation among agents is a basic issue. In order to design and develop a CC system, we have earlier proposed two CC models: the *simple community computing* (SCC) model [2] and *community situation based static* CC model [3]. In this paper, we focus on an extension of the SCC model to incorporate access control requirements.

2.1 Related Cooperation Based Approaches

Many cooperation based approaches have been proposed in the literature with the goal of solving emerging large and complex problems. Several groupwares to support CSCW (Computer Supported Cooperative Work) have been proposed in the literature that effectively perform common tasks through information sharing among all users [4, 5].

Multiagent based approaches have been frequently used to develop complex and intelligent systems. Agents in multiagent systems have features such as *flexibility* and *autonomous* problem solving behavior, and the richness of *interactions* that are useful for solving complex problems. In a typical multiagent system, agents interact with each other in order to achieve their common goals. Zambonelli *et al.* [6] propose Gaia methodology in which a multiagent system is regarded as a collection of computational organizations consisting of various interacting roles, and the cooperation among agents playing different roles aimed towards fulfilling the requirements of the system. PICO (Pervasive Information Community Organization) is a middleware framework for dynamically creating mission-oriented communities of autonomous and ubiquitous software objects, called *delegents*, that offer ubiquitous services [7].

In [8], Ishida *et al.* introduce the notion of community computing to support the process of organizing diverse and amorphous people who are willing to share knowledge and experiences. The objective of their approach is to make a city-scale supporting system to assist a human's everyday life – by creating a community that represents a real human community. Their work supports the process of sharing member's preferences and knowledge so that they can reach consensus.

In [10], Blau emphasizes community computing as an essential emerging technological environment where users share each other's computing capabilities and their identities are spread all over various devices, and points out the need for significant research in this area.

2.2 Community Computing Model

As a cooperative approach to provide ubiquitous services, we have earlier developed an agent based approach called the Community Computing (CC) model [2, 3]. The model helps to realize ubiquitous services by utilizing cooperation among intelligent agents in a ubiquitous environment. In CC approach, services are provided by communities of agents having a common goal. This approach helps to intuitively design ubiquitous services based on agent cooperation. A community consists of agents cooperating with other agents in order to achieve the community's goals, and the problems of ubiquitous computing systems are solved by such communities. We introduce the essential concepts of community computing below.

- *Community* - it is a metaphor to abstract a proactive organization that comprises members cooperating with each others to achieve a particular set of goals. A community has goals, necessary roles, cooperation, and role-member binding information. In the CC model, different types of communities are represented as different community templates. At the execution time, a community instance is dynamically created according to the corresponding community template.
- *Role* - it is a well-defined position in a community, with an associated set of expected capabilities. A role represents a particular responsibility necessary to achieve a community's goal. The capability of a role is represented by actions.
- *Cooperation* - it is a set of cooperative interactions among members assuming the roles defined for a community in order to achieve community's goal(s).
- *Member* - it is a metaphor that abstracts an individual agent involved in a CC system. We can consider a human user as a member by using the agent of his/her personal device. An agent can play different roles in different communities simultaneously.
- *Role-member binding* - in order to create a community instance, we have to find most appropriate members for each role. We refer to this process as role-member binding.
- *Society* - it is a metaphor to abstract a CC system.

```
Platform Independent Community Implementation Description {
    Community EmergencyService {
        Role PATIENT {
            Attribute: LOCATION; BLOOD_PRESSURE; PULSE; BODY_TEMPERATURE;
            Context: EMERGENCY;
            Cast: EMERGENCY; }
        Role AMBULANCE {
            Attribute: AVAILABILITY; DRIVER; LOCATION; PATIENT_LOCATION;HOSPITAL_LOCATION;
            Context: ARRIVE_ON_PATIENT; ARRIVE_ON_HOSPITAL;
            Action: transfer_patient_to_hospital; adjust_temperature; adjust_ambulance_speed;
            Cast: AVAILABILITY=AVAILABLE; LOCATION= nearest(PATIENT.LOCATION);}
        Role MEDICAL_DOCTOR {
            Attribute: AVAILABILITY; MAJOR; FIRSTAID_TREATMENT;
            Action: remote_examine; make_prescripton;
            Cast: AVAILABILITY=AVAILABLE; MAJOR=EMERGENCY; }
        Role PARAMEDIC {
            Attribute: AVAILABILITY; LOCATION;
            Action: save_firstaid_treatment; give_firstaid; bring_patient_to_ambulance; bring_patient_to_hospital;
            Cast: AVAILABILITY=AVAILABLE; LOCATION= nearest(AMBULANCE.LOCATION);}
        Role HOSPITAL_MANAGER {
            Attribute: EMERGENCY_ACCEPTABILITY; LOCATION;
            Action: ready_for_emergency_patient;
            Cast: EMERGENCY_ACCEPTABILITY=ACCEPTABLE; LOCATION= nearest(PATIENT.LOCATION);}
        Role-MemberType Mapping {
            PATIENT:Personal_agent;AMBULANCE:Ambulance_agent;
MEDICAL_DOCTOR:Personal_doctor_agent;
            PARAMEDIC:Personal_paramedic_agent; HOSPITAL_MANAGER:Hospital_agent; }
        Goal Providing_emergency_service(initiator:PATIENT; participant:AMBULANCE,MEDICAL_DOCTOR,
            PARAMEDIC,HOSPITAL) {
            PATIENT{
                PAR{SEND(MsgType="request", ToWhom=AMBULANCE, certificate(Location));
                    SEND(MsgType="request", ToWhom=MEDICAL_DOCTOR, certificate(Healthinfo); ) }
            AMBULANCE{
                IF(RECEIVE(MsgType="request", ToWhom=AMBULANCE, certificate(Location)))
                    transfer_patient_to_hospital; }
            MEDICAL_DOCTOR{
                IF(RECEIVE(MsgType="request", ToWhom=MEDICAL_DOCTOR, certificate(Healthinfo)))
                    SEQ{
                        remote_examine;make_prescripton;
                        PAR{
                            SEND(MsgType="request", ToWhom=PARAMEDIC, certificate(firstaid_treatment));
                            SEND(MsgType="request", ToWhom=HOSPITAL_MANAGER, certificate(firstaid_treatment));}}}
            PARAMEDIC{
                IF(RECEIVE(MsgType="request", ToWhom=PARAMEDIC, certificate(firstaid_treatment)))
                    save_firstaid_treatment;
                IF(AMBULANCE.ARRIVE_ON_PATIENT){
                    bring_patient_to_ambulance;
                    give_firstaid; }
                IF(AMBULANCE.ARRIVE_ON_HOSPITAL;)
                    bring_patient_to_hospital;
                    IF(PATIENT.LOCATION = HOSPITAL.LOCATION) { SUCCESS; }
            HOSPITAL_MANAGER{
                IF(RECEIVE(MsgType="request", ToWhom=HOSPITAL, certificate(firstaid_treatment))
                    ready_for_emergency_patient; } }  }
```

Fig. 1. A part of description for 'EmergencyService' community in a simple community computing model

In the SCC model, a community has a set of roles, one goal, and mapping information between roles and member agents' types. Each role has attributes, contexts, actions, and the condition for membership assignment. A context of a role is implicitly defined by attributes of the role. The role-membertype mapping indicates which agent types can take which roles defined for a community. The goal description part indicates the initiator role and participant roles of cooperation, and the cooperation itself. To describe a cooperation, the SCC framework uses constructs of OCCAM, a parallel computing language, such as SEQ, PAR, ALT, IF, etc.

As a running example, we explain a part of a community description in a simple CC model (see Fig. 1). The example community is based on an emergency service scenario as follows. While an old man is walking in a street, he suddenly falls down. In order to provide an emergency service to him, an instance of 'EmergencyService' community is created. This community type consists of five roles; patient, ambulance, paramedic, medical doctor, and hospital manager. For each role, agents are selected by the casting condition and the role-membertype mapping condition described in the SCC model. After the creation of a community instance, all member agents cooperate to provide the first-aid service to the patient while the patient is transferred to a close by hospital. When the patient falls down on a street, the patient agent interacts with ambulance agent and medical doctor's agent. The patient agent calls the nearest ambulance and requests help for a doctor. At this time, the patient agent should grant the access to patient's information to doctor and ambulance. After obtaining the patient's location, the ambulance moves to where the patient is located. At the same time, a doctor makes a prescription for the emergency patient using patient's health information, and sends it to the paramedic and the hospital. When ambulance arrives, the paramedic brings the patient into the ambulance and then provides first-aid treatment according to the doctor's prescription. Finally, the patient is transferred to the hospital, and the goal of 'EmergencyService' community instance is achieved.

3 Role Interaction-Based Access Control Model

In this section, we propose role interaction based access control (RiBAC) models for the SCC model. Note that agent interaction is a key issue in a CC model. Furthermore, interactions authorized for agents are basically defined by what roles within the community the interacting agents are playing. Such interactions can hence be cast as accesses authorized for agents playing specific roles. For fine-grained role-based policy specification, we categorize agent interactions within a community into two types, as depicted in Fig. 2.

Role-action interaction, shown in Fig.2.a, involves an initiator role (r_i) interacting with a target role (r_t) to indicate that the target role should perform some action it is capable of – in other words, we model this as the initiator role authorized to invoke the target role's action. The pair *role* and its *action invocable* by other roles can be considered as a *role-action permission*.

In *Operation-role interaction*, depicted in Fig.2.b, an initiator role can interact with a target role by performing some operation on the target role itself. In this paper, the pair *operation* and a *target role* is termed as a *role-oriented permission*; we use the term *object-oriented permission* to describe traditional RBAC permission that represents an *operation* over an *object*.

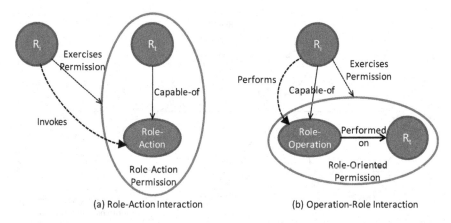

(a) Role-Action Interaction   (b) Operation-Role Interaction

Fig. 2. Two types of Interaction Permissions in Role-based Agent Interaction

It is important to note that in a typical scenario there could exist interdependencies among different types of interactions and *object-oriented* permissions. For instance, a particular *role-action* permission may include several *object-oriented* permissions needed to complete the defined action. If such permission interdependency details could be provided by the underlying environment model, it can be used for access control policy analysis.

In the following subsections, we define the core RiBAC model that extends traditional RBAC with the notion of interaction permissions. We also provide a hierarchical version of the model to leverage hierarchical structures for permission inheritance. It is followed by a constrained RiBAC model.

3.1 Core RiBAC Model

Fig. 3 illustrates the core RiBAC model. Instead of users in standard RBAC model, agents (*AGENTS*) are the entities that can request for access in a MAS environment. Agents are assigned to roles (*ROLES*) and can exercise the permissions assigned to the roles by activating them in a session (*SESSIONS*).

Depending on the application, various objects could exist in the environment which needs to be accessed by agents. The valid pairs objects (*OBS*) and operations on them (*OPS*) form the *object-oriented* permissions (*OOPRMS*). Roles are authorized for object-oriented permissions that are assigned to them through the object-oriented permission assignment relation (*OOPA*).

Interaction permissions include role-action and role-oriented permissions. The valid pairs of roles and their actions (*ROLE-ACTIONS*) invocable by other roles form the role-action permissions (*RAPRMS*). Role-action permissions are assigned to initiator roles according to the policy through role-action permission assignment relation (*RAPA*). An agent that has activated a role is authorized to exercise the assigned role-action permissions (to its role) on any agent that is assuming the target role in the permission. The valid pairs of an operation (*Role-OPS*) and a target role that the operation can be performed on form role-oriented permissions (*ROPRMS*).

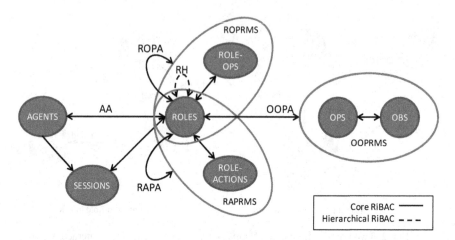

Fig. 3. RiBAC Model

Role-oriented permissions are assigned to authorized initiators using the role-oriented permission assignment relation (*ROPA*).

Note an interaction permission related to a role can also be assigned to the same role; this will allow agents with the same role in the community to interact with each other. For instance, a guarding agent in a patrol community should be able to ask for help from other guarding agents.

The formal definition of the core RiBAC model follows. It consists of the following basic sets:

- *AGENTS*: the set of all participating agents in a community
- *ROLES*: the set of all roles available in a community
- *SESSIONS*: the set of all sessions created for agents in a community
- *OBS*: the set of all objects in the environment
- *OPS*: the set of all applicable operations on objects in the environment
- *OOPRMS* ⊆ *OPS* × *OBS*, the set of all object-oriented permissions
- *ROLE-ACTIONS*: the set of all actions that are defined for community roles and can be invoked through interactions
- *RAPRMS* ⊆ *ROLES* × *ROLE-ACTIONS*, the set of all role-action permissions
- *ROLE-OPS*: the set of all operations that are performable on roles through interactions
- *ROPRMS* ⊆ *ROLE-OPS* × *ROLES*, the set of all role-oriented permissions

The following relations define the access policy in RiBAC:

- *AA* ⊆ *AGENTS* × *ROLES*, the agent to role assignment
- *OOPA* ⊆ *OOPRMS* × *ROLES*, the object-oriented permission to role assignment
- *RAPA* ⊆ *RAPRMS* × *ROLES*, the role-action permission to role assignment
- *ROPA* ⊆ *ROPRMS* × *ROLES*, the role-oriented permission to role assignment

The following relations capture the runtime state of access control through sessions:

- *SessionAgent(s: SESSIONS)* → *AGENTS*, the mapping of session *s* to its corresponding agent
- *SessionRoles(s: SESSIONS)* → 2^{ROLES}, the mapping of session *s* to the set of active roles in it

The following functions retrieve the authorization information according to the policy:

- *authorized_roles(a: AGENTS)* → 2^{ROLES}, the mapping of agent *a* to the set of its authorized roles that it can activate
- *authorized_ooprms(r: ROLES)* → 2^{OOPRMS}, the mapping of role *r* to the set of its authorized object-oriented permissions
- *authorized_raprms(r: ROLES)* → 2^{RAPRMS}, the mapping of role *r* to the set of its authorized role-action permissions
- *authorized_roprms(r: ROLES)* → 2^{ROPRMS}, the mapping of role *r* to the set of its authorized role-oriented permissions
- *authorized_prms(r: ROLES)* → $2^{OOPRMS \cup RAPRMS \cup ROPRMS}$, the mapping of role r to the set of its authorized object-oriented and interaction permissions. Formally: *authorized_prms(r)* = *authorized_ooprms(r)* ∪ *authorized_raprms(r)* ∪ *authorized_roprms(r)*

In order to demonstrate the usage of core RiBAC model, we revisit the the 'EmergencyService' community explained in Section 2 (Fig. 1) in Fig. 4. Fig. 5 illustrates the same example policy using graphical notations.

```
ROLES = {Patient, Doctor, Paramedic, Hospital, Ambulance}
OBS = {hospital_medical_equipment, termometer, ambulance_medical_equipment,
     ambulance_vehicle}
OPS = {operate, read}
OOPRMS = {OOP1=(operate,hospital_medical_equipment), OOP2=(read,termometer),
     OOP3=(operate,ambulance_medical_equipment), OOP4=(operate,ambulance_vehicle)}
ROLE-ACTIONS={give_health_status, give_location, remote_examine, give_prescription,
     provide_firstaid, prepare_for_patient, transfer_patient}
RAPRMS={RAP1=(Patient,give_health_status), RAP2=(Patient,give_location),
     RAP3=(Doctor,remote_examine), RAP4=(Doctor,give_prescription),
     RAP5=(Paramedic,provide_firstaid), RAP6=(Hospital,prepare_for_patient),
     RAP7=(Ambulance,transfer_patient)}
ROLE-OPS={bring_into_ambulance, provide_firstaid}
ROPRMS={ROP1=(bring_into_ambulance,Patient), ROP2=(provide_firstaid,Patient)}
OOPA={(OOP1,Doctor), (OOP2,Doctor), (OOP3,Paramedic), (OOP4,Ambulance)}
RAPA={(RAP1,Doctor), (RAP1,Paramedic), (RAP1,Ambulance), (RAP2,Ambulance), (RAP3,Patient),
     (RAP4,Paramedic), (RAP4,Hospital), (RAP5,Doctor), (RAP6,Doctor), (RAP7,Patient)}
ROPA={(ROP1,Paramedic), (ROP2,Paramedic)}
```

Fig. 4. An example core RiBAC policy specification for 'EmergencyService' community

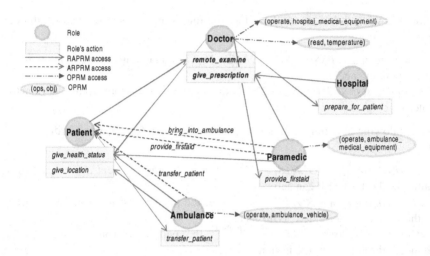

Fig. 5. Graphical representation of the example core RiBAC policy for 'EmergencyService' community

3.2 Hierarchical RiBAC Model (H-RiBAC)

In this section, we propose the hierarchical RiBAC model. One advantage of RBAC model is its ability to leverage hierarchical structure of roles for better permission management. Analogous to standard RBAC, permissions in RiBAC (including object-oriented and interaction permissions) can be inherited through a role hierarchy. We define the role hierarchy *RH* and override the authorization functions in core RiBAC to cope with it as follows:

- *RH* $\subseteq$ *ROLES* × *ROLES* is a partial order relation on *ROLES*, denoted as ≥, where $r \geq r'$ only if all permissions of r' are inherited by r and agents assigned to r can also activate r'. Formally: $r \geq r' \Rightarrow$ *authorized_prms(r')* $\subseteq$ *authorized_prms(r)* $\wedge$ *[r'⊆authorized_roles(a); (a,r) ∈AA]*
- *authorized_roles(a: AGENTS)* $\rightarrow 2^{ROLES}$, the mapping of agent a to the set of its authorized roles that it can activate in presence of role hierarchy. Formally: *authorized_roles(a: AGENTS) = { r ∈ROLES | (a,r') ∈AA, r'≥r}*
- *authorized_ooprms(r: ROLES)* $\rightarrow 2^{OOPRMS}$, the mapping of role r to the set of its authorized object-oriented permissions in presence of role hierarchy. Formally: *authorized_ooprms(r) = {p ∈OOPRMS | r ≥ r', (r',p) ∈OOPA}*
- *authorized_raprms(r: ROLES)* $\rightarrow 2^{RAPRMS}$, the mapping of role r to the set of its authorized role-action permissions in presence of role hierarchy. Formally: *authorized_raprms(r) = {p ∈RAPRMS | r ≥ r', (r',p) ∈RAPA}*
- *authorized_roprms(r: ROLES)* $\rightarrow 2^{ROPRMS}$, the mapping of role r to the set of its authorized role-oriented permissions in presence of role hierarchy. Formally: *authorized_roprms(r) = {p ∈ROPRMS | r ≥ r', (r',p) ∈ ROPA}*

We modify our example to form a role hierarchy among paramedic, doctor, and ambulance, also introducing two new roles. Fig. 6 illustrates a graphical presentation of the hierarchy relation among roles and their assigned permissions. In the hierarchy, the role 'Basic_Medical_Service' and the role 'Medical_Staff' are intermediate roles that are not assigned directly to agents. According to the role hierarchy, 'Paramedic' and 'Doctor' have permissions of 'Medical_Staff' and 'Basic_Medical_Service'. 'Ambulance' also inherits the permission of basic medical service to get the patient health status. Using such patient's health information, an ambulance adjusts the temperature and speed of the vehicle in order to minimize risks to the patient's health. The formal specification of the example policy is shown in Fig 7.

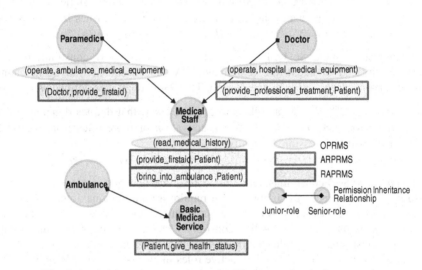

Fig. 6. A role hierarchy example for the 'EmergencyService' community

```
ROLES = {Patient, Doctor, Paramedic, Hospital, Ambulance, Medical_Staff, Basic_Medical_Service}
RH={( Medical-Staff,Basic-Medical-Service), (Ambulance,Basic-Medical-Service),
      (Doctor,Medical-Staff), (Paramedic,Medical-Staff)}
OBS = {hospital_medical_equipment, ambulance_medical_equipment, medical_history}
OPS = {operate, read}
OOPRMS={OOP1=(operate,hospital_medical_equipment),
      OOP2=(operate,ambulance_medical_equipment), OOP3=(read,medical_history)}
ROLE-ACTIONS={give_health_status, provide_firstaid}
RAPRMS= { RAP1=(Patient,give_health_status), RAP2=(Paramedic,provide_firstaid)}
ROLE-OPS={bring_into_ambulance, provide_firstaid, provide_professional_treatement}
ROPRMS={ROP1=(bring_into_ambulance,Patient), ROP2=(provide_firstaid,Patient),
      ROP3=(provide_professional_treatement,Patient)}
OOPA={(OOP1,Doctor), (OOP2,Paramedic), (OOP3,Medical-Staff)}
RAPA={(RAP1,Basic-Medical-Service), (RAP2,Paramedic)}
ROPA={(ROP1,Medical-Staff), (ROP2, Medical-Staff), (ROP3, Doctor)}
```

Fig. 7. An example policy of H-RiBAC for 'EmergencyService' community

3.3 Constrained RiBAC Model (C-RiBAC)

Constrained RiBAC (C-RiBAC) adds separation of duty and cardinality constraints to the core RiBAC model. Separation of duty (SoD) constraints have been discussed in the RBAC literature as a mechanism to minimize the likelihood of fraud and major errors through simultaneous access of users to key organizational tasks or deliberate collusion of users. Community computing environments have similar vulnerabilities as organizations. We propose static and dynamic SoD constraints for RiBAC. In static SoD, no agent can be assigned to a specific number or more of roles in a role set. The *SSoD* relation is defined as follows:

-   *SSoD* $\subseteq 2^{ROLES} \times N$, a collection of pairs *(rs,n)* that defines static SoDs, where for each *(rs,n)* no agent should be assigned to *n* or more roles from the set *rs*. Formally: $(rs,n) \in SSoD \Rightarrow \nexists a \in AGENTS, |authorized\_roles(a) \cap rs| \geq n$.

In contrast to static SoD, dynamic SoD enforces the SoD constraint on role activations instead of agent-role assignments. As a consequence an agent cannot activate certain roles together in one session. The *DSoD* relation is defined as follows:

-   *DSoD* $\subseteq 2^{ROLES} \times N$, a collection of pairs *(rs,n)* that defines dynamic SoDs, where for each *(rs,n)* no agent can activate *n* or more roles from the set *rs* together in one session. Formally:
    $(rs,n) \in DSoD \Rightarrow \nexists s \in SESSIONS, |\{r \in SessionRoles(s)|r \in rs\}| \geq n$.

In addition to SoD constraints, an access control mechanism can enforce cardinality constraints. For instance, a community can require a minimum/maximum number of agents to play some particular role in the community; otherwise the community may fail to achieve its goal. Cardinality constraints can be static or dynamic. Static cardinality constraints are applicable on agent-role assignment relation, while dynamic cardinality constraints are enforced on active roles in agents' sessions. We define four different cardinality constraints as follows:

-   *SMinCardinality* $\subseteq ROLES \times N$, a collection of pairs *(r,n)* that defines static minimum cardinality for roles, where for each *(r,n)* at least *n* agents should be assigned to the role *r*. Formally:
    $(r,n) \in SMinCardinality \Rightarrow |\{a \in AGENTS|r \in authorized\_roles(a)\}| \geq n$.
-   *SMaxCardinality* $\subseteq ROLES \times N$, a collection of pairs *(r,n)* that defines static maximum cardinality for roles, where for each *(r,n)* at most n agents should be assigned to the role *r*. Formally:
    $(r,n) \in SMaxCardinality \Rightarrow |\{a \in AGENTS|r \in authorized\_roles(a)\}| \leq n$.
-   *DMinCardinality* $\subseteq ROLES \times N$, a collection of pairs *(r,n)* that defines dynamic minimum cardinality for roles, where for each *(r,n)* at least *n* agents should have activated the role *r* at a particular time. Formally: $(r,n) \in DMinCardinality \Rightarrow |\{s \in SESSIONS|r \in SessionRoles(s)\}| \geq n$.
-   *DMaxCardinality* $\subseteq ROLES \times N$, a collection of pairs *(r,n)* that defines dynamic maximum cardinality for roles, where for each *(r,n)* at most *n* agents should be allowed to activate the role *r* at a particular time. Formally: $(r,n) \in DMaxCardinality \Rightarrow |\{s \in SESSIONS|r \in SessionRoles(s)\}| \leq n$.

In the presence of various constraints, it is important to ensure that a RiBAC policy is consistent. A static minimum cardinality of m and a static maximum cardinality of n ($n<m$) for the same role are impossible to be enforced at the same time. Respecting the following rule by the model prevents such a conflict:

- $\forall r \in ROLES \; \forall m,n \in N, \; (r,m) \in SMinCardinality \; \wedge \; (r,n) \in SMaxCardinality$
  $\Rightarrow m \leq n$

If we assume the same situation above however with dynamic constraints instead, role r cannot be activated at all. Although, in the latter case the role r becomes useless, but there is no consistency issue for policy enforcement.

The two types of static cardinality and the dynamic maximum cardinality are easily enforceable by keeping a track of assigned or activated roles in a community and avoiding the violation of them. However, the dynamic minimum cardinality is a little tricky to enforce depending on the environment. We assume that there is a proper enforcement mechanism employed in the community to force agents to keep the minimum active roles according to the dynamic minimum cardinality. For instance upon creation of the community, the system can force some agents to activate their roles (even without their discretion), and otherwise can fail the creation.

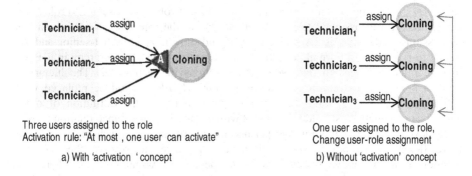

Three users assigned to the role
Activation rule: "At most , one user can activate"

a) With 'activation ' concept

One user assigned to the role,
Change user-role assignment

b) Without 'activation' concept

Fig. 8. Need for the 'activation' concept in community

In fact, the SCC model does not include explicit notion of activation since it assumes that the assigned roles are activated as soon as the agents take the roles. We believe that such an assumption is not adequate enough and need to be removed to support scenarios where explicit notion of activation is required. As an example, consider a biotechnology project community in which there is a role for cloning body tissues and three technicians are able to take the role as shown in Fig. 8. In this case, three technicians can be assigned to the 'cloning' role. However, this job should be performed by a totally isolated technician because it is a very delicate job. If one technician does perform cloning, then we should prevent accesses to cloning task from another technician. In order to enforce that, we can specify a policy that allows at most one user to activate the 'cloning' role at a time (dynamic maximum cardinality constraint). Although an alternative way is to change the role assignments every time a user wants to access the 'cloning' role according to the community's situation as shown in Fig. 8, such an approach would be very cumbersome due to frequent changes in the policy.

3.4 Constrained Hierarchical RiBAC Model (CH-RiBAC)

A comprehensive RiBAC model is formed by combination of hierarchical and constrained RiBAC models. However, the implications of such combination should be precisely captured. For instance, consider role r_1 has dynamic maximum cardinality constraint of 3, and there exist role r_2 which is senior to r_1 ($r_2 \geq r_1$). In such a configuration, if more than 3 agents activate role r_2 it can be interpreted as violation of the cardinality constraint because agents assigned to r_2 can also assume r_1 through the role hierarchy. However, agents acting as role r_2 may not necessarily act as role r_1 all the time (only sometimes require r_1's permissions), which makes the mentioned interpretation too rigid.

In order to provide more flexibility and truly capture the behavior of constraints in the presence of role hierarchy, we adopt the notion of hybrid hierarchy that is originally defined in the context of Generalized Temporal RBAC (GTRBAC) [11]. A hybrid hierarchy differentiates between permission usage and role activation capability in a hierarchy, by taking into account three possible relations: permission inheritance (I), activation (A), and inheritance-activation (IA). If role r_1 is I-senior to role r_2 ($r_1 \geq_I r_2$), it inherits all the permissions r_2 has. If role r_1 is A-senior to role r_2 ($r_1 \geq_A r_2$), then a user assigned to r_1 can activate r_2 but the role r_1 does not inherit r_2's permissions. Finally, r_1 is IA-senior to r_2 if and only if r_1 is both I-senior and A-Senior to r_2 ($r_1 \geq_{IA} r_2$). Formal definitions for semantics of hybrid hierarchy in RiBAC involve minor changes to the overridden functions in Section 3.2. The hierarchy relation ($\geq$) in the definition of function *authorized_roles* should be replaced with activation relation ($\geq_A$), and the hierarchy relation ($\geq$) in the definition of other authorization functions should be replaced with permission inheritance relation ($\geq_I$).

By leveraging the activation and permission inheritance relationships, we achieve more flexibility in policy specification. For instance, to resolve the problem mentioned in the above example we can specify r_2 A-senior to r_1. Therefore, whenever an agent activates the role r_2, the cardinality constraint is respected, and an agent can also activate the role r_1 when it needs but according to the cardinality constraint.

The definitions for dynamic constraints in presence of hybrid hierarchy are overridden as follows (static constraint definitions remain valid):

-   $DSoD \subseteq 2^{ROLES} \times N$, a collection of pairs (rs,n) that defines dynamic SoDs in presence of hybrid hierarchy, where for each (rs,n) no user can activate or use permissions of n or more roles from the set rs together in one session. Formally:
    $(rs,n) \in DSoD \Rightarrow \nexists s \in SESSIONS, |\{r | r \geq_I r, r' \in rs, r' \in SessionRoles(s)\}| \geq n$.

-   $DMinCardinality \subseteq ROLES \times N$, a collection of pairs (r,n) that defines dynamic minimum cardinality for roles in presence of hybrid hierarchy, where for each (r,n) at least n agents should have activated the role r or its I-senior at a particular time. Formally:
    $(r,n) \in DMinCardinality \Rightarrow |\{s \in SESSIONS | r' \geq_I r, r' \in SessionRoles(s)\}| \geq n$.

- *DMaxCardinality* ⊆ *ROLES* × *N*, a collection of pairs *(r,n)* that defines dynamic maximum cardinality for roles in presence of hybrid hierarchy, where for each *(r,n)* at most *n* agents should be allowed to activate the role *r* at a particular time. Formally:

$(r,n) \in DMaxCardinality \Rightarrow |\{s \in SESSIONS| \, r' \geq_l r, \, r' \in SessionRoles(s)\}| \leq n.$

4 Extended Simple Community Computing Model

In this section, we extend the SCC specification framework to allow specifying core RiBAC policies as shown in Fig. 8. We refer the readers to [2] for the complete details of SCC specification language. Based on the formal definition described in Fig. 9, we represent an example of SCC model involving core RiBAC policies for the emergency service scenario in Fig. 10.

```
<RiBAC_policy_description>:= RiBAC Policy { <Role_Policy>* }
<Role_Policy>:= <Role_Name> { <Role_OOPRMSs>*, <Role_ROPRMSs>*, <Role_RAPRMSs>* }
<Role_OOPRMSs>:= OOPRMSs = { <OOPRM>+ },
<OOPRM>:=(<OPS>,<OBS>) , <OPS>:=<String>, <OBS>:=<String>
<Role_ROPRMSs>:=ROPRMS = { <ROPRMS>+ }, <ROPRMS>:= (<Action_Name>,<Role_Name> )
<Role_RAPRMSs>:=RAPRMS = { <RAPRMS>+ }, <RAPRMS>:= (<Role_Name>,<Action_Name>)
```

Fig. 9. BNF definition for describing core RiBAC Policy in the SCC model

```
Platform Independent Community Implementation Description {
   Community EmergencyService {
      Role PATIENT { ...}
      ..........
   Role-MemberType Mapping { .... }
      Goal Providing_emergency_service( ..... ) }
      RiBAC Policy {
         DOCTOR {
            OOPRMSs={(operate,hospital_medical_equipment), (read, temperature)},
            RAPRMSs={(PATIENT,give_health_status),(PARAMEDIC,provide_firstaid),
               (HOSPITAL,prepare_for_patient)} }
         PATIENT {
            RAPRMSs={(DOCTOR,remote_examine),(AMBULANCE,transfer_patient)} }
         AMBULANCE {
            OOPRMSs={(operate,ambulance_vehicle) },
            ROPRMSs={(transfer_patient,PATIENT)}
            RAPRMSs={(PATIENT,give_health_status),(PATIENT,give_location)} }
         PARAMEDIC {
            OOPRMSs={(operate,ambulance_medical_equipment) },
            ROPRMSs={(bring_into_ambulance,PATIENT), (provide_firstaid,PATIENT)}
            RAPRMSs={(PATIENT,give_health_status),(DOCTOR,give_prescription)} }
         HOSPITAL_MANAGER {
            RAPRMSs={(DOCTOR,give_prescription)} }
   }}
```

Fig. 10. An example of the simple community computing model employing core RiBAC

Note that the access control policies for agent interactions are derived from the cooperation definition of communities. Therefore changes in cooperation results in change of access control policies. For the current extension, based on the underlying assumptions in SCC, we consider only predefined cooperation and therefore predefined access control policy. As one of our future works, we leave room for developing more advanced extensions in which policies can be dynamically reconfigured based on changes in cooperation.

In order to enforce RiBAC policies in a CC system, we propose an extension to our existing computation model [2]. In the extended model, policies regarding object-oriented permissions are enforced in a centralized way by the society manager. For policies related to agent interactions, we enforce them in a distributed way. Agents receive the interaction permission specifications in which they are interaction targets from community manager. Based on such specifications, target agents can enforce control over interactions targeted to them. Also note that agents may receive specification about all the permissions they have from community manager, in order to be able to plan based on their accesses. Fig. 11 shows the extended computational model of a community computing system to enforce RiBAC policies.

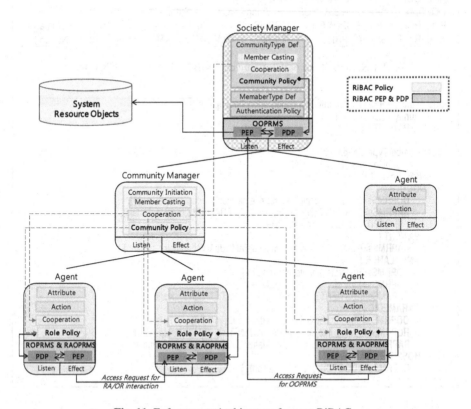

Fig. 11. Enforcement Architecture for core RiBAC

5   Related Works

Many researchers have investigated the security requirements and challenges in multi-agent systems, and pointed out the need for access control in these environments [12, 13]. However, most solutions proposed for access control in MAS are mainly concerned about distributing authorization information using trust management frameworks [14, 15, 16], and less about the access control model itself. These proposals usually adopt SPKI/SDSI (simple public key infrastructure/simple distributed security infrastructure), which is able to manage authorization in a distributed manner using authorization certificates. For instance in [16], Wen *et al.* propose semi-distributed authorization scheme, where agents acquire authorization certificates from an authorization server based on the role certificates their corresponding human users provide.

The closest work to the theme of this paper has been done by Omicini *et al.* in the context of an infrastructure for coordination support in agent-based systems, called TuCSoN [17]. In [18], the authors integrate simple access matrix model (based on agent identity) in a decentralized fashion to authorize exchange of communication tuples among agents. As mentioned, only simple access control lists are allowed by this scheme with an added dimension for controlling tree-structured agents. Later, Omcini *et al.* explore the integration of RBAC into the TuCSoN infrastructure [19]. In order to control the coordination protocol, the authors define a prolog-like role policy definition language. The policies can specify the authorized actions considering the current state of the role and conditions, while determining the next state. The states are managed as part of an alternative for RBAC session. While their approach seems flexible and powerful, the definition of a state-based policy can be very impractical. Also their approach does not include explicit semantics for authorized role interactions, which has been emphasized in this paper, and provides no formal semantics for SoDs and role hierarchy.

Gaia methodology [6] involves role concept and an interaction model among agents. In Gaia, some access control concepts are discussed such as role permissions (on objects), or organizational safety rules that could act as separation of duty constraints. However, we have a more specific approach to specify authorized interaction compared to the interaction notion in Gaia. Our interaction modeling approach is more practical to enable specification and control over interactions in detail. In addition, we provide hierarchical relations among roles to enable more manageable access control policies.

6   Conclusion and Future Work

In order to control accesses to critical data or actions of other agents, , we have proposed a family of RiBAC (Role interaction Based Access Control) models including core RiBAC, H-RiBAC that incorporates role hierarchy, C-RiBAC that incorporates SoD and cardinality constraints, and CH-RiBAC that incorporates constraints and hybrid hierarchy. These are extensions of the standard RBAC models and cover the role interaction as one of the important aspects of MAS. RiBAC models are useful for securing ubiquitous systems characterized by significant agent interactions. We have extended the earlier proposed simple community computing modeling framework to incorporate the proposed RiBAC models.

As future work, we plan to extend the proposed work to cope with context-aware ubiquitous environments by integrating it with time and location based RBAC (LoTRBAC) model [20]. We are currently implementing a working prototype of the proposed work. Moreover, we will investigate models that could support administration and delegation of role interaction permissions in the context of community computing. We also plan to explore security analysis and policy verification method, as well as efficient enforcement techniques for RiBAC policies.

Acknowledgments. This research is supported by Foundation of ubiquitous computing and networking project (UCN) Project, the Ministry of Knowledge Economy (MKE) 21st Century Frontier R&D Program in Korea and a result of subproject UCN 08B3-S2-10M, and by the US National Science Foundation award IIS-0545912.

References

1. Wooldridge, M., Jennings, N.R.: The Cooperative Problem-Solving Process. Journal of Logic Computation 9(4), 563–592 (1999)
2. Jung, Y., Lee, J., Kim, M.: Multi-agent based Community Computing System Development with the Model Driven Architecture. In: Proc. of 5th International Joint conference on Autonomous Agents and Multiagent Systems (AAMAS 2006), pp. 1329–1331 (2006)
3. Jung, Y., Lee, J., Kim, M.: Community Computing Model supporting Community Situation based Cooperation and Conflict Resolution. In: Obermaisser, R., Nah, Y., Puschner, P., Rammig, F.J. (eds.) SEUS 2007. LNCS, vol. 4761, pp. 47–56. Springer, Heidelberg (2007)
4. Wilson, P., et al.: Computer Supported Cooperative Work. Intellect Books, Oxford (1991)
5. Borghoff, U.M., Schlichter, J.H.: Computer-Supported Cooperative Work: Introduction to Distributed Applications. Springer, Berlin (2000)
6. Zambonelli, F., Jennings, N.R., Wooldridge, M.: Developing Multiagent Systems: The Gaia Methodology. ACM Transactions on Software Engineering and Methodology 12(3), 317–370 (2003)
7. Kumar, M., Shirazi, B., Das, S.K., Singhal, M., Sung, B., Levine, D.: Pervasive Information Communities Organization PICO: A Middleware Framework for Pervasive Computing. IEEE Pervasive Computing 2(3), 72–79 (2003)
8. Ishida, T. (ed.): Community Computing and Support Systems. LNCS, vol. 1519. Springer, Heidelberg (1998)
9. Van den Besselaar, P., Tanabe, M., Ishida, T.: Introduction: Digital Cities Research and Open Issues. In: Tanabe, M., van den Besselaar, P., Ishida, T. (eds.) Digital Cities 2001. LNCS, vol. 2362, pp. 1–9. Springer, Heidelberg (2002)
10. Blau, J.: Microsoft: Community Computing is On the Way. InfoWorld Magazine, http://www.infoworld.com/article/05/11/22/HNcommunitycomputing_1.html
11. Joshi, J.B.D., Bertino, E., Latif, U., Ghafoor, A.: A Generalized Temporal Role-Based Access Control Model. IEEE Transactions on Knowledge and Data Engineering 17(1), 4–23 (2005)
12. Beydoun, G., Low, G., Mouratidis, H., Henderson, B.: Modelling MAS-Specific Security Features. In: IEEE 2nd Symposium on Multi-Agent Security and Survivability, pp. 75–84 (2005)

13. Mouratidis, H., Giorgini, P., Manson, G.: Modeling Secure Multiagent Systems. In: Proc. of AAMAS 2003, pp. 859–866 (2003)
14. Hu, Y., Tang, C.: Agent-Oriented Public Key Infrastructure for Multi-agent E-service. In: Palade, V., Howlett, R.J., Jain, L. (eds.) KES 2003. LNCS, vol. 2773, pp. 1215–1221. Springer, Heidelberg (2003)
15. Poggi, A., Tomaiuolo, M., Vitaglione, G.: A Security Infrastructure for Trust Management in Multi-agent Systems. In: Falcone, R., Barber, S., Sabater-Mir, J., Singh, M.P. (eds.) Trusting Agents for Trusting Electronic Societies. LNCS, vol. 3577, pp. 162–179. Springer, Heidelberg (2005)
16. Wen, W., Mizoguchi, F.: An Authorization-based Trust Model for Multiagent Systems. Applied Artificial Intelligence 14(9), 909–925 (2000)
17. Omicini, A., Zambonelli, F.: Coordination for Internet Application Development. Autonomous Agents and Multi-Agent Systems 2(3), 251–269 (1999)
18. Cremonini, M., Omicini, A., Zambonelli, F.: Coordination and access control in open distributed agent systems: The tuCSoN approach. In: Porto, A., Roman, G.-C. (eds.) COORDINATION 2000. LNCS, vol. 1906, pp. 99–114. Springer, Heidelberg (2000)
19. Omicini, A., Ricci, A., Viroli, M.: RBAC for Organisation and Security in an Agent Coordination Infrastructure. In: Proc. of the 2nd International Workshop on Security Issues in Coordination Models, Languages, and Systems, pp. 65–85 (2004)
20. Chandran, S.M., Joshi, J.B.D.: LoT-RBAC: A Location and Time-based RBAC Model. In: Ngu, A.H.H., Kitsuregawa, M., Neuhold, E.J., Chung, J.-Y., Sheng, Q.Z. (eds.) WISE 2005. LNCS, vol. 3806, pp. 361–375. Springer, Heidelberg (2005)

A Constraint and Attribute Based Security Framework for Dynamic Role Assignment in Collaborative Environments*

Isabel F. Cruz, Rigel Gjomemo, Benjamin Lin, and Mirko Orsini**

ADVIS Lab – Department of Computer Science – University of Illinois at Chicago
{ifc,rgjomemo,plin,orsinim}@cs.uic.edu

Abstract. We investigate a security framework for collaborative applications that relies on the role-based access control (RBAC) model. In our framework, roles are pre-defined and organized in a hierarchy (partial order). However, we assume that users are not previously identified, therefore the actions that they can perform are dynamically determined based on their own attribute values and on the attribute values associated with the resources. Those values can vary over time (e.g., the user's location or whether the resource is open for visiting) thus enabling or disabling a user's ability to perform an action on a particular resource. In our framework, constraint values form partial orders and determine the association of actions with the resources and of users with roles. We have implemented our framework by exploring the capabilities of semantic web technologies, and in particular of OWL 1.1, to model both our framework and the domain of interest and to perform several types of reasoning. In addition, we have implemented a user interface whose purpose is twofold: (1) to offer a visual explanation of the underlying reasoning by displaying roles and their associations with users (e.g., as the user's locations vary); and (2) to enable monitoring of users that are involved in a collaborative application. Our interface uses the Google Maps API and is particularly suited to collaborative applications where the users' geospatial locations are of interest.

Keywords: role-based access control, collaborative applications, dynamic environments, Semantic Web, reasoning.

1 Introduction

With the latest trends in collaborative environments, such as Web 2.0 and cooperative projects on grids, more and more resources are being shared by different

---

* Work partially supported by NSF Awards ITR IIS-0326284, IIS-0513553, and IIS-0812258.
** Primary affiliation: Dipartimento di Ingegneria dell'Informazione, Università di Modena e Reggio Emilia, Italy. Work partially supported by MUR FIRB Network Peer for Business project (http://www.dbgroup.unimo.it/nep4b) and Confindustria Modena.

E. Bertino and J.B.D. Joshi (Eds.): CollaborateCom 2008, LNICST 10, pp. 322–339, 2009.

groups and organizations in order to support common tasks. Depending on several factors such as the task, the participants, and data sensitivity, access to these shared resources needs to be controlled and enforced by security policies. The role-based access control (RBAC) model defines roles that have specific privileges on resources and decouples the identity of the users from the resources [15]. In the RBAC model and its variations, constraints can be placed for example on the associations of users with roles or of roles with permissions. When the number of users is high in comparison with the number of roles [1, 2], an automated way to grant permissions is desirable in order to eliminate the burden of manually assigning roles to users. The RBAC model is particularly suited to dynamic task-oriented environments due to its flexibility and policy-neutrality [14], which enables it to express a large range of policies.

In our paper, we investigate a security framework for collaborative applications that relies on the RBAC model. Roles are pre-defined and organized in a hierarchy (partial order). However, we assume that users are not previously identified. Thus, the actions that they can perform are dynamically determined based on their own attribute values and on the values of the attributes associated with the resources. The user's attribute values can vary over time during a session (e.g., the user's location), thus enabling or disabling the user's roles.

We will focus on a scenario associated with the Olympic Games, where not only the venues directly associated with the Olympic Games (e.g., stadiums, gymnasiums) but also tourist attractions in the area (e.g., museums, parks) are resources of interest in our framework. Access to venues and specific places inside the venues depend on the users' types. For example, some spectators can only take part in the opening ceremony, whereas others can access all swimming events or all track and field events, depending on the tickets they have purchased. In addition to visitors, there are many organizations collaborating with one another and sharing information and services (including police forces, hosting companies, media, and sport organizations) who ultimately serve a large range of visitors as well as the competing athletes and their support teams.

Privileges granted to users depend not only on each particular organization but can also differ among members of the same organization. For example, some members of the escort service for teams and athletes may be restricted to escort out of a specific venue but not out of other venues (a situation similar to taxi drivers in some cities, where a taxi that transports passengers from the city to the airport cannot subsequently pick up passengers at the airport).

Different people will have different privileges depending on their status. For example, members of the Olympic Committee, who have VIP status, will have reserved seating in all competitions, while top officials of the local organizing committee, who also enjoy VIP status, may have non-assigned seating. Police officers will be able to enter any area, but without seating privileges. Children or students under a certain age may be able to join tours of the Olympic Stadium for free, while other people will have to pay a fee. For security reasons access to the Olympic Village is restricted to few people besides the athletes and their immediate support teams: for example, employees and volunteers specifically assigned to work in that particular area.

In our approach, the roles of each different collaborating organization are structured in a dominance hierarchy where "higher" roles have all the privileges of "lower" roles. The roles associated with all the organizations can be represented as the union of the hierarchies of roles of the single organizations. Some of the roles have fixed and previously known sets of users, such as police, members of the local organizing committee, or the athletes. Other roles have a large number of possible users that cannot be known a priori, for instance journalists, volunteers, and visitors. In this case, constraints on user attribute values can be used to assign the correct role to each user, based on the values of different attributes (e.g., status, credentials, location, organization). Roles are assigned to users depending on the actual values of their attributes (e.g., VIP, journalist, main stadium, NBC). Constraint values in our framework form partial orders and determine the association of actions with the resources and of users with roles. Therefore, users' actions are dynamically determined based on their own attribute values and on the values of the attributes associated with the resources.

We have designed and implemented a prototype of our access control framework using semantic web technologies. The roles and other entities defined in the RBAC model are represented using the OWL 1.1 language [11], which is a standard language based on Description Logic (DL). Based on previous work, we use two ontologies: the first ontology describes the domain and the second ontology describes the RBAC entities and is partly derived from the first [4]. Reasoning is performed using the Pellet reasoner [5] and is used to implement several functions, such as user to role assignment, separation of duty constraints, symmetry, and class equivalence.

Our model shares some similarities with other approaches including RB-RBAC [1, 2], GEO-RBAC [3, 8], and ROWLBAC [10]. A notable difference is that it has been fully implemented, while the other approaches have not. Therefore, we have leveraged the expressiveness of an actual reasoning mechanism. However, all the other approaches also propose some sort of reasoning. In particular, RB-RBAC uses rules to determine hierarchical roles starting from a partial order of constraints, while GEO-RBAC uses propagation of constraints along the role hierarchy. We extend RB-BAC by starting from individual partial orders of attribute constraints and then unifying them. In comparison with GEO-RBAC, our framework is more general in that it targets all types of constraints, not only spatial constraints. We also consider resource attribute constraints, whose satisfaction enables or disables the privileges defined on the resources. ROWLBAC, even if not implemented, proposes reasoning as performed by OWL. The most similar approach to our current approach is our former approach, which was also fully implemented using semantic web technologies [4]. However, in that approach, we used a simpler constraint framework and did not explicitly consider spatial constraints.

The paper is organized as follows. In Section 2, we present the security model and in particular, the attribute constraints arranged in partially ordered sets and their correspondence with the roles. In Section 3, we describe the different types of entailment that our model supports and give examples of some rules of Description Logic that can be used to express security policies. We also show the process by which users are assigned the correct roles by taking into account constraints. In Section 4 we describe the implementation of the access control model including the design choices we have made. Related work is mentioned in Section 5 and conclusions and future work are discussed in Section 6.

2 Security Model

In this section, we describe the different components that make up our framework. We start by extending our scenario and then we describe the different components that are present in our model. Those components, modeled as classes and as constraints, extend the usual RBAC components.

2.1 Scenario

In our scenario, which is a much simplified version of the kind of considerations needed for the Olympic Games, there are four collaborating organizations: *Media*, *Sports*, *HostingCity*, and *Visitors*. The organizations share the same resources and each of them can be modeled separately. The first organization, *Media*, comprises *MediaOperator* and *Journalist*, where *MediaOperator* has privilege *EnterMediaVillage*, to enter a resource that is reserved for media operators and *Journalist* inherits the privileges of *MediaOperator*. *Journalist* has one additional privilege, *EnterPhotoZone*, to enter a special area that is particularly suitable for taking close up pictures of the athletes.

The second organization, *Sports*, comprises *TeamMember* and *Athlete*. The third organization, *HostingCity*, comprises people who take care of all local organizational tasks. The fourth organization, *Visitors*, comprises all the different people who attend the Olympic Games. We model them as an organization so that we can deal with them similarly to the other groups of people. Visitors can have different degrees of importance, spanning from "VIP" (e.g., members of the Olympic Committee) to "normal" (e.g., common spectators). These different degrees of importance correspond to different privileges. Privileges and the overall role hierarchy of our collaboration scenario is shown in Figure 1. The roles that carry more privileges are shown higher in the hierarchy: for example, the *Manager* role contains all the privileges of the roles that are its descendants in addition to its own, while the role *Volunteer*, which is not a descendant of *Manager*, comprises all the roles of *Employee* and of *NormalVisitor* in addition to its own.

We consider that each organization determines how the roles are assigned to their users depending on their attribute values. For instance, in our scenario, visitors have attributes *Importance*, *Age*, and *Location*. The *Visitor* organization assigns the role *SpecialVisitor* depending on the values of these attributes, for instance if somebody's *Importance* attribute is equal to *VIP*, *Age* is greater than

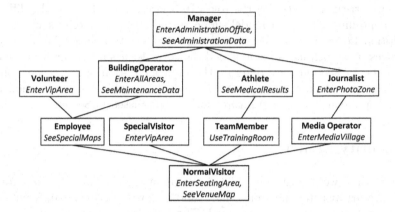

Fig. 1. Roles and privileges for the Olympic Games organizations

21, and *Location* is inside *VIPArea*. In our model, *Location* is both an attribute of users, which is used to associate roles with users, and of resources.

The final role hierarchy shown in Figure 1 is derived using simple inference on a description of the organizations and resources using ontologies. The security administrator checks and validates the inference results. Further description of this step will be given in Section 3.

2.2 Framework Components

In this section, we explain the conceptual components of our system.

Resource class. This class represents the entities on which different actions are or not allowed (e.g., *SeatingArea*). Resources have associated attributes (e.g., *Capacity* of the Olympic Stadium).

Action class. This class represents the actions that can be performed by users on the resources (e.g., *Enter*).

Privilege class. Objects of this class are pairs $\langle Action, Resource \rangle$. For example, the privilege $\langle Enter, SeatingArea \rangle$ allows some users to enter the seating area.

Privilege attribute constraints. These constraints are pairs $\langle p, a \rangle$, where p is a privilege (e.g., $\langle Enter, SeatingArea \rangle$) and a is a pair $\langle attribute, attributeconstraint \rangle$ (e.g., $\langle isOpen, = true \rangle$) associated with the resource that is part of the privilege (in this case, *SeatingArea*). Attribute constraints are recursively defined as follows:

```
attributeconstraint ::= (attributeconstraint)
                      | RELATIONALOPERATOR constant
                      | NEGATION (attributeconstraint)
                      | attributeconstraint BINARYBOOLEANOPERATOR
                        attributeconstraint
```

where a constant can be of different types (e.g., string, number, Boolean, area) and therefore the relational operator (e.g., $=$, $\leq$)) is polymorphic in that it is able to compare different types (for example, $\leq$, when used for areas will be equivalent to set containment, $\subseteq$). Examples of attribute constraints include: $\geq 10 \wedge \leq 18$, and $\neg(\geq 10 \wedge \leq 18)$ and $\leq SeatedArea$. The definition of attribute constraint can be further extended.

Role class. This class is a placeholder for all the roles that are defined. Conceptually, a role is a set of privileges. Roles are assigned to users via sessions.

Role attribute constraints. These constraints are pairs $\langle r,a \rangle$, where r is a role (e.g., *SpecialVisitor*), and a is an attribute pair $\langle attribute, attributeconstraint \rangle$ (e.g., $\langle Importance, = VIP \rangle$), where *attributeconstraint* is defined as previously. There is a many-to-many relationship between roles and attribute pairs. The role *SpecialVisitor* is assigned to a user if the attribute *Importance* has value $= VIP$. When a role attribute constraint refers to spatial attributes, for example, $\langle Journalist, \langle Location, \leq MediaVillage \rangle \rangle$ the role *Journalist* is activated when the user is in the *MediaVillage* (provided that other attribute pairs, if any, are also satisfied).

Session. A user is assigned a session upon entering the system (e.g., *John_680481*). A session is owned by a single user and has a set of roles associated with it. We assume that attribute values associated with resources are not allowed to change during a session. However, attribute values associated with users can change. For example, the location of a user can change during a session, therefore the corresponding attribute *Location* value changes.

2.3   Attribute Constraints

As presented in Section 2.2, role attribute constraints denote a many-to-many relationship between roles and attribute pairs. For a role to be assigned to a user, the user's attribute values must satisfy the attribute constraints. As previously described, the constraints can be expressed in different ways. For instance, a constraint on *Age* can be expressed as a range, for example, ≥ 21, or a constraint on *Importance* can be expressed as a single value, for example $= VIP$. The former constraint would have to be satisfied for someone to have the privilege to enter a bar, whereas the second one would have to be satisfied for someone to access a VIP area.

It is possible to establish a partial order among attribute constraints in the case where an attribute constraint dominates another one. For example, for attribute *age*, ≥ 21 dominates ≥ 18 as someone who is older than 21 is also older than 18. Likewise, for attribute *importance*, $= VIP$ should dominate $= normal$. In our approach, we interpret the dominance relationship between attribute constraints as a satisfiability relationship. Thus, to say that a constraint a dominates a constraint b, written $b \preceq a$ is tantamount to saying that when a is satisfied, b is also satisfied.

Examples of partial orders are shown in Figure 2. Figure 2.1 shows the constraint for user attribute *Age*. The constraint B_3 is dominated by the constraint B_2, and the constraint B_2 is dominated by the constraint B_1 ($(\geq 5) \preceq (\geq 18) \preceq (\geq 21)$). Therefore, if the constraint B_1 is satisfied, then the constraints B_2 and B_3 are also satisfied. Figure 2.2 shows the constraint for user attribute

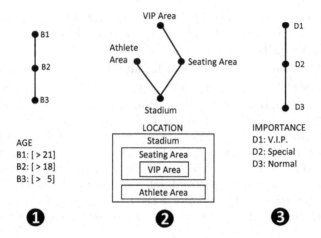

Fig. 2. 1. *Age* partial order 2. *Location* partial order 3. *Importance* partial order

Location, that is, if the coordinates of a user fall inside one of the regions, then the user is located inside the region. In this case, the dominance relationship represents the spatial containment between regions. If the constraint $\leq VIPArea$ is satisfied, meaning if the user is inside location *VIPArea*, then the constraints $\leq SeatingArea$ and $\leq Stadium$ are also satisfied $((\leq Stadium) \preceq (\leq SeatingArea) \preceq (\leq VIPArea))$. If the constraint $\leq AthleteArea$ is satisfied, only the constraint $\leq Stadium$ is also satisfied $((\leq Stadium) \preceq (\leq AthleteArea))$. Figure 2.3 shows the constraint for attribute *Importance*. The constraint D_3 is dominated by D_2, which is in turn dominated by D_1 $(D_3 \preceq D_2 \preceq D_1)$. Therefore, if the constraint D_1 is satisfied by the user *Importance* value, then the constraints D_2 and D_3 are also satisfied.

We argue that in a scenario with different collaborating organizations, each having a different role hierarchy, the definition of partial orders of constraints can play an important role. Each organization will have its attributes and respective constraints. However, some of the attributes may be the same, but with different constraints on them. For instance, with respect to Figure 2.1 it is not difficult to imagine different constraints on the *Age* attribute. If these organizations share their role hierarchies, then they would also share their role attribute constraints. In the next subsection, we discuss the integration of different partially ordered sets of role attribute constraints into one partially ordered set.

2.4   Role-Constraints Partial Order

A role r can be associated with a tuple A of user attribute constraints over distinct attributes. The pair $\langle r, A \rangle$ represents the constraints that must be satisfied to activate the role. Roles are assigned to users, based on the constraints that the user's attribute values satisfy. In Figure 3 we show three roles and their associate attribute constraints, whose partial orders are shown in Figure 2. The role *Journalist* is the dominant role represented in the table. Also, each

Age	Location	Importance	Role	Privilege
>=21	<= VIP Area	= VIP	Journalist	Enter, reserved best seat
>=21	<= VIP Area	= Special	MediaOperator	Enter, reserved seat
>=18	<= Seating Area	= Normal	NormalVisitor	Enter, seat anywhere

Fig. 3. Attribute constraints and roles

attribute constraint of *Journalist* dominates the corresponding attribute constraint of the other roles, that is, the sets of attribute constraints represented in each row are in *componentwise order* [9]. This type of order can be defined on the tuples of the Cartesian product of partially ordered sets. A tuple of the Cartesian product (e.g., $\langle \geq 21, \leq VIPArea, = VIP \rangle$) dominates another tuple (e.g., $\langle \geq 21, \leq VIPArea, = Special \rangle$) if each element of the first tuple dominates the corresponding element of the second tuple (that is, $\geq 21 \preceq \geq 21$, $\leq VIPArea \preceq \leq VIPArea$, and $=Special \preceq = VIP$).

The cardinality of the Cartesian product of the partially ordered sets of constraints can be much higher than the cardinality of the set of roles. For instance, in the example of Figure 2, there are $3 * 4 * 3 = 36$ possible combinations of the different attribute constraints, but likely fewer roles. Therefore, a user may satisfy a set of attribute constraints that does not correspond to any role. For instance, in Figure 3, a user may satisfy the constraints $Age \geq 18$, $Location \leq SeatingArea$, and $Importance = VIP$, which does not correspond to any role. Nonetheless, the user should be assigned the most dominant role possible, that is, *NormalVisitor* [2].

We will discuss later in the implementation part how this feature has been implemented in our framework.

2.5   Transformation Functions

A transformation function can be defined on an attribute to associate the attribute values defined in a certain domain with values on a different domain. For example, given the integer attribute *Age*, the transformation function *child* : $Age \rightarrow Boolean$ associates values greater than 5 to the Boolean *false* and values up to 5 to the Boolean *true*. Transformation functions are total functions. The domain of a transformation function can be the Cartesian product of several attribute domains, associating a set of attributes values with a single attribute value. As in the GEO-RBAC model [3], an example of a transformation function is a location transformation that associates the geographic coordinates of a user with a logical location (e.g., *OlympicStadiumArea*).

With transformation functions applied to a set of user attributes, the constraints can be defined on the target of the transformation function. Applying transformation functions to the user attributes can help in simplifying the computation of the constraints and in preserving privacy [7]. Indeed, if a transformation function is applied on an attribute, only the transformed values (logical values) will be computed over the constraints. The real values will be in a certain sense masked. Moreover, through transformation functions, it is possible to map a set of constraints defined on several attributes into simpler constraints, for example into constraints on Boolean values. In our framework we have implemented only the location transformation function.

3   Reasoning

In the last few years there has been a good amount of research in modeling security models for dynamic environments with the use of Description Logic [4, 10, 17]. Toninelli *et al.* [17] use the OWL language and Logic Programming to model the security policies of a pervasive computing environment. Finin *et al.* consider two approaches for modeling the RBAC model with OWL [10]. Cirio *et al.*, whose work we continue, leverage semantic web technologies to help the security administrator define security policies [4].

The expressiveness of OWL allows for a rich representation of rules and relationships between domain entities and for expressing policies. In particular, it is possible to express:

- Equivalence or disjointness between classes of objects. For instance, it is possible to say that two classes are equivalent and therefore they inherit the properties of each other, or disjoint, therefore an object cannot be an instance of both classes. We use the disjointness feature to implement separation of duty constraints. For instance, it is possible to say that an object belonging to class *TaxiDriver* cannot belong to class *Police*.
- Subclass hierarchies, with multiple inheritance. The subclass inherits the properties of the superclass. We use this feature in two ways: 1) to implement the role constraint hierarchy; 2) to create sets of classes in order to specify a common policy for all of them. The classes of a set are placed under a superclass, to which privileges are attached. Through inheritance, the set of the subclasses inherits the privileges attached to the superclass.
- Properties can be of two types: datatype properties and object properties. We use datatype properties to model the constraints and object properties to assign the privileges to the roles. Object properties, in turn, can also be divided into symmetric, anti-symmetric, transitive, anti-transitive, functional and inverse functional properties.
- New classes can be combined from existing classes using intersection, union, and negation.
- Axioms can be written to express policies. For example, to express the fact that some members of the escort service for teams and athletes may be restricted to escort out of a specific venue but not out of other venues.

We use two types of ontologies in our model: the domain ontology and the RBAC ontology.

The *domain ontology* represents the relationships that hold between the entities of the domain. It can be an existing ontology that describes a particular organization. The domain ontology can contain any of the OWL constructs described

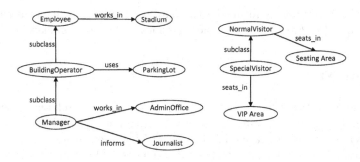

Fig. 4. Domain ontology (portion)

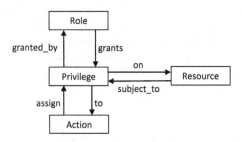

Fig. 5. RBAC ontology

above. We give an example of a portion of our domain ontology in Figure 4. In the figure, we show the ontology classes *Manager, BuildingOperator, Employee,* that are in a class/subclass relationship. Some of the relationships between the different classes are represented by object properties, such as *works*. The *RBAC ontology* (see Figure 5) has four main classes that represent the main concepts of the RBAC model: *Roles, Privileges, Actions,* and *Resources* [4]. These main classes are related to one another by object properties. For example the class *Role* has a relationship named *grants* with the class *Privilege*. These properties are useful during reasoning, because they guide the reasoner in classifying each concept of the ontology under the appropriate class of the RBAC ontology.

Two classification tasks are performed: of the user session and of the classes of the domain ontology into classes of the RBAC ontology. A user session is represented as an instance of the class *Thing* and its attribute values are used by the reasoner to classify the user session in the correct role. The classification of the domain ontology can be performed either by the security administrator or by the the DL reasoner. The latter will classify the different classes of the domain ontology under the classes of the RBAC ontology, following predefined axioms. The axioms are specifications of relationships that must hold between resources [4]. For example, the following rule classifies entities of the domain ontology as subclasses of class *Action* (therefore not in the *Resource, Privilege* or *Role* classes):

$$\exists assign.Privilege \sqcap \neg\{Resource, Privilege, Role\}$$

where *assign* is a property in the domain ontology; therefore, given the assertion *assign(Enter, FreeEnter)*, the reasoner classifies *Enter* as a subclass of *Action*.

4   Prototype

We implemented the security model described in Section 2 relying on semantic web technologies. In particular, the access control model and the features of the application domain are modeled using OWL-DL ontologies. The inference capabilities supported by the OWL-DL language enable the association of the ontology with the Pellet reasoner to perform the classification and reasoning tasks described in Section 3. We used Protege 4.0 to write the ontologies, and the Jena API, as an interface to the ontologies. We used the OWL 1.1 language for complex user-defined data types by means of the new *DataRange* constructors. The Pellet reasoner 1.5.2 supports reasoning on the new constructors. In what follows, we describe the classes that we used in the domain ontologies and in the RBAC ontology.

4.1   Domain Ontology

In the domain ontology, the entities of the domain are described with OWL classes, data type, and object properties. A figure of a portion of our domain ontology was shown in the previous section.

As mentioned in Section 3, the security administrator defines privileges in the domain ontology. Conceptually, the privileges are pairs of *actions* and *resources*. From a practical point of view, this means augmenting the domain ontology by adding new classes to represent the privileges and actions unless they are already in the domain ontology. The security administrator also creates relationships between the classes of the domain ontology and the new added classes. In Figure 6, we show a portion of this process. The figure has three parts. The RBAC ontology is shown at the top. In the beginning, this is a very simple ontology. The domain ontology is shown on the left and on the right is the ontology that specifies the privileges and actions. The latter can be created by the security administrator or be an existing specification of privileges and actions.

In our example, the security administrator creates two OWL classes: *EmployeeEnter*, to represent a privilege, and *FreeEnter*, to represent the associated action. Object property *to* connects the privilege with its action. Privilege *EmployeeEnter* is associated through the object property *on* to the class *Stadium* in the domain ontology. The last object property that is added is the *grants* property that connects a class of the domain ontology, *Employee*, to the privilege *EmployeeEnter* class. As mentioned in Section 3, the reasoner uses the object properties *grants, on, to* to classify each domain ontology class under the correct RBAC ontology class. For instance, *Employee* is classified as a subclass of *Role* and the reasoner places under *Role* the subclasses of *Employee* as well. In this way, the RBAC ontology is extended with all the classes of the domain ontology. The different roles are associated to their privileges through the *grants* object property.

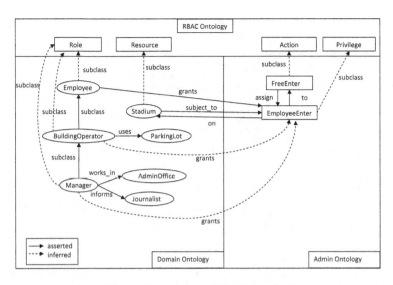

Fig. 6. Domain and RBAC ontology

4.2 RBAC Ontology

We describe now the additions to the RBAC ontology after the reasoning process.
The privileges and actions remain the same as before the reasoning process.
Next, we show how we model the attribute constraints on the user and resource
attributes and how the ontology is used to assign a session to its roles.

- **Constraints.** As mentioned in Section 2 we have attribute, attribute constraint pairs such as (*Importance,* =*VIP*) or (*Age,* ≥ 21). Since the constraints are always used in connection with resources or roles (that is, they
cannot exist by themselves) there are two steps in modeling them:
    (1) Declaration of the attribute as an OWL data type property and
definition of its domain. The domain is the union of the role classes to which
the constraint is associated. The range is the XML data type to which the
constraint value belongs. We have considered only string and integer data
types for now. For instance, to model the constraints on the *Importance*
attribute, we first declare a data type property named *Importance*, whose
domain is the union of all the roles that have *Importance* as a constraint, e.g.,
the set {*SpecialVisitor, NormalVisitor*}. We declare the range of *Importance*
to be the string data type.
    (2) Restriction of the values that the attribute can have inside the classes
that represent roles or resources. For example, in the class for role *SpecialVisitor*, we restrict property *Importance* to assume only value *special.*
- **RoleConstraint class.** As was mentioned in Section 2, the RoleConstraint
represents a role and its constraints. We model every *RoleConstraint* as an
OWL class. The name of the *RoleConstraint* class is the same as the name of
the role, for instance, *SpecialVisitor*. The value of the attribute *Importance*

```
<owl:Class rdf:about="#SpecialVisitor">
    <owl:equivalentClass>
        <owl:Class>
            <owl:intersectionOf rdf:parseType="Collection">
                <owl:Restriction>
                    <owl:onProperty rdf:resource="#hasAge"/>
                    <owl:hasValue>&gt;40</owl:hasValue>
                </owl:Restriction>
                <owl:Restriction>
                    <owl:onProperty rdf:resource="#Importance"/>
                    <owl:hasValue> special </owl:hasValue>
                </owl:Restriction>
            </owl:intersectionOf>
        </owl:Class>
    </owl:equivalentClass>
</owl:Class>
```

Fig. 7. SpecialVisitor role constraint

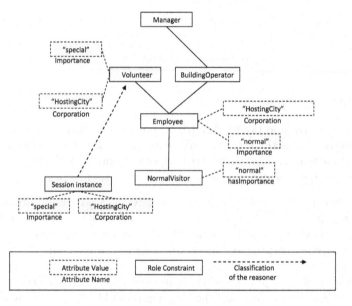

Fig. 8. User session classification

is restricted to assume only the value *special* for the class *SpecialVisitor*. In other words, we are saying that the class *SpecialVisitor* is the class of all objects, whose *Importance* attribute has value *special*. The OWL code for the SpecialVisitor class is shown in Figure 7.

- **Session.** At runtime, we add sessions as instances of the OWL class *Thing*, which is the superclass of all the classes of the domain. These instances are augmented with the attributes and values available from the user. The attributes and values of the instance guide the reasoner in the classification. For instance, in Figure 8 we show an instance of the user session with two attributes *Importance, Corporation* and values *special, HostingCity*, that is classified by the reasoner under the *RoleConstraint* class *Volunteer*.

– **Resource constraints**. With constraints on resource attributes, we have to be able to deal with individual instances, and not with classes of objects anymore. Since each subclass of the class *Resource* can have different instances with different attribute values, we have to identify at instance level the resources that satisfy the constraints. If such resources exist then we can associate them with the instance of the user session. This association happens after the instance of the user session has been classified under a role constraint. OWL-DL does not allow for the specification of conditions about actual instances to identify the resources whose attributes satisfy the constraints. Therefore, we use SPARQL queries to verify that such resources exist [4].

4.3 Transformation Functions

We have implemented the transformation function for the location attribute using the Google Maps API, which allows to define named areas on the map and symbols to represent people. The symbols can be moved around on the map to simulate the movement of people. If a symbol is inside one of the areas, the API returns the area name, which is used as the *Location* attribute of the user. The transformation functions serve also another purpose in masking from the real attribute values of the user. The access decision is performed on the transformed values and not on the real ones, increasing in this way the privacy of the user. For instance, the location attribute values on which the access decision is made do not show the real coordinates of a user, but a larger area. The location privacy of the user is thus increased [3]. Other transformation functions will be implemented in the future.

4.4 Graphical User Interface

For the Olympic Games scenario, we implemented a user interface to illustrate our framework, as shown in Figure 9. It is composed of two parts, the map on the left and a form to retrieve attribute values when new sessions are created on the right. We have defined eight different areas in the map, associated with different values for the *Location* attribute. The form is used to enter attributes and their values. First, the attribute *Organization* is entered and next a pull down menu allows to choose another attribute for which a value will be entered.

Each session is represented by an icon displaying a person. When a session is created, a unique identifier is appended to the session name. The icon can be dragged and dropped in the map, thus changing the location attribute. The other values of the attributes can also be changed and the session attributes updated. Depending on the values of the attributes, the roles in the session may change. Each time the icon is dropped, the dialog window, which can be seen in the figure, is used to show the enabled and disabled roles associated with that person and the privileges associated with that role.

Fig. 9. User interface

4.5   Client Server Architecture

The framework has been implemented in a four-tier client-server architecture:

- **Tier 1: Application web page**. It has been developed with *JavaScript* technology and integrates with the Google Maps API, which also runs JavaScript.
- **Tier 2: Java™ Applet Program**. It is downloaded from the server side and runs on the user's browser. It is responsible for handling the network traffic with the server.
- **Tier 3: Server Side Java™ Program**. It is essentially a network server program, and it is responsible for network server functions, loading the ontology files, and interpreting and processing user requests.
- **Tier 4: Ontologies**. Ontologies are stored in this tier and modeled and maintained independently of the rest of the application.

5   Related Work

Geo-RBAC proposes a model for associating roles with logical location [3, 8]. Logical locations are regions of space defined by real world coordinates and a user can only assume roles that are associated with the location the user is in. In our model, location can be expressed as an attribute of the user along with other attributes, whose values determine the possible roles.

The Proteus system is intended for pervasive computing environments [17]. In Proteus, contexts are defined as intermediaries between entities and operations that they can perform on resources. Contexts are created by data sensed from the environment and reasoning is used to activate permissions on specific resources. Contexts can also inherit constraints from each other. However, Proteus is not role-based.

Kulkarni and Tripathi [13] devise a context-aware access control model. Constraints are defined on different entities of the model, for instance, resources and user attributes. Users can activate personalized permissions in addition to their roles, thus having a somewhat dynamic Role-Permission assignment. Role revocation is also supported, when values of the user attributes no longer satisfy the constraints. Attribute constraints are not arranged in lattices.

ROWLBAC proposes modeling RBAC with OWL [10]. Two different approaches for modeling roles are shown, one where roles are represented as classes and another one where roles are represented as instances. Attribute constraints on role assignments are not modeled, however, and there is no associated system.

RB-RBAC (Rule-Based RBAC) shares some similarity with our approach in that a hierarchy of constraints is mapped to a hierarchy of roles [1, 2]. The rules that associate attributes to roles are arranged in a hierarchy of seniority. When a senior rule is satisfied, the junior rules are automatically satisfied and all the roles produced by the senior rule and the junior ones are assigned to the user. Several other aspects are also considered, including the concept of role hierarchies that are induced by rules. However, they consider just one hierarchy of constraints.

6 Conclusions

The contributions of our paper are summarized as follows:

- We decouple the constraints on the attributes of users from the roles and investigate the relations between hierarchies of attribute constraints and of the roles. Likewise, we decouple the constraints on the resources from their privileges. This simplifies the process of reasoning about users, resources, roles, and privileges.
- We consider dynamic attributes for users, whose values can vary during the same user session. An example includes location, though we offer a unified approach to any attribute type.
- Our model is expressive enough to capture hierarchies both of constraints and of roles and the associated inheritance reasoning as well as reasoning to combine constraints and to infer roles and user sessions.
- We have implemented our framework by exploring the capabilities of semantic web technologies and namely of OWL 1.1 [11] to model our framework and the domain, and to perform reasoning using the Pellet reasoner [5].
- We have adopted a client-server architecture and implemented a user interface whose purpose it twofold: (1) to offer a visual explanation of the underlying reasoning by displaying roles and their associations with users (e.g., as the user's locations vary); (2) to enable monitoring of the users that are involved in a collaborative application. Our interface, which uses the Google Maps API, is particularly suited to collaborative applications where the users' geospatial location is of interest.

Future work includes:

- Adding expressiveness to our framework by allowing other types of constraints, namely temporal [12] or more complex constraints. In addition, further exploration of the consequences of componentwise order (or lack thereof) and of the implementation of transformation functions for attributes other than location can be undertaken.
- Investigating reasoning, conflict resolution, and other aspects of merging ontologies of constraints and roles.
- Considering other privacy aspects, in particular when revealing to other organizations the structure of one's own. Work in privacy-preserving ontology matching [6, 16] needs to be investigated in our particular context.
- Designing a framework for the evaluation of dynamic constraint approaches that will take into account security metrics and the complexity of the evaluation [3] as well as the efficiency of the implementation using semantic web languages and reasoning [10].

References

[1] Al-Kahtani, M.A., Sandhu, R.: A Model for Attribute-Based User- Role Assignment. In: Annual Computer Security Applications Conference (ACSAC), pp. 353–364. IEEE Computer Society, Los Alamitos (2002)
[2] Al-Kahtani, M.A., Sandhu, R.: Induced role hierarchies with attributebased RBAC. In: ACM Symposium on Access Control Models and Technologies (SACMAT), pp. 142–148 (2003)
[3] Bertino, E., Catania, B., Damiani, M.L., Perlasca, P.: GEO-RBAC: A Spatially Aware RBAC. In: ACM Symposium on Access Control Models and Technologies (SACMAT), pp. 29–37 (2005)
[4] Cirio, L., Cruz, I.F., Tamassia, R.: A Role and Attribute Based Access Control System Using Semantic Web Technologies. In: Meersman, R., Tari, Z., Herrero, P. (eds.) OTM-WS 2007, Part II. LNCS, vol. 4806, pp. 1256–1266. Springer, Heidelberg (2007)
[5] Clark & Parsia, LLC. Pellet, http://pellet.owldl.com
[6] Cruz, I.F., Tamassia, R., Yao, D.: Privacy-Preserving Schema Matching Using Mutual Information. In: Barker, S., Ahn, G.-J. (eds.) Data and Applications Security 2007. LNCS, vol. 4602, pp. 93–94. Springer, Heidelberg (2007)
[7] Damiani, M.L., Bertino, E.: Access Control and Privacy in Location- Aware Services for Mobile Organizations. In: International Conference on Mobile Data Management (MDM), pp. 11–20 (2006)
[8] Damiani, M.L., Bertino, E., Catania, B., Perlasca, P.: GEO-RBAC: A Spatially Aware RBAC. ACM Transactions on Information and System Security (TISSEC) 10(1), 2 (2007)
[9] Darnel, M.R.: Theory of Lattice-Ordered Groups, p. 10016. CRC Press, New York (1995)
[10] Finin, T.W., Joshi, A., Kagal, L., Niu, J., Sandhu, R.S., Winsborough, W.H., Thuraisingham, B.M.: ROWLBAC: Representing Role Based Access Control in OWL. In: ACM Symposium on Access Control Models and Technologies (SACMAT), pp. 73–82 (2008)

[11] Horrocks, I., Patel-Schneider, P.F., Motik, B.: OWL 1.1 Web Ontology Language Structural Specification and Functional-Style Syntax (2007)

[12] Joshi, J., Bertino, E., Latif, U., Ghafoor, A.: A Generalized Temporal Role-Based Access Control Model. IEEE Transactions on Knowledge and Data Engineering 17(1), 4–23 (2005)

[13] Kulkarni, D., Tripathi, A.: Context-aware Role-based Access Control in Pervasive Computing Systems. In: ACM Symposium on Access Control Models and Technologies (SACMAT), pp. 113–122 (2008)

[14] Osborn, S.L., Sandhu, R.S., Munawer, Q.: Configuring Role-based Access Control to Enforce Mandatory and Discretionary Access Control Policies. ACM Transactions on Information and System Security (TISSEC) 3(2), 85–106 (2000)

[15] Sandhu, R.S., Coyne, E.J., Feinstein, H.L., Youman, C.E.: Role-Based Access Control Models. Computer 29(2), 38–47 (1996)

[16] Scannapieco, M., Figotin, I., Bertino, E., Elmagarmid, A.K.: Privacy Preserving Schema and Data Matching. In: ACM SIGMOD International Conference on Management of Data, pp. 653–664 (2007)

[17] Toninelli, A., Montanari, R., Kagal, L., Lassila, O.: Proteus: A Semantic Context-Aware Adaptive Policy Model. In: IEEE International Workshop on Policies for Distributed Systems and Networks, pp. 129–140 (2007)

Access Control Model for Sharing Composite Electronic Health Records

Jing Jin[1], Gail-Joon Ahn[2], Michael J. Covington[3], and Xinwen Zhang[4]

[1] University of North Carolina at Charlotte,
jjin@uncc.edu
[2] Arizona State University,
Gail-Joon.Ahn@asu.edu
[3] Intel Corporation,
michael.j.covington@intel.com
[4] Samsung Information Systems America,
xinwen.z@samsung.com

Abstract. The adoption of electronically formatted medical records, so called Electronic Health Records (EHRs), has become extremely important in healthcare systems to enable the exchange of medical information among stakeholders. An EHR generally consists of data with different types and sensitivity degrees which must be selectively shared based on the need-to-know principle. Security mechanisms are required to guarantee that only authorized users have access to specific portions of such critical record for legitimate purposes. In this paper, we propose a novel approach for modelling access control scheme for composite EHRs. Our model formulates the semantics and structural composition of an EHR document, from which we introduce a notion of *authorized zones* of the composite EHR at different granularity levels, taking into consideration of several important criteria such as data types, intended purposes and information sensitivities.

1 Introduction

Healthcare is an increasingly collaborative domain involving a wide range of individuals and organizations. Seamless electronic communication infrastructure that allows patients, physicians, hospitals, public health agencies and other authorized users to share clinical information in real-time, under stringent security and privacy protections, has become extremely important to improve the quality of healthcare while simultaneously reducing costs and administrative complexity [1]. In particular, the adoption of electronically formatted medical records, so called Electronic Health Records (EHRs), has become the primary concern for a broad range of health information technology applications and practitioners.

Critical concerns about the privacy and security of personal medical information remain high in healthcare information sharing systems. More than ever, there is a strong need to define access control models that conform to legal principles and regulations, while limiting access to information to those entities on

E. Bertino and J.B.D. Joshi (Eds.): CollaborateCom 2008, LNICST 10, pp. 340–354, 2009.

need-to-know basis. However, an EHR includes complex health information such as the patient demographics, medical histories, examination reports, laboratory test results, radiology images (X-rays, CTs), and so on. Supporting the authorized and selective sharing of EHRs among several parties with different duties and objectives is indeed a great challenge.

1.1   A Motivation Scenario

In order to better illustrate access control challenges on sharing of EHRs, we consider a typical clinical EHR document, and we demonstrate our proposed approach using the same document throughout the rest of this paper.

Suppose Good Health Clinic is a member of a particular Regional Health Information Organization (RHIO) [2], where health information can be exchanged through an established infrastructure with other involved organizations. Figure 1 illustrates a sample Consultation Note in the clinic for a patient named Henry Levin [3]. The consultation note includes Henry's past medical history, medications, physical examination, labs, etc. The medical information is recorded in various data types such as texts, numbers and images. Some fields inside the document may refer to other external clinical documents. For example, Henry's HIV/AIDS disease history may be maintained in another folder of the patient, and Henry's current medications may be directly linked to the records operated by his pharmacist. Given the complexity of this EHR document, the information contained in the consultation note should be legitimately exchanged to satisfy needs of different parties in RHIO. In particular, the lab orders need to be communicated with appropriate laboratories and specific test codes are used to trigger the billing process. The doctor's prescriptions, on the other hand, are necessary to be filled by the pharmacist, and proper referrals are exchanged with specialists for complex medical problems. However, ensuring the patient's privacy and data security is still vital for the EHR exchange system. The need-to-know

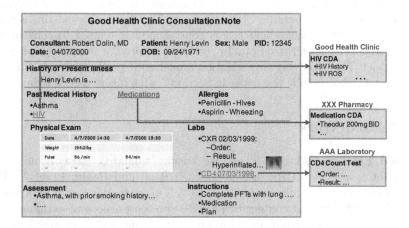

Fig. 1. Motivation EHR Document

principle must be strictly enforced for each responsible party to obtain only the necessary information to carry out its task. For instance, only the test codes and patient's insurance information are necessary for a billing clerk to fulfill her responsibility. The document also has sensitive fields, such as Henry's HIV/AIDS medical history, which may be hidden from general medical information sharing unless a specific treatment purpose is indicated.

The example clinical document has demonstrated several unique characteristics of an EHR, including the composition of various data types, connections among different pieces of information from multiple sources, and navigational aspects of the information linkage and exchange. We thus refer the EHRs with such features as composite EHRs. In supporting partial sharing of a composite EHR, only a portion of the document needs to be shared with authorized users. Without explicitly identifying the *protection objects* and their associations within a composite EHR, the authorization specification referring to specific protection parts is difficult. In addition, these protection objects must be classified with regard to different purposes, data types, and sensitivity levels to guide the selection of specific parts with various protection granularity levels within the document. Finally, as an EHR document may link to other EHRs, the navigation paradigm would affect the authorization model, while the navigational links serve as a visual representation of associations between the EHR documents and need to be protected in a secure manner.

In this paper we propose a novel approach for modeling access control in composite EHRs. Our model first introduces a level of abstraction to formulate the logical structure of a composite EHR in terms of its internal protection objects and relationships among them. The protection objects are categorized by three dimensional properties – sensitivity, intended purpose and object type – to facilitate the authorization model and accommodate the composition and selective sharing requirements. By manipulating the selection criteria of these properties, various *authorized zones* including different protection objects can be dynamically collected to share with recipients.

The rest of the paper is organized as follows. In Section 2, we provide a brief overview of the emerging EHR standards. We also review existing security solutions for EHR systems and access control models related to conventional structured or semi-structured data. In Section 3, we present the logical composite EHR model. The proposed authorization model and specification are discussed in Section 4. We conclude the paper in Section 5 with future research directions.

2   Related Work

Related EHR Standards. There are several standards currently under development to specify EHRs, such as openEHR [4] and Health Level 7 (HL7) Clinical Document Architecture (CDA) [5,3]. These standards aim to structure and markup the clinical content of an EHR for the purpose of exchange. The most important concept introduced in openEHR is the *archetype*, which is used to model healthcare concepts such as blood pressure and lab results. These archetypes serve as fundamental building blocks to form various clinical EHR documents. Meanwhile, these archetypes and the contents contained in them are exactly what need to be protected in the process of information exchange across healthcare systems. Similarly, CDA defines the structure and semantics of medical documents in terms of a set of coded components (called vocabulary) to model basic medical concepts. A common feature of all emerging EHR standards is that the clinical concepts are modeled and expressed independently from how the data is actually stored in underlying database. By implementing or converting to the EHR standards, a "common language" is established between different medical information systems to communicate and share standardized medical information with each other. Therefore, instead of being carried out at the lower level in underlying database, authorization and selective sharing of medical information should be defined and enforced with common understanding of EHR standards. In our motivation example and the rest of the paper, we assume the composite EHR document conforms to CDA standard format.

Access Control for EHR Systems. A number of solutions have been proposed to address the security and access control concerns associated with EHR systems. In [6], the authors propose a set of authorization policies enforcing role-based access control for the electronic transfer of prescriptions. In [7], the paper demonstrates an implementation of EHR prototype system including a basic network and role-based security infrastructure for the United Kingdom National Health Service. In [8], the authors present a trust management and role-based policy specification language, called Cassandra, for expressing access control policies in large-scale distributed systems. A case study discusses how the language can be used to specify security policies for a UK national EHR system. In [9], the paper presents a policy-based security management framework to enforce context based authorizations for federated healthcare databases. Role-based access control [10], with its superior advantages in reducing administration complexity, has become the common theme applied in these approaches. However, the EHR considered in these approaches is either a general abstract object or an isolated primitive object. None of these approaches took into account of the composition feature of EHR documents, and thus cannot support a more fine-grained access control to selectively share composite EHRs as illustrated in our motivational example.

Related Authorization Models for Structured Data. Sharing of composite EHRs requires clear understanding of the internal protection objects/clinical concepts and their structural relationships. There has been a considerable amount of work in regulating access to structured or semi-structured data.

The access control models proposed in [11] and [12] are especially tailored to object-oriented databases storing conventional structured data, where information is represented in the form of objects. These models consider a rich semantic structure of objects incorporating inheritance, aggregation, and composition associations. The relationship of objects in the database is modelled as a hierarchical structure so that the validity of an authorization rule written at some level can be efficiently propagated to its descendants. Such features can be adopted in modelling the logical structure of composite EHRs. However, these models have several shortcomings in providing effective access control for information exchange of EHRs. On the one hand, EHR documents are stored and exchanged based on standards, which are defined independently from underlying database structures. The object relationships and navigational patterns defined in standards may be totally different from the ones enforced by access control mechanisms. On the other hand, as identified in our motivation scenario, the medical information may be distributed at different sites, from which a particular composite EHR document is derived. This unique feature cannot be addressed by a localized object-oriented database.

XML has become the de facto mechanism for sharing data between disparate information systems. It is essentially adopted by HL7 to carry out its standardization efforts to describe, store and exchange health records. Regulating access to XML documents has attracted considerable attentions in recent years [13,14,15]. All these work represent an XML document as a hierarchical tree structure and its authorizations are propagated along with the association links to achieve different granularity levels. However, all these approaches define access control rules for particular elements and attributes of an XML document. The selection of a portion of the document requires a number of authorization rules to be defined and evaluated. This is obviously not effective and efficient in practice to authorize and share a specific part of the document to fulfill the specific functional purpose of the requesting party. In addition, an XML document itself is not semantically enough to represent a variety of data types as encountered in composite EHRs (e.g., image, audio and video). Thus the access control mechanisms proposed for XML documents cannot meet the special requirements for sharing of composite EHRs.

3   Logical Composite EHR Model

In order to enable the selective sharing of specific parts of a composite EHR, we must allow the document to be logically divided into subcomponents so that fine-grained authorization can be applied. Therefore, we consider the basic building blocks of a composite EHR as the pieces of information or clinical concepts that might be individually exchanged. A piece of information is represented as a sub-object within a composite EHR, where each sub-object should be uniquely identified. Sub-objects can be nested at any depth within the EHR and can link to other sub-objects or even other EHRs. In our example, the blood pressure can be modeled as a sub-object in the Good Health Clinic's EHR document and it is nested under the physical examination object category, while the patient's current medication is linked to another EHR document in the pharmacy. We could further differentiate these two types of links between sub-objects and/or composite EHR documents as *inclusion* link and *navigation* link, respectively. The *inclusion* link realizes the typical "is a part of" relation, and the *navigation* link represents the "reference to" relation between sub-objects within or across composite EHR documents.

To cope with the essential features of different object types and their sensitivity levels within a composite EHR, we associate such information as properties for each sub-object within the document. The properties can be categorized into three dimensions: sensitivity, intended purpose and object type. The sensitivity property is designed to label a sub-object based on the sensitivity of the content contained in it, which eventually can prevent sensitive medical information from being disclosed unintentionally. In the practice of Iowa HISPC [16], the sensitivity classifications of medical data include general medical data, drug and alcohol treatment, substance abuse treatment, mental health, communicable disease (HIV, STDs, etc.), decedent, immunizations, and so on. Based on these classifications, the sub-objects representing Henry's *HIV* medical history and the specific *CD4* lab test should be marked with "**communicable disease**" property ("**HIV**" for simplicity). The intended purpose property is necessary to address privacy concerns to guide the exchange of data based on specific purpose(s) and it is also essential to determine necessary pieces of information to fulfill the need-to-know requirement of a specific job function. According to [17], business practices for health information exchange can be organized by 11 purposes including payment, treatment, research, etc. These purposes could be achieved by exchanging different portions of a composite EHR document. The object type property gives another dimension on sub-object selection and protection. The sub-objects can be primitive types such as plain texts, dates and time, images and reference links. They can also be a composite type in the hierarchical structure including other types of sub-objects. Considering the navigational pattern within the document, the starting point of a navigation link should always be associated with an object labelled with the type of reference link.

As a summary, a composite EHR is modeled in terms of the composition of sub-objects and their relationships as links in a hierarchical structure. Each sub-object is labelled with properties of sensitivity, intended purpose and object type. These properties are used along with authorization policies to determine whether a specific sub-object is allowed to be exchanged or not. This can be formally defined as follows.

Definition 1 (*Composite EHR*). *A composite EHR is a tuple* $C = (v_c, V_o, E_o, \gamma_{E_o}, \tau_{V_o})$, *where*

- v_c *is the root representing the whole composite resource object;*
- V_o *is a set of sub-objects within the composite document under protection;*
- $E_o \subseteq V_o \times V_o$ *is a set of edges between sub-objects;*
- $\gamma_{E_o} : E_o \rightarrow \{I, N\}$ *is an edge labelling function indicating whether an edge is inclusion (I) or navigation (N) type;*
- $\tau_{V_o} : V_o \rightarrow P$ *is a sub-object labelling function to specify the property of a sub-object. P is a set of properties defined in Definition 2.*

Definition 2 (*Property*). *Let S, PU, and T be the sets of sensitivity classifications, intended purposes, and object types, respectively.*

- P_s *is a collection of sensitivity classification sets,* $\{ps_1, \ldots, ps_m\}$, *where* $ps_i = \{s_1, \ldots, s_n\} \subseteq S$, $i \in [1, m]$;

- P_p is a collection of intended purpose sets, $\{pp_1, \ldots, pp_m\}$, where $pp_i = \{pu_1, \ldots, pu_n\} \subseteq PU$, $i \in [1, n]$;
- $P = P_s \times P_p \times T$ is a set of three dimensional properties of sensitivity, intended purpose and the type.

Given a property label p for a sub-object, we use the dot notation to refer to a specific property dimension. For instance, $p.ps$ refers to the sensitivity property; $p.pp$ refers to the intended purpose; and $p.t$ refers to the object type. The function $\tau(v_i)$ is used to retrieve the property label for a specific sub-object v_i inside the composition C.

According to Definition 1, a composite EHR can be represented as a labelled hierarchical graph. The root of the tree graph indicates a particular composite EHR document. The nodes represent the sub-objects within the document and specific properties are associated with each node for authorization and selection. Edges represent the inclusion or navigational relationships between the nodes. Within the structure, nodes can be explicitly denoted by their identifiers, or can be implicitly addressed by means of *path* expressions. We apply a simplified XPath [18] expression for the path representation [1]. Simplification comes from the fact that each node is uniformly treated without a type, whereas XPath differentiates between "children" and "attributes" of an object due to the difference between elements and attributes in XML. We do not make such an explicit distinction because nodes in an EHR are the logical representation of clinical concepts under protection. By using our model, the logical structure of an EHR document in Figure 1 can be represented as a rooted tree as shown in Figure 2(a). The links inside the tree are labelled with I and N indicating types of inclusion and navigation, respectively. Figure 2(b) illustrates the example of node labelling for the section of Labs in the document. We use paths to select some of sub-objects in the graph as follows:

- /ConsultationNote: the whole composite EHR document;
- //Labs/CXR: this CXR lab test;
- //Labs/CXR/*: the child nodes of CXR lab test;
- //Labs/CXR//*: all the descendants of CXR lab test.

Another main design issue for the sub-object labelling scheme is the level of granularity an object should be associated with. As sub-objects are managed in a hierarchical structure of the composite EHR document, it enables us to provide a fine-grained labelling scheme yet achieves storage efficiency. In particular, we could explicitly label sub-objects with properties at a certain granularity level and allow the properties to be implicitly labelled through proper propagation and aggregation along with the hierarchical links. As properties are categorized in three dimensions, each has special characteristics for different authorization requirements. Therefore, the property propagation and aggregation for each dimension should be designed individually. We propose the following rules.

---

[1] For brevity, we omit the formal definition of the path specification here.

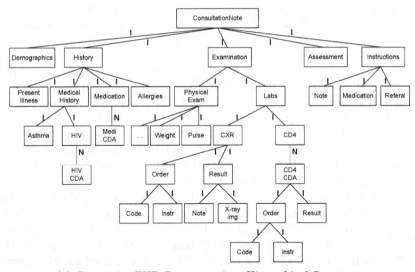

(a) Composite EHR Document in a Hierarchical Structure

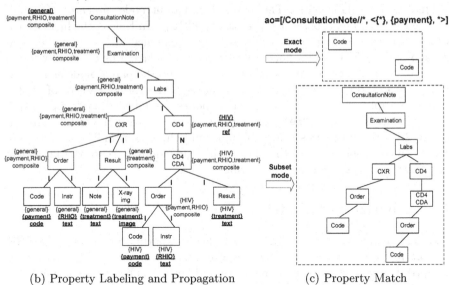

(b) Property Labeling and Propagation   (c) Property Match

Fig. 2. Composite EHR Document Structure

Rule 1. The property of sensitivity is automatically propagated downwards in the hierarchy until a more sensitive label is explicitly specified and overridden. We denote this as $P_s \downarrow$.

Rule 2. The property of intended purpose is aggregated upwards in the hierarchy. We denote this as $P_p \uparrow$.

Rule 3. The property of object type is aggregated upwards along with *inclusion* and *navigation* links and labelled as "composite" and "ref", respectively. We denote these types as $T \uparrow \xrightarrow{I}$ "composite" and $T \uparrow \xrightarrow{N}$ "ref".

In Rule 1, the structure represents an inheritance hierarchy, so that a property defined at the parent can be automatically inherited by its children, and a child may define new properties to override the ones inherited from its parent. In our example, we assume the "general" label is the least-sensitive property, and other labels such as "HIV" and "mental" are more sensitive ones. As shown in Figure 2(b), the root of the clinical consultation note is labelled as "{general}" and this label is implicitly propagated downwards to all sub-objects within the structure. However, as *CD4* is a special lab test related to HIV/AIDS disease, the "HIV" sensitivity is explicitly specified to override the original "general" label. It is then implicitly inherited by its children nodes (e.g., *CD4 CDA*) in the hierarchy. In Rule 2, the hierarchical structure is treated as an aggregation association, where the purposes served by children nodes are aggregated by their parents. In our example, the *code* of the *CXR* lab test is used for "{payment}" purpose and the instruction *instr* is used for "{RHIO}" purpose to be communicated with the laboratory. Therefore, their parent node, *order* of *CXR* lab test, aggregates the purposes as "{payment, RHIO}". In Rule 3, the hierarchical structure reflects both the "is a part of" and "reference to" relations between the sub-objects. The parent node associated with *inclusion* links actually forms a type of "composite" to all its children nodes. And the parent node associated with *navigation* links referring to all its children nodes through a type of "ref". In our example, the root and all internal nodes are labelled as "composite", while *CD4* is labelled as "ref" since it is associated with a navigation link. In Figure 2(b), the properties using bold and underlined font indicate the explicitly specified properties and the ones with regular font indicate the implicitly assigned properties according to the rules.

4   Authorization Model

The fundamental question towards the selective sharing of a composite EHR is *what portion of a document can be exchanged with whom*. The role of an authorization model is then to articulate and specify policies to determine the authorized zone of a source tree that a given subject is permitted to access [2].

4.1   Authorization Subject

The role-based access control model has gained a lot of attention in healthcare security research [19,6,7,8,9] because of its ability to provide practical security administration for a large number of users. Users are authorized through their roles (e.g., patient, physician, nurse) to access EHR documents within a healthcare infrastructure. In our approach, we also adopt a notion of role, considering

---

[2] In this paper, we mainly focus on read-only permission in our authorization model.

authorization subjects as roles directly. We assume a system-wide set of roles (R) has been established within a healthcare system and each individual user is a member of one or more roles. Access control policies are then specified as what role is authorized to access which part of an EHR document.

4.2 Authorization Objects and Property Match

The fine-grained authorization specification should support a set of protection objects with the broader coverage, ranging from a set of interrelated EHR documents to a specific portion of an EHR document. In our hierarchical composite EHR model, XPath like path expressions can be utilized to specify the scope of the sub-objects to which an authorization policy applies. Meanwhile, properties provide the flexibility to group sub-objects and to establish authorized zones within a document scope for meeting various access control requirements. Therefore, the selection of objects can be indirectly achieved by specifying authorized properties. These authorized properties serve as the filtration criteria to be compared with labels of the sub-objects. The matched sub-objects are then selected to share with specific role(s). In specifying authorized properties, we allow patterns to be used instead of enumerating each property. Patterns are expressed by using the wildcard character. Two kinds of patterns are introduced: pattern "*" is to indicate any property type(s) within a property dimension; and pattern "{*}" is to specify any collection(s) of property sets within a property dimension. For example, $<\{*\},\{payment\},*>$ specifies the object(s) that have **any** collections of sensitivity levels, for **payment** purpose with **any** object type(s). The notion of authorized property specification is formally defined as follows.

Definition 3 *(Authorized Property Specification). An authorized property is specified as a tuple prop $=< ps, pp, pt >$, where $ps \in P_s$ or $ps = \{*\}$ is the authorized sensitivity property; $pp \in P_p$ or $pp = \{*\}$ is the authorized purpose property; and $pt \subseteq T$ or $pt = *$ is the authorized object type property.*

As each sub-object is labelled with both explicitly specified properties and implicitly inherited or aggregated properties as the result of property propagation, different semantics must be identified to accommodate such features by incorporating the cascading options to guide the matching process. We further introduce two matching modes as *exact* mode and *subset* mode. The *exact* mode can be utilized to specify access control policies for certain sub-object(s) with specific properties, while the *subset* mode can be specified to select a large collection of sub-objects related to the specified properties, considering the property propagation and aggregation along the hierarchical links.

Definition 4 *(Property Match). Suppose prop $=< ps, pp, pt >$ is an authorized property specification and $p' = (ps', pp', t')$ is the object property label,*

- In **exact** match mode, two properties match if the following is true:
  $[(prop.ps = \{*\})?true : (prop.ps = p'.ps')]\&\&[(prop.pp = \{*\})?true : (prop.pp = p'.pp')]\&\&[(prop.pt = *)?true : (p'.t' \in prop.pt)]$, that is, if patterns are not used, the sensitivity and intended purpose properties must be

exactly equal in the authorized property and the object's label, and the object type must be contained in the authorized types. Otherwise, any pattern used in a property dimension returns a *true* for that property dimension.

- In **subset** match mode, the two properties match if the following is true: $[(prop.ps = \{*\})?true : (prop.ps \supseteq p'.ps')]\&\&[(prop.pp = \{*\})?true : (prop.pp \subseteq p'.pp')]\&\&[(prop.t = *)?true : (p'.t' \in prop.pt)]$, that is, if patterns are not used, the sensitivity property of the object must be contained in the authorized sensitivity property, the authorized purpose property must be contained in the object's purpose property, and the object type must be equal.

We also define an authorization object that is used in an access control policy.

Definition 5 *(Authorization Object Specification). Let scp_expr be a scope expression to denote a set of authorization objects, and prop be an authorized property specification. An authorization object is specified as a tuple ao = (scp_expr, prop).*

Given Definition 4 and the example in Figure 2(b), an authorization object specified as

$$ao = [/ConsultationNote//*, < \{*\}, \{payment\}, * >]$$

means those sub-objects within the whole consultation note with **any** collections of sensitivities, for **payment** purpose, and for **any** object type. In the **exact** match mode, only the two *Code* objects are the matched ones, while in the **subset** match mode, all the parent nodes upwards to the root are additionally included. Figure 2(c) illustrates the property match example.

4.3   Information Sharing Privileges

Our model supports the read-only privilege which allows subjects to read the information in an EHR document and to navigate across EHR documents through navigation links. As identified in our example, navigation links serve as the visual representation of associations between EHR documents and such links should be appropriately protected. In particular, special protection mechanisms can be applied to restrict users' navigational behaviors by not revealing the existence of a navigation link, or by revealing and allowing a subject to explore the objects referenced by a navigation link. Therefore, two different sharing privileges are derived for the protection options, **navi⁻** and **navi⁺**, respectively. By distinguishing these two protection options, it is possible to grant subjects the access permission to a particular EHR document without disclosing links to other EHR documents. For instance, by **navi⁻** privilege, a family physician may be aware of Henry's HIV/AIDS disease from his medical history documented in the consultation note. However, he cannot see the existence of the link to another EHR document for the details of Henry's *HIV/AIDS* treatment history since acquiring such information requires **navi⁺** being assigned. This feature provides another spectrum for the selection of information across composite EHRs.

4.4   Access Control Policy Specification

To summarize the above-mentioned approach, we introduce the definition of an access control policy as follows.

Definition 6 *(Access Control Policy). Let R be the system-wide set of roles in a healthcare system. An access control policy is a tuple acp =< role, ao, match − mode, priv >, where*

- *role ∈ R is a specific role in the system;*
- *ao is an authorization object;*
- *match-mode ∈ {exact, subset} is the match mode for object properties;*
- *priv ∈ {navi⁻, navi⁺} is the sharing privilege for which the authorization is granted.*

The semantics of an access control policy is that, a certain *role* is only authorized with certain *priv* to share the sub-objects whose property labels match the *prop* using the specified *match-mode*. The followings are examples of access control policies and relative authorization zones created against Figure 2(b).

P1: *("billing clerk", [//Labs//*, <{*},{payment}, "code">], exact, navi⁺)*;
P2: *("physician", [//Labs//*, <{general}, {treatment}, *>], subset, navi⁻)*;
P3: *("lab technician", [//Labs//*, <{general}, {RHIO}, *>], subset, navi⁻)*;

These policies select the same scope as the *Labs* category in the clinical consultation note. **P1** states that the billing clerk can only access to the two *Code* objects for both *CXR* and *CD4* lab tests. With **P2**, the physician can access to the CXR lab results, where the content of *CD4* lab test is hidden because of its sensitivity restriction. In **P3**, the lab technician can only access to the *CXR* lab test order with detailed instructions.

With given access control policies, the target scope and corresponding authorization zones are generated as illustrated in Figure 3. The authorization zones are created based on an algorithm as shown in Appendix. The algorithm takes the composite EHR source tree and an access control policy as inputs, and returns the authorized zone including only the authorized portion of the source tree for a given role. The algorithm first retrieves the target subtree from the source tree based on the scope specification and the navigation privilege. Then the properties of each object inside the subtree need to be matched against the authorized property specification in the access control policy, and unmatched ones are pruned from the subtree. Taken the property propagation and aggregation into consideration, the algorithm traverses the target tree in pre-order and post-order, respectively. Overall, the algorithm achieves a time complexity of $O(n)$ for traversing and pruning the target source tree.

5   Concluding Remarks

In this paper, we have presented an access control model for selectively sharing composite EHR documents. Essential features of the model are built with

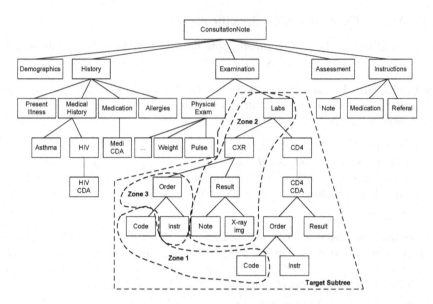

Fig. 3. Authorization Zones

the logical abstraction of a composite EHR through a hierarchical structure, where internal sub-objects are distinguished and organized through their inter-relationships. The design of three dimensional properties for each sub-object addresses the generic concerns for medical data sharing by enabling privacy protection and need-to-know principle for multiple data types, data relationships and access modes. And the property-based authorization zone filtration mechanism provides a flexible yet efficient means to select and authorize a collection of sub-objects with specific property criteria.

Our future work seeks to develop a policy evaluation engine based on our proposed model and standard EHR implementations. Experiments will be conducted on real healthcare systems to demonstrate the applicability and possible extension of our work. Meanwhile, performance and storage efficiency need to be measured and evaluated. Another issue concerns investigating more sophisticated authorization policies to deal with various access types in sharing composite EHRs. For example, a policy may allow a lab technician to directly submit test results to a clinic's EHR, while her access privileges on the medical record should remain intact. Finally, an effective policy propagation and enforcement scheme is necessary to maintain the control power of its original domain after an EHR is distributed and disseminated.

Acknowledgments

The work was partially supported by the grants from National Science Foundation (NSF-IIS-0242393) and Department of Energy Early Career Principal Investigator Award (DE-FG02-03ER25565).

References

1. IEEE-USA's Medical Technology Policy Committee Interoperability Working Group (ed.): Interoperability for the National Health Information Network (NHIN). IEEE-USA EBOOKS (2006)
2. Bartschat, W., Burrington-Brown, J., Carey, S., Chen, J., Deming, S., Durkin, S.: Surveying the RHIO landscape, a description of current rhio models, with a focus on patient identification. J. AHIMA 77(1), 64A–64D (2007)
3. Dolin, R.H., Alschuler, L., Boyer, S., Beebe, C., Behlen, F.M., Biron, P.V.: Hl7 clinical document architecture, release 2.0. ANSI Standard (2004)
4. openEHR Community: openEHR, http://www.openehr.org
5. HL7: Health level 7 (HL7), http://www.hl7.org
6. Chadwick, D.W., Mundy, D.: Policy based electronic transmission of prescriptions. In: Proceedings of the 4th International Workshop on Policyies for Distributed Systems and Networks (POLICY 2003), pp. 197–206 (2003)
7. Eyers, D.M., Bacon, J., Moody, K.: OASIS role-based access control for electronic health records. In: IEE Proceedings – Software, pp. 16–23 (2006)
8. Becker, M.Y., Sewell, P.: Cassandra: flexible trust management, applied to electronic health records. In: Proceedings of IEEE 17th Computer Security Foundations Workshop, pp. 139–154 (2004)
9. Bhatti, R., Moidu, K., Ghafoor, A.: Policy-based security management for federated healthcare databases (or RHIOs). In: Proceedings of the international workshop on Healthcare Information and Knowledge Management, pp. 41–48 (2006)
10. Ferraiolo, D., Sandhu, R., Gavrila, S., Kuhn, R.: Proposed NIST standard for role-based access control. ACM Transactions on Information and System Security (TISSEC) 4, 224–274 (2001)
11. Fernández, E.B., Gudes, E., Song, H.: A model for evaluation and administration of security in object-oriented databases. IEEE Trans. Knowl. Data Eng. 6(2) (1994)
12. Rabitti, F., Bertino, E., Kim, W., Woelk, D.: A model of authorization for next-generation database systems. ACM Transactions on Database Systems (TODS) 16(1), 88–131 (1991)
13. Bertino, E., Castano, S., Ferrari, E., Mesiti, M.: Specifying and enforcing access control policies for xml document sources. World Wide Web Journal 3(3), 139–151 (2000)
14. Damiani, E., di Vimercati, S.D.C., Paraboschi, S., Samarati, P.: A fine-grained access control system for XML documents. ACM Transactions on Information and System Security (TISSEC) 5(5), 169–202 (2002)
15. Gabillon, A., Bruno, E.: Regulating access to XML documents. In: Proceedings of the 15th Annual Working Conference on Database and Application Security (2001)
16. Iowa Foundation for Medical Care: HISPC state implementation project summary and impact analysis report for the state of Iowa (2007), http://www.ifmc.org/news/State%20Impact%20Report_11-27-07.doc
17. Dimitropoulos, L.L.: Privacy and security solutions for interoperable health information exchange: Interim assessment of variation executive summary (2007), http://www.rti.org/pubs/avas_execsumm.pdf
18. Clark, J., DeRose, S.: XML path language (XPath) version 1.0. World Wide Web Consortium (W3C) (1999), http://www.w3.org/TR/xpath
19. Science Applications International Corporation (SAIC): Healthcare RBAC task force charter, v1.1 (2003), http://www.va.gov/RBAC/docs/HealthcareRBACCharterv1_1.pdf

Appendix

```
Algorithm Zone Control
    Input: C = (v_o, V_o, E_o, τ_{Eo}, τ_{Vo})              /* C is the composite EHR source tree */
           acp = <role, ao, match-mode, priv>   /* acp is an access control policy */
    Output: Z     /* Z is the authorized zone for role including a list of nodes from the source tree*/

/* Step 1: Select the scoped subtree for evaluation */
1.  LET scope = acp.ao.scp_expr    /* retrieve the scope specification from the access control policy */
2.  LET Z = select (C, scope, acp.priv)      /* retrieve the subtree Z from C based on the scope and privilege spec */

/* Step 2: Traverse the subtree and match authorized properties */
3.  LET prop = acp.ao.prop          /* retrieve the authorized property specification from the access control policy */
4.  LET N = v_c
/* Step 2.1: Handle exact match mode */
5.  IF match-mode = exact THEN /* handle exact match mode */
6.      IF prop.ps ≠ {*} THEN     /* match sensitivity property label */
7.          WHILE preorder(N).hasnext() DO /* traverse the subtree Z in postorder */
8.              LET ps' = τ(N).ps
9.              IF ps' ≠ prop.ps THEN
10.                 remove N and all its descendant nodes from Z        /* prune unmatched nodes from the tree */
11.     ELSE IF prop.pp ≠ {*} THEN /* match purpose of use property label */
12.         LET N = root of Z
13.         WHILE postorder(N).hasnext() DO /* traverse the remaining tree in postorder */
14.             LET pp' = τ(N).pp
15.             IF pp' ≠ prop.pp THEN
16.                 remove N and all its ancestor nodes from Z      /* prune unmatched nodes from the tree */
17.     ELSE IF prop.pt ≠ * THEN    /* match object type property label */
18.         LET N = root of Z
19.         WHILE postorder(N).hasnext() DO /* traverse the remaining tree in postorder */
20.             LET pt' = τ(N).t
21.             IF pt' ∉ prop.pt THEN
22.                 IF prop.pt contains "composite" THEN
23.                     remove N from Z      /* prune unmatched nodes from the tree */
24.                 ELSE remove N and all its ancestor nodes from Z /* prune unmatched nodes from the tree */
/* Step 2.2: Handle subset match mode */
25. IF match-mode=subset THEN  /* handle subset match mode */
26.     IF prop.ps ≠ {*} THEN    /* match sensitivity property label */
27.         WHILE preorder(N).hasnext() DO /* traverse the subtree Z in postorder */
28.             LET ps' = τ(N).ps
29.             IF ps' ⊈ prop.ps THEN
30.                 remove N and all its descendant nodes from Z            /* prune unmatched nodes from the tree */
31.     ELSE IF prop.pp ≠ {*} THEN /* match purpose of use property label */
32.         LET N = root of Z
33.         WHILE postorder(N).hasnext() DO /* traverse the remaining tree in postorder */
34.             LET pp' = τ(N).pp
35.             IF pp' ⊉ prop.pp THEN
36.                 remove N from Z      /* prune unmatched node from the tree */
37.     ELSE IF prop.pt ≠ * THEN    /* match object type property label */
38.         LET N = root of Z
39.         WHILE postorder(N).hasnext() DO /* traverse the remaining tree in postorder */
40.             LET pt' = τ(N).t
41.             IF pt' ∉ prop.pt THEN
42.                 IF prop.pt contains "composite" THEN
43.                     remove N from Z    /* prune unmatched nodes from the tree */
44.                 ELSE remove N and all its ancestor nodes from Z /* prune unmatched nodes from the tree */
45. RETURN Z
```

Fig. 4. Zone Control Algorithm

Employing Sink Mobility to Extend the Lifetime of Wireless Sensor Networks

Viplavi Donepudi and Mohamed Younis

Department of Computer Science and Electrical Engineering
University of Maryland Baltimore County
Baltimore, MD 21250
{donevip1,younis}umbc.edu

Abstract. Wireless sensor networks (WSNs) often employs miniaturized battery-operated nodes. Since in most setups it is infeasible or impractical to replace the onboard energy supply, the design and operation of WSNs are subject to a great deal of optimization. Among the most popular strategies is the pursuance of multi-hop routes for forwarding collected sensor data to a gateway. In that case, the gateway becomes a sink for all traffic and the close-by nodes relay lots of packets and deplete their battery rather quickly. In this paper, the mobility of the gateway is exploited to balance the load on the sensors and avoid the overload on the nodes in the proximity of the gateway. A novel approach for defining a travel path for the sink is presented. The proposed approach is validated in a simulated environment and is shown to significantly boost the network lifetime.

Keywords: Wireless Sensor Networks, Energy Efficiency, Node Mobility, Network Longevity.

1 Introduction

Wireless sensor networks (WSNs) have been attracting a growing attention from the research community in recent years. A sensor node is equipped with a sensing circuitry to measure ambient conditions such as light, heat and pressure, and a radio for transmitting the collected data. Sensors operate on small batteries and become non-functional when the onboard energy supply gets depleted. A sensor node also has limited computation and memory capacity because of its miniature size. A WSN is composed of a large number of sensor nodes that probe their surroundings and send their data to a gateway for further processing. The gateway interfaces the network to remote command centers. Fig. 1 shows a typical WSN architecture. Applications of WSNs include disaster management, early detection of fires in forests, combat field surveillance and security [1-4]. In these unattended application setups energy consumption is a major concern since a sensor node fails when it runs out of energy and it is impractical to replace its battery in inhospitable environments. Therefore, energy-aware design techniques both at the node and network levels are usually pursued in order to extend the lifetime of the individual sensors.

E. Bertino and J.B.D. Joshi (Eds.): CollaborateCom 2008, LNICST 10, pp. 355–369, 2009.

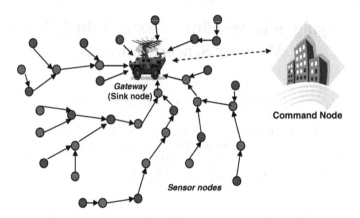

Fig. 1. A sample WSN architecture with the gateway acting as a sink for all traffic and interfacing the network to a remote command center

The quest for maximizing the node lifetime has made multi-hop data routing a very popular optimization scheme. Generally in order to achieve good signal to noise ratio, the output power of a radio at the sender has to be proportional to d^l where d is the distance to the receiver and $l \geq 2$. Therefore, to save energy, sensors data is usually relayed to the sink over multi-hop paths even if a sensor can directly reach the sink. Since in most WSN applications, data is forwarded towards a single sink node, the sensors close to this sink would get heavily involved in packet relaying and consume their energy reserve rather quickly. At the time when a sensor node "S_1" close to the sink runs out of energy, data paths are re-established and a node "S_2" that is further from the sink than S_1 becomes the closet hop. Such a scenario increases the total transmission energy and shortens the node's lifetime. Basically, S_2 will consume more energy to reach the sink than S_1 and dies soon after. Such effect spreads outward and may leave the sink unreachable to many sensors. Fig. 2 illustrates this problem.

The scenario described above is definitely damaging to the application and would cause the network to prematurely partition despite the availability of numerous sensors. This paper investigates means to counter the effect of accelerated energy consumption around the sink node and ensure a longer lifespan for sensors close to the sink node. The problem will be referred to thereafter as having void area around the sink. The proposed approach exploits the mobility of the gateway node. Basically the void problem is caused by the involvement of the neighbors of the gateway in data relaying at all time. Thus, if the gateway location continually changes, it always has new neighbors and the traffic forwarding load will be spread. The main question is what the travel path that the gateway should follow.

Mobility has become a hot research topic in WSN recently. In some of the considered network models, the sink moves around the deployment region and collects data from the sensor nodes. For example, in [5], mobile "Mules" are used as forwarding agents. Another protocol, called SEAD, has been introduced in [6] where access points are defined for the mobile sink to collect the data. In these approaches the sink node moves randomly in the deployment area without a known travel path. In fact, these approaches are geared for handling the sink motion rather than employing

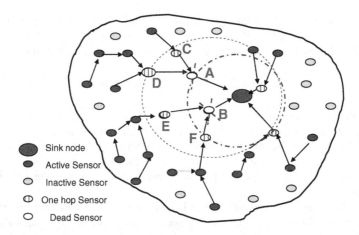

Fig. 2. Sensors close to the sink (inner circle) act as a relay for data sources upstream and deplete their energy at a high rate. Nodes A and B eventually exhaust their batteries and fail, forcing nodes C, D, E and F to become the closest hops to the sink node and to consume their energy at rate higher than before A and B fail given the increased distance. This problem spreads outward quickly creating a void around the sink.

such mobility to enhance the network performance. Unlike such work, this paper promotes mobility as a solution to the void around the sink problem. A novel Density-based Touring Strategy (DTS) is proposed where the sink node is programmed to travel through areas that are highly populated with sensors in order to enhance the performance.

This paper is organized as follows. The next section discusses the related work. The DTS approach is described in section 3. Section 4 describes the simulation setup and the performance results. Finally, the paper is concluded in Section 5.

2 Related Work

The wide variation in the node lifetime across the network has been noted by quite a number of studies [7-8]. The suggested solutions in the literature for tackling this issue can be categorized as precautionary or reactive. Precautionary schemes hope to prevent the problem from happening and often pursue non-uniform node deployment [8-9] and careful topology setup [10-12]. Reactive schemes, as the name indicates, respond to the fact that many sensors die in a particular region. The most notable reactive scheme is the relocation of nodes [13].

Node-placement based solutions strive to increase the sensor population close to the sink in order to ensure the availability of spares. These spares will naturally replace faulty nodes and thus sustain the network connectivity. Ishizuka and Aida [9] have investigated random node distribution functions, trying to capture the fault-tolerant properties of stochastic placement. They have compared three deployment patterns: simple diffusion (2-dimensional normal distribution), uniform, and R-random, where the nodes are uniformly scattered with respect to the radial and angular directions from the sink. The R-random node distribution pattern resembles the effect of an exploded shell and obeys the following probability density function for sensor positions in polar coordinates within a distance R from the sink:

$$f(r,\theta) = \frac{1}{2\pi R}, 0 \le r \le R, 0 \le \theta < 2\pi$$

The simulation results have shown that the R-random deployment is a better placement strategy in terms of fault-tolerance. A similar study has been conducted by Xu et al. [8], where a weighted random node distribution is proposed to account for the variation in energy consumption rate among the nodes. It is worth noting that neither [8] nor [9] has suggested practical means for implementing the proposed distribution.

On the other hand, some have tried to balance the energy consumption among the nodes using careful setup of the routing tree. For example in [10] the node's load, measured by average queue size, is factored in during the route selection. Shah et al. [11] have proposed an occasional use of sub-optimal paths in order to balance the load on nodes and increase their lifetime. Data routes are chosen by means of a probability function, which depends on the energy consumption on the possible paths. Meanwhile, in [12] the energy reserve at the individual nodes is considered in the route selection. However, these techniques cannot prevent the potential of the void around the sink problem since they still involve the sensors around the sink as relays all the time.

The work on sink node relocation [13] is one of the most notable efforts for dealing with the void around the sink problem. The main idea is to move the sink towards the sources of highest traffic. The performance of DTS is compared to this approach in Section 4. A similar idea is explored by Basagni et al. [14], where the sink makes a greedy move to neighboring areas whose sensors collectively have a higher residual energy. Another very recent work on countering the void around the sink problem is reported in [15]. Basically, a number of strategies for node deployment are studied. The main idea is place additional nodes, mainly sensors and gateways, in selected areas in order to prevent overloading some of the existing sensor nodes and to boost their lifetime. It is argued that a deterministic node placement is not feasible in many unattended WSN applications and it may be infeasible to apply such a solution. Nonetheless, the effectiveness of DTS is compared to these approaches through simulation is Section 4.

Employing a mobile sink has been pursued in a number of publications as a means for optimizing the performance of the WSN. Coverage and network longevity are the most popular objectives of the motion. Given the focus of this paper on the void around the sink problem, only work that targets the network lifetime is considered. The proposed approaches in the literature can be categorized based on the travel path into random, predictable and controlled, based on the network state as topology dependent and topology independent, and based on the data collection strategy into employing access points or pursuing direct interaction with sensor nodes. A random travel often fits the category of topology independent schemes and usually yield little benefits relative to the incurred overhead [16, 17]. A way to counter the excessive topology management overhead is to pursue predictable mobility solutions [18-20] where the sink travel path is fixed at the time of network setup. However, this is still topology independent and does not adapt to changes in the network state.

Controlled motion is seen by the research community as the better scheme since the travel path is predictable and the changes in the data dissemination tree due to the sink mobility are deterministic. In addition, the tour can be set based on the network state and the current topology, which makes it feasible to gear the sink motion for maximizing the performance. DTS fits in this category. The two most notable controlled mobility schemes are reported in [21] and [22]. Actually, the approach of [21] resembles those that pursue predictable sink motion. The difference is that the travel path is picked based on the network periphery. The use of network clustering and designating cluster heads are the base for defining the travel path of the sink node in [22]. Cluster heads act as a data storage depot that gets emptied when visited by the sink. In other words, the sink moves from one cluster head to the next and so on. Clearly this approach is mostly influenced by the criteria for clustering and setting intra-cluster data routes. One would argue that the approach in essence leaves the solution of the void around the sink problem to the clustering algorithm to address rather handling it through cleaver selection of the sink travel path.

3 Sink Mobility Strategy

As discussed earlier, the sensors close to the sink node tends to deplete their energy at a high rate and sometimes become traffic bottlenecks. This section describes how a controlled mobility of the sink node can be employed as a means to counter this problem. An algorithm for defining the travel path is presented and its effectiveness in extending the network lifetime is analyzed.

3.1 Design Issues

The essence of employing the sink mobility to counter the potential of the void around the sink problem is to spread the traffic load and prevent relaying bottlenecks from forming. In other words, the sink virtually extends its set of neighboring sensors by being at many spots. There are three major questions that are to be addressed:

1. What travel path to take: This is an intuitive question given the goal of the sink motion. One way to tackle this question is to identify a set of positions that the sink is to visit on a tour. It has been shown that optimal positioning of the sink can be mapped to the 1-center problem, which is NP-hard [23]. Basically, having an infinite solution space complicates the problem. Thus, heuristics ought to be pursued.

2. How fast the sink travels: Changing the sink position introduces two complications to the routing of data. First, the data may be ready while the sink is absent from the neighborhood. This may happen if the sink does not come back on time to the position that the sensors expect it to be at. The alternate option is for the data to follow the sink, which makes the establishment of the data paths unnecessarily complex and imposes significant control packets overhead that diminishes the optimization efforts the sink mobility is geared to achieve. The second complication is that data delivery may be late and the application may get

negatively impacted. Since the sink travel speed may be subject to some physical constraints, e.g., the capabilities of the motors on the sink, the travel path has to be carefully defined in order to cope with the data freshness constraints.

3. How to find the sink: When the position of the sink changes, the sensors may not know how to reach it. Thus, the sink either has to keep broadcasting where it is or the sink position has to be somewhat predictable. Continual update of the sink position makes the network topology too dynamic and unnecessarily complicates the data routing given that the sensors are stationary and the sink motion is to optimize the performance. Predictable sink availability at certain spots makes it easier to establish data routes. Basically, a sensor tries to set up a route to the closest spot that the sink is scheduled to visit.

4. How data is collected: There are potentially two options for the sink to receive the data. In the first some sensor nodes play the role of cluster heads or aggregation nodes. A local routing tree is formed to forward the data to the closest aggregation node. The sink will then harvest the data from aggregation nodes while it is coming within their communication ranges. In other words, the aggregation points act as data access points or data storage depots. This model is not preferred though since it may overload the aggregation nodes and shorten their lifetime. The second option, which is adapted by DTS as explained below, establishes a local routing tree based on a virtual gateway. The virtual gateway basically represents where the sink node will be when it is in the vicinity. Sensors forward their data towards the virtual gateway and the sink will receive the data from the neighbors of the virtual gateway when it comes to the area.

3.2 Density-Based Touring Strategy

The goal of DTS is to find the shortest and most effective travel path for the sink node. To counter the complexity of the sink placement problem discussed above, DTS identifies a set of positions to be visited. As the name indicates, the node density is a main factor considered by DTS for selecting the visited spots on the trip. The rationale is that highly populated areas will have ample routing resources and the relaying load will be split on multiple nodes. Such load sharing will extend the nodes lifetime, which is the objective of the sink mobility. In addition, passing close to nodes that transmit many packets most probably will yield good average delay and energy per packet, network throughput, and reliability [7, 13]. The travel path should actually be a tour after which the sink revisits previously travelled areas. Thus, sensors will wait for the sink to come back to deliver their data reports. Minimizing the travelled distance is important to lower the overhead incurred by the sink node and reduces the latency in data collection. A long tour will delay the sink arrival and affect the freshness of the sensor data and may cause it to miss some important data samples.

Since there are an infinite number of possible paths to be considered, the deployment area is partitioned into a two-dimensional grid of size $m \times n$. In theory the entire deployment area can be a search space. However, in practice it may be desirable to limit the travel distance and to prevent the sink from going too far while moving in order to shorten its tour. The boundary of the allowed travel area can be stretched to enable more flexibility by expanding the search space, especially if the void problem does exist in the network. The size of the cell is a design parameter which can be determined based on sensor's radio range. Sufficiently small cells make it possible for a sensor node to reach the sink when it visits its cell. In addition, appropriate selection of the cell sizes enable nodes in neighboring cells to reach each other and thus a node can pursues few hops to forward its data to the sink while passing a neighbor cell.

The cells in the grid serve as steps on the sink's travel path. In order to set up the path, first the most populated cells are picked. DTS then models the grid as a directed graph G. Each cell c is represented as a node in G. The problem now becomes finding a route that traverse the set of nodes P that corresponds to the picked cells. Two options can be identified. The first option is simply to use the distance between the centers of the cells as link costs on G and then find the minimal spanning tree for the sub-graph involving only the nodes in P. In the second option, DTS estimates a cost factor for each cell c that is inversely proportional to the number the nodes located within the cell c (i.e., $w(c)=\alpha/|c|$). Each cell c_i is connected to all its nine adjacent cells with inbound edges that have a cost $w(c_i)$. Now, the path selection can be easily mapped to the problem of finding the minimal (a least cost) spanning tree (or a cycle) for the nodes in P. In addition to the difference in the link cost calculation, the second option introduces potentially more cells on the travel path and may lengthen the travel distance. As indicated, the sink will travel longer distance and incur overhead. Obviously, selecting the right option is subject to a trade-off.

The intuitive question is how high the sensor population in a cell is in order for the cell to be considered a candidate. One extreme is when all cells are to be visited, which corresponds to the minimum spanning tree or cycle for the entire graph. Obviously this case increases the data collection latency and the motion overhead given the length of the tour that the sink makes. The other extreme is when no cell is

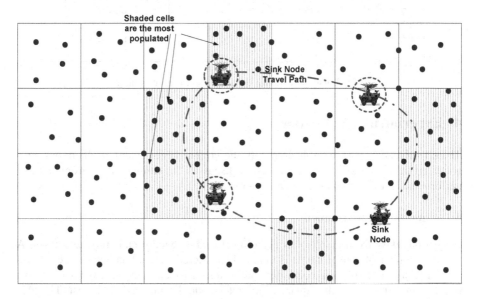

Fig. 3. The sink makes a tour that include the cells that are high populated with sensors

picked which corresponds to a stationary sink that does not move. A reasonable strategy is to set a threshold, i.e., to include the top $x\%$ of the cells in terms of the number of sensors in the cell. In Section 4 the effect of the threshold on the performance is studied through simulation. If a spanning tree is to be identified the sink may have to travel the tree from start to end and back. This may impact the freshness of the data for some sensors. For example, the first cell will be revisited after the sink visits all other cells on the travel path twice. A cycle will be a more appropriate choice. Fig. 3 illustrates the idea.

The DTS works as follows. First the cells that will be visited are identified based on the node population. A travel path is then selected according to the criterion for the inter-cell link cost in the graph representation of the grid. The nodes in the designated cells on the path set routes as if the sink is located at the center of the cell, i.e., by employing the virtual gateway model discussed in the previous section. Nodes in unvisited cells forward their data to the closest cell that is part of the sink tour. When the sink travels to go to the individual virtual gateway positions in the designated cells and receives the data. Fig. 4 shows a pseudo code summary of the DTS algorithm. It should be noted that the sink travel speed and the presence of data collection latency are not factored in this paper for simplicity of the presentation. The DTS algorithm can be easily extended to factor in data freshness constraints.

```
Algorithm Density-based sink touring (x)
 -   Map the deployment area into a grid based on the communication
     range of the individual sensors
 -   Sort the list of cells according to the number of sensors
 -   Identify the set P of the top x% in the sorted list
 -   Model the grid as a graph G and define the link costs
 -   Find the minimal spanning tree for the set P of nodes
 -   Set routes to the closest cell on the tour
 -   Move the sink on the links of the minimum spanning tree
 End;
```

Fig. 4. Pseudo code for the DTS algorithm for sink m

4 Experimental Validation

The effectiveness of DTS in dealing with the void around the sink problem has been validated through simulation. This section discusses the simulation environment and performance metrics and the experiments results.

4.1 Simulation Environment

A Java-based WSN simulator has been developed to handle numerous test cases. A varying number of sensor nodes is randomly scattered over a rectangular area. For a certain position of the sink node, data paths are set by applying Dijkstra's least cost routing algorithm using the square of the inter-node distance as a link cost. The idea of virtual gateways is used to associate sensors to a certain position of the sink on the tour. In that case, a sensor in a cell forwards its data to the closest cell to be visited by the sink. The simulator focuses only on the network layer and assumes collision free medium access.

Once the network has been created, events of interests, such as a rage of fires, are triggered at random spots in the area. The sink will then collect the data from those sensor nodes for which an event falls in their detection range. Sensors that cannot detect an event will not generate any packets. A simulation cycle denotes the time in which each sensor sending its data along the designated path until the data reaches the sink. Each time a packet is transmitted the energy consumed at the sender and receiver is tracked and the remaining battery life is adjusted. When a sensor completely depletes its onboard energy supply, it is considered dead, and the network topology is restructured.

4.2 Experiments Setup and Performance Metrics

In the experiments, the network consists of varying number of sensor nodes (50 to 500) that are randomly placed in a 100×100 m² area. The entire region is divided into cells. The size of the cell is varied to study its impact on the performance. Basically, the area is divided into 9, 16, 25, 36, 49, 64, 81 or 100 equal-sized cells. The mobile sink (gateway) travels through the cells based on the tour devised by the DTS algorithm. A free space propagation channel model is assumed [24]. A node is considered non-functional if its energy gets completely depleted. The maximum transmission and sensing ranges of a sensor node are assumed to be 10m and 20m, respectively. The radio range of the mobile gateway is 100m. All the sensors that can detect an event generate packets at the rate of 1 packet per simulation cycle. Each data packet has an energy field which is updated whenever transmission and reception of a packet takes place. The model of [25] is used for calculating the transmission and reception energy cost.

Simulation experiments have been conducted for different network sizes, grid configurations and selection criteria for the cells to be visited on the sink tour. It should be noted that varying the number of nodes while fixing the radio range and dimensions of the deployment area would capture the effect of the node density and yield topologies with different connectivity characteristics. Each experiment considers a new randomly generated network topology. When comparing to other approaches, each generated topology has been replicated to measure the performance under different parameters. Unless stated otherwise, the sink pursues the shortest travel path between the selected cells. The following metrics are used to assess the performance of DTS:

- *Average energy per packet:* This metric represents the average energy consumed until delivering a data packet to the sink node.
- *Average lifetime of a node:* This metric gives a good measure of the network lifetime by averaging the time a node stay functional.

4.3 Experimental Results

This section presents some of the obtained performance measurements. The results are grouped based on the parameter that is varied. A comparative assessment relative to prior approaches for countering the void around the sink problem is provided at the

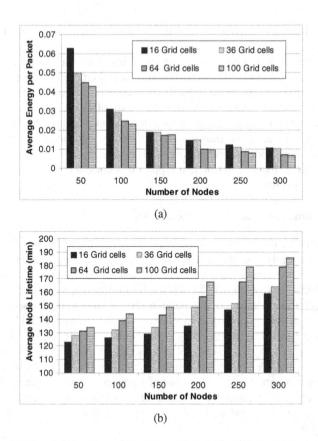

(a)

(b)

Fig. 5. The scalability of the performance gains achieved through the DTS approach and how the cell size influence it

tail of the section. The result of each experiment is the average of five executions. It has been observed that with 90% confidence level, the simulation results stay within 6%-10% of the sample mean.

Effect of the network size: Fig. 5 shows the performance of DTS as a function of the network size and the number of cells in the grid. The results show that the gains achieved through DTS scale very well for large networks. However, the gain appears to saturate for large networks given the increase in node density, which ensures the availability of sufficient routing resources in the network and makes the role of the sink mobility less important. The performance will be compared to other optimization strategies and to the case of stationary sink later in this section.

Fig 5 also indicates that the resolution of the grid, controlled by changing the number of cells, plays a role in the performance. When the cell size is large, i.e., having fewer cells, the performance of DTS is worse than using smaller cells. This is expected since it will be possible to identify the dense areas in the network with a higher resolution. This point will be elaborated in the next.

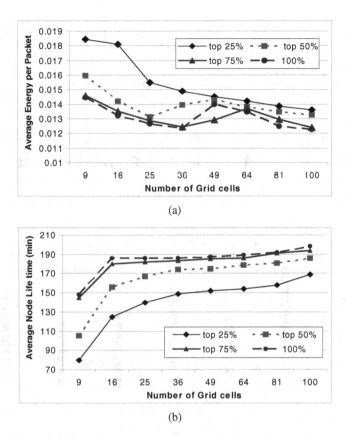

(a)

(b)

Fig. 6. The effect of the cell size and the density threshold for selecting the cells on the sink tour on the achieved performance

Effect of grid related parameters: This set of experiments validates how DTS is affected by the size of the cell and the number of selected cells to be on the sink travel path. The cell size is controlled by changing the number of cells in the grid. Basically, the experiments have considered slicing the grid into 9, 16, 25, ..., 100 cells. In addition, the number of cells considered when setting the sink travel path has been varied. Recall, the DTS sort the cells based on the node density and picks the top $x\%$ of the list. The considered values of x are 25, 50, 75 and 100, which set the threshold for how high the density of a cell in order to be picked. Obviously, selecting 100% of the cells implies touring the entire network and is considered as an extreme case. In these experiments 200 nodes are deployed in the network and the communication range is assumed to be 20m. The simulation results are shown in Fig. 6.

The results indicate that the cell size is an influential parameter. Slicing the grid into few cells does not allow DTS to pinpoint the areas that need attention. The increase in the number of grid cells enables a fine grained analysis and a more accurate identification of highly populated spots that are worthy to be visited by the sink. Nonetheless, increasing the resolution too much does not help. For example,

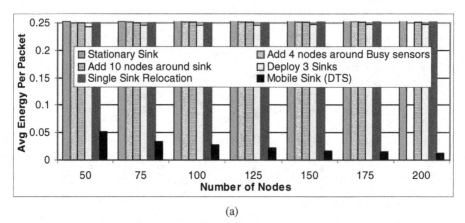

(a)

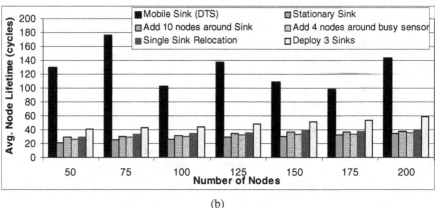

(b)

Fig. 7. When compared to other strategies for countering the void around the sink problem, the effectiveness of DTS is very distinct and its performance significantly dominates them

having 81 cells does not add much gain in performance compared to 49 cells. The performance graphs indicates that for a uniform distribution of nodes having a cell size that equals 2/3 the communication range seems to be a good choice. On the other hand, touring all cells indeed delivers the best performance. However, as discussed earlier, this choice maximizes the overhead incurred by the sink and increases the data latency. Actually, touring 75% of the cells yields a performance that is very close to that of touring all cells. The graphs indicate that selecting 50% of the cells is a very reasonable choice.

Comparison to other solution strategies: To assess the effectiveness of the sink mobility as a solution to the void around the sink problem relative to other solution strategies, the performance of DTS has been compared to the selective node deployment schemes proposed in [15] and the sink relocation approach of [13]. The comparison is based on the two metrics studied above, namely, the Average Energy per packet and the average lifetime of a node. The stationary sink results are used as a baseline. The sensor's communication range has been set to 10m. For DTS the grid is divided into 64 cells and the top 25% of the highly populated cells are visited on the sink tour. The travel path is formed by mapping the grid to a graph with the link costs defined based on the node population, as explained in Section 3. Thus effectively, the sink will visit additional cells during its tour.

The results are shown in Fig. 7. The results demonstrate the significant performance advantage achieved through DTS. Relative to the baseline case, the average energy per packet consumption has been reduced from 0.25 to 0.05, a gain of 400%. In fact, the contribution of the other strategies seems very marginal relative to DTS. The average lifetime of a node is more than doubled in most experiments. It should be noted that the variability in the average node lifetime in this experiments relative to the size of the network is due to the way that path is set compared to the earlier experiments, i.e. the use of a density-base rather than distance-based link cost.

5 Conclusion

This paper has investigated the use of mobile gateway to counter the problem of uneven energy consumption in wireless sensor networks. Basically, the gateway acts a sink for all traffic and their neighboring nodes tend to forward the most packets and thus deplete their energy rather quickly. By moving the sink, the set of neighboring nodes will change and the load is spread throughout the network. A novel approach is presented for defining an effective and efficient travel path for the sink. A density-based touring strategy (DTS) has been promoted for finding the spots that sink will pass to collect data. Each of these spots will be considered by the sensors in the vicinity to build a local routing tree.

The proposed DTS approach been validated through simulation. Two metrics have been pursued to assess the energy efficiency of the network; namely the average energy per packet and the average node lifetime. The simulation results have confirmed the effectiveness of DTS and its scalability for large networks. The experiments also have highlighted the effect of the various parameters on the performance and provided guidelines for the best configuration. The DTS approach is further compared to other strategies for countering the void around the sink problem, namely deploying additional nodes in selected areas and the relocation of the sink when deemed necessary. The comparison has demonstrated the distinction of DTS as a solution and the effectiveness of the sink mobility as a solution if the motion capabilities and overhead can be supported in the network design.

Acknowledgments. This work is supported by the National Science Foundation, contract # 0000002270.

References

1. Akyildiz, I.F., Su, W., Sankarasubramaniam, Y., Cayirci, E.: Wireless sensor networks: a survey. Computer Networks 38, 393–422 (2002)
2. Chong, C.-Y., Kumar, S.: Sensor networks: Evolution, opportunities, and challenges. Proceedings of the IEEE 91(8), 1247–1256 (2003)

3. Biagioni, E., Bridges, K.: The Application of Remote Sensor Technology to Assist the Recovery of Rare and Endangered Species. The International Journal of High Performance Computing Applications, Special issue on Distributed Sensor Networks 16(3), 112–121 (2002)
4. Wireless Network uses "Smart Dust" Technology, Science Applications International Corporation Magazine (Winter 2004/2005), http://www.saic.com/news/saicmag/2005-winter/wireless.html
5. Shah, R.C., Roy, S., Jain, S., Brunette, W.: Data MULEs: Modeling a Three-tier Architecture for Sparse Sensor Networks. In: First IEEE International Workshop on Sensor Network Protocols and Applications (SNPA 2003), pp. 30–41. IEEE Press, New York (2003)
6. Kim, H.S., Abdelzaher, T.F., Kwon, W.H.: Minimum Energy Asynchronous Dissemination to Mobile Sinks in Wireless Sensor Networks. In: First International Conference on Embedded Networked Sensor Systems (SenSys 2003), pp. 193–204. IEEE Press, New York (2003)
7. Akkaya, K., Younis, M.: A Survey on Routing Protocols for Wireless Sensor Networks. Journal of Ad Hoc Networks 3(3), 325–349 (2005)
8. Xu, K., Hassanein, H., Takahara, G., Wang, W.: Relay Node Deployment Strategies in Heterogeneous Wireless Sensor Networks: Single-hop Communication Case. In: IEEE Global Telecommunication Conference (GLOBECOM 2005). IEEE Press, New York (2005)
9. Ishizuka, M., Aida, M.: Performance Study of Node Placement in Sensor Networks. In: 24th International Conference on Distributed Computing Systems Workshops - W7: EC (Icdcsw 2004), vol. 7. IEEE Computer Society, Washington (2004)
10. Younis, M., Youssef, M., Arisha, K.: Energy-Aware management in Cluster-Based Sensor Networks. Computer Networks 43(5), 649–668 (2003)
11. Shah, R., Rabaey, J.: Energy Aware Routing for Low Energy Ad Hoc Sensor Networks. In: IEEE Wireless Communications and Networking Conference (WCNC 2002). IEEE Press, New York (2002)
12. Ma, C., Yang, Y.: Battery-aware Routing for Streaming Data Transmissions in Wireless Sensor Networks. Mobile Networks and Applications 11(5), 757–767 (2006)
13. Akkaya, K., Younis, M., Bangad, M.: Sink Repositioning for Enhanced Performance in Wireless Sensor Networks. Computer Networks 49, 434–512 (2005)
14. Basagni, S., Carosi, A., Melachrinoudis, E., Petrioli, C., Wang, Z.M.: Protocols and Model for Sink Mobility in Wireless Sensor Networks. SIGMOBILE Mobile Computer Communications Reviews 10(4), 28–30 (2006)
15. Younis, M., Pan, Q.: On Handling Weakened Topologies of Wireless Sensor Networks. In: 8th IEEE International Workshop on Wireless Local Networks (WLN 2008). IEEE Press, New York (2008)
16. Chatzigiannakis, I., Kinalis, A., Nikoletseas, S.: Sink Mobility Protocols for Data Collection in Wireless Sensor Networks. In: 4th ACM International Workshop on Mobility Management and Wireless Access (MobiWac 2006), pp. 52–59. ACM, New York (2006)
17. Wang, Z.M., Basagni, S., Melachrinoudis, E., Petrioli, C.: Exploiting Sink Mobility for Maximizing Sensor Networks Lifetime. In: 38th Annual Hawaii international Conference on System Sciences (HICSS 2005) - Track 9, vol. 9. IEEE Computer Society, Washington (2005)
18. Luo, J., Hubaux, J.-P.: Joint mobility and routing for lifetime elongation in wireless sensor networks. In: IEEE INFOCOM 2005. IEEE Press, New York (2005)

19. Gandham, S.R., Dawande, M., Prakash, R., Venkatesan, S.: Energy Efficient Schemes for Wireless Sensor Networks with Multiple Mobile Base Stations. In: IEEE GLOBECOM, pp. 377–381. IEEE Press, New York (2003)
20. Chakrabarti, A., Sabharwal, A., Aazhang, B.: Using predictable Observer Mobility for Power Efficient Design of Sensor Networks. In: Zhao, F., Guibas, L.J. (eds.) IPSN 2003. LNCS, vol. 2634, pp. 129–145. Springer, Heidelberg (2003)
21. Shi, G., Liao, M., Ma, M., Shu, Y.: Exploiting Sink Movement for Energy-Efficient Load-Balancing in Wireless Sensor Networks. In: 1st ACM international Workshop on Foundations of Wireless Ad Hoc and Sensor Networking and Computing (FOWANC 2008), pp. 39–44. ACM, New York (2008)
22. Somasundara, A., et al.: Controllably Mobile Infrastructure for Low Energy Embedded Networks. IEEE Transactions on Mobile Computing 8(8), 958–972 (2006)
23. Kariv, O., Hakimi, S.L.: An Algorithmic Approach to Network Location Problems. I: The p-Centers. SIAM Journal of Applied Mathematics 37(3), 513–538 (1979)
24. Andresen, J.B., et al.: Propagation Measurements and Models for Wireless Communications Channels. IEEE Communications Magazine 33(1), 42–49 (1995)
25. Bhardwaj, M., Garnett, T., Chandrakasan, A.: Upper Bounds on the Lifetime of Sensor Networks. In: IEEE International Conference on Communications (ICC 2001). IEEE Press, New York (2001)

Avoiding Greediness in Cooperative Peer-to-Peer Networks

Matthias R. Brust[1], Carlos H.C. Ribeiro[1], and Jaruwan Mesit[2]

[1] Technological Institute of Aeronautics
Computer Science Division
50, Praça Mal. Eduardo Gomes, 12228-900 Sao Jose dos Campos, Brazil
{matthias.brust,carlos.ribeiro}@ita.br
[2] University of Central Florida
4000 Central Florida Blvd. Orlando, Florida, 32816, USA
jmesit@cs.ucf.edu

Abstract. In peer-to-peer networks, peers simultaneously play the role of client and server. Since the introduction of the first file-sharing protocols, peer-to-peer networking currently causes more than 35% of all internet network traffic—with an ever increasing tendency. A common file-sharing protocol that occupies most of the peer-to-peer traffic is the BitTorrent protocol. Although based on cooperative principles, in practice it is doomed to fail if peers behave greedily. In this work-in-progress paper, we model the protocol by introducing the game named *Tit-for-Tat Network Termination* (T4TNT) that gives an interesting access to the greediness problem of the BitTorrent protocol. Simulations conducted under this model indicate that greediness can be reduced by solely manipulating the underlying peer-to-peer topology.

Keywords: Peer-to-Peer Networks, Topology Control, Cooperation.

1 Introduction

Peer-to-peer networking where the peers simultaneously play the role of client and server becomes more and more popular. In a peer-to-peer network the participants are peers of equal rights that offer and down content.

Since the introduction of the first file-sharing protocols peer-to-peer networking causes more than currently 35% of the overall network traffic with increasing tendency [1]. However, peer-to-peer approaches are not solely used for file-sharing, but also for VoIP, distributed data storage, video streaming, distributed collaboration, and etc. [2, 3].

A remarkable file-sharing protocol using most of the peer-to-peer traffic is the BitTorrent protocol even used by universities to distribute their lecture material [4]. For a file to download in the peer-to-peer mode, one needs the correspondent pointer file called .torrent file. This file contains information of the tracker that is aware of peers sharing the same file. The tracker directs the client on the host machine to this

E. Bertino and J.B.D. Joshi (Eds.): CollaborateCom 2008, LNICST 10, pp. 370–378, 2009.

peer and, generally speaking, manages the file-transfer process on a meta-level. In the BitTorrent protocol, the peer offering the original file ("seed") is called *seeder* and the peer downloading a file is referred as *leecher*. The set of seeders and leechers of one common file are called the swarm of that file. In contrary to many other peer-to-peer file-sharing protocols, the BitTorrent protocol protrudes in the fact to make incomplete downloads available for the swarm to download chunks of the file. This turns the file-sharing process very efficient—in particular for extremely large files— since peers do not have to wait for other peers to finish, before starting to download.

BitTorrent is—as usually any peer-to-peer network—fundamentally based on cooperative behavior and it assumes that leechers turn to be seeders for a file after they have downloaded the file. Although both leechers and seeders are sharing chunks available on their host, seeders still remain most important in the BitTorrent networks because seeders have 100% (all chunks) of a file.

The worst case scenario for the BitTorrent protocol is that leechers leave the network immediately after downloading a file; they simple stop sharing this file. This causes that the remaining peers cannot find missing chunks anymore within the swarm and fragments of incomplete files are left back. This selfish behavior results in successive starvation of the peers, and the swarm dies out. Although based on cooperative principles, in practice the protocol is, thus, failed to doom if peers become greedy. This problem is also known as "the leecher problem".

In order to reduce selfish or greedy behavior, additional mechanisms on the information-flow (network) layer have been suggested and implemented. One strategy, for example, uses the tit-for-tat algorithm that forces cooperation. Hereby, a ratio between the downloaded and uploaded amount of data is calculated and, depending if the ratio is close to one or not, the peer gets preferences by the tracker for downloading with e.g. higher bandwidth.

Summarizing, even considering that the peers maintain a ratio close to one, i.e. the amount of data that has been downloaded is equal to the amount of data that has been uploaded, peers of the swarm can suffer from the problem of starvation and, hence, the dying out of the whole swarm.

The contribution of this work-in-progress paper is to describe a basic mechanism, named T4TNT game (*Tit-for-Tat Network Termination*) which is used to understand the problem of starvation of the swarm, and finally the leecher problem. Based on results from the T4TNT game, we conclude that a crucial impact on the reduction of greedy behavior can be realized by not only providing mechanisms on the information-flow layer, but also on the topology control layer.

Although strongly motivated by the leecher problem caused by the BitTorrent protocol, results of this and future work are not only limited to this field. We see application areas of our research in game theory, social networks, complex networks, and cryptology.

The following section describes the T4TNT game which exhibits some interesting research questions that can partially be reduced to the leecher problem. Section 3 describes the study on the analytical as well as empirical nature of the T4TNT game and relates these to the BitTorrent. Finally, the last section discusses the results and the future work.

2 The T4TNT Game

Given is an undirected network $Net = (N, L)$ with a set of nodes N of size n. The set of links L connects each node with each other, resulting in a clique (later on we change this assumption). Nodes are also referred as participants. We assume that each participant owns a unique chunk item, i.e. nobody else has this item initially. The overall objective of each node is to collect all chunk items which are available in the network to complete e.g. a file or task.

The exchanging of chunks is only permitted in a peer-to-peer mode if both participants are able to exchange interesting chunks to the other. The strategy applied is the tit-for-tat principle where nodes are allowed to exchange also received chunks.

As an additional constraint, if a node terminates, it will immediately leave the network and is not able to exchange any chunk anymore (greedy behavior). This configuration is called the T4TNT game (for *Tit-for-Tat Network Termination*).

2.1 Problem Definition

The constructed scenario creates interesting questions and problem situations. As shown in Fig. 1, consider the case where the number of nodes is $n = 3$. These are some ways of how the nodes can exchange the chunks, but in the end all nodes necessarily reach the terminal state, i.e. each node has all the information available in this network.

The case with n = 4 reveals a more complex nature of the problem (cf. Fig. 1). Not all combinations of steps lead stringently to a final state with all nodes have got all information.

The table in Fig. 1 describes a sequence of steps for the network configuration with n = 4 where finally node B and node C terminate while node A and D do not reach the

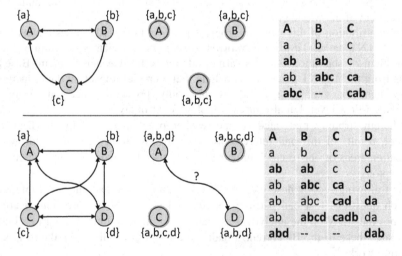

Fig. 1. Network with 3 nodes playing the T4TNT game (above) always terminates. A network with 4 nodes reveals situations where not all nodes are able to terminate.

terminal state. However, the situation is starved because of the remaining nodes A and D cannot exchange additional chunks anymore based on the constraints given before. Thus, the remaining swarm dies out. The questions appearing in context of this example are: How many permutations of all steps lead to a final state where all nodes terminate (for n = 4, 5, 6, ...)? It seems that the final state depends on the topology. Are there topologies that support the concurrent termination of all nodes more effectively than other topologies? How to construct such topologies?

In particular, the last question introduces the area of topology control (TC) in peer-to-peer networking. Topology control is the science of manipulating a topology in order to optimize it according to a certain [5].

2.2 Reducing the T4TNT Game to the Leecher Problem

The mapping from the T4TNT to the BitTorrent peer-to-peer networking is done when interpreting that the network in T4TNT is the swarm in the BitTorrent network. However, there are some differences that do not enter our model (the T4TNT game) so far.

As mentioned in the introduction, the BitTorrent protocol tries to tackle the leecher problem by introducing additional constraints on the network layer. The T4TNT only allows changes on the underlying topology.

The BitTorrent protocol gives the client the option to choose the order of how to download the missing chunks. A default policy is to use random order where as an improved policy is to download pieces in rarest first order. Usually, the client is able to determine this. The described version of T4TNT does not use additional information about the exchanging order of chunks.

Additionally, there are some very specific issues in the BitTorrent protocol. For example, when a download is almost complete, there is a tendency for the last few chunks to trickle in slowly. To speed this up, the client can send requests for all of its missing chunks to all of its peers [6]. The T4TNT game does not use this or similar kind of "end games".

3 Study

In the following study we analyze the behavior of the T4TNT game on different network topologies in particular clique graphs, geometric random graphs and random networks (see Fig. 2).

In the first experiment we run the T4TNT game on a clique graph for different number of nodes as shown in Table 1. The measure *Terminations* means the percent of nodes that reach the termination state, i.e. collecting all chunks. The measure *Exchanges* informs of how many tit-for-tats, i.e. transitions, of all possible transitions have to be completed (in a clique network with n nodes there are exactly $n(n-1)/2$ if all nodes reach the termination state). Both measures are in percentage. All simulations have to done with 10000 simulation results. The data given in Tables 1, 2, and 3 are the average values.

Table 1 shows the probability that all nodes terminate in a game with four nodes is about 81%. In other words, about 81% of all possible transition sequences terminate.

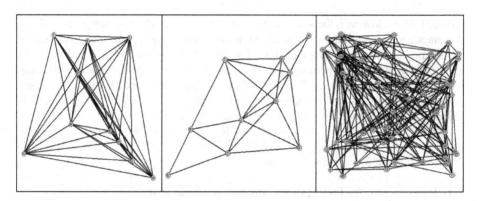

Fig. 2. Clique, geometric random graph and random network

Table 1. Clique networks

	n=4	n=5	n=6	n=10	n=15	n=25
Terminations [%]	81.3	54.6	35.5	16.1	11.9	11.9
Exchanges [%]	97.7	95.9	95.1	95.9	97.5	99.0

(In case of $n = 4$, this are exactly 720 sequences that terminate.) Interestingly, this number is decreasing by increasing the number of nodes while the total number of exchanges is always more than 95%.

In the second experiment we run the T4TNT game on a clique graph with $n = 10$ and a geometric random graph for $n = 10$ (see Table 2). The geometric random graph model is often used in order to model wireless ad hoc or sensor networks [7, 8]. The results show that a typical wireless ad hoc network builds an inappropriate topology for peer-to-peer networking, compared to the clique network.

Table 2. A clique network compared with a geometric random graph

	Clique n=10	GRG n=10
Terminations [%]	16.1	0.1
Exchanges [%]	95.9	63.1

In a next step, we try to estimate if the resources of the network—in particular the links—are used in an efficient manner or if it is possible to obtain similar results by using fewer resources. For this purpose, we introduce the clustering coefficient as local measurement of the clustering of neighbors. The formal definition is given below.

Definition (Local Clustering Coefficient). The *local clustering coefficient CC* of one node v with k_v neighbors is

$$CC_v = \frac{|E(\Gamma_v)|}{\binom{k_v}{2}} \tag{1}$$

where $|E(\Gamma_v)|$ is the number of links in the neighborhood of v and $\binom{k_v}{2}$ is the number of all possible links.

The clustering coefficient CC then is the average local clustering coefficient for all nodes [9]. Many classes of regular networks e.g. square grid networks or the restricted class of circular networks studied in [10] have a high clustering coefficient, i.e. nodes have many mutual neighbors. The opposite extreme to regular networks are random networks, which already have a small clustering coefficient.

However, as we show, the clustering coefficient of a random network can even be more reduced. This corresponds to the fact that randomly appearing groups or cluster have to be deliberately destroyed.

For this purpose, the declustering algorithm "*DeClust*" has been designed and implemented.

DeClust provides a generic approach to implement this general idea of minimizing the clustering coefficient. The basic idea of the algorithm is to verify if a link (u, v) is efficient in terms of the clustering coefficient. In that case, removing the link (u, v) is taken into consideration (lines 3-8). It is not removed immediately because removing might be advantageous for that particular node only. However, since a link removing affects the local clustering coefficients of the 2-hop neighborhood of the set $\{u, v\}$ an additional remove-confirmation phase will be performed (line 11).

In the confirmation phase, nodes exchange the remove-candidate with that corresponding neighbor. For example, if node v calculates that link (v, u) is a remove-candidate, it sends this result to node u. In case that node u has calculated the link (v, u) as remove-candidate as well, the final phase is executed; otherwise the link (v, u) is not removed.

This optimization is justified by the fact that removing a 1-hop link causes a considerably higher impact on the local CC-value than removing a 2-hop link [11]. Since a link removal affects the CC-values of the 2-hop neighborhood of nodes $\{u, v\}$, the final phase calculates the 2-hop neighborhood of $\{u, v\}$. Both the current CC-values of the 2-hop neighborhood as well as the value after a hypothetical removal of (v, u) are calculated. Based on a comparison of those values, it is finally decided whether to remove the link (v, u) (lines 12-18).

As additional criterion, connectivity is guaranteed by line 16 in the pseudo code where removing (u, v) requires that at least one neighbor of u is connected to one neighbor of v.

Furthermore, note that 2-hop synchronization is required before finally removing a link (cf. line 17-18), since 2-hop topological information is required in order to plan the action. Then again, this local link removal affects the 2-hop neighbors. The synchronization procedure is not detailed here.

Algorithm. DeClust (for node v)	

Input:	N: Initial set of neighbor nodes
	$N2$: Neighbors of $u \in N$ (to calc CC)
	RC: Set of remove candidates
Output:	$N_{DeClust}$: Resulting neighbor nodes

01:	$CC(v) \leftarrow |E(\Gamma_v)|/\binom{k_v}{2}$
02:	$RC(v) \leftarrow \emptyset$
03:	**for each** $u \in N$ **do**
04:	$N(v) \leftarrow N(v) \setminus \{u\}$
05:	$CC_{rc}(v) \leftarrow |E(\Gamma_v)|/\binom{k_v}{2}$
06:	**if** $CC_{rc}(v) < CC(v)$ **then**
07:	$RC(v) \leftarrow RC(v) \cup \{u\}$
08:	$N(v) \leftarrow N(v) \cup \{u\}$
09:	$sendRC(v, RC(v))$
10:	$receiveRC(u, RC(u))$
11:	**for each** $w \in (RC(v) \cap RC(u))$ **do**
12:	$CC(uv) \leftarrow \sum_{x \in (N(v) \cup N(u))} CC(x)$
13:	$N(v) \leftarrow N(v) \setminus \{w\}$
14:	$CC_{rc}(uv) \leftarrow \sum_{x \in (N(v) \cup N(u))} CC(x)$
15:	**if** $CC_{rc}(uv) < CC(uv)$ **then**
16:	**if** $N(v) \cap N(u) = \emptyset$ **then**
17:	**if** $permit(v) = $ true **then**
18:	$N(v) \leftarrow N(v) \cup \{w\}$
19:	$N_{DeClust}(u) \leftarrow N(v)$

Applying *DeClust* to a random network given by the number of nodes n and the average node degree k results in the following data given in Table 3.

Table 3. Network characteristics for topologies before and after applying *DeClust*

	n=50 k=5	n=100 k =5	n=50 k=10	n=100 k=10
Terminations before [%]	59.4	57.0	78.8	78.4
Terminations after [%]	54.2	52.4	77.8	74.8
Exchanges before [%]	90.1	90.2	96.8	97.0
Exchanges after [%]	89.3	89.5	97.0	97.0
CC before	0.47	0.45	0.34	0.18
CC after	0.16	0.15	0.12	0.04
k before	9.0	9.5	16.5	18.1
k after	6.8	7.6	11.4	12.5

Table 3 shows the number of terminations, transitions, clustering coefficient and the average node degree for different network configurations for before and after applying *DeClust*. The general conclusion is that for networks with low k *DeClust* reduces the number of termination of about 5% whereby networks with higher k suffer a reduction of between 1% and 4%. The number of transitions for all networks does not change significantly, what means that the information exchange has not been affected at all by *DeClust*. However, looking at the average node degree k, one can see that the *DeClust* networks need up to 30% link resources by having almost the same terminations result as the non-*DeClust* networks.

Saving such an amount of network resources results in the assumption that—if we can find an algorithm that smartly puts about 10% of the saved resources back again in the network—a topology-driven approach can lead to an increase of the number of terminations by using fewer resources.

4 Conclusions and Future Work

This work-in-progress paper introduces the T4TNT game which is used in order to model greedy or selfish behavior in a peer-to-peer network. We show that T4TNT can partially be reduced to the BitTorrent protocol. The BitTorrent protocol is founded upon cooperative concepts. But in practice, cooperation cannot be taken for granted. Thus, this peer-to-peer file sharing protocol suffers efficiency when peers leave the network after finishing their downloads.

We show with empiric studies on T4TNT what the nature of this problem is and propose to use topology control mechanisms in order to reduce the potential greediness factor in the overall system.

For demonstrating, this paper introduces the localized algorithm called *DeClust* which reduces the network resources used while maintaining the efficiency rate of node termination.

The main effect of *DeClust* is to de-cluster the randomized networks regarding to the clustering coefficient. However, *DeClust* can be applied to any other network as well. *DeClust* reduces the clustering coefficient by removing dedicated links, effecting in deliberately destroying groups or local clusters.

DeClust is able to save about 30% of links while maintaining the node termination rate. Saving such an amount of network resources results in the assumption that—if we can find an algorithm that smartly puts about 10% of the saved resources back again in the network—a topology-driven approach can lead to an increasing number of terminations by using considerably fewer resources.

In future works, we plan to extend *DeClust* with the ability to set the saved resources in a smart manner such that more nodes are able to terminate. Additionally, we plan to consider different network types, as small-world and scale-free networks. Furthermore, we think on trying to describe the T4TNT game by regular expressions and to consider the complexity of the problem.

References

1. Izal, M., Urvoy-Keller, G., Biersack, E.W., Felber, P.A., Hamra, A.A., Garces-Erice, L.: Dissecting BitTorrent: Five Months in a Torrent's Lifetime. LNCS, pp. 1–11 (2004)
2. Bharambe, A.R., Herley, C., Padmanabhan, V.N.: Analyzing and Improving a BitTorrent Network's Performance Mechanisms. In: Proceedings of IEEE INFOCOM (2006)

3. Liogkas, N., Nelson, R., Kohler, E., Zhang, L.: Exploiting bittorrent for fun (but not profit). In: Proc. 5th Itl. Workshop on Peer-to-Peer Systems, IPTPS (2006)
4. University, S.: Stanford Engineering Everywhere (2008)
5. Santi, P.: Topology Control in Wireless Ad Hoc and Sensor Networks. ACM Computing Surveys 37, 164–194 (2005)
6. Bharambe, A.R., Herley, C., Padmanabhan, V.N.: Analyzing and Improving BitTorrent Performance. Microsoft Research, Microsoft Corporation One Microsoft Way Redmond, WA 98052, 2005-2003 (2005)
7. Santi, P.: Topology Control in Wireless Ad Hoc and Sensor Networks. Wiley, Chichester (2005)
8. Penrose, M.: Random Geometric Graphs. Oxford University Press, Oxford (2003)
9. Watts, D.J.: Small Worlds - The Dynamics of Networks between Order and Randomness. Princeton University Press, Princeton (1999)
10. Watts, D.J., Strogatz, H.: Collective Dynamics of 'Small World' Networks. Nature 393, 440–442 (1998)
11. Calinescu, G.: Computing 2-Hop Neighborhoods in Ad Hoc Wireless Networks. In: Pierre, S., Barbeau, M., Kranakis, E. (eds.) ADHOC-NOW 2003. LNCS, vol. 2865, pp. 175–186. Springer, Heidelberg (2003)

The Data Interoperability Problem as an Exemplary Case Study in the Development of Software Collaboration Environments

Arturo J. Sánchez–Ruíz[1], Karthikeyan Umapathy[1], Jonathan Beckham[1], and Patrick Welsh[2]

[1] School of Computing
[2] Advanced Weather Information Systems Laboratory
University of North Florida,
1 UNF Drive,
Jacksonville, FL 32224
{asanchez,k.umapathy,jonathan.beckham,pwelsh}@unf.edu

Abstract. The Data Interoperability Problem appears in contexts where consumers need to peruse data owned by producers, and the syntax and/or semantics of such data—at both end points—are not already aligned. This is a very challenging problem whose instances can be found in practically every branch of human knowledge. In this paper we discuss the Data Interoperability Problem as an exemplary case study in the development of software collaboration environments. We define facets which prompt requirements that characterize the development of software systems as enablers of effective collaboration among data stakeholders, and also gauge the extent to which current technologies can be used to implement these software environments.

Keywords: software collaboration environments, aspects, variability axes, requirements, immersion, direct manipulation, second life.

1 Introduction

Consider the following fictitious problem inspired by a real–life scenario. Company 'X' manages human capital (i.e., workforce with different skill levels on a variety of fields) so it can offer services to many different clients on–demand. Each client has its own internal way of classifying human capital based on parameters such as field, education level, years of experience, and hourly rate, to mention just a few. How should 'X' consolidate all these different ways of representing what is essentially the same information across all its clients?

This is an instance of the Data Interoperability Problem, i.e., a collection of clients of 'X' produce data which 'X' needs to consume. However, such consumption cannot be seamlessly implemented because the data models used by 'X' to represent human capital information are not already aligned with those used by its clients.

E. Bertino and J.B.D. Joshi (Eds.): CollaborateCom 2008, LNICST 10, pp. 379–389, 2009.
© ICST Institute for Computer Sciences, Social-Informatics and Telecommunications Engineering 2009

In this paper we propose the Data Interoperability Problem can be considered as an exemplary case study in the development of software environments which enable data stakeholders to solve instances of this problem through collaboration.

Section 2 describes how we envision the collaboration among data stakeholders (i.e., producers and consumers) in order to characterize a model to be supported by software environments. Then, in Section 3, we identify facets associated with the development of software collaboration environments, namely: cross–cutting concerns, variability axes, and functional requirements.

In Section 4 we review various technologies which have the potential of either offering an exemplary perspective to the problem of developing these environments, or being used in their implementation. A comparison matrix, relating elicited requirements to technologies, is offered at the end of this section along with our comments on findings implied by this comparison.

The paper concludes with a discussion of additional related work (cf. Section 5), and our conclusions (cf. Section 6) which include a report of the current status of a project which has motivated us to participate in this workshop with the goal of interchanging points of view with other researchers in the area of collaboration.

2   Our Collaboration Metaphor

The following generic scenario is used to describe our Collaboration Metaphor (CM), i.e., our vision of how data consumers and producers interact with the goal of solving instances of the Data Interoperability Problem, via—what we refer to as—a 'just–in–time' approach.

CM1. Producers explain to consumers the nature of the data they own, including its syntactic structure and intended semantics. Visual representations of the producer's data are used to articulate explanations communicated to the consumer.

CM2. Producers and consumers engage in a question/answer dialog which ends when consumers express they have understood how to peruse the data.

CM3. Using the knowledge acquired from the previous step, consumers manipulate the data to satisfy their interoperability requirements.

This scenario is meant to be a general characterization of how humans approach the problem, not of how collaboration software is to behave. Our intention is to highlight the one–to–many relationship between the former (human approach) and the latter (software system) which is conceived of as an enabler tool. We do not mean to imply the described scenario shows the only—or more important—way humans approach the Data Interoperability Problem. However, we do claim this scenario is very relevant and common.

Consider the following real instance of the Data Interoperability Problem which deals with meteorological data, used to illustrate our metaphor. Given Global Positioning System Integrated Precipitable Water Vapor data (GPS–IPWV), which is typically produced in half–hour intervals, correct it for ambient temperature and pressure in the vicinity of the master station for maximum accuracy. For **CM1**, the producer can explain to the consumer the structure and meaning of data stored (for instance) as a spreadsheet file. This can be accomplished by visualizing the data as a bidimensional array with appropriate labels for rows and columns. If the consumer is trained in meteorology, one would expect the loop in **CM2** to have a short duration. For **CM3**, the consumer uses his/her newly acquired understanding to determine what transformations must be applied to obtain the desired correction. At this point, the consumer might need the services of a software developer to actually implement the task at hand.

3   Facets Associated with the Development of Software Collaboration Environments

Using a problem/solution parlance, Section 2 characterizes the problem. In this section we offer various facets which characterize solutions.

3.1   Cross–Cutting Concerns

A design concern, i.e., an issue of high relevance in the context of the software system under development, is said to be cross–cutting if it affects several layers of this system. We are using the term 'cross–cutting' in the sense presented by Kiczales et alia [10], and the term 'concern' in the sense presented by Hilliard [19]. We have identified the following cross–cutting concerns (CC).

CC1. Target is End–User: This implies empowering users with software tools which allow them to effectively build solutions to their problems without demanding from them skills other than those naturally associated with their domain of expertise, and basic computing literacy. The September 2004 issue of Commnications of the ACM discusses various examples of this approach [1]. A related perspective is that associated with the area of Domain–Specific Software Development, which postulates end–users must be equipped with abstractions that are germane to their domain of application in such a way that solutions can be articulated—by the users—through a language which specifically targets this domain (i.e., a Domain–Specific Language) [3,7].

CC2. Variabilities are organically addressed by the software architecture: Variabilities are defined by axes on which a software system can evolve in the direction of being more generic. For instance, if the software system is a component which searches for an element in a collection, examples of variability axes include: the type of the elements, the data structure used to implement the collection, and properties of the underlying order relation used to determine whether the given element is in the collection or not. Examples of approaches whose raison d'être is to deal with variabilities include Software Product Lines [11,14,18], and Generic Programming [9,12,15]. We say variabilities are organically addressed by a software system if they have been modeled as part of the design of this software system. Examples of practices which organically address variabilities include 'plugins', 'add–ins', 'skins', 'faces', et cetera. Section 3.2 mentions some variability axes for software collaboration environments in the context of the Data Interoperability Problem.

CC3. Visual Models can be Directly Manipulated: Data owned by producers and wanted by consumers can be explained in the context of a model, e.g., a data model. Consider, for instance, a relational model [5]. A visual model is a graphical representation of the data model which can be directly manipulated. In other words, the visual model supports interaction styles such as navigation, and selection/dragging of individual components/regions [4]. These interaction styles have semantics which are defined in terms of the semantics associated with the data model. For instance, in the case of a relational data model, the visual model can be based on the traditional relations–as–tables graphical representations, which would allow users to select cells (i.e., the semantics is a 'select' operation), and a region of the table (i.e., the semantics is a 'project' operation). It could be argued that **CC1** subsumes **CC3**. However, we think it is important to discuss it separately.

CC4. Resources are Automatically Generated: In the context of this paper the word 'Resources' denotes the results of the cooperation among stakeholders. Consider, for instance, the example presented at the end of Section 2. Instances of resources include: an actual software module which computes the appropriate correction transformations (e.g., written in the desired programming language), and maps showing the corrected data. The software module and the maps must be automatically generated by the collaboration environment from specifications that are—essentially—'gestured' by the user as s/he directly manipulates the visual models mentioned in **CC3**. In this case it could also be argued this concern is subsumed by **CC1**, and our reply to such argument is we believe it is important to discuss **CC4** separately.

CC5. Collaboration Decisions are Recorded: Strictly speaking, decisions that are made as part of the collaboration among stakeholders can also be considered as 'Resources', using the meaning discussed in **CC4**. However, we think it is important to differentiate between more 'tangible' resources, such as—for instance—Perl scripts [21], and 'knowledge–like' ones such as decisions made. If we consider again the example presented at the end of Section 2, we would like the collaboration environment to record the fact certain correcting transformations were used, so the environment can suggest them in the future if the same need arises. It could be argued this concern is subsumed by **CC4**, and therefore by **CC1**, but we believe it is important to discuss it separately.

CC6. Collaboration is by Immersion: Our working definition of 'Collaboration by Immersion' is the following. The software collaboration environment must make stakeholders feel as if they were together in a room equipped with various audio/visual tools which promote effective and efficient interactions among them (a.k.a. face–to–face environment). Additionally, our definition requires cooperations enabled by software environments to be as fruitful, if not more so, than those counterparts enabled by face–to–face environments. Finally, our definition also requires for collaborations enabled by software environments to be considerably more efficient than those enabled by face–to–face environments. So far we have identified the following immersion styles: Virtual Reality, Second Life–like, and Elluminate–like. We have used actual commercial names to refer to the last two just because they can be considered as exemplars from the perspective of the concept of 'immersion style' we want to convey, not because we endorse these products. Virtual Reality is discussed in Section 5, while Second Life and Elluminate are discussed in Section 4.

3.2 Variability Axes

We have defined 'Variability Axes', in the context of cross–cutting concern **CC2** (cf. Section 3.1), as those on which a software system can evolve in the direction of being more generic. In this section we discuss the variability axes (VA) we have identified so far.

VA1. Domain of Expertise: Defined by the data model's structure (a.k.a. syntax), and its semantics which define the intended meaning of data and operations on them.

VA2. Type of Resource Generated: Examples of this type include programming language associated with the resource; the type of the resource (e.g., web page, programming module, 'face'[1], 'skin'[2], 'mashup'[3], et cetera); and knowledge (e.g., decisions made through cooperation).

VA3. Visual Models: The way data models are visually represented. For a fixed data model there can be many different ways to visualize it. As mentioned in the context of cross–cutting concern **CC3** (cf. Section 3.1), the visual model must support both the data model's syntax and semantics.

VA4. Type of Data Source: This type describes more 'concrete' representations of data models. Examples include: plaintext structured (e.g. XML[4], CSV[5]), plaintext unstructured, relational (e.g., MySQL, Oracle, MS SQL Server, PostgreSQL, et cetera[6]), and real–time streams of data.

3.3 Functional Requirements

Functional requirements describe relevant interaction scenarios between end–users and the software collaboration environment. We present them using a

---

[1] http://developers.facebook.com/

[2] http://www.winamp.com/

[3] http://www.ibm.com/developerworks/library/x-mashups.html

[4] eXtensible Markup Language. See http://www.w3.org/XML/

[5] Comma-Separated Values.

[6] To mention some well–known database management systems.

format akin to eXtreme Programming's (XP) 'User Stories' as discussed by Wake [23], and to 'Use Case Summaries' as discussed by Larman [6]. Quality Attributes (a.k.a. Non–Functional Requirements), although very important, are not discussed in this paper [16,17]. In the following list each requirement (R) includes, in brackets, the cross–cutting concerns with which it is associated (cf. Section 3.1).

R1. Users, easily, cost–free, and without the aid of a software developer or database administrator, import their data sources into the system [**CC1, CC2, CC6**].

R2. The system dynamically generates visual models from the imported data sources. The underlying software framework should also make it easy for developers to produce these dynamic models [**CC1–CC4, CC6**].

R3. The system allows stakeholders to interact, via direct manipulation, with the models (e.g., by clicking on the visual representations, by showing options, by dragging/selecting elements of the visual representation, by visually inspecting/traversing/navigating the models, et cetera) [**CC1–CC6**].

R4. The system supports a variety of data transformations and manipulations based on the imported data models (e.g., via a menu of options, and gestures such as point–and–click, select–and–drag, et cetera) [**CC1–CC6**].

R5. The system generates resources specified by user's actions [**CC1–CC6**].

R6. The system allows for multiple stakeholders to simultaneously collaborate and manipulate the models in real–time within an immersive environment [**CC1–CC6**].

4   Review of Some Technologies

Previous sections have characterized the task of building software collaborative environments based on our just–in–time collaboration metaphor (cf. Section 2) for the Data Interoperability Problem, according to the restrictions imposed by elicited requirements (cf. Section 3.3), which encompass the discussed cross–cutting concerns (cf. Section 3.1), and variability axes (cf. Section 3.2). In this section we attempt to gauge the extent to which reviewed technologies can be used to accomplish this task.

4.1   Technologies That Do Not Target End–Users Per Se

The following two technologies are worth mentioning even though they do not satisfy cross–cutting concern **CC1** (cf. Section 3.1), embed in all elicited requirements. Altova's Mapforce[7] and Microsoft's SQL Server Integration (SSIS) Services[8] target software developers assisting them on several data mediation

---

[7] http://www.altova.com/products/mapforce/data_mapping.html

[8] http://www.microsoft.com/sql/technologies/integration/default.mspx.

and data mapping tasks approached in a non–collaborative way. Visual interfaces support the graphical specification of data operations with the corresponding automatic generation of implementation code in a variety of programming languages. These two products can therefore be considered as exemplary technologies which address cross–cutting concerns **CC2–CC4**.

Elluminate[9] is a technology that supports our collaboration metaphor (cf. Section 2) and characterizes one of the styles of collaboration by immersion we have identified. It can therefore be considered as an exemplar which aligns with our cross–cutting concern **CC6**.

4.2 Actual Implementation Technologies

Technologies presented in this section have been considered as candidate frameworks which can be used to implement software collaboration environments as per the elicited requirements.

Linden Research Second Life: Second Life[10] supports the construction of online virtual 3D worlds within which users can create and interact with objects, as well as among themselves via their avatars. Users create complex 3D representations from smaller objects (known as 'prims', or primitive objects) combining them to fit the required needs. Second Life possesses its own scripting language, called Linden Scripting Language, which can be used by world designers to add functionality to objects and to manipulate them within previously created inventories. One of the shortcomings associated with Second Life's computational model, however, is that in order to import externally fabricated 3D models into the users inventory, s/he must use the import method from within the environment which charges a monetary fee. Additionally, these imported models must then be manually placed in the environment and scripts have to be manually added to them, once they are imported, in order to provide functionality associated with direct manipulation. This dramatically limits the ability to dynamically create models driven by user–generated events as they manipulate constituting objects and cooperate among themselves. In conclusion, although Second Life's computational model supports collaboration and immersion, it (currently) neither supports the dynamic and event–driven creation of visual objects with which end–users can interact, nor it supports exporting generated resources.

Sun Microsystem Project Wonderland: Project Wonderland[11] is a framework for developing 3D virtual worlds which look similar to those developed in Second Life, although the former is currently not as advanced as the latter. Its open source environment supports multi–channel audio interactions allowing users to move amongst concurrent conversations in an attempt to simulate a real–life office. The framework comes with both server and client components which can be modified by developers to meet their needs. The

---

[9] http://www.elluminate.com
[10] http://secondlife.com/
[11] https://lg3d-wonderland.dev.java.net/

environment provides—much like Second Life—support for the creation of worlds in which users interact and collaborate among themselves in an immersive environment. Additionally, models created with software such as Blender[12] or Maya[13] can be imported into Project Wonderland environments via their World Builder tool. However, it currently does not support the creation of 3D models without the use of external tools. Project Wonderland seems to have the same limitations as Second Life when it comes to dynamically generating event–driven visual models.

ISO X3D: X3D[14] is an XML–based ISO standard which targets the representation of 3D graphic objects allowing users to programmatically create complex worlds. Additionally, it supports object extensions via an API, JavaScript, and Java. Although X3D supports the ability to program interactions with created objects, it does not provide tools that can be used to create a virtual collaboration environment. Further, importing data models would also require a custom solution, for instance written in Java, to interact with the X3D code.

Microsoft Silverlight: Silverlight[15] is a technology that allows users on the web to view high quality video and audio content created using the Microsofts Expressions Studio and the Visual Studio tool suite. The Expression Design tools allow designers to visually create graphics that are then expressed in XAML (Extensible Application Markup Language). XAML supports the generation of human–computer interface elements such as animations, and interactive controls which can be tied to .NET applications via the Windows Presentation Foundation (WPF) and cross–platform, cross–browser Silverlight Plug–ins. This allows developers to tap into the powerful .NET framework through supported programming languages (e.g., C#, Visual Basic, Iron Ruby, Iron Python, et cetera) to create complex applications with dynamic interfaces. The .NET framework provides a large amount of interfaces for various data sources.

Adobe Director: Director[16] is a multimedia authoring tool and plug–in engine that allows developers to create and publish interactive applications on the web, desktop, or to DVD. Commercial add–ins are available for Director to import data from various sources and the ability to export data is also available. Adobe products support SVG (Scalable Vector Graphics)[17], which is an XML–based model used to describe vector graphics.

4.3 Technology Comparison

Table 1 shows the reviewed technologies along with the elicited requirements **R1** to **R6**. A 'Y' in the matrix cell (T_i, R_j) means requirement R_j can be easily

---

[12] http://www.blender.org/
[13] http://usa.autodesk.com
[14] http://www.web3d.org/x3d/
[15] http://silverlight.net/
[16] http://www.adobe.com/products/director/
[17] http://www.w3.org/Graphics/SVG/

Table 1. Comparison Matrix

	Requirements					
Technology	**R1**	**R2**	**R3**	**R4**	**R5**	**R6**
Second Life	N	N	Y	Y	N	Y
Project Wonderland	N	Y	N	Y	Y	Y
X3D	N	Y	Y	Y	Y	N
Sliverlight	Y	Y	Y	Y	Y	N
Director	Y	Y	Y	Y	Y	N

implemented with technology T_i. An 'N' means the requirement cannot be easily implemented with the corresponding technology.

4.4   Characterizing 'Killer Apps'

Clearly none of the reviewed technologies cover all elicited requirements. It therefore makes sense to envision applications that would result if one were to take the best of each of the reviewed tools. These kinds of systems are usually referred to as 'Killer Applications' or 'Killer Apps' for short. In this paper we offer two types of Killer Apps for the Data Interoperability Problem:

Killer App A: Collaboration by immersion is implemented à la Elluminate; direct manipulation and resource generation are implemented à la Mapforce/SSIS but targetting end–users and with the 3D–like quality delivered by Director/Silverlight/X3D/SVG. In this case, support for automatically recording knowledge product of the collaboration among stakeholders would need to be implemented on top of Elluminate, although stakeholders themselves can record this knowledge using ad–hoc methods.

Killer App B: Collaboration by immersion is implemented à la Second Life; direct manipulation and resource generation are implemented à la Mapforce/SSIS but targetting end–users and with the 3D–like quality delivered by Second Life augmented with Director/Silverlight/X3D/SVG. In this case, support for automatically recording knowledge product of the collaboration among stakeholders would need to be implemented on top of Second Life, although stakeholders themselves can record this knowledge using ad–hoc methods.

5   Other Related Work

Alternatives to our collaboration metaphor (cf. Section 2) are discussed in [8,22]. Virtual reality (VR) has been for many years the archetypical approach to immersion. We have not included this approach in our review because we consider the use of typically required 'tethers' impractical and invasive (e.g., googles, glasses, helmets, et cetera). Implementing immersion via 'organic user interfaces' seems like a fascinating idea worth exploring [20]. The collaboration environments for the Data Interoperability Problem we envision are framed by the question "What is the power of computing, by machine and human together?" posed by Wing [13]. Another paper of ours discusses the elements of a generic and extensible architecture for software collaboration environments which target end–users [2].

6   Conclusions and Current Status

Building effective and efficient software collaboration environments is a very complex task. In this paper we have discussed the Data Interoperability Problem as an exemplary case study which can be used to determine the extent to which current technologies possess the level of sophistication required to implement these collaboration environments.

We have characterized a relevant collaboration metaphor and facets associated with the construction of software collaboration environments to support it, including cross–cutting concerns and variability axes. These concepts led to the definition of user–centric requirements which were used to determine whether reviewed technologies could support them. We concluded that none of the reviewed technologies were individually sufficient to implement a system which satifies the elicited requirements. Despite of this, we were able to envision two 'Killer Apps' as collages built from existing technologies.

We argue that, using a ranking of complexity which lists the most complex concern first and the least complex concern last, the complexity ranking of elicited concerns is **CC2**, **CC3**, **CC5**, **CC4**, **CC6**, and **CC1**. This ranking has suggested the project we are currently working on, which is the development of a software collaboration environment with the profile of **Killer App A** (cf. Section 4.4) for meteorological data.

References

1. Sutcliffe, A., Mehandjiev, N. (eds.): Special Issue on End–User Development: Tools that Empower Users to Create their own Software Solutions. Communications of the ACM 47(9) (September 2004)
2. Sánchez–Ruíz, A.J., Umapathy, K., Hayes, P.: Toward generic, immersive, and collaborative solutions to the data interoperability problem which target end–users. In: Proceedings of the 2nd International workshop on Ontologies and Information Systems for the Semantic Web (ONISW 2008) (October 2008)
3. Sánchez–Ruíz, A.J., Saeki, M., Langlois, B., Paiano, R.: Domain–specific software development terminology: Do we all speak the same language? In: Proceedings of the seventh OOPSLA Workshop on Domain–Specific Modeling, ACM–SIGPLAN, New York (October 2007)
4. Shneiderman, B., Maes, P.: Direct manipulation vs. Interface agents. interactions IV(6) (November–December, 1997)
5. Date, C.J.: Database in Depth: Relational Theory for Practitioners. O'Reilly, Sebastopol (2005)
6. Larman, C.: Applying UML and Patterns: An Introduction to Object–Oriented Analysis and Design and Iterative Development, 3rd edn. Prentice–Hall (2005)

7. Domain Specific Development Forum, http://www.dsmforum.org/
8. Stahl, G.: Group Cognition – Computer Support for Building Collaborative Knowledge. MIT Press, Cambridge (2006)
9. Gibbons, J., Jeuring, J. (eds.): Generic Programming, IFIP TC2/WG2.1 Working Conference on Generic Programming, Dagstuhl, Germany, July 11-12, 2002. IFIP Conference Proceedings, vol. 243. Kluwer, Dordrecht (2003)
10. Kiczales, G., Lamping, J., Mendhekar, A., Maeda, C., VideiraLopes, C., Loingtier, J.–M., Irwin, J.: Aspect–oriented programming. In: Aksit, M., Matsuoka, S. (eds.) ECOOP 1997. LNCS, vol. 1241, pp. 220–242. Springer, Heidelberg (1997)
11. Gomaa, H.: Designing Software Product Lines with UML: From Use Cases to Pattern–Based Software Architectures. Addison Wesley, Reading (2004)
12. Jazayeri, M., Loos, R., Musser, D. (eds.): Generic Programming: International Seminar, Dagstuhl Castle, Germany. LNCS, vol. 1766. Springer, Heidelberg (2000) (selected papers)
13. Wing, J.M.: Five Deep Questions in Computing. Communications of the ACM 51(1) (January 2008)
14. Pohl, K., Böckle, G., van der Linden, F.J.: Software Product Line Engineering: Foundations, Principles and Techniques. Springer, Heidelberg (2005)
15. Czarnecki, K., Eisenecker, U.W.: Generative Programming – Methods, Tools, and Applications. Addison Wesley, Reading (2000)
16. Bass, L., Clements, P., Kazman, R.: Software Architecture in Practice, 2nd edn. Addison Wesley, Reading (2003)
17. Barbacci, M., Klein, M.H., Longstaff, T.A., Weinstock, C.B.:Quality Attributes. Technical Report CMU/SEI-95-TR-021, ESC-TR-95-021, Software Engineering Institute, Carnegie Mellon University, Pittsburgh, Pennsylvania, USA (December 1995)
18. Clements, P., Northrop, L.: Software Product Lines: Practices and Patterns. Addison Wesley, Reading (2002)
19. Hilliard, R.: Aspects, concerns, subjects, views, ... In: Proceedings of the 1999 OOPSLA Workshop on Multi–Dimensional Separation of Concerns in Object–Oriented Systems (June 1999)
20. Vertegaal, R., Poupyrev, I. (eds.): Special Issue on Organic User Interfaces. Communications of the ACM 51(6) (June 2008)
21. Cozens, S.: Beginning perl, http://www.perl.org/books/beginning-perl/
22. Kaptelinin, V., Czerwinski, M. (eds.): Beyond the Desktop Metaphor – Designing Integrated Digital Work Ennvironments. MIT Press, Cambridge (2007)
23. Wake, W.: Extreme Programming Explored. Addison Wesley, Reading (2002)

Towards a Framework for Evolvable Network Design

Hoda Hassan, Ramy Eltarras, and Mohamed Eltoweissy

The Bradley Department of Electrical and Computer Engineering, Virginia Tech
{hmhassan,ramy,toweissy}@vt.edu

Abstract. The layered Internet architecture that had long guided network design and protocol engineering was an "interconnection architecture" defining a framework for interconnecting networks rather than a model for generic network structuring and engineering. We claim that the approach of abstracting the network in terms of an internetwork hinders the thorough understanding of the network salient characteristics and emergent behavior resulting in impeding design evolution required to address extreme scale, heterogeneity, and complexity. This paper reports on our work in progress that aims to: 1) Investigate the problem space in terms of the factors and decisions that influenced the design and development of computer networks; 2) Sketch the core principles for designing complex computer networks; and 3) Propose a model and related framework for building evolvable, adaptable and self organizing networks We will adopt a bottom up strategy primarily focusing on the building unit of the network model, which we call the "network cell". The model is inspired by natural complex systems. A network cell is intrinsically capable of specialization, adaptation and evolution. Subsequently, we propose CellNet; a framework for evolvable network design. We outline scenarios for using the CellNet framework to enhance legacy Internet protocol stack.

1 Introduction

Engineering of computer networks has long been influenced by concepts developed during the inchoative stage of computer network design. This resulted in adopting a layered architecture for abstracting network functionalities as well as for engineering network protocols; a methodology that proved to be neither adaptable nor evolvable in response to the continuous change in network operational requirements and technological advancements. As a direct consequence to the layered model limitations, a myriad of alternative network architectures have been proposed targeting computer networks in general and the Internet in particular. While some ingenious proposals were developed at times, we argue that the general trend towards network science and engineering lacks a systematic formalization of core principles that need to guide the process of network design. This research work is an attempt to 1) investigate the problem space in terms of the factors and decisions that influenced the design and development of computer networks 2) extract the core principles for designing a computer network relying heavily on concepts and practices adopted in complex systems modeling, software engineering and computer communications 3) Propose a model and related framework for building evolvable, adaptable and self organizing

E. Bertino and J.B.D. Joshi (Eds.): CollaborateCom 2008, LNICST 10, pp. 390–401, 2009.
© ICST Institute for Computer Sciences, Social-Informatics and Telecommunications Engineering 2009

future networks relying on studies performed on natural complex systems, the structure of their components, and their overall intrinsic behavior specifically studies conducted on primordial communities of bacteria. We will adopt a bottom up strategy primarily focusing on the building unit of the network, which we call the "network cell". We argue that specialization, adaptation and evolution should be intrinsic features of the "network cell" for the network to exhibit intelligent emergent behavior.

The remainder of this paper is organized as follows. Section 2 gives an overview of the problem space; section3 introduces the proposed "network cell"; section 4 explores the evolutionary capability of the network cell; section 5 sketches the CellNet framework within which the network cell will operate; section 6 provides a formal definition of networks and internetworks in terms of the network cell and finally section 7 provides an example for the model realizations. The paper concludes in section 8 with an outline of future work.

2 Computer Network Design

Different computer network concepts, paradigms, and projects were developed before computer internetworking came into being. The most prominent of these projects was the ARPANET. The APRANET was a packet switched store and forward network whose primary mission was to provide distributed data communication network that can withstand almost any degree of destruction to individual components without losing end-to-end communications [1]. The success of the ARPANET to connect isolated computers and the rise of other national networks motivated the idea of inter-connecting networks. It was then realized that a general internetworking protocol is required. This was the motivation for designing the TCP protocol [2]. The adoption of TCP/IP as the "transport protocol" for internetworking could be considered the initiation of the Internet as we know it today. TCP/IP suite abstracts the interconnection functionalities into five layers. The astounding success of the TCP/IP protocol suite in interconnecting desperate networks motivated the adoption of a layered architecture as a reference model for network protocol engineering and development even for protocols running within intranets. The primary motivation of our work is highlighting this misconception; the layered architecture that had long guided network design and protocol engineering was an "interconnection architecture" defining a framework for interconnecting networks rather than a model for network structuring and engineering. We claim that the prevalent approach of abstracting the network in terms of an internetwork hinders the thorough understanding of the network salient characteristics and interactions resulting in impeding design decisions. Hence we embark by clarifying our vision of the network and its relationship to an internetwork. We admit that the presented definitions are already recognized in literature but our contribution is the reasoning that follows the definitions. We define a network as a communication substrate that allows the exchange of data among two or more computers despite the possible heterogeneity in hardware, middleware and software of the attached computers. While an internetwork is defined as a communication substrate that allows the exchange of data among two or more computers by connecting the network communication substrate that connects these computers despite the possible heterogeneity in hardware, middleware and software of both the computers and the communication substratum, i.e. an internetwork is a network of networks connected by internetwork communication substratum. In that sense we reason that the definition of an internetwork is actually a recursive definition of a network with the base case being a network. Thus we reason further that to design an internetwork we need first to design the network that forms the building block for an internetwork.

To design a computer network we note that computer networks are complex by definition. Their complexity can be attributed to the heterogeneous and distributed nature of the technologies adopted, protocols employed, devices used, applications supported, variability of operating conditions and performance requirements, not to mention the unpredictable interactions of all previously mentioned aspects. Hence computer networks stand as a typical example for software intensive complex systems.

Three inherent properties shared by all complex systems are complexity, emergent behavior and composability from autonomous components [3]. Complexity refers to the immense amount of information required to depict the system profile in terms of macro and micro states. Emergent behavior in complex system refers to the ability of the components of the system to change/evolve their structures and/or functions without external intervention as a result of their interactions or in response to changes in their environment. Emergent behavior can be classified as self-organization, adaptation or evolution. Self-organization refers to changes in component individual behavior due to inter-component communication, while adaptation refers to changes in components' behavior in response to changes in the surrounding environment. Both self-organization and adaptation imply information propagation and adaptive processing through feedback mechanisms. Evolution, on the other hand, refers to a higher form of intelligent adaptation and/or self organization of components in response to changes by accounting on previously recorded knowledge form past experience(s). Evolution usually implies the presence of memory elements as well as monitoring functions in evolvable components. Finally composability from autonomous components implies the distributed structure of complex systems where different entities collaborate to perform the global system function. Although delineating the properties of complex systems are rather straightforward, yet designing a system that exhibits these properties is a challenging task. This observation led us to 1) devise a network building block that we coin as the "network cell" by which we build the network in an attempt to imitate natural complex systems' structure behavior and capabilities; and 2) Adopt Separation of Concerns (SoC) as software engineering methodology to tackle functional decomposition in networks yielding our proposed CellNet framework that identifies Application, Communication, Resource and Federation as four functional concerns.

3 The Network Cell

Our research in natural complex systems led us to an interesting study on primordial bacteria that provided us with a vivid representation of the main features that need to be present in entities composing a complex system. In this recent study it has been noted that bacteria is capable of self engineering in the sense that it can "utilize intricate communication capabilities to cooperatively form (self-organize) complex colonies with elevated adaptability—the colonial pattern is collectively engineered according to the encountered environmental conditions." The bacterial cell is described to be "analogous to a complex man-made cybernetic system composed of information-processing systems and at least two thermodynamic machines. Their outer membranes enable them to sense the environment and to exchange energy, matter, and information with it. The internal state and stored information of the cell and the surrounding conditions regulate the membranes." [4].

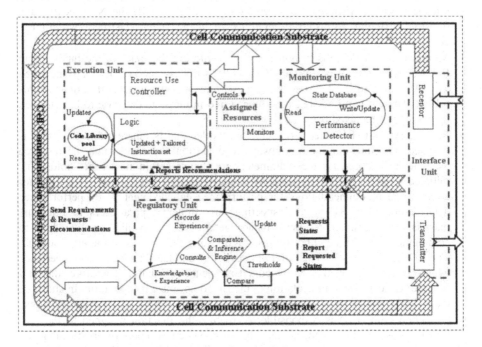

Fig. 1. Generic Network Cell structure

Guided by the previous description, we present the structure of our generic network cell (GNC) whose structure will be common to all network cells (NC) regardless of their assigned responsibilities or roles. As shown in figure 1, the GNC is composed of four units; the Interface Unit (IU), the Monitoring Unit (MU), the Regulatory Unit (RU) and the Execution Unit (EU). A NC has two modes of concurrent operations; intrinsic operation and functional operation. The intrinsic operation is again common to all NCs and represents the NC's genetic blueprint and can be regarded as the sequence of actions and rules that the NC must obey throughout its lifetime. On the other hand, the functional operation of the NC is assigned to it on its creation and prescribes the role that the NC must perform. This includes the behavior realized and instruction set to be executed by all units. For example, the parameters to be monitored and states recorded by the MU, the threshold values to be used by the RU, the library pool out of which the logic to be tailored and executed by the EU. Once the NC is assigned a functional role it turns to be a specialized NC. Therefore the GNC is just a template out of which all specialized NCs can be derived. It is also possible for a specialized NC to change its function during its lifetime or alternate between different functions depending on the role(s) it is assigned. Once a NC materializes by assuming a functional role, it will be assigned, according to its functional needs, a portion of the system resources required for its proper operation. These resources include primarily memory and CPU cycles. Following is an outline for the intrinsic operation of each of the units shown in figure 1 as this will be common to all NCs

- Interface Unit (IU) is the NC boundary allowing it to communicate with the outside world (environment or peer NCs). Through the IU the NCs receive and transmit different forms/representations of data (states, instructions, control, content etc...)
- Monitoring Unit (MU) is responsible for monitoring the states of the input/output flows directed into or out of the NC as well as the assigned recourses usage level. The MU will extract state information and represent these states in a quantifiable format. These quantified states are then stored in the state database to be retrieved upon requests received from the RU
- Regulatory Unit (RU) has two regulatory cycles one is inherent and the other is initiated. The inherent cycle is always in operation and checks that the resource usage levels and performance parameters are always within the set thresholds. The initiated cycle is either triggered by requests received form the EU asking for advices and recommendations for performance enhancement or by performance deterioration. The RU starts inspecting environmental parameters to infer the reasons that accounted for performance deterioration and this step may lead to communication with neighboring peers requesting their views of the environment. The RU has the capability of gaining knowledge and learning from past experience which it records in the Knowledge/Experience database. Therefore the RU provides educated recommendation to the EU to optimize its operation. In addition, the RU may update some of the threshold levels according to its inferred decisions
- Execution Unit (EU) is responsible to execute the function assigned to the NC. Functions assigned to an NC are usually accompanied by a pool of libraries that can be used to formulate different ways of accomplishing the required function. The EU is composed of two main components; the Logic component (LC) and the Resource Use Controller component (RUCC). The logic component is the part responsible for performing the NC function. The Logic component starts by creating a set of instructions that best accomplishes the required function using the library pool. It also requests the RU recommendations thus incorporating both the RU knowledge and experience as well as accounting for environmental alterations. Once the LC receives feedback recommendations form the RU it might update its tailored instruction set to fit the inferred operational status. The RUCC on the other hand is responsible for managing resources assigned to the NC. The RUCC works together with the LC to ensure optimal internal resource usage and distribution. The RUCC is also responsible for estimating the required level of resources for the NC operation as a whole and thus requests the estimated resources form the system.

4 Network Cell Evolution

The capability of network cell (NC) to record its past experience, and use it to infer the future updates required for its software at runtime, in response to internal or external triggers, imply that the NC is capable of evolution. Accordingly a network built of NCs will also be capable of evolution as the network behavior is perceived as the collective behavior of its constituents. We envision the NC experience to be recorded in terms of perceived behavioral patterns, responses to a perceived pattern or a sequence of patterns represented as sequence of updates, and the resulting outcome of each of the adopted decisions in terms of the overall gain in cell performance. The inference engine in the NC's RU will be responsible to pick up the most suitable course of action based on the recorded experience and present NC states. Since each cell can undergo changes independent of its peer cells we need a mechanism to guarantee that evolving cells will maintain communication in spite of any changes applied to their software To allow the independent evolution of cells while maintaining continuous operation of the network, a dynamic interface management technique is required to insure that progressive evolution of cells does not lead to network breakage. A cell publishes one or more local interfaces exposing its services to other cells in the network. When a cell evolution induces changes in the cell local interface, the cell publishes a new interface to support its evolved behavior while retaining the old interfaces to allow other cells that didn't undergo a compatible evolution to continue using the cell services through the older interfaces. Dwelling further into the responsibilities of the interface management capability we foresee that the IU within a cell encompasses the following subunits dedicated for interface management

- Local Interface Manager (LIM): allows the registration/de-registration of local interfaces at runtime. It publishes the local interfaces to other cells, maintains a List of Published Interfaces (LPI), responds to queries requesting available interfaces, and proxies interface invocations to appropriate service implementation.
- Remote Interface Manager (RIM): allows the registration/de-registration of remote interfaces at runtime and maintains a List of Remote Interfaces (LRI). The LRI determines the capabilities of the cell requesting a service from another cell. It also provides stubs to the interfaces listed in LRI to allow the hosting cell to invoke services on other cells.
- Cooperation Interface Manager (CIM): Multiple cell cooperation can be done by implementing cooperation interfaces dictated by the cell managing the cooperation. These interfaces allow the cell responsible of cooperation management to communicate with the participant cells without getting into their implementation details. Like any other cell, the cooperation manager cell is capable of evolution and consequently new cooperation interfaces can be registered. The cooperation participants selects the most appropriate cooperation interface to use in the same way cells select the most appropriate remote interface to use. Accordingly, CIM allows the registration/de-registration of the cooperation interfaces at runtime. It maintains a List of Cooperation Interface when the cells request to cooperate

Using the cell paradigm, we note that the NC, similar to the biological cell, will have a life cycle where NC starts at its infancy with minimal experience, and through learning, the NC experience will mature. This gained experience can be transferred to other naïve NCs introducing the phenomenon of generational learning among NCs.

5 The CellNet Framework

Having derived the structure of the NC, which represents the basic building block out of which the network will be constructed, we embark to define the framework within which the NC will operate in an attempt to formalize a new network design methodology that we refer to as Cell Oriented Architecture (COA). One important thing to emphasize is that a computer network is not a stand alone system but rather a complex distributed system requiring a dual faceted design strategy to address both the vertical functional decomposition and the horizontal functional distribution while paying attention to the different functional dependencies and interactions that exist along these two dimensions. Relying on SE merhods in tackling complexity we adopt the principle of Separation of Concerns (SoC) to derive CellNet framework. SoC is a general problem-solving technique that addresses complexity by cutting down the problem space into smaller manageable, loosely-coupled, and easier to solve sub-problems allowing for better understanding and design. SoC addresses concerns from two different views. The first view defines two types of concerns; core concerns and cross-cutting concerns. Core concerns refer to the core functionalities of a system that can be identified with clear cutting boundaries and hence represented in separable modules. Cross-cutting concerns, on the other hand are behavioral aspects of the system functions that span over multiple modules trying to manage or optimize the core concerns, and if not carefully represented, result in scattering and tangling of system resulting behavior.

The second view of the SoC concept differentiates between concerns, whether core or cross-cutting, representing the loci of functional computations and states, and concern interactions representing the flow of information and state communication. Guided by the first view CellNet abstracts the core network concerns into application-oriented, communication-oriented and resource-oriented functions and allows for concern federation thus addressing the cross cutting functional aspects among the previously identified core concerns. Figure 2 (left) models the CellNet component and for better understanding we present it superimposed on the TCP/IP model in figure 2 (right). Yet we emphasize, as indicated in the figures, that the CellNet framework does not impose layering among its defined abstractions allowing for diverse inter-functional communication.

The CellNet framework can be realized through the instantiation of the following specialized NCs (SNC): Resource Oriented Cell (ROC), Communication Oriented Cell (COC), Application Oriented Cell (AOC), and Federation Oriented Cell (FOC).

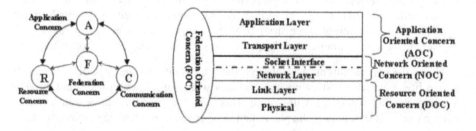

Fig. 2. The CellNet model (left). The CellNet framework superimposed on the TCP/IP model.

Each of these NCs will have the structure of GNC, but each will have its dedicated function that will be executed by the logic in their EU. The instantiation of AOC, COC and ROC is mandatory for the correct operation within a network. In contrast the FOC instantiation is optional, and when in action it acts as a global RU that receives inquiries form and sends recommendations to local RUs within the federating NCs.

For the second view of SoC, we recall our definitions for network and internetworks. Accordingly, we identify three boundaries for NC interactions; within the same computer, on different computers communicating using a network communication substrate, and on different computers communicating using an internetwork communication substrate. NCs instantiated on the same computer form what we call a network component (NComp). The NComp can be composed of any number of specialized NCs but the minimum configuration for an NComp is one instantiation of each of the basic NCs (AOC, COC, and ROC). NComp represent the first interaction boundary. The second interaction boundary is represented by a network hosting two or more NComp communicating using the same homogenous substrate. The third interaction boundary is represented by an internetwork hosting two or more networks, which on turn host the NComps communicating using a heterogeneous internetwork substrate thus requiring an intermediate NComp to act as a translator. The formal definition for this setup is defined in the next section.

The NCs accompanied by the CellNet framework present a new paradigm for building networks. However, to be realized within the present legacy network we propose attaching specialized NCs to existing protocols according to network functional decomposition as dictated by the CellNet framework. For example, the reliable transport service provided by TCP can be encapsulated into an AOC while socket management will be controlled by a COC.

6 Formal CellNet Based Network Definition

In this section we present the formal definition for network structure based on CellNet using EBNF. The definition will use the following notations:

Trailing * means repeat 0 or more times.
Trailing + means repeat 1 or more times

The following abbreviations will be used

INet = Internetwork
Net = Network
IComSub = Internetwork communication substrate
NComSub = Network communication substrate
NComp = Network component
NC = Network Cell

Network Definition

INet = NComp (IComSub NComp)+
IComSub = (NComSub NComp)+ NComSub
Net = NComp (NcomSub NComp)+

NComp = AONE CONE RONE NC*
NC = AONE I CONE I RONE I FONE

7 Network Realization Using CellNet

In this section we present an example to show how a legacy network can be enhanced using CellNet. The CellNet framework introduces monitoring adaptation and learning to enable

1. The TCP protocol to realize the contention level on the links along the path; and
2. The MAC layer to adapt power level to reduce interference, while handling adverse unintended consequences that might occur.

The scenario uses cross layer designs proposed in [5] and [6] and uses the network topology used in [5] and shown in figure 3.

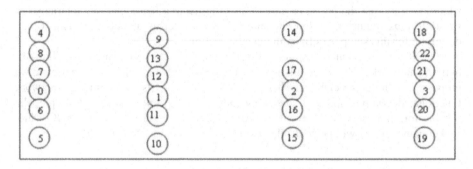

Fig. 3. Network Topology reproduced from [5]

Scenario Assumption
The following NCs are instantiated: TCP-AC an AOC for handling TCP logic, L-RC an ROC for wireless link adaptation, P-RC, an ROC for controlling power, R-CC a COC for handling routing and forwarding, and FC a FOC for federating all previously mentioned specialized cells.

The Scenario Steps
Numbers refer to steps taken by legacy protocols bullets refer to steps taken by the CellNet specialized cells instantiated on the nodes.

1. Node 0 powers up
- FC goal is to provide highest throughput while minimizing power consumption. Let R be the power consumption rate of the link, I be the interference realized, E be the bit error rate attained and T be the throughput achieved, then FC optimization goal can be represented as MIN (R, I, E) and MAX (T). Both R and E can be represented as a scalar value, I can be abstracted in terms of collisions represented as the size of the MAC contention window (CW), and T needs the input of end application in terms of the goodput

- On initialization the P-RC will assign each physical resource on the device a maximum rate for power consumption Rmax which should not be exceeded. Let the rate assigned for the link be LRmax
- The L-RC is responsible to control the PHY layer operation (signal strength) such that the power rate consumptions does not exceed LRmax while achieving required threshold for BER (through adjusting SNR)
- FC requests L-RC to load code for power adaptation and report on BER and contention level
- L-RC instructs PHY to detect the minimum power required to make 1 hop connection to a maximum of 2 neighbors [6]. In case no neighbors are detected then power level is increased and the discovery process is repeated. If power level used hits Pmax (Pmax defined in the thresholds used by the RU) then L-RC assumes that the node is isolated and reports that no connection is available
- Neighbor list is constructed and connection cost is measured in terms of average transmission power required to reach each neighbor
2. Node 0 initiates a TCP connection stating node 3 as the destination.
- TCP-AC on 0 realizes the need for a reliable transmission for the connection
- TCP-AC reports to FC on QoS requirements (reliable transmission, delay tolerant)
- FC recommends that the TCP-AC loads updated code for TCP to operate on wireless links (TCC proposed in [5]) to include consideration contention level along the path and requests TCP-AC to monitor and report on RTT, congestion window, packet error ratw and goodthroughput (these values are already calculated in the TCC protocol)
- Within TCP-AC, RU consults its own KB and communicates, with MU and EU to apply FC recommendations and any other self inferred recommendations (In case contradiction occurs FC recommendations have a higher priority than RU self recommendations)
- TCP-AC on 0 requests route discovery form R-CC to destination 3
- FC requests R-CC to gather path parameters in terms of contention and BER and report on values perceived on node 0
3. AODV initiates route discovery by sending RREQ for destination 3 (In this scenario intermediate replies are prohibited)
- R-CC uses the neighbor list created by L-RC listing 1 hop neighbors
- R-CC record path parameters in terms of contention level and BER in the data exchange unit (DXU) to be sent along the path and exchanged among R-CCs along the path to destination
- Along the path each R-CC will query the respective L-RC for contention level and BER then updates the respective values in the received DXU. The highest values for contention level and BER will be the values reported for path parameters
4. Node 3 will reply with RREP for each RREQ received
- With each returning RREP the path state in terms of highest contention value and BER will be obtained
- R-CC along the path will instruct the AODV to use the path with the least contention and BER even if it is not the shortest path (minimum power transmission is already enforced since the neighbor list is obtained from the L-RC)

- R-CC reports path parameters to FC in terms of expected contention and BER and also reports whether a federation is active on the destination node or not
- FC decides on the best way to handle the flow in terms of fragmentation, FEC etc... and sends recommendation to RUs of TCP-AC and L-RC
5. TCP flow starts (In case there is a FC on 3 steps b & c will be performed through FC to FC communication)
- TCP-AC marks the flow to require a reliable service
- TCP-AC on 0 sends the expected path quality to TCP-AC to be initiated on 3
- TCP-AC on 0 indicates the changes to be made to TCP code on 3
- L-RC along the path instructs LL not to discard packets requesting reliable service
6. First TCP segment reaches 3
- TCP-AC on 3 reads path parameters as indicated by TCP-AC on 0 and loads updates required for TCP
7. During the TCP connection
- TCP-AC on 0 reports on the RTT, congestion window, packet error frame and goodput achieved to FC
- L-RC reports on the BER and contention level seen on the node
- According to the optimization equation employed by FC the decision will be taken as whether to increase power transmission to combat BER and provide shorter routes to enhance throughput

8   Related Work

Limitations induced by the layered architecture have been the focus of several research proposals. These proposals can be classified into two main categories; the first aimed to preserve layering with some modification to allow layer interaction, while the other adopted a clean slate design. Cross Layer Designs are the most prominent example for the former [7]. CLD were applied mainly to wireless networks to enhance network awareness of performance conditions. For clean slate design proposals, these provided radical changes to the network legacy stack. Their main feature is to allow fine grained composition of protocols. An example would be the ANA project aiming to introduce autonomic behavior to the network [8].

9   Conclusion

The design of computer networks needs to account for evolution. Inspired by natural complex systems, we proposed composing the computer network out of Network Cells (NC) capable of evolving through continuous learning and adaptation. We also proposed the CellNet framework within which the NC functions and interactions are defined. CellNet framework is derived based on the concept of separation of concerns that tackle complexity by dividing the problem space into smaller manageable, loosely-coupled, and easier to solve sub-problems allowing for better understanding and design. The CellNet framework abstracts network functions into three main core concerns and one crosscutting concern. These identified abstractions will be the reference model for specializing the NC. Our future work will encompass formalizing a new design methodology that we refer to as Cell Oriented Architecture on which the NC and the CellNet framework are based. We intend to construct a network prototype composed of NC using the CellNet framework to study the performance gains achieved when introducing learning and adaptation to networks.

References

1. 'THINK' protocols, ARPANET, http://www.cs.utexas.edu/users/chris/think/ARPANET/Timeline/#1958
2. Highlights of JF Koh's Honours Programme (1997), http://wwwmcc.murdoch.edu.au/ReadingRoom/VID/jfk/timeline.htm
3. Mitchell, M.: Complex Systems: Network Thinking. Preprint submitted to Elsevier Science, September 8 (2006), http://web.cecs.pdx.edu/~mm/AIJ2006.pdf
4. Ben-Jacob, E.: Social behavior of bacteria: from physics to complex organization. The European Physical Journal B - Condensed Matter and Complex Systems 65(3) (October 2008)
5. Hamadani, E., Rakocevic, V.: A Cross layer Analysis of TCP Instability in Multihop Ad hoc Networks. Journal of Internet Engineering 2(1) (2008),
   http://www.jie-online.org/ojs/index.php/jie/article/view/41
6. Kawadia, V., Kumar, P.R.: A Cautionary Perspective on Cross-Layer Design. IEEE Wireless Communications (February 2005)
7. Srivastava, V., Motani, M.: Cross-Layer Design: A Survey and the Road Ahead. IEEE Communications Magazine (December 2005)
8. D1.4/5/6v1: ANA Blueprint – First Version. Workpackage 1 Deliverable 1.4/5/6v1, ANA Project FP6-IST-27489 (February 2007)

A Comprehensive Comparison of Trust Management Systems for Federation

Zhengping Wu

Department of Computer Science and Engineering,
University of Bridgeport,
221 University Avenue,
Bridgeport, CT 06604, USA
zhengpiw@bridgeport.edu

Abstract. Federation becomes pervasive in information sharing and collaborations over distributed systems, ubiquitous systems, and the Internet. Trust management plays a critical role to smooth collaborations and information sharing across different trust domains. The federation of trust management is a new direction for these networked systems. In this paper, the requirements and a set of evaluation metrics for federated trust management systems are briefly examined, and then a comprehensive comparison of extant trust management systems is made against these metrics. The purpose of this paper is not to provide an ultimate comparison covering all necessary features; instead, its purpose is to initiate a discussion and to offer a context in which to evaluate current and future solutions, in order to encourage the development of proper models and systems for federated trust management.

Keywords: trust management system, federation, comprehensive comparison, evaluation metrics.

1 Introduction

Demand for management of trust in networked systems introduces more complexity than ever when federation activities become pervasive. Many existing research efforts have focused on different aspects of trust management, and they use different criteria and metrics to evaluate their efforts. These criteria and metrics are often applicable only to the researchers' own systems. This paper briefly examines general requirements for federated trust management and a number of existing systems from different aspects, and uses a set of evaluation metrics to comprehensively compare these trust management systems. Using this set of metrics, a system's merits and weaknesses can be more clearly documented for system users and researchers. To illustrate the applicability, the metrics are applied to the comparisons between trust management systems from leading technology companies such as IBM, AT&T, and other extant trust management systems from the research community. However, the metrics introduced in this paper are not ultimate results; rather, they are intended to initiate a broader discussion of what is needed, and to offer a context in which to evaluate current and future solutions and to inspire new directions for federated trust management.

E. Bertino and J.B.D. Joshi (Eds.): CollaborateCom 2008, LNICST 10, pp. 402–415, 2009.

2 Requirements of Federated Trust Management

Ruohomma and Kutvonen [1] discuss the requirements of a trust management system from the viewpoint of trust's life cycle, which include initialization of a trust relationship, observation of the relationship, and actions caused by the relationship. But that is not enough. Wu and Weaver [2] discussed a set of more comprehensive requirements for federated trust management systems. Following this discussion, this section briefly examines the requirements of trust management systems from four different aspects from both fundamental and practical viewpoints. Fulfillment of these requirements will not only provide solid support of the functionalities for trust management proposed by Ruohomma and Kutvonen, but also support new requirements unique from federation activities and federated trust management. Trust representation, trust exchange, trust establishment, and trust enforcement are the four crucial aspects of which a federated trust management system needs to take care.

Trust representation needs a collection of languages to express various factors in federated trust management, plus a set of protocols to make different languages interoperable. Expression of trust facts such as credentials, trust intentions and trust behaviors [3], which describe the identities and their attributes, willingness to act or willingness to accept actions, and the externally observable properties of the actions themselves, is necessary in trust representation. All existing and future authentication technologies need to be supported, and all types of policies describing all possible trust intentions need to be accommodated in trust representation. Meanwhile interoperable protocols need to be provided for all possible expression formats across trust domains.

Trust exchange needs a secure method to communicate trust representations across trust domains. All the communication protocols in the network layers should be supported. And trust exchange is expected to offer not only communication channel security, but also message security. At the same time, users will expect trust exchange to guarantee not only end-to-end security, but also the integrity and privacy of the exchanged information. Although formalization and standardization is desired, no single format can express all types of factors in trust. There is neither a standard syntax nor distribution mechanism by which an authority can make trust-related information available for consumption by all potential relying parties. So trust exchange needs to provide a content interpretation service to translate trust information between different policy languages and message or token formats, and make the final action descriptions easy to understand and enforce.

Trust establishment provides a dynamic and flexible infrastructure to establish and maintain trust relationships across trust domains. Negotiation is a necessary process before trust relationships can be established. Trust establishment needs to support a set of general trust negotiation protocols that permit involved parties to establish and maintain trust relationships, as well as application-specific and content-triggered negotiation protocols. At the same time, privacy control mechanisms are needed in trust establishment to protect negotiating parties' privacy.

Trust enforcement includes a dynamic and flexible infrastructure to publish/discover trust intentions and trust behavior descriptions, and authorize trust behaviors. Trust intentions need to be known and understood by involved parties. Providing a way to publish these trust intentions and making these trust intentions accessible to involved parties or the public are necessary. The trust enforcement infrastructure needs a mechanism to make all trust behaviors consistent with trust intentions. Because trust intentions change from time to time, the trust enforcement infrastructure needs to provide a mechanism to prescribe trust intentions and check the compliance of trust intentions dynamically. In human relationships trust intentions can be uncertain; sometimes they are just derived from feelings. The flexibility to handle this uncertainty is also necessary.

3 Examination of Extant Systems

Examining these requirements of six extant trust management systems from major vendors and international organizations can clearly show the need of an evaluation metrics for federated trust management.

➢ The IBM Trust Establishment Framework [4, 5] is a toolkit for enabling trust relationships between strangers, together with a set of trust enforcement mechanisms and a corresponding representation for policies. Although trust relationships are established in this system, the relationships are merely based on public key certificates, and are manually set by domain administrators. It lacks the capability for on-line negotiation. Its trust enforcement mechanisms are also based on public key certificates. They decide users' roles based on their certificates and certain policies. Enforcement decisions are based on validating certificates and mapping certificates' owners to roles. To represent trust-related information, the system only provides a trust policy language to describe rules that determine how to map entities to roles. IBM did not provide further information about its trust exchange mechanism because that was not the focus of the system.

➢ The AT&T PolicyMaker system [6] integrates trust enforcement and representation in a composite way. The enforcement engine uses certificates only to authorize the holder of the certificate to perform certain actions. It is not convenient to include certain user's attributes in these certificates. The corresponding control policy is expressed in a set of assertions, which can include programs provided by the resource server that are executed as part of compliance checking when a request is made, which makes this system unique. The KeyNote system [7] is a simplified version of the PolicyMaker system with certain extensions for a variety of Internet-based applications. The trust representation in the KeyNote system is a single, unified language for local policies and credentials. These policies and credentials contain predicates that describe the trusted actions permitted by the holders of specific public keys, which are called assertions. The trust enforcement becomes natural when these assertions are essentially small, highly structured programs. Credential assertions, which also serve the role of certificates, have the same syntax as policy assertions but are also signed by the principal delegating the trust. According to their specifications, the trust relationships implied in these systems need to be manually set by administrators. Thus both systems lack negotiation capability.

Exchange mechanisms are not described, but are assumed in the underlying infrastructures.

➢ The REFEREE system [8] is a rule-controlled environment and provides both a general policy evaluation mechanism for web clients and servers and a language for specifying trust policies. In the REFEREE model, trust enforcement is totally under the control of trust representation. REFEREE places all trust decisions under explicit policy control. Every action, including evaluation of compliance with policy, happens under the control of certain policies. That is, REFEREE is a system for writing policies about policies, as well as policies about cryptographic keys, certification authorities, trust delegation, or anything else. Establishment of trust relationships is ignored in this system, so it is not a complete federated trust management system. As with the PolicyMaker and KeyNote systems, exchange mechanisms are assumed in the underlying infrastructures.

➢ The Liberty Alliance is a digital identity standards group. The Liberty Alliance Project [9] is a consortium of technology vendors and consumer-facing enterprises formed "to establish an open standard for federated network identity." It aims to make it easier for consumers to access networked services from multiple suppliers while safeguarding security and privacy. It does not explicitly use trust management methods, but its specifications are closely linked to the SAML (Security Assertion Markup Language [10]) single sign-on standard, and they overlap with certain elements of WS-Security. So the Liberty Alliance has its own representation and enforcement requirement for trust-related activities, and mechanisms for establishment and exchange of trust relationships. Its specifications have been published in three phases: the Identity Federation Framework (ID-FF) came first in early 2003, the Identity Web Services Framework (ID-WSF) followed in late 2003, and the Identity Services Interface Specifications (ID-SIS) document was finalized in late 2004.

➢ Another interesting framework is GAA-API/TrustBuilder [11]. It is an integrated framework with two subsystems: Generic Authorization and Access-control API (GAA-API) [12] and TrustBuilder [13]. Although it uses adaptive trust negotiation and access control as a means to counter malicious attacks and does not offer critical features such as maintenance and updating of trust relationships, it does provide some basic functionalities for federated trust management. TrustBuilder provides functionalities for trust establishment, while GAA-API provides an enforcement engine to control compliance between a user's intentions (represented in policy files) and a system's behaviors. Various trust related information is represented in different formats such as policy files, databases, and credentials. Privacy protection for exchange of trust related information is also addressed. The most important feature of this framework is that it uses trust as its basis to protect security and privacy, and that is the main task of federated trust management systems.

Clearly, an evaluation metrics can be used to reveal the strengths and weaknesses as well as to help users choose a suitable solution from different extant trust management systems.

4 Characteristics of Federated Trust Management

Some characteristics exist in all trust management systems. These characteristics are categorized and summarized from three perspectives in order to offer a set of overall measurements for evaluation purpose.

4.1 Quality of Functionality

Quality of functionality is the most important set of measurements to be considered for evaluation, because it includes the most desirable qualities a user expects from a federated trust management system. Three basic qualities of functionality required for federated trust management are discussed below.

(1) Adaptability. Federated trust management systems need to accommodate the dynamic trustworthiness characteristics of trusted partners' behavior, who might suddenly lose competence or maliciously employ strategies to vary trustworthiness [15]. Federated trust management systems must update themselves frequently to accommodate dynamic trust relationships and evolutionary policies.

(2) Accuracy. Federated trust systems need to include suitable trust factors to correctly model and predict potential partners' future behavior and enforce their behavior. Accuracy of federated trust management systems can be measured in terms of the similarity between the system's calculated trust model or value and the trusted partner's true trustworthiness [14], or in terms of the consistency between a system's behaviors and its users' expectations.

(3) Reputation. Reputation is a measurement and indicator of an entity's (person, service or system) trustworthiness. It mainly depends on partners' experiences of cooperation with that person, using that service, or interaction with that system. Different partners may have different opinions regarding the same entity. The value of a reputation is defined as a comprehensive combination of rankings given to the entity by partners, and that value is the only representative factor of the trustworthiness of that entity.

4.2 Cost of Functionality

All federated trust management systems try to build trust relationships, construct trust models, exchange trust related information, and enforce trust behavior with minimal computational cost and time [16]. Computational efficiency can be gauged by the time needed to complete a specific task, so the time needed for a specific federation task is a useful metric.

(1) Duration. Execution duration measures the expected delay between the moment when a request for a certain trust management operation is sent and the moment when the operation is completed. The execution duration is the sum of the processing time and the transmission time over multiple domains. Execution time can be obtained via active monitoring.

(2) Cost. Cost is something (e.g., money, CPU cycles, time) that users have to pay for the system to fulfill their needs to manage trust across security domains. Users may need management of trust for online collaboration or resource

sharing such as checking credit or determining the amount of money the service requester has to pay to the service provider to get a commodity such as an entertainment ticket or monthly phone service. Providers of trust management either directly advertise the execution price of their services, or they provide means for potential requesters to inquire about it.

4.3 Usability

Usability of federated trust management systems is mainly reflected in user awareness. After a user has deployed a trust management system, operation should be autonomous unless the system actively requires a user's involvement. These two aspects are explained in detail. Other factors such as understandability, operability, user involvement, and user's acceptance will be discussed in the actual comprehensive comparison of existing systems.

(1)   Indicator. Like other security and privacy protection systems that provide a security alert icon (e.g., the SSL icon in web browsers), federated management systems need to provide an indicator of the trustworthiness of a cooperating partner or potential partner in order to explicitly indicate trust and risk.

(2)   User transparency. Since federated trust management handles the non-functional aspects of a system, the workflow and processing of the trust management system should be user-transparent. But when user involvement is needed, the system needs to provide good alert mechanisms to get the user's attention, and employ a good user interface for human machine interactions.

5   Comprehensive Comparisons of Extant Systems

Following the four functional requirement aspects and three important evaluation perspectives discussed in section 2 and 4, a set of comprehensive evaluation metrics will be discussed and used to compare the six major trust management systems, and especially for their support of federation activities. This set of evaluation metrics is divided into four groups and examined from three evaluation perspectives. After this comparison, strength and weakness of each system can then be analyzed. And direction for further improvement of each system can be identified. The evaluation data are collected from a number of server systems. Each system runs on a Xeon 2.80GHz processor, 512MB memory, and the Windows XP professional version.

5.1   Trust Exchange

Since the exchange of trust related information utilizes an underlining communication infrastructure and facilities, evaluation of functionality for trust exchange is focused on other aspects. The most important aspect of trust exchange is secure and reliable transmission of trust related information at the message level. Thus the security token is the cornerstone. Broadly speaking, a number of types of security tokens have been proposed and implemented using different trust models. These trust models include the X.509 standard Public Key Infrastructure (PKI) trust model, the Pretty Good

Privacy (PGP) trust model, the Simple Public Key Infrastructure (SPKI), and the Simple Distributed Secure Infrastructure (SDSI). The capability to accommodate extant security tokens and future token types is an important aspect for any federated trust management system. To measure this aspect, expert judgment needs to be used to answer whether a system's trust exchange facility has an open architecture and to what degree. It is also required to count the number of extant security token types supported and answer "which token types are they"?

Another important aspect for trust exchange is the capability to resolve semantic conflicts. Extant research in information semantic interoperability can be categorized into three types: mapping-based, intermediary-based, and query-oriented approaches. Answering the following questions can measure the semantic interoperability for trust exchange and the measurement can be constructed accordingly.

➢ Are mapping-based interoperation methods supported?
➢ Are intermediary-based interoperation methods supported?
➢ Are query-oriented interoperation methods supported?

The performance measurement is mainly for the overheads of token exchange, semantic interoperation service, and privacy protection.

Ideally, trust exchange is completely automated, but sometimes this is not possible. User involvement refers to whether or not the user is actively engaged in the trust exchange process. A comparison of six major systems' exchange capability is illustrated in table 1. The "yes/no" answers the question of whether a token type or a semantic

Table 1. Comparison of six major systems for trust exchange

Trust exchange		Security token exchange				Semantic interoperation		
		Open archite cture	Token type 1	Token type 2	Token type 3	Mapping-based method	Interm ediary-based method	Query-based method
Quality of functionality	IBM TE	No	PK Cert.	N/A	N/A	Yes	No	No
	PolicyMaker	N/A	N/A	N/A	N/A	N/A	N/A	N/A
	KeyNote	N/A	N/A	N/A	N/A	N/A	N/A	N/A
	REFEREE	N/A	N/A	N/A	N/A	N/A	N/A	N/A
	Liberty	Yes	PK Cert.	X.509	SAML	Yes	No	No
	TrustBuilder	No	PK Cert.	X.509	N/A	Yes	No	Yes
Cost of functionality (overhead)	IBM TE	N/A	1ms	N/A	N/A	N/A	N/A	N/A
	PolicyMaker	N/A	N/A	N/A	N/A	N/A	N/A	N/A
	KeyNote	N/A	N/A	N/A	N/A	N/A	N/A	N/A
	REFEREE	N/A	N/A	N/A	N/A	N/A	N/A	N/A
	Liberty	N/A	3ms	5ms	N/A	N/A	N/A	N/A
	TrustBuilder	N/A	2ms	4ms	N/A	N/A	N/A	N/A
User involvement	IBM TE	No				No		
	PolicyMaker	N/A				N/A		
	KeyNote	N/A				N/A		
	REFEREE	N/A				N/A		
	Liberty	No				No		
	TrustBuilder	No				Yes (when needed)		

method is supported. Overheads of token exchange and interoperation are measured on experiment servers running exchange services within a local network. Liberty Alliance Project can support the most types of tokens, whereas PolicyMaker, KeyNote and REFEREE do not use tokens at all. The overhead for token exchange is almost negligible for each system discussed here if there is any.

5.2 Trust Representation

As for the functionality of trust representation, completeness is the first aspect to be considered; next is the accuracy measurement of trust representation. Because there are diverse trust factors involved in federated trust management, systems' capabilities to accommodate these diverse trust factors are also important. These trust factors can be classified into objective factors and subjective factors. Objective factors include various facts and other objectively measurable elements in federated trust management. Objective factors can be classified into three categories: identity information, privilege information and trust knowledge. Identity information includes a representative element (identification number or name) and other credential information. Privilege information describes allowable actions and behaviors in a system. Trust knowledge covers other supportive information for establishment, monitoring and enforcement of trust relationships. Subjective factors include trust intentions (represented in policies) and reputations (represented in trust values). Two questions need to be answered for these trust factors:

> ➢ Whether a federated trust management system includes these trust factors?
> ➢ What are the representative qualities of these trust factors?

The answer for the first question is yes or no. The answer for the second can be from a fuzzy set {low, medium, high}, or can be a numeric value from an interval such as [0,1]. Extending the work of Klos and Poutré [17], reputation accuracy can be calculated from the difference between the calculated reputation, which is formed using a Beta probability from the action history of the target entity, and the actual reputation from other entities' votes.

Because federated trust management deals with different trust factors across security domains, such a system needs to provide flexibility to allow subjective adjustments to objective trust factors. For example, within one security domain, the system architect can be expected to have access to enough information to assure that a trust representation accurately reflects the accuracy of the underlying authentication technology; but for inter-domain federation, special managerial exceptions should be allowed. For example, if a user from a foreign domain wants to use the fingerprint template obtained at the foreign domain, but the local administrator does not fully trust that template because of lack of knowledge concerning the foreign domain's authentication devices and methods, the local administrator may lower the trust level of that fingerprint template to a password equivalent one in order to reduce risk in the local system. This is an operational or managerial adjustment, and it is subjective. So this question needs to be answered to evaluate a federated trust management system's adaptivity for trust representation:

> ➢ Can users make subjective adjustments to objective trust factors?

Table 2. Comparison of six major systems for trust representation

Trust representation			Objective factors			Subjective factors	
			Identity	Privilege	Trust knowledge	Policy	Reputation
Quality of functionality	Completeness	IBM TE	Yes	Yes	No	Yes	No
		PolicyMaker	Yes	Yes	Yes	Yes	No
		KeyNote	Yes	Yes	No	Yes	No
		REFEREE	Yes	Yes	Yes	Yes	No
		Liberty	Yes	Yes	Yes	Yes	No
		TrustBuilder	Yes	Yes	Yes	Yes	Yes
	Accuracy	IBM TE	High	High	N/A	Yes	N/A
		PolicyMaker	High	High	Medium	High	N/A
		KeyNote	High	High	Medium	High	N/A
		REFEREE	High	High	Medium	High	N/A
		Liberty	High	High	High	High	N/A
		TrustBuilder	High	High	High	High	Medium
	Adjustment	IBM TE	Yes	Yes	N/A	Yes	N/A
		PolicyMaker	No	No	No	N/A	N/A
		KeyNote	No	No	No	N/A	N/A
		REFEREE	No	No	No	Yes	N/A
		Liberty	No	No	No	Yes	N/A
		TrustBuilder	No	Yes	Yes	Yes	No
Cost of functionality	Cost	IBM TE	Low	Low	N/A	Low	N/A
		PolicyMaker	Low	Low	Low	Low	N/A
		KeyNote	Low	Low	Low	Low	N/A
		REFEREE	Low	Low	Low	Low	N/A
		Liberty	Medium	Medium	Medium	Medium	N/A
		TrustBuilder	Medium	Medium	Medium	Medium	Medium
	Duration	IBM TE	Low	Low	N/A	Low	N/A
		PolicyMaker	Low	Medium	Low	Medium	N/A
		KeyNote	Low	Medium	Low	Medium	N/A
		REFEREE	Low	Medium	Low	High	N/A
		Liberty	Medium	Medium	Medium	Medium	N/A
		TrustBuilder	Medium	Medium	Medium	Medium	Medium
Usability	Understandability	IBM TE	Low	High	N/A	Low	N/A
		PolicyMaker	High	Low	Low	Low	N/A
		KeyNote	High	Low	Low	Low	N/A
		REFEREE	High	High	High	High	N/A
		Liberty	Medium	Medium	Medium	Medium	N/A
		TrustBuilder	High	High	High	High	Medium
	User acceptance	IBM TE	High	High	N/A	Medium	N/A
		PolicyMaker	High	Medium	Low	Medium	N/A
		KeyNote	High	High	Low	Medium	N/A
		REFEREE	High	High	High	High	N/A
		Liberty	High	High	High	High	N/A
		TrustBuilder	High	High	High	High	Medium

The evaluation of performance for trust representation is quite straightforward. It consists of measurements of cost and duration. For example, the cost of identity information includes the cost for different authentication technologies deployed within a security domain and the cost needed to train users; the duration measurement needs to cover the time used for different authentication procedures with different technologies and the time used to transform authentication templates into formal representations. The evaluation of usability mainly focuses on user interfaces, which includes the understandability of the user interfaces and the acceptance of users. Table 2 shows a comparison of six major systems' representation capability. The "yes/no" answers the question of whether an objective or subjective factor is supported; the "high/medium/l ow" measures the level of satisfaction for a certain measurement. Using the "quality" and "usability" criteria, table 2 identifies the strengths of TrustBuilder over other systems, which are the support for reputations, the adjustment capability for trust factors, and the usability of the representations for various trust factors such as trust knowledge and policies. Since permitted privileges in KeyNote and PolicyMaker sometimes are small structured programs, it is difficult to understand the actual meaning of these privileges and the entire policy rules. And these small structured programs can also be embedded into credential assertions (a type of trust knowledge), which share the same syntax with privileges. It is even more difficult to understand various types of trust knowledge in policy rules written by administrators and users.

5.3 Trust Establishment

The main functionalities of trust establishment are establishment and maintenance of trust relationships. These two aspects need to be considered simultaneously to evaluate a federated trust management system's capabilities associated with trust establishment. Support of negotiation is the most fundamental requirement, so the questions below need to be answered to measure the generality of a system.

➤ Does the system support negotiation protocols specific for that type of application or that domain?
➤ Does the system support general or user-defined negotiation protocols?

To evaluate the adaptivity of a system's trust establishment capability, its support for different trust models needs to be examined. The questions below are related.

➤ Does the system support direct trust establishment?
➤ Does the system support indirect trust establishment?

Privacy protection is required when a user's private attributes are disclosed. Expert evaluation of this capability will be required. Observation and maintenance of a trust relationship's evolution and update is also one of the main tasks for trust establishment, so it should be included in the evaluation.

The performance of trust establishment for a federated trust management system can be measured by the average time used for the establishment process and its user involvement. The degree of user involvement is also a good measurement of usability. Table 3 shows a comparison of six major systems' establishment capability. The "yes/no" answers the question of whether certain functionality is supported. I simulate the establishment process between a hospital domain and a pharmacy domain using IBM Trust Establishment Framework, Liberty Alliance Project, and TrustBuilder with only one challenge and one verification. The numerical data is obtained from this one-challenge-and-one-verification negotiation protocol. The results show that IBM Trust Establishment Framework can only support direct negotiations, and it is more efficient

Table 3. Comparison of six major systems for trust establishment (A trust establishment simulation with one challenge and one verification)

Trust establishment		Application specific negotiation	General negotiation	Direct establishment	Indirect establishment	Privacy protection
Quality of functionality	IBM TE	Yes	No	Yes	No	No
	PolicyMaker	N/A	N/A	N/A	N/A	N/A
	KeyNote	N/A	N/A	N/A	N/A	N/A
	REFEREE	N/A	N/A	N/A	N/A	N/A
	Liberty	Yes	Yes	Yes	Yes	No
	TrustBuilder	Yes	Yes	Yes	Yes	Yes
Cost of functionality (Duration)	IBM TE	40ms	N/A	40ms	N/A	N/A
	PolicyMaker	N/A	N/A	N/A	N/A	N/A
	KeyNote	N/A	N/A	N/A	N/A	N/A
	REFEREE	N/A	N/A	N/A	N/A	N/A
	Liberty	200ms	200ms	200ms	500ms	N/A
	TrustBuilder	100ms	100ms	100ms	1s	N/A
User involvement	IBM TE	No	N/A	No	N/A	N/A
	PolicyMaker	N/A	N/A	N/A	N/A	N/A
	KeyNote	N/A	N/A	N/A	N/A	N/A
	REFEREE	N/A	N/A	N/A	N/A	N/A
	Liberty	No	No	No	No	N/A
	TrustBuilder	No	No	No	No	No

than Liberty Alliance Project and TrustBuilder for this simple one-challenge-and-one-verification negotiation protocol, because IBM Trust Establishment Framework is implemented in C and does not use web services as its communication interface. On the other hand, compared with IBM Trust Establishment Framework, Liberty Alliance Project and TrustBuilder can support indirect trust establishment and provide more flexibility, which supports adjustments to dynamic trust relationships.

5.4 Trust Enforcement

The most important functionality of trust enforcement is to guarantee compliance between trust behaviors and their corresponding governing policies stating users' trust intentions. This part includes enforcement of trust intentions, definition of trust intentions, revocation of privileges, checking of the validity of identity information and trust knowledge, and privacy protection.

To measure this compliance guarantee, it is important to count the number of compliance failures (or false revocations) within a system running for a certain period of time, and to examine a system's capability to resolve trust intention conflicts with or without human involvement. For example, if two trust intentions describe the constraints for the same trust behavior, the system should either be able to determine which one has superior authority or allow the domain administrator to decide which one is to be used. Thus two questions below need to be answered to measure this functionality.

➢ Is the system able to solve trust intention conflicts?
➢ Does the resolution process need human intervention?

Table 4-A. Comparison of six major systems for trust enforcement (first half)

Trust enforcement			Definition of trust intentions	Enforcement of trust intentions	Revocation of privileges	Validation of trust information	Privacy protection
Quality of functionality		IBM TE	Yes	Yes	Yes	No	No
		PolicyMaker	Yes	Yes	Yes	Yes	No
		KeyNote	Yes	Yes	Yes	Yes	No
		REFEREE	Yes	Yes	Yes	Yes	No
		Liberty	Yes	Yes	Yes	Yes	No
		TrustBuilder	Yes	Yes	Yes	No	No
Usability	User's awareness	IBM TE	Low	Low	Low	N/A	N/A
		PolicyMaker	Low	Low	Low	Low	N/A
		KeyNote	Low	Low	Low	Low	N/A
		REFEREE	Low	Low	Low	Low	N/A
		Liberty	Low	Low	Low	Low	N/A
		TrustBuilder	Low	Low	Low	N/A	N/A
	User interface's acceptance	IBM TE	N/A	N/A	N/A	N/A	N/A
		PolicyMaker	N/A	N/A	N/A	N/A	N/A
		KeyNote	N/A	N/A	N/A	N/A	N/A
		REFEREE	N/A	N/A	N/A	N/A	N/A
		Liberty	N/A	N/A	N/A	N/A	N/A
		TrustBuilder	N/A	N/A	N/A	N/A	N/A
	User interface's operability	IBM TE	N/A	N/A	N/A	N/A	N/A
		PolicyMaker	N/A	N/A	N/A	N/A	N/A
		KeyNote	N/A	N/A	N/A	N/A	N/A
		REFEREE	N/A	N/A	N/A	N/A	N/A
		Liberty	N/A	N/A	N/A	N/A	N/A
		TrustBuilder	N/A	N/A	N/A	N/A	N/A

Due to the dynamic trust relationships and ever-changing contexts for federated trust management, a federated trust management system needs to be able to detect changed trust relationships and updated context information. One performance measurement is the extra time (overhead) used by the trust enforcement processes. Usability can be evaluated by answering below questions.

➢ Are users aware of the trust enforcement process?
➢ Are users comfortable with using the interface?
➢ Do users know how to use the interface?

Table 4 shows a comparison of six major systems' enforcement capability. The two halves (table 4-A and table 4-B) compare different aspects of a systems' enforcement capability. The "yes/no" answers the question of whether certain functionality is supported; the "high/medium/low" measures the level of satisfaction for a certain usability measurement. Although this is only a rough comparison, the difference between Liberty Alliance Project, TrustBuilder, and other systems can be easily identified. Liberty Alliance Project and TrustBuilder provide better quality and usability. Through this comparison, the fact that Liberty Alliance Project provides better usability than TrustBuilder for most trust enforcement capability can also be identified. Validation of trust information and dynamic trust relationship detection are supported by Liberty Alliance Project but not by TrustBuilder.

Table 4-B. Comparison of six major systems for trust enforcement (second half)

Trust enforcement			Compliance check	Trust intention conflict resolution	Human intervention	Dynamic trust relationship detection	Context information update
Quality of functionality		IBM TE	0 failure	No	No	No	No
		PolicyMaker	0 failure	No	No	No	No
		KeyNote	0 failure	No	No	No	No
		REFEREE	0 failure	No	No	No	No
		Liberty	0 failure	Yes	No	Yes	Yes
		TrustBuilder	0 failure	Yes	No	No	Yes
Usability	User's awareness	IBM TE	Low	N/A	N/A	N/A	N/A
		PolicyMaker	Medium	N/A	N/A	N/A	N/A
		KeyNote	Medium	N/A	N/A	N/A	N/A
		REFEREE	High	N/A	N/A	N/A	N/A
		Liberty	High	Medium	N/A	Medium	Medium
		TrustBuilder	Low	Low	N/A	N/A	Low
	User interface's acceptance	IBM TE	N/A	N/A	N/A	N/A	N/A
		PolicyMaker	N/A	N/A	N/A	N/A	N/A
		KeyNote	N/A	N/A	N/A	N/A	N/A
		REFEREE	N/A	N/A	N/A	N/A	N/A
		Liberty	N/A	N/A	N/A	N/A	N/A
		TrustBuilder	N/A	N/A	N/A	N/A	N/A
	User interface's operability	IBM TE	N/A	N/A	N/A	N/A	N/A
		PolicyMaker	N/A	N/A	N/A	N/A	N/A
		KeyNote	N/A	N/A	N/A	N/A	N/A
		REFEREE	N/A	N/A	N/A	N/A	N/A
		Liberty	N/A	N/A	N/A	N/A	N/A
		TrustBuilder	N/A	N/A	N/A	N/A	N/A

6 Conclusion

Again, the purpose of this paper is to initiate discussion of the requirements and evaluation metrics for federated trust management, to offer a context in which to evaluate and compare current and future solutions, and to encourage the development of proper systems for federation in networked systems. A well-defined, general-purpose, federated trust management system cannot be implemented before researchers and developers understand the needs of federation in addition to the needs of traditional trust management. And a comprehensive benchmark is also needed for in-depth comparisons and evaluations.

References

1. Ruohomaa, S., Kutvonen, L.: Trust Management Survey. In: Herrmann, P., Issarny, V., Shiu, S.C.K. (eds.) iTrust 2005. LNCS, vol. 3477, pp. 77–92. Springer, Heidelberg (2005)
2. Wu, Z., Weaver, A.C.: Requirements of federated trust management for service-oriented architectures. International Journal of Information Security 6(5), 287–296 (2007)

3. Grandison, T., Sloman, M.: A survey of trust in internet applications. IEEE Communications Surveys and Tutorials (Fourth Quarter, 2000),
   http://www.comsoc.org/pubs/surveys/
4. IBM: IBM Trust Establishment Policy Language, http://www.hrl.il.ibm.com/TrustEstablishment/PolicyLanguage.asp
5. IBM: Access Control Meets Public Key Infrastructure, or: Assigning Roles to Strangers. In: Proc. of IEEE Symposium on Security and Privacy (2000),
   http://www.hrl.il.ibm.com/TrustEstablishment/paper.asp
6. Blaze, M., Feigenbaum, J., Lacy, J.: Decentralized Trust Management. In: Proc. 1996 IEEE Symposium on Security and Privacy, pp. 164–173 (1996)
7. Blaze, M., Feigenbaum, J., Keromytis, A.D.: KeyNote: Trust Management for Public Key Infrastructures. In: Christianson, B., Crispo, B., Harbison, W.S., Roe, M. (eds.) Security Protocols 1998. LNCS, vol. 1550, pp. 59–63. Springer, Heidelberg (1999)
8. Chu, Y.-H., Feigenbaum, J., LaMacchia, B., Resnick, P., Strauss, M.: REFEREE: Trust Management for Web Applications. World Wide Web Journal 2, 127–139 (1997)
9. Liberty Alliance: Liberty Alliance Complete Specifications ZIP Package (2008),
   http://www.projectliberty.org/resource_center/specifications/liberty_alliance_complete_specifications_zip_package_22_june_2008
10. OASIS Security Services TC: Security Assertion Markup Language (SAML) V2.0 Technical Overview (2008),
    http://www.oasis-open.org/committees/download.php/27819/sstc-saml-tech-overview-2.0-cd-02.pdf
11. Ryutov, T., et al.: Adaptive Trust Negotiation and Access Control. In: Proc. of 11th ACM Symposium on Access Control Models and Technologies, pp. 139–146 (2005)
12. Ryutov, T., Neuman, C.: The Specification and Enforcement of Advanced security Policies. In: Proc. of the 2002 Conference on Policies for Distributed Systems and Networks (2002)
13. Winslett, M., Yu, T., Seamons, K.E., et al.: The TrustBuilder Architecture for Trust Negotiation. IEEE Internet Computing 6(6), 30–37 (2002)
14. Klos, T., Poutre, H.L.: Using Reputation-Based Trust for Assessing Agent Reliability. In: Proc. of the AAMAS-2004 Workshop on Trust in Agent Societies, pp. 75–82 (2004)
15. Fullam, K., Barber, K.S.: A Temporal Policy for Trusting Information. In: Proc. of the AAMAS-2004 Workshop on Trust in Agent Societies, pp. 47–57 (2004)
16. Ghanea-Hercock, R.: The Cost of Trust. In: Proc. of the AAMAS-2004 Workshop on Trust in Agent Societies, pp. 58–64 (2004)
17. Klos, T.B., Poutré, H.L.: Decentralized reputation-based trust for assessing agent reliability under aggregate feedback. In: Proc. of the 7th Workshop on Trust in Agent Societies, pp. 75–82 (2004)

A Model of Bilinear-Pairings Based Designated-Verifier Proxy Signatue Scheme*

Fengying Li[1,2], Qingshui Xue[2], Jiping Zhang[1], and Zhenfu Cao[3]

[1] Department of Education Information Technology, East China Normal University, 200062, Shanghai, China
fyli@sjtu.edu.cn, jpzhang@deit.ecnu.edu.cn
[2] School of Techniques, Shanghai Jiao Tong University, 201101, Shanghai, China
xue-qsh@sjtu.edu.cn
[3] Dept. of Computer Science and Engineering, Shanghai Jiao Tong University, 200240, Shanghai, China
zfcao@cs.sjtu.edu.cn

Abstract. In a proxy signature scheme, one original signer delegates a proxy signer to sign messages on behalf of the original signer. When the proxy signature is created, the proxy signer generates valid proxy signatures on behalf of the original signer. Based on Cha and Cheon's ID-based signature scheme, a model of designated-verifier proxy signature scheme from the bilinear pairing is proposed. The proposed scheme can provide the security properties of proxy protection, verifiability, strong identifiability, strong unforgeability, strong repudiability, distinguishability and prevention of misuse of proxy signing power. That is, internal attacks, external attacks, collusion attacks, equation attacks and public key substitution attacks can be resisted.

1 Introduction

The proxy signature scheme [1], a variation of ordinary digital signature schemes, enables a proxy signer to sign messages on behalf of the original signer. Proxy signature schemes are very useful in many applications such as electronics transaction and mobile agent environment.

Mambo et al. [1] provided three levels of delegation in proxy signature: full delegation, partial delegation and delegation by warrant. In full delegation, the original signer gives its private key to the proxy signer. In partial delegation, the original signer produces a proxy signature key from its private key and gives it to the proxy signer. The proxy signer uses the proxy key to sign. As far as delegation by warrant is concerned, warrant is a certificate composed of a message part and a public signature key. The proxy signer gets the warrant from the original signer and uses the corresponding private key to sign. Since the conception of the proxy signature was brought forward, a lot of proxy signature schemes have been proposed [2]-[14][16-18].

* This paper is supported by the National Natural Science Foundation of China under Grant No. 60673079.

E. Bertino and J.B.D. Joshi (Eds.): CollaborateCom 2008, LNICST 10, pp. 416–424, 2009.
© ICST Institute for Computer Sciences, Social-Informatics and Telecommunications Engineering 2009

Recently, many threshold proxy signature schemes were proposed [2] [6]-[14]. In threshold proxy signature schemes, a group of n proxy signers share the secret proxy signature key. To produce a valid proxy signature on the message m, individual proxy signers produce their partial signatures on that message, and then combine them into a full proxy signature on m. In a (t, n) threshold proxy signature scheme, the original signer authorizes a proxy group with n proxy members. Only the cooperation of t or more proxy members is allowed to generate the proxy signature. Threshold signatures are motivated both by the demand which arises in some organizations to have a group of employees agree on a given message or document before signing, and by the need to protect signature keys from attacks of internal and external adversaries.

In 1999, Sun proposed a threshold proxy signature scheme with known signers [9]. Then Hwang et al. [7] pointed out that Sun's scheme was insecure against collusion attack. By the collusion, any $t-1$ proxy signers among t proxy signers can cooperatively obtain the secret key of the remainder one. They also proposed an improved scheme which can guard against the collusion attack. After that, [6] showed that Sun's scheme was also insecure against the conspiracy attack. In the conspiracy attack, t malicious proxy signers can impersonate some other proxy signers to generate valid proxy signatures. To resist the attack, they also proposed a scheme. Hwang et al pointed out [8] that the scheme in [7] was also insecure against the attack by the cooperation of one malicious proxy signer and the original signer. In 2002, Li et al. [2] proposed a threshold proxy signature scheme full of good properties and performance.

The multi-proxy signature scheme was first proposed in [14]. The multi-proxy signature scheme is a special case of the threshold proxy signature scheme. The multi-proxy signature scheme allows an original signer to authorize a group of proxy members can generate the multi-signature on behalf of the original signer.

In a designated-verifier proxy signature scheme, the proxy signature will be verified only by a designated verifier chosen by the proxy signer. In 1996, Jakobsson et al. designed a designated-verifier proxy signature scheme for the first time [1]. In [21], Dai et al. proposed a designated-verifier proxy signature scheme based on discrete logarithm problems. However, in 2003, Wang pointed out that the original signer alone can forge valid proxy signatures to frame the proxy signer [16]. In 2004, Li et al. proposed a designated-verifier proxy signature scheme from bilinear pairings [17].

In 1984, Shamir proposed identity (ID)-based cryptography to simplify key management and remove the necessity of public key certificates [18]. In 2001, a practical ID-based encryption scheme was found by Boneh and Franklin, who took advantage of the properties of suitable bilinear parings (the Weil or Tate pairing) over supersingular elliptic curves [19].

Designated-verifier proxy signature scheme provides both the security properties of designated verifier signatures and those of proxy signatures. As far as the property of verifiability is concerned, the designated-verifier proxy signature scheme should meet the property of restrictive verifiability which means that only the designated verifier can verifier the validity of proxy signatures.

In 2003, Cha and Cheon [20] designed an ID-based signature scheme using GDH groups. Under the random oracle model, their scheme is proved to be secure against existential forgery on adaptively chosen messages and ID attacks supposing CDHP (Computational Diffie-Hellman Problem) is intractable.

Based on Cha and Cheon's ID-based signature scheme, a model of designated-verifier proxy signature scheme is proposed. The proposed scheme can provide the security properties of proxy protection, verifiability, strong identifiability, strong unforgeability, strong nonrepudiability, distinguishability, known signers and prevention of misuse of proxy signing power. That is, internal attacks, external attacks, collusion attacks and public key substitution attacks can be efficiently resisted.

In the paper, we organize the content as follows. In section 2, we will detail the related knowledge. We will review Cha and Cheon's ID-based signature scheme in section 3. In section 4, we will propose our model of proxy signature scheme using bilinear pairings. The correctness of the proposed scheme will discuss in section 5. Finally, the conclusion is given.

2 Related Knowledge

The In the section, the bilinear pairings and the related mathematical problems are introduced [19].

2.1 Bilinear Pairings

Let G_1 be a cyclic additive group produced by P, with a prime order q, and G_2 be a cyclic multiplicative group with the same order q. Then, $e: G_1 \times G_1 \to G_2$ is a bilinear pairing with the following properties:

(1) Bilinearity: $e(aP, bQ) = e(P,Q)^{ab}$ for all $P, Q \in G_1, a, b \in Z_q$.

(2) Non-degeneracy: There exists $P, Q \in G_1$ such that $e(P,Q) \neq 1$.

(3) Computability: There exists an efficient algorithm to calculate $e(P,Q)$ for all $P, Q \in G_1$.

A bilinear map satisfied the three properties above is said to be an admissible bilinear map. It is well known that Weil and Tate pairings related with supersingular elliptic curves or abelian varieties can be modified to get such bilinear maps.

2.2 Some Mathematical Problems

(1) DLP (Discrete Logarithm Problem): Given two group elements P and Q, find an integer $a \in Z_q^*$ such that $Q = aP$ whenever such an integer exists.

(2) DDHP (Decision Diffie-Hellman Problem): For $a, b, c \in Z_q^*$, given P, aP, bP, cP, decide whether $c \equiv ab \bmod q$. If it holds, (P, aP, bP, cP) is called a valid Diffie-Hellman tuple.

(3) CDHP (Computational Diffie-Hellman Problem): For $a, b \in Z_q^*$, given P, aP, bP, compute abP.

(4) GDHP (Gap Diffie-Hellman Problem): A class of problem where DDHP is easy while CDHP is hard.

When the DDHP is easy but the CDHP is hard on the group G_1, we call G_1 a gap Diffie-Hellman (GDH) group.

2.3 Basic ID-Based Designated-Verifier Proxy Signature Scheme

Usually, the kind of scheme consists of five phases: Setup, Extract, Proxy key pair generation, Proxy signature generation and proxy signature verification. In the phase of Setup, a security parameter k is taken as input and system parameters which include a description of a finite message space M and master key are returned. In general, the system parameters will be publicly known, while the master key will be known only to the Private Key Generator (PKG).

In the phase of Extract, the system parameters, master key and an arbitrary $ID \in \{0,1\}^*$ are taken as input and a corresponding private key d_{ID} is returned as output.

In the phase of Proxy key pair generation, the original signer's private key, a warrant which specifies the original signer, the proxy signer and other application dependent delegation information explicitly, and the proxy signer's identity are taken as input, and a proxy key is returned as output. Only the proxy signer can get the knowledge of the proxy private key, while the proxy public key is public.

In the phase of Proxy signature generation, a message, the warrant, the designated verifier's identity and the proxy private key are taken as input and a designated-verifier signature is returned as output.

In the phase of Proxy signature verification, a signature and the designated verifier's private key are taken as input, and 1 or 0 is returned as output, meaning accept or reject, the information that the signature is valid with respect to a specific original signer and a proxy signer.

3 Review of Cha and Cheon's ID-Based Signature Scheme

The scheme consists of four phases: Setup, Extract, Sign, Verify.

(1) Setup: Select a random integer $s \in Z_q^*$ and set $P_{pub} = sP$. $H_1 : \{0,1\}^* \to G_1^*$ and $H_2 : \{0,1\}^* \times G_1^* \to Z_q^*$ are two cryptographic hash functions. The system parameters are params= $(q, G_1, G_2, e, P, P_{pub}, H_1, H_2)$. $s \in Z_q^*$ is the master key.

(2) Extract: For a given string $ID \in \{0,1\}^*$, the PKG computes $Q_{ID} = H_1(ID)$, and get the corresponding private key $d_{ID} = sQ_{ID}$.

(3) Sign: Given a secret key d_{ID} and a message m, select an integer $r \in Z_q^*$ randomly, compute

$$U = rQ_{ID}, h = H_2(m, U) \tag{1}$$

and

$$V = (r + h)d_{ID}. \tag{2}$$

output a signature $\sigma = (U, V)$.

(4) Verify: To verify a signature $\sigma = (U,V)$ of a message m for an identity ID, check whether

$$e(P,V) = e(P_{pub}, U + H_2(m,U)Q_{ID}).\qquad(3)$$

4 A Model of Bilinear-Pairings Based Designated-Verifier Proxy Signature Scheme

The following participants are involved in the scheme: the original group G_o, the proxy group G_p, the designated verifier or receiver Cindy, etc.

In the scheme, we specify that any t_1 or more out of n_1 original signers $(1 \le t_1 \le n_1)$ can delegate the signing capability to the proxy group on behalf of G_o. Similarly, any t_2 or more out of n_2 proxy signers $(1 \le t_2 \le n_2)$ can represent G_p to sign a message on behalf of G_o. Only designated verifier V can verify the proxy signature.

Throughout the paper, the system parameters are defined as follows: m_w : a warrant that records the identities of the original signers in G_o and the proxy signers in G_p, the parameters (t_1, n_1), (t_2, n_2), the valid delegation period, etc; AOSID: (Actual original signers' ID) the identities of the actual original signers; APSID: (Actual proxy signers' ID) the identities of the actual proxy signers.

In addition, each user U_i has a randomly selected private key d_{Ui} and public key Q_{Ui}. For each user U_i, its identity is ID_i. Suppose that $G_o = \{O_1, O_2, ..., O_{n1}\}$ and $G_p = \{P_1, P_2, ..., P_{n2}\}$ are the groups of n_1 original signers and n_2 proxy signers respectively. The proposed scheme is stated as follows.

The scheme is composed of three phases: proxy share generation phase, proxy signature generation phase and proxy signature verification phase.

4.1 Proxy Share Generation Phase

Step 1. Each of actual original signers O_i $(i = 1,2,...,t_1';t_1' \ge t_1)$ selects a random integer $r_i \in Z_q^*$, calculates

$$U_i = r_i Q_{ID_{Oi}}\qquad(4)$$

and sends U_i to other original signers.

Step 2. After O_i receives $O_j (j = 1,2,...,t_1'; j \ne i)$, O_i computes

$$U = \sum_{i=1}^{t_1'} U_i\qquad(5)$$

and

$$V_i = (r_i + H_2(m_w, AOSID, U))d_{ID_{Oi}} \tag{6}$$

passes $(m_w, AOSID, U, U_i, V_i)$ to all of proxy signers.

Step 3. Each of proxy signers P_j $(j = 1, 2, ..., n_2)$ accepts $(m_w, AOSID, U, U_i, V_i)$ by checking whether the following equation holds:

$$e(P, V_i) = e(P_{pub}, U_i + H_2(m_w, AOSID, U)Q_{ID_{Oi}}) \tag{7}$$

Step 4 If all $(m_w, AOSID, U, U_i, V_i)$'s are valid, P_j computes his proxy key pair as

$$d_{Pj} = \sum_{i=1}^{t_1'} V_i + H_2(m_w, AOSID, U)d_{ID_{Pj}} \tag{8}$$

and

$$Q_{Pj} = U + H_2(m_w, AOSID, U)(\sum_{i=1}^{t_1'} Q_{ID_{Oi}} + Q_{ID_{Pj}}) . \tag{9}$$

Then P_j can sign messages which conforms to m_w on behalf of the original signers.

4.2 Proxy Signature Generation Phase

Step 1. Each of proxy signers P_j $(j = 1, 2, ..., t_2'; t_2' \geq t_2)$ chooses two random integers $a_j, b_j \in Z_q^*$ and calculates

$$X_j = a_j P , \tag{10}$$

$$Y_j = (e(Q_{ID_{Cindy}}, P_{pub}))^{a_j} \tag{11}$$

and

$$B_j = b_j Q_{Pj} . \tag{12}$$

Meanwhile, he/she passes (X_j, Y_j, B_j) to other proxy signers.

Step 2. P_j also computes

$$X = \sum_{j=1}^{t_2'} X_j , \tag{13}$$

$$Y = \prod_{j=1}^{t_2'} Y_j , \tag{14}$$

$$B = \sum_{j=1}^{t_2'} B_j \tag{15}$$

and

$$S_j = (b_j + H_3(m, APSID, X, Y, B))d_{Pj} . \tag{16}$$

H_3 is a secure hash function.

Step 4. P_j sends $(m, m_w, AOSID, APSID, X, U, B, S_j)$ to the signature combiner.

Step 5. Upon The signature combiner receives all of individual proxy signature $(m, m_w, AOSID, APSID, X, U, B, S_j)$ from all of proxy signers, he or she calculates

$S = \sum_{j=1}^{t_2'} S_j$, then the signature combiner passes $(m, m_w, AOSID, APSID, X, U, B, S)$ as

the proxy signature on the message m to the designated proxy signature verifier Cindy.

4.3 Proxy Signature Verification Phase

After receiving the proxy signature $(m, m_w, AOSID, APSID, X, U, B, S)$, the designated verifier Cindy operates as follows.

Step 1. Check whether the message m and parameters t_1', t_2' conforms to the warrant m_w . If not, the scheme stop. Otherwise, continue.

Step 2. Check whether the actual original signers and the actual proxy signers are specified as the original signers and the proxy signers, respectively, in the warrant m_w . If not, stop. Otherwise, continue.

Step 3. Cindy calculates

$$Y' = e(d_{ID_{Cindy}}, X) \tag{17}$$

and

$$Q_P = t_2'U + t_2'H_2(m_w, AOSID, U)(\sum_{i=1}^{t_1'} Q_{ID_{O_i}}) + H_2(m_w, AOSID, U)\sum_{j=1}^{t_2'} Q_{ID_{Pj}}). \tag{18}$$

He or she accepts the proxy signature $(m, m_w, AOSID, APSID, X, U, B, S)$ if and only if the following congruence holds:

$$e(P, S) = e(P_{pub}, B + H_3(m, APSID, X, Y', B)Q_P) . \tag{19}$$

5 Correctness of above Scheme

Theorem 1: If the tuple $(m, m_w, AOSID, APSID, X, U, B, S)$ is a signature by the above scheme, the designated verifier Cindy will accept it.

Proof:

$$S = \sum_{j=1}^{t_2'} S_j$$

$$= \sum_{j=1}^{t_2'} ((b_j + H_3(m, APSID, X, Y, B))d_{Pj}$$

$$= \sum_{j=1}^{t_2'} (b_j d_{Pj} + H_3(m, APSID, X, Y, B)d_{Pj})) \qquad (20)$$

$$= s \sum_{j=1}^{t_2'} (b_j Q_{Pj} + H_3(m, APSID, X, Y, B)Q_{Pj}))$$

$$e(P, S)$$

$$= e(P, s \sum_{j=1}^{t_2'} (b_j Q_{Pj} + H_3(m, APSID, X, Y, B)Q_{Pj}))$$

$$\qquad (21)$$

$$= e(P_{pub}, \sum_{j=1}^{t_2'} b_j Q_{Pj} + H_3(m, APSID, X, Y, B) \sum_{j=1}^{t_2'} Q_{Pj})$$

$$= e(P_{pub}, B + H_3(m, APSID, X, Y, B)Q_P)$$

6 Conclusions

In the paper, based on Cha and Cheon's ID-based signature scheme, a model of bilinear-pairings based designated-verifier proxy signature scheme is proposed.

As far as we know, it is the first model of bilinear-pairings based designated-verifier proxy signature scheme. The proposed scheme can provide the security properties of proxy protection, verifiability, strong identifiability, strong unforgeability, strong nonrepudiability, distinguishability and prevention of misuse of proxy signing power, i.e., internal attacks, external attacks, collusion attacks, equation attacks and public key substitution attacks can be resisted.

References

1. Mambo, M., Usuda, K., Okamoto, E.: Proxy Signature for Delegating Signing Operation. In: Proceedings of the 3rd ACM Conference on Computer and Communications Security, pp. 48–57. ACM Press, New York (1996)
2. Li, J.G., Cao, Z.F.: Improvement of a Threshold Proxy Signature Scheme. Journal of Computer Research and Development 39(11), 515–518 (2002) (in Chinese)
3. Li, J.G., Cao, Z.F., Zhang, Y.C.: Improvement of M-U-O and K-P-W Proxy Signature Schemes. Journal of Harbin Institute of Technology (New Series) 9(2), 145–148 (2002)

4. Li, J.G., Cao, Z.F., Zhang, Y.C.: Nonrepudiable Proxy Multi-signature Scheme. Journal of Computer Science and Technology 18(3), 399–402 (2003)
5. Li, J.G., Cao, Z.F., Zhang, Y.C., Li, J.Z.: Cryptographic Analysis and Modification of Proxy Multi-signature Scheme. High Technology Letters 13(4), 1–5 (2003) (in Chinese)
6. Hsu, C.L., Wu, T.S., Wu, T.C.: New Nonrepudiable Threshold Proxy Signature Scheme with Known Signers. The Journal of Systems and Software 58, 119–124 (2001)
7. Hwang, M.S., Lin, I.C., Lu Eric, J.L.: A Secure Nonrepudiable Threshold Proxy Signature Scheme with Known Signers. International Journal of Informatica 11(2), 1–8 (2000)
8. Hwang, S.J., Chen, C.C.: Cryptanalysis of Nonrepudiable Threshold Proxy Signature Scheme with Known Signers. Informatica 14(2), 205–212 (2003)
9. Sun, H.M.: An Efficient Nonrepudiable Threshold Proxy Signature Scheme with Known Signers. Computer Communications 22(8), 717–722 (1999)
10. Sun, H.M., Lee, N.Y., Hwang, T.: Threshold Proxy Signature. IEEE Proceedings-computers & Digital Techniques 146(5), 259–263 (1999)
11. Zhang, K.: Threshold Proxy Signature Schemes. In: Information Security Workshop, Japan, pp. 191–197 (1997)
12. Hsu, C.L., Wu, T.S., Wu, T.C.: Improvement of Threshold Proxy Signature Scheme. Applied Mathematics and Computation 136, 315–321 (2003)
13. Tsai, C.S., Tzeng, S.F., Hwang, M.S.: Improved Nonrepudiable Threshold Proxy Signature Scheme with Known Signers. Informatica 14(3), 393–402 (2003)
14. Hwang, S.J., Shi, C.H.: A Simple Multi-Proxy Signature Scheme. In: Proceeding of the Tenth National Conference on Information Security, Taiwan (2000)
15. Jakobsson, M., Sako, K., Impagliazzo, R.: Designated verifier proofs and their application. In: Maurer, U.M. (ed.) EUROCRYPT 1996. LNCS, vol. 1070, pp. 143–154. Springer, Heidelberg (1996)
16. Wang, G.: Designated-verifier proxy signatures for e-commerce. In: Proc. IEEE 2004 Int. Conf. on Multimedia and Expo (ICME 2004), vol. 3, pp. 1731–1734 (2004)
17. Li, X., Chen, K., Li, S.: Designated-verifier proxy signatures for e-commerce from bilinear pairings. In: Proc. of Int. Conf. on Computer Communication, pp. 1249–1252 (2004)
18. Shamir, A.: Identity-based cryptosystems and signature schemes. In: Blakely, G.R., Chaum, D. (eds.) CRYPTO 1984. LNCS, vol. 196, pp. 47–53. Springer, Heidelberg (1985)
19. Boneh, D., Franklin, M.: Identity-based encryption from the Weil pairing. In: Kilian, J. (ed.) CRYPTO 2001. LNCS, vol. 2139, pp. 213–229. Springer, Heidelberg (2001)
20. Cha, J.C., Cheon, J.H.: An identity-based signature from gap diffie-hellman groups. In: Desmedt, Y.G. (ed.) PKC 2003. LNCS, vol. 2567, pp. 18–30. Springer, Heidelberg (2002)
21. Dai, J., Yang, X., Dong, J.: Designated-receiverproxy signature scheme for electronic commerce. In: Proc. of IEEE International Confernece on System, Man and Cybernetics, October 5-8, vol. 1, pp. 384–389 (2003)

A Unified Theory of Trust and Collaboration

Guoray Cai and Anna Squicciarini

College of Information Sciences and Technology
Pennsylvania State University, University Park, PA 16802
{cai,asquicciarini}@ist.psu.edu

Abstract. We consider a type of applications where collaboration and trust are tightly coupled with the need to protect sensitive information. Existing trust management technologies have been limited to offering generic mechanisms for enforcing access control policies based on exchanged credentials, and rarely deal with the situated meaning of trust in a specific collaborative context. Towards trust management for highly dynamic and collaborative activities, this paper describes a theory of trust intention and semantics that makes explicit connections between collaborative activities and trust. The model supports inferring trust state based on knowledge about state of collaborative activity. It is the first step towards a unified approach for computer-mediated trust communication in the context of collaborative work.

Keywords: trust communication, access control, information sharing, collaborative work.

1 Introduction

Sharing sensitive information across security domains is almost always a requirement for knowledge intensive collaborative work, but such sharing may impose risks on security and privacy integrity. Research has increasingly recognized the role of trust in minimizing the risk while gaining efficiencies in information sharing. The challenge of trust management is most apparent in digital government applications [14, 25]. Government agencies naturally form multiple security domains (such as DOD, DOE, USDA, USGS) according to different responsibilities of their services and varying sensitivity of information. Some of the most common types of information being shared among government agencies include intelligence, homeland security, law enforcement, and critical infrastructure information. In the literature, the lack of better support for collaboration and the difficulties of information sharing among agencies have been widely recognized in such applications [10, 27]. While each government agency must be responsible for protecting sensitive information they have collected, effective sharing of information among agencies is deemed to be more important when multiple agencies collaborate under high stake missions, such as dealing with large-scale crisis events. As an example, consider the following scenario of bioterrorism investigation.

E. Bertino and J.B.D. Joshi (Eds.): CollaborateCom 2008, LNICST 10, pp. 425–438, 2009.
© ICST Institute for Computer Sciences, Social-Informatics and Telecommunications Engineering 2009

Scenario A: The biological attacks with powders containing *Bacillus Anthracic* sent through the mail during September and October 2001 led to unprecedented public health and law enforcement investigations, which involved thousands of investigators from federal, state, and local agencies. Following recognition of the first cases of anthrax in Florida in early October 2001, investigators from the Centers for Disease Control and Prevention (CDC) and the Federal Bureau of Investigation (FBI) were mobilized to assist investigators from state and local public health and law enforcement agencies. The response to the anthrax attacks required close collaboration because of the immediate and ongoing threat to public safety.   The steps necessary to identify a potential covert bioterrorism attack include a close coordination between those who collect and analyze medical and syndromic surveillance information with the law-enforcement community's intelligence and case-related information.

In this scenario, public health officials and law enforcement agencies must join their knowledge and expertise to identify the sources and consequences of an attack. Collaboration among agencies across CDC and FBI may be difficult for the following reasons: (1) both health and disease information and criminal records are sensitive information to be protected from unintended use; (2) participating parties may not have prior arrangement on trusting relations; therefore trust may need to be developed on demand; (3) the decisions to be made are not 'business as normal'; hence regular security and privacy policies may not apply.

The distinctive feature of this type of applications is that collaboration, trust, and information sharing are tightly coupled and mutually influence each other over extended courses of collaborative activities. These unique characteristics impose new challenges and demand drastically different approaches for trust management. Existing trust management tools for such applications has shown to be cumbersome and are seldom used in real-world applications. Trust management systems, such as PolicyMaker[8], KeyNote[7], and Trust-χ [5], are merely dealing with generic language and mechanisms for specifying and evaluating security policies, credentials, and relationships. They are almost exclusively designed for business transaction applications where stable and uniform policies for security and access control can be enforced. However, managing trust in the contexts of collaboration and information sharing activities is fundamentally different because the meaning of trust always in flux with the situation of the collaboration. Trust is part of the bigger 'picture' of collaborative activities, and can not be understood outside of that context. Methods for supporting this form of trust management must make explicit connection between trust communication and the on-going collaborative activities. For this reason, we need a unified and coherent theory about trust and collaboration, which can serve as the basis for developing computational methods of trust management.

While collaborative activities impose complexities to trust management, we also see collaboration as (potentially) part of the solution to that problem. Trust communication is an inherently complex collaborative activity (to be carried out to support a more primary collaborative activity such as evacuation planning during a crisis). The approach, adopted in this paper, takes advantage of the close coupling among collaborative missions, information sharing, and trust. Our primary objective is to develop an approach for enabling semantic negotiation of trust within the context of collaborative activities.   We see trust communication as a sub-process embedded within a large discourse of the collaborative activity, which allows the knowledge of the ongoing collaboration to be fully utilized. The approach we envisioned uses agent-mediated human-human trust negotiation as a way to encourage human-machine joint problem-solving and to put human in control for trust decisions.

Before the above vision of trust management in collaborative applications can be attempted, we must first address the fundamental question of how exactly collaboration, trust, and data sharing are related. As such, this paper presents a theoretical system that provides a unified characterization of collaboration and trust. The theory imposes a mental-state view on both collaborative work and trust communication. The outcome of this work is a plan-based representation of collaboration and trust state, together with a set of modal operators and reasoning scheme for advancing the state of trust and collaboration.

2 A Theory of Collaborative Activities

For the purpose of this paper, we consider trust in the contexts of collaborative work. The ultimate goal of building a trust is to enable the success of a collaborative activity. For this reason, our framework includes a model of collaborative activity as a way to capture the context around a trust object.

Collaborative activities have been the subject of cognitive and computational studies for many years. Cognitive and social theories, such as activity theory [24], distributed cognition [16], and situated actions [32], provide language and conceptual structure for describing the settings and systems of collaborative work, but they do not deal with the design of systems that support collaboration. A commonly accepted philosophical view of collaborative activity is Bratman's notion of **shared cooperative activity** (SCA) [9]. According to Bratman, three properties must be met for agents to participate SCA: *mutual responsiveness, commitment to the joint activity*, and *commitment to mutual support*. These three properties allow agents to have additional mental attitudes as cognitive resources for communication.

An *activity* consists of a series of actions that are executed by one or more agents to achieve a goal. There actions are related through an underlying intentional structure. For a shared cooperative activity, the intentional structure corresponds to a SharedPlan of the collaboration, according to Grosz and Sidner [15]. A SharedPlan is a formal model of collaborative plans. A SharedPlan for an action includes a mutual belief concerning a way to perform this action / subactions, individual intentions that the action and subactions be performed, and its structure is a hierarchical structure of individual plans and SharedPlans. *Actions* may be basic or complex. Basic actions are performable at will, under certain conditions, while complex actions

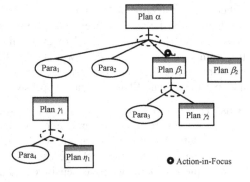

Fig. 1. Structure of an activity represented as a SharedPlan (after[11])

have associated recipes, their performance requiring the performance of each action in their recipe, under certain conditions. *Recipes* represent what agents know when they know a way of doing something. They represent information about the abstract performance of an action, and are composed of a set of constituent acts and associated constraints.

As an example, Figure 1 shows a plan for α, which was elaborated with a recipe that has two parameters (Para$_1$ and Para$_2$) and two subactions β_1 and β_2. Parameters in a recipe are knowledge-preconditions which must be identified before any subactions can be worked on. Identifying a parameter can be a complex process and may need a plan (such as Plan γ_1). A SharedPlan of an activity explains why agents do what they did and is a model of the intentional structure of a collaborative activity. According to Grosz and Kraus [15], a group of agents GR is considered to have a *Full Shared Plan* (FSP) on α when all the following conditions have been established:

---

0.   GR intends to perform action α
1.   GR has a recipe R for action α
2.   For each single-agent constituent action β_i of the recipe, there is an agent $G_{\beta_i} \in GR$, such that

    a. G_{β_i} intends to perform β_i;

       G_{β_i} believes that it can perform β_i;

       G_{β_i} has an individual plan for β_i

    b.   The group GR mutually believes 2.a.

    c.   The group GR is committed to G_{β_i}'s success

3.   For each multi-agent constituent action β_i of the recipe, there is a subgroup of agents $GR_{\beta_i} \in GR$ such that

    a. GR_{β_i} mutually believe that they can perform β_i

    b. GR_{β_i} has a SharedPlan for β_i

    c.   The group GR mutually believes 3.a.

    d.   The group GR is commited to GR_β's success

Otherwise, the agents' plan will only be a *Partial Shared Plan* (PSP).

SharedPlan theory has been a common framework for modeling collaborative activities (see [1, 20, 21, 26]). However, this theory does not consider the issue of trust among agents. In other words, the theory only works in a fully trusted environment. In fact, agents must place great trust on each other when they elaborate and execute a SharedPlan. We can expect two cases where trust can be an issue:

[**Case 1**] *Mutual dependence on sharing sensitive information.* Agent G_1 may require knowledge about a parameter (e.g., para$_1$) to move forward on its part of the duty, but this piece of knowledge may have to be retrieved from another agent G_2. Such knowledge exchange may be a problem if G_2 considers the piece of knowledge as sensitive and does not have trust on G_1 to make fair use of it.

[**Case 2**] *Mutual dependence on each other's capability to perform actions.* Since the success of a larger activity is dependent on the success of component acts which can be executed by different agents, agents place great trust on each other in their capabilities.

Such need for trust was not made explicit as a research topic in previous work, but will be the focus of the next section.

3   A Theory of Trust and Trust Communication

Here we articulate a theory that explains the way in which trust and collaborative activities are coupled and how they become problems and solutions to each other. This theory applies a mental state view to both trust and collaboration, and allows semantic connections through the intentional structures of collaboration and trust communication.

3.1   Definition of Trust

The concept of trust has been intensively investigated in the fields of philosophy, sociology, psychology, management, marketing, ergonomics, human–computer interaction (HCI), industrial psychology and electronic commerce (e-commerce). These disciplines study domain-specific forms of trust to address different types of problems, and they hardly agree on what trust is. When we come to the task of modeling trust in computing systems, we have a 'pudding of trust' [6] to deal with, each emphasizing different sets of issues. Despite such diversity of definitions, many [18, 19] believe that there exists a conceptual core that provides a general construct to model a variety of senses of trust in different application domains. We share the same view in this study. The search for a conceptual core of the trust concept is still an on-going process, but the current literature seems to suggest that trust can be analyzed as a trust relationship (in terms of "A trust B on doing z") and a set of beliefs (e.g. trustor's belief on trustworthiness of the trustee, etc) associated with such a relationship. All the challenges related to managing trust can be eventually translated into the task of representing and reasoning on the trust relations and associated beliefs.

In this study, we limit discussion to the basic form of trust which involves two agents. We use $T(A, B, z)$ to denote the trust object that captures all the information about "A trusts B on achieving the effect of z."

Definition 1. A trust object $T(A, B, z)$ refers to a trust relation together with a set of mental states (see Figure 2). It has three major components.

$T = \{TR(A, B, z), MST(A, TR), MST(B, TR)\}$

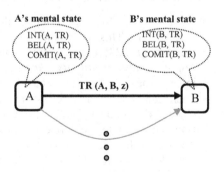

Fig. 2. Triadic relation of trust

(1) **Trust Relation.** A trust object defines a triadic (three place) relation, in the form of 'A trusts B to do z', or TR(A, B, z). Here A stands for the trustor (the peer that trusts someone). B stands for the trustee (the peer being trusted). z is some state of affair that A hopes to achieve. A places some *dependency* on B to achieve z and A is also risked by the possibility that B not do z as expected. A is potentially rewarded if z is achieved.

(2) **Mental States of A towards TR.** Agent A holds a set of individual mental attitudes towards trust relation TR. Such attitudes are constantly in flux, and they change as more evidences are exchanged and taken into account. The state of mental attitude at any given time is called *mental state*. We use MST(A, TR) to refer to the mental state of A towards trust relation TR. For the purpose of this study, we limit the contents of A's mental state to three kinds of mental attitudes: intention, belief, and commitment, represented as INT(A, TR), BEL(A, TR), COMMIT(A, TR), respectively. One important component of A's belief is BEL(A, TW(B, TR)) which refers to "*A's belief on the trustworthiness of B in relation to TR.*" TW(B, TR) is a measure of how much B is able and willing to act in A's best interest. BEL(A, TW(B, TR)) serves as the bases for A to place trust on B. In order to promote A's trust on B, B can manipulate A's belief by communicating the trustworthiness of B, TW(B, TR), to A (through sharing trust-promoting credentials or demonstrating trust-provoking behaviors).

(3) **Mental States of B towards TR.** MST(B, TR) also has three components: INT(B, TR), BEL(B, TR), COMMIT(B, TR), respectively. One important piece of BEL(B, TR is the *trustfulness* of the trustor as perceived by the trustee. This is represented as BEL(B, TF(A, TR)). Trustfulness, TF(A, TR), refers to the capacity of the trustor to take a risk that the trustee will not behave according to a special agreement even if promising to do so [34]. Trustfulness is likely to be influenced by the intentionality, past behavior, social relationship, the risk that is taken by the trustor, and the reward if the trust is realized. The trustee's knowledge on the trustfulness of the trustor may become motivations for the trustee to conform to behavioral rules in place or even form helpful attitude towards the trust relation.

Our definition of trust explicitly recognizes that the mental states of agents are integral part of a trust. Trust communication can be understood as manipulating the mental states of others by communicative actions. A few notes:

- Trust relation TR(A, B, z) implies that A depends on B in some sense in order to accomplish z. This dependency may take one of many possible senses. Based on the literature [13, 23], the most prevalent senses of trust dependencies are *competence, responsiveness, credibility, security, cooperativeness,* etc. Each trust relation can involve one or more of these basic trust dependencies.

- There can be many trust relations between two agents, each characterized as a trust object. We define **T**(A, B) = {T(A, B, *)} as the set of all the trust objects defined from A to B. Also, we define T(A) = { T(A, *, *) } as the set of all the trust objects that A play the role of trustor.

- Our idea of using BEL(A, TW(B, TR)) as the basis of trust is motivated by the work of Bhargava and his colleagues [6] who define trust as 'the trusting peer's belief in the trusted peer's willingness and capability to behave as expected by the trusting peer in a given context at a given time'. Jones [18] identified two kinds of belief: (1) *rule belief* and (2) *conformity belief.* The rule-belief refers to the belief that there exist some rules (pertaining to behavioral regularities, norms, obligations of the trustee) leading to the expectation that the trustee will do z. The conformity-belief states that the trustor holds beliefs on the trustee to actually behave in the way not violating those rules. These beliefs on rules and conformity are necessary basis for establishing belief on trustworthiness based on from observable properties and behavior of the trustee.

The above definition can be re-stated using modal logic notations.

Notations	Meaning
$T(A, B, z) <==>$	"A trust B on achieving z"
a) TR(A, B, z) &	"A has a trust dependency on B to achieve z "
b) MST(A, TR) &	"A's mental state relevant to TR"
c) MST(B, TR) &	"B's mental state relevant to TR"

The recognition of a conceptual core in our framework directly points to the importance of mental beliefs in the theories of trust. This is consistent with prior conception of trust (for recent surveys, see [6, 12, 23, 35]). The variations across these trust definitions can be explained by applying the above core conceptual structure (relation + beliefs) to a specific application context. The generality of this conceptual view lies in the fact that it does not require prior and direct binding of trust with any characteristics of the trustees. Instead, the belief components of a trust serve as the mediator for such binding, and can be done with late-binding. In this way, the concept of trust is allowed to exist in an abstract sense, and will take a concrete meaning only after it is elaborated in a specific situation.

3.2 Trust Communication

Trust communication can be understood as the process of exchanging evidences of trustworthiness and trustfulness. Evidences of trustworthiness are properties of the trustee, but such evidences must be communicated to the trustor and become part of the trustor's belief in order to have an effect on the trust.

Agents begin with a partially developed trust and extend the trust towards a fully developed trust. A *fully developed trust* (FD-Trust) has the following properties:

(i)   The purpose of the trust is known. (This refers to the z component of $T(A, B, z)$);
(ii)   The trustor A and trustee B have been identified;
(iii) The nature of the trust dependency is determined and mutually believed by both the trustor and the trustee;
(iv)   The trustor has established the highest possible belief on the trustworthiness of the trustee based on knowledge about trustee's credentials, observed behavior, reputation, etc;
(v)   The trustee has established the highest possible belief on the trustfulness of the trustor based on knowledge about trustor's risk-taking capacity, goals, risks and rewards, etc.

When the above conditions are not fully met, we say that the trust object is a *partially developed trust* (PDT). In real world situations, agents may have to act based on a partially developed trust, due to lack of knowledge, extra cost of trust communication, or making decisions under urgent conditions. When a trust is perceived as inadequate by the participating agents, they will form a shared intention to further develop the trust. Developing a trust involves elaborating on components of a trust objects. Such elaboration process on a trust will continue until one of the following two conditions is met: (a) the trust becomes adequate for the purpose; or (b) the agents do not have any other ways to advance the trust.

4 Meshing of Collaboration and Trust

In the last two sections, we have presented separate theories for trust and collaboration. Both theories were formulated using mental state operators. Now we are ready to connect these into a larger theory of trust-mediated collaboration. We will focus on two semantic relations between trust and collaboration. At one case, trust is the prerequisite for advancing collaboration on a domain activity. On another case, the state of a collaborative activity serves as trust-requiring situation that guides trust communication. We will discuss these two points in more detail next.

4.1 Trust as Prerequisite for Advancing the State of a Collaborative Activity

As agents develop and execute their collaborative plan, they heavily depend on their collective ability to bring their collaboration to certain desirable state. Such effort often requires two kinds of preconditions to be met, as discussed by Lochbaum [21]. One is called "knowledge preconditions", which are denoted as follows:

- *has.recipe*(G, α, R): a group of agents G has a recipe R for action α
- *Id.Param*$(G, \alpha(p_1, ..., p_n))$: G can identify parameters needed for action α.

Meeting knowledge conditions often requires that agents share their knowledge with each other. When knowledge to be shared is considered sensitive and the environment is not fully trusted, a trust negotiation process must be introduced.

Another set of preconditions for collaboration concerns the ability of agents in executing the collaborative plan. A complex plan is often executed by different agents, each executing some subset of actions in the plan. A requirement for having a SharedPlan is that agents must trust each other in their ability of doing individual share of the task. This kind of trust may not be automatic, but need explicit effort to negotiate.

The SharedPlan theory of collaboration (as described in section 2) does not consider the issue of trust in collaborative work. It works only under the assumptions of a fully trusted environment. We extend such theory of collaboration with the following modal operators:

- *has.recipe.Sensitive*(G, α, R)
- *Id.Param,sensitive*$(G, \alpha(p_1, ..., p_n))$
- *Can,Execute.uncertain*(G, α, R)

When one of these operators is invoked, a trust negotiation process is initiated and inserted as a sub process of the overall collaboration.

4.2 Collaborative Activity as Trust-Requiring Situation

An important property of trust communication within a collaborative activity is that the process of trust negotiation itself is a collaborative activity. As described in Section 3, trust is defined by a set of mental states, which can be concretized only in a real situation. In the context of collaborative work, the goal of a trust communication process is to enable further advances to the larger activity. The state of collaboration on the main activity serves as the motivations behind a trust communication session and determines when and how a trust gets started, developed, and ended. The goal-oriented nature of trust has been widely recognized in the philosophical literature [18], but the articulation of how goals relate to trust has been vague and informal.

The mental-state view of trust serves as a schema with which a trust-requiring situation is recognized, interpreted, acted upon by the agents. *A trust-requiring situation* is a situation that a trust is needed in order to advance the ongoing activity. When a situation is known, an agent will actively interpret the situation in order to decide or update the values/contents of the components in a trust object. At the end of Section 2, we have identified two general classes of situations where trust communication needs to be introduced. Here we will refine that discussion, using the following as an example of a situation:

Scenario B: After a major earthquake disaster, many wounded at the events are moved into The Good Health Hospital (GHH), waiting to be treated and cared. However, the hospital runs short of qualified nurses, and has announced a few temporary positions to be filled quickly. Alice has recently completed her training as a nurse from The Care Hospitals in India, and she is motivated to help local residence in fighting this crisis. She applies on-line for the open position at The Good Health Hospital. The hospital needs to verify her capabilities as a nurse before hiring her while the nurse wants to ensure that the Hospital is of a reputable standing. Further to prove her capabilities, the Hospital requests that she shows her Degree Certificate and her Training Certificate, while the nurse requests that the hospital prove it respects HIPAA (Health Insurance Portability and Accountability Act) rules.

Give the above situation, the following can be inferred.

(1) *A situation determines if a trust object is to be created and when.* In a collaborative activity, there are certain moments when collaboration can not proceed without first establishing trust between entities. In other words, a collaborative activity creates *trust-requiring situations* (following the work of Riegelsberger [28]). In scenario B, there is no need to create (or activate) a trust between GHH and Alice until the moment GHH evaluate Alice's application in order to make a hiring decision.

(2) *A situation determines who are involved in a trust, and what roles they play* (either as trustor or trustee). For example, in Scenario B, Alice needs to gain trust from GHH in order to get the job. Hence, GHH serves as the trustor and Alice serves as the trustee in this relation.

(3) *A situation determines the nature of the trust relation to be established.* In the above, GHH has a concern on the Alice capability in performing a nursing job, while Alice wants to make sure that GHH is a reputable place to work. Depending on what the actual concern was raised, the strategy for elaborating the trust can be quite different.

5   A Running Example

In order to demonstrate the applicability of our theory, we will present a brief walk-through on the analysis of scenario B where a nurse Alice seeks to join medical team at The Good Health Hospital in USA. Using the theory presented in this paper, we can analyze this scenario in two levels.

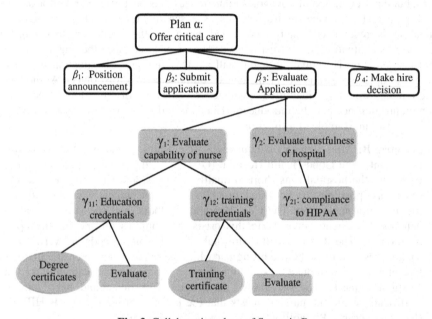

Fig. 3. Collaborative plans of Scenario B

5.1   Intentional Structure of the Domain Activity

The upper portion of Figure 3 shows the intentional structure of the domain activity. The top-level collaborative activity is about finding people who have expertise in providing critical care at an emergency situation. Both Alice and the Hospital share a common goal of providing medical care services to the wounded. To achieve this goal, a process (recipe) adopted by this scenario is that the hospital issued position announcement, and interested candidates are expected to submit applications through an on-line utility, followed by evaluating applications at the Hospital. The hiring decision can not be made until β_1, β_2, β_3 are done. The plan structure of domain level activity is shown in the top part of Figure 3 (none shaded plan nodes).

5.2 Intentional Structure of Trust Communications

When agents elaborate the plan to the point γ_1, the system recognizes that there is a need to create a trust object T_1(GHH, Alice, "qualified nurse"). Following the principles stated in Section 4.2, the system will use the knowledge about the current state of collaboration (specifically, the plan graph that T_1 is rooted) to determine the nature of the trust dependency and the belief components of T_1.

- Determining the trust relation involves identifying trustor and trustee and how the trustor depends on the trustee. Based on the knowledge about plans α and β_3, we can infer that the trustor is GHH and the trustee is Alice. GHH depends on Alice's *capability* of performing a nurse function.
- Determining the mental state components of trust is also relying on the knowledge about α and β_3. Due to emergency situation of this recruiting, the intention to have established trust T_1 is clearly set. The belief component BEL(GHH, TW(Alice, TR)) (i.e., GHH's belief on the trustworthiness of Alice in relation to TR) is zero. TW(Alice, TR) is reflected by two properties of Alice: her degree certificates, and her training certificates. This leads the agents to adopt a recipe for γ_1 that includes two sub actions: γ_{11} and γ_{12}. To contribute these subgoals, Alice shared her degree certificate and training certificate with GHH, and GHH went through an evaluation process.
- Establishing BEL(Alice, TF(GHH, TR)). As part of this trust, Alice would like to insure that GHH is a reputable institution. Based on Alice's request for evidences, GHH shared the certificate of its membership with HIPAA. This will also allow Alice to trust GHH that that information she provided to GHH will not be abused.

6 Discussion and Conclusion

We have presented a unified theory of trust and collaboration using a mental state perspective. As demonstrated by the analysis of scenario B, we have observed that our theory is capable of explaining the way that trust and collaboration are coupled in real activities. Such coupling effect creates opportunities for dealing with difficult semantic issues in trust management. Our work stands at crossroads of two research areas: trust negotiation and theories of collaboration and communication.

The work presented in this paper is conceptual in nature, and is our first step towards effective trust management in collaborative applications. While much research efforts has been placed into the foundations of trust negotiation –such as languages for expressing resource access control policies [3, 4], protocols and strategies for conducting trust negotiations [30, 39], and logic for reasoning about the outcomes of these negotiations [29, 37], little effort has been posed to understanding how the articulated notion of trust fits within negotiations, beyond the access control aspect. Existing trust negotiation theories have formalized the interaction protocols that parties should follow in order to ensure correct negotiation executions. In particular, Yu *et al.* [39] investigated the notion of negotiation strategies which control the exact content of the messages: which credentials to disclose, when to disclose them, and when to terminate a negotiation. Strategies and their interoperability have been further investigated by the same authors

[38, 39] who have proposed a unified scheme, called *Unipro*, to model resource protection, including policies. Additionally, in order to address the need for managing the dynamics of trust, Ma and Orgun [22] proposed a formal theory of trust evolution for multiagent systems. Their theory uses Typed Modal Logic (TML) expressions to represent beliefs and operators on beliefs.

Although relevant, this body of work fails to elaborate on the notion of trust, and to consider how parties' collaboration may substantially alter the negotiation flow. Rather, most of the current trust negotiation approaches have been designed under the assumption that the negotiating parties are inherently not collaborative, although they adhere to the trust negotiation protocol. This motivated a large amount of work focusing on privacy and on cryptographic based negotiations [31, 36]. We believe that this assumption is very restrictive, and that it hindered the deployment of trust negotiation protocols in many real-world domains where collaboration is essential. The only work on negotiation considers the effect of cooperative work on trust negotiation are work by Baselice et al. [2], Jin et al. [17], and Svirskas [33]. However, these works are mostly about interoperability of trust management across domains, and they do not deal with meaning of trust in collaborative applications. Also, a simple collaborative approach for trust negotiations is proposed in [30], where a cooperative strategy is proposed.

Our work fills a gap in the literature by making the connections between theories of collaboration and concepts of trust. Existing theories about collaboration and trust have been isolated. On one hand, theories of collaboration works only with perfectly trusted environment. On the other hand, methods of trust communication assume collaboration-neutral environment, and do not deal with the semantics of trust. Our current work provides a unified theory of trust and collaboration based on the SharedPlan theory of collaboration.

We plan to further validate our theory by investigating more practical scenarios and by conducting extensive case analysis. At the same time, we have been using this theory to guide the design of a new experimental system CollTrust-X. CollTrust-X builds on top of the TRUST-X architecture [5, 30] and adds a semantic layer for managing trust objects and collaborative plans.

Acknowledgement

This work is partially supported by a grant from the National Science Foundation under Grants No EIA-0306845 and by the National Visualization and Analytics Center (NVAC), a U.S. Department of Homeland Security Program, under the auspices of the Northeast Regional Visualization and Analytics Center (NEVAC).

References

1. Balkanski, C., Hurault-Plantet, M.: Cooperative requests and replies in a collaborative dialogue model. International Journal of Human-Computer Studies 53, 915–968 (2000)
2. Baselice, S., Bonatti, P.A., Faella, M.: On interoperable trust negotiation strategies. In: Eighth IEEE International Workshop on Policies for Distributed Systems and Networks (POLICY 2007), Bologna, Italy, June 13-15, pp. 39–50 (2007)

3. Bertino, E., Ferrari, E., Squicciarini, A.: Privacy preserving trust negotiations. In: 4th International Workshop on Privacy Enhancing Technologies, Toronto, Canada (2004)
4. Bertino, E., Ferrari, E., Squicciarini, A.: Trust negotiations: concepts, systems, and languages. Computing in Science & Engineering 6(4), 27–34 (2004)
5. Bertino, E., Ferrari, E., and Squicciarini, A.: Trust-X椹 Peer to Peer Framework for Trust Establishment. IEEE Trans. Knowledge and Data Eng. 16(7), 827–842 (2004)
6. Bhargava, B., Lilien, L., Rosenthal, A., Winslett, M., Sloman, M., Dillon, T.S., Chang, E., Hussain, F.K., Nejdl, W., Olmedilla, D., Kashyap, V.: The pudding of trust. IEEE Intelligent Systems 19(5), 74–88 (2004)
7. Blaze, M., Feigenbaum, J., Ioannidis, J., Keromytis, A.D.: The KeyNote Trust-Management System Version 2 (1999)
8. Blaze, M., Feigenbaum, J., Lacy, J.: Decentralized trust management. In: Proceedings, 1996 IEEE Symposium on Security and Privacy, pp. 164–173 (1996)
9. Bratman, M.E.: Shared cooperative activity. Philosophical Review 101, 327–341 (1992)
10. Butler, J., Mitchell, L.C., Friedman, C.R., Scripp, R.M., Watz, C.G.: Collaboration between Public Health and Law Enforcement: New Paradigms and Partnerships for Bioterrorism Planning and Response. Emerging Infectious Diseases 8, 1152–1156 (2002)
11. Cai, G., Wang, H., MacEachren, A.M., Fuhrmann, S.: Natural Conversational Interfaces to Geospatial Databases. Transactions in GIS 9(2), 199–221 (2005)
12. Corritore, C.L., Kracher, B., Wiedenbeck, S.: On-line trust: concepts, evolving themes, a model. International Journal of Human-Computer Studies 58(6), 737–758 (2003)
13. Grabner-Krauter, S., Kaluscha, E.A.: Empirical research in on-line trust: a review and critical assessment. International Journal of Human-Computer Studies 58(6), 783–812 (2003)
14. Grimes, J.G.: Department of Defense Information Sharing Strategy, Department of Defense (2007)
15. Grosz, B.J., Kraus, S.: Collaborative plans for complex group action. Artificial Intelligence 86, 269–357 (1996)
16. Hollan, J., Hutchins, E., Kirsh, D.: Distributed cognition: toward a new foundation for human-computer interaction research. ACM Transactions on Computer-Human Interaction 7(2), 174–196 (2000)
17. Jin, J., Ahn, G.-J., Shehab, M., Hu, H.: Towards trust-aware access management for ad-hoc collaborations. In: CollaborateCom 2007. International Conference on Collaborative Computing: Networking, Applications and Worksharing, 2007. CollaborateCom 2007, pp. 41–48 (2007)
18. Jones, A.J.I.: On the concept of trust. Decision Support Systems 33(3), 225–232 (2002)
19. Jones, K.: Trust: Philosophical Aspects. In: Smelser, N.J., Baltes, P.B. (eds.) International Encyclopedia of the Social & Behavioral Sciences, pp. 15917–15922. Pergamon, Oxford (2001)
20. Lesh, N., Rich, C., Sidner, C.L.: Using Plan Recognition in Human-Computer Collaboration. In: Proceedings of the seventh international conference on user modelling, Banff, Canada, pp. 23–32 (1999)
21. Lochbaum, K.E.: A collaborative planning model of intentional structure. Computational Linguistics 24(4), 525–572 (1998)
22. Ma, J., Orgun, M.A.: Trust management and trust theory revision. IEEE Transactions on Systems, Man and Cybernetics, Part A 36(3), 451–460 (2006)
23. McKnight, D.H., Chervany, N.I.: The meanings of trust. In: Falcone, R., Singh, M., Tan, Y.-H. (eds.) AA-WS 2000. LNCS (LNAI), vol. 2246, pp. 27–54. Springer, Heidelberg (2001)

24. Nardi, B.A. (ed.): Context and Consciousness: Activity Theory and Human-computer Interaction. MIT Press, Cambridge (1996)
25. Relyea, H.C., Seifert, J.W.: Information Sharing for Homeland Security: A Brief Overview. Congressional Research Service Reports on Homeland Security (2005)
26. Rich, C., Sidner, C.L., Lesh, N.: Collagen: Applying collaborative discourse theory to human-computer collaboration. AI Magazine 22(4), 15–25 (2001)
27. Richards, E.P.: Collaboration between Public Health and Law Enforcement: The Constitutional Challenge. Emerging Infectious Diseases 8(10) (2002)
28. Riegelsberger, J., Sasse, M.A., McCarthy, J.D.: The mechanics of trust: A framework for research and design. International Journal of Human-Computer Studies 62(3), 381–422 (2005)
29. Seamons, K.E., Winslett, M., Yu, T.: Requirements for Policy Languages for Trust Negotiation. In: Third IEEE International Workshop on Policies for Distributed Systems and Networks, Monterey, CA (2002)
30. Squicciarini, A.C., Bertino, E., Ferrari, E., Paci, F., Thuraisingham, B.M.: PP-Trust-X: A system for Privacy Preserving Trust Negotiations. ACM Transactions on Information Systems Security 10(3), 1–50 (2007)
31. Squicciarini, A.C., Bertino, E., Ferrari, E., Ray, I.: Achieving privacy in trust negotiations with an ontology-based approach. IEEE Transactions on Dependable and Secure Computing 3(1), 13–30 (2006)
32. Suchman, L.: Plan担 and Situated Actions: The Problem of Human崩achine Communication. Cambridge University press, Cambridge (1987)
33. Svirskas, A., Isachenkova, J., Molva, R.: Towards secure and trusted collaboration environment for European public sector. In: CollaborateCom 2007. International Conference on Collaborative Computing: Networking, Applications and Worksharing, pp. 49–56 (2007)
34. Tullberg, J.: Trust–The importance of trustfulness versus trustworthiness. Journal of Socio-Economics (2008) (in press)
35. Wang, Y.D., Emurian, H.H.: An overview of online trust: Concepts, elements, and implications. Computers in Human Behavior 21(1), 105–125 (2005)
36. Winsborough, W.H., Li, N.: Protecting sensitive attributes in automated trust negotiation. In: Proceedings of the ACM Workshop on Privacy in the Electronic Society, pp. 41–51. ACM Press, New York (2002)
37. Winsborough, W.H., Seamons, K.E., Jones, V.E.: Automated trust negotiation. In: DARPA Information Survivability Conference and Exposition, Piscataway, New Jersey, pp. 88–102. IEEE Press, Los Alamitos (2000)
38. Yu, T., Winslett, M.: A Unified Scheme for Resource Protection in Automated Trust Negotiation. In: The 2003 IEEE Symposium on Security and Privacy, May 11-14, p. 110. IEEE Computer Society, Los Alamitos (2003)
39. Yu, T., Winslett, M., Seamons, K.E.: Supporting structured credentials and sensitive policies through interoperable strategies for automated trust negotiation. ACM Transactions on Information and System Security (TISSEC) 6(1), 1–2 (2003)

Enabling Interoperable and Selective Data Sharing among Social Networking Sites

Dongwan Shin and Rodrigo Lopes

Computer Science Department,
New Mexico Tech,
Socorro, NM 87801, USA
{doshin,rodrigo}@nmt.edu
http://sislab.cs.nmt.edu

Abstract. With the widespread use of social networking (SN) sites and even introduction of a social component in non-social oriented services, there is a growing concern over user privacy in general, how to handle and share user profiles across SN sites in particular. Although there have been several proprietary or open source-based approaches to unifying the creation of third party applications, the availability and retrieval of user profile information are still limited to the site where the third party application is run, mostly devoid of the support for data interoperability. In this paper we propose an approach to enabling interopearable and selective data sharing among SN sites. To support selective data sharing, we discuss an authenticated dictionary (ADT)-based credential which enables a user to share only a subset of her information certified by external SN sites with applications running on an SN site. For interoperable data sharing, we propose an extension to the OpenSocial API so that it can provide an open source-based framework for allowing the ADT-based credential to be used seamlessly among different SN sites.

Keywords: Privacy, social networking, selective data sharing, interoperability, authenticated dictionary.

1 Introduction

Online social networking (SN) sites have emerged in the last few years as one of the primary sources for information exchange among friends and acquaintances. Typical examples of SN sites are networks of individuals (people in a specific culture, in communities, or in similar working contexts) or networks of organizations (companies, cities, political parties) [12]. Most of them offer the basic features of online interaction, communication, and sharing affinities, by allowing individuals to create digital profiles, which will be then viewed by others. Hence, personal information works as a fundamental building block for the proper operation in online SN sites. As the use of personal information in social networks becomes manifold, including the representation of an individual's identification, so does the abuse or misuse of the information. One of the most important issues

E. Bertino and J.B.D. Joshi (Eds.): CollaborateCom 2008, LNICST 10, pp. 439–450, 2009.
© ICST Institute for Computer Sciences, Social-Informatics and Telecommunications Engineering 2009

to be immediately addressed in this context is the issue of privacy of sensitive personal information, which is generally any type of data which could be used to cause significant harm to the individual.

In addition to that, as the number of different social services provided in a diverse context grows, an individual tends to possess many different profiles across services, each of which contains a range of information that may be duplicate, thus making an issue of data interoperability in SN sites of great importance. This is especially true for the use of third-party applications within SN sites; a new kind of usage of SN sites has developed with the development of small applications that run inside the user profile in a given SN site, many times making use of his/her profile information, thus extending the functionality of the original SN site. Although there have been several proprietary or open source-based approaches to unifying the creation of third party applications, the availability and retrieval of user profile information are still limited to the SN site where the third party application is run, mostly devoid of the support for data interoperability.

In this paper we propose an approach to enabling interopearable and selective data sharing among SN sites. To support selective data sharing for better privacy, we discuss an authenticated dictionary (ADT)-based credential which enables a user to share only a subset of her information certified by external SN sites with applications running on an SN site. Specifically, our approach allows a user to obtain credentials from an SN sites and be able to show that credential for data sharing without the need to contact the SN site again. More importantly, our approach allows the credential to be constructed efficiently using a cryptographic hash function and the user to show and prove any subset of her attributes in the credential. For interoperable data sharing, we propose an extension to the OpenSocial API so that it can provide an open source-based framework for allowing the ADT-based credential to be used seamlessly among different online SN sites. The main contributions of this paper are 1) a novel application of ADT into a social networking domain, 2) the development of a credential based system, not relying on expensive cryptographic constructs, and 3) the extension of the OpenSocial API for data interoperabiliity among SN sites.

The rest of this paper is organized as follows. In Section 2, we discuss background material related to the privacy issues in SN sites and the OpenSocial initiative. Section 3 discusses our approach, followed by the discussion of current implementation based on the proposed approach in Section 4. Section 5 discusses our future work and Section 6 concludes this paper.

2   Background and Related Technologies

2.1   Online Social Networks and Privacy Issues

Online social networks have rapidly emerged, diversified, and adopted in recent years, and the wide adoption of the Internet contributed to the recent thriving popularity of those social networking sites. In general, the privacy issue in online social networking is closely related to the level of identifiability of the information provided, its possible recipients, and its possible uses [12]. The identifiability of information is quite challenging in a sense that even online social networking sites that do not expose their users' identities may provide enough information to identify the profile's owner. According to a recent study [13], for instance, a 15 percent overlap of personal information is observed in two of the major social networking sites, which allows sophisticated viewers to know more about an individual than she may want them to. In addition, since individuals often re-use the same or similar photos across different sites, an identified face can be used to identify a pseudonym profile with the same or similar face on another site. The possible recipients of personally identifiable/identified information are social network hosting sites and third party application hosting sites that may abuse or misuse the information. Our current approach is related to this aspect in that it is based on the notion of user centricity in sharing user profile in a sense that the user will have the ultimate authority to share which data in her profile with what SN sites, thus providing the user more control on her profile.

2.2   OpenSocial and Profile Sharing

The OpenSocial project [3] was born to provide application developers with a single API that would allow the development of applications that would run across different websites, addressing the issue of a different social application API for each SN site. The OpenSocial API, implemented by each provider, would allow a developer to build an application once and deploy it on different websites without any modification to the code. On the other hand, it would also allow upcoming SN sites to have support to a diverse portfolio of applications already developed for popular and established SN websites, and at the same time saving the time and effort of designing and building their own social application API.

The API is divided in three main areas according to the functionality provided. These areas are People and Relationships, Activities and Persistence. People and relationships provide functionality to access users' information and the relations that users have with each other. The activities functionality allows the application developer to access the users' activities in the context of the website and finally the persistence API provides functionality for the application to store and retrieve application specific information. The API views users from three different perspectives: viewer, owner and friends. The viewer is the person in whose browser the application is being rendered and displayed while the owner is the person who owns the profile or information being displayed. Friends refer to the social connections of either the viewer or the owner. The owner and viewer may be the same person if, for example, someone is looking into his own profile and an application is running on that profile, using the owners information who happens to be also the one person looking at the displayed web page.

One of the main limitations in the OpenSocial is the inability for an application to access user information from different websites. Recently, different online SN sites have proposed mechanisms to allow the user profile to be exported to other websites, social networking or not. Some of these initiatives are MySpace Data Availability and Facebook Connect [2,1]. However, the sharing of information on these initiatives is one way, in other words, the information can be shared from the SN website with other websites, but not vice-versa. Also, the source SN website is directly involved with the sharing of user profiles, gaining the knowledge of all the services the user is sharing his information with, and thus having an implication of privacy violation. Our approach put forward in the paper addresses these issues seamlessly through the use of a credential system.

2.3   Credential Systems

A credential system is a system in which a user can obtain credentials (i.e., signed statements) from one organization and demonstrate possession of them to other organizations, and several credential systems based on number-theoretic schemes have been proposed for different purposes in literature. Chaum's approach to designing the digital cash system [9,10], based on blind signature techniques, was one of them, also called an anonymous credential system. This system made it possible to obtain a certified statement from an issuer and show it to a verifier without the possibility of tracing the use of credentials. The credential was built upon the number theory, especially the use of an exponent that defines the type and the value of the credential in the blind signature. One major disadvantage of using this system is that a trusted third party is always required that all participating entities are dependent upon.

Similar to Chaum's system, but a more advanced scheme to design an anonymous credential system was presented by Brands [6]. His credential system could support many features such as expressions of any satisfiable proposition from proposition logic, limitation on the number of times a credential may be used, revocable anonymity, and discouragement of lending credentials. Camenisch et al. [8,7] proposed a credential system that relies heavily on proofs of knowledge like Brands' system. One of the main disadvantages in these credential systems is obviously related to the expensive computational aspect of their cryptographic primitives using number theory and zero-knowledge proof (ZKP).

3   Our Approach

An interoperable and selective data sharing approach is discussed in this section. We first discuss the concept of ADT, then discuss how to construct attribute credentials based on that, and finally present how to integrate the ADT-based credential into OpenSocial-based social networking sites.

3.1   Selective Disclosure Credentials

Authenticated dictionaries (ADTs) have been primarily studied and used in the context of certificate revocation in public key infrastructure (PKI), especially to implement certificate revocation lists (CRLs). One of the best known examples is based on the Merkle hash tree in [15]. We decided to use an authenticated dictionary based on skip lists [5,11] for our purpose of building a credential system that allows the user to selectively share their attributes [14]. A skip list,

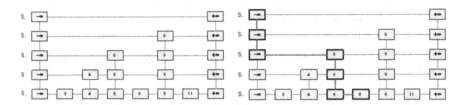

Fig. 1. Skip List (left) and A Value Search in Skip List (right)

shown in Figure 1, is a data structure that allows the effective search and update of elements within a set. It supports the following operations on a set of elements: find(x), insert(x), and delete(x), where x is an element of the set.

Initially, all elements will be ordered and form the first list from the bottom. Subsequent lists are built randomly by selecting elements from the previous list. The elements will be selected with a probability of $\frac{1}{2}$. This will be repeated until there is only one element. The first and last symbols ($-\infty$ and $+\infty$) represent the lower and higher possible boundaries, the last list consisting of only these two symbols. The search of an element in the list is started at the lower boundary symbol on the top list and continues to the right until we find the element being searched or an higher element. If the element is lower, we will descend to the element immediately below; else we will descend to the element below the previous symbol in the list. The search ends when we find our target at the bottom list or two consecutive elements at the bottom list in which the first is lower than our target, and the second is larger. The latter proves that the element being searched is not in the list. The process for searching the value 8 is shown in Figure 1. The data structure described above is very efficient for search, whose cost is $\mathcal{O}(\log n)$.

A special function f is necessary to introduce the *authenticated* skip list. The function is a commutative hashing function, that is, a hashing function that takes two values and returns the same hash independent of the order the values are given. The function is calculated for each element and will depend on all previous elements, as shown in Figure 2. The lower boundary element on the top list will contain a tag as a result of the function on the element that actually depends

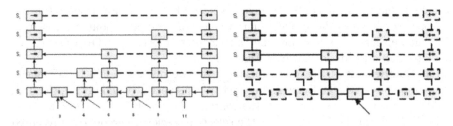

Fig. 2. Commutative hash computation flow (left) and values needed to authenticate the result of search (right)

on the full list. This last tag will be signed and therefore be used to verify the authenticity of the skip list or dictionary. [5,11] has more details on this. The commutative hashing is used to allow the function to be computed independently of the order in which both parameters of the function are entered, making the verification process more efficient, and the right part of Figure 2 shows the values needed to authenticate the result of a search.

The structure of ADT can be used to represent a credential and allow the user to disclose a subset of her attributes to verifiers. The values inside each of the nodes of ADT will be replaced by hashes of user attributes. ADT-based credentials will not contain any user information, either in plain text or encrypted, but only hash values of attributes. Hence, the basic security of this credential system resides in the selection of a good cryptographic hash function. Since the elements in the dictionary are stored in order of the value of their hash, there is no predefined order in which particular attribute values are stored. The issuer will then sign the dictionary.

There are two different ways an attribute can be proved to be an element of ADT. In the first method, the user sends the verifier a set of attributes she wants to disclose, the values in the path from an attribute in the set necessary to compute the f function value for the last element (the lower boundary element in the top list), starting at the element whose presence is to be proved; and finally the signed f function value. Verifier will then hash the attribute and use the values sent from the user to recompute the f function value of the last element, which will in turn be verified to be legitimate with the signature. Note that alternatively, after the user releases the set of her attributes to be disclosed, the verifier can interactively request the values in the path and the signed f function value to the user for each attribute in the set to be proved. A second method uses the full dictionary instead of using the values in a path for proof. The user sends ADT, a set of attributes she wants to disclose, and the signed f function value. The verifier computes function f for each node in the ADT. After verifying the correctness of the f function value of the last element and its signature, the verifier hashes each one of the attributes and searches its value in ADT. If found, the attribute is a legitimate member of the dictionary.

3.2   Extensions to the OpenSocial API

The OpenSocial API allows a third-party application to use a user's profile data available from the container host SN sites. The extension proposed in our approach would allow the application to request information about the user from different websites. To allow this, the DataRequest object of the OpenSocial API needs to be modified, as shown in Figure 3.

The DataRequest object was subclassed by two objects called DataRequestfromRemoteSite and DataRequestfromCredential respectively. Therefore, the data could be retrieved and shared from the container host website, a remote website, and directly from the user through the selective disclosure credential presented in Section 3.1. From the perspective of the application developer, the data from different sources will have the same format as data retrieved from the container

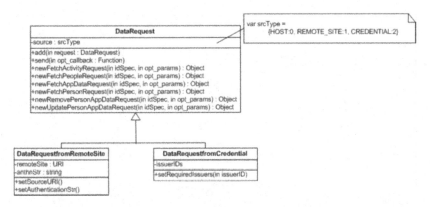

Fig. 3. UML representation of DataRequest, DataRequestfromCredential, DataRequest-fromRemoteSite objects and their relationship

host site. The major difference between the two external data source options is the involvement of the SN website that hosts the data. If the data source is an URI, the host SN website is assumed to know what user information can be disclosed and to whom on the basis of user preference set on the site. If the data source is a credential, the SN site having issued the credential has no knowledge of what information is being shared and with whom. A third-party application may have requirements to which SN sites it supports, and the issuerIDs attribute refers to the SN sites that issue credentials. This field is optional. If set, only credentials issued by the given issuer or set of issuers can be used. If not set, any credential that provides the requested information can be used.

In order to create new data request to not just the container but also the remote site and the credential, the opensocial object also needs to be modified. A new method called newDataRequestEx is added to the object for that purpose, as shown in Figure 4. Depending on the parameter that specifies the source of data, the method will create an appropriate data request object as discussed previously.

Fig. 4. UML representation of opensocial object and the addition of new method called newDataRequestEx

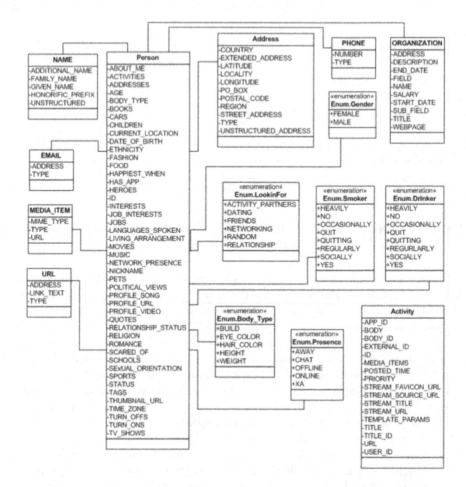

Fig. 5. Representation of the objects as described in the OpenSocial API [4]

3.3   Attribute Mapping from OpenSocial to ADT-Based Credential

All the information that can be retrieved by an OpenSocial-based third party application must be supported as an attribute of the selective disclosure credential. This means that a mapping must exist that allows SN sites to both build and read the credential. The information that can be retrieved from an SN site is limited to two top level objects and the relationship between them. These two top level objects are Person and Activity [3]. Every other object is a part of the top level objects. A more detailed diagram can be seen in Figure 5.

The basic structure of an attribute inside the ADT-based credential is as follows:

[attribute type]:[attribute ownership]:[attribute value]

The attribute type is no more than the type as defined in the OpenSocial API. For the attribute value there can be more than one meaning. If the type is an object, the value will be a set of references to the actual types that constitute it, every object ultimately leading to literal types. If the type is a literal, then the value is the actual literal representation. As previously defined in Section 3.1, attributes in the credential are hashes of the actual attribute values, therefore the value for objects will be sequences of hash values for the actual components of that object. Those components are also part of the credential and can be found in the same credential, if the user chooses to disclose them. The attribute ownership will only have a meaning for top level objects, as it will represent the relationship between the owner of the credential and the owner of the information, that is, the object represented in the attribute. They can be the same user, in which case the information belongs to the owner of the credential, or they can be different users, meaning the owner of the credential has some form of relation to the owner of the information. The OpenSocial API does not specify a limit to how deep in the social graph can information be retreived [4] , it is left up to the container site to define how deep can a user retrieve friends information.

4   Current Implementation

Our implementation phases were divided into two: the first was to develop stand-alone prototypes based on functionalities such as ADT-based credential issuance, management, and verification. The second was to port these prototypes into the OpenSocial-based web environment. As of writing this paper, we finished the first phase of our implementation.

As discussed in previous section, attributes are hashed and then inserted into ADT. The attribute is strongly typed and represented as a concatenation of the attribute type and attribute value, separated by a colon[1]. As a container for the attribute in ADT, we decided to use a four-pointer node. The node will contain pointers to all its neighbors: Up, Down, Left and Right. In addition to the attribute, the f function value will be stored in the node as well. An attribute can be proved to be an element of ADT by finding it inside the skip list and retrieving the path function values. The user is responsible for doing this. The user will send only the attribute's type and value and the corresponding values in the path that allow the re-computation of the signature element. An interesting observation is that the user will most likely disclose several attributes, and these attributes are likely to have overlapping path values. In such cases, the user only needs to send each repeating value once. To allow the user to prove ownership of the credentials there is the need to communicate information to the verifier. This is done through an XML file that includes all different values that will be used, either hashes of attributes or function values and a list of shared attributes,each one including the attribute type, attribute value and list of values needed to calculate the signed value.

---

[1] Note that our current implementation includes only the attribute type and value.

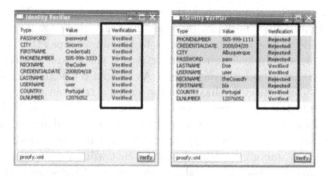

Fig. 6. The User Interface for Verifying ADT-based Credentials

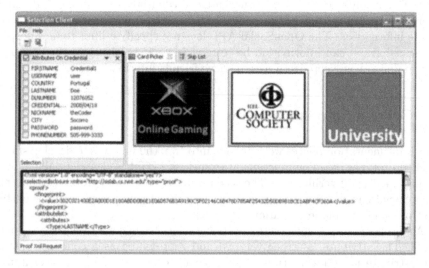

Fig. 7. The User Interface for Managing ADT-based Credentials

Revocation is an important issue in credential-based systems. One intuitive way to support revocation in our design is to have the SN to ask the UAP if any given credential is revoked or not, as typical in current PKI systems. Additionally, the UAP has validity periods associated to credentials it issues.

The standard widget toolkit (SWT) was used for developing the prototype UI for issuing, using, and verifying ADT-based credentials. The credential issuance module was implemented that allows the construction and issuance of credentials. The credential verification module was also implemented to test the functionality required for the verification purpose. This module reads the XML proof request generated by the credential management module and verifies all the attributes disclosed, showing the ones that were correctly verified and those that failed verification, as shown in Figure 6. The credential management module, depicted in Figure 7 includes a card picker and an attribute selector. The list of attributes displayed on the attribute selector matches the selected card on the card picker. In addition, it also includes a graphical representation of ADT that shows the full dictionary. Finally, it includes a simple proof request viewer/editor that shows the request built for the currently selected attributes. The editor allows that request to be manually changed, providing a valuable tool to build invalid requests in an attempt to fool the verifier and test our current prototype system.

5 Future Work

We are currently working on the second phase of our implementation using Apache Shindig and its extension, SUN SocialSite. The open source project Apache Shindig provides a platform that allows us to port our prototypes into a web environment. Shindig has been used successfully as a base for the OpenSocial containers such as Hi5 and Orkut. It implements not only the OpenSocial API but also the gadget engine. The current implementation of Shindig is being modified to accommodate our extension. More specifically, we are working on the changes in the object structures and JavaScript functionality that third party applications can use based on our extension. The server side implementation of Shindig will also be modified. Since Shindig has both Java and php implementations, we are going to focus only on Java version, reusing all the Java code that has already been developed to implement our prototypes in the first phase.

6 Conclusion

With the rapid growth of online social network (SN) sites, there is an increasing demand for sharing user profiles among those sites in a secure and privacy-preserving manner. In this paper we discussed a novel approach to developing an interopearable and selective data sharing solution among such SN sites. Our approach was mainly based on an authenticated dictionary (ADT)-based credential which allows a user to share only a subset of her information certified by external SN sites with applications running on an SN site. Additionally an extension to the OpenSocial API for the purpose of supporting data interoperability was discussed. Finally we presented a proof-of-concept implementation based on our approach, along with our future work.

Acknowledgement

This work was partially supported at the Secure Computing Laboratory at New Mexico Tech by the grants from Sandia National Laboratories (PASP10) and from New Mexico Tech VP Office.

450   D. Shin and R. Lopes

References

1. Facebook Connect, http://developers.facebook.com/connect.php
2. MySpace Data Availability (DA), http://developer.myspace.com
3. OpenSocial Foundation, http://www.opensocial.org
4. OpenSocial pages at Google Code, http://code.google.com/apis/opensocial
5. Anagnostopoulos, A., Goodrich, M.T., Tamassia, R.: Persistent authenticated dictionaries and their applications. In: Proceedings of 4th International Conference on Information Security, Malaga, Spain, October 1-3 (2001)
6. Brands, S.: Rethinking Public Key Infrastructure and Digital Certificates - Building in Privacy. MIT Press, Cambridge (2000)
7. Camenisch, J., Herreweghen, E.V.: Design and implementation of the idemix anonymous credential system. In: Proceedings of 9th ACM Conference on Computer and Communication Security, Alexandria, VA, November 7-11 (2002)
8. Camenisch, J., Lysyanskaya, A.: A signature scheme with efficient protocols. In: Proceedings of 3rd Conference on Security in Communication Networks, Amalfi, Italy, September 12-13 (2002)
9. Chaum, D.: Security without identification: Transaction systems to make big brother obsolete. Communications of the ACM 28(10), 1030–1044 (1985)
10. Chaum, D.: Achieving electronic privacy. Scientific American, 96–101 (August 1992)
11. Goodrich, M.T., Tamassia, R., Schwerin, A.: Implementation of an authenticated dictionary with skip lists and commutative hashing. In: DISCEX II (2001)
12. Gross, R., Acquisti, A., Heinz III., H.J.: Information revelation and privacy in online social networks. In: Proceedings of the 2005 ACM Workshop on Privacy in the Electronic Society, Alexandria, VA, November 7 (2005)
13. Liu, H., Maes, P.: Interestmap: Harvesting social network profiles for recommendations. In: Proceedings of IUI Beyond Personalization 2005: A Workshop on the Next Stage of Recommender Systems Research, San Diego, CA, January 9 (2005)
14. Lopes, R., Shin, D.: Controlled sharing of identity attributes for better privacy. In: Proceedings of the 2nd International Workshop on Trusted Collaboration, White Plains, USA, November 12-15 (2007)
15. Merkle, R.C.: A digital signature based on a conventional encryption function. In: Pomerance, C. (ed.) CRYPTO 1987. LNCS, vol. 293, pp. 369–378. Springer, Heidelberg (1988)

Evaluating the Trustworthiness of Contributors in a Collaborative Environment

Cam Tu Phan Le, Frédéric Cuppens, Nora Cuppens, and Patrick Maillé

Institut TELECOM ; TELECOM Bretagne
2, rue de la Châtaigneraie CS 17607
35576 Cesson Sévigné Cedex, France
firstname.lastname@telecom-bretagne.eu

Abstract. We propose a method to evaluate the contributions of each participant to the development of a document in a collaborative environment. The algorithm proceeds ex post, by analyzing the different steps that led to the final (assumed satisfying) version of the document. Such an evaluation might be considered as a trust or reputation note, and therefore can be used as an input for trust mechanisms aimed at incentivizing users to contribute efficiently.

We implemented this evaluation mechanism in Java, when the document has been developed with Subversion, a version control system used to maintain current and former versions of files.

Keywords: Collaborative work, trust.

1 Introduction

There are more and more digital documents that cannot be elaborated by a single person or entity, because of the prohibitive size of the document, or of the numerous knowledge fields and competences that they require. Thus a whole community or organization is often needed to build a complete document of satisfying quality. For example, online encyclopedies such as Wikipedia [www.wikipedia.org] need contributions from a huge number of persons. Likewise, requests to calls for proposals in industry often imply several (possibly competing) companies joining their efforts in order to build an offer that fulfills the client's needs.

In those contexts, a reliability or trustworthiness evaluation of contributors would be of great help to decide the treatment applied to the contribution: if a participant is known to provide high quality contributions, then a minimum checking might be needed, whereas contributions from untrustworthy participants should be carefully checked or simply ignored. Since deeply checking contributions is necessarily costly, trust or reputation scores of their authors would help improve the document building process.

Moreover, such trust scores could also act as an incentive for participants to perform high quality contributions. Indeed, reputation scores can for example be

E. Bertino and J.B.D. Joshi (Eds.): CollaborateCom 2008, LNICST 10, pp. 451–460, 2009.

used as inputs for access control or usage control policies [3], or even for resource allocation mechanisms (e.g. to share revenues among contributors).

While the notion of trust in networks has recently received quite a lot of attention for peer-to-peer networks (see [4,6] and references therein) or to build social networks [2,5], research on trust mechanisms in collaborative frameworks is only emerging.

In this paper, we propose an objective evaluation scheme for the contributors of a document, that can be used as a trust or reputation score. For sake of simplicity, we restrict our attention to a text document. We assume that the document has reached a stable (final) version, that has been validated, and propose a method to perform trust score calculations.

The remainder of the paper is organized as follows. Section 2 introduces the model considered in terms of participants roles and document development process. Then Section 3 describes our proposal of trust measure. Finally, Section 4 presents our implementation for trust computation, and conclusions and directions for future work are given in Section 5.

2   Model

We present here the assumptions we make regarding the development of the text document. We define three types of agents involved in the development process, and describe that process.

2.1   Roles

We assume that three roles are defined for the elaboration of the document, as described below.

Writers. Those participants have access to the current version of the document. They can add text but cannot delete text written by the other participants. Moreover, they do not see the text that has been deleted (more precisely, proposed for deletion) by reviewers. We denote by W the set of writers.

Reviewers. They can read the current version of the document, and see the parts that have been proposed for deletion by the other reviewers. The possible actions for them are text addition, and proposition of text deletion for parts of the document that have or not already been proposed for deletion. A reviewer can contradict a previous proposition of another reviewer, therefore modifying the text visible to writers. The set of reviewers is denoted by R.

Validator. He sees all the text, including the one that has been proposed for deletion. He can add and delete text to the document, and agree with or contradict deletion propositions of reviewers. In this paper we assume that only one entity is the validator. He is the participant who stops the development process: his choices are definitive and the corresponding version is the final one, that is assumed to be of good quality. Therefore the validator should be the guarantor

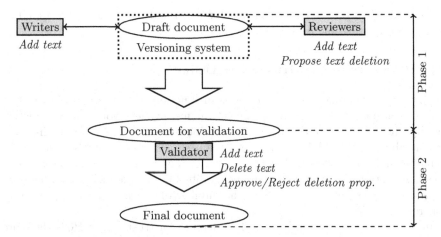

Fig. 1. The document development process, with action rights for each role (in italics)

of the quality of the document, and the reference as regards the trust scores described in the next section.

Notice that we do not enter the rules that determine those roles. The rule to decide whether a participant is a writer or a reviewer may for example take into account the involvement of the contributor in the project (if any), and the trust scores obtained from previous experience and/or recommendation processes [2].

2.2 Document Development

The document development process consists in two phases. First, writers and reviewers work on the document, according to their access rights defined previously. Some collaborative working tools such as versioning softwares can classically be used to manage the evolution of the document. In the second phase, the validator takes the actions that he considers necessary for the document to be of sufficient quality: text deletion, confirmation/cancelling of deletion propositions, and possibly text addition.

The process is illustrated in Figure 1, where actors appear in gray.

If the contributors in the first phase are trustworthy, then the work of the validator should be minimal.

3   Trust Calculation: Algorithm and Implementation

We introduce here a proposal of trust score based on objective measures (still assuming the final validated version is of best quality). We first explain the general principles that we want to apply, and present and justify the mathematical expressions of trust scores for writers and reviewers.

As in most references (e.g. [2,6] and references therein), a trust score will be a real number in the interval $[0, 1]$, the value 0 meaning that the participant has no positive effect on the document development, and the value 1 corresponding to a perfectly trustable participant.

3.1   Principles for the Trust Score Definition

In this paper, we quantify contributions in function of their number of words. This measure is surely imperfect, since changing very few words can completely modify the meaning of the document. A measure based on the signification of contributions would be much better suited, but would involve the use of semantic analysis tools, which is beyond the scope of this paper. Notice that our trust calculation proposals can easily be modified to include such semantic-based measures. Nevertheless we use here the number of words to fix ideas and give concrete examples.

In all this paper, the validator is the reference for trust scores. He is therefore always given a fixed trust score of 1. Therefore we focus here on the trust score definition for writers and reviewers.

We believe that trust scores should respect the following principles.

P1. The trust score of a participant should be increasing with his contribution to the final version. In other words, if a significant part of the validated document comes from his contributions then his trust score should increase.
P2. The trust score of a participant should be decreasing with the proportion of his contributions that have not been kept in the final version.
P3. The trust score of a reviewer should be increasing with his contribution to the deletion propositions that have been validated.
P4. The trust score of a reviewer should be decreasing with the proportion of his deletion propositions that have not been validated.

We actually compute a numerical measure corresponding to each of those principles, and define the trust score as a weighted sum of those measures.

3.2   Trust Score Components

The score associated to Principle P1 should measure the *quantity* of his work with respect to the overall document content. It should answer the question *"How much did this participant contribute to the final version?"*. We therefore simply define it for each participant $i \in W \cup R$ as

$$t_{i,w\_qt} := \frac{n_{i,final}}{n_{final}}, \tag{1}$$

where $n_{i,final}$ is the number of words validated in the final version that come from participant i, and n_{final} is the total number of words in the final document. (w_qt stands for "writing quantity" of the contributions.)

Principle P2 aims to refer to the *quality* of the contributions of participant i, by answering the question *"Were the contributions of i satisfying?"*. The numerical measure we take to answer this question is the proportion t_{i,w_ql} of the words written by i that were validated in the final version.

$$t_{i,w\_ql} := \frac{n_{i,final}}{n_i}, \tag{2}$$

where n_i is the total number of words that participant i has introduced to the document.

While Principles P1 and P2 respectively correspond to the quantity and quality of a participant's writing behavior, the two other principles should have the same meaning as concerns the deleting behavior. Since only reviewer have the right to propose text deletions, the corresponding scores only apply to participants $i \in R$.

If we denote by n_{i,del_prop} the number of words that reviewer i proposed for deletion, and by n_{del_val} the total number of words that were actually deleted in the final version, then we define the numerical measure t_{i,d_qt} associated to Principle P3 as

$$t_{i,d\_qt} := \frac{n_{i,del\_prop}}{n_{del\_val}}. \tag{3}$$

This ratio answers the question *"Does reviewer i delete low-quality text?"*, and reflects the *quantity* of his deletion proposition work.

On the other hand, the *quality* of his deletion proposition work can be evaluated by his degree of accordance with the validator as concerns deletions. This corresponds to Principle P4 and the question *"Does reviewer i delete only low-quality text?"*, which we quantify by defining t_{i,d_ql} as

$$t_{i,d\_ql} := \frac{n_{i,del\_prop}}{n_{i,del\_val}}, \tag{4}$$

where n_{i,del_val} is the number of words that have been proposed for deletion by i, and have effectively been deleted in the final version.

3.3   Definition of Trust Scores

We now propose an overall trust value expression for participants in $W \cup R$, as a weighted sum of the different trust score components defined in the previous subsection.

Writers Trust Score. For a writer $i \in W$, the system designer (possibly the validator) should decide which of Principles P1 or P2 are most important. In other words, he should choose whether to prefer to favor writers who contribute a lot, or those whose contributions are of high quality.

We propose to define the overall trust t_i of writer $i \in W$ as

$$t_i := \alpha_{qt} t_{i,w\_qt} + \alpha_{ql} t_{i,w\_ql}, \tag{5}$$

where α_{qt} and α_{ql} are two positive numbers, with $\alpha_{qt} + \alpha_{ql} = 1$, reflecting the system designer's preferences.

Reviewers Trust Score. For reviewers, we propose the same type of formula, but encompassing Principles P1-P4.

We define the trust score t_i of a reviewer $i \in R$ as

$$t_i := \beta_{w\_qt}t_{i,w\_qt} + \beta_{w\_ql}t_{i,w\_ql} + \beta_{d\_qt}t_{i,d\_qt} + \beta_{d\_ql}t_{i,d\_ql}, \tag{6}$$

where the βs are positive real numbers that sum to 1, and which represent the system designer's priorities in terms of quantity and quality (regarding writing and deletion) in reviewer's work. It would be natural that the weights associated to the writing behaviour have the same relative importance as for writers, i.e. that $\frac{\beta_{w\_qt}}{\beta_{w\_qt}+\beta_{w\_ql}} = \alpha_{qt}$, and $\frac{\beta_{w\_ql}}{\beta_{w\_qt}+\beta_{w\_ql}} = \alpha_{ql}$.

4 Algorithm and Implementation

We intend here to automate the computation on trust scores, based on the history of the versions that have been submitted to the versioning server. We have used Subversion [1] as a versioning tool, and implemented the trust score calculation in Java.

The algorithm proceeds backwards, and compares each version with the previous one using the Subversion command `svn diff`.

4.1 The Command Svn Diff

This command provides three kinds of results, depending whether text has been added "a", deleted "d" or cut "c". As an example, consider the two successive versions of a file given in Figure 2, where lines are numbered.

Then the command `svn diff` would give the result file of Figure 3.

The results interpret as follows:

- 1d0: line 1 of the old version has been deleted, the text of the new version begins at line 0.
- 2a2: some text has been added after line 2 of the old version. In the new version this text is at line 2.
- 4c4,5: line 4 of the old version has been replaced by lines 4,5 of the new one.

Successive comparisons of the versions in the server can therefore be used to deduce the author of a line, or the reviewers that suggested to delete a given line.

file.txt		file.txt	
1	Monday	1	Tuesday Wednesday
2	Tuesday Wednesday	2	added text
3	Thursday	3	Thursday
4	Friday	4	Saturday
		5	Sunday week-end

Fig. 2. Two successive versions of a document

```
diff_file.txt
 1 Index:file.txt
 2 ==========================
 3 1d0
 4 <Monday
 5 2a2
 6 >added text
 7 4c4,5
 8 <Friday
 9 ...
10 >Saturday
11 >Sunday week-end
```

Fig. 3. svn diff applied to the example file of Figure 2

```
del_prop_file.txt
 1 Index:file.txt
 2 =========================
 3 0d1,3
 4 Monday
 5 4d1
 6 Friday
 7 5d3
 8 Sunday week-end
```

Fig. 4. Example of a deletion proposition file

4.2   Management of Deletion Propositions

The management of writers prohibition to delete text is simply made by the versioning server, that refuses to upload a new version if it includes a deletion. Text that has been so far proposed for deletion does not appear in the current version, and therefore is not visible to writers.

To make those (temporary) deletions visible to reviewers, we store them when they are detected at each new version upload (through an svn diff), and indicate them to reviewers in a separate file, together with their position in the text. Remark that those positions are updated at each new version upload, so that an appropriate interface could mix the text file with the deletion proposition file, to show reviewers a unique file (for example using different colors to distinguish deletion propositions). Building such a user-friendly interface is left to future work.

An example of deletion proposition file, refering to our example for the svn diff command, is given in Figure 4. This example reads as follows: we have assumed that the participant that uploaded the new file version of figure 2 has the identifier 1, and that the validator (with identifier 3) has validated that version, but he decided to keep the text Friday that had been proposed for deletion by 1, and to delete the text Sunday week-end that 1 had added. We therefore read

- Od1,3;Monday: that text would be at line 0 of the document if it were not deleted, and it has been proposed for deletion by participants 1,3 (it has thus been deleted in the validated version since 3 is the validator here).
- 4d1,Friday: that text would be at line 4 of the document, it has been proposed for deletion by participant 1, but not by the validator. Therefore the text is reinserted into the final document.
- 5d3,Sunday week-end: that text was at line 5 of the document, and has been deleted by the validator only.

In the document building process, reviewers can choose to read or not the parts proposed for deletion so far, and to confirm or contradict the deletion propositions. In that latter case, the text becomes visible again to writers (it is reinjected in the current version, but still remains in the deletion proposition file to store the fact that some users have proposed it for deletion).

4.3   Computing Trust Scores

We now describe how the trust scores described in Section 3 can be practically calculated after the validator has brought the last changes and validated the final document version.

The total number of words n_{final} in the final version is obviously the most easy index to obtain. Likewise, the total number of words that have been deleted n_{del_val} is simple to compute, simply by counting the words in the last version of the deletion proposition file.

We describe below how we proceed to compute the other indices needed to calculate the trust score of a participant $i \in W \cup R$, namely n_i, n_{i_final} (for writers and reviewers), and $n_{i,del\_prop}, n_{i,del\_val}$ (for reviewers), with the notations of Subsection 3.2.

Indices $n_{i,del}$ and n_{i,del_val} (reviewers). Those indices are respectively the number of words that reviewer i proposed for deletion and the number of words that among those have effectively been deleted. They can be computed quite easily from the deletion proposition file exemplified in Figure 4: $n_{i,del}$ is the number of words of propositions for which identifier i occurs, and n_{i,del_val} is the number of words of propositions for which both identifiers i and V occur, where V is the identifier of the validator.

Indices n_i and $n_{i,final}$ writers and reviewers. Our method uses the text deletion proposition file, and the results of svn diff applied to the successive versions of the document, starting with the latest version, to calculate n_i and the difference $n_{i,bad} := n_i - n_{i,final}$ for each participant i. We proceed by updating a table containing the values of the indices we are looking for, the table being initialized with all values equal to 0. Then the comparison with the previous version allows to determine, for the author of the current version, the number of words that have been added. We moreover use this exploration of the file history to identify the authors of the deleted parts, and update accordingly their index $n_{i,bad}$.

More precisely, the procedure works as follows:

- at each version compared to the previous one, increment n_k where k is the participant that uploaded the version. The value used to increment is simply obtained by counting the words corresponding to the "a"s and "c"s in the svn diff result (see Figure 3).
- for each line of the final deletion proposition fine where the validator appears, increment by the corresponding number of words the $n_{j,bad}$, where j is the author of that line. The text can be tracked via successive svn diff of the latest versions, until its apparition as an addition to the document. The identifier of the uploader of that version is the j we are looking for.

After this scan of the versions, we have the exact values of n_i and $n_{i,final} = n_i - n_{i,bad}$, that can be used to compute the trust scores.

4.4   Why a Reverse Order Processing?

We could also have calculated the indices needed to compute trust scores by comparing the successive document versions in a chronological order. However, we believe that using an anti-chronological method would provide more options.

- We assumed that the versioning system keeps all versions of the document. However we might imagine that very old versions might not be useful and could be deleted. Our procedure could then be easily adapted to that case, simply considering that the text contained in the oldest stored version has no author.
- Following the same ideas, it is possible to imagine that the time component be taken into account in the trust score. For example, early contributions might be preferred to last minute text additions. The trust score formulas we suggest could also be adapted to that case, by adding timing coefficients into the word count of indices $n_i, n_{i,final}, n_{i,del}$, and n_{i,del_val}.

5   Conclusions and Perspectives

In this paper, we have proposed some criteria to evaluate the contributions of each participant in the development of a text document. We have proposed to use a combination of those criteria to compute a trust score for each participant, which can then be used for several purposes (role or revenue distribution, decisions to collaborate or not with that participant in the future...).

We have implemented our proposed procedure to automatically calculate the trust scores, using Java for interfaces and file processing, and Subversion for version management.

Our trust evaluation mechanism stands under quite restrictive assumptions. Relaxing those assumptions gives directions for future work. In particular, we would like to extend our mechanism to the case where there can be more than one validator. Also, it would be useful to allow back-and-forth exchanges between the validator(s) and the writers/reviewers before a version is considered final.

Introducing the time component into the trust scores could also enrich the model, and prevent some problems such as late contributions that are less reviewed. Finally, we aim at using the trust scores (possibly obtained through previous experience) during the document development itself. Indeed, the decision to carefully read or not, to delete or not a text part could rely on the trust score of the author of that part: the efficiency of the document creation process would then be improved, by reducing the reviewing work to the less trustworthy parts.

References

1. Collins-Sussman, B., Fitzpatrick, B.W., Pilato, C.M.: Version control with Subversion. O'Reilly, Sebastopol (2004)
2. Golbeck, J., Hendler, J.: Inferring binary trust relationships in web-based social networks. ACM Trans. on Internet Technology 6(4), 497–529 (2006)
3. Liu, Y.: Trust-based access control for collaborative system. In: ISECS Intl. Colloquium on Computing, Communication, Control, and Management, Guangzhou City, China, pp. 444–448 (August 2008)
4. Marti, S.: Trust and Reputation in Peer-to-Peer Networks. PhD thesis, Stanford University (May 2005)
5. Matthew, R., Agrawal, R., Domingos, P.: Trust management for the semantic web. In: Proc. of 2nd International Semantic Web Conference, Sanibel Island, Florida (2003)
6. Suryanarayana, G., Taylor, R.N.: A survey of trust management and resource discovery technologies in peer-to-peer applications. Technical Report UCI-ISR-04-6, University of California, Irvine (July 2004)

Supporting Agile Development of Authorization Rules for SME Applications

Steffen Bartsch, Karsten Sohr, and Carsten Bormann

Technologie-Zentrum Informatik TZI,
Universität Bremen, Bibliothekstr. 1, 28359 Bremen, Germany
{sbartsch,sohr,cabo}@tzi.org

Abstract. Custom SME applications for collaboration and workflow
have become affordable when implemented as Web applications employing Agile methodologies. Security engineering is still difficult with Agile
development, though: heavy-weight processes put the improvements of
Agile development at risk. We propose Agile security engineering and increased end-user involvement to improve Agile development with respect
to authorization policy development. To support the authorization policy development, we introduce a simple and readable authorization rules
language implemented in a Ruby on Rails authorization plugin that is
employed in a real-world SME collaboration and workflow application.
Also, we report on early findings of the language's use in authorization
policy development with domain experts.

Keywords: Authorization Policy, Agile Security Engineering, End-User
Development, DSL, SME Applications.

1 Introduction

When Small and Medium Enterprises (SME) deploy collaboration and workflow
applications, the applications need to measure up to the established workflows
in terms of efficiency and flexibility. SMEs are often incapable of investing the
required resources into tailoring commercial off-the-shelf software to match the
established workflows. This is further backed by the observation that it is often
the unique selling point of SMEs to implement unconventional processes when
compared to competing larger companies. With the advent of recent technological developments in the Web sector, small and focussed custom applications
have become affordable for implementing SMEs' specific needs in collaboration
and workflow management in *SME applications*.

One aspect of the development of custom SME applications is implementing
authorization. A large amount of research has been invested into the authorization realm resulting e.g. in *Role-based Access Control* (RBAC, [9,15,2]). Specific
solutions have been proposed for collaboration and workflow [4,14,18,16] as well
as high flexibility [19]. Still, with respect to SME applications, the established
approaches are not easily implemented in practice.

E. Bertino and J.B.D. Joshi (Eds.): CollaborateCom 2008, LNICST 10, pp. 461–471, 2009.
© ICST Institute for Computer Sciences, Social-Informatics and Telecommunications Engineering 2009

Typically, SMEs are organisations of limited complexity, but may still depend on task management and collaboration software. When developing custom software for these domains, a few aspects are different from the task in larger companies. First of all, most employed processes are informal and may be modified on a day-to-day basis. Only a fraction of the processes are formally defined. Instead, the process descriptions are present in form of the employees' implicit knowledge. When the processes are captured for requirements engineering, employees will likely fall prey to *process confabulation*. Process confabulation causes domain experts to recount processes not in the way they occur, which is difficult with daily variations, but idealized versions. Thus, if authorization is employed, many restrictions are based on the idealized processes and may be hindering in the execution of day-to-day business. One reason is that employees of SMEs are often unaccustomed to authorization. Typically, most documents are available to a large part of the employees before the implementation of an SME application. On the other hand, with a large amount of data centralized in one application, management will insist on the implementation of fairly strict authorization rules.

One current trend in application development to overcome the problem of fuzzy requirements is employing *Agile development* principles [7]. Agile development focuses on customer needs, implementing in short iterations and allowing modifications of the plan on a regular basis. In Agile development, working applications are preferred over documentation and domain experts are tightly integrated into the process. The focus on constant modification and refinement of requirements makes Agile development suitable for the development of SME applications.

With continuously changing requirements, development environments need to provide an adequate amount of flexibility as well as small development and deployment overhead, as provided by Web applications. *Ruby on Rails*[1] is a current Web development framework that supports Agile development and draws from the meta-programming features of the programming language *Ruby*. Through a plugin architecture, a large community of developers provide other common features, such as authentication, in Rails plugins.

Even with Agile development using Ruby on Rails, implementing security in SME applications remains a challenge, in particular the process-dependent parts of authorization. Flaws in authorization may lead to a loss of efficiency and a lack of acceptance by the end-users, which might even lead to a premature end of the application development. In this paper, we describe Agile security engineering methods to overcome these obstacles. One aspect of our approach is supporting the end-user development of authorization policies. In particular, we introduce an authorization rules *Domain-specific Language* (DSL) for improving authorization policy development. The language is implemented in the `declarative_authorization` Rails plugin. We report on the early feedback of employing the authorization language in a real-world SME application to improve its authorization policy.

---

[1] http://rubyonrails.org/

2 Agile Security Engineering

Security engineering in traditional software development is a heavy-weight process. For example, the ISO 27001 standard structures security engineering into the well-known four phases of *Plan–Do–Check–Act* which are iteratively applied [1]. The planning phase includes systematic approaches to threat analysis and risk assessment. Also, the security architecture is to be designed before any implementation takes place. Such a security engineering process does not fit well into Agile development processes, resulting in several conflicts.

- Security is difficult to retrofit [5], so that security ideally needs to be considered from the beginning. In Agile development, where having modifications of the plan is common, the functional requirements are by definition not clear at the beginning. Thus, security measures cannot be developed initially in sufficient detail.
- With an anticipated shift in functional requirements, security architectures designed at one point will become obsolete in the course of the project. Redoing security engineering as proposed by the classical iterative models before implementing additional functional requirements is no option, either. The heavy-weight nature of the process makes it impossible to fit into the common 2 to 4 week iteration cycle of Agile development.
- Traditional security engineering implies a good measure of security documentation and specification. In Agile development, this is counter-productive with the application being a moving target, causing a mismatch of documentation and code to an even larger extent than in traditional software projects.
- Security objectives are non-functional requirements and thus hard to test. In Agile development, refactoring is an important aspect to constantly adapt to changing plans. Refactoring relies heavily on testing to ensure that deep changes do not break the application. Missing tests of the security requirements could thus lead to the introduction of vulnerabilities through refactoring.

Reviewing the published work on security in Agile development, a few solutions to the above-outlined problems are proposed. A very general proposal is to increase overall security skills of development teams. Ge et al. argue that in Agile development even more than in other development processes, security awareness is necessary for all team members [10]. To comply with formal requirements of security reviews, a security expert might rotate through programming pairs, thus implicitly reviewing the code. Aydal et al. report on a case study of security through refactoring with good results [3]. Tappenden et al. describe security tests which could be employed to secure refactoring [17]. Instead of the usual user stories that provide requirements in many Agile methodologies, *abuser* or *misuser* stories may be employed [13], describing unwanted situations which may be tested. This approach might lack the proper completeness, though, as systematic approaches are needed to capture the wealth of attack vectors. An alternative but less concrete approach is imposing *constraints* on every user story.

For security up front, before any development, Ge et al. propose to have experts agree on overall security principles and a high-level security architecture

[10]. Still, as indicated above, this might prove either quite complex when a suitable security architecture is to be found or might arrive in rather useless too general principles. It is a good idea, though, to begin with system hardening and penetration tests early in the iteration cycles even if the system is not yet set up in the target environment. Thus, security issues may be tackled early [11]. Lastly, Chivers et al. argue that in Agile development, the team should concentrate on providing *good-enough security* as, in practice, security is not absolute [5]. It is arguably correct that even the systematic approaches of traditional security engineering do not guarantee completeness.

While the listed approaches may not serve as a one-size-fits-all solution, a few points may be worth stressing. At one point during development, a systematic threat analysis and risk assessment should be undertaken to provide a good understanding of security aspects to focus on. With the addition of further features in later iterations, the findings certainly need to be adapted with changes in assets and additions of attack vectors. Thus, key to effective Agile security engineering remains the flexibility in implementing changes in the security architecture. A second aspect is that it is hard to capture security requirements for processes in a single iteration. Because of process confabulation, authorization particularly needs adjustment by domain experts later on. Documents derived directly from the code may come to help in discussions with domain experts while preventing additional overhead and the risk of outdated documents. In the next section we describe ways of tightly integrating domain experts into security engineering and authorization policy development, taking the aforementioned aspects into account.

3   End-User Development of Authorization Policies

In the development of custom SME applications, it is even more important to tightly integrate end users into the development process than in software development for large enterprises. Usually, there are no current documents on the company's processes but only implicit knowledge of the employees. Even if there has been an ISO 9001 certification, those documents often do not reflect the actual processes. In *Human-Computer Interaction* (HCI) research, the growing field of *End-User Development* [12] pushes the barrier even further; not only should end users be integrated into the development process, but in addition end users should take part in the development, adapting the application to their needs [6,20].

In the domain of security engineering and authorization policy development, there are three potential actors to design and implement authorization: end users, system administrators and developers. One might argue that authorization configuration should be carried out by administrators. On the other hand, domain knowledge is very important for applying the appropriate measure of restrictions. This means that end users are better suited for the task, at least supporting the administrator. Developers also play an important role in the process by having intimate knowledge of the application. With many authorization decisions being based on the application's underlying data model, which may have to be modified to allow specific authorization rules, it is very important to have the developers take active part in the development. Thus, ideally, an authorization policy development would offer the appropriate level of abstraction to each of these actors [8]. Therefore, the following mechanisms are needed:

- An authorization language and data model primarily for developers to implement authorization policies. The language and data model should be simple enough to help end users to discuss and validate the current policy. It might even be possible for them to correct and develop authorization rules using the language.
- Alternative, e.g. graphical, representations of the effective authorization policy concerning specific objects and users to mitigate the complexity of authorization by offering transparency.
- A UI for overcoming barriers posed by textual specifications to some end users.

4   The Declarative Authorization Plugin

For supporting Agile security engineering and end-user integration in authorization rules development, we developed an authorization rules DSL and supporting development tools. We implemented the DSL and the tools as the Ruby on Rails `declarative_authorization` plugin[2], made available under the MIT Open Source license. Currently, we use the plugin in a real-world collaboration and task management Web application that relies on Ruby on Rails as the underlying Web application framework.

The plugin design was guided by the goal of providing the maximum simplicity and readability of the authorization rules DSL and efficient usage of the plugin in Web application development. Other available Rails authorization plugins usually are based on in-line *Access Control Lists* (ACL) of roles, causing redundant authorization rules in program code. In contrast, the `declarative_authorization` plugin separates program and authorization logic, thus offering a *declarative* approach to authorization. The DSL describes the policy for authorization while the application just defines required permissions for specific actions.

4.1   Authorization Rules DSL

The authorization rules DSL was designed for readability and flexibility. The syntax is derived from natural language that can be read in form of sentences, e.g., *role "admin" has permissions on "employees" to "manage."* Symbols beginning with :, block delimiters **do**, **end** and hash associations through => remain visible indications that the DSL employs Ruby syntax. We decided to implement the language in Ruby because of Ruby's metaprogramming features, which allow a simple, readable DSL while making use of the benefit of the robust Ruby parser.

---

[2] Available at Github: http://github.com/stffn/declarative_authorization

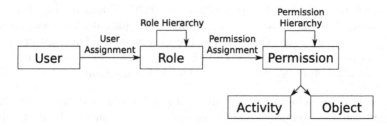

Fig. 1. Role-based access control model

Also, in the target market of SME applications, applications are increasingly based on Ruby on Rails. A simple example of an authorization rule assigning the permission "manage" on objects of type "employee" to role "admin" is given in the following listing:

```
authorization do
  role :admin do
    has_permission_on :employees , :to => :manage
  end
end
```

The authorization data model behind the DSL is similar to RBAC's. One of many extant variations of the RBAC model is shown in figure 1. The model defines *users*, which are assigned to *roles* in an n:m relation. On the other hand, *permissions* are assigned to roles in an n:m relation as well. Permissions are often described as a combination of *activities* on *objects*. Thus, to evaluate the authorization of a user with respect to a specific object, permissions assigned to the user's roles need to be checked.

Instead of defining permissions as activities on objects, the `declarative_` `authorization` data model (figure 2) uses activities on *types* of objects, such as "employees", to increase maintainability. Permissions on individual objects are realized through context authorization constraints [4]. E.g., for restricting "branch admins" to only manage employees of their branch, the statement shown in listing 1.1 in line 9 is employed. Constraints may be nested for more complex cases. A custom language is used for specifying the constraints so that the same conditions may be used not only to restrict access but also to derive the resulting

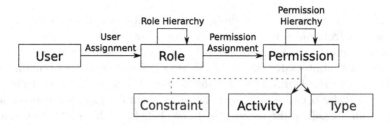

Fig. 2. Authorization rules DSL data model

Listing 1.1. Example authorization rules

```
1   authorization do
2     role :admin do
3       has_permission_on :employees , :to => :manage
4     end
5
6     role :branch_admin do
7       includes :employee
8       has_permission_on :employees , :to => :manage do
9         if_attribute :branch => is {user.branch}
10      end
11    end
12
13    role :employee do
14      # ...
15    end
16  end
```

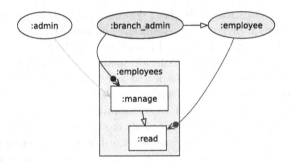

Fig. 3. Graphical representation of authorization rules

constraints on database queries. Role hierarchies are realized using the "includes" statement as demonstrated in listing 1.1 in line 7.

To further improve the usability of the authorization rules language in Agile security engineering, development tools have been implemented. Inside the application, the syntax-highlighted textual representation of the current rules is provided to authorized users. Also, graphical representations have been developed for domain experts to be able to drill down on specific aspects of the authorization rules, as shown in figure 3, while keeping an overview at hand. In the diagram, filled arrows indicate the assignment of permissions to roles, with circles on arrows symbolizing constraints on the assignment. The role hierarchy of "branch admin" including the permissions of "employees" is shown by an unfilled arrow, demonstrating the efficiency of graphical representation for analyzing hierarchical structures.

4.2   Usage in Application Code

In order to support Agile development, ease of implementation in the application
is important. Early in the development process, authorization rarely is of high
priority. Thus, imposing minimal overhead allows for authorization infrastructure to be integrated early-on, resulting in less refactoring being required later.
In Rails, so-called *controllers* are responsible for responding to HTTP requests.
Each URI is routed to a controller's *action*. Thus, for a first line of defense,
restrictions may be imposed on each action. To enable this with the plugin, only
a `filter_access_to` statement in a controller is required to cause all requests
to that controller to be checked for authorization.

```
class EmployeesController
  filter_access_to  :all
  def index
    #  ...
  end
end
```

When the "index" action in the `EmployeesController` is called by an HTTP
request, the authorization rules are consulted. The `declarative_authorization`
plugin considers the roles of the user, which is bound to the current request through
separate authentication measures, to decide on allowing the request. If the permissions for "index" have not been assigned to any of the user's roles, the request is
denied. If the permission is assigned with additional authorization constraints, objects might be examined to evaluate the constraints.

The "index" action in the `EmployeesController` will provide a list of employees, causing a check of "read" permissions according to a preconfigured mapping.
To only display those employees that the current user may read, constraints need
to be imposed on a database query for some roles, according to the authorization
policy. To enable these automatic constraints, the developer only has to use a
`with_permissions_to` call instead of manually constructing the database query
conditions, as shown in the following example.

```
class EmployeesController
  filter_access_to  :all
  def index
    # @employees = Employee.find(:all, :conditions => ...)
    @employees = Employee.with_permissions_to(:read)
  end
end
```

Thus, with the authorization rules shown in listing 1.1, users of role "branch
admin" would only see the intended list of employees in their branch while
minimal extra effort is needed in application development. More importantly,
the code does not need to be changed when authorization conditions change,
allowing developers to focus on functional and security requirements at different
points in time.

5   Early Feedback

In order to evaluate the authorization rules language with respect to its use in Agile security engineering, we employed the `declarative_authorization` plugin in a real-world SME application. The application currently has nine roles and permissions on objects of 35 types. It is a collaboration and task management application that is employed in quality management of automotive parts.

We used the applications authorization rules in discussions with two domain experts. The domain experts use the application regularly as end-users but have not taken part in the programming of the application. In addition to the discussions, we conducted interviews with the domain experts to capture their subjective views on the viability of using textual authorization rules and graphical representations for helping in discussion, finding policy flaws, and allowing end-user modifications.

In both discussions, the textual representation of the authorization rules proved very helpful in improving the current rules. Two flaws within the authorization rules were identified. E.g., an overly narrow restriction on the role of quality inspectors would have prevented their flexible operation for different branches of the SME. The flaws might have hindered the workflow in specific situations by being overly restrictive. In the interviews, the domain experts acknowledged the helpfulness of the textual and graphical representation of the actual authorization rules that are being enforced. Still, for modifications or additions by themselves, both would prefer a user interface.

6   Conclusion and Future Work

When considering custom-built applications for task management and collaboration, Agile development of Web applications helps in efficiently fulfilling SMEs' requirements. To design appropriate security mechanisms, traditional security engineering does not fit well with its heavy-weight processes, though. Agile security engineering processes, as described in this paper, provide an alternative approach by integrating domain experts more tightly into the security engineering process. One important aspect of Agile security engineering is the development of authorization policies. We introduced a tool to support the Agile authorization policy development through a simple and readable authorization rules language and its implementation in the Rails `declarative_authorization` plugin. While certainly not applicable to every kind of application, authorization policies may gain in precision through more intense integration of domain experts and thus improve the effectiveness of the application with only minimal development overhead. Early positive feedback from the evaluation of the authorization language on a real-world SME project demonstrated the potential of our approach.

In addition to broader empirical work, future work will include the development of user interfaces to complement the existing tools. Following the domain experts' suggestions, the UIs should work on a high layer of abstraction, e.g. only allowing the assignment of permissions to existing roles. In another attempt to improve end-user involvement, we will provide measures for test-driven development of authorization rules and an authorization policy development workflow, thus increasing the reliability of authorization policy development.

Taking into account the required flexibility in SME applications' task management, even improved authorization policy development may not prevent occasional missing permissions that degrade efficiency, though. In order to follow the practice of informal processes in SMEs, we will look into a self-regulatory authorization approach that we call *Self-service Authorization*. This mechanism allows end-users to increase their permissions according to certain restrictions on their own while actions are then appropriately audited.

References

1. ISO/IEC 27001:2005. Information technology – Security techniques – Information security management systems – Requirements. ISO, Geneva, Switzerland
2. ANSI INCITS 359-2004. Role-Based Access Control. American Nat'l Standard for Information Technology (2004)
3. Aydal, E.G., Paige, R.F., Chivers, H., Brooke, P.J.: Security planning and refactoring in extreme programming. In: Abrahamsson, P., Marchesi, M., Succi, G. (eds.) XP 2006. LNCS, vol. 4044, pp. 154–163. Springer, Heidelberg (2006)
4. Bertino, E., Ferrari, E., Atluri, V.: The specification and enforcement of authorization constraints in workflow management systems. ACM Trans. Inf. Syst. Secur. 2(1), 65–104 (1999)
5. Chivers, H., Paige, R.F., Ge, X.: Agile security using an incremental security architecture. In: Baumeister, H., Marchesi, M., Holcombe, M. (eds.) XP 2005. LNCS, vol. 3556, pp. 57–65. Springer, Heidelberg (2005)
6. Church, L.: End user security: The democratisation of security usability. In: Security and Human Behaviour (2008)
7. Cockburn, A.: Agile Software Development. Addison-Wesley Professional, Reading (2001)
8. Dai, J., Alves-Foss, J.: Logic based authorization policy engineering. In: The 6th World Multiconference on Systemics, Cybernetics and Informatics (2002)
9. Ferraiolo, D., Kuhn, R.: Role-based access controls. In: 15th NIST-NCSC National Computer Security Conference, pp. 554–563 (1992)
10. Ge, X., Paige, R.F., Polack, F., Brooke, P.J.: Extreme programming security practices. In: Concas, G., Damiani, E., Scotto, M., Succi, G. (eds.) XP 2007. LNCS, vol. 4536, pp. 226–230. Springer, Heidelberg (2007)
11. Kongsli, V.: Towards agile security in web applications. In: OOPSLA 2006: Companion to the 21st ACM SIGPLAN symposium on Object-oriented programming systems, languages, and applications, pp. 805–808. ACM, New York (2006)
12. Lieberman, H.: End user development. Springer, Heidelberg (2006)
13. McDermott, J., Fox, C.: Using abuse case models for security requirements analysis. In: ACSAC 1999: Proceedings of the 15th Annual Computer Security Applications Conference, Washington, DC, USA, p. 55. IEEE Computer Society, Los Alamitos (1999)
14. Oh, S., Park, S.: Task-role-based access control model. Inf. Syst. 28(6), 533–562 (2003)
15. Sandhu, R.S., Coyne, E.J., Feinstein, H.L., Youman, C.E.: Role-based access control models. IEEE Computer 29(2), 38–47 (1996)

16. Sun, Y., Meng, X., Liu, S., Pan, P.: Flexible workflow incorporated with RBAC. In: Shen, W.-m., Chao, K.-M., Lin, Z., Barthès, J.-P.A., James, A. (eds.) CSCWD 2005. LNCS, vol. 3865, pp. 525–534. Springer, Heidelberg (2006)
17. Tappenden, A., Beatty, P., Miller, J.: Agile security testing of web-based systems via httpunit. In: AGILE, pp. 29–38. IEEE Computer Society Press, Los Alamitos (2005)
18. Thomas, R.K., Sandhu, R.S.: Thomas and Ravi S. Sandhu. Task-based authorization controls (TBAC): A family of models for active and enterprise-oriented autorization management. In: Proceedings of the IFIP TC11 WG11.3 Eleventh International Conference on Database Securty XI, London, UK, pp. 166–181. Chapman & Hall, Ltd., Boca Raton (1998)
19. Wainer, J., Barthelmess, P., Kumar, A.: W-RBAC - a workflow security model incorporating controlled overriding of constraints. Int. J. Cooperative Inf. Syst. 12(4), 455–485 (2003)
20. Zurko, M.E., Simon, R.T.: User-centered security. In: NSPW 1996: Proceedings of the 1996 workshop on New security paradigms, pp. 27–33. ACM, New York (1996)

The Application of Human and Social Behavioral-Inspired Security Models for Self-aware Collaborative Cognitive Radio Networks

Jack L. Burbank and William T.M. Kasch

The Johns Hopkins University Applied Physics Laboratory
11100 Johns Hopkins Road
Laurel, Maryland 20723
{Jack.Burbank,William.Kasch}@jhuapl.edu

Abstract. This paper discusses the introduction of anthropology and sociology-inspired approaches to providing security in collaborative self-aware cognitive radio networks. This includes the introduction of not only trust models, but also respect models and 'intuition' models. This paper discusses numerous potential benefits from this type of approach, including benefits to algorithm security, compromise recovery, protection from the Byzantine threat, and policy enforcement.

Keywords: Trust model, respect models, collaborative networking, cognitive networking.

1 Introduction

With the ever-increasing need for wireless network capacity and the simultaneous need to increasingly support performance-sensitive multimedia applications, cognitive radios and cognitive radio networking are expected to become an increasingly important part of the overall wireless networking landscape, both in the commercial and military domain. There are currently multiple CR development and standardization activities. One such effort is the DARPA neXt Generation (XG), which aims to develop technology to utilize unused spectrum, primarily for the United States military [1][2]. In the commercial domain, IEEE 802.22 is the primary commercial CR development activity, which aims to develop technologies to utilize unused television spectrum for broadband wireless services [3]. Furthermore, the IEEE Standards Coordination Committee 41 (SCC41), formerly the IEEE P1900 Standards Group, was established in 2005 to develop supporting standards associated with next generation radio and advanced spectrum management.

However, there is an important technical area that has only recently begun to receive serious attention in the cognitive radio paradigm: wireless security. The cognitive radio paradigm introduces entirely new classes of security threats and challenges, and providing strong security may prove to be the most difficult aspect of making cognitive radio a long-term viable concept. This is true in both the military

E. Bertino and J.B.D. Joshi (Eds.): CollaborateCom 2008, LNICST 10, pp. 472–484, 2009.
© ICST Institute for Computer Sciences, Social-Informatics and Telecommunications Engineering 2009

domain where a deployed network will be potentially subjected to state-sponsored weaponized threats and the commercial domain where the network must protect against both sophisticated and unsophisticated threats. This paper discusses the challenges of providing security in the cognitive radio network paradigm, and discusses the application of a human and social behavior-inspired security framework to these networks to improve overall system security.

2   The Cognitive Network Decision-Making Process

Generally, a cognitive radio exhibits six characteristics [5]:

1. The cognitive radio maintains *awareness* of surrounding and internal state
2. The cognitive radio *adapts* to its environment to meet requirements and goals
3. The cognitive radio uses *reasoning* on ontology and/or observations to adjust adaptation goals
4. The cognitive radio exhibits *learning* from past performance to recognize conditions and enable faster reaction times
5. The cognitive radio *plans* to determine future decisions based on anticipated events
6. The cognitive *collaborates* with other devices to build greater collective observations and knowledge.

Fig. 1 provides a functional decomposition of the general cognitive networking process.

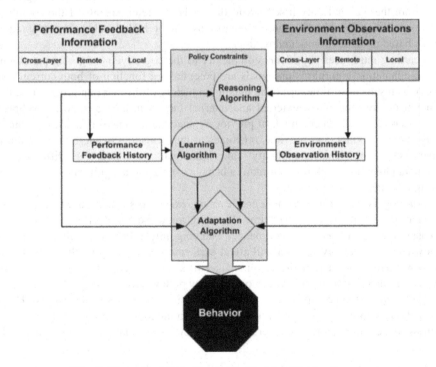

Fig. 1. Generalized Cognitive Radio Decision-Making Process

The cognitive radio maintains *awareness*, which can include observations about its surrounding environment (e.g. spectral density) and observations about its own performance (i.e. error rates). The cognitive radio is *adaptive*, changing some aspect of its behavior based upon observed environment and/or outcome in order to meet its goal (e.g. achieve a certain error rate performance). It should be noted that a radio can maintain awareness without exhibiting any type of adaptivity (e.g. statistics gathering or audit logging for human use). However, these cases are of little interest in the context of this discussion and as such the two functions adaptation and awareness are always co-existent.

It is also important to note that adaptive radios are not necessarily cognitive. There already exist many examples of adaptive radios and techniques that are not considered cognitive [4]. These devices simply adapt based on some pre-defined algorithm or rule-set that does not change over time. Consider the example of adaptive modulation and coding that is based on statically-defined thresholds of link quality. The radio will make some measurement of link quality and adjust its modulation and coding in a pre-defined manner based on pre-defined thresholds. The authors contend that a radio not be considered 'cognitive' unless it employs some degree of *reasoning* and/or *learning*; this position is consistent with that of the larger community.

As shown in the functional decomposition of Fig. 1, reasoning is the function of modifying a radio's adaptation algorithms and rules (which implicitly include objectives and goals) based on current awareness of environment and/or performance in order to best meet the goals of the radio. Algorithms and rules of the cognitive radio are the one and only link back to the goals and requirements of the cognitive radio. Additionally, the function of reasoning might include changing adaptation goals based upon environmental realities.

Learning introduces significant complexity to the cognitive networking paradigm. Now, adaptation algorithms and goals are potentially a function of both current and previous instances of time, up to the maximum history of the learning process (i.e. the amount of time for which external and internal factors influence radio algorithms). The radio notionally keeps track of previously encountered environments, previously attempted behaviors, and previous outcomes to build wisdom of the best decision in given situations. This complexity can dramatically increase the difficulty of understanding and predicting the radio's behavior, creating a significant challenge in forming a stable control system.

Planning is similar to reasoning and learning, except it is making a influencing the adaptation algorithm at a future time. Planning might be based on some history of measured environment or performance. Planning might be the result of a priori knowledge of future events that will affect performance. Planning might be the result of new policy placed into the cognitive network and the cognitive radio wants to provide a smooth transition between old and new policy paradigms.

Collaboration is perhaps one of the easier cognitive functions to understand. Here, the radio is combining its own input functions with the input functions of other radios within the cognitive radio network to form objectives and adaptation criteria. If reasoning and learning processes are employed, then these composite input functions will affect the basic algorithms of the radio, both current and future.

The general cognitive radio is even more complex, as this type of decision-making process can be taking place at multiple places in the protocol stack and that in fact these layers might be cooperating with each other in a cross-layer approach (depicted by the cross-layer inputs of Fig. 1).

2.1 Cognitive Radio Network Security – A New Complex Dimension of Network Security

There are many aspects of cognitive radio network security that are common to non-cognitive wireless networks, such as the desire to provide user authentication and data confidentiality. But there are many aspects that are unique to the cognitive network that require novel approaches to wireless network security. There are numerous new types of threats to the cognitive network that if not accounted for could enable an entire new class of threats and vulnerabilities [5][6]. To enable further discussion, consider Fig. 2.

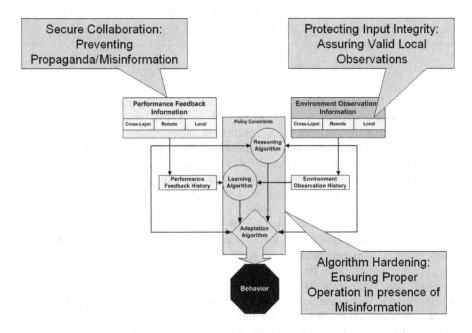

Fig. 2. Required Components of a Cognitive Radio Network Security Architecture

Fig. 3 illustrates the four lines of cognitive network security defense presented in this paper.

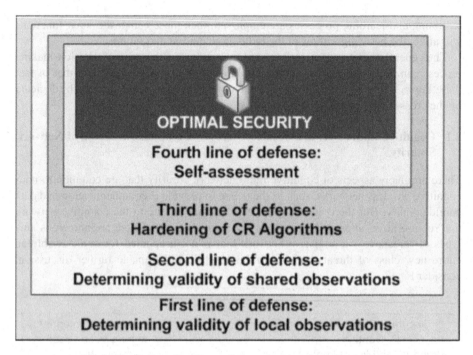

Fig. 3. Cognitive Network Security Lines of Defense

As the first line of defense of the cognitive network, a cognitive radio needs to be capable of judging whether what it is locally sensing is real or falsified. This goes far beyond protecting the network from injection of false messages, as is the focus of traditional network authentication mechanisms. Rather, this means that not only are network messages authenticated, but also that observations of physical phenomena are also authenticated. These physical phenomena include physical attributes of the environment, such as signal presence or channel quality, that do not lend themselves to traditional authentication mechanisms.

Since a CR is utilizing not only its own observations as a basis for decision making but also the observations of others, there is the obvious need to authenticate the shared observations. This is particularly true given the distributed and unseen nature of its peer cognitive radios. Once the authenticity of the source of collaborative CR network messages has been established (which the authors contend is analogous to authentication in traditional non-cognitive networks), the CR needs to be able to judge whether the observations that others within the cognitive radio network are reporting are real or falsified. This, combined with the ability to establish the authenticity of the source, is critical to preventing the propagation of attacker effects within the CR network and is critical for two reasons: 1) to prevent degradation of the greater network because of an individual spoofed cognitive radio element and 2) to protect against the Byzantine (i.e. insider) attack. In this paradigm, the security of each node in the network is dependent upon the security of every other node in the network. This is the second line of cognitive network defense.

Even if mechanisms are put into place to perform authentication of local observations, to perform authentication of collaborative messages, and to determine the validity of remote observations conveyed via collaborative messages, the cognitive radio must still be prepared to properly operate in the presence of malicious information attempting to influence its decision-making process (i.e. the presence of propaganda). This requires that cognitive algorithms be 'hardened' to maximize stability and security (i.e. inability to manipulate or drive the platform into instability because of algorithmic flaws). This includes adaptation algorithms, learning and reasoning algorithms, and planning algorithms. This is the third line of cognitive network defense.

The CR must be able to determine whether it is acting erratically or logically. This self-check is critical to the long-term health of the CR network. If the long-term behavior of the CR has been affected by an attacker, the CR must be capable of identifying itself as an affected node and take self-corrective measures. This aspect is also important because of the envisioned long-term complexity of the CR platform itself. With increasing software complexity, it will be increasingly difficult to test all possible code execution paths to prevent software bugs. Thus, it is important that the CR platform itself is able to perform self-diagnosis to determine if internal problems are present, either because of observation corruption or errors in algorithmic design or implementation. This is the fourth line of cognitive network defense.

Much of the cognitive radio research community is focused primarily on individual problem areas that require maturation. However, as important it is to develop individual protection mechanisms to solve individual portions of the overall problem space, it is equally important to develop an over-arching cognitive network security model to ensure that these individual mechanisms are sufficiently integrated into a single coherent network security approach. This is an area that is receiving little attention in existing research efforts. It is this area in which the remainder of this paper is focused.

3 A Human and Social Behavior Approach

It is important to note that the desired security characteristics previously listed all relate to the need for a cognitive radio to *exhibit good judgment*. It is equally important to recognize that the cognitive radio paradigm imposes human characteristics on the radio device. These radios that now possess human characteristics are then networked together; forming a *virtual cognitive community*, or *virtual cognitive society* and new security threats to this type of network include attempting to manipulate individual networks by influencing the decision-making process. As such, it would appear beneficial to examine social science and human behavior, and consider the characteristics that protect humans from manipulation--primarily relationships, responsibilities, judgment, and wisdom. This is a daunting task, as humanity has not yet mastered these capabilities ourselves. However, it is valuable to consider the human behavioral model in order to isolate protection characteristics that may perhaps be leveraged when beginning to develop a cognitive network security model. Additionally, perhaps the greatest current shortcoming in the area of cognitive radio network security is the lack of a holistic model in which the entire cognitive radio security problem can be viewed, i.e. *a cognitive radio security framework*. This paper contends that human and social behavioral models have the promise of providing the basis for an effective framework in which to view this problem and to bind individual protection mechanisms into a single coherent system protection approach. This is consistent with human concepts of society and community, and it is likely beneficial to think of a CR network as a virtual community. It should be noted that neuroscience-inspired networking research [9] shows promise, but still remains immature and is largely focused in the area of developing localized optimization algorithms.

Human behavior provides protection mechanisms against deceit in two primary forms: 1) a trust model, and 2) a respect model. How much do we trust the person that is sharing information with us? This trust is typically built over time through experience. There is no 'best' equation as to what this trust versus time model looks like, and often effective human decision making can span a wide variety of these models. But what is consistent in effective collaborative human decision making is the model of 1) friends 2) acquaintances, 3) strangers, and 4) adversaries. This proposed Friend-Acquaintance-Stranger-Adversary (FASA) model in Fig. 4 (which is an expanded version of the Friend-Acquaintance-Adversary model proposed in [5]) aims to leverage a key observation of human behavior: both the trust placed in another individual and the respect placed into another individual's opinion is primarily a function of familiarity, history, and stereotype. Individuals build trust and respect in another individual based, in large part, on how well they know them, previous experiences with that individual, and how trustworthy that individual is perceived to be based upon societal stereotype (e.g. the stigma associated with being a 'used car salesman' or a politician).

However, the last aspect is often individual-unique as biases and prejudices such as these are often taught to them or learned through personal experience; this last aspect is likely to be the hardest to implement in software without unintended consequences. It is also unclear if this aspect is desirable in the cognitive network as these biases can lead

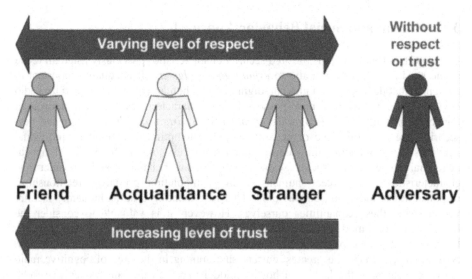

Fig. 4. FASA Model

to poor human decision making. The FASA model is intended to allow the mechanisms to incorporate similar mechanisms into the virtual CR society. Because of factors such as these, the trust an individual is given or the respect that is placed in their opinion can vary greatly across the community population. Another element of the virtual CR society is the law-making body that sets the rules the society must adhere to. In the case of CR, in which policy-based management is envisioned, that law-making body is the CR network designer who develops and configures policies within each CR platform, where each policy can be thought of as a law that must be obeyed.

Friends are elements for which a strong positive trust relationship has been built over time through a deeper level of understanding and familiarity. As such, that understanding can be used to put the conveyed information into a context that can be judged against. The tendency is to trust a friend. Acquaintances are known, but not as well as friends. Here, the tendency tends to remain neutral and not form any type of preconceived notion of trust. Adversaries are the converse of a friend. Here, a deeper level of understanding has been built from which the tendency is to distrust what is being communicated. Strangers are unknown. Here, the tendency generally is to be less trusted. However, the degree of trust placed into strangers can vary greatly across human populations, often influenced by an individual's personal experiences and teachings. Humans achieve this type of understanding over time through gained information, where this information is gained through both direct and indirect communications (i.e. gossip). All of these relationships and the tendency to trust or distrust information are related (at least loosely) to the societal structure and the stated/perceived goals of individuals and individual actions (e.g. custom-based, emotion-based, value-based, etc.). In the cognitive network paradigm, this type of communication represents overhead which is undesirable. So, the goal then is to establish a trust relationship while minimizing the required knowledge to establish the type of peer relationship to be formed with other elements of the cognitive radio network. From a security perspective, it is desirable for a malicious attacker to have as little information as possible to the social values, customs, and motivations of the members of the cognitive radio virtual society. In practical terms, this traces to the need of a malicious attacker to have insight into the goals, methods, and techniques to achieve many of the desired goals (Table 1 from [5]).

3.1 Potential Benefits of a Human-Social Behavioral Approach and Open Research Questions

3.1.1 Trust of Shared Information

Recall the individual CR will eventually make adaptation and perhaps learning decisions based on both locally-collected and remote observations. Thus, the CR platform needs to be capable of judging the validity of observations reported by other CR elements within the CR network. This capability is needed to protect against both the Byzantine threat and the threat of misinformation dissemination amongst the CR network users. This area can take advantage of an overarching model such as the FASA model to determine trustworthiness. Again, there are open research questions that warrant investigation. Should there be designated nodes in the CR network that primarily assess the reasonability of shared observations in an attempt to protect nodes (perhaps a subset) of the network?

Given a set of situational awareness data and desired goals, the algorithms present in the cognitive radio will attempt to make the best decision that will come closest to meeting the set of desired goals. Trust and respect models, such as those enabled by a FASA model, could be employed to police the set of input data that is fed into the decision-making process to provide a line of defense for the algorithms themselves. For example, information that is known to be falsified can be removed from the decision-making process. Information that is more reliable than other information can be weighted differently to have more profound impacts on the decision-making algorithms. It is here that it is believed that behavioral models can be employed to assist in cognitive decision making.

3.1.2 Health and Diagnosis

The CR needs to be able to judge whether it is acting erratically or logically. This self-check is critical to the long-term health of the CR network. At the individual level, humans are typically quite poor at this type of self-diagnostic in an isolated manner. Rather, humans often require communications and interactions with other humans, such as friends ('Is everything OK?') for initial identification of an issue. And even following initial identification, humans often struggle to correct undesired behavior without intervention from friends or paid professionals (e.g. therapists). Reliable isolated self diagnosis may prove difficult to accomplish (if a cognitive radio's algorithms have been compromised how much assurance can be placed that its self-diagnosis functionality is still trustworthy?) and that a distributed approach should instead be considered. Furthermore, a standalone approach may not be desirable because any self-diagnosis function would have to have ultimate access to the rest of the cognitive radio, which could in itself be dangerous.

A FASA model could work well in the CR paradigm to facilitate distributed health diagnosis functions. However, there are numerous ways in which this could potentially be accomplished. Perhaps the cognitive network society is 'friendly and nurturing' and every node helps care for not only itself but for other nodes within the CR network. Or perhaps a 'self-centered' cognitive network approach could be employed, where nodes are not particularly concerned about the health of its neighbors until suspected problems of its neighbors are suspected to be interfering with their own performance. Additionally, the CR could follow the human model even further and have a subset of CR nodes identified as network diagnostic nodes (i.e. therapists) that are charged with analyzing behavior of CR network nodes and assessing the presence of erratic behavior and then assist in the resolution of these issues. Yet another approach would be to assign a subset of CR nodes with the responsibility of policing the CR network, performing assessment of CR node behavior. An approach could also incorporate some combination of all these models. Distributed health diagnosis is a topic that warrants additional research to determine its viability and to assess the strengths and weaknesses of possible approaches.

3.1.3 Byzantine Protection

The Byzantine attack represents the case where a friend or acquaintance has, unbeknownst to the greater cognitive radio network, become an adversary and represents the most difficult subset of this problem space. The Byzantine threat could be substantially more problematic in a collaborative cognitive network. Here, the compromised node can spoof data to its neighbors in an attempt to destabilize or otherwise control or influence learning and reasoning algorithms. Furthermore, the adversary now has potential access to cognitive algorithm software implementations that could perhaps be leveraged into advanced exploits against the cognitive network. Furthermore, the adversary now has potential access to a rich set of network state information that may be useful in further attacks. There are indeed lessons that can be drawn from existing work in the area of Byzantine routing (e.g. [8]). However, we must be careful not to create an overly-paranoid network where nodes are quickly distrusted if behavior of friends or acquaintances becomes inconsistent with expectations. This paranoia itself could be used against the cognitive radio by an attacker to cause a forced effect. In the case of a cognitive radio employing a FASA model, a friend node is likely easier to identify as a Byzantine threat than an acquaintance or stranger. The application of the behavior models for the purposes of Byzantine protection warrants additional research.

3.1.4 Hostility Characterization

In the majority of cognitive networking discussions, the radio is attempting to perceive one or more aspects of its environment. However, there are generally little existing discussions related to building a view of the safety of the environment. Is a particular node currently under attack by a threat? Is the cognitive network operating in an environment known to be hostile? What is the history of hostile acts taken against the network as a whole? Building this type of view of the environment, and sharing this information throughout the cognitive network, could help build context that could potentially be integrated into trust and respect of collaborative information, belief in authenticity of locally-observed environment, and in the hardening of decision-making algorithms by introducing the concept of 'caution' or 'degree of alertness' based on perceived safety of environment. Returning to the human behavioral model, this is analogous to an individual or group of individuals altering behavior based on comfort and perceived personal safety.

3.1.5 The Role of Others in Localized Decision-Making

While this appears a promising model to follow in the cognitive networking paradigm, there are many unanswered questions. In human society, there are individuals designated to enforce the rules of society (i.e. police). Is it beneficial to appoint a subset of cognitive network nodes as the 'police' of the network, to ensure that the policies of the network are being followed? In human society, a large set of human behavior is affected by teachings (parents, teachers, mentors, role-models, etc.). Is it beneficial to have a subset of the cognitive network population act in similar roles?

3.1.6 Non-direct Trust and Respect

In human society, the attitudes individuals develop towards other individuals are formed not only by direct interaction but also from indirectly received information, which may be completely accurate or not. Would this type of 'gossip' prove beneficial to the security of a cognitive network in building trust in members of the cognitive network community? In many cases, humans rely on intangible 'gut instinct' in placing trust and respect in other individuals (e.g. an individual trusts one stronger but distrusts another stranger for no apparent reason). This type of factor could be introduced through an 'intuitive model' where decisions are randomized in some fashion so that behavior is not perfectly deterministic. Here, the degree of importance placed on the 'intuitive' factor would be a function of accumulated wisdom (i.e. cognitive radios learn to either trust or distrust their 'gut instinct' much the same way humans do). Is this type of behavior beneficial in the cognitive network society? Questions such as these, as well as many others, should be addressed as this type of model is explored and matured to assess the viability of this model.

3.1.7 How to Develop Respect

From these research communities there is significant work that can be leveraged to begin developing security solutions for CR networks. For example, researchers have considered the issue of optimally combining advice from a set of experts (e.g. [7]), analogous to CRs sharing their expert advice regarding their environment, and several solutions have been proposed that attempts to optimally combine those expert opinions in a way that is most beneficial (e.g. [7]). However, this begs the question which CRs in a community are considered "experts" as well as "trustworthy?" Perhaps this definition of "expert" is governed by policy loaded into the CR. However, this approach is questionable as cognitive networks will likely accumulate knowledge at non-identical rates. Another approach is to build the ability into a CR to determine who it considers an "expert" as well as building the mechanisms into the cognitive network to enable such determinations. This could be enabled by the respect models of the FASA model. Additionally, perhaps this process of determining "experts" is not done individually but rather nodes build "reputations" in the network and the network as a whole gravitates towards decisions regarding who are "experts" and who are not.

3.1.8 Micro versus Macro Behavior

In human and social behavioral models there is a limit to the number of complex relationships an individual can maintain. Dunbar, an English anthropologist, theorized that there is a limit to human cognitive capacity that limits the number of stable social relationships that can be maintained by a human. This led to Dunbar's Rule of 150 (rounded from 148), which states that the mean group size that can be achieved while maintaining social stability is 148. As a community increases in size, an increasing amount of effort is required in 'social grooming' activities to maintain social cohesion and maintain social and cognitive stability. For groups larger than this, behavior must be restricted through rules and laws to maintain social stability. Furthermore, as the number increases, a hierarchy is generally required where smaller groups of intimate groups are formed with less knowledge of other groups.

It is an intriguing research question as to whether this same type of dynamic holds for the cognitive radio network, as this would have numerous ramifications: 1) it places another dimension on network scalability, cognitive capacity, 2) it places bounds and limits on the way the network is governed (micro vs. macro behavior), and 3) it suggests that hierarchy with differing types of relationships among different groups and levels of that hierarchy will be required for large cognitive networks.

Also of interest is the effect of the decision making process, both from a short-term and long-term perspective. For instance, human models show that decisions often have both short- and long-term consequences—a clear example of this is making the decision to attend college. Generally, those who attend college are sacrificing short-term economic gains and increasing their own short-term workload in order to achieve more desirable, longer-term goals, such as financial security and career stability. One could argue that these longer-term goals provide an increase in the overall "health" of society, which seems like a very reasonable long-term goal for any society to maintain. Cognitive network members and societies may tend toward short-term or long-term goals, and as such, may need to strike a balance in the decision making process, both individually and collectively. More research is warranted in this area to determine the effects of the decision making process on both short- and long-term consequences.

4 Conclusions

This paper proposes that since the cognitive radio paradigm imposes human characteristics on radios that it is appropriate to consider human and social models when considering how to build and protect cognitive networks. This paper contends that there may be valuable lessons from the fields of anthropology and sociology that can be applied to designing secure cognitive networks. Bio-inspired techniques are being applied to the field of cognitive radio, but typically focus on algorithm development rather than considering the macro-level network. This paper does not propose definitive solutions, nor does it benchmark potential solutions. The authors believe that providing security in the cognitive network paradigm may likely prove to be an NP-Complete problem, similar to optimizations in the traditional knapsack problem in a variety of dimensions (time, space, frequency, and power are primary examples). As such, extensive research is certainly necessary before moderately successful solutions emerge. This is believed to be particularly true in the case of an over-arching framework that can bring individual security mechanisms together into a cohesive solution that can enable secure collaborative cognitive networks. Rather, this paper proposes these concepts in hopes that the greater research community will consider these alternate fields of research as sources that can be leveraged.

The authors plan to continue maturing these concepts and to begin implementation of these types of approaches in the form of both modeling and simulation (M&S) and in a Software-Defined Radio (SDR) testbed environment in order to begin answering many of the research questions posed in this paper.

References

1. The XG Vision, Request for Comments, Version 2.0, XG Working Group,
   http://www.darpa.mil/ato/programs/XG/rfcs.htm
2. The XG Architectural Framework, Request for Comments, Version 2.0, XG Working
   Group, http://www.darpa.mil/ato/programs/XG/rfcs.htm
3. Cordeiro, C., et al.: IEEE 802.22: The First Worldwide Wireless Standard based on
   Cognitive Radios. In: 2005 First IEEE International Symposium on New Frontiers in
   Dynamic Spectrum Access Networks (DySPAN), November 8-11, pp. 328–337 (2005)

4. Goldsmith, A.J., Wicker, S.B.: Design Challenges for Energy-Constrained Ad Hoc Wireless Networks. IEEE Wireless Communications Magazine (August 2002)
5. Burbank, J.L.: Security in Cognitive Radio Networks: The Required Evolution in Approaches to Wireless Network Security. In: Proceedings of the Third International Conference on Cognitive Radio Oriented Wireless Networks and Communications (CrownCom), May 15-17 (2008)
6. Burbank, J.L., Roger Hammons Jr., A., Jones, S.D.: A Common Lexicon and Design Issues Surrounding Cognitive Radio Networks Operating in the Presence of Jamming. Accepted for presentation at the 2008 IEEE Military Communications (MILCOM) Conference (November 2008)
7. Cesa-Bianchi, N., et al.: How to use Expert Advice. Journal of the ACM (May 1997)
8. Awerbuch, B., Holmer, D., Nita-Rotaru, C., Rubens, H.: An On-Demand Secure Routing Protocol Resilient to Byzantine Failures. In: ACM Workshop on Wireless Security (WiSe), September 28 (2002)
9. Reggia, J.A., Sutton III, G.G.: Self-processing networks and their biomedical implications. Proceedings of the IEEE (June 1988)

GroupBanter: Supporting Serendipitous Group Conversations with IM

Kori Inkpen[1], Steve Whittaker[2], Mary Czerwinski[1], Roland Fernandez[1], and James Wallace[3]

[1] Microsoft Research, 1 Microsoft Way, Redmond, WA, USA
`{kori,marycz,rfernand}@microsoft.com`
[2] Sheffield University, 211 Portobello St., Sheffield, UK
`s.whittaker@shef.ac.uk`
[3] University of Waterloo, Waterloo, ON, Canada
`jrwallac@uwaterloo.ca`

Abstract. This paper describes GroupBanter, a tool for supporting serendipitous group conversations using instant messaging. We investigated the potential of ephemeral group conversations by providing awareness of friends' IM conversations, serving as an implicit invitation to join a group conversation. We present our vision and describe our prototype system. Results from two field studies carried out in different contexts show that users valued GroupBanter and that it provided new opportunities for communication that aren't well served by traditional IM, email, or face-to-face communication. Our results indicate there is potential in providing a lightweight communication channel that lies between traditional, private IM conversations and more public IRC-like conversations.

Keywords: Instant messaging (IM), chat, group conversations, Internet Relay Chat (IRC), Computer supported Cooperative Work (CSCW), Computer Mediated Communication (CMC).

1 Introduction

Instant Messaging (IM) has become a central part of many people's lives. However, with traditional IM applications, users have no way of knowing who is talking to whom, or what they might be talking about. Unless users are explicitly invited to join a conversation, they will have no awareness of the many conversations that might be of relevance or interest to them, even amongst their own contacts.

This situation contrasts with face-to-face conversations, where multiparty, opportunistic interactions have been shown to be valuable for team building [1], [2]. In face to face situations, nearby people see that the conversation is going on and may also be able to hear parts of it. This information gives people an awareness of the conversation which they can then "join", if desired. Additionally, non-verbal gestures and body language can provide an implicit invitation to others to join the conversation, e.g., making eye-contact with people outside of the conversation, or stepping aside to make room for someone to join [3]. And there are benefits to being

E. Bertino and J.B.D. Joshi (Eds.): CollaborateCom 2008, LNICST 10, pp. 485–498, 2009.

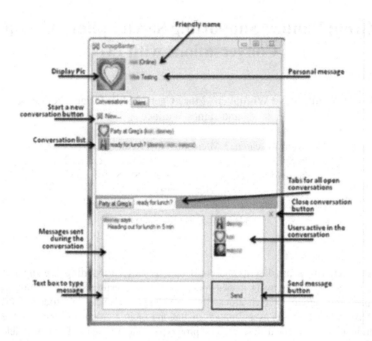

Fig. 1. A screenshot from the GroupBanter prototype. The conversation pane lists all the active conversations including the title and who is participating. The bottom pane provides a tab for each conversation, as well as a list of participants who are currently active in the conversation.

aware of what coworkers are discussing, even if users choose not to participate in the conversation themselves [4].

We developed GroupBanter, a system to encourage serendipitous group conversations. It allows users to publicize conversations as an implicit invitation for others to join the conversation (see Figure 1). It also provides conversational awareness information to users - such as who is talking to whom and the topics of those conversations. These provide opportunities for serendipitous group conversation and awareness like those available in the physical world but which are not supported by most IM clients.

GroupBanter is similar to Internet Relay Chat (IRC) systems where users create discussion threads that others can join. IRC systems enable users to enter a "room" and see who was talking as well as what they are talking about. However, IRC systems tend to be public in nature, with numerous channels persisting for long periods of time. In addition, those frequenting IRC rooms might not be known to the user. In contrast, we hypothesize that having a small number of more transient conversations, started by, and broadcast to people with whom users have an established personal connection can provide value over existing communication channels.

The notion of publicizing IM conversations to enhance group conversations has been explored in previous research such as Babble [5], BackTalk [6], the Community Bar [7] and SWIM [8]. A common theme across many of these systems is that they focus on making conversations persistent and visible to people within a predefined group. We were interested in exploring whether we could achieve some of the same benefits of these systems with more ephemeral conversations while maintaining the lightweight nature of IM.

The goal of this research was to evaluate the utility of a lightweight mechanism to broadcast or receive conversation awareness information within users' social network. We also wanted to explore some of the subtle nuances of ephemeral communication. We conducted two separate short-term deployments where users could explore functionality within GroupBanter and better understand the concept and consequences of broadcasting conversation information. We collected usage data from GroupBanter, as well as user comments and reactions to the system. We also investigated how usage and perceptions differed depending on relationships within the group. Our first deployment was with a large, loosely connected social group, the second with a small, tightly connected team working on closely defined projects.

Results from our in situ field studies showed that users were indeed interested in using the functionality provided in GroupBanter. They found it provided new opportunities that don't exist with other media. In particular, users from the first study stated that GroupBanter enabled them to ask a quick question to a group of people allowing anyone in the group to respond. This freed users from having to decide whom to direct questions to and may have enabled faster responses. In our second study, users found GroupBanter beneficial for quick exchanges and group awareness relating to problems they were working on. The key contributions of this work include results from these field studies, which demonstrated a strong user interest in this kind of software tool, revealed clear conversational usage patterns, and design recommendations that should improve ephemeral conversation sharing.

We first describe related IM literature, focusing on group conversations followed by a description of the GroupBanter system. We next present our field studies along with the results obtained. We conclude with a discussion about the potential for supporting serendipitous group conversations using IM and discuss next steps.

2   Related Work

In 1992, when Dourish and Bly first introduced the notion of Portholes [9] to support distributed work groups, they defined awareness as "knowing who is around, what activities are occurring, [and] who is talking to whom". They went on to state that "Awareness may lead to informal interactions, spontaneous connections, and the development of shared cultures". Jumping ahead sixteen years, we see that although media spaces are not commonplace, Instant Messaging (IM) applications have become an important awareness and communication tool to support distributed work groups; however, most IM systems do not provide awareness of "who is talking to whom". More recently, some systems have explored additional awareness cues such as broadcasting information via display names [10] and whether or not users are currently engaged in IM chat [11], [12]; however, these systems do not disclose who the users are talking to, nor what they are talking about.

Researchers who have studied the use of IM have examined both work contexts [7], [13], and [14] and social settings [15], and have characterized IM use in these environments. Although most messaging systems provide support for group conversations, IM is primarily used for one-to-one conversations [16]. In addition, standard IM systems typically lack support for opportunistic multiparty interactions.

Previous research has identified group IM chat as an important communication component [17]. Herbsleb et al., [17] describes the benefits of group IM as providing "a lightweight communication channel, a way to find out who is available, a trigger for opportunistic communication, some degree of team context, and a way to query one's entire team at once." In our work, we explore techniques to enhance traditional IM clients to better support this type of opportunistic group communication.

A few researchers have also explored extensions to IM to better support group conversations [5], [6], [8], [13], and [16]. Notable here is Babble [5], which provides users with awareness information about ongoing conversations, the participants involved, and user control over their degree of involvement in the conversation. Babble supports persistent conversations, as well as a 'social proxy' to help users visualize conversations and the activities of others within the group. GroupBanter differs from Babble in that Babble was designed to support persistent conversations while GroupBanter conversations are ephemeral in nature. Additionally, the Babble display consumes considerable display space, while GroupBanter was designed to be lightweight, displaying only minimal information until more details are requested.

3   Group Conversations in IM

Group conversations are an important part of chat applications and are supported in most Instant Messaging (IM) clients. However, for most IM clients, group conversations require explicit invitations to all participants. Users must therefore anticipate who is welcome to join a conversation and explicitly send each of those people an invitation. Each invitee must then take action to respond, or dismiss the invitation. This process works well for small, focused group conversations, but becomes onerous if users want to have more large scale conversations, or if the initiator doesn't know exactly who should participate in the conversation. From the recipient's perspective, there may be IM conversations that they want to join, but are unaware that such conversations are taking place. Consider the following scenario:

Scenario. *Bob wants to check out the new Italian restaurant for lunch and is wondering if anyone wants to join him. He starts a new conversation called "Italian for lunch anyone?" and broadcasts the conversation to his work colleagues. Harry (who is from Bob's group) as well as Sarah and Jessica (both of whom work nearby but in a different building) join the conversation and say that they would love to join him. The four decide to meet at 12:15 at the restaurant. Bob keeps the conversation open until he leaves for the restaurant in case someone else decides to come.*

In this scenario, if Bob used a regular group IM feature, he would need to explicitly decide who should be invited, potentially excluding some people and likely disturbing others who may not be interested. Additionally, other people may receive the request after lunch, which would be pointless since lunch was over. Similar issues arise if Bob used email to try to set up this lunch. If Bob's colleagues don't read their email until after lunch, they will have already missed the opportunity for lunch and the email will be irrelevant, yet will still require attention, potentially contributing to email overload.

We define GroupBanter conversations to have the following features:

- Broadcast to a group of people (typically people that already have an established relationship such as those on a buddy list).
- Ephemeral, they only exist as long as someone is interested in the conversation;
- Low overhead. Easy to set up, join, and leave.

These features extend the functionality of IM systems, providing new opportunities for communication. The ability to broadcast conversations to others provides an implicit invitation to those people to join the conversation. Users can maintain an awareness of conversations their friends or colleagues are having and make a personal choice as to whether or not to participate. This is a subtle but useful difference compared to the explicit request-accept model used in traditional IM communication. Additionally, leveraging users' social networks lets people utilize their existing IM relationships.

Having conversations that only persist as long as needed is another GroupBanter feature. Because conversations don't have explicit requests, they disappear seamlessly when the originator (or others involved in the conversation) deem that they are over. Finally, we fit with the current IM model by ensuring interaction is lightweight.

4   GroupBanter Prototype

The GroupBanter prototype (see Figure 1) was developed as a custom stand-alone group conversation application using C#. The interface is divided into three sections: a personal identification section; conversation and user lists section; and a chat section. GroupBanter provides a list of ongoing conversations showing the conversation title and a list of users actively participating in that conversation. Users join GroupBanter conversations by clicking on the conversation title which causes a new conversation tab to open. Once in the conversation they receive all previous messages exchanged in that conversation. Users can leave a conversation by closing the chat window tab and their name is removed from the list of active participants. They can rejoin the conversation at any time if it is still active. Conversations are listed in the conversation pane as long as they remain active (i.e., at least one person has the conversation chat window open). Once all chat windows for a conversation close, the conversation ends and is removed from the conversation list.

5   Field Studies

To better understand the potential of GroupBanter to support ad-hoc serendipitous conversations, and to gain insight into how users would utilize this type of group conversation feature, we conducted two field study deployments. The first was a two week deployment during the summer of 2007 and the second was a four-week deployment during early 2008. We wanted to look at how the prototype was used in two different settings: (a) an informal context with a larger number of participants who did not know each other well, and (b) a work context of a small team whose members were highly familiar with each other and engaged in collaborative work tasks.

5.1 Participants

Phase 1. Sixty-one student interns (18 female) from 39 different Universities at a large software company were recruited to participate in our field study. They ranged in age from 16–29 (median 23). Interns were chosen because they represent a loosely-connected social network of people who often have a desire to interact with each other for work and social purposes; however, there were likely people in the group that didn't know each other. In addition, an established communication channel already existed for the interns (a group email alias). All students who participated were given a $50 honorarium or a piece of software.

Phase 2. Eleven software development engineers at a large software company volunteered to use GroupBanter for 4 weeks. The participants were a tightly integrated work group in their 20's and 30's. All participants were given a $50 honorarium for participating in the study. The team members were distributed across two different buildings, and even for those within the same building, their offices were located in different parts of that building.

5.2 Procedure

Participants in both study phases first completed a background questionnaire which gathered demographic information as well as data related to their use of IM and other communication channels. They then installed and ran the GroupBanter prototype. Data logging recorded all activities related to GroupBanter conversations. In Phase 2 we also conducted a semi-structured interview with six members of the team mid-way through the study to gather usage feedback. At the end of the study, all participants were asked to complete a post-study questionnaire to report GroupBanter use and provide feedback on the communication opportunities GroupBanter provided.

5.3 Data Collection and Analyses

We recorded when a GroupBanter conversation was initiated, along with the name of the user that created the conversation, the conversation title, when users joined or left the conversation, the date, time, and sender for all messages sent within a conversation, and when the conversation ended.

Data logs were used to determine usage patterns, including the number of conversations initiated, the number of users per conversation, the number of messages sent in a conversation, and the conversation duration. In Phase 2 we also logged conversational content. The follow-up surveys were analyzed using descriptive statistics for the frequency, rank, and rating data while qualitative data was clustered into relevant groups

In both phases, users initially spent time exploring the functionality of the system and testing out various features. Additionally, in Phase 2, some participants didn't install and start using the system until the second week of the study. Because we were interested in how people actively used the system for their normal communication, we exclude data from the initial exploration/learning period. Therefore, data is only presented for week 2 of Phase 1, and weeks 3 and 4 of Phase 2.

6 Results

In Phase 1, 61 GB conversations were initiated during the second week (on average, 12 conversations per day). The make-up of the conversations varied widely with the number of users per conversation ranging from 1 to 18 (μ=6), the number of messages sent ranging from 0 to 240 (μ=30), and the duration ranging from less than 1 min to over 71 hours (μ= 8 hours 50 min). The activity level across users also varied widely with some users initiating many conversations (max=9) while 35 others never initiated a single conversation. A high variance was observed for the number of conversations people joined and the number of messages sent, with some users participating in many conversations (max=76) or sending many messages (max=175) while others participated in very few conversations or sent very few messages.

In Phase 2, 25 GroupBanter conversations were initiated during the third and fourth weeks of the study (12 and 13 respectively). The number of users per conversation ranged from 2 to 10 (μ=7), the number of messages sent ranged from 2 to 75 (μ=17), and the duration ranged from 20 min to almost four days (μ=12:29). Although 11 participants participated in the study there were 7 main users who contributed 97% of the messages. Each of these 7 participated in 16-24 conversations. The remaining 4 predominantly observed conversations without sending messages.

Although the number of messages sent and duration of the conversations varied, the overall structure of the conversations was fairly consistent. In most conversations there was an initial burst of highly interactive conversation (~4-20min) followed by a long tail of inactivity, occasionally with a few messages sent later on. For example, in one conversation from Phase 2 (Figure 2), the initial burst of activity was 11 minutes, followed by a day of inactivity (although 4 people dropped in to view the conversation) followed by a second burst of activity which elicited some additional dropping-in to check on the conversation.

Having people drop in and 'lurk' on conversations was common in Phase 1, and occurred in all Phase 2 conversations. Lurkers are people who actively join a conversation (and presumably read the messages) but do not send any messages themselves. In Phase 2, every conversation had at least 1 lurker and several conversations had 6 or 7 lurkers. As the Phase 2 participants were a development team, lurking can be considered a good way to get awareness about what other team members are working on or concerned about. All participants agreed that GroupBanter made them more aware of what other people on their team were discussing - resulting in better overall group awareness.

Figure 3 shows a partial transcript from a representative conversation from Phase 2. It involved 10 participants, with 5 (Jim, Ed, Mitch, Will, Leo) making contributions, and another 5 (Kim, Dave, Mike, Paul and Peter) lurking (all names are pseudonyms).

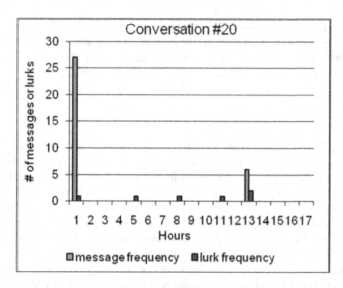

Fig. 2. Activity plot for conversation #20 which shows two spikes of activity (in the first hour and 13 hours later), followed by inactive time with people dropping in to check on the conversation and then leaving.

It involved 37 messages which were an average of 20 words long. The conversation has various interesting properties:

Opportunistic interactions where the respondent is not the person who was addressed. Jim initiated the conversation with a comment to Mike at line 4 which prompted a response from Ed who has done relevant work for Jim. Mitch also contributed an unprompted joke at line 34.

Intermittent fast paced interactive exchanges (lines 4-10, 19-31) interspersed with long periods (excised due to space constraints) when people said little, often 'dropping in' to the conversation without contributing content (lines 12-13).

Informality. Many of the conversations featured highly informal interaction, For example, lines 30-34 discuss cultural differences within the group and a subsequent joke about possible repercussions to a prior comment (lines 33-34).

Lurking. Half the participants were lurkers, who never said anything (although all contributed to other conversations). Lurkers dip into the conversation occasionally to track its progress (e.g., Kim at 12, 18 and 35). Other people alternated between lurking and more active participation.

Active co-ordination. We see GroupBanter being used to resolve co-ordination problems. For example, when a notifying email hadn't arrived (lines 15-17) and when both Mitch and Will accidentally found themselves reviewing the same code (37-42).

1	04/10 09:54	new	Jim	code review tracking
2	04/10 09:54	open	Ed	
3	04/10 09:54	open	Peter	
4	04/10 09:55	msg	Jim	Mike - I have finished reviewing code review #15 - I didn't raise any issues
5	04/10 09:55	msg	Ed	Hey Jim
6	04/10 09:55	msg	Ed	I've yours
7	04/10 09:55	msg	Jim	Kim - I am looking at revew#18 now
8	04/10 09:55	msg	Jim	Hi Ed
9	04/10 09:55	msg	Ed	I've done yours I should say
10	04/10 09:55	msg	Jim	very good - thanks!
11	...			EXCISED MATERIAL
12	04/10 11:51	open	Kim	
13	04/10 13:58	open	Mike	
14	...			EXCISED MATERIAL
15	04/11 12:15	msg	Mitch	Massive Guid - String replace reviewed
16	04/11 12:15	open	Kim	
17	04/11 12:17	msg	Leo	didn't receive any email
18	04/11 12:20	close	Kim	
19	04/11 14:06	msg	Leo	new code review posted.
20	04/11 14:06	msg	Will	what's the focus?
21	04/11 14:06	msg	Leo	I renamed all colo'u'rs to colors for the sake of fxcop
22	04/11 14:06	msg	Leo	no logic changed
23	04/11 14:07	msg	Will	uh...I added the dictionaries already to take care of that
24	04/11 14:07	msg	Leo	:(
25	04/11 14:07	msg	Will	are you still getting FXCop warnings?
26	04/11 14:08	msg	Leo	was not but I decided to do it since it took only 15 mins
27	04/11 14:09	msg	Will	I'd say we should rely on the dictionaries...there are lots of "misspellings" that are actually just unrecognised words. Since we need the dictionaries anyway for those, I say we "fix" all the false positives through the dictionary
28	04/11 14:10	msg	Leo	alright then. i'll revert this one
29	04/11 14:11	msg	Will	(there was one real misspelling, though...and it's in code I'm working on, so I'll fix it with the next checkin)
30	04/11 14:13	msg	Will	we're a mixed-culture team...no reason for us to be draconian about which spellings to use!
31	04/11 14:13	msg	Leo	Heh
32	04/11 14:42	msg	Mitch	I'm not a huge fan of colour myself
33	04/11 14:43	msg	Will	careful, your roommate will get after you
34	04/11 14:43	msg	Mitch	I'm going to need one of those cameras for over my shoulder
35	04/11 15:19	open	Kim	
36	04/11 15:19	close	Kim	
37	04/14 11:01	msg	Will	so, Mitch .... both commented on the same piece of code at the same time (review #29).
38	04/14 11:01	msg	Mitch	did we?
39	04/14 11:01	msg	Mitch	I just did review that one, so its possible :)
40	04/14 11:02	msg	Will	I think Ed will get the msg to make a change there... :)
41	04/14 11:03	msg	Mitch	did you get a concurrency error or did it work?
42	04/14 11:04	msg	Will	it worked -- I think I was in a little earlier than you
42	...			EXCISED MATERIAL

Fig. 3. Transcript from a GroupBanter conversation. Conversation codes are: "new" – new conversation started; "open" – open conversation window; "close" conversation window; "msg" add message to the conversation.

Overall this example illustrates that GroupBanter conversations had many of the features we intended to support. Conversations were often opportunistic with people contributing un-elicited comments and were informal (as evidenced by the jokes and typos). In addition, GroupBanter conversations allowed different levels of contribution (active messaging versus dipping in), different paces of conversation (interactive to intermittent), and were useful in detecting group co-ordination problems.

The main reasons given for why people started GB conversations included:

Didn't know who would be interested: *"I didn't know who in particular would be interested". "wasn't intended for anyone specific". "whoever is interested will join".*

In order to get a quick reply. *"wanted someone to reply right away". "reach a group of people fast". "I would like a quick response". "immediate and real-time feedback".*

Interested in having a group conversation: *"wasn't aimed at an individual ... I wanted to hear other comedic responses". "I didn't really want to talk to one person". "wanted to see what everyone was thinking". "didn't have to ask people individually. We could all discuss it together"*

Just for fun: *"it was there". "just to say hi". "just wanted to talk to some people". "companionship"*

6.1 New Opportunities and Exchanges

Fifty-eight participants in Phase 1 and eight participants in Phase 2 completed the post-study questionnaire. Many respondents saw themselves as active contributors to conversations (Phase 1: 62%; Phase 2: 63%) and initiated conversations that they would not have otherwise engaged in (Phase 1: 41%, Phase 2: 63%). Additionally, 45% of Phase 1 participants indicated they would be more likely to use GroupBanter than the group email list. In Phase 1 (where not all of the participants knew each other), GroupBanter provided opportunities for interaction with new users - 72% of participants indicating they had unexpected conversations and 66% indicating they met new people using GroupBanter.

We also asked whether GroupBanter changed the nature of their communication. Many reported that GroupBanter conversations were more useful than those in other communication channels. When asked *how* communication would have been different without GroupBanter, several participants commented on inclusiveness ("anyone outside the immediate conversation would be blind as to the larger picture involving the code review") and response time ("[it would have taken] a lot longer to get to resolution").

6.2 Attitudes towards GroupBanter

Most participants indicated they would utilize a system like GroupBanter to create conversations that others could see and join (Phase 1: 83%; Phase 2: 100%) and would join GroupBanter conversations others were having (Phase 1: 93%). One participant commented: "My siblings and I use IM a lot to chat since we're spread over the country. I'd like to see and join other conversations that are going on instead of each talking 1-1. This is in addition to just being able to have a multiway chat."

Although GroupBanter was utilized throughout Phase 1, many participants in this group were less interested in GroupBanter for the existing population (Intern group) and instead wanted to use GroupBanter with their close friends. Overall, 49 participants in Phase 1 (84%) reported they would use GroupBanter if it was integrated into their IM application, however, several participants mentioned they would want to know that more people were using it and have more control over whom conversations would be broadcast to. For example, "if I could use it to just communicate within a set of people I know or who are closely related to someone I know."

Users also commented on the benefit of being aware of ongoing conversations and the ability to join conversations they were interested in, as well the ability to socialize, meet new people, and have a sense of community. One participant in Phase 2 commented that: "1) it cut down on the amount of e-mail our team used; 2) I could choose to casually join or leave conversations; 3) there was no immediate pressure to reply to conversations (most of the time); 4) it allowed greater sharing of information - conversations that otherwise would have been hidden were available to "listen to".

6.3   Ephemeral versus Persistent Conversations

GroupBanter was designed to support ephemeral group conversations that can be broadcast to encourage serendipitous group exchanges. We hypothesized that there would be interest in having short-lived, spontaneous conversations similar to hallway conversations. To our surprise, participants tended to keep conversations open for extended periods of time to allow others to see the discussion and provide input if desired. As a result, the duration of conversations was much longer than we anticipated.

We probed the issues of ephemeral versus persistent conversations in the Phase 2 mid-study interviews and the post-study questionnaire. Although GroupBanter conversations persist until everyone closes the conversation window, two people in Phase 2 had specific IM behaviors that conflicted with this approach and contributed to the extended conversation durations. First, one participant never closed any of his IM windows, he just minimized them so that he could maintain an ongoing transcript with each person he IMed with. A second participant wanted to keep the conversations open in case he needed to access the information later. The remaining participants all commented that they would have preferred that conversations end when they became inactive and be removed from the list. Although the participants were interested in having throw-away conversations (i.e., ones that are not archived) they recognized that some conversations contained valuable information and wanted the option of tagging specific conversations for archiving.

7   Design Suggestions and Challenges

Although user reactions tended to be positive, the results from both studies highlighted several design suggestions, suggesting areas for further investigation.

A key concern raised in Phase 1 was who information should be broadcast to. The population we studied in Phase 1 was a group of loosely connected people; however, this type of group interaction was of less interest to our participants. They instead wanted to use GroupBanter with close friends and have control over whom conversations were broadcast to. Tools such as GroupBanter may therefore be better suited to closely connected individuals or those with common interests. This was validated in Phase 2 where GroupBanter was valued more by a group of close work colleagues.

Another important design suggestion relates to the degree to which persistence is supported. If tools like GroupBanter are used in the workplace we need to provide an option to archive some conversations. However, our results indicate that users do not want *all* conversations to persist. Instead, users argued for a semi-persistent, asynchronous tool that enables them to share information with their colleagues for a period of time, and archive the information if desired. This would help reduce 'clutter' resulting from having all conversations persist, while ensuring key information is not lost.

The necessity of good (but still lightweight) awareness and notification features was also evident in Phase 2. Several participants commented that they wanted better awareness of updated conversations, the ability to tag conversations, and an unobtrusive invitation mechanism.

8 Concluding Remarks

Our participants actively used group conversations in GroupBanter and wanted to continue using it after the study was over. The field studies demonstrated the utility of GroupBanter in supporting certain types of conversations that aren't well supported with other tools. GroupBanter has advantages of rapidity, interactivity, and informality over email. We also saw benefits over face to face interaction; GroupBanter allows access to what has happened previously in conversations that can be available longer. These advantages suggest that GroupBanter might usefully augment other media and cut down on email.

Our results also demonstrate the value of GroupBanter compared with other IM systems. GroupBanter offers benefits of lurking, awareness of ongoing conversations, and serendipitous exchanges. Although multi-way IM conversations are reported to occur very infrequently, many of our users' expressed interest in seeing conversation information for people on their buddy list. Participants also reported that GroupBanter provided new opportunities for conversations that wouldn't have otherwise have taken place and that in some instances they would be more likely to utilize GroupBanter than an email list for group conversations.

The usage data revealed that users utilized the system to broadcast conversations, as well as to maintain an awareness of, and join conversations. Not surprising, the activity levels varied greatly across users, with some users initiating and actively participating in conversations, while others sat back and preferred to only interact occasionally. In the work context, participants saw direct team benefits - being more aware of conversations, without feeling the need to interact directly.

Our results show the value of ephemeral group conversation awareness provided by GroupBanter. We also gained insights into the types of conversations that GroupBanter supports, which include: not knowing who to direct a question to; not knowing who is interested in participating in a conversation; needing quick feedback; wanting to have a group conversation; just for fun, and group awareness.

On the issue of persistent versus ephemeral conversations, usage data suggests that users want to allow conversations to persist even after the initial burst of dialog - in case others have anything to add. However, participant feedback also suggests that not all conversations should persist. This argues for a hybrid approach, where ephemeral conversations last long enough for others to provide input, but they eventually disappear, unless someone actively chooses to archive that conversation. Participants also noted that conversations were different with GroupBanter than other media and many participants felt that using GroupBanter made the conversations more useful. Finally, GroupBanter helped increase group awareness, particularly in Phase 2.

We are currently revising our integrated prototype, to incorporate the design suggestions that emerged from this study. We intend to conduct longer term evaluations of GroupBanter and investigate how usage changes over time. In conclusion, despite evaluating an early prototype, we feel that our results provide strong validation for the GroupBanter concept.

Acknowledgements

We would like to thank Jason Cross and all of the participants who took part in our study. In addition, we would like to thank members of VIBE and ASI for their feedback on early versions of GroupBanter.

References

1. Kraut, R.E., Fish, R., Root, R., Chalfonte, B.: Informal communication in organizations: Form, function, and technology. In: Oskamp, S., Spacapan, S. (eds.) Human reactions to technology: Claremont symposium on applied social psychology, pp. 145–199. Sage Publications, Thousand Oaks (1990)
2. Whittaker, S., Frohlich, D., Daly-Jones, O.: Informal communication: what is it like and how might we support it? In: CHI 1994 Conference on Computer Human Interaction, pp. 130–137. ACM Press, New York (1994)
3. Kendon, A.: Conducting interaction, Patterns of behavior in focused encounters. Cambridge University Press, Cambridge (1990)
4. Heath, C., Luff, P.: Collaborative activity and technological design: Task coordination in London Underground control rooms. In: ECSCW 1991, pp. 65–80. Kluwer Academic Publishers, Dordrecht (1991)
5. Erickson, T., Smith, D.N., Kellogg, W.A., Laff, M., Richards, J.T., Bradner, E.: Socially translucent systems: Social proxies, persistent conversation, and the design of "Babble". In: CHI 1999 Conference on Computer Human Interaction, pp. 70–72. ACM Press, New York (1999)
6. Fono, D., Baecker, R.: Structuring and supporting persistent chat conversations. In: CSCW 2006, pp. 455–458. ACM Press, New York (2006)
7. McEwan, G., Greenberg, S.: Supporting social worlds with the community bar. In: Group 2005, pp. 21–30. ACM Press, New York (2005)

8. Tran, M.H., Yang, Y., Raikundalia, G.K.: SWIM: An alternative interface for MSN messenger. In: AUIC 2007, pp. 55–62. Australian Computer Society (2007)
9. Dourish, P., Bly, S.: Portholes: Supporting awareness in a distributed work group. In: CHI 1992, pp. 541–547. ACM Press, New York (1992)
10. Smale, S., Greenberg, S.: Broadcasting information via display names in instant messaging. In: Group 2005, pp. 89–98. ACM Press, New York (2005)
11. Birnholtz, J.P., Gutwin, C., Ramos, G., Watson, M.: OpenMessenger: Gradual initiation of interaction for distributed workgroups. In: CHI 2008, pp. 1661–1664. ACM Press, New York (2008)
12. Gross, T., Oemig, C.: PRIMInality: Towards Human-Centred Instant Messaging Infrastructures. In: M&C 2005, pp. 71–80 (2005)
13. Nardi, B.A., Whittaker, S., Bradner, E.: Interaction and outeraction: Instant messaging in action. In: CSCW 2000, pp. 79–88. ACM Press, New York (2000)
14. Isaacs, E., Kamm, C., Schiano, D.J., Walendowski, A., Whittaker, S.: Characterizing instant messaging from recorded logs. In: CHI 2002, pp. 720–721. ACM Press, New York (2002)
15. Grinter, R.E., Palen, L.: Instant messaging in teen life. In: CSCW 2002, pp. 21–30. ACM Press, New York (2002)
16. Tran, M.H., Yang, Y., Raikundalia, G.K.: Supporting awareness in instant messaging: an empirical study and mechanism deisgn. In: OZCHI 2005, pp. 55–62. Australian Computer Society (2005)
17. Herbsleb, J., Atkins, D.L., Boyer, D.G., Handel, M., Finholt, T.A.: Introducing Instant Messaging and Chat into the Workplace. In: CHI 2002, pp. 171–178. ACM Press, New York (2002)

The Effect of Personality on Collaborative Task Performance and Interaction

Sinéad Mc Givney, Alan F. Smeaton, and Hyowon Lee

CLARITY: Centre for Sensor Web Technologies and
Centre for Digital Video Processing,
Dublin City University, Glasnevin, Dublin 9, Ireland

Abstract. Collocated, multi-user technologies, which support group-work are becoming increasingly popular. Examples include MERL's Diamondtouch and Microsoft's Surface, both of which have evolved from research prototypes to commercial products. Many applications have been developed for such technologies which support the work and entertainment needs of small groups of people. None of these applications however, have been studied in terms of the interactions and performances of their users with regards to their personality. In this paper, we address this research gap by conducting a series of user studies involving dyads working on a number of multi-user applications on the DiamondTouch tabletop device.

1 Introduction

The personality composition of groups of people working collaboratively on shared tasks has been shown to be an important predictor of performance. For instance, a study of 63 virtual teams found that Extraversion was an important personality trait to promote group interaction and teams with lower variances in Extraversion levels did better [6]. Collocated, touch-sensitive, groupware technologies, such as the DiamondTouch [7] and Microsoft's Surface as well as many new applications that support the work of small groups of people, such as photo management and spatial planning applications, are continually growing in sophistication. User studies on such applications and technologies thus far have failed to examine whether the combined personalities of small groups of people, working together on such collaborative technologies, have an impact on their performance and interaction. Here, we address this research gap by conducting a series of three detailed user experiments in order to analyse the effects of the combined personalities of dyads[1] on different collaborative application interface and task constraint variations. From these experiments, we can discover what personality traits significantly impact dyad performance and interaction.

This paper proceeds as follows. Section 2 provides an overview of previous research conducted with regards to the effects of group personality on task performance. In Section 3, we describe the systems that we designed for our user

---

[1] A dyad refers to a group containing two members.

E. Bertino and J.B.D. Joshi (Eds.): CollaborateCom 2008, LNICST 10, pp. 499–511, 2009.

experiments. We follow this with a description of our experimental methodology in Section 4. In Section 5, we outline the results we obtained from our experimentation, in terms of the personality traits, if any, that affect the performance and interaction of dyads. Finally, we list our overall conclusions in Section 6.

2   Group Personality Studies

Much research has been conducted to study the effect of the personality composition of groups on group performance. Rutherfoord [1], conducted a study with groups of people to determine whether those with a heterogeneous personality composition were more productive and enjoyed working together more than those with a homogenous personality composition. Twenty-two students participated in this study, which involved developing a game management system for an Athletic Association. Participants completed the Keirsey Temperament Sorter, which categorises personality along the Myers-Briggs scale [12].

Results showed that the homogenous control groups experienced more problems on a personal level, rather than technical problems. The heterogeneous experimental groups conveyed a broader and more varied style of problem-solving and interacted more. They discussed about alternative solutions, devised more creative and effective ideas, worked together outside class hours more and were generally found to be stronger and more effective.

Gorla and Lam [5] distributed a questionnaire-based survey to 92 employees from 20 small software development teams (from three people to seven people in size), to determine what combinations of personalities resulted in the best-performing teams. The survey elicited information about the amount, quality, effectiveness and efficiency of the work the employees had done, as well as the frequency that their schedule and budget were adhered to. Participants' personalities were profiled using the Keirsey Temperament Sorter.

Results showed that team leaders with *Intuitive*, *Feeling* and *Judging* traits performed better. Heterogeneity of personality between the team leader and the team members, particularly in the *Extravert/Introvert* and *Intuitive/Sensing* dimensions, proved to be more successful, though heterogeneity among team members had no significant effect. *Thinking* type systems analysts performed better, as their roles incorporated more tasks than in a larger team. *Extraverted* programmers performed better than *Introverted* programmers. Diverse expertise and an appropriate means of sharing this information was also important.

Balthazard *et al.* [6] studied the performance of 63 virtual teams, composed of 248 MBA professionals, with respect to each members' level of expertise and *Extraversion*, as well as the interaction style employed by the group. Participants completed a Five Factor Model profile and an online "Ethical Decision Challenge", first individually to determine each person's level of expertise, then as a randomly constructed group. Group members could communicate through an online chat and conference tool. When the task was completed, participants completed a *Group Style Inventory*™, which assessed interaction behaviours within the group, and a group process questionnaire, which assessed process satisfaction and "buy-in" into the consensus solution.

Analysis of the results showed that team performance was best predicted by expertise in the group. In general, it was mostly the interaction style of the groups that had predictive power on the contextual outcomes in virtual environments. Extraversion was found to be an important trait to promote group interaction and teams with lower variance in extraversion levels did better.

A study was conducted in [2] into online communities and the factors that promote participation in these groups. The online community, consisting of eight groups in the study, used a movie recommender system. Uniqueness and similarity combinations were tested to see which condition resulted in the largest participant contribution. Four of the groups were sent a weekly e-mail informing them of the unique perspective they could bring to the current discussion group. The remaining four groups acted as control groups. Groups were defined as "similar" if they typically watched the same movies and agreed on their reviews of these movies. Dissimilar groups either just watched different movies, or disagreed on movies they had watched. Again, there were four similar groups and four dissimilar groups.

Results showed that dissimilar groups that were supplied with uniqueness information contributed more to these online communities. These results were contrary to the authors' hypothesised results and the many theories and studies completed in social psychology e.g. [3], in that dissimilar groups participated more than similar groups and this diversity was significant.

In the studies we carried out and report on, we were not only interested in the effects of dyad personality composition on their performance and interaction styles, but also the effects of the personality traits exhibited by the application interface they used. In the following section, we describe the systems we used for our user-studies.

3   Systems Used

Here, we provide an outline of the technology that we developed our systems on, followed by an outline of three collaborative systems that we designed and used.

3.1   DiamondTouch and DiamondSpin

The **DiamondTouch** is a multi-user, tabletop device designed and developed by researchers at the Mitsubishi Electric Research Labs (MERL) in Boston, Mass. The tabletop's surface is touch-sensitive and the technology can uniquely distinguish the touchpoints of up to four users. This is enabled by placing signal receiver mats under each user and connecting these mats to the underside of tabletop (transmitter). Once the user touches the tabletop's surface, they complete a circuit and are capacitively coupled with the tabletop. A more detailed description of the DiamondTouch can be found in [7].

DiamondSpin[8] is a Java-based Software Development Toolkit, also designed by researchers and collaborators at MERL. The toolkit contains a polar to Cartesian transformation engine, which handles the rotation and orientation of objects displayed on the DiamondTouch's surface. The toolkit has a well-defined API containing 30 Java classes and interfaces. It also uses pure JAVA 2D with JAI (Java Advanced Imaging) and JMF (Java Media Framework).

We now describe three collaborative system variants.

Memory Game

Memory Game is a competitive card game where players try to find matching pairs of cards. For our version, 24 cards are displayed face-down on the tabletop. Each player overturns two cards when it is their turn and if these match, then that player is given one point and another turn. If the cards do not match, control passes to the other player. Scores are displayed at the side of the interface and oriented to each player. The player with the highest number of matching pairs wins the game.

We made this game collaborative by requiring dyads to find pairs together. This game commenced when the first player touched the tabletop screen (Player 1). This player was then required to overturn the first card in this and in subsequent games. Player 2 then had to select a card that they believed matched the already overturned card. Their choice of card was predominantly the result of both players discussing options and sharing potential match location information. We used 4 different sets of cards in this system.

Two different rules or constraints were imposed, the first of which was to find all matching pairs accurately while incurring as few mismatched pairs as possible. The second rule required that users find all matches as quickly as possible, regardless of the number of mismatched pairs they incurred. After the second game was played on each rule, players were asked to switch sides, so that each got a turn at being match-chooser and match-finder for each rule imposed for half the task, making it fairer. Figure 1 illustrates the Accuracy Memory interface.

3.2   Físchlár-DT

Físchlár-DT is a two-person video search system that our research group built on the DiamondTouch for the annual TRECVid (Text Retrieval Conference for

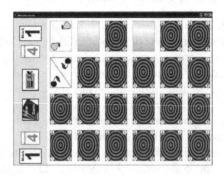

Fig. 1. Accuracy Memory Game interface

Video) 2005 workshop [10]. TRECVid is a benchmarking conference series, where participants compare video retrieval and analysis techniques on a large shared test dataset [13].

The aim of this search task was to find as many video shots (sections of video) as possible out of a supplied repository, that were relevant to a given multimedia topic using a video search system e.g. "Find shots of Tony Blair'. Each shot was represented by an image called a keyframe.

Físchlár-DT was developed using the DiamondSpin SDK, to easily handle the rotation and orientation of objects on the interface. One interface we developed for these experiments had a number of hot-spots which enabled the user to carry out specific actions. Each hot-spot had an associated distinctive sound, which both made their partner aware that a certain function had been invoked and also provided feedback to the user that it was invoked properly. Users could type a text query (using a pop-up keyboard) into a movable search box located in the bottom right-hand corner of the screen. The "search" button then delivered up to 20 keyframes displayed around the table with more relevant keyframes displayed closer to the centre of the screen. This is illustrated in Figure 2.

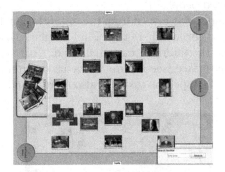

Fig. 2. Físchlár-DT: Awareness interface

Dragging a shot keyframe over the "Play" hot-spot commenced playback of the shot on an external monitor. The "Browse" hot-spot displayed the next ten and previous ten shots in that particular news broadcast, to the shot selected. The "Find Similar" hot-spot displayed keyframes from 20 shots that were similar to the selected shot keyframe, by comparing MPEG-7 descriptors of that keyframe to the rest of the keyframes in the collection. "Remove" deleted the selected keyframe from the screen, not to be retrieved again for that particular search task. Finally, if a keyframe was moved into the "Saved Area", the shot was marked relevant with a yellow border and stamp. Any or all of these functions could be invoked by either user by dragging a keyframe onto the appropriate hot-spot.

Similar to the Memory Game system, one of our user studies involving the Físchlár-DT system imposed different rules on the participating dyads. The first constraint imposed in our our first search-based task (**Físchlár-DT 1**) was a ten minute time-limit, where dyads had to find as many relevant shots as possible to two specified topics – "Find shots of Condoleeza Rice" and "Find shots of people shaking hands". The order of these topics was switched from dyad to dyad to avoid order bias. The other rule demanded that dyads find ten shots in total, that were relevant to two topics (i.e. "Find shots of tanks or other military vehicles" and "Find shots of banners or signs"). The topics used were a subset of the topics used for the TRECVid 2005 interactive video retrieval experiments, since the relevance judgements were known. By this, we mean that we had lists of shots that were deemed relevant to each topic by manual assessors as part of TRECVid.

For our final user experiment, **Físchlár-DT 2**, we altered the interface to the Físchlár-DT system, to give two variations that exploited the *Extraversion* personality trait. Figure 3 shows the Extravert interface. Here, we chose bright, highly saturated colours, boxes and sharp edges [14]. We removed the "Find Similar" hot-spot and instead, when a user saved a keyframe, the system displayed four keyframes representing shots it thought were similar to that saved. These were then displayed in a "Suggested Clips" area, located at the centre of the table. This was in keeping with the idea that system-initiated interaction is preferred by extraverted people [4].

The "Browse" hot-spot was moved from the top right-hand corner of the table, to the bottom left-hand corner where the "Find Similar" hot-spot was originally located, hence making the interface more balanced.

For our *Introvert* interface (see Figure 3), we used softer, pastel colours. The hot-spots were round in shape, the text was also more rounded and we moved the

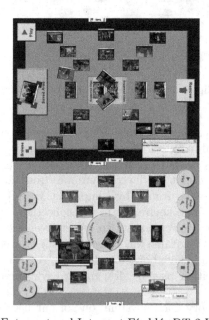

Fig. 3. Extravert and Introvert Físchlár-DT 2 Interfaces

saved area to the centre of the table [14]. Each of the functions were duplicated for each user, allowing them to work more independently and quietly, which was in keeping with the introverted personality type. This however, did result in users being less aware of each others' actions. The "Find Similar" hot-spot was brought back into this version.

Dyads searched for 3 topics on each of these interfaces, totaling 6 topics altogether for the entire session. These again, were a subset of the TRECVid 2005 topics. There was a 5-minute limit imposed on dyads for each topic to find as many shots as possible that were relevant to that topic. The order of presentation of the interfaces was changed for each dyad.

4   Experimental Methodology

Here, we give an overview of how we conducted our user experiments, from how our experiment participants were recruited to the experimental procedure we followed. We also outline how the participants' personalities were profiled.

4.1   Participant Recruitment

Participants were recruited from the general university student population via email. This email requested the participation of pairs of users, whom if selected, would be financially rewarded in return for completing our user-studies.

We used the Five Factor model of personality to profile the personalities of our participants, which is the most widely accepted model of personality in the personality psychology community. This model describes the personality of individuals in terms of five personality traits i.e. *Openness to Experience, Conscientiousness, Extraversion, Agreeableness and Neuroticism – OCEAN* [11]. The strength of these traits present in an individual are measured based on the responses of the individual to a specially designed personality questionnaire. Analysing these answers enables a percentage to be calculated for each trait e.g. 35 % Extravert.

In this study, we believed that *Extraversion* would have the greatest impact on both the performance and the interaction of the group. Hence, when people initially responded to the recruitment email, we requested them to answer 6 short questions from the IPIP-Neo online personality questionnaire [15] which appeared to prevalently measure the *Extraversion* trait. After the first experiment, participants were asked to complete the short version (i.e. 60 questions) of an online IPIP-Neo personality questionnaire. 36 people in total took part in the studies, with just three females. Other females who had responded to the recruitment email, failed to show up at the experiments. There were no female/female dyads.

There was at least one week between each of the tasks, with each one lasting between 30 minutes and one hour. Before starting each task, dyads were introduced to the system interface variations or rule variations, as well as completing some pre-task training. Each participant also completed pre and post study questionnaires which elicited information about their age, background, prior experience and their opinions on the task they had just completed.

Footage of the user studies was captured using a CCTV camera, placed at a height above the tabletop. We subsequently annotated the interaction of dyads from this footage. We logged and time-stamped four types of communication – requests (which could be verbal, gestural or both), responses (which could be verbal, gestural or both), comments and coordination errors. A coordination error was an action that one user took that interrupted their partner's work e.g. invoking an action without warning, that entirely changed the display. The recording of the studies was approved by our University's Ethics committee. In total, we recorded approximately 55 hours of video footage.

4.2 Data Gathered

We gathered a substantial amount of data in carrying out our user studies, which we categorised under two main headings:

Explicitly Supplied User Data

1. Questionnaire responses from users (both pre and post-study questionnaires), which elicited information regarding participant's age, course, familiarity with web searching and the DiamondTouch, frequency of working in groups, as well as their opinions on the systems used (i.e. ease of use, opinion of interface colours and layout etc.).
2. Personality Questionnaire responses (i.e. users' scores for the Big Five personality traits).

System Recorded Data:

3. Performance Data (i.e. user scores in the game experiments and the number of relevant shots saved in the search tasks).
4. User touchpoints on the tabletop (meaning exactly where on-screen each user touched).
5. CCTV footage of the user experiments and associated annotations.

Our analysis of this data involved identifying relationships between each of these data sources to study the effects of personality traits on performances and interactions on our collaborative tasks. We explain this in the next section.

5 Results

5.1 Personality and Performance

In order to explore whether correlations exist between the personalities of dyads and their performance, it was necessary to combine the trait scores of both dyad members. For the *Extraversion* trait, we tested a number of orderings, including a metric which we called "E-Dist". This measured the absolute difference between the *Extraversion* scores of both dyad members, as reported on their completed personality questionnaires. The idea here was that the closer each person's level

Table 1. Correlations between performance and dyad personality traits

Task	Related Traits	r_s value
Accuracy Memory	*Least Cons*	-0.53
	Least Agree	-0.53
	Avg. Agree	-0.53
Speed Memory	—	—
Fís-DT 1 (10 min)	*O-Dist*	-0.49
Fís-DT 1 (Find 10)	—	—
Fís-DT 2 (Int)	*Least Open*	-0.54
	Least Consc.	-0.47
Fís-DT 2 (Ext)	*O-Dist*	-0.64
	Most Open.	-0.47

of *Extraversion* was to that of their partner, the more similar and compatible they would be [3]. Hence, we anticipated a correlation between low *E-Dist* values and high levels of performance.

Our other metrics included "Avg. Extra", "Most Extra" member and "Most Intro" member. For "Avg. Extra", we simply averaged both dyad member's scores for the *Extraversion* trait. In the case of the "Most Extra" measure, we examined the *Extraversion* results for each dyad member and chose the more extravert member's result. Similarly, we noted the member of each dyad who had the lowest percentage of *Extraversion* for "Most Intro". We applied the same combination schemes to the other four personality traits (*Openness to Experience (O-Dist, Avg. Open, Most Open, Least Open), Conscientiousness (C-Dist, Avg. Cons, Most Cons, Least Cons), Agreeableness (A-Dist, Avg. Agree, Most Agree, Least Agree)* and *Neuroticism (N-Dist, Avg. Neur, Most Neur, Least Neur)*).

We used the Spearman rank correlation method (a special, non-parametric case of the Pearson product-moment rank correlation) to identify statistical relationships between the orderings of each of our personality trait combination metrics and ordering of dyad performance, which we decided was the most appropriate metric given the characteristics of our dataset. Table 1 displays the statistically significant relationships between dyad personality traits and performance (given a critical value of $\pm$ 0.476 at $\alpha = 0.05$ for a two-tailed test). Column 1 lists the tasks studied; column 2 lists the personality trait combination schemes that had a statistically significant effect on dyad performance and column 3 gives the respective correlation coefficients (r_s) calculated from our Spearman rank correlations. We note here that the combined dyad *Extraversion* and *Neuroticism* trait did not affect performance on any of our tasks – a surprising result, given the social nature of the tasks.

It is interesting to note that none of the personality traits affected performance on either of the 2 systems that required users to complete the task quickly, namely Speed Memory and the Físchlár-DT 1 (Find 10) system both of which required users to complete their respective tasks as quickly as possible. In terms of Físchlár-DT 1 (10 minute), and both Físchlár-DT 2 interfaces, we see that *Openness to Experience* is an important trait in relation to performance, though the correlations calculated indicate that dyads containing at least one person with a much lower *Openness to Experience* score than their partner perform better.

The strong negative correlation along the *Least Cons* combination scheme for Físchlár-DT 2 (Introvert interface) is also a surprising finding, since we believed that this system required both users to think before they acted. Since the functions were duplicated on this interface, there was more potential for users to interrupt their partner's work e.g. playing over each others' videos.

Both *Conscientiousness* and *Agreeableness* were important in the Accuracy Memory system where the *Least Cons, Least Agree* and *Avg. Agree* trait combination schemes all produced negative correlations. This implies that low Conscientiousness and low Agreeableness produced lower performances (the performance ranks of Accuracy Memory differed since a lower figure for performance indicated better performance/fewer mismatches). These resulting correlations were much more intuitive, since it would be important that dyad members were both conscientious (i.e. they lacked impulsiveness and thought before they acted) and agreeable, so that they made the fewest errors possible.

5.2   Personality and Interaction

We conducted a similar type of analysis for our interaction data for all dyads and all systems – that being the touchpoints recorded and the interactions annotated from the CCTV footage of the experiments. Again, we used the personality trait combination metrics that we listed in the previous subsection. Since the length of some of the tasks differed (i.e. Accuracy Memory, Speed Memory and Físchlár-DT 1 (Find 10)), we had to normalise the number of interactions per dyad so that they could be fairly compared. Hence, we took one minute of time as our normalising unit.

We look first at our **touchpoint data**. From Table 2, we see that *Conscientiousness* and *Extraversion* have a significant effect on the number of touchpoints for both Collaborative Memory game rules. This indicates that dyad members, whose level of *Conscientiousness* was similar (i.e. a low *C-Dist*), had fewer touchpoints per minute than those who had very different levels when working on Accuracy Memory. However, for Speed Memory, the r_s values obtained implied that dyads who had a high average *Conscientiousness* or where both members had high levels of *Conscientiousness* had fewer touchpoints. This was a logical finding, since a lack of impulsiveness and a more thoughtful approach to the game would be important here.

We also see that the *Neuroticism* personality trait is significantly correlated to the number of touchpoints in Speed Memory, where dyads who have similar levels of *Neuroticism* have fewer touchpoints. In addition, dyads containing at least one member with a high level of *Neuroticism* had significantly more touchpoints than those dyads whose members had lower levels. *Neuroticism* also has a significant negative correlation on Físchlár-DT 1 along the *N-Dist* metric i.e. dyads whose members' level of *Neuroticism* was similar had more touchpoints. *Openness to Experience* produced a negative correlation on Físchlár-DT 2

Table 2. Traits significantly related to touchpoints for each system and associated combination metric

	Related Traits	r_s value
Accuracy Memory	*C-Dist*	0.49
Speed Memory	Avg. Cons	-0.62,
	Least Cons	0.48
	N-Dist	0.53
	Most Neur	0.5
Fís-DT 1	*N-Dist*	-0.59
Fís-DT 2 (Int)	*Most Open*	-0.49
Fís-DT 2 (Ext)	*Most Agree*	-0.51
	A-Dist	-0.48

(Introvert Interface) along the *Most Open* metric i.e. dyads where at least one dyad member had a relatively high level of openness had fewer touchpoints.

Finally, on Físchlár-DT 2 (Extravert interface), negative correlations were calculated for the *Most Agree* and *A-Dist* metrics. These results imply that dyads with at least one more agreeable member had fewer touchpoints, while dyads whose members had more similar levels of *Agreeableness* had more touchpoints.

Finally, we look at the **annotations** (interactions) that we made from the CCTV recordings of the experiments. Due to the fact recordings were corrupted for some dyads in some systems, our sample sizes and subsequently our critical values were different for each system. For both Collaborative Memory systems and both Físchlár-DT 1 rules, our sample size was n=17. With an α of 0.05 (two-tailed test), our critical value here was 0.507. Our sample size for Físchlár-DT 2 Extravert interface was 16, with a critical value of 0.507. Lastly, our Físchlár-DT 2 Introvert system had an n of 15 and a critical value of 0.545.

It is clear from Table 3 that the strong significant positive correlation between the *Avg. Extra* metric and interactions indicates that users with higher average *Extraversion* values have a greater number of interactions (communication) on the Accuracy Memory game and Físchlár-DT 1 (both rules) and Físchlár-DT 2 (Introvert Interface). Físchlár-DT 2 (Extravert) shows a highly significant

Table 3. Traits significantly related to interactions and associated combination metric for each system

	Related Traits	r_s value
Accuracy Memory	*Avg. Extra*	0.63
	Most Intro	0.63
Speed Memory	—	—
Fís-DT 1 (10 min)	*Avg. Extra*	0.51
Fís-DT 1 (Find 10)	*Avg. Extra*	0.56
Fís-DT 2 (Int)	*Least Neur*	-0.59
	Avg. Extra.	0.70
Fís-DT 2 (Ext)	*Avg. Agree*	0.55
	Most Extra.	0.74

correlation between *Most Extra* and interactions, indicating that dyads with at least one highly extraverted member communicated more. This would appear to support previous psychological research showing that people with high levels of *Extraversion* are talkative and sociable.

The *Most Intro* metric, which also showed a significant positive r_s value of 0.63 for the Accuracy Memory system, indicates that those dyads that contained at least one very introvert member were less likely to communicate than those with more extraverted members. Físchlár-DT 2 (Introvert interface) displays a significant negative correlation alog the *Neuroticism* personality trait i.e. dyads where both members were highly neurotic had fewer interactions. Físchlár-DT 2 (Extravert interface) showed a significant, positive correlation between increasing *Avg. Agree* and increasing interactions i.e. dyads whose members were on average more agreeable, had more interactions. These were intuitive findings.

6   Conclusions

From the results presented above, we can see that the combination of dyad members' personalities does impact their performance and interaction. However, the personality traits that most prevalently have an impact differ from task to task. One very obvious trend was that *Extraversion* had an impact on tasks that did not enforce very short time constraints. *Openness to Experience* had an impact on performance on search tasks, while *Agreeableness* was important for tasks where tight collaboration was required (in our case, the Accuracy Memory system). *Conscientiousness* was also found to have an impact on performance, though there was no apparent trend across the systems it impacted. All personality traits aside from *Extraversion* had some impact on the number of touchpoints that each dyad incurred. *Conscientiousness* impacted the number of touchpoints incurred on both our collaborative Memory Game systems. However, there were no other obvious trends concerning trait impact on touchpoints and interface or task type.

Collaborative tasks, such as tagging on the net, both for work and for leisure pursuits, are growing and becoming more widespread through the use of devices like the DiamondTouch and Microsoft's Surface. From our rather mixed results we can conclude that as this growth happens, system designers do need to be made aware of findings such as ours as they will influence, in one way or another, the effectiveness of systems built to support collaboration.

Interesting future experiments may look at a comparison of the performance of one person executing these tasks against the performance of dyads working on such a collaborative technology; or determining whether similar trends can be observed when users are collaboratively working together in a distributed/virtual environment.

Acknowledgements

The authors gratefully acknowledge the support of Mitsubishi Electric Research Labs. Thanks also to Emilie Garnaud for the use of original Memory Game system. This work is supported by the Irish Research Centre for Science, Engineering and Technology (IRCSET) and Science Foundation Ireland under grant numbers 03/IN.3/I361 and 07/CE/I1147.

References

1. Rutherfoord, R.H.: Using personality inventories to form teams for class projects: a case study. In: SIGITE 2006, pp. 9–14. ACM, Minnesota (2006)
2. Ludford, P.J., Cosley, D., Frankowski, D., Terveen, L.: Think different: increasing online community participation using uniqueness and group dissimilarity. In: CHI 2004, pp. 631–638. ACM, Vienna (2004)
3. Byrne, D., Nelson, D.: Attraction as a Linear Function of Proportion of Positive Reinforcements. Journal of personality and social psychology (4), 240–243 (1965)
4. Reeves, B., Nass, C.: The Media Equation. In: Media and Personality, P.75. CSLI Publications (1996)
5. Gorla, N., Lam, Y.W.: Who should work with whom?: building effective software project teams. Communications of the ACM 47, 79–82 (2004)
6. Balthazard, P., Potter, R.E., Warren, J.: Expertise, extraversion and group interaction styles as performance indicators in virtual teams: how do perceptions of IT's performance get formed? In: ACM SIGMIS Database, vol. 35, pp. 41–226. ACM, NY (2004)
7. Dietz, P., Leigh, D.: DiamondTouch: a multi-user touch technology. In: UIST 2001, pp. 219–226. ACM, Orlando (2001)
8. Shen, C., Vernier, F.D., Forlines, C., Ringel, M.: DiamondSpin: an extensible toolkit for around-the-table interaction. In: CHI 2004, pp. 167–174. ACM, Vienna (2004)
9. Pickford, R.W.: Psychology and Visual Aesthetics. Hutchinson Educational LTD, London (1975)
10. Foley, C., Gurrin, C., Jones, G., Lee, H., Mc Givney, S., O'Connor, N., Sav, S., Smeaton, A.F., Wilkins, P.: TRECVID 2005 Experiments at Dublin City University. In: TRECVID 2005: - Text REtrieval Conference TRECVID Workshop, Gaithersburg, Maryland (2005)
11. Costa, P.T., McCrea, R.R.: Revised NEO Personality Inventory (NEO PI-R) and NEO Five-Factor Inventory (NEO-FFI). Psychological Assessment Resources (1937)
12. Moad, J.: Psych Tests for MIS Staff: Is This Nuts? Datamation (1994)
13. Smeaton, A., Over, P., Kraaij, W.: Evaluation campaigns and TRECVid. In: MIR 2006, pp. 321–330. ACM, Santa Barbara (2006)
14. Karsvall, A.: Personality preferences in graphical interface design. In: NordiCHI 2002, pp. 217–218. ACM, Aarhus (2002)
15. Short Form for the IPIP-Neo (International Personality Item Pool Representation of the NEO PI-R),
    http://www.personal.psu.edu/faculty/j/5/j5j/IPIP/ipipneo120.htm

Replication in Overlay Networks: A Multi-objective Optimization Approach

Osama Al-Haj Hassan, Lakshmish Ramaswamy, John Miller, Khaled Rasheed, and E. Rodney Canfield

Computer Science Department, University of Georgia,
Athens, GA 30602, USA
{hasan,laks,jam,khaled,erc}@cs.uga.edu

Abstract. Recently, overlay network-based collaborative applications such as instant messaging, content sharing, and Internet telephony are becoming increasingly popular. Many of these applications rely upon data-replication to achieve better performance, scalability, and reliability. However, replication entails various costs such as storage for holding replicas and communication overheads for ensuring replica consistency. While simple rule-of-thumb strategies are popular for managing the cost-benefit tradeoffs of replication, they cannot ensure optimal resource utilization. This paper explores a multi-objective optimization approach for replica management, which is unique in the sense that we view the various factors influencing replication decisions such as access latency, storage costs, and data availability as objectives, and not as constraints. This enables us to search for solutions that yield close to optimal values for these parameters. We propose two novel algorithms, namely multi-objective Evolutionary (MOE) algorithm and multi-objective Randomized Greedy (MORG) algorithm for deciding the number of replicas as well as their placement within the overlay. While MOE yields higher quality solutions, MORG is better in terms of computational efficiency. The paper reports a series of experiments that demonstrate the effectiveness of the proposed algorithms.

Keywords: Replication, Multi-Objective Optimization, Evolutionary Algorithms, Greedy Approach.

1 Introduction

Overlay networks have evolved as scalable and cost-effective platforms for hosting several collaborative applications. Examples of overlay-based collaborative applications include instant messaging [1], content sharing [2] and Internet telephony [3]. However, the very fact that most of the overlays are formed from personal computers rather than powerful servers implies that collaborative applications running on top of them have to constantly deal with a variety of resource limitations such as storage and bandwidth constraints. Furthermore, the

E. Bertino and J.B.D. Joshi (Eds.): CollaborateCom 2008, LNICST 10, pp. 512–528, 2009.
© ICST Institute for Computer Sciences, Social-Informatics and Telecommunications Engineering 2009

overlay networks experience significant *churn* with end-hosts constantly entering and exiting the network.

For collaborative applications to yield acceptable quality of service (qos), it is essential that the individual nodes of the system are able to access data-items in an efficient, scalable, and reliable manner. Replication of data-item is known to be an effective strategy for achieving better performance, scalability, and availability [4], and it has been utilized in a number of applications. However, data replication does not come for free; it consumes various resources like storage and network bandwidth. Replication imposes additional storage costs, and these costs are especially high in environments comprising of memory-scarce devices such as PDAs and cell phones [5]. Similarly, ensuring that replicas are consistent imposes communication overheads [6]. Thus, designing replication strategies involves balancing a variety of tradeoffs.

Two important questions in replicating data in overlay networks are: *(1) How many replicas of each data item should be maintained within the overlay?*; and *(2) Where (on which nodes of the overlay) should these replicas be placed?*. These two related challenges are collectively referred to as the *replica-placement problem*. Although replica placement in overlay networks has been previously studied [7][8][9][10][11], very few of the existing strategies take a holistic view of the various costs and benefits of replication. Many of them are limited by the fact that they consider only a small number of performance parameters. Even the ones that are sensitive to larger sets of performance factors, use simple rule-of-thumb strategies to manage the various tradeoffs. These schemes fail to optimally utilize the various resources available in the overlay.

In this paper, we propose a multi-objective optimization framework for the overlay replica placement problem. Our framework is characterized by several unique features. First, it takes into account several factors such as access latency, storage costs and availability. Second, these factors are regarded as *objectives for optimization* rather than constraints. This provides us with the advantage that we can *search* for solutions that yield close to optimal values for these parameters instead of just attempting to keep them within certain bounds. Third, our framework is inspired by evolutionary computing paradigm, and each solution is represented as a chromosome.

As a part of this framework, we propose two algorithms, namely, *multi-objective Evolutionary (MOE)* algorithm and *multi-objective Randomized Greedy (MORG)* algorithm. MOE algorithm is based upon the NSGA-II algorithm [13]. While MOE yields higher quality solutions, it is computationally intensive. To mitigate this concern, we propose the novel MORG algorithm, which is not only very efficient, but also yields solutions that are comparable in quality to those produced by the MOE algorithm.

We have performed series of experiments to study the costs and benefits of the proposed techniques. The results demonstrate the effectiveness of our multi-objective optimization framework in determining the locations for placing the replicas.

2   Background and Related Work

Replication techniques for overlays have been an active area of research. master-slave replication model has been adopted by several systems. For example, Sacha and Dowling [7] utilize a gradient technique for designing a master-slave repli-cation for peer-to-peer networks. Replica placement problem has also received considerable research attention in recent years. In the Gnutella P2P system [2], only the nodes which request and retrieve a data-item hold a copy of that ob-ject. Freenet [8], however, allows replicas to be created on nodes other than the ones that requested the data-item. Cohen and Shenker [9] propose the path replication scheme, wherein replicas are placed along the path traversed by a data request. They also discuss random placement scheme where the replicas are placed on randomly chosen nodes in the overlay network. Some researchers have also addressed the question of how many replicas of a given data-item need to be maintained in the overlay. Proportional replication, wherein the number of replicas of a data-item increase with its usage has been discussed by Lv et al. [10]. They also contrast this scheme with a uniform replication scheme where the same number of replicas is created for all data-items. Benayoune and Lancieri [11] survey several replication techniques including the idea of replicating refer-ences of data-items instead of the data-items themselves.

Some of the existing techniques optimize the number of created replicas [16], while others optimize the locations in which to place replicas [17]; still others optimize how often replicas should be updated [18]. However, many of these techniques have the shortcoming that they only consider a limited set of param-eters affecting the replication decision. The works by Loukopoulos and Ahmad [12] has the same objective as ours. They design a genetic algorithm to find the optimal replication strategy. In that work, two versions of the algorithm, a static version and a dynamic adaptive version are proposed. However, they model the problem as a single objective optimization problem. Specifically, they optimize latency, while storage, bandwidth and other parameters are considered as con-straints. One of the limitations of this approach is that it can only maintain the constraint parameters within certain bounds, but cannot explicitly optimize them. Further, their work did not take into account the reliability of the sys-tem. Thus, we believe that there is a need for a holistic approach to the overlay replica placement problem which not only takes all the important factors into ac-count but also explicitly optimizes them. Motivated by this need, we propose the MOE and MORG algorithms, both of which are based upon the multi-objective optimization paradigm.

3   Architectural Overview

Our system is based upon unstructured P2P overlays. Unlike their structured counterparts, unstructured overlays do not provide distributed hash table (DHT) support. In these networks, content searching happens purely by ad-hoc messag-ing among neighbors. In our architecture, a data-item and its replicas are viewed

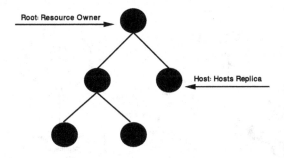

Fig. 1. Logical tree of nodes hosting replicas

as a logical tree. We build a replication tree for each data-item in the system in which the root would be the owner of the original copy of the data-item , and the other nodes of the tree would have replicas. Fig. 1 illustrates the replication tree. The replication tree is constructed using a scheme similar to the one proposed by Zhang et al. [15].

When a node in the system wants to *read* a data-item it accesses the closest replica of the data-item. However, updates of a data-item are always initiated at root of the tree. A node that wants to update a data-item, sends it to the root, which is then propagated down the tree-hierarchy. The root node as well as the other nodes holding replicas collect various statistics such as the frequency at which a replica is used, frequency at which the data-item is updated, ratio of reads to writes for a data item, failure statistics of the node holding the replica, and storage availability and utilization at each node. The information collected at various nodes will be aggregated at the root of the tree. These statistics will be fed into our optimization engine which produces solutions to the replica placement problem, indicating which nodes should hold additional replicas and which of the existing replicas need to be de-commissioned. The replication tree is then modified accordingly. Fig. 2 illustrates the functioning of our system.

4   Problem Formulation

The problem on hand consists of optimizing a set of objectives, some of which might be conflicting with one another. For example, achieving better latency might require creating additional replicas. However, doing so would invariably increase storage and consistency maintenance costs. Similarly, placing the replicas on most stable nodes might not be ideal from latency minimization perspective. Multi-objective optimization deals with these conflicting objectives by evolving a set of solutions that compromise these conflicting objectives.

The quality of solutions obtained by multi-objective optimization is inherently dependent upon how well the objectives are formulated. In this section, we first model each of the objectives following which we discuss their conflicts.

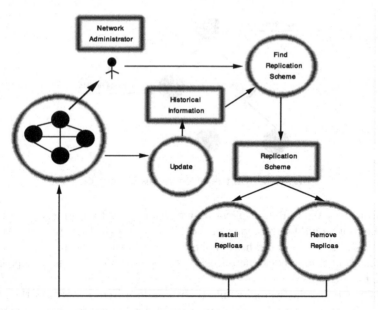

Fig. 2. System functionality overview

4.1   Latency

Minimizing latency is important for any collaborative system. Minimizing latency depends on utilizing high bandwidth channels, as high bandwidth channels yields lesser latency. Thus, it is better to avoid nodes with low-bandwidth connections. Furthermore, if a node frequently accesses a data-item, then minimizing its latency in retrieving the data-item should naturally take priority over those nodes that occasionally access the same data-item. Taking these aspects into account, we model the latency objective function D as the following:

$$D = R + W \tag{1}$$

where

$$R = \sum_{i=1}^{n} \sum_{j=1}^{m} E(i, s_j) * \frac{Z(s_j)}{B(i, H(s_j))} * RP(i, s_j) \tag{2}$$

and

$$W = \sum_{i=1}^{n} \sum_{j=1}^{m} (1 - E(i, s_j)) * \frac{Z(us_j)}{B(i, O(s_j))} * WP(i, s_j) + \sum_{k=1}^{x} \frac{Z(us_j)}{B(O(s_j), k)} * WP(i, s_j) \tag{3}$$

Where
R: Total read cost in the system
W: Total write cost in the system
i: index for nodes of the system

j: index for data-items of the system

x: index for nodes holding replicas of data-item j

s_j: is the data-item for which we are trying to find read cost.

$E(i,s_j)$: equals to 0 if data-item j exists on host i, otherwise it equals to 1

$H(s_j)$: is the machine that hosts replica of data-item j

$RP(i, s_j)$: is the percentage of read requests coming from node i asking for data-item j

$WP(i, s_j)$: is the percentage of write requests coming from node i updating data-item j

us_j: is the updated version of data-item j

$O(s_j)$: is the owner of data-item j

$B(a,b)$: Minimum bandwidth along the path from node a to node b

$Z(s)$: is the size of the data-item 's'

We assume that the system is fully active, which means that each node in the system attempts read and write requests, each node according to its read requests percentage (RP) and write requests percentage (WP). Basically, what happens in a read operation is that a data item needs to be transferred in chunks to the requester; this is determined by dividing the size of the data item on the minimum bandwidth along the path from source to requester. With regard to write requests, the first part of the equation before the plus sign models transferring the data item in chunks to its master copy owner and the second part of the equation after the plus sign models the propagation of the data item in chunks from the master copy owner to all nodes holding a replica of the data item.

4.2   System Reliability

Network churn is an inherent characteristic of a P2P overlay. While nodes continuously enter and exit the network, some nodes are more stable than others. For example, machines that are connected through wireless links are more likely to disconnect from the network than those that are on wired connections. Naturally, it is preferable to place replicas on more stable nodes. In our system, replica reliability is expressed through the failure probability of the node hosting it, and reliability maximization is achieved by minimizing replica failure probability. Hosts failure probabilities are drawn randomly and they can be updated by tracking the history of hosts in the system. Reliability objective function SR is modeled through the following function:

$$SR = \prod_{i=1}^{n} \prod_{j=1}^{m} E(i, s_j) * F(i) \tag{4}$$

Where

i: index for nodes of the system

j: index for data-items of the system

$E(i,s_j)$: equals to 0 if data-item j exists on host i, otherwise it equals to 1

$F(i)$: failure probability of node i

4.3 Storage

In a heterogeneous network, nodes can have different storage capacity constraints. Usually each node has an upper limit on the storage that can be utilized by the overlay applications. This makes our objective here is to minimize storage consumption on each node of the overlay taking into consideration the total storage available at the node. Storage objective function SC is given by the following:

$$SC = \sum_{i=1}^{n} SC(i) + \sum_{j=1}^{m}(1 - E(i, s_j)) * Z(s_j)$$ (5)

Where
i: index for nodes of the system
j: index for data-items of the system
SC(i): is the storage consumption on node i.
$E(i,s_j)$: equals to 0 if replica j exists on host i, otherwise it equals to 1
Z(s): is the size of the data-item 's'

4.4 Conflicting Objectives

Multi-objective optimization is most appropriate when the objectives conflict. If there are no conflicts, we will end up with one solution. Conflict among objectives results in a set of compromise solutions. Basically, the conflict in our system occurs whenever we have good values for one objective and bad values for another objective. If we have good values in both objectives or bad values in both objectives, then these are the best case and the worst case scenarios respectively, which do not usually exist in overlay networks. Two types of conflicts exist in our system. The first conflict is latency-reliability conflict. The second conflict is storage-reliability conflict. The former conflict occurs because as more replicas are installed in the system, latency tends to increase and reliability tends to increase. Latency tends to increase as more replicas are installed in the system because the propagation update cost resulted by write requests tends to overwhelm read cost savings resulted by read requests. For sure, reliability increases as more replicas are installed in the system because whenever a failure occurs, the system functionality is preserved because of the replicas we have. Fig. 3 shows conflicts between objectives. The cross mark indicates that a conflict does not exist and a tick mark indicates that a conflict exists.

Conflict Matrix	Delay	Consumed Storage	Reliability
Delay		✗	✓
Consumed Storage	✗		✓
Reliability	✓	✓	

Fig. 3. Conflicts between objectives

	N1			N2			⋯				Nn	
S1	⋯	Sm	S1	⋯	Sm	⋯	⋯	⋯	S1	⋯	Sm
0	⋯	1	0	⋯	0	⋯	⋯	⋯	1	⋯	1

Fig. 4. Binary representation of a replication scheme

5 Our Approach: Multi-objective Optimization

Our approach depends on taking the historical system information and feed it to an engine where we try not only to keep latency, reliability, and storage within constraints, but in addition we try to optimize latency, reliability, and storage in order to find different trade offs between these objectives. Since we are using more than one objective, we are doing multi-objective optimization.

5.1 Solution (Chromosome) Representation

A solution in our system is a combination of nodes that will hold replicas of a given data-item. We use a binary representation in which a value of 1 means hosting a replica and the value of zero means no hosting of a replica. Fig. 4 shows the binary representation of one chromosome for a system of n nodes and m data-items. The first row has nodes labels, the second row has data-items labels, and the third row has the general binary representation of the chromosome.

5.2 Multi-objective Evolutionary (MOE) Optimization

In this technique, we apply multi-objective optimization to the problem at hand. Specifically, we use an existing algorithm called NSGA-II [13]. Multi-objective optimization is one of several techniques in evolutionary computing. Evolutionary computing is the branch of science that takes randomness as a mean of problem solving; it also considers solutions of the problem as chromosomes. Mating between different chromosomes could yield a better breed or better solutions. Using evolutionary computing techniques is very helpful in situation where the search space of a problem is huge; searching this huge space in sequential search techniques takes exponential times. Evolutionary computing jumps in the search space in such away that explores areas in which a potential good solution can be found. Many of evolutionary computing techniques rely on operators such as crossover operator which is used for mating between chromosomes, mutation operator which is used to alter genes of the chromosomes, parent selection operators which is responsible of choosing chromosomes for mating. Doing the mating process continues over and over until specific conditions are met such as accuracy of solution or no change over the best solution.

NSGA-II Multi-objective Optimization. This algorithm is a low computation, elitist approach, parameter-less niching, and simple constraint handling strategy algorithm. A non-dominated based sorting technique is used in the algorithm. Furthermore, a selection operator that selects parents based on fitness and spread of mating pool members is adopted. Having solutions of the replication problem as chromosomes, the algorithm selects solution for mating from a set of previously initialized solution set, the chosen solutions mate together and produce more solutions, the new solutions are added to the solution set, the solution set is cut to fronts based on comparisons between solutions, a solution is better than another if it dominates the other solutions. Solution 'A' dominates solution 'B' if solution 'A' is better or equal to solution 'B' in terms of all criterions, namely, delay, reliability, and consumed storage. For our system, we care about the first front which contains the set of solutions that are not dominated by any other solutions. This process continues until a specific number of fitness evaluations are attempted. It can also be set to continuous execution until a specific time expires or until there is no further improvement.

The core part of NSGA-II algorithm is listed below. The intuition behind using this algorithm is the ability to find several fronts of solutions using ranking and crowding. This will give us a variety of solutions, which is done in lines 6,7, and 8 of the while loop. In our experiments we used binary representation of solutions, binary tournament selection, single point crossover for mating with a probability of 0.9 to perform crossover and bit flip mutation for mutation operation with a probability of (1/number of nodes) to make mutation.

The complexity of this algorithm is $O(MN^2)$. Where M is number of objectives and N is the population size.

Chore loop of NSGA-II multi-objective evolutionary approach

```
set initial population size pSize
set maximum number of evaluations maxEval
for ( i iterations from 1 to pSize)
   initialize a solution Sol i
   calculate Soli fitness
   add soli to population pool
   evaluations = evaluations + 1
end-for
while (evaluations < maxEvaluations)
   select parent P1 from population pool
   select parent P2 from population pool
   perform crossover between P1 and P2 and get child C1,C2
   evaluate C1 fitness and C2 fitness
   add C1, C2 to population pool
   perform ranking on population pool
   assign crowding distance to individuals of population
   get the front of individuals of the population pool
   add the front to the solution set solSet
   evaluations = evaluations + 2
end-while
return solSet
```

(Chore loop of NSGA-II multi-objective evolutionary approach)

5.3   Multi-objective Randomized Greedy (MORG) Optimization

One of the characteristics of the evolutionary multi-objective approach is that it takes significant time to converge. So, we need algorithms that can converge in reasonable amount of time. In general, the greedy algorithms are good candidates when it comes to fast execution. Ordinary greedy algorithms do not use dominance as criteria of deciding the best among individuals. So, we use dominance to drive the greedy decisions. Also, greedy algorithms generate one solution. But, in our system, the notion of conflicts between objectives implies that there is no one best solution, so we use a multiple random starting points to generate different solutions. A pseudo code is listed below for the multi-objective randomized greedy approach. The intuition behind using this algorithm is its fast execution time which could be necessary sometimes if we need to generate quick solutions when the network is not in a good shape. The uniqueness of this algorithm relies in the several starting points that give us a variety of solutions and relies in the use of dominance as criteria of comparing solutions. The first for loop of the algorithm generates different starting points to generate solutions from. Each starting point is basically a node in the system. In each starting point, the algorithm considers replicating on neighbors. Here, two cases may happen, if replicating on any of the neighbors does not dominate the current solution, then the current solution is the final solution. Otherwise, we replicate on one of the neighbors which dominate the current solution and the process will be repeated from that neighbor until no further improvement can be found.

Multi-objective randomized greedy approach

```
set number of desired solutions solDesired
for (n iterations from 1 to solDesired)
   current node currNode = random node
   initialize current solution currSoln by having 1's on
     data-item owners positions.
   for(i iterations from 1 to number of data-items)
// Tests if replicating data-item i on currNode is better
  than current solution
      testResult = dominanceTest(currSoln,currNode,i)
      if  (testResult = 1)
add replicating data-item i on node currNode to currSoln
      end-if
      progress=true
      while (progress=true)
progress=false
neb = neighbor list of currNode
solk is the solution coming from replicating data-item i
  on node nebk
         // Tests if replicating data-item i on currNode is
           better than current solution
         testResult = dominanceTest(currSoln,nebk,i)
```

```
    if (testResult =  1)
      save the best nebk of the neighbors in terms of
       dominance
      progress = ture
end-if
   end-while
  end-for
  add soln to set of final solution solSet
end-for
return solSet
```

(Multi-objective randomized greedy approach)

6   Experiments and Results

6.1   Experimental Setup

The code we used for NSGA-II implementation is available on jMetal [14] which is an object-oriented java-based framework that eases the development, testing, and working with metaheuristics for solving multi-objective optimization problems (MOPs). Our experiments were done over unstructured peer-to-peer overlay with 50, 75 and 100 nodes and 1 data-item. Experiments can be extended to incorporate larger numbers of data-items. In each experiment we study the trade-off between two factors, because it is difficult to clearly visualize the results if several factors are simultaneously varied in a single experiment.

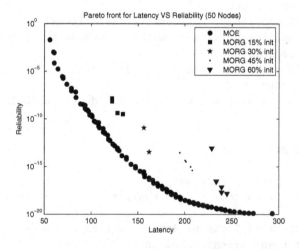

Fig. 5. Pareto front of latency VS reliability (50 Nodes)

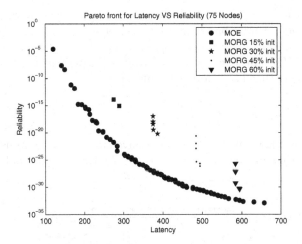

Fig. 6. Pareto front of latency VS reliability (75 Nodes)

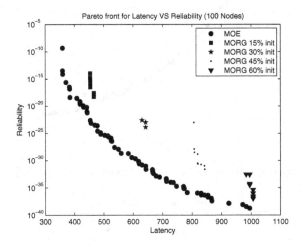

Fig. 7. Pareto front of latency VS reliability (100 Nodes)

6.2   Latency-Reliability Tradeoff

Fig. 5, 6 and 7 show the pareto front of latency against reliability in experiments
that involved 50, 75, 100 nodes respectively. latency values are better when they
are low, and because reliability is expressed in terms of node failures, lower
failure values mean better reliability. It is clear how the MOE approach gives
a variety of solutions that include a trade off between latency and reliability.
The system administrator can choose a solution based on the network status.
For example, if the network is not reliable because of nodes departures, he can
pick a replication scheme that increases network reliability. If the network suffers

from high latencies, a replication scheme with low latency is good. The MORG
approach gives good values based on the percentage of nodes that get initialized
with replicas in advance of running the algorithm, but still, it does not give as
good values as MOE approach. It is good to use MORG when the network is in
a critical condition that needs a quick solution.

6.3   Storage-Reliability Tradeoff

Fig. 8, 9 and 10 show the pareto front of available storage against reliability
in experiments that involved 50, 75, 100 nodes respectively. Available storage

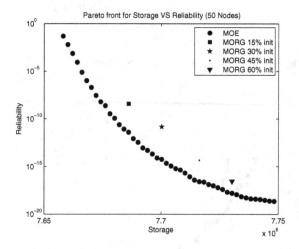

Fig. 8. Pareto front of storage VS reliability (50 Nodes)

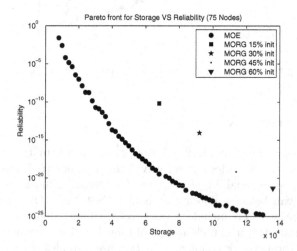

Fig. 9. Pareto front of storage VS reliability (75 Nodes)

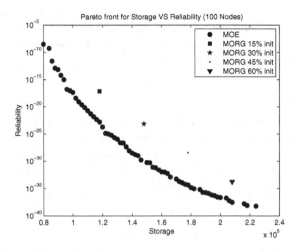

Fig. 10. Pareto front of storage VS reliability (100 Nodes)

values are better when they are high, reliability are expressed in terms of node failures, so lower failure values means better reliability. It is clear how the MOE approach gives a variety of solutions that include a trade off between available storage and reliability. The system administrator can choose a solution based on the network status. For example, if the network is not reliable because of nodes departures, he can pick a replication scheme that increases network reliability. If the network nodes suffer from lack of storage, then the priority changes to selecting a replication scheme with high available storage. The MORG approach

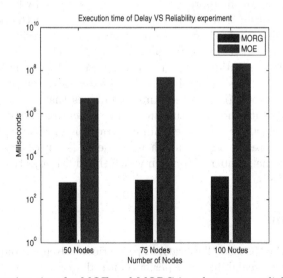

Fig. 11. Execution time for MOE and MORG in a latency vs reliability experiment

gives good values based on the percentage of nodes that get initialized with replicas in advance of running the algorithm, but still, it does not give as good values as MOE approach. It is good to use MORG when the network is in a critical condition that needs a quick solution.

6.4   Execution Time

Fig. 11 shows the execution time for the 2 algorithms in the 3 experiments. The downside for the multi-objective evolutionary approach is the long time it needs to give us good results; this is why we choose to run it overnight when the network activity is low. Nevertheless, MOE gives better results than MORG approach with respect to execution time.

7   Discussion

In [12], the authors deal with the replication problem as a single objective optimization; they optimize latency taking into consideration satisfying constraints related to some parameters like storage availability. Dealing with these parameters as constraints will ensure that the constraints are met. But they did not find the best value for those parameters. This is not the right approach. A justification of that is the following. In many cases, nodes of the system are not dedicated to a specific service, and they might host different services. Those services might consume nodes resources such as storage, each node according to its behavior. At some point, the system could suffer from lack of storage, which means that storage in this case is a vital resource, and we should maximize it as much as possible instead of keeping it under a certain level using a constraint. This is why the multi-objective optimization approach is better than the single objective genetic algorithm approach. If we are in a situation where the network is in a critical condition that requires a quick solution, then the best approach to be used is MORG. Sometimes, a system can have low traffic during certain overnight hours, and in this case the best approach to choose is MOE because of the wide variety of solutions that give us the best optimization for our objectives. Since the multi-objective evolutionary approach takes long execution time, one thing to be done is to use forecasting techniques that help us to estimate a good time to execute the algorithm instead of executing the algorithm regularly. Also, in cases where the system administrator is monitoring the network, he can simply execute the algorithm whenever he finds a necessity to do so and this can minimize the number of times in which the multi-objective evolutionary algorithm needs to be executed.

8   Conclusion

While many overlay-based collaborative applications rely upon data-replication for achieving better scalability and performance, data replication also involves various overheads. Replica placement is one of the key problems in overlay-based replication schemes. This paper proposes a novel multi-objective optimization approach for replica-placement in an overlay. One of the key strengths of our approach is that we view various factors influencing replication decisions such as access latency, storage costs, and data availability as objectives, and not as constraints, which allows us to search for solutions that optimize these parameters. Specifically, we propose two multi-objective optimization algorithms. The multi-objective evolutionary (MOE) algorithm is based on the NSGA-II algorithm, and it has the advantage of providing us with very high quality solutions albeit a longer execution time. On the other hand, multi-objective randomized greedy (MORG) algorithm is characterized by its superior computational efficiency, and it yields solutions that are of comparable quality. We report several experiments to study the effectiveness and performance of the proposed algorithms.

References

1. Minar, N., Hedlund, M., Shirky, C., O'Reilly, T., Bricklin, D., Anderson, D., et al.: Peer-to-Peer: Harnessing the Power of Disruptive Technologies. O'Reilly Media Inc., Sebastopol (2001)
2. Gnutella Protocol Specification,
   www9.limewire.com/developer/gnutella_protocol_0.4.pdf
3. Baset, S., Schulzrinne, H.: An Analysis of the Skype Peer-to-Peer Internet Telephony Protocol. In: 25th IEEE International Conference on Computer Communications, Spain, pp. 1–11 (2006)
4. Yu, H., Vahdat, A.: The Costs and Limits of Availability for Replicated Services. In: 18th ACM symposium on Operating systems principles, Canada, pp. 29–42 (2001)
5. Teuhola, J.: Deferred maintenance of replicated objects in single-site databases. In: 7th International Workshop on Database and Expert Systems Applications, Finland, p. 476 (1996)
6. Chun, B., Dabek, F., Haeberlen, A., Sit, E., Weatherspoon, H., Kaashoek, M.F., Kubiatowicz, J., Morris, R.: Efficient replica maintenance for distributed storage systems. In: 3rd Symposium on Networked Systems Design and Implementation, California, p. 4 (2006)
7. Sacha, J., Dowling, J.: The Physiology of the Grid: an Open Grid Services Architecture for Distributed Systems Integration. In: Databases, Information Systems, and Peer-to-Peer Computing, International Workshops, pp. 181–184. IEEE Press, New York (2005)
8. Clarke, I., Sandberg, O., Wiley, B., Hong, T.W.: Freenet: A distributed anonymous information storage and retrieval system. In: ICSI Workshop on Design Issues in Anonymity and Unobservability, pp. 181–184. IEEE Press, California (2000)
9. Cohen, E., Shenker, S.: Replication Strategies in Unstructured Peer-to- Peer Networks. In: ACM SIGCOMM Computer Communication, pp. 181–184. IEEE Press, New York (2002)
10. Lv, Q., Cao, E., Cohen, E., Li, K., Shenker, S.: Search and Replication in Unstructured Peer-to-Peer networks. In: 16th ACM International Conference on Supercomputing, pp. 181–184. IEEE Press, New York (2002)
11. Benayoune, F., Lancieri, L.: Models of Cooperation in Peer-to-Peer Networks, A Survey. In: 3rd European Conference on Universal Multiservice Networks, pp. 181–184. IEEE Press, New York (2004)

12. Loukopoulos, T., Ahmad, I.: Static and Adaptive Distributed Data Replication using Genetic Algorithms. Journal of Parallel and Distributed Computing 64, 1270–1285 (2004)
13. Deb, K., Pratap, A., Agarwal, S., Meyarivan, T.: A fast and elitist multiobjective genetic algorithm NSGA-II. IEEE transactions on evolutionary computation 64, 182–197 (2002)
14. Metaheuristic Algorithms in Java, http://mallba10.lcc.uma.es/wiki/index.php/JMetal
15. Zhang, J., Liu, L., Ramaswamy, L., Zhang, G., Pu, C.: A Utility-Aware Middleware Architecture for Decentralized Group Communication Applications. In: ACM/IFIP/USENIX Middleware Conference. New port beach, California (2007)
16. Chen, Y., Katz, R.H., Kubiatowicz, J.D.: Dynamic Replica Placement for Scalable Content Delivery. In: Druschel, P., Kaashoek, M.F., Rowstron, A. (eds.) IPTPS 2002. LNCS, vol. 2429, pp. 306–318. Springer, Heidelberg (2002)
17. Mansouri, Y., Monsefi, R.: Optimal Number of Replicas with QoS Assurance in Data Grid Environment. In: Second Asia International Conference on Modelling and Simulation, Kuala Lumpur, pp. 168–173 (2008)
18. Tu, M., Tadayon, T., Xia, Z., Lu, E.: A Secure and Scalable Update Protocol for P2P Data Grids. In: 10th IEEE High Assurance Systems Engineering Symposium, Texas, pp. 423–424 (2007)

An Undo Framework for P2P Collaborative Editing

Stéphane Weiss, Pascal Urso, and Pascal Molli

Nancy-Université, LORIA,
F-54506, Vandoeuvre-lès-Nancy Cedex, France
{weiss,urso,molli}@loria.fr
http://www.loria.fr/~{weiss,urso,molli}

Abstract. Existing Peer to Peer (P2P) collaborative editing systems do not allow any user to undo any modification. However, in such systems, users are not aware of others' modifications, hence, they could obtain duplicate work, conflicting modifications or malicious contents. In this paper, we propose a new undo framework called "UNO: Undo as a New Operation" in the Operational Transformation approach which does not limit the scalability of P2P algorithms. As a proof of concept, we apply our framework to build a P2P collaborative editor with undo capabilities in which any user can undo any modification.

Keywords: Group undo, P2P Collaborative Editing, Operational Transformation.

1 Introduction

Collaborative editing systems allow people distributed in time and space to work together on shared documents. The major benefits of collaborative writing include reducing task completion time, reducing errors, getting different viewpoints and skills, and obtaining an accurate document [1,2].

Nowadays, collaborative editing systems are becoming Peer to Peer (P2P): Version Control Systems (VCS) turn into Distributed Version Control Systems (DVCS), Wiki systems become P2P Wiki system [3,4,5] and even softphones change into P2P softphones such as skype. P2P architecture provides massive collaboration, resistance to failure and censorship. Such systems could also increase data availability and allow off-line work.

In a P2P environment, users are not immediately aware of others' concurrent modifications. Therefore, a site merging its document with another peer could obtain duplicate work, conflicting modifications or malicious contents. In such a context, an undo feature is mandatory. Every user must be able to revert any undesired change. Moreover, the modification to undo is not necessary the last received one, hence, users must be able to undo any operation in their history. Therefore, we need to provide the most general model of undo mechanism which allows any user to undo any edit operation at any time.

All existing undo approaches in the literature [6,7,8,9,10] are specific to a collaborative editing system. Unfortunately, none of these systems is designed to support P2P architectures. Therefore, none of the existing approaches could provide an undo for P2P systems. On the other hand, some existing collaborative softwares such as Wiki or DVCS propose an undo mechanism. However , wiki systems may fail to undo any

E. Bertino and J.B.D. Joshi (Eds.): CollaborateCom 2008, LNICST 10, pp. 529–544, 2009.

operation. Moreover, such systems are centralized, hence, they cannot be used in P2P environment. DVCS allow any user to undo any operation. Nevertheless, DVCS do not bring any warranties about data consistency.

The Operational Transformation (OT) [9,11] framework, purposes a consistency model (CCI) to preserve Causality, Converge and Intention. OT is recognized as a suitable approach to maintain consistency of shared documents. This approach is applied to develop both real-time and asynchronous collaborative editors [12,13]. It consists of two main components: a generic integration algorithm which manages concurrent operations and transformation functions specific to a data model. For instance, MOT2 [13] is an integration algorithm designed for P2P architecture.

In this paper, we propose an undo in the OT framework that respects P2P algorithms' constraints. We call our approach UNO : *Undo as a New Operation*, because it aims to treat undo operation as any other operation newly generated by users. This approach, inspired from well established collaborative tools, allows building a generic schema which can be introduced in any OT approach without affecting its scalability.

As a proof of concept, we apply our framework on the TTF functions which are also the only published set of transformation functions which can be used with MOT2 (See appendix section A). Therefore, in this paper, we obtain a P2P collaborative text editor with undo features.

The structure of the paper is as follows. We first motivate the need of a novel undo approach for P2P systems in Section 2. We explain the main idea of the UNO in Section 3. Then, we briefly describe the OT approach in Section 4. We present our approach in Section 5 and apply it on the TTF functions in Section 6. Section 7 deals with the UNO framework correctness. Finally, we compare our approach with existing undo approaches in Section 9.

2   Motivation

P2P collaborative systems bring several exciting features:

- Massive editing: thousand of users can work on the same project and reduce drastically the task completion time,
- Off-line work: users edit their own copy, hence, they can work online or off-line,
- Privacy: users decide when they want to publish their modifications,
- Mobilibity: such systems support ad-hoc collaboration.

However, merging data over a P2P network implies some inconvenient behaviors:

- Obviously, each user cannot know what other users are doing: we can have duplicate work or conflicting modifications,
- Malicious peers could degrade existing work, merging with such peers will propagate this alteration to the whole network.

Such scenarios are not problematics as soon as users are capable of quickly reverting undesired changes. Therefore, in such systems, the undo feature is mandatory.

In OT, several approaches allow undoing any operation at any time such as GOTO-ANYUNDO[14], COT [10]. The GOTO-ANYUNDO approach uses state vectors (aka vector clocks [15]) while the COT approach uses extended state vectors [10] called "context vectors". A state vector is a vector which contains a logical clock entry per host present in the network. As a consequence, state vector's size grows linearly with the number of site in the system. In P2P networks, the number of site is potentially unbounded and not even known by network participants. Therefore, state vectors are not compatible with P2P constraints such as scalability or churn.

Finally, we need to design an undo approach which does not limit the integration algorithm's scalability.

3   UNO Idea

The main idea of our approach is to treat undo operations as any other operation generated by users. To illustrate this idea, assume that a text document is replicated (Figure 1). At the beginning, the document contains only "Rendezvous". Then a first user inserts the sentence "at nine." at line 2. Concurrently, a second user inserts "At 8 in the park:" at the beginning of the document. And finally, a user wants to undo the operation "ins(2, at nine.)".

Existing OT undo approaches roughly consist in forming do-undo-pair by coupling the undo operation with the undone operation (Figure 1(a)). Unfortunately, integration algorithms are designed to generate and integrate operations only on the current state. Thus, specific mechanisms, such as "context vectors" [10], are designed to support such insertion. As a result, these undo mechanisms are tightly coupled to a specific integration algorithm that may not scale.

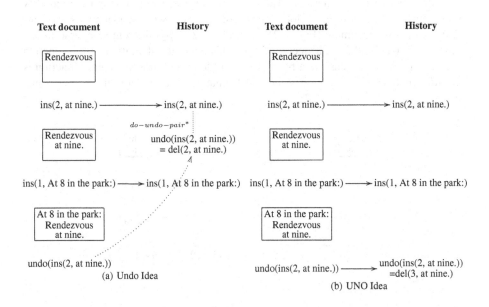

Fig. 1. UNO idea

To obtain a generic undo mechanism, we propose to use the same schema as massively used in collaborative tools such as VCS or Wiki. For instance, in SVN ([16] page 91), undoing a previous revision consists in applying a modification and then committing it normally. In the UNO, we produce a new operation that has the wished effect on the current state, then we integrate it as any other user's operation. *Therefore, the undo operation will be placed in the history according the user's real schedule (Figure 1(b)).*

Thus, we obtain an undo mechanism that can be introduced in any OT collaborative editing system without modifying the way operations are integrated. Consequently, the scalability of the targeted OT system is not limited by the undo mechanism.

In the Figure 1, when we want to undo the operation "insert(2, at nine.)", we want to remove the third line "at nine.". Our idea is simply to generate a new operation which removes the third line instead of undoing the insertion (see Figure 1(b)). This new operation is generated on the current state, hence, all integration algorithms can handle it.

In the following sections, we give the details required to implement this idea.

4   The Operational Transformation (OT) Approach

In the OT approach, shared documents are replicated. Each site contains its own copy of the document, and a user is supposed to work at one site. OT approach allows any user to modify at any time his own copy of the document. Therefore, different copies of the same document can be modified in parallel. In the OT model, a modification is represented as an operation. Each site sends all the locally generated operations to the other sites. On these other sites, such operations are seen as remote operations which have to be integrated for execution.

To allow convergence, these algorithms use a transformation function T to modify remote operations according to local ones. For instance, we consider two sites sharing the same text document (Figure 2). We call $T(op_1, op_2)$ the remote operation op_1 transformed against the local operation op_2. Of course the definition of the function T is specific to the targeted data type. However, defining a transformation function is not sufficient to ensure correctness, the transformation function must also respect some formal properties (see Section 7).

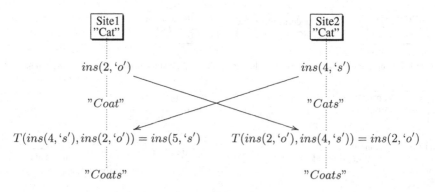

Fig. 2. Transformations

5   Proposition: Undo as a New Operation

The main advantage of our undo scheme is that undo operations are treated as regular ones, i.e. do-operations, when integrated on local and remote sites. Thus, undo operations do not require any special treatment on remote sites.

Given a set of operations, an instance of the UNO framework is built in three steps. First, we define the (possibly new) operations that counterbalance original ones. Second, we define the transformation functions for these new operations, if any. Third, we formally verify the properties required by the targeted integration algorithm.

Then, a simple algorithm is used to provide the undo feature.

Algorithm. We call $undo(op)$ the undo operation of op, i.e. the operation which counterbalances the effect of op, if op is the last executed operation. $undo(op)$ can be either a newly defined operation or an operation from the initial set.

However, since op may not be the last executed operation, we need to compute an operation $undo(op)'$ which is defined on the current state. $undo(op)'$ is the transformation of $undo(op)$ according to all operations which have been executed on the local site since the execution of op. To compute $undo(op)'$, we use the following algorithm (also illustrated in Figure 3):

```
UNO(HB, i):
op:= undo(HB.get(i))
j:=i+1
while(j <= HB.size)
do
  op:= T(op, HB.get(j))
  j:=j+1
endwhile
return op
```

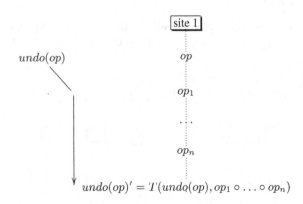

Fig. 3. Naive undo Algorithm

Therefore, $undo(op)'$ is defined on the current state of the document. Thus, $undo(op)'$ is considered as a normal operation directly done by a user when it will be integrated and transformed on remote sites.

Since undo operations are treated as normal operations, these transformation functions are standard transformation functions, and thus must be proven correct according to CCI criteria, see Section 7 about correctness of the approach.

Complexity of the UNO Framework. The UNO algorithm's time complexity is linear with the number of operation received. The space complexity is constant, indeed, the algorithm does not require any data structure except one operation. Since the UNO framework complexity does not depend on the number of site, it can be applied to P2P architecture.

6   Instantiation

Now, we want to apply our undo framework to provide the undo feature in a P2P collaborative text editor built with MOT2 and TTF.

6.1   The Tombstones Transformation Functions

The TTF approach is divided in two parts: the model and the transformation functions. A detailed explanation of the TTF approach and its correctness can be found in [17].

The main idea of the model is to keep deleted characters as tombstones. The document's view only shows visible characters: tombstones are hidden. Consequently, the model differs from the view. Figure 4 illustrates this. Assume that a document is in a state "abcd". Now, a user deletes the character 'b'. In the TTF model, the character is replaced by a tombstone (i.e. the character with a visibility flag set to false). The view differs from the model as the view only contains "acd" while the model contains "a̸bcd". Since tombstones are necessary to achieve consistency, they cannot be removed and thus, the operation "Ins" is not inversible.

6.2   Undo Operation

The first step in applying the UNO framework is to define the undo operations and their effects. Undoing an operation must return the system to a state on which the undone

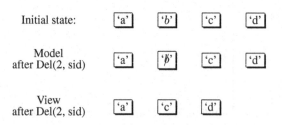

Fig. 4. Model in the TTF approach

operation was never performed. In our context, this definition implies that a character deleted concurrently by N sites should not be visible unless each of these N delete operations are undone.

To achieve such a behavior, we simply propose to replace the visibility flag of each character by a visibility level. This visibility level is an integer. Initially, an inserted character has a visibility level of 1. Each time we undo an insertion operation, the visibility level of the corresponding character is decreased. Each time we undo a deletion, we increase the visibility level of this character.

A character is said "visible" and appears in the document's view if its visibility level is at least 1. Similarly, a character is said "invisible" and does not appear in the document's view if its visibility level is less than 1. Since characters are just marked as invisible, we introduce a new operation "Undel(p,sid)" which effect is to increase the visibility level of the character at position "p". The use of visibility levels is illustrated in Figure 5.

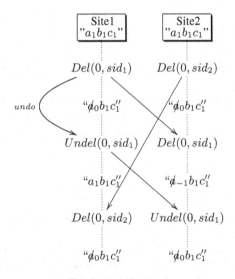

Fig. 5. Visibility level

The function $undo(op)$ links normal operations to undo operations. As we have defined undo operations, we can now write the function $undo(op)$.

```
undo(op):
IF op = Ins(p, c, sid) THEN undo(op) := Del(p, sid)
IF op = Del(p, sid) THEN undo(op) := Undel(p, sid)
IF op = Undel(p, sid) THEN undo(op) := Del(p, sid)
```

The second step is to write transformation functions for all operations. The definition of the transformation functions for the operations "Ins" and "Del" are the same as in original TTF approach.

T(Ins(p_1, c_1, sid_1),Undel(p_2, sid_2)):
    return Ins(p_1, c_1, sid_1)
end

T(Del(p_1, sid_1), Undel(p_2, sid_2)):
    return Del(p_1, sid_1)
end

T(Undel(p_1, sid_1), Ins(p_2, c_2, sid_2)):
    if $(p_1 < p_2)$ **return** Undel(p_1, sid_1)
    else return Undel$(p_1 + 1, sid_1)$
end

T(Undel(p_1, sid_1), Undel(p_2, sid_2)):
    return Undel(p_1, sid_1)
end

T(Undel(p_1, sid_1), Del(p_2, sid_2)):
    return Undel(p_1, sid_1)
end

Moreover, since these transformation functions are bijective, they can easily be reversed. Consequently, we can apply this approach with integration algorithms as SOCT2, GOTO which require reversible transformation functions.

7   Correctness

An OT system is considered as correct if it respects the CCI [9] criteria:

Causality: This criterion ensures that all operations ordered by a precedence relation, in the sense of the Lamport's *happened-before* relation [18], will be executed in the same order on every copy.

Convergence: The system converges if all copies are identical when the system is idle.

Intention: The expected effect of an operation should be observed on all copies. It must be ensured by the transformation functions and by the integration algorithm.

In [13], the authors show how MOT2 ensures Causality. Convergence is achieved if the transformation functions satisfy two properties [19]:

* $TP1$: The transformation property $TP1$ defines a state equality. The state obtained by the execution of an operation op_1 on a state S followed by the execution of the operation $T(op_2, op_1)$ should be equal to the state obtained by the execution of op_2 on a state S followed by the execution of $T(op_1, op_2)$:

$$TP1: S \circ op_1 \circ T(op_2, op_1) = S \circ op_2 \circ T(op_1, op_2)$$

* $TP2$: The property $TP2$ ensures that the transformation of an operation against a sequence of operations does not depend on the transformation order of operations in this sequence.

$$TP2 : T(op_3, op_1 \circ T(op_2, op_1)) = T(op_3, op_2 \circ T(op_1, op_2))$$

Based on some problematic scenarios called "undo puzzles", prior works expressed the need of additional properties to obtain a correct undo. Two properties $IP2$ and $IP3$ are proposed [7,20] to solve these scenarios. However, none shows that these properties are necessary and sufficient to ensure a correct undo. For instance, the property $IP2$ is not respected by our transformation functions while the corresponding problematic scenario does not appear (Figure 6).

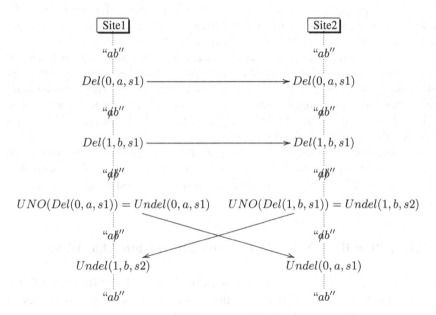

Fig. 6. IP2 undo puzzle

The condition $IP3$ is formally defined as:

$$IP3 : T(undo(op), T(seq, op)) = undo(T(op, seq))$$

To illustrate this condition, Figure 7, two sites make concurrent operations. Site1 generates op while site 2 generates a sequence of operations seq. Both sites receive remote operations, transform and integrate them. Now, they are on the same state. Consequently, if they want to undo the same operation on the same state, they must obviously generate the same operation. Site1 generates $undo(op)$ and transforms it against following operations $T(seq, op)$. Site2 undoes the last received operation which is $T(op, seq)$. These two undo operations are defined on the same state, they undo the same operation, so the resulting operation must be the same. The verification of this property ensures that whenever an operation is undone, the undo effect remains the same.

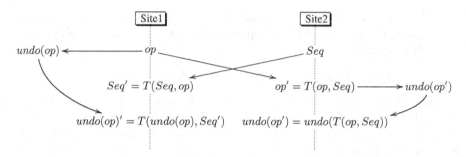

Fig. 7. Respect of the undo effect

So, there are properties to verify in order to ensure a correct OT system with undo. Due to their conciseness, these properties are theoretically easy to prove. However, one of the particularity of the OT approach is the huge numbers of cases to check.

In such conditions, a hand proof is error-prone. Indeed, many hand-proven transformation functions were finally revealed false (all counter examples can be found in [17]).

On another hand, each of the cases to check can be easily handled by an automated formal theorem prover. Consequently, we choose to use the proof environment VOTE [21] based on the theorem prover Spike [22,23] which generates all the cases and ensures the verification of all properties.

Using the proof environment VOTE [21], we have proven that our transformation functions verify the properties $TP1$, $TP2$ and $IP3$. The system specification given to the theorem prover Spike[1] can be reviewed and tested at the following url: `http:// graveyard.sf.net/`.

8   Integrating the UNO with Existing Integration Algorithms

In the OT framework, integration algorithms (SOCT2, SOCT4, GOTO, COT, MOT2) are defined for operations (with no assumption about the number or the kind of operations) and need transformation functions to deal with these operations.

The UNO framework extends a set of operations and transformation functions to support a recovery mechanism. We obtain a new set of operations and transformation functions. Consequently, the resulting set can be handled by any existing integration algorithm.

Our framework also requires the UNO algorithm. To undo an operation op, we generate an undo operation $undo(op)$. The UNO algorithm transforms $undo(op)$ against all operations which have been executed after op. For this stage, $undo(op)$ is considered as concurrent to all operations after op. Fortunately, the main goal of every integration algorithm is to transform an operation against a set of concurrent operations.

Consequently, any OT integration algorithm can determine the undo operation. The resulting operation is treated as a normal operation. Thus, the UNO algorithm can be easily integrated in any integration algorithm. Of course, this requires to remove the

---

[1] `http://lita.sciences.univ-metz.fr/~stratula`

undo dedicated treatment from these algorithm (such as the "mirror" and "fold" functions of adOPTed or "ensure-IPXSafety" of COT).

As a proof of concept, we build the Graveyard prototype[2]. Graveyard is an open-source collaborative text editor that allow any user to undo any operation. It relies either on the MOT2 algorithm or on the SOCT2 algorithm for integrating concurrent operations and it uses the TTF transformation functions with related undo operations. However, we can replace MOT2 by SOCT4, adOPTed or GOTO and obtain the same result.

9   Related Work

The first selective undo was proposed in [7]. To undo an operation, the authors propose to swap it with following operations in the history. Then, the resulting operation's inverse is applied. However, swapping two operations in the history is not always possible, hence, the authors also add the notion of conflict. If a conflict occurs, the undo is aborted. Therefore, this framework does not allow undoing any operation.

In [24], the authors introduce an undo specific to the adOPTed algorithm by adding two functions called "mirror" and "fold". This solution allows undoing operations in the inverse chronological order, i.e. from the last operation to the first one without skipping one. This approach does not allow undoing any operation. Since the adOPTed algorithm requires transformation functions satisfying $TP1$ and $TP2$, we can use the TTF functions in association with our undo approach to provide an undo for any operation.

The GOTO-ANYUNDO approach [20] is associated with the GOTO integration algorithm. This approach introduces a new undo algorithm called ANYUNDO-X. This undo approach is the first to solve known undo problematic scenarios while allowing any user to undo any operation at any time. GOTO-ANYUNDO treats specifically undo operations: undone and undo operations are grouped to create do-undo pairs. While integrating an undo operation, the history buffer is modified in order to remove the undone operation effect from the history. The GOTO-ANYUNDO approach is designed for real-time editing. In such a context, state vectors are adequate, however they are not compatible with P2P environment.

In [25], the authors define two properties $C3$ and $C4$ which are similar to $IP2$ and $IP3$. To ensure the verification of these two properties, the authors introduce a specific operation "undo(op)". This approach defines generic transformation functions for this operation "undo(op)" using the proposed transformation functions. The main idea to enforce $C4$ is to swap the operations and undo the resulting operation. Unfortunately, the authors do not discuss the case of causally dependent operations. This leads to incorrect results.

The COT approach [10] is an OT system designed for real-time editing which introduces the notion of "context vector". A context vector is associated to each operation and represents the operations executed before its generation. Unlike state vectors, context vectors captures undo operations causality and concurrency. As state vectors, the cost of context vector is compatible with real-time editing, however, they are not suitable in a P2P environment.

---

[2] http://graveyard.sf.net

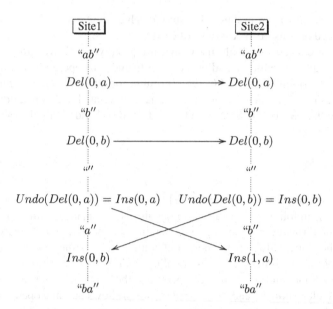

Fig. 8. IP2 undo puzzle

Distributed version control systems (DVCS) as Git [3] are P2P collaborative systems mainly used for source code editing. They propose an undo comparable to the UNO approach: they compute a new patch to remove the effect of a previous one and treat it as a new patch. However, DVCS lack of a formal framework, indeed, there is no property to validate DVCS' correctness. On the contrary, the UNO approach is based on the CCI framework.

Repliwiki, Distriwiki and Wooki are P2P wiki systems. Unfortunately, they do not provide an undo mechanism.

Discussion. Algorithms similar to the UNO algorithm already appear in the literature. For instance, [25] calls it the naive undo algorithm. However, it was never supported as a correct undo algorithm. The reason is its apparent inability to solve known undo-puzzles.

In this paper, we have shown that it provides a correct undo

- even if the $IP2$ condition is relaxed
- and if the operation set and the transformation functions are able to respect the CCI criteria including the undo intentions.

For instance, the operation "Ins" does not realize exactly the undo intention of the operation "Del", in Figure 8, this leads to swap the characters 'a' and 'b'. The intention of "Ins" is *"insert a new element"*. On the other hand the operation "Undel" realizes the intention *"makes a deleted element reappear"*. Thus, if a framework wants to use the operation "Ins" to undo the operation "Del", it is forced to introduce complex integration

---

[3] http://git.or.cz/

mechanisms to avoid undo-puzzle to occurs. On the contrary, using an operation expressing the undo intention solves this puzzle as show in Figure 6.

We thus strongly claim, that operations and transformation functions which ensure undo intention preservation allow building more generic, more efficient and correct undo mechanism.

10 Conclusions

In all existing OT approaches, undo is designed for real-time editing. In this paper, we introduced our undo framework which provides undo feature for all integration algorithms even P2P ones.

In this paper, we propose:

- a generic undo framework: This framework can be applied to all set of transformation functions to provide an undo mechanism on several date type. An important feature of our approach is that the resulting transformation functions remain generic towards integration algorithms. Consequently, we can apply these functions with COT, SOCT2, SOCT4, MOT2, GOTO and adOPTed.
- a CCI compliant framework: The CCI criteria is a formal framework for collaborative editing correctness. The UNO framework uses the CCI to ensure its correctness.
- a scalable framework: The UNO approach time and space complexity is constant with the number of site. Therefore, it is particularly adequate for P2P environment. The UNO algorithm is efficient since it is only linear in time with the number of operation received. We also show that a simple and efficient algorithm considered incorrect can be instantiated to provide a correct undo.
- an implementation: We have a complete solution to build correct P2P text editors with a flexible undo capability. The TTF transformation functions with the undo proposed in this paper are implemented in the Graveyard[4] collaborative text editor. Graveyard is a prototype which can be used with MOT2 for P2P or SOCT2.

The CCI framework includes the Intention definition which is not formally defined in the general case. In the UNO, the undo behavior depends on the Intention criterion. Therefore, as future work, we will try to formally defined the Intention. We plan also to implement a DVCS and a wiki system using the UNO approach.

References

1. Tammaro, S.G., Mosier, J.N., Goodwin, N.C., Spitz, G.: Collaborative Writing Is Hard to Support: A Field Study of Collaborative Writing. Computer-Supported Cooperative Work - JCSCW 6(1), 19–51 (1997)
2. Noël, S., Robert, J.-M.: Empirical study on collaborative writing: What do co-authors do, use, and like? Computer Supported Cooperative Work - JCSCW 13(1), 63–89 (2004)

---

[4] http://graveyard.sf.net

3. Morris, J.C.: Distriwiki: a distributed peer-to-peer wiki network. In: Int. Sym. Wikis, pp. 69–74 (2007)
4. Kang, B.B., Black, C.R., Aangi-Reddy, S., Masri, A.E.: Repliwiki: A next generation architecture for wikipedia (unpublished), http://isr.uncc.edu/repliwiki/repliwiki-conference.pdf
5. Weiss, S., Urso, P., Molli, P.: Wooki: a p2p wiki-based collaborative writing tool. In: Web Information Systems Engineering, December 2007, Springer, Nancy (2007)
6. Berlage, T., Genau, A.: A framework for shared applications with a replicated architecture. In: ACM Symposium on User Interface Software and Technology, pp. 249–257 (1993)
7. Prakash, A., Knister, M.J.: A framework for undoing actions in collaborative systems. ACM Trans. Comput.-Hum. Interact. 1(4), 295–330 (1994)
8. Choudhary, R., Dewan, P.: A general multi-user undo/redo model. In: ECSCW, pp. 229–246 (1995)
9. Sun, C., Jia, X., Zhang, Y., Yang, Y., Chen, D.: Achieving convergence, causality preservation, and intention preservation in real-time cooperative editing systems. ACM Transactions on Computer-Human Interaction (TOCHI) 5(1), 63–108 (1998)
10. Sun, D., Sun, C.: Operation Context and Context-based Operational Transformation. In: Proceedings of the ACM Conference on Computer-Supported Cooperative Work - CSCW 2006, November 2006, pp. 279–288. ACM Press, Banff (2006)
11. Ellis, C.A., Gibbs, S.J.: Concurrency control in groupware systems. In: Clifford, J., Lindsay, B.G., Maier, D. (eds.) SIGMOD Conference, pp. 399–407. ACM Press, New York (1989)
12. Molli, P., Oster, G., Skaf-Molli, H., Imine, A.: Using the transformational approach to build a safe and generic data synchronizer. In: Proceedings of the ACM SIGGROUP Conference on Supporting Group Work - GROUP 2003, November 2003, pp. 212–220. ACM Press, Sanibel Island (2003)
13. Cart, M., Ferrié, J.: Asynchronous reconciliation based on operational transformation for p2p collaborative environments. In: CollaborateCom (2007)
14. Sun, C., Chen, D.: Consistency maintenance in real-time collaborative graphics editing systems. ACM Transactions on Computer-Human Interaction (TOCHI) 9(1), 1–41 (2002)
15. Mattern, F.: Virtual time and global states of distributed systems. In: Cosnard, M. (ed.) Proceedings of the International Workshop on Parallel and Distributed Algorithms, October 1989, pp. 215–226. Elsevier Science Publishers, Château de Bonas (1989)
16. Collins-Sussman, B., Fitzpatrick, B.W., Pilato, C.M.: Version Control with Subversion. O'Reilly Media, Sebastopol (2007), http://svnbook.red-bean.com/
17. Oster, G., Urso, P., Molli, P., Imine, A.: Tombstone transformation functions for ensuring consistency in collaborative editing systems. In: The Second International Conference on Collaborative Computing: Networking, Applications and Worksharing (CollaborateCom 2006), November 2006. IEEE Press, Atlanta (2006)
18. Lamport, L.: Time, clocks, and the ordering of events in a distributed system. Commun. ACM 21(7), 558–565 (1978)
19. Ressel, M., Nitsche-Ruhland, D., Gunzenhäuser, R.: An integrating, transformation-oriented approach to concurrency control and undo in group editors. In: CSCW, pp. 288–297 (1996)
20. Sun, C.: Undo as concurrent inverse in group editors. ACM Transactions on Computer-Human Interaction (TOCHI) 9(4), 309–361 (2002)
21. Imine, A., Molli, P., Oster, G., Urso, P.: Vote: Group editors analyzing tool: System description. Electr. Notes Theor. Comput. Sci. 86(1) (2003)
22. Nieuwenhuis, R. (ed.): RTA 2003. LNCS, vol. 2706. Springer, Heidelberg (2003)
23. Stratulat, S.: A general framework to build contextual cover set induction provers. J. Symb. Comput. 32(4), 403–445 (2001)

24. Ressel, M., Gunzenhäuser, R.: Reducing the problems of group undo. In: GROUP, pp. 131–139 (1999)
25. Ferrié, J., Vidot, N., Cart, M.: Concurrent undo operations in collaborative environments using operational transformation. In: Meersman, R., Tari, Z. (eds.) OTM 2004. LNCS, vol. 3290, pp. 155–173. Springer, Heidelberg (2004)

Appendix

A MOT2 and TTF

In [13], the authors claim that MOT2 only require the $TP1$ property. Therefore, we could use the following transformation functions since they satisfy $TP1$.

```
T( Ins(p1, c1) , Ins(p2, c2) ):
if  p1 < p2 or ( p1 = p2 and c1 < c2 )
   Ins(p1, c1)
else  Ins(p1 + 1, c1)

T( Ins(p1, c1), Del(p2, c2) ):
if  p1 <= p2
   Ins(p1, c1)
else  Ins(p1 − 1, c1)

T( Del(p1, c1), Ins(p2, c2) ):
if  p1 < p2
  Del(p1, c1)
else  Del(p1 + 1, c1)

T( Del(p1, c1), Del(p2, c2) ):
if  p1 < p2
  Del(p1, c1)
else  Del(p1 − 1, c1)
```

Unfortunately, Figure 9 illustrates a divergence scenario which can occur. This problem is an instance of the $TP2$ puzzle [17].

Finally, MOT2 requires transformation functions which satisfy the properties $TP1$ and $TP2$. Therefore, the TTF transformation functions are particularly adequate for MOT2 since they are the only published set of transformation functions satisfying $TP1$ ant $TP2$.

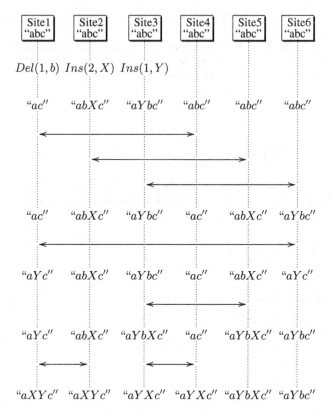

Fig. 9. Divergence scenario

A Contract Language for Service-Oriented Dynamic Collaborations

Surya Nepal, John Zic, and Shiping Chen

CSIRO ICT Center, P.O. Box 76,
NSW 1710, Australia
FirstName.LastName@csiro.au

Abstract. Dynamic collaborations are built using contributed resources that have come across the organizational boundaries. These resources include data, application, software, tools as well as infrastructures, and are typically subject to a rich set of access policies. The automated instantiation of a collaboration using such resources including their interoperability is a difficult problem. Existing systems are either built for specific resources, or use manual and ad-hoc approaches. This problem has attracted the Web Services community, where Web Services standards such as WSLA and WS-CDL have been proposed to address similar problems. These approaches are designed to deal with scenarios involving two parties: a service provider and a service consumer. They do not scale well to multiparty nature of dynamic collaborations. This paper proposes a contract language for dynamic multiparty collaborations that captures the contributed resources and negotiated agreements on them, as well as the mechanisms for instantiation and termination of the collaboration. The language itself has been defined using XML Schema and has been implemented in a dynamic collaboration platform to provide a connectivity service.

1 Introduction

Recently, there has been much interest in forming on-demand dynamic collaborations between autonomous, competitive organizations to collaborate on occasion [4]. Such collaborations are built for a specific purpose. For example, a dynamic collaboration among researchers in eResearch domain may be required so as to study a specific climate change problem. The idea of collaborating in this way, however, is not new. For example, the area of virtual organizations [1][2][3] explores mechanisms that enable entities from different organizations to collectively create such virtual enterprises or organizations. This goal is typically achieved through open service discovery, negotiation and execution based on service level agreements (SLAs). A trend is developing, however, where collaborations are much more dynamic and the resources contributed by each organization to the collaboration are governed by a set of complex policies [5][4][18] constructed upon each separate organization's policies. In this situation, open service discovery mechanisms cannot be used, as resource information is deliberately hidden through the use of organizational policies. Collaborations built around this concept are termed *dynamic collaborations*.

E. Bertino and J.B.D. Joshi (Eds.): CollaborateCom 2008, LNICST 10, pp. 545–562, 2009.

One of the key features of a dynamic collaboration is an on-demand contribution of resources from participating autonomous organizations. Recently, resources such as storage and networking infrastructures, tools, software and data are implemented using Web Services technologies so that they can be made available as services. For example, the concept of Software-as-a-Service (SaaS) is introduced for providing software [19] and Infrastructure-as-a-Service (IaaS) [11] for storage and networking infrastructures. Therefore, it is possible to define and share *resources as services* in the context of dynamic collaborations.

The management of workflows of contributed resources during a dynamic collaboration is a critical issue. The management workflows include negotiation of resources, validation of resources, instantiating of resources/collaboration, monitoring resources and releasing resources when the collaboration terminates or when a partner leaves the collaboration. Existing dynamic collaborations deal with these issues either in an ad hoc manner or manually. There is a need of a framework that enables the definition of collaborations in such a way that it can be unambiguously and automatically instantiated and managed.

The problem of interoperability becomes evident while managing the workflows of resources due to involvement of a variety of autonomous organisations as well as the resources contributed by them. This problem has attracted the Web Services community, where standards such as WSLA and WS-CDL have been developed. Keller and Ludwig [17] defined a Web Service Level Agreement (WSLA) [10] framework for defining and monitoring Service Level Agreements (SLAs) between service providers and service consumers in an electronic commerce scenario. Kavantzas et al. [27] define the Web Services Choreography Description Language (WS-CDL) that describes peer-to-peer collaborations of Web Services participants by defining their common and complementary observable behavior.

These languages work well in a type of scenarios that involve only two parties with distinct roles; the service provider offering a service and the service consumer requesting and consuming the service. However, in the context of dynamic collaboration, this does not work well due to the following reasons:

- Dynamic collaborations have *complex policies* defining the interactions, access and use of resources.
- *Multiple parties* are involved in dynamic collaborations;
- *Multiple resources (services)* are contributed to the collaboration by multiple parties;
- *Both roles* of service provider and service consumer are often played by a single party;
- *All parties* must agree with each other's contributions and obliged with their agreements.

In order to start to address this problem, we recently [28] proposed an extension to WSLA, called WSLA+, for dynamic collaborations. However, the extended language involves semantic interpretations of WSLA elements different than what they were intended for as well as could not fulfill all the above requirements specifically on specifying policies on services. In order to fulfill these requirements, this paper presents a framework for Web Service Collaborative Context Definition Language for dynamic collaboration, called WS-CCDL. It enables collaborating partners to unambiguously define the requirements for the collaboration as well as agreements for all the resources contributed to the collaboration. The semantics of the framework is defined briefly as a short paper in [29]. In this paper, we describe the language itself, which is defined using XML Schema and an implemented prototype system in an environment to deliver a connectivity service between multiple partners in a collaboration.

The rest of the paper is structured as follows. Section 2 describes the background and motivation of this work using examples from a variety of applications. We then describe the framework and its runtime model in Sections 3 and 4, respectively. Section 5 describes the connectivity service implemented using the framework. The final section draws the concluding remarks and future works.

2 Background and Motivation

Dynamic collaborations bring together complementary sets of competencies from competing enterprises to address new market opportunities in a rapidly evolving services economy [4]. In addition to enterprise applications, dynamic collaborations between cross-organizational entities occur in other application domains such as Global Command and Control Systems in military application [5], coalitions formed among civilian organizations as responses to emergency situations, coalitions between researchers in different institutions for eResearch applications and health care facility and practitioners' coalitions for eHealth applications. The valuable contributions of dynamic collaboration technologies have been recognized by both industries and governments as evident from the special issue Journal on Dynamic Collaboration by NEC [4], the Australian Government's funding support for collaborative platforms within eResearch [18], European collaborative project ECOSPACE [23] and DARPA funded research in dynamic collaboration [14][15][16]. We next describe three motivating examples of collaboration from different application domains.

Post-production industry - Figure 1 shows an example of a dynamic collaboration formed between three distributed, autonomous postproduction houses in order to produce a movie [6]. As can be seen in the figure, three companies contribute

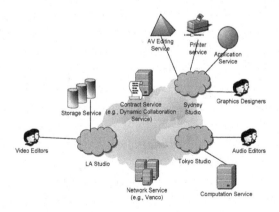

Fig. 1. An Example of Dynamic Collaboration in a movie postproduction industry

different resources as services in the collaboration. The contributed services include Audio Visual editing service, Audio Visual application service, storage service, printer service, computation service as well as the services of audio video specialists. The collaboration also uses external third party provided services such as contract service and network service.

Retail enterprise - [20] explains the scenarios in retail and hospitality industries where collaborations with partners provide effective ways of gaining competitive advantages by making use of existing resources. They include streamlining the product recall process, online web conferencing and virtual war room. The partners within the retail industries include retail outlets, suppliers, transport companies, etc.

eHealth – Collaborative eHealth programs such as Baltic eHealth [21] and Kentucky eHealth [22] are taking advantage of collaboration in health care sectors. The aim of these programs is to provide secure, private and confidential healthcare services by taking advantages of expertise within the regions.

3 WS-CCDL Framework

Figure 2 shows the main concepts and their relationships within WS-CCDL. As a convention throughout this paper, we denote sets of entities using upper-case letters, with the entities themselves in lower-case letters. The main entity, called *contract*, captures the entities requirements, participants, contributions and agreements. The resources, activities, policies and attributes are used to describe these entities.

A *contract* is a collaborative context that specifies not only the requirements for the collaboration but also captures the contributions made by the participants as well as the agreements between them for contributed resources. The contract includes collaboration requirements, contributions by participants, agreements among participant and the list

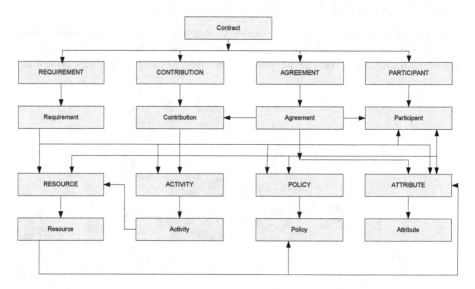

Fig. 2. Overview of main WS-CCDL concepts and relationships

of participants. The high-level elements of the contract are shown in a snapshot of XML-schema below.

```
<xs:element name="econtract" type="ccdl:econtractType"/>
<!-- high level element -->
<xs:complexType name="econtractType">
 <xs:sequence>
    <xs:element ref="ccdl:participants"/>
    <xs:element ref="ccdl:requirements"/>
    <xs:element ref="ccdl:contributions"/>
    <xs:element ref="ccdl:agreements"/>
 </xs:sequence>
 <xs:attribute name="econtractId" type="xs:anyURI" use="required"/>
 <xs:attribute name="Version" type="ccdl:VersionType" default="1.0"/>
 <xs:attribute name="contractAgreementProtocol" type="xs:anyURI" use="required"/>
</xs:complexType>
```

In addition to the four core elements, the contract must also specify the negotiation and agreement protocol.

A dynamic collaboration is built among a number of participating organizations. In general, we categorize the participants as follows:

Initiator is a participant who initiates the collaboration. The initiator specifies the initial requirements for the collaboration.

Invited participants are the participants that are invited by the initiator to participate in the collaboration.

These participants are further categorized as follows.

Signatory participants are authorized by the collaborating organisations to negotiate on their behalf. Both initiator and invited participants are signatory participants.

Contributing participants are contributed by the signatory participant to participate in the collaboration. For example, a participant can delegate a storage service provider to provide a storage service to the collaboration. We capture such participants as resources in our framework. We do further discussion on resources later in this section.

The signatory participants are defined using their identity, role, addressing mechanism, etc. as follows. Also, the participants must be specified with an authentication algorithm.

```
<xs:element name="participants" type="ccdl:participantsType"/>
 <xs:complexType name="participantsType">
    <xs:sequence>
       <xs:element ref="ccdl:participant" maxOccurs="unbounded"/>
    </xs:sequence>
 </xs:complexType>
<xs:complexType name="participantType">
    <xs:sequence>
       <xs:element ref="ccdl:identity"/>
       <xs:element ref="ccdl:role"/>
       <xs:element ref="ccdl:organisation"/>
       <xs:element ref="ccdl:addressing"/>
       <xs:element ref="ccdl:section"/>
```

```
        </xs:sequence>
        <xs:attribute name="authenticationAlg" type="xs:anyURI" use="required"/>
        <xs:attribute name="name" type="xs:string" use="required"/>
        <xs:anyAttribute namespace="##any" processContents="lax"/>
    </xs:complexType>
```

As discussed earlier, an initiator – the participant who initiates the collaboration - expresses the need of the collaboration through requirement. The requirements specify not only the purpose of the collaboration, but also durations, activities and resources needed for establishing and continuing the collaboration. In order to capture these initial statements about the collaboration, we define the requirement as follows.

```
    <xs:element name="requirement" type="ccdl:requirementType"/>
    <xs:complexType name="requirementType">
        <xs:sequence>
            <xs:element ref="ccdl:activities" minOccurs="0"/>
            <xs:element ref="ccdl:resources" minOccurs="0"/>
            <xs:element ref="ccdl:policies" minOccurs="0"/>
        </xs:sequence>
        <xs:attribute name="name" type="xs:string" use="required"/>
        <xs:attribute name="date" type="xs:date" use="required"/>
        <xs:attribute name="time" type="xs:time" use="required"/>
        <xs:anyAttribute namespace="##any" processContents="lax"/>
    </xs:complexType>
```

It is also important to note that these requirements are negotiable. That is, a participant may disagree with some of the requirements and may negotiate the changed requirements with other participants using negotiation protocols. Examples of such negotiation protocols will be discussed in the next section.

Within a collaboration, participants may engage in a number of activities, and each activity may need different set of participants and resources. For example, a collaboration in the post-production industry may have activities like video enhancing, audio enhancing, audio-visual mixing, preparing scenes, etc. In our framework, we represent such activities as follows.

```
    <xs:element name="activities" type="ccdl:activitiesType"/>
    <xs:complexType name="activitiesType">
        <xs:sequence>
            <xs:element ref="ccdl:activity" minOccurs="0" maxOccurs="unbounded"/>
        </xs:sequence>
    </xs:complexType>
    <xs:complexType name="activityType">
    <xs:sequence>
        <xs:element name="activityid" type="ccdl:idType"/>
        <xs:element name="activityname" type="xs:string"/>
        <xs:element name="resources" type="ccdl:resourceType"/>
        <xs:element ref="ccdl:policies" minOccurs="0" maxOccurs="unbounded"/>
        <xs:element name="participant" type="xs:string" minOccurs="0"
                maxOccurs="unbounded">
            <xs:keyref name="activityref" refer="ccdl:participantKey">
                <xs:selector xpath="ccdl:econtract/participants/identity"/>
                <xs:field xpath="id"/>
```

```
            </xs:keyref>
        </xs:element>
    </xs:sequence>
    <xs:attribute name="date" type="xs:date" use="required"/>
    <xs:attribute name="time" type="xs:time" use="required"/>
    <xs:attribute name="duration" type="xs:time" use="required"/>
    <xs:anyAttribute namespace="##any" processContents="lax"/>
</xs:complexType>
```

It is important to note here that the activity definition includes both the description for the activity as well as the resources required to perform these activities. Whether the overall resource requirements may capture these resources depends on what kind of resource satisfaction algorithm would be used and this will be discussed in the next section in details.

A unique characteristic of a dynamic collaboration is that it is formed by combining each participant's contributed resources. In our framework, signatory participants contribute resources towards the collaboration. The resources are contributed at both activity and collaboration levels. That is, one participant may choose to contribute resources in such a way that it can be used by all activities within a collaboration, whereas other participants may choose to contribute resources only for a specific activity. The resources include contributing participants, software, data, tools and information resources. The resources are formally represented as follows.

```
<xs:element name="resources" type="ccdl:resourcesType"/>
<xs:complexType name="resourcesType1">
    <xs:sequence>
        <xs:element ref="ccdl:resource" minOccurs="0" maxOccurs="unbounded"/>
    </xs:sequence>
</xs:complexType>
<xs:element name="resource" type="ccdl:resourceType">
    <xs:key name="resourceKey">
        <xs:selector
            xpath="ccdl:econtract/collaborationcontext/resources/resid/identity"/>
        <xs:field xpath="@id"/>
    </xs:key>
</xs:element>
<xs:complexType name="resourceType">
    <xs:sequence>
        <xs:element name="resid" type="ccdl:idType"/>
        <xs:element name="resname" type="xs:string"/>
        <xs:element ref="ccdl:policies" minOccurs="0" maxOccurs="unbounded"/>
    </xs:sequence>
    <xs:anyAttribute namespace="##any" processContents="lax"/>
</xs:complexType>
```

A collaborator must provide enough information about any contributed resources so that they can be accessed by other collaborating participants such as addresses, interfaces and protocols. With the emergence of Web Services, it is now possible to define these resources as services and contribute them to the collaboration. The details on how to model and define *a resource as a service* is outside the scope of this paper.

However, we refer readers to the implementation of storage and networking *infrastructures as services* in [11] for further details.

Fundamentally, we maintain that collaborations are driven by policies, and this is presented in the above formalization. Different organizations participating in the collaboration each operate under their own set of policies. Furthermore, the collaboration is built and operated under a set of policies defined for different entities and activities. For example, a collaborator can define policies that determine who can participant in the video editing activities. Similarly, a participant contributing resources can specify a set of policies for their contributed resources. For example, only project leaders can access the edited videos. In order to represent policies within our framework, we define policy as follows.

```
<xs:element name="policies" type="ccdl:policiesType"/>
<xs:complexType name="policiesType">
    <xs:sequence>
        <xs:element ref="ccdl:policy" minOccurs="0" maxOccurs="unbounded"/>
    </xs:sequence>
</xs:complexType>
<xs:element name="policy" type="ccdl:policyType"/>
<xs:complexType name="policyType">
    <xs:sequence>
        <xs:element name="PolicySet" type="xacml:PolicySetType"/>
    </xs:sequence>
</xs:complexType>
```

Different Digital Right Management and access policy expression languages such as XACML [24][25] can be used to describe policies.

One of the key elements specified in the requirements is resources. The requirement of resources is fulfilled through contributions from the participating parties. The contribution can be done at a specific activity level or at the collaboration level. Also, the contributions need to satisfy the corresponding policies specified in the requirement. Therefore, the contribution of the resources by participants depends on the resource needs specified in the requirements as well as the corresponding policies. We define such contribution as follows.

```
<xs:element name="contributions" type="ccdl:contributionsType"/>
<xs:complexType name="contributionsType">
    <xs:sequence>
        <xs:element ref="ccdl:contribution" minOccurs="0" maxOccurs="unbounded"/>
    </xs:sequence>
</xs:complexType>
<xs:element name="contribution" type="ccdl:contributionType" id="string"/>
<xs:complexType name="contributionType">
    <xs:sequence>
        <xs:element ref="ccdl:contributor"/>
        <xs:element ref="ccdl:activitityName" minOccurs="0"
                maxOccurs="unbounded"/>
        <xs:element ref="ccdl:resourceName" minOccurs="0"
                maxOccurs="unbounded"/>
        <xs:element ref="ccdl:policies" minOccurs="0" maxOccurs="unbounded"/>
    </xs:sequence>
</xs:complexType>
```

As mentioned earlier, in the Web Services and SOA environment, such resources can be contributed as services, i.e., Resource-as-a-Service (RaaS).

The contributed resources are negotiated among participants. One of the important requirements of the dynamic collaboration is that all participants must agree with each others' contributions. In the Web Services environment, this means agreement with the contributed services. We define agreement using a digital signature as shown below.

```
<xs:element name="agreements" type="ccdl:agreementType"/>
<xs:complexType name="agreementTypeType">
    <xs:sequence>
        <xs:element ref="ds:Signature" maxOccurs="unbounded"/>
    </xs:sequence>
</xs:complexType>
```

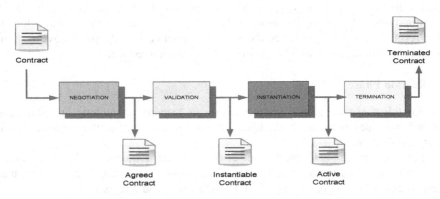

Fig. 3. Different phases of the contract in a runtime environment

4   WS-CCDL Runtime Framework

In the above section, we define a contract language along with its associated elements. The contract goes through the different phases in its lifecycle as shown in Figure 3. This section describes the four different phases of the contract namely negotiation phase, validation phase, instantiation phase and termination phase.

Negotiation Phase

During this phase, the participants negotiate the terms and conditions of the collaboration, including contributed resources and policies attached to them. Each party may contribute a set of resources along with associated access policies. A party in the collaboration may, however, disagree with the terms and conditions of the collaboration or some particular contributed resources or access policies. In such scenarios, participants may need to re-negotiate the content in the contract. This is facilitated using contract negotiation algorithms.

A set of Web Services standards for negotiations have been proposed for this purpose: WS-AgreementNegotiation [7], WS-Negotiation [8], and WS-Agreement [9]. WS-Negotiation is a domain independent language for generating agreements between a service provider and a service consumer. WS-Negotiation only considers two parties: a provider and a consumer. WS-Negotiation supports a simple one to one negotiation protocol. Though the objective of WS-Agreement is to have a language and a protocol that creates agreements, publicizes a service offer and provides a monitoring service, it also specifies a very simple negotiation protocol. As this protocol does not allow offer refinement, WS-AgreementNegotiation was defined so as to overcome this shortcoming by allowing negotiation and re-negotiation of agreements between two parties.

As mentioned earlier, these work well in two party scenarios but are not suited for use in multi-party, multi-service negotiation in the context of dynamic collaborations. We have defined protocols for dynamic collaboration in [12]. The unique characteristic of such protocols is that all parties must agree with each others' contributions. The negotiation phase ends when the contract meets this characteristic and results in an *agreed* contract. An agreed contract is such all parties have seen the final contributions from all other parties and all have agreed with it.

Validation Phase

During this phase, the agreed contract is validated against two criteria first of all, and if both are successful, a determination is then made whether the collaboration is instantiable or not.

The first criterion is to check whether the resources required for the collaboration as well as activities are met by the contributions made by the participants. Contributed resources can be categorized into the following two broad categories:

- Collaboration specific – includes resources contributed to the whole collaboration and not tied to a specific activity.
- Activity specific – includes resources contributed for specific activities.

That means resources specified for the collaboration can be used for a particular activity if the resources contributed for an activity do not satisfy the requirements specified for that activity. We also need to ensure that the resource satisfaction for a contract meet the policy conditions. For example, if a printer is available for a week and the collaboration requires the printer for one month, then the contributed resource can not meet the required resource. We define this check as follows. The contract is said to be *resource satisfied* if the contributed resources meet all the resource requirements of the contract under the given policy.

The second criterion is to check whether different set of policies specified within the contract conflict with each other or not. Policies are specified at the level of requirements, participants, resources, activities and contributions. Some of these policies may conflict with each other. For example, a policy may state that participants can access all information related to the collaboration at the requirement level, but the policy specified at the contribution by a participant may prevent certain participants accessing some information. The policies need to be checked and any conflicts arises need to be resolved. The final set of policy must satisfy the requirements for the collaboration and activities within it. We define this process formally as follows. The contract is said to be *policy satisfied* if the policies expressed in the contract are not conflicting each other.

After the successful checking of the two criteria above, we need to check whether the contract is instantiable or not. We define the contract is *instantiable* if it is agreed by all participant and satisfies both policy and resource requirements. It is important to note that the above definition does not cover some of the technical aspects such as all resources specified must have a valid address and they are online. These aspects are dynamic and included in the monitoring of contract, which is outside the scope of this paper.

Instantiation Phase

Once the contract has been validated, it is then interpreted by an engine (the instantiation engine) that results in an instantiation of the collaboration. The instantiation engine extracts the information from the contract and sends to relevant services. For example, the network specific requirements are extracted and sent to the network service provider. Once the collaboration is established (and has not been terminated), the contract is said to be *active*. The contract is *active* if it has been successfully instantiated and has not been terminated.

Termination Phase

The last phase of the runtime environment is called termination, where the collaboration is terminated as per contract. We have previously defined one such termination protocol using WS-BusinessActivity [12]. Other distributed termination protocols can be used. There are a lot of activities that need to be performed at the time of termination such as logging, archiving and destroying. The agreed policies for termination determine what actions need to be taken for which piece of information. The contract is said to be terminated if all parties agreed to terminate the instantiated collaboration and the termination protocol is run successfully.

We discussed the four different phases that the contract goes through during a runtime environment. The discussion of these phases above also raises a number of research questions such as: determination of both resource and policy satisfaction, the definition of policies for a party to join an already existing collaboration, and how exceptions are handled, such as a partner failing to comply with an agreement. We are actively perusing these issues as part of the future works.

5 Connectivity Service

This section describes a prototype contract based connectivity service that we have implemented and deployed in order to demonstrate the usage of the proposed contract language in dynamic collaborations. In our prototype system, we have made an assumption that this contract service will be provided by a trusted third party, whose sole business is to provide secured, managed network connectivity to clients for the purpose of collaboration. One of the main features of this service is that the connectivity is abstracted to the user level so that any number of users can connect to each other by using computer connected to the Internet and can use any collaborative applications. The connectivity between collaborators is established when they agree to the terms and conditions specified in the contract.

Figure 4 shows the overall architecture for the implemented prototype connectivity service driven by contract. Our architecture consists of two services: the contract service itself, and a VPN service. The contract service provides the management of the contract and includes a registration and discovery service for the use of its clients. The VPN service is used by the contract service provider to provide connectivity once the contract is agreed. All these services as well as users (from different administrative domain such as home office, university and government office) are connected to the Internet. Initially, all of them communicate with each other using an open Internet connection. When all users agreed with the contract and the contract is deployed into the Internet, a dynamic Intranet is created (the intranet is referred to as dynamic because the connectivity is established at the user level rather than the machines used by the users). We next describe the major implemented components of the architecture and the interactions among them.

Initially, each collaborator resides within its own administrative domain and may be unknown to the other collaborators. In order to initiate the collaboration, each collaborator needs a contract service. All collaborators first subscribe to the contract service so that they can either initiate or be invited to join into a dynamic collaboration. The collaborators use a service to register themselves and make them available for collaborations. Once the registration process is completed, the collaborator then downloads and installs a client application which then enables them to process the contract through each of the negotiation, validation, instantiation and termination phases described above.

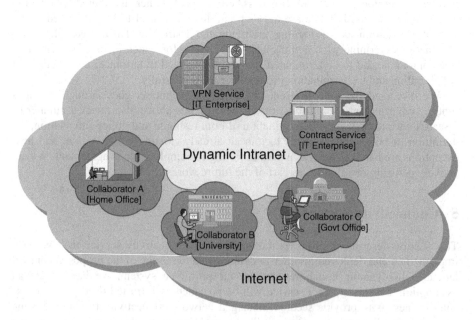

Fig. 4. Overall architecture of eContract service for dynamic collaborations

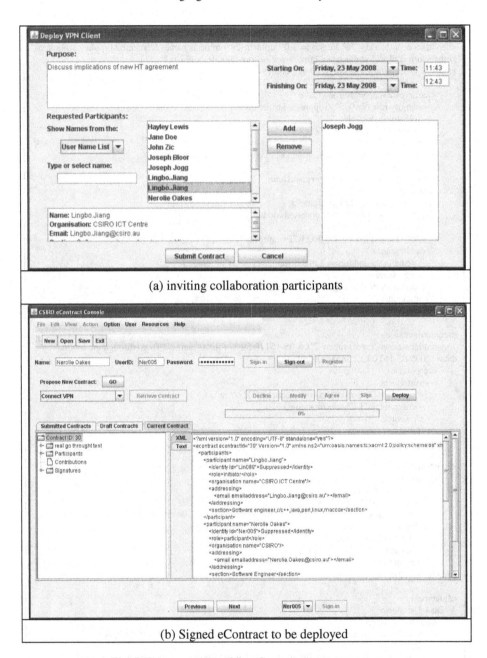

(a) inviting collaboration participants

(b) Signed eContract to be deployed

Fig. 5. The screenshots of the eContract prototype system

We next describe the process of creating a dynamic collaboration between three parties A, B and C. Suppose A wishes to set up a dynamic collaboration with B and C and use a document sharing application called Virtual Terminal (VT). First, all three

```
<?xml version="1.0" encoding="UTF-8" standalone="yes"?>
<econtract econtractId="26" Version="1.0" xmlns:ns2="urn:oasis:names:tc:xacml:2.0:policy:schema:os"
xmlns="urn:ccdl:v1" xmlns:ns4="http://www.w3.org/2000/09/xmldsig#"
xmlns:ns3="http://www.w3.org/2004/12/addressing">
  <participants>
    <participant name="Nerolie Oakes">
      <identity id="Ner005">Suppressed</identity>
      <role>initiator</role>
      <organisation name="CSIRO"/>
      <addressing>
        <email emailaddress="Nerolie.Oakes@csiro.au"></email>
      </addressing>
      <section>Software Engineer</section>
    </participant>
    <participant name="Lingbo.Jiang">
      <identity id="Lin089">Suppressed</identity>
      <role>participant</role>
      <organisation name="CSIRO ICT Centre"/>
      <addressing>
        <email emailaddress="Lingbo.Jiang@csiro.au"></email>
      </addressing>
      <section>Software engineer,c/c++,java,perl,linux,macosx</section>
    </participant>
  </participants>

<requirements>
    <collaborationContext time="2008-05-16T10:59:58+10:00" name="To go through the routine"
date="2008-05-16T09:59:58+10:00"/>
    <resources>
      <resource>
        <resid id="http://www.xmlspy.com">0002</resid>
        <resname>VT Client</resname>
      </resource>
    </resources>
  <requirements>

<contributions>
    <contribution>
        <id>Lin089</resid>
        <resname>VT Client</resname>
    </contribution>
    <contribution>
        <id>Ner005</resid>
        <resname>VT Client</resname>
    </contribution>
</contributions>

<agreements>
  <ns4:Signature>
    <ns4:SignedInfo>
        <ns4:CanonicalizationMethod Algorithm="http://www.w3.org/TR/2001/REC-xml-c14n-
20010315"/>
        <ns4:SignatureMethod Algorithm="http://www.w3.org/2000/09/xmldsig#rsa-sha1"/>
        <ns4:Reference URI="">
          <ns4:Transforms>
            <ns4:Transform Algorithm="http://www.w3.org/2000/09/xmldsig#enveloped-signature"/>
          </ns4:Transforms>
          <ns4:DigestMethod Algorithm="http://www.w3.org/2000/09/xmldsig#sha1"/>
```

Fig. 6. An eContract signed by two participants in our prototype system

```
        <ns4:DigestValue>+llp4pVrVBr3h/RnIAdIXTDas+Y=</ns4:DigestValue>
      </ns4:Reference>
    </ns4:SignedInfo>
<ns4:SignatureValue>DZn8HWsXBtc5rUM9Os5SHWpOQ3/gcqGfO1FPtxwk+g8FnU7n3xztLsLubMu
St5BLbP.......</ns4:SignatureValue>
      <ns4:KeyInfo>
        <ns4:X509Data>

<ns4:X509SubjectName>CN=Ner005,OU=Unknown,O=Unknown,L=Unknown,ST=Unknown,C=Unkn
own</ns4:X509SubjectName>

<ns4:X509Certificate>WCZBfPsCl+7r2//Z76DiEFCrLZgDn0GYNPFBBZr2aY4V2MTSAy3xi......</ns
4:X509Certificate>
        </ns4:X509Data>
      </ns4:KeyInfo>
    </ns4:Signature>
    <ns4:Signature>
      <ns4:SignedInfo>
        <ns4:CanonicalizationMethod Algorithm="http://www.w3.org/TR/2001/REC-xml-c14n-
20010315"/>
        <ns4:SignatureMethod Algorithm="http://www.w3.org/2000/09/xmldsig#rsa-sha1"/>
        <ns4:Reference URI="">
          <ns4:Transforms>
            <ns4:Transform Algorithm="http://www.w3.org/2000/09/xmldsig#enveloped-signature"/>
          </ns4:Transforms>
          <ns4:DigestMethod Algorithm="http://www.w3.org/2000/09/xmldsig#sha1"/>
          <ns4:DigestValue>+llp4pVrVBr3h/RnIAdIXTDas+Y=</ns4:DigestValue>
        </ns4:Reference>
      </ns4:SignedInfo>

<ns4:SignatureValue>FlGysAmLkxw/oAFk6I2Y0yig/c3wctle+9pr8xvVpMAZv35DfGQ4nXB..........
</ns4:SignatureValue>
      <ns4:KeyInfo>
        <ns4:X509Data>

<ns4:X509SubjectName>CN=Ner005,OU=Unknown,O=Unknown,L=Unknown,ST=Unknown,C=Unkn
own</ns4:X509SubjectName>

<ns4:X509Certificate>MIICTTCCAbagAwIBAgIESCkMWjANBgkqhkiG9w0BAQUFADBrMRAwDg
Y......</ns4:X509Certificate>
        </ns4:X509Data>
      </ns4:KeyInfo>
    </ns4:Signature>
  </agreements>
</econtract>
```

Fig. 6. (*continued*)

collaborators must have previously and successfully registered themselves with the contract service, and download and install the client application. Collaborator A runs the client application and initializes contract by first discovering, and then adding the collaborators B and C as participants as shown in Figure 4 (a).

As an initiator, collaborator A also specifies the resources required for the collaboration such as the VT application, as well as any of A's contributed resources in the contract. Once the requirement and contribution are specified, the contract is submitted to the contract service which will then go through the different phases as discussed earlier. During the negotiation phase, collaborators B and C will be informed that they are invited to participate in the collaboration and can negotiate the resources with A. They can decide to accept or decline the invitation. If they decide to join the collaboration, each can negotiate the content in the eContract with all the other participants following a negotiation protocol [12]. Once all participants agree upon and sign the eContract as shown in Figure 4(b), the eContract becomes agreed contract.

The agreed contract then goes through the validation phase, where resources and policies are checked. It should be noted that we have not yet implemented the validation part in our prototype system and for the purposes of this prototype, we assume that all agreed contracts are valid. The validated contract is then executed during the insanitation phase. As part of the execution, the contract service extracts the necessary information and sends it to the VPN service. The VPN service then establishes a dynamic intranet whose behavior is determined by the defined and agreed upon contract between the participants. The VPN service then automatically sends and installs a VPN driver into each of the participants' machines, and if required, dispatches the VT application as well. The collaborators are then ready to use VT to share documents and files. Figure 5 shows an example contract generated by our implemented system. Here, the aim is to establish network connectivity, allowing the collaboration using the VT between the participants to proceed. When the collaboration is completed and all parties agreed to terminate the contract, a termination protocol is executed resulting in the contract being terminated.

In our prototype, there are three major components that are implemented as follows. We use Sun Glassfish v2.0 to implement the contract Web Service with the support of MySQL v5.122 as a backend database. The VPN server was implemented using OpenVPN v2.1. The client application is implemented using Sun's JDK 1.6, including Swing and JAXB.

Through the implementation of above discussed connectivity service, we have shown how one can use our contract language as a template to (a) capture the requirements of the collaboration, (b) contribute resources as services in the collaboration, (c) negotiate resources for the collaboration, (d) capture agreements between collaborators, and (e) instantiate and terminate the collaboration.

6   Conclusions and Future Work

The paper presented a contract language for defining a context for a dynamic collaboration between partners. The language is used to generate the templates that can be used to automatically configure the collaboration. The templates, which we refer as electronic contracts, are also used to negotiate resources (that can be expressed as Web Services) and policies. Hence, the language is called Web Service Collaborative Context Definition Language (WS-CCDL). The language has been defined using XML Schema. We have also developed a service-oriented prototype system for an instance of a collaborative environment to provide connectivity service to the collaborating partners. The prototype system provided us evidence that it is feasible to develop a contract driven dynamic collaboration using our proposed language. We have finally devised a runtime framework for the contracts consisting four phases: negotiation, validation, instantiation and termination.

The proposed language in its current form only captures some core elements for negotiation, validation and instantiation. We plan to extend the language and propose a Quality of Service (QoS) model for it. The QoS model is expected to captures obligations in terms of security, privacy, trust, performance and availability. We then plan to propose a mechanism for monitoring those obligations. With regard to validation of contract, we are also working on defining formal models as well as algorithms for checking resource and policy satisfactions so that all participants' requirements needed for the completion of tasks within the collaboration are met. Finally, we are also looking at the specification of different termination protocols within the contract similar to that of negotiation and agreement protocols.

References

[1] Mowshowitz, A.: Virtual Organization: A vision of management in the information age. The Information Society 10(4), 267–288 (1994)

[2] Foster, I., Kesselman, C., Tuecke, S.: The Anatomy of the Grid: Enabling Scalable Virtual Organizations. International Journal of High Performance Computing Applications 15(3), 200–222 (2001)

[3] Globus, http://www.globus.org/grid_software/monitoring/

[4] Yamazaki, Y.: Dynamic Collaboration: the model of new business that quickly responds to changes in the market through The integrated IT/Network Solutions provided by NEC. NEC Journal of Advanced Technology 1(1), 9–16 (2004)

[5] Handley, H.A.H., Wentz, L., Levis, A.H.: Continuity in Dynamic Coalition Operations. In: Proc. 7th Int'l Command and Control Research and Technology Symposium, Monterey, CA (June 2002)

[6] Chan, J., Rogers, G., Agahari, D., Moreland, D., Zic, J.: Enterprise Collaborative Contexts and their Provisioning for Secure Managed Extranets. In: Proc. of IEEE WETICE 2006, pp. 313–318 (2006)

[7] Andrieux, A., Czajkowski, K., Dan, A., Keahey, K., Ludwig, H., Pruyne, J., Rofrano, J., Tuecke, S., Xu, M.: Web Services Agreement Negotiation Specification (WS-AgreementNegotiation), version 1,
http://forge.ogf.org/sf/go/doc6092?nav=1

[8] Hung, P.C.K., Li, H., Jeng, J.J.: WS-Negotiation: An overview of research issues. In: Proc. of the 37th Hawaii International Conference on System Sciences (2004)

[9] Andrieux, A., Czajkowski, K., Dan, A., Keahey, K., Heiko, L.: WS-Agreement Specification (2005),
http://www.gridforum.rg/Meetings/GGF11/Documents/draft-ggf-graap-agreement.pdf2005

[10] Ludwig, H., Keller, A., Dan, A., King, R.P., Franck, R.: Web Service Level Agreement (WSLA) Language Specification (2003),
http://www.research.ibm.com/wsla/WSLASpecV1-20030128.pdf

[11] Nepal, S., Chan, J., Chen, S., Moreland, D., Zic, J.: An Infrastructure Virtualisation SOA for VNO-based Business Models. In: IEEE International Conference on Services Computing (SCC 2007), July 2007, pp. 41–51 (2007)

[12] Nepal, S., Zic, J., Chan, J.: A distributed Approach for Negotiating Resource Contributions in Dynamic Collaboration. In: The Eight International Conference on Parallel and Distributed Computing, Applications and Technologies (PDCAT 2007), December 3-6, 2007, pp. 82–86 (2007)

[13] Chen, S., Nepal, S., Chan, J., Moreland, D., Zic, J.: Virtual Storage Services for Dynamic Coalitions. In: Proceedings of IEEE International Workshops on Enabling Technologies: Infrastructures for Collaborative Enterprises, WETICE (2007)

[14] Khurana, H., Gligor, V.D.: A Model for Access Negotiations in Dynamic Collaborations. In: Proc. of the 13th IEEE WETICE, 2004, pp. 205–210 (2004)

[15] Freudenthal, E., Pesin, T., Keenan, E., Port, L., Karamcheti, V.: dRBAC: Distributed Role-Based Access Control for Dynamic Collaboration Environments. In: Proc. of the ICDCS 2002, pp. 411–420 (2002)

[16] Patz, G., Condell, M., Krishnan, R., Sanchez, L.: Multidimensional Security Policy Management for Dynamic Collaborations. In: DARPA Information Survivability Conference and Exposition (2001)

[17] Keller, A., Ludwig, H.: Defining and Monitoring Service-Level Agreements for Dynamic e-Business. In: 16th System Administration Conference, pp. 189–204 (2002)

[18] Department of Education, Science and Training, Australia. An Australian e-Research Strategy and Implementation Framework. Report, 4/2006

[19] Ma, D.: The Business Model of "Software-as-a-Service". In: SCC 2007, pp. 701–702 (2007)

[20] Microsoft Enterprise Collaboration,
     http://download.microsoft.com/download/c/6/0/c6003d74-2f58-4868-a8ff-172576303864/CollaborationBizOverview.pdf

[21] Baltic eHealth,
     http://www.ehealthconference.info/StockholmConferenceBrochure.pdf

[22] Kentucky eHealth,
     http://ehealth.ky.gov/NR/rdonlyres/DE96BBFC-6AE5-4A80-BA62-44B1D233514C/0/PrivacySecurityFinalReport.pdf

[23] ECOSPACE, http://www.ip-ecospace.org/

[24] XACML, http://www.oasis-open.org/committees/tc_home.php?wg_abbrev=xacml

[25] EPAL,
     http://www.zurich.ibm.com/security/enterprise-privacy/epal/

[26] SecPAL, http://research.microsoft.com/projects/secpal/

[27] Kavantzas, N., Burdett, D., Ritzinger, G.: Web Services Choreography Description Language, http://www.w3.org/TR/2004/WD-ws-cdl-10-20040427/

[28] Nepal, S., Zic, J., Chen, S.: WSLA+: Web Service Level Agreement Language for Collaborations. In: IEEE International Conference on Service Computing (SCC), Hawaii, USA, July 8-11 (2008) (to appear)

[29] Nepal, S., Zic, J., Chen, S.: WS-CCDL: A Framework for Web Service Collaborative Context Definition Language for Dynamic Collaborations. In: IEEE International Conference on Web Services (ICWS), Beijing, China, September 23-26 (2008)

Monitoring Contract Enforcement within Virtual Organizations

Anna Squicciarini[1] and Federica Paci[2]

[1] College of Information Sciences and Technology
The Pennsylvania State University
asquicciarini@ist.psu.edu
[2] Computer Science Department
Purdue University
paci@cs.purdue.edu

Abstract. Virtual Organizations (VOs) represent a new collaboration paradigm in which the participating entities pool resources, services, and information to achieve a common goal. VOs are often created on demand and dynamically evolve over time. An organization identifies a business opportunity and creates a VO to meet it. In this paper we develop a system for monitoring the sharing of resources in VO. Sharing rules are defined by a particular, common type of contract in which virtual organization members agree to make available some amount of specified resource over a given time period. The main component of the system is a monitoring tool for policy enforcement, called Security Controller (SC). VO members' interactions are monitored in a decentralized manner in that each member has one associated SC which intercepts all the exchanged messages. We show that having SCs in VOs prevents from serious security breaches and guarantees VOs correct functioning without degrading the execution time of members' interactions. We base our discussion on application scenarios and illustrate the SC prototype, along with some performance evaluation.

Keywords: Virtual Organizations, Monitoring, Access Control, Collaboration.

1 Introduction

The Internet and the Web have enabled new ways for users, enterprises, and organizations to collaborate in a large number of application domains–from service provisioning and e-commerce to collaborative e-learning, entertaining, and cultural heritage. Virtual organizations (VOs for short) represent a new collaboration paradigm where the participating entities (enterprises or individuals) pool resources, services, information, and knowledge in order to achieve a common goal. Researchers as well as practitioners have recognized the advantages of VOs and have explored a number of possible approaches to facilitate their formation and management, especially in grid computing systems [2,4].

VOs vary tremendously, according to the specific goals, context and infrastructure. As such, a single architecture is not sufficient to fit all the possible organization types. Nevertheless, despite the many differences among VOs, research studies have identified

E. Bertino and J.B.D. Joshi (Eds.): CollaborateCom 2008, LNICST 10, pp. 563–577, 2009.

a broad set of common concerns and technology requirements. For example, Foster et al. in [4], identify a number of relevant requirements, the first of which is the need for highly flexible sharing relationships. They also pointed to the need of sophisticated and precise levels of control over how shared resources are used, including fine-grained and multi-stakeholder access control, delegation, and application of local and community policies and issues of quality of service, scheduling, and accounting. With regards to issues related to access controls, several approaches have been proposed [10,11,14].

A widely adopted approach, that we take into account in this work, is to share services and/or resources according to a set of policies of two main types, global to the VO and local to the VO members. The VO community policies are specified in the VO *contract*, representing the collaboration agreement established among all the VO members. Members join the VO aware of the contract regulating the system, and define their own local policies accordingly. The local policies represent the plan according to which the VO members will collaborate within the VO, and they must be compliant with the VO contract. Because many relevant operations by members depend on such policies, monitoring that they are properly enforced is crucial for the development of safe and well grounded VOs. In fact, it is possible that, unless strict enforcement mechanisms are in place, VO members do not act as stated and thus violate such contract.

Previous work has tackled the issue of policy enforcement within VOs from different angles, resulting in new access control mechanisms [10,11] and monitoring systems [9,14]. However, most of the proposed approaches either rely on a centralized entity, causing bottlenecks and scalability issues, or they are specific to a given domain, and cannot be easily applied to others.

In this paper we propose a new decentralized mechanism to monitor VO members' behaviors and compliance with global policies. Our work builds on a framework for secure specification and distribution of VO contracts previously proposed by us [9,11]. The framework includes a model for specifying VO contracts and policies of VO members, along protocols addressing integrity and confidentiality of the policy publication process [11], and is completed by the protection mechanism discussed in this paper.

The core component of our solution introduced in this paper is the Security Controller (SC), a fully implemented monitoring system, developed using SOA architecture. The SC has a number of interesting features. First, the SC enables secure distribution of the VO contract in a private fashion and ensures that VO members' local policies are compliant to the VO contract. Second, it monitors messages among VO members and ensures that entitled members receive the services as promised by the provider members; third it ensures non-repudiation, in that VO members cannot deny having receiving a request or a certain service and claim for additional ones (if not entitled). The SC is realized in a completely decentralized fashion, in that each VO member has an associated SC, which verifies if service requests are to be satisfied, To the best of our knowledge this is the first comprehensive solution for access control policy specification, monitoring and enforcement specific to VOs.

The paper is organized as follows. Section 2 introduces the concept of VO contract, while Section 3 overviews the main phases of the VO lifecycle. Section 4 describes the VO creation process and how the rules specified in the contract are enforced. Section 5 describes the SC architecture, possible application scenarios and some relevant

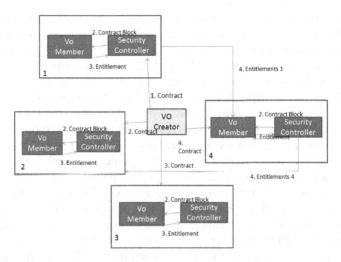

Fig. 1. Contract Publishing and Entitlements Distribution

implementation details. It also shows results of experiments we carried out to bench-mark the overhead of the system. Section 6 gives an overview of related works. Section 7 concludes the paper.

2   Contract Specification and Local Policy Representation in Virtual Organizations

In this section we present an overview of a framework for regulated sharing of compu-tational resources in a Virtual Organization[9] (VO). The type of organization we focus on is characterized by VO members, denoted as $VoSet$ representing groups of end users, also referred to as enterprises. We do not make any assumption about enterprise internal regulation and structure, and assume that the entities interested in participating to the VO are represented by service providers (SP). In a VO, different $VoSet$ members are pooled together for sharing a set of resources, referred to as $ResSet$, according to a community policy, also referred to as a *contract* among VO members.

The building block of a contract is represented by obligations. Obligations dictate exactly when and for what amount a member has the right to use the resources provided by the other members and the obligations a member has in terms of resources it has to provide to other community members. Precisely, we represent an *obligation* by a logic predicate of the form $Obl(VoM, VoS, R, I)$, where $VoM, VoS \in VoMSet$, R is a resource in $ResSet$ and I is a temporal expression. A VO member VoM has to make available to members VoS a total amount of a resource R over a time interval I. The resource can also be made available to all possible members, in which case Vos is omitted. We represent contracts in terms of two building blocks: the *obligation sequence* and the *contract block*.

An obligation sequence is a sequence of obligations $Obl(VoM, Vos, R_1, I_1, ..., R_k,$ $I_k)$, such that $R_1,...,R_k$ are all instances of the same resource type and each $I_i, i =$ $1, \ldots, k$, is an ordered, contiguous time interval. Each contract block lists a set of obligation sequences, in order to allow the bearer VoM to choose which component of the obligation sequences to fulfill. A contract is a finite set of contract blocks $\{CB_1,...,CB_n\}$ $(n \geq 1)$, specified in such a way that it is not possible for a resource bearer to fulfill several obligations at once.

Each VO member, upon joining the VO, agrees on sharing its resources with other partners. The starting point for the fulfillment of a VO contract by a VO member is the publishing of a local policy for its resources. Indeed, the VO member keeps control of its resources and it autonomously decides which is the policy to use for them. As such, a local policy serves two main purposes: specifying how the VO member intends to grant access to its resources and, second, publishing the VO member's plan to comply with its obligations in a contract. Vo members define such local policies as strong permissions to a set of entitled members, denoted by expressions of the form $Ent_{VoM_k}(VoM_i, R, I)$. By publishing an entitlement the VoM_k promises that it will make R available over time interval I to the VO member VoM_i. The local policy is publicly available for other VO members. A local policy has to comply with community policies, that is, with the obligation sequences of the contract blocks referring to the resource bearer.

We say that a set of entitlements Ep *complies* with an obligation $Obl(VoM, VoS,$ $R, I)$ if, for every enterprise $E \in VoS$ and every time point $t \in I$ there exists an entitlement $Ent'(E, R', [t_s, t_e])$ such that $t_s \leq t \leq t_e$ and $R \subset R'$. We denote with $R \subset R'$ as two comparable instances of a certain resource of the same type, wherein R is less than or equal to R' according to a given metric. Finally, we say that an access request is *supported* if there is a corresponding entitlement granting it.

Example 1. We consider a VO called Genome where the members are enterprises Hospital of Chicago (HPC), Department of Biochemistry California University (UBC), Hospital of Seattle (HSE), Department of Computer Science of University of Illinois (CSI) and cooperate for a project whose goal is to study the structure of human genomes. The resources to be shared are two databases conveying human genome data, called DB_1 (provided by the HPC) and DB_2 (provided by the HSE) and two servers $Serv_1$ and $Serv_2$ (provided by the CSI) where special software implementing dynamic programming techniques to elaborate data runs. Further, assume that DB_1 and DB_2 can be accessed either with read(r), or write(w) option, while $Serv_1$ and $Serv_2$ can be accessed for running (e) existing software or for updating(u)/deleting(d) software components[1]. The following is HPC's contract block: CB_1= $(Obl(HPC, \{HSE, UBC\}, \{DB_1, w\},$ [(1-05-2007,10:00:00),(5-05-2007,22:15:00)]). Once received CB_1, HPC defines its own local policies by specifying the following set of entitlements: $Ent_{HPC}(HSE,$ $\{DB_1, r\}$,[(1-05-2007,10:00:00),(1-05-2007,15:10:00)]),
$Ent_{HPC}(HSE, \{DB_1, a\}$,[(1-05-2007,15:20:00),(1-05-2007,22:15:00)]),
$Ent_{HPC}(UBC, \{DB_1, r\}$,[(1-05-2007,13:16:00),(2-05-2007,15:10:00)]),
$Ent_{HPC}(UBC, \{DB_1, r\}$,[(2-05-2007,15:11:00),(5-05-2007,21:36:00)]).

---

[1] Here, we assume that access rights follow the following order: $r < w$ for databases, whereas $e < u < d$ for server management.

3 Virtual Organization Lifecycle

In order to discuss the role of SCs in the VO management, we summarize the main phases in a VO lifecycle.

- *Preparation for participation in the VO.* This is a preliminary phase and reflects the necessary steps that a SP has to take in order to participate to the VO. SPs publish their resources' functionalities in a public repository. The resources' description provides detailed information about resources' capabilities, the resources' interaction means and other information like the resource quality. This information allows one to select a SP for inclusion in the VO.
- *Identification.* This phase is considered as the first major phase in the VO lifecycle and starts when an organization, referred to as VO Creator, identifies a business goal and thus defines a contract to fulfill it. The contract, as discussed in the previous section, states the roles and the requirements that each member has to fulfill in order to be part of the VO.
- *Formation.* The VO Creator queries public repositories to retrieve the information published during the Preparation phase. The Creator uses such information to select a set of potential VO members that match the contract's requirements. The VO Creator then sends them an invitation to join the VO containing the terms of the contract they have to fulfill. If they accept the invitation, they become members of the VO.
- *Operation.* Once the VO is set up, its members cooperate according to the collaboration rules specified in the contract. The operation phase has several critical security issues. VO members may exploit their privileges and misuse the resources available, gather information about other enterprises for personal gain or fail to fulfill the contract rules, and even take advantage of the resources made available to perpetrate crimes. All the interactions must be monitored, ruled by security policies and any violation must be notified.
- *Dissolution.* This phase takes place when the objectives of the VO have been fulfilled. The VO structure is dissolved and final operations are performed to nullify all contractual binding of the VO members.

4 Security Enhanced Virtual Organization Lifecycle

The SC monitors and coordinates the main operations of each of the VO lifecycle's phases. In particular, the SC has two main functions 1) during the creation phase, it distributes the VO contract in a selective manner and it controls compliance of the VO member's local policies, and 2) during the operational phase it monitors VO member's message exchanges to detect contract breaches. We elaborate on such functions in the remaining of this section.

4.1 Virtual Organization Creation and Contract Distribution

In this section we focus on the main operations of the VO creation phase in the in case the SC is set up. The SC interleaves with the conventional contract distribution and policy publishing operations, so to ensure that the VO members access only the correct amount of data and that the members publish local policies compliant with the VO contract.

Upon defining the contract, the VO Creator is in charge of setting up the VO. It thus invites a number of potential members, selected on the basis of the services (or resources) they could offer to the VO. Potential members are selected based on the information related to the provided resources made available during the preparation phase.

If the potential member accepts, the VO Creator requests to a Certificate Authority (CA) to issue an identity certificate to it. This certificate is typically encoded by an X.509 credential that binds the VO's public key to the VO member identity. At this point, in conventional VO systems, the contract is distributed and the related local policies published by the new VO members. To ensure the correctness and compliance of VO contracts, we require the VO Creator to publish a list of endpoints where the SC components are up and running[2]. Each VO member then selects the SC that will monitor its message exchanges during the whole VO lifetime. The same SC can be the monitor of more than one VO member. Once all VO members have been identified, the VO creator distributes the contract to the VO members through a software component that selectively distributes obligations and entitlements [1]. Distribution is performed in such a way that members will access only the obligations of which they are bearers and the entitlements that grant them the access to other VO members' resources (Figure 1-step 1).

Each SC component facilitates the tasks of the VO members, in that it intercepts the contract and forwards to the associated VO member only the contract blocks of its interest (Figure 1-step 2). Upon receiving the contract blocks, the VO member defines the set of entitlements specifying how it will fulfill its obligations towards the community (Figure 1-step 2) and returns them to the SC component (Figure 1-step 3). The SC is in charge of verifying that the entitlements fulfill the member's obligations, and of distributing these entitlements (Figure 1-step 4) to the guaranteed members-identified by the VOs field of the entitlement (see entitlement definition in Section 2). Once obligations and entitlements have reached all the respective VO members, the VO set up process is complete and the VO enters the operational phase. SC components play a crucial role in this phase of the VO lifecycle: they check that their VO member submits only requests supported by entitlements, and in case of VO provider members that the provided resources respect the entitlements in place.

We elaborate on how SC components guarantee that there are no VO contract breaches in the subsequent section.

4.2 Contract Enforcement and Monitoring

Within the operational phase, the VO members' interaction consists of resources and services provided upon request, according to the specified entitlements. Intuitively, if no monitoring system is in place, a number of security breaches could arise. For example, a VO member could simply deny supported requests, or it could falsely claim of not having received the requested services. A trivial solution to avoid these issues would be

---

[2] SCs are by assumption trusted software components that run on trusted platforms.

to rely on a centralized controller. However, this would likely result in delays and the centralized monitor be a bottleneck. When the SC components are employed, instead, these type of situations are prevented without causing significant overhead.

The interaction among VO members can proceed with no third party in between. When a request is rejected, two different -and trusted- SCs double-check it, to ensure that the denial is grounded. Furthermore, a requesting member cannot claim of not having received a service, if this was actually granted, as by the data logged by the SC. Figure 2 summarizes how the SC components affect the message flow between two VO members. The SC filters intercepts the messages exchanged, to detect potential contract breaches. Precisely, a SC accepts two types of incoming messages:

- a message $msg = (Cert, Resource)$ that requests a resource $Resource$ that is provided by the monitored VO member;
- a fault message $msg = (Resource, FaultReason)$ that communicates that the monitored VO member's request of $Resource$ cannot be granted because is not available.

As shown in Algorithm 1, If SC receives a resource request message $msg = (Cert, Resource)$ it first verifies the validity of $Cert$ in msg. Then, it derives from $Cert$ the identity of the resource requester and controls the existence of an entitlement Ent_{VoM_i} (VoM_k, R, I) that obliges the monitored VO member to provide the resource $Resource$ to requester VO member for the whole time interval I, where I includes the time in which the request is received. If such an entitlement exists, SC forwards the resource request to VO member it controls that, in turn, returns the $Resource$ to the requester VO members (lines 1-11, Algorithm 1). On the contrary, if SC receives a fault message $msg = (Resource, FaultReason)$ it checks if the denial of Resource is motivated or not. SC looks for an entitlement Ent_{VoM_i} $(VoM_k, Resource, I)$ that grants to the monitored VO member the access to $Resource$. If such an entitlement does not exist, then the denial was motivated and the SC forwards the fault message to the

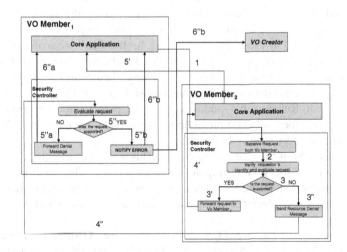

Fig. 2. Contract monitoring flow

controlled VO member. Otherwise, the provider's VO member violated the entitlement and the SC forwards the message $msg = (Resource, FaultReason)$ to the VO member it monitors, and to the VO Creator, which can apply some punishing actions[3].

The SC also detects the situation in which a requested $Resource$ that is available, is not released to a requestor whose request is granted by entitlement $Ent_{VoM_i}(VoM_k, R, I)$. The SC stores locally all the messages received and sent by the monitored VO member within a certain time frame (e.g., a few sessions). Such message history can be consulted at any time by the VO member, as it is made available to it upon request.

In this case, the SC checks that a reply message has been sent by the VO member providing resource R within the time interval I. If this is not the case, the SC notifies to thirds, typically the VO Creator. This simple mechanism ensures non-repudiation; the VO member cannot claim it has been denied a resource that it has actually received.

Example 2. UCB wants to examine some data contained in the database DB_1 of HPC. It decides to access the database DB_1 the 2nd of May 2007 at 10 p.m. The HPC's SC checks if there are entitlements granting the access to UCB. The access to DB_1 is granted to UBC in times different from the time of the request as stated by the following entitlement: $Ent_{HPC}(UBC, \{DB_1, r\}, [(1-05-2007,13:16:00), (2-05-2007, 15:10:00)])$, Ent_{HPC} $(UBC, \{DB_1, r\}, [(2-05-2007,15:11:00),(5-05-2007,21:36:00)])$. Thus, the HPC's controller sends a fault message to the UBC's controller to communicate the denial of the request. UBC's SC verifies that the denial was well motivated and forwards the fault message to UBC.

5   System Implementation

In this section we provide a sketch of the architecture which implements the proposed SC along with interesting details of the SC monitoring component.

The SC component is realized by three main modules. First is the *message handler* that handles incoming and outcoming messages during the distribution phase of the contract and the VO operational phase. The second component is the *distribution module* that is realized by the $\mathcal{X}$-Seal system [1], for the distribution of signed contract blocks and encrypted documents. Last but not least is the *compliance checker* module. The compliance checker module is used for checking whether the received entitlements at the time of contract distribution or contract update are actually fully compliant with obligations or not. Running this module is a crucial precondition for ensuring monitoring correctness since only compliant entitlements and obligations must be usefully distributed and enforced within the VO [11].

The core of the SC is the monitoring system. This module is activated during the VO formation phase and it is used during the operational phase. The monitoring system is realized as a proxy that enforces the local entitlements on the incoming messages. We focus on technical details related to this component in the remainder of this section.

---

[3] Punishing actions can be of several type, from banning to the VO to decreased reputation and services' availability. We do not further elaborate on this aspect as it is out of the scope of the current work.

Algorithm 1. Monitor Contract Enforcement

Require: A resource request message $msg = (Cert, Resource)$ where $Cert$ is the sender's identity certificate and $Resource$ is the requested resource **OR** a fault message $msg = (Resource, FaultReason)$ where $Resource$ is the resource requested but not available and $FaultReason$ specifies the reason why $Resource$ is not granted

1: **if** msg is a $msg = (Cert, Resource)$ **then**
2:    **if** $Cert$ is valid **then**
3:       $VOMemberID := ExtractIdentity(Cert)$;
4:       **if** $(Ent_{VoM_i}(VoM_k, R, I)$ s.t $VoM_k, == VOMemberID \wedge R == Resource \wedge t_{msgsend} \in I)$ **then**
5:          Send $msg = (Cert, Resource)$ to Resource's provider Member
6:       **else**
7:          $FaultReason :=$ "No Entitlement Supports Resource Request";
8:          Send $msg = (Resource, FaultReason)$ to Resource VOMemberID 's SC
9:       **end if**
10:    **end if**
11: **end if**
12: **if** msg is a $msg = (Resource, FaultReason)$ **then**
13:    **if** $(Ent_{VoM_i}(VoM_k, R, I)$ s.t $VoM_k, ==$ VOMemberMonitored $\wedge$ R $==$ Resource $\wedge t_{msgsend} \in I)$ **then**
14:       $FaultReason :=$ "Resource's provider violates the contract";
15:       Send $msg = (Resource, FaultReason)$ to VOMemberMonitored and VO Creator
16:    **else**
17:       Send $msg = (Resource, FaultReason)$ to VOMemberMonitored
18:    **end if**
19: **end if**
20: **if** !(Receive $msg \wedge t_r \in I)$ **then**
21:    Send $msg = (Resource, Contract\_Violation)$ to VO Creator
22: **end if**

Fig. 3. Security Controller main interface

Security Controller Monitoring System. The SC monitoring system has been implemented in Java (JDK 1.5) and Java Server Pages (JSPs), the Apache Tomcat Application Server and MySQL database to store the entitlements and certificates. We have deployed the SC component in a SOA-based VO infrastructure where the services provided by the VO members are Web services and the messages exchanged are SOAP messages. The three most relevant operations of the monitoring system are realized by the `checkRequestResource`, `checkReplyMessage` and `checkReceivedMessage` java methods. `checkRequestResource` is executed upon receiving of the SOAP message from a VO member to invoke a Web service operation. This method implements the checks performed on a resource message listed in Algorithm 1 (lines 1-11). We report the code snippet of the `checkRequestResource` method in Appendix. `checkReplyMessage`, on the contrary, is executed when the request of a Web service's operation cannot be granted and hence a SOAPFault message is received or when no reply SOAP message is received. The method implements the second half (lines 12-21) of Algorithm 1. `checkReceivedMessage` controls that for a given request message, the corresponding reply message has been received (see Figure 4).

Entitlements and information about the VO Web service providers and the url to locate them are stored respectively into the ENTITLEMENTS and RESOURCES tables. Table CERTIFICATES contains the VO membership certificate and the certificate of the issuer CA. The messages intercepted by the SC are stored in the table MESSAGES.

The monitoring system has been suited with a JSP interface that displays the SOAP messages sent from or to its VO member. Possible displayed messages are: the SOAP message sent by the VO to invoke the operations of a Web service of another VO member, the reply received to the VO member as output of an executed operation request, and

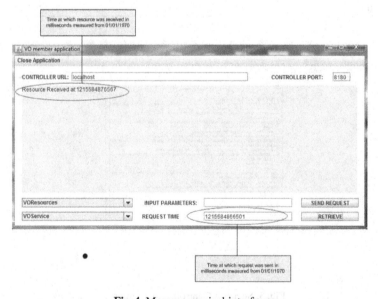

Fig. 4. Message receival interface

the reply SOAPFault message, if the operation cannot be invoked. Figure 3 represents an example of SOAP message sent by the VO member 123456 to invoke the operation `query` offered by the Web service `DataStorageWS`. The message Header contains an Authentication element including a Certificate which includes the VO member's 123456 identity certificate, while the Body of the message contains an element query specifying the name of an XML file name and the XPath query to execute on the file. The entitlement that supports this request states the VO member 123456 is allowed to invoke any of the `DataStorageWS`' operations between 10:00 a.m to 11:00 p.m.

Notice that the SC implementation is modular: checking if a resource message request is supported by an entitlement is independent from the type of message. Therefore, our SC could be integrated in any VO infrastructure -like grid infrastructure- by only implementing the necessary parsers to comply with the format exchanged in that VO, if it does not support SOA messages. Similarly, to facilitate future integrations we chose not to encode the entitlements in any proprietary format. To this extent, we also used the standard and well established X.509 encoding for our VO member identity certificates. This certificate should be released on behalf of the VO Creator by a CA. In order to verify the validity of this certificate, also the CA public key certificate is needed. Both the certificates have to be sent with the resource request messages to authenticate the resource requester. For testing purposes, we assumed that both the membership certificate and the CA certificate are stored locally into the database of the VO member.

Monitoring System Evaluation. We present different test cases to evaluate the performance of the SC component. For each scenario we have compared the interaction time between two VO members with and without the intervention of the SC Components. In all the test cases we have assumed that: a) VO member HPC provides the `DataStorageWS` Web service; b) HBC previously defined an entitlement that grants to VO member UCB the right to invoke the query operation between 10:00 a.m. and 3:00 p.m. Specifically, we have conceived the following cases:

1. UCB requests the operation query within 10:0 a.m-3:00 p.m. a. HPC's SC allows the execution of query operations and the query result is returned to UCB b.

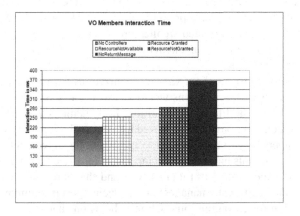

Fig. 5. VO Members Interaction Times

HPC's SC allows the execution of query operations but the `DataStorageWS` is not available due to a deployment error. Therefore, the query result is not returned to UCB.

2. UCB requests the operation query at 4:15 p.m. HPC's SC does not grant query operation invocation. It returns a SOAP fault message to UCB's SC. It double-checks that the request to invoke query operation is in fact not supported and forwards the message to UCB.

3. UCB requests the operation query at a time t within 10:0 a.m-3:00 p.m. a. HPC's SC allows the execution of query operations but the query result is not returned to UCB. UCB's SC checks that a return message with the query results has been received by UCB in the time interval that goes from t to 3:00 p.m.

4. UCB invokes directly the query operation and receives the result. In this case the SC components are not involved.

We have performed our experiments on a Genuine Intel CPU T2300@ 1.66 GHz processor and with 1 GB of RAM, under Microsoft Windows XP Home Edition. The performances have been measured in terms of CPU time (in milliseconds) and are reported in Figure 5.

We notice that the interaction time is always between 200 and 400 ms, regardless of the considered case. The variance for each case is relatively small, and it is about 22. Therefore we can conclude that having SCs which mediate the collaborations among the VO members is worth the cost of the added overhead as it prevents from serious security breaches and guarantees the correct functioning of a VO. Additionally, we expect the time required for the monitoring process to become lower once the SC will be deployed in a real setting, where more efficient and faster processors can be used.

6   Related Work

Virtual Organizations have been thoroughly explored in the realm of grid computing systems [4,2], where technology and resources enable the formation of virtualized environments of users and relative resources belonging to different administrative domains.

The TrustCom project [12] have produced a framework for trust, security and contract management of service oriented architectures, web services and grid technologies to manage the formation, operation and dissolution of virtual organisations and supply chain business relationships.

Another interesting project about virtual organizations is [5]. The project focus on dynamic coalitions, namely, coalitions where member domains may leave or new domains may join during the life of the coalition. In dynamic coalitions, the sharing of resources by autonomous domains is achieved by the distribution of access permissions to coalition members based on negotiated resource-sharing agreements. In the context of the project, a set of tools have been developed that integrate security services for dynamic coalitions, namely, services for (1) private and shared resource management, (2) identity and attribute certificate management, (3) secure group communication, and (4) joint administration for enforcing joint-action policies on shared critical resources. A number of tools and techniques to support the monitoring of network performance and

Grid resources and services have been proposed: for example, NetLogger[13], Autopilot [8] and Remos [3]. These systems incorporate a range of often sophisticated sensor interface, instrumentation, data collection, data filtering, and data summarization techniques that have proven invaluable in a range of application experiments. These systems differ from ours in their main goals and application domains. We do not require specific underlying infrastructure and do not focus on monitoring performance of distributed applications. Rather our goal is to create a self-monitored VO, where members' fulfillment to security and sharing policies is proactively executed. Our SC could be integrated with a performance monitoring tool, to also tackle the problem of monitoring services performance and quality of service. A related contract monitoring system intended to provide automated checking of business to business contracts has been proposed in [6]. It introduces a novel modeling approach to obligations, unifying the treatment of both permissions and obligations by refyining both. The closest work to ours is the Law governed interaction (LGI) proposed by Minsky et al. [14]. LGI is a decentralized coordination and control mechanism for distributed systems. It enables a distributed group of software actors, which may be heterogeneous, open, and large, to engage in a mode of interaction governed by an explicitly specified policy, called the interaction law of this group. The law-enforcement is done in a logically decentralized manner, by associating with each actor a generic component called controller, which is trusted to mediate the interaction of its actor with others. The implementation of this coordination and control mechanism is called Moses [7]. Similarly to our work, the community is governed by global policy and each actor is governed by a local policy, which must conform to. Our concept of contract is however different. In [14] local laws are obtained as refinements of community laws, whereas we consider local policy as a plan for enterprises to allocate resources under their own control while complying with coalition policy as expressed in the contract. Moreover, the implementation of the Moses' controller and of our SC differs in two aspects: 1) the Moses controller allows the member/actor to chose the law that he wants to be applied, while in our controller this is not possible, since it is the single member that has the ability to specify its own entitlements; 2) the Moses controller applies a law enforcing strategy that prevents contract violations, while our controller lets the members autonomy to operate, and detects entitlements violations.

7   Conclusions

Virtual Organization represents a new collaboration paradigm in which the participating entities pool resources in order to achieve a common goal. Ensuring trustworthiness of the members is a fundamental aspect for the VO success. In this paper, we addressed two main problems related to Virtual Organizations's secure deployment: the VO policies' enforcement and the monitoring of VO members' interactions. We have proposed a decentralized monitoring system realized by a software component called Security Controller. We have also evaluated the system overhead introduced by the presence of SC components. The overhead introduced by the SC is reasonably low. Therefore we conclude that having SCs in VOs prevents from serious security breaches and guarantees VOs correct functioning without degrading the time required for members' interactions. We plan to extend the SC implementation with new components to provide monitoring of service performance. We are investigating which of the existing performance monitoring tools could possibly be employed for integration. We also plan to deploy our SC component in the realm of grid environment.

References

1. Bertino, E., Ferrari, E., Paci, F., Parasiliti Provenza, L.: System for Securing Push Based Distribution of XML Documents. International Journal of Information Security 6(4), 255–284 (2007)
2. Czajkowski, S., Foster, I., Kesselman, C., Sander, V., Tuecke, S.: Snap: A protocol for negotiating service level agreements and coordinating resource management in distributed systems. In: Feitelson, D.G., Rudolph, L., Schwiegelshohn, U. (eds.) JSSPP 2002. LNCS, vol. 2537, pp. 153–183. Springer, Heidelberg (2002)
3. Dewitt, T., Gross, T., Lowecama, B.: Remos-A Resource Monitoring System for Network Aware Applications. Carnegie Mellon School of Computer Science, CMU-CS-97-194
4. Foster, I., Kesselman, C., Tuecke, S.: The Anatomy of the Grid: Enabling Scalable Virtual Organizations. International J. Supercomputer Applications 15(3) (2001)
5. Integrated Security Services Dynamic Coalition Management, http://www.ece.umd.edu/gligor/ISSDCM2003/ISSDCM2003.html
6. Linington, P., Neal, S.: Using policies in the checking of business to business contracts. In: Proceedings of the 4th IEEE Workshop on Policies for Distributed Systems and Networks, Como, Italy, June 2003, pp. 207–218 (2003)
7. Moses-Law Governed Interactions (LGI), http://www.moses.rutgers.edu/
8. Nastel AutoPilot Overview White Paper. Published by Nastel Technology
9. Sadighi Firozabadi, B., Sergot, M., Squicciarini, A.C., Bertino, E.: A Framework for Contractual Resource Sharing in Coalitions. In: Proceedings of IEEE 5th International Workshop on Policies for Distributed Systems and Networks, New York, USA, pp. 117–126 (2004)
10. Sadighi Firozabadi, B., Sergot, M.: Contractual Access Control. In: Proceedings of IEEE Security Protocols,10th International Workshop, Cambridge, UK, pp. 96–103 (2002)
11. Squicciarini, A.C., Bertino, E., Paci, F.: A Secure framework for Virtual Community Contracts. International Journal of Web based Communities (IJWBC), Inderscience 2(2), 237–255 (2006)
12. TrustCom project, http://www.eu-trustcom.com/
13. Tierney, B., Gunter, D.: NetLogger: A Toolkit for Distributed System Performance Tuning and Debugging, http://dsd.lbl.gov/publications/NetLogger.overview.pdf
14. Xuhui, A., Minsky, N.H.: Flexible Regulation of Distributed Coalitions. In: Snekkenes, E., Gollmann, D. (eds.) ESORICS 2003. LNCS, vol. 2808, pp. 39–60. Springer, Heidelberg (2003)

A   CheckRequestResource's Code

In this appendix we report code snippet of method CheckRequestResource introduced in Section 5.

```
public boolean checkRequestResource() {

   settings = Proxy.getInstance().serverSettings;
   this.direction = "IN";
   this.destinationHost = settings.getHost();
   this.senderHost = settings.getSenderHost();
   boolean result = false;
   boolean valid;
   try {
    (SOAPobject.getCertificate()).checkValidity(new Date());
    valid=true;
   } catch (CertificateExpiredException e1) {
    valid=false;
    e1.printStackTrace();
   } catch (CertificateNotYetValidException e1) {
    valid=false;
    e1.printStackTrace();
      }

   if(valid==false){
    msg="Error: Your Certificate is not Valid!";
    result = false;
   }else{
    result = findEnt(SOAPobject.getResource(), memberID);
      }
   if(result){
    Proxy.getInstance().getInfoServer().add(getInfoLog());
      }
   return result;
}
```

Using Epidemic Hoarding to Minimize Load Delays in P2P Distributed Virtual Environments

Ingo Scholtes[1], Jean Botev[1], Markus Esch[2], Hermann Schloss[1],
and Peter Sturm[1]

[1] Systemsoftware and Distributed Systems, University of Trier, D-54286 Trier,
Germany
{scholtes,botev,schloss,sturm}@syssoft.uni-trier.de
http://syssoft.uni-trier.de
[2] Faculty of Sciences, Technology and Communication, University of Luxembourg,
L-1359 Luxembourg-Kirchberg, Luxembourg
markus.esch@uni.lu

Abstract. Distributed Virtual Environments (DVEs) have grown popular in various fields of application. Apart from providing great collaborational opportunities in an immersive setting, large-scale DVEs pose severe scalability challenges. Although P2P approaches have proven to be effective for tackling many of these issues, still load delay problems remain in regions with high object or avatar density. In this article we present and evaluate a hoarding approach that is suitable to minimize such delays in P2P-based DVEs with a real-time distribution of dynamic data. The prediction of what data shall be hoarded is based on an epidemic aggregation algorithm working solely with local knowledge. Evaluation results that have been obtained using a DVE simulation environment will be presented.

Keywords: DVE, P2P, Hoarding, Gossiping, Epidemic Aggregation.

1 Introduction

The potential of Distributed Virtual Environments (DVEs) for facilitating immersive and intuitive user collaboration is well-recognized. Until now being predominant in the form of Massively Multiplayer Online Games (MMOGs), they are increasingly used for other purposes like e.g. learning or telepresence. While today MMOGs with several thousand concurrent players constitute the largest DVEs, it is justifiable to think about future environments with hundreds of millions of concurrent participants. An interesting example for such a global-scale future DVE is a 3D representation of the real world in which all kinds of information are embedded. In analogy to Neal Stephenson's novel "Snow Crash", this vision of a virtual environment as major future Internet application is often called "MetaVerse".

E. Bertino and J.B.D. Joshi (Eds.): CollaborateCom 2008, LNICST 10, pp. 578–593, 2009.

The realization of this scenario poses severe technical challenges. Current MMOGs usually rely on several gigabytes of pre-supplied data. This approach is not practicable when considering future environments with huge amounts of dynamic objects. While the real-time distribution of these data is alluring, it poses severe scalability issues to any centralized infrastructure. Even with today's - comparably moderate - user numbers and pre-supplied data, server-based DVEs are suffering from scalability problems. In order to overcome these issues, P2P-based approaches have been proposed over the last few years. While these have effectively addressed server-side scalability issues, in crowded virtual regions there remain problems that result from inevitable limitations of the clients' bandwidth. Having motivated the resulting load delay issues in more detail in the following section 2, we describe a scalable probabilistic solution in section 3. It has been implemented within the HyperVerse project[1] [4], which investigates a P2P-based infrastructure for global-scale DVEs providing flawless user experience in face of unlimited user numbers and population densities. The proposed algorithm has been implemented in a simulation environment for DVEs. Evaluation results will be presented in section 4 of this article.

2 Motivation

In order to achieve scalability in face of an unlimited amount of objects and participants, it is crucial for P2P-based DVEs to minimize the state required in each component. Interest management (IM) schemes have been developed for this purpose [20]. Due to the implicit locality of interest, usually space-based approaches are used in which a client's knowledge about objects and other users is limited to a certain surrounding area. In the following we intend to motivate load delay problems that arise from the usage of a dynamic, space-based IM scheme in the HyperVerse infrastructure. Similar ones are widely deployed in many other DVEs. The scheme is based on Euclidean distance and defines two spheres around a user's position p in the virtual world. A sphere with radius d defines the user's Field of View (FoV), i.e. the range within objects and other avatars shall be visible. A second sphere with radius $d + \Delta$ is called Area of Interest (AoI) and represents the range within a client is aware of objects and other avatars. The motivation for using an AoI is to make clients aware of nearby objects and avatars before they enter the FoV so that there remains enough time to prefetch data necessary for rendering.

We assume that the AoI remains static unless the user moves more than a certain distance Λ away from its center. In this case (see e.g. position p'' in Figure 1) a new AoI centered around the user's current position will be computed and objects therein will be retrieved. Depending on the client's capabilities, motion speed and object density, the sizes of the FoV and the AoI as well as the threshold Λ need to be adapted. Since it minimizes a client's knowledge about its environment, the AoI size should be as small as possible. It must however be large enough to provide sufficient time for data retrieval.

---

[1] http://hyperverse.syssoft.uni-trier.de

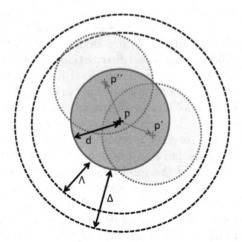

Fig. 1. Area of Interest (AoI) and Field of View (FoV) of a client

Using the IM scheme described above, load delays may occur when approaching densely populated areas, so-called hot spots. Such a situation is illustrated by the following example. Let's assume a client becomes aware of a hot spot within its AoI at time t_1. Let's further assume at t_2 the client has moved to a point where these objects are within its FoV. This situation can be observed in the simulation snapshots in Figure 2. The outer circle is the client's AoI, the inner circle represents its FoV.[2]

If - based on the client's downlink bandwidth - the time taken to retrieve data for all objects in the client's FoV at time t_2 exceeds $t_2 - t_1$, there will necessarily occur a load delay, even assuming unlimited resources at the data provider. Consequently, the question arises how such situations can be avoided. For this, clients must be made aware of hot spots at time $t_0 < t_1$, so that $t_2 - t_0$ is sufficient to retrieve all relevant data. As can be seen in Figure 2(b), at time t_0 the client has however no knowledge about the nearby hot spot.

One possible solution would be to increase the client's AoI, so that the hot spot can be identified at time t_0. Since it conflicts with the minimization of a client's knowledge horizon, this is however not a scalable solution. This becomes especially clear when considering dynamic objects and users. A hot spot resulting for instance from a user crowd can exist at the same position for a long time regardless of the dynamics of its constituents. Tracking a huge number of dynamic entities in a wide range in order to identify hot spots clearly is not a scalable solution. Since in P2P DVEs there is no central instance with global knowledge the question arises how the "crowd wisdom" of peers can be utilized to solve these issues. In the following section we describe a scalable solution for this problem.

---

[2] As can be seen in Figure 2(b), in the simulated situation the client is aware of some objects outside it's direct awareness radius: These are cached objects that have been discovered on its way towards the current position.

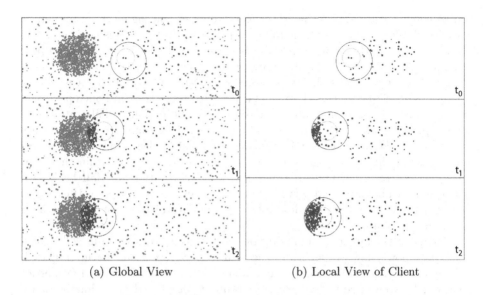

(a) Global View   (b) Local View of Client

Fig. 2. Problem Motivation

3   Epidemic Hoarding

The basic idea that can be used to prevent load delays when entering hot spot regions is to get rid of the inherently bursty traffic pattern that results from the IM scheme described in section 2: Traffic bursts occur whenever the AoI changes. In the following we will answer the question whether it is possible to distribute traffic across time better and thus equalize these bursts. For this we propose a hoarding mechanism in which a certain fraction of a client's bandwidth is constantly dedicated to speculatively prefetch data regardless of a client's AoI. If this bandwidth is used to selectively prefetch data only from within hot spot areas, load delays can be minimized or totally anticipated. For this, hot spots need to be identified based on a peer's local knowledge. In the following we will show how this information can be efficiently retrieved using a modification of the epidemic algorithm described in [15]. Since for this the P2P overlay topology of the HyperVerse infrastructure is used, we will briefly describe it in the following section.

3.1   P2P Overlay Topology and Data Distribution

For the sake of scalability in the face of a potentially unlimited number of users, within the HyperVerse infrastructure data are exchanged directly between peers whenever possible. For any communication between clients, a P2P overlay topology is used. An interesting property of DVEs is that communication most likely occurs between peers that are close to each other in respect of the virtual geography. Reasons for this include direct avatar to avatar interaction, mutual visibility or an exchange of data with geographic reference. Consequently, by maintaining direct connections between "nearby" peers, complex routing mechanisms can be avoided. Besides supporting scalability, a positive effect of this is that no deterministic structure for routing needs to be maintained. This allows for high peer dynamics and avoids network maintenance overhead.

The P2P topology of the HyperVerse infrastructure is built in a way that maintains direct connections between peers with intersecting AoI. Such peers will most likely have a common interest in data or can potentially collaborate via an object present in both of their AoI and might thus be required to communicate. In order to make real-time distribution of data scalable, clients in the HyperVerse infrastructure first ask neighbored peers whenever data from within their AoI needs to be retrieved. Only if this fails, data distribution will fall back to a federated backbone of seed servers. Since it is beyond the scope of this paper, we refer to [4] for a detailed description of the data distribution and neighbor discovery mechanism.

Currently, the application of additional rules (as e.g. described in [22]) which effectuate power law properties in the resulting overlay are being investigated. The main motivation for using such schemes are the favorable global properties that can be attributed to the power law property of networks [10]. Furthermore, the theory of critical phenomena in complex networks [11] provides means for a self-organized monitoring and adaptation of these properties [23].

3.2   Epidemic Hot Spot Aggregation

In this section we will present an algorithm that utilizes the P2P overlay described above in order to identify hot spots within a definable range based on a client's local knowledge. The algorithm uses an epidemic aggregation mechanism similar to the one described in [15]. The main advantage of this scheme is that it does not require any network structure, making it suitable for networks with highly dynamic constituents and topologies. The basic idea of our epidemic hot spot aggregation approach is to consider objects and avatars as particles with a certain mass, their mass reflecting the transmission effort involved when retrieving associated model and texture data. In order to describe the algorithm in more detail, we rely on the following definitions.

Definition 1. *Let p_i be a client with n renderable objects and users within its AoI. With $s_1, \ldots, s_n$ denoting their transmission sizes in bytes, we define the mass M_i of the client's AoI as $M_i = \sum_{j=1}^{n} s_j$. With $r_1, \ldots, r_n$ being the objects' (or users') positions in virtual space, a peer p_i's center of mass C_i is defined as*

$$C_i = \frac{\sum_{j=1}^{n} r_j \cdot s_j}{M_i}.$$

Our aggregation scheme involves peers computing cumulative mass and center of mass for objects and avatars in their AoI as well as exchanging this information with a random neighbor. For this, we assume that each peer p_i keeps a local fixed-size vector S_i of "most crowded spots". Each entry (C_k, M_k) in S_i consists of an AoI mass M_k and the associated center of mass C_k. Furthermore, each peer p_i defines a maximum lookahead distance L_i which determines the range for which it desires to aggregate the most densely populated hot spots.

The algorithm requires each client to be aware of its nearest neighbors (according to the overlay topology described above) along with their AoI and lookahead radii. Each peer p_i applying the epidemic scheme as described in [15], in random intervals the entry in S_i with maximum mass is exchanged with a random neighbor p_j in the overlay. The following algorithm describes the aggregation scheme when information is exchanged between two peers p_i and p_j:

1. p_i selects the entry (C_k, M_k) from its local vector S_i with $dist(C_k, p_j) < L_j$ and maximum mass M_k. If there is no such entry or the mass M' of p_i's current AoI (with center of mass C') is bigger than M_k, (C', M') will be sent to p_j, otherwise (C_k, M_k) will be sent.

2. On reception of (C, M), p_j will add it to the size-constraint vector S_j, possibly replacing an existing entry with smaller mass. It will then select the entry (C_k, M_k) from its vector S_j with maximum mass M_k and with $dist(C_k, p_i) < L_i$. If such an entry does not exist or if the mass M' of p_j's current AoI (with center of mass C') is bigger than M_k, the local information (C', M') will be sent back to p_i. Otherwise (C_k, M_k) will be sent.

The scheme resembles the decentralized gossip-based maximum aggregation as proposed in [16] but it has been extended by some additional rules. First of all information that is aggregated is dynamic, since a client's AoI as well as the objects and avatars within (and thus the total mass as well as the center of mass) can change at any time. In order to account for this dynamics, on each gossip iteration clients check whether the mass of their current AoI is bigger than their currently known maximum. Furthermore, range constraints have been introduced: By having a client check whether the maximum center of mass falls within the random neighbor's lookahead range, only information from within the client's lookahead will be aggregated.

The main advantage of using epidemic aggregation is that is has proven to produce fast-converging results in highly dynamic networks [16] with constant communication cost. In our case, each client will retrieve a fixed-size set of most crowded places that are within its lookahead radius and which are known to some peer in its connected component. For this, only a small number of information exchanges is required. Since only aggregated information are exchanged in regular intervals, this involves only a small constant communication overhead. In particular, in each gossip iteration a 3D position and a mass value needs to be exchanged with a single neighbor.

From a "thermodynamic" argumentation, one can infer that aggregate information on hot spots is likely to remain stable in spite of the dynamics of its constituents. Thus an important contribution of our algorithm is that it allows clients to efficiently retrieve stable, aggregate information on hot spot areas without being burdened with dynamic details on objects or users within.

3.3 Hoarding of Hot Spot Data

A peer p_i's vector S_i resulting from above epidemic aggregation scheme can be utilized to prevent load delays. Entries of S_i representing the most crowded areas within p_i's lookahead radius, their aggregate mass and center of mass provide an estimation of required bandwidth and loading time. The fact that users exhibit a high probability to go to these most crowded (and thus most popular) areas calls for a foresighted hoarding of data from within these regions. In order to prioritize the hoarding of data for multiple hot spots in S_i, additional client-side information like motion trajectories, speed and history can be used.

We propose that clients dedicate a certain fraction of idle downlink bandwidth for speculatively hoarding data from hot spots and thus mitigating delays. This fraction needs to be adapted to the client's lookahead radius: A larger lookahead radius provides for smaller hoarding bandwidth, since there is more time for prefetching data. It is important to note that, by virtue of the epidemic scheme described above, increasing the lookahead radius does not involve additional communication overhead. Further arguments on which lookahead radii and thus hoarding bandwidths are suitable to be used in practice are currently under investigation.

4   Evaluation Results

In order to implement and evaluate the proposed hoarding scheme, comprehensive simulation support is required. For this, TopGen[3] [24] - an open-source topology generator created within our working group - has been extended by DVE simulation facilities. For realistically simulating large-scale distributed virtual environments it provides a deterministic, event-based simulation of avatar mobility based on different models. For the following simulations, a DVE-specific model has been used which will be described in more detail in the following section. Apart from users with simulated mobility, objects with different transmission sizes can be placed in the virtual world. By this means it is possible to realistically simulate the object retrieval traffic resulting from different mobility patterns, IM and prefetching schemes.

An important feature of TopGen is the possibility of extending it by so-called experimental modules. By hooking into certain simulation events (join and exit of clients, avatars becoming mutually visible, refresh of AoI, etc.), simulations can be extended with own code. For the evaluations in this section we have created an experimental module which implements interest management, object retrieval and epidemic hoarding as described in sections 2 and 3. In each simulation step, every peer was allowed to transfer a limited amount of data in order to simulate client-side bandwidth limitations.

---

[3] http://syssoft.uni-trier.de/~scholtes/

4.1   Preferential Way Point Mobility Model

An important aspect when performing DVE simulations is the choice of a realistic model for avatar mobility. The most simple model known e.g. from the field of ad hoc networks is random way point [19]. Here each simulated agent selects a random point with uniform probability. The agent then starts moving towards this point and selects a new target once having reached it. Due to lacking a notion of Points of Interest (PoIs), the model is not very realistic. Since it seems intuitive that users move to certain PoIs with higher probability, we propose a variation of the random way point model that respects objects, users and their distribution. For this we assume that DVE users are collaborative by nature, i.e. that they are primarily interested in interacting with objects and other users.

Our "preferential way point" mobility model is identical to the random way point model, except for the fact that movement targets are selected among all possible object and user positions with a probability proportional to the object and user density in the surrounding region. Users will thus preferentially move to densely populated hot spot regions. The name has been chosen in resemblance of the "preferential attachment" generation model for power law graphs [1] in which newly added nodes create links to existing nodes with probability proportional to the target's link number. While here every new edge will further increase the "attractiveness" of a node, a similar effect occurs in our mobility model: Each user that moves towards a certain position increases the probability that other users go there and thus further the attractiveness of the surrounding region.

4.2   Simulation Results

In this section we provide simulation results of the hoarding scheme that have been retrieved using the TopGen simulation environment. For this a background set of 200 objects is randomly distributed in a virtual region of 1000 x 350 pixels in size. Additionally two hot spots consisting of 400 objects each are created. Synthetic data transmission sizes between 1 and 5 units are randomly assigned to objects and the users' avatars. The simulation comprises 200 randomly distributed avatars moving according to the preferential way point model. In each simulation step, each of the simulated clients can download a maximum of 15 data units from a fictional data provider. Furthermore each client uses a cache limited in size to 3000 data units. As described in section 3.1, clients with intersecting AoI are interconnected via an edge in the overlay topology. The initial distribution of objects and peers in the simulated setting is shown in Figure 3.

Two simulations consisting of 1250 iterations have been performed. For these, the IM scheme described in section 2 is used with a FoV radius of $d = 50$ pixels, an AoI radius of $d+\Delta = 75$ and $\Lambda = 12$ pixels. The motion speed of peers is set to a maximum of one pixel per simulation step, i.e. the AoI of a client is refreshed at most every 12 simulation steps. The simulated traffic arising from object retrievals is recorded for each peer. In order to capture and evaluate situations with visible load delays, the amount of object data from within the FoV which could not be loaded in time is recorded for each peer in every simulation step.

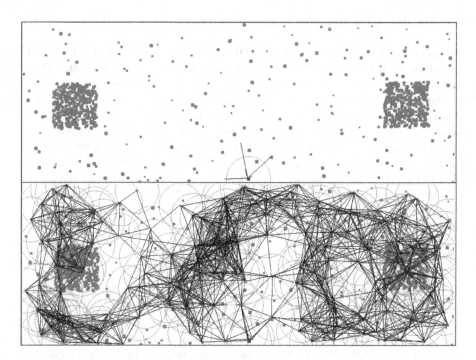

Fig. 3. Initial situation with all clients and P2P overlay (bottom) and selected peer only (top)

This value can be used to identify situations as motivated in section 2, i.e. where the client's bandwidth is not sufficient to retrieve data in time. The following paragraphs present results of a single random client. The initial position of this client can be seen in the top part of Figure 3.

Simulation without Epidemic Hoarding. Figure 4 shows simulation results of a random client with no epidemic hoarding being used. For the sake of clarity only the selected client is shown in Figure 4(a) at three selected simulation steps. Links to peers in the overlay topology (i.e. nearby clients with intersecting AoI) are indicated by edges. Based on the preferential way point mobility model, the selected client first moves towards the hot spot which can be seen in the left part of the simulated area in Figure 4(a). Having reached this in step 316 of 1250, it proceeds to the hot spot that can be seen in the right part of the simulated area. The client reaches this hot spot in step 1048. A video of the simulation can be found at the website of one of the authors[4].

Looking at the client's bandwidth that is utilized for retrieving data within its AoI, in the bottom part of Figure 4(b) one recognizes numerous peaks which occur whenever the AoI changes. Usually - because the AoI is bigger than the FoV - there remains enough time to load objects coming into the FoV shortly. In this case there are no objects with unloaded data in the client's FoV. In the

---

[4] http://syssoft.uni-trier.de/~scholtes/VideoA.avi

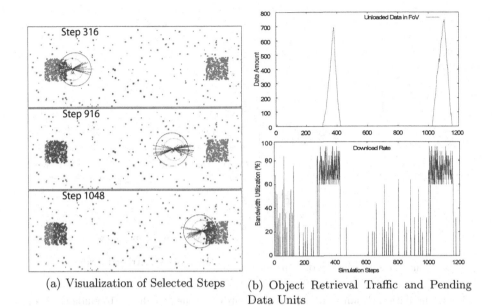

(a) Visualization of Selected Steps   (b) Object Retrieval Traffic and Pending Data Units

Fig. 4. Simulation Results without Epidemic Hoarding (Lines are drawn to guide the eye)

top part of Figure 4(b), one recognizes that this is the case during the first 315 simulation steps. In step 316, the client's FoV enters the crowded area. Due to the density of objects, now data can not be retrieved in time. The amount of unloaded data in the FoV that is shown in the upper part of Figure 4(b) exhibits two sharp peaks when the client enters the hot spot areas in simulation steps 316 and 1048. The maximum value of pending data was 750 units. Based on the maximum download bandwidth of 15 units per simulation step, in this situation at least 50 additional time steps would have been required to load all objects within the FoV in time. In a real setting this would have resulted in visible delays. Another effect than can be seen in Figure 4(b) is that beginning in simulation step 280, the client's available download bandwidth is saturated until it leaves the hot spot in simulation step 410. In reality this can affect other communication protocols (voice chat, avatar interaction, etc.) and thus degrade user experience over a long period.

Simulation with Epidemic Hoarding. Figure 5 shows the results of another simulation run for the same client using the same random seed. Here the epidemic hoarding algorithm described in section 3 is used. No client-side information (like e.g. movement trajectory) is utilized to improve the prediction which data shall be preloaded, i.e. all data from within predicted hot spot areas are hoarded. Pending data transfers resulting from the IM scheme are prioritized, i.e. only

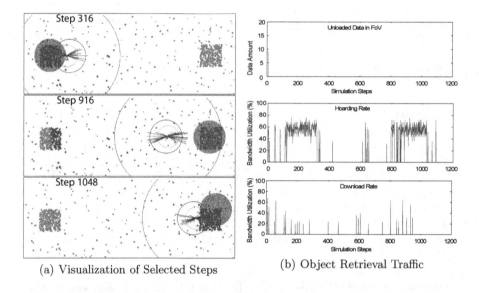

(a) Visualization of Selected Steps

(b) Object Retrieval Traffic

Fig. 5. Simulation Results with Epidemic Hoarding (Lines are drawn to guide the eye)

otherwise unused bandwidth is used for hoarding. Clients use a lookahead range of 5 times their AoI size. The maximum bandwidth utilization for hoarding is set to 70 %. In case of a full client cache, an additional rule disables the hoarding of objects that are farther away than all objects in the cache. This prohibits thrashing situations in which hoarding displaces entries in the cache that are repeatedly required for rendering. Again, a video of this simulation can be retrieved from the website of one of the authors[5].

Figure 5 shows results obtained in this simulation. In Figure 5(a), the same selected simulation steps as in 4(a) are visualized. The lookahead radius is indicated by the outermost circle around the selected client. The client's local hot spot prediction resulting from epidemic aggregation is visualized by the shaded circle. Due to hoarding, all data have already been retrieved when the client enters the left hot spot in step 316. As soon as the right hot spot is in the client's lookahead range in step 916, the hot spot is correctly identified by the epidemic aggregation algorithm and hoarding of data begins. Finally, when the client's FoV enters the hot spot region in step 1048, again all data have already been retrieved and no load delays occur.

These claims are substantiated by the results shown in Figure 5(b). The middle diagram shows the rate at which data have been speculatively hoarded. Comparing both diagrams to Figure 4(b), one recognizes that periods with saturated bandwidth could be avoided. A positive side-effect of this is that it leaves more resources for other communication protocols. The most interesting result, the amount of unloaded data in the client's FoV, is shown in the topmost diagram.

---

[5] http://syssoft.uni-trier.de/~scholtes/VideoB.avi

	Data Transferred	Unloaded Data in FoV	Canceled Transfer Data
without hoarding	5794	85109	94
with hoarding	6462	9	0

Fig. 6. Integral Transfer Statistics

Due to epidemic hoarding, load delays could be avoided since at no moment there are objects with unloaded data in the client's FoV[6].

Although these results look promising, an important question is the overall additional cost resulting from data hoarding. In order to assess this, the integral amount of data retrieved in both simulation has been recorded for the client considered above. The result is shown in Figure 6. One recognizes a roughly 11% increase in the total amount of data that have been transferred. An important question is how much of this difference results from situations in which a client not using epidemic hoarding leaves a hot spot before all objects have been loaded. This results in any queued downloads being canceled, thus underestimating the amount of total data that actually need to be transferred. A further evaluation of simulation data has shown that this accounts for a difference of 94 data units. After accounting for canceled transfers, one concludes that hoarding leads to a 9 % overhead in transferred data for the simulated setting.

5   Related Work

An important characteristic of DVEs is the locality of access with respect to virtual geography that results from human cognition. The main motivation for the geography-based overlay topology presented in section 3.1 is to respect this fact and thus guarantee that required data are available in a peer's neighborhood. Similar techniques have been investigated to improve search performance in general P2P systems [21] [2] [9]. The basic idea of these approaches is to adapt overlay topologies with respect to content that peers provide or are interested in.

Several P2P-based approaches to improve the scalability of large-scale DVEs have been proposed. Some of these approaches specifically address non-uniform access patterns. The P2P framework ATLAS [18] introduces a user-specific object popularity based on repeated access which is used to improve prefetching and caching. While this can mitigate delays for frequently visited areas, it does not work for hot spots that have not yet been accessed or that form dynamically. Another way of minimizing load delays is to predict avatar behavior. The utilization of local knowledge (e.g. motion trajectory) to predict future object access has been investigated in [17] and [7]. Although the proposed schemes do not consider heterogeneous distributions of dynamic objects, they might be suitable to prioritize hot spots predicted by our epidemic aggregation approach.

Most solutions to problems related to hot spots - or flash crowds - have been developed with a focus on the data provider side. Dynamic partitioning schemes

---

[6] The reason for the small peak in the first simulation step is, that in the initial situation the client was set to a position where some objects were in its FoV already.

like the one presented in [6] can e.g. be used to equally distribute objects or avatars from densely populated regions across data providers. The approach presented in [26] combines octrees with the Chord [25] protocol to achieve the same task. In order to maintain a minimum quality of service for at least a limited number of users in server-based MMOGs, [8] propose an "early warning system" that detects hot spots by monitoring performance degradations. In case a hot spot is identified, no more users are admitted to the identified crowded regions. None of the aforementioned approaches addresses the problem of the limited bandwidth of clients resulting in load delays regardless of the data provider's resources. The work that has been done in this area focuses on traffic resulting from mutual avatar visibility. [3] deals with avatar interactions in crowded DVEs and introduces a scheme that aggregates individual avatars to crowds in order to maintain scalability. [12] describes a group-based filtering mechanism that minimizes motion updates of nearby avatars in crowded areas.

Another active field of research are scalable interest management schemes for large-scale DVEs. A survey of such schemes for MMOGs has been performed in [5]. A common practice for scalable IM schemes is to reduce the AoI size when object or avatar density reach a certain threshold. This technique is e.g. used in the Voronoi-based clustering that can be found in VON [14]. Without the usage of AoI-independent hot spot detection mechanisms like the one presented in this article, reducing the AoI will however worsen the problem of delays resulting from object retrieval traffic. The usage of adjustable AoI shapes is another direction of research, being investigated e.g. for the P2P DVE infrastructure FLoD [13].

6   Conclusion and Future Work

In this article we have presented an efficient probabilistic and localized approach to identifying hot spot regions in DVEs that rely on real-time data distribution. It can be used to enrich interest management with hot spot predictions, so data can be speculatively hoarded before clients are too close for data still being retrieved in time. The only knowledge required for this prediction is a list of objects and avatars in the client's AoI. By virtue of using an epidemic aggregation approach, the communication overhead involved is limited by a small constant. Another advantage is the fact, that neither user mobility nor peer dynamics constitute a problem, since epidemic aggregation makes no assumptions about the structure of the overlay topology. In DVEs, hot spot regions most likely remain at a certain position even though the constituting objects and avatars can be highly dynamic. The approach presented in this article is well-suited to efficiently retrieve inertial aggregate hot spot information without burdening clients with the details of the underlying dynamics. A disadvantage of existing prediction-based prefetching schemes is the fact that they do not consider dynamic hot spots. Rather than requiring an exact prediction of user mobility, our approach efficiently yields those regions that will potentially incur load delays. Prioritizing hot spots retrieved by means of prediction is considerably easier than obtaining an exact prediction of the user's movement.

From our simulations we draw the conclusion that the proposed scheme can efficiently be used to avoid load delays in DVEs with real-time data transfer and thus improve user experience. In the simulated setting the hoarding scheme resulted in a 9 % increase of a client's total data traffic while totally eliminating load delays. It remains to investigate how local knowledge like movement trajectories, motion speed or favorite venues can be used to further improve predictions and thus minimize this overhead. Since avatar traces of real-world DVEs are slowly becoming available, we plan to investigate the usage of such heuristics as well as the viability of our mobility model.

Another future direction is the optimization of what regions are treated as hot spots by clients. For this, we plan to apply a second epidemic aggregation algorithm which efficiently determines the average mass density within the virtual world. By this, only those hot spots that significantly exceed average density can be advertised by gossiping, thus improving prediction quality. While the scheme currently only works for a continuous avatar motion, we plan to investigate extensions that consider avatar relocation through teleportation. Finally, another direction for improvements is the consideration of additional information while aggregating information: When moving in a certain direction, e.g. gossip messages received from peers in this direction can be prioritized.

Ultimately, it has to be investigated whether interest management as a whole can be replaced in favor of a self-organizing and probabilistic prediction similar to the hot spot identification presented in this article. For this a fixed fraction of bandwidth could be dedicated to hoarding while a self-organizing process ensures that all required data are available in time.

References

1. Barabasi, A.-L., Albert, R.: Emergence of scaling in random networks. Science 286, 509–512 (1999)
2. Bawa, M., Manku, G.S., Raghavan, P.: Sets: search enhanced by topic segmentation. In: SIGIR 2003: Proceedings of the 26th annual international ACM SIGIR conference on Research and development in informaion retrieval, New York, USA, pp. 306–313. ACM, New York (2003)
3. Benford, S., Greenhalgh, C., Lloyd, D.: Crowded collaborative virtual environments. In: CHI 1997: Proceedings of the SIGCHI conference on Human factors in computing systems, New York, USA, pp. 59–66. ACM, New York (1997)
4. Botev, J., Esch, M., Hoehfeld, A., Schloss, H., Scholtes, I.: The hyperverse - concepts for a federated and torrent based "3d web". In: Proceedings of the First International Workshop on Massively Multiuser Virtual Environments at IEEE Virtual Reality 2008 (March 2008)
5. Boulanger, J.-S., Kienzle, J., Verbrugge, C.: Comparing interest management algorithms for massively multiplayer games. In: NetGames 2006: Proceedings of 5th ACM SIGCOMM workshop on Network and system support for games, 6 p. ACM, New York (2006)
6. Bouras, C., Giannaka, E., Tsiatsos, T.: Partitioning of distributed virtual environments based on objects' attributes. In: DS-RT 2007: Proceedings of the 11th IEEE International Symposium on Distributed Simulation and Real-Time Applications, Washington, DC, USA, pp. 72–75. IEEE Computer Society, Los Alamitos (2007)

7. Chan, A., Lau, R.W.H., Ng, B.: Motion prediction for caching and prefetching in mouse-driven dve navigation. ACM Trans. Interet Technol. 5(1), 70–91 (2005)
8. Chen, X., Heidemann, J.: Flash crowd mitigation via adaptive admission control based on application-level observations. ACM Trans. Interet Technol. 5(3), 532–569 (2005)
9. Chiou, H., Su, A., Yang, S.: Interest-based peer selection in p2p network. In: International Conference on Sensor Networks, Ubiquitous, and Trustworthy Computing, pp. 549–554 (2008)
10. Dorogovtsev, S., Mendes, J.: Evolution of Networks: From Biological Nets to the Internet and WWW. Oxford University Press, Oxford (2003)
11. Dorogovtsev, S.N., Goltsev, A.V., Mendes, J.F.F.: Critical phenomena in complex networks (2007)
12. Han, S., Lim, M., Lee, D.: Scalable interest management using interest group based filtering for large networked virtual environments. In: VRST 2000: Proceedings of the ACM symposium on Virtual reality software and technology, pp. 103–108. ACM, New York (2000)
13. Hu, S.-Y.: A case for 3d streaming on peer-to-peer networks. In: Web3D 2006: Proceedings of the eleventh international conference on 3D web technology, New York, USA, pp. 57–63. ACM, New York (2006)
14. Hu, S.-Y., Chen, J.-F., Chen, T.-H.: Von: a scalable peer-to-peer network for virtual environments. IEEE Network 20, 22–31 (2004)
15. Jelasity, M., Montresor, A.: Epidemic-style proactive aggregationin large overlay networks. In: Proceedings of the 24th International Conference on Distributed ComputingSystems (ICDCS 2004), Tokyo, Japan, pp. 102–109. IEEE Computer Society, Los Alamitos (2004)
16. Jelasity, M., Montresor, A., Babaoglu, O.: Gossip-based aggregation in large dynamic networks. ACM Trans. Comput. Syst. 23(3), 219–252 (2005)
17. Lau, R.W.H., Chim, J.H.P., Green, M., Leong, H.V., Si, A.: Object caching and prefetching in distributed virtual walkthrough. Real-Time Syst. 21(1/2), 143–164 (2001)
18. Lee, D., Lim, M., Han, S.: Atlas: a scalable network framework for distributed virtual environments. In: CVE 2002: Proceedings of the 4th international conference on Collaborative virtual environments, pp. 47–54. ACM, New York (2002)
19. Lin, G., Noubir, G., Rajaraman, R.: Mobility models for ad hoc network simulation. In: INFOCOM 2004. Twenty-third AnnualJoint Conference of the IEEE Computer and Communications Societies, vol. 1 (2004)
20. Morse, K.L., Bic, L., Dillencourt, M.: Interest management in large-scale virtual environments. Presence: Teleoper. Virtual Environ. 9(1), 52–68 (2000)
21. Ramanathan, M.K., Kalogeraki, V., Pruyne, J.: Finding good peers in peer-to-peer networks. In: IPDPS 2002: Proceedings of the 16th International Parallel and Distributed Processing Symposium, Washington, DC, USA, P. 158. IEEE Computer Society, Los Alamitos (2002)
22. Rozenfeld, A.F., Cohen, R.: Scale-free networks on lattices. Physical Review Letters 89, 218701 (2002)
23. Scholtes, I., Botev, J., Esch, M., Hoehfeld, A., Schloss, H.: Awareness-driven phase transitions in very large scale distributed systems. In: Proceedings of the Second IEEE International Conferences on Self-Adaptive and Self-Organizing Systems (SaSo). IEEE, Los Alamitos (2008)

24. Scholtes, I., Botev, J., Esch, M., Hoehfeld, A., Schloss, H., Zech, B.: Topgen - internet router-level topology generation based on technology constraints. In: Proceedings of the First International Conference on Simulation Tools and Techniques for Communications, Networks and Systems (SIMUTools) (February 2008)
25. Stoica, I., Morris, R., Karger, D., Kaashoek, M.F., Balakrishnan, H.: Chord: A scalable peer-to-peer lookup service for internet applications. In: SIGCOMM 2001: Proceedings of the 2001 conference on Applications, technologies, architectures, and protocols for computer communications, pp. 149–160. ACM Press, New York (2001)
26. Tanin, E., Harwood, A., Samet, H.: Using a distributed quadtree index in peer-to-peer networks. VLDB 16(2), 165–178 (2007)

A Battery-Aware Algorithm for Supporting Collaborative Applications

Sami Rollins and Cheryl Chang-Yit

University of San Francisco, San Francisco, CA, 94121, USA
{srollins,cchangyit}@cs.usfca.edu

Abstract. Battery-powered devices such as laptops, cell phones, and MP3 players are becoming ubiquitous. There are several significant ways in which the ubiquity of battery-powered technology impacts the field of collaborative computing. First, applications such as collaborative data gathering, become possible. Also, existing applications that depend on collaborating devices to maintain the system infrastructure must be reconsidered. Fundamentally, the problem lies in the fact that collaborative applications often require end-user computing devices to perform tasks that happen in the background and are not directly advantageous to the user. In this work, we seek to better understand how laptop users use the batteries attached to their devices and analyze a battery-aware alternative to Gnutella's ultrapeer selection algorithm. Our algorithm provides insight into how system maintenance tasks can be allocated to battery-powered nodes. The most significant result of our study indicates that a large portion of laptop users can participate in system maintenance without sacrificing any of their battery. These results show great promise for existing collaborative applications as well as new applications, such as collaborative data gathering, that rely upon battery-powered devices.

1 Introduction

Battery-powered devices such as laptops, cell phones, and MP3 players are becoming ubiquitous. One study, conducted in the US, estimates that 73.7 percent of University students own laptop computers and 83.1 percent of 18- to 19-year-olds own an MP3 player [8]. Some Universities even require all incoming freshman to have laptops[21]. With the interest surrounding devices like the iPhone [1] and platforms such as Google's Android [7], this trend is unlikely to reverse.

There are several significant ways in which the ubiquity of battery-powered technology impacts the field of collaborative computing. First, new applications, such as collaborative data gathering, become possible. These applications enable end-user devices, such as phones and laptops, to gather and report information about their surrounding environments [3] and can be used for a variety of purposes including environmental monitoring and entertainment. Additionally, the performance applications that depend on collaborating devices for system maintenance tasks, such as communication, is impacted. Consider an application, such as Skype [18], that relies on collaborators to help connect parties that wish

E. Bertino and J.B.D. Joshi (Eds.): CollaborateCom 2008, LNICST 10, pp. 594–608, 2009.
© ICST Institute for Computer Sciences, Social-Informatics and Telecommunications Engineering 2009

to engage in a conference. Users of battery-powered devices may be hesitant to provide a service that requires them to devote precious battery, but for which they see no direct benefit. Similarly, users who do allow their battery-powered devices to provide such a service may see a decrease in the performance of the device, for example, its lifetime.

Fundamentally, the problem lies in the fact that collaborative applications often require end-user computing devices to perform tasks that happen in the background and are not directly advantageous to the user. This is in stark contrast to the underlying principle of most battery-saving techniques: enter a low-power state when possible. In this work, we seek to better understand how laptop users use the batteries attached to their devices and explore how these usage patterns can be used to guide how aggressively a device should participate in tasks from which the user does not derive direct benefit.

In particular, we focus our attention on a battery-aware alternative to Gnutella's ultrapeer selection algorithm that determines which collaborating peers are responsible for maintenance tasks such as routing and caching. The goal of our algorithm is to devote system maintenance tasks to devices that have the most stable battery characteristics. Our results are not only applicable to building a Gnutella-style overlay, but also provide insight into how to integrate battery-awareness into applications such as collaborative data gathering.

The remainder of this paper is organized as follows. First, we analyze battery data collected from 41 laptop users over a period of roughly 7 months. Our primary finding is that laptop users are often plugged into a power outlet during periods of active use. Based on this finding, we evaluate a battery-aware modification of Gnutella. Our results show that this algorithm consumes significantly less battery than the standard Gnutella algorithm and still ensures that over half the network can participate in maintenance tasks over 90 percent of the time.

2   Data Collection

The goal of this work is to understand the usage patterns of battery-powered devices and analyze the impact of those patterns on collaborative applications. Our analysis is based on data collected by 41 laptop users during the months of January through August 2007. Unlike previous studies that either collect data at a central collection point, such as a base station [11], or ask users to carry special-purpose devices for data collection [15], we asked the participants to install our data collection software on their personal laptop computers. As a result, we were able to gather a significant amount of information about the real usage patterns of our participants.

Our software is written in Java and runs on both Windows and Mac OSX. It periodically records information about the status of the laptop on which it runs, including the percentage of the battery remaining, whether the device is on AC power, and whether the device is connected to the Internet. Once per day, it uploads the information collected to our data collection server. Our software is completely passive and only collects data during periods when the laptop is already on.

We advertised our software among colleagues and friends, and on several mailing lists. The characteristics of the data are shown in Table 1.

Table 1. Characteristics of the data collected

	Total Days Participating	% Days Reporting
Minimum	16	.1%
Maximum	216	96%
Mean	190	62%
Median	158	56%

All of our participants downloaded and installed the software at different times, therefore the *Total Days Participating* column indicates the minimum, maximum, mean, and median for the total number of days from the time a participant installed the software until the end of the data collection period (August 8, 2007). The *% Days Reporting* column indicates the ratio of the number of days a participant recorded data to the participant's *Total Days Participating*.

3   Churn and Battery Characteristics

Our analysis considers two elements that impact the ability of battery-powered devices to participate in maintenance tasks to support collaborative applications: the churn rate of the nodes and the battery constraints of the devices. If nodes are only briefly online, the overhead, for example network traffic, required to allocate the appropriate maintenance tasks may be too cumbersome. Further, nodes without sufficient battery are unlikely to want to contribute this valuable resource to tasks that do not directly benefit the user. Our results suggest that laptop users demonstrate rather stable usage patterns: often staying online for over 1 hour and often charging their laptops for the entire duration of their session.

Figure 1 examines the length of the *sessions* observed in our data set. A session begins when a node first reports being on and connected to the Internet and ends when it no longer reports data or when it reports being no longer connected to the Internet. Because we sample the data at 10-minute intervals, there is a small margin of error in our results. If a node records a state of disconnected at 2:00, a state of connected at 2:10, and a state of disconnected at 2:20, we assume that the node was on for 10 minutes from 2:10 to 2:20, though it is possible that the node was on for up to 20 minutes or as little as a few seconds. The figure plots the cumulative distribution function (CDF) of the percentage of sessions of a given length for all sessions observed during the data collection period.

We observe that the sessions in the 25th to 75th percentile are roughly 10 minutes to 2.5 hours in length. Roughly 22 percent of sessions are 10 minutes or shorter, and the longest sessions are well over 5 days in length. While it is clear that allocating system tasks to nodes that are online for only 10 minutes must be avoided, our results demonstrate ample opportunity to identify nodes that can support longer-lived applications.

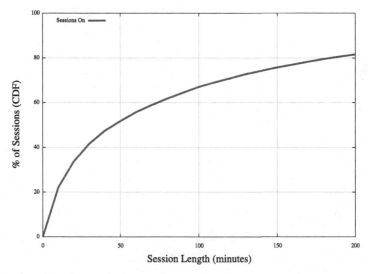

Fig. 1. CDF of the length of time a laptop user is typically online

Because our analysis shows that session lengths are longer than 3 hours in only about one-fifth of cases, we suspected that there may be a correlation between session length and laptop battery lifetime. Figure 2 shows this assumption to be false. It plots the CDF of the percentage of nodes online at each 10-minute time sample. Recall that not all of the participants started recording data on the same day. The percentage of nodes online is the number of nodes online at a given time divided by the total number of nodes who have reported data prior to that time. As expected, for a given percentage of nodes (x), the CDF shows that there is a higher probability that x or fewer nodes will be on and plugged in than simply on.

Examining the 25th to 75th percentile, we find that the percentage of nodes online varies from approximately 16% to 34% and the percentage of nodes online and on AC power varies from 14% to 30%. This indicates that only a small percentage of nodes are typically online and *not* plugged in. Our previous work [2] suggests that (1) the devices in our study are rarely on and not online and (2) nearly half of all recharges happen when the battery is at less than 50 percent capacity. This combination of data suggests that most battery is spent when laptops are in a suspended state.

Figure 3 takes a closer look at the number of sessions observed where the node is either on AC power the entire session, not on AC power the entire session, or plugs in or unplugs during the session. There are nearly 3 times as many sessions where a node is on AC power versus not on AC power for the entire session. We also note that further analysis indicated that for the sessions that exhibited a state change, in about half of all cases over 80 percent of the session was spent on AC power. This suggests that there is ample opportunity to design systems that run on battery-powered nodes yet only utilize battery of those nodes that can spare it.

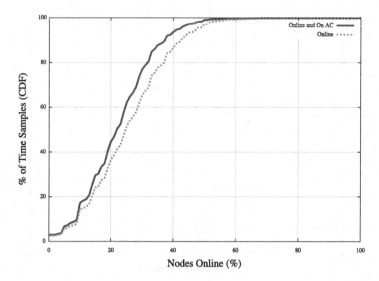

Fig. 2. CDF of the percentage of nodes online and the percentage of nodes online and plugged in at each time sample

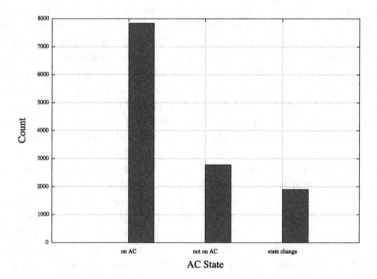

Fig. 3. Count of the number of sessions where a node is (a) plugged in for the entire session, (b) unplugged for the entire session, or (c) plugs in or unplugs at least once during the session

3.1 Discussion

The interesting result of this study is that while the laptops often exhibited what we refer to as *desktop replacement* behavior, for example often running on AC power during times of use, their behavior does differ from a traditional desktop.

Sessions are shorter than would be expected from an always-connected desktop and there are situations where the nodes do drain their batteries during times of use. The question remains, is it prudent to assume that laptops should be exempt from maintaining the infrastructure to support collaborative applications, or can we design the system such that a laptop contributes only a reasonable set of resources? The remainder of this paper addresses this question by evaluating a battery-aware algorithm for building a Gnutella overlay.

4   Battery-Aware Supernode Selection

Resource constraints are a concern for any distributed system in which end-user devices are called upon to contribute to the whole of the system. One technique used by the P2P community is to balance system load by creating a hierarchical network where resource-plentiful nodes are promoted to *ultra* or *super* status [6,14]. Gnutella [13], for example, supports two types of peers: ultrapeers and leaves. Ultrapeers are full participants in the network and must relay messages, perform searches, and cache information. Leaves merely consume the services of the network through ultrapeers. When a node joins the Gnutella network, it is initially designated as a leaf. If a node has the appropriate bandwidth and connectivity characteristics, it will try to promote itself to ultrapeer status after it has been online for at least 1 hour.

In this section, we explore a battery-aware alternative to Gnutella's mechanism for selecting ultrapeers. Our algorithm favors selection of supernodes that are likely to be plugged in, and attempts to avoid choosing supernodes that will be unplugged for any portion of their session. Our results indicate that this algorithm nearly always selects nodes that will remain plugged in for the entire period they serve as a supernode.

In this work, we focus exclusively on the construction of the overlay; application-layer metrics are the subject of future work. In addition, we do *not* assume that our underlying network is a mobile, ad-hoc network. Our data does not provide location information, therefore our nodes are either connected to the Internet and can reach all other connected nodes, or are disconnected from the Internet and unable to participate in overlay construction. Finally, we assume that our nodes meet the bandwidth and connectivity characteristics required to serve as a supernode.

4.1   Experimental Setup

Our evaluation is based on simulated analysis of the data discussed in Section 2. We have developed our own simulator that operates on the following types of events:

- **join** a - A join for node a is generated at the time that a first reports being connected to a network.
- **leave** a - A leave for node a is generated if a fails to report data or reports being disconnected from the Internet.

- **acchange** *a* - An acchange for node *a* is generated if *a* goes from a plugged in to an unplugged status or vice versa.
- **batpercentchange** *a* - A batpercentchange for node *a* is generated if *a*'s percentage of battery remaining changes.
- **superstatuschange** *a* - A superstatuschange for node *a* is generated if *a* promotes itself to be a supernode or demotes itself from supernode status to leaf status. We consider several algorithms for promotion and demotion of supernodes in the following section.

4.2   Supernode Selection Algorithms

Periodically, a node determines whether to promote itself to supernode status or demote itself to leaf status. Our evaluation compares three algorithms: random, uptime, and battery. The random algorithm gives us a baseline for comparison. We consider two uptime algorithms: the standard Gnutella approach and a slightly modified and more aggressive Gnutella-style algorithm. Finally, the goal of the battery algorithm is to choose nodes with the most stable battery characteristics. The intuition is that nodes with higher battery are more likely to exhibit *desktop replacement*-style behavior and will be online and plugged in for significant periods of time; nodes with lower battery, though they may be plugged in, may be less stable.

- **Random** - At five-minute intervals each online node determines randomly, using a uniform distribution, whether to change its supernode status.
- **Uptime** - At five minute intervals each online node will promote itself to supernode status if it has been up (online) longer than a given threshold. Our results compare an aggressive threshold of 5 minutes and the 1-hour threshold used by Gnutella [13]. Once a node has promoted itself, it will remain a supernode until it goes offline.
- **Battery** - At five minute intervals each online node executes the following algorithm:

```
if(!supernode and (on ac power and bat > threshold))
    become supernode
elif(supernode and !(on ac power and bat > threshold))
    become leaf
```

Unless otherwise noted, we use a threshold of 75 percent.

4.3   Results

Our primary goal is to minimize the amount of time a supernode spends unplugged. Figure 4 illustrates the amount of time a supernode spends on battery power. It plots the CDF of the percentage of time a supernode spends in an

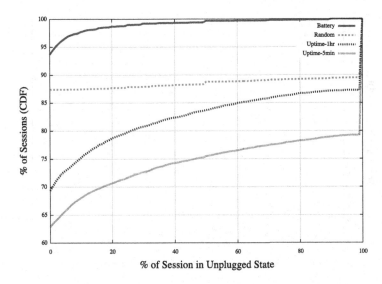

Fig. 4. CDF of the percentage of time that a supernode is not plugged in

unplugged state. Over 62 percent of the time, a node is plugged in during the
entire period that it serves as a supernode. The Battery algorithm significantly
outperforms the others; over 93 percent of the time a supernode is plugged in
during its entire session. Using the Battery algorithm, the only time a supernode
can be unplugged is the 5-minute interval between the periodic checks of battery
status. By reducing the interval to 1-minute, we can actually ensure that a
supernode is never unplugged.

Interestingly, the Uptime algorithm with a threshold of 5 minutes performs
worst; using this algorithm, nearly 22 percent of the time a supernode is unplugged for greater than 80 percent of its session. The Uptime algorithm with a
threshold of 1 hour performs much better, but still not as well as Random. In
other words, it is safer to choose randomly from nodes that are online than to
select the node that has been up the longest. Further analysis of the data indicates that the reason for this behavior is that a small number of nodes are online
for long periods of time, but alternate between a plugged in and unplugged state
during that time. The Uptime algorithm favors these nodes, but the Random
algorithm does not select them. Improvements to the Uptime algorithm, such
as enabling a node to demote itself once its battery drops below a certain level,
yield better performance. However, the Uptime algorithm with these battery-
aware improvements still does not match the performance of the straightforward
Battery algorithm.

Though the Battery algorithm is the clear choice for minimizing battery spent
by supernodes, the potential concern is that too few nodes will ultimately promote themselves and the system maintenance tasks will be neglected. Figure 5
considers the ratio of supernodes to non-supernodes in the network. It plots the
CDF of the percentage of time a given ratio of supernodes is seen in the network.

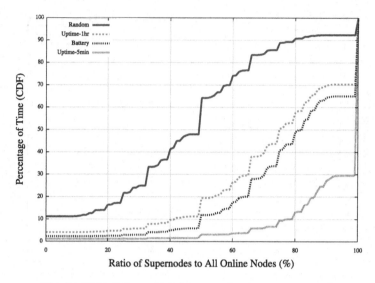

Fig. 5. CDF of the ratio of supernodes to non-supernodes

The Uptime algorithm with a 5-minute threshold performs best. Using this algorithm the probability with which fewer than 80 percent of the online nodes will carry supernode status is just over 10 percent, which means that nearly 80 percent of the network carries supernode status nearly 90 percent of the time. This ratio is a bit extreme; ideally, the number of supernodes should be just large enough to handle the burden of maintaining the network.

In the case of the Battery algorithm, only a small percentage of the time, less than 3 percent, are there no supernodes in the network. In fact, over 90 percent of the time there is at least a 1-to-1 ratio of supernodes to non-supernodes. This demonstrates that, even using a battery-conservative algorithm, a significant number of laptops can contribute to the system at low cost.

We also note that we ran our experiments using a Battery algorithm with a threshold of 90 percent and a Battery algorithm that used no threshold—it simply promoted a node when it was plugged in and demoted a node if it unplugged. The only metric where the threshold had a noticeable impact was the ratio of supernodes metric. The 90 percent algorithm performed slightly worse and the no threshold algorithm performed slightly better. This suggests that it may be useful to use threshold as a parameter to tune the supernode ratio to meet the demands of a given application.

Our final experiment considers the impact of the supernode selection algorithm on the churn rate of the network. Figure 6 illustrates the length of the time a node typically serves as supernode. It plots the CDF of the length of time between the promotion of a supernode and the demotion of the same supernode. The Uptime algorithm with a threshold of 1 hour performs best; roughly 35 percent of the sessions are shorter than an hour. In the Battery case, only 55

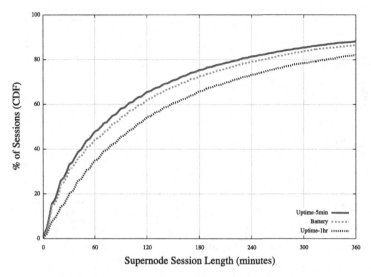

Fig. 6. CDF of the length of the session for a supernode

percent of sessions exceed the 1-hour mark. As we observed in Figure 4, the behavior of the Uptime algorithm is such that a few long-running nodes are selected as supernodes, but are unplugged and plugged back in several times during the session. Therefore, the churn rate is lower, but the battery used during the session is potentially detrimental to the node. Further, the improved churn rate may not be sufficiently significant to warrant the risk.

We investigated further to determine the percentage of the battery remaining at recharge for the long-running supernodes. For each node that transitioned from an unplugged to plugged-in state more than once during a single session, we record the percentage of the battery remaining each time the laptop is plugged in. In some cases, the battery gets as low as 3 percent, with a mean of 71 percent and a median of 80 percent. Though those nodes that only unplug briefly would presumably not be impacted by any additional battery devoted to overlay maintenance, there are a number of cases where additional battery usage would likely impact the user. The conservative, battery-aware approach yields a slightly higher churn rate, but ensures that the battery life of the device is not impacted and produces acceptable supernode-to-non-supernode ratios.

4.4   Additional Observations

We also considered an algorithm that uses *global knowledge* of the battery and uptime characteristics of all online nodes to select supernodes such that a ratio of 1 supernode to 4 non-supernodes is maintained. The intuition behind this algorithm is that the *local-knowledge* Uptime and Battery algorithms described above select more supernodes than necessary (see Figure 5). By maintaining a fixed ratio, fewer nodes will be promoted to supernode status and, as a result, fewer nodes will spend battery on supernode duties.

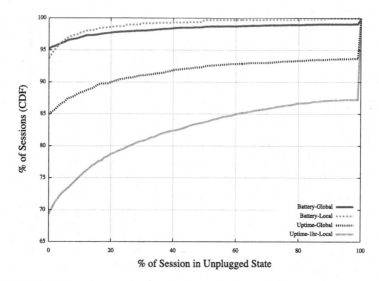

Fig. 7. CDF of the percentage of time that a supernode is not plugged in using a global-knowledge algorithm

To elect a new supernode, the global-knowledge algorithm chooses the online node with the highest battery, for the Battery algorithm, or longest uptime, for the Uptime algorithm. Once a node becomes a supernode, it remains so until it goes offline. Clearly, this algorithm requires more overhead since global state must be collected before any change to the network topology.

Figure 7 considers the amount of time a supernode spends on battery power. It plots the CDF of the percentage of time a supernode spends in an unplugged state for both the global-knowledge and local-knowledge Battery and Uptime algorithms. Despite the increased complexity of the global algorithm, the local Battery algorithm performs best overall. The global Uptime algorithm does perform significantly better than the local Uptime algorithm, because the ratio of supernodes to non-supernodes is lower. However, it is clearly advantageous to integrate battery characteristics into the supernode selection algorithm.

4.5   Discussion

The most significant result of our study is that a large portion of the laptop users we have observed can participate in P2P overlay maintenance and construction without sacrificing any of their battery. Additionally, the top-performing battery-aware algorithm is a straightforward algorithm that uses local knowledge to determine whether a node should choose to promote itself to supernode status. These results demonstrate significant potential to support collaborative applications in mobile environments where the participating nodes are also responsible for the maintenance of the system.

This work introduces a number of additional questions we would like to further explore. First, our current data set does not enable us to quantify the negative impact of promoting to supernode status those nodes which are running on battery. In other words, we cannot quantify how much battery a node would devote to its supernode duties, nor can we determine the impact on the overall lifetime of the device. Our results indicate that even our extremely conservative approach performs well. However, we plan to explore less conservative algorithms that *predict* how much battery a node will have to devote to the system as a whole, for example using prediction strategies similar to those proposed by Mickens and Noble [16].

We also plan to evaluate the performance of our strategy in the context of a real application. In particular, we would like to implement our algorithm in the context of a collaborative data gathering application that enables mobile nodes to share information they have witnessed with other interested parties.

5   Related Work

This work is the first, to our knowledge, that uses real traces to analyze a battery-aware algorithm for building a P2P infrastructure to support collaborative applications. Our primary goal is to bridge the gap between studies of battery usage and studies that use purely synthetic data to analyze the performance of P2P algorithms for mobile environments.

The goal of the Hybrid Chord Protocol (HCP) [22] is to enable resource-constrained nodes to participate in P2P networks. Their approach is to build a structured P2P network that differentiates between *static* and *temporary* nodes. Resource-plentiful static nodes then take on the bulk of the network maintenance overhead. Unlike our work, this work does not consider battery as a metric for differentiating between nodes. Our analysis, based on real data, provides additional insight into how battery impacts the behavior of *temporary* nodes. An interesting extension of our work would be to investigate how our battery-aware metrics could be integrated into HCP.

Approaches such as Ekta [17] and the approach proposed by Landsiedel, Gotz, and Wehrle [12] are also related to our work. Both projects address the problems associated with building distributed hash tables in mobile ad-hoc networks, but neither directly addresses the challenge of dealing with the limited battery lifetime of the mobile nodes. The body of work on sensor networks and disruption tolerant networks (DTNs) is also related to our work, and much of this work focuses on energy constraints. For example Jun et al. [9] consider power management in DTNs and Span [4] proposes an energy-efficient algorithm for overlay maintenance in ad hoc wireless networks. However, these approaches are exclusively designed for a MANET environment. We take a different view by considering the real usage patterns of laptop users.

There is a broad body of work that considers overlay maintenance and supernode selection for P2P applications. Lo et al. [14], compare several algorithms for scalably selecting supernodes in P2P networks and Garces-Erice et al. [6] investigate hierarchical DHTs. However, this work does not consider performance in the context of real usage patterns. Stutzbach and Rejaie [20] consider the impact of churn by analyzing usage data for several existing P2P networks. However, this work, as well as the work of Lo et al., is targeted toward non-battery powered, standard desktop computers. It does not consider how to integrate battery as a metric for overlay maintenance.

Several studies have attempted to capture usage patterns of mobile users. Kim and Kotz [10] investigate ways in which to model user mobility based on traces of user visits to a set of access points. Similarly, Song and Kotz [19] use realistic traces to simulate several opportunistic routing algorithms. In both of these cases, the goal is to investigate mobility patterns of users, not battery usage patterns. In fact, the trace data collected for the studies is collected via an access point and does not contain battery usage data.

There have been a few studies that specifically collect traces of battery usage. The study conducted by McNett and Voelker [15] collects mobility and battery data from a set of PDA devices given to a class of college freshmen. However, the results of the study again focus on mobility of the users, not their battery usage. MyExperience [5] more carefully considers battery usage of mobile phone users, but does not address the impact with respect to building systems.

6   Conclusion

In this work, we investigate the impact of battery life on the infrastructure to support collaborative applications. We identify the unique characteristics of laptop users by analyzing data collected by 41 users over a period of 7 months. Our results suggest that laptop users often behave similar to desktop users—staying online and plugged in to a power outlet for long periods of time—but also demonstrate periods of running on battery power or staying online for short stretches. We then evaluate a conservative, battery-aware alternative to the Gnutella ultrapeer selection algorithm. The key element of our approach is the selection of battery-plentiful supernodes that can bear the brunt of the system maintenance and overhead. Our results indicate that, using this algorithm, battery-powered nodes sacrifice little or none of their limited battery resources for the sake of overlay construction and maintenance. These results show great promise for existing collaborative applications as well as new applications, such as collaborative data gathering, that rely upon battery-powered devices.

Acknowledgments

We would like to thank Mark Corner, Nilanjan Banerjee, Ahmad Rahmati, and Lin Zhong for many prior discussions of adaptive energy management and for their collaboration in the collection of the empirical data. We would also like to thank Nitin Ramamurthy for his help with developing and deploying the data collection software. We would like to thank Karlo Berket for this comments on early drafts of the work. We would also like to thank all of the participants of our study. This work was supported by NSF grant number CNS-0724027.

References

1. Apple, http://www.apple.com/iphone/
2. Banerjee, N., Rahmati, A., Corner, M.D., Rollins, S., Zhong, L.: Users and batteries: Interactions and adaptive energy management in mobile systems. In: Krumm, J., Abowd, G.D., Seneviratne, A., Strang, T. (eds.) UbiComp 2007. LNCS, vol. 4717, pp. 217–234. Springer, Heidelberg (2007)
3. Burke, J., Estrin, D., Hansen, M., Parker, A., Ramanathan, N., Reddy, S., Srivastava, M.B.: Paticipatory sensing. In: World Sensor Web Workshop, Boulder, Colorado, USA (October 2006)
4. Chen, B., Jamieson, K., Balakrishnan, H., Morris, R.: Span: an energy-efficient coordination algorithm for topology maintenance in ad hoc wireless networks. Wirel. Netw. 8(5), 481–494 (2002)
5. Froehlich, J., Chen, M.: MyExperience: A system for in situ tracing and capturing of user feedback on mobile phones. In: Proc. Int. Conf. Mobile Systems, Applications, and Services (MobiSys) (June 2007)
6. Garces-Erce, L., Biersack, E., Felber, P., Ross, K.W., Urvoy-Keller, G.: Hierarchical peer-to-peer systems. In: Euro-Par 2003, Klagenfurt, Austria (2003)
7. Google, http://code.google.com/android/
8. Inside Higher Ed. Students 'evolving' use of technology (September 2007), http://www.insidehighered.com/news/2007/09/17/it
9. Jun, H., Zhao, W., Ammar, M.H., Zegura, E.W., Lee, C.: Trading latency for energy in densely deployed wireless ad hoc networks using message ferrying. Ad Hoc Netw., 5(4), 444–461 (2007)
10. Kim, M., Kotz, D.: Modeling users mobility among wifi access points. In: WiT-MeMo 2005: Papers presented at the 2005 workshop on Wireless traffic measurements and modeling, Berkeley, CA, USA, pp. 19–24. USENIX Association (2005)
11. Kotz, D., Essien, K.: Analysis of a campus-wide wireless network. Wirel. Netw. 11(1-2), 115–133 (2005)
12. Landsiedel, O., Götz, S., Wehrle, K.: A churn and mobility resistant approach for dhts. In: MobiShare 2006: Proceedings of the 1st international workshop on Decentralized resource sharing in mobile computing and networking, pp. 42–47. ACM, New York (2006)
13. Limewire, http://wiki.limewire.org/index.php?title=Ultrapeers
14. Lo, V., Zhou, D., Liu, Y., GauthierDickey, C., Li, J.: Scalable supernode selection in peer-to-peer overlay networks. In: HOT-P2P 2005: Proceedings of the Second International Workshop on Hot Topics in Peer-to-Peer Systems, Washington, DC, USA, pp. 18–27. IEEE Computer Society, Los Alamitos (2005)
15. McNett, M., Voelker, G.M.: Access and mobility of wireless pda users. SIGMOBILE Mob. Comput. Commun. Rev. 9(2), 40–55 (2005)
16. Mickens, J.W., Noble, B.D.: Exploiting availability prediction in distributed systems. In: NSDI 2006: Proceedings of the 3rd conference on 3rd Symposium on Networked Systems Design & Implementation, Berkeley, CA, USA, P.6. USENIX Association (2006)
17. Pucha, H., Das, S.M., Hu, Y.C.: Ekta: An efficient dht substrate for distributed applications in mobile ad hoc networks. In: WMCSA 2004: Proceedings of the Sixth IEEE Workshop on Mobile Computing Systems and Applications, Washington, DC, USA, pp. 163–173. IEEE Computer Society, Los Alamitos (2004)

18. Skype, http://www.skype.com/
19. Song, L., Kotz, D.F.: Evaluating opportunistic routing protocols with large real-
    istic contact traces. In: CHANTS 2007: Proceedings of the second workshop on
    Challenged networks CHANTS, pp. 35–42. ACM, New York (2007)
20. Stutzbach, D., Rejaie, R.: Understanding churn in peer-to-peer networks. In: IMC
    2006, Rio de Janeiro, Brazil (October 2006)
21. University of Oregon, http://engr.oregonstate.edu/students/wireless/
22. Zoels, S., Schubert, S., Kellerer, W., Despotovic, Z.: Hybrid DHT design for mobile
    environments. In: Joseph, S., Despotovic, Z., Moro, G., Bergamaschi, S. (eds.)
    AP2PC 2006. LNCS, vol. 4461, pp. 19–30. Springer, Heidelberg (2008)

Collaborative Graphic Rendering for Improving Visual Experience

Xiaoxin Wu and Guodong Pei

Intel China Research Center Ltd, Beijing, China
{xiaoxin.wu,guodong.pei}@intel.com

Abstract. Handheld devices such as UMPC, though convenient, bear weakness of size constraint for display. To mitigate such a problem and enhance user experience for owners of small devices, in this paper we design a collaborative rendering platform. When running game graphic applications at a handheld, the generated OpenGL graphic commands are intercepted and then delivered to a device with a larger display. The graphics are rendered and displayed at that device. The performance of the collaborative rendering platform is determined by graphic computing resources and network bandwidth. Analysis and simulation prove that other than providing a better display, the collaborative system can improve game experience also by increasing frame rates. In particular, at a low computing cost, a further collaboration between GPUs of collaborators can improve frame rate by eliminating the negative impact from network delay on applications that require GPU feedback.

1   Introduction

Collaborative computing accomplishes tasks that may be difficult or even impossible for individual device to handle, by jointly utilizing resources such as computing components [1,2], storage [3,4], and services [5,6] provided by collaborative parties. As a typical collaborative computing case, Grid Computing [7] has been widely investigated and implemented for different applications. Grids are built up by a group of network-connected servers, providing computing services and data services. To support user mobility and more dynamic grid membership, wireless grid computing [8] has been proposed, where wireless networks are used for connection among grid members for convenience.

Handheld computing devices such as UMPC are becoming popular. Compared to larger devices, e.g., laptops, UMPC has comparable CPU computing capability and same comunication interfaces including wireless communication interfaces for WiFi and Bluetooth. Yet it is much easier to carry a UMPC because it is only $1/5$ of the size of a laptop and weights much lighter. A shortcoming of handheld devices, however, is that the small-sized body may result in a worse user experience. In particular, as UMPC has a much smaller display, for applications such as game and video that require good visual effect, it can not bring users as much joy as a laptop does. In addition, UMPC generally does not have strong display card or GPU. It then may not process complicated graphic calculations that are required for, e.g., $3D$ graphic applications at all.

E. Bertino and J.B.D. Joshi (Eds.): CollaborateCom 2008, LNICST 10, pp. 609–622, 2009.
© ICST Institute for Computer Sciences, Social-Informatics and Telecommunications Engineering 2009

We apply the concept of collaborative computing and build small-sized grids to enhance visual experience of handheld users. Closely located collaborative parties, e.g., a UMPC and a laptop, are connected by networks so that graphic or video results generated at UMPC can be shown at the laptop's display. The network can be either wired (e.g., cable or USB) so that a high bandwidth, reliable communication is applicable, or wireless (e.g., WLAN, UWB, etc.), which supports mobility and convenient usage models. Since OpenGL [9] is a strong and well established graphic tool for generating pictures with sophisticated visual effect (For example, it creates $3D$ graphics in computer games and virtual life), we investigate how to display OpenGL games through collaborative systems and design a platform that supports sharing of displays and GPUs among collaborative parties.

Such a collaborative display can be implemented at different layers. It can be implemented at a very high layer, where the display side does almost everything including game execution. The UMPC then works only as a user interface for game operation inputs. Although the approach can maximumly free UMPC and fully utilize the computing resources including both CPU and GPU from its collaborator, it requires that the collaborative parties have exactly the same game environment. This means the display side has to be very powerful and load all the games that a UMPC user may play with. Therefore, the solution lacks flexibility and scalability, and is less practical. On the other hand, the collaboration can also be done at a very low layer. The UMPC executes the games, renders the graphic, and generates low-layer graphic elements (e.g., pixels, color units). It then sends the elements to its collaborator where graphics can be reconstructed. The display side only needs the computing capability for graphic generation (probably with a graphic card installed) and networking interface. The drawback for this approach is that the bandwidth requirement for delivering graphic results from UMPC to the display side is too high. This limits the use of wireless collaboration because it may jam the wireless link, which itself is a scarce resource that has to be shared with a lot of other users. Another drawback of the approach is regarding to power. Because the UMPC has to go through the entire graphic display process and transmit a large amount of data, the load is too heavy and it may soon run out of battery.

To address the problems in both of the above approaches, we propose collaboration at a relatively middle layer. In particular, we "outsource" the display role to a stronger device by first intercepting OpenGL calls for graphic rendering and then sending these calls to that device, where OpenGL is supported so that graphics can be rendered and displayed. Other than obtaining, generally, a much larger display, such a collaboration may also help to improve game performance in terms of frame rate if good sets of computing resources and network is applied.

Related work of rendering graphics by intercepting graphic commands can be found in [10,11,12,13]. Other than building a real game remote rendering system, in this work we design mechanisms for performance improvement and develop analysis model that can be used as platform design guide. In summary, our major contributions are summarized as follows:

– We apply the concept of collaborative computing to enhance visual experience for users of small devices. We design and implement a collaborative rendering platform that intercepts and transmits OpenGL calls, so that any OpenGL based graphic applications executed at a device can be rendered and displayed at other destined devices. The platform is flexible and supports usage models such as multi-view games and large-scale display wall.

- We develop mathematical models for analyzing system performance of different settings, to theoretically evaluate the gain of collaborative system. We conduct extensive experiments and present detailed data from real case study as well.
- Based on analysis and simulation study we identify the potential performance bottlenecks for the collaborative rendering platform, and determine the collaborative settings that may improve game performance. To eliminate the negative impact of slow network on games with GPU feedback requirement, we design a mechanism that utilizes extra GPU resources to reach a desired frame rate at a balanced communication and computation cost.

The rest of the paper is organized as follows. In Section 2 we present platform architecture and a few performance improvement mechanisms. In Section 3 we build mathematical model to analyze game improvement through the collaborative systems. In Section 4 we show experimental results and data analysis. We conclude in Section 5.

2 Collaborative Graphic Rendering Design

2.1 Architecture

A collaborative rendering system is built up by client and server(s), plus the network connecting them. Generally, the client has a small display and probably, a weaker GPU. A server, on the other hand, should have a larger display and a stronger GPU. When executing OpenGL graphic applications such as games over the collaborative rendering system, the client executes the games by itself and generates the OpenGL commands for game graphics. It then sends the OpenGL commands to the server. Installed with OpenGL environment, the server can render the graphics by executing the received OpenGL commands and display. Since transmitting OpenGL commands requires a much less bandwidth than transmitting graphic elements, the requirement for network is less stringent. Either high-speed cable network or low-bandwidth WLAN (802.11g) can be used for system connectivity. In this platform TCP is used as the transport layer for communication reliability.

The collaborative rendering architecture is shown in Fig. 1. The key function block is the OpenGL Command Intercepter block at the client. It gets all the graphic rendering commands and sends them to the server. When graphics have to be rendered at multiple displays, this function block also determines which of the OpenGL command streams will be sent, and to which servers the different streams should be sent. For example, for a multi-view game, the OpenGL Command Intercepter block finds the OpenGL commands for a particular view and then sends the commands regarding to that view to a destined server. By doing so, different views will be shown on different displays for an impressive game experience.

2.2 Potential Performance Bottlenecks

The most important criteria for game performance is frame rate, or the number of frames per second (FPS). In the collaborative rendering platform, frame rate depends on the

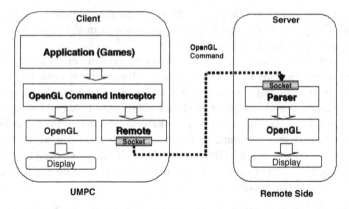

Fig. 1. Collaborative rendering system architecture

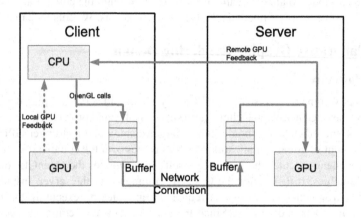

Fig. 2. Remote rendering flow

performance of a few components. As shown in Fig. 2, the remote rendering may involve CPU at client, GPU at server, and network connecting them. It may also involve GPU at client side, depending on how to generate GPU feedback that is required for game computing. The dash lines in the figure illustrates a scenario that the local GPU generates some of GPU results and sends the results to the local CPU. The reason for doing this will be explained in 2.3.

Here we summarize in more details on how the capability of above mentioned components may slow down the game as follows.

– A slow CPU at the client will slow down the game. This is obvious because it will take longer time to execute the game and generate OpenGL commands.
– A slow GPU at the server will slow down the game. This is because a slow GUP will cause the buffer at the server to be filled very soon. Consequently, the buffer at the client will be full as well. In our design, when client buffer is full, an interrupt has to be sent to the CPU so that no new commands will be generated.

- A slow network will slow down the game. A slow network will result a filled buffer at the client side. No more frames are generated until some of generated OpenGL calls are delivered to the server.

To speed up games running over the collaborative rendering platform, a strong CPU at the client, a high-performance GPU at the server, and a good network connection are needed. In case when system settings and network can not be changed, other techniques can be developed to most efficiently utilize the available resources for obtaining the best game experience.

2.3   Improve Game Performance

Game FPS can be improved by reducing the bandwidth requirement for delivering OpenGL calls, and therefore reducing the communication delay over the network. FPS can also be improved by program optimization, and by selectively using the available computing resources at client and server to minimize the overall frame generation time that consists of communication and computing delay.

Reducing Bandwidth Requirement. To reduce the impact of communication delay, a straightforward solution is to reduce the data amount required to be transmitted for every game frame. The techniques adopted in the collaborative rendering platform are as follows:

- *Object Caching.* To reduce the data amount transmitted from client to server during a game, objects (most time an object is a texture) that will be used in the game will be transmitted from the client to the server at the game setup stage. The server will cache the objects, and sync with the client through agreed object index. Later during the game when a specific object is called by an OpenGL command, the object itself will not be delivered to the server. Instead, an object index number is transmitted. The server then can render the graphics by calling the correct object based on the received number. As in our platform, objects are delivered and cached at the server at game set-up stage, during the game there is no object delivery. The bandwidth for collaborative rendering during the game then can be significantly reduced.
- *Command Labelling.* Index is also used for indicating commands (including parameters) that have been transmitted in the previous frame(s). The client checks whether any command has been transmitted previously. If so, it will transmit an index number for that command. Because there are not many types of OpenGL commands, the index requires only a few bits. Transmitting command index can result in a much smaller load for the network. To further reduce the bandwidth requirement, sophisticated data compression technique such as Huffman code can be used for index compression. The compression gain, however, will be traded off by the increased computing load and the corresponding larger delay.

Program Optimization. We use multi-threaded game computing in the collaborative OpenGL rendering platform to reduce the impact of communication overhead. The OPenGL commands are generated at the client and then sent to the server. If a single thread is used and OpenGL command interception and delivery are executed in a series manner, before calculating further game operations, the game engine will wait until the delivery for previous command finishes. This will decrease the frame rate. In the multi-thread platform, we add a thread for command delivery, so that the game engine will continue calculation while the previous results are delivered to the server. This program optimization speeds up the overall process, and increases the frame rate for a better game view.

GPU Collaboration for Computing and Communication Resource Optimization.
In most games, CPU has to take some of the previous GPU results for future frame generation. In the collaborative rendering platform, GPU data required for game calculation has to be generated at server GPU and sent back from the server to the client. The corresponding delay on feedback transmission will cause significant performance degradation in particular when a large amount of feedback is required, because the computation gain obtained at GPU has been offset by the communication loss at the network. The longer the network delay is, the worse the performance is.

To solve this problem, we propose partially utilizing GPU on the client side, to locally generate the data required for client CPU. The results generated at the server GPU then do not have to be sent back to the client side. This solution is also called GPU collaboration, as server GPU and client GPU work together to resolve the problem.

In the GPU collaboration, as the first step, we identify the OpenGL calls that require feedback from GPU, and test how frequent these calls are generated in the game. In the typical car racing game Torcs, we identify five OpenGL calls that have to use previous GPU results. We further identify that three of these commands are only needed at the beginning of the game, and will not have much impact on game performance. For the rest of two, one command is especially used for error correction which seldom happens and can be neglected. Then for only one of these commands the client GPU has to execute the related commands to generate the required feedback data. Compared to the entire game, such a calculation load is small. In the GPU collaboration the client GPU will not be a bottleneck for game performance. As the negative impact from feedback delay has been removed, the frame rate can be significantly increased.

3   Frame Rate Analysis: Mathematical Models

For analysis tractability, we assume that each game frame consists of n OpenGL calls, and for each of these calls, the CPU computing time is the same, which is denoted as T_{cpu}. We further assume that the GPU rendering time for each call at either client side or server side is the same. In particular, for each of the calls, the GPU rendering time at the client is denoted as T_{gpu1}, and the GPU rendering time at the server is denoted as T_{gpu2}. In general, as server has a stronger GPU, $T_{gpu2} < T_{gpu1}$.

We assume that the processing time for CPU to fetch data (e.g., the feedback from GPU) from the GPU located at the same device can be neglected. The CPU generates a new OpenGL commands when it receives the required feedback information. In the case that no feedback is required, the CPU generates a new OpenGL command if the previous generated command has been executed, i.e., transmitted from client to server. For analysis simplicity, we assume that the buffer depth at both of the client and server is zero. As when rendering graphics, CPU and GPU work in a pipeline manner, the component that takes a longer time to accomplish its task is the performance bottleneck.

Denote T_{round} as the average round trip delay between the client and the server. Let t_1 be the average frame interval when game is executed at client itself, t_2 be the average frame interval when game is rendered through the collaborative rendering platform, and t_3 be the average frame interval when game is rendered through the collaborative rendering platform where GPU collaboration is applied (i.e., local GPU is partially on for generating feedback data for client CPU). The corresponding frame rates for these three settings then are $1/t_1$, $1/t_2$, and $1/t_3$. Denote p as the probability that in a game when generating the next OpenGL command, the CPU needs GPU feedback.

3.1 Basic Collaborative Rendering Platform

We calculate when client and server have different settings (i.e., CPU and GPU), the average frame interval in the local graphic rendering system and the collaborative rendering platform.

We first neglect the network factor (e.g., we assume a high speed network is in use). When client CPU is the bottleneck for game frame generation, i.e., when $T_{cpu} > T_{gpu1}$ and $T_{cpu} > T_{gpu2}$,

$$t_1 = ((1-p)T_{cpu} + p(T_{cpu} + T_{gpu1})) \times n, \tag{1}$$
$$t_2 = ((1-p)T_{cpu} + p(T_{cpu} + T_{round} + T_{gpu2})) \times n.$$

For this case, the collaborative rendering platform brings computation gain in frame generation when $t_1 > t_2$, i.e., when $T_{gpu1} > T_{round} + T_{gpu2}$.

When client GPU is the performance bottleneck for rendering graphics locally at the client, i.e., $T_{cpu} < T_{gpu1}$, and client CPU is the performance bottleneck for rendering graphics through the collaborative rendering platform, i.e., $T_{cpu} > T_{gpu2}$,

$$t_1 = ((1-p)T_{gpu1} + p(T_{cpu} + T_{gpu1})) \times n, \tag{2}$$
$$t_2 = ((1-p)T_{cpu} + p(T_{cpu} + T_{round} + T_{gpu2})) \times n.$$

For this case, the collaborative rendering platform brings performance gain when $T_{gpu1} > (1-p)T_{cpu} + p(T_{round} + T_{gpu2})$.

When client GPU is the performance bottleneck for rendering graphics locally, i.e., $T_{cpu} < T_{gpu1}$, and server GPU is the performance bottleneck for rendering over the collaborative rendering platform, i.e., $T_{cpu} < T_{gpu1}$,

$$t_1 = ((1-p)T_{gpu1} + p(T_{cpu} + T_{gpu1})) \times n, \tag{3}$$
$$t_2 = ((1-p)T_{gpu2} + p(T_{cpu} + T_{round} + T_{gpu2})) \times n.$$

For this case, remote rendering platform brings computation gain only when $T_{gpu1} > T_{gpu2} + pT_{round}$.

For all of the above cases, if we consider a slow network and communication round trip time is the bottleneck, i.e., if $T_{round} > max\{T_{cpu}, T_{gpu2}\}$,

$$t_2 = ((1-p)T_{round} + p(T_{cpu} + T_{round} + T_{gpu2})) \times n. \tag{4}$$

3.2   Collaboration with Local GPU Partially on

When GPU feedback is required for CPU to generate OpenGL commands, GPU at the client can be partially on and collaborate with the GPU at the server to improve the game performance. If CPU is the performance bottleneck, the average frame interval for collaborative system, t_3, can be calculated as

$$t_3 = ((1 - p)T_{cpu} + p(T_{cpu} + T_{gpu1})) \times n. \tag{5}$$

If the server GPU is the bottleneck,

$$t_3 = ((1 - p)T_{gpu2} + max\{p(T_{cpu} + T_{gpu1}), pT_{gpu2}\}) \times n \tag{6}$$
$$= ((1 - p)T_{gpu2} + p(T_{cpu} + T_{gpu1})) \times n.$$

If the communication delay is the bottleneck,

$$t_3 = ((1 - p)T_{round} + max\{p(T_{cpu} + T_{gpu1}), pT_{round}\}) \times n. \tag{7}$$

4   Performance Evaluation

4.1   Numerical Results

Based on the above analysis, we evaluate the frame rate per second (FPS) increase in the collaborative rendering system. We use the frame increase ratio, i.e., the ratio between the FPS obtained in a collaborative system and the FPS obtained when client executes the game individually for performance gain evaluation. We set the average CPU computing time for generating an OpenGL call as the basic unit, i.e., $T_{cpu} = 1$. We assume the GPU at server is stronger than that at client, and $T_{gpu1} = 5T_{gpu2}$. For round trip delay, we use $T_{round} = 10T_{cpu}$ for a shorter round trip delay, and $T_{round} = 20T_{cpu}$ for a longer one. We assume the average number of OpenGL commands for generating a frame is 10^4, and the probability that an OpenGL command generation depends on GPU feedback, p, is 1.0×10^{-5}.

Figure 3 shows the performance gain in the collaborative rendering system. The x-axis indicates the computing speed of client CPU referred to client GPU. The collaboration brings computation gain only when the y-axis, i.e., the frame increase ratio has a value greater than 1. Basically, the collaborative rendering system helps to improve FPS gain when the client GPU becomes computation bottleneck, i.e, when $T_{gpu1} > T_{cpu}$. In the system where the client GPU is off, the collaborative system brings performance gain when compared to the client GPU, the client CPU is fast enough. The gain from a system with a longer round trip delay is less than that with a shorter one. When applying GPU collaboration and have client GPU partially on, the FPS in the collaborative system is at least the same as that obtained on a single device. GPU collaboration helps to achieve a much better gain especially when CPU gets stronger. However, when CPU is strong enough and server GPU becomes the bottle neck (i.e, $T_{gpu2} > T_{cpu}$), speeding CPU no longer results in much more gain.

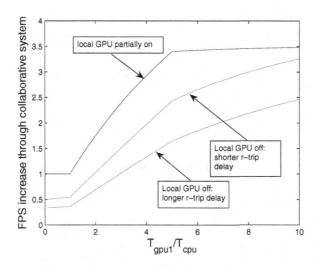

Fig. 3. FPS improvement through collaborative system

4.2   Measurement: Tocrs over Collaborative Rendering Platform

Unless otherwise specified, we use Sony UMPC as the client and $T61p$ laptop as the server in the collaborative rendering system. On UMPC, CPU is Intel core (TM)solo $u1500@1.33GHZ$. Graphic card is Intel 945 card. The OpenGL version is mesa library 6.5. $T61p$ has an Intel core 2 Due $L7700$ CPU, and a Graphic card NVIDIA Quadro FX $570M$. The OPenGL version on $T61$ is 7.5. A car racing game Torcs is loaded and executed at UMPC. The game pictures are rendered at $T61$ and shown on its larger display. In the experiment we only measure the game that a single view has been displayed at the server. We use 100Mb/s wired network for connection between client and server.

Figure 4 shows FPS statistics under different system scenarios. Their correspondent average FPS over a time period is shown in Figure 5.

Figure 4 (a) shows the FPS when game runs locally on UMPC. This reference performance is used to find out whether collaborative rendering can help to improve game performance. When exporting OpenGL commands to a stronger GPU for rendering the graphics, as shown in Figure 4 (b), if p, the probability that generating an OpenGL command requires feedback from GPU, is a small value, the performance for the collaborative rendering platform is better. Compared to the reference case, collaborative rendering can help to improve the game performance because the gain of high-speed rendering at the server (thanks to its stronger GPU) overwhelms the lost on the delay caused by GPU feedback. However, the obtained FPS is bursty. When p increases, as shown in Figure 4 (c), the collaborative rendering platform results in a very poor performance, because the round trip delay at each of feedback from the server GPU to the client CPU will significantly delay the frame generation.

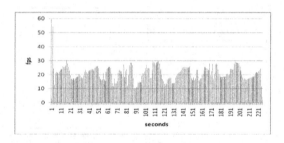

(a) Local Rendering

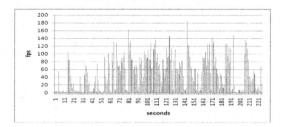

(b) Remote rendering ($p = 0.0002$)

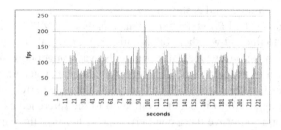

(c) Remote rendering ($p = 0.0016$)

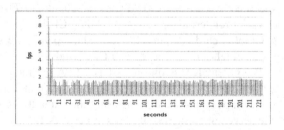

(d) Remote rendering with GPU collaboration

Fig. 4. Frame rate per second under cases of a)game rendered locally, b)game rendered remotely with a low feedback probability, c)game rendered remotely with a high feedback probability, and d)game rendered remotely with GPU collaboration

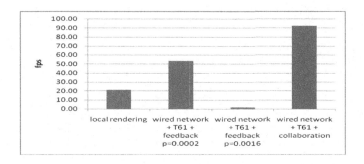

Fig. 5. Average frame rate for different cases

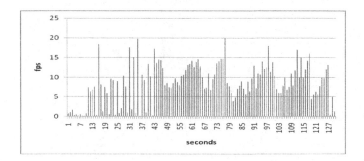

Fig. 6. FPS when having a slower network

To deal with the problem observed from Figure 4 (c), we use our proposed GPU collaboration scheme and turn on the GPU at the client as well, to calculate the graphic results that are required by OpenGL command generations. As shown in Figure 4 (d), through GPU collaboration the average frame rate is much higher than the reference case. The reason is that no feedback from the server is needed. Therefore, the negative impact from the feedback delay has been removed. The load on client GPU, on the other hand, is small so that it will not take much time for it to accomplish its assignment. Actually in this setting the CPU at the client is the bottleneck. Another observation is that as there is no feedback from remote side, the FPS statistics are smooth and not bursty at all.

Figure 6 shows when wireless network (802.11g) has been used instead of wired network, the FPS will be low even when client GPU is partially on. Compared to the system with a wired network, the average FPS has decreased to 8.57, a significant decrease compared to the average FPS 92.36 in the wired system. The results indicate that though wireless network does have advantages of convenience, its limited bandwidth slows down the frame generation.

Figure 7 shows when server has a relatively weaker GPU, how the collaborative rendering performance suffers. When using $T43$ laptop that has a slower GPU than $T61$, the average FPS decreases to 55.5.

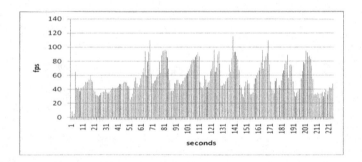

Fig. 7. FPS when having a weaker server

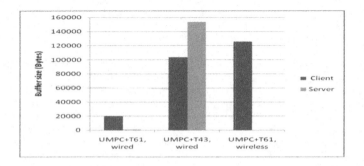

Fig. 8. Buffer size for different settings

Finally, we measure the buffered data at both client and server to further analyze the results we have obtained, thus to figure out the performance bottlenecks. As shown in Figure 8, in the setting when a UMPC collaborates with a T61, the buffered data at both client and server sides is not much. This indicates that neither network nor server is the performance bottleneck. When the computing capability at the client increases, a FPS improvement in the system should be expected. Not shown in the paper, this has been proved in our test when using T43 as a client, under which the FPS increases. The figure also shows when server has a weaker GPU (a T43 instead of a T61), there will be more buffered data at the server side. The server then is the performance bottleneck as the relatively long GPU processing time on OpenGL calls delivered to the server will make the server buffer full, which results in a full buffer at the client as well because the generated OpenGL calls from the client CPU cannot be delivered to the server. The full buffer at the client consequently impedes the frame generation. In this case, using a stronger sever can improve the game performance. When using wireless network, there is a large amount of data buffered at the client yet little data buffered at the server. This means the network should be the performance bottle neck, as for each second, only a small number of OpenGL commands can be delivered to the server. In this case, using a faster network can improve the game performance.

5   Conclusion

In this paper we design and evaluate a collaborative rendering platform, under which OpenGL graphics generated at a device can be rendered at a network-connected device with a larger display and a better GPU. Such a collaborative system can help to overcome the size limit of small devices (e.g., UMPC). Based on analysis and real system experimental results, we prove that the collaborative rendering system can improve game performance in frame rate, and identify the factors that may affect the platform performance, which may be a slow CPU at client, a slow GPU at server, and a slow network. We also find that in a game if a large amount of GPU feedback is required for game calculation, the performance will significantly degrade. To deal with this problem, we propose to partially turn on the GPU at the client to collaborate with the GPU at the server for speeding up the games. Experiment results show that the GPU collaboration can greatly improve frame rate by avoiding the impact of feedback delay. The GPU collaboration can smooth the game FPS as well.

Acknowledgement

We thank Lakshman Krisnurmathy for his guide on architecture design of remote rendering platform. We also thanks Khanh Nygeun and Zan Ding for their contribution to code development.

References

1. Abramson, D., Giddy, J., Kotler, L.: High Performance Parametric Modeling with nimrod/g: Killer Application for the Global Grid? In: Proceedings of the 14th International Parallel and Distributed Processing Symposium, IPDPS 2000 (2000)
2. Buyya, R., Abramson, D., Nimrod/G, G.J.: An architecture for a resource management and scheduling system in a global computational Grid. In: Proceedings of the International Conference on High Performance Computing in Asia–Pacific Region (2000)
3. Chervenek, A., Forster, I., Kesselman, C., Salisbury, C., Tuecke, S.: The Data Grid: Towards an Architecture for the Distributed Management and Analysis of Large Scientific Datasets. Journal of Network Computer Applications 23(3), 187–200 (2000)
4. Vazhkudai, S., Ma, X., Freeh, V., Strickland, J., Tammineedi, N., Simon, T.A., Scott, S.L.: Constructing Collaborative Desktop Storage Caches for Large Scientific Datasets. ACM Transaction on Storage, TOS (2006)
5. Georgakopoulos, D., Schuster, H., Cuchoicki, A., Baker, D.: Managing Process and Service Fusion in Virtual Enterprises. Information System, Special Issues on Information System Support for electronic Commerce 24(6), 429–456 (1999)
6. Zeng, L., Benatallah, B., Dumas, M., Kalagnanam, J., Sheng, Q.Z.: Quality Driven Web Services Composition. In: Proceedings of WWW 2003 (2003)
7. Krauter1, K., Buyya, R., Maheswaran, M.: A taxonomy and survey of grid resource management systems for distributed computing. Software–Practice and Experience 32, 135–164 (2002)
8. Ahuja, S.P., Myers, J.R.: A Survey on Wireless Grid Computing. The Journal of Supercomputing 37, 3–21 (2006)

9. OpenGL - The Industry Standard for High Performance Graphics,
   `http://www.opengl.org/`
10. Lamberti, F., Zunino, C., Sanna, A., Fiume, A., Maniezzo, M.: An accelerated remote graphics architecture for PDAS. In: Proceedings of the Eighth international Conference on 3D Web Technology (2003)
11. Yang, S.J., Nieh, J., Selsky, M., Tiwari, N.: The Performance of Remote Display Mechanisms for Thin-Client Computing. In: Proceedings of the General Track of the Annual Conference on USENIX Annual Technical Conference (2002)
12. Humphreys, G., Houston, M., Ng, R., Frank, R., Ahern, S., Kirchner, P.D., Klosowski, J.T.: Chromium: a stream-processing framework for interactive rendering on clusters. In: Proceedings of the 29th Annual Conference on Computer Graphics and interactive Techniques (2002)
13. Stegmaier, S., Magallón, M., Ertl, T.: A generic solution for hardware-accelerated remote visualization. In: Proceedings of the Symposium on Data Visualisation (2002)

Analytics and Management of Collaborative Intranets

Peter Géczy, Noriaki Izumi, Shotaro Akaho, and Kôiti Hasida

National Institute of Advanced Industrial Science and Technology (AIST)
Tokyo and Tsukuba, Japan

Abstract. We present analytic framework for evidence-based management, design, and engineering of collaborative intranet environments. The analytics target elucidation of essential elements of human-system interactions. Temporal segmentation of human behavior in digital environments permits identification of crucial navigational points as well as higher order abstractions. Explorations of these elements provide fertile grounds for assessment of usability and behavioral characteristics that directly translate to actionable knowledge indispensable for improvements of collaboration portals. We extrapolate the analytic findings from a case study of a large scale collaborative organizational intranet; in order to identify three crucial domains facilitating alignment between observed evidence and best management and engineering practices.

Keywords: Collaborative Intranets, Web-based Portals, Analytics, Logs.

1 Introduction

"The overwhelming majority of organizations, however, have neither a finely honed analytical capability nor a detailed plan to develop one." [1] The absence of analytics deployment in organizations has limiting consequences on operational and management efficiency. Despite significant investments in organizational information and collaborative platforms, their usability remains low [2],[3].

The key to advancing usability of organizational collaborative information systems is the alignment of natural human behavior in electronic environments with the design and engineering. Investigation of human behavior in digital spaces has been attracting significant attention from corporate sector [4]. Corporations are eagerly collecting interactive and behavioral data about their web customers. Employed predictive modelling techniques of user behavior aim at converting visitors into customers—leading to increased revenues [5],[6]. Unfortunately, the usability improvements of their internal information and collaborative systems are undervalued.

We introduce an analytic framework addressing the needs of evidence-based management and design of collaborative intranets. The framework enables detailed analytics of human-system interactions. The analytics highlight knowledge pertinent to usability improvements and identification of high priority management domains.

E. Bertino and J.B.D. Joshi (Eds.): CollaborateCom 2008, LNICST 10, pp. 623–631, 2009.
© ICST Institute for Computer Sciences, Social-Informatics and Telecommunications Engineering 2009

2   Analytics Deployment

The implementation of analytics in organizational intranets is generally a multi-stage process. Four essential stages are: data collection, cleaning, preprocessing, and analysis. The processing flow is fundamentally sequential (as illustrated in Figure 1), however, it cyclically repeats whenever new data is collected. Ideally, on-the-fly analytics would be the most desirable. This requires availability of a computing power matching the data volumes and complexity of processing. In practice, periodical processing is often implemented (e.g. data collected during daytime is processed overnight).

Data collection in organizational intranets can be managed directly by the servers. Web servers have capability to record every arriving and served request to substantial detail. The information is stored in a predefined format—facilitating automated processing. The servers, however, record both human and machine generated requests. Hence the collected data requires cleaning.

Cleaning should eliminate the machine generated traffic (e.g. automated network monitors checking responsiveness of serves, crawlers, indexers, etc.) and preserve the human generated traffic. Machine traffic is often voluminous. Cleaning may substantially reduce the data volume—easing the following processing.

Preprocessing prepares clean data for analytic processing. Server log records contain several information fields. The log records need to be parsed for individual fields. The extracted information should be suitably organized; preferably structured and databased for further analysis.

Analysis targets various explorations of human behavior in intranet environments; such as usability analysis, user profiling, collaborative filtering, etc. The analytics play a vital role in intranet management, personalization, service deployment, and business process (re-)engineering.

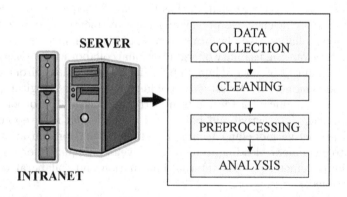

Fig. 1. Depiction of sequential intranet analytics implementation consisting of four stages: data collection, cleaning, preprocessing, and analysis

3   Analytic Framework

Human dynamics in electronic environments have temporally specific features [7]. Users exhibit periods of activity followed by longer inactivity periods. The human-web interactions can be segmented with respect to these temporal indicators. The temporal segmentation framework of human browsing behavior has been introduced in [2]. We concisely recall relevant constructs.

The page transition sequences are segmented into *sessions* and *subsequences*. The segmentation is illustratively outlined in Figure 2. The sessions represent more complex tasks undertaken by the users. They are further divided into the subtasks indicated by the subsequences. Consider the sequence of the form: $\{(p_i, d_i)\}_i$ where p_i denotes the visited page URL_i and d_i denotes a delay between the consecutive views $p_i \rightarrow p_{i+1}$. **Session** is a sequence $B = \{(p_i, d_i)\}_i$ where each $d_i \leq T_B$. **Subsequence** $S = \{(p_i, d_i)\}_i$ consists of pairs (p_i, d_i) with delays satisfying the conditions: $d_i \leq T_S$.

Pertinent issue in segmenting the human browsing interactions into sessions and subsequences is the appropriate determination of the separating delays—the values of T_B and T_S. Explorations of student web behavior revealed that their browsing sessions last on average 25.5 minutes [8]. Analysis of knowledge worker browsing interactions on the organizational intranet portal exposed longer session duration: 48.5 minutes on average [2]. The study used empirically determined minimum inter-session delay $T_B = 1\ hour$. The subsequence delay separator T_S was calculated dynamically as an average delay in the session bounded from below by 30 seconds.

Consider the following example of interactions on the organizational intranet. At the beginning, a user logins into the intranet system—subsequence 1. Successful login process will lead to a display of the initial portal page. Navigating from the opening page, a user accesses a bulletin board of an organizational interest group he/she belongs to—subsequence 2. On the bulletin board a user locates and reads the latest announcement concerning a group meeting—subsequence 3. Then he/she leaves the environment for another work-related activity.

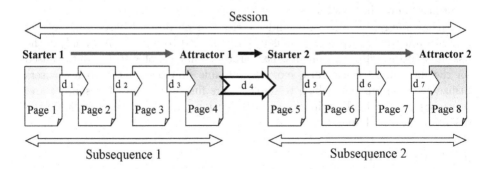

Fig. 2. Segmentation of web interactions and identification of navigation points

The example of user's interactions on an organizational intranet portal illustrates a potentially typical session consisting of three subsequences. Each subsequence corresponds to a distinct task: 1–login, 2–accessing a bulletin board, 3–locating and reading an announcement. Each subsequence exhibits relatively dynamic transitions from the initial page to the target. At the target page the user's attention is required. The attention takes time. Hence, there are longer delays recorded prior to initiating the next browsing task.

Important navigation points are the points where users initiate their browsing actions—*starters*, the resources they target—*attractors*, and the single action behaviors—*singletons*. **Starters** are the first points of subsequences or sessions with length greater than 1. **Attractors** are the last points of subsequences or sessions with length greater than 1. **Singletons** are the points of subsequences or sessions with length equal to 1.

In the formerly presented example of user interactions on the intranet portal, the *starter* of the first subsequence is the login page, and the *attractor* is the opening portal page (after successful login). Singletons outline a single action behaviors surrounded by longer delays. They generally relate to the use of hotlists, such as history or bookmarks, where users access the desired resource directly without proceeding throughout several transitions [9].

Subsequences constitute the elemental tasks and browsing segments. Users can take various navigational paths from the initial point to the target. Since the intermediate points between the starter and the attractor are only transitional, tracking the multitudes of all navigational pathways may be a waste of resources. It is more efficient to focus on the abstractions of the segments. Starter-attractor pairs, denoted as **SA elements**, are suitable abstractions of subsequences. The connecting elements of subsequences are represented by attractor-starter pairs. Formation of more complex browsing patterns can be observed from sequences of SA elements and connectors.

Segmented user behavior, into sessions and subsequences, identification of important navigation points, and higher order abstractions provide valuable information enabling analysis of collaborative intranet environments. Analytic findings often translate into actionable knowledge for managers, administrators, and designers. This enables continual improvement of the existing services and identification of the novel ones.

Various analytics, measures, and metrics can be derived based on the presented framework. In practice, it is often beneficial to explore and analyze the usability of digital environments. Exploratory analysis of web log data, based on the introduced framework, exposes valuable findings related to how users utilize the environment, which resources users find useful, which resources and processes pose difficulties in access or execution, etc. This study explores the essential statistical analytics.

4 Case Study

The investigated organizational collaborative intranet is a large-scale system implemented at The National Institute of Advanced Industrial Science and

Technology. The system is significantly complex and distributed. The web core comprises of six servers connected to the high-speed backbone in a load balanced configuration. Users access the system via local subnets with infrastructures ranging from high-speed optical to wireless.

The collaborative intranet portal incorporates a large number of resources and services in a decentralize and distributed manner. A rich spectrum of resources span across documents in various formats, multimedia, software, etc. The extensive range of implemented services support the organizational business processes; cooperation with industry, academia, and other institutes; internal collaboration; localization of resources, etc. Local networking and blogging services within the organization are also implemented. Visible web space is in the excess of 1 GB, and deep web space is considerably larger, however, it is difficult to estimate its size due to the distributed architecture and constantly changing back-end data.

The collaboration intranet portal manages considerable traffic. The peak traffic is primarily during the working hours. There are also few cyclical traffic peaks. Collected web log data by the servers is voluminous and contains details of portal utilization and users' browsing features. The web logs contain records of both human and machine generated traffic. Cleaning, preprocessing, and segmentation of human-web interactions has been presented in [2]. The resulting working data, together with the essential intranet statistics, are described in Table 1.

Table 1. Information and basic data statistics of the organizational intranet portal

Web Log Volume	~60 GB
Average Daily Volume	~54 MB
Number of Servers	6
Time Period	1 year
Log Records	315 005 952
Resources	3 015 848
Sessions	3 454 243
Unique Sessions	2 704 067
Subsequences	7 335 577
Unique Subsequences	3 547 170
Valid Subsequences	3 156 310
Unique Valid Subsequences	1 644 848
Services	855

5   Analytic Findings and Managerial Implications

Exploratory analysis of data revealed significant statistical usability pattern. Essentially all analyzed aspects of user interactions on the large-scale organizational collaborative intranet indicated long tailed characteristics. The typically observed pattern is depicted in Figure 3. It displays the access statistics of portal services.

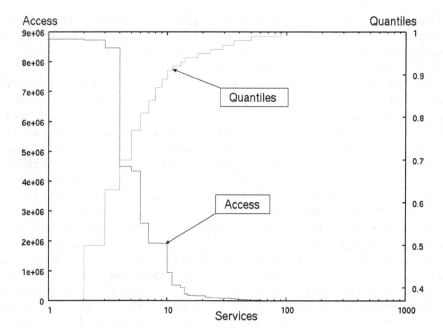

Fig. 3. Histogram and quantile characteristics of services access. X-axis is in logarithmic scale. Left y-axis refers to access histogram and right y-axis refers to quantiles.

It is noticeable that relatively few services were frequently used (note that x-axis is in a logarithmic scale, in order to visualize the head of the distribution). Only approximately ten services (out of 855) were frequently used. Over half of the services were accessed less than ten times. Top three services, that is 0.35%, accounted for 50% of use. These were: bulletin boards (containing organizational and other announcements), attendance service (recording, verifying, and altering the presence, business trip, and holiday records), and information service from human resources division (finding information about the members of the organization, such as e-mail, phone numbers, location, etc.). Bulletin boards were accessed most frequently. It indicates that users were generally interested in organizational and personal announcements.

Frequently used services should be easily accessible, highly optimized and suitably personalized. Unfortunately, majority of organizations do not pay sufficient attention to analytics, optimization, and personalization of internal web-based environments that should foster collaboration and higher working efficiency. They often use one-fit-all templates resulting in low portal usability. Following are concise highlights of further principal findings.

– **Underutilization of resources and services.** Evidence of service underutilization has been described in the former paragraphs. Analogous situation has been observed also in the case of other resources. Knowledge workers have generally utilized a small set of starters and attractors. The size of the starter and attractor sets amounted for approximately 3.84% and 9.55% of the total navigation points, respectively.

- **Few useful resources.** Number of unique single user actions—represented by singletons–have been minuscule. The unique singletons have accounted for only 1.92% of navigation points. Only about ten navigation points have been found substantially useful by users to be included in their hotlists and recurrently accessed.
- **Short attention span.** The average attention span at the target has been observed to be only approximately 6.5 minutes. This has been indicated by the detected delays between subsequences.
- **Rapid transitions.** The peak interval of subsequence duration has been between four to six seconds. During this time, the users have made four to five page transitions–on average. This implies rapid pace—approximately one second per page transition.
- **Task subdivision.** The observed peak interval of number of subsequences in session has been $< 2, 4 >$. The browsing sessions have contained, on average, three subsequences. This suggests that the users have divided their more complex browsing and interaction tasks into three simpler and less complex subtasks.
- **Pattern formation.** Knowledge workers have formed elemental and complex interaction patterns. This has been indicated by a relatively small number of frequently repetitive SA elements and connectors. Frequent repetition of elemental patterns interconnected by frequent connectors exposes formation of more complex patterns.
- **Common browsing pattern.** Smaller number of starters have repeated substantially more frequently than the adequate number of attractors. The starter-attractor frequency ratio has been approximately one-to-ten. This implies that the general browsing strategy reflected the knowledge of the starting navigation point and familiarity with the traversal pathway to the target.
- **Behavioral habituation.** Knowledge worker browsing behavior has gradually habituated. At early stages of use, the resource access has been more 'ballanced'. Users' familiarity with the environment has resulted in gradually shrinking set of frequently accessed resources. Furthermore, they have exhibited faster navigational transitions.

The management of the organizational collaborative intranet portals should inevitably take into account the presented analytic evidence. It exposes the actionable knowledge related to several crucial usability aspects. The implications of the findings extend to various managerial domains. The three essential domains to be addressed are highlighted in the following paragraphs.

Process Engineering. Organizations are increasingly transferring internal collaborative and business processes to their information platforms. Design and engineering of business and collaborative processes should be aligned with the fundamental elements of human interactions. The elements of human interactions are rarely accounted for during the design and engineering. This decreases the user working efficiency and induces the negative experience effects. It is often the case that the actual implementations of processes result in multistage extended human-system interactions. The analytic findings indicate that the users naturally divide their browsing tasks into three subtasks–on average. This implies that the extensive and prolonged processes should be re-engineered, so that they can be segmented into approximately three sub-processes. Furthermore, each stage should require less than seven minutes of human attention.

Assistance Services. Proficiency in use of organizational collaborative platforms requires practice–which can be time and resource consuming. To accelerate the learning, the users should be systematically assisted during their interactive experiences. Conversely, the extensive use and increased proficiency is linked with habituation and lack of exploratory behavior. Suitable assistance services can facilitate steeper learning curves and improved attention management. Assistance services should at least incorporate technologies such as collaborative filtering, recommendations, and localized search. The effective search enables fast location of closely relevant resources. The recommendation systems utilize the knowledge of use histories, preferences, and other analytics to offer suitable recommendations on resources and services of potential interest to the users [10]. The collaborative filtering technologies leverage the correlations among 'like-minded' users in providing assistance and recommendations [11],[12]. All these services can efficiently (re-)use the analytics.

Personalization. Different users have different interaction and browsing styles. Conventionally, the interactivity of organizational information systems with the human users has followed the one-fit-all style; possibly with exceptions of few optional adjustments. This interfacing is inadequate and often leads to underutilization. Human interactivity should be approached in a personalized manner. Personalization should be realized essentially on two levels: group and individual. The group personalization underlines the interface adjustments for a set of users with similar behavioral and/or working characteristics. The personalization on the individual level allows delivery of personalized interfaces for individual users. Personalization is closely linked with profiling. Each user, or group, should have a well formed profile incorporating the essential elements of human-system interactions. Based on the profile characteristics, the interface adjustments should be carried out adaptively and on-the-fly.

6   Conclusions

We presented the significant analytic findings of a large scale organizational collaborative intranet case study. The analysis revealed important usability and behavioral characteristics of users that translate into actionable knowledge for managers, administrators, and designers of collaborative intranet systems. The findings advocate effective deployment of appropriate system analytics as a necessary precursor for evidence-based management. The analytics provide a vital source of knowledge for decision making. Efficient collaborative intranet platforms require alignment of design, engineering, and management of the systems with usability and behavioral characteristics of users. The alignment demands covering the three high priority domains: process engineering, assistance services, and personalization. Further extensions and improvements of collaborative intranet environments can suitably utilize and build upon these three essential bases.

References

1. Davenport, T.H., Harris, J.G.: Competing on Analytics: The New Science of Winning. Harvard Business School Press, Boston (2007)
2. Géczy, P., Akaho, S., Izumi, N., Hasida, K.: Knowledge worker intranet behaviour and usability. Int. J. Business Intelligence and Data Mining 2, 447–470 (2007)
3. Huntington, P., Nicholas, D., Jamali, H.R.: Website usage metrics: A re-assessment of session data. International Journal of Information Processing and Management 44(1), 358–372 (2008)
4. Petre, M., Minocha, S., Roberts, D.: Usability beyond the website: an empirically-grounded e-commerce evaluation for the total customer experience. Behaviour and Information Technology 25, 189–203 (2006)
5. Park, Y.-H., Fader, P.S.: Modeling browsing behavior at multiple websites. Marketing Science 23, 280–303 (2004)
6. Moe, W.W.: Buying, searching, or browsing: Differentiating between online shoppers using in-store navigational clickstream. Journal of Consumer Psychology 13, 29–39 (2003)
7. Barabasi, A.-L.: The origin of bursts and heavy tails in human dynamics. Nature 435, 207–211 (2005)
8. Catledge, L., Pitkow, J.: Characterizing browsing strategies in the world wide web. Computer Networks and ISDN Systems 27, 1065–1073 (1995)
9. Thakor, M.V., Borsuk, W., Kalamas, M.: Hotlists and web browsing behavior–an empirical investigation. Journal of Business Research 57, 776–786 (2004)
10. Adomavicius, G., Tuzhilin, A.: Toward the next generation of recommender systems: A survey of the state-of-the-art and possible extensions. IEEE Transactions on Knowledge and Data Engineering 17, 734–749 (2005)
11. Symeonidis, P., Nanopoulos, A., Papadopoulos, A.N., Manolopoulos, Y.: Collaborative recommender systems: Combining effectiveness and efficiency. Expert Systems with Applications 34(4), 2995–3013 (2008)
12. Jin, R., Si, L., Zhai, C.: A study of mixture models for collaborative filtering. Information Retrieval 9, 357–382 (2006)

Mashup Model and Verification Using Mashup Processing Network

Ehtesham Zahoor, Olivier Perrin, and Claude Godart

LORIA, INRIA Nancy Grand Est Campus Scientifique
BP 239 54506 Vandoeuvre-lès-Nancy Cedex, France
{zahooreh,operrin,godart}@loria.fr

Abstract. Mashups are defined to be lightweight Web applications aggregating data from different Web services, built using ad-hoc composition and being not concerned with long term stability and robustness. In this paper we present a pattern based approach, called Mashup Processing Network (MPN). The idea is based on Event Processing Network and is supposed to facilitate the creation, modeling and the verification of mashups. MPN provides a view of how different actors interact for the mashup development namely the producer, consumer, mashup processing agent and the communication channels. It also supports modeling transformations and validations of data and offers validation of both functional and non-functional requirements, such as reliable messaging and security, that are key issues within the enterprise context. We have enriched the model with a set of processing operations and categorize them into data composition, transformation and validation categories. These processing operations can be seen as a set of patterns for facilitating the mashup development process. MPN also paves a way for realizing Mashup Oriented Architecture where mashups along with services are used as building blocks for application development.

Keywords: Mashups, Service Composition, SOA.

1 Introduction

Mashups are defined to be lightweight Web applications aggregating data from different sources such as Web services. In the literature [1,2,9,4], it has been suggested that mashup principles can be the new wave for composing Web services. In this new agile programming paradigm, component services can be assembled with very little or no programming effort, without requiring heavy orchestration techniques such as WSBPEL [7]. Moreover, freely available mashup creator tools ease the process of creating mashups by integrating content from more than one Web services and mashups can be created and published in minutes.

The mashups principles, initially targeted to end-users, can also be used within an enterprise context, called enterprise mashups, to facilitate the process of service composition within an enterprise. Enterprise mashups lack the formalizations and concepts needed to properly describe, model and validate Mashups.

E. Bertino and J.B.D. Joshi (Eds.): CollaborateCom 2008, LNICST 10, pp. 632–648, 2009.

In this paper, we present an approach for facilitating the creation, modeling and the validation of enterprise mashups, introducing the Mashup Processing Network (MPN) approach. The idea is based on Event Processing Network [6,8]. Mashup Processing Network provides a view of how different actors interact for the mashup development namely the producer, mashup processing agent, consumer and the communication channels. It also illustrates the role of mashup application, which acts both as mashup processing agent and as a data flow consumer.

The Mashup Processing Network approach supports modeling transformations and validations of data, and offers validation of both functional and non-functional requirements, such as reliable messaging, security, and fault-tolerance, that are key issues within the enterprise context [10]. We have also enriched the model with a set of processing operations and categorize them into data composition, transformation and validation categories. These processing operations can be seen as a set of patterns for facilitating the mashup development process. MPN also paves a way for realizing Mashup Oriented Architecture (MOA) where mashups along with services are used as building blocks for application development.

The rest of this paper is organized as follows. Section 2 discusses background and related work, then we will present a sample health-care scenario in Section 3 as the basis for discussing processing operations. We introduce mashup processing network in Section 4. Mashup processing operations can be classified into three categories: composition (Section 5), transformation (Section 6) and validation of data (Section 7). Section 8 models the sample scenario using the mashup model presented earlier, while we discuss implementation details in Section 9. Finally, Section 10 concludes.

2   Related Work and Motivation

Classically, a Web service is defined as a self contained and modular unit of application logic which permits communication and data transfer between heterogeneous systems in a distributed environment such as Internet. Using Web services as the basic building blocks for application development results in a totally decentralized architecture called Service Oriented Architecture (SOA). In SOA, individual services may need to be composed to form composite services and WSBPEL [7] is the most commonly used method for services composition. WSBPEL, though very powerful and widely used, lacks the primitives to easily handle data validations and transformations. This makes it difficult to build mashups using WSBPEL because of the data inherent nature of mashups, in contrast to the control flow oriented nature of WSBPEL.

Mashups in an Enterprise context aim at enabling the users to dynamically compose and interconnect their own operational environments and processes in a very flexible fashion. An Enterprise mashup architecture will facilitate flexible, useful, and effective user interaction and management with all kind of resources (SOAP or REST-based Web services, Atom or RSS data sources, or other mashups), and in this sense, such an architecture can be seen as a real collaboration tool. In contrast to the developer centric approach of traditional service composition, data driven mashup programming is a new agile application development paradigm in which knowledge workers, who do not have previous coding skills but do have extensive domain expertise, visually assemble and combine off-the-shelf components or services with both development and runtime rendering capabilities. Then, traditional service composition is an interface level composition and relies on composing operations while mashups are an application level service composition and focus on composing the data from Web services.

There are various freely and commercially available mashup tools for creating mashups using service composition without requiring technical expertise. These include Microsoft Popfly[1], Yahoo Pipes[2], Google Mashup editor[3] and IBM DAMIA[4]. Using these efficient frameworks, it becomes possible to rapidly develop applications and to remove dependence on IT staff. Focus is on simplicity and on creating the mashup application with minimal expertise, effort and time. However, in an Enterprise context, validation is very important, and the mashup tools introduced above lack the advanced customizations to handle validations/synchronization modes and some transformations. Google's Mashup Editor or IBM DAMIA are relatively more powerful and customizable as they are targeted to users with technical expertise, but still lacks handling of advance features such as synchronization modes and validation. Further, their usage within an enterprise context is limited due to the fact that they lack the primitives to manage validations and transformations which can be of critical importance, or primitives to handle security. In this paper, we propose an extension of Enterprise Integration Patterns [5] to take into account the classical problems of data integration, but also the problem of validation of Enterprise mashups.

As mashups are dedicated to data level composition, they introduce the classical data related challenges. Thus, the proposed MPN model will take into account following challenges:

- data heterogeneity and integration: data from different services can be of different format (XML, JSON, data localization, date or currency formats).
- service heterogeneity: as similar to data heterogeneity, services being used can be either RESTful, SOAP based, or using some other protocols.
- streaming data: data provided by different services can be streaming and thus mashup application should be able to handle streaming data.
- data quality: data quality is of high importance in enterprise context. Data returned from services should be valid and well-formed and should be according to constraints imposed by the service consumer.
- data security: some data can be confidential any breach in data security can be critical in the enterprise context. Data exchanged between service providers and consumers should be secure.

---

[1] http://www.popfly.com/
[2] http://pipes.yahoo.com/pipes/
[3] http://editor.googlemashups.com/editor
[4] http://services.alphaworks.ibm.com/damia/

– data reliability: data stream from service provider should be reliable and in case of non availability, alternatives reliable sources should be provided.

3 Patients Checkout Handling Mashup Example

In order to illustrate enterprise mashups, we consider the example of a Health Care System (HCS) implementing SOA, with services for various redundant operations and systems which use these services. Let us consider a mashup being set up for handling patients checkout within SOA based HCS (Figure 1).

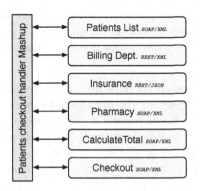

Fig. 1. Patients checkout handling mashup

For the example mashup, there exists a streaming Web service which will provide the social security number for patients checking-out on a particular day. Our mashup application will first fetch this streaming data from patients list Web service (*patientsList*) and for each patient, it will collect outstanding dues from *pharmacy* and billing department (*billingDept*) Web services and will also request the amount to reimbursed by the insurance company Web service (*insuranceCompany*). Our example mashup will then forward this information to *calculateTotal* Web service for calculating the amount to be paid by patient. Finally, it will checkout the patient.

SOA based implementation in HCS can be of great advantage as different systems can be built on top of these services without replicating the functionality. Moreover, community-based collaborations can be fostered, thanks to the introduction of a share, reuse and assembly culture of collaboration. However, it remains important to validate the application obtained by composition, in order to guarantee data reliability, data security and data quality, but also the consistency of the entire mashup.

Before going further, lets us discuss how mashup can ease service composition within the proposed scenario. Implementing the above scenario using traditional service composition techniques such as WSBPEL, will require the end user (domain expert but without technical expertise) to learn the language, and have some knowledge about Web service concepts such as their interfaces and APIs.

On the other hand, a mashup tool will allow end-user to create mashups on the fly without very little or no programming skills. The popularity of mashups thus stems from their ease of usage and flexibility in contrast to the traditional service composition techniques. However, mashup application, when used within an enterprise context such as the example above, requires modeling and validation which may or may not be left to the end user.

4   Modeling Mashups

4.1   Introduction

In our mashup model, a *data flow* – response message from a Web service – is obtained by sending a message to a service (a universal resource identifier, URI). Different types of data flows can be obtained based on different synchronization modes, that can be:

- **synchronous** - synchronous data flow mode requires mashup to suspend its execution after requesting the data from the service providers until it receives the data. Thus, mashup has a data existence dependency on requested data. Synchronous data flow is normally used when the response is of high importance and response time is known to be short.
- **asynchronous** - asynchronous data flow mode requires mashup to continue its execution after requesting the data from the service providers. Thus it has no dependency on requested data and it can later "pull" the data from provider or alternatively data is "pushed" to mashup by service providers, when it is ready. Asynchronous data flow is normally used when the requests take a long time to produce response.
- **streaming data** - mashups can process streaming data. Streaming data transfer can be either service driven or mashup driven [3]. We assume services to be continuously supplying data and mashup can "pull" data from the Web services whenever mashup is ready to process that data. In this case mashup can never be overloaded with data. On the other hand, services can continuously "push" the data to mashup and thus it should have capacity for the storage and the processing of data.

4.2   MPN: Mashup Processing Network

In this section, we will introduce the concept of Mashup Processing Network (MPN) based on Event Processing Network approach as presented in [8]. Event Processing Network is based on Event Driven Architecture (EDA) [11] which is defined to be a pattern promoting the production, detection, consumption and reaction to events. Event producers asynchronously broadcast events as they occur to be later consumed by some receiving system resulting in a totally decoupled architecture. EDA also supports Complex Event Processing (CEP) [6], which enables event driven applications to react not only to a single event but a complex composition of events happening in different times and contexts.

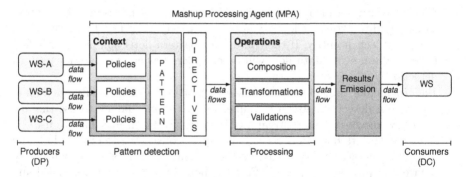

Fig. 2. Mashup processing network: components and stages

Our MPN model consists of four components: Dataflow Producer (DP), Dataflow Consumer (DC), Mashup Processing Agent (MPA) and the communication channels to send requests to and receive responses from Web services (see Figure 2).

In MPN, Dataflow Producers, or just producers, are the Web services producing data to be consumed. Communication protocols are used to invoke the Web services and to receive responses. The data flows are the response messages from the Web services. Mashup application acts as both the Mashup Processing Agent (MPA) and as a Consumer by considering mashups as both service composition and as service providers (Mashup-As-Service); they can aggregate data from multiple sources and provide aggregated data to other mashups while acting as a service. Formally, an MPN is a graph $G = (Vertices, Edges)$ where:

$$Vertices = DP \cup CC \cup MPA \cup DC \text{ and } Edges = \{(u, v)|$$
$$(u \in (DP \vee MPA) \rightarrow v \in CC) \wedge (u \in CC \rightarrow v \in (DC \vee MPA))\}$$

Mashup Processing Agent (MPA) is the core component of the model, and is divided into following three stages (see Figure 2):

- *Pattern*[5] *detection* stage is responsible for selecting data flows matching a particular pattern.
- *Processing* stage is responsible for applying processing functions to patterns detected in pattern detection phase and thus resulting in derived data flows.
- *Results/Emission* stage, which is responsible for either emission of derived data flows or storing them as results.

The **Pattern detection** stage is further divided into following components:

- *Context*, which specifies relevance of participating data flows and can be either *temporal*, *spatial* or *semantics* based. Temporal context may restrict for example, to consider only the data flows received in some specific amount of time. Spatial context may restrict to consider only data flows received

---

[5] Patterns in a MPN are the relations between data flows, not to be confused with design patterns in general.

from Web services in specific geographical locations while semantics context can be used to express relevance between participating data flows through a mutual object or entity. If the context for pattern detection is not specified (*None* value), every data flow will be considered as a candidate for pattern detection.

– *Policies* include decisions to either use *first*, *last* or *each* of dataflow in stream for pattern detection. As an example, we can specify policy to use the *last* data flow received from a streaming Web service to ensure that we use the most recent data flow. Policies can also apply constraints to only include the data flows satisfying a predicate on their attributes, for example to use only secure and reliable data flows. Further, policies can be used for specifying expiry time for data flows.

– *Patterns* specify the relationship among data flows complying policies and that are within specified context. The MPN model, as similar to EPN model, neither restricts operators used for pattern detection nor the semantics given to them. Some examples of operators include the operator *any*, meaning that any data flow within context and complying policies results in pattern detection and the operator $all(df_1, df_2...df_n)$ requiring that all data flows $(df_1, df_2...df_n)$ need to exist for pattern detection.

– *Directives* specify the directives for reporting pattern detection to processing stage. For instance, the directive *immediately* specifies to report immediately to the processing stage as the pattern is detected. Other directives include to report the pattern detection at the end of the detection interval or to report pattern detection at specifiable periods.

The **Processing** component is responsible for processing the data flows contributing to pattern detection and it is the core of Mashup application. Processing operations can be of *data composition*, *data transformation* or *data validation*. We will describe these three categories in sections 5, 6, and 7.

The **Results/Emission** component is responsible for either emission of derived data flows or storing them as results. It also supports data validations in the form of post conditions before emitting the data flows.

5   Data Composition Operations

Mashup is the composition of data flows extracted from Web services. There exist many ways to compose these flows and the *data composition operations* are further divided into *routing* and *aggregate* sub-categories.

5.1   Routing

The *data routing* operations characterizes the manner in which data flows (and their multiple parts) can influence the operation of other aspects of the mashup, particularly the control flow perspective (each part can be processed in a different way). We identify the following operations.

- **Sequence** - the *sequence* operation is the most basic operation for routing information. Given a service, and a message sent to this service, a data flow is obtained and this data flow is used to call a new service.
- **Content based routing** - mashups can route the input data to different services based on their content. If the data flow content matches a given criteria, it is routed to the output of the mashup, otherwise, it is discarded.
- **Data routing** - similar to the content based routing operation, the data routing operation splits the incoming data to different services. However, in contrast to above mentioned operation, this splitting does not have to be content based. For an example consider that the mashup application decides to split different incoming request to different Web services as a form of load-balancing to avoid over-loading a single service.

For the content based routing and data routing operations listed above, actual split can take one of three forms: **AND-Split**: same input data is routed to **all** services, **OR-Split**: same input data is routed to **at-least one** of the services, and **XOR-Split**: same input data is routed to **exactly one** of the services. We ensure that every *split* operation must be later followed by an *aggregator* operation, which we describe below.

5.2   Aggregator

The *Aggregator* is an operation that receives a stream of data flows and identifies data flows that are correlated. Once a complete set of data flows has been received, the Aggregator collects information from each correlated data flow and publishes a single, aggregated data flow to the output channel for further processing. In order to decide that a set is complete, we introduce the following aggregation schemes: **all** – all the data flows should be considered in order to consider the set complete, **exactly-one** – one the data flows should be considered in order to consider the set complete, **at-least-one** – the first data flow that is received is considered, and **subset** - only a subset of data flows is merged.

We earlier mentioned that any *split* operation must be later followed by an *aggregate* operation, however the converse is not true. We can aggregate different data flows which may not be obtained as an result of a split operation.

Let us review the scenario presented in section 3 and focus on how different data composition operations fit into the example scenario. For the checkout handler mashup (see Figure 3), response from **all** of *billingDept*, *pharmacy* and *insuranceCompany* Web services will be sent to *calculateTotal* service, and a **subset** of responses from source services will be used to checkout the patient. Further, data from *patientsList* service is **routed** to *billingDept*, pharmacy and *insuranceCompany* Web services using **AND-split**. As we discussed earlier, split operation is followed by an **aggregation** operation, and here we later aggregate these data flows using **aggregate-all** operation. Similarly **content based routing** on data from the source service can be used to decide to which insurance company the claim request should be sent.

6   Data Transformation Operations

Mashups receive data from different Web services that expose their data in different formats (JSON, XML,...). Thus the mashup may need to *translate* input data to some common format. Mashups may also need to *transform* the input messages even if they have the same binding, for example to normalize or filter the input messages. In order to manage this transformation, we have introduced data transformation operations:

Translator. Mashups provide an abstraction layer for dealing with heterogeneous data from different sources. The translator function converts data from one format to some other common format decided by the mashup application.

Wrapper. To wrap data inside an envelope that is compliant with the infrastructure. The *wrapper* operation can be used to include encryption facilities or QoS properties.

Data enricher. Mashup may enrich the input data to append new data to the data flow. Examples of this kind of operation may include expanding acronyms, including metadata or other similar transformations.

Filter. This operation is the dual of data enricher operation. The *filter* operation can be used to remove unwanted data elements from a data flow leaving only necessary items. The *filter* operation can be useful to simplify the structure of the XML document, thanks to a SAX parser for instance.

Normalizer. Mashup may require to normalize the input data from different sources to handle localized information such as currency rates, date formats and so on. We can associate a *normalizer* with a *translator* so that the resulting data flows match a common format.

Resequencer. The *resequencer* can receive a stream of data flows that may not arrive in order. The role of *resequencer* is twofold; to re-order the data flows and secondly, to re-order message parts within a data flow (for instance, re-ordering the nodes in the XML tree of the response message).

For the sample scenario presented earlier, responses from different services are in different formats and service calls are based on different protocols (see Figure 3). **Translator** is thus needed for data transformation to some common format. Response from different services need to be **filtered** to include only the relevant information, before forwarding data to other services. Finally, data from different services may require to be **normalized** before use: the **normalizer** may be needed to convert currency formats before sending data to *calculateTotal* Web service if the patient is covered by some foreign insurance company.

7   Data Validation

Validation for mashups is of high importance. This validation may include checking data accuracy, security checks or some other data level properties. In our

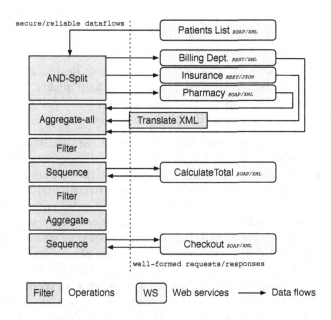

Fig. 3. Mashup operations for the motivating example

model, data validation for mashups can occur at three different levels and consequently it is handled at three different levels in MPN: **pre-conditions** which are constraints imposed by mashup before pattern detection (they can be specified as constraints on data flows in the *policies* for pattern detection), **validations** which are the constraints imposed by the mashup after pattern detection, possibly after applying processing operations such as transformations (they can be specified as validation functions in *processing* phase after pattern detection), and finally **post-conditions** which are the constraints on data being sent by the mashup application and they can be specified as constraints before emitting data flows. In our model, we consider the following validation operations.

Existence. Mashups can put constraints on existence of data and it acts as a **pre-condition** for the mashup. Mashups have constraints on existence from either one specific data source or from a set of data sources. Existence constraint is handled by specifying the appropriate policies description in mashup processing network model presented earlier.

Format. Constraints on format of input data may also be needed. Although the *translate* processing operation provides abstraction layer for different data formats, it will allow transformation for some specific (already known) data formats. This constraint thus acts as a **pre-condition** for the mashup and is handled by specifying the appropriate policies description in mashup processing network model presented earlier. As an example, consider now that our mashup application sets constraints input to be only XML based, as it may not be able to handle JSON based data.

Value. Mashups can also impose constraints on data values. This constraint may require translation processing operation and thus can be validated after data transformation; it is thus considered as a **validation** constraint.

Quality. Mashups can have some restrictions on data quality and in terms of a HCS, it is of critical importance for data to be of high quality. As an example, mashup application may impose constraint to receive only well formed and valid XML by demanding DTD or XML Schema file in response for data validation.

Streaming Data Constraints. Different type of data constraints can be imposed by mashup applications for streaming data. These constraints partially depend on the approach used by mashup to handle the streaming data.

On one hand, data availability can be **mashup driven** and it can "pull" the data from streaming data source, whenever data is needed and mashup is ready to process the data. Different types of constraints can be imposed when using this approach, these include **Max idle time** constraint, which require timely reception of data and specifies the maximum amount of time mashup application should wait for data before concluding that data stream has ended.

On the other hand, data availability can be **source driven** and data from streaming data source can be continuously "pushed" to mashup. The constraints using this approach include **Update rate** constraint which specifies the rate at which data should be pushed to mashup by data source. It is important as it can help avoiding data overloading/over-writing at mashup.

Some other constraints are independent of "mashup driven" or "source driven" approaches discussed above. These include **Data Size** constraint, which is the maximum amount of data mashup can process at a time, and data should be pushed or pulled from data source in chunks based on data size specified by mashup. These constraints may also include **Freshness** constraint, which specify the time interval during which data is considered "fresh" or valid.

Finally, these constraints can be imposed on both requests to and responses from Web services, so they can either be in the form of **pre** or **post** condition.

Data Security. Constraints can also specify that data from the service providers should be on secure channels or should use some security standards. In case of HCS it is of critical importance as health records are confidential, similar is the case when, for example, using credit cards to make payments. Data Security constraints can be imposed on both requests to and responses from Web services, so they can either be in the form of **pre** or **post** conditions.

Data Reliability. Mashups can also impose reliability constraints on data flow that can be in the form of **pre** or **post** conditions.

For the patients checkout handler mashup, application has **data existence pre-condition** on data from *patientsList* Web service (see Figure 3). Let us assume that mashup application can only handle REST/ SOAP based XML and JSON data thus it has **data format pre-condition** on data from all Web services. Then, *patientsList* Web service is streaming and thus different temporal pre-conditions can be imposed as well. Mashup application **pulls** data for each patient from *patientsList* Web service thus it has **data size pre-condition** on input data. Similarly **freshness pre-condition** can be added to specify that the data is valid for a given amount of time. For each contributing data flow, we can also have **pre/post conditions** to only use secure/reliable data flows, and requiring well-formed requests/responses as a form of **data quality** constraint.

8   Mashup Validation

In this section, we will attempt to model and validate patients checkout handler mashup using Mashup Processing Network (MPN) as presented earlier. We will use the processing operations identified in Figure 3 and will model them using the template below.

A1 - Handle response message from patientsList Web service
Detection:
-Context: *None* - every data flow is considered for pattern detection
-Policies: *secure/reliable* data flows - *last* df_patientsList as PL
-Pattern: *Any*
-Directives: *Immediate*
Processing:
Operation : *Validate*
-If *invalid* patient record then *Reject and terminate* processing
Operation : *Split*
-df_billingDept, df_insuranceCompany, df_Pharmacy
Emission/Results
Post Conditions - use *secure/reliable* channels
-*Emit* PL.social_security_no to billingDept service
-*Emit* PL.social_security_no to insuranceCompany service
-*Emit* PL.social_security_no to Pharmacy service

Mashup application first fetches the patient record from the *patientsList* streaming Web service. We have modeled the role of mashup application (acting as MPA) in agent A1. In this template, we first specify the name of agent, and brief description of its role. Below we discuss different phases of the pattern detection:

- first, we specify the *context*, which in this case is *None* meaning that every data flow arriving to mashup application will be considered as a candidate. However, the *context* can be either temporal, spatial or semantic based as discussed earlier. As an example of *temporal* context, we can specify to consider all the data flows arriving in a specific time interval. In the example above, we can specify the *maximum idle time* streaming data constraint by specifying the time interval in which data flow should be received.
- in the *policies* part of pattern detection we have specified predicates on data flows within specified context. In the example above we have specified preconditions to use secure/reliable data flows, we can also specify the expiry time for data flows as an example of *freshness* streaming data constraint.

Further, we have specified to use the *last* data flow we have received from *patientsList* Web service; this will ensure that we use the most recent data flow as the *patientsList* Web service is a streaming Web service.

- then, for the pattern part we specify the relation between data flows that are within specified context and which comply the specified policies. MPN model neither restricts operators used for pattern detection nor the semantics given to them, some examples of operators include *Any* meaning that any data flow within context and complying policies results in pattern detection, it can also be of the form $all(df_1, df_2...df_n)$ requiring that all data flows $(df_1, df_2...df_n)$ need to exist for pattern detection. In the example above, we have specified pattern to be *any*, thus the last data flow we received from *patentsList* Web service (context) and is reliable and secure (policy) will mark pattern detection.

- finally, we specify the directive to be *immediate*, meaning that as soon as we will detect the pattern, we will move on to processing phase.

In the processing phase, we specify the processing operations on data flows detected in the pattern detection phase. In the example above, we first perform a validation operation to check if the message we have received is well-formed and valid and in case of invalid record, processing by this agent will be terminated. Then, we perform a split operation and specify the targets to which the data flow should be split. Finally, in the processing phase we will emit the social_security_no field from *patientsList* service to the targets identified in the split operation. We will then aggregate these splitted data flows later in agent run A2 and we will use the same template to model the MPA functionality. Further, we have modeled the *calculateTotal* Web service invocation in agent run A3 and finally patient checkout is modeled in agent run A4 (see Figure 4).

Now we will briefly discuss how can we validate a mashup using the mashup model presented earlier. We define a mashup to be valid, if constraints for every data flow in mashup are satisfied and dependence between operations and/or there usage conditions are respected. From the above mashup model for checkout handler mashup presented earlier, we can say that a mashup is valid if all the constraints (pre/post conditions and validations) are satisfied i.e secure/reliable channels are used for sending requests and to receive responses. To illustrate the dependence between operations and its application to mashup validation, we take the case of *routing/splitting* and *aggregation* operations. We believe that every *routing/splitting* of data flow should be followed by aggregation somewhere later in mashup flow. For illustrating the usage conditions for an operation, we cannot perform an aggregation of data flows of different format; for every such instance we first need to translate the data flow(s) and then aggregate. Similar is the case with possible data flow ordering and filtering to match target Web service input, before performing sequence operation.

9   Implementation

To illustrate how the proposed set of processing operations can be used as patterns for mashup development, we have implemented a Java based server side

A2 - Process response from billingDept, insuranceCompany, and Pharmacy Web services
Detection:
-Context: *None* - every data flow is considered for pattern detection
-Policies: *secure/reliable* data flows, *first* df_billingDept as BD,
first df_insuranceCompany as IC, *first* df_Pharmacy as PH
-Pattern: *all*(BD,IC,PH)
-Directives: *Immediate*
Processsing
Operation : *Validate*
- If *invalid* BD, IC, PH then *Reject and terminate* processing
Operation: *Translate*
df_insuranceCompany' := translate(df_insuranceCompany, XML)
Operation: *Aggregate*
df_calculateTotal := df_billingDept.gross_total ∪ df_Pharmacy
.gross_total ∪ df_insuranceCompany'.amount_rembursed
Emission/Results
Post Conditions - use *secure/reliable* channels
-Emit df_calculateTotal to calculateTotal Web service

A3 - Process response from calculateTotal Web service
Detection:
-Context: *None* - every data flow is considered for pattern detection
-Policies: *secure/reliable* data flows, *first* df_calculateTotal as CT
-Pattern: *any*
-Directives: *Immediate*
Processsing
Operation : *Validate*
- If *invalid* CT then *Reject and terminate* processing
Operation: *Aggregate*
df_patientCheckout := df_calculateTotal.gross_total ∪ df_patientsList
.name ∪ df_patientsList.id_number ∪
df_patientsList.social_security_no ∪ current_date
Emission/Results
Post Conditions - use *secure/reliable* channels
-Emit df_patientCheckout to patientCheckout Web service

A4 - Process response from patientCheckout Web service
Detection:
-Context: *None* - every data flow is considered for pattern detection
-Policies: *secure/reliable* data flows, *first* df_patientCheckout as PC
-Pattern: *any*
-Directives: *Immediate*
Processsing
Pattern : Validate
- If *invalid* PC then *Reject and terminate* processing
Emission/Results
Post Conditions - use *secure/reliable* channels
-Store df_patientCheckout Result

Fig. 4. Patients checkout handler mashup - Model

mashup application for patients checkout scenario presented in section 3 (see Figure 5). We have programmed Web services which return sample data for patients from different systems including billing department, insurance company,

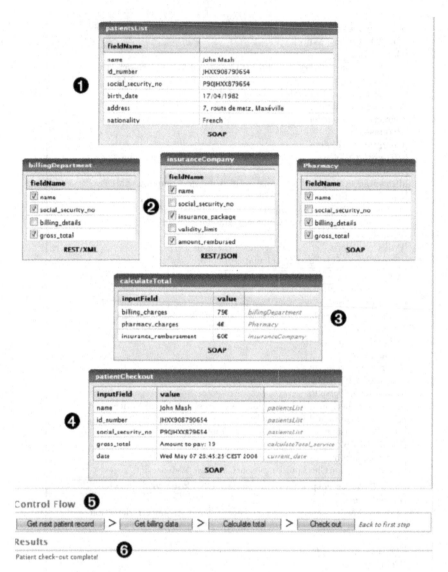

Fig. 5. Patients checkout handler mashup - Implementation

pharmacy and others. These Web services are intentionally programmed to support different data formats (XML, JSON) and access protocols (SOAP, REST).

To simulate a streaming based service, we have programmed a SOAP based *patientsList* Web service which provides data for one patient at a time. This web service is pull based and our mashup application will pull the next patient record after checking out current patient. So in the first step, mashup application fetches the patient record from *patientsList* Web service and it then splits this information(using AND-split) to REST/XML based *billingDepartment*, REST/JSON based *insuranceCompany* and SOAP based Pharmacy Web services. The data returned from these services will include billing amount for *billingDepartment* and *Pharmacy* Web services and amount reimbursed information from *InsuranceCompany* Web service. This information will then be aggregated (using aggregate-all) and sent to SOAP based *calculateTotal* Web service, which will return the amount to be paid by the patient. Finally, the information from before mentioned Web services will be merged and will be sent to *patientCheckout* service to checkout the patient. User can then move on to processing next patient record from the *patientsList* Web service.

The patients checkout handler mashup discussed above uses the sample data from Web service written specifically for this purpose. In order to test our implementation on publicly available Web services, we have programmed a search-Mashup which can search user specified query from various Web services, including del.icio.us Web service, Yahoo search services, YouTube Web service and others. The services we have chosen for the mashup application are heterogenous as they support different data formats (XML/JSON) and support different API formats (SOAP/RESTful). In addition some services are being called asynchronously. Users are given option to select Web services and constraint, transform, filter the data returned. Space limitations restrict us to discuss these options in detail.

10   Conclusion

In this paper,we have proposed an approach for building, modeling and validating enterprise mashups. We introduce the concept of Mashup Processing Network (MPN) which illustrates how different actors interact for the development of mashup. The MPN model consists of four components: Dataflow Producer (DP), Dataflow Consumer (DC), Mashup Processing Agent (MPA) and the communication channels to send requests to and receive responses from Web services.

We further enriched this model with a set of processing operations that can be used to process data flows. These operations are divided into three categories: composition operations (routing and aggregation operations), transformation operations (operations to update data flows such as translator, wrapper, filter, data enricher. . .), and validation operations.

Data validation operations are divided into pre/post-conditions and validations. They are necessary in order to express data level properties and they are handled at three different stages in the MPN: before using data, after processing data, and before emitting data.

We have also presented a sample scenario for the SOA based Health Care System to illustrate these concepts, and we have modeled patient checkout handler mashup using the MPN model introduced in the paper. We have also implemented the sample scenario to discuss how we can use the proposed processing operations as patterns for mashup development and have also tested our implementation on freely "real life" Web services to create a search mashup application, which allows content to be searched using various search Web service including Yahoo search Web service, YouTube Web service and others.

In our future work, we will focus on finding the sufficient conditions to consider a mashup application to be Valid and Well-formed: we will also work on providing a management framework for enterprise mashups and we will work on the security aspects and the runtime management of enterprise mashups.

References

1. Liu, X., Sun, W., Hui, Y., Liang, H.: Towards Service Composition Based on Mashup. In: Proc. of the SCW 2007 International Workshop at ICWS 2007, Salt Lake City (July 2007)
2. Bioernstad, B., Pautasso, C.: Let it flow: Building Mashups with Data Processing Pipelines. In: Di Nitto, E., Ripeanu, M. (eds.) ICSOC 2007. LNCS, vol. 4907, pp. 15–28. Springer, Heidelberg (2009)
3. Bioernstad, B., Pautasso, C., Alonso, G.: Control the Flow: How to Safely Compose Streaming Services into Business Processes. In: Proc. of the 2006 IEEE International Conference on Services Computing (SCC 2006), Chicago (September 2006)
4. Pautasso, C., Alonso, G.: Parallel Computing Patterns for Grid Workflows. In: Proc. of the HPDC2006 Workshop on Workflows in Support of Large-Scale Science (WORKS 2006), Paris, France (June 2006)
5. Hohpe, G., Woolf, B.: Enterprise Integration Patterns: Designing, Building, and Deploying Messaging Solutions. Addison-Wesley, Boston (2004)
6. Luckham, D.: The Power of Events: An Introduction to Complex Event Processing in Distributed Enterprise Systems. Addison-Wesley Professional, Boston (2002)
7. OASIS, Web Services Business Process Execution Language (WSBPEL) 2.0 (2006)
8. Sharon, G., Etzion, O.: Event-processing network model and implementation. IBM Systems Journal (2008)
9. Merrill, D.: The new breed of Web app - An introduction to mashups, http://www-128.ibm.com/developerworks/xml/library/x-mashups.html
10. Hinchcliffe, D.: The quest for enterprise mashup tools, http://blogs.zdnet.com/Hinchcliffe/?p=59
11. Hohpe, G.: Programming Without a Call Stack - Event-driven Architectures, http://www.eaipatterns.com/docs/EDA.pdf

Automatic Categorization of Tags in Collaborative Environments

Qihua Wang[1,*], Hongxia Jin[2], and Stefan Nusser[2]

[1] Purdue University, West Lafayette, Indiana
[2] IBM Almaden Research Center, San Jose, California

Abstract. Tagging allows individuals to use whatever terms they think are appropriate to describe an item. With the growing popularity of tagging, more and more tags have been collected by a variety of applications. An item may be associated with tags describing its different aspects, such as appearance, functionality, and location. However, little attention has been paid in the organization of tags; in most tagging systems, all the tags associated with an item are listed together regardless of their meanings. When the number of tags becomes large, finding useful information with regards to a certain aspect of an item becomes difficult. Improving the organization of tags in existing tagging systems is thus highly desired. In this paper, we propose a hierarchical approach to organize tags. In our approach, tags are placed into different categories based on their meanings. To find information with respect to a certain aspect of an item, one just needs to refer to its associated tags in the corresponding category. Since existing applications have already collected a large number of tags, manually categorizing all the tags is infeasible. We propose to use data-mining and machine-learning techniques to automatically and rapidly classify tags in tagging systems. A prototype of our approaches has been developed for a real-word tagging system.

Keywords: Tagging, Web 2.0, Social Network, Categorization, Machine Learning.

1 Introduction

Tagging has gained popularity as a lightweight and flexible approach to classifying and retrieving information. It enables individuals to use whatever terms they think are appropriate to describe an item without the burden of selecting the term from a pre-defined taxonomy. Tagging has been applied in a variety of applications ranging from desktop applications for photo organization (F-Spot [3]) to email systems (Gmail [6]). Tagging becomes most compelling when it is used in a collaborative environment, where tags from different people can be aggregated and combined. This social tagging approach has been used to manage bookmarks (Del.icio.us), images (Flickr), and products (Amazon.com).

In addition to characterizing items, tagging has also been applied to describing people. Fringe Contacts (or Fringe for short) [4] is a reference system designed to augment

---

* This work was done when the author was an intern at IBM Almaden Research Center.

E. Bertino and J.B.D. Joshi (Eds.): CollaborateCom 2008, LNICST 10, pp. 649–662, 2009.

Fig. 1. Fringe profile page of Edward Forelli. Note the tagger widget on the left hand side, as well as incoming (received) and outgoing (assigned) tag clouds.

employee profiles with tagging in a corporate enviornment. In Fringe, people are allowed to tag each other with arbitrary terms. A person's incoming tags and outgoing tags are viewable in the form of tag clouds on a user's employee profile page. Figure 1 shows a Fringe profile page. The tagging functionality of Fringe is useful in keeping certain profile information such as projects, expertise, and interests, up-to-date. According to system records, most employees do not update their profile in a timely manner [5]. Fringe enables a small group of active users to update the information of the people they know through tagging. It has been shown that, in most cases, the tags one received adequately describes oneself [5]. Thus, we may make use of tags to learn more about a person, such as her projects and skills, or search for expertise in a certain field within a corporate environment.

As of May 14, 2008, 53844 people has been tagged by a total of 170137 tags in Fringe. In particular, 557 people have been tagged by 20 or more distinct terms [1]. Currently, the distinct terms from tags are listed alphabetically in a tag cloud on one's Fringe profile (see Figure 2). These terms may describe different aspects of a person. For example, the terms "fringe" and "sonar" are project names, which probably indicate the projects the person works on; the terms "ajax" and "perl" describe the programming skills the person has; the terms "blogger" and "innovator" describe the person himself.

---

[1] In Fringe, a user may be tagged with the same term by multiple users. For example, a software developer may be tagged the term "Java" ten times.

Fig. 2. Tag cloud showing tags used by other people on a person. Tags with the same term are shown only once; and the larger the font size of a term, the more times the person is tagged by the term.

To learn about all the skills the person has, one has to go over all the terms in the tag cloud on the person's profile one by one and collect those terms that are relevant to skills. When the number of terms one has been tagged is large, scanning all the terms in the tag cloud is time-consuming. Other popular websites/applications that provide tagging functionality, including Flickr and Amazon.com, do no better in organizing and displaying tags to users.

Grouping tags into categories such as "Project-related" and "Skill-related" will facilitate information retrieval from tags and enhance the usability of tagging systems. Tag categorization can also help alleviate the problem of naming collisions, which is considered to be an open issue in existing tagging systems [5]. For example, some users in our corporate are working on a project codenamed "vista", which is also the name of an operating system. There are 30 tags with the term "vista" in Fringe, and it is hard to tell the actual meaning of these tags without referring to other information. If such tags were classified into categories such as "Internal Projects" and "Operating Systems", the meaning of each tag would be clarified by its category.

Unfortunately, the importance of tag-organization is largely ignored by existing tagging systems.

In this article, we propose to organize tags in a hierarchical manner. Similar to creating a tag, users may create a category or a sub-category under another category using whatever term they consider appropriate. They may then place new or existing tags into the created categories. The effect of categorization activities from different users will be combined and shared in the system. Allowing users to create categories preserves the spirit of freedom in tagging and avoids the need of a pre-defined taxonomy.

Since tagging systems such as Fringe have collected a large number of tags, it is infeasible to manually classify the existing tags into different categories. An automatic approach is needed to categorize the tags with minimum human-intervention. A challenge for automatic categorization is that, unlike words in an article, tags are individual words with very limited context information. Also, users may use different terms to refer to the same thing. For example, "tim", "itim", and "tivoli-identity-manager" all mean the same product. A categorization approach has to find out the synonyms used in tagging activities. In this article, we propose an approach that makes use of data-mining and machine-learning techniques to reliably and rapidly categorize tags based on user-inputs and feedbacks. Even though our discussion will be mainly based on Fringe, our techniques can be applied to other tagging systems as well.

The contributions of this paper are summarized as follows.

- We propose to organize tags in a hierarchical manner. Our approach allows users to create categories and sub-categories, which preserves the spirit of freedom in tagging systems.
- We design an automatic method to categorize tags using data-mining and machine-learning techniques. Our approach is efficient and effective in practice.
- We propose to solve the problem of naming collisions using user-connection graphs generated from tagging relations. We observed that tags with the same term in the same connected component of the connection graph normally mean the same thing; while tags with the same term from different connected components could have different meanings.
- We developed a prototype of our approach for a real-world tagging system, Fringe. Our prototype demonstrates the efficiency and effectiveness of our approach. Our prototype also enables one to learn about a tag whose meaning is unknown by referring to categorized related tags.

The rest of this paper is organized as follows. We describe the problem of tag categorization in detail in Section 2 and present our solutions in Section 3. After that, we describe our prototype for Fringe in Section 4. Finally, we discuss related work in Section 5 and conclude in Section 6.

2   Problem Description

In this section, we describe the problem of tag-categorization in details. We first give the representation of tags and categories, and then we define the categorization problem and discuss goodness metrics for its solutions.

Definition 1 (Tagging Relation). The *tagging relation* of a system is represented as $TR \subseteq \mathcal{U} \times \mathcal{U} \times \mathcal{W}$, where $\mathcal{U}$ is the set of all users in the system and $\mathcal{W}$ is the set of all possible terms. A *tagging tuple* (or a *tag* for short) $(u_1, u_2, t) \in TR$ indicates that user u_1 has tagged u_2 using the term t.

Intuitively, the tagging relation is the set of all the tags in the system. In Fringe, a term used in a tag may consist of a single word, such as "java" and "perl", or multiple words connected by the symbol "-", such as "java-developer" and "tivoli-identity-manager". A term consisting of a single word is called a *simple term*, while a term consisting of multiple words is called a *complex term*. Among the 170137 tags in Fringe, 22540 distinct terms have been used and 12033 (or 53%) of them are complex terms.

Definition 2 (Category). A *category* is represented as a term $c \in \mathcal{W}$. Let C be the set of categories in the system, the hierarchical relation of categories is denoted as $CH \subseteq C \times C$, where $(c_1, c_2) \in CH$ indicates that c_2 is a *subcategory* of c_1.

For example, the category "research areas" may contain subcategories such as "theory" and "database". We assume that there is a special category *unknown*. Those tags that have not been classified are placed in the category *unknown*.

Next, we define the tag-categorization problem.

Definition 3 (Tag-Categorization Problem). A state of a *tagging system* is given as $\langle TR, C, CH, FC \rangle$, where TR is a tagging relation, C is a set of categories, $CH \subseteq C \times C$ is the category hierarchy, and FC is a function that maps every tag in TR to a category in C.

The input to the *tag-categorization problem (TCP)* is an initial state $\langle TR, C, CH, FC \rangle$ such that $unknown \in C$ and $\forall_{t \in TR} FC(t) = unknown$. We are asked to output $\langle TR, C', CH', FC' \rangle$ such that $\forall_{t \in TR} FC'(t) = c, c \in C'$ and $c \neq unknown$.

The above definition does not require $C' = C$. In other words, new categories can be created in solutions to the categorization problem.

Definition 3 only defines what is a solution to an instance of TCP without stating what is a good solution. When the set of possible terms is infinite, we we may have infinitely many solutions for a TCP instance. It is clear that all the solutions are not equally good. For example, we may come up with a trivial solution by creating a category "xyz" and map all tags to such a category. But such a trivial solution is useless in practice. Intuitively, the categorization of tags should match the expectation of human users so as to be useful. A naive approach to get a good solution is to ask a human user to categorize all the tags in the system. But when the number of tags is large, manual categorization is infeasible.

3   A Tag-Categoration Approach

In this section, we describe our approach for tag categorization. The overview of our approach is as follows.

- First of all, we find the synonyms used in tags based on statistics and the similarity between words. When a term is placed into a category, its synonyms should be placed into that category as well.
- Second, the system learns how to categorize tags from human users in a collaborative environment. Users train the system by creating categories and placing tags into such categories. The knowledge from different users are combined, and conflicts are resolved using a voting mechanism. The system also derives rules from classified tags and applies such rules to categorize other tags.

Finding Synonyms. As we have mentioned in Section 1, since tagging systems grant users the freedom to use whatever terms they like in tags, different terms may be used to refer to the same thing. A common practice is to use initials instead of full project or title names in tags. For example, in Fringe, "de" is short for "distinguished-engineer" and both terms are used in tags. For another example, "itim" is short for "ibm-tivoli-identity-manager", which is equivalent to "tivoli-identity-manager". Finding the synonyms used in tags can speed up the categorization process, as once the category of a term is known, tags using the synonyms of the term can be automatically placed in that category as well.

A natural approach to determine if the meanings of two terms are equivalent is to see if the two often appear together. Intuitively, if users who have been tagged t_1 are usually tagged t_2 as well, and vice versa, then it is likely that t_1 and t_2 are synonyms. Let $|t_1|$ and $|t_2|$ be the number of tags using term t_1 and t_2, respectively, and $|(t_1, t_2)|$ be the number of users being tagged both t_1 and t_2. The function $g(t_1, t_2) = \langle |(t_1, t_2)|/|t_1|, |(t_1, t_2)|/|t_2| \rangle$ computes the *statistical likelihood* that t_1 and t_2 are synonyms. If both $|(t_1, t_2)|/|t_1|$ and $|(t_1, t_2)|/|t_2|$ are close to 1, we have high confidence that t_1 and t_2 mean the same thing. For instance, "bsa" is the initial of "business-solutions-architect" and the two terms are synonyms. Let t_1 = "bsa" and t_2 = "business-solutions-architect". We have $|(t_1, t_2)|$ = 9 and $g(t_1, t_2) = \langle 100\%, 90\% \rangle$ in Fringe.

Even though a large number of pairs of synonyms in Fringe have high statistical likelihood, we found that using statistical likelihood alone to determine synonyms will lead to relatively high false positive rate. For example, "ns-staff" and "buddylist" appear together 206 times and $g(\text{ns-staff}, \text{buddylist}) = \langle 99\%, 94\% \rangle$, which is higher than most other pairs of terms. But apparently, "ns-staff" is not a synonym of "buddylist". Also, many pairs of synonyms have relatively low statistical likelihood. For instance, the statistical likelihood of "wempe" and "websphere-everyplace-mobile-portal-enable" is only $\langle 60\%, 60\% \rangle$, but they are probably equivalent as the former is the initial of the latter and no other terms in Fringe has initial "wempe".

To complement the statistical approach, we take the syntactically similarity between words into account when finding synonyms. For example, two terms are syntactical similar if one is the initial of the other, one is the prefix/suffix of the other, or they are complex terms sharing some single terms. In general, we compute the confidence score measuring the likelihood that two terms are synonyms by combining the statistical likelihood of the pair and the level of similarity between the words used in the terms.

As we will see in Section 4, our approach is effective in finding synonyms used in tags.

Learning in a collaborative environment. In our system, categories are created by users. The system learns how to place tags into different categories by observing how human users classify tags. For example, assume that a user is browsing an employee's profile and finds that a tag with the term "business-solutions-architect" remains unclassified. Then, the user may drag the tag to the category "Job Title", which was created earlier by another user. The system learns that other tags with the same term probably belong to the same category (except in the cases of name collisions, which will be discussed later). Also, tags with the term "bsa", which is found to be a synonym of "business-solutions-architect", should be placed in the category "Job Title" as well.

Fringe works in a collaborative environment, where a large number of users browse employee profiles through Fringe every day. Every user may contribute to the learning process of tag categorization. Conflicts may occur when we combine the opinions of all users, as different users may have different opinions on how to categorize a term. For instance, some users think that tags with term t should be placed in category c_1, while some others consider category c_2 to be more appropriate. Sometimes, users may make mistakes as well, like placing t into c_1 while t should belong to c_2. To resolve conflicts and correct errors, we employ a voting mechanism, i.e. if the number of users who prefer t to be in c_1 is larger than the number of those who prefer c_2, then t will be put in the category c_1.

Fringe has collected 170137 tags, and 22540 distinct terms are used in those tags. To speed up the categorization process, the system must be able to guess the categories of those tags whose terms have not been categorized by human users based on what it has learned. The system thus needs to link terms that are likely to belong to the same category together. Unlike words extracted from articles, which can be linked by topics, tags are individual terms and there are not obvious semantic links between them. Here, we consider linking tags syntactically through complex terms.

As we have mentioned in Section 2, more than 50% of the terms used in Fringe tags are complex terms, which consist of more than one words. An important observation is that the category of a complex term is determined by its subterms. For example, if "tivoli" is a product, then complex terms such as "tivoli-identity-manager" and "tivoli-workload-scheduler" are likely to be products too. Furthermore, by knowing that "tivoli-workload-scheduler" is a product, the system may infer that other terms containing the word "workload" and/or "scheduler" could be a product as well. In general, the system may derive categorization rules from what it has learned from human users.

Definition 4 (Categorization Rule). A *categorization rule* is represented as $\langle t \rightarrow c, T \rangle$, where t is a term, c is a category, and T is a set of terms called the *supports* of the rule. We say that $\langle t \rightarrow c, T \rangle$ is a rule for term t.

The system maintains the following two types of rules for tag classification.

- *User-specified rules*: if the combined effort of human users indicates that term t (which can be a simple or complex term) belongs to category c, then a user-specified rule $t \rightarrow c$ is added to the system and $\{t\}$ is the supports of the rule.
- *Derived rules*: if the combined effort of human users indicates that complex term t belongs to category c, then for every single subterm t' of t, a derived rule $t' \rightarrow c$ is added to the system (if such a rule does not exist yet) with $\{t\}$ as its supports. This indicates that it is possible that t' belong to category c, because one of its superterms belongs to c. If the rule $t' \rightarrow c$ is derived again from another complex term t_1 in future, then t_1 will be added to the supports of the rule. Derived rules with larger supports will be given more weights when they are applied.

    For instance, if the system is told that "tivoli-identity-manager" is a product, then derived rules "tivoli $\rightarrow$ product", "identity $\rightarrow$ product" and "manager $\rightarrow$ product" are added to the system (if they do not exist). And "tivoli-identity-manager" is added to the supports on these rules.

Note that a single term may have multiple derived rules targeting different categories. For example, in addition to the rule ⟨manager → product, {tivoli-identity-manager}⟩, we may have another rule ⟨manager → job title, {sales-manager, people-manager}⟩. Intuitively, the two rules indicate that a complex term containing "manager" could be a product or a job title, and the latter case is more likely than the former as the latter has more supports. Also, a term may be removed from the supports of a rule in the future, if its category changes later. Term t will be removed from the supports of rule $t \rightarrow c$ when its category is no longer c (for example, more users vote that t should be in c'). A rule will be removed if its supports becomes empty.

Next, we describe how to apply the categorization rules to guess the category of a new term. Given a term t, let $S_t = \{t_1, \ldots, t_m\}$ ($m \geq 1$) be the set of single terms in t. The algorithm that outputs a category for t is described in Figure 3. The high-level idea of the algorithm is that, for every sub-term $t_i \in S_t$, we compute the probability that t_i falls into a certain category c based on the supports of its rules (if t_i does not have a rule regarding c, it is ignored). Note that user-specified rules have higher priority over derived rules. We then determine the probability that t falls into c by combining the results of its subterms. Finally, we select the category c' with the largest probability that t falls into it [2]. Furthermore, when guessing the category of t, we prefer to use rules whose terms are closer to t. For example, assume that we have rules for both "manager" and "identity-manager". To guess the category of "tivoli-identity-manager", rules for "identity-manager" will be used while rules for "manager" will not. This is because "identity-manager" is a subterm of "tivoli-identity-manager" that subsumes "manager", which indicates that the rules for "identity-manager" should be more precise with respect to "tivoli-identity-manager" than those for "manager".

The following example illustrates how the algorithm works.

Example 1. Assume that we are given a term "social-network-computing", which has not been categorized by human users. We have the following rules in the system.

- ⟨social → c_1, S_1⟩, where $|S_1| = 30$.
- ⟨social-network → c_1, S_2⟩, where $|S_2| = 9$.
  ⟨social-network → c_2, S_3⟩, where $|S_3| = 1$.
- ⟨computing → c_1, S_4⟩, where $|S_4| = 2$.
  ⟨computing → c_2, S_5⟩, where $|S_5| = 2$.
  ⟨computing → c_3, S_6⟩, where $|S_6| = 6$.

According to our algorithm, the rule for "social" will not be used as we have rules for "social-network" which subsumes "social". We then compute the probabilities that "social-network-computing" does not fall into c_1, c_2, and c_3, using the rules for "social-network" and "computing". We have

- $M(c_1) = (1 - 9/(1+9)) \times (1 - 2/(2+2+6)) = 0.1 \times 0.8 = 0.08$
- $M(c_2) = (1 - 1/(1+9)) \times (1 - 2/(2+2+6)) = 0.9 \times 0.8 = 0.72$
- $M(c_3) = 1 \times (1 - 6/(2+2+6)) = 1 \times 0.4 = 0.4$

---

[2] In the algorithm described in Figure 3, we actually select the category with the smallest probability that t does not fall into it.

Input: A set R_u of user-specified rules; a set R_d of derived rules; a term t.
Output: A category c_t.

Begin
    Let $T = \{t_1, \ldots, t_m\}$ be the set of single subterms of t;
    Let M be a hashmap that maps a category to a real number;
      (Initially, M maps every category to 1)
    For every term $t_i \in T$ do
        Find term t' with the largest number of subterms that satisfies the follows:
          - There is at least one rule for t' in R_u or R_d
          - t_i is a subterm of t'
          - Every single subterm of t' is in T
        If such a t' does not exist, continue to process the next subterm in T;
    EndFor;
    Let R be the set of rules for t' in R_u;
    If R is empty, let R be the set of rules for t' in R_d;
    Let x be the sum of the size of supports of rules in R;
    For every rule $r_j = \{t' \rightarrow c_k, S\} \in R$ do
      $M(c_k) = M(c_k) \times (1 - |S|/x)$;
    EndFor;
    Return the category c_t such that $M(c_t)$ is the smallest;
End

Fig. 3. The algorithm for guessing the category of a term t based on a set of categorization rules

Since $M(c_1)$ is the smallest, the algorithm returns c_1 as the most likely category for "social-network-computing".

As shown in the experimental results in Section 4.1, our learning approach allows the system to categorize a large number of tags with a small number of rules. And the correctness rate of the categorization is satisfactory.

Handling Naming Collisions. As stated in Section 1, naming collisions is an open issue in tagging systems. With naming collisions, it is possible that tags with the same term should belong to different categories, depending on their context. In our approach, we detect and handle naming collisions using tagging-relation graphs.

    Our observation is that, when naming collisions occur, it is almost always the case that two disjoint sets of people use the same term to mean different things. It is very rare that a person would use the same term for different meanings as that would confuse herself. Also, it is unlikely that a term has different meanings to a group of closely connected users in the tagging system. We say that a group of users are closely connected if they often tag each other. In particular, if a group of users tag each other using term t, then t probably means the same thing in the group. A tagging-relation graph with respect to t can be constructed in such a way: the nodes of the graph represent users, and there is an edge from node n_1 to n_2 if and only if user u_1 has tagged u_2 using term t.

    A potential naming collision on term t is detected when the system finds that several users vote category c_1 for some tags with term t, while several others vote category c_2

for some other tags with the same term. When this happens, we construct a tagging-relation graph with respect to t. If those tags being voted as c_1 and those as c_2 are associated with users in different connected components of the graph, we may conclude that t means something belonging to c_1 in some connected components, while it means another thing belonging to c_2 in other connected components. In this case, the system uses different internal representations of t to distinguish it from one connected component to another. The difference of internal representations of term t in different tags is invisible to end-users. In that case, instead of categorizing all tags with t into either c_1 or c_2, we may now place some of the tags in c_1 and the others in c_2. And placing a tag under a category makes it less likely for users to confuse its meaning with a tag with the same term in another category.

4   A Prototype for Fringe

We have implemented a prototype for our tag-categorization approach in Fringe. In this section, we first show that how categorization may facilitate the retrieval of information from tags by presenting screenshoots of our tool, and then we present experimental results to demonstrate the effectiveness of our method.

As we can see in Figure 4, tags are grouped into different categories for display in our tool, which makes it much easier to learning about different aspects of a person, when compared to the current tag cloud showed in Figure 2. We may find out the skills the user has and the projects he is working on at a glance, instead of having to go over all the tags to pick out relevant information.

Tag categorization also makes it easier to learn about those tags that are unknown to a user who is browsing a profile. By double-clicking a tag on an employee's profile, our tool pops up a window containing the tags that may be related to the targeted tag. Such related tags are selected from those tags, which often appear together with the targeted tag on employ profiles. For instance, Figure 5 shows the tags related to "fringe". We can quickly find out that "fringe" is probably developed in Almaden Research Center (as it is related to the term "almaden" in the category "Location"), it is about collaboration and social-network (as it is related to such terms in the category "Skills"), and the personnel related to Fringe also work on projects such as Bluemail and Dogear.

In general, in a people-tagging system such as Fringe, a person's tags describe the person, while a tag's related tags describe the tag itself. Tag categorization makes it easier to learn about both people and tags in the system.

4.1   Experimental Results

In this subsection, we demonstrate the effectiveness of our tag-categorization approach by presenting experimental results. Our implementation is on Fringe and we use the dataset collected by Fringe for experiments. Fringe is a tagging system used in our corporate and its dataset represents a real-world scenario.

First of all, we would like to evaluate our approach on finding synonyms used in tags. As stated in Section 3, the approach we designed takes into account statistical likelihood and word similarities.

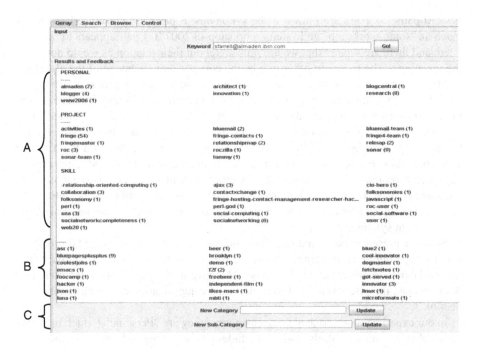

Fig. 4. The tags on an employee's profile as displayed in our tag categorization tool. (A) Tags that have been classified into three categories, "Personal", "Skills", and "Projects". (B) Tags that have not been categorized yet. (C) Feedback area where users can create a category, categorize an unclassified tag, or try to correct the category of a tag.

Fig. 5. Tags related to "fringe" as displayed by our tag categorization tool

In Fringe, there are 22540 distinct terms used in the 170137 tags. We set the selection threshold of our algorithm to a such value that it outputs 312 pairs of potential synonyms. To evaluate the correctness of the results, we ranked the pairs based on their confidence scores and manually examined the first 50 and the last 50 pairs. Out of the first 50 pairs, 37 pairs are known to be synonyms, 8 pairs are closely related terms (such as "soma-workshop" and "soma-workshop-dk2007"), 1 pair appears to be unrelated, and there are 4 pairs that we are not sure about their relation as we do not know the meaning of the terms. In other words, the correctness percentage of the algorithm is 74%, and if we take closely related terms into account, the correctness percentage is 90%. In contrast, in the last 50 pairs, 6 pairs are synonyms, 21 of them are related, 7 are unrelated, and we are not sure about the remaining 16. If we take pairs of related terms into account, the correctness rate of the algorithm is 54%. Since two closely related terms are likely to be placed in the same category, it does not do much harm on the correctness of categorization, even if the algorithm takes closely related terms as synonyms and automatically classifies them together. Note that we can always increase the threshold to make the results more accurate (in that case, less pairs will be outputted). Also, our tool provides an interface that allows users to correct the mistakes made by the system in synonym discovery.

Next, we present experimental results of our categorization algorithm. Our prototype has not been deployed in Fringe yet, so we are unable to evaluate our approach in a real collaborative environment. The major objective of the experiments reported here is to evaluate the effectiveness of the rule-based categorization approach proposed in Section 3.

In our experiment, we created three categories; they are "Personal" (which indicates personal information), "Skills" (which includes programming and research skills), and "Projects" (which are name of projects). To train the tool, we manually categorize 36 tags with distinct terms. Among the 36 tags we classified, 8 of them are placed into "Personal", 16 of them are "Skills", and 12 belong to "Projects". We then ask our tool to classify all the tags in the system. It took about 15 seconds for our tool to finish the classification. Among the 170137 tags, 141557 (or 83%) of them have been categorized by the tool. And those tags that have been classified have 21664 distinct terms (i.e. 96% of the total 22540 distinct terms). Of all the classified terms, 4371 (or 20%) of them are categorized as "Personal", 9145 (or 42%) of them are "Skills", and 8148 (or 38%) of them are "Projects". To evaluate the correctness rate of the approach, we examined 10 employee profiles, 5 of which were selected manually as they contain a large number of tags (more than 60), and the other 5 were picked randomly. Among the 1107 tags with 476 distinct terms in the selected profiles, 467 distinct terms (or 98%) are classified. Through manual examination, we estimate that 300 (or 64%) distinct terms have been classified correctly. Most of the incorrectly-categorized terms have been mistakenly placed into the category "Skills". The major reason is that several terms we manually classified as "Skill", such as "machine-learning" and "social-network-analysis", are complex terms, while all the terms we manually classified as "Personal" and "Projects" are single terms. Since the categorization of complex terms would lead to more derived rules, the tool tends to place terms into the category "Skills".

In general, the performance our rule-based category algorithm is satisfactory. We have only classified 36 tags in the training process, but our rule-based algorithm is able to spread such limited categorization knowledge to most other tags in the system with a decent correctness rate. After our tool is deployed in our corporate websites, it will be able to learn and derive a lot more categorization rules from many users. We expect the accuracy of tag categorization will improve significantly with the growing number of rules.

5   Related Work

Tagging in collaborative environments has attracted significant amount of interests in the research community [8,2,7,11,4,5,10].

Research has been done on tags visualization [8,2] so as to facilitate the browsing of resources with tags, or allow users to figure out the important tags associated with an item quickly. However, existing tag visualization work does not provide automatic tag-classification functionality. In order to select tags describing a certain aspect of an item, users still have to go over all the tags and do the selection themselves.

In tagging systems, users have the freedom to choose whatever terms they like in tags. As we have seen earlier, this results in non-uniform usage of terminology (e.g. synonyms), naming collisions, and other problems. There has been work on improving the quality of tags in collaborative environments. In [11], Xu et al. defined a set of general criteria for a good tagging system. They also proposed a collaborative tag suggestion algorithm using those criteria to spot high-quality tags. Similar to [11], the goal of our paper is to improve the usability of tagging systems. However, instead of suggesting tags based on existing ones, we focus on automatic organization of tags so as to make it easier for users to find the information they want. In [10], Razavi and Iverson proposed to allow users to control access to their information using people-tagging. But they did not study the categorization of tags.

Our tag categorization work is related to research on documentation clustering [1]. In documentation clustering, topics are extracted from text-documents, and those documents are classified based on their topics. The major difference between our tag-categorization work and documentation clustering is that text-documents contain a large number of words while tags are individual terms. When given a text-document, people may extract frequently-appeared words in the document to serve as its topic (or category). However, tags do not have an article as its context, and thus there is little contextual information we can use to link together different terms used in tags.

6   Conclusion and Future Work

Tagging has gained popularity in collaborative systems, such as online photo sharing, webpage bookmarking, and employee profiling systems. Since different tags may describe different aspects of an item, placing tags into different categories will improve the usability of tagging systems, especially when the number of tags in the system is large. In this paper, we have proposed an approach to automatically categorize tags in tagging systems. Our approach look for synonyms used in tags by combining statistical data and the syntactical similarity between words. Whenever human users classify a tag, categorization rules may be derived to classify more tags. Also, we have proposed to use tagging-relation graph to handle the issue of naming collisions. Finally, we have implemented a prototype of our approach for Fringe, which is a real-world tagging system. Our experiments on the data collected by Fringe demonstrated the effectiveness of our approach.

Our next step is to develop a user-friendly interface for our tool and deploy it on Fringe. We will perform user-study with the deployed tool and make improvements. Also, we will explore other ways, such as searching and recommendation, to make use of the tags collected by Fringe. We would also like to test our tag-categorization approach on other enterprise-oriented tagging systems for webpages and resources, such as Dogear [9].

References

1. Andrews, N., Fox, E.: Recent developments in document clustering. Technical Report TR-07-35 (2007)
2. Dubinko, M., Kumar, R., Magnani, J., Novak, J., Raghavan, P., Tomkins, A.: Visualizing tags over time. In: International World Wide Web Conference (WWW), Edinburgh, Scotland (2006)
3. F-Spot, http://www.gnome.org/projects/f-spot/
4. Farrell, S., Lau, T.: Fringe contacts: People-tagging for the enterprise. In: Workshop on Collaborative Web Tagging in conjuction with WWW 2006, Edinburgh, Scotland (2006)
5. Farrell, S., Lau, T., Nusser, S., Wilcox, E., Muller, M.: Socially augmenting employee profiles with people-tagging. In: UIST 2007: Proceedings of the 20th annual ACM symposium on User interface software and technology, pp. 91–100. ACM, New York (2007)
6. GMail, http://www.gmail.com
7. John, A., Seligmann, D.: Collaborative tagging and expertise in the enterprise. In: Workshop on Collaborative Web Tagging in conjuction with WWW 2006, Edinburgh, Scotland (2006)
8. Kaser, O., Lemire, D.: Tagcloud drawing: Algorithms for cloud visualization. In: International World Wide Web Conference (WWW), Banff, Canada (2007)
9. Millen, D.R., Feinberg, J., Kerr, B.: Dogear: Social bookmarking in the enterprise. In: CHI 2006: Proceedings of the SIGCHI conference on Human Factors in computing systems, pp. 111–120. ACM, New York (2006)
10. Razavi, M.N., Iverson, L.: Supporting selective information sharing with people-tagging. In: CHI 2008: CHI 2008 extended abstracts on Human factors in computing systems, pp. 3423–3428. ACM, New York (2008)
11. Xu, Z., Fu, Y., Mao, J., Su, D.: Towards the semantic web: Collaborative tag suggestions. In: Workshop on Collaborative Web Tagging in conjuction with WWW 2006, Edinburgh, Scotland (2006)

A New Method for Creating Efficient Security Policies in Virtual Private Network

Mohammad Mehdi Gilanian Sadeghi[1], Borhanuddin Mohd Ali[1], Hossein Pedram[2],
Mehdi Deghan[2], and Masoud Sabaei[2]

[1] Faculty of Engineering, Universiti Putra Malaysia, Malaysia
mmgsadeghi@yahoo.com, borhan@eng.upm.edu.my
[2] Faculty of Computer Engineering and IT, Amirkabir University, Iran
{pedram,dehghan,sabaei}@ce.aut.ac.ir

Abstract. One of the most important protocols for implementing tunnels in order to take action of secure virtual private network is IPsec protocol. IPsec policies are used widely in order to limit access to information in security gateways or firewalls. The security treatment, namely (Deny, Allow or Encrypt) is done for outbound as well as inbound traffic by security policies. It is so important that they adjust properly. The current methods for security policies creation as seen in given security requirements are not efficient enough i.e. there are much more created policies than requirements. In this paper, we define a new method to decrease adopted security policies for a specific set of security requirements without any undesirable effect. Our measurement shows that security policies creation will be improved efficiently, and their updating time will be decreased.

Keywords: IPsec policies, security policy, security requirement, virtual private network.

1 Introduction

Virtual Private Network (VPN) is a group of techniques which makes implementation of an organization's private network on public and dynamic and scalable Internet. Many protocols are used for the creation of virtual private networks (VPN) [1] and IPsec protocol is one of the best for making security. IPsec policies [2] which are placed on Security Policy Database (SPD) and Security Association Database (SAD) consist of two parts, namely condition and action. The part of condition considers any header field in IP packet for each policy. Generally, the part of action includes three modes: Deny, Allow and IPsec_action. By mixing the properties of condition and action, the policies would be represented. For example Packet with A source and B destination addresses would pass in src=A, dst=B->Allow.

An inappropriate policy would possibly cause communication deficiency or serious security breach [3, 4]. Some problems are due to manager's carelessness for policies adjustment, while some others might arise from interactions that cannot be easily detected even with careful and experienced administrators. In the following, we study one scenario of policies problem [5].

E. Bertino and J.B.D. Joshi (Eds.): CollaborateCom 2008, LNICST 10, pp. 663–678, 2009.

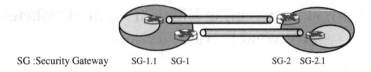

SG :Security Gateway   SG-1.1   SG-1   SG-2   SG-2.1

Fig. 1. Example of Policy Problem

In figure 1, there are financial department 1.1 in location 1 and financial department 2.1 in location 2. Suppose that each department has a unique security gateway as well as security policies in order to protect data. For example, department 1.1 decides to encrypt all traffic from 1.1 to 2 with a tunnel SG-1.1 to SG-2. At the same time, the administrator for location 1 decides that whole traffic from location 1 to financial department 2.1 must be encrypted through a tunnel from SG-1 to SG-2.1 because of its importance. Thus, traffic from SG-1.1 to SG-2.1 would be covered using two separate policies.

But such a scenario has a problem, i.e. with this configuration, a new header would be encapsulated to packet in SG-1.1, and then another new header would be encapsulated to these data in SG-1 again, finally they will be sent to SG-2.1 destination. When packets arrived at SG-2.1, the new header in second step is decapsulated, so it is clear to determine SG-2 destination. Hence, SG-2.1 returns traffic to SG-2. Finally, the new header in the first step is decapsulated in SG-2 and traffic is sent to its real destination. Although our aim is to encrypt the traffic from SG-2 to SG-2.1, there are some interactions between tunnels, so the real traffic will be sent from SG-2 to SG-2.1 without any encryption.

The disadvantage of Figure 1 is solved in Figure 2 by choosing appropriate policy. In Figure 2, the traffic is encrypted in SG-1.1. Again, it is encrypted in SG-1. The destination for both tunnels is SG-2. They are decrypted there and changed into plain text and then the traffic is encrypted in SG-2 and sent to the next tunnel between SG-2 and SG-2.1. If SG-2 is trusted in the second requirement, then the three-tunnel plan can well satisfy both requirements.

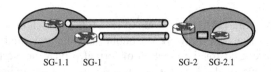

SG-1.1   SG-1   SG-2   SG-2.1

Fig. 2. IPsec policies to satisfy Security Requirements

In policy hierarchy [6], requirements (high level policy) are objectives while implementation policies (low level policies) are specific plans to meet the objectives. Each requirement may be met by a set of implementation policy. Thus, the process of policy creation is to meet the demands of targets in such a way that it transforms the requirements to implementation policies. So, it is necessary to choose policies very carefully to meet all requirements.

2   Related Works

A working group on IP security policy (IPSP) formed in IETF has addressed complex IPsec security policy problems. The requirements that we define in this paper basically follow the IPSP requirement draft [7]. There is no complete solution found up to now to meet all the objectives specified in the requirement and no interference between policies has been considered. Moreover, many different studies have been done on security policies [8, 9, 10] to standardize the policy specifications, which currently address only low-level policy specifications. Similarly, other proposed drafts regarding policy information base [11, 12] and data model [7] have also focused on low-level policies while [13] analyzed policy management problem and introduced global policies. [14]-[19] focus on finding an automated approach of IPsec policy configuration. In these two papers [18,19], "Filtering rules" refer to security requirements, while "IPsec policies" represent security policies. [20] presents an extension to Ordered-Split algorithm that analyzes the traffic probability together with the original algorithm to optimize the solution. Other research focuses on the policy management alone. [21] demonstrates an algorithm for distributing policies among a number of management stations, while [22] discusses an approach to conflict handling relying on a priori models. In order to avoid firewall policy anomalies, [23] proposes an approach to perform symbolic model checking of the firewall configurations for all possible IP packets and along all possible data paths to provide a complete solution.

The necessity of separation between high-level policies and low-level requirements has been studied in [24, 6]. There are two levels of policy hierarchy described in [14, 15] and this led to high level policies and low level security requirements that we use in this research.

In [5] a method to create appropriate policies in order to meet their requirements automatically has been presented. They guarantee the policy accuracy plus the interference among policies as much as possible. But, this would not be useful any longer because the number of security policies is more than security requirements. In this paper, we present a method to decrease the number of created security policies that will lead to increased efficiency as well as saving updating time for creating those policies.

In section 2, we review related works. We discuss current methods for creating policies in section 3. In section 4 a method is proposed to solve the problems of current security policies and then analyze them. Our research conclusion is finally in section 5.

3   Creating Security Policies to Meet Security Requirements

In total, there are four main security requirements for IPsec policies [14, 15].

✓   **Access control requirement (ACR):** One fundamental function of security is to conduct access control that is to restrict access only to trusted traffic. A simple way to specify an ACR is: flow id.->deny | allow

✓ **Security Coverage Requirements (SCR):** using security functions for the whole area (between two locations) to prevent traffic from illegal access during data transfer. A simple way to specify a SCR is to protect traffic from *"from"* to *"to"* by a security function with certain strength: *flow id.-> protect (sec_function, strength, from, to, trusted_nodes)* The requirement is satisfied only if the traffic is with sufficient security protection on every link and node in protection area from *"from"* to *"to"*, except that the trusted nodes can be left uncovered by the function.

✓ **Content Access Requirement (CAR):** Some nodes like firewalls with an intrusion detection system (IDS) would need to examine traffic content in order to decide how to manage passing traffic characteristic. CAR can be expressed as denying certain security function to prevent the nodes from accessing certain traffic. This is expressed as follows: *flow id.-> deny_sec (sec_function, access_nodes).* The requirement is satisfied only if the traffic is not secured with the function *"sec_function"* on any node specified in *"access_nodes"*.

✓ **Security Association Requirement (SAR):** Security Association (SA) [2] needs to perform encryption as well as authentication. There might be needs to specify that some nodes desire or not desire to set up SA of certain security function with some other nodes because of public key availability, capability match/mismatch etc. A simple way to specify a SAR could be: *flow id.->deny_SA (SA_peer1,SA_peer2, sec_function).* The requirement is satisfied only if none of the nodes specified in *"SA_peer1"* forms SA with any of nodes specified in *"SA_peer2"* with function *"sec_function"*.

Some security requirement characteristics have been mentioned above. Characteristics of security policies; they include *Deny, Allow, IPsec_action (sec_ port, algorithm, mode, from A, to A)* for selected traffic. s*ec_port* determines *AH* or *ESP* protocols. *Algorithm* determines all possible algorithms of Internet Key Exchange (IKE). *Mode* determines whether it is transfer or tunnel mode. *From A to A* determines two factors to create security Association. Policies perform security operations on passing traffic.

In [5], **Bundle Approach** was presented to create security policies, but the major problem is non efficiency. In other words the rate of security policies would be increased more than security requirements. In this way, the entire traffic would be divided into some sub set of separate Bundles. Each Bundle includes one set of security requirements. For one particular bundle, the condition part of policies contains bundle selectors and action part contains appropriate security actions to satisfy all requirements for the bundle. From Figure 3, there are a set of three security requirements [5]:

Three_Reqs = { Req1 (src=1.*, dst=2.*→ weak, ENC, 1.*, 2.*), Req2 (src=1.1.*, dst=2.*→ Strong, ENC, 1.1.*, 2.*), Req3 (src=1.*, dst=2.1.*→ Strong, AUTH,1.*, 2.1.*)}

They include F1, F2 and F3 filters (they can be 2-tuple, 3-tuple or 5-tuple). Also SG-1 and SG-2 security gateways are assumed as CAR nodes. Black, Gray and white lines in Figure 3 are determined for Req1, Req2 and Req3 respectively.

SG-1.1   SG-1   SG-2   SG-2.1

Fig. 3. Three_Reqs Example

The problem of using Bundle Approach is solved in two phases. In the first Phase, the entire traffic flow will be divided into separate bundles and then a set of requirements will be calculated for each of them. In the second phase for every bundle, appropriate policies (for action part) are selected according to the given requirements. In addition, the bundle's selectors will be calculated. Next, we discuss both the calculation selectors for each Bundle and the action part for creating the policies as follows:

3.1 Selection Decision

A Relationship Tree is used for calculating the requirements as well as their order. Figure 4 shows the relationship among **three_Reqs** filters. Filter F2 with Req2 has been used as a child of Filter F1 with Req1 in relationship tree, because it is contained by F1. Filter F3 with Req3 has overlap with F2. Thus, a new filter called F4 with Req3 generate which is combined by two filters F2 and F3 and inset as child of F2 since F4 is contained by F2. F3 would be inserted to the relationship tree as a child of F1, because it is contained by F1.

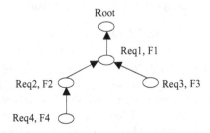

Root

Req1, F1

Req2, F2   Req3, F3

Req4, F4

Fig. 4. Relationship Tree

As a result, it is clear that four policy sets are generated namely: {policy_set 1, policy_set2, policy_set3, policy_set4} to satisfy requirement set {{Req1}, {Req1, Req2}, {Req1, Req3} and {Req1, Req2, Req3}, respectively. The filters of the policy sets are {F1, F2, F3, F4}. So, they include the following addresses, they are four bundles {(1.1.*.*, 2.1.*), (1.*-1.1.*, 2.1.*), (1.1.*, 2.*-2.1.*), (1.*-1.1.*, 2.*-2.1.*)}.

3.2 Policies Decision

In this stage, the aim is to decide how to use a set of appropriate policies according to requirements. If the inner most paths to carry packets is called **primary tunnels**, and the corresponding SA is called **primary SA**, then the primary tunnels need to be chained together across an area to provide security coverage for the area.

Our aim of tunnel creation is to satisfy Security Coverage Requirement (SCR), Content Access Requirement (CAR) and Security Association Requirement (SAR). Eligible Security Associations are confirmed by CAR and SAR. SCR has two major functions: encryption and authentication. A primary tunnel can only provide the coverage for just one function. The rest of the tunnels may be placed on top of primary tunnel to provide the necessary coverage for the other functions, so they are called *Secondary Security Association*. Finding Eligible SA is solvable using Algorithms and Graphs. To find eligible primary SAs, we need three graphs: **ENC secondary graph, AUTH secondary graph** and **Primary graph**, in which ENC and AUTH graphs are needed to determine secondary SA paths [5].

As discussed in previous section, there are four bundles for Three_Reqs example. If SG-1 and SG-2 security gateways are considered as Access Control Requirement (ACR) except the three Security Coverage Requirements, we can start finding policies using filter F1which contains Req1. Req1 has only encryption so it does not need AUTH secondary graph. Primary graph and ENC secondary graph are based on Figure 5. The edge 2-3 is called E1 that identify encryption for Req1.

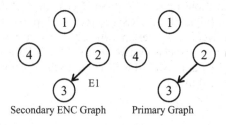

Secondary ENC Graph   Primary Graph

Fig. 5. Graphs of Filter F1

Then policies of Filter F2 with Req1 and Req2 are calculated. In this case these requirements contain only encryption so they do not need AUTH secondary graph. The only graph which can satisfy Req1 and Req2 is according to Figure 6.a. The edges are labeled as E2 because E2 is the stronger encryption Algorithm. (There are two encryption security coverage called E1 and E2 between two nodes 2 and 3 but E2 is stronger than E1, so E2 is selected). Node 2 has been chosen as a Content Access Requirement; therefore we would remove the edge between nodes 1-3 in order to break down the tunnel in node 2. All graphs will be formed like Figure 6.b after removing Edge.

Next we calculate policies of filter F3 with Req1 and Req3 according to Figure 7.a. Both AUTH and ENC secondary graph are necessary in this case because Req1 acts as encryption, and Req3 acts as authentication. Since there is no necessity for security coverage for ENC between nodes 3-4, there would be no edge in ENC secondary graph for these nodes. Node 3 has Content Access Requirement; consequently all passed association from the node will be removed. Thus, the processed graphs are formed as in Figure 7.b.

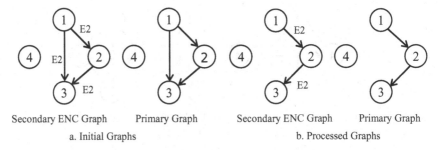

Secondary ENC Graph   Primary Graph   Secondary ENC Graph   Primary Graph

a. Initial Graphs   b. Processed Graphs

Fig. 6. Graphs of Filter F2

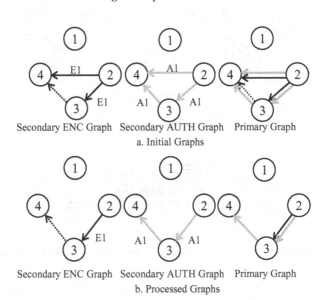

Secondary ENC Graph   Secondary AUTH Graph   Primary Graph

a. Initial Graphs

Secondary ENC Graph   Secondary AUTH Graph   Primary Graph

b. Processed Graphs

Fig. 7. Graphs of Filter F3

Finally, there is a filter F4 to calculate policies based on Req1, Req2 and Req3 like figure 8.a. In such a case, nodes 2 and 3 are Content Access Requirement and edges have to be removed. Final graphs will be formed like figure 8.b after removing edges. Also, the edge 3-4 in ENC secondary graph needs no ENC security coverage and the edge 1-2 in AUTH secondary graph needs no AUTH security coverage.

Figure 9 shows four groups of policies (tunnels) for four bundles with different colors using Bundle Approach [5]. There is a hatching tunnel set which is placed between traffic (1.1.*, 2.1.*). All these three satisfy the requirements of {Req1, Req2,Req3}. Gray tunnels apply for traffic (1.1.*, 2.*-2.1.*) and satisfy the requirements of {Req1,Req2}. White tunnels apply for traffic (1.*-1.1.*, 2.1.*) and satisfy the requirements of {Req1,Req3}. Black tunnels satisfy the requirements of Req1. In Total, 10 tunnels are necessary to satisfy the requirements of Three_ Reqs example. It should be noted that there are no distrusted nodes (tunnels cannot break

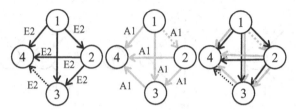

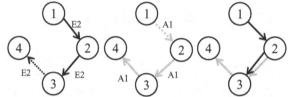

a. Initial Graphs

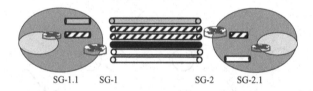

b. Processed Graphs

Fig. 8. Graphs of Filter F4

SG-1.1   SG-1   SG-2   SG-2.1

Fig. 9. Solutions (Policies) for Three_Reqs Example Using Bundle Approach

down among these nodes) in this case; otherwise they will have to consider in tunnel configuration.

4 Proposed Method

In the previous section, we observed that there are many created policies using *Three_Reqs* example and in some cases are more than the actual requirements. Thus, created policies are labeled as E1, E2 and A1 for each filter individually. But the problem is to increase policies (repetitive policies) that cause overloading and decreases efficiency because of the high costs of tunnels. On the other hand, if we use a new requirement with a new filter that contains some of the previous filters, then we have to consider these filters as children of the new filter in the relationship tree. Furthermore, we have to change the policy of these filters because their requirements have been changed. (Requirements of every node in the relationship tree equal its requirements plus parents requirements.) Changing filters policy waste time since we have to create new policies according to new requirements, and as a result policy updating time will be increased.

The most important issue in order to reuse policies is how to adjust **Selectors**. There was no problem in Bundle Approach because the policies have been created individually for each selector (policies were generated recurrently). On the other hand, if we want to use the previous policies for generating policies of the new filters, then adjusting selector is not easy.

In our proposed approach, we use two *recursive binary tree data structure* [25] which plays the role of adjusting selectors as well as using previous policy. Two binary tree data structures accomplish each other so we can use them to remove repetitive policies. Simply, we call them **NP** for New Policies and **TP** for Total Policies. In TP tree there is a set of bundle policies plus selectors whereas in NP tree, there are only new policies. First, the inputs of our algorithm are policies of each filter that generate in Bundle Approach. Then we place these policy selectors in TP tree. Next, we search NP tree to scrutinize how we can use previous created policies for the new filter policies coverage. If there are no corresponding policies for policies of the new filter, then we create new filter policies individually and put them as new nodes in NP tree. Afterwards , we create an appropriate link among present nodes in NP tree (new policies) and present node in TP tree (Filters selector), but If there are some needed policies for the new filter in NP tree, we can put only one required link between these nodes and the present node in TP tree.

So, all needed policies are accessible to each bundle with traverse TP tree data structure. Also, we can also use this structure to adjust selectors. New policies would be placed on NP tree and there are no repetitive policies there. On the other hand, if a new filter which contains some previous filters is added, then in Bundle Approach the policies of these filters that change requirements must be recreated, leading to an increase in updating time. However in our proposed approach, the updating time is reduced because some policies have been used again (We would be able to get access to all the required policies for each filter while searching in TP tree).

We explained the proposed approach using Three_Reqs example: we assume that security gateways addresses are SG-1.1= 00*, SG-1=0*, SG-2=1*, SG-2.1=11*. Filter F1 has (scr =0*, dst=1*) address and Req1. First, we put a new node according to F1 selectors (0*, 1*) in TP tree. F1 required policy consists only (scr=0*, dst=1*, alg=E, strg=1). Then, we search through all previous created policies in NP tree again to examine whether there is any policy according to F1 new filter or not. Since NP tree is empty and there is no node, no policy is in it yet. Therefore, we created a new node in NP tree according to (scr=0*, dst=1*, alg=E, strg=1) policy. There is an association between this node and present node in TP tree. Figure 10 shows how to make NP and TP trees. F1 policies are accessible from TP tree.

Now, F2 enters with (scr=00*, dst=1*) addresses and Req2 and Req1. In the first stage, we add F2 selector (00*, 1*) as a new node to TP tree. After that we search NP tree to scrutinize previous policies to know if it is based on new policies such as (scr=00*, dst=0*, alg=E, strg=2) or (scr=0*, dst= 1* ,alg=E, strg=2). In this case, there is a policy for (scr=0*, dst=1*) in NP tree but encryption algorithms power is totally adverse due to security coverage, so we can not use the previous policies. Figure 11 shows two tree data structure for F2. It is accessible from TP to get filter F2 policies.

We add filter F3 with (src=0*, dst=11*) Address and Req1 and Req3 in the next step. In this case, we add a new node (0*, 11*) to TP tree. All filter F3 policies are as

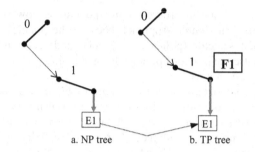

a. NP tree   b. TP tree

Fig. 10. Filter F1

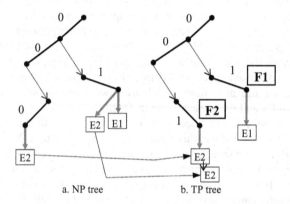

a. NP tree   b. TP tree

Fig. 11. Filter F2

the following: (src=0*, dst=1*, alg=E, strg=1), (src=1*, dst=11*, alg=A, strg=1), (src=0*, dst=1*, alg= A, strg=1).While searching in the NP tree, we find a policy corresponding to (src=0*, dst=1*, alg=E, strg=1). (in the first step the policy is created for filter F1). But there are not two policies in NP tree and must be created as well. Figure 12 shows TP and NP trees. We can also get F3 policies using TP tree.

In the final step, we put filter F4 with the following characteristics: (src=00*, dst=11*) and {Req1, Req2, Req3}. Likewise, a new node will be added to TP tree with (00*, 11*) addresses. The F4 policies are as follows: (src=0*, dst=1*, alg=A, strg=1), (src=0*, dst=1*, alg=E, strg=2), (src=00*, dst=0*, alg=E, strg=2), (src=1*, dst=11*, alg=A, strg=1). We note that all needed policies are available for searching NP tree. Figure 13 shows the association between TP and NP trees for filter F4. We can reach F4 policies using TP tree.

Using the proposed approach (e.g. Three_Reqs), as we used some policies again, they will be decreased to five policies. Since creating each policy involves high costs (e.g: SA key discussion, etc.), thus we optimize expenses as well as efficiency in comparison with Bundle Approach. On the other hand, Updating time will be decreased. Since in Bundle Approach we have to create all new policies according to change each filter requirements at the first. (With changing filter requirements, their old policies will be deleted and their new policies will be created according to new

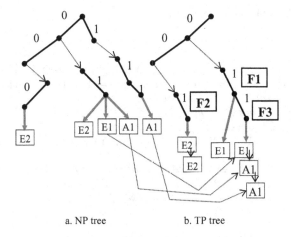

a. NP tree   b. TP tree

Fig. 12. Filter F3

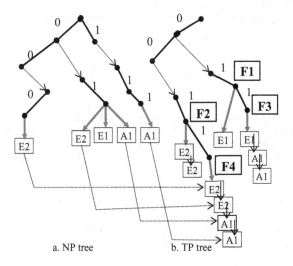

a. NP tree   b. TP tree

Fig. 13. Filter F4

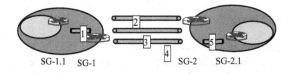

SG-1.1   SG-1   SG-2   SG-2.1

Fig. 14. Solutions (Policies) for Three_Reqs Example Using New Approach

requirement). But in this new approach we reuse some policies, so there is no time to create policies and we only calculate new policies time. Figure 14 shows the policies using new approach.

New algorithm is based on Figure 15.

```
Algorithm DeleteRepeatedPolicies(new-policies){
    selector ← CalculateSeclector(new-policies)
    InsertTreeTP(Selector)
    for every newpolicy i,i+1 in new-policies
        if (SearchInTreeNP(new-policy i,i+1))
            LinkTPNP(Selector, new-policy i,i+1)
        else
            InsertTreeNP(new-policy i,i+1)
        LinkTPNP(selector, new-policy i,i+1)
        CalculatePolicies(NP)
}

CalculateSelector(new-policies){
    Selector ←(new-policy1,new-policyn)
    if selector is in TP
        UpdateTP(new-policies, selector)


else
        Return selector
}

UpdateTP(new-policies, selector){
    RemoveLinkTPNP(New-policies, selector)
    RemoveTreeTP(selector)
    DeleteRepeatedPolicies(new-poliocies)
}

LinkTPNP(selector, new-policy i,i+1){
    TraverseTP(selector)
    TraverseNP(new-policy i,i+1)
    selector←ADRS(new-policy i,i+1)
}
```

Fig. 15. New algorithm

4.1 Analyses and Simulation

We wrote our algorithm in C++ Language and Linux OS. The input to the algorithm is the requirements file whereas output is the policies file which consists of automatically created policies. Requirements will are created in the input file randomly. In other words, one random set of sources would like to get secure connect to one random set of destinations and its encryption algorithm power will be chosen randomly. Simulation environment has been organized based on Figure 16.

Fig. 16. Relationship between domains

We assumed that there are three levels in each domain and three levels in each sub-domain. Security gateways are the same in domains and sub-domain. Movement route in security gateways is linear, for example for connecting from 1.1.*.* to 2.2.*.* the route in security gateways is as follows: 1.1.*.*, 1.*.*.*, 2.*.*.* and 2.*.*.*. The number of nodes in the route is equal to 3*2= 6 using three hierarchical levels of domains. We created 5, 10, 15, 20... 60 requirements randomly. Then we compared Bundle and New approach based on these Requirements. Figure 17 shows the number of created policies between the two approaches.

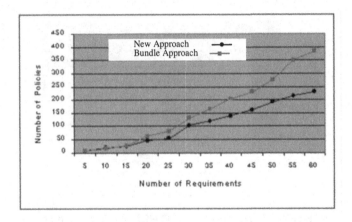

Fig. 17. Comparing the number of created policies in Bundle Approach and New Approach

In Bundle Approach, there are many policies (tunnels) to satisfy different requirements. So, increasing the number of requirements will lead to an increase in the number of policies, however this comes at the expense of scalability. In the proposed approach, there are fewer policies since we reuse the previous policies as much as possible.

On the other hand, when we add new requirements and they contain previous requirements, the policies of previous requirements should be reproduced because new requirement affect their policies. In Bundle Approach, all policies must be created again so the updating time for policies is high while in the our proposed approach, we only calculate new policies time. As a result, the entire traffic time will be as short as the time we spent to create each bundle policy. Figure 18 shows a comparison of the updated policies.

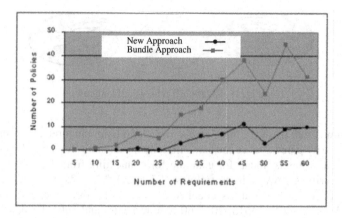

Fig. 18. Comparing the number of updated policies in Bundle Approach and New Approach

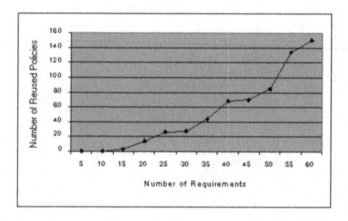

Fig. 19. The number of Reused Policies in New Approach

Figure 19 shows the proposed approach and the number of reused policies. In other words, it shows its decreased policies. There is a high expense to create each policy (e.g. SA key discussion), so we can decrease costs through less policies.

5   Conclusion and Future Work

IPsec/VPN policies are used widely in security gateways or firewalls where security treatment (Deny, Allow or Encrypt) is done for outbound as well as inbound traffic through security policies. It is so important that they should be adjusted properly. On the other hand, efficiency is a very important issue which is not considered in the present methods. In this paper, we presented a new approach which optimizes the creation of new policies. In fact we used these policies together with old policies so that organizations or people would be able to determine easily their requirements at a high level and they will no longer be concerned about efficiency loss as well as the increase of updating time. Repetitive policies cause scalability problem such that with increasing requirements it does not run and this will lead to less efficiency. In this paper, we proposed integrated policies. We can use this approach not only for distributed policies but also for other parameters such as routing and QoS. Moreover, we can scrutinize how to reach the requirements from policies.

References

1. Doraswamy, N., Harkind, D.: IPSEC, The New Security Standard for Internet, Intranets, Virtual Private Network. Prentice Hall PTR, Englewood Cliffs (1999)
2. Kent, S., Atkinson, R.: Security Architecture for the Internet Protocol. RFC 2401 (1998)
3. Lupu, E.C., Sloman, M.: Conflict Analysis for Management Policies. In: 5th IFIP/IEEE International Symposium on Integrated Network Management, pp. 430–443 (1997)
4. Lupu, E.C., Sloman, M.: Conflicts in Policy Based Distributed Systems Management. IEEE Transaction on Software Engineering 25(6), 852–869 (1999)
5. Fu, Z., Wu, S.F.: Automatic Generation of IPsec/VPN policies in an Intra-Domain Environment. In: 12th International Workshop on Distributed System: operation & management (DSOM 2001), Nancy, France (2001)
6. Moffett, J.D., Sloman, M.S.: Policy Hierarchies for Distributed Systems Management. IEEE Journal on Selected Areas in Communication 11, 1404–1414 (1993)
7. Blaze, M., Keromytis, A., Richardson, M., Sanchez, L.: IP Security Policy Requirements. Internet draft, draft-ietf-ipsp-requirements-02.txt, IPSP Working Group (2002)
8. Condell, M., Lynn, C., Zao, J.: Security Policy Specification Language. Internet Draft, draft_ietf_ipsp_spsl_00.txt (2000)
9. Jason, J.: IPsec Configuration Policy Model. Internet Draft, draft_ietf_ipsp_config_policy_model_00.txt (2000)
10. Pereira, R., Bhattacharya, P.: IPSec Policy Data Model. Internet Draft, draft_ietf_ipsec_policy_model_00.txt (1998)
11. Law, K.L.E.: Scalable Design of a Policy-Based Management System and its Performance. IEEE Communication Magazine 41(6), 72–97 (2003)
12. Zao, J., Sanchez, L., Condell, M., Lyn, C., Fredette, M., Helinek, P., Krishnan, P., Jackson, A., Mankins, D., Shepard, M., Kent, S.: Domain Based Internet Security Policy Management. In: Proceedings of DARPA Information Survivability Conference and Exposition (2000)
13. Baek, S., Jeong, M., Park, J., Chung, T.: Policy-based Hybrid Management Architecture for IP-based VPN. In: Proceedings of 7th IEEE/IFIP Network Operations and management Symposium (NOMS 2000), Honolulu, Hawaii (2000)
14. Fu, Z., Wu, S.F., Huang, H., Loh, K., Gong, F.: IPSec/VPN Security Policy: Correctness, Conflict Detection and Resolution. In: IEEE policy 2001 Workshop (2001)
15. Yang, Y., Martel, C., Fu, Z., Wu, S.F.: IPsec/VPN Security Policy Correctness and Assurance. In: Proceedings of Journal of High Speed Networking, Special issue on Managing Security Polices: Modeling, Verification and Configuration (2006)
16. Yang, Y., Martel, C., Wu, S.F.: On Building the Minimum Number of Tunnels – An Ordered-Split approach to manage IPsec/VPN policies. In: Proceedings of 9th IEEE/IFIP Network Operations and Management Symposium (NOMS 2004), Seoul, Korea (2004)
17. Yang, Y., Fu, Z., Wu, S.F.: BANDS: An Inter-Domain Internet Security Policy Management System for IPSec/VPN. In: Proceedings of 8th IFIP/IEEE International Symposium on Integrated Network Management (IM 2003), Colorado (2003)

18. Al-Shaer, E., Hamed, H.: Taxonomy of Conflicts in Network Security Policies. Proceedings of IEEE Communications Magazine 44(3) (2006)
19. Hamed, H., Al-Shaer, E., Marrero, W.: Modeling and Verification of IPsec and VPN Security Policies. In: Proceedings of 13th IEEE International Conference on Network Protocols, ICNP 2005 (2005)
20. Chang, C.L., Chiu, Y.P., Lei, C.L.: Automatic Generation of Conflict-Free IPsec Policies. In: Wang, F. (ed.) FORTE 2005. LNCS, vol. 3731, pp. 233–246. Springer, Heidelberg (2005)
21. Sheridan-Smith, N., Neill, T.O., Leaney, J.: Enhancements to Policy Distribution for Control Flow, Looping and Transactions. In: Schönwälder, J., Serrat, J. (eds.) DSOM 2005. LNCS, vol. 3775, pp. 269–280. Springer, Heidelberg (2005)
22. Kempter, B., Danciu, V.: Generic policy conflict handling using a priori models. In: Schönwälder, J., Serrat, J. (eds.) DSOM 2005. LNCS, vol. 3775, pp. 84–96. Springer, Heidelberg (2005)
23. Yuan, L., Mai, J., Su, Z., Chen, H., Chuah, C.N., Mohapatra, P.: FIREMAN: A Toolkit for Firewall Modeling and Analysis. In: Proceedings of IEEE Symposium on Security and Privacy (2006)
24. Moffett, J.D.: Requirements and Policies. In: Position paper for Policy Workshop (1999)
25. Adiseshu, H., Suri, S., Parulkar, G.: Detecting and Resolving Packet Filter Conflicts. In: INFOCOM (2000)

Data Quality and Failures Characterization of Sensing Data in Environmental Applications*

Kewei Sha[1], Guoxing Zhan[2], Safwan Al-Omari[2], Tim Calappi[2], Weisong Shi[2], and Carol Miller[2]

[1] Oklahoma City University, Oklahoma City OK 73106, USA
ksha@okcu.edu
[2] Wayne State University, Detroit MI 48202, USA
{gxzhan,somari,tcalappi,weisong,cjmiller}@wayne.edu

Abstract. Environmental monitoring is one of the most important sensor network application domains. The success of those applications is determined by the quality of the collected data. Thus, it is crucial to carefully analyze the collected sensing data, which not only helps us understand the features of monitored field, but also unveil any limitations and opportunities that should be considered in future sensor system design. In this paper, we take an initial step and analyze one-month sensing data collected from a real-world water system surveillance application, focusing on the data similarity, data abnormality and failure patterns. Our major findings include: (1) Information similarity, including pattern similarity and numerical similarity, is very common, which provides a good opportunity to trade off energy efficiency and data quality; (2) Spatial and multi-modality correlation analysis provide a way to evaluate data integrity and to detect conflicting data that usually indicates appearances of sensor malfunction or interesting events; and (3) External harsh environmental conditions may be the most important factor on inflicting failures in environmental applications. Communication failures, mainly caused by lacking of synchronization, contribute the largest portion among all failure types.

1 Introduction

As new fabrication and integration technologies reduce the cost and size of wireless micro-sensors, we are witnessing another revolution that facilitates the observation and control of our physical world [3,12], just as networking technologies have changed the way individuals and organizations exchange information. Environmental monitoring, targeting at discovering and understanding the environmental laws and changes, is one of the most important sensor network application domains.

With the increasing number of deployments of sensor systems, in which the main function is to collect interesting data at the sink, it is becoming crucial to carefully analyze the large amount of collected data. However, this problem is neglected in previous research, which mainly focuses on energy efficient, reliable sensor systems design and optimization. Although data quality management attracts more and more attention in

---

* This work is in part supported by NSF grant CNS-0721456. The work was done when the first author was a graduate student at Wayne State University.

the last two years [10,15], proposing novel data quality management mechanisms is still an important and interesting research topic. We argue that sensor system optimization and data quality management are closely related to the characteristics of collected data, in other words, sensor system optimization and data quality management should take data characteristics into consideration. Thus, in this paper, we take an initial step to characterize the data quality and failures using a set of one-month data collected by a real-world water system surveillance application. The data set consists of water level, precipitation, and gauge voltage measurements from 13 gauges located around Lake Winnebago, St. Clair River and Detroit River in January 2008.

Our data analysis focuses on two aspects: *quality oriented data analysis* and *failure pattern analysis*. In quality oriented data analysis, we intend to discover two types of data, namely similarity data and abnormal data, whereas, in failure pattern analysis, we try to classify the common failure type and record failure time. The significance of our discovery is two-fold. On one hand, it helps us understand the laws and changes in the monitored field. On the other hand, it unveils the limitations in the current sensor system design, and provides us with a strong ground upon which we can base our future WSN systems design.

Our study reveals several interesting facts. First, information similarity, including pattern similarity and numerical similarity, is very common, which provides a good opportunity to trade off energy efficiency and data quality. Second, different parameters exhibit different data characteristics, which suggests that adaptive protocols using variable sampling rates can bring in significant improvements. Third, spatial correlation analysis and multi-modality correlation analysis provide a way to evaluate data integrity and to detect conflicting data that usually indicates appearances of sensor malfunction or interesting events. Fourth, abnormal data may appear all the time, and continuous appearance of abnormal data usually suggests a failure or an interesting event. Finally, external harsh environmental conditions may be the most important factor on inflicting failures in environmental applications. Communication failures, mainly caused by lack of synchronization, contribute the largest portion among all failure types.

The rest of the paper is organized as follows. A brief background of the targeting application and data is described in Section 2. We conduct quality oriented data analysis in Section 3, followed by failure pattern analysis in Section 4. Finally, related work and conclusion are listed in Section 5 and Section 6 respectively.

2   Background

The United States Army Corps of Engineers (USACE) in Detroit District, has 22 data collection platforms commonly referred to as sensor nodes or gauges, deployed around the St. Clair and Detroit rivers in southeast Michigan as well as the Lake Winnebago watershed southwest of Green Bay, Wisconsin. One month data in January 2008 from 13 of the 22 gauges were made available for this study. Each sensor node collects battery voltage, water level and precipitation except the Dunn Paper gauge (G1) which collects battery voltage, air temperature and water temperature. However, precipitation data for the St. Clair/Detroit river system is not used in this work, because that "data" in the raw files is simply an artifact of the gauge programming. For convenience, we name each

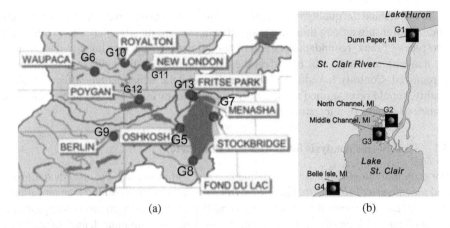

Fig. 1. Map of: (a) Lake Winnebago Watershed, (b) St. Clair River and Detroit River

sensor node as G1, where 'G' stands for "gauge." The gauge locations of G1, G2 and G3 are on the St. Clair River, G4 is located on the Detroit River, and G5 through G13 are spread around the Lake Winnebago watershed. Gauges G5 through G13 are shown in Figure 1(a), and the remaining gauges are shown in Figure 1(b). It is worth mentioning that G8 and G10 suffered many failures throughout the period of study. Therefore, any data analysis on G8 or G10 will mostly look like "weird" or at least different from the other gauges.

Data samples are sent from each gauge to the GOES satellite, once every hour or every four hours, depending on whether the station has a high baud rate transmitter or not. High baud rate transmitters send data every hour. Data is then sent from the satellite to a central location in Wallops Island in Virginia, where the data samples are collected and arranged in files for later download through a regular ftp service. We conducted our analysis directly using the un-decoded files. This raw data set has not been subject to any quality control procedure, and thus provide a good opportunity to study failures happening in sensor network. Water level and precipitation are sampled once every hour, whereas voltage is sampled once every hour or every two hours. Water level is measured against the IGLD Datum 1985, which works as the base to measure current water level. So negative water level means it is below the local IGLD Datum 1985, though that does not happen often. Precipitation data is supposed to be constantly increasing (except when the gauge resets as part of its normal operation). To figure out how much precipitation fell over a one-hour period, the difference between consecutive samples are calculated and reported. The measurements for voltage and precipitation are in volts and inches respectively. Water level is reported in meters, centimeters and feet. For convenience, we converted the readings for water level in meters.

3   Quality-Oriented Sensing Data Analysis

In this section, we focus on quality-oriented sensing data analysis. How to define data quality is still an open problem. Here, We define high quality data as the data that contains the most information from the monitored field.

To understand the quality of the collected data, we try to discover the spatial and temporal relationship among those data; specifically, we are mostly interested in detecting two types of data, redundant data and abnormal data. Usually, redundant data, which we name as similarity, will not affect the overall quality of the collected data when it is removed. Contrary to redundant data, abnormal data, which largely affects the data quality, should be examined more carefully, because it usually denotes sensor failures, malicious attacks or interesting events.

3.1 Time Series Analysis for Individual Parameter

For each individual parameter, we define two types of similarity, *the pattern similarity* and *the numerical similarity*. Here, we define a pattern as the continuous reappearance of the same value sensed by one sensor, and the number of continuous reappearance is called pattern length. Note that a pattern must have a minimum length of 2. Thus, each pattern is a two tuple $< key, length >$. For example, if the sensor reads a series of $4, 4, 4, 5, 5, 4, 5$, we detect the patterns as $< 4, 3 >$ and $< 5, 2 >$, and the number of appearance of each pattern is 1. We use the pattern reappearance ratio, which is the ratio of the pattern data in the whole data, to measure the pattern similarity among the data. The numerical similarity records the number of reappearance of the same numerical value. For example, if a sensor reads a series of $4, 4, 4, 5, 5, 4, 5$, we get numerical similarity as 4 times of appearance of value 4 and 3 times of appearance of value 5. Similarly, the numerical similarity ratio is used to evaluate the value similarity, which is defined as the ratio of the reappeared sensor readings in all sensor readings.

Pattern Similarity. We detect all patterns for all monitoring parameters in 13 gauges. Here, we pick up gauge G5 as a typical example to show the patterns we detected as well as reappearance times of the pattern, which is shown in Figure 2.

From the figure, we do find specific patterns in the collected data, and the number of total patterns is small for all three parameters. Water level of gauge G5 has the largest number of patterns, which is 33, whereas, precipitation has the smallest number of patterns, which is 19. Some patterns have very large pattern length. For example, the largest pattern length for water level and for precipitation are 77 and 139 respectively. This indicates that water level and precipitation values stay constant for a long period of time at the area where G5 located. The number of appearances of each pattern is mostly small, especially for patterns with large length. This is because we set up endurance interval as $[0.00, 0.00]$, thus, very small difference between two keys, such as 14.66 and 14.67, are distinguish. Here endurance interval is an interval within which the difference between two readings can be ignored, for example, if the endurance interval is $[-0.02, 0.02]$, 14.67 and 14.66 can be regarded as the same. Because of unavoidable system error in measurement and applications lowered requirements on accuracy, it is reasonable to set up an endurance interval for each monitoring parameter. Another reason is that we define different patterns even when they have the same key value but different lengths.

Figure 3(a) shows the pattern reappearance ratio, where "-" means there is no available data. In the figure, we find that voltage has the smallest pattern reappearance ratio, which suggests that the changes of the voltage are very frequent. This is also because

V Pattern	Appearances	W Pattern	Appearances	P Pattern	Appearances
<14.09, 2>	1	<0.67, 2>	1	<1.67, 2>	1
<14.58, 2>	1	<0.68, 2>	1	<1.77, 2>	1
<14.59, 2>	1	<0.69, 2>	2	<2.28, 2>	1
<14.63, 2>	2	<0.70, 2>	1	<2.50, 2>	1
<14.64, 2>	1	<0.71, 2>	2	<2.52, 2>	1
<14.66, 2>	2	<0.72, 2>	1	<2.30, 5>	1
<14.67, 2>	2	<0.68, 3>	1	<2.47, 5>	1
<14.68, 2>	3	<0.69, 3>	2	<2.24, 7>	1
<14.69, 2>	1	<0.70, 3>	2	<2.34, 7>	1
<14.71, 2>	1	<0.71, 3>	4	<2.40, 8>	1
<14.73, 2>	1	<0.72, 3>	2	<1.69, 16>	1
<14.57, 3>	1	<0.70, 4>	2	<2.36, 22>	1
<14.60, 3>	1	<0.71, 4>	1	<2.20, 38>	1
<14.67, 3>	3	<0.72, 4>	3	<2.36, 44>	1
<14.72, 3>	1	<0.69, 5>	2	<2.11, 49>	1
<14.65, 4>	1	<0.70, 5>	4	<2.53, 67>	1
<14.67, 4>	2	<0.70, 9>	1	<2.41, 97>	1
<14.68, 4>	3	<0.72, 9>	1	<2.51, 102>	1
<14.69, 4>	2	<0.71, 11>	1	<1.29, 139>	1
<14.61, 5>	1	<0.71, 14>	1		
<14.64, 5>	1	<0.68, 16>	1		
<14.67, 5>	1	<0.71, 16>	1		
<14.68, 5>	2	<0.71, 18>	1		
<14.68, 6>	1	<0.71, 22>	1		
<14.70, 6>	1	<0.67, 28>	1		
<14.67, 7>	2	<0.68, 29>	1		
<14.69, 7>	1	<0.71, 30>	1		
<14.68, 8>	2	<0.70, 34>	1		
<14.68, 9>	2	<0.70, 38>	1		
<14.68, 10>	1	<0.69, 45>	1		
<14.68, 11>	1	<0.69, 47>	1		
<14.67, 12>	1	<0.68, 69>	1		
		<0.72, 77>	1		

Fig. 2. Detected patterns and the number of appearance in gauge G5

Gauge ID	Voltage Pattern Reappearance Ratio	Water Level Pattern Reappearance Ratio	Precipitation Pattern Reappearance Ratio
G1	0.07	-	-
G2	0.85	0.64	-
G3	0.78	0.43	-
G4	0.38	0.57	-
G5	0.50	0.88	0.92
G6	0.17	0.84	0.89
G7	0.96	0.69	0.93
G8	-	-	-
G9	0.23	0.87	0.89
G10	0.04	0.44	0.77
G11	0.10	0.83	0.90
G12	0.87	0.94	0.91
G13	0.05	0.88	0.89

Gauge ID	Voltage Pattern Reappearance Ratio [-0.1, 0.1]	Water Level Pattern Reappearance Ratio [-0.02, 0.02]	Precipitation Pattern Reappearance Ratio [-0.02, 0.02]
G1	0.59	-	-
G2	1.00	0.85	-
G3	1.00	0.74	-
G4	0.96	0.78	-
G5	0.88	0.99	0.95
G6	0.98	0.94	0.92
G7	1.00	0.99	0.95
G8	-	-	-
G9	1.00	0.94	0.92
G10	0.64	0.72	0.79
G11	0.78	0.93	0.94
G12	1.00	0.99	0.94
G13	0.80	0.95	0.94

(a)   (b)

Fig. 3. Pattern reappearance ratio with: (a) zero endurance interval, (b) increased endure intervals

we distinguished the pattern keys in extremely fine granularity; however, even in such a fine granularity, both patterns in water level and precipitation show a large ratio of pattern similarity. For example, the smallest pattern reappearance ratio is 0.43 in G3, and the largest pattern reappearance ratio is 0.94 in G12. While precipitation shows the largest pattern similarity, which can be seen not only from the least number of patterns in Figure 2, but also from the fact that it has all pattern reappearance ratio larger than 0.77; actually, most pattern reappearance ratio of precipitation is about 0.99 for all gauges. We can expect precipitation to stay stable at most time. It may change suddenly, however, after this sudden change, it goes back to normal and stabilizes for a long period of time. Voltage has the most varying pattern reappearance ratios, which ranges from 0.04 to 0.96, showing that the performance of the power supply is really independent and highly dynamic.

The goal of the sensor network applications is to collect meaningful data, thus, most of those applications can endure a certain level of data inaccuracy, which will not affect our discovery of the rules and events in the monitoring field. We reexamine the pattern reappearance ratio after we lower the accuracy requirements on the collected data and set up different endurance intervals for three parameters. The resulted pattern reappearance ratio is depicted in Figure 3(b), where the three numbers under the title are the endurance intervals, which are mostly 10% of possible largest changes, i.e., we allow voltage to endure 0.2 volts changes, water level to endure 0.04 meter changes, and precipitation to endure 0.04 inch changes. Note that different units are used for water level and precipitation, i.e., meter for water level and inch for precipitation, which we keep the original units as in the raw data.

Comparing Figure 3(b) to Figure 3(a), we can find that almost all pattern reappearance ratios increased by increasing the endurance interval, especially for those with small reappearance ratio in Figure 3(a). After we increase the endurance interval, we can see that 50% of the voltage data pattern reappearance ratio is larger than 0.95, while water level and precipitation pattern reappearance ratio do not change too much compared to that in voltage; however, most of them are still larger than those in Figure 3(a). From both figures, we can see that there is a big pattern reappearance ratio.

In our definition, pattern length means the number of continuous appearance of the same sensor reading. Thus, we try to figure out the distribution of the pattern length in terms of variable endurance interval, as shown in Figure 4, where the x-axis is the length of the pattern and the y-axis is the CDF of the pattern length. From the figure, we find that most patterns have short patten length. For example, when the endurance interval is set to be [0.00, 0.00], 90% of voltage patterns have length less than 10, and about 70%

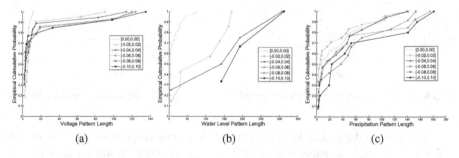

Fig. 4. CDF of pattern length: (a) Voltage, (b) water level, (c) precipitation

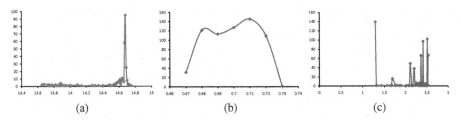

Fig. 5. The number of appearances for each numerical values: (a) Voltage, (b) water level, (c) precipitation

of water level patterns and about 60% of precipitation patterns have length less than 10. However, different parameters have different pattern lengths. In the figure, we can see that voltage, which has almost all pattern length less than 20, has more short length patterns than water level and precipitation, while precipitation has the longest length among the three parameters, where about 30% of the precipitation pattern has length longer than 20. This observation shows that precipitation is stable at most of the time, but the reading of the voltage has high dynamics. By increasing the endurance interval, more patterns have longer length appear. For example, when water level endurance interval is increased to $[-0.04, 0.04]$, more than 30% of the patterns have length between 140 to 180.

Numerical Similarity. Having studied pattern similarity, we move on to check the numerical similarity. Numerical similarity focuses on the numerical value reappearance of the sensing data, which differs from pattern similarity in that numerical similarity does not intend to detect any pattern. For the numerical similarity, we identify the number of appearance for each individual value. Figure 5 shows the numerical distribution of the collected data, where the x-axis is the numerical value of the sensing reading and the y-axis denotes the number of appearance of the corresponding numerical value. Note that we pick up the data collected by gauge G5 as an example.

In the figure, we find that those three parameters exhibit totally different distributions. The reading of the voltage and water level are very close to normal distribution with $\mu = 14.22, \sigma = 0.38$ and $\mu = 0.7, sigma = 0.02$ respectively. The voltage readings are more centralized to value 14.7, while water level readings are more broadly distributed from 0.68 to 0.72 and centralized at 0.71. The reading of precipitation shows no obvious distribution. It spreads from about 1.25 to 2.55. Some precipitation values such as 1.29 and 2.51, appear much more times than others, which means no rain or snow falls for a long time after the precipitation value is read, while other precipitation readings only appear several times, which mainly depicts some transitional states during a continuous rain or snow falling. Like the pattern similarity ratio, numerical reappearance ratio is used to evaluate the numerical similarity.

Figure 6(a) presents the numerical reappearance ratio of the sensing data at all gauges. We can see that all parameters exhibit very high reappearance ratio. Compared to pattern reappearance ratio, numerical reappearance ratio is much larger for voltage, fairly larger for water level, and comparable for precipitation. For example, the voltage pattern reappearance ratio in G1, G10 and G11 is less than 10%, while the voltage numerical pattern reappearance is close to 80%. The large difference implies that

Gauge ID	Voltage Numerical Reappearance Ratio	Water Level Numerical Reappearance Ratio	Precipitation Numerical Reappearance Ratio
G1	0.84	-	-
G2	0.99	0.64	-
G3	0.97	0.43	-
G4	0.91	0.57	-
G5	0.82	0.88	0.92
G6	0.94	0.84	0.89
G7	0.99	0.69	0.93
G8	-	-	-
G9	0.97	0.87	0.89
G10	0.77	0.44	0.77
G11	0.82	0.83	0.90
G12	0.99	0.94	0.91
G13	0.89	0.88	0.89

Gauge ID	Voltage Numerical Reappearance Ratio [-0.1, 0.1]	Water Level Numerical Reappearance Ratio [-0.02, 0.02]	Precipitation Numerical Reappearance Ratio [-0.02, 0.02]
G1	0.95	-	-
G2	0.99	0.97	-
G3	0.99	0.94	-
G4	0.97	0.95	-
G5	0.94	0.99	0.95
G6	0.98	0.98	0.93
G7	1.00	1.00	0.95
G8	-	-	-
G9	0.99	0.96	0.93
G10	0.89	0.93	0.90
G11	0.92	0.96	0.94
G12	1.00	0.99	0.95
G13	0.95	0.97	0.94

(a)   (b)

Fig. 6. Numerical reappearance ratio with: (a) endurance interval [0.00, 0.00], (b) increased endurance intervals

although the numerical readings of the voltage have a large similarity, they fluctuate very frequently and there are no obvious patterns in voltage readings. The two reappearance ratios of precipitation do not differ too much, which suggests that reappearance patterns play an important role in precipitation.

Similar to what we have done in the pattern similarity analysis, we increase the endurance interval to a certain level. Here, we set the endurance interval to the same value as we did in the pattern similarity analysis. As a result, most numerical appearance ratios are increased by increasing the endurance interval; however, the increasing rate is not as big as the one in pattern similarity analysis. From Figure 6(b), we really find that the numerical redundancy is very high in all three types of sensing data. For instance, after we increase the endurance interval, the numerical reappearance ratio is mostly over 90%. We also try to mine the pattern of the data change in terms of the time series. We calculate the coefficiency in the time series with different time periods such as 24 hours, 48 hours and so on, however, we find that all the coefficiencies are very low, thus, we believe that there is no strong clues showing the periodically reappearance pattern in data changes.

Abnormal Data Detection. Abnormal data may result from sensor malfunction, data loss during the communication, faked data inserted by malicious nodes, or the appearance of an interesting event. We try to detect abnormal data based on the presented numerical value of the data. Basically, two types of abnormal data can be detected. One is the out-of-range data, and the other is dramatic changing data.

Figure 7 shows the appearance of the out-of-range data, which is the data out of the possible valid range defined by the domain scientists. Based on the figure, we figure out that most sensing data are within the normal range. We find out-of-range data only at two gauges, G6 and G10, and G6 only has one invalid reading. Considering the failure patterns to be discussed in Section 4, we find that G10 has a maximum number of failures as well. So, we believe there are some relations between the probability of abnormal readings and the probability of failures.

Gauge ID	Parameter	Position	Value
G6	Water Level	Reading # 45	62.79
G10	Voltage	Reading #47	1.00
G10	Voltage	Reading #119	1.00
G10	Voltage	Reading #126	1.00
G10	Voltage	Reading #127	1.00
G10	Voltage	Reading #323	1.00

Fig. 7. Detected out-of-range readings

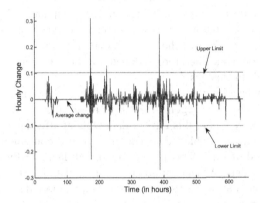

Fig. 8. Limit control of G3's hourly water level changes

Figure 8 explains hourly water level changes in gauge G3, where we find that their distributions are close to normal distribution based on normal probability plot, which is a graphical technique for assessing whether or not a data set is approximately normally distributed. For such data, 3-sigma limits is a common practice to base the control limit, i.e., whenever a data point falls out of 3 times the standard deviation from its average value, it is assumed that the process is probably out of control. In the figure, two horizontal lines depict the upper and lower 3-sigma limits. We find that only several points are out of the two limits, which means domain scientists do not need to check the cause of water level changes at most time. The similar patterns are detected in all gauges as shown in Figure 9, where most gauges have water level changes within 3-sigma limits. Investigation is deserved when out-of-limit changes are detected to find the cause of the abnormality.

Implications. Learned from above similarity and abnormal analysis, we argue that we need to revisit system protocol design by integrating the intrinsic features of the monitoring parameters.

First, we can take advantage of the large amount of data similarity. Because data similarity is common, it is not necessary to transfer all the collected data to the gateway.

G2	G3	G4	G5	G6	G7	G9	G10	G11	G12	G13
2.17%	1.55%	2.95%	0.00%	0.31%	0.16%	0.00%	1.40%	0.16%	6.06%	1.86%

Fig. 9. Out-of-Limit ratio for hourly water level changes

Quality-assured local data processing, aggregation and compression algorithms are necessary to remove redundant data and reduce overall data volume but keep the quality of the collected data at a satisfactory level. By enduring a certain level of data inaccuracy, we can reduce the total amount of collected data up to 90% according to the pattern and numerical reappearance ratios. In addition, strong patterns are helpful to estimate the future data and detect abnormal data.

Second, we can use different data sampling rates for different monitoring parameters. For example, we discover that the changes in voltage is much more frequent than those in precipitation. Thus, we need to increase the sampling rate to sense voltage data more frequently, whereas, decrease the sampling rate for precipitation. Furthermore, in the sensor readings for precipitation, some of them reappear a large amount of times, while others only appear once. Usually, the readings that only appear once or twice imply a high dynamic environment. Therefore, it is better to increase sampling rate so that we can detect the details in changes.

Third, there may be a lot of abnormal data existing in the sensor reading. Basically, they can be classified to two categories. One type is transitional, which disappears very quickly. We can mostly ignore this type of data without affecting overall data quality by replacing it with a reasonable value. The other type is continuous, which typically lasts a longer period of time. This type of abnormal data usually implies malicious data or interesting events. When continuous abnormal data is detected, more attention should be paid to them at the early stage. For example, more data should be sampled and reported to the gateway as fast as possible.

Finally, various data sampling rates may result in different amount of data traffic. Samplings for different parameters and detected abnormal data may have different priorities in their delivery to the gateway. A well designed data collection protocol is necessary to achieve this goal.

3.2   Multi-Modality and Spatial Sensing Data Analysis

In this subsection, we analyze the relationship between two types of sensing data, water level and precipitation. Moreover, we try to explore the spatial relationship at different locations.

Although water level can be affected by many factors, including moisture when it starts raining, rainfall intensity, and even temperature and slope of the land, we believe

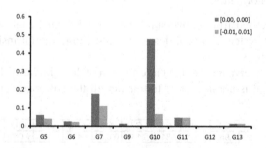

Fig. 10. Conflict ratio of water level and precipitation

that there is a relationship between water level and precipitation. Mostly when precipitation increases, water level should also increase. We count the ratio of the conflict, which is defined as the appearance when precipitation increases but water level decreases, to verify this relationship. Figure 10 records the conflict ratio between water level and precipitation. In the figure, the x-axis depicts the gauge ID, and the y-axis shows the conflict ratio. The dark blue bar and the gray bar denote the conflict ratio with endurance interval $[0.00, 0.00]$ and $[-0.01, 0.01]$ independently. From the figure we observe that in most cases the conflict ratio is less than 6%, which verifies that water level is closely related to precipitation; however, there are two gauges with conflicts larger than 10%, i.e., G7 has conflict ratio of 18% and G10 has conflict ratio of 48%. After a carefully examination, we figure out that G10's high conflict ratio is related with lots of failures it has. While G7's high conflict ratio may be caused by other reasons, because when precipitation increases only a little, other factors, such as moisture and temperature, may play major roles to determine water level. This is verified by the fact that when we increase the endurance interval a little, the conflict ratio decreases very fast, and it eventually disappears when we set endurance interval to $[-0.01, 0.01]$ for water level and $[-0.02, 0.02]$ for precipitation.

We analyze spatial correlation for all of the three parameters. Because there are no direct communications among sensors at different locations in this application, we do not expect spatial correlation among voltage readings at the different gauges, which is validated by the collected data. The calculated co-efficiency value between any two gauges is less than 0.54 and 99% of them is less than 0.32. However, we do find some spatial correlation for both water level and precipitation based on the data sensed from various gauges. The results are depicted in Figure 11(a) and 11(b) respectively.

In the figure for precipitation, we only have data for listed gauges. We can see that all gauges with precipitation data have very large co-efficiency value because they are all located at Lake Winnebago, which means that the weather in that area is pretty uniform. When there is a rain fall at the location of one of the gauges, it is most probably raining at the locations of the other gauges as well. Water level also exhibits the similar pattern. In Figure 11(a), gauges located closely usually have high co-efficiency values, which results in similarity in water level changes, while gauges located far away usually have no obvious similarity in terms of water level changes. For instance, gauges can be grouped into several small groups with similar water level changes based on the calculated large co-efficiency values. Thus, gauge G2 and G3 are within one group with co-efficiency value larger than 92%. We can see that both of them are located in St. Clair River. G4 is the only gauge in Detroit River, so it has no high co-efficiency

Water Level	G2	G3	G4	G5	G6	G7	G9	G11	G12	G13
G2	1	0.924	0.174	0.344	0.083	0.314	0.64	0.471	0.513	0.569
G3	0.924	1	0.306	0.428	0.254	0.377	0.601	0.505	0.525	0.591
G4	0.174	0.306	1	0.486	0.413	0.35	0.35	0.54	0.436	0.528
G5	0.344	0.428	0.486	1	0.159	0.916	0.699	0.888	0.875	0.555
G6	0.083	0.254	0.413	0.159	1	0.113	-0.1	0.002	-0.01	0.32
G7	0.314	0.377	0.35	0.916	0.113	1	0.659	0.832	0.848	0.474
G9	0.64	0.601	0.35	0.699	-0.1	0.659	1	0.825	0.835	0.7
G11	0.471	0.505	0.54	0.888	0.002	0.832	0.825	1	0.909	0.627
G12	0.513	0.525	0.436	0.875	-0.01	0.848	0.835	0.909	1	0.652
G13	0.569	0.591	0.528	0.555	0.32	0.474	0.7	0.627	0.652	1

Precipitation	G5	G6	G7	G9	G11	G12	G13
G5	1	0.977	0.996	0.995	0.985	0.996	0.996
G6	0.977	1	0.959	0.99	0.996	0.967	0.968
G7	0.996	0.959	1	0.983	0.969	0.999	0.998
G9	0.995	0.99	0.983	1	0.992	0.988	0.988
G11	0.985	0.996	0.969	0.992	1	0.975	0.975
G12	0.996	0.967	0.999	0.988	0.975	1	0.999
G13	0.996	0.968	0.998	0.988	0.975	0.999	1

(a)   (b)

Fig. 11. Spatial correlation of: (a) water level, (b) precipitation

with any other gauges. Moreover, gauge G5, G7, G11, and G12 show high similarity because they are located closely. Thus, we believe that geographical similarity exists in the sensed data for water level and precipitation.

Implication: Multi-modality and spatial sensing data analysis helps us to find the correlation between different parameters and geological correlation of the same parameter. Therefore, data collected by the correlated sensors can be used as a reference to calibrate the sensing data. For example, an increase in precipitation mostly results in an increase in water level. When there are some conflicts between them, we need to take a close look and figure out the reason of the conflict. Furthermore, we can take advantage of similarity in different parameters or sensors located in different locations. Quality-assured aggregation can be applied in this scenario to reduce the volume of sensing data. Thus, multi-modality models and spatial models are very useful in quality-assured data collection protocol design.

4   Failure Analysis

In this section we study the failure patterns of the sensor system including communication related failures and sensing hardware related failures. First, we present a few important definitions.

TTF denotes Time To Failure and represents the time between two consecutive failures. Mean TTF (MTTF) is a measure of the system reliability.
TTR denotes Time to Repair that is the time it takes the system to recover from a failure. A system that exhibits a small Mean TTR (MTTR) typically maintains high availability.
Total time: represents the total system lifetime including functioning as well as failing periods.
Uptime: the total time a system is in the functioning mode, in contrast, **Downtime** is the total time, in which the system is un-available. The following two equations illustrate the relationship between these values:

$$MTTF = \frac{Total\ time}{number\ of\ failures} \tag{1}$$

$$Downtime = MTTR \cdot number\ of\ failures \tag{2}$$

4.1   Methodology

For each sensing parameter (i.e., Water level or Precipitation), we organize the readings as a discrete time series and locate missing or corrupted readings. Each missing or corrupted reading is considered a failure. For each time series, we record the **Number of Failures**, **TTFs**, and **TTRs** for each individual failure type independently.

In our investigation of the raw data traces, we discovered several failure types. Some of these failures are related to communication failures, while others are pertinent to the sensing hardware itself. Figure 4.1 lists all the failure types we encountered in the raw data along with a simple description for each one of them. The first four failures in the figure (i.e., Comm-T1 to Comm-T4) are communication failures between the

Failure Type	Message in the raw traces	Description
Comm-T1	"ADDRESS ERROR CORRECTED"	Unknown reasons. We could not reach technical people who could provide explanation.
Comm-T2	"MISSING SCHEDULED DCP MESSAGE"	Communication failure due to lack of time synchronization between the gauge station and the satellite unit.
Comm-T3	"MESSAGE RECEIVED ON WRONG CHANNEL"	The message was not received on the channel that has been assigned to that particular gauge station.
Comm-T4	"MESSAGE OVERLAPPING ASSIGNED TIME WINDOW"	Communication failure due to lack of time synchronization between the gauge station and the satellite unit.
H/W-T1	Blank	Sensor failure, no reading was reported by the sensor on time. This represents a fail-stop sensor failure
H/W-T2	Corrupted reading	Sensor failure, the data format is corrupted, unreadable reading

Fig. 12. Failure types and their description

gauge station and the satellite unit. The last two failures (i.e., H/W-T1 and H/W-T2) are sensing hardware malfunctioning. H/W-T1 represents a fail-stop failure, where the sensor simply fails to report a reading on time, whereas, in H/W-T2, the sensor reports a corrupted reading (i.e., unreadable values).

4.2 Failure Analysis by Type

To understand the relative importance of these failure types, we draw their relative occurrence in the raw data traces for all locations combined in Figure 13(a) and the total downtime due to the particular failure type in Figure 13(b). Figure 13(a) gives an idea of how frequent a particular failure type is, whereas, Figure 13(b) clarifies how severe that failure is, in other words, how long it takes to recover from the failure.

In Figure 13(a), we observe that 56% of the total number of failures are of type Comm-T2 communication failure, all other communication related failures (i.e., Comm-T1, Comm-T3, and Comm-T4) collectively account for only 6% of the total number of failures. Comm-T2 as well as Comm-T4 are directly related to the lack of time synchronization between the gauge station and the satellite unit, thus, the lack of time synchronization constitutes 58% of the total number of failures. Failure to report measurements by the sensor hardware on time (i.e., H/W-T1 failure) accounts for 34% of the total number of failures, in contrast, reporting corrupted data (i.e., H/W-T2 failure) accounts for only 4%. This observation suggests that fail-stop failures are more common in the real world environmental applications.

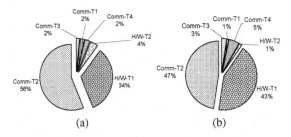

(a)   (b)

Fig. 13. Understanding relative importance of different failure types. (a) shows their relative frequency (b) shows their contribution to system total downtime.

Figure 13(b) allows us to observe the importance of the different failure types from a different perspective, in particular, how long it takes to recover from a particular failure type. For example, Although Comm-T4 and Comm-T1 failure types account for the same percentage of the total number of failures (i.e., 2% as shown in Figure 13(a)), it seems that recovering from a Comm-T4 failure takes more time compared to recovering from a Comm-T1 failure, which allows us to conclude that Comm-T4 failures are more important than Comm-T1 failures, in other words, Comm-T4 failures contribute 5% to the system total downtime, whereas, Comm-T1 contributes only 1% as shown in Figure 13(b). We also, observe that sensing hardware failures (i.e., H/W-T1 and H/W-T2 failures) account for 44% of the total system downtime.

We observe in Figure 13 that we have two equally important major failure types, communication related failures and sensing hardware failures. Based on these findings and after consultation with field experts, we decide to merge these failure categories and abstract them into two failure classes: communication failures and sensing hardware failures in the rest of this section.

4.3   Failure Analysis by Location

In this subsection, we study failure characteristics at different locations, which allows us to understand the effect of the environment on inflicting failures on the system. At each location, we record the Number of failures and MTTR for each failure type and draw them in Figure 14(a) and Figure 14(b) respectively. Note that MTTF is directly proportional to the Number of failures (refer to Equation 1), therefore, including MTTF offers no insight in our analysis.

Figure 14 allows us to observe that gauge G10 experience much more failures compared to the other gauges, because of the hostile environment surrounded G10. This suggests that the external environment plays a significant role in the failure frequency and pattern of the system. We also observe in Figure 14(a) that the environmental impact is uniform in inflicting different failure types. For example, Figure 14(a) shows that gauge G10 suffered around 26 communication failures, 26 water level sensor failure, and 28 precipitation sensor failures, whereas, Gauge G3 experienced 1 water level sensor failure, 1 precipitation sensor failure, and 0 communication failures.

In Figure 14(b), we observe that different failure types need different recovery time. For example, at gauge G10 in Figure 14(b), precipitation sensor failure takes more time

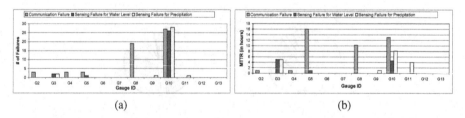

(a)   (b)

Fig. 14. Understanding effect of external environment on inflicting failures. (a) effect of environment on failure frequency (b) effect of environment on MTTR.

on average to recover from a failure compared to water level sensor failure. Surprisingly, communication failures exhibit much longer repair time.

4.4 Summary and Implications

Based on our findings, we believe that the lack of time synchronization is a major source of communication failures, this makes time synchronization algorithms of particular importance in remotely deployed environmental monitoring sensor applications. Sensor hardware failures are also a major source of failures in these applications, we found that fail-stop failure is the most common failure pattern in this category. We further observed that different sensor hardware exhibit different failure characteristics, in particular, different repair times. Finally, we found that external environmental factors, perhaps, are the most important factor on inflicting failures in environmental applications. This makes deployment-based failures particularly important, in which failures are independent of aging.

5   Related Work

The work presented in this paper is inspired by many previous work in WSNs, although, to our knowledge, it is the first work on detailed data quality and failures characterization of sensing data in WSNs. Next, we will list the most relevant previous efforts.

SenseWeb [14] has provided a venue for people to publish their data, but we have not seen any analysis yet. Our next step will use more data set from SenseWeb. Data aggregation is an important way to reduce the volume of the collected data. A few data aggregation approaches have been proposed. These approaches make use of cluster based structures [6] or tree based structures [2,5,7,11,18]. Tang and Xu propose to differentiate the precisions of data collected from different sensor nodes to balance their energy consumption [16].

Adaptive sampling has been proposed to match sampling rate to the properties of environment, sensor networks and data stream. Jain and Chang propose an adaptive sampling approach called backcasting [8]. Gedik and Liu proposed a similar way of data collection, selective sampling [4]. Although many approaches have been proposed to reduce energy while maintaining data quality, there exists rare study on the pattern of raw data collected by sensor nodes in the real world. In addition, most studies adopt the way of simulation, whereas, our quality-oriented sensing data analysis gives a chance to take a fresh look at how the data behaves.

Failure pattern is another important issue for WSNs. There have been a few efforts that focus on understanding failure patterns of computer hardware components, in particular hard disks [9,13]. Our work employs similar techniques and investigates a different type of system that is deployed in an open environment, therefore, we believe that its failure behavior is totaly different from classical computer systems. To the best of our knowledge, there is no prior work that specifically studies and analyzes real sensor failure traces so that our work is a leading exploration step in this direction. Most existing work on WSN reliability assumes exponential lifetime distribution of sensor nodes [1,17], and here we take a second look of such assumption by investigating real sensor system failure traces. Although the current data set spans a short period of time and does not permit us to draw strong conclusions regarding lifetime distributions, we believe that our work brings new insights in understanding sensor device failure patterns.

6 Conclusion

In this work, we use real sensor data sets collected by 13 sensor nodes to study and analyze data quality properties as well as failure patterns.We found that data redundancy is very high in the water level and precipitation data sets. This provides us with an opportunity to design more aggressive energy-efficient data collection protocols. We also found that the lack of time synchronization is a major source of communication failures in the system, which suggests that we should pay more attention to time synchronization protocols in remotely deployed WSN environmental applications. In our future work, we will focus on designing energy-efficient sensor networks with high-quality data taking advantage of what we have learned here about information redundancy, similarity between data series, and abnormal data detection.

References

1. Al-Omari, S., Shi, W.: Availability modeling and analysis of autonomous in-door wsns. In: Proceedings of IEEE MASS 2007 (September 2007)
2. Ding, M., Cheng, X., Xue, G.: Aggregation tree construction in sensor networks. In: Proceedings of the 58th IEEE Vehicular Technology Conference 2003 (October 2003)
3. Estrin, D., Culler, D., Pister, K., Sukhatme, G.: Connecting the physical world with pervasive networks. IEEE Pervasive Computing 1(1), 59–69 (2002)
4. Gedik, B., Liu, L.: Energy-aware data collection in sensor networks: A localized selective sampling approach. Technical report, Georgia Institute of Technology (2005)
5. Goel, A., Estrin, D.: Simultaneous optimization for concave costs: Single sink aggregation or single source buy-at-bulk. In: Proceedings of the 14th Annual ACM-SIAM Symposium on Discrete Algorithms 2003 (2003)
6. Heinzelman, W., Chandrakasan, A., Balakrishnan, H.: An application-specific protocol architecture for wireless microsensor networks. IEEE Transactions on Wireless Communications 1(4), 660–670 (2002)
7. Intanagonwiwat, C., Estrin, D., Govindan, R., Heidemann, J.: Impact of network density on data aggregation in wireless sensor networks. In: Proceedings of IEEE ICDCS 2002 (July 2002)
8. Jain, A., Chang, E.: Adaptive sampling for sensor networks. In: Proceedings of the First Workshop on Data Management for Sensor Networks(DMSN 2004) (August 2004)
9. Jiang, W., Hu, C., Zhou, Y., Kanevsky, A.: Are disks the dominant contributor for storage failures? a comprehensive study of storage subsystem failure characteristics. In: Proceedings of USENIX FAST 2008 (January 2008)
10. Li, M., Ganesan, D., Shenoy, P.: PRESTO: Feedback-driven data management in sensor networks. In: Proc. of the NSDI 2006 (May 2006)
11. Luo, H., Luo, J., Liu, Y.: Energy efficient routing with adaptive data fusion in sensor networks. In: Proceedings of the Third ACM/SIGMOBILEe Workshop on Foundations of Mobile Computing 2005 (August 2005)

12. Pottie, G., Kaiser, W.: Wireless integrated network sensors. Communications of the ACM 43(5), 51–58 (2000)
13. Schroeder, B., Gibson, G.: Disk failures in the real world: What does an MTTF of 1,000,000 hours mean to you? In: Proceedings of USENIX FAST 2007 (February 2007)
14. Microsoft research
15. Sha, K., Shi, W.: Consistency-driven data quality management in wireless sensor networks. Technical Report MIST-TR-2007-001, Wayne State University (January 2007)
16. Tang, X., Xu, J.: Extending network lifetime for precision-constrained data aggregation in wireless sensor networks. In: Proc. of IEEE International Conference on Computer Communications (INFOCOM 2006) (April 2006)
17. Yu, S., Yang, A., Zhang, Y.: Dada: A 2-dimensional adaptive node schedule to provide smooth sensor network services against random failures. In: Workshop on Information Fusion and Dissemination in Wireless Sensor Networks (2005)
18. Zhang, W., Cao, G.: Optimizing tree reconfiguration for mobile target tracking in sensor networks. In: Proceedings of INFOCOM 2004 (March 2004)

Security through Collaboration in MANETs

Wenjia Li, James Parker, and Anupam Joshi

Department of Computer Science and Electrical Engineering,
University of Maryland, Baltimore County (UMBC),
1000 Hilltop Circle, Baltimore MD 21250
{wenjia1,jparke2,joshi}@cs.umbc.edu

Abstract. It is well understood that Mobile Ad Hoc Networks (MANETs) are extremely susceptible to a variety of attacks, and traditional security mechanisms do not work well. Many security schemes have been proposed that depend on cooperation amongst the nodes in a MANET for identifying nodes that are exhibiting malicious behavior such as packet dropping, packet modification, and packet misrouting. We argue that in general, this problem can be viewed as an instance of detecting nodes whose behavior is an outlier when compared to others. In this paper, we propose a collaborative outlier detection algorithm for MANETs that factors in a nodes reputation. The algorithm leads to a common outlier view amongst distributed nodes with a limited communication overhead. Simulation results demonstrate that the proposed algorithm is efficient and accurate.

Keywords: outlier detection, mobile ad hoc network, misbehavior, gossiping.

1 Introduction

Outliers are generally defined as data points that are very different from the rest of the data with respect to some measure [1, 2]. Outlier detection can be used for two purposes. The first is to eliminate outliers to potentially reduce the noise in the data. The other usage of outlier detection is to expose the outliers for further analysis, for example in intrusion detection [3, 4], fraud analysis [5] and habitat monitoring for endangered species [6].

Several factors make Mobile Ad Hoc Networks (MANETs) extremely susceptible to various attacks such as intrusions [7], greyholes [8], and blackholes [9]. First of all, data in MANETs are transmitted via RF broadcasts, which can be easily eavesdropped on or even modified. Second, nodes in MANETs have limited power supply, and consequently their performance is severely degraded when power is exhausted. Third, when they are used for security and military purposes, nodes in MANETs are vulnerable to compromise and manipulation by adversaries. Hence, it is obvious that misbehavior detection should be an indispensable component of any security solution that aims to safeguard the mobile ad hoc networks. The misbehavior typically observed includes dropping of packets, misroutes, false Requests/Clears in the MAC layer etc. However, many of these events can also happen due to environmental and mobility related reasons, not just malicious intent. Most of the current misbehavior detection

E. Bertino and J.B.D. Joshi (Eds.): CollaborateCom 2008, LNICST 10, pp. 696–714, 2009.
© ICST Institute for Computer Sciences, Social-Informatics and Telecommunications Engineering 2009

mechanisms rely on a predefined threshold to decide if a node's behavior is malicious or not. However, it is rather difficult to set an appropriate threshold because the network is quite dynamic and unpredictable, and environmental conditions such as ambient RF noise can vary. In contrast, we do not need to rely on any previous knowledge to find anode that is an outlier with respect to a given observable. Given the fact that a malicious node will behave differently when compared to other nodes, we can detect the node misbehaviors by means of outlier detection.

In this paper, we propose and evaluate a collaborative, gossip-based outlier detection algorithm for mobile ad hoc networks. In our approach, as in many others [22,24,28,33], all the nodes in MANETs observe the behavior of their neighbors. Unlike most existing approaches however, each node calculates its local views of outliers amongst the neighboring nodes. In the next step, the nodes exchange their local views with their immediate neighbors. Then they will update their local views if they find that outlier lists from other nodes are more accurate than theirs. This process continues, with each node updating its neighbors when its current view of the outliers changes, and halts when there are no more changes. Some important features of our algorithm are: (1) it is compatible with different outlier detection heuristics; (2) it is resilient to attempts by misbehaving nodes to defeat it; (3) it is resilient to the motion and failure of nodes in MANETs; (4) it is efficient in terms of communication overhead; and (4) all the nodes will ultimately have a coincident view of outliers unless the nodes change their behaviors very fast.

2 Related Work

2.1 Outlier Detection

Outlier detection is a hot topic in the data mining research, and various definitions of outliers have been proposed in the literature. Our proposed algorithm takes two popular distance-based definitions into account: (1) distance to the nearest neighbor (NN) [10], and (2) average distance to k nearest neighbors (k-NN) [11].

One major motivation of outlier detection research is to efficiently identify outliers in a large-scale database [10, 12, 13, 14]. Nevertheless, the situation in mobile ad hoc networks is significantly different from that in large-scale central databases: in mobile ad hoc networks, data are generated and stored in scattered nodes and transmitted via wireless channels, which are unreliable and bandwidth and power-constrained. Outlier detection methods for the large-scale databases cannot be seamlessly used in mobile ad hoc networks because they will cause a large communication overhead.

Several outlier detection algorithms have been recently proposed for wireless sensor networks (WSNs) [6, 19, 20, 21]. Palpanas et al. propose a model-based outlier detection algorithm in sensor networks [20]. In their algorithm, normal behaviors are first characterized by predictive models, and then outliers can be detected as the deviations. Subramaniam et al. [21] propose an online outlier detection mechanism for sensor networks. In this mechanism, every sensor node will keep a sliding window of the historic data and approximate the data distribution to detect the outliers. In a recent paper by Sheng et al. [6], a histogram-based outlier detection algorithm is studied, and sensor data distribution is estimated by the histogram-based method. This method can reduce communication cost under two different detection schemes. Moreover, a histogram refinement technique for some crucial portion of data distribution has been applied to obtain more information about outliers. Branch et al. [19] propose an in-network outlier detection scheme to detect the outliers based on data exchange among neighbors. In this scheme, all the sensor nodes will first calculate the local outlier(s). Then some messages, which contain the local outlier(s) as well as some other supportive information, will be exchanged among all the nodes. The message exchanging process will not halt until all the nodes have the same global view of outlier(s). Our proposed outlier detection algorithm is somewhat similar to the method proposed by Branch et al. However, there are two significant differences between the two methods. First, the method by Branch et al. does not consider the mobility of the nodes, whereas our proposed method takes the mobility issue in consideration. Second, there is no malicious behaviors in the discussion of the method by Branch et al., i.e., the nodes will not deliberately fabricate fake local views or alter incoming local views in their method. On the contrary, we have considered the malicious behaviors of the nodes, and applied the knowledge of trust and reputation as the countermeasure to the malicious behaviors.

2.2 Misbehavior Detection in Mobile Ad Hoc Networks

In mobile ad hoc networks, all network operations such as routing and forwarding rely on cooperation of the nodes because there is no centralized infrastructure. Hence, if some nodes choose not to participate in the network operations, then these network services may be incomplete or even unavailable. These non-cooperative nodes are generally called *selfish nodes* [22]. Besides selfishness, ad hoc network misbehavior may also be conducted by malicious nodes, which aim to harm the whole ad hoc networks. A malicious node can perform different attacks to either compromise individual node(s) or degrade the performance of the overall network [23]. The existence of selfishness and malicious behaviors has motivated research in the area of misbehavior detection for mobile ad hoc networks.

Intrusion Detection Systems (IDS) are an important means to detect node misbehavior. Several mechanisms have been proposed to build IDS on individual nodes due to the lack of a centralized infrastructure [24, 25, 26, 27]. In these mechanisms, every node is equipped with an IDS, and each IDS is assumed to be always on, which is not energy-efficient given the limited battery power of nodes in ad hoc networks. On the other hand, Huang et al. [28] propose a cooperative intrusion detection framework in which clusters are formed in ad hoc networks and all the nodes in one single cluster will cooperate in intrusion detection operation.

Routing misbehavior is another kind of malicious activity that is common in ad hoc networks. When an adversary aims to degrade the network service of ad hoc network, he can try to compromise some nodes in the ad hoc network, and use them to disturb the routing service so as to make part of or the entire network unreachable. Marti et al. [22] introduce two related techniques to detect and isolate misbehaving nodes, which are nodes that do not forward packets. In the "watchdog" approach, a node forwarding a packet verifies whether the node in the next hop also forwards it or not. If not, a failure tally is incremented and misbehavior will be recognized if the tally exceeds a certain threshold. The "pathrater" module then utilizes this knowledge of misbehaving nodes to avoid them in path selection. There are also some other proposed solutions that aim to handle the routing misbehavior [29, 30, 31].

3 Gossip-Based Outlier Detection Algorithm

In this section, we describe our gossip-based distributed outlier detection algorithm. The goal of the algorithm is to find the top k outliers in terms of some observed behaviors (such as packet drops or misroutes) from all the nodes in mobile ad hoc networks (Here k is a user-defined parameter). The algorithm leads to a coincident global view of the top k outliers in all the nodes as long as these nodes do not change their behavior significantly during the convergence time of the algorithm. By using constrained gossiping, the algorithm avoids flooding the network.

3.1 Algorithm Description

The proposed outlier detection algorithm contains the following four steps, namely local view formation, local view exchange, local view update, and global view formation. We have adopted two local view update methods in our algorithm: one is the simple averaging method, in which all the local views are merged by simply averaging them; the other method is the trust-based weighted method, in which the local views are merged incorporating the trust in other nodes.

The first step of our algorithm is the formation of local views. The nodes monitor and record the possible malicious behaviors of other nodes within their radio range. Each node generates its local view of outliers based on their own observations.

Once all the nodes form their local views, they will broadcast the local views to all of their immediate neighbors, i.e., all the nodes that are one hop away from them. Upon reception of a local view from another node, the recipient will update its local view based on the received view. The first local view update method we employ is the simple averaging method, which is shown in the Subroutine 1 below. Here n_i denotes the i-th node in the mobile ad hoc networks. V_i denotes the initial view of n_i. V_i' denotes the updated view of n_i.

Subroutine 1 Update of Local View for node i Using the *Simple Averaging* Method

Input of n_i: V_i

Output of n_i: V_i'

Upon reception of V_j from node n_j:

if $V_j \neq V_i$

—merge the V_i and V_j according to the following rules:

——if node m is in BOTH V_i AND V_j, then calculate the average of the corresponding columns for node m in BOTH V_i and V_j, and store the average of node m to an intermediate list $TEMP_i$ as an entry.

——if node m is in EITHER V_i OR V_j, but NOT BOTH, then add a virtual entry of node m to the view that previously does not contain m, and set all the columns of this virtual entry as 0. Then calculate the average between the true entry of m and virtual entry of m for each column, and then store the average values of node m to an intermediate list $TEMP_i$ as an entry.

—calculate the top k outliers from $TEMP_i$, and assign these k top outliers to V_i'.
—broadcast V_i' to all of its immediate neighbors (number of hop = 1).
else keep V_i unchanged, and not send any message out

The averaging is necessary due to the existence of malicious nodes that may produce false views to mislead other nodes. Suppose a malicious node randomly generates some entries reporting large misbehaviors for a good node, and sends this false view to others. If the recipients simply take the false view it will miss the true outliers. Averaging the information from all neighbors helps avoid this. Another heuristic is that if a recipient receives information about any node that has never been seen before, it will use only half of the reported value in computing the average. In other words, it will treat this new information conservatively. On the other hand, the true outliers will not be influenced by either of the heuristics because several nodes will report their observed outlier values. Of course, this scheme will be vulnerable in a locality where most of the nodes are malicious, but in such circumstances most misbehavior detection algorithms fail anyway.

Another possibility is to use the trust-based weighted method during the local view update process. Unlike the simple averaging method, the trust-based weighted method relies on the reputation of a node to determine how to merge the view it sends out with the local view of the receiver. The trust-based weighted method is listed in the Subroutine 2 below. Again, n_i denotes the i-th node in the mobile ad hoc networks. V_i denotes the initial view of n_i. V_i' denotes the updated view of n_i. w_{ik} denotes the weight of local view sent from node k to node i.

Subroutine 2 Update of Local View for node i using the *Trust-based Weighted* Method

Input of n_i: V_i
Output of n_i: V_i'
Upon reception of V_k from node n_k:
if $V_j \neq V_k$
—merge the V_i and V_k according to the following rule:
——if node m is in BOTH V_i AND V_k, then calculate the weighted average WA_i of the corresponding columns for node m in BOTH V_i and V_k according to the following formula:

$$WA_i = (w_{ii} * m_i + w_{ik} * m_k)/(w_{ii} + w_{ik})$$

and then store the weighted average WA_i of node m to an intermediate list $TEMP_i$ as an entry.
——if node m is in EITHER V_i OR V_k, but NOT BOTH, then we simply set m_i or m_k to be zero, and the calculation of WA_i follows the formulae below:

$$WA_i = \begin{cases} w_{ii} * m_i, \text{ when } m_k = 0 \\ w_{ik} * m_k, \text{ when } m_i = 0 \end{cases}$$

and then store the weighted average WA_i of node m to an intermediate list $TEMP_i$ as an entry.
—calculate the top k outliers from $TEMP_i$, and assign these k top outliers to V_i'.
—broadcast V_i' to all of its immediate neighbors (number of hop = 1).
else keep V_i unchanged, and not send any message out

Note that unlike traditional gossiping, the more the nodes that accept the same view of outliers, the less the number of new messages that are sent out. Ultimately, when all the nodes hold the same view of outliers, the algorithm will halt, and the view that all the nodes hold is regarded as the global view of outliers.

The pseudo-code of the algorithm is given in Table 1 and uses the same notation as described earlier. In addition, GV denotes the ultimate global view.

Algorithm 1. Gossip-based Outlier Detection

Input of n_i: V_i
Output of n_i: GV
For each node n_i:
broadcast V_i to all of its immediate neighbors
Upon reception of V_j from node n_j:
invoke **Subroutine1** *OR* **Subroutine 2**
When no more message exchange occurs:
$\forall k$, $GV = V_k$

3.2 Trust Establishment and Management

Several trust and reputation management schemes have been proposed in the past decades [34, 35, 36]. Any of them can be used in our system. For our experiments, we chose a simple approach that starts with a default trust for unknown nodes, and modifies it upon each encounter with that node.

Initially, we define all the trust value to be 1. Whenever the node observes any misbehavior of its neighbors, the node reduces the trust value of the entry for the misbehaving neighbor according to the punishment factors. We set different reduction factors for different misbehaviors when we adjust the trust value. For example, packet dropping and packet modification are both misbehaviors. However, packet dropping may be caused either by intentional malicious behavior or by power failure. On the other hand, when we find that a node is modifying the incoming packets, we can safely conclude that it is malicious. Hence, we set a higher reduction factor for packet modification than packet dropping.

During the local view update process, when a node i gets local view from its neighbor k, the node uses the trust value of its neighbor as the weight w_{ik}, and its own weight w_{ii} will always be 1. In this way, we apply the knowledge of trust and reputation to the local view update process, and we can ensure that the fake local views spread by the malicious nodes will not influence the formation of the global view.

3.3 An Example Scenario

To help better understand the proposed algorithm, an example is presented in Fig. 1. In Fig. 1a, node A observes all the misbehaviors of it neighbors, and then forms its local view based on its own observation. Node A will also construct its initial trust table based on its observation to its neighbors. All other nodes are simultaneously collecting their neighbors' misbehavior information, and generate their local views as well as trust tables. The outlier candidates in the local views are sorted according to the distances

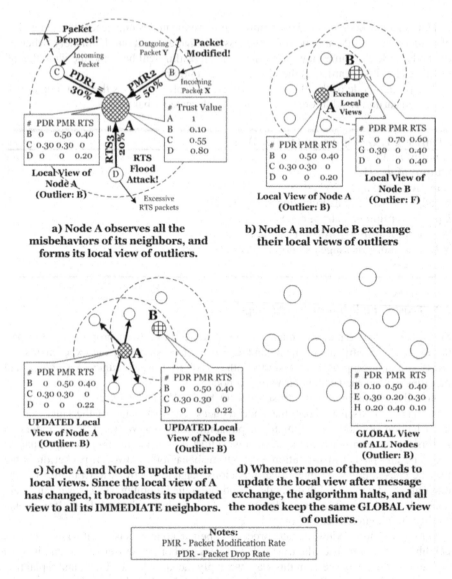

Fig. 1. Gossip-based Outlier Detection Algorithm

between their nearest neighbors and themselves, and the top three outliers are picked in this example. We note that as long as all the nodes are observing the same set of behaviors, our approach can handle anything defined as a misbehavior.

The next step is the initial exchange of the local views, which is demonstrated in Fig. 1b. In this step, all the nodes send their local views to all of their *immediate* neighbors, which are defined as the nodes that are located one hop away from them. From Fig. 1b we find that the local views of node A and node B are not consistent.

Fig. 1c exhibits the view update and optional rebroadcast step. Both node A and node B update their local views according to the view they have received. We note that node A applies the knowledge of trust to the local view update process. In this way, node A ensures that its updated local view contains the least fake information from node B, who is likely to be a malicious node since its trust value is quite low. Then, they rebroadcast their updated views to all the immediate neighbors. We should also be aware that node B may send out any arbitrary view to its immediate neighbors regardless of the true updated view it gets, because node B seems to be malicious.

The view update and optional rebroadcast process will continue until all the nodes hold the same view of the top three outliers, and this final state is shown in Fig. 1d. We find from Fig. 1d that the composition of the outliers has been significantly altered for both node A and B when compared to their initial views.

4 Evaluation

In this section, we present the experimental evaluation results to verify the performance of the algorithm. There are two goals for the performance evaluation: the first is to compare the performance of our algorithm with that of a centralized outlier detection algorithm; the other is to observe the performance of our algorithm under different parameter configurations.

4.1 Experimentation Setup

We use Glomosim 2.03 [32] as our simulation platform, and the simulation setup is shown in Table I. We use three parameters to assess the correctness and efficiency of our algorithms: Correctness Rate (*CR*), Total Number of Packet for Outlier Detection (*TNPOD*), Communication Overhead (*CO*), and Convergence Time (*CT*). They are defined as follows:

$$CR = \frac{\text{Number of } \textit{True} \text{ Outliers Found}}{\textit{Total} \text{ Number of Outliers}}$$

$$TNPOD = \textit{Total Number} \text{ of Packets for Outlier Detection}$$

$$CO = \frac{TNPOD}{\textit{Total} \text{ Number of Packets in the network}}$$

$$CT = \textit{Time} \text{ taken to form a } \textit{consistent} \text{ global view of outliers}$$

Here we want to keep track of *CO* since we want to see the ratio of network traffic that outlier detection consumes over the whole network traffic. However, we also have interest in exploring the possible relationship between *TNPOD* and the number of nodes in the network.

We compare the performance of our collaborative outlier detection algorithm with that of a centralized algorithm. All nodes send their observations of misbehaviors to a designated *fusion* node, which then calculates the global outliers and floods the results out to all nodes in the network. An example of the centralized algorithm is shown in Fig 2.

Table 1. Simulation Setup

Parameter	Value
Simulation area	150m × 150m, 300m × 300m, 450m × 450m, 600 m × 600m
Number of nodes	15, 25, 50, 100, 200
Transmission range	45m, 60m, 90m, 120m
Simulation duration	900 s
Mobility pattern of nodes	random waypoint
Maximum motion speed	5m/s, 10m/s, 20m/s
Number of bad nodes	5

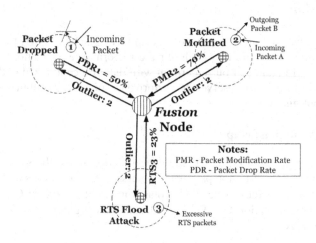

Fig. 2. Centralized Outlier Detection Algorithm

4.2 Experimentation Results

The first series of the experiments aim to compare the performance of our algorithm with that of the centralized algorithm. We use two different definitions to the outliers, which are distance to the nearest neighbor (NN) and average distance to k nearest neighbors (k-NN) in our experiments. All the experiments are simulated for thirty runs. The results are shown in Fig. 3 and Fig. 4.

From Fig. 3 we find that the Correctness Rate of our algorithm is higher than that of the centralized algorithm. This is true because of the robustness introduced by local gossiping in our algorithm. The centralized algorithm requires reliable communication links between the fusion node and other nodes, which cannot be guaranteed due to the node mobility and limited radio range. Moreover, the misbehavior of some nodes will also prevent some observations from successful delivery to the fusion node. Hence, the calculation of the global outliers ends up being based on a subset of the observations that the fusion node gets. In contrast, our algorithm is more resilient to various

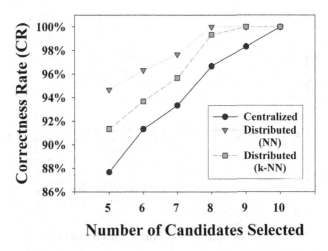

Fig. 3. CR of Various Algorithms in a 50-node MANET

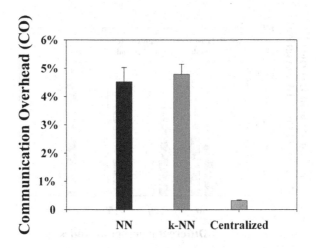

Fig. 4. CO of Various Algorithms in a 50-node MANET

misbehaviors. By use of gossiping method, a node can receive the observations of its neighbors through different routes. Even if some of the observation messages are blocked by malicious nodes, a node may still get the blocked observations that are forwarded by some other nodes in its neighborhood. We also note that the Correctness Rate of *NN* is slightly higher than that of *k-NN*. By definition, *k-NN* finds *k* distinct supporting points to identify one outlier, whereas *NN* simply looks for the nearest neighbor to get one outlier. Hence, *k-NN* is more prone to the noise brought by multiple supporting points, and consequently it will produce a lower Correctness Rate that *NN*.

Fig. 4 shows that while our algorithm produces higher communication overhead than the centralized algorithm, it is still within 5% of the total messages. Given that our algorithm produces higher correctness rate, and is more resilient to misbehaviors, the communication overhead of our algorithm is acceptable.

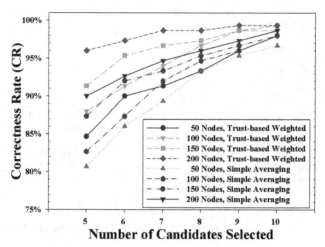

Fig. 5. CR with Different Amounts of Nodes (Area: 600m ×600m, Radio Range: 120m, Speed: 5m/s)

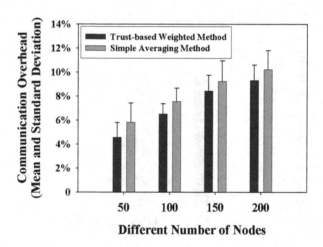

Fig. 6. CO with Different Amounts of Nodes (Area: 600m ×600m, Radio Range: 120m, Speed: 5m/s)

The second series of experiments are designed to observe the performance of our algorithm under different parameter configurations. We have compared the performance of our algorithm under the following four conditions: different number of nodes, different simulation areas, different radio ranges, and different adversary strategies. The experimentation results are displayed in Fig. 5 through Fig. 19.

There are two adversary strategies that are used in our experiments. The first is called the *Comprehensive* strategy, in which the adversary simultaneously conducts several kinds of misbehaviors. This is used as a default in our simulations. In the second strategy, which is called the *Dedicated* strategy, the adversary conducts merely one

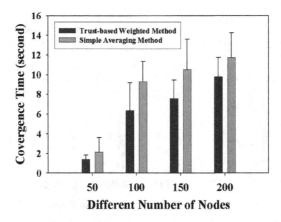

Fig. 7. CT with Different Amounts of Nodes (Area: 600m ×600m, Radio Range: 120m, Speed: 5m/s)

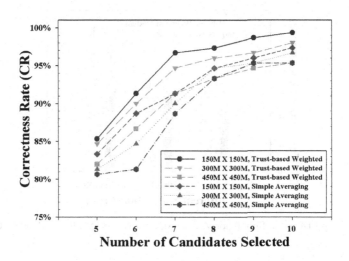

Fig. 8. CR with Different Simulation Areas (Num. of Nodes: 50, Radio Range: 60m, Speed: 5m/s)

kind of misbehavior at a time. Whereas most of the studies in the security area make the assumption that an adversary conducts one malicious behavior at a time, a recent study has shown that there may be cross-layer attacks [33] that involve misbehaviors at several layers of the protocol stack. In the *Dedicated* attack strategy, the malicious behaviors are less distinctive compared to other normal behaviors. In addition, the adversary may switch from various malicious behaviors from time to time, which makes it harder to keep track of each malicious behavior the adversary has conducted. Therefore, it is more difficult to identify an adversary if it deploys the dedicated attack strategy. We run experiments to compare the behavior of our approach against both.

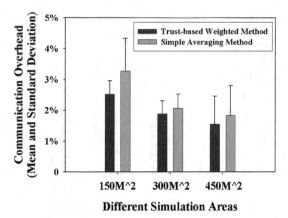

Fig. 9. CO with Different Simulation Areas (Num. of Nodes: 50, Radio Range: 60m, Speed: 5m/s)

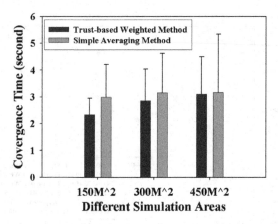

Fig. 10. CT with Different Simulation Areas (Num. of Nodes: 50, Radio Range: 60m, Speed: 5m/s)

From Fig. 5 through Fig. 7, we find that with an increase in the number of the nodes, the correctness rate increases, and the communication overhead also rises for both simple averaging method and trust-based weighted method. This is true because the information gathered to identify the outliers is generally more accurate if there are more observers. At the same time, more messages need to be exchanged amongst all the nodes to reach a consistent view when there are a larger amount of nodes. We also note that the trust-based weighted method yields better performance than the simple averaging method. Through the use of trust in the local view update process, a higher correctness rate can be produced in a shorter period of time together with a lower communication overhead.

Fig. 8, Fig. 9, and Fig. 10 illustrate the results with different simulation areas. It is obvious that the correctness rate decreases as we increase the simulation area for the both methods. We also find that the communication overhead is reduced as the simulation area becomes larger. Since the nodes have a lower probability to

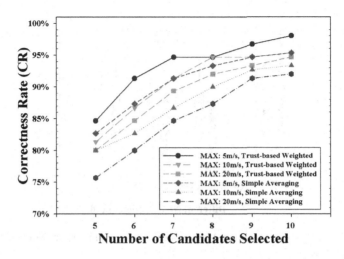

Fig. 11. CR with Different Maximum Motion Speed (Area: 600m ×600m, Num. of Nodes: 100, Radio Range: 60m)

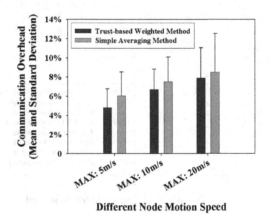

Fig. 12. CO with Different Maximum Motion Speed (Area: 600m ×600m, Num. of Nodes: 100, Radio Range: 60m)

communicate with other nodes if the simulation area becomes larger, the correctness rate will surely become lower. Moreover, there will also be less communication overhead. As we have expected, the trust-based weighted method can also achieve better performance than the simple averaging method in different simulation areas.

The experimental results under different node motion speeds are demonstrated in Fig. 11 through Fig. 13. We find that with the increase to the maximum speed of nodes, the performance for both methods decreases. This is true because it is harder for the nodes to exchange their views when they are moving in a higher speed.

Fig. 14 through Fig. 16 shows how the experiment results differ with respect to different radio ranges. We conclude that the correctness rate significantly decreases as

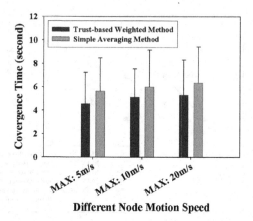

Fig. 13. CT with Different Maximum Motion Speed (Area: 600m ×600m, Num. of Nodes: 100, Radio Range: 60m)

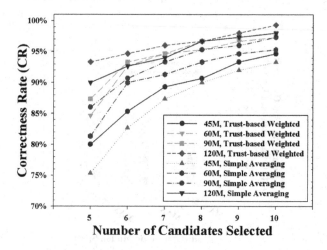

Fig. 14. CR with Different Radio Ranges (Num. of Nodes: 100, Area: 600m ×600m, Speed: 5m/s)

the radio range decreases. When it is more difficult for the nodes to exchange their local views when the radio range is smaller, the correctness rate of the final global view will surely be degraded. However, even if the radio range has been halved, the trust-based weighted method still yields a good performance.

In Fig. 17 through Fig. 19, the experiment results with two different attack strategies are discussed. We find that the algorithm will achieve a slightly higher correctness rate when the dedicated strategy is deployed. It is also clear that the communication overhead for the dedicated strategy will be lower than that for the comprehensive strategy. Nevertheless, our algorithm can achieve a satisfactory performance with both of the attack strategies.

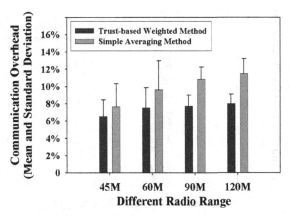

Fig. 15. CO with Different Radio Ranges (Num. of Nodes: 100, Area: 600m ×600m, Speed: 5m/s)

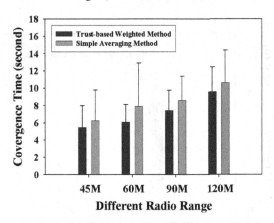

Fig. 16. CT with Different Radio Ranges (Num. of Nodes: 100, Area: 600m ×600m, Speed: 5m/s)

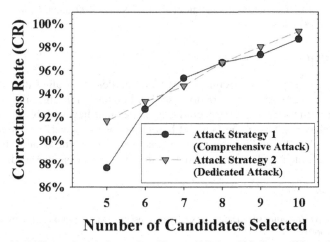

Fig. 17. CR with Different Attack Strategies (Num. of Nodes: 100, Area: 600m ×600m, Range: 90m, Speed: 5m/s)

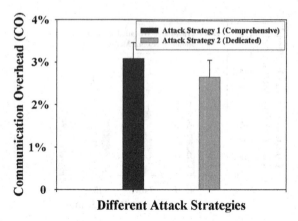

Fig. 18. CR with Different Attack Strategies (Num. of Nodes: 100, Area: 600m ×600m, Range: 90m, Speed: 5m/s)

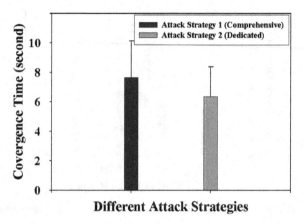

Fig. 19. CT with Different Attack Strategies (Num. of Nodes: 100, Area: 600m ×600m, Range: 90m, Speed: 5m/s)

5   Conclusion

In this paper, we propose a collaborative outlier detection algorithm for securing mobile ad hoc networks. The gossip-based outlier detection algorithm can help us identify the outliers, which are generally the nodes that have exhibited some kind of abnormal behaviors. Given the fact that benign nodes rarely behave abnormally, it is highly likely that the outliers are malicious nodes. Simulation results show that our algorithm is efficient and accurate with a small communication overhead.

References

[1] Grubbs, F.: Procedures for Detecting Outlying Observations in Samples. Technometrics 11(1), 1–21 (1969)
[2] Barnett, V., Lewis, T.: Outliers in Statistical Data. John Wiley and Sons, New York (1994)

[3] Lazarevic, A., Ertoz, L., Ozgur, A., Srivastava, J., Kumar, V.: A Comparative Study of Anomaly Detection Schemes in Network Intrusion Detection. In: Proceedings of the Third SIAM International Conference on Data Mining, San Francisco, CA, USA (May 2003)

[4] Zhang, J., Zulkernine, M.: Anomaly Based Network Intrusion Detection with Unsupervised Outlier Detection. In: Proceedings of IEEE International Conference on Communications (ICC 2006), Istanbul, Turkey, pp. 2388–2393 (2006)

[5] Ferdousi, Z., Maeda, A.: Unsupervised Outlier Detection in Time Series Data. In: Proceedings of the 22nd International Conference on Data Engineering Workshops (ICDEW 2006), Atlanta, GA, USA (April 2006)

[6] Sheng, B., Li, Q., Mao, W., Jin, W.: Outlier Detection in Sensor Networks. In: Proceedings of the 8th ACM international symposium on Mobile ad hoc networking and computing (MobiHoc 2007), Montreal, Quebec, Canada, pp. 219–228 (2007)

[7] Zhang, Y., Lee, W.: Intrusion detection in wireless ad-hoc networks. In: Proceedings of the 8th International Conference on Mobile Computing and Networking (MobiCom), Atlanta, GA, USA, pp. 275–283 (2002)

[8] Hu, Y., Perrig, A., Johnson, D.: Ariadne: A Secure on-demand routing protocol for ad hoc networks. In: Proceedings of the 8th International Conference on Mobile Computing and Networking (MobiCom), Atlanta, GA, USA, pp. 12–23 (2002)

[9] Sun, B., Guan, Y., Chen, J., Pooch, U.W.: Detecting black-hole attack in mobile ad hoc networks. In: Proceedings of 5th European Personal Mobile Communications Conference, Glasgow, Scotland, UK, pp. 490–495 (2003)

[10] Ramaswamy, S., Rastogi, R., Shim, K.: Efficient Algorithms for Mining Outliers fromLarge Datasets. In: Proceedings of the 2000 ACM SIGMOD international Conference on Management of Data, Dallas, Texas, USA, pp. 427–438 (2000)

[11] Anguilla, F., Pizzuti, C.: Fast Outlier Detection in High Dimensional Spaces. In: Elomaa, T., Mannila, H., Toivonen, H. (eds.) PKDD 2002. LNCS, vol. 2431, pp. 15–26. Springer, Heidelberg (2002)

[12] Knorr, E.M., Ng, R.T.: Algorithms for Mining Distance-Based Outliers in Large Datasets. In: Proceedings of the 24th international Conference on Very Large Data Bases (VLDB 1998), New York, USA, pp. 392–403 (1998)

[13] Knorr, E.M., Ng, R.T.: Finding Intensional Knowledge of Distance-Based Outliers. In: Proceedings of the 25th international Conference on Very Large Data Bases (VLDB 1999), Edinburgh, Scotland, UK, pp. 211–222 (1999)

[14] Bay, S.D., Schwabacher, M.: Mining Distance-based Outliers in Near Linear Time with Randomization and a Simple Pruning Rule. In: Proceedings of the Ninth ACM SIGKDD international Conference on Knowledge Discovery and Data Mining (KDD 2003), Washington, D.C., USA, pp. 29–38 (2003)

[15] Aggarwal, C., Yu, S.: An Effective and Efficient Algorithm for High-dimensional Outlier Detection. The VLDB Journal 14(2), 211–221 (2005)

[16] Aggarwal, C.C.: Re-designing Distance Functions and Distance-based Applications for High Dimensional Data. ACM SIGMOD Record 30(1), 13–18 (2001)

[17] Aggarwal, C.C., Yu, P.S.: Outlier Detection for High Dimensional Data. In: Proceedings of the 2001 ACM SIGMOD international Conference on Management of Data (SIGMOD 2001), Santa Barbara, California, USA, pp. 37–46 (2001)

[18] Lazarevic, A., Kumar, V.: Feature Bagging for Outlier Detection. In: Proceeding of the Eleventh ACM SIGKDD international Conference on Knowledge Discovery in Data Mining (KDD 2005), Chicago, Illinois, USA, pp. 157–166 (2005)

[19] Branch, J., Szymanski, B., Giannella, C., Wolff, R., Kargupta, H.: In-network Outlier Detection in Wireless Sensor Networks. In: Proceedings of the 26th IEEE International Conference on Distributed Computing Systems (ICDCS 2006), Lisbon, Portugal (2006)

[20] Palpanas, T., Papadopoulos, D., Kalogeraki, V., Gunopulos, D.: Distributed Deviation Detection in Sensor Networks. ACM SIGMOD Record 32(4), 77–82 (2003)

[21] Subramaniam, S., Palpanas, T., Papadopoulos, D., Kalogeraki, V., Gunopulos, D.: Online Outlier Detection in Sensor Data Using Non-parametric Models. In: Proceedings of the 32nd international Conference on Very Large Data Bases (VLDB 2006), Seoul, Korea, pp. 187–198 (2006)

[22] Marti, S., Giuli, T.J., Lai, K., Baker, M.: Mitigating Routing Misbehavior in Mobile Ad Hoc Networks. In: Proceedings of the 6th Annual international Conference on Mobile Computing and Networking (MOBICOM 2000), Boston, MA, USA, pp. 255–265 (2000)

[23] Liu, Y., Comaniciu, C., Man, H.: A Bayesian Game Approach for Intrusion Detection in Wireless Ad Hoc Networks. In: Proceeding of the 2006 Workshop on Game theory For Communications and Networks (GAMENET 2006), Pisa, Italy (2006)

[24] Zhang, Y., Lee, W.: Intrusion Detection in Wireless Ad-hoc Networks. In: Proceedings of the 6th Annual international Conference on Mobile Computing and Networking (MOBICOM 2000), Boston, MA, USA, pp. 275–283 (2000)

[25] Deng, H., Zeng, Q., Agrawal, D.P.: SVM-based Intrusion Detection System for Wireless Ad Hoc Networks. In: Proceedings of the IEEE Vehicular Technology Conference (VTC 2003), Orlando, FL, USA, vol. 3, pp. 2147–2151 (2003)

[26] Kachirski, O., Guha, R.: Intrusion Detection Using Mobile Agents in Wireless Ad Hoc Networks. In: Proceedings of the IEEE Workshop on Knowledge Media Networking, Kyoto, Japan, pp. 153–158 (2002)

[27] Tseng, C., Balasubramanyam, P., Ko, C., Limprasittiporn, R., Rowe, J., Levitt, K.: A Specification-based Intrusion Detection System for AODV. In: Proceedings of the 1st ACM workshop on Security of ad hoc and sensor networks(SASN 2003), Fairfax, VA, USA, pp. 125–134 (2003)

[28] Huang, Y., Lee, W.: A Cooperative Intrusion Detection System for Ad Hoc Networks. In: Proceedings of the 1st ACM Workshop on Security of Ad Hoc and Sensor Networks (SASN 2003), Fairfax, VA, USA, pp. 135–147 (2003)

[29] Kefayati, M., Rabiee, H.R., Miremadi, S.G., Khonsari, A.: Misbehavior Resilient Multi-path Data Transmission in Mobile Ad-hoc Networks. In: Proceedings of the Fourth ACM Workshop on Security of Ad Hoc and Sensor Networks (SASN 2006), Alexandria, VA, USA, pp. 91–100 (2006)

[30] Xue, Y., Nahrstedt, K.: Providing Fault-Tolerant Ad hoc Routing Service in Adversarial Environments. Wireless Personal Communication 29(3-4), 367–388 (2004)

[31] Anderegg, L., Eidenbenz, S.: Ad hoc-VCG: A Truthful and Cost-efficient Routing Protocol for Mobile Ad Hoc Networks with Selfish Agents. In: Proceedings of the 9th Annual international Conference on Mobile Computing and Networking (MOBICOM 2003), San Diego, CA, USA, pp. 245–259 (2003)

[32] Glomosim 2.03, http://pcl.cs.ucla.edu/projects/glomosim/

[33] Parker, J., Patwardhan, A., Joshi, A.: Cross-layer Analysis for Detecting Wireless Misbehavior. In: Proceedings of the IEEE Consumer Communications and Networking Conference(CCNC 2006), Las Vegas, Nevada, USA (January 2006)

[34] He, Q., Wu, D., Khosla, P.: SORI: A Secure and Objective Reputation-based Incentive Scheme for Ad hoc Networks. In: Proceedings of the IEEE Wireless Communications and Networking Conference (WCNC), vol. 2, pp. 825–830 (2004)

[35] Patwardhan, A., Perich, F., Joshi, A., Finin, T., Yesha, Y.: Active Collaborations for Trustworthy Data Management in Ad Hoc Networks. In: Proceedings of the 2nd IEEE International Conference on Mobile Ad-Hoc and Sensor Systems (November 2005)

[36] Srinivasan, V., Nuggehalli, P., Chiasserini, C.-F., Rao, R.R.: An analytical approach to the study of cooperation in wireless ad hoc networks. IEEE Transactions on Wireless Communications 4(2), 722–733 (2005)

A Hybrid Key Predistribution Scheme for Sensor Networks Employing Spatial Retreats to Cope with Jamming Attacks

Korporn Panyim and Prashant Krishnamurthy

Graduate Program in Telecommunications and Networking
University of Pittsburgh
{kop1,prashk}@pitt.edu

Abstract. In order to provide security services in wireless sensor networks, a well-known task is to provide cryptographic keys to sensor nodes prior to deployment. It is difficult to assign secret keys for all pairs of sensor node when the number of nodes is large due to the large numbers of keys required and limited memory resources of sensor nodes. One possible solution is to randomly assign a few keys to sensor nodes and have nodes be able to connect to each other with some probability. This scheme has limitations in terms of the tradeoffs between connectivity and memory requirements. Recently, sensor deployment knowledge has been used to improve the level of connectivity while using lesser amounts of memory space. Jamming attacks are an easy and efficient means for disruption of the connectivity of sensors and thus the operation of a sensor network. One solution for mobile sensor nodes to overcome the impact of jamming is to perform spatial retreat by moving nodes away from jammed regions. However, deployment based key predistribution schemes may cause a large number of nodes to be cryptographically isolated after they move out of the jammed area. Moved nodes may not be able to reconnect to the network because they do not have any shared secret with new neighbors at new locations. In this paper, we propose a hybrid key predistribution scheme that supports spatial retreat strategies to cope with jamming attacks. Our scheme combines the properties of random and deployment knowledge based key predistribution schemes. In the presence of jamming attacks, our scheme provides high key connectivity (similar to deployment knowledge based schemes) while reducing the number of isolated nodes. We evaluate the performance of our scheme through simulations and analysis.

1   Introduction

Sensor networks applications have been constantly diversifying to include environmental sensing, object detection, structural health monitoring, patient health monitoring, and goods tracking. In many of these scenarios it is important to preserve confidential the data exchanged by sensors. For these purposes, sensor nodes must share cryptographic keys (typically secret (symmetric) keys because

E. Bertino and J.B.D. Joshi (Eds.): CollaborateCom 2008, LNICST 10, pp. 715–731, 2009.

public-key schemes are computationally expensive for sensors). There are several challenges here. At one end of the spectrum, assigning a single master key to every node results in a lack of resilience to node compromise. A single node, if compromised, can enable communications of all pairs of nodes to be compromised. It is difficult to assign and manage *pairwise* secret keys for all pairs of sensor nodes when the number of nodes is large due to the large numbers of keys and limited memory resources of sensor nodes (the number of keys stored is $n-1$ for a group of n nodes). Pairwise keys also limit deployment of additional sensors. One possible solution is to randomly predistribute a subset of keys from a big pool of keys to sensor nodes and have nodes be able to securely connect to each other with some probability [5]. In this approach sensors in communicating range can securely connect only if they share at least one key from the randomly pre-distributed set they each carry. This probability (a related measure of which is called local connectivity) depends on the key pool size and the number of keys stored in each sensor. Recently, sensor deployment knowledge has been used to improve local connectivity while using a smaller memory space [4] by partitioning the pool of keys such that nodes that are deployed together spatially are more likely to share keys as against nodes that are far away from each other.

Jamming attacks form efficient means for disruption of the connectivity of sensors and thus the operation of a sensor network. One solution for mobile sensor nodes to overcome the impact of jamming is to perform *spatial retreats*[6,11] by moving nodes away from jammed regions. With spatial retreats and deployment based key predistribution a large number of sensor nodes can be isolated from the rest of the network after they move out of the jammed area. This is because moved nodes may not be able to find share secret keys with new neighbors at new locations. The random key predistribution scheme [5] is not affected by movement of nodes, but it has a lower *a priori* connectivity than the one that employs deployment knowledge given the same number of keys stored in sensor nodes. Similar problems of isolation can be anticipated with other techniques to combat jamming (e.g., increasing transmit power to reach nodes that are beyond the jammed region) although we do not consider them in this paper.

In this paper, we propose a *hybrid key predistribution scheme* that supports spatial retreat strategies to cope with jamming attacks. This scheme combines the properties of random and deployment knowledge based key predistribution schemes. In the presence of jamming attacks, the scheme provides high local connectivity (similar to deployment knowledge based schemes) while reducing the number of isolated nodes (like the random scheme) due to node's movement. We evaluate the performance of our scheme through simulations and analysis. We organize our paper as follows: Section 1.2 provides the background of key predistribution schemes for sensor networks and jamming models for attacks; Section 1.3 describes the impact of jamming on key connectivity of sensor nodes that adopt a spatial retreat strategy. We introduce the hybrid key predistribution scheme in Section 1.4; Section 1.5 presents an evaluation of the hybrid key predistribution scheme using simulations; Section 1.6 provides some discussions and limitations of the work; and finally Section 1.7 presents the conclusions.

2 Background

In this section, we present some basic background of key predistribution schemes for wireless sensor networks and an overview of jamming attacks. This section is necessary for understanding the hybrid scheme and its performance.

2.1 Key Predistribution for Sensor Networks

Unique characteristics of wireless sensor networks introduce challenges in providing security services. A sensor has limited size of memory but the number of sensor nodes involved in one application can be large (1,000 to 10,000 nodes). A possible approach for providing security services in wireless sensor networks is to install cryptographic keys in sensor nodes prior to deployment. If a single master key is installed in all sensors (which will then be used to bootstrap secure communications), a single node compromise can impact the entire network. When the number of sensors is large, installing pairwise keys (where each pair of nodes has a unique shared secret key) becomes unmanageable. Each node has to keep $n-1$ keys in an n-node network and rekeying if nodes are added becomes a problem. Finally, since sensors typically communicate locally with direct neighbors, it may not be necessary to install pairwise keys between all pairs of sensors. However it is hard to determine which sensors will be eventual neighbors after deployment.

To overcome the above challenges, Eschenauer and Gligor proposed a random key predistribution scheme (EG scheme) [5]. The EG scheme (also called "basic" random key predistribution) relies on probabilistic key sharing among nodes in a random graph. The EG scheme consists of three phases: key distribution phase, shared-key discovery phase, and path-key establishment phase. In the key distribution phase, an off-line key distribution center generates a key pool consisting of large number of keys. Each node randomly picks k keys from this global key pool S of size $|S|$ and stores them in its memory. Each key is associated with a key identification (key-ID). The set of keys drawn from the key pool with associated key-IDs is called a key ring. In the shared-key discovery phase, each node exchanges, with its neighbor, information used to establish a shared key. The goal of this phase is to find a common key between two neighboring nodes. The common key(s) can be used to establish a secure link between two nodes by encrypting all messages with their shared key (or performing local key establishment using these keys). A secure link exists between two nodes if they share a key and can communicate directly. The simplest way to do this is to have each node broadcast, in clear text, its list of key IDs in the key ring. To add security to exchanged information, a challenge-response protocol can be used to hide key sharing patterns among nodes from an adversary [5]. However, since keys in node's key ring are randomly drawn from the key pool, it is possible that a pair of nodes may not have any common key. The path-key establishment phase allows a pair of nodes that do not have common key to establish a secure path through two or more links. The graph of sensor nodes is connected (securely) if each sensor node has enough neighbors even though k is small compared to $|S|$.

Typically, k is on the order of a hundred while $|S|$ is on the order of several tens or hundreds of thousands. From [5], the probability that any two sensor nodes share a key given $|S|$ and k is:

$$1 - \frac{((|S| - k)!)^2}{(|S| - 2k)!|S|!} \qquad (1)$$

The above equation considers the number of possible sets of size k drawn without repetition from a set of size $|S|$ that have no overlap to compute the probability that two nodes do not share a key and subtracts this from 1 to determine the probability that two nodes do share at least one key. We will refer to the fact that two nodes within transmission range share at least one key as constituting "secure connectivity" in this paper.

The use of *deployment knowledge* is proposed as an improvement to the EG scheme. The deployment knowledge based key predistribution scheme (we shall call it *EGD scheme* throughout this paper), proposed by Du, et al [4], is based on the idea that the way that sensor nodes are deployed can be use to improve secure connectivity. One practical way to deploy sensor nodes is to divide sensors into small deployment groups or clusters. These groups are deployed sequentially so that the sensors in groups that are next to each other have a better chance to be within each other's radio transmission range. Knowing which pair of nodes is "likely" to comprise of neighbors is valuable in assigning keys from the key pool. The clustered deployment of sensor nodes is modeled by using probability density functions. In EG scheme, nodes are deployed uniformly in the entire sensor field – therefore there is no information on clustering. Every pair of nodes has the same chance to be neighbors. The EGD scheme uses a two dimensional Gaussian distribution to model node deployment in clusters where a mean (μ) is the targeted deployment point of each group. Next, multiple key pools are used in the EGD scheme as opposed to a single global key pool in the EG scheme. Each deployment group has its associated group key pool of size $|S_c|$ which is generated from the larger key pool of size $|S|$. Keys from the global key pool are assigned to group key pools in a way that the group key pools that are deployed nearby have a certain number of common keys. Overlapping factors denoted by a and b determine the fraction of shared keys between two adjacent group key pools. Assuming that clusters of sensors are arranged in a grid, of the $|S_c|$ keys in a given group key pool, $a|S_c|$ keys are shared between its horizontal and vertical neighboring clusters. The number of keys shared with its diagonal neighbors is $b|S_c|$. If two clusters are not neighbors, the group key pools do not share any keys. Given a global key pool of size $|S|$, number of deployment group, and overlapping factor, one can calculate $|S_c|$ by using a method described in [2]. For a memory size of k, a node randomly picks k keys from its associated *group* key pool of size $|S_c|$. The scheme has been shown to improve the network connectivity over the EG scheme for the same number k of keys installed in each node's memory. The probability of finding at least one common key between two nodes n_i and n_j that belong to deployment groups G_i and G_j respectively can be determined as in [4] as follows. Let $\delta(i, j)$ denote the number of shared keys between the deployment groups G_i and G_j and the overlapping factors between vertical-horizontal and diagonal groups be a and b respectively. The value of $\delta(i,j)$ changes as follows:

- When $i = j$, $\delta(i,j) = |S_c|$
- When i and j are horizontal or vertical group neighbors, $\delta(i,j) = a|S_c|$
- When i and j are diagonal group neighbors, $\delta(i,j) = b|S_c|$
- When i and j are not neighbors, $\delta(i,j) = 0$

The probability that two nodes share at least one key is:

$$1 - \frac{\sum_{m=0}^{min(k,\delta(i,j))} \binom{\delta(i,j)}{m}\binom{|S_c|-\delta(i,j)}{k-m}\binom{|S_c|-m}{k}}{\binom{|S_c|}{k}^2} \tag{2}$$

The computation of the above probability again considers the chance that two sets of k keys (now drawn differently as described) have no overlap (and subtract this probability from 1). To calculate Pr[two nodes do not share any key], first sensor node with a key ring of size k selects m keys from the intersecting keypool of size $\delta(i,j)$ and $k - m$ keys from its non-intersecting group key pool. The second node, in order to avoid selecting k keys that already selected by the first node, can pick only $|S_c| - m$ keys from its group key pool where m is the number of overlap keys between both node's group key pool that already picked by first node.

Instead of sharing keys, it is possible to share "key spaces" (e.g., using Blom's approach [3][1], that increases the resiliency of the network to multiple node compromise). While the proposed hybrid scheme can be changed to include this, we only consider sharing of keys in this paper. Both (1.1) and (1.2) ignore the fact that two sensor nodes may not be in transmission range. So the probability that two sensor nodes can securely communicate is actually conditional on the fact that they are within range of one another.

2.2   Jamming Attacks

Jamming attacks can disrupt communications in any wireless network quite easily. Xu, et al [11] has classified jammers into the following types: 1) Constant jammers that constantly emit a radio signal 2) Deceptive jammers that constantly inject fake (but valid otherwise) packets into the network without following the medium access protocol 3) Random jammers (also considered energy efficient jammers) that randomly choose a period of time to sleep and a random period of time to jam and 4) Reactive jammers that sense the channel and when they sense valid traffic being exchanged in the network they start jamming. To detect the presence of jamming attacks, [11] proposed to use packet delivery ratios as the main metric along with carrier sensing time and the signal strength. The results are promising, but not conclusive. In this paper we assume that jamming can be detected accurately.

Solutions to cope with jamming attacks include adjusting transmit power [10], data rate, or hopping to another frequency channel [13]. For a sensor node that has an ability to move, one convenient solution is to physically move the sensors away from the jammer [6]. We assume a constant or deceptive jammer and spatial retreats for combatting the attack in this paper.

To the best of our knowledge there is no publication that has looked at the effects of jamming attacks over connectivity of secure links, and how this problem can be solved. In the next section we explain the impact of jamming on secure connectivity and also describe the solution we propose to cope with the low level of secure connectivity due to jamming attacks.

3   Impact of Jamming on Secure Communications in Sensor Networks

In this section, we demonstrate the impact of a constant jammer on the probability of secure links in sensor networks. We use *local connectivity* (defined as the fraction of neighbors with whom at least one key is shared) and *number of moved nodes that are isolated* (nodes that share no keys with any neighboring nodes after spatial retreat) as our performance metrics. Then, we present our hybrid key pre-distribution scheme to cope with jamming attacks.

Jamming versus node compromise: The node compromise attack is usually considered when designing key pre-distribution schemes. When a node is captured, sensitive information including encryption keys stored in node's memory may be disclosed. Jamming attacks may not be able to expose information inside a jammed node. However, in the worst case, it is essentially incommunicado and cannot help in the application objectives. An adversary may find it is more convenient to launch an jamming attack remotely using a powerful transmitter; rather than being in deployment area to capture a node.

A successful jammer can prevent the victim nodes from transmitting and receiving data. It is not necessary that a jammer should jam the whole network. A jammer can launch targeted jamming which focuses only specific victim nodes, links or flows. A jammed node may transmit a signal to a non-jammed node, thus creating an asymmetric link in the network [7]. However, due to MAC protocols that use carrier sensing, jamming attacks may be successful in preventing legitimate nodes from accessing the channel to send data. When a node senses a channel, it will see the channel as busy all the time [8].

Jamming Attack Model: Here we describe the model of the jamming attacks that will be used in this paper.

- The jammer performs constant jamming or deceptive jamming. Any node that lies in jammed area is assumed to be affected completely by the jamming attack.
- The jammed region is assumed to be a circle centered at the jammer's location, the size of jammed region is measured by transmission range of the jamming device.
- The jammer interferes with part of the deployment area. As a result, there will be some nodes that are jammed and some nodes that are not jammed.

We will analyze the performance of the key pre-distribution schemes under this jamming model.

Strategy for Spatial Retreat: The first step is to detect the presence of jamming attacks. We assume that sensor nodes use various statistical methods to detect the presence of jamming [12]. Once jamming is detected, nodes can identify jammed and non-jammed areas and map them [9]. One possible solution to overcome jamming is for a jammed node to evacuate from the jammed area (spatial retreat) [13]. The main goal of the evacuation process is to move jammed nodes out of the jammed region. The solution proposed by [6] is to move the jammed nodes in a random direction out of jammed area. Upon moving, each node continuously runs its detection algorithm until it reaches the border of the jammed region. After the node is outside the jammed area, it tries to connect to the sensor nodes nearby (finding new neighbor nodes). If there is no node within its radio range, the node will move along the jammed perimeter until it connects to other nodes.

We use a simpler strategy for node evacuation. If a node is deployed within a jammed area, the node will move out from the jammed region by randomly selecting its new location within the sensor field (it random picks a new x and y coordinate). This can be accomplished by the node moving a random distance in a random direction. Once the node moves to new location, it will check if its new location is also jammed. If so, it will randomly pick another location. After that, node will try to connect with sensor node nearby. In our simulations, we repeat the move till the node moves out of the jammed area. It is possible to improve the approach by increasing the distance moved from the current location in subsequent tries or to use the original approach in [6].

Demonstration of the Impact of Jamming on the Secure Connectivity after Spatial Retreat: A secure link can be established between two sensor nodes under these two conditions: 1) sensor nodes are within each others' communication range 2) there is a common key between two nodes. After a node moves to its new location, it tries to find whether it has a common key with its new neighbors. A neighbor node that has at least one shared key will be able to establish a secure link with the moved node. The probability of having at least one common key with the new neighbor node depends on the type of key predistribution that was employed. If the sensor nodes select keys from a single key-pool as in the EG scheme, each node will have (on average) the same chance as in (1.1) to have a common key with its neighbor because the keys stored in the node's memory are selected regardless of the location of the nodes.

However, when the key pre-distribution scheme employs multiple key pools with deployment knowledge, each node will select its keys according to its associated key pool which depends on the deployment group that the node belongs to. Two nodes that picked their keys from the same key pool (they are from the same deployment group) will have a greater probability of finding a common key than two nodes that chose their keys from different key-pools (they are from different deployment groups). If the jammed node moves far enough to enter a

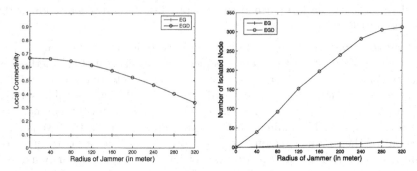

Fig. 1. (a) Local connectivity of EG and EGD schemes and (b) number of moved nodes that are isolated in EG and EGD schemes with different jamming radii

completely different deployment area, the chance of finding some common keys to establish secure links with the new set of neighbors will be reduced.

To see what impact jamming has on the local connectivity and the number of moved nodes that are isolated, we ran simulations that used $|S| = 100000$ keys, $|S_c| = 1760$ keys, number of keys installed in a node's memory $k = 100$ keys, overlap factors $a = 0.15$ and $b = 0.1$ in a 10000 node network in a 1000m $\times$ 1000m sensor field. The clusters of sensors in the deployment based multiple key pool approach are arranged a 10×10 grid, where each grid cell is of size 100m $\times$ 100m. The transmission range of a sensor is 40m. The numbers and scenario used here are very similar to the ones in [4,5]. The jammer is placed at the center of the sensor field.

Figure 1a shows the local connectivity after the nodes evacuate from the jammed region. We show the results of key connectivity for the whole network for different sizes of the jamming region. When the size of jamming hole is 0, it is equivalent to a network with no jamming. We compare the random scheme (EG) with the deployment knowledge scheme (EGD). Under jamming, we calculate the average connectivity of the whole network after all jammed nodes move away from jamming hole. It is clear that the local connectivity with the EGD scheme decreases while connectivity for EG scheme remain at the same level. Note however that the EG scheme already has poor connectivity (in this case, only 10% of neighbors share a key which implies that a high node density is mandatory for a securely connected network).

When a jammed node moves out of its deployment location, it will see a new set of one-hop neighbors at its final destination. With the EGD scheme, a node may travel beyond its deployment group to non-neighboring deployment groups. Nodes will have a slim chance of finding common keys with new neighbors since the selected keys are from non-overlapping group key pools. Thus, these nodes may be isolated from the network as they cannot connect to other sensors securely. By isolated we mean the node that is isolated because of jamming evacuation. Such a node cannot connect because it does not have any shared key with its new neighbors even though it is within their communication range. In Figure 1b, we plot the number of isolated nodes with different sizes of jamming area. When the jamming radius increases, the number of isolated nodes also increases at least up to a jamming radius of 320m (we have more discussion in Section 1.5). The number of isolated nodes with the EGD scheme is significantly larger than the number of isolated nodes with the EG scheme.

4   Hybrid Key Predistribution Scheme

In this section, we present a *hybrid* key predistribution scheme (HB scheme) designed to support the spatial retreat strategy to cope with jamming attacks. It makes use of the beneficial features of both the EG and EGD schemes. The goal of our scheme is as follows: When there is no jamming, the new scheme should show better connectivity compared to the random (EG) scheme. The new scheme should have an acceptable level of local connectivity even when the nodes have moved away from their original locations and fewer nodes should be isolated. All of this must be achieved without increasing the number of installed keys in a sensor node.

We adopt the group-based deployment model as in [4]. A group of N sensor nodes is divided into equal sized groups arranged in a grid of size $t \times n$. A sensor node that belongs to a group $G_{i,j}$ for $i = 1, \ldots, t$ and $j = 1, \ldots, n$ is deployed according to a target deployment point (x_i, y_j). The deployment points are arrange in grid as in [4]. Note that deployment points can be differently arranged depending on the method of deployment and application objective. We use a two-dimensional Gaussian distribution (Normal distribution) as in [4] for modeling deployment where the target deployment point is the mean of the distribution. The actual location of a sensor node will be around the associated target deployment point. The standard deviations are $50m$, which is similar to the number used in [4].

Like other existing key pre-distribution schemes proposed in the literature, the hybrid scheme comprises of 3 phases: a key distribution phase, a shared key discovery phase, and a path-key establishment phase.

Step 1: Key Distribution Phase: Each sensor node randomly selects keys from 2 types of key pools and installs them into the node's memory. We define two types of keypool. A *global keypool* that consists of large number of cryptographic keys and *group keypools* that consist of subsets of keys selected from a second global keypool. It is possible to create group key pools from the first global keypool, but we keep the two key pools separate to simplify the analysis presented next. Simulations (not shown here) show little difference between the two approaches since the group key pool is typically smaller than the global key pool (by two orders of magnitude – $|S_c| \ll |S|$ – for the 10×10 grid). Each deployment group has one associated group key pool. Given a global keypool S of size $|S|$, we divide S into $t \times n$ group key pools $S_{i,j}$ (for $i = 1, 2, \ldots, t$ and $j = 1, 2, \ldots, n$) each of size $|S_c|$. Each group key pool shares some amount of keys with adjacent group keypool (vertically, horizontally and diagonally) as previously described with overlapping factors a and b (see [4] for more details).

We further define a hybrid threshold τ. This threshold τ indicates the distribution of keys that a node selects from the first global keypool and its group keypool. The value of τ ranges from 0 to 1 ($\tau = 0, \ldots, 1$). When $\tau = 0$, a node will select keys only from its group keypool. This is equivalent to the EGD scheme. When $\tau = 1$, a node will select no key from the associated group key pool but will select all keys from the first global key pool. By doing this, the scheme is converted to the EG scheme (each node selects keys from the same key pool). Our scheme benefits from both key predistribution methods by selecting an appropriate value of τ as seen later in the simulations. Each sensor will select some amount of keys from its group keypool and some portion of keys from global keypool. For instance, given a memory size of $k = 100$ keys, when τ is set to 0.25, a node will select 25 keys from the first global keypool and 75 keys from its group keypool.

Step 2: Shared Key Discovery Phase: After the nodes are deployed, they find some common keys with their neighbors. Each node does this by broadcasting a message containing the indices of the keys that they hold. Each node uses these broadcast messages with its neighbors to find out if they share a common key. If a common key exists between a pair of nodes, both nodes can establish a secure link using the shared key as a link key.

Step 3: Path-Key Establishment Phase: Since the distribution of keys to each node is done randomly, it is possible that some nodes may not be able to find any common key with a subset of neighbors. In this case, as long as the key sharing graph of the entire sensor network is connected, the nodes can always establish secure links with neighbors through their shared-key neighbors. Note that step 2 and 3 are similar to EG and EGD schemes.

Analyzing Secure Connectivity: Given that two sensor nodes are neighbors, we can calculate the probability that they share a key by using (1.1) and (1.2). This is simply 1 minus the probability that two nodes do not share a key from the first global key pool nor do they share a key from the group key pools. A node picks $k\tau$ keys from the first global key pool and $k(1-\tau)$ keys from its group key pool. Since the two key pools are independent, given τ, this probability can be written as:

$$1 - \left\{ \frac{((|S| - k\tau)!)^2}{(|S| - 2k\tau)!|S|!} \right\} \times \left\{ \frac{\sum_{m=0}^{min(k,\delta(i,j))} \binom{\delta(i,j)}{m} \binom{|S_c| - \delta(i,j)}{k(1-\tau)-m} \binom{|S_c|-m}{k(1-\tau)}}{\binom{|S_c|}{k(1-\tau)}^2} \right\} \quad (3)$$

Note that this probability is for the situation when there is no jamming. Under jamming and spatial retreat, the equation will change only in terms of the value of $\delta(i,j)$ which could be 0 in the worst case where nodes are from non-adjacent group or $|S_c|$ in the best case where nodes are from the same group.

5   Performance Evaluation

In this section, we evaluate the performance of the hybrid key predistribution scheme through simulations. The metrics considered are local connectivity and the the number of moved nodes that are isolated after detecting jamming and performing spatial retreat. We compare our results to the random scheme (EG scheme) [5] and the deployment knowledge based scheme (EGD scheme) [4]. Simulation parameters are the same as those in Section 1.3 unless otherwise stated. Each simulation is run 10 times with different seeds of the random number generator, and the results represent the average value of the 10 runs. We consider a range of values for the hybrid threshold τ, namely $\tau = 0, 0.25, 0.50, 0.75, 1$, to assess the performance. Under jamming, nodes perform spatial retreat as previously described in Section 1.3.

Performance with a Single Jammer: Here the jammer is placed at the center of the sensor field. We vary the size of jammer by changing transmission range of jammer from 0 to 320 meters. The simulation results are shown in Figure 2. When $\tau = 1$, all keys stored in the node memory are picked from the first global keypool. Thus, the scheme converts to a random key distribution scheme (EG scheme). The only difference between the original EG scheme and the HB scheme with $\tau = 1$ is the nodes deployment method. The EG scheme uses a uniform deployment method while the HB scheme uses two dimensional gaussian deployment as in the EGD scheme. However, the local connectivity is not impacted by the deployment method as seen in Figure 2(a). At the other end, when τ is equal to 0, the scheme acts like the EGD scheme since all the keys installed in a node's memory are from the node's associated group key pool. Nodes that are from different groups will have a smaller chance of finding common keys as they select keys from different group key pools.

From the results in Figure 2(a), the local connectivity level decreases when the size of the jamming radius increases. This is to be expected. It is important to look at the the number of moved nodes that are isolated as well since local connectivity excludes those nodes that cannot connect to any neighbors. The results show that although the EGD scheme or HB scheme with $\tau = 0$ achieve high local connectivity, the the number of moved nodes that are isolated is also high. This is because when the size of the jamming region is increased, the number of jammed nodes increases. Since there are more sensor nodes that

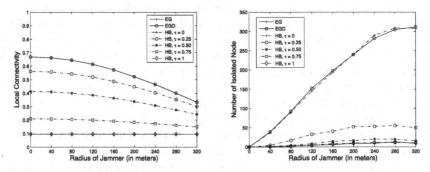

Fig. 2. (a) Local connectivity and (b) number of moved nodes that are isolated for EG, EGD, and Hybrid (HB) schemes with different sizes of jamming areas

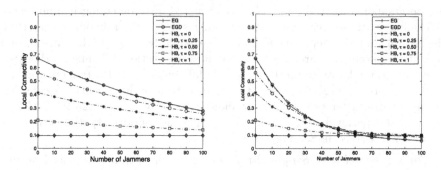

Fig. 3. Local connectivity of EG, EGD, and Hybrid (HB) scheme with multiple jammers (a) radius of jammer = 40m (b) radius of jammer = 80m

need to move out of the jammed area, there will be a larger chance that moved nodes will not be able to find a common key with their new neighbors. If nodes are finally surrounded by neighbors that are from different groups, they will have a small chance of finding common keys with them. However, the hybrid scheme performs in between the EG and EGD schemes depending on the value of τ. Clearly, the hybrid scheme outperforms the EGD scheme in that even with $\tau = 0.25$ when only 25% of the keys installed are from first global key pool, the the number of moved nodes that are isolated is reduced significantly while level of connectivity does not reduce much.

Performance with Multiple Jammers: In the case of multiple jammers, we randomly place jammers in the deployment area (using a uniform distribution). The number of jammers is varied from 0 to 100. In some cases there may be overlap between jammed areas. In such a case, as long as a node is covered by at least one jammer, it is considered to be jammed. Figure 3 shows the local connectivity in the case of multiple jammers for the different schemes. In Figure 3(a), the individual jammers have a jamming radius of 40m (the same as the transmission range of a single sensor). In Figure 3(b), the jamming radius is doubled. Clearly, multiple jammers impact the local connectivity more significantly, especially if they have a larger radius. The performance of the various schemes show a similar trend as that with a single jammer for smaller numbers of jammers (i.e., the HB scheme is in between the EG and EGD schemes). Note that the jammed area could be much larger than the jammed area in the single jammer case, such that for more than 60 jammers with a jamming radius of 80m, the local connectivity of the EGD scheme drops below that of the EG scheme.

The the number of moved nodes that are isolated for the two cases is shown in Figure 4 (a) and (b) respectively. The number of isolated nodes can be as high as 10% of all nodes in the network if only the EGD scheme or HB scheme with $\tau = 0$ are used. Simply changing τ to 0.25 can reduce this number to 2% or lower indicating the benefits of the hybrid scheme. When the jamming radius is 80m and the number of jammers increases, at one point (around 20 jammers), the number of isolated nodes starts to decrease with the EGD scheme and the HB

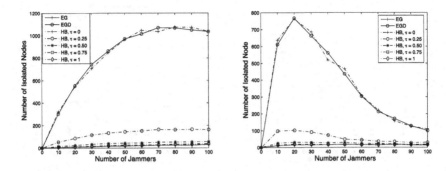

Fig. 4. Number of moved node that are isolated for EG, EGD, and Hybrid (HB) schemes with multiple jammers (a) radius of jammer = 40m (b) radius of jammer = 80m

scheme with $\tau = 0$ and $\tau = 0.25$. This is because the large number of jammers renders the total jammed area to be a significant fraction of the sensor field. Although it is hard to calculate the total jammed area (since the locations of each jammer is random and there could be overlaps), with 20 jammers and and a jamming radius of 80m, the jammed area is approximately $\frac{20 \times \pi \times 80^2}{1000^2} \approx 40.21\%$ of the deployment area. Consequently, sensor nodes are more likely to move close to each other so that the network becomes very dense resulting in a better chance for moved nodes to share keys with some new neighbors. A similar effect is seen with a single jammer when the jamming radius is much larger than 320m (results are not shown here).

Impact of Grid Size and Node Density: In the previous results, a 10×10 grid of sensor clusters was used in the EGD and hybrid schemes. This means there are 100 group key pools, and each cluster of sensors is deployed in a 100m×100m grid. With a transmission range of 40m, sensors in a cluster (deployment group) will have a good chance of being in each other's transmission

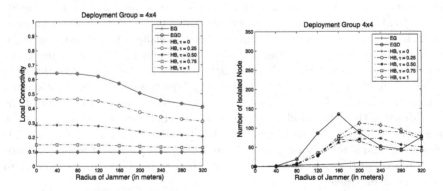

Fig. 5. (a) Local connectivity and (b) number of moved node that are isolated for EG, EGD, and HB schemes with different size of jamming areas for 4×4 grid size

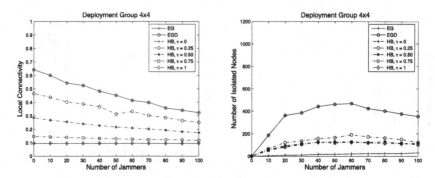

Fig. 6. (a) Local connectivity and (b) number of moved node that are isolated for EG, EGD, and HB schemes with multiple jammers for 4×4 grid size

range. The work in [4] does not look at the sensitivity of the key predistribution scheme to changes in the size of the grid. With the same size of deployment area ($1000m \times 1000m$), we run simulations using a 4×4 grid – there are 16 clusters of sensors and a grid is $250m \times 250m$ in size. The group key pool size increases to $|S_c| = 9433$ keys while it is 1760 keys in the 10×10 grid. There are 10000 sensors deployed in the field as before. We show the average of 5 simulation runs. Figures 5 and 6 show the local connectivity and the number of moved nodes that are isolated for single and multiple jammers respectively for various schemes. The drop in local connectivity of the EGD scheme or HB schemes compared to the 10×10 grid is not significant, and is in fact stable with increase in jamming radius. Moreover, the the number of moved nodes that are isolated is much smaller. This can be expected since a greater number of sensors derive keys from the same key pool (about six times more sensors than before). There is more chance that moved node will still be surrounded by neighbors that are from the same group. It is thus better to deploy fewer clusters of grids to provide resilience to jamming.

The node density will influence the connectivity and the ability to create a securely connected graph in the network. This is an issue that has not received much attention in the literature on key predistribution. We ran simulations to obtain some understanding of the impact of node density. The averages for 5 simulation runs are shown here. Figure 7 shows the results of the local connectivity and the number of moved nodes that are isolated as the number of deployed sensors changes in the 10×10 grid. We picked 50 jammers for illustration and compare the EG, EGD, and HB ($\tau = 0.5$) schemes. An interesting result of the simulations is that the number of moved nodes that are isolated drops as the node density increases with the EG and HB ($\tau = 0.5$) schemes while the EGD scheme continues to perform poorly. This is because the EGD scheme is optimized to exploit deployment and lacks the ability to be robust under changes to the initial deployment.

Summary: By picking appropriate values of τ and the grid size, it is possible to balance the level of local connectivity and the number of moved nodes that are

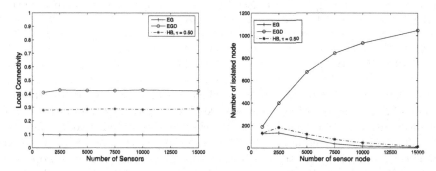

Fig. 7. (a) Local connectivity and (b) number of moved node that are isolated for EG, EGD, and HB (with $\tau = 0.50$) with different size of node density when number of jammers is 50. The jamming radius of each jammer is 40m.

isolated. For example (Figure 3(a) and 4(a)), when there are 50 jammers, the hybrid scheme with τ set to 0.25 has 12.03% lower connectivity than the EGD scheme but has an 85.04% decrease in the number of isolated nodes. Even ignoring the grid size, we can recommend the use of the hybrid scheme with $\tau = 0.25$ for good robustness to jamming and maintaining reasonable local connectivity.

6   Discussions, Limitations, and Ongoing Work

We clarify the limitation of the definition of isolation that we use here which does not guarantee that the network is not partitioned. For instance, two sensor nodes may securely connect to one another as they share common keys, but together, they may not be able to securely connect to any other sensor. Still, it provides a lower bound on the number of nodes that are disconnected from the largest securely connected part of the network. Ongoing work is considering quantifying the partitioning of the network.

Some limitations of this work are as follows. Another measure of connectivity used in [4,5] is the number of hops required to securely reach a direct neighbor. We have not looked at this measure in our work. We also would like to explore performance of our hybrid scheme with different evacuation strategies proposed in literature [6]. Other approaches to overcome jamming (e.g., reducing rate or increasing power) create longer links and the hybrid scheme may be useful there, but the actual tradeoffs are not clear. The assumption that a node that lies in jammed area will be completely affected can be relaxed as sensor nodes that lie at the border of jammed region may be able to retain transmission functionality.

Since a sensor node has limited memory space for storing cryptographic keys, it is desirable to use to the extent possible all of the keys stored in node's memory as link keys to neighbor nodes. A key stored in node's memory that is not useful is wasting memory space. If a link between two node A and B is jammed, it is not necessary for A and B to store a shared key. Information of areas that are more susceptible to jamming could be useful for network operators in predistributing keys to sensor nodes. This is also part of ongoing work.

7   Conclusion

In this paper, we described our study on the performance of key pre-distribution schemes in the presence of jamming attacks. We proposed a solutions for robust key distribution to cope with jamming attacks while maintaining good connectivity even when there is no jamming. We present an analysis and results from our simulations that show the benefits of the proposed scheme. A network operator can use our results to decide an appropriate value of τ that gives a satisfactory level of connectivity and number of isolated nodes under jamming attacks.

Acknowledgments

This work was funded in part by the National Science Foundation Award No. CNS-0721183. The authors would like to thank the anonymous reviewers for their comments and suggestions to improve the paper.

References

1. Blom, R.: An optimal class of symmetric key generation systems. In: Beth, T., Cot, N., Ingemarsson, I. (eds.) EUROCRYPT 1984. LNCS, vol. 209, pp. 335–338. Springer, Heidelberg (1985)
2. Du, W., Deng, J., Han, Y.S., Chen, S., Varshney, P.K.: A key management scheme for wireless sensor networks using deployment knowledge. In: IEEE INFOCOM, vol. 1, pp. 586–597 (2004)
3. Du, W., Deng, J., Han, Y.S., Varshney, P.K.: A pairwise key pre-distribution scheme for wireless sensor networks. In: Proceedings of the 10th ACM conference on Computer and Communications Security CCS 2003 (2003)
4. Du, W., Deng, J., Han, Y.S., Varshney, P.K.: A key predistribution scheme for sensor networks using deployment knowledge. IEEE Transactions on Dependable and Secure Computing 3(1), 62–77 (2006)
5. Eschenauer, L., Gligor, V.D.: A key-management scheme for distributed sensor networks. In: 9th ACM Conference on Computer and Communication Security, pp. 41–47 (November 2002)
6. Ma, K., Zhang, Y., Trappe, W.: Mobile network management and robust spatial retreats via network dynamics. In: 1st International Workshop on Resource Provisioning and Management in Sensor Networks (RPMSN 2005) (November 2005)
7. Noubir, G.: On Connectivity in Ac Hoc Networks under Jamming Using Directional Antennas and Mobility. In: Langendoerfer, P., Liu, M., Matta, I., Tsaoussidis, V. (eds.) WWIC 2004. LNCS, vol. 2957, pp. 186–200. Springer, Heidelberg (2004)
8. Pelechrinis, K., Iliofotou, M.: Denial of service attacks in wireless networks: The case of jammers, http://www.cs.ucr.edu/~kpele/Jamming.pdf

9. Wood, A., Stankovic, J., Son, S.: Jam: A jammed-area mapping service for sensor networks. In: 24th IEEE Real-Time Systems Symposium, pp. 286–297 (2003)
10. Xu, W.: On adjusting power to defend wireless networks from jamming. In: MobiQuitous: Mobile and Ubiquitous Systems: Networking and Services, pp. 1–6 (August 2007)
11. Xu, W., Ma, K., Trappe, W., Zhang, Y.: Jamming sensor networks: Attack and defense strategies. IEEE Network 20(3), 41–47 (2006)
12. Xu, W., et al.: The feasibility of launching and detecting jamming attacks in wireless networks. In: MobiHoc 2005: Proceedings of the 6th ACM international symposium on Mobile ad hoc networking and computing, pp. 46–57. ACM, New York (2005)
13. Xu, W., Wood, T., Trappe, W., Zhang, Y.: Channel surfing and spatial retreats: Defense against wireless dinal of service. In: ACM workshop on wireless security, pp. 80–89 (2004)

Location-Based Mapping Services to Support Collaboration in Spatially Distributed Workgroups

Eike Michael Meyer[1], Daniel Wichmann[1], Henning Büsch[1], and Susanne Boll[2]

[1] OFFIS Institute for Information Technology, Oldenburg, Germany
{emm,wichmann,buesch}@offis.de
[2] University of Oldenburg, Oldenburg, Germany
susanne.boll@uni-oldenburg.de

Abstract. Mobile devices and systems reached almost every part of our daily life. Following the mobile computing trend, also business logics of distributed, cooperative applications started to move into the mobile client applications. With this shift, the cooperation aspect may also exploit the user's location and situation context and capabilities of the mobile device and integrate it into the actual cooperation and collaboration. In this paper, we present an approach for a Collaborative Map that exploits the spatial context of the member of a distributed group as a means to visualize and provide collaboration functionality. Then, a number of location-related cooperation methods become feasible such as getting an overview of the spatial distribution of the team members, identify an ad-hoc meeting place nearby, or chat with a group member who has a certain expertise in his or her profile. With CoMa, we move from standard collaboration tools that marginally consider spatial information towards context-aware mobile collaborative systems that can support a wide range of applications such as emergency response, maintenance work or event organization where human resources have to be coordinated in a spatial context and tasks need to be assigned dynamically depending on capabilities and situation context.

Keywords: mobile collaborative working environments, location-based services, map visualization, spatial distribution.

1 Introduction

Collaborative Working Environments (CWEs) are designed to support the work on collaborative tasks within groups of users. These workgroups may be either co-located or spatially distributed. However, people were used to remain at the same place for work in both cases. Through increasing dynamics in today's working world, the mobility of working people becomes more important every day. This not only includes people working from multiple locations but also potential movement during their activities, which implies a dynamically changing context. Advances in technology and an increasing number of available mobile

E. Bertino and J.B.D. Joshi (Eds.): CollaborateCom 2008, LNICST 10, pp. 732–745, 2009.

devices with sufficient computing power for collaborative working promote this development. Beyond that, more and more mobile devices provide appropriate hardware for spatial positioning. Recent approaches in research consider the increasing mobility of today's workpeople. They focus on collaborative solutions based on mobile network technologies, but they do not yet address the utilization of location-awareness in spatially distributed workgroups. This leads to the question of how to benefit from location-awareness in a CWE. Traditional collaborative tools like file sharing, discussion boards, chat or calendar hardly offer fitting means to make use of a user's location.

The idea presented in this paper is to bring the location aspect into CWEs by integrating maps with location-aware collaborative functionalities for the use on mobile devices. Using a map in a collaborative context enables to visualize the location of a user, the locations of others who participate in the related workgroup as well as points of interest (POIs). Furthermore such a map can link the users' position and POIs to traditional collaborative tools within the CWE to support a location- and context-related interaction. This approach allows to work collaboratively with other people on spatially located tasks. The approach of a location-aware mobile collaboration supported by an interactive map is applicable for a wide range of application scenarios with a spatial context. Potential professional application areas are, e.g., the coordination of workforce in emergency response, disaster management, construction and maintenance works or event organization scenarios where human resources have to be collaboratively coordinated in a spatial context and tasks need to be assigned dynamically within workgroups. The following scenario is presented exemplarily as it shows a potential application case for a CWE that incorporates spatial information:

The organization of public events is always a big challenge for the involved actors and groups. E.g., open-air music festivals of several days' duration take place in terrain that is not familiar to all participating workers. Additionally the masses of visitors make it difficult to keep the overview on everything that happens. During the actual event many different activities have to be performed by different professional groups. For example, members of the organizational staff arrange performing the festival program and take care for the general coordination. Technicians re-arrange the stage set up and fix technical problems. Security forces react in case of trouble and support emergency services. The involved professional groups are coordinated by team leaders in different granularities while the whole event is headed by the festival coordinator. In certain cases tasks are assigned to workers by the coordinator or by team leaders, in other cases self-coordination is applied within the groups. Furthermore, the members of the professional groups interact with each other to solve appearing problems. So the members of all involved professional groups form a number of redundant workgroups. An established way to coordinate the working at such events is by radio. This offers no visual representation of the people and the area as well as no meta-information for the tracking of tasks like, e.g., a task priority. Furthermore, the communication is complicated by noise. The high dynamics of emerging work in the heavy-crowded event area require for spontaneous assignment of tasks to the performing and supporting workers.

A mobile collaborative application with dynamic location- and context-aware assignment of tasks would help to improve the coordination task. The involved people would receive a real-time spatial overview of teams and workers, their current tasks and the work progress as well as additional information like a worker's profession. Coordinators would be able to assign specific work tasks to teams or workers by their availability, location and profile information. This would improve the collaboration between teams and workers among each other and with the coordinators.

The next section presents related work in the field of mobile and dynamic collaboration as well as map-based location-aware systems where people can meet. In Section 3 we present our concept of a Collaborative Map. Section 4 introduces the mobile CWE platform POPEYE upon which the prototype for a Collaborative Map is built. The realization of the Collaborative Map is described in Section 5. Before we conclude this paper Section 6 illustrates ideas for potential future development of the Collaborative Map.

2   Related Work

Currently, both computer supported collaborative work and mobile applications based on location-aware services are active research areas. In the following, we present related projects and approaches.

The aim of the C@R (Collaboration at rural) project [9] is to provide collaboration tools for rural communities to support and catalyze the development of and in rural regions. As result a flexible worker-centric collaborative platform is envisaged. The definition of the platform will happen in cooperation with other CWE communities.

The POPEYE (Peer to Peer Collaborative Working Environments over Mobile Ad-Hoc Networks) project [14] aims to allow collaboration over mobile ad-hoc networks. Within its scope a middleware was developed that is extensible through plug-ins and allows to collaborate without any present network infrastructure.

The main objective of the WORKPAD (An Adaptive Peer-to-Peer Software Infrastructure for Supporting Collaborative Work of Human Operators in Emergency/Disaster Scenarios) project [16] is to develop an innovative software infrastructure for supporting the collaboration of human operators in emergency situations. A major focus of this project lies on the adaption to connection problems and task deviations of team members in these scenarios equipped with mobile handheld devices. In this context Bortenschläger presents in [4] a concept for geo-spatial collaboration on mobile devices based on geo-data provided by external GIS servers. The paper mainly concentrates on connectivity issues between the mobile client devices. Collaborative aspects of this approach and the user interaction are not further elaborated.

New collaboration models will be developed in the CoSpaces (Innovative Collaborative Work Environments for Design and Engineering) project [8] and a distributed software framework will be realized. By means of this framework users in industrial environments will be able to easily create CWEs for collaboration of distributed workers and teams. The focus of the project lies on support for complex processes in order to produce complex products.

The inContext project [12] aims to enable dynamic collaboration of knowledge workers in a number of different projects at the same time. Therefore, a very flexible form of collaboration and the spontaneous emerging of new teams with dynamic interaction have to be supported. New techniques and algorithms are explored in this project to allow for such kind of collaboration.

The project GeoCollaborative Crisis Management [5,6,13] aims at supporting the management of large scale and distributed crises as it is a priority for government agencies. It uses geospatial map applications to display crisis events, affected resources and actions taken to handle these critical situations. While its approach is very domain specific, it does not consider overall collaboration areas.

Location based services represent an emerging class of computer systems nowadays, as the authors of GeoHealth [7] state. Their approach is to take advantage of this evolution by combining geographical location information, provided by mobile devices, with home healthcare services. Their prototype is providing distributed healthcare workers with a spatial view on their co-workers and patients and, if needed, further information about their patients' illnesses and injuries. While their prototype is web based, mobile devices are used in order to update the current position of each user.

The goal of BuddySpace [11] is to combine instant messaging and geo-referenced map presentation in order to solve problems involving collaborative group work practices. Through having the online status of other users and these users themselves displayed on a geographic reference, the actual user of BuddySpace is always aware of the presence or absence of his buddies. Though the online status of the user's buddies is updated in real-time, their location isn't.

Mobile G-Portal [15] is a client application for Personal Digital Assistants (PDAs) to collect, to temporarily store and to transfer data from geography fieldwork. The main focus lies on collaborative collection of data and learning of the fieldwork. The system takes advantage of positioning and maps based on raster data to record and display the location of collected data.

Besides these research approaches, there are commercial navigation and mapping solutions such as Qiro[1] and TomTom[2]. In addition to map-based navigation, these platforms allow their users to see their buddies on the map and allow for limited interaction with them. Mostly, this interaction is restricted to writing short messages. Thus, they do not enable real collaboration in working environments.

Most of the projects and approaches presented above focus on collaboration of stationary users and systems but they do not consider spatial information and mobility. Some first projects already combine collaboration and mobility. However, they are not location-aware in the sense of taking advantage of information about the current position of the user. They are not able to provide

---

[1] http://www.myqiro.de/

[2] http://www.tomtom.com/

location-based services or to react on the contextual changes resulting from workers' movement. One of these few projects that already address both collaboration and mobility is GeoHealth [7]. Its use is restricted to its application domain and it is for this reason not applicable for a broad variety of different scenarios. The devices used in the GeoHealth project are Laptops integrated in cars, while there is no support for mobile handheld devices such as PDAs that are ready to hand at any time.

3   Concept of the Collaborative Map

The goal of this work is to support collaborative workers and groups in dynamic distributed working environments in which the status of the workers, the tasks, and the locations are not static but changing over time. To efficiently collaborate, the current situation and the location have to be considered when working on common objectives, coordinating tasks, or communicating with each other. This can be supported by context-aware and location-based services on digital maps which allow interaction and collaboration while keeping the spatial overview.

We propose the concept of a **Collaborative Map**, in the remainder also called **CoMa**, which is not tailored to any specific domain to be applicable in a wide variety of application areas. The main goal of CoMa is to provide a spatial view on a collaborative workgroup and to offer location-based functions for collaboration within this workgroup. It is also designed to be capable for integration with other collaborative tools within an underlying mobile CWE system. CoMa enables collaboration support in highly mobile and dynamic environments in which persons do not have access to stationary computers or can not carry Tablet PCs or notebooks along. Therefore, CoMa focuses on mobile handheld devices such as PDAs or cell phones.

In the context of CoMa, a *workgroup* is a group of persons collaboratively working together on a shared task or a common topic. The members of such a group can be spatially distributed. The workgroup itself has a profile which describes its tasks or the topics the members work at. Each member of a workgroup has a certain role. One person is the creator of the workgroup and is able to invite others as well as to define its goals and profile information including the assignment of roles to members of the workgroup. Furthermore this person can define the set of tools which will be available for the group and grant additional rights for administration and coordination to other members. A workgroup consists of workers, also called *members*, that can be spatially distributed. Besides a location, each of the members has an own profile with information in different categories, e.g., research areas, topics of interest or skills. The profile data entries of these profiles can be set as private or as public. The public subset of the profile information can be accessed by other workgroup members. *Tasks* that the workers work at currently or in the future do have certain locations and corresponding conditions and parameters. They are specific objects that can have a state such as *unassigned* or *delayed*, a time interval in which they are valid, and further the task describing information. These information can be entered manually or be generated automatically based on the current situation. Besides tasks, specific locations such as meeting points, dangerous places, or POIs are important objects within CoMa. They also do have a location and can be enriched with additional data such as a title or a short description.

The Collaborative Map allows for support of collaboration and coordination within a workgroup. This is achieved by a map-based visualization of a workgroup considering the location and dynamics of mobile working environments. CoMa visualizes all of its objects on a geo-referenced map. In the case of a displayed worker, both the location and status is represented. Members can be presented differently according to their activities such as *on the way to task's location, working at task* or *unassigned*. A task's visualization considers its current state. At a glance coordinators and other members of the workgroup can see whether a task has been assigned or not. Specific locations' representations give the viewer a general idea about what type that location is of. Thus, a meeting point is displayed in another way than a dangerous place is.

CoMa allows to interact with all entities visualized on the map. By exploring the map, users are able to learn these entities' locations and states, and monitor changes of those. Users can communicate with other members of the workgroup by means of a chat. This chat can either be one-to-one or one-to-many. Also, further information about each member can be retrieved as long as the member's profile is publicly available. Tasks can be created, modified or deleted. When a task is created or modified, the task can be described with a title and a description, its initial state can be chosen, and it can be assigned to a member of the workgroup. As a shortcut, tasks can be assigned to workers depending on the situation's context. Either the closest member can be assigned or the nearest member whose profile fits with the task's description. This assignment can either depend on the location or the task's description. The user can also mark specific locations on the map. They offer the same functionality as tasks except they cannot be assigned to members.

Collaboration is supported by these interaction possibilities. Coordinators are supported in decision making through having access to the profiles of the workgroup's members. The profiles enable them to assess who can be assigned to tasks depending on, e.g., availability, proximity, current activity, or skills. Users can arrange meetings, talk about shared tasks, or ask for help by using the one-to-many chat. Contrariwise they are able to use the one-to-one chat in situations where bothering the others is inappropriate or a private matter has to be discussed such as discussing a specific task and resolving unclear issues. The context aware assignment of tasks to the nearest or the most appropriate member supports and simplifies the self-coordination of the workgroup. Members can create tasks and relay the assignment decision to the system. This also allows the coordinator to quickly response on changing situations. Besides tasks, users are able to place meeting points on the map. These meeting points can be either made visible to all other members or to a specific subset of the workgroup. They are thus able to collaboratively plan their further actions such as the next physical meeting.

4   The POPEYE Platform for Collaborative Applications

The work of CoMa is embedded in a larger context. The idea evolved within the POPEYE [14] project. In Section 5.4 this paper will show how CoMa is realized based on the POPEYE platform.

POPEYE is a Specific Targeted Research Project (STREP) in the New Working Environment of the European Commission's 6th Framework Programme which aims to enable dynamic, spontaneous, peer-to-peer collaborative group working environments, over heterogeneous mobile ad hoc networks (MANETs). The result of the project is a middleware called POPEYE [10] that offers collaborative services for frameworks that aim to enable spontaneous collaboration over P2P wireless ad hoc groups. POPEYE integrates a communication platform and context-aware, secure and personalized core services to enable the design and the usability of collaborative applications in mobile environments. The platform offers different kinds of basic services, such as group management, communication within groups of peers as well as between single peers and data sharing services while considering the flexibility and spontaneous character of mobile ad hoc networks. Furthermore, it provides extensibility by its plug-in infrastructure.

In POPEYE users meet in so called Workspaces. The term Workspace (WS) designates a group of users and the data and applications they share. The Workspace corresponds with the workgroup presented in the concept section. Users can search for and join existing WS or create new ones and invite other available users to join for collaboration. Sharing of data between all members of the WS is supported by the Shared Space which is associated to each WS. The applications the users employ for collaboration (e.g. file sharing, group calendar, whiteboard, etc.) can be plugged into the POPEYE environment at runtime. In POPEYE those applications are called plug-ins and their instances each associated to one specific Workspace and having a specific configuration are named (plug-in) Sessions. Based on the characteristics presented above, POPEYE offers suitable conditions to realize the CoMa concept.

5   CoMa Realization

To test the approach, the Collaborative Map has been realized as a POPEYE plug-in. It builds up on the infrastructure and system components provided by the POPEYE platform. In the following, the realization of CoMa is described. The concepts of the map-based visualization as well as the interaction possibilities of the user are presented. In Section 5.3 the implementation of collaboration aspects is illustrated. In the last step a detailed view on the technical aspects of the integration of CoMa with POPEYE is given.

5.1   Map-Based Visualization

The design approach of CoMa was to identify a graphic presentation of the map that is common to most users. Major decisions were taken based on our previous experiences in location-based pedestrian applications [1,2,3]. It had to be decided what type of map would be displayed. One option is to use vector maps. There are several data formats for vector maps that allow storing different information such as plain geographic data or, in addition, topological relationship information. Besides, vector maps allow a fully scalable presentation. As semantically enriched maps are not necessary for the purpose of CoMa and most open and standardized vector data formats such as Geography Markup Language [3] have a comparatively big overhead, it was decided to use raster maps at the cost of continuous zoom but with the benefit of performance increase. The position of users is crucial for a map application whatever it is used for. CoMa gathers the user's current position from a position receiver connected to the mobile device. It is automatically sent to the other Workspace members to enable them to see the position on their device. The position data is currently based on GPS (Global Positioning System) signals. When developing software for mobile devices such as PDAs the screen's resolution and size are both crucial for the user interface design. Because of the small display, the user has to have the possibility to toggle what is shown and what is hidden from the current presentation. Therefore, different visualization layers have to be implemented to present different types of information that can be added to or removed from the view. Besides a map layer, there is a user layer and a POI layer. Here users, tasks and specific locations are displayed by appropriate icons that change according to their state.

5.2   Interaction with CoMa

The Collaborative Map plug-in was realized as application for mobile handheld devices with touch screen interaction. Hence, the users are able to pan the map by dragging it. This is a very popular operating method at common mobile location-based systems, such as TomTom.

Also, users are able to center the map view on them and will thus not lose track of their own position. Also, they are able to zoom in and out of the map according to their personal preferences. These functionalities are accessible by using the buttons on the main interface (see Figure 1(a)). As described in Section 3, users can interact with CoMa by clicking on every position on the screen. This results in a context sensitive popup window that reacts on what was clicked on. As example, Figure 1(b) shows the window that pops up after a click on the map. Here the users can select to either start a chat or to set a new object on that position of the map.

If users choose to set a new object, they firstly can select what type of object they want to use, e.g., a task or a POI. After that, they can enter a title which is visible directly on the map. If users wish to provide further information, they are also allowed to enter a description. As Figure 2(a) shows, the map will be hidden and a new view is presented to the user if the *create POI*-option has been chosen. In this view the title (*Label*) and the description (*Description*) can be entered. Besides this, the users are able to select to make the object visible either

---

[3] http://www.opengeospatial.org/standards/gml

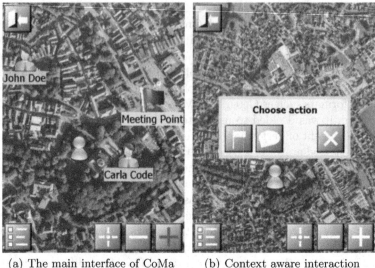

(a) The main interface of CoMa   (b) Context aware interaction

Fig. 1. CoMa's main presentation to the user

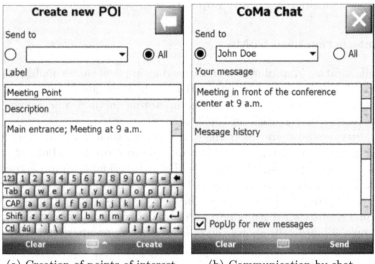

(a) Creation of points of interest   (b) Communication by chat

Fig. 2. Two types of interaction with CoMa

to all other users or just to one specific. If, contrariwise, the *create Task*-option
has been chosen, the creator is able to manually or automatically assign the task
to a member of the Workspace. Also, the task can stay unassigned. When the
user chooses the chat option from the popup window, another view is brought
up that is shown in Figure 2(b). Common unicast chat (one-to-one) as well as
information broadcast by multicast chat (one-to-many) is supported within the

related Workspace. Thus, the users have to select whom to send the message to, right in the same manner as when choosing the visibility of a new object. Besides chatting and creating POIs, users are able to request further information about other members of the Workspace. In order to do this, they have to select the *receive Profile*-option from the popup window that shows up when clicking on another user's icon on the map. All profile information about this user, which is publicly available in that Workspace, will then be presented to the inquirer.

5.3   Implementation of Collaboration

Collaborative work is supported by the afore-mentioned interaction possibilities. The user has got a spatial overview of the workgroup, its tasks and other specific locations based on a reference map. This allows for the assessment of the spatial aspects of the current working environment and the location-based assignment of tasks. Also, the arrangement of meetings is simplified. On one hand, it is eased by being able to discuss all of the meeting's circumstances via chat. This discussion can be done privately between two coordinating persons or publicly between all Workspace members. On the other hand, meeting points can be placed on the map and be provided with a title. At a glance all Workspace members can see where the meeting will take place and what its topic will be. Tasks can be created and assigned to members of the Workspace. Through this, the workgroup is supported in its self-coordination. Members of the workgroup are able to create new tasks if needed or let the system choose whom to assign these tasks based on the current context. Also coordinators of the workgroup are supported in their work. They no longer have to concentrate on finding workers with appropriate skills but can focus on identifying the actual tasks. Users can retrieve profile information about other members of the Workspace. This supports coordinators in decision makings and planing further actions. Members benefit from becoming aware of the profession and skills of other workgroup members and thus know whether they can request help from that person or not. Furthermore, objects displayed by the Collaborative Map can refer to other tools within the surrounding CWE for perfoming specialized collaborative tasks.

5.4   Integration of CoMa with POPEYE

The architecture of the POPEYE platform presented in Figure 3 is designed as a layered architecture with vertical macro-components for security and context. The layers group the components for network abstraction, middleware, application level and user interfaces. The plug-in concept that has been integrated in the POPEYE architecture allows easy extensibility of the platform's functionalities. So, being implemented as a POPEYE plug-in, CoMa is able to make use of the infrastructure provided by the POPEYE platform. To add a new functionality to POPEYE a new plug-in has to extend the basic *Plug-in* class and must provide an appropriate *Plug-in-specific UI* component. In Figure 3 the box named *CoMa* shows where a Collaborative Map plug-in takes place within the POPEYE architecture.

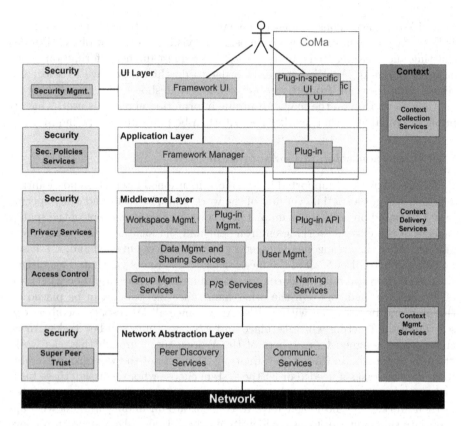

Fig. 3. The location of CoMa within the POPEYE architecture

The *Plug-in API* represents a well defined interface that encapsulates the set of those lower level functions which are to be accessed by (third party) application plug-ins like CoMa. Application plug-ins are not allowed to use all administrative functions of POPEYE components like, e.g., the *Workspace Management*, which controls the lifecycle of Workspaces and Sessions. The *User Management* component provides profile information about participating users of all Workspaces. CoMa consumes these information from the local instance of the User Management component, which acquires the information from other peers over the MANET. Which data is provided by each user is managed in association with the POPEYE Security modules.

As application plug-ins run within Sessions each CoMa instance is associated to one specific Workspace. Consequently, the access rights defined for this Workspace are also applied to CoMa. The communication between two instances of a CoMa plug-in Session on different peers occurs by means of the *Communication Services* component. The main part of this component is the Communication Channels that are associated with Workspaces. Named Communication Channels represent a dedicated way for sending messages for a specific purpose, i.e., they enable Workspace-specific and Session-specific communication between different peers. CoMa employs Communication Channels to broadcast messages to all peers in the Workspace as well as to send messages to single peers. In that way CoMa distributes the profile and position information of users, POI information and chat messages to all members of the Workspace or just to specified ones. Building up on the Communication Services the *Publish/Subscribe Services* component offers a fully-decentralized topic-based subscription mechanism, where durable and non durable topic subscriptions are supported. It is suited for instance for plug-ins' synchronization, i.e., in future work CoMa will be able to forward to other application plug-ins and to interact with them within POPEYE by means of Publish/Subscribe Services.

6   Future Work

For the future development of CoMa a number of extensions of the current prototype is planned. One idea to emphasize the collaborative character of CoMa is to create a whiteboard overlay for the map so that users can use a "paint"-feature to show routes, areas or locations on the map to others in an intuitive way. Another collaborative approach is to allow users an interactive geo-referencing of plain pictures that are shared within a Workspace, e.g., a building plan where users can mark their own location and in that way annotate a valid position. From a certain number of annotated positions CoMa would be able to calculate the necessary data to generate a geo-referenced map from the picture. In a similar approach also users without valid location information may be allowed to appear on the map by placing themselves manually, even if no GPS signal or indoor positioning is available. A further option is to allow POIs to be associated with additional data like, e.g., external sensor or inventory information. Finally, the usability and the interaction have to be evaluated in detail.

7   Conclusion

In this paper, we have shown how the Collaborative Map (CoMa) allows for enhanced interaction and mobile collaboration of spatially distributed workgroups by means of location-based services. CoMa is targeted towards mobile handheld devices which are at hand in most situations, even in very mobile and dynamic environments. The provided tools for collaboration and coordination of common tasks are quickly accessible via an easy-to-learn map-based interface with an interaction designed and adapted to the challenges of mobile devices and environments. The realization is based on top of POPEYE which is a platform for the development of mobile collaborative applications. CoMa extends the POPEYE functionality with location-based services and sets the existing plug-ins for typical CWE tasks in a spatial context for the workgroup. In return, CoMa takes advantage of the functionality already provided by POPEYE. The integration of the CoMa map-based view can thus be used to support mobile collaboration scenarios.

Acknowledgments

This work is supported by the POPEYE project: Peer to Peer Collaborative Working Environments over Mobile Ad-Hoc Networks. POPEYE is part-funded by the EU under the 6th Framework Program, IST priority Contract No. IST-2006-034241. http://www.ist-popeye.org. We would like to acknowledge each member of the POPEYE consortium.

References

1. Ahlers, D., Boll, S., Wichmann, D.: Virtual Signposts for Location-based Storytelling. In: GI-Days 2008, Münster, Germany (2008)
2. Ahlers, D., Pielot, M., Wichmann, D., Boll, S.: GNSS Quality in Pedestrian Applications - A Developer Perspective. In: Kaiser, T., Jobmann, K., Kyamakya, K. (eds.) 5th Workshop on Positioning, Navigation and Communication WPNC 2008, Hannoversche Beiträge zur Nachrichtentechnik, pp. 45–54. Shaker (2008)
3. Baldzer, J., Boll, S., Klante, P., Krosche, J., Meyer, J., Rump, N., Scherp, A., Appelrath, H.-J.: Location-Aware Mobile Multimedia Applications on the Niccimon Platform. In: IMA 2004, Brunswick, Germany (2004)
4. Bortenschläger, M., Leitinger, S., Rieser, H., Steinmann, R.: Towards a P2P-Based GeoCollaboration System for Disaster Management. In: GI-Days 2007, Münster, Germany (2007)
5. Cai, G., Bolelli, L., MacEachren, A.M., Sharma, R., Fuhrmann, S., McNeese, M.: Geocollaborative crisis management: Using maps to mediate eocmobile team collaboration. In: Proceedings of the 2004 annual national conference on Digital government research, Seattle, WA, USA, pp. 1–2. Digital Government Society of North America (2004)
6. Cai, G., MacEachren, A.M., Sharma, R., Brewer, I., Fuhrmann, S., McNeese, M.: Enabling geocollaborative crisis management through advanced geoinformation technologies. In: Proceedings of the 2005 national conference on Digital government research, Atlanta, Georgia, USA, pp. 227–228. Digital Government Society of North America (2005)
7. Christensen, C.M., Kjeldskov, J., Rasmussen, K.K.: GeoHealth: a location-based service for nomadic home healthcare workers. In: OZCHI 2007: Proceedings of the 2007 conference of the computer-human interaction special interest group (CHISIG) of Australia on Computer-human interaction: design: activities, artifacts and environments, pp. 273–281. ACM, New York (2007)
8. CoSpaces.: Innovative Collaborative Work Environments for Design and Engineering. Integrated Project, IST programme of the European Commission's 6th Framework, http://www.cospaces.org
9. C@R.: Collaboration at Rural. Integrated Project, IST programme of the European Commission's 6th Framework, http://www.c-rural.eu
10. Duong, H.D.H., Melchiorre, C., Meyer, E.M., Nieto, I., Paris, G., Pelliccione, P., Tastet-Cherel, F.: A Software Architecture for Reliable Collaborative Working Environments. In: 3rd International Conference on Collaborative Computing: Networking, Applications and Worksharing (CollaborateCom 2007), November 15 (2007)
11. Eisenstadt, M., Komzak, J., Dzbor, M.: Instant messaging + maps = powerful collaboration tools for distance learning. In: Proceedings of TelEduc 2003, Havana, Cuba, May 19-21 (2003)

12. Truong, H.-L., Dustdar, S., Baggio, D., Dorn, C., Giuliani, G., Gombotz, R., Hong, Y., Kendal, P., Melchiorre, C., Moretzky, S., Peray, S., Polleres, A., Reiff-Marganiec, S., Schall, D., Stringa, S.: InContext: a Pervasive and Collaborative Working Environment for Emerging Team Forms. IEEE Saint (2008)
13. MacEachren, A.M., Cai, G., McNeese, M., Sharma, R., Fuhrmann, S.: Geocollaborative crisis management: Designing technologies to meet real-world needs. In: Proceedings of the 2006 international conference on Digital government research, San Diego, California, USA, pp. 71–72. ACM, New York (2006)
14. POPEYE.: Peer to Peer Collaborative Working Environments over Mobile Ad-Hoc Networks. Specific Targeted Research Project (STREP) in the New Working Environment, European Commission's 6th Framework, http://www.ist-popeye.eu
15. Theng, Y.-L., Tan, K.-L., Lim, E.-P., Zhang, J., Goh, D.H.-L., Chatterjea, K., Chang, C.H., Sun, A., Yu, H., Dang, N.H., Li, Y., Vo, M.C.: Mobile G-Portal supporting collaborative sharing and learning in geography fieldwork: an empirical study. In: JCDL 2007: Proceedings of the 7th ACM/IEEE-CS joint conference on Digital libraries, pp. 462–471. ACM, New York (2007)
16. WORKPAD: An Adaptive Peer-to-Peer Software Infrastructure for Supporting Collaborative Work of Human Operators in Emergency/Disaster Scenarios. Specific Targeted Research Project (STREP), European Commission's 6th Framework, http://www.workpad-project.eu

Serial vs. Concurrent Scheduling of Transmission and Processing Tasks in Collaborative Systems

Sasa Junuzovic and Prasun Dewan

Department of Computer Science, University of North Carolina at Chapel Hill
Chapel Hill, NC 27599, USA
{sasa,dewan}@cs.unc.edu

Abstract. In collaboration architectures, a computer must perform both processing and transmission tasks. Intuitively, it seems that these independent tasks should be executed in concurrent threads. We show that when multiple cores are not available to schedule these tasks, a sequential scheme in which the processing (transmission) task is done first tends to optimize feedback (feedthrough) times for most users. The concurrent policy gives feedback and feedthrough times that are in between the ones supported by the sequential policies. However, in comparison to the process-first policy, it can noticeably degrade feedback times, and in comparison to the transmit-first policy, it can noticeably degrade feedthrough times without noticeably improving feedback times. We present definitions, examples, and simulations that explain and compare these three scheduling schemes for centralized and replicated collaboration architectures using both unicast and multicast communication.

Keywords: collaboration architecture, scheduling policy, response time, feedback time, feedthrough time, unicast, multicast, simulations.

1 Introduction

An important issue in collaborative systems is the architecture of the implementation, which has an impact on the performance, the level of sharing, and correctness of the system. This area has been studied extensively [3] and has identified several important dimensions. In this paper, we focus on two related questions that have been largely ignored previously – the manner in which the tasks needed to implement collaborative systems are scheduled and the impact of the scheduling policy on local and remote response times. We refer to local response times as *feedback times* and remote response times as *feedthrough times*. Feedback times are also sometimes called simply response times [4].

Two mandatory tasks performed by a collaborative system are processing and transmission of user commands. The nature of these tasks depends on (a) whether computation is centralized or replicated and (b) whether the commands are unicast or multicast. We consider all four cases in the evaluation of policies for scheduling these tasks.

The implementation and evaluation of scheduling schemes depend on how many cores are available for scheduling. For example, if two cores are available for

E. Bertino and J.B.D. Joshi (Eds.): CollaborateCom 2008, LNICST 10, pp. 746–759, 2009.

scheduling, it is possible to carry out processing and transmission tasks in parallel. Thus, additional cores have the potential to improve feedback and feedthrough times. However, we assume only one core is available to execute the tasks of a collaborative application, leaving multi-core scheduling as future work.

The rest of this paper is organized as follows. We first describe more precisely the processing and transmission tasks. We then motivate, illustrate, and qualitatively compare the sequential and concurrent policies for scheduling these tasks. Following this, we present simulation results that quantitatively compare these policies in realistic collaborations and give brief conclusions and directions for future work.

2 Processing and Transmission Tasks

The processing and transmission tasks in collaborative systems depend on the underlying architecture. Two popular collaboration architectures are the centralized and replicated architectures. In both cases, it is assumed that an application is logically separated into a program and user-interface components. The program component manages the object that is shared by all of the users. The user-interface component allows interaction with the shared object by manipulating state that is not shared by the users. A separate user-interface component runs on each user's machine.

In the centralized architecture, all of the user-interface components are mapped to a single program component. The computer running the program component is called a *master* and the other computers are called *slaves*. A master computer receives input commands from and sends output commands to all of its slaves. In addition, a master is responsible for processing all input commands and their outputs. A slave, on the other hand, is responsible for transmitting input commands from its user to the master and processing the output of all input commands. A centralized architecture with six users in which $user_1$ is the master is shown in Fig. 1 (top). The figure shows the transmission of an output for an input entered by $user_1$. In the replicated architecture, each user-interface component is mapped to the program component running on the local computer. Thus, all of the computers are masters. To keep the program components on different masters in sync, whenever a master receives an input command from the local user, it transmits the command to all of the other computers. A replicated architecture with six users is shown in Fig. 2 (top). The figure shows the transmission by $user_1$'s computer to all of the other computers after $user_1$ enters an input command.

One issue with the traditional architectures is that if inputs or outputs are large and the number of users is high, then the cost of transmitting an input or output to many users is also high. As a result, master computers can become performance bottlenecks. It is possible to overcome this problem by using the bi-architecture model [4], in which a collaborative system is separated into two sub-architectures. As in the traditional architecture case, the user-interface components are still mapped to program components; however, the mapping in this case is not bi-directional. In particular, a slave computer sends input commands to the master computer to which it is mapped, but the master computer does not have to directly send input and output commands to all of the other masters and its slaves, respectively. Instead, multicast is used allowing more than just the master to transmit the commands.

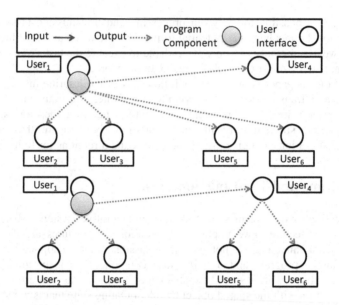

Fig. 1. (top) Traditional centralized architecture and (bottom) the bi-architecture model with a centralized architecture in which multicast is used for communication

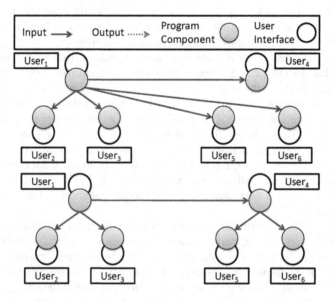

Fig. 2. (top) Traditional replicated architecture and (bottom) the bi-architecture model with a replicated architecture in which multicast is used for communication

The idea of multicast requires, for each source of messages, the construction of a multicast overlay that defines the paths a message takes to reach the destinations. The bi-architecture model makes several assumptions regarding multicast. First, because

IP-multicast is not widely deployed, the model assumes an application-layer multicast in which end-hosts form the overlay. Second, the model assumes that only the users' computers can be used in the overlay. This is consistent with the notion of peer-to-peer sharing systems.

With multicast, every computer may perform some part of the transmission task. For example, if multicast is used in the centralized architecture, then a slave computer, in addition to processing any outputs that it receives, may also need to forward the outputs to other slaves as shown in Fig. 1 (bottom). Fig. 1 (bottom) shows the transmission after $user_1$'s computer, which is the master, computes the output for a command entered by $user_1$. The master transmits the output only to computers belonging to $user_2$, $user_3$, and $user_4$. $User_4$'s computer, which is a slave, then forwards the output to the computers belonging to $user_5$ and $user_6$. Similarly, if multicast is used in the replicated architecture, a master computer that receives an input command from another master may, in addition to processing the command, have to forward it to other masters as shown in Fig. 2 (bottom). Fig. 2 (bottom) shows the transmission of an input command entered by $user_1$. $User_1$'s computer transmits the command only to computers belonging to $user_2$, $user_3$, and $user_4$. $User_4$'s computer forwards the command entered by $user_1$ to computers belonging to $user_5$ and $user_6$. When unicast is used for communication among the computers, the bi-architecture model reduces to the traditional model.

3 Scheduling of Tasks

While the bi-architecture model specifies the tasks that the users' computers will carry out, it leaves as an implementation issue the scheduling of these tasks on each computer. In this section, we motivate, illustrate, and qualitatively analyze three useful scheduling policies.

3.1 Running Example

To illustrate and compare the policies we consider in this paper, we will use the replicated-multicast architecture shown in Fig. 2 (bottom) with the following additional properties: (a) $user_1$'s computer transmits commands first to $user_4$, then to $user_2$, and finally to $user_3$, while $user_4$'s computer forwards the commands first to $user_5$ and then to $user_6$; (b) $user_1$ enters all of the commands; (c) the users all have the same computers; (d) the network latency between any two computers is D; (e) the time the computers require to process an input and output command is 3T and T, respectively; and (f) the time the computers require to transmit an input command to a single destination is T. The relationships between the various times were carefully selected to allow this theoretical example to be used to easily compare all of the policies. In our simulations, we use realistic values for all of these parameters, which do not assume, for instance, that the network latencies among the users are the same.

For all of the scheduling policies we consider, we illustrate $user_1$'s feedback time and $user_6$'s feedthrough time. The reason we consider $user_6$ instead of other users is because $user_6$ is the "farther" from the source than any other user. As Fig. 2 (bottom) shows, the path from $user_1$ to $user_6$ is longer than the path from $user_1$ to any other user, except $user_5$. The paths from $user_1$ to $user_5$ and $user_6$ both go through $user_4$. Since $user_4$ transmits first to $user_5$ and then to $user_6$, we consider $user_6$ to be farther away than $user_5$ is from $user_1$. Once the calculation of $user_6$'s feedthrough time is understood, the feedthrough times of other users are easy to derive. Therefore, these feedthrough times are presented without derivation in Table 1.

3.2 Process-first and Transmit-First Scheduling Policies

One way of scheduling the processing and transmission tasks it to execute them sequentially. There are two sequential policies possible in which either the processing or the transmission task is performed first.

The process-first policy provides better feedback times than the transmit-first policy because, unlike the transmit-first policy, it does not delay the processing of a command until the transmission task completes. Comparing the feedthrough times of the two policies is more complicated. Transmitting first from a source seems to improve the feedthrough times of the destinations. However, as each destination may also be a source, delaying the processing of the received command can increase the feedthrough time seen by the local user.

To understand the influence of these factors on the relative feedthrough performance of the two policies, consider the feedthrough time of $user_6$ in our running example. In all policies, this time consists of four components: (1) the total network delay the command experiences, (2) the time taken by $user_6$'s computer to process the command, (3) $user_1$'s delay, and (4) $user_4$'s delay, where $user_1$'s ($user_4$'s) delay is equal to the time that elapses from the moment $user_1$'s ($user_4$'s) computer receives a message to the moment it transmits it to $user_4$'s ($user_6$'s) computer. The first two components have the same values in all policies. A command always traverses the network twice, which requires 2D time. Since $user_6$'s computer does not transmit commands to other computers, once it receives the command, it always processes the command and the corresponding output in 4T time. The values of the other two components are policy-specific.

The calculation of the policy-specific components when process-first and transmit-first scheduling are used is shown in Fig. 3 (top) and Fig. 3 (bottom), respectively. As Fig. 3 (top) shows, with the process-first policy, $user_1$'s delay is equal to the time $user_1$'s computer requires to process the input command and the corresponding output, 4T, plus the time it takes to transmit the input to a single destination, T. Thus, $user_1$'s delay is equal to 5T. As Fig. 3 (top) also shows $user_4$'s delay is equal to the time $user_4$'s computer requires to process the input command and the corresponding output, 4T, plus the time it takes to transmit the input to two destinations, 2T. Thus, $user_4$'s delay is equal to 6T. Hence, $user_6$'s feedthrough time with the process-first policy is 4T+2D+5T+6T=15T+2D. On the other hand, as Fig. 3 (bottom) shows, when transmit-first scheduling is used, $user_1$'s delay is equal to the time $user_1$'s computer requires to transmit the input command to a single destination, T, while $user_4$'s delay is equal to the time $user_4$'s computer requires to transmit the command to two destinations, 2T. Hence, $user_6$'s feedthrough time is 4T+2D+T+2T=7T+2D. The feedthrough times for the remaining users are given in Table 1.

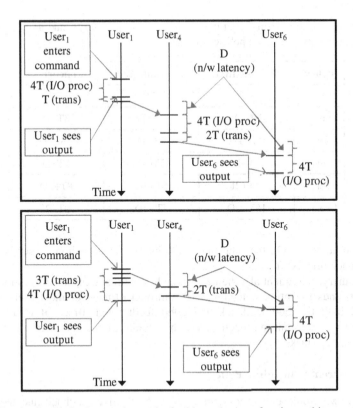

Fig. 3. User₁'s feedback time and user₆'s feedthrough time for the architecture in Fig. 2 (bottom) when the (top) process-first and (bottom) transmit-first scheduling is used

Table 1 shows that *in this theoretical example* the transmit-first policy gives better feedthrough times than the process-first policy for all of the users. However, this is not true in all cases. For instance, suppose there were five more users in our example, and the multicast overlay was organized so that these five users all receive inputs from user₄'s computer. In this case, user₄'s computer would still receive the command 4T earlier with the transmit-first than with the process-first policy but would have to transmit for 5T longer before processing it. Hence, the benefit from receiving input early can, theoretically, get outweighed by the transmission cost; in this example, user₄'s feedthrough time would increase by T. Such an increase can only happen when multicast is used. However, in our experience with a state of the art multicast scheme, such an increase does not really occur because usually a small number of computers actually forward commands. Moreover, an even smaller number of computers forward commands to many destinations. As a result, the number of destinations a computer forwards to is usually small enough that the total transmission cost for a node is smaller than the benefit the node receives when the transmit-first policy is used. Hence, we expect that the transmit-first policy will provide better feedthrough times than the process-first policy to most, if not all, of the users.

Our running example also shows that the process-first policy gives better feedback times than the transmit-first policy. As Fig. 3 (top) shows, user₁'s process-first

Table 1. User$_1$'s feedback times and user$_2$'s, user$_3$'s, user$_4$'s, user$_5$'s, and user$_6$'s feedthrough times under the three scheduling policies

Policy	Process-first	Transmit-first	Concurrent
User$_1$	4T	7T	7T
User$_2$	10T+D	6T+D	8T+D
User$_3$	11T+D	7T+D	10T+D
User$_4$	9T+D	7T+D	8T+D
User$_5$	14T+2D	6T+2D	8T+2D
User$_6$	15T+2D	7T+2D	10T+2D

feedback time is 4T. On the other hand, as Fig. 3 (bottom) shows, user$_1$'s transmit-first feedback time is 7T.

In summary, a sequential scheme in which the processing (transmission) task is done first tends to optimize feedback (feedthrough) times for most users If we are interested in both good feedback and good feedthrough times, it is attractive to investigate a concurrent approach in which separate threads perform the processing and transmission tasks.

3.3 Concurrent Scheduling Policy

Intuitively, we would expect a concurrent policy to give feedback and feedthrough times in between those supported by the two sequential policies. In fact, in this policy, it is possible to get feedback times that are as bad as those of the transmit-first policy and feedthrough times that are as bad as those of the process-first policy.

Let us analyze what happens on user$_1$'s computer in our running example when the computer receives an input command. As described above, in this case, the processing and transmission task require 4T and 3T time, respectively. We assume that neither task blocks because it is difficult to predict their behavior, otherwise. The non-blocking task assumption is consistent with assumptions made in real-time systems when tight performance bounds are required. While results exist for blocking tasks, the upper-bounds for the performance in this case are extremely loose. Moreover, the non-blocking task assumption is realistic as a well-designed application can help ensure that the processing and transmission tasks do not block by using separate threads and asynchronous communication, respectively. In addition, we consider context switch times negligible as we have found that they are no more than a few microseconds on modern operating systems running Pentium 4 desktops, which is several orders of magnitude lower than processing and transmission costs we have observed in real collaboration scenarios. Finally, for illustration purposes, we assume here that the length of the scheduling quantum is much less than the processing and transmission costs. In our simulations, we in fact, use a much more realistic value of 10ms for the quantum size. Given these assumptions and our earlier assumption that a single core is available for scheduling, the execution of these tasks for the concurrent and the two sequential policies is illustrated in Fig. 4. As Fig. 4 shows, with the

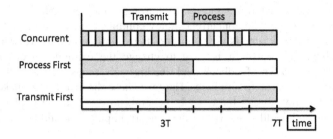

Fig. 4. Process and transmission task completion times for user₁'s computer for the concurrent, process-first, and transmit-first scheduling policies

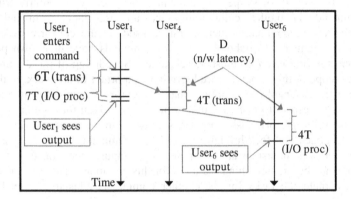

Fig. 5. User₁'s feedback time and user₅'s feedthrough time for the multicast communication architecture in Fig. 2 (bottom) when the concurrent scheduling is used

concurrent policy, the shorter transmission task completes in 6T time, which is twice the time it takes to complete when the task runs standalone. As Fig. 4 also shows, with the concurrent policy, the longer processing task completes in 7T time, which is equal to the total time required to process the processing and transmission tasks sequentially. We can generalize the figure as follows: when the processing and transmission tasks are executed concurrently, (a) the shorter of the two will complete in exactly twice the time it would complete were it running standalone, and (b) the longer of the two will complete in exactly the time required to run the two tasks sequentially. In this example, the processing task is the longer one, so user₁'s feedback time is $3T+4T=7T$.

As mentioned earlier, user₆'s feedthrough time equals $4T+2D$ + user₁'s and user₄'s delays. As Fig. 5 shows, user₁'s delay with the concurrent policy is equal to the time user₁'s computer requires to transmit the command to a single destination while concurrently processing the command. Since transmitting to a single destination takes T time and the processing task takes 4T time, the transmission to a single destination completes in 2T time since it is the shorter of the two tasks. Similarly, as Fig. 5 also shows, user₄'s delay is going to be 4T. Thus, user₆'s feedthrough time equals $4T+2D+2T+4T=10T+2D$. The feedthrough times of all users are shown in Table 1.

Based on the feedback times and the feedthrough times in Table 1, it seems that *in this theoretical example* the concurrent policy combines the worst of both sequential policies as its feedback time is no better and its feedthrough times are worse than the transmit policy. Of course, it is easy to change the example to ensure that the concurrent policy offers feedback and feedthrough times between those of the transmit-first and process-first policies. Here we chose the example to make the subtle point that this is not always the case. In general, however, if the goal is to equally favor feedback and feedthrough times, the concurrent policy should be used.

3.4 Simultaneous Commands

One issue we have not addressed so far is the scheduling of multiple simultaneous commands. In general, two types of commands can occur concurrently with $user_1$'s input command: 1) another collaboration-unaware user input command, or 2) a collaboration-aware command, such as one caused by the concurrency control or awareness mechanisms. Collaboration-aware commands have their own processing and/or transmission tasks that must be scheduled. Scheduling of these commands is beyond the scope of this paper and we leave it as important future work. In this paper, we make the reasonable assumption that tasks for a command are completed atomically with respect to tasks for other commands. Given this assumption, once a computer begins to perform tasks for $user_1$'s input command, other commands cannot affect the feedback and feedthrough times of the command. However, it is possible that when $user_1$'s input arrives at a computer, the computer performs tasks for several other commands before beginning the tasks for this command. The time the computer takes to complete the tasks for these other commands adds to the feedback and feedthrough times of $user_1$'s command.

Collaboration-aware commands simply add some time to the feedback and feedthrough times that is independent of the user command scheduling policies. Hence, the differences in feedback and feedthrough times illustrated above stand. User input commands also add some time to the feedback and feedthrough times of $user_1$'s command that is independent of our choice of scheduling policy. The reason is that regardless of the scheduling policy, the time that elapses from the moment a computer begins performing the first task for a user command to the moment it completes the final task for the command is the same. Consider $user_1$'s computer in our running example. The time it takes to process $user_1$'s input command and output and transmit the input command is 7T in all cases. Thus, the illustrated feedback and feedthrough time differences in our running example for the three scheduling policies again stand.

4 Simulations

Our work so far has made several conclusions about the relative performance of the three scheduling policies based on theoretical arguments. While these results are a contribution on their own, it is important to see if the differences shown through a theoretical evaluation can be significant when the policies are evaluated in practical scenarios.

We determined the performance of the scheduling policies in practical scenarios using bookkeeping or accounting mathematical equations that simulate a collaborative system. Such simulation approaches are popular in other fields such as networking and real-time systems. Because of lack of space, we omit the equation details.

4.1 Parameter Values

To perform meaningful simulations we need realistic values for the parameters that influence the performance of the three scheduling policies: (a) input and output processing and transmission costs; (b) the number of users; (c) the types of the users' computers; and (d) the network latencies.

To obtain realistic input and output processing and transmission costs, we identified user-commands in logs of actual application use and measured the costs of these commands. We logged three different applications, but as we have space to talk about the results with only one these applications, we focus only on it.

We analyzed recordings of two PowerPoint presentations. These recordings contain actual data and users' actions – PowerPoint commands and slides. We assumed that the data and users' actions in the logs are independent of the number of collaborators, the processing powers of the collaborators' computers, and network latencies. PowerPoint turned out to be a good choice of an application for which to analyze actual logs for two reasons: 1) the parameter values we measured in the associated logs were fairly wide spread, and 2) it is frequently used in presentations.

To obtain the processing and transmission time parameter values, we created a collaborative session with several computers. We designated one of the computers as the source of the commands, and then we replayed the PowerPoint logs using a Java-based infrastructure that has facilities for logging and replaying commands.

We measured the processing and transmission times on the source computer. We used a P3 866MHz desktop and a P4 2.4 GHz desktop as sources, both of which were running Windows XP. The P3 desktop is used to simulate next generation mobile devices. We recorded the average processing and transmission times of each machine for PowerPoint. We removed any "outlier" entries from the average calculation, caused for instance, by operating system process scheduling issues. To reduce these issues, we removed as many active processes on each system as possible. Ideally, while we replay the recordings, we should run a set of applications users typically execute on their systems. However, the typical working set of applications is not publicly available so we would have to guess which applications to run. For fear of incorrectly affecting transmission times by running random applications, we used a working set of size zero, a common assumption in experiments comparing alternatives.

We had to assign the values of the number of collaborators and the processing powers of their machines. In the collaboration recordings that we analyzed, the number of users ranged from thirty to sixty. Unfortunately, this is not a wide enough range of values; in particular, the maximum value of the parameter needs to be much bigger to be representative of large collaborations, such as a company-wide PowerPoint presentation. Therefore, we chose synthetic but not unrealistic values for the number of observers. As observers do not input commands, they do not influence the logs. Moreover, the talks we observed had tight time constraints which did not allow questions. Thus, they were independent of the number of observers. We randomly assigned the type of computer of each observer to be a P3 or P4 desktop.

Based on pings done on two different LANs, we use 0ms to simulate half the round-trip time between two computers on the same LAN. Similarly, based on pings done between computers on different LANs, we use 15ms and 177ms to simulate half the round-trip time between a Northwest and a Southwest U.S. LAN and an East-coast U.S. and an Indian LAN, respectively. These values defined the minimum and maximum network latencies in our evaluation.

4.2 Simulations

Using these parameter values, we simulated the feedback and feedthrough times for all of the policies for both centralized and replicated architectures when unicast and multicast are used for communication. Of all of the existing multicast algorithms, we know of only one that that considers the time the users' computers require for transmitting on the network in the building of such a tree, which is the HMDM algorithm [2]. In our experience, the cost of transmitting commands can be high in data-centric applications such as PowerPoint. Thus, we implemented HMDM in Java and used it to create our multicast overlays.

4.3 Process-First vs. Transmit-First

Our theoretical results predict that the process-first policy gives better feedback times but worse feedthrough times than the transmit-first policy, and vice versa. To check if this difference can be significant in practical circumstances, we consider a scenario in which a PowerPoint presentation is being given to 200 audience members around the world. Based on the ping times we reported earlier, we assume that the latencies between all of the users are between 15ms and 177ms. The lecturer is using a next generation PDA device. Moreover, the users are organized in a centralized architecture in which the lecturer's computer is the master. Finally, we assume that multicast is used for communication.

Previous work has shown [6] that users can notice feedback times greater than 50ms. We consider a 50ms increment in feedback times significant. Moreover, since we know of no feedthrough thresholds, we assume that 50ms increments in feedthrough times are also significant. In this scenario, the process-first policy feedback time, 650.4ms, is significantly better than the transmit-first feedback time is, 761.2ms. The difference between the process-first and transmit-first feedthrough times are shown in Fig. 6. As Fig. 6 shows, the process-first feedthrough times results are significantly worse, by as much as 2804ms. Hence, there are cases when the process-first policy can provide significantly better feedback times and significantly worse feedthrough times than the transmit-first policy. The results of another simulation, which we do not have room to present, show that the process-first feedthrough times can be significantly better than the transmit-first feedthrough times. However, for a large majority of the users (99%), the feedthrough times were actually either noticeably lower or not noticeably higher with the transmit-first than the process-first policy.

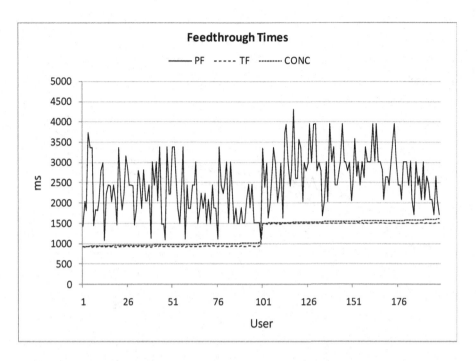

Fig. 6. Feedthrough times for the process-first (PF), transmit-first (PF), and concurrent (CC) scheduling policies

4.4 Concurrent vs. Sequential

Our second theoretical result was somewhat counter-intuitive. It showed the concurrent policy can be as bad as the transmit-first policy in terms of feedback times and worse than the transmit-first policy in terms of feedthrough times. To find out if the feedthrough time differences can be significant, we consider the same scenario as in the previous result.

The scenario simulation results confirm that the concurrent policy feedback times can be the same as those of the transmit-first policy (761.2ms for both). Moreover, the simulation feedthrough times are shown in Fig. 6 and they show that the concurrent policy feedthrough times can be significantly worse, by as much as 110.0ms, than the transmit-first feedthrough times. Even worse is the fact that more than one quarter of the users experience these significant feedthrough time degradations.

Another theoretical result regarding the concurrent scheduling policy is that it is useful if both feedback and feedthrough times are equally favored because with the concurrent policy, these times can be in between those provided by the process-first and transmit-first scheduling policies. It turns out that these differences can be significant in the following practical scenario.

Consider again the PowerPoint scenario described earlier with three differences: (a) there are only 100 users watching the presentation, (b) they are all in the same LAN as the lecturer and thus experience only LAN network latencies (i.e. 0ms), and (c) unicast is used for communication.

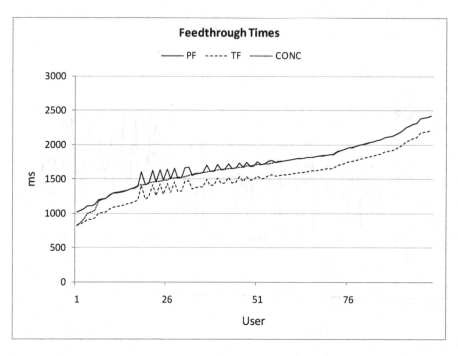

Fig. 7. Feedthrough times for the process-first (PF), transmit-first (PF), and concurrent (CC) scheduling policies

In this case, the concurrent policy feedback time, 860.4ms, is significantly worse than the process-first policy feedback time, 650.4ms, but is significantly better than the transmit-first feedback time, 1502.4ms. Moreover, the concurrent policy feedthrough times are significantly better than those of the process-first policy for some users. In addition, for those same users, the concurrent policy feedthrough times are significantly worse than those of the transmit-first policy, as shown in Fig. 7. As Fig. 7 shows, the feedback time for user 6 is (a) 105.2ms better with the concurrent than with the process-first policy and (b) 100.0ms worse with the concurrent than with the transmit-first policy.

5 Conclusions and Future Work

We show that scheduling of processing and transmission tasks can significantly influence interactivity. As these are independent tasks, intuitively, it seems that they should be executed in concurrent threads scheduled by the operating system. However, we show that, when a single-core is available for processing, this policy is dominated in several realistic collaborations by sequential policies that are aware of the nature of these two tasks. This result also has an implication for multi-core scheduling systems. These systems tend to require an application to decompose its processing into one or more concurrent threads and schedule these threads on as many physical cores/processors as available. Our results show that when the processing and transmission tasks cannot be scheduled simultaneously on multiple cores/processors, it may be better, in many scenarios, to execute them in a single thread using process-first or transmission-first scheduling rather than in multiple threads. Thus the main conclusion of our work is that a generic collaboration infrastructure must support all three scheduling policies and allow them to be dynamically switched based on system and task parameters.

Certain collaborative applications adapt the amount of processing work done to ensure tolerable feedback times. For example, certain game playing applications [1] adapt the level of detail presented based on the scene and processing power of the computer. Moreover, in many applications, several independent tasks can be performed in the processing phase, and in multicast, sends and receives can be performed in different threads [5]. Therefore, it would be useful to consider new scheduling policies that take into account the fact that the processing/communication task can be adapted and broken into independent work units. It would also be useful to study the (potentially application-specific) scheduling policies used in current commercial collaborative systems, which we have not been able to determine so far. Future work is also needed to consider concurrent scheduling on multiple cores, better and more formally characterize scenarios in which various scheduling policies should be used, create an infrastructure that automatically adapts the policy based on the various system and task parameters identified here, and most importantly, study how the feedback/feedthrough tradeoff should be made in different collaborations.

Acknowledgements

This research was funded in part by a Natural Science and Engineering Research Council of Canada scholarship, a Microsoft Research fellowship, and NSF grants ANI 0229998, IIS 0312328, IIS 0712794, and IIS-0810861.

References

1. Brockington, M.: Level-of-detail AI for a large role-playing game. AI Game Programming Wisdom, Charles River Media (2002)
2. Brosh, E., Shavitt, Y.: Approximation and heuristic algorithms for minimum delay application-layer multicast trees. In: INFOCOM (2004)
3. Dewan, P.: Architectures for collaborative applications. Trends in Software Computer Supported Co-operative Work 7 (1998)
4. Junuzovic, S., Dewan, P.: Multicasting in groupware? CollaborateCom (2007)
5. Ostrowski, K., Birman, K.: Implementing High Performance Multicast in a Managed Environment. Technical Report. Cornell University (2007)
6. Shneiderman, B.: Response time and display rate. Designing the User-interface: Strategies for Effective Human-computer Interaction. Addison-Wesley, Reading (2004)

Ontology Support for Managing Top-Down Changes in Composite Services*

Xumin Liu[1] and Athman Bouguettaya[2]

[1] Department of Computer Science, Virginia Tech, USA
xuminl@vt.edu
[2] CSIRO ICT Center, Canberra, ACT, Australia
Athman.Bouguettaya@csiro.au

Abstract. We present a foundational framework to manage changes in composite services. The framework takes as input a change specification and reacts to the change in an automatic and efficient manner. We propose a service ontology that provides systematic support for the change management process. We also propose a set of algorithms that enable us to efficiently query the proposed service ontology. With the ontology support, desired service functionalities can be accurately, efficiently retrieved and composed to react to changes. We use a Service-Oriented Enterprise (SOE) as an application of composite services to motivate and illustrate the proposed solution. We evaluate the performance of the proposed algorithms with a set of experiments.

Keywords: top-down changes, change management, composite service, ontology, service oriented enterprises.

1 Introduction

The emerging service oriented computing and the enabling technologies facilitate efficient functionality outsourcing on the Web. This is enabling a paradigm shift in business structures allowing them to outsource required functionality from third party Web-based providers through service composition [3]. A *composite Web service* is therefore an on-demand and dynamic collaboration between autonomous Web services that collectively provide a value added service. Each autonomous service specializes in a core competency, which reduces cost with increased quality and efficiency for the business entity and its consumers. While there has been a large body of research in the automatic composition of Web services, managing the changes during the lifecycle of composite Web services has so far attracted little attention [3,19,4].

We use a *Service Oriented Enterprise* (SOE) as a typical application of composite services to motivate and illustrate our work. An SOE is a Web-based Virtual Enterprises [11]. It outsources the functionalities from autonomous Web services, whose providers may be geographically distributed and organizationally

* This work was supported by the National Science Foundation under the CNS - Cyber Trust program with contract 0627469.

E. Bertino and J.B.D. Joshi (Eds.): CollaborateCom 2008, LNICST 10, pp. 760–777, 2009.

independent. It is expected to promote entrepreneurship and introduce new business opportunities through dynamic alliances.

Example 1.1. We use an application from the travel domain as a running example throughout this paper. Consider a travel SOE that aims to provide a comprehensive travel package by outsourcing functionalities from different service providers, including Airline services, Hotel services, and Car rental services. Suppose that a new market report shows that Point of Interest (POI) services are very popular recently. A POI service is expected to retrieve the local attractions based on user interests given a geographical location. Using this service, a traveler can very easily get the information, like restaurants, museums, music centers, around the hotel he/she chooses to stay in during the trip. Therefore, the owner of a travel agency SOE, say John, wants to add a new POI service into the travel package to attract more market interests. To react to this change, a POI service needs to be added and composed with other services. Meanwhile, suppose that another market report shows that users put more attention to the service's reputation when they choose a travel package. In this case, John wants to ensure that all the outsourced service providers have a high reputation.   □

Fully realizing SOEs lies in providing support to improve their adaptability to the dynamic environment, i.e., to deal with changes during the life-time of an SOE as rules and not as exceptions [2,11]. For instance, market conditions may change, business regulations may evolve, individual Web services may come and go at will, or new technologies may emerge over time. These all may trigger a change in an SOE with respect to the functionality it provides, the way it works, the partners it is composed of, and the performance it offers. Unlike traditional enterprises, where changes are "exceptions", in SOEs changes are likely the norm. Therefore, a systematic solution for handling changes is a fundamental issue in SOEs.

Changes in SOEs can be classified into two categories: *top-down changes* and *bottom-up changes* [12]. Top-down changes refer to those that are initiated by an SOE owner. These are usually the result of new business requirements, new regulations, or new laws. For example, the owner of a travel agency SOE may want to add a taxi service to the travel package. Bottom-up changes refer to those that are initiated by the outsourced Web service providers. For example, an airline reservation service provider may change the functionality of the service by adding a new operation for checking a flight status, or a traffic service provider may decide to increase the invocation fee of the service. In this paper, we focus on dealing with top-down changes.

Change management in the context of composite services poses a set of research issues. A composite service outsources its functionality from independent service providers. There are no central control mechanisms that can be used to monitor and manage these service providers. Therefore, the challenge of managing changes lies in providing an end-to-end framework to introduce, model, and manage a top-down change in a way that best reacts to the change.

Among the most challenging issues is the automation of the process of change reaction. We expect that changes in an SOE occurs frequently due to the dynamic business environment it interacts with. Thus, it is challenging to manage all changes in a manual way. There are existing frameworks proposed for managing changes in other fields, such as software systems, database systems, and workflow systems [8,14,16]. In these frameworks, automating change reaction mainly relies on predefined schemas or policies, whose availability cannot be guaranteed in an SOE.

Therefore, it is not sufficient to manage changes in an SOE by simply applying the approaches adopted in existing frameworks.

In this paper, we leverage the machine-processable semantics delivered by a Web service ontology to support automatic change management in an SOE. Web service ontologies have been proposed to semantically enrich the description of Web services, such as their functionality, invocation, quality, etc [18,5]. They also capture the semantics of the interactions between different communities of Web services. The semantics enable software agents to automatically locate, access, and compose Web services without human interference. Therefore, we expect that the semantic support will also play a key role in the automatic change management process. We assume that the development, agreement, and management of ontologies can be achieved through the existing ontological supporting tools [9].

We summarize our major contributions as follows.

- First, we propose an integrated change management framework that enables an SOE to systematically react to a top-down change. The framework takes a change specification as input and reacts to the change by modifying the composition of the member services of an SOE.
- Second, we enrich the change management framework with ontology support for automatically reacting to the changes. This has the effect of transforming a change specification into a corresponding service ontology query. By answering the query, the desired functionality related to the change can be efficiently retrieved from the tree-structured service ontology.

The reminder of this paper is organized as follows. In Section 2, we introduce three-layer top-down changes based on an SOE's architecture. In Section 3, we propose an ontology-based framework that manages top-down changes in an SOE. In Section 4, we define a service ontology with a tree-like structure to provide the sufficient semantics for change management. In Section 5, we propose a set of algorithms to efficiently query the service ontology. We report our experimental results in Section 6. We briefly overview some related work in Section 7 and conclude in Section 8.

2   Preliminary

In this section, we briefly introduce a supporting infrastructure of an SOE by identifying its key components. Based on this infrastructure, we then describe a layered top-down changes that might occur to an SOE. Top-down changes are initiated at the top components and propagated to the lower ones.

2.1 A Supporting Infrastructure of an SOE

There are two key components and two supporting components in an SOE infrastructure. The key components include an *SOE schema* and an *SOE instance*. An SOE is associated with an SOE schema, which describes its high-level business logic. An SOE schema consists of a set of abstract services and the relationships among these services. An abstract service specifies one type of functionality provided by Web services. It is not bounded to any concrete service. It is defined in terms of a Web service ontology. An SOE instance is an orchestration of a set of concrete services, which instantiates an SOE schema. It actually delivers the functionality and performance of an SOE. The two supporting components include *ontology providers* and *Web service providers*. The ontology provider manages and maintains a set of ontologies that semantically describe Web services. An SOE outsources ontologies from an ontology provider to build up its schema. The Web service providers offer a set of Web services, which can be outsourced to form SOE instances.

The underpinning of the proposed supporting infrastructure is a standard *Service Oriented Architecture* (SOA) [7]. The service providers use WSDL to describe their services. Web service registries, such as UDDI, can be used as a directory for an SOE to look for Web services. After locating a Web service, SOAP messages are exchanged between an SOE and the service providers for invoking the service. Beyond this, semantic Web service technologies can be used by the ontology providers to define their service ontology, such as OWL-S and WSMO [5,18]. The composition between selected services can be defined using service orchestration language, such as BPEL [10].

2.2 The Change Layers

Changes in an SOE can be categorized into three layers: *business requirement changes*, *SOE schema changes*, and *SOE instance changes*. The uppermost layer reflects the dynamic environment that an SOE is exposed to. An SOE schema gives a high-level abstraction of an SOE's functionality and invocation. An SOE instance consists of a set of concrete Web services, which are composed together to instantiate an SOE's schema. A business requirement change could be led by new technologies, new business strategies, new market requirements, or new regulations and laws. In our running example, the owner of the travel agency SOE wants to add a POI service to the travel package. The business requirement change can be interpreted as the modification of SOE's functionality, invocation, (i.e., an SOE schema change) and the updated performance requirement (i.e., an SOE instance change). That is, the travel agency SOE needs to add a POI functionality. At the same time, the invocation among the member services (i.e., the airline service, the hotel service, and the taxi service) needs to be modified, respectively. An SOE schema change will be propagated to the SOE instance changes, to implement the changes in practice. An SOE instance change can be specified as the modification of the list of the concrete services and the way they cooperate.

3   Ontology-Based Framework for Change Management

In this section, we propose an ontology-based framework to support automatic change management. We first propose a formal model that captures the key features of top-down changes. Based on this model, we then propose our framework (depicted in Figure 1). The framework consists of two major components: a *change manager* and an *ontology manager*. The change manager is used for managing changes in an SOE. It takes a change specification as input and generates a new SOE schema and instance as output. The ontology manager is used for managing ontologies to provide semantic support for the change manager. It also provides an interface to query the semantics.

3.1   Top-Down Change Model

Generally, the process of change reaction is modifying an SOE's functionality and/or performance to fulfill the requirement introduced by the change. Therefore, we model a change by specifying its functional and non-functional (i.e., performance) requirement.

Definition 3.1. *A top-down change C is a binary $\{C_{\mathcal{F}}, C_{\mathcal{P}}\}$, where $C_{\mathcal{F}}$ is the functional requirement enforced by introducing the change (referred to as a* functional change*), and $C_{\mathcal{P}}$ is the performance requirement enforced by introducing the change (referred to as a* non-functional change*).* □

In the above definition, $C_{\mathcal{F}}$ specifies the requirement on the modification of an SOE's functionality enforced by introducing C, such as adding a new functionality and/or removing an existing functionality. In our running example, $C_{\mathcal{F}}$ refers to that an SOE should add a POI service.

To fulfill the requirement defined in $C_{\mathcal{F}}$, the first step is to change the SOE's schema, which defines the SOE's functionality. Therefore, the change analyzer

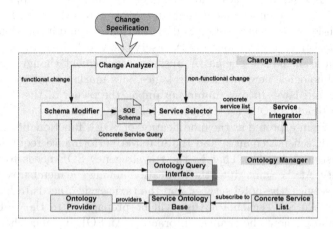

Fig. 1. An Ontology-based Framework For Change Management in SOEs

needs to specify $C_{\mathcal{F}}$ in the same way in defining an SOE's functionality. Since an SOE outsources its functionality from one or more Web services, it is natural to use the combination of a set of abstract services to define an SOE's functionality [12]. Each abstract service defines a type of functionality, such as transportation, lodge, information, etc. Therefore, we have the formal definition of $C_{\mathcal{F}}$ as follows.

Definition 3.2. *A functional change* $C_{\mathcal{F}}$ *is a binary* $\{\mathcal{S}_{\mathcal{A}}, \mathcal{S}_{\mathcal{D}}\}$*, where* $\mathcal{S}_{\mathcal{A}}$ *is the set of abstract services that define the functionality required to be added to an SOE, and* $\mathcal{S}_{\mathcal{D}}$ *is the set of abstract services that define the functionality required to be removed from an SOE.* □

$C_{\mathcal{P}}$ specifies the requirement on the modification of an SOE's performance enforced by introducing C, such as improving the SOE's reliability, reducing the cost, reducing the invocation duration, increasing the service provider's reputation, etc. In our running example, $C_{\mathcal{P}}$ refers to that all the outsourced service providers should have a reputation with the degree of high.

$C_{\mathcal{P}}$ can be defined in terms of a set of quality constraints. These constraints can be enforced on a single outsourced service or the SOE. Examples of such constraints include: *the charge of the* Lodge *service should be less then 80 dollars per night; the reputation of each service provider in the SOE should be high; the overall reliability of invoking the SOE should be high.* We have the formal definition of $C_{\mathcal{P}}$ as follows.

Definition 3.3. *A functionality change* $C_{\mathcal{P}}$ *is a set* $\{\gamma_1,..., \gamma_i, ..., \gamma_n\}$*, where each* γ_i *is a quality constraint and defined as a triple* $\{p_i, c_i, S_i\}$*. p_i is a quality parameter, such as reputation, reliability, cost, etc; c_i is a conditional formula, such as "$< \$80$", "$= high$", etc. S_i is a set of abstract services whose performances are enforced by* γ_i*. Since a quality constraint can be enforced on either single service or an SOE, we use* $\mathcal{E}$ *to represent the SOE. Therefore, if $S_i = \mathcal{E}$, it means that γ_i is enforced on the entire SOE.* □

Example 3.1. In our travel SOE example, the functional change can be specified as $C_{\mathcal{F}}=\{ \{POI\}, \{\}\}$ based on Definition 3.2. Similarly, based on Definition 3.3, the non-functional change can be specified as $C_{\mathcal{P}}=\{\gamma_1\}$, where $\gamma_1=\{$"reputation", "=high", {Airline, Hotel, Car rental, POI} $\}$. □

3.2   Change Manager

The change manager consists of a set of components, including a *change analyzer*, a *schema modifier*, a *service selector*, and a *service integrator*. The change analyzer takes as input a change specification in the format that can be understood and processed by other components. A change specification conveys the information about the requirement on modifying an SOE's functionality and/or performance, which are determined by the SOE's schema and the outsourced Web services respectively. Therefore, the schema modifier may need to update the SOE's schema to fulfill the functional requirement of the change. The service selector may need to locate Web services to fulfill both the functional and performance requirement of the change. Finally, the service integrator may compose the outsourced Web services to generate the new SOE instance.

A **change analyzer** provides a user interface that takes as input a top-down change specification. The information contained in a change specification is used for reacting to the change, including functional requirement ($C_{\mathcal{F}}$) and performance requirement ($C_{\mathcal{P}}$) of a change. $C_{\mathcal{F}}$ will be used as the input of the schema modifier to update the functionality of an SOE. $C_{\mathcal{P}}$ will be used as the input of the service selector to locate the service that delivers the desirable quality.

The **schema modifier** changes an SOE's schema to fulfill the requirement specified in $C_{\mathcal{F}}$. A set of SOE schema templates can be predefined and stored in a domain-specific knowledge base to facilitate the schema updating process. Thus, once there is a requirement on changing an SOE's schema, a schema modifier first searches the knowledge base for a predefined SOE schema that matches the requirement. If there is not such a match, the schema modifier will automatically generate a new semantically correct service schema based on $C_{\mathcal{F}}$ to compose different services [13].

The **service selector** locates Web services to generate an instantiation of the new SOE's schema. It takes as the input of the SOE's new schema and $C_{\mathcal{P}}$ to guarantee that the newly generated SOE's instance meets both the functional and the performance requirement of C. Specifically, a service selector follows two steps: *functionality-based Web service discovery* and *quality-based service selection*. The first step is to find Web services that provide the functionality specified in the new SOE's schema. It requires a functionality-based service registry to achieve this purpose. Since there might be competing providers that offer the similar functionality, the service selector may get multiple services. Thus, it needs to select a service based on the quality requirement. The service selector first removes the services that do not meet $C_{\mathcal{P}}$. It then chooses the service with the best quality. The output of the service selector is a list of Web services (referred to as CS) whose composition is expected to meet both $C_{\mathcal{F}}$ and $C_{\mathcal{P}}$.

The **service integrator** generates a new SOE's instance by composing the services in S. It takes as input the service list CS and the updated SOE's schema. It specifies the execution order and data flow among the services in S that conforms to the cooperation patterns defined by the updated SOE schema. It also coordinates the interaction between different services. Some existing Web service standards such as WS-Coordination, BPEL, etc, can be leveraged to implement the service integrator [15,10].

3.3   The Ontology Manager

The ontology support components include a *service ontology base* and an *ontology query interface*.

The **service ontology base** stores the ontology definitions of Web services within a specific domain. A node in a service ontology defines a type of functionality offered by a service. Examples of the nodes in a travel domain include Airline, Taxi, and Hotel. By the nature of ontology, Web services can be classified into categories based on their functionalities. Therefore, each node in a service ontology is associated with a list of services that provide the defined functionality. This association enables a service selector to perform functionality-based service discovery by first locating the corresponding node in a service ontology, then locating the Web services that subscribe to the node. Beside of functionality, a service ontology also models the relationship between different Web services, which can be used to guide their composition.

The **ontology query interface** supports two types of queries in the ontology base: *functionality query* and *Web service query*. The functionality query is to locate a node in the service ontology and retrieve the related information, such as its relationships with other nodes. It can be performed in the following ways: (1) operation-based query, (2) data-based query, and (3) the combination of (1) and (2). An operation-based query is to traverse the service ontology and retrieve the related information about the nodes which provide the operation. A data-based query is to traverse the ontology and retrieve the related information about the nodes which provides the matched input and output. The Web service query is to find a list of Web services that provide a specific functionality, which is identified by a certain node in a service ontology. The corresponding Web services can be retrieved by checking whether they are subscribing to the node.

Ontology support components are central for automatic change management process. We will elaborate them in the following sections.

4   Web Service Ontology

In this section, we propose a *Web service ontology* that provides semantic support for automatic change management. We first identify a set of key semantics that are described by the service ontology. We then define the structure of the service ontology which will be used as the basis for ontology querying.

4.1   Ontology Definition

The semantics provided by the service ontology aims to help automatically generate a new SOE's schema. Generating the new schema requires two steps. First, it needs to identify the functionality being added to or removed from an SOE. Second, it needs to gracefully compose the newly updated service list. To achieve this, a service ontology needs to capture two types of semantics: *service functionality* (which helps achieve the first step), and *service dependency* (which helps achieve the second step).

The functionality of a service can be modeled from two aspects: the operations that a service provides (i.e., *service operation*) and the data that a service operates on (i.e., *service data*), which also corresponds the two type of functionality query we proposed in Section 3.3.

A service functionality is collectively delivered by a set of operations. The process of accessing a service is actually invoking one or more operations provided by the service. The operations consume the service input and generate the output of the service. It is worthy to note that there may be dependent relationships between different service operations. For example, an Airline service may provide several operations, such as `user_login`, `airline_reservation`, etc. Typically, an user needs to login before (s)he can reserve an air ticket. Therefore, there is a dependency between `user_login` and `airline_reservation`. The dependencies between service operations (referred to as *operation-level dependencies*) need to be strictly enforced when accessing a service.

A service data is also an essential aspect of a service functionality. A service is affected by the outside with a set of input and responses with a set of output [1]. From the external perspective, a service data therefore consists of two data sets: *input ($\mathcal{I}$)* and *output ($\mathcal{O}$)* data.

A service ontology also needs to capture the dependent relationships defined in term of composite services. A Web service is independent and autonomous in nature. A user can directly access a Web service without relying on other services. However, when multiple services are composed together by an SOE, certain dependency constraints can be defined within the generated composite service. For example, the Hotel service usually depends on the Airline service when they are both included in a travel package since the city and the check in-and-out dates of the Hotel service are usually determined by the flight information. As a result, the invocation of the Hotel service should be performed after the Airline service is invoked.

4.2   Ontology Structure

The structure of ontology is hierarchical and extensible by nature. Each node in this structure corresponds to a type of service functionality. Once the ontology structure becomes large with the increment of the available service functionalities, the process of identifying a proper piece of functionality would turn out to be time consuming. It is of importance and beneficial for change management to make this process efficient and accurate. An intuitive way is to leverage the relationship between a node and its children to guide the search of the ontology. We identify two types of *parent-child* relationships in a service ontology: *Is-a* and *Has-Of*, as depicted in Figure 2.

An *Is-a* relationship lies in between a node and its parent node if the node is one type of the parent node. That is, the child node has all the properties (i.e., operations and service data) of its parent node. Beside, it may also has the properties that the parent node does not have. For example, in Figure 2, an Airline service is a child of a Transportation service. It provides the transportation service with a special feature, i.e., through a flight. Therefore, there is an *Is-a* relationship between the Airline service and the Transportation service, shown by a line between them.

A *Has-of* relationship lies in between a node and its parent node if the node is one part of the parent node. That is, the child node has part of the properties of its parent node. For example, in Figure 2, a Flight Quote service is a child of an Airline service. It only provides the service of getting the quote of a flight, but not other airline-related services, such as checking flight status, reserving a flight,

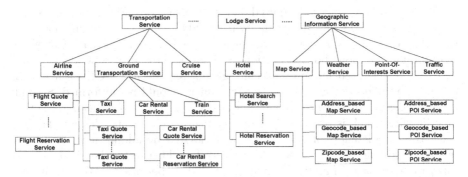

Fig. 2. A Travel Domain Ontology

electronic check in, etc. Therefore, there is a *Has-of* relationship between the Flight Quote service and the Airline service, shown by a dashed line between them.

5   Service Ontology Query Infrastructure

As stated in Section 3, reacting to a change requires to refer back to the hierarchical structure of the corresponding service ontology. As the ontology structure may become very large due to the increase of the services in the domain, there is a need to efficiently query the service ontology to retrieve the required service nodes and locate Web services that subscribe to them at the same time. Considering the tree-like structure of the service ontology we proposed in Section 4, we leverage *path expressions* as an effective tool to declaratively and efficiently query the service ontology [17].

To use path expression in the service query, we add a root node to our ontology to make it have a well-formed tree structure. The root node is an abstract one that does not have any properties. For any service node that does not have a parent node will take the root node as its parent. An *Is-a* relationships lies in between the root node and its child nodes. By using the abstract node, it is guaranteed that the query can be specified and performed from the root of the ontology tree.

5.1   Processing the Service Ontology Queries

We present algorithms to process the queries on the service ontology for the purpose of change management. As discussed in Section 3, there are mainly two types of ontology queries needed to be performed: Web service query and functionality query.

The Web service query is required when a service selector needs to find a list of Web services that provide the specific functionality. In this case, the query process takes a service node as a input and return the list of Web services that subscribe to it. It can be easily performed through the subscription between the ontology base and the Web service list in our proposed framework. Therefore, we will focus on functionality query in this section.

The functionality query is required under two situations. First, when an SOE's owner wants to add a new functionality to the SOE, the corresponding node and the related operation in the service ontology need to be retrieved. Meanwhile, the information about both operation-level and service-level dependencies also needs to be retrieved for automatically generating the new SOE's schema. In this case, an operation-based functionality query should be performed. Second, the composition of the new member services may need to outsource another functionality which is not specified in a change requirement. This will happen when the completeness of the data flow is violated by adding new services or removing existing ones. New services need to be added to fill the blank [12]. In this case, data-based functionality query should be performed. We will present algorithms for these two types of functionality queries as follows.

Operation-based Functionality Query. In an operation-based functionality query, the tree-like structure of an ontology is traversed to find the node that matches the given functionality. The query is specified in terms of a path expression. It returns the required service node and the operation as well as both the service-level and operation-level dependencies if there is any.

As depicted in Algorithm 1., the input is a service ontology tree and a path expression, which is specified in terms of a string. It first extracts the elements from the path expression, such as the path variables($\mathcal{C}$), the service nodes($\mathcal{S}$), and the operation($\mathcal{OP}$). It then takes different steps for different path variables. If the path variable is '/', the algorithm leverages a simple search procedure (line 7-17), which only looks up the immediate children of the current node being processed. On the other hand, if the path variable is '//', the algorithm leverages a heuristic breath first search procedure (line 18-25 and line 32-38), which only searches the child nodes that potentially have the desired operation. For example, if the parent node does not provide the targeted operation, its *Has_of* children will not provide it either. In this case, the algorithms will not explore these children. This will greatly improve the performance of the search process. When the algorithm hits a path variable of '[', it gets the target operation. Then the information of the node and the operation will be retrieved (line 26-29).

Data-based Functionality Query. The data-based functionality query takes as input the desired service data (i.e., input and output). It then traverses the ontology tree to locate the service node that provides the specified service data. Instead of exhaustively going through the entire ontology tree, the algorithm takes advantage of the two types of relationships between a node and its children to effectively narrow down the searching scope.

As shown in Algorithm 2., we use a recursive procedure to query the tree-like structure of a service ontology. The data-based functionality query is performed by matchmaking between two sets of data: service data (including S_I and S_O) of the node in an ontology and the required data (including D_I and D_O) given by the schema modifier. The matching criteria can be defined as: a node is matched if it's output covers the required output, i.e., $S_O \supseteq D_O$, and it's input can be covered by the given input, i.e., $S_I \subseteq D_I$.

Algorithm 1. Operation-based Service Functionality Query

Require: a service ontology query $\mathcal{Q}$ (a path expression); a service ontology tree $T(r)$
Ensure: a service node N_S; N_S's depending service nodes L_S; an operation op; op's depending
operation L_{op}
1: $\mathcal{C} = \mathcal{Q}.\mathcal{C}$; $\mathcal{S} = \mathcal{Q}.\mathcal{S}$; $\mathcal{OP} = \mathcal{Q}.\mathcal{OP}$;
2: $N = r$;
3: **while** $\mathcal{C} \neq \phi$ **do**
4:      $c = \mathcal{C}.pop()$;
5:      **if** $\mathcal{S} \neq \phi$ **then**
6:          $s = \mathcal{S}.pop()$;
7:      **if** $c == '/'$ **then**
8:          find=false,
9:          **for all** $n \in N$ **do**
10:              **if** n.name matches s **then**
11:                  $N = n$; find=true;
12:              **end if**
13:          **end for**
14:          **if** find==false **then**
15:              return ERROR; {Fail to find the specified service}
16:          **end if**
17:      **end if**
18:      **if** $c == '//'$ **then**
19:          **for all** $n \in N$ **do**
20:              N=HBFS($s, OP, T(n)$); {Heuristically breath first search s in subtree $T(n)$}
21:              **if** N=null **then**
22:                  return ERROR; {Fail to find the specified service}
23:              **end if**
24:          **end for**
25:      **end if**
26:      **if** $c = '['$ **then**
27:          $N_S = N$; L_S=N.getDependingService();
28:          $op = N.getOperation(OP)$;
29:          L_{op}=N.getDependingOperation(op);
30:      **end if**
31:      **end if**
32: **end while**
33: **Function** HBFS($s, OP, T(n)$)
34: N=get_Children(n);
35: **if** $OP \notin n.OP$ **then**
36:      N=get_Is_a_Children(n);
37: **end if**
38: **for all** $t \in N$ **do**
39:      **if** t.name matches s **then**
40:          return t; {Find the service}
41:          Else HBFS($t, OP, T(t)$)
42:      **end if**
43: **end for**
44: return NULL;

The query starts at the root node. It first checks whether the current node matches the requirement. If so, it will return the current node as the result (Line 3-9). If not, there will be two cases. First, the current node requires more input than the specified one. In this case, the child nodes that follow an *Is-a* relationship will be pruned since they require no less input than the current node (Line 10-17). Second, the current node does not fully provide the specified output. In this case, the child nodes that follow a *Has-of* relationship will be pruned since they provide no more output than the current node (Line 18-25). By leveraging the two types of relationships to guide the search, the algorithm performs more efficient by only checking the potential nodes that provide the specified service data.

Algorithm 2. Data-based Service Functionality Query

Require: Required input $\mathcal{D}_I$; Required output $\mathcal{D}_O$, a service ontology subtree $\mathcal{T}(r)$
Ensure: a service node $\mathcal{S}$; the related operation list L_{OP}
 1: **Function** CHECK(s,$\mathcal{D}_I$,$\mathcal{D}_O$, $\mathcal{T}(s)$)
 2: **if** $s.Input \subseteq \mathcal{D}_I$ **then**
 3:     **if** $s.Output \supseteq \mathcal{D}_O$ **then**
 4:         $\mathcal{S} = s$; {Find the matched service node}
 5:         L_{OP}=s.get_Operation_By_Output($\mathcal{D}_O$)
 6:         return L_{OP};
 7:     **end if**
 8: **end if**
 9: **if** ($s.Input \subseteq \mathcal{D}_I$)==true **then**
10:     **if** ($s.Output \supseteq \mathcal{D}_O$)= false **then**
11:         C_L=get_Is_a_Children(s);
12:         **for all** $s' \in C_L$ **do**
13:             return CHECK(r, $\mathcal{D}_I$,$\mathcal{D}_O$,$\mathcal{T}(r)$)});
14:         **end for**
15:     **end if**
16: **end if**
17: **if** ($s.Input \subseteq \mathcal{D}_I$)==false **then**
18:     **if** ($s.Output \supseteq \mathcal{D}_O$)= true **then**
19:         C_L=get_Has_of_Children(s);
20:         **for all** $s' \in C_L$ **do**
21:             return CHECK(s', $\mathcal{D}_I$,$\mathcal{D}_O$,$\mathcal{T}(s)$)})
22:         **end for**
23:     **end if**
24: **end if**
25: return ERROR; {Fail to find a matched service node}

5.2   Automatic SOE Schema Modification

In this section, we propose an integrated process to automatically modify an
SOE's schema. The updated schema is guaranteed to fulfill $\mathcal{C}_{\mathcal{F}}$. This process
is essentially enabled by the proposed service ontology and the corresponding
query support.

As depicted in Figure 3, the process starts from generating the new function-
ality list, taking $\mathcal{C}_{\mathcal{F}}$ as its input. The functionality that is expected to add to an
SOE is specified in terms of a path expression.

In the second step, it performs an operation-based service ontology query (i.e.,
algorithm 1.) to retrieve the related service node and the operations for each

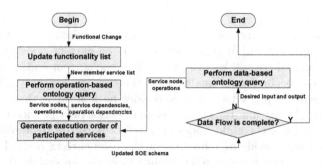

Fig. 3. The Diagram of Modifying an SOE's Schema

path expression. The query result will be used for service selection. Meanwhile, the related service dependencies and operation dependencies are also retrieved. These dependencies will be enforced when composing different services together.

In the third step, the invocation order of the member services and their operations are generated based on their dependencies. Specifically, it first follows the service-level dependencies to generate a service-level order. For example, if invoking a service A depends on the invocation of service B, A will be invoked after the invocation of B. It then follows the operation-level dependencies to generate an operation-level order. As a result, the member services are compose together, which actually defines the new SOE's schema.

In the fourth step, it checks whether the data flow of the updated schema is complete. If not, it performs a data-based query on the service ontology to find the service node which can fill the blank of the data flow (refers to algorithm 2. for details). The returned service nodes are then added to the SOE and composed with other services (i.e., by taking the third step). If the data flow is complete, the process terminates with the output of a new SOE's schema.

6   Experiments

We conducted a set of experiments to assess the performance of the proposed service ontology query algorithms. We run our experiments on a cluster of Sun Enterprise Ultra 10 workstations under Solaris operating system. In order to evaluate the query efficiency, we need to first build a complete service ontology, referred to as $\mathcal{O}$, upon which the query can be applied. We describe the key parameters and illustrate how each of these parameters are used to construct the service ontology. Table 1 shows the definitions of the parameters and their values.

6.1   Constructing the Service Ontology

We define two key parameters to determine the size of $\mathcal{O}$: depth d and total number of service nodes n. We will evaluate the effect of both d and n on the query efficiency. We construct the service ontology level by level. The construction starts from the root, which is a dummy node with an id of 1, representing the entry point of the ontology. The fanout of each node is a randomly generated number with an upper bound of f. For instance, if the fanout is 3, the root node will have three child nodes, whose ids are 11, 12, and 13. The parent-children

Table 1. Parameter Settings

Parameter	Meaning	Values
d	Ontology depth	[6, 12]
n	Total nodes	$[10^3, 10^6]$
f	Node fanout	[5, 10]
k_1	Number of new operations	[1, 5]
k_2	Number of inherited operations	[1, 4]

relationship has two types: $t_1 = is$-a and $t_2 = has$-of. We randomly assign t_1 or t_2 between a child node and its parent. If a child node cn holds an is-a relationship with its parent pn, cn will inherent all the operations from pn. In addition, k_1 randomly generated new operations will also be assigned to cn. If cn holds an has-of relationship with pn, k_2 operations will be randomly selected from the operation set of pn and assigned to cn. We assign no operations for the root node since it is just an entry point of the service ontology.

We leverage a FIFO queue Q to facilitate the process of building the service ontology $\mathcal{O}$. We start by generating the root node and inserting it into Q. The root node is then extracted from Q. All its child nodes are generated based on the rationale we described above. These child nodes are then inserted into Q. The node generation stops when the depth or the maximum number of nodes are reached. After that, we continue to extract the node from the queue until it becomes empty.

6.2   Performance Study

We study the performance of the service ontology query algorithm (referred to as OntoQuery) in this section. We also implemented a Depth First Search (referred to as DFS) on the service ontology for comparison purpose. By performance, we report both the node accesses (referred to as NA), which is independent of hardware settings, and the actual running time on our experiment machines. We run our experiments on a cluster of Sun Enterprise Ultra 10 workstation with 512 Mbytes Ram under Solaris operating system.

Depth of the Service Ontology. We study the effect of the depth of the service ontology in this section. We keep the maximum fanout as 5, i.e., $f = 5$, and vary the depth from 6 to 12. Figure 4 shows how the number of node accesses varies with the depth of the service ontology. OntoQuery accesses much less number of nodes than DFS. The smallest difference is almost two orders of magnitude. Generally, DFS accesses more nodes as the depth of the service ontology increases. This increase is in line with the increase in the size of the service ontology (in terms of the total nodes). It is worth to note that the size of the created service ontology does not necessarily increase with its depth. This is because that we only specify the upper bound of the fanout of each node and the actual fanout of most nodes in a deeper ontology may be smaller than those in a shallower ontology. The number of node accesses does not necessarily increase with the depth, either. This is because OntoQuery only picks either is-a or has-of to proceed. Since these two relationships are randomly generated, they may not necessarily increase with the depth. This also accounts for the larger performance difference when the depth increases. Figure 5 shows the actual CPU time, which demonstrates a very similar trends as the number of node accesses.

Fanout of the Service Nodes. We investigate the effect of the maximum node fanout f in this section. We keep the depth of the ontology as 6, i.e., $d = 6$, and vary the maximum fanout from 6 to 15. Figure 6 and 7 show the number of

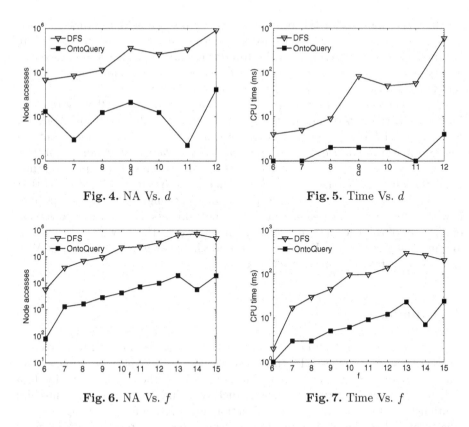

Fig. 4. NA Vs. d **Fig. 5.** Time Vs. d

Fig. 6. NA Vs. f **Fig. 7.** Time Vs. f

node accesses and the CPU time, respectively. The results are fairly consistent with those from Section 6.2. The results also further confirm the efficiency of the proposed algorithm.

7   Related Work

Change management is an active research topic in database management, knowledge engineering, and software evolution. Research efforts are also underway to provide change management in a Web service community and adaptive workflow systems [2,6]. In this section, we will elaborate some representative works and differentiate them with our work.

In [2], it focuses on managing bottom-up changes in service-oriented enterprises. Changes are distinguished between service level and business level: *triggering* changes that occurs at the service level and *reactive* changes that occur at the business level in response to the triggering changes. A set of mapping rules are defined between triggering changes and reactive changes. These rules are used for propagating changes. A petri-net based change model is proposed as a mechanism for automatically reacting changes. Agents are employed to assist in detecting and managing changes to the enterprises. [2] mainly focus on devising handling mechanisms for exceptional changes. An example of such mechanisms is that the system will switch to use an alternative service if a sudden failure occurs to a service. We focus on the top down changes, which are initiated by an SOE's owner in case of the occurrence of new business requirements or new business regulations.

In [6], it focuses on modeling dynamic changes within workflow systems. It introduces a Modeling Language to support Dynamic Evolution within Workflow System (ML-DEWS). A change is modeled as a process class, which contains the information of *roll-out time*, *expiration time*, *change filter*, and *migration process*. The roll-out time indicates when the change begins. The expiration time indicates when the change ends. The change filter specifies the old cases that are allowed to migrate to the new procedure. The migration process specifies how the filtered-in old cases migrate to the new process. In [6], the new version of the workflow schema is predefined. In our work, the new SOE schema is automatically generated. We also propose mechanisms to efficiently select Web services to instantiate the new schema.

8   Conclusion

We presented an ontology-based framework that enables an SOE to efficiently adapt to top-down changes. The proposed service ontology provides sufficient semantic support for automatically updating an SOE's schema when reacting to a change. The tree-like service ontology structure defines two types of parent-child relationships: Is-a and Has-of. The functionalities relevant to a change can be efficiently and accurately identified by following these two types of relationships in the ontology tree. Our experimental results demonstrated the efficiency of the proposed service ontology query algorithms.

References

1. Abiteboul, S., Vianu, V., Fordham, B., Yesha, Y.: Relational transducers for electronic commerce. In: PODS 1998, pp. 179–187. ACM Press, New York (1998)
2. Akram, M.S., Medjahed, B., Bouguettaya, A.: Supporting Dynamic Changes in Web Service Environments. In: First International Conference on Service Oriented Computing, Trento, Italy, pp. 319–334 (December 2003)
3. Baghdadi, Y.: A Web services-based business interactions manager to support electronic commerce applications. In: ICEC 2005: Proceedings of the 7th international conference on Electronic commerce, pp. 435–445. ACM Press, New York (2005)
4. Casati, F., Shan, E., Dayal, U., Shan, M.-C.: Business-Oriented Management of Web Services. ACM Communications (October 2003)
5. Coalition, T.O.S.: Owl-s: Semantic markup for web services. Technical report (July 2004), http://www.daml.org/services/owl-s/1.1B/owl-s/owl-s.html
6. Ellis, C.A., Keddara, K.: A workflow change is a workflow. In: Business Process Management, Models, Techniques, and Empirical Studies, London, UK, pp. 201–217. Springer, Heidelberg (2000)

7. Erl, T.: Service-Oriented Architecture: A Field Guide to Integrating XML and Web Services. Prentice Hall PTR, Upper Saddle River (2004)
8. Francisco-Revilla, L., Frank Shipman III, M.S., Furuta, R., Karadkar, U., Arora, A.: Managing change on the web. In: Joint Conference on Digital Libraries, Roanoke, United States, June 2001, pp. 67–76 (2001)
9. Gomez-Perez, A., Corcho, O., Fernandez-Lopez, M.: Ontological Engineering: with examples from the areas of Knowledge Management, e-Commerce and the Semantic Web. Springer, Heidelberg (2004)
10. Khalaf, R., Nagy, W.A.: Business Process with BPEL4WS: Learning BPEL4WS, Part 6. Technical report, IBM (2003),
    http://www-106.ibm.com/developerworks/webservices/library/ws-bpelcol6/
11. Khoshafian, S.: Service Oriented Enterprises, 1st edn. Auerbach (October 2006)
12. Liu, X., Bouguettaya, A.: Managing top-down changes in service-oriented enterprises. In: ICWS 2007, Salt Lake City, Utah (July 2007)
13. Liu, X., Bouguettaya, A.: Reacting to functional changes in service-oriented enterprises. In: CollaborateCom 2007, White Plains, NY (November 2007)
14. Nickols, F.: Change management 101: A primer. Technical report, Distance Consulting (September 2004), http://home.att.net/~nickols/change.htm
15. Orchard, D., Cabrera, F., Copeland, G., Freund, T., Klein, J., Langworthy, D., Shewchuk, J., Storey, T.: Web Service Coordination (WS-Coordination) (March 2004)
16. van der Aalst, W.M.P., Basten, T.: Inheritance of workflows: an approach to tackling problems related to change. Theoretical Computer Science 270(1–2), 125–203 (2002)
17. W3C. XML Path Language (XPath) (November 1999),
    http://www.w3.org/TR/xpath
18. WSMO Working Group. Web Service Modeling Ontology (WSMO) (2004),
    http://www.wsmo.org/
19. Zeng, L., Benatallah, B., Dumas, M., Kalagnanam, J., Sheng, Q.: Quality-driven Web Service Composition. In: Proc. of 14th International Conference on World Wide Web (WWW 2003), Budapest, Hungary, May 2003. ACM Press, New York (2003)

Trusted Translation Services

Yacine Atif, Mohamed Adel Serhani, Piers Campbell, and Sujith Samuel Mathew

College of Information Technology
UAE University
{Yacine.Atif,serhanim,P.Campbell,s.mathew}@uaeu.ac.ae

Abstract. Administering multilingual Web sites and applications reliably, involves interconnected and multipart tasks, where trust in the involved parties and content translation sources is paramount. Published Web sites may reflect content from databases, content management systems and other repositories to manage related Web content. But a Web site mirrored wholly or selectively onto a target language version requires streamlined trusted processes. Traditionally, files are translated and transferred via FTP, e-mail, or other communication means. Similarly, translation instructions are communicated between involved parties through verbal instruction, e-mail, and instruction files lead to a variety of inconsistencies and lack of trust in the translation process. This paper proposes a Web service approach to streamline the translation processes and an integration of trust properties in the proposed translation Web services. Web Services have been instrumental in handling problems inherent to systems integration, allowing web-based systems to converse and communicate data automatically. The OASIS Translation Web Services Technical Committee has released a standard way for Web Services to serve the translation and localization business. This article proposes a framework to centralize translation services at a reputable source providing a workflow and a mechanism to quantify service trust. An implementation of the framework is also described in the context of a localization case study.

1 Introduction

Any multilingual site owners would realize the soaring cost in translating content, as well as the opportunity cost of having it localized and culturally adjusted. The substantial effort involved in integrating a translated content to produce target language pages entails a certain challenge in making sure the translated sites meet localization standards, particularly when the source language sites are dynamic. Furthermore, given the regional operations' requirements on regional sites to reflect in a timely manner offshore content, one may need to define a model of trust whereby these operators can accomplish some of their processes themselves in updating their own content. The need for language translation in the appearance and operations of web contents and services is as appealing as challenging to modern industries. Yet, those aspirations have to respond also to a certain level of trust as they involve Web exposure of businesses and client-facing interfaces. A framework for a reliable and

E. Bertino and J.B.D. Joshi (Eds.): CollaborateCom 2008, LNICST 10, pp. 778–791, 2009.

automatic translation processes using current infrastructure, to respond to today and future trusted localization requirements of global web contents, forms the scope of this paper.

Our particular collaborative internet-based translation framework, involves dozens of expert researchers to translate prominent web contents from source languages into a targeted language. It allows multilingual content site owners to translate source-language articles to a target-language destination which is relevant to localized content for prominent regional market. The Translation Management System (TMS) isolates the effected articles and invokes a translation Web service [1] which route the translation request across trusted translation parties. Thus our framework is based on a Web services translation engine which is compliant with OASIS Translation [2] standards. The need to design standard Web Services for translation was highlighted at several instances in the context of web content with global reach intent. For example, the Olympics Web site [4]. Yet, Web content owners are reluctant to solicit translation services due to the long term partnership requirements to translate dynamic content reliably. TMS provides an on-line translation factory based on standard document tagging structure and involving field expert translators.

Earlier, Oasis standardization body developed XLIFF (XML Localization Interchange File Format), an "XML-based format that enables translators to concentrate on the text to be translated" [6]. XLIFF supports a full localization process by providing tags and attributes for review comments and tracking translation status. XLIFF aggregation recognizes several source document formats, and will translate them to XLIFF counterpart destination. Any translation service or application that understands XLIFF can open and change the communicated content. XLIFF grew as a result of significant work from the industry to develop localization within OASIS. Created at the beginning of 2003, the OASIS Technical Committee includes representatives from major IT industries including Oracle, Microsoft and IBM. This standardization embracement facilitates the propagation of translation engines such as the one proposed in this paper.

While web services technology's short span of life has seen extensive applications in business information, with rich content such as airline reservation, its exploitation in globalizing reliably web contents has not been fully investigated. The approach adopted in this paper aims at reducing cost of translation and localization process when globalizing web contents. The proposed framework mediates the interaction instances between a translation solicitor and provider using standard translation related web services. These interactions may involve contract agreement on translation terms and the actual translation job itself, in trust-building environment. The proposed architecture empowers corporate with worldwide operations to meet effectively a global audience. TMS is a business partner providing this far-reaching audience to corporate and businesses.

Traditional localization processes incur lack of trust because notorious issues such as redundancy, communication overheads, high translation costs, errors and delays have created reluctance to translation and Web content globalization. To alleviate these shortcomings, we propose TMS, a Web portal giving clients quick access to a wide range of trusted translation services. TMS offers Web Service interfaces with simple and direct programmatic access to existing content repositories (such as CMS). This seamless integration increases further level of trust in the translation process and reliability of the translated content. TMS Web Services use XLIFF to specify the organization of translation content, and Translation Web Services. This approach streamlines the communication between translation clients and service providers. Using these services, web source content is translated and republished directly into the production website, while translation status can be tracked during translation until completion is unveiled. All data retrievals are handled without tedious manual intervention. In addition, once extracted from a CMS, TMS employs a variety of QoS processes to ensure the reliability, precision, and speed of the translation process. For example, translated resources may be referred to a translation review service prior to commit the delivered translations. This added-value service further strengthens the level of trust in the translation process.

The remaining sections of this paper are organized as follows. First, we discuss some earlier related work to justify the proposed web translation model in this paper. Then, we reveal the translation workflow and related processes followed by the communication architecture of the proposed TMS framework. We then present a case study of an ongoing TMS-based implementation named Murshid, which aims at validating the proposed model in producing Arabic web content out of existing prominent web sources. Finally, we conclude the paper with a summary of results and suggestions for future work.

2 Background and Related Work

There are a number of different approaches to translating a website, each with its own advantages and disadvantages. To successfully cross the language translation divide, many suggestions have been reported [7] for both writing clear, translatable content as well as choosing a suitable translation service. In many cases, it is not simply enough to translate words into another language. Languages with scripting systems that read from right to left, for example, should have layouts and menus adjusted accordingly when translated. Furthermore, cultural dimensions may be considered in replicating interfaces for countries of different cultures as look and feel may differ from one country to the other [8]. Actually, designing interfaces for international use has been extensively addressed in the past [9, 10] where usability principles and cultural issues are considered in translating an interface.

There are a number of ways to go about providing translations of websites. One such way is to perform translation with an automated translation program, though quality of these results can vary greatly. An example of such an automatic system is AltaVista's Babel Fish Translation [11] in which users may receive translations for words, sentences, or paragraphs by entering these directly, or translating a full web page by providing a URL to a page. However, automatic translation is still in its infancy, especially when multimedia contents is involved [13].

Another approach to web content translation is for the designer of a website to perform translation of content and interfaces by hand, which can be a cumbersome and time-consuming. The problems which can arise in this approach are discussed in 'Internationalizing Online Information' [12]. Furthermore, developers tend to ignore internationalization issues when designing a website and must reconsider these at the time of deployment.

A third option for Web content translation is to appeal to a site's user-base and allow this select community of volunteers or professional translators to translate a website. This approach has been successful in translating online newsletters and entire websites. This approach depends on an online community of users to volunteer their time to do the translation. One example of community-based translation can be found in TidBITS [14], and SOL [15]. Teams of translators and editors work on the translation process. One team member may acts as coordinator to assign articles to the other four, and assemble the finished work. This administrative hierarchy has been found to work well, allowing an extra level of style and quality checking. The coordinator is in charge of maintaining the quality of the translation. Similar initiatives prove the effectiveness of the community-based approach. OmniWeb [16], a browser created for Mac OS X which includes support for more languages than any other web browser. Another example is the Translation Project [17] which aims to translate free software packages into various languages. "Google in your language" [18] is another example of community-based translation. Users of Google register to translate into one of one hundred and forty-eight languages, and are then presented with items (strings of words) which appear on Google's pages that could need translation.

Community-based translation presented above appears to be most prominent and advocated by several initiatives as it uses a wide source of human translation expertise. However, these are ad-hoc approaches suitable for specific Website or tool. The processes are slow due to the absence of a common translation specification standard and a system that streamlines translation workflows. In this paper, we introduce a general approach to community-based translation where the Web acts as a natural middleware linking translation client and service providers. The proposed Translation Management System or TMS has a suite of remote translation-authoring, content reviewing and approving in integrated workflows. This framework allows content editors from different locations to request for language translations and for translators to perform translation online. The Translation Management System lowers the overall cost, reduces the administrative overhead and streamlines the entire operations. Furthermore, the adoption of open standards leads to the construction of powerful translation services. The proposed model represents a translation aid platform that content providers can use, with the prospects to offer translation web services to their clients, without the need to transfer valuable multilingual content. Finally, the implementation approach enables the integration of such service into larger business information applications with superior multilingual processing capabilities.

3   Translation Workflows and Web Services

The proposed service architecture is an attempt to increase the level of performance of producing correct translations. It joins a persistent translation engine to a dynamic source for translations on the fly. For every thematic domain, participants cooperate around the TMS-provided services to accomplish a domain-related translation. TMS participants include six categories of roles: guests, translators, editors, translation project managers (or managing editor), reviewer and administrator, for every translation service project. Relevant translation-related web services are triggered for each participant category. Members of each category are able to access appropriate TMS services available to that category and all the preceding categories. Hence the scope of services increase hierarchically.

XLIFF is used as communication medium between clients and TMS, whereas Translation Web Services define the nature of translation related services for a given translation project. Our standards-supported approach allows source content of any media type to be posted directly into TMS's translation production process from the client CMS. Translations can also be tracked from the CMS engine to facilitate automatic integration into the client's portal when translation completes, without additional manual intervention. Further QoS attributes can include a variety of translation productivity tools such as accuracy, and timeliness of the translation. Figure 1 includes typical TMS and client modules of the framework architecture. This framework is applied to our TMS design and instantiated to our translation case study.

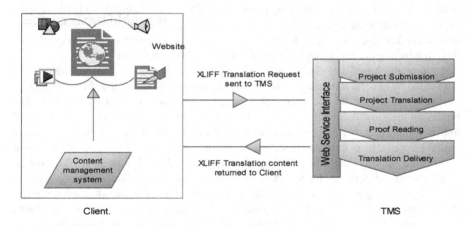

Fig. 1. TMS Architecture

This is the model which we have used for translating prominent web source to Arabic language as a case study of the proposed framework. Typical websites use a content management system (CMS) to store media and articles displayed on the website. Translation is processed through the TMS, an online translation service provider. Initially, content is taken from the source web site CMS and integrated into an XLIFF document (with relevant translation-related tags). Following a Service-Oriented Architecture, SOAP protocol wraps each XLIFF document and sends it to TMS via Web Services invocation. At the TMS side, Web service interfaces represented by corresponding WSDL define how the available services are invoked as

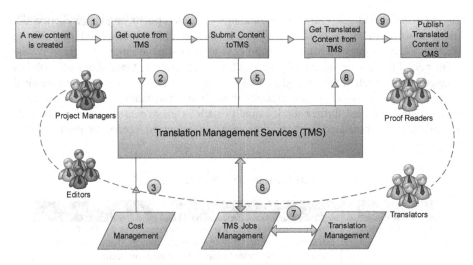

Fig. 2. Translation Workflows

well as their properties. A request carrying the XLIFF-wrapped document reach the TMS, where the translation process is managed and a translated version of the document is returned to the web site CMS via web services. Typical workflows are described in Figure 2. The execution of translation projects involves several document transfers between the project members whose roles are described in the subsequent section. These transfers are vulnerable to errors because they are processed manually. The proposed translation workflows are more effective than traditional email communications when the translation content is substantial. It controls the transfer of translation requests and returning back translated documents, while permitting members involved in the translation development to follow-up the state of every resource as well as identifying errors and delays punctually. Another advantage of this framework is its provision of accounting applications with respect to the size of a translation job (in terms of word count) as show in Figure 2 (Steps 2 and 3). The translation workflow is integrated with translation-related databases (Steps 6 and 7), and client CMS (Steps 8 and 9).

Web services offer several advantages in this translation processes streamlining framework [19]:

- Universal service repository available to anyone
- Selective access to any translation process
- Client can communicate with any translation vendor who support the service (such as the proposed TMS)

The details of the advertised Web Services used in TMS have some of the basic functionality that one might expect from a translation vendor service. Table 1 below illustrates the standard Web services used in TMS, and which specifications are reported in [3] and [5]. Our implementations of these specifications are carried out along a workflow to be elaborated later in this article. As described in Table 1, submitJob initiates the translation process after cost negotiations triggered by the sequence of methods requestQuote and acceptQuote. Once status of a job has changed to completed, the method retrieveJob is called to integrate the translated contents into the client's CMS. Besides these basic translation web services, other mechanisms provided further service quality such as reviewJob which proofreads the quality of a translated content and returns an enhanced version of the translated resource.

Table 1. Translation Web services

Web Service	Specification
requestQuote	This request initiates the translation process by returning an estimated cost to the translation source. Rates may vary according to the translation volume and on volume and media type rates.
retrieveQuote	This call facilitates the retrieval of a quote.
acceptQuote	Using the proposed Job reference assigned when a request for quote has been issued, a translation request may be accepted, at which point translation process starts.
submitJob	Eventually combines requestQuote & acceptQuote, when a relationship between client and service provider has pre-established, or translation fees have been prepaid. Alternatively, this web service may be invoked when translation is deployed internally and hence bypassing quotes negotiation phase. This is the case for our case study implementation (i.e. Murshid) of the TMS discussed in this paper.
retrieveJob	When a translation is complete, this service is called to retrieve the translated resource.

This process maximizes automation the translation process and the communication between involved stakeholders, and therefore shortens the turnaround times. Access to TMS via web services is also made available to service provider personnel. For example, TMS typically uses a range of translators, who may be internal or remote. Translators use a Web service to retrieve pending translation documents. Using this service translation requests could be checked out, retrieved and later on submitted back, from within a translation service provider context. TMS actually involved a number of personnel to fulfill the requirement of a translation (as shown in Figure 2). These include:

a) *Guests*: Guests are allowed to browse parts of TMS translation database. Since the translated documents are meant to be published anyway, guests may search for text phrases, Boolean combinations of phrases, particular keywords, and various field-specific searches to index translated articles or resources. These resources are returned with their target URI links, to invite guests to visit the target websites for which the articles were translated. TMS maintains two translation databases: the test and production database. The test database provides translators with an experimental environment of translation jobs. Committed translation works are sent to the production database. While the test database could be considered as a temporary working memory, which will be erased upon committing translation jobs, the production database is a sustained memory environment of all delivered translation by TMS.

b) *Project Managers*: Maintain interaction with a client and also get the source for translation, ensures that the translations are complete, reviewed and the final version is published. They also have the responsibility of assigning the translation work to editors. This hierarchy provides a modular approach for large translation contents. For example, Murshid involves a large Web source partners which are candidate for translation. In one specific source, contents is a collection of scientific articles in various domains but categorized into say Geography, Chemistry, Computer, etc.. Murshid assigns an expert Editor for each domain area. A project manager can view the current progress of the entire Website translation project. They have a view over each editor's section. Once the collection of content in each section of the website has been vetted by the Editor, the translation project is said to be complete.

c) *Editors*: They are best seen as area consultants and subject experts in the area and the target language for translation. Their job is to receive content from project manager and examine translations returned by translators. This operation is labeled as "vetting". Editors have expertise in specific areas. Multiple translations may be vetted by a single editor. Editors can examine the history of a candidate article, including all translations, revisions, and vetting. However, their vetting only applies to the most recent version of the translation. Editors can view the current progress of the Website translation project in their particular area. They can see which articles have been translated but not yet vetted, and they can pinpoint exactly which translated article they wish to vet. Editors are also responsible to assign source content to translators. Content is shown to editors in both input and output format. They may then make changes to the translation or send back to the original translator. So the editor and translator can discuss the changes in a cyclic process. Once the editor approves the translation, he states the resource as "vetted". A vetting mark is made in the translation database and a notice is sent to the translator. Translators work is stored in test version of the translation database. Once materials have been vetted by an editor, they are stored in the production version of the translation database. Subsequent emendation or expansion of a vetted article can occur in a new workflow.

d) *Translators*: They must be subject experts i.e. they are experts in the content to be translated. Translation can be carried out in a Push or Pull process. A translator may be assigned a set of article entries by the editor. Alternatively, translators may request assignments either in the form of a range (of pending articles for translation), or in the form of a topic, such as "Biology". This request indicates whether the translator wants to work in the test or the production database. Web services are invoked upon requests generation. Editors are notified and may subsequently initiate or modify translation assignments. Given an assignment the corresponding translator proceeds with the actual translation task. The translator sees a placeholder to upload his translation in the expected format. The input is initially checked for completeness before giving an opportunity to make last changes prior to storing the translated item in the translation database. A translator may not modify a translation previously submitted. A submitted translation is vetted by an editor. Prior to submit a translation, translators may solicit the service of proofreaders or reviewers.

e) *Reviewers*: They are responsible for ensuring the quality of translation. They will proofread content and make grammatical or other linguistic or cultural amendments to the translated content. Eventually reviewers may instead make suitable comments and suggestions to be considered by translators. Reviewer may either approve or reject the translation.

f) *TMS Administrator*: The TMS Administrator would have overall responsibility of the TMS environment. He provides user access rights, sets up new user accounts and roles, supports and trains TMS related personnel.

4 Trust Specification

Trust remains a crucial component in any system. It is essential that users be able to appraise service reputation. This is particularly important in a translation service, where the quality of the service outcome can often be measured only after the content deployment. To this end we propose a reputation metric to measure trust of our proposed TMS services. We define reputation to be a quality property, composed of three sub-properties: Service Availability, Quality of Translation and Frequency of Service Invocation. Each of these components is associated to a weighted value. All values are then aggregated to produce a measure of reputation. Service availability represents the probability that the Web Service is accessible (available for use) quantified by the percentage of time the service is operating. Quality of translation is based on the speed, accuracy and presentation of translated material and is a composite value based on end users feedbacks. The frequency of invocation represents the number of times a service operation is invoked. The higher the level of invocation, the higher is the level of customers' trust in the service provider reputation.

Based on the value of the reputation, we classify the Web service into three qualitative categories: Strong, Satisfactory, and Weak. We specify reputation property of a translation Web service by aggregating composing sub-properties, which are embedded in an XML representation that is included in the WSDL document of the TMS Web service. The properties' values are defined for each operation provided by the TMS Web service. The figure below presents the XML description of these quality properties for TMS Web service.

```
<Trust-WS name= "TMS">
        <Category name="Strong">
                <operation        name= "Translate"
                                  Availability = 95%
                                  Quality of Translation = Excellent
                                  Frequency of Invocation = 1
                </operation>
                <operation        name= "Review"
                                  Availability = 90%
                                  Quality of Translation = Very Good
                                  Frequency of Invocation = 1
                </operation>
        </Category >
        < Category name="Satisfactory">
                <operation        name= "Translate"
                                  Availability =80 %
                                  Quality of Translation = Very Good
                                  Frequency of Invocation =1
                </operation>
                <operation        name= "Review"
                                  Availability = 75%
                                  Quality of Translation = Good
                                  Frequency of Invocation = 2
                </operation>
        </ Category >
        <Category name="Weak">
                ......
        </Category >
</Trust-WS >
```

Fig. 3. XML representation of TMS Web service: Trust property

5 Prototype and Case Study

To validate some of the features of our TMS based Web services model, we provide a brief illustration of a case study for translating web content stored in CMS or content repository into Arabic language. We first show the XML specifications of implemented web services and the structure of the exchange XLIFF messages.

5.1 Murshid Web Service

Translation web services provide a range of operations such as submitJob and retrieveJob where the first operation allows a client to request a translation from a web service and the second operation allows a client to get the translated content from a web service. An excerpt of WSDL specification of Murshid Web service is illustrated in Figure 4. It describes the set of available operation interfaces, and their related binding information.

```
<?xml version="1.0" encoding="utf-8" ?>
- <wsdl:definitions xmlns:http="http://schemas.xmlsoap.org/wsdl/http/" ... >
- <wsdl:types>
- <s:schema elementFormDefault="qualified" targetNamespace="http://www.Murshid.ae">
- <s:element name="Translate">
- <s:complexType>
    ..........
  </wsdl:types>
- <wsdl:message name="TranslateSoapIn">
    ......
  </wsdl:message>
- <wsdl:message name="TranslateSoapOut">
    .....
  </wsdl:message>
- <wsdl:portType name="TranslateServiceSoap">
- <wsdl:operation name="Translate">
  <documentation xmlns="http://Murship.ae/wsdl/"> Convert text from one language to Arabic language.
      Supported language is English to Arabic. </documentation>
  <wsdl:input message="tns:TranslateSoapIn" />
  <wsdl:output message="tns:TranslateSoapOut" />
    </wsdl:operation>
    </wsdl:portType>
- <wsdl:binding name="TranslateServiceSoap" type="tns:TranslateServiceSoap">
  <soap:binding transport="http://schemas.Murshid.ae/soap/http" style="document" />
- <wsdl:operation name="Translate">
  <soap:operation soapAction="http://www.Murshidwebservice.ae/Translate" style="document" />
- <wsdl:input> .... </wsdl:input>
- <wsdl:output> ..... </wsdl:output>
  </wsdl:operation>
  </wsdl:binding>
- <wsdl:binding name="TranslateServiceHttpPost" type="tns:TranslateServiceHttpPost">
  <http:binding verb="POST" />
    ..........
  </wsdl:operation>
  </wsdl:binding>
    .......
  </wsdl:port>
  </wsdl:service>
  </wsdl:definitions>
```

Fig. 4. A part of WSDL document of Murshid Web services

5.2 XLIFF Specification for Murshid Web Service

To illustrate an example of XLIFF specification used to translate Web content to Arabic language, Figure 5 presents an itemized menu together with a login frame and sign up a new account as obtained by the proposed TMS web service implemented in Murshid case study.

Fig. 5. Example of source content in English translated to Arabic using XLIFF specification

6 Conclusion

This paper has addressed many of the problems inherent to web content globalization through the provision of Translation Management Services (TMS). We also introduced a measure of trust to quantify the Quality of Service of the proposed translation services. Based on standardized web service specifications, this paper presented a streamlined approach to translating and localizing web content based on a consistent workflow and well defined stakeholders roles. We first introduced the TMS model, as a systematic management of translating source web material to a given target language. We validated an instance of the TMS where the target language is Arabic in the context of a case study to demonstrate the operations TMS web services. The case study has further illustrated how TMS services could be used to effectively manage complex translation processes, while maintaining QoS attributes pertaining to a translation process, such as proof reading, traceability and transparency. Our solution presents a comprehensive enterprise approach to web translation, which seamlessly interoperates CMS functions with our proposed translation workflows, leading all the way to translation personnel whose roles have been defined in this paper.

To further specify trust, we plan to integrate the standard WS-Policy framework [20], which allows web services to advertise their Quality of Service (QoS), and for web service consumers to specify their QoS requirements. WS-Policy defines a policy to specify requirements and capabilities that manifest on the wire (for example, authentication scheme and transport protocol), as well as capabilities which are critical to proper service selection such as QoS characteristics. The advertised policy contributes to match a service requesters with the expected service quality, and hence the expected level of trust from the service outcome. Our future work explores further extensions of the TMS to provide mechanisms for trust based on WS Policy standard to further adhere to the OASIS prescribed standards.

References

1. Antonopoulios, V., Demiros, I., Cafatalayannls, G., Piperidis, S.: Integrating Translation Technologies Towards a Powerful Translation Web Service. In: Proceedings of the 2004 IEEE Conference on Cybernetics and Intelligent Systems Singapore, December 1-3 (2004)
2. OASIS Translation Web Services Technical Committee, http://www.oasis-open.org/committees/tc_home.php?wg_abbrev=trans-ws
3. Translation Web services specification, Standard Specification Draft (June 2008), http://www.oasis-open.org/committees/workgroup.php?wg_abbrev=trans-ws
4. Reynolds, P.: Web Services and Globalization Management: A Case Study. Multilingual Computing & Technology, num. 73 16(5), July/August (2005)
5. Using Web Services for Translation, A white paper on the Translation Web Services standard (April 2006), http://www.oasis-open.org/committees/download.php/21054/TWS%20Whitepaper.doc
6. XLIFF Specification, http://docs.oasis-open.org/xliff/xliff-core/xliff-core.html
7. Dilts, D.: Successfully Crossing the Language Translation Divide. In: (ACM) Proceedings of the 19th Annual International Conference on Computer Documentation (2001)
8. Marcus, A., Gould, E.W.: Crosscurrents: Cultural Dimensions and Global Web User-Interface Design. ACM Interactions 7(4) (July 2000)
9. Levanthal, L., et al.: Designing for Diverse Users: Will Just a Better Interface Do? In: SIGCHI, pp. 191–192. ACM Press, New York (1994)
10. Nielsen, J.: Usability Testing of International Interfaces. Elsevier Science Publishers Ltd., UK (1990)

11. AltaVista Babel Fish Translation, `http://babelfish.altavista.com`
12. Merrill, C.K., Shanoski, M.: Internationalizing Online Information. In: SIGDOC, pp. 19–25. ACM Press, New York (1992)
13. Volk, M.: The Automatic Translation of Film Subtitles. In: A Machine Translation Success Story? Proceedings of Languages amd the Media, 7th International Conference and Exhibition on Language Transfer in Audiovisual Media, Berlin, Germany (2008)
14. TidBITS Translations,
    `http://www.tidbits.com/about/translations.html`
15. SOL: Byzantine Lexicography, `http://www.stoa.org/sol/`
16. OmniWeb, The Omni Group,
    `http://www.omnigroup.com/applications/omniweb/`
17. The Translation Project,
    `http://www.iro.umontreal.ca/contrib/po/HTML/index.htm`
18. Google in Your Language, `http://services.google.com/tc/Welcome.html`
19. Globalize your On Demand Business, IBM, `http://www-01.ibm.com/software/globalization/topics/webservices/translation.jsp`
20. Web Services Policy, `http://www.w3.org/Submission/WS-Policy/`

Enabling Meetings for "Anywhere and Anytime"

Alison Lee and Umesh Chandra

Nokia Research Center – Palo Alto
{Alison.Lee,Umesh.1.Chandra}@nokia.com

Abstract. Mobile technologies and services are playing critical roles in mobile work. One area is mobile collaboration where mobile telephony and data sharing are in high demand. This paper explores and demonstrates that enabling meetings for the mobile context to support "anywhere and anytime" collaboration poses new opportunities, challenges, and tools. EasyMeet incorporates four novel additions, compared to traditional, electronic, meeting tools that support these scenarios and opportunities. They include s60 widget, synchronous voice and data sharing, remote content access, and access to mobile phone platform capabilities through web services. Initial feedback from a pilot has provided insights and improvements about usability and system performance.

Keywords: AJAX, mobile meeting, phone platform capabilities, remote file access, S60 Web Runtime widget, simultaneous voice and data sharing, user feedback, Web 2.0.

1 Introduction

As Web 2.0 took shape in enterprises, organizations increasingly pushed for services to be hosted on the Web. With widespread use of and improvements in mobile devices and connectivity, there is an increasing demand to access these services with mobile devices. This demand is particularly strong for services in communication and collaboration. An informal poll of mobile workers reveal the need to participate in meetings using mobile phones; the simplest being to see shared slides. This request is not surprising given that meetings are commonplace within organizations.

The interest in mobile collaboration can also be attributed to the prevalence of mobile work and large numbers of mobile workers. For many, the need to carry a mobile phone for communication and a laptop for computing is burdensome but necessary. Mobile phones are unlikely to supplant laptops in the immediate future. Collaboration, however, is a natural extension of using mobile phones; when they are used to conference into meetings.

In response to the numerous requests for a mobile meeting service within our company, we created EasyMeet. Its initial functionality was modeled around simplified, traditional PC-based meeting tools like slide sharing, chat, people awareness, highlighter, and meeting minutes recording. People using and seeing this first prototype were excited; particularly as it enables them to conduct meetings "anywhere and anytime." Through a small, limited deployment, we gained many insights and feedback about use scenarios, usability and system performance. In

E. Bertino and J.B.D. Joshi (Eds.): CollaborateCom 2008, LNICST 10, pp. 792–804, 2009.

addressing them, we have identified some key differences with a mobile meeting tool compared to traditional electronic meetings.

In this paper, we describe four new additions to traditional meeting tools for meetings using mobile phones. They facilitate several "anywhere and anytime" use cases that are not adequately supported with PC-based meeting tools. The next section uses several scenarios to illustrate the new use cases and functionalities. We then present the initial version of EasyMeet, a mobile meeting service for mobile phones. We introduce and describe the four new add-ons in version 2: S60 widget, synchronous voice and data sharing, remote content access, and access to mobile phone platform capabilities. We share experiences, challenges, and informal feedback with this service.

2 Meeting Opportunities Enabled by Mobility

Mobility adds a new dimension to electronic meetings. The most salient aspect is that individuals are not restricted in where they can conduct or participate in meetings. This was first evident for telephony when people were able to make phone calls "anywhere and anytime." The same potential exists for mobile meetings. First, mobile phones are the primary entry to the Internet in emerging markets [17]. Second, fieldwork is underserved by synchronous collaboration technologies where "points of inspiration" or "no opportunity better than the present" are at play [1, 11, 22]. Third, traditional electronic meeting tools are typically used to enable meetings for virtually co-located people. While mobile collaboration is useful in those situations, it also enriches face-to-face interactions. O'Hara et al. (2001) found extensive talk around document use and vice versa; be it on a mobile phone or in person.

We give several use scenarios of mobile collaboration for meetings, collected in talks with business groups and users.

Scenario 1
Sue is a real-estate agent. Occasionally, her clients are from out-of-town and cannot review properties in-person. In such cases, Sue visits the properties alone. When she sees one of interest to her client, she starts a mobile conference. Her client receives the EasyMeet URL through an SMS. Both of them meet on EasyMeet and communicate using voice and sharing of slides and photos; the latter compiled on-site by Sue. Sue creates a permanent EasyMeet conference for each client she works with. Over the course of a client engagement, a number of EasyMeet sessions typically occur. Both or either one of them can return to this permanent conference to have further discussions or to review the uploaded content from the various sessions.

Scenario 2
Robert is a healthcare technician who travels to different villages in Kenya as part of a mobile health clinic. Occasionally, Robert encounters medical cases that require remote consultation with doctors and specialists. Using the capture capabilities of his mobile phone's camera, Robert is able to provide pictures, notes, etc. to a doctor in Nairobi. As a doctor's on-site examiner, he can provide his assessment and measurements that help to diagnose the problem. Doctors can review and update the case file.

Scenario 3
Miika is traveling by train from Helsinki to Tampere. He joins a scheduled meeting by clicking a EasyMeet conference URL that he received via email. Using his mobile phone's voice and data connections, he can converse and view the meeting slides. He participates in the ongoing text chat and contributes minutes for the meeting. He observes, from the location and participant list, that several other participants are remote; including one person located near him. He sets out and finds his co-located colleague and sits through the rest of the meeting together.

Scenario 4
Janet is visiting a colleague in an adjoining office building. En-route, she bumps into Henry, a co-worker on a joint project. As part of a status update, Henry mentions new results that he obtained. Janet, eager to see them, pulls out her mobile phone and invites Henry to a permanent conference created for such ad-hoc interactions. Henry remotely uploads the PowerPoint file from his office PC to the conference using EasyMeet's file upload feature. Once uploaded and shared, they review the results.

3 Related Work

CSCW researchers noted that people are often mobile to meet others and to solve problems. Bergqvist et al. (1999) examined meetings occurring outside of meeting rooms. They found how such meetings took place (i.e., multi-threaded, work-related, situated and opportunistic) and how they are initiated and re-established. They recommended two tools to support such meetings: a dynamic ToDo list to support the establishment of mobile meetings and a portable project database to provide users with easy access to potentially relevant information in a mobile situation. Our scenarios reflect the structured as well as ad-hoc, serendipitous, and opportunistic nature of meetings and highlight EasyMeet capabilities to support them. We have also found the need for remote access to documents to be important and integrated EasyMeet with a service to access a user's various remote computers for files. In addition, the availability of a persistent meeting space and a Web-based handle to it supports not only ToDo lists as well as other resources related to a project (e.g., participants, document artifacts, chat logs).

Tamaru et al. (2005) examined the influence of cell phones in the way work is unconstrained by time and space in three mobile-work domains. They found that workers creatively and constructively restructured their work and communication to leverage social and human resources using mobile telephony and mobile email-for-chat. They argue that mobile phones are a fundamental element of CSCW technology for mobile workers. Additionally, O'Hara et al. (2001) studied mobile workers and found a relationship between talk and text. These studies point to the importance of mobile phones for both its voice and data sharing capabilities and the ability of mobile workers to leverage them to enhance mobile meetings. Smart phones are central and primary device targeted in the development of EasyMeet.

There is a long line of research dating back to Doug Englebart's famous 1968 demo and plurality of research and commercial (Microsoft NetMeeting, IBM Sametime, Webex) systems developed to support desktop-based electronic meetings and meeting capture [5,14,15]. Building off this long history, EasyMeet's initial version was seeded with a number of basic functionality common to all these systems but optimized for the mobile phone form factor [12].

In the specific area of developing systems to support mobile meetings, Wiberg (2001) found that it was critical to seamlessly integrate interaction from mobile meetings. Mobile meetings were defined as informal face-to-face meetings, with those interactions that are in-between meetings [20]. This was based on his field study work that found that work occurred in all four squares of a 2x2 matrix with axes of "time" (i.e., any time and particular time) and "space" (i.e., any place and particular place) and that the vision of work occurring "anytime, anywhere" is not easy to realize for mobile workers. He argued that the integration should address situations for divided use rather than divided user attention, for invisible computer support, and for seamless ongoing interaction across physical and virtual meetings. Roamware leverages three technologies (PDA, proximity sensor, and PC application) to enable seamless integration and re-establishment of different threads of interaction by offering to convert personal and public interaction histories into project contexts. Our work primarily focuses on the four zones with less attention to the in-between aspects.

PDAs have been used in meetings for taking personal notes. Myers et al. (1998) used PalmPilot PDAs to control a meeting PC and to draw [13]. Kobayashi et al. (1998) described a service from IBM involving Web-based synchronous voice and data sharing service for collaborative customer service. It is most similar in spirit to EasyMeet because of its integration of voice and data sharing and its notion of bringing virtually co-located people into a meeting. Most meeting support tools do not support voice directly, opting to use audio conference system or VOIP to do that. However, there have been efforts to bring data sharing to audio conferences (e.g., [21] provides out-of-band communication features such as text chat).

There have been several research projects to develop meeting tools for mobile devices [1, 10, 14, 19, 20] but none that are deployable for diverse set of mobile devices. EasyMeet aims to be both a practical tool as well as research testbed to study mobile meeting usage. Furthermore, while there have been studies on mobile work, mobile meetings, and mobile phone use, none have examined mobile phones for simultaneous voice and data sharing.

4 EasyMeet V1.0: Design and Implementation

EasyMeet is a Web-based, meeting service for mobile phones. It was seeded with basic capabilities found in other electronic meeting tools such as NetMeeting, Sametime, and Webex. Feedback and requests in pilot of this service have led to several additions and refinements that differentiate EasyMeet from traditional electronic meeting tools. In this section, we present the initial version of the service. The next section introduces the extensions and refinements.

4.1 Features and Capabilities

Leveraging on prior experiences with electronic meeting tools, EasyMeet V1.0 supports the following capabilities and illustrated in Figure 1.

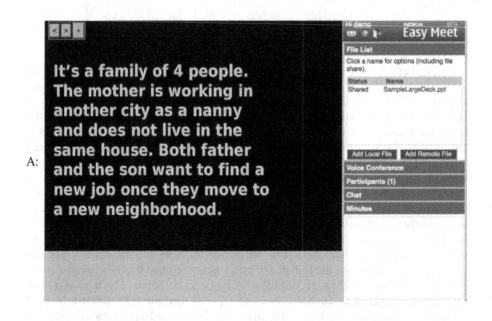

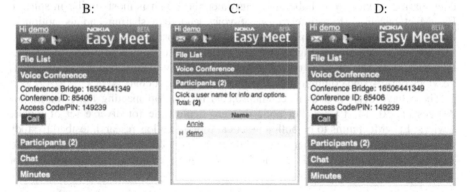

Fig. 1. Large screen layout using accordion on right of A: slide-sharing with file list, B: voice conference, C: participant awareness, and D: chat

- Meetings may be *scheduled* events or *permanent* events. Scheduled events have designated date, time, and length while permanent events are available at all times.
- Meetings may include a number of files that are uploaded before or during a meeting (see *files list* in Figure 1A).
- Image and powerpoint files may be shared simultaneously to all participants by the meeting host using *slide-sharing,* Figure 1A. For files with a content format that is not supported by EasyMeet's slide-sharing capability, participants can download the files to their device for individual viewing or safekeeping.
- A highlighter tool allows the meeting host to highlight contents of the slide being shared. These highlights are updated on all participants' view of the slide.

- A *participant list,* see Figure 1C, provides an awareness mechanism for all meeting participants of who is present and contact information.
- A *chat tool,* see Figure 1D, permits all participants to chat. While not all mobile phones make text chat easy, we opted for it over voice chat for many of the reasons identified by [14].
- A *meeting minutes tool* permits a designated meeting scribe to record textual notes about the meeting.
- Registered users can access their meetings through their *meeting list.* Invited participants, who are not registered users of EasyMeet, may also join the meeting. The latter lowers the barrier to meeting participation by not requiring registration to use the service.

4.2 Implementation of EasyMeet

EasyMeet is accessible from any mobile device with a standards-compliant Web browser; Nokia devices, Apple iPhone, Samsung Blackjack, Blackberry Bold and Storm, and GooglePhone. AJAX 2.0 technologies (CSS, HTML, Javascript, XMLHttpRequest) are used to develop client-side functionality. Apache and Django (high-level python Web framework) are used to develop the server-side functionality. A wide variety of mobile devices and laptops can access EasyMeet using these technologies.

A key challenge with developing applications for mobile phones is the lack of large displays, full QWERTY keyboard, or two-dimensional pointing device like a mouse [11]. EasyMeet supports two different screen layouts to accommodate different mobile phone screen resolutions (see Figure 1 and Figure 2). The screen layout used is determined by a simple heuristic – mobile browser display width. Widths that are

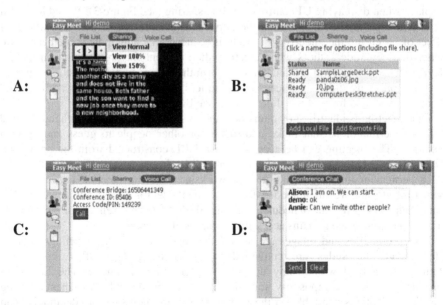

Fig. 2. Small screen layout with tab widget to access functionality (A: slide sharing, B: file list, C: voice conference, D: chat)

Next Slide

Slide Control
Expand/Contract

Slide List

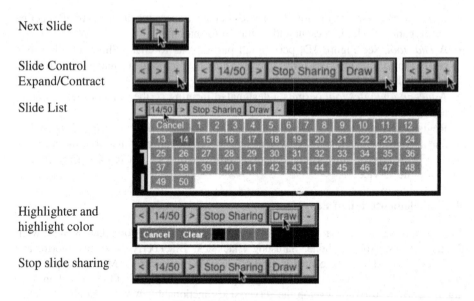

Highlighter and
highlight color

Stop slide sharing

Fig. 3. Slide sharing control

QVGA (320x240 or 240x320) or smaller use the small, tab layout and larger mobile displays use the large, accordion layout.

Display real estate and device interactions on mobile phones are constrained and can access-challenge able-bodied people. These issues surfaced in the case of small displays when displaying UI controls for slide sharing (see Figure 3). We addressed it by overlaying the slide controls on the upper left-hand corner of the slide where its effect of obscuring the underlying content is reduced. We anticipate some behavioral adaptations by slide authors when creating slide content for presentation on mobile devices. The slide control has a contracted form that allow common functions such as next and previous slide to be accessed while less frequently used tools are accessed from the expanded form of the slide control (see Figure 3).

Each meeting is identified by a unique, randomly generated 8-byte alphanumeric id with 38^8 permutations that make it difficult for other people to guess and crash a meeting. The meeting can be accessed via a URL constructed from the unique id. This URL is sent to participants via email and SMS. In permanent meetings, the URL for a permanent meeting is a persistent workspace for the meeting participants in which all artifacts (chat, uploaded files) are available for access and review at all times and days. After the scheduled meeting, the minutes are sent to all participants and the meeting space remains accessible to the meeting creator.

PowerPoint files and images are uploaded to and shared in the meetings. During file upload, the slides are converted to JPEG using OpenOffice converters. Participants may download any uploaded content to their phone. The EasyMeet meeting serves as a repository for sharable and non-sharable documents. Using viewer applications available on the mobile phone, the non-sharable documents can be viewed.

5 EasyMeet V2.0: Design and Implementation

We obtained user feedback and feature requests from pilot of EasyMeet 1.0 that are incorporated in the current version. Several issues related to usability and system performance were highlighted.

5.1 S60 Web Runtime Widget

First, many early users had to key in the URL to the service on their mobile phone web browser. This was unwieldy for those without a QWERTY keyboard. While email and SMS were different ways to share the meeting URL with other participants and enable them to access the meeting with click on the URL, they were not sufficient. We redesigned and shortened the URL to reduce the amount of keying operations. The short URL consists of the domain name, a single command character and the unique meeting id.

However, the most effective solution was the S60 Web Runtime widget that we created for EasyMeet [1]. The S60 Web Runtime allows building mobile applications using Web technologies: HTML, CSS, JavaScript, and AJAX. S60 widgets are lightweight Web applications that are installed on the device (see Figure 4A). They use the same underlying technology that powers their Web browser counterparts. Mobile widgets give users a full Web experience with instant access to Web 2.0 services and content from their mobile devices.

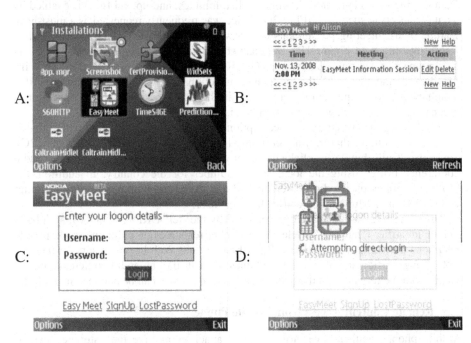

Fig. 4. S60 Web Runtime widget for EasyMeet. A: Looks like any other native application on mobile phone. B: Meeting list for user. C: Widget configuration of user id and password. D: Subsequent auto-login to service.

Our EasyMeet widget uses the same AJAX code that powers EasyMeet's web application. Once launched, the widget connects to the EasyMeet service (see Figure 4C,D) and refreshes the user's meeting list (see Figure 4B). This list replicates the functionality available from the EasyMeet service but is always accessible. The widget can be left running on the mobile phone, in the background. The user can refresh the list by clicking the 'Refresh' button (see Figure 4B). From the meeting list, the user can join the desired meeting by clicking the respective meeting link. This launches the mobile phone browser and navigates the user to the EasyMeet service for the selected meeting. Thus, the user never needs to key in the URL for EasyMeet or the meeting.

Widgets also enable users to personalize the content and experience through preferences. We use this personalization feature to enable users to configure their widget with their EasyMeet user id and password (see Figure 4C).

Thus, the widget provides a number of key user experience enhancements to EasyMeet. The enhancements provide users with a personal on-ramp to the EasyMeet service. With about two clicks, the user can join a meeting without having to key in URLs or remember meeting ids. Finally, the widget provides users with personalized access to EasyMeet and allows them to refresh their meeting list with a click.

5.2 Simultaneous Voice and Data Sharing

EasyMeet supports simultaneous voice and data sharing as alluded to in the scenarios. Data sharing (text chat, slide sharing, file list, minutes, and upload files) is enabled by a data connection such as WIFI or 3G. Voice was frequently requested as a must-have feature. Thus, meeting participants can now initiate audio teleconference once they join a meeting (see Figure 1B). 3G-enabled mobile phones support both voice and data connection simultaneously. For 2G/2.5G mobile phones, users need to use WIFI for data connection and the cellular connection for voice. The reason is that simultaneous voice and data is not allowed in these networks and voice connection is given priority over the data connection that is put on hold.

By clicking the 'voice conference' option, participants are presented with a dialog to select the country that they are currently located in (see Figure 1B and Figure 2C). Once the 'Call' button is clicked, the browser initiates a voice call to an audio conference bridge using the local access number for the country. In addition, the browser supplies the 'audio conference' id and pin along with appropriate delimiter codes without any further key entries from the user.

The voice telephony capability is enabled by the 'tel' URI (RFC 3966); a globally unique identifier ("name") for telephone number resources on public network, private telephone network, or the Internet [7]. All Nokia S60 Web browsers support the 'tel' URI. Thus, participants with mobile phones can call into an audio conference bridge where both the number and the authentication information can be encoded in the URI.

5.3 Remote Content Access from Mobile Phone

Mobile phones neither have large storage capacities nor are they storage devices. Meeting participants who use mobile phones and want to share files typically need to upload these files from their remote PCs rather than their mobile phones [16]. To

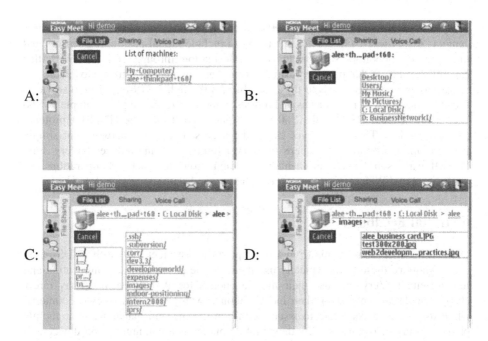

Fig. 5. EasyMeet directory and file browser of remote content. It incorporates breadcrumb (see content to right of computer icon in C) that allow users to pop up during drill downs. Lists that are longer than those displayable are paged with the first sequence of characters for the first item of the page identified (see box under Cancel button in C). Directories are colored light gray (see A, B, C) and files are colored green (see D).

upload such content to a meeting, we integrated a remote content access service (OVI Files) into EasyMeet. Each PC or desktop that a user wishes to access remotely must be registered with this service and a connector application installed. Thereafter, users may access their content from a mobile phone.

Our integration of this service involved creating a file browser UI for the mobile phone and server enhancements (see Figure 5). The latter includes the development of a number of JSON-based Web services that the file browser calls via asynchronous requests to login, authenticate, and request remote directory and file information. In addition, the EasyMeet server serves as a proxy to the OVI File service, forwarding login, authentication, and remote directory and file information. Once the remote file is selected, the EasyMeet server uploads the remote file from OVI File and stores it on the server; it converts the file if it is a Powerpoint document.

5.4 Leveraging Mobile Phone Platform Capabilities as Web Services

Beyond just voice and SMS capabilities, EasyMeet can leverage content and functionality from the user's mobile device (e.g., contacts and calendar for data and GPS and camera functionality). In our scenarios, we allude to the use of camera and GPS for enriching the content that can be shared in a meeting and the meeting experience. These platform capabilities are becoming commonplace features of smart phones. Estimates are that by 2009, 90% of mobile phones worldwide will integrate a camera. Also, mobile phones are beginning to include global positioning sensors and many phone operators support location information through cell ids. With this capability, services that provide positioning, navigation, and tracking are available.

EasyMeet provides access to these capabilities through JSON-based Web services. It can invoke these services as asynchronous requests. We developed a simple PyS60 Web server (S60HTTP) for the S60 mobile phones that uses the HTTP1.1 protocol (see Figure 4A). The Web server cannot be accessed from the network but simply from the mobile phone. This keeps the server lightweight and reduces battery drain [11]. If care is not taken in managing computations and network operations, an application or a Web service can drain the battery and shutdown the mobile phone.

6   Initial Feedback

Our early user feedback came from a small pilot of EasyMeet V2.0 with 25 US-based users. Many of these users typically use their mobile phones for communication and reading email. Very few use their mobile phones for Web browsing. They rarely change the default settings of their mobile phones. Many issues that they encountered while using EasyMeet relate to issues with configuring and managing their mobile phones. Many of our users view their mobile phone as a communication device and not a computing device; smart phones are more complex than a telephony device. As mobile computing becomes commonplace and users become more sophisticated with using their mobile phones, we anticipate that these issues will arise less frequently.

While our two UI layout seemed to be a useful approach to addressing heterogeneous display sizes, early feedback suggests that the UI should be greatly simplified. Complex and highly interactive UIs like our tabbed and accordion interfaces are challenging because of the small screen real estate and reduced input capabilities. Most mobile phone users are casual, consumers of information and only a few are sophisticated mobile computing users. In general, it is important that application UIs are contained in one screen. Screens requiring scrolling increase search and panning. Mobile phones lack a full-fledge 2D pointing device for effective UI navigation; very few current mobile phones support touch or point interface. One way to improve accessibility of EasyMeet and other mobile applications is to develop keyboard navigation. The ideas underlying AxsJAX, a framework for making AJAX applications accessible, are useful for mobile Web applications [3].

We discovered that an hour-long meeting drains the battery due to network and processing of updates. We developed an Ajax broker to aggregate client-server messages and to adapt poll frequencies [9]. A resulting benefit was improved UI responsiveness and a reduction of flashing due to network activity.

Delays due to network bandwidth and load time impacted user experience. We improved load times for the meeting screen by compressing large JavaScript files; a 5-fold reduction in size. Our current download for the conference screen is approximately 225KB. Making greater use of XMLHttpRequest, popularized by Web 2.0, mitigate page reloads for any action requiring server capabilities and thus data transferred.

We have just completed an incremental rollout of EasyMeet2.0 in our company. Though it is too early to share behavioral usage data, users have requested integration of EasyMeet with other company productivity tools (i.e., IBM SameTime for collaboration needs, Microsoft Outlook for email and calendar, in-house built conference room and voice bridge booking system). Specifically, users feel it would be more productive if EasyMeet would allow them to do everything – create a meeting, book a voice bridge and conference room, add the meeting entry into the calendar and use SMS to send the meeting URL.

It is also worth noting that compared to rollouts of other internal, non-mobile phone-based, collaboration services where interest (i.e., registration) is less than 2%; our pilot has garnered 4% interest. Furthermore, while many users initially register and explore the system with desktop browsers, our more recent rollouts have seen increased numbers of registrants and returning users using their mobile phones.

7 Conclusion

We presented four new additions to traditional meeting tools that facilitate "anywhere and anytime." They include S60 widget, synchronous voice and data sharing, remote content access, and access to mobile phone platform capabilities. These arose from insights and feedback with using EasyMeet Version 1.0. We are presently engaged in company-wide pilot of EasyMeet 2.0. We anticipate that usability and system performance remain primary and ongoing challenges. Findings from this pilot will offer valuable insights about issues and challenges with designing and developing collaborative mobile phone applications.

References

1. Ajaxian. JSONP: JSON with Padding (2005),
   http://ajaxian.com/archives/jsonp-json-with-padding
2. Bergqvist, J., Dahlberg, P., Ljungberg, F., Kristoffersen, S.: Moving Out of the Meeting Room: Exploring Support for Mobile Meetings. In: Bodker, S., et al. (eds.) Proceeding of 6th ECSCW Conference, pp. 81–98. Kluwer, Dordrecht (1999)
3. Chen, C., Raman, T.V.: Introducing AxsJAX – Access-Enabling AJAX (2007), http://google-code-updates.blogspot.com/2007/11/introducing-axsjax-access-enabling-ajax.html
4. Forum Nokia. Widgets, http://www.forum.nokia.com/main/resources/technologies/browsing/widgets.html
5. Geyer, W., Richer, H., Fuchs, L., Frauenhofer, T., Daijavad, S., Poltrock, S.: A Team Collaboration Space Supporting Capture and Access of Virtual Meetings. In: Proceedings of the 2001 International ACM SIGGROUP Conference on Supporting Group, pp. 188–196. ACM, New York (2001)
6. IETF. URI Scheme for GSM Short Message Service: draft-wilde-sms- uri-15 (2008), http://tools.ietf.org/html/draft-wilde-sms-uri-15
7. IETF. IETF RFC 3966: The tel URI for Telephone Numbers (2004), http://www.rfc-archive.org/getrfc.php?rfc=3966

8. Kobayashi, M., Shinozaki, M., Sakairi, T., Touma, M., Daijavad, S., Wolf, C.: Collaborative Customer Services Using Synchronous Web Browser Sharing. In: Proceeding of ACM Conference on CSCW, pp. 99–109. ACM, New York (1998)

9. Li, D., Anand, M.: Improving Resource Management for Web-Based Applications on Mobile Devices. In: Proceeding of MobiSys 2009. ACM, New York (to appear) (2009)

10. Luk, R., Ho, M., Aoki, P.M.: Asynchronous Remote Medical Consultation for Ghana. In: Proceeding of Conference on Human Factors in Computing Systems, pp. 743–752. ACM Press, New York (2008)

11. Machin, A., Dominguez, C.: Integrating mobile services and content with the Internet. In: MobEA VI Workshop on Empowering the Mobile Web, in conjunction with WWW 2008 Conference (2008),
http://www.research.att.com/~rjana/Program2008.htm

12. Mark, G., Grudin, J., Poltrock, S.E.: Meeting at the Desktop: An Empirical Study of Virtually Collocated Teams. In: Bodker, S., et al. (eds.) Proceeding of 6th ECSCW Conference, pp. 159–178. Kluwer, Dordrecht (1999)

13. Myers, B.A., Stiel, H., Gargiulo, R.: Collaboration Using Multiple PDAs Connected to a PC. In: Proceeding of ACM Conference on CSCW, pp. 285–294. ACM, New York (1998)

14. Nijholt, A.: Meetings, Gatherings, and Events in Smart Environments. In: Proceedings of the 2004 ACM SIGGRAPH International Conference on Virtual Reality Continuum and its Applications in Industry, pp. 229–232. ACM, New York (2004)

15. Nunamaker, J.F., Dennis, A.R., Valacich, J.S., Vogel, D.R., George, J.F.: Electronic Meeting Systems to Support Group Work. Communications of ACM 34(7), 40–61 (1991)

16. O'Hara, K., Perry, M., Sellen, A., Brown, B.: Exploring the Relationship Between Mobile Phone and Document Use During Business Travel. In: Brown, B., Green, N., Harper, R. (eds.) Wireless World: Social and Interactional Aspects of the Mobile Age, pp. 180–194. Springer, Heidelberg (2001)

17. Roto, V.: Web Browsing on Mobile Phones – Characteristics of User Experience. PhD Dissertation, Helsinki University of Technology (2006),
http://lib.tkk.fi/Diss/2006/isbn9512284707/

18. Tamaru, E., Hasuike, K., Tozaki, M.: Cellular Phone as a Collaboration Tool that Empowers and Changes the Way of Mobile Work: Focus on Three Fields of Work. In: Gellersen, H., et al. (eds.) Proceeding of Ninth ECSCW, pp. 247–266. Springer, Heidelberg (2005)

19. Wiberg, M.: RoamWare: An Integrated Architecture of Seamless Interaction In Between Mobile Meetings. In: Proceedings of the 2001 International ACM SIGGROUP Conference on Supporting Group Work, pp. 288–297. ACM, New York (2001)

20. Wiberg, M.: In Between Mobile Meetings: Exploring Seamless ongoing interaction support for Mobile CSCW. PhD Dissertation, Umea University (2001)

21. Yankelovich, N., McGinn, J., Wessler, M., Walker, W., Kaplan, J., Provino, J., Fox, H.: Private Communications in Public Meetings. In: CHI 2005 Extended Abstracts on Human Factors in Computing Systems, pp. 1873–1876. ACM, New York (2005)

22. Yeh, R.B., Liao, C., Klemmer, S.R., Guimbretiere, F., Lee, B., Kakaradov, B., Stamberger, J., Paepcke, A.: ButterflyNet: A Mobile Capture and Access System for Field Biology Research. In: Proceeding of the SIGCHI Conference on Human Factors in Computing Systems, pp. 571–580. ACM, New York (2006)

Collaboratively Sharing Scientific Data

Fusheng Wang[1] and Cristobal Vergara-Niedermayr[2,*]

[1] Integrated Data Systems Department, Siemens Corporate Research, Princeton,
New Jersey, USA
fusheng.wang@siemens.com
[2] Freie Universität, Berlin, Germany
vergara@mi.fu-berlin.de

Abstract. Scientific research becomes increasingly reliant on multi-disciplinary, multi-institutional collaboration through sharing experimental data. Indeed, data sharing is mandatory by government research agencies such as NIH. The major hurdles for data sharing come from: i) the lack of data sharing infrastructure to make data sharing convenient for users; ii) users' fear of losing control of their data; iii) difficulty on sharing schemas and incompatible data from sharing partners; and iv) inconsistent data under schema evolution. In this paper, we develop a collaborative data sharing system *SciPort*, to support consistency preserved data sharing among multiple distributed organizations. The system first provides Central Server based lightweight data integration architecture, so data and schemas can be conveniently shared across multiple organizations. Through distributed schema management, schema sharing and evolution is made possible, while data consistency is maintained and data compatibility is enforced. With this data sharing system, distributed sites can now consistently share their research data and their associated schemas with much convenience and flexibility. SciPort has been successfully used for data sharing in biomedical research, clinical trials and large scale research collaboration.

Keywords: Scientific Data Sharing, Scientific Data Integration, Biomedical Data Management, Computer Supported Collaborative Work, Schema Sharing, Schema Evolution.

1 Introduction

With increased complexity of scientific problems, scientific research is increasingly a collaborative effort across multiple institutions and disciplines. Scientific researchers need an effective infrastructure to share their complex data, results, and the experiment settings that generate the results. Therefore, researchers are able to reuse experiments, pool expertise and validate approaches. As stated in the NIH roadmap and blueprint initiatives [1], to achieve the need to develop new partnerships of research, we need to represent and record clinical research

---

* Work done while visiting Siemens Corporate Research.

E. Bertino and J.B.D. Joshi (Eds.): CollaborateCom 2008, LNICST 10, pp. 805–823, 2009.
© ICST Institute for Computer Sciences, Social-Informatics and Telecommunications Engineering 2009

information, exchange and share such information through standard information protocol, provide a modern information technology platform.

For example, NIH provides large-scale collaborative project awards for a team of independently funded investigators to synergize and integrate their efforts, and the awards mandate the research results and data to be shared [2,3]. As another example, Siemens Medical Solutions has research collaborations with hundreds of research sites distributed across the US, each providing Siemens marketing support by periodically delivering white papers, case reports, clinic methods, clinic protocols, state-of-the-art images, etc. In the past, data were delivered through media such as emails, CDs and hard copies. As a result, deliverable content was non-centralized, therefore difficult to manage, integrate, search, and reliably archive.

Besides, clinical trials are often distributed among multiple hospitals or medical research institutes. For example, University of California, Irvine is leading a group of universities to conduct Diffuse Optical Spectroscopy based clinical trials. Patients are recruited at distributed institutions and experiments are performed on these patients. These require a platform to collect both clinical data and experiment data at multiple distributed institutions, and integrate and share them together for patient study and data analysis.

While the user demands for scientific data sharing have only increased with time, it is still difficult for researchers to find data sharing solutions to support their collaborative research. Given the strong demand, the lack of viable solutions can be attributed to the following reasons. i) The lack of data sharing infrastructure for convenient data sharing. Cyberinfrastructures such as Grid based systems (CaBIG [4], Biomedical Informatics Research Network (BIRN) [5]) focus on large scale data sources and are heavy weight for regular research sites; ii) Users' fear of losing control of their data. Researchers would rather have maximal control of their data on a server located on their own labs, instead of "outsourcing" them somewhere else. Each Principle Investigator and its collaborators will naturally form a research unit and produces a data source. Even when data are shared, the researchers may still want to have flexible sharing control – they keep the ownership of the data, and can revoke the sharing of the data at any time. iii) Difficulty on sharing data under the same or compatible schemas and incompatible data formats from sharing partners. Each site may use different schemas and represent data in different formats; and iv) Inconsistent data under schema evolution. As schemas can keep evolving as applications change, data consistency can be broken at either the same site or across multiple sites.

To meet these demands and solve the problems, we develop SciPort [6], a scientific data management and sharing system for collaborative scientific research. SciPort brings together the following essential components to support scientific data sharing:

- Generic XML based scientific data management which provides a unified data model to represent scientific data (Section 2);
- Lightweight and fully controlled data sharing architecture through a Central Server (Section 3);

- Flexible schema sharing for multiple distributed research sites (Section 4);
- Distributed uniform schema management to keep data and schema consistent across multiple sites (Section 5);
- Distributed multiform schema management to provide flexible schema evolutions at each Local Server while maintaining data compatibility on Central Servers (Section 6); and
- a schema change detection tool to detect and visualize changes between schemas to support schema management (Section 7).

2   Overview of Scientific Data Management with SciPort

SciPort was first developed as a scientific data management system for scientific data modeling, data authoring, management, viewing, searching and exchange. SciPort takes an XML based approach for data modeling, schema representation, and storage and queries.

2.1   Scientific Data Modeling

Scientific experiments often consist of complex steps or processes. A complex scientific experiment can be modeled as a set of atomic objects. The context information of such objects can then be represented through a unified document model, *SciPort Document*. SciPort Document can represent both (nested) structured data, files and images.

A SciPort document includes several objects: i) Primitive Data Types/Fields. Primitive data types are used to represent structural data, including *integer*, *float*, *date*, *text*, and Web-based data types such as *textarea*, *radiobutton*, *checkbox*, *URL*, etc.; ii) File. Files can be linked to a document through the file object; iii) *Reference*. A reference type links to another SciPort document; iv) Group. A group is similar to a table, which aggregates a collection of fields or nested groups. There can be multiple instances for a group, like rows of a table; and v) Category. A category relates a list of fields, e.g., "patient data" category, "experiment data" category, etc. Categories are used only at the top level of the content, and categories are not nested (Figure 1).

2.2   XML Based Implementation

The model can be best implemented as XML. The hierarchical nature of the data model fits very well with the tree based XML data model. Users can also easily define their own schemas which are internally represented with an XML-based schema definition language. Here we take the native XML database approach to manage scientific documents, where standard XML query language XQuery [7] is supported. We provide two options: Oracle Berkeley DB XML [8], an open source embedded XML database, and IBM DB2 with pureXML^{TM} support. SciPort provides comprehensive Web-based tools to support authoring and searching [6].

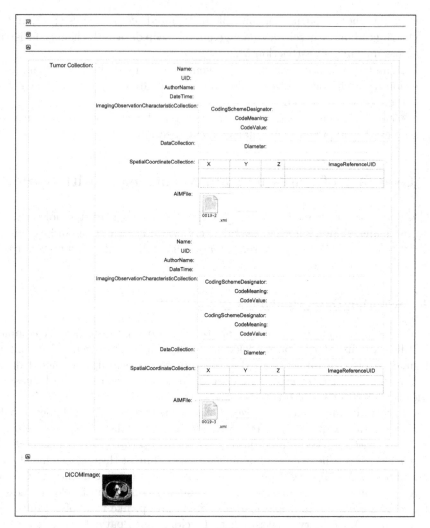

Fig. 1. A Sample SciPort Document

3   Sharing Distributed Scientific Data

As scientific research increasingly becomes a collaboration activity, researchers frequently need to collaborate through sharing their data. There are several common requirements for the data sharing: i) Convenience: data sharing should be a single step action; ii) Data ownership: researchers own and have full control of their data; iii) Flexible Sharing Control: while data can be shared, data sharing can also be revoked by researchers at any time; iv) Up-to-date of shared data. As data are updated or removed, corresponding shared data also need to be synchronized accordingly to stay current.

3.1 Sharing Data through a Central Server

To meet the above requirements and support closer collaboration and integration, we develop a distributed architecture to share and integrate data through a Central Server (Figure 2). In this architecture, each research site will have their own Local Server which itself functions as an independent Server for data collection, management, search, and report. In addition, there will be an additional Central Server upon which Local Servers are able to selectively publish their data (structured documents) (Figure 3). Images/files, which are often the major source of data volume, are still stored on corresponding Local Servers but are linked from the published documents on the Central Server. Once a user on the Central Server tries to download a document from the Central Server, actual data files are downloaded from the corresponding Local Server that holds the data.

Thus, the Central Server provides a global view of shared data across all distributed sites, and can also be used as a hub for sharing schemas among multiple sites. Since data are shared through the metadata (SciPort Documents), the integration is lightweight. Users on the Central Server will only have read access to the data.

Figure 2 illustrates an example SciPort sharing architecture formed by four Local Servers at four universities: UCI, UCSF, Dartmouth and Penn. Each Local Server is used for data collection and management of clinical trial data at its local institution. Since these clinical trials are under the same research consortia,

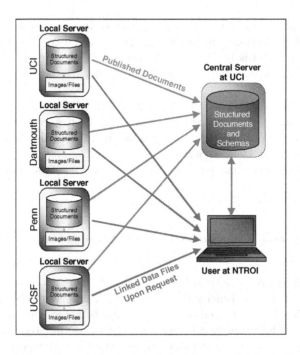

Fig. 2. The Central Server Based Architecture for Data Sharing

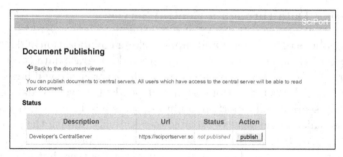

Fig. 3. An Example of Publishing an Existing Document

they would share their data together by publishing their data (documents) to the Central Server located at UCI. Members at NTROI research consortia are granted read access on such shared data through the Central Server. Once the user identifies a data set from the Central Server and wants to download it, the user will be redirected to the corresponding Local Server that hosts the data to download the data to the client.

3.2 Data Synchronization

One requirement for the data sharing is to keep shared data up-to-date. The following operations are related to document synchronization.

- Create. When a document is created, the author or publisher has the option to publish this document (Figure 4). Once the document is published, a "published" status is added to the document. A user can also set up an automatic publishing flag so all new documents will be automatically published;
- Update. When an update is performed on a published document, the document will automatically be republished to the Central Server;
- Delete. When a published document is deleted, it will also be automatically removed from the Central Server;
- Unpublish. A user can also stop sharing a document by unpublishing the document.

3.3 Security and Trust between Local Servers and the Central Server

Server Verification. The trust between Local Servers and the Central Server is implemented through security tokens. For a Local Server to be accepted into the network, it will be granted a security token to access the Central SciPort Server services. The token will be imported at the setup step. When a Local Server tries to connect to the Central Server, the Central Server verifies if the token matches.

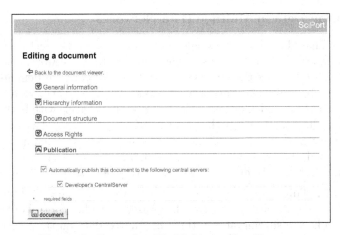

Fig. 4. An Example of Publishing a New Document

Single Sign-on and Security. One issue for sharing data from distributed databases is that it is not feasible for Central Server users to login to every distributed database. Since once a user publishes a document, the user grants the read access of the document (including the files attached to the document) to the users on the Central Server, thus it is unnecessary for another authentication. Therefore, users on the Central Server should be able to automatically access shared data from a Local Server in a transparent way.

To support this, the Local Server Document Access Control Manager has to make sure that the remote download requests really come from Central Server users who are currently logging on. We develop a single sign-on method to guarantee the security of the data sharing, consisting of the following steps as shown in Figure 5.

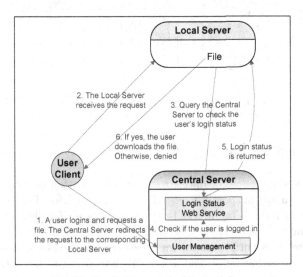

Fig. 5. Single Sign on for Central Server

3.4   Sharing Data in Multiple Data Networks

Data can be shared not only in a single data network through one Central Server, but also in multiple data networks through multiple data networks. One organization may want to share the same data in multiple networks, as demonstrated in an example (Figure 6). There are two networks one centered at UCI, and another one centered at Stanford. One institution UCI is collaborating with both networks and needs to share data with both networks. UCI will be granted as a partner site and its Local Server will be configured for both networks. When a document is being published, the target Central Server can be either of them or both of them. This sharing architecture make it possible for very flexible data sharing.

The Benefits. This data sharing architecture provides many benefits: i) data sharing is as convenient as a single click; ii) users have full control of their data, and can revoke the sharing at any time; iii) shared data on the Central Server always remain updated, and iv) the Central Server based sharing architecture makes it possible to conveniently share schemas, as discussed next.

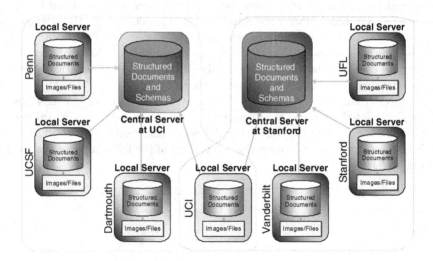

Fig. 6. Sharing Data in Multiple Data Networks

4   Sharing Schemas

Schemas are used to define the data structures and constraints of documents. The former includes a mix of (possibly nested) object types defined in the data model, and the latter includes i) number of instance constraints for file and group types, ii) minimal and maximal value constraints; and iii) controlled values (Figure 7).

Schemas are an essential component since they are used for i) data validation; ii) document authoring form generation; iii) data presentation – templates are defined based on schemas; iv) search form generation. Sharing schemas are critical

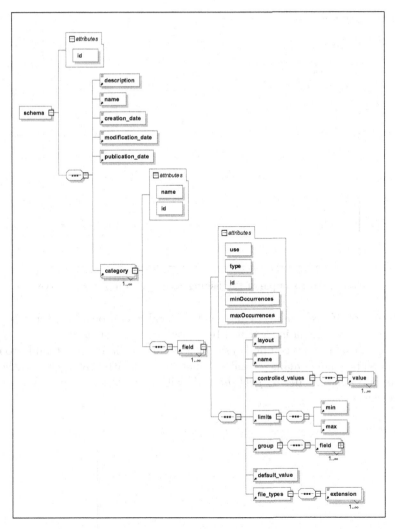

Fig. 7. Schema Model Diagram

for sharing data, since the Central Server glues data together using shared schemas to present and search data. How to keep data from multiple Local Servers coherent is also dependent on at what level and how schemas can be shared.

4.1 Publishing Schemas

Schemas can be shared by publishing them to the Central Server. From a Local Server *Schema Management* menu, schemas created on the Local Server can be selectively published to target Central Servers, as shown in the example in Figure 8. When a new document is being published to the Central Server, the availability of the corresponding schema will be checked. If not, the schema will also be published.

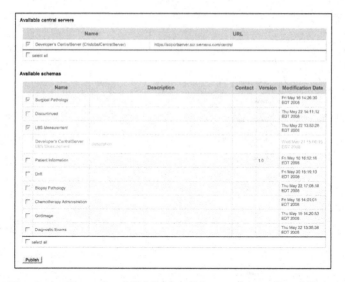

Fig. 8. An Example of Publishing Schemas from a Local Server

The *owner of a schema* is defined as the Local Server on which the schema is first created. A schema is identified by its owner and schema ID.

SciPort also provides comprehensive access control management, and two roles are related to schema management: i) *organizer* role with privileges to authoring and update schemas and ii) *publisher* role with privileges to publish documents and schemas.

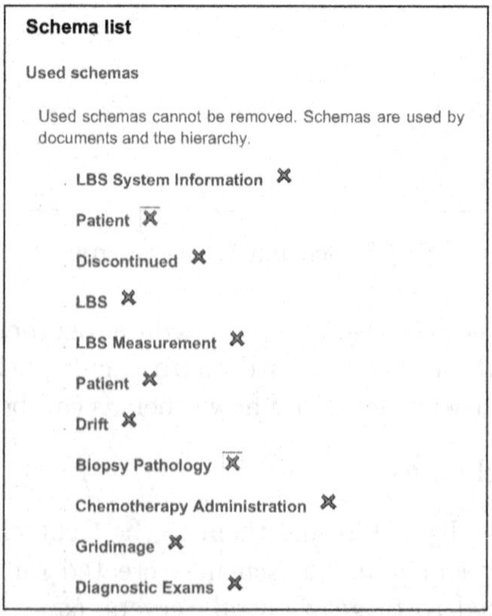

Schema list

Used schemas

Used schemas cannot be removed. Schemas are used by documents and the hierarchy.

. LBS System Information ✖

Patient ✖

Discontinued ✖

LBS ✖

LBS Measurement ✖

Patient ✖

. Drift ✖

Biopsy Pathology ✖

Chemotherapy Administration ✖

Gridimage ✖

Diagnostic Exams ✖

Fig. 9. An Example of Schemas Shared on a Central Server

Once a schema is published, it can be shared through the Central Server. Figure 9 shows a sample list of schemas published from Local Servers. Schemas can also be removed from the Central Server to stop the sharing.

Other Local Servers can reuse schemas by importing schemas from the Central Server, as shown in Figure 10.

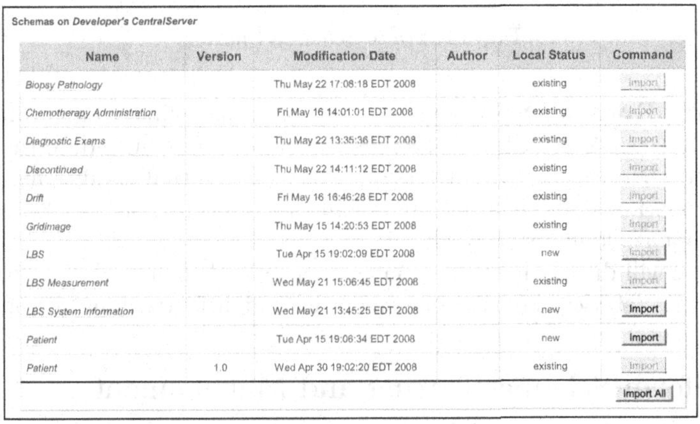

Schemas on Developer's CentralServer

Name	Version	Modification Date	Author	Local Status	Command
Biopsy Pathology		Thu May 22 17:06:18 EDT 2008		existing	Import
Chemotherapy Administration		Fri May 16 14:01:01 EDT 2008		existing	Import
Diagnostic Exams		Thu May 22 13:35:36 EDT 2008		existing	Import
Discontinued		Thu May 22 14:11:12 EDT 2008		existing	Import
Drift		Fri May 16 16:46:28 EDT 2008		existing	Import
Gridimage		Thu May 15 14:20:53 EDT 2008		existing	Import
LBS		Tue Apr 15 19:02:09 EDT 2008		new	Import
LBS Measurement		Wed May 21 15:06:45 EDT 2008		existing	Import
LBS System Information		Wed May 21 13:45:25 EDT 2008		new	Import
Patient		Tue Apr 15 19:06:34 EDT 2008		new	Import
Patient	1.0	Wed Apr 30 19:02:20 EDT 2008		existing	Import

Import All

Fig. 10. An Example of Importing Schemas to a Local Server

Unpublish. A schema can be unpublished from a Central Server by a Local Server, thus the schema is not available on the Central Server for further sharing.

Remove from Central Server. Users on the Central Server with an "organizer" role can remove a schema from the Central Server if no document on Central Server is using this schema. This can be used to cleanup non-used schemas.

4.2   Three Scenarios of Schemas Sharing

Based on the use cases, there are three typical scenarios of schema sharing:

Static Schema. A schema is fixed and will not be changed. For example, some common standard based schemas are not likely to change. Once a schema is authored and changed to the fixed status, it can be published to the Central Server to be shared by every Local Servers (Figure 11). This is the simplest scenario, as schemas can be created once and shared directly through the Central Server.

Uniform Evolving Schema. A Schema can be changed and a uniform version is shared by all Local Servers, thus data consistency is maintained across all sites. The schema is owned by its original creating Local Server, and the owner can make certain changes.

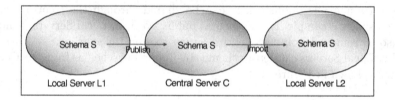

Fig. 11. Static Schemas Sharing

Multiform Evolving Schema. A "seed" schema is first created and shared as public – every Local Server becomes the owner and can update the schema. The Central Server maintains a version of the schema that conditionally merges updates from Local Servers, thus all documents published on the Central Server will be compatible under this schema.

Next, we will discuss how to manage schemas and their evolution for the last two scenarios (static schema management is straightforward and ignored here.)

5   Uniform Schema Sharing and Management

Since schemas can be shared and used across multiple distributed data sources, one challenging issue is how to manage schema evolution while keeping the document consistent and compatible with their schemas in a distributed environment. To solve this problem, we first define the following principles for distributed schema management and sharing:

- Minimal administration: no central management on schemas, and the Central Server serves as an information exchange hub;
- Data consistency: schema evolution has to be backward compatible otherwise the integrity of documents will be broken;
- Control of schemas: only the owner of a schema can update a schema;
- Current of Schema: the Central Server always has the up-to-date version of compatible schema if that schema is shared by the owner;
- Sharing Maximization: Only the last time publisher can unpublish a schema from the Central Server.

On a Local Server, schemas can be created, updated, deleted, imported, and published or unpublished. Schemas can also be removed from the Central Server to stop the sharing. To enable data consistency, each schema operation has to be carefully defined.

5.1   Uniform Schema Management

Next we discuss schema operations and their conditions.

Creation. A schema can be created on a Local Server if the user has the organizer role. This Local Server will become the owner of this schema.

Incompatible Update. Incompatible update is the one that can lead to inconsistency between the new schema and existing documents if any. Incompatible updates are forbidden unless the following conditions are met: i) only the owner of a schema can make updates to the schema; ii) there are no existing documents created using this schema on this Local Server; and iii) the schema was never published, i.e., there will no other Local Servers using the schema to create documents. A publishing status is associated with each schema.

Compatible Update. A user updates an existing schema and such updates will not lead to inconsistency between the new schema and existing documents if any. The following conditions are required for compatible update:

- *Ownership.* The Local Server is the owner of the schema, and the user is the organizer on this Local Server.
- *Field Containment.* All the fields in the last schema are present in the new schema, belong to same category, and belong to the same group if any. There can be new categories and fields added.
- *Type Compatibility.* All the fields in the new schema have the same type or a compatible type, i.e., a more general type. For example, an integer type can be updated to a float type.
- *Relaxed Value Range Constraints.* No new value constraints are permitted for existing fields which do not have any constraint. Value constraints can be updated with more relaxed ranges. i.e., the new maximal limit should be greater than or equal to last one, and the new minimal limit should be less than or equal to last one. Constraints on new fields are permitted.
- *Relaxed Controlled Values.* For field with controlled values, the extent is enlarged with more options. Similarly for radiobuttons and checkboxes, more options are added.
- *Relaxed Constraints on Number of Instances.* For group field or file field, there can be a constraint on the minimal and/or maximal number of instances. No instance number constraint is permitted on existing fields, and instance number constraint can be updated with more relaxed range. i.e., the new maximal limit should be greater than or equal to last one, and the new minimal limit should be less than or equal to last one. Constraints on new fields are permitted.

Change of a field's order within its sibling is not considered incompatible.

Once a schema is updated on the Local Server, it will be automatically republished to the Central Server (if any) onto which the schema has been published. This will ensure the Central Server always maintains up-to-date versions of schemas.

Delete. A schema can be deleted if the user has the organizer role, and there are no documents using this schema on this Local Server. If the Local Server is the owner of the schema, and the schema is never published, deleting a schema will eliminate the schema forever. If the schema was once published, it may be still alive and used on other servers.

Publish. A schema can be published to one or multiple Central Servers if the user has a publisher role and there is no newer version of this schema on the Central Server. There are three scenarios of schema publishing:

– Schemas can be manually published from the schema publishing interface;
– The schema of a document is automatically published when a document is published. When a document is published, the Local Server will check the Central Server if the schema is available or up-to-date. Otherwise the schema is republished;
– If a schema was published and is then updated with compatibility, the new version schema will be automatically republished on the Central Server and replace the last version. This will keep the schemas on the Central Server up-to-date.

Unpublish. A schema can be unpublished by a Local Server with the following conditions: i) the user has the "publish" role on the Local Server; ii) there is no document associated with it on the Central Server, and iii) the Local Server is the last publisher of the schema. The last condition is necessary. Otherwise if the schema is used at multiple Local Servers, every Local Server can easily stop the publishing which can be against the sharing goal of the last publisher.

Import. A Local Server can import a shared schema from the Central Server if the user has the organizer role. When there is a new version of a schema on the Central Server, it will be automatically detected by a Local Server when there is a document being published from that Local Server.

Remove from Central Server. Users on the Central Server with the organizer role can remove a schema from the Central Server if no document on Central Server is using this schema. This can be used to cleanup non-used schemas.

5.2   An Example of Uniform Schema Management

A user with organizer privilege on a Local Server L1 creates a schema S(V1) (Figure 12). The user may later find the schema not accurate, and makes changes to the schema. Since no document has been created and the schema has never

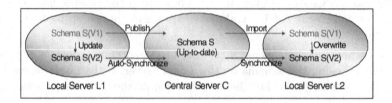

Fig. 12. Uniform Schema Sharing

been shared yet, the user may make arbitrary changes, including incompatible updates. Once the user has a stable usable version of the schema, the user begins to author documents based on this schema, and publishes documents to the Central Server C. Schema S(V1) will be automatically published to the Central Server. After some time, the user may need more information for their data or adjust existing fields, and need to update schema S. Since there are existing documents using the schema, and the schema was also published, the user can make compatible update to schema S(V1). (If compatible update is not sufficient, the user has to create a new schema.) Once schema S(V1) is updated as S(V2), it will be automatically propagated to the Central Server to replace the last version S(V1).

A user with organizer privilege on a Local Server L2 imports schema S(V1) after S(V1) is published on the Central Server, and documents then are create on L2 on this schema. Later S(V2) replaces S(V1) on the Central Server, which is detected when a document of schema S(V1) is published to C. The user at L2 will be prompted to synchronize the schema, and S(V1) is replaced by S(V2) on L2.

6   Distributed Multiform Schema Sharing

Uniform schema sharing provides data compatibility through a single uniform version of schemas across all servers, and maintains the ownership of schemas and provides controlled schema evolution. There can also be cases that multiple sites need to adapt certain schema to their own needs, and a uniform schema may not be feasible. To provide flexible schema evolution at each Local Server and support data compatibility on the Central Server, we provide a multiform schema sharing approach.

As shown in Figure 13, a "seed" schema S will be first created and made as public owned, and then published onto the Central Server. Each Local Server will be able to import this schema, and adjust the schema for its local use (S_{L1}, S_{L2}, etc.) Schema updates from each site will be conditionally merged on the Central Server as S_M. The goal of the merging is to keep the schema version on the Central Server mostly relaxed, through the following merging conditions:

– If the changes are incremental structural changes, they will be merged. These include adding of new fields or new categories;

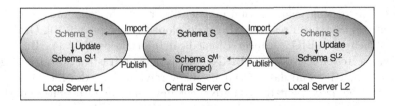

Fig. 13. Multiform Schema Sharing

- If the constraints on the Central Server in the central server are more permissive than the new or updated constraints that the modification suggests, then the suggested changes are ignored by the Central Server;
- Structural removal changes such as field removal or category removal will be ignored and not merged.

In this way, each Local Server will maintain its local schema evolution while the Central Server will maintain a merged schema for shared data compatibility.

7   Schema Change Detection

To support schema management, schema change detection tool is needed to detect changes (structural changes and constraint changes, compatible and incompatible changes) and visualize changes for users. SciPort uses XML based schema representation to represent both complex data structures and constraints, as shown in Figure 7. The schema has two types of objects: category and field. Category is the top level object, and a field can be nested if it is of group type. Each object is represented with an unique ID. We develop a schema change detection tool, thus changes can be easily visualized through XSLT.

The algorithm is shown in Algorithm 1. It compares nodes from the base schema ($NODE\_B$) and nodes from the target schema ($NODE\_T$). For the child nodes of two comparing nodes, the child nodes are ascendingly sorted based on their IDs (S1 and S2 respectively), thus the comparison will be on two sorted lists. Starting from the root, the algorithm will walk through each node S1, and try to identify target node with the same ID. For nodes with smaller IDs on the target S2, they will be identified as new nodes; for target node with identical ID, for non-group fields, compatibility is checked; for group fields, they are further recursively compared. If identical ID node is not the last one on S2, next node in S1 is picked up and the process is repeated until the end. The changes generated include structural changes (NEW, DELETE), incompatible constraint changes (INCOMPATIBLE_CHANGE), and compatible constraint changes (COMPATIBLE_CHANGE). Changes are ordered based on the schema hierarchy, thus they can be easily visualized through applying an XSLT template.

8   Related Work

With the increasing collaboration of scientific research, collaborative cyberinfrastructures have been researched and developed in the past [9,10]. Grid-based systems(such as caBIG – cancer Biomedical Informatics Grid [4], Biomedical Informatics Research Network (BIRN) [5]) provide infrastructures to integrate existing computing and data resources. They rely on a top down common data structure. This is difficult to get agreement upon and requires much effort and cost to setup and maintain such systems. SciPort is lightweight and can be quickly customized for either research labs or research networks.

Algorithm 1. schema_node_comparison (*NODE_B, NODE_T, CHANGE*)

```
 1: L1 ← List of child nodes of NODE_B
 2: L2 ← List of child nodes of NODE_T
 3: NEW = NULL
 4: DELETE = NULL
 5: INCOMPATIBLE_CHANGE = NULL
 6: COMPATIBLE_CHANGE = NULL
 7: if NODE_B is root then
 8:     CHANGE = NULL
 9: end if
10: if L1 = NULL then
11:     NEW = L2;
12:     CHANGE += NEW;
13: else if L2 = NULL then
14:     DELETE = L1
15:     CHANGE += DELETE;
16: else
17:     S1 = SORT L1 in ascending order by ID
18:     S2 = SORT L2 in ascending order by ID
19:     P = first node in S2
20:     for  N = first node in S1 to N = last node in S1  do
21:         if id(N) = id(P) then
22:             if N is a group then
23:                 CHANGE' = NULL
24:                 CALL schema_node_comparison (N, P, CHANGE')
25:                 CHANGE += CHANGE'
26:             else
27:                 if P != N then
28:                     INCOMPATIBLE_CHANGE = incompatible changes
29:                     COMPATIBLE_CHANGE = compatible changes
30:                 end if
31:             end if
32:         else if id(N) < id(P) then
33:             DELETE = F
34:         else if  id(N) > id(P)  then
35:             NEW = P
36:             while  P = P → next and id(N) > id(P)  do
37:                 NEW += P
38:             end while
39:             P = P → next
40:             if id(N) = id(P) then
41:                 if N is a group then
42:                     CHANGE' = NULL
43:                     CALL schema_node_comparison (N, P, CHANGE')
44:                     CHANGE += CHANGE'
45:                 else
46:                     if P != N then
47:                         INCOMPATIBLE_CHANGE = incompatible changes
48:                         COMPATIBLE_CHANGE = compatible changes
49:                     end if
50:                 end if
51:             end if
52:         end if
53:         CHANGE += NEW + DELETE + INCOMPATIBLE_CHANGE + COMPATI-
            BLE_CHANGE
54:     end for
55: end if
```

A context-based sharing system is proposed in [11], which focuses on tools instead of data as in SciPort.

While Grid based systems are more used on sharing computing and storage resources, P2P is more used on sharing data [12]. MIRC [13] is a popular pure-P2P based system for authoring and sharing teaching files, which is hard to extend for generic data management. SciPort provides much generality on scientific data management and supports much more powerful integration.

A publish and subscribe architecture for distributed metadata management is discussed in [14], which focuses on the synchronization problems. In [15], an approach of bottom-up collaborative data sharing is proposed, where each group independently manages and extends their data, and the groups compare and reconcile their changes eventually while tolerating disagreement. Our approach takes an approach in between the bottom-up and top-down approaches, where each group manages their data, but also achieves as much agreement on schemas as possible through controlled schema evolution.

Extensive work has been done in data integration and schema integration [16,17]. Our system takes a proactive approach where schema and data consistency is enforced during data authoring and schema authoring.

9   Conclusion

Contemporary scientific research is moving towards multi-disciplinary, multi-institutional collaboration. These lead to strong demand for tools and systems to manage and share the data. This drives the development of SciPort – a Web-based data sharing system for collaborative scientific research. Through a lightweight Central Server based sharing architecture, SciPort provides convenient ways for not only data sharing, but also schema sharing, where data owners still have full control of the data. SciPort further provides flexible approaches to manage schemas and their evolution while maintaining data consistency. Besides static schema sharing, SciPort makes it possible to share a uniform evolving schema across multiple sites, or even site-varied multiform evolving schemas while compatibility is maintained on the sharing server. The system is being well received by research communities, and has been successfully deployed in many research organizations.

References

1. NIH Roadmap Initiatives, http://nihroadmap.nih.gov/initiatives.asp
2. NIH Statement on Sharing Scientific Research Data,
   http://grants2.nih.gov/grants/guide/notice-files/NOT-OD-03-032.html
3. Piwowar, H., Becich, M., Bilofsky, H., Crowley, R.: Towards a Data Sharing Culture: Recommendations for Leadership from Academic Health Centers. PLoS medicine 5(9) (September 2008)
4. caBIG: cancer Biomedical Informatics Grid, http://caBIG.nci.nih.gov/
5. Biomedical Informatics Research Network, http://www.nbirn.net/

6. SciPort Wiki, https://sciportserver.scr.siemens.com/mediawiki
7. XQuery 1.0: An XML Query Language, http://www.w3.org/TR/xquery/
8. Oracle Berkeley DB XML, http://www.oracle.com/database/berkeley-db/xml/
9. Arzberger, P., Finholt, T.A.: Report on Data and Collaboratories in the Biomedical Community Workshop (2002), http://nbcr.sdsc.edu/Collaboratories/CollaboratoryFinal2.doc
10. Revolutionizing Science and Engineering Through Cyberinfrastructure: Report of the National Science Foundation Blue-Ribbon Advisory Panel on Cyberinfrastructure (2003), http://www.communitytechnology.org/nsf_ci_report/report.pdf
11. Chin, Jr.,G., Lansing, C.S.: Capturing and Supporting Contexts for Scientific Data Sharing via the Biological Sciences Collaboratory. In: CSCW (2004)
12. Foster, I., Iamnitchi, A.: On Death, Taxes, and the Convergence of Peer-to-Peer and Grid Computing. In: IPTPS 2003 (2003)
13. MIRC, http://mirc.rsna.org
14. Keidl, M., Kreutz, A., Kemper, A., Kossmann, D.: A Publish & Subscribe Architecture for Distributed Metadata Management. In: ICDE (2002)
15. Taylor, N.E., Ives, Z.G.: Reconciling while Tolerating Disagreement in Collaborative Data Sharing. In: SIGMOD (2006)
16. Halevy, A., Rajaraman, A., Ordille, J.: Data integration: the teenage years. In: VLDB (2006)
17. Doan, A., Halevy, A.Y.: Semantic integration research in the database community: A brief survey. AI Magazine 26(1), 83–94 (2005)

IT Incident Management as a Collaborative Process: A Visualization Tool Inspired to Social Networks

Claudio Bartolini

HP Laboratories
1501 Page Mill Rd, Palo Alto, CA 94304
claudio.bartolini@hp.com

Abstract. Dynamics of IT support organizations can be quite complex to analyze. We introduce a prototype visualization tool that exploits similarities of support organizations with social networks. Our tool borrows techniques from social network visualization and analysis to help IT manager better understand dynamics of their organization in the incident management process.

Keywords: IT service management, IT infrastructure library, incident management, social networks, visualization.

1 Introduction

The IT Infrastructure Library (ITIL [1]) is a comprehensive set of concepts and techniques for managing IT infrastructure, development, and operations. Developed by the UK Office of Government Commerce (OGC), ITIL is today the de facto best practice standard for IT service management. Among the processes that ITIL defines, *Incident Management* is the process through which IT support organizations manage to restore normal service operation after a disruption, as quickly as possible and with minimum impact on the business.

IT support organizations are structured as complex networks of support groups, each comprising of a set of skilled technicians. Incident management can therefore be seen as a very complex collaborative process. With the complexity of IT support organizations and staff working around the clock in disparate geographies, it is hard to understand the dynamic of the organization.

In this paper, we present ITSupportster, a visualization tool that takes inspiration from graph-like representation of social networks. The remainder of this paper is structured as follows: in section 2 we present an abstraction of the IT incident management process, which we used as a basis to build the model behind our visualization tool; in section 3 we describe our visualization tool, ITSupportster; in section 4 we present empirical and anecdotal evidence of the usefulness of our tool; we review related work in section 5 and conclude in section 6 mentioning the next steps in continuing development of our prototype tool.

E. Bertino and J.B.D. Joshi (Eds.): CollaborateCom 2008, LNICST 10, pp. 824–830, 2009.

2 The IT Incident Management Process

An IT support organization (fig. 1) consists of a network of support groups, each comprising of a set of skilled technicians, with their work schedule. Support groups are divided into support levels (usually three to five). The helpdesk is assigned level zero, support groups at lower levels may be are able to deal with generic issues such as "user forgot password", while groups at higher levels are more specialized and able to deal with harder tasks. Support groups are further specialized by category of incidents that they treat (network, server, etc...) and divided into geographies, to ensure a more prompt handling of incidents especially at lower support levels.

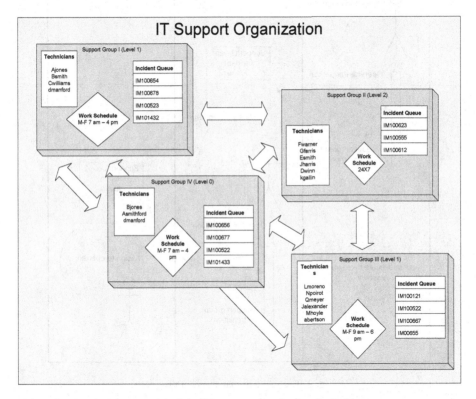

Fig. 1. Conceptual model of the IT support organization for incident management

When a customer experiences a disruption in an IT service, he or she interfaces with a help desk, which opens an incident, also sometimes called troubleticket (simply ticket in the rest of our paper). The incidents are worked on by different support groups throughout their lifetime, as technicians in a given support group can either resolve the incident or pass it on to a different support group (usually escalating to a higher level of support). We model the support organization as a queue system, each support group having a queue of incidents that it is working on at a given time. This process is exemplified in fig. 2.

826   C. Bartolini

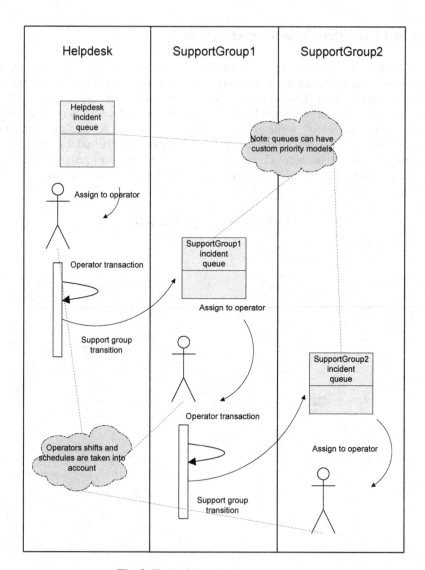

Fig. 2. The incident management process

The incident lifecycle (fig. 3) is described as the progression of an incident from its initial occurrence to detection, then to the diagnosis of the cause of failure, the repair of the issue, recovery of the component that was at fault, and finally restoration of service. Throughout the lifetime of an incident, the incident gets "opened" by the helpdesk, then assigned to a support group which is going to work on it and either mark it "closed" or "reassign" it to a different support group. At each of these states, the incident record is updated with the pertinent information, such as the troubleshooting that has taken place, which team is responsible for action, which engineer on the team, and what the current status of the incident is. Figure 3

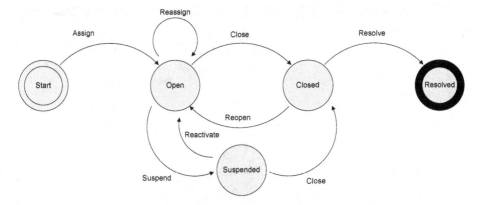

Fig. 3. Incident lifecycle

demonstrates the progression between these different states: An incident is opened when a call comes in to the call center after an issue is detected.

Once the incident is assigned to the appropriate team that will handle the issue, it is updated numerous times to reflect the progression of troubleshooting that the engineers attempt. If, for some reason, the end-users requests that the engineer stops working on the issue, it is placed in a "suspended" state so as not to incur SLO penalty while not being worked on. Once the disruption is repaired, the incident is placed in "closed" state until the end-user confirms that service has been restored and all is well. Once the restoration is confirmed, the incident is "resolved" and its lifecycle ends.

3 ITSupportster

ITSupportster is a visualization tool that provides insight into the structure and the dynamics of an IT support organization.

The main view of ITSupportster is a map of the workgroups that compose the IT support organization, as shown in figure 4. Workgroups are laid out on the map according to inter-group communication dynamics: workgroups that communicate often – i.e. redirect tickets from one another – are near to each other on the map. This is similar to the concept of social networks where entities that are marked as "friend" are drawn near to one another. All of the data necessary to populate the ITsupportster social network map is collected through off-the-shelf IT help desk software products. To develop our prototype, we gathered data from installations of HP Service Manager [2].

Various pictorial features on the map are used to convey information. A prominent feature of the visualization is that the size of the node is proportional to the number of tickets that the workgroups process. In this way it is immediate to get an impression of what workgroups see the most traffic. The thickness of the directed edges connecting nodes is used to represent the ticket throughput between the workgroups. A thicker edge represents a higher number of tickets being passed from one group to the next. In this edges come to represent "information highways". The thickness of

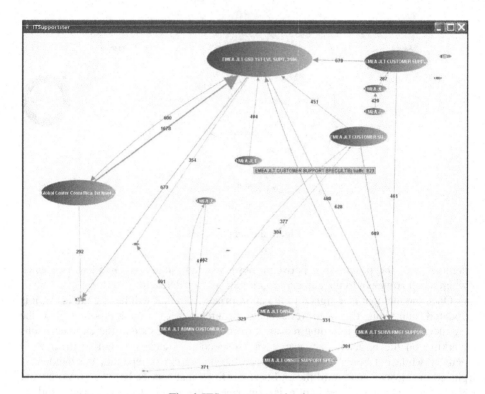

Fig. 4. ITSupportster main view

the node border is proportional to the number of tickets resolved by the support group represented by the node. The coloring is used to represent the level of support (helpdesk, first line of support, etc.)

It has to be noted that the mapping of visual features to metrics for support group dynamics is highly customizable. For example a user may want the dimension of the node to indicate the staffing level of the workgroup, or the coloring to indicate the geography that the workgroup belongs to. Finally, node vicinity (the map layout) could also be customized to represent other features. For example, the nodes could be layered as to represent to support level hierarchy or even drawn on a geographic map.

Given the elevated number of nodes on the graph (the number of workgroups in an IT large support organization can be up to thousands), the map is represented through a hyperbolic graph [3]. The main feature of a hyperbolic graph is that the region of the map that is in focus is rendered with greater detail, while still giving a picture comprising of the whole map. Zoom-in and zoom-out are supported.

Because of the extremely high density of information that it conveys, the main ITSupportster map is the ideal starting point for IT performance analysis, business impact analysis and assisted optimization (re-design) of the IT support organization.

Highlighting a node representing a workgroup on the map, a side pane (workgroup view) shows structural information about the workgroup (name, manager, contacts, location, technicians, etc...), and collates information useful for IT performance analysis that is collected through a separate decision support module, SYMIAN described in more detail in [4, 5]. The architecture of ITSupportster follows the Model-View-Controller architectural pattern. The social network map that is used as a view in the IT performance analysis and business impact analysis modalities, is also used as controller in the guided optimization (or assisted organization design) that is available through the sister tool SYMIAN.

4 Validation of the Prototype

We built several visualization examples from real life data derived from installations of HP Service Manager in an outsourcing context. When we shared the examples with the IT managers, they immediately recognized their organization, and in more than one case were able to suspect workgroups to be bottlenecks in the network. In one example, one major flow identified by ITSupportster as a possible red herring, was already suspected to be an issue. However they had no quantitative data to support this, and the diagram and associated metrics helped to focus the dialog between the two workgroups involved, contributing to the issue resolution.

5 Related Work

Our work on visualization of incident management dynamics can be seen as part of a recently emerged research area that focuses on the two IT management dimensions of people and processes. The interest for this topic arose as researchers started analyzing the relationships between people, processes and technological optimization and the impact of automation and process complexity on labor cost. As a representative example, we cite Diao et al.'s recent research effort addressing the very important question of when does it make sense to automate processes based on metrics of process complexity [6, 7]. The main difference of our approach and theirs is that make similar modeling considerations to achieve significant improvements in the performance of the organization through visualization, decision support and simulation techniques.

The analysis of the incident management process and the IT support organization model presented in this paper shares common aspects with what we described in [8] and then again in [4]. In this paper, however, we build on those abstractions to build a tool that is able to visualize the dynamics between the various support groups that we began to describe there.

Social network analysis has been used as an analysis technique applied to various domains ranging from information science, organizational behavior, economics, and other. Social network analysis explores the relationships and ties between actors within the network, rather than the individual aspects of each actor. Visual representation of social networks is deemed important to understand the network data and convey the result of the analysis. See for example Freeman's work [9]. Our ITSupportster tool can be seen as an application of these ideas to the IT support organization seen as social network of support workgroups.

6 Conclusion and Future Work

Dynamics of IT support organizations can be quite complex to analyze. We presented ITSupportster, a prototype visualization tool that exploits similarities of support organizations with social networks and borrows techniques from social network visualization and analysis to help IT manager better understand dynamics of their organization in the incident management process.

Our next steps will be to closely couple the ITSupportster visualization prototype with a decision support tool that we have developed for optimizing the performance of IT support organizations through simulation techniques (SYMIAN, described in [4]).

References

1. IT Infrastructure Library, ITIL Service Delivery and ITIL Service Support, OGC, UK (2003)
2. HP ServiceManager, http://www.hp.com/software
3. Herman, I., Melançon, G., Marshall, M.S.: Graph Visualization and Navigation in Information Visualization: A Survey. IEEE Transactions on Visualization and Computer Graphics (2000)
4. Bartolini, C., Stefanelli, C., Tortonesi, M.: SYMIAN: a Simulation Tool for the Optimization of the IT Incident Management Process. In: De Turck, F., Kellerer, W., Kormentzas, G. (eds.) DSOM 2008. LNCS, vol. 5273. Springer, Heidelberg (2008)
5. Bartolini, C., Stefanelli, C., Tortonesi, M.: Business-impact analysis and simulation of critical incidents in IT service management. In: Proceedings of IEEE Integrated Management Conference IM (2009)
6. Diao, Y., Keller, A., Parekh, S., Marinov, V.: Predicting Labor Cost through IT Management Complexity Metrics. In: Proceedings of the 10th IEEE/IFIP Symposium on Integrated Management (IM 2007), Munich, Germany (2007)
7. Diao, Y., Bhattacharya, K.: Estimating Business Value of IT Services through Process Complexity Analysis. In: Proceedings of the 11th IEEE/IFIP Network Operation and Management Symposium (NOMS 2008), Salvador de Bahia, Brazil (2008)
8. Barash, G., Bartolini, C., Wu, L.: Measuring and Improving the Performance of an IT Support Organization in Managing Service Incidents. In: Proc. 2nd IEEE Workshop on Business-driven IT Management (BDIM 2007), Munich, Germany (2007)
9. Freeman, L.C.: Visualizing Social Networks. Journal of Social Structure, JoSS 1(1) (2000)

Author Index

Printed in the United States
By Bookmasters